TWO WEEKS FREE TO *Antique Trader* W9-CSU-135

☐ **YES!** Send me two **FREE** issues of *Antique Trader*.

Each week *Antique Trader* delivers thousands of Antique & Collectible items to your door. Use the classified listings to add to your collection, sell off duplicate pieces, or monitor prices in the marketplace. Also use the auction and show listings to plan your travels.

Each issue also provides you with in-depth editorial coverage on the Antique & Collectible hobby you need to make informed decisions about your collecting.

Send in the card today to receive your two **FREE** issues.

Name _____

Address _____

City _____ State _____

| Source |
| BPG97 |

Zip + 4 _____ Phone _____

TWO WEEKS FREE TO *Antique Trader*

☐ **YES!** Send me two **FREE** issues of *Antique Trader*.

Each week *Antique Trader* delivers thousands of Antique & Collectible items to your door. Use the classified listings to add to your collection, sell off duplicate pieces, or monitor prices in the marketplace. Also use the auction and show listings to plan your travels.

Each issue also provides you with in-depth editorial coverage on the Antique & Collectible hobby you need to make informed decisions about your collecting.

Send in the card today to receive your two **FREE** issues.

Name _____

Address _____

City _____ State _____

| Source |
| BPG97 |

Zip + 4 _____ Phone _____

ANTIQUE TRADER WEEKLY

BUSINESS REPLY MAIL
FIRST CLASS MAIL   PERMIT NO. 50   DUBUQUE, IA

POSTAGE WILL BE PAID BY ADDRESSEE

ANTIQUE TRADER WEEKLY
PO BOX 1050
DUBUQUE IA 52004-9969

ANTIQUE TRADER WEEKLY

BUSINESS REPLY MAIL
FIRST CLASS MAIL   PERMIT NO. 50   DUBUQUE, IA

POSTAGE WILL BE PAID BY ADDRESSEE

ANTIQUE TRADER WEEKLY
PO BOX 1050
DUBUQUE IA 52004-9969

Fourteenth Edition
Antique Trader Books
ANTIQUES & COLLECTIBLES
PRICE GUIDE

1998 ANNUAL EDITION

ANTIQUE TRADER BOOKS
Antiques & Collectibles
Price Guide

Edited by
Kyle Husfloen

An illustrated comprehensive price guide to the entire field of antiques
and collectibles for the 1998 market

ISBN: 0-930625-13-7
ISSN: 1083-8430

Editor: *Kyle Husfloen*
Editorial Assistants: *Ruth Willis, Pat B. Scott*
Book Designer: *Virginia Hill*
Design Assistants: *Lynn Bradshaw, Aaron Wilbers, Barb Brown,
    Jill Hohmann, Janell Edwards*
Cover Design: *Jaro Sebek*

Cover photo credits:
Front cover: top left to top right: "Big Loo" plastic robot, 1960s, $1,052.00,
    Courtesy of Just Kids Nostalgia; Pennsbury Pottery Red Rooster pattern 10" d.
    plate, $48.00, Courtesy of Susan N. Cox; Hopalong Cassidy plastic radio, 1950s,
    $518.00, Courtesy of Christie's East; Graniteware Emerald Ware coffeepot, 10"
    h., $500.00, Courtesy Jo Allers; Toy windup celluloid Santa with bell, Japan, ca.
    1950s, $75.00. Bottom: Ornately carved Victorian Baroque-Style partner's desk,
    ca. 1880-1900, $6,875.00.

Back cover: Victorian sapphire blue blown glass bowl ornately decorated with overall small enameled floral sprigs, 6 x 9½", 5¼" h., $345.00, Courtesy of Temples
    Antiques, Eden Prairie, Minnesota.

Printed in the United States of America

To order additional copies of this
book or a catalog please contact:

Antique Trader Books
P.O. Box 1050
Dubuque, Iowa 52004
1-800-334-7165

 Antique Trader Books
A division of Landmark Specialty Publications

A WORD TO THE READER

It has been over a quarter of a century since the Antique Trader published its first price guide to the antiques and collectibles field. In 1984 we introduced our new annual edition, the Antiques & Collectibles Price Guide, a comprehensive reference covering all the major fields of collecting.

Since the beginning, each of our annual editions has contained completely new, updated pricing information and over the years we have changed our category listings to more accurately reflect current collecting trends. We continue that tradition with this 1998 edition.

All of the staff of Antique Trader's Antiques & Collectibles Price Guide work diligently to compile and prepare the most accurate, detailed and up-to-date pricing information available. We have also, with this volume, added a number of pricing sections specially prepared for us by expert consultants. We are grateful for their assistance and the added scope of expertise it brings to our guide. You will find their names and addresses listed elsewhere in this book.

Another new feature this year is our "Antiques & Collectibles Market Survey," which we're certain all our readers will find of interest and value. For this initial survey we have asked for the input of four large, well-established antique malls from across the United States. We wanted to see how regional trends in collecting might vary or overlap. In the following pages you'll find information on many of the "hottest" antiques and collectibles as noted in a mall on the West Coast, Midwest, Southeast and Northeast.

In using this price guide we ask you to remember that it should be used as only a guide to evaluating and pricing items. Many factors such as condition, rarity and, of course, regional demand, will play a part in what a piece may bring in your area.

Our Antiques & Collectibles Price Guide follows a basically alphabetical format for most categories. However, we have arranged the larger categories of Ceramics, Furniture and Glassware into their own section where each specific type or maker will be listed alphabetically within that section. Our comprehensive Index at the conclusion of our listings will help you locate specific categories also. Many of our individual categories are provided with a brief introduction to their history and origins and in the Ceramics and Glass sections we also include sketches of many of the markings used on items listed.

Please keep in mind that although our descriptions and prices have been double-checked and every effort has been made to assure accuracy, neither the editor nor publisher can assume responsibility for any losses that might be incurred as a result of consulting this guide, or of errors, typographical or otherwise.

Photographers who have contributed to this issue include: E. A. Babka, East Dubuque, Illinois; Stanley L. Baker, Minneapolis, Minnesota; Donna Bruun, Galena, Illinois; Herman C. Carter, Tulsa, Oklahoma; Robert Cohen, Albertson, New York; J. D. Dalessandro, Cincinnati, Ohio; Bill Freeman, Smyrna, Georgia; Louise Paradis, Sparta, Wisconsin; Joyce Roerig, Waltersboro, South Carolina; Ruth Eaves, Marmora, New Jersey, and Tom Wallace, Chicago, Illinois.

For other photographs, artwork, data or permission to photograph in their shops, we sincerely express appreciation to the following auctioneers, galleries, museums, individuals and shops: Donna Bauerly, Dubuque, Iowa; Bertoia Sales, Vineland, New Jersey; Brown Auctions, Mullinville, Kansas; Burns Auction Service, Bath, New York; Butterfield & Butterfield, San

Francisco, California; The Cedars - Antiques, Aurelia, Iowa; Christie's, New York, New York; Cincinnati Art Galleries, Cincinnati, Ohio; Collector's Auction Services, Oil City, Pennsylvania; Collector's Sales & Services, Middletown, Rhode Island; DeFina Auctions, Austenburg, Ohio; William Doyle Galleries, New York, New York; Garth's Auctions, Inc., Delaware, Ohio; Mary Frank Gaston, Bryan, Texas, Glass-Works Auctions, East Greenville, Pennsylvania; Glick's Antiques, Galena, Illinois; Morton M. Goldberg Auction Galleries, New Orleans, Louisiana; Robert Gordon, San Antonio, Texas; Grunewald Antiques, Hillsborough, North Carolina; and Guyette and Schmidt, West Farmington, Maine.

Also to Vicki Harmon, San Marcos, California, the Gene Harris Antique Auction Center, Marshalltown, Iowa; the late William Heacock, Marietta, Ohio; The House in the Woods Gallery, Eagle, Wisconsin; Leslie Hindman Auctioneers, Chicago, Illinois; Jackson's Auctions, Cedar Falls, Iowa; James Julia, Fairfield, Maine; Agnes Koehn Antiques, Cedar Rapids, Iowa; Peter Kroll, Sun Prairie, Wisconsin; Leland's Sporting Life, New York, New York; Jim Ludescher, Dubuque, Iowa; Joy Luke Gallery, Bloomington, Illinois; Clarence and Betty Maier, Montgomeryville, Pennsylvania; Mastro and Steinbach Auctions, Oak Brook, Illinois; Randall McKee, Kenosha, Wisconsin; McMasters Doll Auctions, Cambridge, Ohio; Dr. James Measell, Berkley, Michigan; North Shore Sports, L.L.C., Northbrook, Illinois; O'Gallerie, Inc., Portland, Oregon; Pacific Glass Auctions, Sacramento, California; Dave Rago Arts & Crafts, Lambertville, New Jersey; Jane Rosenow, Galva, Illinois; Skinner, Inc., Bolton, Massachusetts; Slawinski Auction Company, Felton, California; Sotheby's, New York, New York; Doris Spahn, East Dubuque, Illinois; Stanton's Auctions, Vermontville, Michigan; Michael Strawser, Wolcottville, Indiana; Temples Antiques, Eden Prairie, Minnesota; Treadway Gallery, Cincinnati, Ohio; Lee Vines, Hewlett, New York; Bruce & Vicki Waasdorp, Clarence, New York; Witherell Ent., Healdsburg, California; Wolf's Auctioneers and Appraisers, Cleveland, Ohio; Woody Auctions, Douglass, Kansas; and Yesterday's Treasures, Galena, Illinois.

We hope that everyone who consults our Antiques and Collectibles Price Guide will find it the most thorough, accurate and informative guide on the ever-changing world of collecting.

The staff of Antique Trader's Antiques & Collectibles Price Guide welcomes all letters from readers, especially those of constructive critique, and we make every effort to respond personally.

—Kyle Husfloen, Editor

SPECIAL CATEGORY CONTRIBUTORS

GENERAL CATEGORIES

Bootjacks
Harry A. Zuber
Houston, TX

Bottle Openers
Charles Reynolds
Reynold's Toys
2836 Monroe St.
Falls Church, VA 22042

Bottles
Cecil Munsey
Poway, CA

Cash Registers
William Heuring
Hickory Bend Antiques
2995 Drake Hill Rd.
Jasper, NY 14855

Cat Collectibles
Marilyn Dipboye
33161 Wendy Dr.
Sterling Heights, MI 48310

Christmas Collectibles
Robert Brenner
Princeton, WI

Costume Jewelry
Marion Cohen
P.O. Box 39
Albertson, NY 11507

Currier & Ives Prints
Robert L. Searjeant
Box 23942
Rochester, NY 14692

Kitchenwares
General
Carol Bohn
Don Simmons
KOOKS (Kollectors of Old
Kitchen Stuff)
Mifflinburg, PA 17844

Margaret "Bunny" Upchurch
Boyce, VA

Coffee Mills
Mike White, Editor
The Grinder Finder
2518 County Rd. 5
P.O. Box 483
Fraser, CO 80442

Eggbeaters
Don Thornton
Beat Books
1345 Poplar Ave.
Sunnyvale, CA 94087

Egg Timers, Pie Birds, Sprinkling Bottles & String Holders
Ellen Bercovici
5118 Hampden La.
Bethesda, MD 20814
(301) 652-1140

Irons
Jimmy & Carol Walker
Iron Talk
P.O. Box 68
Waelder, TX 78959-0068

Juice Reamers and Napkin Dolls
Bobbie Zucker Bryson
1 St. Eleanores La.
Tuckahoe, NY 10707
Napkindoll@aol.com

Graniteware
Jo Allers
Cedar Rapids, IA 52410

Nutting Books, Prints & Furniture
Michael Ivankovich Auction Co., Inc.
P.O. Box 2458
Doylestown, PA 18901
(215) 345-6094

Old Magazines, Parrish (Maxfield) & Pin-ups
Denis C. Jackson
P. O. Box 1958
Sequim, WA 98382
(360) 683-2559
ticn@olypen.com

Orientalia
Sandra Andacht
P.O. Box 94
Little Neck, NY 11363
Editor, The Orientalia Journal

Razor Blade Banks
Deborah Gillham
47 Midline Ct.
Gaithersburg, MC 10878
dgillham@erols.com

Sports
Steve Ryan
27 Cameo Dr.
Aliso Viejo, CA 92656

Vending & Gambling Machines
Jack Kelly
(616) 983-0311

CERAMICS

Blue & White Pottery
Stephen E. Stone
18102 East Oxford Dr.
Aurora, CO 80013

Flow Blue & Mulberry
Ellen R. Hill
Mulberry Hill North
P.O. Box 56
Bennington, New Hampshire 03442
(603) 588-4099

Lefton China
Loretta DeLozier
1101 Polk St.
Bedford, IA 50833

Pennsbury Pottery
Susan N. Cox
237 E. Main St.
El Cajon, CA 92020

Red Wing Pottery
Charles W. Casad
801 Tyler Ct.
Monticello, IL 61856

Stoneware
Vicki & Bruce Waasdorp
P.O. Box 434
Clarence, NY 14031

Watt Pottery
Dennis M. Thompson
P.O. Box 26067
Fairview Park, OH 44126

GLASS

American Cameo Pilgrim Glass
The Pilgrim Glass Corp.
P. O. Box 395
Ceredo, WV 25507
(304) 453-3553

Carnival Glass
Edward L. Radcliff
603 Columbia Avenue
Williamstown, WV 26187

ANTIQUES & COLLECTIBLES MARKET SURVEY

featuring
ANTIQUES MALLS ACROSS AMERICA

As a special feature for our readers, this year we are presenting a survey of the most popular antiques and collectibles which have been selling at large, well-established antiques malls across the country.

We asked each mall to provide a listing of the top selling categories they have noted in recent months, together with a price listing of typical examples they have sold. We have even included some photographs of the pieces listed.

Although antiques malls certainly aren't the only major marketplace for buying and selling antiques and collectibles, they do see a great deal of traffic from collectors and dealers, not only from their own area but often from visitors from other regions of the country.

Check out our survey below and see if your favorite category is included. Our special thanks to the four antiques malls who helped us with the survey. So here, from West to East, is our 1998 Malls Across America Antiques & Collectibles Market Survey:

WEST COAST

Vintage Bank Antiques
101 Petaluma Blvd. N
Petaluma, CA 94952
(707) 769-3097
Daily: 10 a.m. to 5:30 p.m.
Owner: Warren Davis
fax: (707) 431-7545

ANTIQUE & COLLECTIBLE GLASS

Fine Moser Vase

Moser vase w/enameled chrysanthemums, shading from emerald green to clear, stems in applied gold, some wear to gold, 15½" h (ILLUS.)............................**$850.00**

Cambridge, signed, 12" Caprice patt., Moonlight Blue **56.00**

Fostoria
June cereal bowl, topaz **39.00**
June center handled tray,
   topaz...**64.00**
Heisey
Signed, Crystolite creamer &
   sugar...**135.00**
Signed, punchbowl, Colony
   patt., 15"......................................**225.00**
Imperial
Candlewick, center-handled
   develed egg server **135.00**
Candlewick, punch set w/cups &
   underplate....................................**275.00**
Candlewick, lemon server.................**40.00**
Sandwich Glass Co., dolphin base
   candlesticks, canary yellow,
   ca. 1850-1870, 10" h., pr...............**1,995.00**

EARLY AMERICANA

Glass dish, blown-three-mold,
   Diamond & Ray patt. (GII),
   ca. 1820-1840, 7" d., 1" h...............**$125.00**

Blue & White spongeware pitcher,
   Diamond & Flower patt.,
   mid-19th c., 9½" h. **325.00**

Tavern table, fruitwood, 18th c.,
   27 x 43"...**1,200.00**

Oil lamps, blue, hand-blown centers,
   mid-19th c., pr. **695.00**

Flex cart, late 19th c., original
   paint **375.00**

Jacquard, blue & white coverlet,
   double woven, wool, ca. 1850..........**450.00**

Mirror, beveled oval, folding-type
   w/fretwork & detailed inlaid
   frame **235.00**

FURNITURE

Ornate Renaissance Revival Table

Dutch kas, ornately carved &
ebonized, original hardware & key,
late 18th-early 19th c.,
80 x 80 x 23" **7,500.00**

**Federal manor chest of four
drawers,** cherry & tiger maple,
ca. 1830, 47 x 43 x 20"...................**1,490.00**

**Victorian Renaissance Revival
substyle table,** marble & walnut,
original base, original finish, possibly
by Thomas Brookes, ca. 1875
(ILLUS.)...**4,500.00**

Jelly cabinet, painted green,
19th c., some peeling **850.00**

Arts & Crafts-style library table,
solid burl redwood, signed "C.L.
Roberts," dated 1914 ....**1,500.00**

Doughbox, pine, red milk paint,
ca. 1880, 16 x 27" **385.00**

Charles X-style chairs, maple
w/inlaid arabesques, ca. 1830,
set of 4 ....**4,900.00**

ORIENTALIA

**Chinese blue & white dragon
design temple jar w/lid,** Qianlong
period, ca. 1800, 11" d., 17" h. **$1,400.00**

Tansu-Somo dansu, 1869, Japan,
Edo period, chest on chest,
Paulownia wood, hand-made
hardware, 17 x 45", 45" h. **1,950.00**

Chinese cloisonné duck, 19th c.,
9" l., 12" h. **425.00**

Japanese inro, lacquered, four-part,
signed, w/netsuke, ca. 1890...........**1,250.00**

**Japanese cloisonné vase w/silver
base,** signed, 19th c., 2"deep,
5½" h. **900.00**

Korean blanket chest, crypomeria
wood w/brass, ca. 1870, 16 x 32",
32" h. **800.00**

PAINTINGS

Fine Wm. Keith Oil Painting

William Keith, oil on canvas, signed
"Portola Valley," dated 1881,
22 x 36" (ILLUS.).......................**$19,500.00**

Mary Deneal Morgan, oil on artist's
board, signed, "Clearing with Oaks,"
in the style of Arthur Mathews,
ca. 1920, 16 x 22" **7,000.00**

Giuseppe Cadenasso, oil on canvas,
signed "Cows in Misty Landscape,"
ca. 1910 ....**12,500.00**

Margaret Bruton, oil on canvas
board, "Acacia," modernist still-life,
1927, 16 x 20" **4,500.00**

S. Kolesnikoff, oil on canvas, signed,
"Russian Church in Village," oval,
4 x 6" **1,450.00**

POTTERY

Roseville "Fuschia" Vase

Bauer oil jars, red-orange color, 22" h., pr. **$1,500.00**

Fulper vase w/handles, ringed & bulbous, 9 x 10" **275.00**

Gladding McBean, large handled oil jar, mottled blue-green, 31" h. **900.00**

Roseville Fuschia patt. vase, two handles, 9½" h. (ILLUS.) **275.00**

Roseville Snowberry patt. vase, 10" h. (chips to base) **95.00**

Weller Lilac patt. vase, unsigned, hand-painted Hudson-type...............**495.00**

Weller Hudson vase, signed "Pillsbury," morning glories, excellent, 9" h. **1,200.00**

MIDWEST

Antique America
1316 E. 9th St.
Davenport, IA 52803
(319) 326-3233
Director: Bill Mergenthal

CHILDREN'S DISHES

Creamer, china, chicken wearing bonnet decoration, Czechoslovakia ..**$60.00**

Creamer, china, children on beach scene decoration, Japan **35.00**

Kitchen set, "Like Mothers," aluminum, by Mirra, in box **165.00**

Tea set, American Maid, Akro Agate Co., in box, service for 4 ....**325.00**

Tea set, Cherry Blossom patt., no box, 14 pieces **275.00**

Tea set, Delphite blue glass, no box, 14 pcs..**325.00**

Tea set, Little Hostess, flowered pattern, Japan, in box, service for 4 ....**95.00**

Tea set, Little Hostess, flowered pattern, Japan, in box, service for 6 ....**65.00**

Tea set, rabbit figures decoration, Japan, in box, service for 3 ....**295.00**

Tea set, woodland scene decoration, marked Noritake, no box, service for 6 ....**275.00**

CLOCKS

Ansonia, large cast-iron mantel clock **$235.00**

Ansonia, statue clock w/fisherman & hunter, Crystal Palace award **695.00**

Ingraham eight-day movement mantel clock **150.00**

Long-drop octagon-style, seconds bit **295.00**

New Haven Clock Company, standing cupid model **135.00**

Novelty clock, boy on top of world **175.00**

Seth Thomas ogee-style case w/columns, reverse-painted door panel, 28" h. **250.00**

Wurttenberg, Germany, one-day movement clock **165.00**

FISHING LURES

Creek Chub Co. Pikie Minnow **$36.00**

Chock Club Injured Minnow...............**24.00**

Heddon Tadpolly Spook.....................**22.00**

Heddon Vamp Spook..........................**30.00**

Kautzy Lazy Ike **15.00**

Pflueger Musky Globe **40.00**

Rascal Brass Spoon **15.00**

Robert's Mud Puppy **42.00**

South Bend Babe-O-Reno (wood).......**10.00**

FURNITURE

Ornate Victorian Barber's Chair

Baker's Cabinet (Hoosier-type), oak, Seller's brand, enameled work surface w/tambour roll door..........**$1,975.00**

Barber's Chair, Victorian, ornately carved oak, new upholstery (ILLUS.)..**998.00**

Bookcase, turn-of-the-century, oak, lawyer stack-type, four sections & base w/drawer, original finish............**900.00**

Pressed-back Oak Side Chair

Chairs, turn-of-the-century, side-type, oak, pressed-back w/rabbits ears, new fiber seats, refinished, set of 4 (ILLUS. of one) **595.00**

Hall seat, turn-of-the-century, oak w/lift seat, fill mirror & hooks **1,150.00**

Music cabinet, early 20th c., oak, plain form w/one door opening to shelves, refinished **200.00**

Plant stand, Mission-style, oak w/long cylindrical wicker basket insert **275.00**

Secretary-bookcase, fall-front-type, turn of the century, drawers below **1,350.00**

Table, square, oak, quarter sawn, five legs, turned & carved **595.00**

Oak Step-back Wall Cupboard

Wall Cupboard, turn-of-the-century, oak, step-back-type, two-piece w/crown, two doors over three drawers & two doors, refinished (ILLUS. bottom previous column)...**1,450.00**

TEDDY BEARS

Brown, jointed, very long nose, 7" **$165.00**

Billiken, mohair, Horsman, ca. 1909, 12" **625.00**

Brown mohair, long arm, long feet, rare, 16" l. **350.00**

Grey mohair, jointed red ears, paws, 15" **175.00**

Pink mohair, straw-stuffed, 12" (worn condition)...**195.00**

Red mohair, electric-eye, 22" (non-working condition) **450.00**

Red mohair, straw-stuffed, 12" **250.00**

Steiff, golden brown, straw-stuffed, 10" **300.00**

Steiff, "Lotty," mohair, w/collar, ca. 1960s...**195.00**

TOYS

Mickey Mouse ice skates **$225.00**

Lewis Mark windup tank, w/recoil cannon **259.00**

Buddy L firetruck, wooden ladder......**198.00**

Buddy L Army supply truck **165.00**

Hubley cast-iron motorcycle cop, 3½" **125.00**

Line Mar windup Donald Duck drummer..**595.00**

Unique art windup tin "Rodeo Joe" **345.00**

Windup robot, Japan, ca. 1960, 5" h. **195.00**

Murray peddle car, restored............**1,150.00**

SOUTHEAST

The Gas Works Antique Mall
818 N. McKenzie
Foley, AL 36535
(205) 943-5555
Manager: Rita McNair

BLUE RIDGE POTTERY
Chocolate Pot, cov. **$145.00**
Cup, "Darcy" patt. **7.00**

Cup & Saucer, "Stanhome Ivy" patt. **8.00**
Plate, "Crab Apple" patt., 9½" d. **15.00**
Plate, "Falling Leaves" patt., 10¼" d. **13.00**
Plate, "Spray" patt., 6" d. **7.00**
Platter, "Poinsettia" patt., 11" d. **38.00**
Saucer, "Crab Apple" patt.....................**7.00**

COCA-COLA
Bingo card, Florence Bottling Plant,
1941 ....**$40.00**
Bottle, Alabama National Champs,
1992 ....**7.00**
Bottle, Bear Bryant...............................**8.00**
Bottle, brown....................................**50.00**
Bottle, Disney World 25th Anniversary ...**5.00**
Bottle, 1996 Olympics...........................**7.00**
Cooler, chest, 1950s **165.00**
Jug, syrup, clear glass, 1960s..............**15.00**
Ornament, Christmas, 1963.................**10.00**

FURNITURE
Armoire, Acadian pine, double door,
early 1800s...............................**$2,250.00**
Bed, double, four-poster canopy,
mahogany, 1920s...........................**850.00**
Bench, hired man's, mahogany,
w/settle end, early 1800s, 8' l. **2,200.00**
Center table, piecrust edge, carved
Queen Anne legs **450.00**
Couch, Victorian Rococo substyle,
medallion back, mahogany,
mid-19th c. **1,200.00**
Desk, S-curve oak roll-top, seven
drawers, turn-of-the century **1,800.00**
Parlor set, four pieces, shells &
pearls, Fantasy Furniture, silver on
gesso, the set................................**5,500.00**
Pie safe, ten punched-tin panels,
dated 1883 ....**425.00**
Server, oak, Empire Revival, early
20th c. **495.00**
Sideboard, Gothic Revival, flame
mahogany **1,250.00**
Washstand, walnut, black marble top,
dated 1815, Austrian **1,300.00**

FOSTORIA
Bowl, Baroque patt., clear.................**$32.00**
Candy, cov., Coin patt., amber.............**38.00**
Creamer, Coin patt., amber..................**18.00**

Goblet, American patt. **12.00**
Pitcher, single-serving size, American
patt. **35.00**
Punch bowl on pedestal base,
12 cups, American patt. **560.00**
Sandwich tray, Colony patt., clear,
12½"...**38.00**
Sugar, cov., American patt., 6¼" h........**47.00**

MAJOLICA

Etruscan Majolica Leaf Dish

Figural busts, man & woman, 6" h.,
pr. (man as-is) **$275.00**
Figural, Gypsy (chip on nose) **95.00**
Leaf dish, Etruscan line, ca. 1880s
(ILLUS.)...**150.00**
Leaf dish, early 1900s (some chips) **65.00**
Pitcher, w/birds, nest & twig handle,
8" h..**275.00**
Pitcher, corn design, 12" h. **375.00**
Wine jug, fish figural............................**85.00**
Umbrella stand, h.p. flowers in
panels..**700.00**

MCCOY POTTERY
Ashtray, pink bird on blue flower.........**$15.00**
Cache pot, green, 1948 ....**42.00**
Creamer, "Ivy" patt., 1925 ....**25.00**
Mixing bowl, brown, 8" d. **18.00**
Model of a deer, pink...........................**18.00**
Novelty dish w/bird, blue, 1950 ....**33.00**
Planter, figural turtle **24.00**
Planter, model of a spinning wheel,
1953 ....**32.00**
Shoe, Mary Ann, blue, 1941 ....**20.00**
Vase, rustic, greens & browns, 1943.....**33.00**

MILITARIA
Badge, WWI, shipbuilders' **$78.00**
Bars, captain's, sterling, pair **20.00**

Belt, web w/brass buckle, WWII **12.00**
Broach, Bronze Star, WWII...................**32.00**
Pin, British Aid, WWII **22.00**
Pin, Naval, WWII **20.00**

PATTERN GLASS

Liberty Bell Signer's Platter

Bread tray, Liberty Bell patt.,
Signer's-type (ILLUS.) **$45.00**
Cake stand, U.S. Coin patt. w/clear
coins, 10" d......................................**275.00**
Spooner, Fan & Bubble patt..................**35.00**
Spooner, Grasshopper patt...................**65.00**
Spooner, Persian patt. **32.00**
Spooner, Pressed Leaf patt. **38.00**

ROSEVILLE POTTERY
Apple Blossom patt. teapot,
No. 371P **$350.00**
Columbine patt. vase, blue,
No. 655-4" **115.00**
Dahlrose patt. vase, slimform, angled
handles..**250.00**
Donatello patt bowl.............................**65.00**
Freesia patt. bowl, blue, No. 464-6"...**160.00**
Iris patt. bowl, brown, No. 360-6".......**175.00**
Magnolia patt. ewer, No. 13-6" **125.00**
Peony patt. ashtray, No. 27 ....**155.00**
Pine Cone patt. match holder, blue ..**325.00**
Silhouette patt. vase, green, 12" h. ...**165.00**
Velmoss patt. vase, green, 12½" h. ...**175.00**

NORTHEAST

Old Glory Antique Marketplace
5862 Urbana Pike
Frederick, MD 21704
(301) 662-9173
e-mail: oldglory@fred.net
Manager: Janice Cooney

ADVERTISING ITEMS
Beer tray, round, picture of lady
holding beer wearing green dress on
blue background, "Ortlieb's,"
11½" d. **$100.00**
Box, wooden w/label, Borden
Condensed Milk, 13 x 20" **43.00**
Clock, electric, reads "Drink Coca-
Cola," tin, brown & red w/gold
numbers, 18" d. **140.00**
Sign, tin, "Enjoy Grapette," green &
orange, 27" oval..................................**80.00**

Old Coca-Cola Vending Machine

Vending machine, Coca-Cola,
10 cent bottle-type, red & white,
reads "Drink Coca-Cola," 32 x 63"
(ILLUS.)..**795.00**

DEPRESSION-ERA GLASS
Bowl, Fostoria, footed, pink,
1928-1944 ....**$60.00**
Cup & saucer, Horseshoe patt.
(#612), green, Indiana Glass Co. **12.00**
Plate, Jane Ray patt., Anchor Hocking
1945-1963, Jadite green, 9" d. **8.00**
Platter, Bubble patt., Anchor Hocking
1940-1965, blue **16.00**
Punch set: 15 cups & ladle; Fostoria
American, crystal, 1915-1986,
the set **295.00**

FURNITURE, MAHOGANY
Beds, twin size, low-poster, pineapple
finials, pr...**$545.00**
Buffet, brass pulls, Hepplewhite-Style,
5' l...**595.00**

Corner cupboard, curved front, two
glass doors, one drawer, two door
cabinet at bottom, 3' w. **975.00**

Desk, slant-front, four drawers, ball &
claw feet, Maddox **275.00**

Highboy, Queen Anne-Style, bonnet
top-type, eleven drawers, 5' 5" h. **775.00**

LIONEL TRAINS & ACCESSORIES

Lionel Train Engine GG1

Catalog, 1957, paper, 7½ x 11" **$17.00**

Flattop train car, red, transporting
brown & white boat, cat. no. 6511.......**65.00**

Town station, painted tin, cream,
green & yellow w/red roof, No. 137 ...**110.00**

Train engine, GG1, metal, green, five
stripes in gold, cat. no. 2330
(ILLUS.)...**790.00**

Transformer, RW, 110 watt, original
in box...**95.00**

MCCOY POTTERY

Bowl, glossy green, old stoneware
mark (shield in circle), #4 large size,
11¼" d...**$72.00**

Cookie jar, black & cream kitty on
basket, marked, 10" h. **126.00**

Flowerpot, w/saucer, green, diamond
w/leaves design, marked, 6" h. **25.00**

McCoy Figural Planter

Planter, double figural, two flowers
cups in two tones of green w/black
& white bird, marked, 1949
(ILLUS.)...**54.00**

Vase, soft blue matte finish, marked,
9¼" h. **39.00**

PRIMITIVES

Bench, mortised, construction, old
paint, 4' l. **$118.00**

Birdhouse, Adirondack-type,
w/chimney **150.00**

Bowl, dough-type, hand-hewn,
16 x 23"..**265.00**

Cupboard, two door, green paint,
36" w., 17" deep, 5' h. **748.00**

Pie safe, blue paint on white wood,
diamond & circle tin panels, 31" w.,
14¼" deep, 4' 8½" h. **750.00**

ROSEVILLE POTTERY

Bowl, Florentine patt., earthtones,
"RV" ink stamp, 1924-28, 9" h. **$80.00**

Double cornucopia, Bushberry patt.,
green w/rust berries, matte finish,
marked in relief, 1948, No. 155-8".....**134.00**

Vase, Dahlrose patt., light brown
w/cream flowers, green leaves,
black paper label, 1924-28...............**257.00**

Vase, Primrose patt., blue w/white
flowers, matte finish, marked in
relief, 1930, No. 767-8" **190.00**

STERLING SILVER

Sterling Candlesticks

Candlesticks, simple etched design,
by Albert J. Gannon, Philadelphia,
Pennsylvania, 1907-1986, the set
(ILLUS.)...**$295.00**

Dresser set: eight pieces including
three brushes, comb, button hook,
nail file & shoehorn; ca. 1915,
the set **250.00**

Mustard pot, cov., cobalt glass insert,
Birmingham, England hallmark,
1946-47 ....**169.00**

Tablespoon, Gorham, Lancaster
patt. **79.00**

Thimble, plain.....................................**19.00**

ADVERTISING ITEMS

Thousands of objects made in various materials, some intended as gifts with purchases, others used for display or given away for publicity are now being collected. Also see various other categories.

Sinclair Dino Ashtray

Advertisement, "A & P Baking Powder," colorful street scene outside the Great Atlantic & Pacific Tea Co., w/three inset images of a package of backing powder, a woman baking bread, & a Mammy, all of this above "The Above Picture Shows - The Great Demand - For A & P Baking Powder - At The Atlantic & Pacific Tea Co.'s Stores - A Want Long Felt Supplied At Last - By A & P Baking Powder - Everybody Wants It.," 6½ x 8½" (bent corner tips, minor soiling) **$94.00**

Advertisement, "Climax Coffee," paper, lithographed, reads "No Better Coffee - At Any Price - Ask the Clerk - Climax Coffee - Sold Only in Sealed Cartons," to the left of a package of coffee, done in red, yellow, black & white, 39½ x 54" (folds, tears & soiling) **121.00**

Advertisement, "Empress Chocolate," celluloid, multicolor full-length portrait of a queen in robe, in gold-painted frame, 16 x 20" (minor paint chipping) **358.00**

Advertisement, "Our Trademark Ham," paper, shaped like a packaged ham w/shield-shaped label reads "Our - Trademark - Ham - F.A. Ferris & Co. - New York," text on reverse, 2¾" w., 4½" h. (creases & soiling)............**11.00**

Ashtray, "Sinclair Gas," chromed metal, long shallow oblong dish w/a narrow center raised platform supporting a full-figure dinosaur above the embossed wording "Go Dino," ca. 1950s-60s, scratches, 7" l., 2" h. (ILLUS.) **77.00**

Bank, "Amoco," commemorative, Model T, for 100th anniversary, w/original box marked "100th - Anniversary - Commemorative - Edition - 1917 Model T Bank," 3 x 6", 3½" h. (box w/soiling) **39.00**

Bank, "Ralston Cereal," Batman bank, box not opened, 1989........**20.00**

Baseball, "Skelly," styrofoam **25.00**

Blotter, "Badger Tires," full-color printed cardboard, a large tire & red innertube in the foreground w/a large factory in the background all on a medium blue ground w/a black border, printed "Badger - Double Duty Tire - Winning With Quality," 3½" w., 6" h. (edge wear) **17.00**

Blotter, "Gulf Supreme Motor Oil," cardboard, rectangular, a full-color scene of boys iceskating in the foreground w/a 1920s touring car in the background, a large orange circle overprinted in black w/"Supreme Motor Oil" in the upper left w/small white lettering across the bottom "Smooth Running - Low Cold Test - Gulf Refining Company," 6¼" l., 3" h. **55.00**

Blotter, "Kellogg's Toasted Corn Flakes," cardboard, image of young boy holding spoon sitting in front of bowl to the left of "Kellogg's - The Original - Toasted Corn Flakes - The Best Liked - Cereal - Always Light, Dainty - and Appetizing in Flavor - W.K. Kellogg - Look For This Signature" w/box of Corn Flakes to the right, done in blue, green, red & black, 3 x 5½" (corner crease) **28.00**

Blotter, "Morse & Rogers Shoes," celluloid button & cloth, a central button w/a yellow ground printed in black w/"Morse & Rogers Shoes for Men, Women & Children - All Leather for All Weather," button framed by in inner ring of deep red cloth & an outer ring of black cloth, 3¼" d. **17.00**

Sunoco Gas Blotter

Blotter, "Sunoco Gasoline," rectangular, printed in color at one end w/a man filling a car w/gas, on the left side a large billboard reading "Only ONE Quality - Blue Sunoco - No Second Grade - No Third Grade," printed small advertising for a Philadelphia firm below, 9" l., 4" h. (ILLUS.).....................**61.00**

Box, "Barnum's Animal Crackers," cardboard, w/colorful images of different animals in cages, w/"Barnum's Animals" above, w/shoestring handle, 3 x 5" **22.00**

Bottle carrier, "Pepsi-Cola," wood & pressed board, narrow oval form w/upright sides & wide carrying strap, black ground, the front w/white stripes behind a white oval w/red lettering reading "Drink Pepsi-Cola," 19" l., 6" h. (scratches, soiling, scuffs) **193.00**

Bottle opener, "Canada Dry," wall-mount style, painted cast iron, curved top flange w/raised red-painted wording "Canada Dry," rounded backplate w/holes

for mounting, lower flange impressed "Starr x Brown Co." 2¾" w., 3¼" h. (scratches, soiling, paint wear) **55.00**

Bottle opener, "Dr. Pepper," flat metal hand-held style, long handle in the form of the bottle w/the prying end in the form of a lion's head w/open jaws, the incised w/wording "Dr. Pepper....," by Crown T & D Co. Chicago, Ill., 3" l. (scratches, soiling & rust on chain) **94.00**

Bottle opener, "Dr. Pepper," wall-mount style, painted cast iron, curved top flange w/raised red wording "Drink Dr. Pepper," rounded backplate w/holes for mounting, 2¾" w., 3¼" h. (scratches, soiling, paint chipping) **66.00**

Bottle opener, "Royal Crown Cola," wall-mount style, painted cast iron, curved top flange w/raised red-painted wording "Drink Royal Crown Cola," rounded backplate w/holes for mounting, 2¾" w., 3¼" h. (scratches, soiling, paint wear) **66.00**

Brochure, "Columbia Bicycles," paper, colorful Art Nouveau-style lithographed cover, top w/swirls above image of classically dressed woman w/arm raised kneeling by bicycle below "Columbia," flanked by Greek-style columns, all above "The Pope Manufacturing Co. - Westfield, Mass.," ca. 1915, 24 pgs., 7¼ x 8¾" (creases, minor soiling) **61.00**

Brochure, "Harley-Davidson," paper, colorful lithographed cover scene of motorcycle & sidecar driving by tent & trees, upper right corner reads "1923 - Harley-Davidson - Motorcycles - and Sidecars," lower left corner reads "The - Open Road - Calls You!," 12 pgs., 8 x 9¼" (crease down middle) **83.00**

Brochure, "Singer," paper, black & white lithographed image of two women dressed in 19th c. clothing standing by a sewing machine looking at a picture on the wall, marked "The Singer Manu'f'g. - Co.'s - Exhibit Of - Family Sewing Machines and - Art - Embroidery - Liberal Arts - Building - North Gallery.," & "World's Columbian Exhibition - Chicago 1893." across bottom, 4¼ x 5¼" (minor soiling) **39.00**

Hood's 1892 Calendar

Calendar, 1892, "Hood's Sarsaparilla," color lithographed paper, a round disc w/a ring of charming children shown sewing around the border framing the center full calendar pad, titled at the base "The Sewing Circle," printed Hood's advertising & date at the top, soiling, 6¾" d. (ILLUS.) **110.00**

Calendar, 1936, "Louella Butter," color lithographed paper, the large top panel w/a oval reserve showing a young girl in a yellow dress holding the collar of a brown & white calf, the reserve flanked by small pictures of the product w/a landscape scene w/cows below, the large complete calendar pad

1938 Richfield Calendar

below printed in black & red on white, 12" w., 25" h. **44.00**

Calendar, 1938, "Richfield," cardboard, rectangular, the upper half printed to resemble a brown & white frame surrounding a black & white photograph of a Richfield truck above printed advertising for "Newcomer's Service Stations," the red, black & white complete calendar pad below, w/a series of compartments for bills, soiling, rough edges, 10½" w., 14½" h. (ILLUS.) **83.00**

Calendar, 1947, "Bear Wheel Alining," die-cut color paper, a standing yellow bear smiling & holding a complete calendar pad for 1947, a narrow rectangular deep red panel across the bottom w/advertising for "Collier Body & Paint Co....," soiling, creased ear, 3½" w., 6" h. (ILLUS. top next page) **33.00**

Chair, "Cross-Cut Cigarettes," wooden, folding-type, the back w/a colored bust portrait of a young woman, the reverse

1947 Bear Calendar

Pepsi-Cola Chalkboard

showing a packet of the cigarettes, late 19th - early 20th c. **275.00**

Chair, "Piedmont Cigarettes," wooden, folding-type, the back w/a a dark blue porcelain panel printed in white "Smoke - Piedmont - 'The Cigarette of Quality'," (chipping, small piece of wood missing on back) **209.00**

Chalkboard, "Pepsi-Cola," painted tin, rectangular w/rounded corners painted to resemble an old-fashioned school slateboard, red & black string-wrapped printed border around printed wooden frame, rectangular panel at the top printed in black, red & white "Drink - Pepsi-Cola - Bigger-Better" above the rectangular chalkboard area, soiling, scratches, denting, paint chipping, 19½" w., 30" h. (ILLUS. top next column) **275.00**

American Express Wall Clock

Clock, "American Express," electric light-up wall-type, plastic & metal, a blue, red & white metal rectangular case w/a plastic face w/Arabic numerals, advertising in the lower half reads "American Express Money Orders - Since 1882," some paint chippings & minor scratches, 13½" w., 24½" h. (ILLUS. bottom previous page) **83.00**

Clock, "Campbell Soup," kitchen-type, w/Campbell Soup Kids, made by New Haven Clock Co., 1987 .... **25.00**

Clock, "Dr. Pepper," electric lighted wall-type, plastic w/a metal back, modeled as a large bottle cap, white w/ black Arabic numerals except oversized red numbers "10," "2" & "4," wide red center band w/"Dr. Pepper" in large white letters, 11½" d. (scratches, soiling) **149.00**

Fisk Tire Clock

Clock, "Fisk Tires," electric wall-type, round black rubber tire frame surround the round center dial w/Arabic numerals & a small orange toddler & tire logo framed by the words "Time To Retire - Buy Fisk" in black, soiling, 7" d. (ILLUS.) **176.00**

Clock, "Forst's Foremost Franks," electric wall-type, reverse-painted glass face w/Arabic numerals & reads "Forst's - Foremost - Franks" in red & black on white ground, made by Pam Clock Co., Inc., New Rochelle, New York, 15" d. (metal band on outside of clock repainted, paint chips) **121.00**

Clock, "Kendall Oil," electric neon wall-type w/spinner, metal & glass, black tire-form outer frame around a white band w/Arabic numerals around a red inner circle w/a white hand logo & wording "Kendall - the 2000 Mile Oil," lights white, 22" d. (soiling, paint loss, rust & paint chipping to glass front) **660.00**

Clock, "NuGrape Soda," salesman's sample, electric wall-mount style, metal & glass, rectangular metal frame w/domed glass front, white dial printed w/red Arabic numerals & a large red bottle behind an orange & red oval printed "NuGrape Soda," sweep seconds hand, Swinhart Products - USA - Indiana, 2¾ x 6½", 8" h. (scratches, fading) **149.00**

Clock, "Pepsi-Cola," plastic, electric wall-type, square face w/clear plastic cover, cover w/Pepsi logo & Arabic numerals, 17 x 47" (wear to number, scratches to edges) **303.00**

Clock, "Pontiac," electric countertop-type, round painted tire-form metal frame w/a center round metal white dial w/Arabic numerals & a large red Pontiac Indian chief logo across the center, sweep seconds hand, glass front, chip at top glass front, soiling, paint chipping, new wire & plug, 21" d. **1,430.00**

Valvoline Motor Oil Clock

Clock, "Valvoline Motor Oil,"
electric neon wall-type, metal &
glass, octagonal outer frame
around a wide yellow band
w/delicate white lined designs
encircling the black round dial
w/white Arabic numerals, hands
& sweep seconds hands, yellow
lettering reads "ask for
VALVOLINE Motor Oil," some
peeling to outside glass border
decal, works, 18" w., 18" h.
(ILLUS.) **660.00**

Wear-Ever Frying Pan Clock

Clock, "Wear-Ever," electric wall-
type, metal, model of a frying
pan w/the dial w/Arabic
numerals in the center, working,
8½" d., 14¾" h. (ILLUS. bottom
previous column) **88.00**

Early Pepsi-Cola Cooler

Cooler, "Pepsi-Cola," store-type,
painted wood w/a tin sign &
cast-iron bottle opener, the large
rectangular case w/a hinged lid
raised on four tall slender
square legs, the rectangular tin
sign on the front reads "Drink
Pepsi-Cola 5¢ - Refreshing and
Healthful" in red & black on
white, worn silvered paint, early,
rust, scratches & dents to sign,
edge wear & soiling on cooler,
rust to hinges, 19 x 35½", 32" h.
(ILLUS.) **396.00**

Cooler, "Whistle," picnic-type,
painted metal, a red rectangular
container w/rounded corners & a
lift-off top, double wire swing bail
handles & latch closure, the side
w/a large decal w/a white dot
showing an elf pushing a
handcart w/a bottle of Whistle
soda, printed in black, white &
red across the top "Thirsty? Just
- Whistle," made by the
Progress Refrigerator Co.,
Louisville, KY, 8 x 17½", 11¾" h.
(scratches, soiling, paint
chipping & rust) **176.00**

Counter display, "Armor Plate Hosiery," die-cut cardboard, cut-out image of man in suit of armor in front of circle, outside of circle reads "Armor - Plate - Hosiery," bottom reads "Des Moines Hosiery Mills - Des Moines, Iowa, U.S.A.," done in blue, yellow, black, grey & red, 3½ x 5¾" **33.00**

Counter display, "Bickmore's Gall Cure," color-printed die-cut cardboard, three-fold, the large center panel w/a bust portrait of a smiling man w/his horse above a red rectangular panel reading "Bickmore's Gall Cure - Be Sure and Work the Horse - For Wounds and Sores Upon Animals," the narrower side wings w/rounded top corners printed w/color scenes, one of a horse-drawn wagon in town & the other w/a farmer w/cows in a pasture, further advertising printed in each wing, 50" w., 33" h. (scratches, repair to ears of center horse, tears at folds)..**275.00**

Blony Gum Display Truck

Counter display, "Blony Gum," cardboard w/wooden wheels, model of an angular pick-up truck printed in red, yellow, blue & white, the cab showing a boy, girl & dog, the side of the cab door reading "Biggest Piece of gun in the World for a Penny,"

the bed of the truck printed in red, yellow & blue w/"Blows Bigger Bubbles - Blony," creases, soiling, tears, 13½" l., 8" h. (ILLUS.)............................**385.00**

Keen Kutter Cutlery Display

Counter display, "Keen Kutter Cutlery," a shallow hinged wooden box holding six knives & six forks, the inside of the lid w/a colorful label centered by the "E.C. Simmons Keen Kutter Cutlery" logo in red, white & yellow again a pale yellowish ground, cutlery somewhat tarnished, the set (ILLUS.) **121.00**

Counter display, "Maytag," composition, figure of the Maytag Man standing w/one hand on a washing machine, the other hand on his cheek, cone in white, red, blue & grey, all on a wood block, 6 x 7½", 10" h. (minor soiling & chipping, plaque from wood block missing) **209.00**

Counter display, "No-Tair Hair Net," tin, tiered rack, front marked "Perfect Hair Nets, - No-Tair Guaranteed - Perfect Hair Nets," black, 7 x 18", 9" h. (Dents to sides) **50.00**

Counter display, "Sherwin-Williams," top w/semi-circle w/scene of old convertible above "Sherwin-Williams" flanked by logos, above "Auto Enamels," all above various paint samples, 12 x 16" (soiling, scratches & paint chips) **220.00**

Counter display, "Winchester Batteries," cardboard box, top flap reads "Sight Test Top - Winchester" above gun above image of globe all above "Leakproof," of w/Winchester logo flanked by "If It's Blue - .....It's New" & "Exclusive - Sight-Test Top," done in red, yellow & blue, together w/pack of D batteries, 5½ x 10", 8" h. (soiling & edge wear)................**303.00**

Counter display, "Wrigley's," lithographed paper over cardboard, reads "Use Daily-Insure Attractive Smile - Sweet Inoffensive Breath-Millions Do" above arrow marked "Healthful Refreshing Delicious - Wrigley's" arrow points toward stylized image of smiling woman, 9 x 12", 6½" h. (minor wear) **215.00**

Counter display case, "Beeman's Pepsin Gum," wooden frame w/glass top & two sides, rectangular, deep wooden base w/shallow display case, front glass panel w/decal showing a large red dot behind a large black & white pack of gum, 20½" sq., 11¾" h. (overall minor wear, decal w/chipping & loose pieces) **231.00**

Counter display figure, electric company, "Reddy Kilowatt," die-cut cardboard, printed in red & cream, 8½" w., 10" h. (scratches, soiling, thumbtack & nail marks)..**127.00**

Counter display globe, "Blake's Milk and Cream," milk white glass, model of a large bottle of milk, the front printed in red & black w/"We Sell- Blake's - Milk and Cream - 'Better Milk For Particular People'," scratches, some minor soiling, 7½" d.,20" h. (ILLUS. top next column) **1,100.00**

Blake's Milk Globe

Counter display jar, "Planters 5¢ Peanuts," clear glass w/cover, six-sided, embossed across the top "Planters" above a panel embossed w/"Pennant 5¢ Salted Peanuts," alternating panels w/an embossed figure of Mr. Peanut, Dutch girl decal on one side, very minor edge cracks, 8" w., 12" h. (ILLUS. top next page) **94.00**

Counter display rack, "Packard Battery Cables," metal, black rectangular ground w/yellow wording w/a yellow curved upper border w/black working, an applied paper label showing the sizes available along the bottom edge, center reads "Genuine Packard Korelug Battery Cables - S.A.E. and Car Equipment Standard," outer border reads

Planters Peanuts Jar

Ovens Bakery Crate

U.S. Baking co. - Crackers,
Cakes, Biscuits - Buffalo, NY,"
wording overprints on designs of
flowers & wheat w/a small round
reserve at the center showing a
buffalo head, narrow end panels
w/the black ground printed
w/tiny round reserves against
tall leafy flowering branches,
scratches, soiling, tears, pieces
of label missing, lid missing,
14 x 21", 10" h. (ILLUS.)............**303.00**

Doll, "Gerber," stuffed cloth,
image of Gerber Baby on cloth,
done in blue, yellow & white,
8" h. (minor soiling)..................**220.00**

Door push, "Crescent Flour," tin,
embossed & painted in cream
"Push - and - Try A Sack - of"
above image of sack of flour
w/Crescent logo on it, above
"Crescent - Flour - Sold Here,"
all on blue ground, 3¾ x 9½"
(nail hole at top).......................**440.00**

Door push, "Dr. Caldwell's Syrup
Pepsin," porcelain, rectangular,
top has yellow rectangle that
reads "Push" in black letters
above "You Can Depend On" in
yellow, all above yellow shield
marked "Dr. Caldwell's - Syrup -
Pepsin - The - Family Laxative"
in black all on black ground, 3¾
x 6½" (scratches & chipping).....**231.00**

Door push, "Junge's Bread,"
porcelain, blue lettering reads
"Junge's - Bread - For Better
Health" on yellowish green
ground, 3¾ x 9¼" (minor
chipping & crazing).....................**66.00**

"Faster Cranking Speeds -
Quicker Starts," 20" l., 8" h.
(scratches, soiling) **110.00**

Counter display stand, "Canada
Dry," metal, green three-tier,
tiers read "Canada Dry," "Pale
Ginger Ale" & "Chlemsford" in
black on cream ground, 17 x
24", 43" h. (scratches & minor
surface rust) **61.00**

Crate, "Dwinell-Wright Co.
Coffee," wood w/paper label,
reads "Most Modern - and
Complete - Coffee Roasted -
Establishment - In The World"
above image of the factory, all
above "Dwinell-Wright -
Company - Boston - Chicago,"
accented by twigs w/leaves &
berries, 16 x 15", 20" h. **242.00**

Crate, "R. Ovens Branch Cakes -
Crackers - Biscuits," wooden
w/paper labels, rectangular, the
colorful front label w/a large
rectangular reserve w/a black
background printed w/wording in
white "The R. Ovens Branch

Door push, "Salada Tea," metal, red lettering reads "Delicious 'Salada' Tea Flavor" on yellow ground w/black ends, reverse reads "Thank You - Call Again," 3 x 32" (minor wear, soiling on reverse) **66.00**

Door push, "Sunbeam Bread," porcelain, dark blue ground printed w/small red words "Reach for" & large white words "Sunbeam Bread," 26½" l., 2¾" h. **110.00**

Fan, "Peters Shoes," cardboard, decorated w/Art Deco-style lady **55.00**

Fan, "Royal Crown Cola," cardboard w/image of Shirley Temple **55.00**

Fan, "Worcester Salt," cardboard folding-type w/flat wooden stick handle, deeply creased folds forming a round fan in white printed w/black advertising, framed, 9½" w., 12½" h. (creases, soiling & edge wear) **33.00**

Flour sack, "Sleepy Eye Flour," cloth, long narrow white sack printed in red, yellow & black w/the wording "Sleepy Eye Flour - A Mark of Quality - Sleepy eye Milling Co., Sleepy Eye Minn.," color bust portrait of Chief Sleepy Eye at the center, 16 x 36" (soiling, some fading) ..**231.00**

Socony Fly Swatter

Fly swatter, "Socony Kerosene Oil," long wire loop handle w/a wire mesh blade w/a vinyl edge, printed advertising at the base of the blade in white & blue on red, scratches, soiling, rust & some edge wear, 3" w., 17" l. (ILLUS.) **132.00**

Handbook, "Harley-Davidson," black drawing of man driving motorcycle w/sidecar, above "Harley-Davidson - Rider's Hand Book" above Harley-Davidson logo, above "Harley-Davidson Motor Co. - Milwaukee, Wis., U.S.A. - 74 train Model," all on yellow ground, 40 pgs., 4¾ x 6¾" (crease down middle)..........**55.00**

Keychain, "Texaco," bronzed metal, round, relief-cast w/two Scottie dogs in a listening pose w/the Texaco star logo beside them & "Listen" embossed at the bottom, marked on back "A.E. Co., Utica, NY," 1" d. (soiling)......**44.00**

Letter opener, "Uneeda Bisquits," die-cut metal figure holding a box of Uneeda Bisquits above blade, done in red, black, gold, yellow & silver, 1½" w., 8¼" h. (paint ships & scratches, minor surface rust) **66.00**

Map, "Greyhound," paper, colorful lithograph of map of the United States showing Greyhound routes, dated November 1, 1934, 20 x 30½" (some wear to edges, minor soiling) **44.00**

Menu chalkboard, "Kayo Chocolate Drink," painted tin, rectangular, a yellow rectangular panel at the top printed w/a portrait of Kayo & a bottle of the product flanking the red & blue wording "Tops in Taste - Kayo - It's REAL Chocolate Flavor," the lower portion in black w/the small white wording at the top "Specials Today," scratches, soiling, denting, 13½" w., 27" h. (ILLUS. top next column)...........**110.00**

Kayo Menu Chalkboard

Mug, "Hilliard Oil & Gas," clear glass, footed cylindrical form w/long squared handle, the side etched w/lettering & a scene of an oil derrick, 5½" h. (scratches) ..**55.00**

Pencil, "Lion Head Motor Oil," mechanical-type, plastic, white ground w/black "Lion Head" wording flanking the orange lion head logo, a calendar around the lower end in black & orange, 5¾" l. **72.00**

Pillow, "Alka-Seltzer," box-shaped......................................**98.00**

Pin, "Welch's Grape Juice," celluloid on metal, in the shape of a bunch of grapes centered w/bottle of grape juice below "Welch's," ½ x ¾" **110.00**

Pinback button, "Berry Brothers Varnish," celluloid over metal, centered w/image of can of varnish, rim reads "Berry Brothers - Varnishes," done in red, orange, black & grey, ¾" d. (minor scratches)......................**22.00**

Pinback button, "Bill Dugan Cigar," celluloid over metal, colorful bust portrait of Bill Dugan below "Bill Dugan Cigar.," top half of rim w/stars on blue ground, bottom of rim w/red & white stripes, ¾" d. (minor soiling) **55.00**

Pinback button, "Domestic Vacuum Sweeper Company," celluloid over metal, w/image of woman demonstrating vacuum flanked by "217 Masonic - Temple" & "Peoria - Ill.," reads "Domestic - Vacuum Sweeper Company," done in blue, yellow, red, brown, black & orange, 1¼" d. (minor scratches) **44.00**

Pinback button, "Liquozone," celluloid over metal, shows two children flanking a bottle of Liquozone, flanked by "Gives - Life" and above "Destroys Disease Germs," all below "Liquozone," rim decorated w/stars & stripes, done in red, white, blue, gold & green, 1¼" d. (reverse w/rust) **50.00**

Pinback button, "National Lead Co.," celluloid over metal, centered w/seated boy w/paint bucket & brush, rim reads "I Am A White-Leader - National Lead Co.," done in yellow, red, blue, brown & black, ¾" d. (minor soiling) **44.00**

Pinback button, "Sharples Tubular Cream Separator," celluloid over metal, centered w/image of woman using separator above "The Tubular Cream Separator," rim reads " 'Different From The Others' - The Sharples Co. Chicago, Ill. - P.M. Sharples West Chester, PA.," 1½" d. (minor water stain)......................................**50.00**

Pinback button, "Worchester Salt," celluloid over metal, w/image of bag of salt in front of factory, reads "Worchester Salt" at top & "The Standard For Quality" at bottom, done in blue, cream & black, 1½" d. (crazing) ..**33.00**

Plate, "Ford," china, round w/flanged rim, black on white, the rim printed w/"Ford," the center w/a round vignette building scene, base marked "Shenango China New Castle, Pa.," 9⅛" d. (scratches, minor wear) **50.00**

Pocket watch, "Harley-Davidson Motor Cycles," open-faced w/embossed metal frame & top winding stem, white dial w/Arabic numerals & the company logo in black & orange, seconds dial, w/a blue, gold & red fob, overall 7" l. (not working, new stem & fob) **264.00**

Puzzle, "Hoods," 'Rainy Day & Balloon,' reversible, one side full-color, ca. 1890s, complete in original box **150.00**

Radio, "Abbotware," figural cast metal, a model of a standing horse w/copper-overlaid mane, hooves, tail & edge of the low rectangular radio base w/dials, minor scratches, saddle & bridle missing, working, 5 x 12½", 14" h. (ILLUS. top next column).....................................**176.00**

Abbotware Horse Radio

Recipe booklet, "Elsie the Cow," 1948 ....**18.00**

Rug, "Red Goose Shoes," cloth, rectangular w/a yellow border band around the olive green center w/two red & yellow geese marked "Red Goose Shoes" flanking central yellow wording "Half The Fun of Having Feet," minor soiling & wear, 27½ x 60" (ILLUS. below)..........................**413.00**

Safety marker, "Grapette," sidewalk-type, painted metal, round w/embossed lettering reading "Enjoy - Grapette - Walk

Red Goose Shoes Rug

Grapette Safety Marker

Safely," worn gold paint, soiling, crack at registered trademark symbol, 4" d. (ILLUS.) **28.00**

Service pin, "Esso," silvered metal & enamel, a rectangular narrow frame around space to insert name tag, the top edge w/a long oval impressed w"Esso" enameled in red above "Service" enameled in black, incised fanned trim, 1½" l., 2¼" h. **303.00**

Store bin, "Dayton Spice Mills," wooden, tall rectangular crate w/a slanted lift-lid, nailed construction, old worn surface w/traces of several colors of paint, black stenciled label on the front "Dayton Spice Mills - Company's - Choice - Roasted Coffee," late 19th - early 20th c., 24" h. **116.00**

Store display globe, "Fellow - Society of American Florists," hanging-type, metal w/glass lenses, the wide dark round metal frame w/a rolled tab hanger at the top encloses milk white glass lenses printed w/a large black diamond w/a horizontal red center band printed in white "Say it with Flowers" overprinted on a stylized oblong yellow vase printed in black w/"Fellow -

Society of American Florists," 16½" d. (scratches to body & lens, soiling, paint loss & rust to frame) **550.00**

Store display rack, "Quaker Oats," metal, a tall metal lattice rack w/solid metal open shelves, a narrow rectangular metal sign at the top printed in color w/a red long narrow oval printed w/"Quaker Oaks Quality Products," black background w/yellow wording above & below oval reading "The Best Cereal Foods - Alternate to Suit Your Taste," an oval reserve at each end of the sign showing a color portrait of the standing Quaker man, early, 28" w., 5' 10" h. (scratches, soiling, paint loss) ...**715.00**

Straight razor & pouch, "Gargoyle Marine Oils," folding-type w/creamy celluloid handle & steel blade, leather pouch printed w/"Vacuum Oil Company - Oils That Lubricate Most," 6" l., 2 pcs. (soiling, rust to pouch) **259.00**

Rare King Midas String Holder

String holder, "King Midas Flour," painted tin & metal, two-sided, a rectangular metal sheet w/an arched cut-out center supporting the tall roll of string, printed in orange blue & white, advertising reads "Buy King Midas - The Highest Priced - Flour - in America" & "Worth All It Costs," a small circle at one side reads "It's A Thirsty Flour," minor scratches & some surface rust, 15" w., 20" h. (ILLUS.) **1,540.00**

Thermometer, "Carter White Lead Paint," porcelain, rectangular, reads "Carter White Lead" in red above "The All Weather - Paint" in black above thermometer, below is an image of black paint can below banner, can marked "Carter - Strictly - Pure - White Lead" in white, banner reads " 'Save the surface and - you save all'," all on white ground, 7¼ x 27½" (minor chipping) **22.00**

Thermometer, "Ex-Lax," porcelain, rectangular, reads "Ex-Lax - the - chocolated - laxative" above thermometer, all above "millions - prefer - Ex-Lax," done in orange, white, blue & black, 8 x 36" (minor chips) **220.00**

Thermometer, "Hills Bros. Coffee," porcelain, tall rectangular form w/a rounded top, red ground w/a yellow-garbed Arab man drinking a cup of coffee beside the thermometer, printed in white lettering at the bottom "Hills Bros. Coffee," scratches, 8½" w., 21" h. (ILLUS. top next column) **550.00**

Thermometer, "Jaeger Butter Tub Co.," tin, round, painted "Established 1888 - Jaeger - Butter Tub Company, Inc. - Manufacturer - Butter Tubs" above image of factory, above "Where 'Jaeger Quality' Tubs are Made - Dyersville, Iowa," to the right of thermometer, done in

Hills Bros. Coffee Thermometer

blue, red, orange & black, 9" d. (minor soiling & scratches) **44.00**

Thermometer, "Prestone Anti-Freeze," porcelain, long slightly tapering rectangle w/stepped edges, a black trapezoid at the top w/white lettering "Prestone Anti-Freeze" above the thermometer, a raised red oval near the base w/white lettering reads "You're Safe and You Know It," 9" w., 36" h. (chipping, water stain, white paint drops).....**94.00**

Thermometer, "Raybestos Brake Lining," painted metal, rectangular, yellow, red, black, white & blue, a yellow ground w/a red panel at the top w/white lettering "Check Brakes!" above the thermometer & a small comic figure of a stout man wearing a checked jacket above a black panel showing a colored box of the product & wording "Reline with Raybestos - America's Biggest Selling Brake Lining," 9½" w., 30½" h. (scratches, paint chipping, denting, edge rust) **121.00**

Thermometer, "Vernor's Ginger Ale," round, w/image of a winking leprechaun above dial, all above "Drink - Vernor's - Ginger Ale," on half green, half yellow ground, green side marked "Serve Hot in Cold Weather" & yellow side marked "Serve Cold in Hot Weather," 12" d. (thermometer broken, edge & back has rust) **88.00**

Thermometer, "Wishing Well Soda," self-framed tin, long rectangular form w/a rounded top, bright yellow ground printed in large black & red letters at the top "Drink - Wishing Well Orange" above the thermometer w/an orange & black bottle of the product against a large black dot at the bottom, ca. 1961, 10½" w., 40½" h. (minor scratches) **215.00**

Tie Bar, electric company, metal, w/figural "Reddy Kilowat".............**35.00**

Watch, "Harley-Davidson," rounded sides w/impressed decoration, dial w/Arabic numerals, second hand dial & Harley-Davidson logo, black leather band, Elgin, face 1¼ x 1½" (minor wear to edges) **660.00**

Knox Gasoline Water Set

Water or lemonade set, "Knox Gasoline," consisting of a frosted glass pitcher & eight tumblers each w/a different color scene of a Native American, all fitted into rectangular wooden tray w/raised end handles, the tray also w/Native American designs, a 1957 promotional set, artwork by Ace Blue Eagle, tray 7½ x 27", the set (ILLUS.) **165.00**

ARCHITECTURAL ITEMS

In recent years the growing interest in and support for historic preservation has spawned a greater appreciation of the fine architectural elements which were an integral part of early buildings, both public and private. Where, in decades past, structures might be razed and doors, fireplace mantels, windows, etc., hauled to the dump, today all interior and exterior details from unrestorable buildings are salvaged to be offered to home restorers, museums and even builders who want to include a bit of history in a new construction project.

Building finial, copper, a slender shaft decorated w/large looping scrolls below a crown-form ring centers by for curved ball-tipped arms centering a tall pole w/a knob finial, 19th c., 7' 8" h. (ILLUS. bottom next page) ...**$3,450.00**

Building grate, exterior-type, cast iron, rectangular w/a pierced rectilinear design, brown paint finish, designed by George Washington Maher, from Rockledge, early 20th c., 14 x 48" **99.00**

Door knob plates, cast iron, oblong flattened form w/three intersecting circular designs w/the initials "CSEB," designed by Louis Sullivan for the Chicago Stock Exchange Building, 3 x 9", pr. **275.00**

Fireplace mantel, painted wood, Federal style, the rectangular molded shelf above a cove-molded edge over a central

Early Painted Mantel

American Building Finial

painted panel depicting a landscape scene flanked by grey-painted pilasters, possibly New York, ca. 1830, 62" w., 4' 3" h. (ILLUS.) **805.00**

Fireplace mantel, painted pine, Federal style, the reverse-breakfronted mantel above a conformingly-shaped & paneled frieze, on molded, raised-panel stiles, ca. 1810, 81" w., 5' 1" h. (paint flaking, central tablet once fitted w/an ornament).................**690.00**

Louvres, painted wood, a demi-lune frame enclosing angled, fanned slats, painted yellow, Midwest, late 19th c., 40" w., 22" h., pr. **690.00**

Register cover, interior, metal, a square composed of nine hinged segments each w/a Greek key design, designed by George Washington Maher, from Rockledge, probably done after

Fine Federal Fan Light

a remodeling, early 20th c.,
30 x 36" **110.00**

Window, Federal fan-light type,
white-painted pine, tole & cast
lead, the demi-lune frame fitted
w/glazed panels secured by tole
dividers mounted w/lead
rosettes, pineapples, acorns &
oak leaves, the lower section
mounted w/a central eagle
w/outspread wings, New
England, ca. 1800, bottom board
replaced, 33½" w., 11" h.
(ILLUS.) **3,162.00**

Windows, leaded glass, Prairie
School-style, rectangular, a
central geometric design in
amber, green & frosted clear
glass, surrounded by clear glass
set in brass caming, early 20th
c., 16 x 45", pr. (some breaks in
caming, new frame)..................**440.00**

ART DECO

Interest in Art Deco, a name given an art movement stemming from the Paris International Exhibition of 1925, continues to grow today. This style flowered in the 1930s and actually continued into the 1940s. A mood of flippancy is found in its varied characteristics - zigzag lines resembling the lightning bolt, sometimes steps, often the use of sharply contrasting colors such as black and white and others. Look for prices for the
best examples of Art Deco design to continue to rise. Also see JEWELRY, MODERN.

Bar set, an open chrome rotating
framework in a cylindrical form
w/a central double bar rack
supporting four tapering
cylindrical clear glass cocktail
glasses, 20" l., 4" h., the set **$88.00**

Carpet, handwoven wool,
rectangular, an abstract design
of rust bars & angles on a cream
field, 55 x 76"............................**385.00**

Clock, mantel, 'telechron,' upright
rectangular case of chrome
w/radiating alternating bands of
colored enamel on the top &
sides, polished & brush-
burnished gold & silver face
w/Arabic numerals, designed by
Paul Frankl, ca. 1929, 3 x 5",
8" h. (cord replaced) **468.00**

Lamp, table, bronze & shell, a
figure of a woman, nude except
for a beaded girdle, standing on
one leg w/the other raised
ahead of her & her arms raised
above her head holding a metal
frame supporting a large spiral
shell shade, the figure raised on
a stepped cylindrical black onyx
base, Germany, 4"d., 19" h. **770.00**

Lamp, table, wrought iron, the
hammered shade & base in the
form of a series of graduated

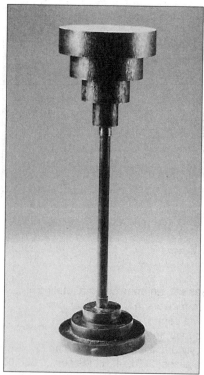

Wrought-iron Art Deco Lamp

Bronze Art Deco Wall Mirror

concentric discs conjoined by a rod standard, France, ca. 1925, 37" h. (ILLUS.)......................**2,300.00**

Mirror, hand-held, nephrite & coral, circular outline set w/carved & pierced jade plaque accented by coral & black enamel w/a black silk tassel **575.00**

Mirror, wall-type, hammered bronze, the arching frame wrought w/a flower-filled urn & scrolling leafage, grapes & stylized eagle heads w/open beaks, the lower border w/a scallop shell & scrolling leafage, impressed "Oscar Bach," ca. 1925, 30" w., 4' 8¼" h. (ILLUS. top next column)........**2,875.00**

Pen & pencil set, fountain-type, in yellow gold (14k), one w/seal, signed "Cartier".......................**1,725.00**

Plaque, rectangular, carved bronze decoration of leaves &

flowers on both sides, 11½" x 14½" (some discoloration).........**413.00**

Torchere, miniature, chrome, a triple-tiered trumpet-form top on a slender stem to a tall pedestal w/three graduated discs above the ringed disc foot, alternating black & chrome decoration & a chrome base, ca. 1930s, 6"d., 19" h. **495.00**

Tray, rectangular, a metal frame w/a raised thin bar gallery on posts & hinged end handles w/black wood grips, tray of reverse-painted glass decorated in green, black & white w/a random geometric arrangement of arcs, bars, & overlapping circles, 12 x 19" **330.00**

ART NOUVEAU

Art Nouveau's primary thrust was between 1890 and 1905 but commercial Art Nouveau productions continued until about World War l. This style was a rebellion against historic tradition in art. Using natural forms as inspiration, it is primarily characterized by undulating or wave-like

*lines and whiplashes. Many objects were
made in materials ranging from glass to
metals. Figural pieces w/seductive maidens
with long, flowing hair are especially popular
in this style. Interest in Art Nouveau remains
high with the best pieces by well known
designers bringing strong prices. Also see
JEWELRY, ANTIQUE.*

Dish, gilt-metal, figural, scalloped
shallow flower-form cast in the
center w/a female bust & flowers
amid gently swirling waters,
inscribed "Compliments of - The
Cincinnati Aluminum Casting
Co. - Cincinnati, O.," ca. 1900,
5½" d. **$690.00**

Figural Art Nouveau Shell Dish

Dish, carved ivory, bronze &
abalone, the wide oblong shell
mounted on one edge w/a
figural mermaid & seaweed cast
in bronze w/a carved ivory head
& upper torso, ca. 1900, 9½" w.,
(ILLUS.) **3,450.00**

Fireplace surround, stoneware,
in three sections; a central
section cast w/a female masque
w/Medusa-like hair, flanked on
either side w/flowing stylized
leafage, glazed in shades of
white, orange, green & yellow,
restorations, probably by Xavier
Schoellkopf, ca. 1902, 9½ x 52",
46" h. (ILLUS. top next
column)..................................**5,750.00**

Art Nouveau Stoneware Mantel

Inkwell, metal w/glass insert,
depicts young woman reading
book on base, ornate floral
design.......................................**180.00**

Tea tray, brass-mounted curly
maple & mahogany marquetry,
oval, the foliate-cast gilt-metal
frame w/pointed end handles &
pairs of curved & pointed leaves
overlapping the tray of inlaid
mahogany w/stylized flowers &
whiplash leafage, by Maurice
Dufrene, France, ca. 1900,
22" l. **5,175.00**

Art Nouveau Bronze Vase

Vase, bronze, figural, squatty
cushion base w/tapering
cylindrical sides & an uneven

rim, cast w/stylized nudes & flowers in swirling water in high-relief around the sides & rim, after a model by Maurice Bouval, incised artist's signature & impressed "The Henry-Bonnard Bronze Co. Founders, N.Y. 1900, No. 2," ca. 1900, patina loss, varnished, 9" d., 8½" h. (ILLUS.)..........................**863.00**

Vase, pottery, figural, large flaring cylindrical form molded in full-relief at opposite sides of the rim w/busts of Art Nouveau maidens, the flowing tresses forming the rim & continuing down the sides, integral lower loop handles ending in swirling scrolls continuing around the lobed foot, molded leaf & blossom trim, cream matte glaze w/orange highlights, Northwestern Terra Cotta Company, Chicago, Illinois, marked "Norweta," ca. 1900, 16" w., 20" h. **1,320.00**

AUDUBON PRINTS

John James Audubon, American ornithologist and artist, is considered the finest nature artist in history. About 1820 he conceived the idea of having a full color book published portraying every known species of American bird in its natural habitat. He spent years in the wilderness capturing their beauty in vivid color only to have great difficulty finding a publisher. In 1826 he visited England, received immediate acclaim, and selected Robert Havell as his engraver. "Birds of America," when completed, consisted of four volumes of 435 individual plates, double-elephant folio size, which are a combination of aquatint, etching and line engraving. W. H. Lizars of Edinburgh engraved the first ten plates of this four volume series. These were later retouched by Havell who produced the complete set between 1827 and early 1839. In the 1840s, another definitive work, "Viviparous Quadrupeds of North America," containing 150 plates, was published in America. Prices for Audubon's original

double-elephant folio size prints are very high and beyond the means of the average collector. Subsequent editions of "Birds of America," especially the chromolithographs done by Julius Bien in New York (1859-60) and the smaller octavo (7 x 10 1/2") edition of prints done by J.T. Bowen of Philadelphia in the 1840s , are those that are most frequently offered for sale.

Anyone interested in Audubon prints needs to be aware that many photographically-produced copies of the prints have been issued during this century for use on calendars or as decorative accessories so it is best to check with a print expert before spending a large sum on an Audubon purported to be from an early edition.

American Crossbill - Plate CXCVII, hand-colored engraving by Robert Havell, Jr., London, 1827-38, framed, 21¼ x 26½" **$1,092.00**

American Flamingo - Plate CCCCXXXI, hand-colored engraving by Robert Havell, Jr., London, 1827-38, 25¼ x 38⅛" (few spots of foxing, tiny skinned area, faint discoloration, few tiny losses at extreme edges, repaired tear in left corner, stitch holes on disbound edge) **46,000.00**

American Green Winged Teal - Plate CCXXVIII, hand-colored engraving by Robert Havell, Jr., London, 1827-38, 26⅝ x 39⅛" (tiny spots of foxing, minor margin discoloration, few small tears & losses at edges).........**5,750.00**

American Ptarmigan and White-tailed Grous - Plate CCCXVIII, hand-colored engraving by Robert Havell, Jr., London, 1827-38, framed, 17½ x 24" (creasing) **1,380.00**

American Snipe - Plate CCXLIII, hand-colored engraving by Robert Havell, Jr., London, 1827-38, 24⅞ x 37½" (faint mat stain, small printer's crease, few fox marks & slight edge staining).................................**4,312.00**

Rare Eider Duck Print

Black American Wolf - Plate LXVII, hand-colored lithograph by J.T. Bowen, Philadelphia, 1845, framed, 20 x 26" (few fox marks, faint water staining, small tear in lower edge, discoloration & few tiny losses in extreme edges) **1,380.00**

Canada Goose - Plate CCI, hand-colored engraving by Robert Havell, Jr., London, 1827-38, framed, 26½ x 39½" (minor soiling & discoloration in margins, tiny back tears & edge losses) **21,850.00**

Canada Lynx - Plate XVI, hand-color lithograph by J.T. Bowen, Philadelphia, ca. 1843, framed, 19⅞ x 26" (minor foxing & soiling, three short backed tears in top edge, discoloration & tiny loss on edges) **3,335.00**

Chestnut-backed Titmouse. Black-capt Titmouse. Chestnut-crowned Titmouse - Plate CCCLIII, hand-colored engraving by Robert Havell, Jr., London, 1827-38, 25¼ x 38" (minor foxing, tape staining, faint discoloration, few repaired tears in edges, trimmed unevenly along disbound edge) **1,955.00**

Common American Skunk - Plate XLII, hand-colored lithograph by J.T. Bowen, Philadelphia, ca. 1845, framed, 19¾ x 25¾" (unobtrusive creasing)....................................**920.00**

Eider Duck - Plate CCXLVI, hand-colored engraving by Robert Havell, Jr., London, 1827-38, occasional foxing, few tiny abrasions, minor edge soiling & discoloration, small loss at extreme lower edge, framed, 25¼ x 38⅛" (ILLUS.) **12,650.00**

Gadwell Duck - Plate CCCXLVIII, hand-colored engraving by Robert Havell, Jr., London, 1827-38, 27 x 39¾" (few spots of foxing, minor margin discoloration & tears)..**4,600.00**

Glossy Ibis - Plate CCCLXXXVII, hand-colored engraving by Robert Havell, Jr., London,

1827-38, framed, 26⅝ x 39⅜"
(very faint mat stain, minor
soiling & discoloration in edges,
two small holes at bottom
edge) **7,475.00**

Great Auk - Plate CCCXLI, hand-
colored engraving by Robert
Havell, Jr., London, 1827-38,
framed, 25 x 37½" **4,370.00**

**Hutchin's Barnacle Goose -
Plate CCLXXVII,** hand-colored
engraving by Robert Havell, Jr.,
London, 1827-38, 25¼ x 37¾",
framed **3,162.00**

**Maria's Woodpecker. Three-
toed Woodpecker. Phillips'
Woodpecker. Canadian
Woodpecker. Harris's
Woodpecker. Audubon's
Woodpecker. - Plate
CCCCXVII,** hand-colored
engraving by Robert Havell, Jr.,
London, 1827-38, framed, 25⅜ x
37⅞" (faint off-print, minor
discoloration on edges, stitch
holes along disbound edge) ...**3,737.00**

Mocking Bird (The) - Plate 21,
hand-colored engraving by

The Mocking Bird

Robert Havell, Jr., London,
1827-38, framed, slightly
darkened paper, minor soiling,
repaired & other tears, 26⅜ x
39" (ILLUS.).........................**14,950.00**

Musk Ox Males - Plate CXI,
hand-colored lithograph by J.T.
Bowen, Philadelphia, ca. 1845,
framed, 20¾ x 26¾" (mat
staining, unobtrusive creasing)..**863.00**

Passenger Pigeon

Passenger Pigeon - Plate 62,
hand-colored engraving by
Robert Havell, Jr., London, 1827-
38, faint mat stain, light margin
discoloration, small tear at left
edge, framed, 26¼ x 38⅞"
(ILLUS.) **11,500.00**

**Pinnated Grouse - Plate
CLXXXVI,** hand-colored
engraving by Robert Havell, Jr.,
London, 1827-38, framed, 25¼ x
36⅝" (faint spots of foxing, laid
down)....................................**6,900.00**

Raccoon - Plate LXI, hand-
colored lithograph by J.T.
Bowen, Philadelphia, 1845,
framed, 20 x 26" (minor foxing &
soiling in margins, crease & pin
holes in upper left, backed tear &
pin holes in upper right,
discoloration & tiny tears &
losses in edges) **5,175.00**

**Republican or Cliff Swallow -
Plate 68,** hand-colored
engraving by Robert Havell, Jr.,
London, 1827-38, 26¼ x 39¼"
(mat stain, minor soiling, tape
stain, tears & horizontal
crease)....................................**1,265.00**

**Ruby-Throated Humming Bird -
Plate XLVII,** hand-colored
engraving by Robert Havell, Jr.,
London, 1827-38, minor
discoloration, stitch holes on
disbound edge, framed, 25⅝ x
38⅛" **10,925.00**

Sanderling - Plate CCXXX, hand-
colored engraving by Robert
Havell, Jr., London, 1827-38,
25⅝ x 38¼" (few tiny fox marks,
minor soiling, stitch holes & small
disbound edge, faint off-print).....**805.00**

Says Least Shrew - Plate LXX,
hand-colored lithograph by J.T.
Bowen, Philadelphia, ca. 1845,
matted, unframed, 21½ x 27¼"
(unobtrusive handling marks,
foxing).......................................**230.00**

**Sharp-shined Hawk - Plate
CCCLXXIV,** hand-colored
engraving by Robert Havell, Jr.,
London, 1827-38, framed, 25½ x
38⅛" (faint mat stain &
discoloration in margins, few fox
marks, stitch holes & tiny tears
along disbound edge).............**1,150.00**

Song Sparrow - Plate 25, hand-
colored engraving by Robert
Havell, Jr., London, 1827-38,
26¼ x 37⅝" (few fox marks,
tears & losses at edges, tape
stains) **920.00**

**Trumpeter Swan - Plate
CCCCVI,** hand-colored
engraving by Robert Havell, Jr.,
London, 1827-38, 26 x 38⅞"
(slight discoloration, few fox
marks, tiny repaired tear in
upper edge, minor soiling &
discoloration in extreme edges,
stitch holes on disbound
edge) **37,375.00**

**White-Fronted Goose - Plate
CCLXXXVI,** hand-colored
engraving by Robert Havell, Jr.,
London, 1827-38, framed, 25⅛ x
37¾" (spots of foxing, pinholes
in top corners, discoloration &
few tiny tears & losses on
edges) **6,325.00**

White-Headed Eagle ,
chromolithograph by J. Bien,
New York, 1860, framed, 25⅝ x
38⅞" (light stain, water staining,
small tear in lower edges, tape
stains along edges on verso,
small paper label on verso) **747.00**

Winter Hawk - Plate 71, hand-
colored engraving by Robert
Havell, Jr., London, 1827-38,
framed, 25 x 37⅞ (overall
foxing, short creases, lower
water stains) **4,312.00**

**Worm Eating Warbler - Plate
XXXIV,** hand-colored engraving
by Robert Havell, Jr., London,
1827-38, 25⅜ x 37⅞" (minor
foxing, discoloration & tiny
losses to edges) **1,495.00**

AUTOGRAPHS

*Value of autographs and autographed
letters depend on such factors as content,
scarcity and the fame of the writer. Values of
good autograph material continue to rise.
A.L.S. stands for "autographed letter signed,
L.S. for "letter signed," D.S. for "document
signed," and S.P. for "signed photograph."*

Barnum, Phineas T. (1810-91),
American showman, signed on
ruled paper "London Feb. 7
1890 Truly yours, P.T. Barnum,"
fold lines, 2½ x 4½" **$176.00**

Barton, Clara (1821-1912),
founder of the American Red
Cross, one-page typed poem,
signed "Sister Clara,"
ca. 1905..................................**275.00**

Burr, Aaron (1756-1836), Vice-
President of the United States,

part of an 1819 document w/light signature, plus an engraved portrait, 2 pcs.............................**352.00**

Davis, Jefferson (1808-89), President of the Confederacy, LS, U.S. War Dept., Aug. 6, 1856, lengthy inscription, fold lines **770.00**

Dickens, Charles (1812-70), English writer, signed "Faithfully yours, Charles Dickens, Tremont House, Boston, Fourth February 1842," on a small sheet w/an embossed painted flower, framed, sheet 4¾ x 6¾" **110.00**

Doubleday, Abner (1819-93), purported inventor of baseball, signed note w/real photograph **2,150.00**

Dumas, Alexander (1802-70), French writer, a note in French describing his feelings on the marriage of his daughter, framed, 7 x 8½" **138.00**

Garfield, James A. (1831-81) President of the United States, ALS, letter dated 1880 on Committee of Ways and Means, House of Representatives stationery, signed "J.A. Garfield," fold lines **275.00**

Grant, Ulysses S. (1822-85), Union General & President of the United States, signed card ..**495.00**

Grant, Ulysses S. (1822-85), Union General & President of the United States, S.P. **2,000.00**

Hancock, John (1737-93), Revolutionary War leaders & Signer of the Declaration of Independence, DS, Revolutionary War part-printed document as President of the Continental Congress, appointment of John Justice as "Ensign of a company of foot in the Eleventh Pennsylvania Regiment," dated May 10, 1777, bold signature, light stains on

folds, remnants of tape stain, archivally-backed....................**4,950.00**

Howe, Julia Ward (1819-1910), author of "The Battle Hymn of the Republic," note on slip of paper inscribed "I did not write 'Columbia' I did write the 'Battle Hymn of the Republic'," signed "J.W. Howe," remnants of mounting tissue on two corners, 2 x 4" **275.00**

Jay, John (1745-1829), early American Statesman & First Chief Justice of the Supreme Court, ALS, one-page letter written to a Mrs. Izard dated Paris, May 8, 1783, while Jay was one of the Commissioners negotiating an end to the American Revolution, some bleeding, minor staining, framed w/a portrait..............................**1,100.00**

Lee, Robert E. (1807-70), Confederate General, S.P. **3,950.00**

Longstreet, James (1821-1909), Confederate General, signed check **475.00**

Nixon, Richard M. (1913-1994), Vice President & President of the United States, signed "Best wishes from Dick Nixon" on front free end paper of book Nixon by Ralph deToledano, 1st edition, 1956, foxing on spine, no dust jacket, plus 5 x 7" photo of Nixon shaking hands w/supporter, 2 pcs. **99.00**

Roosevelt, Franklin D. (1882-1945), President of the United States, signed book, Records of the Town of Hyde Park, Dutchess County, NY, 1928, signed on front free end-paper "No. 45 of 100 copies Franklin D. Roosevelt - Hyde Park, 1928," faded spine, slightly shaken **1,045.00**

Sherman, William Tecumseh (1820-91), Union General, L.S. **900.00**

Twain, Mark (Samuel Clemens), (1835-1910), American author & humorist, card signed "Yours truly, Mark Twain, Apl. 1880," very slight smudging **385.00**

Washington, Booker T. (1856-1915), American black leader & founder of the Tuskegee Institute, 1907 letter signed on Tuskegee Institute stationery, a lengthy thank you for a $100 donation, one inch left margin tear **176.00**

Wharton, Edith (1862-1937), American author, L.S. **650.00**

Whitman, Walt (1819-92), American poet, photograph of Whitman seated at a table leaning on one arm, signed in lower right "Walt Whitman born May 31, 1819," mount imprinted "Photo'd from life, Sept., '72, Brooklyn N.Y. by G.F.E. Pearsall, Fulton St." (printed by C.F. Spieler, Phila.), image size 4 x 6" **540.00**

AUTOMOTIVE COLLECTIBLES

Anti-freeze advertising kit, contains a large metal rectangular sign in yellow, black & white w/a black panel at the top w/yellow & white wording "Super Pyro Anti-Freeze," the long lower section w/a yellow background w/a long stick & a round dial-form thermometer w/two measuring charts at one side & at the bottom center, a narrow black band at the bottom w/white wording "No Boil-Away....," also includes posters, banners, etc., in original box, 17½ x 34", the set (ILLUS. of part, top next column) **$468.00**

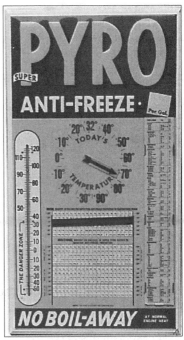

Pyro Anti-Freeze Kit

Blanket, flannel, rectangular, printed w/a full-color service station scene, ca. 1950s, w/the wording in red across the top "Remember When?," ca. 1970s, 44½ x 68" (soiling) **60.00**

Blotter, "Kelly Springfield Tires," cardboard, rectangular, printed in full color w/a nighttime scene of a yellow 1920s sedan racing past the silhouette of a broken-down auto against a dark blue sky w/large orange full moon & green clouds, a large image of the tire on the left side, yellow wording on the right "Kelly Springfield Tires," Maine dealer's name & address printed in black at the bottom, 3¼ x 6¼" **50.00**

Blotter, "Parkway Ford," paper, colorful lithograph of 1920s woman to the left of "It pays to 'Patronize the Parkway' - Sales

Ford Service" above written advertisement above "1065 Wisconsin Ave. West 163 - Washington D.C. - One Half Block Below 'M' Street," 3¼ x 6" (minor soiling) **55.00**

Blotter, "Tydol Veedol Service Station," paper, rectangular, white ground printed in color w/a large bust portrait of a flapper-type young lady wearing a white hat & jacket & yellow scarf & gloves & holding a steering wheel, black & red wording "A Swell Date ...to Change to VEEDOL Motor Oil," printed along the bottom edge "Tydol - Veedol Service Station - Sixth & Union Streets, Allentown, Pa.," 3½ x 6" (soiling)..........................**50.00**

Bottle carrier, "Veedol Motor Oil," wire, rectangular wire framework w/a center upright handle w/handgrip, holds eight clear glass quart bottles, seven w/white, black & red applied "Veedol Motor Oil" labels & screw-on pointed metal spout lids, eighth an Amoco bottle, carrier 8 x 17", 14" h., the set (soiling, rust, pieces of labels missing) **468.00**

Calendar, 1908, "Holsman Automobiles," paper cardboard, printed in dark green, orange & black on white, the top w/a large running red-costumed elf beside sections of advertising reading "Holsman Automobiles - 'The Buggy Kind' - They Set the Pace and KEEP IT UP" above the name & address of the Rochester, New York dealer, printed along the bottom of the upper page " 'Get A Flying Start To-day,' " long rectangular full bottom calendar pad printed in white on black, 7" w., 9¾" h. (scratches, fading) **231.00**

Change purse, model of a chauffeur's hat, leather & silvered metal, the leather cap fitted w/a metal rim w/visor & a disc cover embossed w/an early autoing scene, marked "Islip, NY," 3" d. (scratches, soiling) **72.00**

Concept car model, carved wood w/metal bumpers & rubber tires, two-tone sedan in red over white paint w/streamlined mid-1950s design, marked on the bottom "4496 Mich.," paint chipping, cracking paint & wood, 6½ x 17", 3½" h. (ILLUS.)..........**275.00**

Costume, nylon & metal framework, life-sized "Michelin Man," white fabric, consists of pants, top, sash, head & boots, complete (ILLUS. bottom next page) **990.00**

1950s Concept Car Model

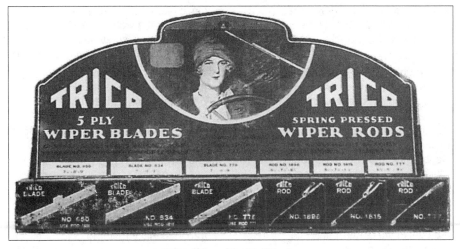

Trico Wiper Blades Display

Michelin Man Costume

Counter display, "Gulf Solar Heat," cardboard cut-out, colorful lithographed bird w/large bill wearing top hat & shorts w/suspenders & a bow tie, hat marked "Gulf - Solar Heat," legs marked "T Plan," bottom half of bill marked "No Large Bills," bill

opens & closes, 5½" w., 8" h. (minor creases) **61.00**

Counter display, "Schrader Tire Gauge," metal, cylindrical model of a tire gauge printed in red w/black wording "Schrader Tire Gauge" & black & white images of gauges, the top rim tapering slightly to a short black cylinder printed w/white gauge numbers, inside w/ "Schrader Gauge box, Cornell - GMC - Schrader & Allstate Valve Cores," 6" d., 15" h. (scratches, soiling, paint chipping, denting, fading & rust) **308.00**

Counter display, "Trico Wiper Blades," painted metal, high stepped & arched backplate w/a central color vignette of a 1920s lady driving a car above a wide red panels printed w/white wording on each end "Trico 5 Ply wiper Blades...," above a row of boxes of the various blades, scratches, soiling, paint chipping, 18¼" l., 10" h. (ILLUS.) **990.00**

Counter display case, "Goodyear," glass top w/open front & wood base, framed in metal, front reads "Insure

Against Delay - Goodyear - Tire Accessories," 20 x 23" (some scratches & wear).....................**165.00**

Fan, "Skelly," cardboard, colorful lithograph of Skelly gas station at intersection w/two cars & a stoplight, holder reads "Go With" above Skelly logo above "Quality Has No Substitute," reverse reads "Dodge City Cooperative - Oil Dept. - Dodge City, Kansas," 8½ x 13" (minor soiling & creasing) **242.00**

Flag, "Indianapolis Speedway," cloth, black & white check w/a red oval in the center printed in white w/"Indianapolis Speedway" centered by a black & white racing car, 17½" sq. (soiling) **149.00**

Game, "Red Crown Gasoline," cardboard, 1937 ....**65.00**

Gasoline pump globe, "American Gas," glass, black metal band surrounding blue lens w/red center, outside of lens marked "American - Gas," 13½" d. (paint loss to metal band, minor fading, soiling, minor chipping to base) **231.00**

Gasoline pump globe, "Amoco," glass, black metal bands surrounding red lens w/black center stripe marked "Amoco" in white, 13½" d. (chip & scratches to base, scratches) **353.00**

Gasoline pump globe, "Coreco Gas," three-piece glass, round white framed enclosing a single lens w/a yellow background printed in large red letters "Coreco Gas" & centered by a Pennsylvania-shaped logo in black printed in white "Established 1885," 13½" d. (scratches & soiling) **605.00**

Gasoline pump globe, "Crescent," red metal frame around a yellow lens printed w/black lettering "Crescent

Gasoline" w/fanned thin red lines over the wording, 15" d. (only one lens, scratches to lens & paint chips to frame).......**660.00**

Gasoline pump globe, "Esso," glass, oval, centered by "Esso - Extra" in blue & red, 20" d., 15" h. (chips at base, soiling, fading, paint loss) **385.00**

Gasoline pump globe, "Gulf Gasoline," round one-piece milk white glass w/raised lettering, printed w/red borders enclosing the black words "That Good Gulf Gasoline" (professionally restored, scratches) **770.00**

Gasoline pump globe, "Hancock Cock O The Walk," black metal round high profile body w/milk glass lenses printed black wording "Hancock" across the top & "Cock O The Walk" across the bottom, a large red & black strutting rooster in the center, 15" d. (reverse lens cracked)..**3,025.00**

Gasoline pump globe, "Johnson Time Tells Gasolene," round black metal high profile body, glass lenses printed w/an outer orange ring around a black ring printed in white w/"Johnson Gasolene" flanking a central black, white & orange hourglass w/white wings printed in black "Time Tells," 15" d. **3,300.00**

Gasoline pump globe, "Marathon," round green metal high profile body, milk glass lenses printed w/an orange racing athlete behind the word "Marathon" printed in dark green, 15" d. (one lens cracks, repainted) **770.00**

Gasoline pump globe, "Pennzoil," milk glass printed w/a gold bell overprinted in red w/"PENNZOIL," one-piece, fired-on lettering (ILLUS. top next page) **2,420.00**

Rare Pennzoil Gas Globe

Gasoline pump globe,
"Plymouth," black high-profile
round metal frame, milk glass
lens printed w/a pale blue
rectangular enclosing an early
sailing ship in blue & white
above the word "PLYMOUTH" in
white, 16½" d. (body paint
chips) **968.00**

Gasoline pump globe,
"Republic," three-sided one-
piece, milk glass w/each side
mounted w/an American shield
w/a blue band at the top w/small
stars & the word "Republic" in
white above a red lower section
w/thin white stripes, raised
lettering (scratches, paint
loss) **2,420.00**

Gasoline pump globe,
"Shamrock," plastic, white oval
w/thin green stripe around edge,
centered w/green shamrock
marked "Shamrock" in white,
16" w., 12" h. (soiling)................**660.00**

Gasoline pump globe, "Shell,"
milk glass, in the shape of a
shell marked "Shell" in red,
19" w., 18" h. (paint missing on
lettering) **358.00**

Gasoline pump globe, "Skelly,"
capcolite, red lens centered by

white "S" in blue diamond
marked "Skelly" above
"Gasoline" above three stars,
13½" d. (minor scratches) **187.00**

Rare Texaco Pump Globe

Gasoline pump globe, "Texaco,"
star-shaped glass, red-painted
star centered by a large gold "T"
above the word "Texaco" in
black, completely repainted,
raised lettering, paint scuffing
(ILLUS.) **5,170.00**

Gasoline pump globe, "Utility,"
Gill body, a red border around a
dark blue & white world globe
overprinted w/a blue band
printed in red "UTILITY," the
word "Gasoline" in blue at
bottom of the globe, 13½" d.
(scratches to lens, chips to
base) **660.00**

Gasoline pump sign, "Mobiloil,"
porcelain, red Pegasus above
"Mobilgas" in blue on white
ground outlined in blue, 12 x
12½" (chips at edges, minor
scratches) **94.00**

Hat box, cover & original hat,
"Packard," round cylindrical
cardboard w/a flat fitted brown
cover, the sides printed in tones
of pale green, cream & dark
brown w/a continuous rural

Packard Hat Box

Hood ornament, Chevrolet, gold-painted pot metal, figural quota trophy-type, a half-length semi-nude woman holding aloft an early airplane, behind her is a round medallion w/raised lettering & the Chevrolet logo reading "Quota Trophy - October 1927," on a round leaf-embossed base, cracking in the metal, 6¼" w., 4" h. (ILLUS. bottom previous column) **1,430.00**

1908 Pennsylvania License Plate

landscape w/large touring cars, a cartouch-form label printed in white & black "The Packard Hat" above a size notation panel, also marked "Created by Adam - America's Famous Hatter," size, 6⅞, ca. 1920s, soiling, tape repair to box, creases & tears in cover, hat excellent, the set (ILLUS. of box) **132.00**

Hood ornament, Cadillac, chromed metal, figural, a horizontal figure of an Art Nouveau-style lady w/flowing gown, her heads behind her head holding a long flowing scarf, marked "08352" & "Design Patent 81303," 9½" l., 5" h. (minor pitting) **248.00**

License plate, 1908, Pennsylvania, porcelain, rectangular, yellow ground printed in black w/"Penn 1908" in small letters above the large numbers "22117," 10½" l., 6½" h. (ILLUS.) **220.00**

License plate, 1913, Massachusetts, porcelain, blue on white **83.00**

License plate, 1914, California, red & white porcelain, narrow rectangle, white letters on red w/"CAL" at one end & "1914" at the other end, in the center the large numbers "101725," also marked "ING-RICH Mfg. Co., Beaver Falls, PA," 16" l., 5½" h. (scratches, chipping) **165.00**

License plate, 1914, Pennsylvania, porcelain, black on white **22.00**

License plate, 1915, Maine, porcelain, blue on white...............**28.00**

License plate, 1920, Rhode Island, hand-painted metal, nearly square w/rounded

Early Chevrolet Hood Ornament

corners, black ground w/lettering & numbers in white "293 - R.I. 1920," 8" w., 6" h. (soiling, paint chipping, rust spotting) **55.00**

License plate, undated, early Ohio pre-dated era, rectangular leather w/large metal letters reading "3030," 5 x 15" (soiling, ragged edges) **330.00**

License plate attachment, "Farm Bureau," painted metal, reads "Insurance - Farm - Bureau - Companies" red & blue on cream, 3½" w., 4¾" h. (minor scratches)...**17.00**

Lighter, "Chevrolet School Bus," porcelain, w/scene of school bus in neighborhood, marked "Chevrolet School Bus," done in light blue, blue & gold, Ronson, 1½ x 2¼" (minor scratches).........**61.00**

Lighter, "Firestone," silver w/Firestone logo, bottom right corner engraved "W.A.M." (some scratches) **11.00**

Lighter, "Texaco," silver body w/gold emblem, in original box, 2" h. (minor scratches & wear) ..**176.00**

Mileage chart, "Grapette," 1970, 7 x 9" **85.00**

Motorcycle license plate, painted & embossed metal, nearly square w/a dark green ground w/raised lettering in silver "M - 3311 - Maine 1949," w/original mailing envelope, 4½ x 6" **110.00**

Motor oil bottle, "Huffman Mfg. Co.," 1 qt., Duraglass, cylindrical form tapering to cylindrical neck, w/metal spout, w/Huffman logo in red & blue, 3½" d., 14¾" h. (minor soiling, minor dents to spout) **55.00**

Motor oil bottle, "Shell Motor oil," 1 pt., glass, thin cylindrical form tapering to short cylindrical neck, embossed w/Shell Logo above "Shell-Penn - Motor Oil - 100% Pure Pennsylvania," 3" d., 14¾" h. (minor scratches) **72.00**

Motor oil bottle, "Socony Motor Oil," 1 qt., glass w/metal spout, cylindrical body tapering to cylindrical neck, embossed "Socony - Motor - Oil" on both sides, 3⅓" d., 16½" h. (some scratches, minor denting to spout) **88.00**

Motor oil can, "Archer Lubricants," 1 qt., tan can w/image of American Indian w/bow & arrow above "Archer - lubricants - Archer Petroleum Corp.," 4" d., 5½" h. (rust, dented on side)............................**28.00**

Motor oil can, "Galena Processed Motor Boat Oil," 1 gal., reads "Galena - Processed - Motor Boat Oil - Galena Oil Corporation," done in red, black & cream (scratches & minor rust spots)..**28.00**

Motor oil can, "Shell Oil," 1 qt., red can reads "Shell - X-100 - Motor Oil" above Shell logo above "Premium," 4" d., 5½" d. (opened at bottom, minor scratches & dents)......................**17.00**

Pail w/bail handle, toy-size, "Indianapolis Speedway," tin w/a large round black label printed w/large white & red wording "Indianapolis 500 Mile... Auto Classic Speedway" flanking a long red racing car, 6" d., 5¼" h. (scratches, creases, soiling)......**105.00**

Pocket knife, "Chevrolet," yellow plastic ground w/red Chevrolet logo, closed 3" l. (scratches, soiling) **83.00**

Pocket knife, "Chevrolet," cream plastic ground w/blue Chevrolet logo, 3½" l. (minor scratches & wear) **22.00**

Pocket knife, "Essolube," metal, in the shape of old gas pump, side impressed "Essolube," 3" l. (heavy wear, blade rusted)........**253.00**

Pocket knife, "Ford," white plastic handles w/blue "Ford" logo &

Early Ford Pocket Knife

blue sketch of a Model A sedan,
closed, scratches, soiling, fading
& rust, 3" l. (ILLUS.)...................**138.00**

Pocket knife, "Ford," blue ground
w/red lettering "Ford," 3½" l.
(minor scratches & wear) **44.00**

Pocket knife/key chain,
"Marathon," cylindrical form, side
w/Marathon logo & "Marathon -
Gasoline-Lubricant - Tires-
Batteries-Accessories" in blue,
red end w/key chain, 3" l. (minor
wear) **39.00**

Amoco Gas Pump Radio

Radio, "Amoco," model of a gas
pump in silver, red, blue, white &
gold w/earphone, in original box
w/original packings, minor
scratches, 2½" w., 4¼" h.
(ILLUS.) **77.00**

Restroom key holders,
"Texaco," metal, T-shaped, top
w/Texaco logo, bottom of one
reads "Ladies," other "Mens,"
done in red, black & white,
3½" w., 5¾" h., pr. (minor
scratches)................................**160.00**

Shock absorber fluid can,
"Permatex," 1 gal., decorated
w/striped swirl centered by circle
reading "Permatex," marked
"Permatex - Shock Absorber
Fluid - For Houdialle and Ford
Types," done in blue, oranges &
black, 6½ x 9½" (minor
scratches, denting & fading) **22.00**

Thermometer, "Marathon," metal,
rectangular, Marathon logo
above thermometer above "In
Case of An Oil Leak - In The
Line Please Phone - Office
Below Collect," all above local
advertisement, red & blue on
white, 5 x 16" (minor scratches
& soiling).....................................**99.00**

Thermometer, "Mobilgas,"
porcelain, rectangular, top
w/Pegasus above "Mobilgas"
above thermometer, all above
"Friendly - Service," done in
white, red & blue, 4¼ x 32½"
(colors faded) **385.00**

Thermometer, "Prestone Anti-
Freeze," porcelain, marked
"Prestone - Anti-Freeze" above
thermometer, all above "with
Exclusive - Magnetive Film -
Prevents Rust," done in red,
blue & white, minor rust at
edges, 9½ x 36½"......................**110.00**

Thermometer, "Red Crown
Gasoline," porcelain,
rectangular, white circle at the
top w/red lettering reading "Red
Crown Gasoline" above the
wording "for Power Mileage"
over the thermometer, red &
black-outlined triangle at the

Large Red Crown Thermometer

bottom around "Polarine - Made in Five Grades," mounted on a wood frame, chipping, 18" w., 6' h. (ILLUS.) **990.00**

Thermometer, "United Motors," wood, top centered by logo above "Specialized Electrical - Service - For Motor Cars," above local advertisement, all above thermometer, done in red & black on white, 4 x 15" (fading & some damage) **50.00**

Ticket, "Grand Prix de Monoco" sweepstakes ticket, paper printed in white, green, black & red w/a racing car in the center, dated "August 8, 1937," 2¾ x 5½" **149.00**

Tie tack, "Mobil," metal, figure of flying horse **40.00**

Tire inflator, "Tireflator," service station-type, upright cast-iron

casing painted red, an oblong top section w/a round dial & the black-painted embossed wording "Eco Tireflator," a large flat-sided round body raised on a slightly flaring squared pedestal base, marked "Service Station Equipment Co., Conshonocken, PA, U.S.A.," 24½" w., 4' 3" h. (restored, gauge aging & paint-chipped) **1,430.00**

Visor-Mount Picture Frame

Visor-mount picture frame, cast metal, flattened relief-cast stylized version of a Model T sedan w/a square opening for a photo in the center of the body, raised white-painted wording across the top & bottom "Remember Me" & "Drive Safely" painted black w/gold center frame & wheels, soiling, paint chipping, rust, 3½" w., 2½" h. (ILLUS.) **176.00**

Watch fob, "AAA," celluloid, circular, centered by "AAA" on top of bell, outside reads "Automobile Club - Southern California," done in blue, gold & red, 1¾" d. (minor crazing) **44.00**

Watch fob, "Buick Motor Cars," enameled metal on a leather strap, rectangular white enameled border w/the large script "Buick" name diagonally across the center, silver letters in top border read "Valve In Head," lower border w/"Motor Cars," early 20th c., 5" l. (band wear, soiling & scratches to fob).............**28.00**

Presto, Cabin & Liliput Banks

BANKS

Original early mechanical and cast-iron still banks are in great demand with collectors and their scarcity has caused numerous reproductions of both types and the novice collector is urged to exercise caution. The early mechanical banks are especially scarce and some versions are seldom offered for sale but, rather, are traded with fellow collectors attempting to upgrade an existing collection. Numbers before mechanical banks refer to those in John Meyer's Handbook of Old Mechanical Banks. However, another book Penny Lane—A History of Antique Mechanical Toy Banks, by Al Davidson, provides updated information and the number from this new volume is indicated in parenthesis at the end of each mechanical bank listing.

In past years, our standard reference for cast-iron still banks was Hubert B. Whiting's book Old Iron Still Banks, but because this work is out of print and a beautiful new book, The Penny Lane Bank Book—Collecting Still Banks by Andy and Susan Moore pictures and describes numerous additional banks, we will use the Moore numbers as a reference preceding each listing and indicate the Whiting reference in parenthesis at the end. The still banks listed are old and in good original condition with good paint and no repair unless otherwise noted. An asterisk (*) indicates this bank has been reproduced at some time.

Clown on Globe Bank

49 Clown on Globe, PL 127 (ILLUS.) **6,325.00**

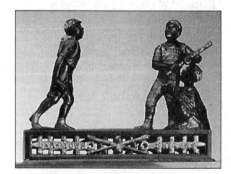

Darktown Battery Bank

MECHANICAL

16 Bird on Roof (PL 36) **$575.00**

33 Cabin, cast iron, J. & e. Stevens Co., ca. 1885, 4³⁄₁₆" h., PL 93 (ILLUS. center)................**748.00**

56 Darktown Battery, PL 146
(ILLUS. bottom previous
page) **2,300.00**

**63 Dog - Bulldog bank - Coin on
Nose,** one glass eye missing,
jaw inoperable (PL 64) **6,325.00**

Dog on Turntable Bank

67 Dog on Turntable, PL 159
(ILLUS.).....................**450.00 to 525.00**

69 Dog - Speaking
(PL 447) ....**1,000.00 to 1,500.00**

Trick Dog Bank

71 Dog - Trick, PL 481
(ILLUS.).....................**750.00 to 950.00**

Elephant Mechanical Bank

80 Elephant w/howdah, pull tail,
Hubley Mfg. Co., PL 174
(ILLUS. bottom previous
column).....................................**259.00**

Elephant w/howdah, w/tusks,
pull tail (PL 175) **403.00**

**146 Hall's Liliput Bank with
Tray,** cast iron, J. & E. Stevens
Co. , light green paint, 4½" h.,
PL 230 (ILLUS. right, top
previous page).........................**920.00**

I Always Did 'Spise a Mule

4 I Always Did 'Spise a Mule,
boy on bench, PL 250
(ILLUS.) **3,738.00**

129 Indian Shooting Bear
(PL 257)..................................**1,725.00**

134 Jolly Nigger Bank, "Butterfly
Tie," cast iron, John Harper &
Co., England, 6½" h. (PL 276)...**345.00**

135 Jolly Nigger with Top Hat,
John Harper & Co., England, red
shirt, blue tie, white hat w/black
stripe, surface shellacked, 8" h.
(PL 277)....................................**403.00**

138 Jonah and the Whale
(PL 282)................................**2,875.00**

Lion Hunter Bank

143 Leap Frog
(PL 292) ....**3,800.00 to 4,800.00**

148 Lion Hunter, PL 301 (ILLUS.
bottom previous page)...........**8,050.00**

182 Owl - turns heads
(PL 375).....................................**575.00**

Trick Pony Bank

196 Pony - Trick, PL 484
(ILLUS.)..................**900.00 to 1,200.00**

199 Presto Bank, model of a
building, cast iron, attributed to
Kyser & Rex Co., ca. 1892,
4¼" h., PL 397 (ILLUS. left
w/Cabin bank) **690.00**

203 Punch and Judy
(PL 404)..................................**1,265.00**

The Record Money Bank scale,
tin, upright w/dial, Germany,
ca. 1906 (similar to PL 487) **518.00**

Try Your Weight scale, tin,
upright w/dial at top, Germany,
ca. 1906 (PL 487) **518.00**

237 William Tell, cast iron,
PL 565 (ILLUS. below) **431.00**

STILL

20 Baseball player, cast iron,
A.C. Williams Co., Ohio, 1901-
34, 5¾" h (W. 10) ......**150.00 to 175.00**

693 Bear Stealing Pig, standing
animal holding pig, cast iron,
American-made, 5½" h. (ILLUS.
bottom left, top next page)......**1,093.00**

1125 Building - Crown bank,
building w/crown on roof &
"Bank" over entrance, cast iron,
J&E Stevens 1873-1907 & Grey
Iron Casting Co. 1903-1928,
3¼ x 4⅜", 5" h. **2,243.00**

1145 Building - Cupola Bank,
cast iron, Vermont Novelty

William Tell Mechanical Bank

A Group of Fine Still Banks

Works 1869 & J. & E. Stevens 1872, 3⅜ x 4½", 5½" h. (W. 305)....................................**345.00**

1201 Building - "Home Savings Bank" Dog Finial, cast iron w/silver repaint over original red & blue, J. & E. Stevens, 1891, 3⁵⁄₁₆ x 4⅜", 5¾" h. (W. 375) **225.00**

1176 Building (mosque) - domed "bank" (combination door), cast iron, Grey Iron Casting Co., 1903-28, 3⅛ x 5⅛", 5⅛" h. (W. 417) **288.00**

1124 Building - Roof Bank, cast iron, J. & E. Stevens, 1887, 3¼ x 3¾", 5¼" h. **259.00**

1078 Building "State Bank," cast iron, Kenton Hardware Mfg. Co., ca. 1900, 5½ x 7" (W. 441)....................................**403.00**

157 "Mutt & Jeff," cast iron, A. C. Williams, 1912-31, repainted

silver, 3½" w., 4¼" h., W. 13 (ILLUS. left, top next page) **115.00**

241 Buster Brown & Tige, cast iron, A.C. Williams, 1910-32, 5½" h., W.2 (ILLUS. right, top next page) **201.00**

442 Dog - Puppo on Pillow, cast iron, Hubley, ca. 1920s, 5⅝ x 6" **240.00**

616 Duck on Tub ("Save for a Rainy Day"), cast iron, Hubley, 1930-36, 5⅜" h. (W. 323) **345.00**

54 General Butler, cast iron, frog w/man's head, J. & E. Stevens, 1884, 6½" h., W. 294 (ILLUS. next page) **2,185.00**

1313 "Our Kitchener," bust portrait of Lord Kitchener within wreath, bronze-plated cast iron, Sydenham & McOustra, England, ca. 1914, 6¹¹⁄₁₆" h. * **144.00**

Mutt & Jeff & Buster Brown Banks

Rare General Butler Bank

561 Possum, cast iron, Arcade, 1910-13, 4⅜" l., 2⅜" h., W. 205 (ILLUS. top right, previous page) **288.00**

Professor Pug Frog, seated frog wearing jacket, cast iron, A.C. Williams, 1905-12, 3¼" h. (ILLUS. top left, previous page) **403.00**

61 Santa with Tree, cat iron, Hubley, 1914-30, 5⅞" h. W. 62 (ILLUS. bottom right, previous page) **431.00**

1165 Statue of Liberty, cast iron, Kenton Hardware Mfg. Co., 1910-31, 2⅜ x 2½", 6⅜" h. **86.00**

1459 Steamboat, cast iron, cast iron, A.C. Williams, 1912-20s, 7⅝" l., 2⁷⁄₁₆" h., W. 148 (some paint chipping) **201.00**

1437 Tank - "U.S. Tank Bank 1918," model of a World War I Tank, cast iron, A.C. Williams, 1920s, 4¼" l., 2⅜" h. (W. 162)...**115.00**

1437 Tank - "U.S. Tank Bank 1918," model of a World War I Tank, cast iron, A.C. Williams, 1920s, 3¹¹⁄₁₆" l., 3" h **144.00**

POTTERY

Building, model of an oblong hexagonal structure w/a steeply pitched roof & center chimney, multiple small impressed windows & a center front door, dark brown glazed roof & tan sides, Staffordshire, England, 19th c., 4¼" h. **110.00**

Cottage, model of a double-cabled small house w/long double windows in each bay, center chimney, raised on an oval base w/applied floral trim, polychrome decoration, Staffordshire, England, 19th c., 4½" h. **165.00**

Dog's head, a Spaniel's head covered in an overall mottled brown Rockingham glaze, incised details for the collar, eyes, ears & muzzle, 19th c., 3½" h. **165.00**

Dog's head, a Spaniel's head decorated w/black enamel ears, spots & collar w/orange & black eyes & a gold neck chain, late 19th c., 4⅛" h. **209.00**

BARBERIANA

A wide variety of antiques related to the tonsorial arts have been highly collectible for many years, especially 19th and early 20th century shaving mugs and barber bottles and, more recently, razors. We are now combining these closely related categories under one heading for easier reference. A selection of other varied pieces relating to barbering will also be found below.

BARBER BOTTLES

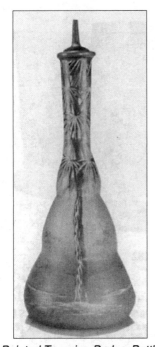

Painted Tapering Barber Bottle

Amber, Hobnail patt., Hobbs.....**$249.00**

Amber, frosted, footed bulbous base tapering to lady's leg neck, heavy white enamel floral decoration, ground & polished lip, smooth base, ca. 1885-1925, 8¼" h. **187.00**

Amber, long tapering cylindrical, tooled mouth w/broad rounded ring below thickened plain lip, embossed w/emblem & "Reddington & Co., San Francisco"................................**413.00**

Amethyst, Mary Gregory-style, white enamel little boy in ring of flowers **195.00**

Blue opalescent, Hobnail patt., polished pontil **185.00**

Clear, frosted, tapering bulbous w/green & white painted landscape decoration, tooled mouth, metal stopper, smooth base, ca. 1885-1925, 8" h. (ILLUS. previous column).........**743.00**

Clear opalescent, ovoid w/long cylindrical neck, Spanish Lace patt., rolled lip, polished pontil, ca. 1885-1925, 7⅛" h. **99.00**

Clear opalescent w/pinkish tones, bulbous base w/three Hobnail rings on neck, Hobnail patt., rolled lip, polished pontil, ca. 1885-1925, 6⅞" h. (two Hobnails chipped).......................**94.00**

Cobalt blue, squatty bulbous base w/long slightly tapered cylindrical neck, Optic Rib patt., decorated w/white & gold enamel, sheared mouth, pontil-scarred base, ca. 1885-1925, 6¾" h. **88.00**

Cobalt blue, squatty bulbous base under swollen ringed shoulder tapering to knobbed neck, Optic Rib patt. w/white, yellow & gold enamel floral design, sheared lip, pontil-scarred lip, ca. 1885-1925, 7¾" h. **220.00**

Cranberry, Optic Rib patt., decorated w/fine enameled florals................................**225.00**

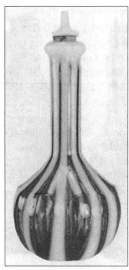

Cranberry Opalescent Barber Bottle

Cranberry opalescent, melon-lobed, bulbous base w/long cylindrical neck, Stripe patt., rolled lip, smooth base, ca. 1885-1925, 7¼" h. (ILLUS.) **142.00**

Emerald green, ovoid base tapering to lady's leg neck, white & gold gilt Art Nouveau decoration, rolled lip, pontil-scarred base, ca. 1885-1925, 7⅞" h. **242.00**

Cone-shaped Barber Bottle

Emerald green, cone-shaped w/green, pink, & red thistle decoration, ca. 1885-1925, 7⅝" h. (ILLUS. bottom previous column) **523.00**

Golden yellow, long slender tapering cylindrical, tooled mouth w/broad rounded ring below thickened plain lip, embossed "Crane & Brigham, San Francisco" in bayleaf **660.00**

Purple w/gold "oilspot" iridescent design, ovoid base tapering to lady's leg neck, swirled Loetz-style decoration, ground & polished lip, smooth base, ca. 1885-1925, 8⅛" h. **413.00**

Green, bulbous base w/three Hobnail rings on neck, Hobnail patt., tooled mouth, smooth base, ca. 1885-1925, 7" h. **83.00**

Milk Glass Barber Bottle

Milk glass, slightly tapering cylindrical body w/thin ring above & below center band depicting cottage in forest, thin rings on cylindrical neck, ground lip, "W.T. & Co." on smooth base, made for "Harold Crowe Tonic," ca. 1885-1925, 9½" h. (ILLUS. bottom previous page) **688.00**

Milk glass, slightly tapering cylindrical body w/thin ring above & below center band depicting two cranes, thin rings on cylindrical neck, ground lip, original pewter screw, "W.T. & Co." on smooth base, made for "A.H. Matlock Tonic," ca. 1885-1925, 9½" h. **358.00**

Milk glass, slightly tapering cylindrical body w/thin ring above & below center band depicting bird in bird's nest, thin rings on cylindrical neck, ground lip, original pewter screw, "W.T. & Co." on smooth base, ca. 1885-1925, 9½" h. **358.00**

Milk glass, slightly tapering cylindrical, "Cologne" & clover decoration, long cylindrical neck, rolled lip, metal stopper, pontil-scarred base, ca. 1885-1925, 9⅛" h. **121.00**

Milk glass, slightly tapering cylindrical, "Cologne" & floral decoration, long cylindrical neck, rolled lip, stamped "Melchior Bros. Decorators Chicago and Omaha" on smooth base, ca. 1885-1925, 8⅞" h. ("Cologne" worn) **154.00**

Milk glass, slightly tapering cylindrical w/floral decoration encircling "Bay Rum," long cylindrical neck, tooled mouth, "Koken - St. Louis Mo" on smooth base, ca. 1885-1925, 9⅛" h. **176.00**

Milk glass, footed squatty bulbous base w/Bohemian-style decoration, polished lip, smooth base, ca. 1885-1925, 8½" h. **110.00**

Pinkish amethyst, barrel-shaped base w/long cylindrical neck, Optic Rib patt., decorated w/white, orange, & gold enamel, sheared lip, pontil-scarred base, ca. 1885-1925, 7⅝" h. **413.00**

Purple, ovoid base tapering to lady's leg neck, white enamel decoration of grist mill & "Bay Rum," rolled lip, pontil-scarred base, ca. 1885-1925, 7⅝" h. **231.00**

Purple, frosted, ovoid base w/lady's leg neck, Optic Rib patt. w/white & gilt Art Nouveau floral decoration, rolled lip, pontil-scarred base, ca. 1885-1925, 7⅞" h. **264.00**

Diamond Optic Pattern Barber Bottle

Sapphire blue, cylindrical, Diamond Optic patt., enamel floral decoration, rolled lip, polished pontil, ca. 1885-1925, iridescent bruise on edge of base, 8⅝" h. (ILLUS.) **413.00**

Sapphire blue, ovoid melon-ribbed body tapering to lady's leg neck, Coin Spot patt., rolled lip, smooth base, 8½" h. **110.00**

Yellow, ovoid base tapering to lady's leg neck, Coin Spot patt. w/white enamel Art Nouveau "cameo" decoration, rolled lip, pontil-scarred base, ca. 1885-1925, 8" h. **275.00**

Yellowish green, squatty bulbous base w/white, pink & green enameled water lily floral decoration, sheared lip, pontil-scarred base, ca. 1885-1925, 6¾" h. **110.00**

Yellowish green, frosted, bulbous base tapering to lady's leg neck, Optic Rib patt. w/enamel floral decoration, sheared lip, polished pontil, ca. 1885-1925, 7⅞" h. **220.00**

Barrel-shaped Barber Bottle

Yellowish green, barrel-shaped w/long cylindrical neck, Optic Rib patt. w/white & orange floral decoration, sheared mouth, original stopper, pontil-scarred base, ca. 1885-1925, 7⅝" h. (ILLUS.) **231.00**

Yellowish green, bulbous base w/rib patt. decorated in white, yellow & green daisy enamel, tooled mouth, pontil-scarred base, ca. 1885-1925, 6⅛" h. **176.00**

Yellowish green, squatty bulbous base under swollen ringed-shoulder tapering to knobbed neck, Optic Rib patt. w/white, yellow & green enamel floral decorations, sheared lip, pontil-scarred base, ca. 1885-1925, 7⅝" h. **121.00**

RAZORS

Straight razor, "Clause Tremont O., U.S.A.," black plastic handle w/a molded woman on both sides, ca. 1890-1935 ....**215.00**

Straight Razor Set

Straight razor set: seven razors in case; celluloid handles inlaid w/"Gondola" marked "Gondola Made In Germany," each blade marked w/different German town & coat of arms, hard blue case lined in pink felt w/tag marked "Souvenir of Solingen," ca. 1890-1930 (ILLUS.) **358.00**

RAZOR BLADE BANKS

Razor blade banks were invented as a safety device to dispose of used razor blades. Even though disposable razor blades date back as far as 1903, razor blade banks can only be traced as far back as the early 1930s. Electric razors, and later disposable razors, made the need for these whimsical receptacles unnecessary by the 1960s. Shapes include barbers, animals, barber chairs and barber poles. Some banks were distributed by shaving-related companies, like Listerine, as promotions for shaving cream. Listerine banks that are most commonly found are a white frog, donkey and elephant. The donkey and elephant were sold by Listerine in 1936 and carried political overtones. Most razor blade banks are ceramic.

Looie Razor Blade Bank

Occupied Japan Razor Blade Bank

Barber holding pole, white coat w/red bow tie, striped towel over right arm, Occupied Japan, 4" h. (ILLUS.).........................**50.00 to 60.00**

Barber, wooden, Woodcroft, ca. 1950, "Gay Blade" marked bottom unscrews, 6" h................................**65.00 to 75.00**

Barber, wooden, key & metal holder for razor & brush, 9" h...............................**85.00 to 95.00**

Barber, "Looie" holding razor, dressed in red & white striped shirt w/blue bow tie, blue pants, blue suspenders w/red clips,

black shoes, marked "Looie - Razor Bank" on white apron, 7" h. (ILLUS.) ....**85.00 to 100.00**

Barber Stroking Chin

Barber, "Tony", dressed in blue coat accented w/black buttons & comb in front pocket, white towel w/two red stripes on right arm &

right hand stroking chin, left hand holding razor, 5¾" h. (ILLUS. bottom previous page) ....**75.00 to 80.00**

Barber chair, small, 4¾" h. ....**75.00 to 100.00**

Barber Chair Blade Bank

Barber chair, large, 5¾" h. (ILLUS.) ....**100.00 to 125.00**

Barber's Head Razor Blade Bank

Barber's head, brown hair & mustache, red polka-dotted white tie, white collar & blue jacket, Clemenson, 4" h. (ILLUS. bottom previous column)..........................30.00 to 35.00

Tony Razor Blade Bank

Barber's head, "Tony," grey hair, white barber's coat accented w/two buttons, scissors & comb in front pocket, Ceramic Arts Studio, 4¾" h. (ILLUS.)....**85.00 to 95.00**

Barber poles, red & white w/various designs, each (ILLUS. top next page) ....**25.00 to 30.00**

Clemenson Razor Blade Bank

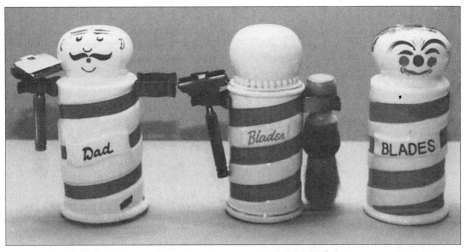

Barber Pole Razor Blade Banks

Bell-shaped, depicts man shaving, Clemenson (ILLUS. bottom previous page)..............................**25.00 to 30.00**

Blade box, metal, shows policeman holding up hand, marked "Used Blades," 4" h...............................**50.00 to 65.00**

Blade safe, green, embossed "Blade Safe" on front, 2¾" h. (ILLUS. right)................**45.00 to 55.00**

Donkey, Listerine, 2¼" h. (ILLUS. below, left) ......**20.00 to 30.00**

Blade Safe Razor Blade Bank

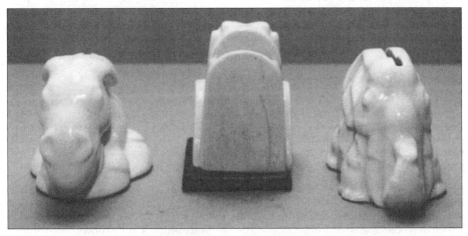

Listerine Razor Blade Banks

Elephant, Listerine, 2½" h.
(ILLUS. bottom right, previous
page) ....**25.00 to 30.00**

Frog, Listerine, 3" h. (ILLUS.
bottom center, previous
page) ....**15.00 to 20.00**

Half-Shaving Cup, marked "Gay
Old Blade" w/quartet, hangs on
wall ....**65.00 to 75.00**

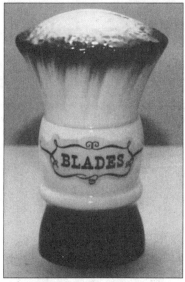

Shaving Brush Razor Blade Bank

Shaving brush, "Blades" decal
on cream body, black base, 4½" h.
(ILLUS.).........................**50.00 to 60.00**

SHAVING MUGS

Fraternal
**American Order of United
Workmen,** decorated
w/emblem, marked "Mark
Greely" below, stamped "J.O.
Thomas Co. Barber's Supplies
Ottumwa, Iowa" on base, gilt
trim, ca. 1885-1925, 4" h. **55.00**

**Brotherhood of Locomotive
Firemen,** depicts locomotive &
tender w/letters "B. of L.F." on
side of tender, stamped "Aug.
Kern Barber Supply Co. St.

Louis Trade Mark Always
Upright" on base, gilt trim, ca.
1885-1925, 3⅞" h. **330.00**

**Brotherhood of Railroad
Trainmen,** decorated
w/emblem, marked "W.A.
Crawshaw" above, stamped
"East St. Louis Barber's Supply
Co. East St. Louis, Ill." on base,
gilt trim, ca. 1885-1925, 4" h......**143.00**

Foresters of America, shows
"Foresters of America" emblem,
marked "John R. Martin" on
sides, stamped "T & V Limoges
France" & "J. Price" on base, gilt
trim, ca. 1885-1925, 3⅝" h. **578.00**

Grand Army of the Republic,
depicts "G.A.R." medal, marked
"Hollis Cook" on sides, gilt trim,
ca. 1885-1925, 3 3/8" h. **440.00**

**Independent Order of Odd
Fellows,** depicting emblem
w/"Samuel Jacob" marked
above, gilt trim, ca. 1885-1925,
3¾" h. **77.00**

**Independent Order of Odd
Fellows,** decorated w/various
emblems of the "Odd Fellows
Lodge," marked "F.W. Wielder"
above, gilt trim, ca. 1885-1925,
3⅝" h. (re-attached chip on
side of lip) **220.00**

Triple Fraternal Shaving Mug

**Junior Order of United Auto
Mechanics, Odd Fellows,
Knights of Templer,** decorated

w/three Fraternal emblems, "John Smith" marked above, stamped "T & V Limoges France" on base, gilt trim, ca. 1885-1925, 3⅝" h. (ILLUS. bottom previous page)...........**1,265.00**

Loyal Order Of Moose Shaving Mug

Loyal Order of Moose, showing "Order of Moose" emblem & "No. 30" below "Vic Chamar," stamped "T & V Limoges France" on base, gilt trim, ca. 1885-1925, 3⅝" h. (ILLUS.) **688.00**

Modern Woodsmen of America, decorated w/emblem, marked "W.K. Butrick" below, stamped "V x D Austria" on base, gilt trim, ca. 1885-1925, 3⅞" h. **72.00**

Order of the Redmen, depicting Indian chief emblem w/"Philip Buhl" marked above, gilt trim, ca. 1885-1925, 3⅝" h. **253.00**

Patriotic Order of Sons of America, full black wrap w/emblem, marked "Chas. C. Fenstermaker" above, stamped "Austria" on base, gilt trim, ca. 1885-1925, 3⅝" h. **523.00**

Woodsmen of the World, showing "W.O.W." in emblem below "Emil F. Rudert," stamped "Germany" on the base, gilt trim, ca. 1885-1925, 3⅝" h. **154.00**

Occupational

Artist Shaving Mug

Artist, shows artist's pallet & brushes, "E. Ratellier" marked above, ca. 1885-1925, 3½" h. (ILLUS.) **385.00**

Baker, depicts three men working in bakery, "J. Marianski" marked below, gilt trim, ca. 1885-1925, 3⅞" h. **385.00**

Bartender, depicts bartender in barroom scene w/cigar counter to the left of customers, "Thos. Wooley" marked above, stamped "M.R. France" on base, ca. 1885-1925, 3½" h. **495.00**

Bartender, shows barroom scene w/"E.G. Fox" marked above, stamped "Limoges W.G. & Co. France" on base, gilt trim, ca. 1885-1925, 3⅝" h. **187.00**

Beer wagon driver, depicts a man driving a horse-drawn "Lager Beer" wagon, marked "Sig. Propst" above, gilt trim, ca. 1885-1925, 3¾" h. **550.00**

Blacksmith, shows blacksmith standing at his anvil, "Wm Johnson" marked above, stamped "Limoges W.G. & Co. France" & "The World Our Field Koken St. Louis Trade Mark" on base, gilt trim, ca. 1885-1925, 3⅝" h. **413.00**

Blacksmith, depicts blacksmith shoeing a horse, "J.W. Morrical" marked below, stamped "Limoges W.G. & Co. France" & "C. Dehaan & Co. Des Moines, Iowa" on base, gilt trim, ca. 1885-1925, 3⅝" h. **523.00**

Brick Mason Shaving Mug

Brick mason, depicts brick mason laying up a wall, "W.A. Parkins" marked above, gilt trim, ca. 1885-1925, professional repair in handle area, 3⅝" h. (ILLUS.) **253.00**

Buggy driver, depicts a man driving a horse-drawn buggy, "John A. Budgeon" marked above, stamped "Aug. Kern Barber Supply Co. St. Louis Trade Mark Always Upright," on base, ca. 1885-1925, 3¾" h. (name & other gold decoration redone) **209.00**

Buggy driver, depicts man driving horse-drawn buggy, "Phil Dooley" marked above, stamped "T & V France" on base, ca. 1885-1925, 3½" h. **275.00**

Butcher, shows steer's head & crossed butcher's tools, marked "R.J. Hynes" above, 3½" h. **132.00**

Butcher, shows man ready to slaughter steer, "D. McDonald" marked above, gilt trim, ca. 1880-1925, 3⅜" h. **275.00**

Butcher, depicts butcher carving ribs at butcher block, "H.E. Appley" marked above, stamped "Leonard Vienna Austria" & "M.E. Waite Barber Supplies Utica, N.Y." on base, gilt trim, ca. 1885-1925, 4" h. (hard to see hairline crack from rim to letter "y") **264.00**

Cabinetmaker, depicts cabinetmaker ripping a piece of wood, "B.W. Riley" marked above, stamped "T & V Limoges France" on base, "Cochran Bros, Ottumwa Iowa" written in gold gilt, ca. 1885-1925, 3⅝" h. **330.00**

Carpenter, depicts carpenter planing a board at his bench, "H. Ebelin" marked above, stamped "Leonard Vienna Austria" & "A. Kern B.S. Co. St Louis" on base, gilt trim, ca. 1885-1925, 4" h. **358.00**

Carpenter, depicts carpenter notching a corner of a board, "J.H. Adams" marked above, stamped "J & C Bavaria" on base, gilt trim, ca. 1885-1925, 3⅞" h. **413.00**

Carpenter, shows carpenter's tools, "Linn Thomas" marked below, gilt trim, ca. 1880-1925, 3⅝" h. **105.00**

Delivery wagon driver, depicts man driving a horse-drawn delivery wagon, "Jno. H. Trone" marked above, stamped "T & V Limoges France" on base, gilt trim, ca. 1885-1925, 3⅝" h. **358.00**

Delivery wagon driver, horse-drawn delivery wagon w/"H.C. Fricken Baker - Pastry" on the side, "K.C. Fricken" marked above, stamped "H & Co." on base, ca. 1885-1925, 3⅜" h. **550.00**

Druggist, shows a mortar and pestle, "J.G. Scraggs" marked

below, stamped "Made by A.L.
Undeland Omaha" on base, gilt
trim, ca. 1880-1925,
3⅝" h. **275.00**

Farmer, depicts farmer plowing
field behind a two-horse team
w/house in distance, marked
"Geo. Stratton" below, stamped
"A.L. Undeland & Co.
Decorators, Omaha" on base,
gilt trim, ca. 1885-1925,
3⅝" h. **605.00**

Fireman, depicts fireman driving
a horse-drawn fire engine,
marked "W. H. Torrance" above,
stamped "C.F.H. G.D.M." on
base, ca. 1885-1925,
3¼" h. **778.00**

Hardware store clerk, depicts a
sales clerk & customer in
hardware store, "K. Raftshal"
marked above. gilt trim, ca.
1885-1925, 3⅝" h. **258.00**

Iceman, shows block of ice and
tongs with "C.M. Mohler" marked
below, stamped "T & V Limoges
France" on base, ca. 1885-1925,
full black wrap, 3⅝" h. **468.00**

Livery stable owner, depicts
livery stable scene w/"Oake's
Stable" in arch above "Office,"
gilt trim, ca. 1185-1925, 3¾" h.
(professional repair to top of
base) **688.00**

Milk wagon driver, shows man
driving a horse-drawn delivery
wagon w/"Milk" on side panel,
"M. Wentworth" marked above,
gilt trim, ca. 1885-1925,
3¾" h. **688.00**

Musician, shows coronet w/"G.
Jochem" marked below, ca.
1885-1925, 3½" h. **303.00**

Sportsman, depicting hunter
shooting at three ducks w/dog
on point, marked "F.J. Mitschke"
above, stamped "The World Our
Field Koken St. Louis Trade
Mark" on base, ca. 1885-1925,
3⅞" h. **194.00**

Stake Wagon Driver Shaving Mug

Stake wagon driver, shows a
man driving horse-drawn stake
wagon, marked "Charley Cross "
below, gilt trim, ca. 1885-1925,
3½" h. (ILLUS.).........................**550.00**

Stake wagon driver, depicts man
driving horse-drawn stake
wagon, marked "Joseph
Richards" above, full maroon
wrap w/gilt trim, ca. 1885-1925,
3½" h. **243.00**

Sulky driver, shows man driving
a racing sulky, "A.O. Courtright"
marked above, stamped "T & V
France" on base, ca. 1885-1925,
gilt trim, 3⅝" h...........................**468.00**

Telegraph Operator Shaving Mug

Telegraph operator, depicts
hand operating a telegraph key,
"J.A. Brownlee" marked below,

gilt trim, ca. 1880-1925, 3⅝" h.
(ILLUS. bottom previous page) **413.00**

Telegraph operator, depicts
telegraph key encircled w/floral
decorations surrounding a full
black wrap, "Jacob Darst"
marked above, stamped "G.D.A.
France" on base, ca. 1885-1925,
3⅝" h. **770.00**

Tinsmith, depicts tinsmith
working at his bench with five
teakettles underneath bench,
made for "Math. Koob " marked
below, gilt trim, ca. 1885-1925,
3⅘" h. **633.00**

Train engineer, depicts
locomotive & tender w/full
maroon wrap, "J.M. Elliott"
marked above, ca. 1885-1925,
3⅞" h. **330.00**

Trolley driver, depicts electric
trolley w/operator & conductor,
"Harry Kelly" marked above,
stamped "Koken Barbers'
Supply St. Louis Mo." on smooth
base, gilt trim, ca. 1885-1925,
4" h. **605.00**

General

American Flags Shaving Mug

Ceramic, American flags, depicts
two crossed American flags on
front w/46 stars, marked
"Williams Shaving Soap Healing
Antiseptic" on back, gilt trim,
4⅝" h. (ILLUS.).........................**125.00**

Bust of Woman Shaving Mug

China, shows bust of woman in
cameo, "James M. Koons"
marked above, gilt trim, ca.
1885-1925, 3½" h. (ILLUS.).......**715.00**

China, depicts cottage & bridge
w/church in distance, "Meggs V.
Cole" marked above, gilt trim,
ca. 1885-1925, 3⅝" h. **220.00**

China, depicts two horse heads,
marked "Wm Pohlman" above,
stamped "Koken Barbers' Supply
St. Louis U.S.A." on base, gilt
trim, ca. 1885-1925, 4" h...........**253.00**

China, patriotic design shows
eagle w/shield & crossed
American flags, marked "C.T.
Wilcox" above, stamped "Felda
China Germany" on base, gilt
trim, ca. 1885-1925, 3⅝" h. **154.00**

China, depicts howling wolf &
"Louis" w/full maroon wrap, "Elite
L. France" & "L. Venettisch"
stamped & written on base, gilt
trim, ca. 1885-1925, 3⅞" h. **187.00**

Jasper ware, greyish-olive
background w/white relief
decoration, showing various
barber scenes around entire
mug, ca. 1885-1925, 3¾" h. **165.00**

Redware, tall cylindrical
w/conjoined shorter cylindrical
compartment for soap at the
back just below the top strap
handle, brownish-green mottled
glaze, 19th c., 5¾" h..................**286.00**

GENERAL ITEMS

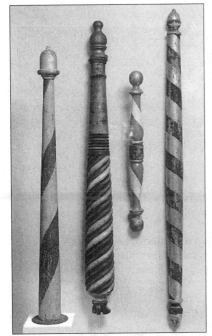

Barbershop Poles

Barber pole, carved & painted wood, cylindrical w/spiraling stripes, 19th c., 5' h. (some losses) **748.00**

Barber pole, carved & painted pine, a block base section below two long rod-turned sections divided by a baluster-turned section, ring-turned at the top w/a ball finial, a harlequin design of red, white & blue diamonds trimmed w/stenciled stars, now mounted on a flat black metal stand, late 19th c., 7' 5" h. **7,475.00**

Barber pole, tapering carved, painted & gilted pole w/spiraling red & white stripes, gilt-painted acorn finial, 1880s, 45" h. (ILLUS. left) **1,380.00**

Barber pole, carved, painted & gilted pine pole w/tapering & fluted baluster-turned & ring-carved form w/spiraling red, white & blue stripes, bands of gold, ball & acorn finial, inscribed "5¢," 49½" (ILLUS. second from left)....................**4,312.00**

Barber pole, carved, painted, stenciled & baluster-turned pole, orange & white spiraling stripe, blue center-carved painted band w/ stenciled star, ball finials, 28" h. (ILLUS. second from right) **3,450.00**

Barber pole, carved, painted & gilded pine pole tapering w/molded rings & acorn finials, covered in gilding w/black stripes, 1800s, 57½" (ILLUS. right) **977.00**

Barber Pot Lid

Pot lid w/original pot, depicts man shaving, black transfer reading "Wright's Gold Metal Saponaeous Shaving Compound", ca. 1850-1865, 4¼" d. (ILLUS.)............................**83.00**

Pot lid, white porcelain w/black transfer reading "Genuine Beef Marrow For the Hair Jules Hauel Perfumer 120 Chestnut St. Philadelphia," ca. 1855-1865, 2⅞" d. **116.00**

Pot lid, white porcelain w/black transfer reading "Genuine Beef Marrow Pomatum X. Bazin Succor to E. Roussel 114 Chestnut St. Philadelphia," ca. 1855-1865, 3" d. **358.00**

Razor Sharpening Stone

Razor sharpening stone, black, marked "Koken's (bust of black man) Moor," aluminum embossed "The moor" on lid top, paper litho inside, ca. 1890-1925 (ILLUS. above) **425.00**

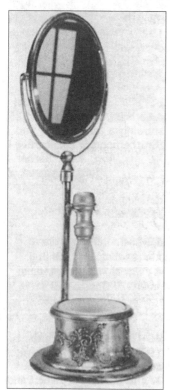

Barber Shaving Stand

Shaving stand, silver plated w/raised floral decoration, beveled glass mirror, shaving brush & milk glass pot, ca. 1900-1935, 15¼" h. (ILLUS. bottom previous column) **275.00**

Shaving stand on adjustable standard, beveled glass mirror w/magnifier mirror on reverse, copper pedestal holding two round shelves, cast-iron base w/feet, ca. 1900-1930, adjustable to 50" h.....................**121.00**

BARBIE DOLLS & COLLECTIBLES

At the time of her introduction in 1959, no one could have guessed that this statuesque doll would become a national phenomenon and eventually the most famous girl's plaything produced.

Over the years, Barbie and her growing range of family and friends have evolved with the times, serving as an excellent mirror on the fashion and social changes taking place in American society. Today, after almost 40 years of continual production, Barbie's popularity goes on unabated among both young girls and older collectors. Early and rare Barbies can sell for remarkable prices and it is everyone's hope to find mint condition "#1 Barbie."

DOLLS

Allan, 1964, painted red hair, pink lips, straight legs, striped jacket, blue swim trunks, cork sandals w/blue straps (some clothing wear) **$35.00**

Allan, 1964, painted red hair, beige lips, straight legs, "Touchdown" outfit w/red "7" shirt, pants w/lacings, red & blue knee socks, black cleats, football, red plastic helmet & shoulder pads (black dot on side of hair) **40.00**

Allan, 1964, painted red hair, beige lips, straight legs, original striped jacket, blue swim trunks, corks sandals w/blue straps, in box w/black wire stand, "Exclusive Fashions by Mattel Book 1" booklet (slightly discolored jacket, box discolored & worn) **65.00**

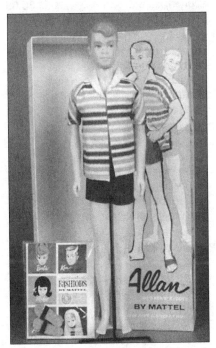

1964 Allan

Allan, 1964, painted red hair, pink lips, straight legs, original striped

jacket, blue swim trunks, black wire stand, "Exclusive Fashions by Mattel book 1" booklet, cork sandals w/blue straps in cellophane bag, in box (ILLUS. bottom previous column) **110.00**

Allan, 1965, painted red hair, dark beige lips, straight legs, sailor outfit w/white shirt, decal on sleeve & necktie, matching pants, white cotton socks, black shoes, plastic sailor cap, duffel bag w/drawstring (outfit discolored) **35.00**

Barbie, "#3 Ponytail Barbie," 1960, light blonde hair in original topknot, brown eyeliner, red lips, finger & toe paint, straight legs, black & white striped swimsuit, pearl earrings, in , box w/black open-toe shoes (overall light fading w/some dark fade spots, faded dark area on hair, box slightly aged & faded) **850.00**

Barbie, "#3 Ponytail Barbie," brunette, red lips, brown eyeliner, faint cheek blush, finger & toe paint, straight legs, black & white striped swimsuit, pearl earrings, white-rimmed glasses w/blue lenses, black No. 1 open-toe shoes w/holes, pedestal stand, pink cover Barbie booklet, cardboard neck insert, in box (slight fading & wear on clothing & box) **1,000.00**

Barbie, "#4 Ponytail Barbie," brunette hair in original ponytail, full red lips, nostril paint, finger & toe paint, black & white striped knit swimsuit in , box w/black wire stand, blue cover booklet , black open-toe shoes, in box (ILLUS. top next page) **375.00**

Barbie, "#5 Ponytail Barbie," blonde, red lips, finger & toe paint, straight legs, black & white striped swimsuit (hair loose & flat, right eyelash rub, some fading & discoloration) **140.00**

#4 Ponytail Barbie

Barbie, "#5 Ponytail Barbie," titian hair in original set, full red lips, finger & toe paint, black & white striped one-piece swimsuit, pearl earrings, black open-toe shoes (right side bottom curl loose, top of hair lightly soiled, faint green spots on ears, faint red stain on upper front of left leg, swimsuit slightly worn) **475.00**

Barbie, "#6 Ponytail Barbie," titian, coral lips, finger & toe paint, straight legs, black & white striped swimsuit, black open-toe shoes (loose ponytail, strap broken on one shoe) **290.00**

Barbie, "American Girl Barbie," 1966, titian, beige lips w/orange in center finger & toe paint, bendable legs, original one-piece swimsuit, aqua open-toe shoes, (faint dark stain on lower back of right leg) **575.00**

Barbie, "American Girl Barbie," 1966, brunette, dark pink lips, cheek blush, finger & toe paint, bendable legs, original one-piece swimsuit (faint ink dot on forehead, faint ink spots on both legs, loose left leg at torso attachment) **2,900.00**

Barbie, "Applause Barbie," 1991, No. 3406, never removed from box (box slightly discolored w/tear on bottom flap)..................**40.00**

Barbie, "Barbie as Scarlett O'Hara," 1994, Hollywood Legends Collection, No. 12997, Bar-B-Que dress, Timeless Creations Collection, never removed from box (box slightly scuffed)..**35.00**

Barbie, "Barbie as Scarlett O'Hara," 1994, Hollywood Legends Collection, No. 13254, New Orleans dress, Timeless Creations Collection, never removed from box (box slightly scuffed)..**35.00**

Barbie, "Barbie as Scarlett O'Hara," 1994, Hollywood Legends Collection, No. 12815, red dress, Timeless Creations Collection, never removed from box (box slightly scuffed, top flap creased) **40.00**

Barbie, "Barbie with Growin' Pretty Hair," 1971, blonde, pink lips, rooted eyelashes, bendable legs, original pink satin dress, pink shoes, curled hair piece w/pink ribbon (original rubberband broken w/most missing) **105.00**

Barbie, "Benefit Ball Barbie," 1992, Classique Collection, No. 1521, Timeless Creations, never removed from box (small crease right side of box) **145.00**

Barbie, "Blossom Beautiful Barbie," 1992, Sears Special Edition, No. 3817, never removed from box **240.00**

Barbie, "Bubblecut Barbie," 1961-1962, titian, pink lips, finger &

toe paint, straight legs, black & white striped swimsuit, black open-toe shoes, in box w/wire stand, white cover booklet.........**115.00**

Barbie, "Bubblecut Barbie," 1964, brunette, coral lips, finger & toe paint, straight legs, "Lunch Date" dress (faint green dots on both ears, green outline on lips) **110.00**

Bubblecut Barbie

Barbie, "Bubblecut Barbie," 1986, blonde, Japan, pink lips, black & white dress, white shoes, in light pink box w/Barbie logo & plastic wire stand (ILLUS.)...................**625.00**

Barbie, "Bubblecut Barbie" & "Barbie's Sparkling Pink Gift Set," 1963, blonde, bright pink lips, finger & toe paint, straight legs, pink nylon one-piece swimsuit, pearl earrings, wrist tag, includes pink satin jacket w/silver glitter, blouse w/single shoulder strap & bow accent, wrap skirt, long coat w/diamond accents, pillbox hat, diamond stud earrings in small cellophane bag, clear open-toe shoes w/gold glitter in small cellophane bag, white cover booklet in cellophane bag, pale pink open-toe shoes, gold wire stand, in box, the set (wristband worn & creased, torn cellophane booklet bag, loose pink shoes, box shows fading & wear) **1,050.00**

Barbie, "Busy Gal Barbie," 1995, brunette, Limited Edition Reproduction, No. 13675, Timeless Creations, never removed from box, cardboard shipping box (small section of plastic window loose) **45.00**

Barbie, "Christian Dior Barbie," 1995, Limited Edition, No. 13168, never removed from box, cardboard shipping box (small tear on upper flap closure) **75.00**

Barbie, "Circus Star Barbie," 1994, FAO Schwarz, Limited Edition, No. 13257, never removed from box **90.00**

Barbie, "City Style Barbie," 1993, Classique Collection, No. 10149, never removed from box (box edges slightly creased)................**65.00**

Barbie, "Donna Karan New York Barbie," 1995, Bloomingdale's Department Store Special, Limited Edition, No. 14545, blonde, never removed from box (box lightly scuffed & right side slightly creased) **85.00**

Barbie, "Empress Bride Barbie," 1992, Bob Mackie, fifth in series, No. 4247, cardboard shipping box (box worn & damaged) **700.00**

Barbie, "Enchanted Evening Barbie," 1991, J.C. Penny, Limited Edition, No. 2702, never removed from box (small crease on right side of plastic window) ...**45.00**

Barbie, "Evening Extravaganza Barbie," 1993, Classique Collection, No. 11622, Timeless Creations, never removed from box..**55.00**

Barbie, "Evening Flame Barbie," 1991, No. 1895, never removed from box (torn side flap) **100.00**

Barbie, "Evergreen Princess Barbie," 1994, The Winter Princess Collection, Limited Edition, No. 12123, never removed from the box (crease front left side of box & on insert)..**80.00**

Fashion Queen Barbie

Barbie, "Fashion Queen Barbie," 1963, painted brunette hair, pink lips, finger & toe paint, gold & white one-piece swimsuit w/matching hat, blonde, brunette & titian wig (ILLUS.)...................**105.00**

Barbie, "Fashion Queen Barbie," 1964, painted brunette hair w/blue head band, pink lips, finger & toe paint, straight legs,

"Fancy Free" dress, blonde wig (small faded dots on both ears, discolored area on upper back, small green area inside wig)........**75.00**

Barbie, "Feelin' Groovy Barbie," 1986, No. 3421, designed by BillyBoy, Limited Edition, never removed from box (box lightly scuffed) **165.00**

Barbie, "1920's Flapper Barbie," 1993, The Great Eras Collection, No. 4063, Timeless Creations, never removed frombox (back of box creased) **155.00**

Barbie, "Gibson Girl Barbie," 1993, The Great Eras Collection, No. 3702, Timeless Creations, never removed from box (box edges & corners creased)............**85.00**

Barbie, "Goddess of Sun Barbie," 1995, Bob Mackie, eighth in series, No. 14056, signed fashion illustration, cardboard shipping box..............................**115.00**

Barbie, "Gold Barbie," 1990, Bob Mackie, first in series, in clear plastic case w/black plastic trim & back w/signed fashion illustration, plastic case insert, boa stole in plastic bag, stand, booklet, no wear or discoloration, in box, cardboard shipping box...**580.00**

Barbie, "Gold Jubilee Barbie," 1994, Limited Edition D4313/5,000, Timeless Creations, never removed from box, cardboard shipping box......**750.00**

Barbie, "Golden Greetings Barbie," 1989, FAO Schwarz, No. 7734, never removed from box (small crease upper right corner of box)............................**175.00**

Barbie, "50th Golden Anniversary Barbie," 1995, Limited Edition No. 20399, Timeless Creations, never removed from box, cardboard shipping box **275.00**

Barbie, "Holiday Memories Barbie," 1995, Hallmark Special Edition, No. 14106, never removed from box.......................**45.00**

Barbie, "Jeweled Splendor Barbie," 1995, FAO Schwarz, Signature Collection, No. 14061, never removed from the box, cardboard shipping box **200.00**

Barbie, "Kool-Aide Barbie," 1992, Collector's Edition, No. 10309, never removed from box (box corners slightly creased) **60.00**

Barbie, "Le Nouveau Theatre De La Mode Barbie," 1985, BillyBoy, No. 2807, no fingernail polish, never removed from box, cardboard shipping box **160.00**

Barbie, "Little Debbie Barbie," 1992, Collector's Edition, No.10123, never removed from box..**100.00**

Barbie, "Live Action Barbie," 1971, blonde, pink & orange lips, rooted eyelashes, faint cheek blush, bendable legs & arms, original one-piece jumpsuit w/fringe on waist, flat brown shoes, two fringe bracelets (faded pink stain on right wrist, small plastic section of one bracelet is broken)............**65.00**

Barbie, "Living Barbie," 1970, brunette, pink lips, rooted eyelashes, cheek blush, bendable arms & legs, original orange net cover-up, one-piece swimsuit (ILLUS. bottom previous column) **155.00**

Barbie, "Loop Scoop Barbie," No. 1454, yellow dress w/crochet trim, yellow shoes, "Living Barbie" booklet, cellophane bag, paper label, never removed from carton (missing cardboard box)...**30.00**

Barbie, "Madison Avenue Barbie," 1991, FAO Schwarz, Limited Edition, No. 1539, never removed from box (crease in upper edge of box) **170.00**

Barbie, "Mardi Gras Barbie," 1987, American Beauties Collection, No. 4930, never removed from box **70.00**

Barbie, "Masquerade Ball Barbie," 1993, Bob Mackie, sixth in series, No. 10803, booklet, signed fashion illustration, cardboard shipping box (torn box flap)....................................**250.00**

Living Barbie

Mermaid Bride Barbie

Barbie, "Mermaid Bride Barbie,"
35th Anniversary Barbie
w/blonde ponytail restyled in a
braid, redressed in antique lace,
glass beads & pearls, 14"
(ILLUS. bottom previous page) **210.00**

Barbie, "Medieval Lady Barbie,"
1994, The Great Eras
Collection, No. 12791, never
removed from box **30.00**

Barbie, "Midnight Gala Barbie,"
1995, Classique Collection, No.
12999, Timeless Creations,
never removed from box (box
corners & cover creased) **70.00**

Barbie, "Mink Minx," hand-rooted
restyled Sidepart American Girl
hairstyle, real fur coat, strapless
sheath, glitter mules, necklace,
MiKelman wrist tag, enclosed in
black box w/clear plastic window
w/MiKelman sticker **175.00**

Barbie, "Neptune Fantasy
Barbie," 1992, Bob Mackie,
fourth in series, No. 4248,
Timeless Creations, in box,
cardboard shipping box (top flap
creased) **657.00**

Barbie, "Night Sensation Barbie,"
1991, FAO Schwarz, No. 2921,
never removed from box,
cardboard shipping box
(small crease on front left
side of box)..............................**135.00**

Barbie, "Opening Night Barbie,"
1993, Classique Collection, No.
10148, Timeless Creations,
never removed from box (crease
in box insert & on back)..............**60.00**

Barbie, "Pepsi Spirit Barbie,"
1989, No. 4859, never removed
from box (box lightly scuffed &
corners slightly creased) **65.00**

Barbie, "Pink Sizzle," festive pink
lame strapless bodice
w/multicolored "shag" lame shirt,
tulle petticoat, blue lame gloves,
metallic pink pumps to match
bodice, h.p. face & chignon
hairstyle designed by MiKelman,

Pink Sizzle Barbie

MiKelman wrist tag , enclosed in
"Happy New Year Barbie" box
(ILLUS.) **175.00**

Barbie, "Platinum Barbie," 1991,
Bob Mackie, third in series, No.
2703, Timeless Creations,
booklet, signed fashion
illustration, in box, cardboard
shipping box (creased
box flap)....................................**525.00**

Barbie, "Platinum Barbie," 1991,
Bob Mackie, third in series, part
of initial run of only 1,000 dolls
w/slight blue tint to sequins, sold
privately & carry different stock
number on shipping box, Mattel
employee newsletter included
offering doll to Mattel employees
only, in box, cardboard shipping
box, no wear.............................**725.00**

Barbie, "Queen of Hearts Barbie,"
1994, Bob Mackie, seventh in
series, No. 12046, booklet,
signed fashion illustration, in
box, cardboard shipping box **120.00**

Barbie, "Regal Reflections Barbie," 1992, Spiegel Department Store Special, No. 4116, never removed from box...**220.00**

Barbie, "Rockettes Barbie," 1992, FAO Schwarz, No. 2017, never removed from box ...**175.00**

Barbie, "Royal Invitation Barbie," 1993, Spiegel Department Store Special, No. 10969, never removed from box ...**95.00**

Barbie, "Ruffles 'N Swirls," No. 1783, blue, pink & white print dress, belt, aqua shoes, "Living Barbie & Skipper" booklet, cellophane bag, paper label, never removed from carton (missing cardboard box) ...**50.00**

Barbie, "Satin Nights Barbie," 1992, Service Merchandise, No. 1886, never removed from box (box lightly scuffed & worn) ...**50.00**

Barbie, "Savvy Shopper Barbie," 1994, Bloomingdale's Department Store Special, No. 12152, designed by Nicole Miller, never removed from box (small crease on left side of box) ...**105.00**

Barbie, "Silver Screen Barbie," 1993, FAO Schwarz, No. 11652, never removed from box (worn box edges) ...**175.00**

Barbie, "Snow Princess Barbie," 1994, Enchanted Seasons Collection, Limited Edition, No. 11875, includes crystal drop earrings, in box, cardboard shipping box ...**115.00**

Barbie, "Southern Belle Barbie," 1991, Sears Special Edition, No. 2586, never removed from box ...**55.00**

Barbie, "1850s Southern Belle Barbie," 1993, The Great Eras Collection, No. 11478, never removed from box (box edges & corners creased) ...**65.00**

Barbie, "Starlight Splendor Barbie," 1991, Bob Mackie, second in series, No. 2704, black doll, Timeless Creations, booklet, in box, cardboard shipping box (box upper left corner dented) ...**515.00**

Barbie, "Starlight Waltz Barbie," 1994, Ballroom Beauties Collection, Limited Edition, No. 14070, never removed from box ..**55.00**

Barbie, "Super Size Barbie," 1976, No. 9828, includes Wear 'n Share jewelry, never removed from box (box slightly discolored & worn, small section on upper window is loose) ...**100.00**

Barbie, "Sweet Valentine Barbie," 1995, Hallmark Special Edition, No. 14800, never removed from box ...**40.00**

Barbie, "Swirl Ponytail Barbie," 1964, golden blonde hair, beige lips w/tint of orange, finger & toe paint, straight legs, red nylon swimsuit (near mint condition w/hair in original topknot, dark green discolored dot on left ear, face slightly darker than body) ..**295.00**

Barbie, "Theater Elegance Barbie," 1994, Spiegel Department Store Special, No. 12077, never removed from box (side flap closure torn & taped, several small creases on upper section of box insert) ...**135.00**

Barbie, "Twist 'N Turn Barbie," 1967, blonde, pink lips, rooted eyelashes, cheek blush, finger & toe paint, bendable legs, orange one-piece nylon swimsuit w/original net cover suit (slightly frayed swimsuit seams, rubs on finger & toe paint) ...**135.00**

Barbie, "Uptown Chic Barbie," 1993, Classique Collection Barbie, No. 111623, never removed from box (small crease on rights side of box) ...**70.00**

Barbie, "Victorian Elegance Barbie," 1994, Hallmark Special Edition, No. 12579, never removed from box ...**70.00**

Barbie, "Winter Fantasy Barbie," 1990, FAO Schwarz, Limited Edition," No. 5946, includes extra head w/silver earrings, never removed from box (faint blue on ears from earrings, crease in lower front box) **260.00**

Barbie, "Winter Princess Barbie," 1993, Limited Edition, No. 10655, never removed form box.............**300.00**

1966 Francie

Talking Brad

Brad, "Talking Brad," 1971, painted black hair, bendable legs, original print shirt, orange vinyl swim trunks, wrist tag, non-working, creased wrist tag (ILLUS.) **90.00**

Christie, "Live Action Christie," 1970, print outfit, wrist tag, stand, in box (box discolored & slightly aged) **180.00**

Francie, 1966, blonde hair w/original stringing, pink lips, rooted eyelashes, cheek blush, bendable legs, original two-

piece red & white swimsuit, white soft shoes w/heels, Francie booklet, wrist tag, gold wire stand, cardboard insert, in box (ILLUS.) **260.00**

Francie, 1966, brunette, pink lips, rooted eyelashes, cheek blush, one-piece swimsuit w/green bottoms (ends of eyebrows slightly faded, faint green dot above left eye, cheek blush rubs) **125.00**

Francie, "Growin' Pretty Hair," 1970, blonde, pinks lips, rooted eye lashes, original pink dress (missing rubberband from hair, faded satin dress) **50.00**

Francie, "Hair Happenin' Francie," 1970, blonde, pink lips, rooted eyelashes, cheek blush, Twist 'N Turn-style, bendable legs, blue dress w/lace trim, two blonde & one brunette hair piece (lace on dress worn, pin hole & light colored spot on left ear) **105.00**

Francie, "Twist 'N Turn Francie," 1967, blonde hair w/original stringing, pinks lips, rooted eyelashes, cheek blush, bendable legs, original one-piece swimsuit (some body discoloration, otherwise near mint condition) **75.00**

Kelly, "Quick Curl Kelly," 1972, red hair, green & white dress, wrist tag, accessories, never removed from box (box & front cardboard slightly discolored)............................... **105.00**

Quick Curl Kelly

Kelly, "Quick Curl Kelly," 1973, titian, pink lips, bendable legs, wrist tag, original dress w/accessories, white plastic stand, never removed from box (ILLUS.) **90.00**

Ken, 1961, medium brown flocked hair, beige lips, straight legs, red swim trunks w/stripe,

cork sandals w/red straps (hair rubs, split on one sandal) **60.00**

Ken, 1962, painted blond hair, beige lips, straight legs, red & white striped jacket, red cotton shorts, cork sandals w/red straps (right leg slightly shorter than left) **30.00**

Ken, 1963, painted brunette hair, beige lips, straight legs, print short sleeve shirt w/button accents, brown pants, yellow cotton socks, brown shoes (faint pink lines on both legs)...............**50.00**

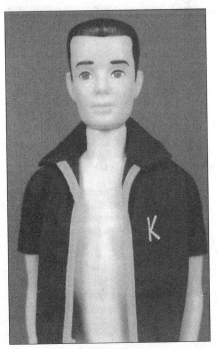

1965 Ken

Ken, 1965, painted brunette hair, pink lips, cheek blush, bendable legs, original jacket marked "K," red shorts, cork sandals w/red straps, faded ink stain on front upper right leg (ILLUS.) **125.00**

Ken, "Ken as Rhett Butler," 1994, Hollywood Legends Collection, No. 12741, never removed from box (box slightly scuffed w/creased top flap) **45.00**

Live Action Ken

1964 Midge

Ken, "Live Action Ken," 1971, painted brown hair, original print nylon shirt, yellow satin pants, brown fringe vest, brown shoes, wrist tag (ILLUS.).......................**65.00**

Midge, 1963, titian, pink lips, finger & toe paint, straight legs, original two-piece chartreuse & orange swimsuit (rubs on inside eye & eyebrows).........................**55.00**

Midge, 1963, brunette, coral lips w/teeth, finger & toe paint, two-piece pink & red nylon swimsuit (loose bottom stitching on swimsuit, snag on swimsuit bottom) **105.00**

Midge, 1964, blonde, pink lips, finger & toe paint, straight legs, original two-piece blue swimsuit, in box (hair slightly mussed, faint pink stain on back of swimsuit top, box slightly discolored & worn) **70.00**

Midge, 1964, titian, pinks lips, finger & toe paint, straight legs,

original two-piece chartreuse & orange swimsuit (ILLUS.) **80.00**

Midge, 1964, brunette, pink lips, finger & toe paint, straight legs, wearing "Barbie in Hawaii" outfit w/two-piece red & white swimsuit, "grass" skirt, flower lei, plastic pineapple, travel pamphlet (clothes discolored, small hole in pineapple).............**125.00**

Midge, 1965, brunette, pink lips, bendable legs, original one-piece striped swimsuit (frayed & worn swimsuit, eyebrows slightly faded, small lip rub) **305.00**

P.J., "Live Action," 1971, blonde hair w/original braids & beaded accents, pink lips, rooted eyelashes, faint cheek blush, bendable arms & legs, original jumpsuit & purple fringe vest..**100.00**

Ricky, 1965, painted red hair, beige lips, straight legs, striped

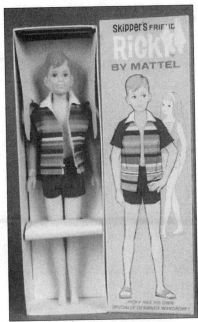

Ricky, Skipper's Friend

Skipper, Barbie's Little Sister

jacket, blue swim trunks, wrist tag, in box w/black wire stand, box insert, some slight aging & discoloration (ILLUS.) **100.00**

Skipper, 1964, pale blonde hair, bright beige lips, straight legs, red & white one-piece swimsuit, red flat shoes, brass headband (near mint condition w/faded green discoloration along hairline, some fading of clothes) **50.00**

Skipper, 1964, titian, pink lips, pink skin, one-piece swimsuit, yellow brush, red flat shoes (light discolored area on left from temple to ear, slightly worn swimsuit) **35.00**

Skipper, 1964, blonde, pink lips, straight legs, original red & white one-piece swimsuit, red flat shoes, headband, gold wire stand, white cover "Skipper" booklet, in box (elastic on swimsuit legs stretched, box slightly discolored & worn, damage to upper flap) **85.00**

Skipper, 1964, brunette, pink lips, straight legs, original one-piece red & white swimsuit, red flat shoes, white plastic comb, white cover booklet, gold wire stand, in box, (ILLUS.) **90.00**

Skipper, 1970, "Living Skipper," blonde hair in original set w/pink ribbon ties, pink lips, rooted eyelashes, cheek blush, bendable legs, one-piece nylon swimsuit (arms do not bend, small hole right arm at elbow from bendable mechanism, few right eyelashes bent) **25.00**

Skipper, 1974, Japan, short red hair w/ribbon ties, red dress w/butterfly decal, cardboard "wings," pink plastic comb, brush hair curler, hair ribbons & pins, never removed from package(discolored & worn cardboard package, dent in lower left plastic corner) **95.00**

Skipper Party Time Gift Set

Skipper, "Skipper Party Time Gift Set," blonde, pink lips, straight legs, original red & white one-piece swimsuit, headband, flat red shoes, white plastic brush, white cover Skipper booklet, bottom of box w/cardboard liner, cellophane over doll's head, No. 1902 Silk 'n Fancy dress, No. 1906 Dress Coat w/button accents & matching hat w/bow accents, purse w/button closure & braid handle, white nylon socks, short gloves, white flat shoes, gold elastic headband attached to cardboard backing & cellophane covering, in box (ILLUS.) **600.00**

Skooter, 1964, titian hair w/ribbon ties, pink lips, straight legs, wearing Skipper's red & white one-piece swimsuit, red flat shoes, wrist tag, gold wire stand, yellow cover booklet, in box (torn wrist tag, box discolored & worn) **80.00**

Skooter, 1965, light blonde hair w/ribbon ties, pink lips, faint cheek blush, straight legs, two-piece red & white swimsuit (near mint condition w/slight wear on swimsuit top) **55.00**

Skooter, 1965, brunette hair w/replaced ribbons, pink lips, straight legs, original red & white two-piece swimsuit, yellow booklet, gold wire stand, in box w/cardboard liner......................**100.00**

Stacey, "Talking Stacey," titian, pink lips w/painted teeth, rooted eyelashes, bendable legs, wrist tag, two-piece swimsuit w/clear plastic stand, never removed from box (box slightly discolored, scuffed & worn w/small crease on both sides) **285.00**

Stacey, "Twist 'N Turn Stacey," 1968, blonde hair pulled back w/ribbon tie, rooted eyelashes, pink lips w/painted teeth, finger & toe paint, bendable legs, red nylon swimsuit w/button accents, red open-toe shoes (two small dots on lower leg cheek, both arms yellowed).......**155.00**

Steffie, "Busy Steffie," 1972, brunette, pink lips, bendable arms & legs, original long dress, instruction booklet, brown travel

case w/stickers, brown side tray
w/twos cuts, brown record
player & record w/decals, brown
telephone, broken left arm,
discolored booklet, record arm
missing **85.00**

Walk Lively Steffie

Steffie, "Walk Lively Steffie,"
1972, No. 1183, print outfit
w/scarf, shoes stand, certificate,
in box, box slightly worn &
discolored (ILLUS.)...................**145.00**

HAPPY HOLIDAYS BARBIE

Barbie, "Happy Holidays Barbie,"
1988, No. 1703, red dress
w/silver design, never removed
from box (box slightly
discolored, scuff on plastic
window) **775.00**

Barbie, "Happy Holidays Barbie,"
1989, No. 3523, white gown
w/fur trim, never removed from
box (slight age
discoloration) **225.00**

Barbie, "Happy Holidays Barbie,"
1990, No. 4098, fuchsia gown
w/silver design, in box (slight
wear on right side box
corners) **130.00**

Barbie, "Happy Holidays Barbie,"
1990, No. 4098, fuchsia gown
w/silver design, never removed
from box (lightly scuffed plastic
window) **175.00**

Barbie, "Happy Holidays Barbie,"
1991, No. 1870, green velvet
gown w/sequin design, never
removed from box (slight
discoloration of box) **210.00**

Barbie, "Happy Holidays Barbie,"
1991, black, No. 2696, green
velvet gown w/sequin design,
never removed from box (box
discolored, partially loose plastic
bottom, small cut on top
plastic) **45.00**

Barbie, "Happy Holidays Barbie,"
1992, No. 1429, silver gown
w/sequin & bead design, never
removed from box (crease
inplastic window) **110.00**

Barbie, "Happy Holidays Barbie,"
1993, No. 10824, red gown
w/gold glitter, bead & sequin
design, never removed from
box, cardboard shipping box **100.00**

Barbie, "Happy Holidays Barbie,"
1994, No. 12155, gold gown
w/fur & sequin design, never
removed from box **80.00**

Barbie, "Happy Holidays Barbie,"
1995, No. 14123, green gown
w/sequin & bead design, never
removed from box **50.00**

Barbie, "Happy Holidays Barbie,"
1995, No. 14124, black, green
gown w/sequin & bead design,
never removed from box **40.00**

Barbie, "Happy Holidays Gala
Barbie," 1994, Special Edition,
No. 13545, never removed from
box..**85.00**

INTERNATIONAL BARBIE

Barbie, "Canadian Barbie," 1987,
No. 4928, never removed from
box (box slightly discolored
w/wear to corners) **50.00**

Barbie, "Czechoslovakian Barbie," 1990, No. 7330 (box scuffed w/wear & creases to corners) **65.00**

Barbie, "English Barbie," 1991, No. 4973, never removed from box (box corners slightly creased) **40.00**

Barbie, "Eskimo Barbie," 1981, No. 3898, never removed from box (box discolored w/slight wear to corners & edges, upper left corner on plastic loose, crease in lower front corner)........**80.00**

Barbie, "German Barbie," 1986, No. 3188, never removed from box (lightly scuffed & discolored box w/slightly worn corners) **50.00**

Barbie, "Greek Barbie," 1985, No. 2997, never removed from box (box corners slightly worn w/some damage)......................**40.00**

Barbie, "Hispanic Barbie," 1979, No. 1292, never removed from box (slight wear to box, upper section cardboard worn & creased, upper & lower sections of plastic window loose) **25.00**

Barbie, "Icelandic Barbie," 1986, No. 3189, never removed from box (box corners slightly worn)....**50.00**

Barbie, "India Barbie," 1981, No. 3897, never removed from box (box discolored w/edges & corners worn, several small tears, lower front slightly dented) **45.00**

Barbie, "Irish Barbie," 1983, No. 7517, never removed from box (box slightly discolored w/slight wear to corners & edges, plastic window cracked w/extending tears) **55.00**

Barbie, "Italian Barbie," 1979, No. 1602, never removed from box (box worn, scuffed & slightly discolored, crease in cardboard, taped split in upper back edge) ..**130.00**

Barbie, "Japanese Barbie," 1984, No. 9481, never removed from

box (box worn w/slight discoloration, dent to left side of cardboard, bottom flap opened & taped, plastic window slightly creased) **55.00**

Barbie, "Korean Barbie," 1987, No. 4929, never removed from box (box lightly scuffed w/slightly worn corners) **45.00**

Barbie, "Mexican Barbie," 1988, No. 1917, never removed from box (box slightly discolored w/wear to corners, upper front cardboard & corners slightly dented) **35.00**

Barbie, "Nigerian Barbie," 1989, No. 7376, never removed from box (box lightly scuffed w/slightly worn corners, bottom flap has been opened) **35.00**

Barbie, "Oriental Barbie," 1980, No. 3262, never removed from box (box slightly worn, scuffed & discolored, crease on lower right front) **50.00**

Barbie, "Parisian Barbie," 1979, No. 1600, never removed from box (box worn, scuffed & discolored, crease in front cardboard, edges worn) **55.00**

Barbie, "Peruvian Barbie," 1985, No. 2995, never removed from box (slight wear to box corners) ..**45.00**

Barbie, "Royal Barbie," 1979, No. 1601, never removed from box (box worn, scuffed & discolored, crease in front cardboard, wear on corners) **85.00**

Barbie, "Russian Barbie," 1988, No. 1916, never removed from box, (slight wear & discoloration on box, dent in lower front right side, flap opened & taped) **45.00**

Barbie, "Scottish Barbie," 1980, No. 3263, has been opened (box slightly worn, scuffed & discolored, shoe package retaped to inside of box, stand loose in box) **80.00**

Barbie, "Spanish Barbie,"
1982, No. 4031, never removed
from box (box discolored w/wear
to corners & slightly
scuffed)..............................**60.00**

Barbie, "Swedish Barbie," 1982,
No. 4032, never removed from
box (slight wear & discoloration
to box, yellowed plastic
window) **45.00**

Barbie, "Swiss Barbie," 1983,
No. 7541, never removed from
box (box slightly worn, scuffed &
discolored, bottom flap opened
& taped) **45.00**

PORCELAIN DOLLS

Barbie, "Benefit Performance
Barbie," 1988, certificate No.
01697, in box, cardboard
shipping box (box slightly
discolored w/worn corners, wear
on upper flap closure)..............**200.00**

Barbie, "Blue Rhapsody Barbie,"
1986, certificate No. 00591, in
box (box discolored & worn
w/crease in flap) **215.00**

Barbie, "Crystal Rhapsody
Barbie," 1992, certificate
No. 07259, in box w/cardboard
shipping box **360.00**

Barbie, "Enchanted Evening
Barbie," 1987, certificate
No. 004986, in box, cardboard
shipping box (box slightly
discolored w/worn & creased
flap) **185.00**

Barbie, "Gay Parisienne Barbie,"
1991, brunette, certificate
No. 08406, in box, cardboard
shipping box **120.00**

Barbie, "Gay Parisienne Barbie,"
1991, Disney issue w/titian hair,
certificate No. 15986, Disney
certificate No. 016/300, "Disney
World Gay Parisienne Barbie"
ribbon & Showcase of Dolls
1991 pin, box signed by Carol
Spencer, in box, cardboard
shipping box (shoes & purse

loose, upper front corners
slightly dented) **235.00**

Barbie, "Gold Sensation Barbie,"
1993, certificate No. 12448, in
box (several small creases in
right side of box) **375.00**

Barbie, "Plantation Belle Barbie,"
1992, red hair, certificate
No. 03043, in box (hat, shoes &
purse loose in box) **155.00**

Barbie, "Royal Splendor Barbie,"
1993, certificate No. 01876, in
box, cardboard shipping box **185.00**

Barbie, "Silken Flame Barbie,"
1993, brunette, certificate No.
07810, in box (box flap closure
worn & slightly torn) **95.00**

Barbie, "Silver Starlight Barbie,"
1993, certificate No. 05224, in
box, cardboard shipping box
(shoes are loose)..................**115.00**

Barbie, "Solo in Spotlight Barbie,"
1990, certificate No. 00156, in
box, cardboard shipping
box(slight wear to box corners,
several small cuts to top flap)....**120.00**

Barbie, "Solo in Spotlight Barbie,"
1990, certificate No. 20422, in
box (box slightly scuffed)..........**140.00**

Barbie, "Sophisticated Lady
Barbie," 1990, certificate
No. 05193, in box (box slightly
discolored) **85.00**

Barbie, "Sophisticated Lady
Barbie," 1990, certificate
No. 07216, in box, cardboard
shipping box (box slightly
discolored) **115.00**

Barbie, "Star Lily Bride Barbie,"
1994, certificate No. 12172, in
box, cardboard shipping box
(shoes are loose)..................**115.00**

Barbie, "Wedding Day Barbie,"
1989, certificate No. 6500, in
box, cardboard shipping box(box
slightly discolored & worn
w/small faded spots)................**200.00**

Barbie, "Wedding Party Barbie,"
1989, certificate No. 0952, in

box, cardboard shipping box (box slightly discolored w/loose left side seam) **275.00**

Ken, "30th Anniversary Ken," 1991, certificate No. 06494, in box, cardboard shipping box(dent left back box corner).....**80.00**

Midge, "30th Anniversary Midge," 1992, certificate 03226, new in box, cardboard shipping box **115.00**

Skipper, "30th Anniversary Skipper," 1993, certificate No. 00478...................................**95.00**

CLOTHING & ACCESSORIES

Apron & utensils, 1962, Barbie pak item, blue apron, never removed from package (cardboard backing discolored, torn cellophane above spatula) **75.00**

Brush & mirror set, brush w/nylon bristles & pale pink plastic w/plastic lacework edging, plastic covering on backs w/brunette Ponytail Barbie wearing "Orange Blossom" outfit dated 1962, child-size (bent bristles on brush, small crack in edging on picture side of mirror) **105.00**

Clothing set, Barbie, "American Airlines Stewardess," No. 984, blue jacket w/wings & button accents, matching skirt & hat w/metal insignia, white nylon bodyshirt w/button accents, black vinyl shoulder purse black open-toe shoes, blue fight bag w/zipper & insignia, blue cover booklet, no wear or soil **70.00**

Clothing set, Barbie, "Arabian Nights," No. 0874, pink satin blouse, long skirt w/gold trim, matching shawl, gold vinyl slippers, gold lamp, gold earrings, beaded necklace, three bracelets (slightly frayed blouse tag, frayed edges of shirt & shawl)....................................**150.00**

Clothing set, Barbie, "Barbie Baby-Sits," No. 953, pink & white apron, painted face baby w/diaper & flannel sacque, pink plastic bassinet w/floral liner, pillow, extra diaper, bottle, cola bottle, white telephone, book strap, three books, alarm clock, black-rimmed eye glasses w/clear lenses, telephone number list, blue cover booklet, never removed from box (paper label missing, box slightly discolored w/split edges) **145.00**

Clothing set, Barbie, "Barbie Learns to Cook," No. 1634, print dress w/button accents & pink belt, pale blue pointed-toe shoes, toaster, two slices of toast, teakettle, three pans in various sizes w/matching lids, double broiler, potholder, "Barbie's Easy-As-Pie Cookbook" (slight age discoloration of dress, pans, toaster, teakettle & book) **185.00**

Clothing set, Barbie, "Beautiful Blues," Sears Exclusive, blue short dress w/bow accent, blue satin coat w/fur trim, blue vinyl clutch purse w/button closure, turquoise pointed-toe shoes (coat slightly faded w/frayed arm inseams, slightly frayed dress tag, bow accent slightly worn) ...**725.00**

Clothing set, Barbie, "Black Magic Ensemble," No. 1609, black sheath dress, black tulle cape w/ribbon trim, black nylon short gloves, black open-toe shoes **145.00**

Clothing set, Barbie, "Campus Sweetheart," No. 1616, white satin gown w/red pink tulle panels, silver trophy (pin holes along hem of gown)..................**285.00**

Clothing set, Barbie, "Candy Striper Volunteer", No. 0889, red & white striped pinafore, white hat, white tennis shoes, plastic soap, wax, watermelon slice, orange drink w/fizz, Kleenex tissues, white plastic tray, (slight general wear) **45.00**

Clothing set, Barbie, "Career Girl," No. 954, black & white jacket w/button accents, matching skirt & hat w/velvet band & rose accent, red sleeveless cotton bodyshirt, black nylon long gloves, black open-toe shoes, (frayed jacket tag) **95.00**

Clothing set, Barbie, "Cheerleader Barbie," No. 0876, white sweater marked "M," red shirt, white cotton socks, red tennis shoes in small cellophane bag, red & white pompons, megaphone marked "M" (discolored sweater & socks) **65.00**

Clothing set, Barbie, "Commuter Set," No. 916, navy knit jacket & matching skirt, white satin bodyshirt, blue & white checked bodyshirt w/button accent, rose colored flower hat, , hat box w/string handle, white nylon short gloves, crystal two-strand necklace & bracelet, navy open-toe shoes (slightly frayed edges on hat, small stain on one glove, bottom of hat box worn, shoes different shades of navy)..**300.00**

Clothing set, Barbie, "Debutante Ball," No. 1666, aqua gown w/flower accent, fur stole w/ties, clear open-toe shoes w/gold glitter, single pearl necklace, gold clutch purse w/button closure (slightly frayed inseams & flowers on gown, fade spots, slightly worn button closure on purse) **215.00**

Clothing set, Barbie, "Dinner at Eight," No. 946, jumpsuit, net hostess coat, cork wedgies w/gold uppers, blue cover booklet (small pull in fabric on front of jumpsuit at bodice gathering) **55.00**

Clothing set, Barbie, "Dog 'n Duds," No. 1613, grey poodle w/felt features, braid & chain leashes attached to vinyl collars, red velvet & plaid coats, pink tutu w/ribbon ties, white plastic collar w/ribbon ties, felt hat w/elastic strap, red & white ear muffs, plastic bone, dog food box, wooden bowl w/dog food, white cover booklet (dog partially flat, ends frayed on ribbon, discolored dog food box) **90.00**

Clothing set, Barbie, "Drum Majorette," No. 0875, red velvet jacket w/gold trim, white skirt, nylon tights, white nylon short gloves, white boots w/molded tassel, red hat w/gold trim & elastic chin strap, baton (elastic stretched on hat chin strap & skirt waistband, elastic missing on tights).....................................**60.00**

Clothing set, Barbie, "Enchanted Evening," No. 983, pink satin gown w/sequins at waist, pink lined stole, white long gloves, clear open-toe shoes w/gold glitter, three-strand pearl necklace & matching earrings w/drops (inseams slightly frayed, reconstructed earrings) **105.00**

Clothing set, Barbie, "Evening Splendour," No. 961, gold & white brocade dress, matching coat w/fur trim, fur hat w/pearl trim, turquoise corduroy clutch purse, pearl necklace, brown open-toe shoes (frayed coat tag, discolored necklace, slightly soiled purse w/button missing) **110.00**

Clothing set, Barbie, "Formal Occasion," No. 1697, long dress w/gold trim, gold long coat w/neckties, white pointed-toe shoes (dress slightly discolored, frayed area below zipper, slightly frayed tag & ends of neckties) **125.00**

Clothing set, Barbie, "Friday Night Date," No. 979, corduroy jumper w/appliqués, white underdress, black open-toe shoes, two orange drinks w/fizz & two plastic straws, black plastic tray w/Barbie logo (jumper w/loose snap & soiling) ..**65.00**

Clothing set, Barbie, "Gay Parisienne," No. 964, navy & white dot dress w/bow accents, white fur stole, navy tulle hat w/bead accents, blue open-toe No. 1 shoes w/holes, gold corduroy clutch purse w/button closure, white nylon long gloves, pearl necklace & earrings (frayed dress tag, discolored metal on necklace, discolored stole, several small stains) **700.00**

Clothing set, Barbie, "Glimmer Glamour," No. 1547, blue dress w/gold trim & design, gold lame coat, gold belt & clutch purse w/button closure, clear open-toe shoes w/gold glitter, ca. 1968 (missing some glitter on dress, slightly worn button closure on belt & purse) **900.00**

Clothing set, Barbie, "Golden Groove," pink & gold jacket w/fur trim & button & chain accents, matching short skirt, gold thigh-hi boots (some silver discoloration on boots) **250.00**

Clothing set, Barbie, "Guinevere," No. 9873, blue velvet gown w/embroidery trim & chain belt, red nylon armlets, brocade crown w/nylon snood & neck strap, one brocade slipper (belt loose on front of gown, discolored neck strap on crown)....................................**60.00**

Clothing set, Barbie, "Barbie in Japan," No. 0821, kimono, obi, three hair ornaments, thongs w/white nylon socks, fan, samisen, travel pamphlet, yellow cover booklet, cellophane covering **300.00**

Clothing set, Barbie, "Knitting Pretty," No. 957, royal blue sweater, sleeveless shell, skirt, black open-toe shoes, scissors, bowl w/red, yellow & green yarn & two needles, "How to Knit" book, blue cover booklet, paper label, box dated 1962, never removed from box (light age discoloration on box) **165.00**

Clothing set, Barbie, "Let's Dance," No. 978, blue dress w/print design, white clutch purse, black open-toe shoes, single pearl necklace (fraying tag on dress, discolored necklace) **75.00**

Clothing set, Barbie, "Let's Have a Ball," No. 1879, gown w/attached belt & metal flower w/jewel, matching velvet coat w/fur trim, turquoise shoes (small brown spots on dress over-shirt) **65.00**

Clothing set, Barbie, "Little Red Riding Hood and the Wolf," No. 0880, blue & white dress, corset, cape, black vinyl shoes, woven straw basket, red & white checkered napkin, wax rolls, black & red checked cap, dotted hat, wolf's head, theater program, "Exclusive Fashions by Mattel" booklet, never removed from box (box discolored w/worn edges & corners) **450.00**

Clothing set, Barbie, "Magnificent Midi," No. 3418, red velvet coat w/fur trim & button & tab closures, matching hat & dress w/attached belt, black vinyl boots w/fur trim (several small dents on boots)` **265.00**

Clothing set, Barbie, "Masquerade," No. 944, black & yellow bodysuit w/tulle & glitter trim & ribbon ties, black nylon tights, felt hat w/elastic chin strap, black mask w/elastic head strap, black open-toe shoes, yellow pompons, party invitations (loose pompons, otherwise near mint) **50.00**

Clothing set, Barbie, "Midnight Blue," No. 1617, blue & silver gown, matching long coat w/fur collar, white nylon long gloves, pearl necklace, silver clutch purse w/button closure (slightly frayed tag, pinholes in gown & coat) **225.00**

Clothing set, Barbie, "Mini Print," No. 1809, print short dress w/zipper, matching stockings, blue bow shoes (frayed tag on dress) **90.00**

Clothing set, Barbie, "Open Road," No. 985, coat w/toggle buttons, striped pants, beige knit sweater, straw hat w/attached red scarf & hat band, red rimmed eye glasses w/blue lenses, cork wedgies w/red uppers, Mattel Road Map (Road Map slightly discolored & worn, coat tag slightly frayed) **155.00**

Clothing set, Barbie, "Party Date," No. 958, white satin dress w/gold glitter, gold belt & clutch purse w/button closure (dress slightly discolored, wear on belt & purse) **65.00**

Clothing set, Barbie, "Patio Party," No. 1692, floral print jumpsuit, green & blue satin cover-up, medium blue pointed-toe shoes, blue round earrings w/four gold accents (several pin holes on cover-up, discolored metal on earrings) **115.00**

Clothing set, Barbie, "Peachy Fleecy Coat," No. 915, beige coat stitched to hold sides in place, brown felt hat w/feather & pearl accent, tan vinyl gloves, brown open-toe shoes, shows no fading or wear........................**50.00**

Clothing set, Barbie, "Picnic Set," No. 967, red & white checked bodysuit w/button accent, denim jeans, cork wedgies w/red upper

& woven straw straps, straw hat w/flower & frog accents & ribbons ties, fishing pole w/handle, line sinker & fish, woven straw hat, no fading or wear...**170.00**

Clothing set, Barbie, "Pink Sparkle," No. 1440, pink dress w/pink design, pink nylon cape w/ties, dark pink pointed-toe shoes (slightly frayed dress tag) **135.00**

Clothing set, Barbie, "Plantation Belle," No. 966, pale pink dot dress w/lace trim, petticoat w/tulle & bow accents, straw hat w/flower accent, pink woven straw purse w/sequin & bead design, white nylon short gloves, pale pink open-toe shoes, pink pearl necklace & bracelet (frayed ends of bow on petticoat, missing metal headband on hat, discolored gloves) **115.00**

Clothing set, Barbie, No. 1491, "Red, White n' Warm," white vinyl coat w/fur trim & button & tab closure, belt, matching boots w/fur trim & button & chain accents, orange & pink dress (slightly discolored vinyl pieces, chain loose on boot, sides of belt are slightly stretched) **85.00**

Clothing set, Barbie, "Riding in the Park," No. 1668, plaid jacket w/button accents, yellow jodhpurs, white bodyshirt, brown nylon short gloves, brown plastic hat, boots & riding crop, "Exclusive Fashions by Mattel Book 3" booklet, plastic covering (plastic covering cracked over hat) **325.00**

Clothing set, Barbie, "Scene Stealers," No. 1845, pink ruffled skirt w/green trim, green lame shirt w/pink trim, sheer pink coat, bright pink pointed toe shoes, sheer pink nylon stockings (loose elastic button closure on skirt, inseams frayed)...................**85.00**

Clothing set, Barbie, "Sheath Sensation," No. 986, red dress w/button accents, woven straw hat w/ribbon band, white open-toe shoes, shows no wear or fading..**45.00**

Clothing set, Barbie, "Shimmering Magic," No. 1664, silver lame sheath dress, red satin coat, hat w/silver tulle & rose accents, red pointed-toe shoes (rose slightly faded & beginning to fray along edges, faded leaves, pin holes in hem of coat)...............................**450.00**

Clothing set, Barbie, "Slumber Party," No. 1642, pink robe w/attached belt, two-piece satin pajamas, one pink open-toe scuff w/blue pompon, bath scales w/pink top, "How to Lose Weight" book, blue plastic comb & brush, six pink plastic curlers & "Barbie" pins in original plastic bag w/paper label (bath scales top slightly soiled).......................**85.00**

Clothing set, Barbie, "Solo in the Spotlight," No. 982, black sequin gown w/tulle & rose accent, pink scarf, black nylon long gloves, black open-toe shoes, crystal four-strand necklace, microphone (rose edges slightly frayed, scarf slightly discolored, missing attachment piece to microphone) **130.00**

Clothing set, Barbie, "Sophisticated Lady," No. 993, pink satin sown w/silver trim, velvet long coat w/button accents, pale pink open-toe shoes w/silver glitter, white nylon long gloves, solid grey plastic tiara, pink pearl necklace, (coat tag slightly frayed) **110.00**

Clothing set, Barbie, "Sorority Meeting," No. 937, brown dress, vest, hat, brown open-toe shoes, pearl necklace & earrings, blue cover booklet, never removed from box (light age & wear on box) **155.00**

Clothing set, Barbie, "Sparkle Squares," No. 1814, pink, yellow & silver coat w/diamond button accents & ruffle, matching dress w/attached silver belt & nylon over-skirt, sheer white stockings (small discolored area & wear to edge of back ruffle near neck, right shoulder strap loose on front of dress) **115.00**

Clothing set, Barbie, "Student Teacher," No. 1622, red & white dress w/attached belt & button accents, black-rimmed eye glasses w/clear lenses, geography book, black pointer w/silver tip, red pointed-toe shoes (dress slightly discolored, book slightly worn)....................**100.00**

Clothing set, Barbie, "Velveteens," No. 1818, Sears Exclusive, pantsuit w/red velvet pants & crepe top w/ruffle trim, matching coat w/diamond button closure, red pointed-toe shoes (frayed tag on jacket, discolored pantsuit)....................................**350.00**

Clothing set, Barbie, "Winter Wow," No. 1486, orange jacket w/button accents & fur trim, matching pleated skirt, gold belt, fur hat w/gold braid ties, gold metallic thigh-hi boots (bent braid ties on hat, boots discolored) **95.00**

Clothing set, Barbie, "The Yellow Go," yellow coat w/button accents, yellow hat w/pompon & attached checked scarf, yellow lacy stockings, blue vinyl purse w/chain shoulder strap & metal closure accent, blue & grey flat shoes w/buckle (slightly frayed coat tag, small mended area on a stocking) **270.00**

Clothing set, Francie, "Bells," No. 1275, red, white & blue print sleeveless shirt w/button closure & cardboard form, matching blue & white bell bottom pants & cap, red vinyl purse w/strap, blue flat shoes w/molded buckle, no fading or wear............................**135.00**

Clothing set, Francie, "Check This," No. 1291, black, white & yellow dress w/vinyl & plastic daisy accents, yellow chiffon scarf w/daisy, white nylon short gloves, white pointed-toe soft shoes, no fading or wear.............**90.00**

Clothing set, Francie, "Clear Out!," No. 1281, red, white & blue striped knit dress, clear plastic coat w/red trim & vinyl tab closures, matching hat, red hatbox w/decal (front of dress slightly faded, hatbox decal discolored)................................**255.00**

Clothing set, Francie, "Dreamy Wedding," No. 1217, white satin gown, white nylon over-dress w/embroidered flowers, white tulle veil w/bow accent & metal headband (slightly discolored dress & bow on veil)....................**75.00**

Clothing set, Francie, "In Print," No. 1288, w/paper label, ca. 1965, never removed from package (box discolored & damaged) **80.00**

Clothing set, Francie, "Summer Coolers," No. 1292, yellow dress w/button accents & print pockets & trim, matching print two-piece swimsuit w/bow accents, matching tote bag w/ribbon drawstring, cork sandals w/attached red ribbon leg ties, blonde hair braid w/attached red ribbon & gold barrette, plastic granny glasses, paper umbrella w/wooden handle (some hair stands loose from braid).............**260.00**

Clothing set, Ken, "Army and Air Force," No. 797, tan shirt w/decal on pocket & button accents, matching pants, blue tie w/elastic strap, shoes, belt & hat, tan tie, shoes, belt, hat & socks, black socks, metal "wings," color card, blue cover booklet, ca. 1961, never

removed from card (plastic over blue shoes dented, box aged & discolored w/wear to edges) **90.00**

Clothing set, Ken, "Dreamboat," No. 785, olive blazer, pants, print shirt w/button accent, hat w/hatband, yellow cotton socks, brown shoes, blue cover booklet, paper label, ca. 1961, never removed from box (slight wear & yellowing of box) **90.00**

Clothing set, Ken, "Going Huntin'," No. 1409, plaid shirt w/button accents, denim jeans, red plastic hat, black boots, red cotton socks, plastic rifle, yellow cover booklet (hat loose from cardboard backing, discolored paper on backing).......................**45.00**

Clothing set, Ken, "Graduation," No. 795, black robe, black felt hat w/tassel, diploma w/ribbon tie, blue cover cardboard booklet, cardboard backing (items loose from original cardboard backing).....................**30.00**

Ken In Holland

Clothing set, Ken, "Ken in Holland," 1961, No. 0777, w/paper label, never removed from box, box worn & discolored, top edge torn near perforation, bottom edge creased (ILLUS.) **175.00**

Clothing set, Ken, "In Training," No. 780, white shirt & briefs, red & white shorts, two black plastic dumbbells, "How to Build Muscles" book, pink cover "Barbie" booklet, ca. 1961, never removed from box (box slightly discolored & worn).......................**30.00**

Clothing set, Ken, "Ken in Mexico," No. 0778, brown jacket & pants w/braid trim, matching hat, white shirt, green cummerbund, tie w/elastic neck strap, black boots, travel pamphlet, "Exclusive Fashions by Mattel Book 2" booklet, never removed from box label (missing label, slight age & discoloration to box) **135.00**

Clothing set, Ken, "The Prince," No. 0772, green cape w/gold lining, green & gold brocade jacket w/lace trim & diamond accents, white lace collar, velour pantaloons w/attached nylon tights, green slippers, pillow w/tassel accents, clear pointed-toe shoes, gold velour hat w/feather & emerald & gold velour hat w/feather & emerald & pearl jewels (stretched elastic on pantaloons, worn & frayed gold edging, slightly discolored collar)......................................**125.00**

Clothing set, Ken, "Ken in Switzerland," No. 0776, lederhosen w/attached suspenders & button accents, white shirt, white cotton-ribbed knee socks, felt hat, black boots, pipe, stein w/metal lid, travel pamphlet (shirt & travel pamphlet slightly discolored)...................................**85.00**

Clothing set, Ken, "King Arthur," No. 0773, silver lame armor, red satin surcoat w/gold griffin, belt, silver plastic helmet, cardboard shield, spurs, plastic sword &

scabbard, theater program, "Exclusive Fashions by Mattel Book 4," booklet, additional plastic covering on box, ca. 1964, never removed from box (box slightly discolored w/dented corners) **225.00**

Clothing set, Ken, "Play ball," No. 792, two-piece outfit w/marked "M" & attached belt, red cotton knee-socks, black cleats & ball in separate small cellophane bags, bat, yellow cover booklet, ca. 1961, additional plastic covering shrink-wrapped over box for protection, never removed from box (red cap loose, box discolored w/slight wear) **80.00**

Clothing set, Ken, "Sailor," No. 796, white shirt w/decal on arm & black tie, white cotton socks, black shoes in small cellophane bag, white plastic cap, blue cover booklet, cellophane cover (cellophane shoe bag has been opened, small tear near opening & loose from cardboard backing, paper on back of package discolored & taped closed) **45.00**

Ken "Shore Lines"

Clothing set, Ken, "Shore Lines," 1969, No. 1435, w/paper label, never removed from box, box slightly discolored & worn (ILLUS. bottom previous page) ...**55.00**

Clothing set, Ken, "Ski Champion," No. 798, red coat w/zipper, black pants & hat, brown plastic skis w/rubberbands, ski poles w/handles & "stops," green goggles, black cloth mittens, black boots, yellow cover booklet, paper label, additional plastic covering over box for protection, ca. 1961, never removed from box (box slightly discolored, small tear in original cellophane over ear end of goggles) **80.00**

Clothing set, Ken, "Tuxedo," No. 787, black jacket w/boutonniere, matching pants, white tuxedo shirt, burgundy cummerbund & bowtie, black nylon socks, black shoes, flower corsage, yellow cover booklet, paper label, never been removed from box (box lightly discolored & worn) **100.00**

Clothing set, Ricky, "Little Leaguer," No. 1504, red & blue shirt, matching socks, denim jeans, red plastic cap marked "M," white tennis shoes, ball, plastic glove, yellow cover booklet, paper label, never removed from box (glove loose in box, box slightly discolored w/some wear to corners) **45.00**

Clothing set, Skipper, "Ballet," No. 1905, tutu, black nylon leotard on cardboard form w/tights, flower headband, shoes, pink bag, ballet program, white cover booklet, never removed from box (missing label, box lightly aged & discolored) **65.00**

Clothing set, Skipper, "Dress Coat," No. 1906, red velvet coat w/button accents, matching hat

w/bow accent, purse w/button accent & braid handle, white nylon short gloves, white flat shoes in small cellophane bag, yellow cover booklet, paper label, ca. 1963, never removed from box (box slightly discolored & worn)......................**75.00**

Clothing set, Skipper, "Flower Girl," No. 1904, yellow dress w/ribbon accents, flower bouquet, flower headband, white nylon short gloves & socks, white flat shoes, white cover Skipper booklet, ca. 1964, never removed from box (discolored & worn box).............**145.00**

Clothing set, Skipper, "Learning to Ride," No. 1935, black & white checked jacket w/button accents, black plastic hat & knee boots, no wear or fading.............**35.00**

Clothing set, Skipper, "Lemon Fluff," No. 1749, yellow fur robe w/ribbon & daisy accents, matching slippers, yellow two-piece pajamas w/lace trim, "Living Barbie" booklet, paper label, ca. 1969, never removed from box (box slightly discolored & worn)......................**65.00**

Clothing set, Skipper, "Rain or Shine!," No. 1916, yellow rain coat w/matching belt & hat, yellow umbrella w/tassel, white knee-hi boots, white cover Skipper booklet, paper label, ca. 1963, never removed from box (box slightly discolored w/no wear) **110.00**

Clothing set, Skipper, "Red Sensation," No. 1901, red dress, straw hat, white nylon short gloves & socks, red flat shoes, white cover booklet, paper label, never removed from box (box discolored w/slightly worn edges) **60.00**

Clothing set, Skipper, "Skating Fun," No. 1908, red velvet skirt w/attached suspenders, red &

Skipper on Wheels Set

white jumpsuit, fur hat, white skates w/plastic blades, "Fashion & Play Accessories by Mattel" booklet, ca. 1964, never removed from box (box slightly discolored & worn)....................**150.00**

Clothing set, Skipper, "Skimmy Stripes," No. 1956, knit dress w/matching knee socks, orange felt hat w/ribbon trim, orange soft ankle boots, English & Arithmetic books, two pencils & black boot strap (edges slightly worn on Arithmetic book).............**95.00**

Clothing set, Skipper, "Skipper on Wheels," No. 1032, blue jacket & matching pants, embroidered blue blouse, "Barbie" print shirt, red wrapskirt, pairs of blue & red shoes, red hat, red yo-yo, red plastic goggles, red roller skates, red plastic skateboard & Skooter, "Exclusive Fashions by Mattel Book 1" booklet, goggles, Skooter, skateboard, skates, & booklet resewn on cardboard, box discolored, stained & worn on edges (ILLUS.) **505.00**

Clothing set, Skipper, "Under-pretties," No. 1900, white nylon slip, panties, pink plastic comb, brush & mirror, four pink plastic rollers in small cellophane bag, white cover Skipper booklet, ca. 1963, paper label, never removed from box (box slightly discolored & worn w/split on top of right side, paper label creased)....................**35.00**

Cologne, Barbie, 4 oz. gold colored cologne, pink plastic top, paper label on front w/blonde Ponytail Barbie, marked "Roclar Company, Beverly Hills, Calif.," ca. 1961, 5½" h. **35.00**

Convention items, 1994, "The Magic of Barbie in Birmingham 1994 Convention Package," canvas tote of American Girl Barbie, souvenir book, activity sheets, flyers, magazines, advertising items, souvenir Barbie doll wearing magician outfit, box w/convention logo, stand, never removed from box, limited to 650, extra outfit never removed from box (ILLUS. top next page) **160.00**

Barbie 1994 Convention Set

Convention items, 1996, black canvas tote bag w/Barbie & Bandstand print decals, black vinyl Barbie Tune Tote w/can of Aqua Net hair spray, American Bandstand Collector's Cards in packages, record-shaped pin, pen, comb, miniature Barbie Beat magazine, Barbie Autograph Book, six 45 RPM records in paper sleeves, black gift box w/small gold charm, most items w/Barbie or Convention logos, Bandstand Beauty Barbie convention doll in box (no wear or damage) **215.00**

Doll stand, twenty-four stands in two boxes for 11½"-12½" dolls, plastic coated metal w/base, never removed from boxes..........**20.00**

Hair Fair Barbie items, blonde hair head, blonde wig with elastic strap & bow, long blonde curls w/attached blue hair barrette & hair pin, brunette flip, white plastic comb & brush, two flower accents & two hair pins

attached to blue cardboard oval (cardboard worn & slightly torn) ..**50.00**

Tea set, "35th Anniversary Barbie Tea Set," 1994, 25 piece set in black velvet covered box w/pink lined insert & clasp closure, cardboard shipping box **35.00**

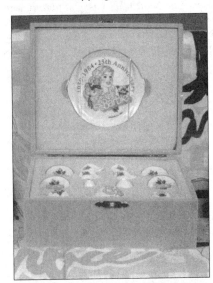

25th Anniversary Barbie Tea Set

Tea set, "25th Anniversary Barbie Tea Set," 1984, 14 piece set in grey velvet covered box w/pink lined insert & clasp closure, photocopy of Certificate of Authenticity No. 1252/25,000, in box (ILLUS. bottom previous page) **30.00**

View-Master Reels, "Barbie's Around the World View-Master Reels," 1965, includes reels 1-3 w/reel sleeve, envelope & "Diary" story booklet, Sawyer's (paper discolored, reel sleeve edges worn).................................**55.00**

Wrist watch, "Fossil Barbie Watch," No. 08878/20000, first edition, in hatbox w/scarf, no wear..**110.00**

BASKETS

The American Indians were the first basket weavers on this continent and, of necessity, the early Colonial settlers and their descendants pursued this artistic handicraft to provide essential containers for berries, eggs and endless other items to be carried or stored. Rye straw, split willow and reeds are but a few of the wide variety of materials used. The Nantucket baskets, plainly and sturdily constructed, along with those made by specialized groups, would seem to draw the greatest attention to this area of collecting.

A "Buttocks" & Storage Basket

"Buttucks" basket, fourteen-rib construction, eye-of-God handle design, bentwood handle, good color, some damage, 15 x 16½", 6½" h. plus handle (ILLUS. top, w/storage basket) **$72.00**

Early Leather Key Basket

Key basket, leather, black oval w/upright flat sides decorated in silver & gold stitches w/stylized scrolling foliage, the interior in red leathers, the underside inscribed illegibly, worn, probably Richmond, Virginia, early 19th c., 3⅝ x 5⅞", 4¾" h. (ILLUS.).......................**2,070.00**

Knife basket, woven splint, rectangular upright sides w/rounded corners, center wooden divider w/a bentwood handle, old patina w/some stains, minor damage, 8½ x 11", 3¾" h. plus handle.............**370.00**

Nantucket "Lightship" basket, finely woven splint, oval, w/the tapering body having a molded swing handle, on a turned plank base, Nantucket Island, Massachusetts, 20th c., 5¼ x 5¾" **575.00**

Nantucket "Lightship" basket, finely woven splint & cane, round w/turned wooden bottom, bentwood swivel handle, worn old varnish finish, 10" d., 5½" h. plus handle **880.00**

Three Figural Brass Bells

Storage basket, woven splint, rounded w/wooden bottom & rim band w/wire bail handle w/a wooden hand grip, old worn light green paint, 10" d., 6" h. plus handle......................................**523.00**

Sewing basket, woven splint, round tapering sides w/a rectangular base, bentwood rim handles, poplar w/red stain, small oval basket on interior, attributed to the Shakers, minor damage, 8" d., 3¼" h. **394.00**

Storage basket, woven splint, deep rounded sides w/a wide wrapped rim & swivel bentwood handle, thirty-three rib construction, 15" d., 10" h. (some damage & repair)............**138.00**

Storage basket, cov., woven splint, rectangular w/rounded corners, dark stain w/reddish orange 7 blue, wear & damage, 19½" l. (ILLUS. bottom, previous page) **72.00**

Utility basket, woven splint, thirty-three rib construction, shallow wide rounded sides on a small footring, the wrapped rim w/a bentwood handle, good age & color, 8" d., 3¼" h. plus handle (minor break in rim) **116.00**

Utility basket, half-basket, woven splint, deep rounded ribbed sides w/bentwood handle, attributed to Pennsylvania, 9" h. plus handle .**358.00**

BELLS

Figural bell, brass, two full-figure pixies sitting atop a large ribbed mushroom, 3" d., 3" h. (ILLUS. above center) **$40.00**

Figural bell, brass, figural head of an angry bearded god on each side w/a hand & bar top handle, 2¼" d., 3½" h. (ILLUS. above left) **65.00**

Figural bell, brass, standing figure of a young girl wearing a hat & standing w/her arms outstretched, 1½" d., 3¾" d. (ILLUS. above right) **65.00**

Figural bell, brass, figural Jacobean head finial, the sides embossed w/figure above a rim inscription, 3¼" d., 4" h. (ILLUS. top next page) **118.00**

Figural bell, brass, standing Dutch boy w/umbrella & jug, 2" d., 4¼" h. (ILLUS. right, with counter bell, bottom next page).................**55.00**

Jacobean Head Figural Bell

Figural Bell with Knight

Figural Counter-type & Dutch Boy Bells

Figural bell, brass, the handle in the form of a standing armored knight, the sides embossed w/figures & the flaring rim w/wording & "Hemony," 3⅜" d., 6¾" h. (ILLUS.)..........................**118.00**

Figural bell, brass, counter-type, the domed bell w/push knob finial supported by a nude standing cherub on a domed & scroll-pierced three-legged base, 3½" d., 10" h. (ILLUS. left, previous column) **135.00**

BIRDCAGES

Although probably not too many people specialize in just collecting birdcages, many who keep birds as pets enjoy keeping them in old or antique cages. The shiny brass birdcages widely produced earlier in this century by firms such as Hendryx are also popular decorative accent pieces in the homes of antiques lovers who may use them to hold a fern or potted plant rather than a live bird. Note that the very large and elaborate cages produced in the 19th century are the ones which today bring the highest prices on the collecting market. Readers should also be aware that a great many antique-style wooden and wire birdcages are currently on the market as simply decorative accessories but they might fool the unwary buyer in the antiques market.

Early Faience Birdcage

Faience, painted & decorated, of domed square form, painted in blue w/Iznik-style foliate scroll panels & an arched, domed roof surmounted by an hexagonal spiral capitol, the sides finely pierced w/vertical bars between broader painted horizontal panels, flanked by six vertical pillars issuing from square sectional peg feet & terminating in pentagonal spiral capitols w/painted decoration, the sides fitted w/two removable urn-form feeders & the front w/a metal-hinged door above a small rectangular removable sliding panel, some chips & major restorations, Europe, probably France, 19th c., 22" h. (ILLUS.) **$1,840.00**

Painted metal, Victorian-style w/a domed top & flattened paw feet, early 20th c., 27½" h.................**115.00**

Painted tole, rectangular shaped form w/a crenulated roof line beneath a pair of pointed roofs flanking a circular turret w/conical roof, each surmounted by flying flags, Europe, 32" h. **368.00**

Painted wood, plywood & wire, duplex-style, the two-story form w/wire sides & a small upper & lower door, a low-pitched four-gable roof, worn orange paint over yellow, 20th c., 30" h. **85.00**

Wood & wire, the large bulbous onion-form woven wire top w/ornate delicate scrolling wire above a square lower cage w/delicate scrolling wire panels & attached feeding compartments on two sides, pull-out tray in the base, white repaint trimmed in blue, 25½" h. **128.00**

BLACK AMERICANA

Over the past decade or so, this field of collecting has rapidly grown and today almost anything that relates to Black culture or illustrates Black Americana is considered a desirable collectible. Although many representations of Blacks, especially on 19th and early 20th century advertising pieces and housewares, were cruel stereotypes, even these are collected as poignant reminders of how far American society has come since the dawning of the Civil Rights movement, and how far we still have to go. Other pieces related to this category will be found from time to time in such categories as Advertising Items, Banks, Character Collectibles, Kitchenwares, Cookie Jars, Signs and Signboards, Toys and several others. For a complete overview of this subject see Antique Trader Books' Black Americana Price Guide with a special introduction by Julian Bond.

Elaborate Black Cloth Doll

Ashtray, chalkware, shows black boy eating watermelon **$50.00**

Book, "Little Black Sambo," Whitman, 1959 ....**35.00**

Book, "Sambo & Twins," H. Banerman, 1936, hardcover........**60.00**

Book, "Topsy Turvy & The Easter Bunny," 1941 ....**60.00**

Boot scraper, cast iron, scraper flanked by two black jockeys wearing red cap & vest w/white shirt & pants & black boots, all on rectangular base, embossed "BB" on lower right of base, underside of base embossed "B.B. Butt - Balto. MD," base 7 x 15½", 11" h. (chipping & wear) **1,210.00**

Bowl, cereal, "Robertson's," image of Gollywog on bottom, ca. 1960s.....................................**75.00**

Doll, cloth girl, stockinette head w/ivory eyes w/shoe button pupils, embroidered mouth & eyebrows, black astrakhan hair, cotton twill body & limbs, dressed in period clothing, late 19th c., 20" h. (some fiber loss & repairs) **1,955.00**

Doll, cloth girl, the flattened rounded head w/embroidered upward glancing eyes, eyebrows, nose & open oval smiling mouth, looped hair w/a blue silk bow, the fabric body clothed in a period blue, red, ochre & cream wool flannel dress over a white lacy petticoat, red stockings & high-button leather boots, hair possibly later, early 20th c., 37" h. (ILLUS.) ..**2,300.00**

Doll, Julia, vinyl, wearing a one-piece nurse's outfit w/white shoes, wrist tag, booklet, never removed from box, 1968 ....**155.00**

Drawing, water-color & pen & ink on Bristol board, a stylized portrait of a standing black girl w/her hands to her front, wearing a long red & yellow dress, inscribed in pencil along the bottom edge "Ellen Luthen. The Bridesmaid," in an early beveled giltwood frame, American School, 19th c., drawing, 3¾" sq........................**575.00**

Three Various Black Figurals

Figure of a black girl, majolica, modeled stretched out on her stomach, wearing a pale blue hat, pink dress, purple bodice, white blouse & yellow apron, France, ca. 1890s, 2 x 5", 3½" h. (ILLUS. right, bottom previous page) **95.00**

Figure of a black man, cast metal, standing figure wearing knee-length gold pants w/a red waistband, holding a removable basket of finely woven brass wire w/a bring around his neck, on a round brass base, ca. 1890, 2⅜" d., 5⅜" h. (ILLUS. left, bottom previous page) **145.00**

Figure of a black man, carved & decorated wood & cloth, the full-bodied male w/turning head, articulated hair, eyes, cheeks, nose & mouth, above a wood body w/hinged shoulders & elbows & carved hands, clothed w/a red cotton neckerchief, a blue & white checkered V-neck long-sleeved cotton shirt over draw-string cotton pants, black leather shoes, on a blue trapezoidal base, Tonawanda, New York, late 19th - early 20th c., 11¾ x 15", 5' 5½" h. (right hand replaced) **11,500.00**

Figure of a black man, carved & painted pine, circus-type figure of a pugilist, free-standing full-length figure carved in the round w/arms extended, wearing red-and-white-striped shorts, on a rectangular base w/small wooden wheels, ca. 1870, cracks, overall 5' 4" h. (ILLUS. top next column)........**4,600.00**

Figure of a black princess, bisque, allegorical figure standing wearing a blue tunic, red & gold belt, pink scarf over her shoulders & a striped, feathered turban, holding a cornucopia of flowers in one hand, the other arm raised

Carved Figure of a Black Pugilist

Carved African Colonial Solider

holding a parrot, on a round platform base decorated w/gold scrolls & bands, France, late 19th c., 3½" d., 11" h. (ILLUS. center w/other figures)..............**495.00**

Figure of a black soldier, carved & painted wood, the African Colonial soldier standing wearing a separately carved red-dyed fez w/tassel atop a carved cylindrical head resting on a flat body form w/intricately carved uniform detail & displaying an applied carved wooden cartridge box & bayonet, w/aluminum buttons, the shorts carved w/a side satchel, tubular legs mounted separately & w/separately carved & attached bare feet, Europe, ca. 1900, 19" h. (ILLUS. bottom previous page)...........................**495.00**

Figure group, porcelain, modeled as three black boys seated on a log eating corn-on-the-cob, polychrome decoration, ca. 1890, 5½" l., 5" h. **303.00**

Film, 8mm, Little Black Sambo, Castle film, boxed........................**65.00**

Hitching post, hollow cast iron, figure of black jockey wearing red cap & jacket, white pants & black boots w/outstretched hand holding hoop, on rectangular base, base 15 x 20", 47" h. (minor rust & wear)...................**880.00**

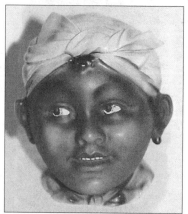

Figural Tobacco Humidor

Humidor, cov., bisque china, figural head of a young black girl w/a green & white striped head scarf, Europe, early 20th c., 3¾" d., 4¾" h. (ILLUS. bottom previous column).......**250.00 to 300.00**

Humidor, cov., majolica, figural race car driver w/cap, ...**350.00**

Incense burner, cast iron, black boy screaming on potty **95.00**

Marionette, composition, black man w/red lips & top hat.............**60.00**

Pincushion, bisque, black bellhop..**50.00**

Salt & pepper shakers, ceramic, Mammy & chef, 5" h., pr. **50.00**

Salt & pepper shakers, ceramic, Mammy & chef, 8½" h., pr. **110.00**

Spoon rest, ceramic, chef w/bobbing head (minor paint wear) **95.00**

Teapot, cov., black boy on lid, figural elephant body w/lustre glaze...**70.00**

Towels, linen, w/embroidered & appliqué images of a Mammy & chef, pr. **50.00**

Boy on Velocipede Clockwork Toy

Toy, clockwork, tin & cloth, figural black boy riding a velocipede, Stevens & Brown, New York, New York, late 19th c. (ILLUS.) **2,310.00**

Toy, clockwork, carved wood & cloth, Jubilee dancers, three

Early Clockwork Toys

small jointed carved wood black figures atop a round disc raised on a waisted pedestal & the dovetailed box base w/a colored bust profile of a gypsy, w/original box, late 19th c. (ILLUS. left)..**9,570.00**

Toy, clockwork, carved wood & cloth, preacher, carved & jointed figure w/cloth outfit atop a double-stepped box base painted red w/scrolled decoration, by Ives Corp., Bridgeport, Connecticut, late 19th c. (ILLUS. right) **2,310.00**

Ventriloquist's dummy, carved wood, movable head & mouth, glass eyes, includes trunk & six outfits, doll 45" h., the group...**1,500.00**

Violin & case, carved wood, the violin w/carved body w/f-shaped resonance holes, solid carved & polychromed tailpiece in the form of a reclining dog, a one-piece carved neck surmounted w/a pegbox carved in the form an African-American male head wearing a kepi w/turned-up bill, the bill inscribed in red paint "SAMBO," eyes & teeth of inlaid ivory or bone, the handcrafted casket-form case of walnut w/square nail construction, decorated w/15 light colored

Early Violin with Black Man's Head

wood heart-shaped inlays & two large star-shaped inlays, metal bail handle w/hook & eye latch on hinged lid, w/a horse hair bow, violin 7½" x 28", case 9 x 31", the group (ILLUS. of violin) **2,299.00**

BOOK ENDS

Albert Berry Book Ends

Copper, hand-hammered, Arts & Crafts style, wide rectangular upright plates w/a design of five cut-out vertical small rectangles & delicate linear tooling surrounding the edges, original dark brown patina, impressed mark of the Forest Craft Guild, 6" w., 4¼" h., pr. **$176.00**

Copper, hand-hammered, Arts & Crafts style, a flat pointed backplate w/the base rest supporting a cast infant's shoe including detailed laces, stitching & creases, original dark brown patina, impressed mark, impressed mark of Dirk van Erp, early 20th c., 6¼ x 7", 5" h. pr....**990.00**

Copper, hand-hammered, Arts & Crafts style, upright rectangular plate w/rounded corners & a reticulated design of pine cones in one corner, original dark brown patina, impressed Albert Berry mark, early 20th c., 4 1/4" w., 5¼" h., pr. (ILLUS.) **468.00**

Copper, hand-hammered, Arts & Crafts style, heavily embossed arched plate decorated w/a large flower blossom, riveted edges, original dark brown patina, Roycrofters, early orb mark, pr. **715.00**

Copper, hand-hammered, Arts & Crafts style, large applied walrus tusk on an irregular oval design w/crimped edges, marked by Albert Berry, early 20th c., 9¼" w., 5¼" h., pr. **1,210.00**

Pewter, hand-worked, Arts & Crafts style, rectangular backplate w/gently arched top, the sides inset w/a green malachite stone surrounded by stacks of repoussé rectangular panels w/crisscross designs, Forest Craft Guild, early 20th c., 5¼" w., 7" h., pr. **468.00**

Wrought iron, figural, Art Deco style, each cast as a stylized pelican w/its beak wide open catching streams of arching water from a fountain, designed by Edgar Brandt, impressed "E. BRANDT," ca. 1925, 7" h., pr....**6,037.00**

BOOTJACKS

"Foxy Grandpa"

Brass, figural "Foxy Grandpa," ca. 1900-1910, 12" (ILLUS).....**$900.00**

Advertising Bootjack

Cast iron, advertising, original gold paint, geometric & scroll design w/embossed words "Use - Musselmans - Bootjack - Plug - Tobacco," early 20th c., 9½" (ILLUS.) **165.00**

"Boss" Lettered Bootjack

Cast iron, cut-out lettering "BOSS," ca. 1880s, 15" (ILLUS. bottom previous column) **300.00**

Cast iron, embossed lettering "Wittier's" above & "American Centennial Boot Jack - 1876" around a cut-out star, above another star circled by "Hyde Park" all above "Mass - 1776," 13" **350.00**

Figural Devil Bootjack

Cast iron, figural Devil w/painted white horns & arms, cut-out circular eyes & triangular nose above a painted red mouth & cut-out stomach, w/some original paint, ca. 1880-90, 10½" (ILLUS.) **275.00**

Cast iron, figural mermaid w/outstretched arms lying atop green seaweed, w/original paint, ca. 1900, 11" (ILLUS. top next page) **450.00**

Cast iron, figural "Naughty Nellie" w/hands away from her head, painted gold, date unknown, crude casting, 10" **500.00**

Figural Mermaid Bootjack

Figural Folding Pistol Bootjack

Cast iron, model of a folding
pistol, marked "Phelps Dodge -
Palmer - Chicago," ca. 1890,
8½" (ILLUS.) **275.00**

Cast iron, model of a lobster,
marked "Keen Kutter" on
underside, w/some original
paint, 10¼" **125.00**

Cast iron, model of a lyre,
ca. 1890, 12" **275.00**

Cast iron, model of a pair of
upside-down dress boots above
two scrolls, ca. 1870s, 13"........**375.00**

Figural Cricket Bootjack

Cast iron, model of a cricket
w/original paint, decorated in
brown, red, blue & yellow on a
black ground, ca. 1900
(ILLUS.) **125.00**

Figural Snail Bootjack

Cast iron, model of a snail, date unknown, 13" (ILLUS. bottom previous page)..........................**125.00**

Cast iron, model of the Tree of Life w/unusual vulture heads, cut-out heart at base, ca. 1890, 11¾" **125.00**

Cast iron, original red paint, elaborate floral & scroll designs w/inverted heart in center & hole at bottom, ca. 1880-90, 12¼" **250.00**

Cast iron, traveling-type, pivoting arms fit size of heel, cut-out vine design, style pat'd. Oct. 29, 1867 by A.P. Seymour, Hecla Works, N.Y., 8¾" open, 5⅛" closed.........**95.00**

Victorian Scroll Design Bootjack

Cast iron, Victorian scroll design, ca. 1900, 11" (ILLUS.) **400.00**

Wooden, folding-type, long narrow boards w/brass hinges & pins, possibly Shaker, ca. 1870-80, 10½" **250.00**

Wooden, walnut, folding, ladies' legs w/pointed toes, brass hinges & pins, ca. 1860-70, 10" **350.00**

BOTTLE OPENERS

Corkscrews were actually the first bottle-openers and these may date back to the mid-18th century, but bottle openers as we know them today, are strictly a 20th century item and came into use only after Michael J. Owens invented the automatic bottle machine in 1903. Avid collectors have spurred this relatively new area of collector interest. Our listing encompasses the four basic types sought by collectors; advertising openers, full figure openers which stand alone or hang on the wall; flat figural openers such as the lady's leg shape; and openers with embossed, engraved or chased handles.

The numbers used at the end of the entries refer to Figural Bottle Openers Identification Guide, *a new book printed by the Figural Bottle Opener Collectors Club (F.B.O.C.)*

BOTTLE OPENERS BY TYPE:

Type 1 – Figural bottle openers, free-standing or in its natural position or wall-mounted, the opener an integral part of the figure.

Type 2 – Figural openers with corkscrew, lighter or nutcracker, etc.

Type 3 – Figural openers, three-dimensional on both sides but do not stand.

Type 4 – Figural openers with loop openers an integral part of design.

Type 5 – Figural openers with a loop inserted in the casting process. The loop or opener is not part of the casting process.

Type 6 – Same as Type 5 with an added can punch.

Type 7 – Same as Type 5 with an added corkscrew or lighter.

Type 8 – Flat, back not three-dimensional, loop part of casting.

Type 9 – Same as Type 8, loop inserted in the casting process.

Type 10 – Same as Type 8 with a corkscrew.

Type 11 – Openers are coin or medallion shape, one or two sided, with an insert or cast integral loop opener. (These are very common.)

Type 12 – Figural stamped openers, formed by the stamping process (steel, aluminum, or brass).

Type 13 – Extruded metal openers.

Type 14 – Johnny guitars or figural holders; Johnny Guitars are figures made of wood, shells, string, etc. They have a magnet that holds a stamped steel (Type 12) opener. Figural holders or display holders are cast holders that have a clip that holds one or two cast figural openers.

Type 15 – Church keys with a figure riveted or cast on the opener. Some do not have a punch key.

Type 16 – Figural church key openers with corkscrew.

Type 17 – Decorated church key openers. (Church key loop or wire loop openers with names and jewels attached).

Type 18 – Base opener (opener molded in bottom as integral part).

Type 19 – Base opener added (opener added to bottom by brazing or soldering).

Type 20 – Base plate opener (opener screwed in base of figure).

Type 21 – Wooden openers/Syroco openers (metal insert, cast stamped or wire type).

Type 22 – Knives, hatches, scissors, etc., with openers.

RARITY

A - Most Common
B - Difficult
C - Very difficult
D - Very hard to find
E - Rare
Rare to Very Rare (few known)

FIGURAL (Full-Dimensional)

• Type 1

All-American, cast iron, figure of a man in an orange football jersey w/the letters "Z B T" across his chest, standing on base marked "Joe Alexander," rarity E, 4¼" h.,
F-38..........................**$350.00 to 550.00**

Alligator w/boy, cast iron, figural group of black boy being bitten in the behind by an alligator, rarity B, 3" h., F-133
(ILLUS. left, below) .....**75.00 to 150.00**

Alligator & boy w/hands up, cast iron, figural group of black boy w/his hands raised above his

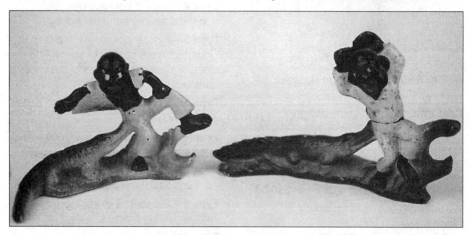

Alligator and Boy Bottle Openers

head, being bitten in the behind
by an alligator, rarity B, 2¾" h.,
F-134 (ILLUS. right, bottom
previous page) ....**75.00 to 150.00**

Barking at the moon, aluminum,
figural group, a barking brown &
white dog sitting at the base of a
crescent moon, 2" h.,
N-529 ....**75.00 to 150.00**

Figural Caddy Bottle Opener

Figural Bear Bottle Openers

Bear, baby, aluminum, model of
Baby Bear wearing a red top,
blue pants & holding a cap in his
hand, rarity C, 3" h., N-562
(ILLUS. right).............**150.00 to 250.00**

Bear, mama, aluminum, model of
Mama Bear wearing a yellow &
green dress, rarity C, 4" h., N-
561 (ILLUS. center)...**150.00 to 250.00**

Bear, papa, aluminum, model of
Papa Bear wearing a blue
jacket, red vest & grey pants,
rarity C, 4⅝" h., N-560
(ILLUS. left)..............**150.00 to 250.00**

Bear at fence, aluminum, model
of a bear standing at a fence
marked "FIGURAL-BOTTLE-
OPENERS," rarity B, 4⅝" h.,
N-582 ....**75.00 to 150.00**

Bird's Birch Beer, aluminum,
model of a grey bird perched
atop a branch, the bird marked
"Birds," the branch marked "Birch
Beer," 3" h., N-574 ....**50.00 to 75.00**

Caddy, cast iron, figure of a black
boy wearing a red shirt, black
pants & red shoes, holding a
golf bag w/clubs & resting his
hand on a white sign that reads
"19," rarity D, 5⅞" h.,
F-44 (ILLUS.) ....**250.00 to 350.00**

Cathy Coed, cast iron, figure of a
young woman wearing a yellow
hat, blue V-neck blouse, short
flared yellow shirt & black Mary
Jane-type shoes, standing on a
base marked "Women's
Weekend," rarity E, 4⁵⁄₁₆" h.,
F-39.........................**350.00 to 550.00**

Chili pepper '93, cast Iron, model
of a red chili pepper, rarity B,
5⅝" h., N-658 ....**75.00 to 150.00**

Cool penguin, zinc, model of
walking penguin wearing a top
hat, rarity C, 4" h. ......**150.00 to 250.00**

Cowboy w/cactus, pot metal,
figural group of cowboy wearing
cowboy hat & plaid shirt
clutching a cactus, rarity D,
4⅝" h., F-23 ....**250.00 to 350.00**

Figural Devil, Skeleton and Pumpkin Head

Devil, aluminum, figure of Devil dressed in red robes holding pitch fork, rarity B, 4" h., N-563 (ILLUS. above left) ......**75.00 to 150.00**

Dolphin, aluminum, model of stylized goldish green dolphin w/tail curled over its head, 4" h., N-616 ....**75.00 to 150.00**

Donkey, aluminum, w/3" ears, rarity D, 3⅜" h., F-59 (ILLUS. below center) ....**250.00 to 350.00**

Donkey, brass, body of donkey marked "Phila. - 1948," rarity D, 3¾" h., (ILLUS. below right).................**250.00 to 350.00**

Donkey, brass, base marked "Norwood," rare, 4⅛" h. (ILLUS.below left) ....**550.00 and up**

Figural Dragon

Donkey Bottle Openers

Dragon, cast iron, model of dragon w/open mouth, arched back & curled tail, rarity E, 5" h. (ILLUS. middle previous page) ....**350.00 to 550.00**

Elephant, cast iron, model of walking elephant w/mouth open & truck raised, rarity D, 4¼ l., N-616 ....**250.00 to 550.00**

Figural Aluminum Bottle Openers

Father Time, aluminum, figure of Father Time dressed in grey robe, holding a sickle & an hour glass, rarity B. 4¾" h., N-599 (ILLUS. right)...............**75.00 to 150.00**

Flying fish, aluminum, model of a trout atop a wave, rarity B, 4¾" h., N-656 (ILLUS. left).................**75.00 to 150.00**

Gobbler, aluminum, model of gold-painted turkey w/stern look on his face, wearing suit w/arms crossed, 3" h., N-625 ..**75.00 to 150.00**

Good luck, aluminum, model of a hand in the form of a fist w/forefinger overlapping thumb, wrist marked "Good Luck," rarity A, 3¼" h., N-624 (ILLUS. with Father Time) ....**50.00 to 75.00**

Heart in hand, cast iron, model of an upturned hand w/a cut-out heart in the palm, rarity E, 4¼" h., F-203 ....**350.00 to 550.00**

Indian chief, aluminum, figure of Chief wearing full headdress, standing w/legs spread & hands on hips, 5" h., N-598 .....**50.00 to 75.00**

Key (large), stainless steel, marked "Powell-White-Star

Large Figural Key

Valves-are-Closers," rare, 9" l. (ILLUS.) ....**550.00 and up**

Lady in the wind, aluminum, figure of woman wearing royal blue dress & hat, she is leaning into the wind clutching her hat, 4" h., N-598 ....**50.00 to 75.00**

Lamp post drunks, cast iron, figural, common, 4⅛" ....**10.00 to 25.00**

Mexican w/cactus, cast iron, figural group of Mexican wearing sombrero sitting beside cactus, rarity E, 2⅞" h., F-24...**350.00 to 550.00**

Miner, FBOC '95, cast iron, figure of miner wearing blue pants, yellow shirt & brown hat holding pan & pick on base marked "FBOC 1995," rarity A, 4⅛", N-670 ....**50.00 to 75.00**

Mother goose, aluminum, figure of woman in a green dress & white apron holding a goose, rarity A, 3¾" h., N-573...**50.00 to 75.00**

New Year baby, aluminum, figure of Baby New Year holding a parrot & wearing a black top hat, diaper & sash marked "1989," 4⅝" h., N-567 ....**75.00 to 150.00**

Old pal, aluminum, model of a dog w/head turned & paw raised, rarity B, 2¾" h., N-570...**75.00 to 150.00**

Oriental clown, aluminum, figure of Oriental man w/hands in pockets dressed in brown, black & red clown suit, rarity C, 4⅜" h., N-559 ....**150.00 to 250.00**

Owl, cast iron, rarity E, 2" (F-127) ....**350.00 to 550.00**

Parrot on perch, cast iron, figure of yellow, blue, green & red parrot on elaborate perch, rarity E, 4⅞" h., F-114 ....**350.00 to 550.00**

Pelican, cast iron, model of a pelican w/orange eyes, 3⅜" h., F-131 ....**250.00 to 350.00**

Polar bear, aluminum, model of polar bear standing on its hind legs holding a brown stick, rarity C, 3¾" h., N-557 ....**250.00 to 350.00**

Cast-Iron Pretzel Bottle Openers

Pretzel, cast iron or aluminum, rarity A, 3⅜" w., F-230 (ILLUS. left) ....**50.00 to 75.00**

Pretzel, cast iron, black, marked "Hauenstein Beer," rarity D 2⅞" w., F-231 (ILLUS. right) .... **250.00 to 350.00**

Pumpkin head, aluminum, figure of a person w/pumpkin head wearing black robe, rarity B, 4¼ h., N-565 (ILLUS. w/Devil) ....**75.00 to 150.00**

Red Riding Hood, aluminum, figure of Red Riding Hood holding a basket w/the wolf at her feet, 4" h., N-568 .....**50.00 to 75.00**

Rhino, cast iron, rarity E, 4," F-76 ....**350.00 to 550.00**

Rooster, cast iron, rarity A, 3⅛" h., F-97 (ILLUS. below left) ....**50.00 to 75.00**

Rooster (large), cast iron, tail down, rarity B, 3¾" h., F-98 (ILLUS. below right) ....**75.00 to 150.00**

Rooster (tail down), cast iron, rarity B, 3¾" h., F-99 (ILLUS. below center) ....**550.00 and up**

Sea horse, cast iron, 4" h., F-140 ....**75.00 to 150.00**

Skeleton, aluminum, rarity B, 4⅞" h., N-566 (ILLUS. w/Devil) ....**75.00 to 150.00**

Teen girl, cast iron, figure of a teen-aged girl lying on her stomach w/her chin in her hands & her feet in the air, wearing black pants, white shirt & a red ribbon in her blond hair, 2" l., N-577 ....**250.00 to 350.00**

Totem pole, aluminum, rarity B, 3¾" h., N-573 ....**75.00 to 150.00**

WALL MOUNT

• Type 1

Amish man, cast iron, w/long beard wearing Amish-style hat, rare, 4⅛" h., F-422 (ILLUS. top next page).....................**550.00 and up**

Bear head, cast iron, 3" h., F-426 ....**150.00 to 250.00**

Cast-Iron Rooster Bottle Openers

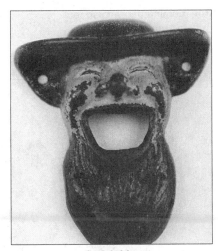

Amish Man

Winking Boy

Cast-Iron Wall Mount Bottle Opener

Boy winking, cast iron, freckle-faced winking boy w/two large front teeth, rare, 3⅞" h., F-418 (ILLUS.) ....**550.00 and up**

Bronze pirate, pirate head wearing a red scarf on his head, an eye patch & holding a knife between his teeth, 5" h., N-512 ....**75.00 to 150.00**

Cast-Iron Bulldog

Bulldog, cast iron, rarity B, 4" h., F-425 (ILLUS.) ....**75.00 to 150.00**

Coyote, cast iron, gold-painted, rare, 3½" h., F-429 (ILLUS. top next page).....................**550.00 and up**

Beer drinker, cast iron, model of older man wearing cap, white shirt & orange vest holding a mug of beer, surrounded by cast-iron frame w/banner at the bottom marked "Spencer Brewing Co. - Lancaster, Pa.," rarity E, 6⅜" h., F-406 (ILLUS.)....................**350.00 to 550.00**

Cast-Iron Coyote

Sun, aluminum, orangish red-painted smiling sun w/black eyebrows, rarity B, 4" h., N-663 (ILLUS. below left) ......**75.00 to 150.00**

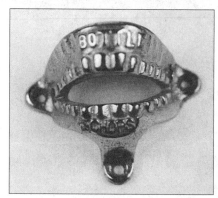

Brass Teeth

Four-eyes man, cast iron, four-eyed man w/mustache, rarity B, 3¹⁵⁄₁₆" h., F-413 ....**75.00 to 150.00**

Miss Two Eyes, zinc, two-eyed woman w/short hair & hoop earrings, rarity C, 3⅜" h., F-409 ....**150.00 to 250.00**

Moon, aluminum, smiling & winking black painted moon face w/silver painted eyebrows, eyes, nose, cheeks, teeth & chin, rarity B, 3½" h., N-664 (ILLUS. below right) ....**75.00 to 150.00**

Teeth, brass, model of teeth & gums marked "Bottle Chops," rarity B, 3¼" w., F-420B (ILLUS.)......................**75.00 to 150.00**

• Type 2

Old Snifter, zinc, turns head & corkscrew comes out (ILLUS. left, top next page)....................**125.00**

Old Snifter, zinc, w/lighter & corkscrew (ILLUS. right, top next page) **200.00**

Aluminum Sun and Moon

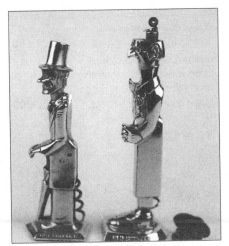

Old Snifter Bottle Openers

• Type 3

Various Cast-Iron Animals

Dachshund, Wilton Flats cast iron, three-dimensional but does not stand (ILLUS. bottom) ....**50.00 to 100.00**

Donkey, Wilton Flats, cast iron, three-dimensional but does not stand (ILLUS. top) ....**50.00 to 100.00**

Elephant, Wilton Flats, cast iron, three-dimensional but does not stand (ILLUS. left) ....**50.00 to 100.00**

Fish, Wilton Flats, cast iron, three-dimensional but does not stand (ILLUS. center) ..**50.00 to 100.00**

Scottie Dog, Wilton Flats, cast iron, three-dimensional but does not stand (ILLUS. right) ....**50.00 to 100.00**

• Type 4

Drunk, Wilton, cast iron, three-dimensional drunk wearing black top hat & suit, w/loop top **50.00**

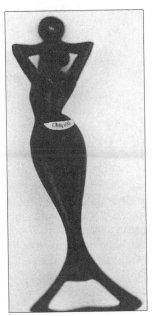

Cast-Iron Mermaid

Mermaid, cast iron, three-dimensional, marked "Chiquita," loop tail (ILLUS.) **90.00**

• Type 8

Gemini Bottle Opener

Gemini, zinc, flat back (ILLUS.) **20.00**

Lobster, cast iron, flat back, red, claws serve as loop **35.00**

Mad Man, zinc, flat back, depicts man bending at the knees w/hands clasped, legs serve as loop..**45.00**

• Type 9

Figural Winston Churchill

Winston Churchill, aluminum & steel, shows Churchill in front of hand giving a victory sign, fingers of hand hold loop, loop inserted in casting process (ILLUS.) **65.00**

• Type 11

Coins, cast iron, three Oriental coins joined together w/loop cut-out of top coin **15.00**

• Type 12

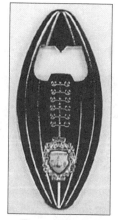

Figural Football

Ax, stamped steel & wood, rectangular wood handle, opener cut-out of blade **10.00**

Fist, stamped steel, w/opener cut-out of palm, wrist reads "Kung-Fu" **8.00**

Football, stamped steel, w/opener cut-out of top, small medallion at bottom reads "Clearwater" (ILLUS.) **8.00**

• Type 13

Aluminum Shark

Shark, aluminum, mouth serves as opener, marked "Ocean City, MD," attached to key ring (ILLUS.) **3.00**

• Type 14

Golf bag & caddie, golf bag holder holds figural caddie opener..........................**50.00 to 75.00**

Shield & knight, shield holds figural knight opener .....**50.00 to 75.00**

• Type 15

Violin Case

Violin case, attached to church key-type opener, case marked "Beethoven's Fifth" (ILLUS. bottom previous page)................**20.00**

• Type 17

Church Key and Wire-Type Bottle Openers

Church keys & wire-type, w/scrolls, medallions & decorations, each (ILLUS.)........................**15.00 to 20.00**

• Type 18

Bronze Bull's Head

Bull's head, bronze, full-figured, opener in bottom (ILLUS.) **35.00**

• Type 19

Various Bronze Hats

Hats, bronze, opener soldered in bottom, each (ILLUS.) **30.00**

• Type 20
Horse's head, zinc, base plate opener screwed in bottom **35.00**

•Type 21

Man by Lamppost

Man by Lamppost, wooden, carved, figure of man w/suitcase standing next to lamppost, music box in suitcase, metal opener attached to head inside body (ILLUS.) **150.00**

Figure, wooden, figure of golfer w/wooden golf club serving as opener, Danish.............**10.00 to 30.00**

Wooden, metal opener attached, marked "Wartime Bottle Opener - With nail-head under cap, pull up . . . your bottle is open!" World War II era **45.00**

BOTTLES

BITTERS

Augauer Bitters

African - Stomach - Bitters, cylindrical w/applied mouth, smooth base, ca. 1875-1885, yellowish olive, 9⅜" h. (two½" cooling cracks in base) **132.00**

Aimar's - Sarracenia - Bitters, rectangular w/beveled corners, tooled square collar mouth, smooth base, ca. 1860-1880, aqua, 7⅛" h. **83.00**

Allen's (William) - Congress Bitters, rectangular w/tooled round collar mouth, pontil-scarred base, purple, 7⅝" h. **303.00**

Amazon Bitters - Peter McQuade, New York, square w/tooled sloping collar mouth, smooth base, ca. 1870-1890, golden amber, 9¼" h. (pinhead flake on mouth).........................**154.00**

Andrews (David) - Vegetable - Jaundice - Bitters - Providence - R.I., rectangular tombstone-form w/applied sloping collar mouth, pontil-scarred base, ca. 1840-1855, aqua, 8⅛" h. **385.00**

Augauer Bitters - Augauer Bitters Co, Chicago, rectangular, tooled lip, wide bevels w/three narrow vertical ribs, smooth base, ca. 1900-1910, green, 8" h. (ILLUS.) **88.00**

Ayer (Dr. M.C.) - Restorative Bitters - Boston Mass, rectangular w/tooled square collar mouth, smooth base, ca. 1870-1890, clear w/grey overtones, 8⅝" h. **88.00**

Bancroft's Bitters - D.W. Bancroft - Marshfield Vt, rectangular w/applied square collar mouth, smooth base, ca. 1860-1880, aqua, 8¾" h. **94.00**

Banker's (Dr.) - Home Bitters - New York, rectangular w/applied sloping collar mouth, ca. 1865-1875, aqua, 9" h. **110.00**

Bell's (Dr.) Liver & Kidney Bitters, square w/applied sloping collar mouth, smooth base, ca. 1860-1880, greenish aqua, 9" h. ..**83.00**

Bell's (Dr.) - The Great English Remedy - Blood Purifying - Bitters, rectangular, applied mouth, smooth base, ca. 1860-1880, amber, 9⅜" h..................**102.00**

Bengal Bitters, square w/applied sloping collar mouth, smooth base, ca. 1860-1880, golden amber, 8⅞" h. **94.00**

Big Bill Best Bitters

Bouvier Buchu Bitters

Big Bill Best Bitters, tapering square w/tooled mouth, smooth base, ca. 1900-1910, amber, 12" h. (ILLUS.)............................**110.00**

Bismarck - Bitters, rectangular w/rounded corners & fluted shoulders, tooled double collar mouth, smooth base, ca. 1880-1900, 8⅝" h. **154.00**

Boerhaves Holland Bitters - B. Page Jr & Co - Pittsburgh PA., rectangular w/ applied double collar mouth, smooth base, ca. 1860-1880, aqua, 8" h. **66.00**

Boozer's Liver & Kidney Bitters - Oscar W. Olson, Danville, Ill., square, tooled sloping collar mouth w/ring, smooth base, ca. 1880-1900, golden amber, 10½" h. (¼" bruise on base) **154.00**

Bouvier Buchu Bitters, Bouvier Specialty Co, Louisville, KY., Incorporated, oval w/connecting label panels, ca. 1906-1915, amber, 10⅝" h. (ILLUS. top next column)......................**605.00**

Bowe's Cascara Bitters Has No Equal - P.F. Bowe, Waterbury, Connecticut, square w/rounded corners, tooled sloping collar mouth, smooth base, ca. 1880-1900, clear, 9⅝" h. **94.00**

Brady's Nerve Bitters, rectangular w/beveled corners, applied double collar mouth, smooth base, ca. 1860-1880, aqua, 9⅛" h. **165.00**

Brophy's Bitters, (five-pointed star), Trade Mark, Nokomis Illinois, square w/beveled corners, tooled mouth, smooth base, ca. 1880-1900, aqua, 7⅜" h. **77.00**

Brown's Catalina, cylindrical lighthouse-shaped w/applied square collar mouth, smooth base, ca. 1860-1880, yellowish amber, 10⅞" h. **176.00**

Brown's Celebrated Indian Herb Bitters, Patented Feb 11, 1868, Indian Queen shape w/sheared & rolled lip, smooth base, ca. 1868-1875, yellow w/amber, 12⅛" h. **2,530.00**

Buchan's (A. Harvard) Bitters,
Toronto, rectangular w/applied
double collar mouth, smooth
base, ca. 1860-1880,
aqua, 7⅞" h. **50.00**

Bull's (Dr. John) Cedron Bitters,
Louisville, Kentucky-Patented,
square semi-cabin shaped
w/applied sloping collar, smooth
base, ca. 1865-1870, golden
amber, 10⅝" h. **688.00**

Bull's Compound Cedron Bitters

**Bull's (Dr. John) Compound
Cedron Bitters,** Louisville, KY.,
square w/applied sloping collar
mouth, smooth base, ca.
1865-1875, yellowish olive
green, 9⅜" h. (ILLUS.)..............**880.00**

Bull's Luxury Bitters, Louisville,
KY, applied mouth, lady's leg
neck, smooth base, amber,
9⅛" h. **220.00**

**Bull's (Dr) Superior Stomach
Bitters** - W.H. Bull & Co., St.
Louis, square w/applied sloping
collar mouth, smooth base, ca.
1860-1880, golden amber,
9" h. **121.00**

**Burton's - Ginger - Wine -
Bitters,** square w/tooled mouth,
smooth base, ca. 1885-1895,
aqua, 4⅛" h. **550.00**

**Caldwells The Great Tonic Herb
Bitters,** tapering rectangular
w/applied mouth, iron pontil,
bold embossing, ca. 1870-1875,
medium amber, 12⅝" h. **231.00**

Dr. Cambells Scotch Bitters

Campbells (Dr.) Scotch Bitters,
strapside flask w/tooled mouth,
smooth base, ca. 1885-1895,
golden yellow amber, 6⅝" h.
(ILLUS.) **275.00**

Canteen Bitters, For All
Disorders Of The Stomach -
John Hart & Co, Lancaster, PA,
square w/applied double collar
mouth, smooth base, ca. 1870-
1880, medium blue green,
10" h. **1,595.00**

Carmeliter Stomach Bitters Co.,
New York, "S.J." monogram &
"Registered" on reverse, square
w/beveled corners, applied
sloping collar mouth, smooth
base, ca. 1860-1880, yellowish
olive, 9⅛" h..............................**303.00**

Carpathian Herb Bitters, square
w/tooled sloping collar mouth,
smooth base, ca. 1870-1890,
amber, 7¾" h. **44.00**

**Chevalier (F. & Co) Sole Agents
Celebrated Crown Bitters,**
square w/tooled sloping collar
mouth, smooth base, ca. 1880-
1900, golden amber,
9" h. **231.00**

Clarke's - Constitution Bitters -
London, rectangular, tooled
sloping collar mouth w/ring,
smooth base, ca. 1880-1900,
aqua, 7⅝" h. **39.00**

Clark's Giant Bitters, Philada
PA., rectangular w/tooled square
collar mouth, smooth base, ca.
1880-1900, aqua, 6¾" h. **66.00**

Coca Bitters, square w/beveled
corners, applied sloping collar
mouth, smooth base, ca. 1860-
1880, reddish amber, 8⅜" h. **88.00**

**Cocamoke - Cocamoke Bitters
Co.,** Hartford, Conn., square
w/applied sloping collar mouth,
smooth base, ca. 1860-1880,
golden amber, 9¾" h. **154.00**

Compound Cathartic Bitters,
Andrew Lee, Manchester, Mass,
rectangular w/applied square
collar mouth, smooth base, ca.
1860-1880, aqua, 7⅞" h. **88.00**

Congress - Bitters, rectangular
w/applied sloping collar mouth,
smooth base, ca. 1860-1880,
reddish amber, 9⅝" h. **121.00**

Cook's - Crystal - Bitters,
rectangular w/beveled corners,
applied double collar mouth,
smooth base, ca. 1860-1880,
aqua, 8⅜" h. **94.00**

Corwitz - Stomach Bitters,
square w/tooled sloping collar
mouth, smooth base, ca. 1880-
1900, light yellowish
amber, 7⅝" h. **61.00**

Curran's Herb Bitters,
Pepsinized - The Napa Valley
Wine Co, Minneapolis, Minn.,

rectangular w/tooled mouth,
smooth base, ca. 1880-1900,
yellowish green, 8⅝" h. **176.00**

**Curtis & Perkins - Wild Cherry -
Bitters,** cylindrical w/applied
sloping collar mouth, pontil-
scarred base, ca. 1840-1860,
aqua, 6¾" h. **66.00**

Dansby's Cotton Patch Bitters,
square w/tooled sloping collar
mouth, smooth base, ca.
1880-1900, yellowish amber,
8¾" h. **242.00**

**De Andries - Sarsaparilla
Bitters -** E.M. Rusha, New
Orleans, rectangular w/applied
mouth, smooth base, ca. 1860-
1880, golden amber, 10" h. **165.00**

**De Long's (Dr.) Plantation
Bitters,** square w/tooled sloping
collar mouth, smooth base, ca.
1870-1890, reddish amber,
9⅝" h. **132.00**

Demuth's - Stomach Bitters -
Philada, square w/applied
sloping collar mouth, smooth
base, ca. 1860-1880, golden
amber, 9⅜" h. **55.00**

Digestine Bitters, P.J. Bowlin
Liquor Co. Sole Proprietors, St.
Paul, Minn., rectangular
w/rounded corners, tooled
sloping collar mouth, smooth
base, amber, 8⅜" h. **176.00**

Doyles - Hop - Bitters, square
modified cabin-shaped, tooled
mouth w/ring, smooth base, ca.
1870-1890, golden
amber, 9⅝" h. **143.00**

**Drakes (ST) 1860 Plantation X
Bitters -** Patented 1862, cabin-
shaped, six-log w/applied
sloping collar mouth, smooth
base, copper puce, 10" h. **231.00**

**Drakes (ST) 1860 Plantation X
Bitters -** Patented 1862, cabin-
shaped, six-log w/applied
sloping collar mouth, smooth
base, ca. 1862-1870, strawberry
puce, 9⅞" h. **303.00**

Dromgoole - English Female Bitters - Louisville, KY., rectangular w/tooled mouth, smooth base, ca. 1875-1885, aqua, 8⅜" h. **121.00**

Egerton's (R.L.) - Stomach Bitters - Louisville, KY, square w/applied mouth, smooth base, ca. 1870-1875, medium honey amber, 10⅞" h. **303.00**

Eureka Bitters - Granger & Co., Titusville Pa, square w/applied sloping collar mouth, smooth base marked "Wm.McC&Co.," ca. 1860-1880, golden amber, 9⅞" h. **523.00**

Fenner's (Dr. M. M.) - Capitol Bitters - Frendonia, N.Y., rectangular w/tooled sloping collar mouth, smooth base, ca. 1880-1900, aqua, 9" h. **39.00**

Fixner (John P.) Stomach Bitters, Mfr. & Prop. Of Bonekamp, Springfield Ills., square w/beveled corners, sloping collar mouth w/ring, smooth base, ca. 1880-1900, clear, 8⅝" h. **99.00**

Dr. Forest's Tonic Bitters

Forest's (Dr.) Tonic Bitters - Bacon and Miller, Harrisburg, Penna., square w/applied double collar mouth, smooth base, ca. 1870-1875, yellowish amber, 9⅞" h. (ILLUS. bottom previous column) **180.00**

4 In 1 Bitters Co., square w/rounded corners, tooled sloping collar mouth w/ring, smooth base, ca. 1880-1990, clear, 10⅝" h. **105.00**

Frazier's Root Bitters For The Blood, Depot Cleveland Ohio, rectangular w/applied sloping collar mouth, smooth base, ca. 1870-1890, aqua, 7¾" h. **83.00**

Gentiana Root and Herb Bitters - Seth Clapp & Co, Sole Proprietors - Boston, Mass, square case gin shaped, applied mouth, smooth base, ca. 1865-1870, aqua, 9⅞" h. **138.00**

Godfrey's Celebrated Cordial Bitters, rectangular w/applied double collar mouth, iron pontil, ca. 1840-1860, aqua, 10" h. **176.00**

Gotthard (St.) Herb Bitters, Mette & Kanne Pros, St Louis, Mo, square w/applied sloping collar mouth, smooth base marked "M.G.Co.," ca. 1860-1880, amber, 8⅞" h. **55.00**

Graves & Son - Tonic Bitters - Louisville, KY., square semi-cabin shaped w/applied sloping collar mouth, five-pointed star on smooth base, ca. 1865-1875, light ice blue, 10⅝" h. **413.00**

Graves (Dr Jas.) - Tonic Bitters - Louisville, KY, square semi-cabin shaped w/applied sloping collar mouth, smooth base, ca. 1865-1875, aqua, 9⅞" h. **358.00**

Great Western. Tonic. Bitters, Patented. Jany. 21. 1868, square w/applied sloping collar mouth, smooth base marked "L & W," ca. 1860-1880, deep golden amber, 9" h. (⅛" flake on side of mouth) **121.00**

**Greene (C.F.) - Rome New York
- Anti Bilious or - Tonic
Bitters,** rectangular w/beveled
corners, applied collar mouth,
smooth base, ca. 1860-1880,
aqua, 8⅝" h. **84.00**

Greenhut's Bitters, Prepared By
S. Greenhut, Cleveland, O.,
square w/rounded corners,
tooled sloping collar mouth,
smooth base, golden amber,
11" h. **83.00**

Greer's Eclipse Bitters, square
w/applied sloping collar mouth,
smooth base, ca. 1870-1880,
amber, 8¾" h. **127.00**

Greer's Eclipse Bitters -
Louisville, KY., square,
w/applied mouth, smooth base,
ca 1870-1880, medium amber,
9⅜" h. **105.00**

Griel's Herb Bitters, Griel &
Young, Mf'trs, Lancaster, PA.
U.S.A., tooled w/round mouth,
smooth base, ca. 1890-1900,
aqua, 9⅛" h. **132.00**

*Hardmann's Good Samaritan
Stomach Bitters*

**Hardmann's (Dr.) - Good
Samaritan Stomach Bitters,**
square w/applied sloping mouth,
smooth base, ca. 1875-1885,
golden yellowish amber, "S"
letter & both "N" letters are
backwards in embossing,
9⅝" h. (ILLUS.).........................**468.00**

Hagan's Bitters

Hagan's - Bitters, triangular-form
w/applied mouth, smooth base,
ca. 1865-1875, medium amber,
9⅝" h. (ILLUS.)..........................**523.00**

Hellman's Congress Bitters

Hellman's - Congress Bitters -
St. Louis, MO, square w/applied
sloping collar mouth, smooth
base, ca. 1865-1870, root beer
amber, 9" h. (ILLUS. bottom
previous page)..........................**303.00**

**Henley's (Dr.) Wild Grape Root
IXL (in oval) Bitters,** round,
tooled mouth, smooth base, ca.
1870-1880, bluish aqua, 12⅝" h...**77.00**

**Hibbard's (Dr. R.F.) Wild Cherry
Bitters,** cylindrical w/applied
square collar mouth, smooth
base, ca. 1860-1880, aqua,
8⅝" h. (¼" chip on side of
mouth) **88.00**

**Hopkins (Dr. A.S.) Union
Stomach Bitters,** Hartford
Conn, square w/applied sloping
collar mouth, smooth base, ca.
1870-1875, yellow w/strong olive
tone, 9⅞" h. **303.00**

Hops & Malt Trade Mark Bitters

Hops & Malt Trade, (sheaf of
hops), Mark Bitters, square
semi-cabin shaped w/applied
sloping collar mouth, smooth
base, ca. 1875-1880, reddish
amber, 10" h. (ILLUS.)..............**300.00**

Horse Shoe Bitters, square
w/beveled corners, applied
sloping collar mouth, smooth
base, ca. 1860-1880, amber,
8⅞" h. **121.00**

**Hostetter's (Dr. J.) Stomach
Bitters,** square w/applied
sloping collared mouth, pontil-
scarred base, ca. 1860-1880,
dense olive green,
9⅞" h. **1,210.00**

Hunkidori Stomach Bitters -
H.B. Matthews, Chicago, Ill,
square w/beveled corners,
tooled sloping collar mouth,
smooth base, ca. 1860-1880,
golden amber, 9" h. **105.00**

**Huntington's (Dr) Golden Tonic
Bitters,** square w/applied
sloping collar mouth, smooth
base, ca. 1860-1880, golden
amber, 9⅞" h. **193.00**

**Hurley Bros - Pepsinized
Bitters,** rectangular w/tooled
sloping collar mouth, smooth
base, ca. 1880-1900,amber,
8" h. **154.00**

Jacob's (Dr.) Bitters - New
Haven, CT. - S.A. Spencer,
rectangular w/applied sloping
collar mouth, smooth base, ca.
1850-1860, deep bluish aqua,
10⅝" h. **231.00**

**Jewitt's (Dr. Stephen) -
Celebrated Health Restoring
Bitters -** Rindge, N.H.,
rectangular w/applied square
collar mouth, pontil-scarred
base, ca. 1840-1860, ice blue,
7⅞" h. **132.00**

Johnson's Calisaya Bitters,
square w/beveled corners,
applied sloping collar mouth
w/ring, smooth base, ca. 1860-
1880, yellowish amber, 10" h. **94.00**

Johnson's - Tonic Bitters,
rectangular w/beveled corners,
tooled double collar mouth,
smooth base, ca. 1880-1890,
aqua, 8⅝" h. **66.00**

King Solomon's Bitters -
Seattle, Wash., rectangular,
tooled sloping collar mouth
w/ring, smooth base, ca. 1880-
1900, golden amber, 7⅝" h. **50.00**

King's 25 Cent Bitters, oval
w/tooled square collar mouth,
smooth base, ca. 1880-1900,
aqua, 6¾" h. **50.00**

Lambert's (A.) Bitters, Philada,
square w/applied double collar
mouth, smooth base, ca. 1860-
1865, amber, 11" h. **798.00**

Lamot's - Botonic Bitters,
square w/applied sloping collar
mouth, smooth base, ca. 1860-
1900,golden amber, 8⅝" h. **99.00**

**Langley's (Dr.) Root & Herb
Bitters,** cylindrical, tooled
square collar mouth, smooth
base, ca. 1860-1890, golden
amber, 5⅞" h. **88.00**

**Langley's (Dr.) Root & Herb
Bitters,** cylindrical w/applied
square collar mouth, smooth
base, ca. 1860-1890, bluish
green, 6⅞" h. (pinhead flake on
top of mouth) **121.00**

**Langley's (Dr.) Root & Herb
Bitters,** cylindrical w/applied
square collar mouth, smooth
base, ca. 1860-1890, yellowish
amber, 7" h. **66.00**

**Langley's (Dr.) Root & Herb
Bitters,** cylindrical w/applied
square collar mouth, smooth
base, ca. 1860-1890, apple
green, 8⅞" h. **132.00**

Litthauer Stomach Bitters,
Invented By Josef Loewenthal,
Berlin, square case gin shaped
w/applied mouth, smooth base,
Germany, ca. 1875-1885, milk
glass, 9⅞" h. **94.00**

Litthauer Stomach Bitters,
Invented By Josef Loewenthal,
Berlin, square case gin shaped
w/tooled square collar mouth,
smooth base, ca. 1880-1900,
clear, 9⅞" h. **154.00**

Lorimer's Juniper Tar Bitters

Lorimer's - Juniper Tar - Bitters,
Elmira, N.Y., square w/applied
sloping collar mouth, ca. 1875-
1885, bluish green, 9⅞" h.
(ILLUS.) **1,540.00**

Lyman's Dandelion Bitters,
rectangular w/tooled square
collar mouth, smooth base,
ca. 1860-1880,aqua,10⅞" h. **55.00**

Mahan Bitters Co., St. Louis.
Mo., cylindrical w/tooled square
collar mouth, smooth base, ca.
1880-1900, clear, 8⅜" h. **88.00**

Maryland Tonic Bitters, oval
w/tooled square collar mouth,
smooth base, ca. 1880-1900,
aqua, 6¾" h. (½" chip on
mouth) **132.00**

**Maton's (Dr.) Celebrated
Stomach Bitters,** square,
applied sloping collar mouth
w/ring, smooth base, ca. 1860-
1880, golden amber, 9⅝" h. **209.00**

**McClintock's (Dr. J.R.B.)
Dandelion Bitters,** rectangular
w/applied square collar mouth,
smooth base, ca. 1860-1880,
aqua, 8⅛" h. **55.00**

McHenry (Dr. M.) Stomach Bitters, rectangular w/tooled square collar mouth, smooth base, ca. 1880-1900, aqua, 7¾" h. **83.00**

McKleever's Army Bitters

McKleever's Army - Bitters, round drum-shaped body w/applied mouth, shoulders covered w/cannonballs, smooth base, ca. 1865-1875, amber, 10⅞" h. (ILLUS.).........**2,145.00**

Medicine (N.W.) Co Bitters, oval w/tooled square collar mouth, smooth base, ca. 1880-1900, yellowish amber, 7⅞" h. **61.00**

Mishler's Herb Bitters, square, applied sloping collar mouth w/ring, smooth base, 98% original label, ca. 1860-1880, yellowish amber, 9⅛" h. **121.00**

Moffat (John) & Cos Phoenix Bitters - New York - Price $1,00, rectangular w/applied round collar mouth, smooth base, ca. 1860-1880, aqua, 6⅜" h. (light interior haze) **77.00**

Montgomery's (Dr.) Vegetable Bitters, rectangular w/tooled square collar mouth, smooth base, ca. 1880-1900, aqua, 8⅝" h. **55.00**

Morning (five-pointed star) Bitters, Inceptum 5869, triangular w/applied sloping collar mouth, red iron pontil, eighteen diagonal ribs, ca. 1870-1875, root beer amber, 11⅞" h. **1,210.00**

Nibol - Kidney and Liver - Bitters, square w/rounded corners, tooled sloping collar mouth, smooth base, ca. 1870-1890, golden amber, 9⅝" h. (¼" bruise on one corner) **44.00**

Normandy Herb & Root Stomach Bitters - Normandy Medicine M'F'G. Co., Louisville. KY., rectangular w/rounded corners, tooled square collar mouth, smooth base, ca. 1880-1900, topaz, 7⅝" h. **99.00**

Olgaro (D.) Bitters., cylindrical, applied sloping collar mouth w/ring, smooth base, ca. 1860-1880, olive green, 9⅛" h..............**83.00**

Old Homestead Wild Cherry Bitters

**Old Homestead Wild Cherry
Bitters -** Patent, square cabin
w/applied sloping collar mouth,
smooth base, ca. 1865-1875,
root beer amber, 9⅝" h. (ILLUS.
bottom previous page)..............**308.00**

**Old Sachem Bitters and
Wigwam Tonic,** barrel-shaped,
ten-rib w/applied mouth, smooth
base, ca. 1860-1870, pinkish
puce, 9⅞" h. **853.00**

**Old Sachem Bitters and
Wigwam Tonic,** barrel-shaped,
ten-rib w/applied mouth, smooth
base, ca. 1860-1870, light
pinkish topaz, 9⅝" h. **3,410.00**

**Old Sachem Bitters and
Wigwam Tonic,** barrel-shaped,
ten-rib w/applied mouth, ca.
1860-1870, pinkish amethyst,
9⅞" h. **633.00**

Oswego 25¢ Bitters, oval
w/tooled square collar mouth,
smooth base, ca. 1870-1890,
yellowish amber, 7" h. **77.00**

Penn's Bitters for the Liver,
square w/tooled mouth, smooth
base, ca. 1880-1900, golden
amber, 6⅞" h. **99.00**

Pepsin Bitters, rectangular
w/rounded corners & fluted
shoulders, tooled sloping collar
mouth, smooth base, ca. 1880-
1900, yellowish green, 8⅜" h. **55.00**

Peruvian Bitters - W.K.
(monogram in shield), square
w/applied mouth, smooth base,
ca. 1875-1885, medium amber,
9⅝" h. (ILLUS. top next
column)......................................**94.00**

**Pierce's (Dr Geo) - Indian
Restorative Bitters, -** Lowell
Mass, rectangular w/beveled
corners, applied sloping collar
mouth, iron pontil mark, ca.
1845-1860, aqua, 7⅝" h. **154.00**

Prune Bitters - Gives Strength
Quickly, rectangular w/tooled
sloping collar mouth, smooth
base, ca. 1880-1900, golden
amber, 9⅝" h. **231.00**

Peruvian Bitters

Rex Kidney & Liver Bitters

Red Cloud Bitters - Vowinkle &
Theller, square w/applied
sloping collar mouth, smooth
base marked "A.& DHC," ca.
1860-1880, golden amber,
9⅞" h. **154.00**

Rex Kidney and Liver Bitters -
The Best Laxative and Blood
Purifier, square w/tooled mouth,
smooth base, ca. 1890-1910,
golden yellow amber,
6¾" h. (ILLUS. bottom
previous page)..........................**137.00**

Richardson's (S.O.) - Bitters -
South Reading - Mass.,
rectangular w/wide beveled
corners, tooled mouth, pontil-
scarred base, ca. 1840-1860,
aqua, 6⅝" h. **39.00**

Richardson's (W.L.) - Bitters -
South Reading - Mass.,
rectangular w/wide beveled
corners, tooled mouth, pontil-
scarred base, ca. 1840-1860,
aqua, 6⅞" h. **110.00**

Root's Bitters

Root's (John) Bitters - 1834 -
Buffalo, N.Y., rectangular
w/beveled corners, modified

cabin shaped, applied mouth,
smooth base, ca. 1865-1870,
bluish green, 10⅛" h. (ILLUS.
bottom previous column) **2,970.00**

Rothery's Bitters

Rothery's Bitters, The Great
English Tonic, Chicago, U.S.A.,
rectangular w/tooled mouth,
smooth base, ca. 1890-1900,
amber, 8⅛" h. (ILLUS.)...............**83.00**

Royce's Sherry Wine Bitters,
rectangular w/applied sloping
collar mouth, pontil-scarred
base, ca. 1840-1860, aqua
8⅝" h. **127.00**

Russ' St. Domingo Bitters - New
York, square w/beveled corners,
applied sloping collar mouth,
smooth base, ca. 1860-1880,
yellowish amber, 9⅞" h. **83.00**

Russell Bitters, square w/tooled
sloping collar mouth, smooth
base, ca. 1880-1900, amber,
8⅞" h. **83.00**

Ryder's (Dr.) - Clover Bitters,
rectangular w/rounded corners,
tooled mouth, smooth base, ca.
1870-1890, amber, 7⅝" h.........**121.00**

S & S Bitters, Der Doktor, square w/rounded corners & swirled neck, tooled sloping collar mouth w/ring, smooth base, ca. 1880-1900, clear, 9⅞" h. **176.00**

Saint Jacob's Bitters, square w/applied sloping collar mouth, smooth base marked "KYGWCO," ca. 1860-1880, golden amber, 8⅝" h. (⅛" flake on mouth) **44.00**

Sazerac Aromatic Bitters, cylindrical w/lady's leg neck, applied mouth w/ring, smooth base, ca. 1860-1880, yellowish amber, 10" h. **198.00**

Scheetz - Celebrated Bitter Cordial - Philada, square w/beveled corners, tooled sloping collar mouth, smooth base, ca. 1880-1900, aqua, 9⅞" h. **77.00**

J.H. Schroeder Bitters

Schroeder (J.H.), 28 Wall Street, Louisville, KY., square w/sloping collar mouth, smooth base, ca. 1860-1870, deep olive green, 10" h. (ILLUS.)...........................**578.00**

Schroeder, (J.H.), 58 Water Street, Louisville, KY., square w/applied sloping collar mouth, smooth base, ca. 1860-1870, golden yellowish amber, 9" h. **330.00**

Schroeder's (motif of rooster) Bitters, Louisville, KY., cylindrical w/applied mouth, lady's leg neck, smooth base, amber, 4⅞" h. **990.00**

Schroeder's Bitters, Established 1845, Louisville and Cincinnati, cylindrical w/tooled mouth, lady's leg neck, smooth base, amber, 5⅜" h. **330.00**

Schroeder's Bitters, Established 1845, Louisville and Cincinnati, round w/tooled mouth, lady's leg neck, "S.B. & G. Co." on smooth base, amber, 9" h. **226.00**

Schroeder's Bitters, Established 1845, Louisville and Cincinnati, round w/tooled mouth, lady's leg neck, "S.B. & G. CO." on smooth base, ca. 1875-1885, amber, 11⅝" h. **264.00**

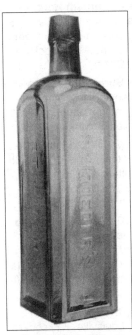

Schroeder's Bitters

Schroeder's Bitters, Louisville (embossed vertically), round w/applied mouth, "K.H. & G." on smooth base , ca. 1875-1885, amber, 8⅞" h. (ILLUS. bottom previous page)...........................**193.00**

Schroeder's Bitters, Louisville, KY, cylindrical w/tooled mouth, lady's leg neck, smooth base, ca. 1870-1880, amber, 5⅝" h. **550.00**

Schroeder's Bitters, Louisville, KY., round w/applied double collar mouth, lady's leg neck, "KY.,G.W. CO." on smooth base, ca. 1875-1885, golden amber, 12" h. **330.00**

Schroeder's Stomach Bitters, square w/applied sloping collar mouth, smooth base, golden amber yellow, 9¾" h. (½" shallow open bubble on shoulder) **209.00**

Schwab. Pieters & Co Red Jacket Bitters, square w/applied sloping collar mouth smooth base, ca. 1860-1880, amber, 9⅞" h. **110.00**

Sharp's - Mountain Herb - Bitters, square w/applied sloping collar mouth, smooth base, ca. 1860-1880, golden amber, 9¾" h. **110.00**

Shedd's Spring Bitters, square, tooled sloping collar mouth w/ring, smooth base, ca. 1890-1900, medium amber, 9¾" h. **182.00**

Simon's (Dr. W.) Indian Bitter, round w/tooled mouth, smooth base, letters read base to shoulder, ca. 1885-1895, yellowish green, 5⅝" h. **578.00**

Smith's (Dr. A.H.) Celebrated Old Style Bitters - The Standard Tonic And Purifier, square w/applied sloping collar mouth, smooth base, ca.1860-1880, golden amber, 9" h. **99.00**

Smith's (Dr. M.) - Stomach Bitters, Louisville, KY, square semi-cabin shaped w/applied

sloping collar mouth, smooth base, ca. 1865-1875, root beer amber, 9⅞" h. **550.00**

Snyder's Celebrated Bitter Cordial, H.G. Leisenring & Coy, Philada PA, applied double collar mouth, smooth base, ca. 1870-1875, yellowish amber, 9⅝" h. **165.00**

Soule (Dr.) - Hop - Bitters, square modified cabin form, applied sloping collar mouth w/ring, smooth base, ca. 1860-1880, topaz, 8" h. **259.00**

Sperry's (Dr.) - Rheumatic Bitters - Hartford, CT., rectangular w/applied sloping collar mouth, smooth base, ca. 1860-1880, aqua, 10⅛" h. **88.00**

Staake's Original Vital-Tonic Bitters, oval w/tooled square collar mouth, smooth base, ca. 1880-1900, clear, 8⅛" h. **66.00**

Steinfeld's French Cognac Bitters, cylindrical, applied sloping mouth w/ring, smooth base, ca. 1860-1880, light yellowish amber, 11⅝" h. **413.00**

Stoever's (Dr.) Bitters - Established 1837 - Kyder & Co, Philadelphia, square w/applied sloping collar mouth, smooth base, ca. 1860-1870, yellowish amber w/hint of olive, 9⅝" h. **110.00**

Strassburger Krauter Bitter, square w/beveled corners, applied sloping collar mouth, smooth base marked "A& D.H.C.," ca. 1860-1880, reddish amber, 9" h. **132.00**

Sulphur and Iron Bitters, rectangular w/tooled sloping collar mouth, smooth base, ca. 1880-1900, yellowish amber, 8⅜" h. **39.00**

Sun Kidney And Liver Bitters, Vegetable Laxative Bowel Regulator And Blood Purifier, square, sloping collar mouth w/ring, smooth base, ca. 1900-1910, golden amber 9⅝" h. **28.00**

Tonola Bitters, (motif of eagle), Trade Mark, Philadelphia, square w/tooled square collar mouth, smooth base, ca. 1880-1900, aqua, 8⅝" h. **99.00**

Tyler's Standard American Bitters, square w/ applied sloping collar mouth, smooth base, ca. 1860-1880, amber, 9⅝" h. **55.00**

Tyree's - Chamomile - Bitters, oval w/square tooled collar mouth, smooth base, ca. 1880-1900, golden amber, 6⅝" h. **165.00**

U.S. - Gold - Bitters, square modified cabin form, tooled sloping collar mouth w/ring, smooth base, ca. 1870-1890, aqua, 9⅝" h. **935.00**

Van Ness Golden Bitters, (motif of tree), Manufactured By E.A. Van Ness, Ravenna Ohio, oval w/tooled square collar mouth, smooth base, ca. 1880-1900, clear, 8⅝" h. **66.00**

Von Hopf's Curaco Bitters

Von Hopf's (Dr.) Curaco Bitters - Chamberlain & Co, Des Moines Iowa, square w/tooled mouth, long tapered collar, smooth base, ca. 1890-1900, medium amber, 9⅛" h. (ILLUS. bottom previous column) **72.00**

Von Koster Stomach Bitters, Fairfield Conn., square w/tooled sloping collar mouth, smooth base, ca. 1870-1890, amber, 9" h. **110.00**

Dr. Washington's American Life Bitters

Washington's (Dr) American Life Bitters, square w/tooled mouth, multi-sided neck ,smooth base, ca. 1890-1900, amber, 9⅛" h. (ILLUS.).........................**231.00**

Watson (W.M.) & Co., German Balsam Bitters, Sole Agents For U.S., square w/applied mouth, smooth base, ca. 1900-1904, milk glass, 9" h. **385.00**

Wear Upham & Ostrom, Julien's Imperial, Aromatic Bitters, N.Y., round w/applied mouth, lady's

Wear Upham & Ostrom Bitters

leg neck, smooth base, ca.
1865-1875, yellowish amber,
12⅞" h. (ILLUS.)....................**2,695.00**

**Webb's Improved - Stomach
Bitters -** C.W. Webb & Bro.,
Jackson, Mich., square
w/beveled corners, applied
sloping collar mouth, smooth
base, ca. 1860-1880, 9" h. **88.00**

West India Stomach Bitters,
square w/applied sloping collar
mouth, smooth base marked
"B.F.G. Co.," ca. 1860-1880,
golden, amber, 8⅞" h. **143.00**

Wheatley's Hop Bitters, W.J.
Stevens, St. Pauls Bristol,
cylindrical, applied sloping collar
mouth w/ring, smooth base,
England, ca. 1860-1880,
yellowish olive, 7⅜" h. **50.00**

**Wheeler's (Dr) Sherry Wine
Bitters,** oval w/applied double
collar mouth, smooth base, ca.
1860-1880, aqua, 8" h. **50.00**

Whitcomb's (Faith) - Bitters,
Boston, Mass. U.S.A. - Faith

Whitcomb's Agency, rectangular
w/applied double collar mouth,
smooth base, ca. 1860-1880,
aqua, 9⅜" h. **39.00**

Whitney's (Dr.) - Bitters, Olean,
N.Y - U.S.A., oval w/tooled
square collar mouth, smooth
base, ca. 1880-1900, golden
amber, 7" h. **83.00**

Willard's Golden Seal Bitters,
oval w/tooled square collar
mouth, smooth base, ca. 1870-
1890, aqua, 7¾" h. **50.00**

Wilmerding & Company Peruvian Bitters

Wilmerding & Co., Sole Agents
For, Peruvian Bitters, 214 & 216
Front St, S.F., flask w/tooled lip,
smooth base, ca. 1878, amber,
6" h., ⅞ pt. (ILLUS.)...............**6,930.00**

**Winfree's (H.N.), Aromatic,
Stomach Bitters,** Chester, VA,
oval w/tooled mouth, smooth
base, ca. 1880-1890, aqua,
6⅞" h. **303.00**

Winter's - Stomach Bitters,
square w/beveled corners,
tooled sloping collar mouth,
smooth base marked "AB Co.,"
ca. 1870-1890, amber, 9⅞" h. **84.00**

Wolf's Stomach Bitters, square
w/applied sloping collar mouth,
smooth base, ca. 1860-1880,
golden amber, 9" h. **132.00**

Wonser's (Dr.) Bitters - USA,
square w/applied sloping collar
mouth, smooth base, ca. 1860-
1880, light bluish green,
9" h. **105.00**

Wonser's Indian Root Bitters

Wonser's (Dr.) Bitters - USA
Indian Root Bitters, round w/blob
top, two neck rings & sixteen
shoulder flutes, ca. 1870s,
yellowish amber, 11" h.
(ILLUS.) **3,960.00**

XXX Dandelion Bitters - Chicago
Ill, square w/beveled corners,
applied square collar mouth,
smooth base, ca. 1870-1890,
amber, 8⅞" h. **121.00**

Yerba Buena - Bitters S.F. Cal.,
rectangular flask-shaped, tooled
sloping collar mouth, smooth
base, ca. 1870-1890, golden
amber, qt. **61.00**

**Youngs (Dr.) Wild Cherry
Bitters,** Brooklyn, N.Y.,
rectangular w/tooled double
collar mouth, smooth base, ca.
1880-1900, yellowish amber,
8⅝" h. **58.00**

Zoeller's Stomach Bitters

Zoeller's, Stomach Bitters - The
Zoeller Medical Co., Pittsburgh,
PA., rectangular, two sides
folded, w/tooled mouth, smooth
base, ca. 1890-1900, amber,
9⅞" h. (ILLUS.).........................**275.00**

Zu Zu Bitters (on three panels),
square w/applied mouth, smooth
base, ca. 1870-1880, medium
amber, 9⅞" h. **110.00**

CONTEMPORARY

Jim Beam
Baggage Car (1981) **50.00**

Caboose, grey (1988) **65.00**

Coal Tender, No. 197 ....**75.00**

Combination Car (1988) **45.00**

Dining Car (1982) **85.00**

Fire Engine, 1867 Mississippi
Steam Engine (1978) **150.00**

Flat Car (1988) **75.00**

Locomotive, Casey Jones
w/tender (1989) **50.00**

Locomotive, Grant (1979) **95.00**

Locomotive, J.B. Turner (1982)
(no box) **100.00**

Locomotive, The General
(1988) **115.00**

Log Car, J.B. Turner RR
(1984) **75.00**

Lumber Car (1987) **50.00**

Observation Car (1987) **50.00**

Passenger Car (1981) **50.00**

Tank Car, J.B. Turner RR
(1983) **55.00**

Water Tower (1987).....................**45.00**

Wood Tender, J.B. Turner RR,
No. 249 ....**95.00**

FIGURALS

Bear Bottle

Bear, smooth base, tooled mouth,
ca. 1890-1910, deep olive
amber, 9⅝" h. (ILLUS.)..............**550.00**

Bust of La Tsarine, embossed
"La Tsarine, Bonbons, John
Tavernier" around base, ground
base opening, original tin lid on
base, French, ca.1895-1910,
milk glass, 13⅛" h. **413.00**

Bust of wiseman, ground base
opening, orginial tin lid on base,
ca. 1890-1915, clear, 11⅛" h. ...**605.00**

Clock, embossed "Here Is To
You, Merry Christmas, Happy
New Century, And Many Of
Them," Roman numeral clock
w/hands at a quarter to twelve,
ground lip with screw threads,
smooth base, ca. 1900, 4⅞" h.
(cap is missing) **231.00**

Clown, pontil-scarred base,
ground lip, correct glass head
stopper, ca. 1890-1910, clear,
12⅞" h. **55.00**

Coal piece, flask-type, smooth
base, ground lip, metal screw
cap, ca. 1890-1910, black
amethyst, 3⅞" h..........................**88.00**

Duck, "Patd April 11th 1871" on
smooth base, ground lip, milk
glass, Atterbury Glass Co., ca.
1871-1880, 11⅝" h. **303.00**

Hand Holding Dagger Bottle

Hand holding dagger, polished pontil, tooled mouth, ca. 1890-1910, deep cobalt blue, 14⅝" h. (ILLUS. bottom previous page)..........................**523.00**

Hat, embossed "Dr. Fox's Sarsaparilla For The Blood," tooled lopped rim, footed w/smooth base, ca. 1890-1910, clear, 1⅞" h. **77.00**

Heart, embossed "John Hart & Co," applied double collar mouth, smooth base, ca. 1875-1885, cobalt blue, 5⅞" h............**358.00**

Japanese Man Blacking Bottle

Japanese man, embossed "J.C.F. - Indestructible - Trade Mark - Japanese - Polish - Gloss - Primicerio & Co - Sole Proprietors & Manufacturers, Baltimore, MD," smooth base, tooled lip, medium amber, 6¾" h. (ILLUS.).........................**358.00**

Pickle or cucumber, rolled lip, ca. 1885-1900, light bluish green, 4⅞" l. **143.00**

Pig, smooth base, tooled lip, ca. 1880-1890, clear, 9⅞" l. **253.00**

Pineapple, round, applied double collar mouth, smooth base, ca. 1865-1875, amber, 9" h. **176.00**

Statue Of Liberty, metal statue marked "Liberty Enlightening The World. Pat. Feb. 18, 1879, July 16, 1885," milk white statue 7⅜" h., base 8" h. **750.00**

FLASKS

Flasks are listed according to the numbers provided in American Bottle & Flasks and Their Ancestry *by Helen McKearin and Kenneth M. Wilson.*

GI-2 - Washington bust below "General Washington" - American Eagle w/shield w/seven bars on breast, head turned to right, edges w/horizontal beading w/vertical medial rib, sheared lip, pontil-scarred base, ca. 1825-1830, pale greenish aqua, pt.......**253.00**

GI-20 - Washington bust (facing right) below "Fells," "Point" below bust - Baltimore Monument w/"Balto" below, vertical medial rib, sheared lip, pontil-scarred base, ca. 1825-1835, pinkish amethyst, pt. **1,430.00**

GI-21 - Washington bust (facing right) below "Fells," "Point" below bust - Baltimore Monument w/"Balto" below, vertical medial rib, sheared lip, pontil-scarred base, ca. 1825-1835, pinkish amethyst, qt. **853.00**

GI-24 - "Washington" above bust - Taylor bust below "Bridgeton (star) New Jersey," sheared lip, pontil-scarred base, ca. 1825-1835, bluish green, pt. **468.00**

GI-36 - Washington bust - tree, calabash, applied sloping collar mouth, open pontil, ca. 1855-1865, aqua. **165.00**

GI-37 - Washington bust below "The Father of His Country" - Taylor bust, "Gen. Taylor Never Surrenders, Dyottville Glass

Works, Philada.," sheared lip, pontil base, ca. 1850-1860, cobalt blue, qt. **2,090.00**

GI-40a - Washington bust below "The Father of His Country," - Taylor bust, "Gen. Taylor Never Surrenders," sheared lip, pontil-scarred base, ca. 1850-1860, cobalt blue, pt. **2,365.00**

GI-57 - Washington bust - Sheaf of rye on crossed rake & pitchfork, sloping collar mouth w/ring, pontil-scarred base, ca. 1840-1860, aqua, qt. **55.00**

GI-72 - Taylor bust facing left, "Rough and Ready" below - Ringgold bust, facing left w/"Major" in semicircle above bust & "Ringgold" in semicircle beneath bust, heavy vertical ribbing, sheared lip, pontil-scarred base, ca. 1825-1835, smoky amethystine, pt...............**187.00**

GI-79a - Grant bust in medallion - American Eagle on shield & carrying ribbon in beak all above oval frame, smooth edges, crudely applied mouth & band, amber streak base & back, smooth base, aqua, pt. **88.00**

GI-99 - "Jenny Lind" above bust - View of Glasshouse w/"Glass Works" above & "Huffsey" below, calabash, smooth sides, broad sloping collar, pontil-scarred base, ca. 1850-1860, aqua **99.00**

GI-102 - "Jenny" above bust obverse - "Glass Factory" w/six-point star & glasshouse shown on reverse, calabash w/ribbed sides, applied sloping collar mouth, iron pontil, aqua.............**176.00**

GII-11a - American Eagle on oval w/head turned to left & eleven tiny stars in semicircle above eagle - inverted Cornucopia with Produce, horizontally beaded w/vertical medical rib, sheared lip, pontil-scarred base, ca. 1825-1835, yellow, ⅞ pt. **3,190.00**

GII-21 - American Eagle w/head turned to right & w/stars above & "My Country" below - "For Pike's Peak" above prospector w/staff & pack, applied collar mouth w/ring, smooth base, ca. 1860-1880, bluish aqua, pt. **94.00**

GII-35 - American Eagle in oval above panel w/"Louisville Ky. Glass Works," entire flask covered w/vertical ribbing, applied collar mouth w/ring, smooth base, ca. 1860-1873, aqua. qt. **110.00**

GII-36 - Eagle in oval panel above rectangular panel w/"Louisville Ky. Glass works," entire flask except two panels on obverse covered w/vertical ribbing, applied mouth, smooth base, ca. 1855-1865, aqua, pt. **99.00**

GII-55 - American Eagle w/shield & thirteen stars - Bunch of Grapes, vertically ribbed edges, sheared mouth, pontil-scarred base, ca. 1825-1835, greenish aqua, qt. (four ⅛" flakes on mouth) **83.00**

GII-55 - American Eagle w/shield & thirteen stars - Bunch of Grapes, vertically ribbed edges, sheared lip, pontil-scarred base, ca. 1836-1847, golden amber, qt. **2,255.00**

GII-61 - American Eagle below "Liberty" - inscription in four lines, "Willington - Glass Co. - West Willington - Conn.," applied mouth, smooth base, olive green, qt. **258.00**

GII-63 - American Eagle below "Liberty" - inscription in five lines "Willington - Glass - Co - West Willington - Conn," smooth edges, applied double collar mouth, ca. 1860-1870, yellowish olive amber, ⅞ pt. **132.00**

GII-83 - American Eagle above oval obverse & reverse, sheared lip, pontil-scarred base, medium yellowish amber, pt. (ILLUS. top next page) **121.00**

American Eagle Flask

GII-86 - American Eagle above oval & obverse & reverse, vertically ribbed edges, sheared lip, pontil-scarred base, olive amber, ⅞ pt. **121.00**

GII-92 - American Eagle above oval, pronounced beak & eye, pennant in beak w/slender forked end obverse & reverse, smooth edges, sheared lip, open pontil, ca. 1835-1845, yellowish olive amber, pt. **83.00**

GII-103 - American Eagle above oval obverse & reverse w/"Pittsburgh, Pa." in oval on obverse, narrow vertical rib on edges, applied mouth, smooth base, ca. 1860-1870, dark green, qt. **275.00**

GII-126 - Small American Eagle above a large laurel wreath w/stems crossed below large ribbon obverse & reverse, smooth edges, applied mouth, smooth base, ca. 1865-1875, amber, ⅞ pt. **303.00**

GIII-14 - Cornucopia with Produce & curled to right - Urn with Produce, vertically ribbed edge,

sheared lip, open pontil, ca. 1830-1840, emerald green, ⅞ pt...........**468.00**

GIII-16 - Cornucopia with Produce & curled to right - Urn with Produce & w/"Lancaster.Glass Works, N.Y." above, sheared mouth, vertically ribbed edges, iron pontil, ca. 1835-1845, bluish aqua, pt. **253.00**

GIII-17 - Cornucopia with Produce & curled right - Urn with Produce, plain lip, double rounded collar, open pontil, ca. 1835-1845, deep bluish green, pt. **605.00**

GIV-42 - Clasped hand above square & compass above oval w/"Union inside shield - American Eagle above "A.R.S.," calabash, fluted edges, broad sloping collar mouth, pontil-scarred base, ca.1865-1870, light yellowish green **330.00**

All Seeing Eye Flask

GIV-43 - All Seeing Eye, "A D" - bent arm inside six-point star, "GRJA," sheared lip, pontil-scarred base, yellowish amber, pt. (ILLUS.) **132.00**

GV-1 -"Success to the Railroad" around embossed locomotive - similar reverse, sheared tooled lip, open pontil, ca. 1825-1835, golden yellow amber, pt. **4,510.00**

"Railroad" - American Eagle Flask

GV-10 - "Railroad" above horse-drawn cart on rail & "Lowell" below - American Eagle lengthwise & thirteen five-point stars, vertically ribbed edges, sheared lip, pontil-scarred base, yellowish olive green, ⅞ pt. (ILLUS.) **154.00**

GVI-4 - "Baltimore" below monument - "Corn For The World" in semicircle above ear of corn, smooth edges, applied mouth, iron pontil, yellow amber, qt. **688.00**

GVIII-9 - Sunburst w/"Keen" - Sunburst w/"P.&W.," horizontal ribbed sides, sheared lip, pontil-scarred base, yellowish amber, ⅞ pt. (ILLUS. top next column) ..**258.00**

GVIII-10 - Sunburst w/"Keen" & "P. & W.," ribbed sides, olive green, ⅞ pt. **215.00**

Sunburst Flask

GVIII-16 - Sunburst w/twenty-one triangular sectioned rays obverse & reverse, sheared lip, open pontil, yellowish olive green, ⅞ pt. **303.00**

GVIII-16 - Sunburst w/twenty-one triangular sectioned rays obverse & reverse, sheared lip, pontil-scarred base, ca. 1810-1820, moss green, ⅞ pt.............**424.00**

GIX-12 - Scroll w/two seven-point stars above "Louisville" in straight line near base obverse & reverse, vertical medial rib, rough sheared lip, pontil-scarred base, ca. 1845-1855, deep olive moss green, pt..........................**770.00**

GIX-29 - Scroll w/two eight-point large stars in upper & mid-space w/slightly sunken rectangular panel near base obverse & reverse, sheared lip, open pontil, ca. 1845-1855, aqua, ½ gal.......**413.00**

GIX-31 - Scroll w/two six-point stars, larger star above smaller star obverse & reverse, sheared lip, pontil-scarred base, ca. 1835-1845, lime green, ⅞ pt. **990.00**

GIX-32 - Scroll w/five-point star above large fleur-de-lis obverse & reverse, vertical medial rib on edge, tooled rounded collar w/lower bevel, applied disc-type mouth, red iron pontil, ca. 1845-1855, yellowish olive green, ⅞ pt. **1,540.00**

GXI-34 - "For Pike's Peak" above prospector w/tools & cane standing on oblong frame - American Eagle w/pennant above frame "Ceredo," applied mouth, smooth base, ca. 1870-1875, yellowish olive, qt. **853.00**

GXI-41 - "For Pikes Peak" above prospector w/tools & cane - American Eagle w/pennant above oval frame, applied mouth, smooth base, ca. 1870-1875, bluish aqua, pt. **88.00**

GXI-46 - "For Pike's Peak" above prospector w/tools & cane - Hunter shooting at stag, sheared lip, smooth base, aqua, pt. **94.00**

GXII-2 - Thirteen stars & "Waterford" in arch above clasped hands & oval - American Eagle & oval reverse, applied collar mouth, smooth base, ca. 1860-1880, aqua, qt.....**55.00**

GXII-13 - Clasped hand above oval w/"L.F. & Co" all inside shield w/"Union" above - American Eagle above frame w/"Pittsburgh Pa.," applied collar mouth w/ring, smooth base, ca. 1860-1880, aqua, qt. **77.00**

GXII-29 - Clasped hands above oval all inside w/shield below "Union" - American Eagle w/shield w/nine vertical bars in talons & pennant in beak, applied collar mouth w/ring, smooth base, ca. 1860-1880, aqua, ⅞ pt. **50.00**

GXII-37 - Clasped hands above oval all inside shield w/"Union" above shield obverse & reverse, applied mouth, iron pontil, ca. 1860-1870, aqua, qt. **110.00**

GXII-42 - Clasped hand above w/"FA & Co" near top of oval all inside shield w/"Union" above - Cannon w/American flag, tooled mouth, smooth base, ca. 1870-1880, aqua, ⅞ pt. **85.00**

GXIII-3 - Girl wearing a full-length skirt & hat & riding a bicycle - American Eagle w/head turned right above oval frame embossed w/"A & DH.C," applied mouth, smooth base, ca. 1865-1875, aqua, pt. **166.00**

GXIII-7 - Hunter - Hounds, applied double collar mouth, pontil-scarred base, ca. 1865-1870, aqua, pt. **198.00**

GXIII-12 - Soldier standing on patch of ground holding rifle & pointing to drum above bevel-edged narrow rectangular bar inscribed "BALT. MD." - Ballet dancer on patch of ground holding tambourine above bevel-edged narrow rectangular bar inscribed "CHAPMAN," applied mouth, smooth lip, deep bluish aqua, pt. **176.00**

GXIII-14 - Soldier wearing spiked helmet - w/rectangular frame enclosing "Balt. MD." below, applied mouth, smooth base, ca. 1860-1870, yellowish-olive, pt. **935.00**

GXIII-15 - Soldier - Daisy, calabash w/ribbed edges, applied sloping collar mouth, iron pontil, deep bluish aqua, qt. (ILLUS. top next page) **303.00**

GXIII-19 - "Flora Temple" above motif of horse w/"Harness Trot 2.19¾" & "Oct. 15, 1859" below obverse, applied mouth, smooth base, ca. 1859, deep burgundy puce, qt.....................................**253.00**

GXIII-23 - "Flora Temple" above motif of horse w/"Harness Trot 219¾" below obverse, applied mouth, smooth base, ca. 1859, bluish green, pt. **715.00**

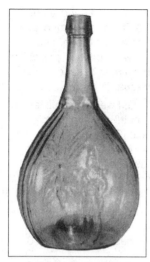

Soldier - Daisy Flask

GXIII-29 -"Will You Take" in shallow arc above "A Drink" w/duck & "Swim?" below, tooled mouth, pontil-scarred base, ca. 1820-1830, bluish green, 7/8 pt.....**83.00**

GXIII-40 - Sheaf of Grain w/rake & pitchfork crossed behind sheaf - small-five-point star, sheared lip, pontil-scarred base, ca. 1850-1860, yellowish grass green, 7/8 pt. **2,090.00**

GXIII-48 - Anchor w/forked-ended pennants inscribed "Baltimore" & "Glass Works" - Sheaf of Grain w/rake & pitchfork crossed behind sheaf, applied mouth, smooth base, ca. 1865-1875, deep amber, qt. **633.00**

GXIII-55 - Anchor w/fork-ended pennants inscribed "Isabella" & "Glass Works" on obverse - three-quarter view of glasshouse reverse, plain lip, smooth edges, aqua, qt. **165.00**

GXIII-83 - five-pointed star - "Ravenna" in arc above "Glass - Works," applied mouth, smooth base, ca. 1855-1865, yellowish olive, pt. **1,595.00**

GXIV-2 - "Traveler's Companion" arched above & below star formed by a circle of eight small triangles obverse - Star & "Ravenna" above & "Glass Co" below reverse, applied collar w/ring, iron pontil base, ca. 1845-1860, aqua, qt. **94.00**

GXIV-2 - "Traveler's Companion" arched above & below formed by a circle of eight small triangles obverse - Star & "Ravenna" above & "Glass Co" below reverse, applied mouth, pontil-scarred base, ca. 1865-1875, yellowish amber, qt.........**688.00**

GXIV-3 - "Traveler's Companion" arched above & below star formed by a circle of eight small triangles - Sheaf of Grain w/rake & pitchfork crossed behind, applied mouth, smooth base, ca. 1860-1870, aqua, pt. **132.00**

GXIV-27 - "Traveler's Companion - Railroad Guide," pontil-scarred base, ground lip with period screw cap added at later time, light bluish green, 7/8 pt. **176.00**

GXV-15 - "Newburgh Glass Co." upper half of circle & "Patd Feb 27th 1866" in lower half of circle - plain reverse, applied double collar mouth, smooth base, ca. 1865-1875, black amber, 7/8 pt. **1,760.00**

Newburgh Glass Company Flask

GXV-15 - "Newburgh Glass Co."
upper half of circle & "Patd Feb
27th 1866" in lower half of circle
- plain reverse, applied mouth,
smooth base, ca. 1866-1870,
yellowish olive, pt. (ILLUS.
bottom previous page)............**1,870.00**

GXV-28 - "Zanesville City Glass
Works" on oval, applied mouth,
smooth base, ca. 1875-1885,
aqua, pt. **99.00**

Chestnut, 14 vertical ribs, cobalt
blue, sheared lip, pontil-scarred
base, ca. 1820-1832, 4¾" h. **220.00**

Chestnut, 18 swirled ribs to left,
aqua, sheared lip, pontil-scarred
base, ca. 1820-1830, 6⅝" h. **55.00**

Chestnut, 20 ribs swirled to right,
sapphire blue, sheared & flared
lip, pontil-scarred base, ca.
1820-1830, 3⅞" h. **523.00**

Chestnut, 20 vertical ribs, cobalt
blue, sheared lip, pontil-scarred
base, European, ca. 1830-1850,
4⅞" h. **231.00**

Chestnut, 24 vertical ribs,
Zanesville, Ohio, golden amber,
4⅞" h. **220.00**

Chestnut, 24 vertical ribs, yellow
w/olive tone, sheared lip, pontil-
scared base, ca. 1820-1835,
5⅝" h. **495.00**

Chestnut, 24 ribs swirled to left,
medium amber, sheared lip,
pontil-scarred base, ca. 1820-
1830, 4⅞" h. **176.00**

Chestnut, ten-Diamond patt.,
Zanesville, Ohio, golden amber,
5⅞" h. **935.00**

Chestnut, twenty-Diamond patt.,
deep purple amethyst, sheared
& tooled lip, pontil-scarred base,
ca. 1770-1790, 6" h. **1,430.00**

Chestnut, light olive green,
partially rolled lip, pontil-scarred
base, ca. 1780-1800, 6⅝" h.
(ILLUS. top next column).............**99.00**

Chestnut, free-blown, yellowish
olive, applied string mouth,
pontil-scarred pontil, ca. 1780-
1800, 6⅛" h. **165.00**

Early Chestnut Flask

Chestnut, flattened, yellow
w/olive tone, rolled lip, pontil-
scarred base, ca. 1780-1820,
5⅜" h. **143.00**

Chestnut, deep cherry puce,
applied mouth & handle, pontil-
scarred base, ca. 1870-1880,
8" h. **60.00**

Chestnut, flattened Nailsea-type,
greenish aqua w/red & white
splotches, applied sloping collar
mouth, pontil-scarred base, ca.
1830-1850, 7⅞" h. **132.00**

Chestnut, aqua, embossed "L.
Gerstle, Bluff City, Tenn.," tooled
mouth, smooth base, ca. 1885-
1900, 4¾" h. **330.00**

Nailsea, milk white glass w/red &
white loop patt., sheared lip,
pontil-scarred base, applied
berry-type rigaree on both
shoulders, ca. 1840-1865,
7⅝" h. **143.00**

Pitkin, 23-vertical rib patt., clear,
sheared lip, pontil-scarred base,
ca. 1790-1820, 4⅝" h. **105.00**

Pitkin, 36-broken rib patt.,
medium root beer amber,
sheared lip, pontil-scarred base,
ca. 1815-1825, 5¾" h.
(ILLUS. top next page) **495.00**

Pitkin Broken-Rib Pattern Flask

Pitkin, 36-broken rib patt. swirled to left, medium yellow amber, sheared lip, pontil-scarred base, ca. 1780-1820, 5⅛" h. **578.00**

Pitkin, 36 ribs swirled to left, light green, sheared lip, pontil-scarred base, New England, ca. 1780-1810, 6⅜" h. **688.00**

INKS

Carter's Cathedral-Style Ink Bottle

Cathedral, six Gothic arch panels, cobalt blue, embossed "CA-RT-ER," ABM lip, "Carter's" on smooth base, 99% original labels, ca. 1920-1935, 6⅝" h. **264.00**

Cathedral, six Gothic arch panels, cobalt blue, embossed "CA-RT-ER," ABM lip, "Carter's" on smooth base, 99% original labels, ca. 1920-1935, 7⅞" h. **176.00**

Cathedral, six Gothic arch panels, cobalt blue, embossed "CA-RT-ER," ABM lip, smooth base, 99% original labels, ca. 1920-1935, 9¾" h. (ILLUS. bottom, previous column) **88.00**

Cone-shaped, clear, tooled mouth, embossed "Hodgson-Philada" around pontil-scarred base, ca. 1845-1855, 1⅞" h. **303.00**

Cone-shaped, cobalt blue, rolled lip, open pontil **495.00**

Cone-shaped, light emerald green, rolled lip, open pontil, ca. 1845-1855, 2⅝" h. **99.00**

Cylindrical w/24 vertical ribs, clear, tooled & pressed funnel lip, pontil-scarred base, ca. 1810-1830, 1⅞" h. **242.00**

Cylindrical, deep cobalt blue, embossed "Harrison's Columbian Ink," rolled lip, open pontil, ca. 1840-1855, 2⅛" h. **770.00**

Cylindrical footed globe, aqua, embossed w/world continents, tooled mouth, smooth base, ca. 1885-1895, 2⅛" h. **110.00**

Cylindrical, cobalt blue, embossed "Harrison's Columbian Ink," applied mouth, open pontil, ca. 1840-1855, 4⅝" h. **468.00**

Cylindrical, master size, amber, embossed "Hohenthal Brothers & Co Indelible Writing Ink N.Y.," applied mouth w/pour spout, pontil-scarred base, ca. 1845-1860, 8⅞" h. **688.00**

Hexagon, cobalt blue, embossed clover design, ABM lip, "Carter's" on smooth base, ca. 1920-1935, 2⅞" h. (ILLUS. bottom previous column) **121.00**

Octagonal, aqua, embossed "Harrison's Columbian Ink," rolled lip, open pontil, ca. 1845-1855, 1¾" h. **88.00**

Pitkin-type, deep olive amber, 36 ribs swirled to left, tooled disc-type mouth, pontil-scarred base, ca. 1780-1820, 1⅞" h. **83.00**

Twelve-sided, bluish aqua, embossed "Harrison's Columbian Ink," applied mouth, open pontil, ca. 1840-1855, 5¾" h. **176.00**

Twelve-sided, aqua, marked "Harrison's Columbian Ink," applied flared collar mouth, pontil-scarred base, ca. 1840-1860, 6" h. **88.00**

Twelve-sided, aqua, marked "Harrison's Columbian Ink," applied flared collar mouth, iron pontil base, ca. 1845-1860, 7⅞" h. **121.00**

Twelve-sided, large master size, light clear green, applied mouth, iron pontil, 9⅛" h. (¼" shallow chip on base) **240.00**

Umbrella-type (8-panel cone shape), golden amber, rolled lip, open pontil **275.00**

Umbrella-type (8-panel cone shape), cobalt blue, inward rolled lip, smooth base, ca. 1860-1880, 2⅝" h. **220.00**

Umbrella-type (8-panel cone shape), emerald green, rolled lip, open pontil, 2⅞" h. (ILLUS. top next page) **143.00**

Umbrella-type (8-panel cone shape), deep green, sheared top, open pontil.........................**330.00**

Umbrella-type (8-panel cone shape), olive green, sheared lip, open pontil...............................**165.00**

Cylindrical Ink Bottle

Cylindrical, light green, embossed "S. Fine Blk. Ink," rolled lip, open pontil, 3" h. (ILLUS.) **330.00**

Cylindrical, large master size, amber, applied mouth, smooth base, New England, ca. 1855-1875, 9⅝" h. **83.00**

Domed w/offset neck, yellowish amber, embossed "J & IEM," ground lip, smooth base, ca. 1880-1890, 1⅝" h. **215.00**

Carter's Hexagon-Shaped Ink Bottle

Umbrella Ink Bottle

Umbrella-type (8-panel cone
  shape), purple puce, rolled lip,
  open pontil..............................**1,100.00**

Umbrella-type (8-panel cone
  shape), root beer puce, rolled
  lip, open pontil **550.00**

MEDICINES

Allan's Anti-Fat - Botanic
  Medicine Co. - Buffalo, N.Y.,
  rectangular, applied mouth,
  smooth base, ca. 1875-1885,
  deep teal blue, 7⅝" h.................**440.00**

Bach's - American Compound -
  Auburn, N.Y., rectangular
  w/beveled edges, applied
  mouth, open pontil, ca. 1840-
  1855, bluish aqua, 7½" h...........**132.00**

**Bettison's English Horse
  Liniment,** 11th & Market,
  Louisville, cylindrical w/rolled lip,
  open pontil, ca. 1840-1855,
  aqua, 4" h. **413.00**

Bitter Witch (embossed
  horseshoe) Trademark, oval
  flask-shaped, tooled collar
  mouth w/lower bevel, ca. 1870s,
  yellowish olive **523.00**

**Bull's (Dr. John) - Compound
  Pectoral -** Wild Cherry -
  Louisville, KY & New York,
  rectangular w/applied double
  collar mouth, iron pontil, ca.
  1840-1855, aqua, 7½" h.
  (ILLUS. top next column)...........**231.00**

Bull's Compound Pectoral

**Burkhardt's - Fever & Ague
  Remedy -** Louisville, KY,
  rectangular w/applied sloping
  collar mouth, pontil-scarred
  base, ca. 1840-1855, aqua,
  6¾" h. **413.00**

Citrate Of Magnesia, H.P.
  Wakelee & Co., Druggists,
  cylindrical, tooled collar mouth
  w/lower bevel, ca. mid 1870s,
  cobalt, 7¼" h..............................**770.00**

**Connell's Brahaminical
  Moonplant East Indian
  Remedies** (embossed w/ten
  stars encircling two feet) Trade
  Mark, oval flask-shaped, tooled
  collar mouth w/lower bevel, ca.
  early 1870s, yellowish olive,
  8¼" h. **495.00**

Crooke's (Dr. C.) - Never Fail -
  Louisville, KY, rectangular
  w/rolled lip, pontil-scarred base,
  ca. 1840-1855, aqua, 4¼" h. **330.00**

Daily's Pain Extract - Louisville,
  KY, rectangular w/rolled lip,
  open pontil, ca. 1840-1855,
  bluish aqua, 5½" h. (ILLUS.
  top next page) **385.00**

Daily's Pain Extract

Force's Asthmanna

Daily's Pain Extractor -
Louisville, rectangular w/rolled
lip, pontil-scarred base, ca.
1840-1855, deep bluish
aqua, 4⅝" h. **83.00**

Daily's Pain Extractor -
Louisville, KY, rectangular
w/applied mouth, pontil-scarred
base, ca. 1840-1855, bluish
aqua, 6¾" h. **605.00**

Force's Asthmanna, Trade Mark
Reg. Asthma, Bronchitis, Colos,
Etc. S. B. Force Mf'g. Chemist
San Francisco, Cal., tooled lip,
smooth base, 98% original label,
ca. 1890-1900, amber, 8⅞" h.
(ILLUS. top next column)...........**303.00**

Gibbs Bone Liniment, 6-sided,
applied collar mouth, open
pontil, ca. 1840-1855, olive
amber, 6¼" h. **1,155.00**

Grave's (Dr.) Worm Syrup -
Louisville, KY, square semi-
cabin shaped w/tooled mouth,
"A. & D.H." on smooth base, ca.
1880-1885, clear, 4½" h. **105.00**

Hall's Balsam For The Lungs -
F.J. Henry Curran & Co - 8 & 9
Collage Place, N.Y., rectangular
w/beveled edges, tooled mouth,
smooth base, ca. 1880-1890,
medium cobalt blue, 7⅞" h. **72.00**

Henion's Malaria Cure

Henion's (Dr. J. B.) - Sure Cure For Malaria, square, applied mushroom-style lip, smooth base, ca. 1886, cobalt blue, two pinhead-size flakes on base & panel edge, 5 3/4" h. (ILLUS. bottom previous page).........**11,000.00**

Huff's (W.W.) Linament, cylindrical w/applied mouth, open pontil, ca. 1845-1855, light green, 4½" h. **220.00**

Hunt's (J.J.) Modern Remedy, rectangular w/applied mouth, open pontil, ca. 1845-1855, bluish aqua, 6½" h. **88.00**

Hyatt's - Infallible - Life Balsam N.Y., rectangular w/applied sloping double collar mouth, iron pontil, ca. 1845-1855, emerald green, 9½" h. **578.00**

Indian Cough Syrup - Warm Springs, Oregon, rectangular w/tooled lip, smooth base, ca. 1890-1900, clear, 6¾" h. **55.00**

Kelling's (Dr.) Pure Herb Medicines, cylindrical w/applied disc-type mouth, open pontil, ca. 1840-1855, aqua, 6½" h. **88.00**

Kellinger's (Dr. D.C.) - Remedies - New York, rectangular w/beveled edges, applied sloping collar mouth, open pontil, 8¾" h.....................**220.00**

Lane's (Dr.) - Headache & Liver Regulator - Louisville, KY, rectangular w/rolled lip, pontil-scarred base, ca. 1840-1855, aqua, 5⅛" h. **61.00**

Lewis' (M.L.) - Mothers Friend - Louisville, KY, rectangular w/applied mouth, iron pontil, ca. 1845-1855, deep bluish aqua, 9" h. **1,210.00**

Lull's Anti Spasmodic For Coughs, San Francisco Cal., tooled lip, smooth mouth, ca. 1885-1895, aqua, 4⅝" h. **110.00**

McDonald & Levy (Drs.) Compound Fluid Extract of Manzanita, Sacramento City

California, rectangular w/rolled lip, open pontil base, ca. 1853, aqua, 4½" h. **1,210.00**

McGown's (Dr. T) Ess. Tar, rectangular w/rolled lip, open pontil, ca. 1835-1845, aqua, 5¼" h. **99.00**

Merchant (G.W.) Lockport N.Y., rectangular w/applied sloping collar mouth, open pontil, ca. 1845-1855, aqua, 4⅞" h. **99.00**

Merchant (G.W.) Lockport N.Y. - small star on reverse, rectangular w/applied sloping collar mouth, open pontil, ca. 1845-1855, deep emerald green, 5" h. **176.00**

G.W. Merchant Chemist

Merchant (G.W.) Chemist. - From The Laboratory Of - Lockport N.Y., rectangular w/applied sloping collar mouth, iron pontil, ca. 1840-1855, medium bluish green, 5½" h. (ILLUS.) **204.00**

Newell's - Pulmonary Syrup - Reddington & Co., rectangular, crudely applied mouth, smooth base, ca. 1865-1875, aqua, 7⅝" h. **83.00**

Nutt's (Doctor N.M.) Cough Mixture, rectangular w/wide

beveled corner panels, applied mouth, open pontil, aqua, 5⅞" h. **231.00**

Perry's Magnetic Wine of Iron - Manchester N.H., rectangular w/applied mouth, smooth base, ca. 1870-1880, cobalt blue, 7⅛" h. **303.00**

Pratt (Lucien) - Le Renovateur De La Femme - Waterbury Conn., rectangular w/tooled mouth, smooth base, ca. 1880-1895, cobalt blue, 9½" h...........**198.00**

Reed, Carnrick & Andrus Pure Cod Liver Oil, (motif of fish) - Chemist - New York, rectangular w/tooled mouth, smooth base, ca. 1880-1890, deep cobalt blue, 9¼" h. **303.00**

Richardson's (S.O.) - Pectoral - Balsam, rectangular w/beveled edges, flared lip, open pontil, ca. 1840-1855, aqua, 5⅞" h. **88.00**

Robert's (M.B.) Vegetable Embrocation, cylindrical w/applied sloping collar mouth, pontil-scarred base, ca. 1840-1855, medium bluish green, 5½" h. **121.00**

Robert's (M.B.) Vegetable Embrocation, cylindrical w/applied sloping collar mouth, smooth base, ca. 1855-1865, golden amber, 9⅝" h. **121.00**

Rohrer's Expectoral Wild Cherry Tonic, Lancaster, PA, tapered square w/roped corners, applied sloping collar mouth, iron pontil, ca. 1860-1870, medium amber, 10½" h. (ILLUS. top next column) **385.00**

Schenck's - Seaweed - Tonic, rectangular, applied sloping double collar mouth, iron pontil, ca. 1845-1855, bluish aqua, 8⅞" h..**165.00**

Scott & Stewart - United States Syrup - New York, rectangular w/applied sloping collar mouth, iron pontil, ca. 1840-1855, deep ice blue, 9⅝" h.......................**1,320.00**

Rohrer's Expectoral Wild Cherry Tonic

Secor (Mrs. Dr.) Boston Mass, square w/tooled mouth, smooth base, ca. 1880-1890, cobalt blue, 9⅝" h. **143.00**

Smith's - Green Mountain - Renovator - East Georgia, VT., rectangular, pontil-scarred base, applied mouth, olive amber, 7" h. **1,430.00**

Smith's Sex-O-Tine The Great Tonic For Men Prepared By Smith's Sex-O-Tine Medicine Co Mobile Ala. - Sex-O Tine, rectangular w/tooled mouth, smooth base, ca. 1890-1905, clear, 6⅝" h. **330.00**

Such's - California Cure For Asthma - & Lung Disease, rectangular w/applied mouth, smooth base, ca. 1865-1875, bluish aqua, 8⅛" h. (ILLUS. top next page) **495.00**

Sutcliffe & Hughes - Druggists - Louisville, KY, rectangular w/applied sloping collar mouth, iron pontil, ca. 1845-1855, greenish aqua, 10¼" h. **176.00**

Such's California Cure Medicine Bottle

Warner & Company's Tippecanoe Bottle

Tippecanoe - Warner (H.H.) & Co, log-shaped cylindrical w/ringed neck & short sloping shoulder, applied mouth, mushroom stopper, marked "Pat Nov 20 83 Rochester NY" on smooth base, ca. 1875-1885, 9⅛" h. (ILLUS.)............**77.00**

Warner's Safe Cure (motif of safe) Trade Mark Melbourne, oval w/applied mouth, smooth base, Australia, ca. 1885-1900, deep red amber, 9½" h.............**72.00**

Warner's Safe Cure Medicine Bottle

Warner's Safe Cure (motif of safe), Frankfort A/M, oval w/applied mouth, smooth base, Germany, ca. 1885-1900, yellowish olive green, 9" h. (ILLUS.) **257.00**

Warner's Safe Nervine (motif of safe) Trade Mark Rochester, N.Y., oval w/single collar mouth, embossed "A. & D.H.C." on smooth base, ca. 1880-1890, deep amber, 7⅜" h. **110.00**

Warner's Safe Rheumatic Cure (motif of safe), London, oval w/applied mouth, smooth base, England, ca. 1885-1900, yellow topaz, 9¼" h. **187.00**

Warner's Safe Rheumatic Cure (motif of safe), Melbourne, oval w/tooled lip, smooth base, Australia, ca. 1885-1900, red amber, 9½" h. **176.00**

Weaver's (Dr. S.A.) Canker &
Salt Rheum Syrup, oval
w/applied mouth, iron pontil, ca.
1845-1855, aqua, 9⅛" h. **105.00**

Wilder (Edward & Co.)
Wholesale Druggists -
Mother's Worm Syrup - (motif of
five story building), square semi-
cabin w/tooled mouth, smooth
base, ca. 1880-1890, clear,
4¾" h. **143.00**

Wilder's (Edward) Compound
Extract of Wild Cherry - (motif
of five story building) - Edward
Wilder & Co, Wholesale
Druggists, Louisville, KY, square
semi-cabin w/tooled mouth,
smooth base, ca. 1880-1890,
clear glass with smoky tint,
7½" h. **209.00**

Wilder's (Edward), Chill Tonic -
(motif of five story building) -
Edward Wilder & Co, Wholesale
Druggists, Louisville, KY, square
semi-cabin w/tooled mouth,
smooth base, ca. 1880-1890,
clear glass w/amethystine tint,
6¼" h. **209.00**

Wilder's - Vermifuge, square
w/rolled lip, open pontil, ca.
1840-1855, bluish aqua, 5⅞" h. ...**176.00**

Wistar's (Dr.) - Balsam of - Wild
Cherry - John D. Park,
Cincinnati, Ohio, octagonal,
applied sloping collar mouth,
iron pontil, ca. 1840-1855, deep
blue aqua, 6¼" h. **83.00**

MINERAL WATERS

Adirondack Spring Co,
Whitehall, N.Y., cylindrical,
applied double collar mouth,
smooth base, ca. 1865-1875,
deep emerald green,
9⅜" h., qt. **1,100.00**

A.P. New Almadan Vichy Water,
Trade Mark, California, cylindrical
w/tooled mouth, ca. 1870s,
medium green, 13" h., qt. (3½"
hairline crack along left seam) **165.00**

A.P. New Almadan Vichy Water,
Trade Mark, California,
cylindrical w/tooled mouth, ca.
1870s, deep olive amber,
10" h., pt. **770.00**

A.P. New Almadan Vichy Water

A.P. New Almadan Vichy Water,
Trade Mark, California,
cylindrical w/tooled mouth, ca.
1870s, green, 10" h., pt.
(ILLUS.) **825.00**

B&G, San Francisco - Superior
Mineral Water, cylindrical
w/tooled mouth, ten-sided base,
iron pontil, ca. 1852-1856, cobalt
blue...**880.00**

Blount Springs Natural Sulphur
Water - Trade BS (monogram)
Mark, cylindrical w/applied
mouth, smooth base, ca. 1865-
1875, medium cobalt blue,
7⅜" h., pt. **86.00**

Blount Springs Natural Sulphur
Water - Trade BS (monogram)
Mark, cylindrical, applied
mouth, smooth base,
cobalt blue, 9" h.......................**187.00**

Bolen Waack & Co., New York,
Mineral Spring Water,
cylindrical w/applied mouth,
smooth base, ca. 1870-1880,
emerald green, 6¾" h., ½ pt. **120.00**

Borgman (H.) Mineral Water Manufacturer, Cumberland. MD, ten-pin form, applied blob-type mouth, iron pontil, ca. 1845-1860, 8½" h. **1,320.00**

Chase & Co. Mineral Water, San Francisco, Stockton And Maryville, Cal., cylindrical w/blob top, iron pontil, ca. 1853-1855, green **880.00**

Clarke (John), New York, cylindrical, applied sloping collar, pontil-scarred base, ca. 1855-1865, deep olive amber, 7⅜" h., pt. **143.00**

Clarke & Co, New York, cylindrical, applied sloping double collar mouth, iron pontil, ca. 1855-1860, medium teal green, 7¾" h., pt. **138.00**

Clarke & White, New York, cylindrical, applied sloping double collar mouth, pontil-scarred base, ca. 1855-1865, medium olive green, 9½" h., qt....**99.00**

Cooper's Well Water, Miss, cylindrical w/applied double collar mouth, "B.G.Co." at side of smooth base, ca. 1870-1880, orange amber, 8" h., pt. **132.00**

Cooper's Well Water, Miss, cylindrical w/applied double collar mouth, "B.G.Co." at side of smooth base, ca. 1870-1880, orange amber, 9⅝" h., qt. **121.00**

Congress & Empire Spring Co, E Saratoga. N.Y., cylindrical w/applied double collar mouth, smooth base, ca. 1865-1875, dark olive green, 7¾" h., pt........**138.00**

Cudworth (A.W.) & Co., San Francisco, cylindrical w/blob top, iron pontil, ca. 1856-1861, green, 7½" h. (ILLUS. top next column).....................................**715.00**

Cudworth (A.W.) & Co., San Francisco, Cal., cylindrical w/blob top, ca. 1856-1861, green, 7½" h. **523.00**

Cudworth & Company Soda Water

John Diehl's Mineral Water

Diehl's (John), D Mineral Water Philada This Bottle D To Be Returned, eight-sided w/tooled sloping collar mouth, iron pontil, blue, 7¼" h. (ILLUS.) **825.00**

Hart (E.S. & H.), Superior Mineral Union Glass Works, cylindrical w/blob top, iron pontil, cobalt blue, 7½" h. **220.00**

Highrock Congress Spring (motif of rock) C.&W., Saratoga, N.Y., cylindrical w/applied mouth, smooth base, deep teal blue, 7⅝" h., pt. **440.00**

Jackson's Napa Soda Springs Mineral Water, cylindrical w/blob top, ca. 1873-1885, medium bluish w/olive green striations **825.00**

Kimball & Co., cylindrical w/blob top, iron pontil, ca. 1853-1856, cobalt blue **605.00**

Lansing Mineral & Magnetic Well At The Capital Of Michigan, cylindrical w/applied sloping collar mouth, smooth base, ca. 1875-1885, amber, 9¾" h., qt. **440.00**

Lippencott (B.R.) & Co., Stockton, embossed "Superior Mineral Water Union, Glass Works" reverse, cylindrical w/blob top, ten-sided base, iron pontil, ca. 1852-1858, cobalt ..**1,870.00**

Lynde & Putnam Mineral Waters, San Francisco, Cal.A Union Glass Works, cylindrical w/blob top, iron pontil, ca. 1850-1851, cobalt..........................**1,210.00**

Massena Spring (monogram) Water, cylindrical, applied collar mouth, smooth base, ca. 1865-1875, deep emerald green, 9⅜" h. **132.00**

Mills Seltzer Springs, cylindrical w/applied double collar mouth, ca. 1874, golden amber (ILLUS. top next column)........**4,180.00**

Napa Soda Phil Caduc Natural Mineral Water, cylindrical w/blob top, ca. 1873-1881, aqua **220.00**

Natural Mineral Water T.A.W. Napa Soda, cylindrical w/blob top, ca. 1861-1862, emerald green **550.00**

Mills Seltzer Springs

Pacific Congress Springs, cylindrical w/applied double collar mouth, smooth base, black **3,740.00**

Pacific Congress Springs, cylindrical w/applied double collar mouth, smooth base, cobalt blue **6,050.00**

Pacific Congress Water, cylindrical w/blob top, ca. 1869-1876, medium green **1,870.00**

Pacific Congress Water, P. Caduc, cylindrical w/blob top, ca. 1868-1881, bluish aqua **110.00**

Pacific Congress Water Springs, (embossed running deer), Saratoga California, cylindrical w/applied double collar mouth, ca. 1872-1874, olive amber............................**1,760.00**

Pacific Congress Water Springs, (embossed running deer), Saratoga California, cylindrical w/applied double collar mouth, ca. 1872-1874, medium lime green................**4,400.00**

Pacific Congress Water Springs, (embossed running deer), Saratoga California, embossed "Sage's" reverse, ca. 1874-1875, yellowish olive **550.00**

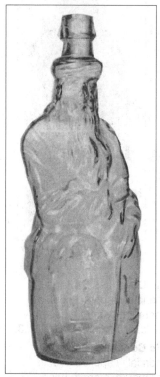

Poland Mineral Spring Water

Poland Water - Poland Mineral Spring Water (in banner around) P.M.S.W. (monogram) - H. Ricker & Sons Proprietors, figural Moses, applied sloping mouth, smooth base, ca. 1880-1890, aqua, 11" h. (ILLUS.) **182.00**

Reiners (C.A.) Improved Mineral Water, San Francisco, cylindrical w/blob top, ca. 1873-1975, green **715.00**

Rockbridge Alum Water - Alum Springs, Virginia, rectangular, applied mouth, smooth base, ca. 1855-1865, emerald green, crude & highly whittled glass, 13¼" h. (ILLUS. top next column)................................**12,100.00**

Rockbridge Alum Mineral Water

Ryan (John) Excelsior Mineral Water, Savannah, Ga., 1859 - Union Glass Works, Phila, This Bottle Is Never Sold, cylindrical w/applied mouth, smooth base, ca. 1845-1855, cobalt blue, 7⅛" h. **121.00**

Sage's Pacific Congress Water, embossed deer reverse, cylindrical w/blob top, ca. 1874-1875, aqua **330.00**

Shasta (W.&B.) - Union Glass Works, Philada. Superior Mineral Water, cylindrical w/applied blob mouth, iron pontil, ca. 1850-1857, cobalt blue, 7⅜" h. (³⁄₁₆" chip on base) **8,250.00**

Shasta (W.& B.) - Union Glass Works, Philad Superior Mineral Water, cylindrical w/applied blob mouth, iron pontil, ca. 1850-1857, cobalt blue **12,100.00**

Strumatic Mineral Water N P.S.M. Co., cylindrical, applied sloping double collar mouth, smooth base, ca. 1870-1880, deep red amber, 7⅜" h., pt. (ILLUS. top next page) **550.00**

Strumatic Mineral Water

Syracruse Springs Excelsior Bottle

Syracuse Springs D Excelsior,
A.J. Delatour, New York,
cylindrical, applied sloping collar
mouth, smooth base, ca. 1870-
1880, golden yellow amber,
7¾" h., pt. (ILLUS.)...................**440.00**

Syracuse Springs Excelsior,
cylindrical, applied sloping
double collar mouth, smooth
base, ca. 1870-1880, deep red
amber, 7⅞" h., pt. **160.00**

Syracuse Springs Excelsior,
cylindrical w/applied mouth,
smooth base, yellowish amber,
7⅝" h., pt. **264.00**

Victoria Springs Mineral Water

Victoria Springs, A Frelichburg,
Canada, cylindrical, applied
double collar mouth, smooth
base, Canada, ca. 1875-1885,
deep bluish aqua, 9½" h.
(ILLUS.) **935.00**

Washington Spring , Saratoga,
N.Y., cylindrical, applied sloping
collar mouth, smooth base, ca.
1870-1880, emerald green, 8" h.,
pt. (ILLUS. top next page) **220.00**

**W & W New Almaden Mini
Water,** ten-sided w/blob top, iron
pontil, ca. 1854-1860, aqua....**1,430.00**

Washington Spring Water Bottle

PICKLE BOTTLES & JARS

Milwaukee Pickle Company Pickle Jar

Amber, cylindrical, embossed "Milwaukee Pickle Co.," applied mouth, cylindrical ringed neck & shoulder, "D.S.G. Co." on smooth base, ca. 1880-1895, 9¾" h. (ILLUS.) **99.00**

Aqua, four-sided cathedral-type, tooled lip, "D.O.C." on smooth base, 95% original label for "Arrow Brand Pickles," ca. 1890-1900, 7¼" h. **165.00**

Aqua, cylindrical w/vertical panels, embossed "W. Numsen & Son - Baltimore" on neck, rolled lip, open pontil, ca. 1850-1860, 10½" h. **715.00**

Aqua, six-sided cathedral-type, rolled lip, smooth base, ca. 1865-1875, 13¼" h. **121.00**

Pioneer Pickle Works Pickle Jar

Bluish-aqua, square, rolled lip, shoulder collar tapering to square body, smooth base, ca. 1880-1890, 99% original label marked "Pioneer Pickle Works, Sacramento, Cal., Mixed Pickles," 10¾" h. (ILLUS.) **55.00**

Bluish-green, four-sided cathedral-type, applied mouth, iron pontil, ca. 1855-1865, 11¾" h. **220.00**

Emerald green, four-sided cathedral-type w/Gothic arch windows, rolled lip, open pontil-scarred base, ca. 1850-1860, 9¼" h. **578.00**

Catherdral-Type Pickle Bottle

Emerald green, four-sided cathedral-type w/Gothic arch windows, rolled lip, iron pontil, ca. 1850-1860, 11¾" h. (ILLUS.) **798.00**

POISONS

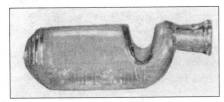

Martin Poison Bottle

Amber, square, embossed "Poison," tooled lip, smooth base, 70% original label on reverse for "Antiseptics Bernays," ca. 1890-1910, 10" h. **121.00**

Aqua, cylindrical, embossed "Poison - The Martin Poison Bottle - Patented," tooled mouth w/deeply indented shoulder recess below neck, smooth base, England, ca. 1890-1915, 4½" l. (ILLUS.) **143.00**

Aqua, cylindrical, embossed "Poison Not To Be Taken - The Martin Poison Bottle - Patented," tooled mouth w/deeply indented shoulder recess below neck, smooth base embossed "S.S.A. LTD. Manchester," England, ca. 1890-1915, 6½" l. **176.00**

Submarine-Shaped Poison Bottle

Cobalt blue, submarine-shaped, embossed "Poison," tooled mouth, "Registered No 336907" on smooth base, England, ca. 1890-1910, 4⅝" l., 3" h. (ILLUS.) **440.00**

Skull-Shaped Poison Bottle

Cobalt blue, figural skull, embossed "Poison - Pat. Appl'd For," tooled mouth, smooth base, ca. 1885-1910, several pinhead-size flakes, 4¼" h. (ILLUS. bottom previous page) **1,265.00**

Cobalt blue, figural skull, embossed "Poison - Pat. Appl'd For," tooled mouth, "Pat June 26th 1894" on smooth base, ca. 1885-1910, 3⅝" h. (professional repair on neck of skull) **743.00**

Cobalt blue, figural skull, embossed "Poison - Pat. Appl'd For," tooled mouth, "Pat June 26th 1894" on smooth base, ca. 1885-1910, 2⅞" h. (small repairable hole tip of nose) **853.00**

Cobalt blue, square, embossed "Poison (skull and crossbones) Bews Pharmacy, Revelstoke," tooled mouth, "W.T. & Co. U.S.A." on smooth base, Canada, ca. 1890-1910, 6½" h. **3,850.00**

Cobalt blue, square, embossed "Poison (skull and crossbones) Demert Drug & Chemical Co., Spokane," tooled mouth, "W.T. & Co. U.S.A.." on smooth base, ca. 1890-1910, 4½" h. **4,070.00**

Cobalt blue, coffin-shaped w/overall raised diamond design, embossed "Poison," tooled lip, smooth base, l00% original label and contents, ca. 1890-1910, 3⅜" h. **220.00**

Cobalt blue, cylindrical lattice and diamond pattern, embossed "Poison" in large letters across label panel, tooled mouth, "Poison" stopper, smooth base, ca. 1890-1910, 9¼" h. (ILLUS. top next column) **2,035.00**

Cobalt blue, cylindrical lattice and diamond pattern, tooled mouth, "U.S.P.H.S." on smooth base, ca. 1890-1910, 13⅛" h. **963.00**

Lattice & Diamond Pattern Poison Bottle

Cobalt blue, cylindrical lattice and diamond pattern, tooled mouth, smooth base, correct "Poison" stopper, ca. 1890-1910, 11¼" h. **467.00**

Cobalt blue, cylindrical lattice and diamond pattern, tooled mouth, correct "Poison" stopper, smooth base, ca. 1890-1910, 9¼" h. **385.00**

Cobalt blue, cylindrical lattice and diamond pattern, tooled mouth, correct "Poison" stopper, smooth base, ca. 1890-1910, 7⅛" h. **204.00**

Cobalt blue, cylindrical lattice and diamond pattern, tooled mouth, correct "Poison" stopper, "H.B. Co." on smooth base, ca. 1890-1910, 5⅛" h. **121.00**

Cobalt blue, embossed "Poison - Not To Be Taken," side ribbing, tooled mouth, smooth base, England, ca. 1890-1915, 13¼" h. **187.00**

Bowman Drug Store Poison Bottle

Cobalt blue, embossed "Poison - Bowman - Drug Store - Poison," side ribbing, tooled mouth, smooth base marked "G.C.G.Co.Patent Applied For," ca. 1890-1901, 6¼" h. (ILLUS.) **770.00**

Cobalt blue, triangular, embossed "Poison - The Owl Drug Co." - motif of owl on mortar and pestle, tooled mouth, smooth base, 90% original label and I.D. tag, ca. 1890-1915, 9⅝" h. **605.00**

Cobalt blue, triangular, embossed "Poison - The Owl Drug Co." - motif of owl on mortar and pestle, tooled mouth, smooth base, 100% original label for "Denatured Alcohol," ca. 1890-1915, 7⅞" h. **358.00**

Cobalt blue, triangular, embossed "Poison - The Owl Drug Co.," - motif of owl on mortar and pestle, tooled mouth, smooth base, 97% original label for "Denatured Alcohol," ca. 1890-1915, 4⅞" h. **121.00**

Cobalt blue, triangular, embossed "Poison - The Owl Drug Co." - motif of owl on mortar and pestle, ABM lip, smooth base, 100% original label for "Stronger Ammonia Water USP," ca. 1915-1925, 6½" h **220.00**

Cobalt blue, triangular, motif of owl on mortar and pestle, "T.O.D.Co.," tooled mouth, "W.T. Co. U.S.A." on smooth base, ca. 1890-1915, 6¼" h. **198.00**

Cobalt blue, star-form w/flat back label panel, embossed "Poison, Not To Be Taken," tooled lip, smooth base, England, ca. 1890-1910, 6¾" h. **110.00**

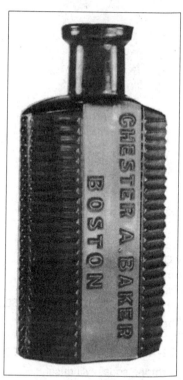

Hexagon Poison Bottle

Cobalt blue, hexagon (irregular), "Chester A. Baker, Boston," tooled lip, smooth base embossed "C.L.G.Co. Patent Applied For," 4⅛" h. (ILLUS.) **275.00**

SODAS & SARSAPARILLAS

Babb & Co., San Francisco Cal., soda, cylindrical w/blob top, iron pontil, ca. 1852-1854, medium green **605.00**

Bay City (five-point star) Soda Water Co S F, cylindrical w/blob top, ca. 1871-1880, sapphire blue...**110.00**

Bay City Soda Works Bottle

Bay City (five-point star) Soda Works Co S F, cylindrical w/blob top, ca. 1871-1880, teal blue (ILLUS.) **468.00**

Billings (E.L.) Geyser Soda, Sac City, cylindrical w/blob top, ca. 1872-1879, yellowish green **990.00**

Boardman., soda, cylindrical w/applied heavy collar mouth, red iron pontil mark, ca. 1845-1860, cobalt blue, ½ pt. **94.00**

Boley & Co., Sac City, Cal. Union Glass Works, Philad., soda, cylindrical w/blob top, iron pontil, ca. 1850-1862, cobalt...............**303.00**

Bull (John) - Extract of Sarsaparilla, Louisville, KY, rectangular, applied mouth, open pontil, ca. 1840-1855, aqua, 6½" h. **275.00**

Bull (John) - Extract of Sarsaparilla, Louisville, KY, rectangular, applied sloping collar mouth, open pontil, ca. 1845-1855, bluish aqua, 9¾" h...**138.00**

Burt (W.H.), San Francisco, soda, cylindrical w/blob top, iron pontil, ca. 1852, green **605.00**

California Natural Seltzer Water, (embossed bear), H&G, cylindrical w/blob top, ca. 1875-1885, cobalt blue **1,320.00**

Cantrell's Compound Medicated - Syrup of Sarsaparilla or Antiscorbutic Syrup, rectangular w/beveled edges, applied sloping collar mouth, open pontil, aqua, 6" h...**495.00**

Casey & Cronan Eagle Soda Works, cylindrical w/applied top, gravitating stopper, green.........**220.00**

Casey (Owen) Eagle Soda Works, cylindrical w/blob top, ca. 1867-1871, sapphire blue....**143.00**

Casey (Owen) Eagle Soda Works, cylindrical w/blob top, ca. 1867-1871, medium green ..**303.00**

Classen & Co. Pacific Soda Works, San Francisco, cylindrical w/blob top, ca. 1863-1868, aqua **143.00**

Classen & Co. Sparkling, (motif of crossed anchors), cylindrical w/tooled mouth, ca. 1864-1868, aqua **176.00**

Connoly And Bro, S.F., soda, cylindrical w/blob top, ca. 1862-1868, cobalt blue **990.00**

Cottle, Post & Co (eagle w/outstretched wings), Portland OGN, soda, cylindrical, applied mouth, smooth base, ca. 1877-1887, teal, 7¼" h. (ILLUS. top next page) **440.00**

Cottle, Post & Company Soda Bottle

C&R Eagle Works, Sac City,
soda, cylindrical w/blob top, ca.
1860, cobalt blue **1,650.00**

Crystal Soda Water Co.,
cylindrical w/tooled folded
mouth, smooth footed base, ca.
1873-1886, light cobalt **220.00**

Crystal Soda Water Co.,
cylindrical w/blob top, smooth
footed base, ca. 1873-1886,
bluish green **330.00**

Crystal Soda Water Company Bottle

Crystal Soda Water Co. -
Patented Nov. 12. 1872, U.S. Pl,
cylindrical w/wide applied
mouth, smooth base, ca. 1873-
1886, aqua, 7¾" h. (ILLUS.
bottom previous column) **55.00**

Cudworth (A.W.) & Co., San
Francisco, Cal., cylindrical
w/applied mouth, iron pontil, ca.
1858-1861, green, 7¼" h. (⅜"
diameter open bubble on
shoulder) **66.00**

*Dietz & Ellerkemp San Francisco
Soda Works*

**Dietz & Ellerkemp San
Francisco Soda Works,**
cylindrical w/blob top, ca. 1868-
1872, medium bluish aqua
(ILLUS.) **1,980.00**

D.S. & Co., San Francisco,
cylindrical w/tooled sloping collar
mouth, ca. 1861-1864, cobalt
blue..**358.00**

D.S. & Co., San Francisco,
cylindrical w/blob top, ca. 1861-
1864, emerald green **440.00**

El Dorado, soda, cylindrical
w/blob top, ca 1860-1880,
emerald green **358.00**

Empire Soda Works, Vallejo,
embossed w/eagle holding two
arrows in talon reverse,
cylindrical w/blob top, ca. 1874-
1890, aqua **231.00**

**Ficken (H.), California Soda
Works,** S.F., cylindrical,
embossed eagle w/snake in
beak and arrows in talons,
applied mouth, smooth base, ca.
1878-1879, aqua, 7" h. **275.00**

Ghirardelli's Branch, Oakland,
soda, cylindrical w/blob top, ca.
1863-1869, cobalt blue **715.00**

Golden Gate, cylindrical w/blob
top, ca. 1850-1870, emerald
green **132.00**

**Gooch's - Extract Of
Sarsaparilla -** Cincinnati O,
rectangular w/tooled sloping
collar mouth, smooth base, ca.
1880-1900, clear, 9¼" h. **66.00**

**Guysott's (Dr) Yellowdock &
Sarsaparilla,** rectangular
w/applied sloping collar mouth,
pontil-scarred base, ca. 1845-
1860, aqua, 9⅞" h. **77.00**

Hair's (Dr. B.W.) - Sarsaparilla,
square w/applied mouth, open
pontil, ca. 1845-1855, bluish
aqua, 9⅝" h. **578.00**

Hogan & Thompson, San
Francisco Cal., soda, cylindrical
w/blob top, iron pontil, ca. 1854,
cobalt **3,300.00**

**Hurley' (Thos. A.) - Compound
Syrup of Sarsaparilla -**
Louisville KY., rectangular
w/applied mouth, iron pontil,
bluish aqua, 9½" h. **908.00**

**Hurley' (Thos. A.) - Compound
Syrup of Sarsaparilla -**
Louisville KY., rectangular
w/applied sloping collar mouth,
"S.G.W. Lou, KY" on smooth
base, ca. 1875-1885, amber,
10" h. (ILLUS. top next column) ..**413.00**

Hurley' Compound Syrup of Sarsaparilla

**Italian Soda Water Manufactory
San Francisco Union Glass
Works,** cylindrical w/blob top,
iron pontil, ca. 1856-1863, deep
green **550.00**

Log Cabin Sarsaparilla, irregular
hexagonal, applied heavy collar
mouth, smooth base, ca. 1860-
1880, golden amber, 9" h. **94.00**

Masury's Sarsaparilla Cathartic,
rectangular w/applied mouth,
pontil-scarred base, ca. 1845-
1855, aqua, 6⅝" h. **440.00**

McEwin Ten-Sided Soda Bottle

Mc Ewin, San Francisco, soda,
ten-sided w/blob top, light aqua
(ILLUS. bottom previous page) ..**110.00**

Monier (J.) & Co. CL-FR-NA,
soda, cylindrical w/blob top, iron
pontil, ca. 1856-1858, greenish
aqua **715.00**

Monier (J.) & Co. CL-FR-NA,
soda, cylindrical w/blob top, iron
pontil, ca. 1856-1858, cobalt
blue......................................**4,400.00**

**Morley's (Dr.) - Sarsaparilla And
100 Potass -** St. Louis.,
rectangular w/tooled square
collar mouth, smooth base, ca.
1880-1900, aqua, 9¼" h. **121.00**

**Morison's Comp'd Syr of
Sarsaparilla,** rectangular
w/applied sloping collar mouth,
smooth base, ca. 1860-1880,
golden amber, 9⅝" h. **83.00**

**M R Sacrimento (sic) Union
Glass Works,** soda, cylindrical
w/blob top, iron pontil, California,
ca. 1851-1853, deep aqua **2,860.00**

**M R Sacrimento (sic) Union
Glass Works,** soda, cylindrical
w/blob top, iron pontil, California,
ca. 1851-1853, cobalt blue **6,600.00**

**Old Dr. Townsend's
Sarsaparilla,** square w/applied
sloping collar mouth, pontil-
scarred base, ca. 1845-1860,
bluish green, 9½" h...................**209.00**

**Old Dr. J. Townsend's
Sarsaparilla,** square w/tooled
sloping collar mouth, smooth
base, ca. 1880-1900, yellowish
green, 10¼" h. **94.00**

Phoenix Bottling Works,
Phoenix, Arizona, cylindrical
w/tooled lip, smooth base, ca.
1900-1910, aqua, 6⅞" h.
(ILLUS. top next column).............**83.00**

Phoenix Genuine Sarsaparilla -
Louisville, KY, rectangular
w/applied sloping collar mouth,
iron pontil, ca. 1845-1855, bluish
aqua, 8⅞" h. **1,430.00**

Phoenix Bottling Works Bottle

Phoenix Genuine Sarsaparilla

Phoenix Genuine Sarsaparilla -
Louisville, KY, rectangular
w/applied sloping mouth,
smooth base, yellowish grass
green, 9" h. (ILLUS.)...............**1,375.00**

Pioneer Soda Works Bottle

Pioneer Soda Works,
(embossed shield w/"PSW"),
San Francisco, cylindrical w/blob
top, ca. 1877-1896, light aqua
(ILLUS.) **77.00**

Ray (James), Savannah Geo. -
Ginger Ale, cylindrical w/tooled
collar mouth, smooth base,
ca.1870-1890, cobalt blue,
7¾" h. **154.00**

R & H Soda Water

R & H, Columbia Cal;, soda,
cylindrical w/applied blob top,
ca. 1852-1856, greenish aqua
(ILLUS. bottom previous
column)....................................**4,840.00**

Ryan (John), Savannah Geo.,
cylindrical w/applied collar
mouth, iron pontil base, ca.
1845-1860, cobalt blue, ½ pt......**121.00**

Ryan (John), S. 1852 T.,
Columbus, Ga. - This Bottle Is
Never Sold 1883, cylindrical
w/tooled collar mouth, smooth
base, ca. 1880-1900, cobalt
blue, 7¾" h. **209.00**

Sacramento Eagle, (embossed
w/eagle), soda, cylindrical
w/tooled mouth, iron pontil, ca.
1852-1863, teal green **303.00**

San Jose Soda Wors (sic),
cylindrical w/blob top, ca. 1870-
1886, deep bluish aqua **198.00**

Schmuck's (Geo.) Ginger Ale,
Cleveland, O., twelve-sided
w/tooled collar mouth, smooth
base, ca. 1880-1900, golden
amber, 7¾" h. **83.00**

Turner's Sarsaparilla

Turner's Sarsaparilla, Buffalo,
N.Y., applied sloping mouth,
smooth base, ca. 1865-1870,
deep bluish aqua, 12¼" h.
(ILLUS.) **523.00**

Woods (Dr.) Sarsaparilla & Wild Cherry Bitters, rectangular w/applied double collar mouth, open pontil, ca. 1845-1855, aqua, 8⅝" h. **303.00**

Williams & Severance, San Francisco, Cal., Soda & Mineral Waters, cylindrical, applied mouth, iron pontil, ca. 1852-1854, green **330.00**

Williams & Severance, San Francisco, Cal., Soda & Mineral Waters, cylindrical w/blob top, iron pontil, ca. 1852-1854, cobalt blue..**358.00**

William's (B.F.) - Syrup of Sarsaparilla & Iodid of Potass - Louisville, KY, rectangular, w/applied sloping collar mouth, iron pontil, ca. 1845-1855, greenish aqua, 9¾" h. **1,375.00**

Wright (W.S.) Pacific Glass Works, soda, cylindrical w/blob top, ca. early 1860s, turquoise ..**715.00**

XLCR Soda Works, San Francisco, cylindrical w/blob top, ca. 1861-1872, deep bluish aqua **3,740.00**

WHISKEY & OTHER SPIRITS

Buffalo Br'g Company Beer Bottle

Beer, "Ainslie Leeds Street Brewery, Liverpool," cylindrical w/applied mouth, pontil-scarred base, English, ca. 1790-1810, olive amber, 8¾" h....................**578.00**

Beer, "This Bottle - Buffalo Br'g Co - Sacremento - Not To Be Sold," cylindrical w/applied mouth, smooth base, red amber, 12⅛" h. (ILLUS. bottom, previous column) **138.00**

Beer, "Chattanooga Ice & Beer Co, Chattanooga. Tenn. - This Bottle Is Never Sold," cylindrical w/tooled mouth, smooth base, ca. 1890-1905, medium amber, 7" h. 1,375.00

Golden Gate Bottling Works Beer Bottle

Beer, "Golden Gate Bottling Works - Trade (motif of bear w/mug) Mark - San Francisco," cylindrical w/tooled mouth, smooth base, ca. 1880-1900, deep reddish amber, 7½" h. (ILLUS.) **55.00**

Beer, "Jamaica Champagne Beer, S.F. - D.L. Fonseca & Co.," cylindrical w/blob top, ca. 1885-1886, cobalt blue.............**358.00**

Bourbon, "Brickwedel (H.) & Co. Wholesale Liquor Dealers 298 & 210 Front Street S.F.," flask-shaped w/applied mouth, ca. 1880-1883, amber, ½ pt. **413.00**

Bourbon, "Brickwedel (H.) & Co. Wholesale Liquor Dealers 208 & 210 Front Street S.F.," flask-shaped w/tooled top, ca. 1880-1883, amber, pt. **605.00**

Bourbon, "Cutter (J.F.) Extra Trade (shield w/star) Mark Old Bourbon," cylindrical w/applied mouth, smooth base, ca. 1880-1891, amber w/olive tone, 11¾" h. **183.00**

Bourbon, "Cutter (J.F.) Extra Trade (shield w/star) Mark Old Bourbon," cylindrical w/tooled mouth, deep chocolate **165.00**

Bourbon, "Cutter (J.F.) Old Bourbon (embossed crown) E. Martin & Co. Sole Agents," cylindrical, tooled double collar mouth, ca. 1874-1879, golden amber **385.00**

Bourbon, "Hilderbrandt, Posner & Co. S.F." (w/monogram), cylindrical w/tooled mouth, ca. 1884-1890, medium amber **176.00**

Bourbon, "McKenna's Nelson County Extra Kentucky Bourbon Whiskey W&K Sole Agents," marked "W&K" on reverse shoulder, cylindrical w/tooled mouth, ca. 1880s, amber..........**495.00**

Bourbon, "McKenna's Nelson County Extra Kentucky Bourbon Whiskey W & K Sole Agents," cylindrical w/applied mouth, ca. 1874-1878, amber **1,100.00**

Bourbon, "Naber, Alfs & Brune, Wholesale (embossed phoenix bird w/upstretched wings) Liquor Dealers San Francisco," cylindrical, applied mouth, smooth base, ca. 1880-1883, amber, 11½" h. **1,485.00**

Bourbon, "OPS (monogram) Bourbon Whiskey From A.P.

Hotaling's Bourbon Whiskey Bottle

Hotaling's Old Private Stock San Francisco," cylindrical w/tooled mouth, ca. 1879-1885, medium amber (ILLUS.) **440.00**

Bourbon, "The Rothenberg Co Old Judge (embossed picture of a judge) Kentucky Bourbon Trade Mark Registered San Francisco Cal.," cylindrical, tooled lip, smooth base, ca. 1890-1900, 11½" h. **88.00**

Bourbon, "Simmond's Nabob (picture of Nabob) Pure Kentucky K.Y. Bourbon Whiskey," cylindrical w/double collar mouth, amber................**1,980.00**

Bourbon, "Teakettle (picture of teakettle) Trade Mark Old Bourbon Shea, Bocqueraz & McKee Agents San Francisco," applied mouth, smooth base, 1871-1878, golden amber **825.00**

Bourbon, "Van Bergen (N.)& Co (standing horse) Gold Dust Kentucky Bourbon" (circular) w/"Trade Mark" above "N. Van Bergen & Co Sole Agents," cylindrical, applied mouth, smooth base, ca. 1880-1882, aqua, 12" h. **825.00**

Early Case Gin Bottle

Case gin, free-blown, applied mouth, open pontil, Dutch, ca. 1770-1800, yellowish olive, 11¼" h. (ILLUS.)........................**143.00**

Case gin, free-blown, applied mouth, open pontil, Dutch, ca. 1770-1800, yellow w/olive tone, 10⅛" h. **176.00**

Case gin, tapered gin-form, tooled flared mouth, pontil-scarred base, Netherlands, ca. 1750-1800, olive amber, 9" h. **88.00**

Case gin, tapered gin-form, flared & rolled mouth, pontil-scarred base, Netherlands, ca. 1750-1800, yellowish green, 9¾" h. (⅛" sandgrain crack) **77.00**

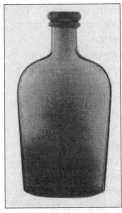

Wormer Brothers Fine Old Cognac

Cognac, "Wormer's Bro's S.F. - Fine Old Cognac," flask-shaped w/double collar mouth, ca. 1870-1872, olive amber, 6¾" h. (ILLUS. bottom previous column).................................**11,000.00**

Schnapps, "Patten & Samson. Samson's Schiedam Aromatic Schnapps," square w/beveled edges, applied top, smooth base, ca. late 1860s, dark amber, 9½" h. **550.00**

Wolfe's Aromatic Schnapps

Schnapps, "Udolpho Wolfe's - Schiedam - Aromatic Schnapps," square w/applied sloping collar mouth, ca. 1865-1870, pinkish puce, 8¼" h. (ILLUS.) **523.00**

Spirits, free-blown, globular, tall neck, unpatterned, Zanesville, Ohio, deep amber, 11½" h. (very minor surface wear)...................**413.00**

Spirits, free-blown, irregular cylindrical, applied string lip, pontil-scarred base w/unusual "clover", England, ca. 1740-1750, deep olive amber, 8⅛" h. (ILLUS. top next page) **121.00**

Early Free-Blown Spirits Bottle

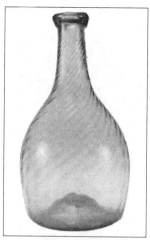

Mold-Blown Spirits Bottle

Pancake Onion Spirits Bottle

Spirits, free-blown, pancake onion, applied "up-side-down" string lip, pontil-scarred base, England, ca. 1690-1700, olive amber, 5¾" dia. at widest point, 5½" h. (ILLUS.) **303.00**

Spirits, mold-blown, globular, twenty-four swirled to right rib pattern, ca. 1820-1830, rolled lip, pontil-scarred base, aqua, 7⅞" h. (ILLUS. top next column) **110.00**

Spirits, mold-blown, globular, sixteen vertical rib pattern, ca. 1820-1830, applied mouth, pontil-scarred base, aqua, 8⅛" h. **176.00**

Spirits, mold-blown, globular, tall neck, twenty-four swirled ribs, Zanesville, Ohio, golden amber, 7½" h. **468.00**

Spirits, mold-blown, globular, tall neck, twenty-four swirled ribs, Zanesville, Ohio, amber, 8⅞" h. (some interior stain & residue) ..**275.00**

Spirits, mold-blown, globular, tall neck, twenty-four swirled ribs, Zanesville, Ohio, amber, 9⅝" h. (light interior residue) **523.00**

Spirits, mold-blown, rectangular w/rolled & flared lip, pontil-scarred base, ca. 1800-1830, Stiegel-type, clear 7½" h. **94.00**

Spirits, squat cylinder, applied string rim, pontil-scarred base, Netherlands, ca. 1740-1760, yellowish olive, 6⅜" h. (string rim w/some chips) **110.00**

Spirits, cylindrical, sheared mouth w/thin string rim, long neck, pontil-scarred base, Netherlands, ca. 1770-1790, 2⅞" d., 8½" h. **44.00**

Spirits, cylindrical, tooled mouth w/applied string rim, pontil-scarred base, "A.S/C.R" on applied seal, England, ca. 1770-1800, dark olive amber, 3½" d., 11" h. (½" spider crack on shoulder) **66.00**

Spirits, cylindrical, applied sloping collar mouth w/ring, pontil-scarred base, marked "G.S.C." on seal, England, ca. 1820-1840, dark olive green, 8¾" h. (two ¼" chips on applied seal) **99.00**

Spirits, elongated cylinder, applied double collar mouth, pontil-scarred base, marked "P.F. Heering" on applied seal, ca. 1800-1840, reddish amber, 8¾" h. **143.00**

Whiskey, "Bennett & Carrol 120 Wood St Pittsburgh," barrel w/horizontal ribbing, applied mouth, iron pontil, ca. 1855-1865, olive, 9½" h. **770.00**

Whiskey, "Bennett & Carroll No 120 Wood St. Pitts, PA," chestnut-type, applied mouth, iron pontil, ca. 1855-1865, yellow with slight olive tone, 8½" h. **880.00**

Whiskey, "California 1866 Whiskey (embossed w/two barrels) Miller Steward & Co. Distillers Louisville, Kentucky," cylindrical w/tooled lip, ca. 1880s, amber **770.00**

Whiskey, "Caster's Whiskey Made By Honest North Carolina People," cylindrical w/raised ribbing on shoulders & neck, tooled lip, smooth base, ca. 1885-1895, cobalt blue, 12" h....**440.00**

Whiskey, "Chapin & Gore Chicago Sour Mash 1867," flask-shaped w/applied collar mouth, interior screw stopper, smooth base, ca. 1860-1880, amber, pt. **50.00**

Whiskey, "Fleckenstein & Mayer (monogram) Portland, Oregon.," knife-edge style flask w/tooled lip & double roll collar, ca. 1877-1885, amber **888.00**

Whiskey, "Fleckenstein & Mayer. (monogram) Portland, Oregon.," cylindrical w/applied double

Fleckenstein & Mayer Whiskey Bottle

collar mouth, ca. 1877-1885, golden amber (ILLUS.) **1,650.00**

Whiskey, "Goudie & McKelvy Peppertree Saloon Ats For Louis Hunter Rye San Pedro Cal.," shoe-fly flask, tooled double collar mouth, ca. early 1900s, medium amber **1,320.00**

Whiskey, "Graef's (H.A.) Son N.Y. Canteen," canteen-form, tooled square collar mouth, smooth base, ca. 1860-1880, dark yellowish olive, 6½" h. (manufactured missing one handle) **143.00**

Whiskey, "Lilienthal & Co. S.F.," oval flask-shaped, double collar mouth, ca. 1870-1880, partial original blue lick label, olive amber **1,100.00**

Whiskey, footed Lilienthal Teardrop flask w/crosshatching behind shield, metal screw cap, ca. 1876-1880, medium amber **495.00**

Whiskey, "Macfarlane & Co. (emblem & slugplate) Honolulu," cylindrical w/tooled mouth, ca. 1890s, amber **440.00**

Whiskey, "Non Pareil Trade (embossed elk) Mark Kolb & Denhard San Francisco," jug-shaped, tooled mouth w/broad rounded ring below plain lip, applied handle, ca. 1895-1902, red amber **8,800.00**

Spears Old Pioneer Whiskey Bottle

Whiskey, "Spears (Wm. H.) & Co. Old Pioneer Whiskey. (embossed walking bear) A Fenkenkhausen & Co. Sole Agents," cylindrical, applied mouth, smooth base, America, ca. 1875-1893, amber, 12" h. (ILLUS.) **1,815.00**

Whiskey, "Star Whiskey New York W.B. Crowell Jr.," tapering ovoid w/vertical ribbing, small applied flaring spout, applied handle curling at bottom, deep root beer, 8" h. (ILLUS. top next column)...........**468.00**

Whiskey, "Wormser Bros. San Francisco," flask-shaped, tooled mouth w/lower bevel, ca. 1860-1870, golden amber **143.00**

Star Whiskey Bottle

Wine, "I. Hessefsy Park 1774" on impressed seal, large cylindrical w/applied string lip & seal, pontil-scarred base, English, ca. 1774, olive amber, 13⅛" h. **1,540.00**

Wine, "I.T. 1787" on impressed seal, cylindrical w/applied string lip & seal, pontil-scarred base, English, ca. 1787, olive amber, 10½" h. **853.00**

Wine, "John Key 1727" below star on impressed seal, squatty bulbous body w/applied string lip & seal, open pontil scar, English, ca. 1726, olive green, 7½" h. **4,070.00**

BOXES

Apothecary box, painted pine, rectangular w/old green paint, hinged lid opens to a fitted interior, early 19th c., 13½ x 19¾", 8¾" h. (imperfections) ...**$431.00**

Band box, painted & decorated, round w/a removable lid, the lid decorated w/a man & woman & a basket of fruit within a floral & foliate border, American-made, late 19th c., 6½" d., 3" h. **345.00**

Band box, wallpaper-covered poplar, oval, deep oblong form w/the sides covered w/the original early floral paper covering in two shades of blue & white, wear & stains, bottom & lid renailed, first half 19th c., 13½" l. **237.00**

Rare Early Band Box

Band box, wallpaper-covered, oval, deep sides w/the fitted tin lid cover in a blue, white & beige-glazed wallpaper depicting Castle Garden, New York harbor & a hunting scene, the edges trimmed w/contemporary chintz fabric, the sides w/a continuous scene of blue houses, churches & trees on a creamy tan ground w/shaded golden brown leafage, minor tears & losses, New England, ca. 1830, 17⅝ x 21⅜", 16¼" h. (ILLUS.) **6,900.00**

Bentwood box, oval, deep hardwood & pine sides decorated w/original crewel-like floral decoration in black, blue, white & pink on a natural brown patina, dated at bottom center of the design "1808," attributed to Old Saybrook, Connecticut, 22½" l. (lid rim damaged, glued & incomplete) **4,510.00**

Bentwood box, round, decorated pine & hardwood, original stylized floral decoration in red, green & black on a natural varnished ground, 19th c., 8½" d. **990.00**

Bible box, walnut, Chippendale style, low rectangular dovetailed sides w/old finish, hinged two-board thumb-molded lid w/added interior cleats, molded base on simple bracket feet, original lock & brass bird head keyhole escutcheon, Pennsylvania, late 18th - early 10th c., 14¼ x 22¾", 8½" h. (hinges replaced) **908.00**

Bride's box, pine bentwood w/laced seams, oval, fitted cover & sides decorated w/a polychrome floral decoration on a light blue ground, probably Europe, 19th c., 14½" l. (edges of lid & rim incomplete) **413.00**

Bride's box, pine bentwood w/laced seams, painted & decorated, the sides w/worn original decorated of flowers, the fitted cover decorated w/a parrot-like bird, 19th c., 15¼" l...**726.00**

Fine Decorated Bride's Box

Bride's box, decorated bentwood, oval, the sides painted in orange, yellow, iron red, brown, black & cream w/bands of stylized blossoms, the fitted lid decorated w/a

Rare Early Candle Box

scene of a standing lady & gentleman in formal attire above an inscription & surrounded by scrolls & foliage, Europe, late 18th - early 19th c., 18½" l., 7½" h. (ILLUS. bottom previous page)......................**1,495.00**

Candle box, painted & decorated pine w/sliding lid, incised compass flower designs picked out in red & black w/traces of white in the incised lines, natural 19th c., 10 x 14", 8¼" h. **743.00**

Candle box, painted & decorated pine, rectangular dovetailed sides w/a slide lid, original red graining w/white initials & dated "M.E.D. 1818," the lid w/floral decoration in red, black & white on a blue ground, top edge molding restored, lid w/nailed edge repair, 12½ x 18½", 7¼" h. (ILLUS. above) **2,145.00**

Document box, inlaid mahogany, rectangular, deep sides hinged at the center, the figured mahogany veneer w/crossbanded edge inlay & thin herringbone banding, large oval

Fine Hepplewhite Document Box

inlaid shell medallions, one on the lid & one on the front, original stamped round brasses w/round bails at the ends, Hepplewhite style, late 18th - early 19th c., minor age cracks, 9 x 10½", 7¼" h. (ILLUS.).......**1,320.00**

Figural box, miniature, carved wood, in the shape of a comical stout man wearing a long coat, tiny brass buttons & horn eyes, hinged door in back, made from one piece of wood, inserted feet, 3⅜" h. **770.00**

Amethyst Box with Enameled Florals

Glass box w/hinged cover,
round, footed, rich amethyst
decorated on the domed cover
w/white enameled flowers &
leaves & around the sides w/a
band of tiny leaves, 4⅛" d.,
3⅝" h. (ILLUS.)..........................**195.00**

Ornately Enameled Glass Box

Glass box w/hinged cover,
round, sapphire blue ornately
decorated w/a gold ground &
white bands & lacy white
palmettes, raised on a gilt-metal
base w/embossed scroll feet,
4¼" d., 4" h. (ILLUS.)................**265.00**

Paint box, mahogany, low
rectangular form w/a slide lid,
opens to a compartment
w/original watercolor paint
blocks in unused condition &
paper label "Osborne's
American toy Water
Colours...Philada.,"
19th c., 5¼" l..............................**165.00**

Early Decorated Painter's Box

Painter's box, square, low sides
w/blind dovetailed construction,
hinged lid to a divided interior,
poplar or bass wood w/ornate
floral & grapevine decoration
around the sides & the lid w/a
large drapery wreath, swags &
classical columns, all in red,
gold, green, olive green & black
on a dark bluish ground, lighter
blue showing beneath, attributed
to Rufus Cole, 19th c., 12" sq.,
5" h. (ILLUS.)........................**1,760.00**

Patch box, carved maple, in the
shape of an ovoid fish w/delicate
chip-carving & a varnish finish,
chip on tail glued,
19th c., 6½" l..............................**303.00**

Pipe box, wall-hanging, carved &
painted pine, two-tier form,
upright rectangular for, the
arched backrail carved w/a fan &
an inverted heart behind two
tiered, scalloped deep

compartments, the front fitted at the bottom w/a small drawer, painted black, probably New England, 5¾ x 5⅞", 17½" h. **2,185.00**

Early Hat Shipping Box

Shipping box for hats, painted wood, tapering rectangular deep sides pierced overall w/almond-shaped openings, old red paint accented by black, Amish, underside stamped "3 Doz. Black Style...6¾, 7¼... Deep Brim ," imperfections, 19th c., 17½ x 33¾", 21" h. (ILLUS.)......**805.00**

Staffordshire china box, cov., w/mirror, crowns, sword, cross..**125.00**

Staffordshire china box, figural cover of baby in basin holding oars, "Paddling His Own Canoe"...**165.00**

Staffordshire china box, figural cover w/a child, Griffins, 2" h. **150.00**

Staffordshire china box, figural cover w/a crawling child **140.00**

Staffordshire china box, figural cover w/a monkey wearing a hat **140.00**

Storage box, carved & painted pine, heart-shaped, fitted w/a sliding hinged lid, bears the initials & dated "C R 1741," 3½ x 4", 1¾" h. **517.00**

Storage box, domed lid, rectangular sides, pine

w/original black paint w/blue edge striping & overall stenciled decoration of trees in vases in red & silver w/free-hand red & yellow flowers on the lid, brass bail lid handle & lock w/hasp, New England, possibly Massachusetts, minor edge wear, 19th c., 9¾" l................**3,905.00**

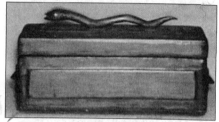

Folk Art Box with Snake

Storage box, carved wood, rectangular, brown lacquer & worn gilded trim, the low rectangular sides w/raised narrow panels & small applied end handles, the fitted lid w/a full-relief carved undulating snake, 12" l. (ILLUS.) **121.00**

Storage box, painted & decorated wood, rectangular w/hinged lid, original decoration w/pumpkin color ground & black fanciful graining, Pennsylvania, early 19th c., 9 x 13¼", 9¼" h. **3,737.00**

Fine Decorated Presentation Box

Storage box, painted & decorated dovetailed pine,

original brown paint w/red striping, geometric designs & a rose in red, white, yellow, green & dark blue, presentation inscription on the lid "To Mrs. M.J. Pollard from G.W. Rines, A present 1874" w/"Friendship" on the front panel, inside the lid decorated w/a landscape painting of cows & ducks, rosebud on lid w/some old repaint, hinged lid rail w/nailed repair, 10¼ x 13½", 6¼" h. (ILLUS. bottom previous page)..........................**1,100.00**

Storage box, painted & decorated pine, rectangular w/domed top, original red, yellow & green fanciful graining accented by simulated stringing, New England, ca. 1830, 9⅛ x 16", 8¼" h. **2,990.00**

Storage box, painted pine & poplar, rectangular w/slightly domed lid, original overall red vinegar graining on a light ground, wrought-iron lock & hasp, 19th c., 19¼" l..................**770.00**

Storage box, painted & decorated pine, rectangular dovetailed case w/molded-edge lid w/staple hinges & oval brass bail end handles, interior baffle removed, decorated w/red paint w/stylized floral decoration in red, black, yellow & green, two painted panels on the front & two on the lid w/hearts on corners, lid exposed to heat causing alligatoring & flaking of paint to lighter red ground, some old touch-up on edges, back w/stenciled & free-hand inscription "J.K. Hoadle, So. Woodstock, Jan. 1816," 10⅝ x 20½", 10½" h. **3,030.00**

Storage box, painted & decorated pine, rectangular w/hinged lid, original black freehand marbleizing on a white ground, inside of the flat lid signed in pencil "Samuel Jackson," initials "AG" & "1823" hidden in the painted design, wrought-iron lock w/hasp, found in New Hampshire, 14 x 26¾", 10½" h. **1,430.00**

Storage box, painted & decorated, rectangular w/low-domed hinged lid, original red paint w/trailing yellow & blue vines, initialed similarly "J.D.," brass end carrying handles, probably Scohaire County, New York, late 18th c., minor imperfections, 15 x 35¼", 13¼" h. (ILLUS. below) **748.00**

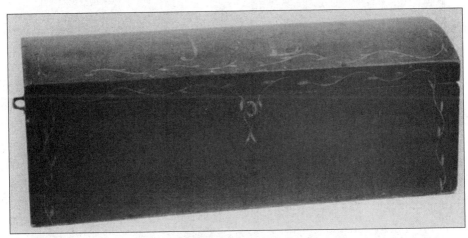

Large Decorated Storage Box

BREWERIANA

Beer is still popular in this country but the number of breweries has greatly diminished. More than 1,900 breweries were in operation in the 1870s but we find fewer than 40 major breweries supply the demands of the country a century later. Although micro-breweries have recently sprung up across the country.

Advertising items were used to promote various breweries, especially those issued prior to prohibition, now attract an ever growing number of collectors. The breweriana items listed are a sampling of the many items available.

Ashtray, "Old Faithful Beer," round, center w/rectangular image of Old Faithful above "Old Faithful - Beer," rim marked "Gallatin Brewing Co. - Bozeman, Mont. - Bozeman Beer," painted orange, blue, cream & yellow, 4½" d. (minor paint chips) **$44.00**

Beer can, "Fitzgerald's Lager," cone-top-type, black label w/Fitzgerald's logo above "Fitzgerald's Lager Beer" all on white ground, 3" d., 5½" h. (small dent)................................**39.00**

Beer can, "Rupert Knickerbocker Beer," marked "Ruppert" above Knickerbocker logo above "Draft Beer," from Ruppert Knickerbocker Brewing Co., New York, New York, 1 gal., 6¼" d., 9" h. (scratches) **105.00**

Beer glass, "Al's Beer," Bloomer Wisconsin, red enamel w/picture of bottle, tall flaring sides (ILLUS. second from left) **105.00**

Beer glass, "Anheuser-Busch" w/flying "A" logo in black, pre-Prohibition (ILLUS. second from right, top next page) **40.00**

Beer glass, "Atlantic Draft Beer," red enamel wording "We Feature Atlantic Draft Beer," tall flaring sides (ILLUS. second from right, below)........................**80.00**

Beer glass, "Black Dallas Beer," black & red enamel wording "Drink Black Dallas Beer," clear cylinder w/silver rim bands (ILLUS. far right, below) **25.00**

Beer glass, "4-X Beer," red enamel wording "Enjoy 4-X Pilsner Beer," New Orleans, cylindrical (ILLUS. far left, below)..**66.00**

Beer glass, "Muenchner," white wide band printed w/"B/and/B Muenchner - The Imperial

Four Collectible Beer Glasses

Pre-Prohibition Beer Glasses

Bottling Works, Denver, Colorado," w/vignette of Munich Child, gold band trim, pre-Prohibition (ILLUS. far left, above) **616.00**

Beer glass, "Standard Export Beer," wide white printed center band w/logo & wording in red & black "Purity Guaranteed - Standard Export Beer - Anaconda Brewing Co. - Anaconda, Mont.," gold band trim, pre-Prohibition (ILLUS. second from left, above) **930.00**

Beer glass, "The Union Brewing Co. - Denver, Colo.," frosted band w/black letter & a red, white & blue flag & black & white eagle, cylindrical, pre-Prohibition (ILLUS. far right, above) **772.00**

Beer glass, "Saazer Crown," Cincinnati, Ohio, round gold, black & red eagle emblem above wording in red enamel, tapering footed form (ILLUS. left, top next column) **100.00**

Beer glass, "Tally-Ho Beer," Ridgewood, New York, red enamel lettering w/black coaching scene, tapering footed form (ILLUS. right, top next column) **61.00**

Two Footed Beer Glasses

Beer glass, "Top Hat," Cincinnati, Ohio, black top hat w/red lettering & red cane above red & black wording "A Premium Brew - by Schoenling," tapering footed form (ILLUS. left, next page) **61.00**

Beer glass, "Walter's Beer," Pueblo, Colorado, red enamel lettering w/"5¢" near the base, tall slender waisted shape (ILLUS. right, next page) **39.00**

Top Hat & Walter's Beer Glasses

Bottle opener, "Anheuser Busch," shaped like a beer bottle, ca. 1897...........................**70.00**

Early Beer Advertising Chair

Chair, oak, advertising item for "Valley Forge Beer," tall slender balloon-form back carved w/facing heads of two men above a small beer keg, rectangular seat on square slightly canted legs joined by stretchers, ca. 1933 (ILLUS.) **154.00**

Counter top display, "Anheuser-Busch," chalkware, waiter dressed in yellow apron w/white shirt & black pants wearing Anheuser-Busch medal around neck, 20" h. (minor crazing & chipping) **189.00**

Counter top display, "Miller," chalkware, figure of young woman w/long dark hair wearing wide-brimmed hat, short flared dress & knee-high boot, on base marked "Miller High Life," done in red, yellow, blue, cream, black & brown, 6½" h. (crazing & minor chipping) **72.00**

Counter top display, "Progress Brand Beer," tin, die-cut, painted image of portly man dressed in Renaissance-style clothing sitting in a chair holding glass of beer, he is next to keg of beer w/ "Gold Medal - Paris 1900," lower left-hand corner marked "Indianapolis Brewery," lower right-hand corner "Progress Brand Beer," 10" w., 14¼" h. (minor scratches & surface rust, some dents)...............................**138.00**

Mug, pottery, Budweiser series, Bud Girl w/filigree, Ceramarte of Brazil, CS21 (ILLUS. far left, top next page) **427.00**

Mug, pottery, Budweiser series, Bud Girl, no filigree, Ceramarte of Brazil, CS 21 (ILLUS. second from left, top next page) **413.00**

Mug, pottery, Budweiser series, "Natural Light" variation, Ceramarte of Brazil, CS43 (ILLUS. second from right, top next page) **199.00**

Mug, pottery, Budweiser series, "Busch," Ceramarte of Brazil, CS44 (ILLUS. far right, top next page) **200.00**

Mug, pottery, Budweiser "Americana" series, Ceramarte of Brazil, CS 17, ½ liter (ILLUS. center left, next page)...............**462.00**

Four Modern Budweiser Beer Mugs

Two Collectible Budweiser Mugs

Mug, pottery, Budweiser "Label" model, Ceramarte of Brazil, ½ liter (ILLUS. above right) **521.00**

Logo & Bud Man Mugs

Mug, pottery, Budweiser "A" & eagle logo design, Ceramarte of Brazil, CS 24, ½ liter (ILLUS. left) **455.00**

Mug, cov., pottery, Budweiser original figural "Bud Man," cover hinged at jaw, Ceramarte of Brazil (ILLUS. right) **375.00**

Notepad, "Malt Turine," leather cover, Anheuser Busch, ca. 1904 ....**20.00**

Pinback, "Anheuser-Busch," plastic, centered w/Anheuser-Busch logo, rim reads "Help Yourself With Budweiser - Anheuser-Busch, Inc.," done in red, white, brown, blue & yellow, 1½" d. (minor scratches) **66.00**

Postcard, black & white image of five identified Beaver County Oklahoma lawmen & captured contraband, Prohibition era, ca. 1920s...**75.00**

Rare California Brewing Company Sign

Sign, "California Brewing Co. Beer - San Francisco, Cal.," oval, reverse-painted on glass, vignette of a brown bear at the top on a white ground w/yellow California poppies above a wide red center band w/gold lettering above a lower white section w/gold hops & green leaves above gold & red lettering, narrow gold frame, ca. 1910 (ILLUS. bottom previous page)......................**18,700.00**

Two Heidelberg Modern Steins

Stein, pottery, Budweiser "German Cities" series, short cylindrical shape, gold, black, green & red city crest & scrolls above "Heidelberg,", Ceramarte of Brazil, CS16 (ILLUS. left) **281.00**

Stein, pottery, Budweiser "German Cities" series, tall tapering cylindrical shape, molded narrow & wide bands around the top & base in tan & brown, a molded central city crest in gold, black, green & red above a banner w/"Heidelberg," Ceramarte of Brazil, CS16 (ILLUS. right) **385.00**

BUTTER MOLDS & STAMPS

While they are sometimes found made of other materials, it is primarily the two-piece wooden butter mold and one-piece butter stamp that attract collectors. The molds are found in two basic styles, rounded cup-form and rectangular box-form. Butter stamps are usually round w/a protruding knob handle on the back. Many were factory-made items w/the print design made by forcing a metal die into the wood under great pressure, while others had the design chiseled out by hand. An important reference book in this field is Butter Prints and Molds, *by Paul E. Kindig (Schiffer Publishing, 1986).*

Cow mold, cased-type, carved animal standing below an overhanging branch, notched border band, round case w/old color & varnish, print w/old scrubbed finish, 4¼" d. **$242.00**

Cow & tree stamp, carved poplar, a cow standing in tall grass beneath an arched, leafy tree, zipper-cut rim band, dark patina, one-piece turned handle, 4½" d. **193.00**

Eagle stamp, scrubbed poplar, spread-winged bird w/crosshatched body above blossom & leafy sprigs, zipper-cut border, one-piece turned handle, 4¼" d. **385.00**

Flower stamp, carved wood, a single large teardrop-form blossom w/feathering along each side above wide pointed leaves below, hand-whittled inserted handle, 3½" d...............**116.00**

Pinwheel stamp, carved wood, deeply carved four-petal pinwheel within zipper-cut rim bands, old worn patina, inserted turned handle, good wear, 19th c., 4¼" d. (small hole)........**149.00**

Starflower "lollipop" stamp, scrubbed poplar, six-petal star framed by a circle of pointed notched, long flattened handle w/hanging hole, 9" l. **248.00**

Tulip stamp, scrubbed poplar, a large stylized blossom flanked by leaves & w/a three-petal loop design at the top, zipper-cut rim band, one-piece turned handle, 4¼" d. (some wear) **275.00**

CANDLESTICKS & CANDLEHOLDERS

Louis XV-Style Candelabrum

Candelabra, gilt-bronze, Louis XV-Style, three-light, rounded triangular foot w/raised scrolls between ribbed bars to the scroll-embossed baluster-form standard w/a tulip-form socket support three scrolled & swirled leafy arms ending in flattened ruffled bobeches below swirled tulip-shaped candle sockets, Europe, late 19th c., pr. (ILLUS. of one) $3,737.00

Candelabra, silver, Louis XVI-style, two-light, the stems in the form of sheathless arrows, detachable nozzles, A. Aucoc, Paris, France, ca. 1900, 12¾" h., pr. 5,750.00

Candelabra, silver, George III-style, two or three light, of plain vase form, engraved w/arms & crests, reeded borders,

detachable branches, nozzles & finials, fully marked, John Green & Co., Sheffield, England, 1794, 17½" h. 9,200.00

Candelabra, silver, George II rococo-style, three-light, the baluster stems cast w/flowers & shellwork in low & high relief, detachable branches spreading from a wrythen finial, removable nozzles, fully marked & stamped "R.& S. Garrard Panton St. London," R. & S. Garrard & Co., London, England, 1851, 18" h., pr. 19,550.00

Candelabra, silver-gilt, five-light, triform bases supporting infant bacchus figures within asymmetrical grapevine stem, leafy detachable nozzles, ca. 1840-50, Wilkins, Bremen, Germany, 25" h., pr. 5,462.00

Candelabra, silver, seven-light, in German rococo style, chased & applied w/water plants on a waved ground, detachable nozzles, monogrammed, ca. 1895, Adolf Czokolly, Vienna Austria, 27¾" h., pr. 16,100.00

Candelabrum, brass, Arts & Crafts style, three-light, a widely flaring thin round foot tapering to a slender tall standard supporting a pair of slender upturned arms w/bulbous sockets flanking a central bulbous socket, two sockets w/original bobeches, original patina, signed "only four of these candlesticks made - this being number one," by Jarvie, early 20th c., 14" h. (ILLUS. top next page) 9,900.00

Candleholder, brass, single-light, a tall slender standard w/a ring top supporting an adjustable cylinder w/an extending conical copper shade above an adjustable cylinder w/an extended arm supporting a cylindrical candle socket w/a

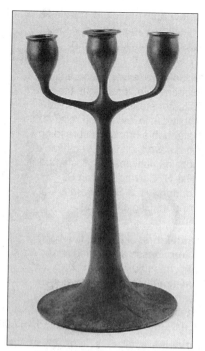

Rare Jarvie Candelabrum

Unusual Stickley Electric Candlestick

flattened drip pan, on a round flaring lead-filled domed foot, signed by James S. Davis, Boston, Massachusetts, second half 18th c., 19⅞" h. (some repairs) **7,475.00**

Candlestick, brass, Arts & Crafts style, a wide round disc foot supporting a very slender waisted standard w/a trumpet top & flaring socket rim, early cleaning, by Jessie Preston, impressed "Anderson Foundry" mark, 7"d., 14" h. **385.00**

Candlestick, bronze, Art Nouveau design, a wide diamond-shaped leaf-form base issuing a curved & forked stem w/an upright stem w/a curved hook end & a side-curved stem supporting a bulbous candle socket on three small prongs, original bobeche on socket, original brown patina, Tiffany Glass & Decorating mark, early 20th c., 8" h..........**1,430.00**

Candlestick, hand-hammered copper, Arts & Crafts style, electric, a tapering cylindrical socket above a slender shaft flanked by three tightly arched straps from the top to the widely flaring round foot, original dark patina, impressed Gustav Stickley mark, Model No. 233, 8¾" h. (ILLUS.)......................**1,610.00**

Candlesticks, brass, Arts & Crafts style, wide round disc foot supporting a very tall & slender standard below the bulbous socket w/original bobeche cup & liner, incised "Jarvie - 17," 14" h., pr. **990.00**

Candlesticks, brass, "Prince of Diamonds" design, a tall cylindrical candle socket w/flattened flaring rim above a ring-turned shaft section above a swelled diamond-design section over further ring-turning & a stepped, flaring base on a

"Prince of Diamonds" Candlesticks

square foot w/cut-corners, England, late 19th - early 20th c., 11⅞" h., pr. (ILLUS.).....**395.00**

Candlesticks, brass, William & Mary style, a flattened flared candle socket above a ring standard w/a wide flat circular mid-drip plate above a widely flaring low domed foot, probably England, ca. 1690, 9" h., pr. **6,900.00**

Candlesticks, hand-hammered copper, Arts & Crafts style, a four-sided base supports two nicely riveted heavy gauge standards & a flaring round drip pan below a short cylindrical candle socket, original dark brown & black patina, marked "KK," Karl Kipp, early 20th c., 8" h. pr. **1,045.00**

Candlesticks, hand-hammered copper, Arts & Crafts style, four flat tall straps joined by a small ring near the top & base form the shaft and continue down to form arched outswept legs, the shaft topped by a wide dished

drip pan centered by a cylindrical candle socket, lightly cleaned original patina, 11½" h., pr. **440.00**

Candlesticks, hand-hammered copper, Arts & Crafts style, heavy gauge twisted standard above domed & dished undulating base, the top w/a stepped flaring drip pan below the flaring cylindrical candle socket, overall hammer marks, original dark brown patina, unmarked Old Mission Copperkraft, early 20th c., 11⅞" h., pr. **880.00**

Candlesticks, silver, George II-Style, on shaped octagonal bases w/conforming baluster stems & molded borders, marked on bases & sconces, James Gould, 1735, 6¼" h.. pr. **4,312.00**

Candlesticks, silver, George II-Style, on shell decorated shaped square bases, fluted baluster stems, engraved w/crests & coronets, repeated on detachable nozzles, marked on bases & nozzles, William Brown, London, 1822, 10" h., pr. **2,300.00**

Candlesticks, silver, square bases, draped column stems & campana-shaped sconces, marked w/maker's mark "BHC," Germany, 7⅝" h., set of 4.....**3,450.00**

Candlesticks, silver, George II-Style, on square bases decorated w/classical profiles & swags, Corinthian column stems & detachable nozzles, crested bases & nozzles, marked on base rims & nozzles, John Carter, London, England, 1770, 12¼", set of 4 .....**18,400.00**

Candlesticks, silvered-metal, octagonal baluster form standard cast & chased w/military trophies, profiles, lyres & patriotic emblems, conforming

Early French Silvered-Metal Candlesticks

tall candle socket, raised on a dished chased square foot w/cut-corners, Regence era, France, ca. 1715., silvering worn, 9" h., pr. (ILLUS.) **3,680.00**

Candlesticks, silver plated, George III-Style, each domed lid w/acorn finial reversing to form a candle socket, the columnar shaft on a stepped circular base on tiny bun feet, 19th c., 8¾" h., set of 4 (some rubbed areas) **2,300.00**

Chamberstick, hand-hammered copper, Arts & Crafts style, round dished base centered by a tall slender cylindrical shaft w/a wide flaring socket rim, C-scroll strap handle at side of shaft, rich original dark brown patina, impressed mark of Gustav Stickley, 9" h. (three drill holes for electric conversion)..............................**330.00**

Chamberstick, hand-hammered copper, Arts & Crafts style, a wide circular base supporting a tapering cylindrical shaft w/a gently flared rim & a delicate stylized shoulder handle, original rich dark brown patina, Stickley Brothers, early 20th c., 9⅞" h. **440.00**

CANS & CONTAINERS

The collecting of tin containers has become quite popular within the past several years. Air-tight tins were first produced by hand to keep foods fresh and, after the invention of the tin-printing machine in the 1870, containers were manufactured in a wide variety of shapes and sizes with colorful designs.

Anti-freeze, Eveready 1 gal. can, reads "Eveready - Prestone - The Perfect Anti-Freeze - Does Not Boil Off - Prevents Rust" above image of thermometer & the front half of a snow covered car, all above "National Carbon Company, Inc. - Unit of Union Carbide and Carbon Corporation - New York, N.Y.," done in grey, blue, orange & white, 6½ x 9½" (minor dents, scratches & paint wear, opened at top) **$55.00**

Ford Anti-Freeze Gallon Can

Anti-freeze, Ford 1 gal. can, upright rectangular form w/large black oval w/red lettering reading "Genuine Ford Anti-Freeze" against a bright yellow ground w/further wording including "Contains Rust Inhibitor," black bands around the top & bottom, handle & opening in the top, scratches, soiling, denting, 8" w., 11½" h. (ILLUS. previous page) **94.00**

Anti-freeze, Kodiac 1 qt. can, has image of standing polar bear in winter scene next to "Danger" label, marked "Kodiak - King Of The North - Menthol - Anti-Freeze" in white, all on blue ground, 4" d., 5½" h. (rust to can & lid) **88.00**

Cylinder Lubricant Can

Auto cylinder lubricant, Primrose Speedoil Upper Cylinder Lubricant cylindrical can, wide white upper band w/black & red wording above a red & black racing car, a narrower black lower band w/white lettering, scratches, w/contents, 2¼" d. 2¾" h. (ILLUS.) **204.00**

Auto gear lubricant, Pure as Gold Gear Lubricant 5 lb.

cylindrical can, red, yellow, black & blue w/a printed "Guarantee - by the Pep Boys," w/caricature of the boys in a circle, w/contents, 6½" d., 5¼" h. (scratches, soiling, rust) **44.00**

Coffee, Royal Dutch 1 lb. can, white lettering "Royal Dutch - Coffee" on red ground, 4" d., 6¼" h. (minor scratches) **66.00**

Coffee, Tru-Cup 1 lb. can, marked "1 Lb. Net Weight - Tru-Cup" above image of coffee cup & saucer, all above "Perfection - Coffee," red, gold & white on brown ground, 4" d., 6" h. **50.00**

Coffee, Wish Bone 1 lb. can, marked "Regular Grind - Wish Bone - Combination - Coffee," w/a wishbone in the background, painted green, cream & black (wear, scratches, lid may have been replaced) **22.00**

Engine oil additive, MoPar 1 qt. can, cylindrical, red, yellow & blue bands printed w/yellow, blue & red wording, Chrysler Corporation of Canada, Ltd., w/contents, 4" d., 5½" h. (scratches, dents) **55.00**

Gum, Adams Pepsin tin, rectangular w/hinged flat lid, yellow ground w/white & red lettering & simulated side openings showing packs of gum, flared base band, scratches, chipping & fading, 4¾ x 6½", 6" h. (ILLUS. next page, top left) **495.00**

Gum, Yucatan tin, rectangular w/hinged flat lid, yellow ground w/red bands & white lettering, top w/oval red reserve w/white wording "Chew Yucatan Gum," front & sides w/simulated openings showing packs of gum, scratches, chipping, rust at bottom, 4¾ x 6½", 6" h. (ILLUS. next page, top right) **468.00**

Two Early Chewing Gum Tins

Pure Honey 5 lb. Pail

Household Lubricant Can

Honey, Pure Honey 5 lb. pail, cylindrical w/wire bail handle, red ground w/white curved banners above & below a vignette of an orchard w/beehives, long red bottom rectangle w/black wording "William Garwood, Jr. - Batavia, N.Y.," scratches, soiling, 5" d., 6" h. (ILLUS.).....................**39.00**

Household lubricant, Household Lubricant - Standard Oil Company cylindrical can w/spray nozzle on top, the sides w/a yellow ground decorated w/green brackets at the top above an arched green reserve w/white lettering, scratches, soiling, 2½" d., 5½" h. (ILLUS.) **121.00**

Carnation Malted Milk Can

Buffalo Motor Oil Can

Malted milk, Carnation container, cylindrical, red, cream & green metal w/debossed lettering & embossed white carnations in the center, fitted metal cover w/high round finial, 6" d., 9" h. (ILLUS.) **413.00**

Motor oil, Buffalo ½ gal. can, upright rectangular form w/pour opening at one end of top, dark yellow side label printed w/brown & black lettering & a vignette of a grazing bison, Prairie Cities Oil Co., Limited, Canada, scratches, soiling, fading, denting (ILLUS.) **204.00**

Early Metal Polish Can

Rare Conoco Oil Can

Metal polish, Blue Ribbon Metal Polish cylindrical can w/cone top, wide white label w/blue, black & red lettering arching above & below a sketch of an early racing car, some contents, scratches, soiling, denting & paint chipping, 6½" d., 10" h. (ILLUS.) **149.00**

Motor oil, Conoco ½ gal. can, upright rectangular form w/handle, opening at one end of top & pouring spout at other end, yellow ground w/ white stripes, a green & white standing figure of a Minute Man standing to the side w/green wording "Conoco Motorine Light - The Continental Oil Company," pour spout patented Sept. 13, 1898, scratches, soiling, chipping & denting, 8" w., 6" h. (ILLUS.) **413.00**

Group of Collectible Motor Oil Cans

Motor oil, Diamond Special 1 qt. can, cylindrical, shiny gold ground w/wide red band w/white & black lettering above a stylized diamond above black & white lettering, Diamond Head Oil Refining Co., w/contents, scratches, rust, 4" d., 5½" h. (ILLUS. far left) **165.00**

Motor oil, Hi Value 1 qt. can, cylindrical, white background w/orange lettering & a black oil derrick in the background, scratches, soiling, denting, 4" d., 5½" h. (ILLUS. second from right) **88.00**

Motor oil, Husky 1 qt. can, cylindrical, yellow, blue & white upper band w/the head of a Husky dog above a lower white band w/blue & yellow lettering, Western Oil and Fuel Company, 4" d., 5½" h. (rust, scratches, fading) **303.00**

Motor oil, Mobiloil 1 qt. can, white can w/a gargoyle below "Gargoyle," all above "Mobiloil," above red stripes & "Socony-Vacuum Oil Company - Made in U.S.A.," 4" d., 5½" d. (no cover, faded, scratches) **33.00**

Motor oil, Pennelene ½ gal. can, rectangular, marked "⅞ Gallon Net - Pennelene - Auto Oil - Penn Soo Oil Co. - Sioux Falls, South Dakota," 3 x 8", 5½" h. (scratches, soiling & minor denting) **28.00**

Motor oil, Pennzoil can, w/image of prop airplane in flight, w/three owls at bottom of can, marked "United Air Lines Uses Pennzoil Exclusively" at top of can, below plane is a quote from United Air Lines engineer, all above Pennzoil logo, done in yellow, black & red, 4" d., 5½" d. (opened at bottom) **66.00**

Motor oil, Pure As Gold 1 qt. can, cylindrical, geometric yellow, black & red design w/white & red lettering above a circle vignette w/a caricature of "The Pep Boys," w/contents, scratches, denting, 4" d., 5½" h. (ILLUS. second from left).......................**215.00**

Motor oil, Sho-Me 1 qt. can, ribbed cylinder, white over red ground w/a red, white & blue shield w/"MFA" in the top half above white & black wording below reading "Sho-Me Non-Detergent Motor Oil - MFA Oil Company," w/contents, scratches, denting, 4" d., 5½" h. (ILLUS. far right) **28.00**

Motor oil, Skelly 1 qt. can, red ground fading to white, centered w/Skelly logo, bottom w/silhouette of oil field, 4" d., 5½" d. (minor dents & scratches, opened at bottom) **50.00**

Motor oil, Texaco Marine Motor Oil 1 qt. can, w/image of several boats at sea w/seagulls flying above, marked "Texaco - Marine

Rare Vanderbilt Oil Can

Light House Peanut Butter Pail

- Motor Oil" above Texaco logo, 4"
d., 5½" d. (minor scratches &
denting, rust at top & bottom) **176.00**

Motor oil, Vanderbilt 1 qt. can,
cylindrical, wide black center
band w/yellow & black leopard
jumping through a large red "V,"
yellow bands at top & base
w/red & black lettering,
w/contents, scratches,
4" d., 5½" h. (ILLUS. above)......**468.00**

Peanut butter, Light House pail
w/wire bail handle, cylindrical
w/fitted flat metal lid, red ground
w/silvered wording "Light House
- Peanut Butter" above & below
a oval lighthouse vignette,
narrow silver banner near the
bottom w/black wording
"Distributed by National Grocer
Co., General Offices, Detroit,
Mich.," some scratching (ILLUS.
top next column) **200.00**

Peanut butter, Ox-Heart pail,
metal, label on front reads
"Contents 16 ozs. - Lang's - Ox-
Heart - Brand - Wholesome -
Delicious - Peanut Butter -
Oswego Candy Works Inc. -
Oswego, N.Y." all surrounding
logo, done in yellow, brown,

gold, red, green & cream, 4" d.,
3½" h. (minor paint chips).........**105.00**

Peanut butter, Sunny Boy pail,
red lettering reads "Net Wt. 16
ozs. - Sunny Boy - Peanut
Butter - The Brundage Brothers
Co. Toledo, Ohio" surrounding
image of young boy holding
sandwich w/sun behind him, all
on cream ground, 4" d., 3" h.
(soiling, scratches & fading) **132.00**

Shortening, Crisco 50 lb. can,
metal, blue lettering reads
"Crisco - For Frying For
Shortening - For Cake Making"
on white ground, 12½" d.,
15½" h. (scratches,
rust & dent) **77.00**

Syrup, Bee Hive 2 lb. can, reads
"Bee Hive - Golden - Corn
Syrup" surrounding an image of
beehive surrounded by corn,
3¼" d., 5¼" h. (minor scratches,
surface rust to top & bottom) **17.00**

Talcum powder, Jergens
Oriental tin, cylindrical w/low
domed shoulder & short central
neck w/cap, the sides w/color
lettering & a half-length vignette
of a Japanese geisha,
w/contents, chips & soiling,
2½" d., 4½" h. (ILLUS.
next page) **88.00**

Jergens Oriental Talcum Powder Tin

Talcum powder, Watkins Egyptian Bouquet tin, slightly pyramid-shaped, colorfully painted & embossed w/Egyptian-style decorations w/image of the Sphinx below "Watkins - Egyptian - Bouquet - Talcum - Powder," all above "The Sphinx - Container Made In U.S.A.," 1½ x 3", 5½" h...............**50.00**

Tea, Rington's, green & black on gold ground, reads "Rington's - Tea" above horse & carriage, all above "Renowned for - Purity, Strength - & Flavor - See Analysts' Report.," 4 x 4", 7" h. (minor scratches).......................**55.00**

Tobacco, Ojibwa Fine Cut store tin, upright rectangular container w/a flat hinged cover, the sides w/a colorful scene of a canoe of Native Americans paddling towards a standing warrior on shore, Scotten Dillon Co., Detroit, Michigan, early 20th c. (ILLUS. below)..........................**375.00**

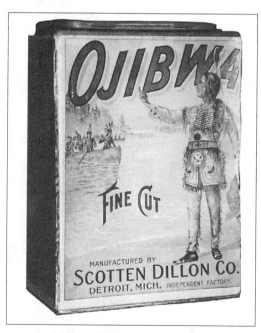

Ojibwa Fine Cut Tobacco Store Tin

CASH REGISTERS

James Ritty of Dayton, Ohio, is credited with inventing the first cash register. In 1882, he sold the business to a Cincinnati salesman, Jacob H. Eckert, who subsequently invited others into the business by selling stock. One of the purchasers of an early cash register, John J. Patterson, was so impressed with the savings his model brought to his company, he bought 25 shares of stock and became a director of the company in 1884, eventually buying a controlling interest in the National Manufacturing Company. Patterson thoroughly organized the company, conducted sales classes, prepared sales manuals, and established salesman's territories. The success of the National Cash Register Company is due as much to these well organized origins as to the efficiency of its machines. Early "National" cash registers, as well as other models, are deemed highly collectible today.

National Model 63 with Sign

National Model 313

National Counter-Top Cash Registers

Model No. 1, extended base ..**$4,000.00**

Model No. 2, inlaid wood case **3,000.00**

Model No. 3, narrow scroll case **1,000.00**

Model No. 4, fine-scroll case....**1,800.00**

Model No. 5, fine-scroll case....**2,000.00**

Model No. 6, extended base, fleur-de-lis **3,500.00**

Model No. 8, fleur-de-lis case **900.00**

Model No. 11, cast-iron case .. **1,600.00**

Model No. 35 through 49, Renaissance case **700.00**

Model No. 50, Renaissance case **1,600.00**

Model No. 52, dolphin case **1,500.00**

Model No. 63, cast-iron case, w/top sign (ILLUS. top, next column) **800.00**

Model No. 78, scroll case.........**1,200.00**

Model No. 87, empire case **700.00**

Models No. 225 or 226 ....**700.00**

Model No. 313 (ILLUS.) **800.00**

Model No. 314............................**800.00**

Model No. 324............................**700.00**

Models No. 500 through 599, single drawer **1,000.00**

Models No. 1054 & 1064 ....**600.00**

National Floor Models

National Model 572

Models No. 500 through 599,
floor model, metal case atop set
of wood drawers, each
(ILLUS.) **2,000.00**

Other Manufacturers

American Model 50

American Cash registers
(ILLUS.)..............**1,000.00 to 3,000.00**

**Michigan Cash
registers** ....**200.00 to 700.00**

**St. Louis Cash
registers** ....**200.00 to 700.00**

**Weller Cash
registers** ....**300.00 to 800.00**

CASTORS & CASTOR SETS

Pickle castor, art glass insert in
amethyst craquelle glass
enameled w/gold orchids, ornate
silver plate frame & tongs
w/large full figural bird in flight
on cover...................................**$595.00**

Pickle castor, cobalt blue
enameled w/gold scrolls &
florals insert, lovely silver plate
frame & tongs **385.00**

Pickle castor, Coralene
decoration in green & pink on
unusual Inverted Thumbprint
rubina insert w/wavy lines,
Forbes 255 silver plate frame,
10½" h. **920.00**

Pickle castor, Coreopsis patt.
insert in white satin w/colored
flowers, ornate silver plate
footed frame, tongs **395.00**

Pickle castor, cranberry Cone
patt. cylindrical insert, original
cover, tongs & ornate silver
plate frame w/a wide flaring
base, scrolls at top of handle,
marked "Britannia Metal Co.,"
4½" d., 10¾" h., all resilvered
(ILLUS. top left, next page) **425.00**

Pickle castor, deep red mother-
of-pearl satin glass Diamond
Quilted patt. insert, footed silver
plate Empire frame, complete
w/fork, 9¾" h.............................**850.00**

Pickle castor, white satin
embossed Heart Arches patt
insert, enameled w/rose colored
apple blossoms & green leaves
on back, sides & front, silver
plate frame **395.00**

Cranberry Pickle Castor

Unusual Frosted Crystal Castor

Pickle castor, frosted crystal barrel-shaped insert w/relief-molded blue floral decoration, ornate footed silver plate frame w/tongs, marked "Stevens Silver, Portland, ME.," 9¾" h. (ILLUS. next column)................**620.00**

Pickle castor, frosted & pink satin w/opalescent swirled stripes, Mt. Washington, polished pontil silver plate frame & cover (small chip on rim under cover) **350.00**

Pickle castor, Royal Ivy patt. frosted to clear insert in lovely silver plate frame w/tongs..........**325.00**

Pickle castor, Wave Crest insert, decoration of pink shasta daisies, silver plate frame, cover & tongs **395.00**

Pickle castor, white decorated satin Open Heart Arches patt. insert, silver plate frame & tongs...**350.00**

CAT COLLECTIBLES

Books

"A Cat Came Fiddling and Other Rhymes of Childhood," by Paul Kapp, New York, 1956, introduction by Burl Ives, illustrations by Irene Hass, song book, fine condition, 80 pp. **$40.00**

"Archy and Mehitabel," by Don Marquis, New York, 1936, tenth edition, drawings by George Herriman, fine condition, 196 pp. **30.00**

"**Babette,**" by Claire Turlay Newberry, New York, 1937, second edition, pictures by the author, very good condition, 30 pp. **95.00**

"**Cat Calls,**" a book of poems, drawings by author Peggy Bacon, New York, 1935, first edition, very good condition, 87 pp. **75.00**

"**Cat Royal,**" by Charles Brady, New York, 1947, first edition, illustrated by Rosemarie Renkis, very good condition, 72 pp. **45.00**

"**Golden Book of Cat Stories,**" by Era Zistel, New York, 1946, second edition, illustrations by Rod Ruth, fine condition **30.00**

"**The Stout-Hearted Cat: A Fable for Cat Lovers,**" New York, 1947, first edition, drawings by Hans Fischer, very good condition, 140 pp. **30.00**

Bottles

Avon, "Curious Kitten," cat beside goldfish bowl, 1979.....................**10.00**

Avon, "Kitten Little," white glaze, 1972-76 ....**7.00**

Jim Beam, "Katz," black & white or yellow & white, 1963, 14¾" h., each..**50.00**

Cookie Jars

California-made pottery, reclining cat w/closed eyes & curled-up tail, golden yellow ground decorated w/h.p. brown & caramel florals, ca. 1930s, 10½" l., 9¼" h. (ILLUS. top next column) **75.00**

McCoy, Kitten on Coal Bucket, brown kitten on black bucket, introduced in 1983.....................**350.00**

McCoy, Kitten on Coal Bucket, white kitten on tan & black bucket, introduced in 1983 ....**395.00**

McCoy, Three Kittens atop a Ball of Yarn, yarn in yellow, maroon or green, each...........**100.00 to 125.00**

California-made Cat Cookie Jar

Turner, The Cowardly Lion, from the Wizard of Oz, modern limited edition dated "1939," the year of the original movie release.......................................**195.00**

Figurals: Ceramic & Glass

Tabitha Twitchett w/Miss Moppet Figure

Ceramic, Beswick, England, Beatrix Potter characters: **Ginger**....................................**1,000.00**

Miss Moppet............................**250.00**

Simpkins (old version)..............**900.00**

Susan (old version)..................**375.00**

Tabitha Twitchett w/Miss Moppet (ILLUS. bottom previous page)..........................**250.00**

Ceramic, Empire Porcelain Company, England, model of a cat, the seated, smiling stylized animal in the manor of Emile Gallé, gilt & enamel-decorated w/floral designs w/a blue ground blanket on its back, green glass eyes, printed mark ca. 1900, 13¼" h. (leg repair)...................**920.00**

Ceramic, Kay Finch, California:
"Do No Evil," No. 4834, 1948, 3" h. **55.00**

"See No Evil," No. 4835, 1948, 3" h. **125.00**

"Hear No Evil," No. 4836, 1948, 3" h. **125.00**

"Hannibal," No. 180, 10¼" h....**100.00**

Ceramic, Royal Doulton, "Cook and Cheshire Cat," large size jug, discontinued, 1989 ....**265.00**

Ceramic, Royal Doulton, flambé glaze, experimental piece modeled after a white cat called "Shadow Play"........................**1,425.00**

Ceramic, Royal Haeger pottery, model of an Art Deco style stylized seated cat, gold-painted textured finish, one eye open, one closed, ca. 1938, 15½" h. (ILLUS. next column)................**140.00**

Porcelain, Limoges, model of a grey & white cat sitting upright on a white base, marked "Limoges, France," 3" l., 2¾" h. **85.00**

Porcelain, Royal Copenhagen, figure of a girl in a blue dress grooming a white cat, No. 4631, 5⅞" h.......................**450.00**

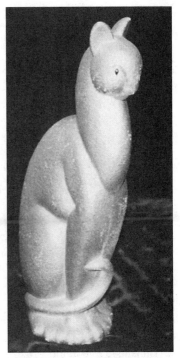

Royal Haeger Art Deco Cat

Glass, Fenton Art Glass, model titled "Alley Cats," produced in various colors w/Velva Rose among the more expensive, 1970- current, each.....**30.00 to 100.00**

Figurals: Metal

Brass, pipeholder, modeled as arched-back cats at each end, the base holds five pipes, marked "England," 10" l., 4¼" h. (ILLUS. top next page) **225.00**

Bronze, model of a long-haired Persian, painted grey w/a pink bow, ca. 1880-90, 2" h...............**125.00**

Pewter, model of a kitten in a cream pitcher, licking one paw, marked "1983 Hudson Pewter USA," 1¼" h................................**24.00**

Pewter, model of a kitten & a pair of high-heeled shoes, from "Little Gallery Hallmark Cards," 1¾" h. **27.00**

Brass Pipeholder with Cats

Miscellaneous Items:

Bell, porcelain, Bing & Grondahl, traditional Danish blue & white, titled "Christmas Eve at the Farmhouse," in original box, 1985 ....**42.00**

Coasters, tin, decorated w/black cats wearing colorful bows, ca. 1940, 3" d., set of 8 ....**24.00**

Plastic Jewelry Box

Jewelry box, cov., plastic, rectangular, various colors used for the bottom & a clear cover featuring embossed kitten designs, various sizes, ca. 1950s, each (ILLUS.) ....**25.00 to 30.00**

Spoon dish, ceramic, lavender w/pink flowers, ca. 1960, 6½" h. **10.00**

TV lamp, ceramic, figural, modeled as a mother & baby Siamese seated side by side, shaded browns, ca. 1950s, 13¾" h. (ILLUS. below) **95.00**

1950s Cats TV Lamp

CERAMICS

Also see Antique Trader Books American & European Art Pottery Price Guide; 20th Century American Ceramics Price Guide; *and* Pottery and Porcelain Ceramics Price Guide, 2nd Edition.

ABINGDON

Daisy Cookie Jar

From about 1934 until 1950, Abingdon Pottery Company, Abingdon, Illinois, manufactured decorative pottery, mainly cookie jars, flowerpots and vases. Decorated with various glazes, these items are becoming popular with collectors who are especially attracted to Abingdon's novelty cookie jars.

Abingdon Mark

Cookie jar, Daisy, No. 677
(ILLUS.) **$55.00**

Cookie jar, "Humpty Dumpty" **375.00**

Cookie jar, Wigwam....................**725.00**

Model of a penguin, No. 573D,
5" h. **23.00**

Sugar bowl, cov., lemon finial.......**35.00**

Vase, 10" h., Swirl, No. 513,
white **20.00**

Vase, No. 522, Barre **15.00**

Vase, seashell-shaped, No. 507,
yellow **25.00**

BELLEEK

Belleek china has been made in Ireland's County Fermanagh for many years. It is exceedingly thin porcelain. Several marks were used, including a hound and harp (1865-1880), and a hound, harp and castle (1863-1891). A printed hound, harp and castle with the words "Co. Fermanagh Ireland" constitutes the mark from 1891. Belleek-type china also was made in the United States last century by several firms, including Ceramic Art Company, Columbian Art Pottery, Lenox Inc., Ott & Brewer and Willets Manufacturing Co.

AMERICAN

Coffee set: cov. coffeepot, creamer & cov. sugar bowl; decorated w/pink roses & gold garlands on turquoise ground, 3 pcs., unmarked (Lenox)........**$325.00**

Creamer, Undine patt.
(Willetts) **55.00**

Mug, figural lizard handle, undecorated, 5½" h.
(Willets) **115.00**

Pitcher, cider, 9" h., apples decoration, artist-signed, (Lenox, Inc.) **125.00**

IRISH

Bowl, 9½" d., reticulated basketweave w/applied floral rim & lilies-of-the-valley, impressed "Belleek Fermanagh" (minor damage to applied work) **303.00**

Creamer, Cleary patt., green mark **50.00**

Creamer, Lotus patt., black mark ..**65.00**

Creamer & open sugar bowl, Ribbon patt., green mark, pr........**75.00**

Cup & saucer, Neptune patt.,
   green mark **75.00**

Dish, heart-shaped, , 3rd black
   mark, 6" **85.00**

Flowerpot, swirled sides
   w/scalloped rim & applied
   flowers, 4" h., 3rd black mark **75.00**

Model of a dog, green mark **65.00**

Model of a harp, decorated
   w/shamrocks, 6½" h,
   3rd green mark **165.00**

Plate, 6" d., Tridacna patt., pink
   tint, 2nd black mark **60.00**

Plate, 8" d., Tridacna patt.,
   green mark **55.00**

Salt dip, three-lobed, scalloped,
   pink trim, realistic leaf veining on
   exterior, 3" d., black mark............**85.00**

Tea cup & saucer, Neptune patt.,
   green tint, 3rd black mark..........**135.00**

Tumbler, indented ribs around
   bottom half, all-white, 1st black
   mark, 3⅝" d., 4⅜" h. **110.00**

Vase, 8½" h., ewer-style,
   Aberdeen patt., 2nd black
   mark ....**400.00 to 600.00**

BLUE & WHITE POTTERY

The category of blue and white or blue and grey pottery includes a wide variety of pottery, earthenware and stoneware items widely produced in this country in the late 19th century right through the 1930s. Originally marketed as inexpensive wares, most pieces featured a white or grey body molded with a fruit, flower or geometric design and then trimmed with bands or splashes of blue to highlight the molded pattern. Pitchers, butter crocks and salt boxes are among the numerous items produced but other kitchenwares and chamber sets are also found. Values vary depending on the rarity of the embossed pattern and the depth of color of the blue trim; the darker the blue, the better. Some entries refer to several different books on Blue and White Pottery. There books are: Blue & White Stoneware, Pottery & Crockery *by Edith Harbin (1977, Collector Books, Paducah, KY);* Stoneware in the

Dragonfly & Flower Butter Crock

Blue and White *by M.H. Alexander (1993 reprint, Image Graphics, Inc., Paducah, KY); and* Blue & White Stoneware *by Kathryn McNerney (1995, Collector Books, Paducah, KY).*

Baking dish, Peacock patt.,
   9" d. **$750.00**

Batter jar, cov., Wildflower patt.,
   7" d., 8" h. **300.00**

Bowl, Apricot with Honeycomb
   patt., 7½" d., 2¾" h. **135.00**

Bowls, Wildflower patt., 4" to 14"
   d., nesting-type, the set **250.00**

Butter crock, cov., Dragonfly &
   Flower patt., small (ILLUS.).......**500.00**

Butter crock, cov., Indian patt.,
   2 lbs. **650.00**

Butter crock, cov., Printed Cows
   patt., 6½" d., 5" h. **195.00**

Canister, cov., Basketweave &
   Morning Glory (Willow) patt.,
   "Beans," average
   5½ to 6½" h. **325.00**

Canister, cov., Basketweave &
   Morning Glory (Willow) patt.,
   "Tea," average
   5½ to 6½" h. **325.00**

Canister, cov., Snowflake patt.,
   5¾" d., 6½" h. **235.00**

Beaded Rose Chamber Pot

Chamber pot, Beaded Rose patt., 9½" d., 6" h. (ILLUS.)........**250.00**

Chamber pot, Open Rose & Spear Point Panels patt., 9½" d., 6" h. **300.00**

Cider cooler, cov., w/spigot, 13" d., 15" h. **425.00**

Coffeepot, cov., molded vertical bands of bull's-eyes................**1,000.00**

Coffeepot, cov., Diffused Blue patt., oval body, 11" h. **1,700.00**

Cold fudge crock w/tin lid & ladle, marked "Johnson Cold Fudge Crock," 12" d., 13" h., the set.....................................**300.00**

Flying Bird Cookie Jar

Cookie jar, cov., Flying Bird patt., 6¾" d., 9" h. (ILLUS.)..............**1,050.00**

Cuspidor, Snowflowers patt., 9¾" d., 9" h. **200.00**

Custard cup, Fishscale patt., 2½" d., 5" h. **100.00**

Custard cup, Peacock patt., 2⅞" h. **245.00**

Ewer & basin, Apple Blossom patt., the set................................**575.00**

Ewer & basin, Feather & Swirl patt., ewer 8½" d., 12" h., basin 14" d., 5" h., the set..........**550.00**

Ewer, Apple Blossom patt., 12" h. **350.00**

Ewer, Bowtie (Our Lucile) patt., w/rose decal, 11" h. **175.00**

Ewer, Wildflower patt., 7½" h. **300.00**

Foot warmer, signed Logan Pottery Co. **250.00**

Iced tea cooler, cov., w/spigot, Maxwell House, 13" d., 15" h.....**325.00**

Jardiniere & pedestal base, Tulip patt., jardiniere 7½" h., pedestal 7" h., 2 pcs. **1,100.00**

Match holder, model of a duck, 5½" d., 5" h. **250.00**

Measuring cup, Spearpoint & Flower Panels, 6 ¾" d., 6" h. **450.00**

Meat tenderizer, Wildflower patt., 3½" d. **370.00**

Mixing bowl, Flying Bird patt., 8" d. **340.00**

Mug, Cattail patt., 3" d., 4" h........**130.00**

Mustard jar, cov., 3" d., 4" h. **200.00**

Pitcher, 6¼" h., 6¾" d. Capt. John Smith & Pocahontas patt. **350.00**

Pitcher, 7" h., 7" d., Old Fashioned Garden Rose patt. ...**400.00**

Pitcher, 8½" h., 5½" d., Swan patt. **450.00**

Pitcher, 8" h., 4" d., Tulip patt. **350.00**

Pitcher, tankard, 9" h., 6½" d., Willow patt. **245.00**

Ramekin, Peacock patt., 4".........**300.00**

Rolling pin, Wildflower patt., large **300.00**

Salt box, Wildflower patt., w/hinged wooden lid, 4½" h., 6" d. **170.00**

Salt, cov., Daisy patt., 6" d., 6½" h. **235.00**

Salt, cov., Flying Bird patt.,
6½" d., 6" h. **450.00**

Salt, cov., Raspberry patt.,
5½" d., 5½" h. **200.00**

Soap dish, Wildflower patt.,
3⅝" w., 5¼" l. **225.00**

Spice jar, cov., "Cloves,"
Wildflower patt. **200.00**

Stein, Grape Leaf Band patt.,
5" h. **125.00**

Stewer, cov., Wildflower patt.,
4 qt. **285.00**

Swirl Teapot

Teapot, cov., Swirl patt.,
6" d., 6" h. (ILLUS.)...................**800.00**

Tobacco jar, cov., Berry Scrolls
patt., 5" d., 6½" h. **300.00**

Waste jar, cov., Willow patt. **325.00**

Water cooler, cov., Apple
Blossom patt., w/spigot, 13" h. ..**850.00**

Water cooler, cov., Polar patt.,
w/spigot, 8 gal. **975.00**

Water cooler, cov., Polar patt.,
w/spigot, 10 gal. **1,250.00**

BLUE RIDGE DINNERWARES

The small town of Erwin, Tennessee was the home of the Southern Potteries, Inc., originally founded by E.J. Owen in 1917 and first called the Clinchfield Pottery.

In the early 1920s Charles W. Foreman purchased the plant and he revolutionized the company's output, developing the popular line of hand-painted wares sold as "Blue Ridge" dinnerwares. Free-hand painted by women from the surrounding hills, these colorful dishes in many patterns, continued in production until the plant's closing in 1957.

Tulips Pattern Ashtray

Ashtray, advertising, two
cigarette rests, Tulips patt.,
"compliments of Southern
Potteries, Inc., Erwin, Tenn."
(ILLUS.) **$65.00**

Bonbon, flat shell shape, French
Peasant patt. **110.00**

Cake lifter, Leaf patt. **30.00**

Celery tray, Leaf patt. **125.00**

Pitcher, figural Betsy patt., china,
brick..**180.00**

Pitcher, Grace shape **135.00**

Plate, 9" d., Green Briar patt. **5.00**

Plate, 10" d., Chrysanthemum
patt. **15.00**

Plate, dinner, French
Peasant patt. **35.00**

Plate, square, Nocturne patt..........**13.00**

Salt & pepper shakers, figural
mallards, model of male &
female, male 4" h., female
3½" h., pr. **200.00**

Teapot, cov., Sunflower patt.,
Piecrust shape............................**95.00**

Tray, Maple leaf-shaped,
Chintz patt. **75.00**

Tray, Maple leaf-shaped,
Verna patt.................................**75.00**

CARLTON WARE

The Staffordshire firm of Wiltshaw & Robinson, Stoke-on-Trent, operated the Carlton Works from about 1890 until 1958, producing both earthenwares and porcelain. Specializing in decorative items like vases and teapots, they became well known fro their lustre-finished wares, often decorated in the Oriental taste. The trademark Carlton Ware was incorporated into their printed mark. Since 1958, a new company, Carlton Ware Ltd., has operated the Carlton Works at Stoke.

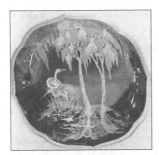

Rouge Royale Bowl

Bowl, 7½" d., 1¾" h., Rouge Royale line, shallow irregular-shaped, decorated w/scene of exotic birds & trees in multicolored enamels, gold trim (ILLUS.) **$145.00**

Jar, cov., footed baluster form body, domed lid w/gold finial, decorated w/multicolored "Chinoiserie" scene of Oriental home & temple w/fine outlining in gold, man & woman at table on reverse, blue lustre ground, gold trim on foot & cover rim, 3⅝" d., 9⅜" h. **395.00**

Potpourri jar, cov., bulbous ovoid body w/domed fitted lid, deep yellow background w/large medallion scene of Oriental buildings & person in multicolored enamels on black satin ground, bordered w/gold, matching scene on reverse w/smaller scenes on each side & on cover, 7½" d., 9¾" h..........**495.00**

Relish dish, Rouge Royale line, irregular oval shape, decorated w/multicolored enamel plants, leaves, spider & web & butterflies, part of original label still intact, 5¼ x 8½"..................**110.00**

Vase, 7" h., 4¼" d., footed bulbous ovoid body w/short slightly flaring rim, decorated w/exotic landscape scene of Art Deco trees & long-tailed flying birds in multicolored enamels & gold on deep blue ground, enameled flowers & gold around top & mother-of-pearl lustre interior w/gold trim on rim **450.00**

Tall Oriental-style Vase

Vase, 12½" h., footed cylindrical body w/flattened shoulder, centered cylindrical neck w/cupped rim, decorated w/scene of Oriental man & woman w/fans standing in front of house & background scene of homes, bridge, temple & small boats, pale blue lustre ground, blue floral border w/green bank around neck, mother-of-pearl lustre inside top (ILLUS.)...........**395.00**

CLEMINSON CLAY

"The World Is Our Oyster" Dish

Betty Cleminson, a hobbyist living in Monterey Park, California, began using her garage during World War II to form what would later become known as Cleminson Clay, one of the most successful companies in the United States.

Betty and George, her husband who took care of the business of running the small operation, started with only a few items such as the now sought after pie bird and many other kitchen-related items. Most of these early pieces were simply marked with a lower case "b" in an upper case "c," but new collectors sometimes mistake the mark for a copyright symbol. Later pieces would bear a stamp mark with a girl on one side, a boy on the other side of what resembles a plate and inside it are the words, "The California Cleminsons" and the older "b" inside a "c". Below the mark is "Hand Painted." Sometimes this mark will not include the boy and girl.

A line known as Galagray features an overall grey background with deep red accents or designs. Most often found are the man and woman salt and pepper shakers. At this time, the line is not a priority for collectors. Only time will prove whether or not the line becomes more popular with other generations. Another line which is more popular is the Distlefink. It was a large group of items with either a white or light brown glazed bird with brown and green accents. This line, made two years after the opening of Cleminsons in 1941, was created in a new facility in El Monte, California. After the move the firm expanded eventually having up to 150 employees which enabled the Cleminsons to expand their lines. Included were butter dishes, canisters, cups and saucers, cookie jars, cleanser shakers, ring holders, recipe holders, wall plaques, and decorative plates, to name but a few.

In the late 1950s business was still prospering due, in part, to the free-lancing Hedi Schoop did at the Cleminson plant when Schoop's operation was destroyed by fire. However, by 1961 and facing, as did so many other businesses, the importation of cheaper gift and housewares, George and Betty decided to close the operation.

Cleminson Clay Marks

Oyster dish, easel shape w/"The World Is Our Oyster" & picture of the world & an oyster, white ground w/red, blue, black & pink glazes, 6½" d. (ILLUS.) **$35.00**

Plate, 5¼" d., assorted glazed flowers, grey scalloped rim, two holes for hanging **15.00**

Plate, 6½"d., pale blue ground w/white & black silhouettes, woman sitting at spinning wheel, two holes for hanging **18.00**

Salt & pepper shakers, model of the Distlefink, 6¼" h., pr. **23.00**

String holder, model of a house w/lettering "Friends from afar and nearabout will find our latchstring always out," string comes out through a portion of the door, string holder is also a wall plaque, 6½" h. **65.00**

Wall pocket, model of a scoop, white body w/blue & red flowers & green leaves, second mark without boy & girl on each side, also has "hand painted" & a copyright symbol, 9" l. **35.00**

Delft Candlestick & Chargers

DELFT

In the early 17th century Italian potters settled in Holland and began producing tin-glazed earthenwares, often decorated with pseudo-Oriental designs based on Chinese porcelain wares. The city of Delft became the center of this pottery production and several firms produced the wares throughout the 17th and early 18th century. A majority of the pieces featured blue on white designs, but polychrome wares were also made. The Dutch Delftwares were also shipped to England and eventually the English copied them at potteries in such cities as Bristol, Lambeth and Liverpool. Although still produced today, Delft peaked in popularity by the mid-18th century.

Candlestick, a tall ringed & baluster-turned standard raised on a high domed foot, the top w/a widely flaring candle socket, decorated overall w/delicate stylized floral designs in blue on white, marked, damage, repairs, 15" h. (ILLUS. bottom center) ..**$303.00**

Charger, a central scene of an Oriental figure standing near benches or tables, the flanged rim w/floral sprigs, blue on white, edge chips, 12" d. (ILLUS. top right) **138.00**

Charger, decorated w/a central garden scene of large blossoms, the wide border w/a ring of round medallions w/various emblems, blue on white, chips, 12" d. (ILLUS. top left) **330.00**

Charger, a center decoration of a covered jar beside a large vase of vining flowers, the scalloped rim w/bianco sopra bianco decoration, blue on white center, edge chips, 13⅝" d. (ILLUS. bottom left) **523.00**

Charger, a central Oriental landscape scene w/several temples centered by a tall willow tree all within a narrow inner border band, the outer rim w/a narrow border band of diaper panels alternating w/leaf panels, blue on white, chips & hairlines, 13¾" d. (ILLUS. bottom right) **330.00**

Plate, 5¼" d., center polychrome decoration of floral fan in vase, Oriental cloud border design (edge chips & drilled hole above fan) **$165.00**

Plate, 8⅝" d., blue on white center decoration of bluster of stylized flowers, buds & leaves, floral sprays on border (edge chips & crazing)........................**116.00**

Plate, 8¾" d., center decoration of standing figure surrounded by large flower blossoms, sgraffito border, attributed to Bristol or Lambeth, England (edge chips)..............................**275.00**

Plate, 10½" d., decorated in blue on white, center decoration of floral fan in vase w/Oriental cloud design on border, yellow edge, initial mark (small chips & hairline)....................................**303.00**

Plate, 11½" d., blue on white central scene of tree & birds, border decorated w/alternating wide & narrow panels of stylized flowers & feathery leaf branches (edge chips)..............................**385.00**

Plates, 8⅞" d., blue Oriental landscape scene on white, house & stylized trees & bushes w/boat on water, attributed to Bristol, England, pr. (edge chips)..............................**440.00**

Plates, 9" d., center polychrome decoration of stylized flowers & leaves in flowerpot, buds & leafy branches on border, pr. (edge flakes)..............................**605.00**

Plates, 9½" d., blue & white center Oriental landscape design w/pagoda & mountains & "A.M." beneath scene, oval reserves w/stylized scenes of buildings & trees & purple marbling in border, pr. (edge chips)..............................**880.00**

Stein, cov., baluster-form body, decorated w/large stylized flowers, leaves & bird, blue on white, pewter lid w/pointed thumb-rest & foot rim, C-form handle, initials engraved on lid, 10¼" h. (small chips & hairlines in rim & handle)..........**495.00**

Tea caddy, cov., rectangular w/angled corners, blue on white center design of trees & Oriental figure w/parasol, corner panels w/diamond lattice design, mismatched pewter lid, "Art Institute of Chicago" exhibition sticker, 5" h. (chips & yellowed repair along bottom edge) **468.00**

Tray, 4⅞ x 7¼", rectangular, blue on white center Oriental landscape scene of trees & homes & bridge, floral & diamond lattice design border (edge chips)..............................**193.00**

DOULTON & ROYAL DOULTON

Doulton & Co., Ltd., was founded in Lambeth, London, about 1858. It was operated there till 1956 and often incorporated the words "Doulton" and "Lambeth" in its marks. Pinder Bourne & Co., Burslem was purchased by the Doultons in 1878 and in 1882 became Doulton & Co., Ltd. It added porcelain to its earthenware production in 1884. The "Royal Doulton" mark has been used since 1902 by this factory, which is still in production. Character jugs and figurines are commanding great attention from collectors at the present time.

Royal Doulton Mark

ANIMALS

Dog, Bulldog Puppy, tan w/dark brown patches over eye & back, K 2, 1931-77, 2" h.....................**$90.00**

Dog, Cocker Spaniel Chewing Handle of Basket, white w/dark brown ears & patches on back, light brown patches over eyes, light brown basket, No. HN 2586, 1941-85, 2¾" h..................**80.00**

Dog, Dachshund, golden brown w/dark brown markings, K 17, 1940-77, 1¾ x 2¾".....................**90.00**

Dog, Springer Spaniel Ch. "Dry Toast," white coat w/dark brown markings, HN 2516, 1938-68, 5" h...........................**175.00 to 225.00**

CHARACTER JUGS

Albert Saggar the Potter, small, 4" h..**115.00**

Angler (The), small, 4" h...............**39.00**

Busker (The), large, 6½"..............**65.00**

Capt. Ahab, miniature, 2½" h.......**70.00**

Captain Hook Mug

Captain Hook, small, 4" h. (ILLUS.).....................**300.00 to 325.00**

Cardinal (The), tiny, 1½" h........................**195.00 to 225.00**

Catherine Howard, large, 7" h............................**90.00 to 100.00**

Cavalier, large, 7" h......................**75.00**

Chief Sitting Bull & George Armstrong Custer, Chief Sitting Bull on forward side of jug & Custer on the reverse, 1984, limited edition **110.00**

D'Artgnan, small, 4" h.................**45.00**

Falconer (The), small, 3¾" h........**55.00**

Falstaff, small, 3½" h. **39.00**

Gladiator, small, 3½" h........................**400.00 to 450.00**

Granny Mug

Granny, miniature, 2¼" h. (ILLUS.) **35.00**

Jockey (The), small, 4" h. **49.00**

John Shorter, small, 4¼" h...........**99.00**

Lawyer (The), small, 4" h..............**39.00**

Leprechaun, large, 7½" h. **65.00**

Long John Silver, miniature, 2½" h.............................**50.00 to 60.00**

Lord Mayor of London, large, 7¼" h. **99.00**

Master/Equestrian (The), small, 4" h. **45.00**

Merlin, small, 3¾" h......................**39.00**

Night Watchman, miniature, 2¼" h. **100.00**

North American Indian, Canadian Centennial series, large, 7¾" h. **225.00**

Old Charley, large,
5½" h. ....**70.00 to 75.00**

Old Salt, miniature, closed arm,
2½" h. **55.00**

Owd Mac, large,
6¼" h. ....**275.00 to 300.00**

Pied Piper, large,
7" h. ....**100.00 to 150.00**

Sam Weller, tiny, 1¼" h.................**60.00**

Santa Claus, plain handle, small,
3¼" h. **39.00**

Toby Philpots, large, 6¼" h. **110.00**

Ugly Duchess, small,
3½" h. ....**275.00 to 300.00**

Wizard, small, 3¾" h. **39.00**

Yeoman of the Guard (The),
large, 7" h. **75.00**

FIGURINES

Autumn Breezes

Autumn Breezes, HN 2147,
black & white, 1955-71
(ILLUS.) **285.00**

Baby Bunting, HN 2108, brown &
cream, 1953-59.........**200.00 to 225.00**

Ballad Seller, HN 2266, pink
dress, 1968-73 ....**260.00 to 275.00**

Bess, HN 2003, pink dress,
purple cloak, 1947-50 ....**525.00**

Delight, HN 1772, red dress,
1936-67 ....**175.00**

Delphine

Delphine, HN 2136, blue &
lavender, 1954-67
(ILLUS.).....................**255.00 to 275.00**

Invitation, HN 2170, pink dress,
1956-75 ....**140.00**

Goody Two Shoes, M 80, blue
skirt, red overdress,
1939-49 ....**975.00**

Gypsy Dance (A), HN 2230,
purple & white dress,
1959-71 ....**275.00 to 325.00**

Minuet, HN 2019, white dress,
floral print, 1949-71 ....**255.00**

Jill, HN 2061, pink & white,
1950-71 ....**155.00**

Noelle, HN 2179, orange, white &
black, 1957-67 ....**300.00 to 350.00**

Pantalettes, M 15, shaded blue
dress, red hat, 1932-45 ....**450.00**

Patchwork Quilt (The), HN 1984,
green dress, 1945-59 ....**350.00**

Penelope, HN 1901, red dress,
1939-75.....................**275.00 to 300.00**

The Polka

Polka (The), HN 2156, pale pink dress, 1955-69 (ILLUS.).....................**300.00 to 350.00**

Polly Peachum, M 21, red gown, 1932-45 ....**450.00**

Sweet Anne

Sweet Anne, HN 1496, pink & purple dress & hat, 1932-67 (ILLUS.)....................**200.00 to 225.00**

Prue, HN 1996, red, white & black, 1947-55 ....**300.00 to 325.00**

Top o' the Hill, HN 1849, 1938-75 ....**250.00**

Young Master, HN 2872, purple, grey & brown, 1980-89.....................**200.00 to 250.00**

MISCELLANEOUS

Ashtray, porcelain, round, beige ground w/figural white hound dog with grey & beige trim laying on the edge, marked "Modeled by Doris Lindner," 4¼" d., 1¾" h. **125.00**

Flask, figural, "Kingsware," Uncle Sam **500.00**

Plaque, oval, pierced to hang, flow blue, Babes in Woods, scene of two little girls w/pixie man, 7½ x 9½" **1,500.00**

Plate, 8¾" d., Burslem Wares series, pastel flowers decorate center, ornate gold scrolls & flowers highlighted w/white enamel around rim **125.00**

Plate, 10¼" d., Burslem Wares series, Dr. Johnson at The Cheshire Cheese.......................**105.00**

Plate, 10¼" d., Fox-Hunting series **115.00**

Sandwich tray, decorated w/h.p. pansies, 7½ x 18" (tight hairline & some crazing)............**195.00**

Vase, 3¾" h., 1¾ x 5" pillow-shaped, "Babes in the Woods" line, flow blue, decorated w/a girl comforting a crying toddler **600.00**

FLOW BLUE

Flow Blue ironstone and semi-porcelain was manufactured mainly in England during the second half of the 19th century. The early ironstone was produced by many of the well known English potters and was either transfer-printed or hand-painted (Brush stroke). The bulk of the ware was exported to the United States or Canada.

The "flow" or running quality of the cobalt blue designs was the result of introducing certain chemicals into the kiln during the final firing. Some patterns are so "flown" that it is difficult to ascertain the design. The transfers were of several types: Asian, Scenic, Marble or Floral.

The earliest Flow Blue ironstone patterns were produced during the period between about 1840 and 1860. After the Civil War Flow Blue went out of style for some years but was again manufactured and exported to the United States beginning about the 1880s and continuing through the turn-of-the-century. These later Flow Blue designs are on a semi-porcelain body rather than heavier ironstone and the designs are mainly florals.

AMOY
(Wm. Davenport & Co., ca. 1844)

Cup & saucer, handleless $25.00

Plate, 7½" d. 70.00

Plate, 8½" d. 80.00

Plate, 9½" d. 100.00

Plate, 10½" d. 150.00

Soup plate 150.00

Teapot, cov. 650.00

ARGYLE
(W.H. Grindley & Co., ca. 1896)

Argyle Cup & Saucer

Cup & saucer, handled (ILLUS.) ..85.00

Plate, 7" d. 65.00

Plate, 8" d. 75.00

Plate, 9" d. 85.00

Plate, 10" d. 95.00

Platter, 14" l. 250.00

Soup plate, 9" d. 85.00

Vegetable bowl, open, small 165.00

CASHMERE
(F. Morley & Co., ca. 1850)

Cashmere Cup & Saucer

Cup & saucer, handleless
(ILLUS.).....................................300.00

Plate, 7½" d. 90.00

Plate, 8½" d. 100.00

Plate, 9½" d. 150.00

Plate, 10½" d. 175.00

Soup plate, 10" d. (ILLUS.).........225.00

Wash bowl & pitcher, 2 pcs....3,000.00

Cashmere Soup Plate

CHAPOO
(John Wedgwood, ca. 1850)

Cup & saucer, handled...............150.00

Cup & saucer, handleless 125.00

Plate, 8½" d. 80.00

Plate, 10½" d. 150.00

Platter, 16" l..............................450.00

Soup plate, 10" d. 150.00

FLORIDA
(W.H. Grindley or Johnson Bros., ca. 1895)
Cup & saucer, handled..............175.00

Plate, 7½" d...............................125.00

Plate, 8½" d...............................100.00

Plate, 9½" d.................................85.00

Plate, 10" d................................135.00

Soup plate, flanged rim, 8" d. 125.00

JAPAN
(T. Fell & Co., ca. 1850)

Japan Water Pitcher

Cup & saucer, handleless 125.00

Pitcher, water, hexagonal
  (ILLUS.)....................................500.00

Plate, 10½" d..............................150.00

LA BELLE
(Wheeling Pottery Co., West Virginia, 1879-1910)

La Belle Cracker Jar

Cracker jar, cov., 7½" h.
  (ILLUS.).....................................550.00

Chocolate mug..........................600.00

Cup & saucer, handled..............175.00

Plate, 7" d.................................125.00

Plate, 8" d................................100.00

Plate, 9" d..................................85.00

Plate, 10" d...............................135.00

Soup plate, flanged rim, 8" d. 125.00

MANILLA (Podmore, Walker & Co., 1840s-50s)
Cup & saucer, handled..............155.00

Plate, 8½" d.................................80.00

Plate, 9½" d...............................100.00

Plate, 10½" d..............................150.00

Platter, 12" l..............................300.00

Relish, mitten-shaped 200.00

MARBLE
(maker unknown, ca. 1850)

Rare Marble Pepper Pot

Pepper pot, panelled sides, very
  rare, 5" h. (ILLUS.) 1,400.00

NON PAREIL
(Burgess & Leigh, 1889-1910)
Bone dish 80.00

Cup & saucer, handled..............165.00

Pitcher, 2 qt...............................300.00

Plate, 8" d................................100.00

Plate, 9" d..................................80.00

Plate, 10" d...............................120.00

Sauce tureen, cover, ladle &
  undertray, 4 pcs.......................950.00

Soup plate, flanged rim, 8"d. 120.00

OREGON
(T. J. & U. Mayer, ca. 1850)

Creamer 300.00

Plate, 7½" d. 70.00

Plate, 9½" d. 100.00

Plate, 10½" d. 150.00

Sugar bowl, cov. 450.00

Teapot, cov. 650.00

Waste bowl 300.00

SCINDE
(J. & G. Alcock, 1839-46)
*(Note: Scinde by T. Walker
is an entirely different pattern)*

Scinde Handled Cup & Saucer

Cup & saucer, handled, large
(ILLUS.) 250.00

Cup & saucer, handleless 125.00

Plate, 7½" d. 70.00

Plate, 8½" d. 80.00

Plate, 9½" d. 100.00

Plate, 10½" d. 150.00

Scinde Potato Bowl

Potato bowl, panelled, 11" d.
(ILLUS.) 750.00

Scinde Sauce Tureen

Sauce tureen, cov. (ILLUS.) 1,200.00

Soup plate, 10½" d. 150.00

Scinde Teapot

Teapot, cov., pumpkin-shaped
(ILLUS.) 750.00

Wash bowl & pitcher, 2 pcs. 2,000.00

Scinde Waste Bowl

Waste bowl, round (ILLUS.) 350.00

TEMPLE (Podmore, Walker & Co., 1849-59)

Cup & saucer, handleless **120.00**

Temple Gothic Water Pitcher

Pitcher, water, classic Gothic
   shape, 8" h. (ILLUS.) **700.00**
Plate, 10½" d. **150.00**

TONQUIN (Wm. Adams & Son or Joseph Heath, ca. 1850)

Plate, 7½" d. **70.00**
Soup plate, 10" d. **150.00**

Tonquin Teapot

Teapot, cov., full-panelled Gothic
   shape (ILLUS.) **650.00**

TOURAINE
(H. Alcock & Co., ca. 1898)

Chocolate cup & saucer............**400.00**
Cup & saucer, handled.................**75.00**

Plate, 7" d. **65.00**
Plate, 8" d. **70.00**
Plate, 9" d. **80.00**
Plate, 10" d. **135.00**
Soup plate, flanged rim, 9" d. **85.00**

FRANCISCAN WARE

A product of Gladding, McBean & Company of Glendale and Los Angeles, California, Franciscan Ware was one of a number of lines produced by that firm over its long history. Introduced in 1934 as a pottery dinnerware, Franciscan Ware was produced in many patterns including "Desert Rose," introduced in 1941 and reportedly the most popular dinnerware pattern ever made in this country. Beginning in 1942 some vitrified china patterns were produced under the Franciscan name also.

After a merger in 1963 the company name was changed to Interpace Corporation and in 1979 Josiah Wedgwood & Sons purchased the Gladding, McBean & Co. plant from Interpace. American production ceased in 1984.

Franciscan Mark

Ashtray, individual, rose-shaped,
   Meadow Rose patt., ca. 1977,
   3½" d. **$22.00**
Ashtray, Apple patt., 4¾" sq. **135.00**
Bowl, cereal or soup, 6" d.,
   Desert Rose patt., ca. 1941..........**9.00**
Box, heart-shaped, Desert Rose
   patt., 4½" l., 2½" h. **145.00**
Butter dish, cov., Apple patt. **35.00**
Butter dish, cover & liner,
   Ivy patt......................................**95.00**
Candleholders, Desert Rose
   patt., 3" h., pr. **100.00**
Candy dish, oval, Desert Rose
   patt., 6½ x 7", 1" h. **125.00**

Casserole, cov., Apple patt.,
1½ qt. **95.00**

Casserole, cov., Ivy patt.,
ca. 1948, 1½ qt., 8" d., 4" h. **195.00**

Casserole, cov., Madeira patt.,
ca. 1967, 2½ qt.....................**55.00**

Chip & dip plate, Madeira patt.,
ca. 1967.....................................**30.00**

Coffeepot, cov.,
Desert Rose patt. **110.00**

Coffee server, cov., demitasse,
Desert Rose patt. **350.00**

Coffee server, cov., Apple patt. ..**175.00**

Coffee server, cov.,
Desert Rose patt. **175.00**

Cookie jar, cov., Apple patt.,
11½" h. **225.00**

Cookie jar, cov., Desert Rose
patt., 11½" h. **265.00**

Creamer & cov. sugar bowl,
demitasse, Desert Rose patt,
pr. **160.00**

Cup & saucer, Desert Rose patt.,
ca. 1941......................................**8.00**

Cup & saucer, Desert Rose patt.,
ca. 1941, extra large...................**35.00**

Egg cup, Desert Rose patt............**27.00**

Ginger jar, cov.,
Desert Rose patt. **35.00**

Gravy boat, California Poppy
patt. **90.00**

Gravy boat, Desert Rose patt. **35.00**

Gravy boat, Ivy patt. **45.00**

**Gravy boat w/attached
undertray,** Desert Rose patt.......**40.00**

**Gravy boat w/attached
undertray,** Fruit patt.,
ca. 1949.....................................**150.00**

Gravy boat & undertray,
Apple patt., 2 pcs.........................**45.00**

Jam jar, cov., Desert Rose patt.,
5" h. **75.00**

Mug, chocolate, Apple patt.........**125.00**

Mug, Apple patt., ca. 1940,
10 oz., 4¼" h. **25.00**

Mug, Apple patt., 12 oz. **48.00**

Mug, Desert Rose patt., 12 oz.......**45.00**

Napkin ring, Desert Rose patt. **35.00**

Pepper shaker & underplate,
Apple patt., apple-shaped,
2 pcs...**20.00**

Pitcher, water, Desert Rose patt.,
2½ qt. **125.00**

Plate, side salad, 4½" w., 8" l.,
crescent-shaped, Apple patt........**25.00**

Plate, bread & butter, 6½" d.,
Apple patt., ca. 1940 ....**6.00**

Plate, salad, 8½" d., Apple patt.,
ca. 1940......................................**10.00**

Plate, luncheon, 9½" d., Apple
patt., ca. 1940.............................**12.00**

Plate, luncheon, 9½" d., Desert
Rose patt., ca. 1941 ....**12.00**

Plate, dinner, 10½" d., Apple
patt., ca. 1940.............................**12.00**

Plate, dinner, 10½" d., Desert
Rose patt. **16.00**

Plate, dinner, 10½" d., Meadow
Rose patt. **18.00**

Plate, dinner, Mesa patt. **8.00**

Plate, dinner, 10½" d.,
October patt..................................**14.00**

Plate, chop, 12" d., Apple patt. **55.00**

Plate, chop, 12" d., Ivy patt..........**150.00**

Plate, chop, 14" d., Apple patt. **125.00**

Platter, 14" l., Apple patt. **49.00**

Platter, 14" l., Meadow Rose
patt. **65.00**

Platter, turkey, Apple patt............**350.00**

Platter, turkey, Desert Rose
patt. **145.00**

Platter, turkey, Ivy patt. **295.00**

Relish dish, oblong, three-part,
Apple patt., ca. 1940, 11¾" l. **60.00**

Salt & pepper shakers, Apple
patt., 6¼" h., pr. **60.00**

Salt & pepper shakers, Desert
Rose patt., 6¼" h., pr...................**55.00**

Salt shaker & pepper mill,
Meadow Rose patt., 6" h., pr. **195.00**

Sherbet, footed, Desert Rose
patt., 4" d., 2½" h. **23.00**

Soup plate w/flanged rim, Apple patt., ca. 1940, 8½" d., ...**17.00**

Sugar bowl, cov., Apple patt.........**40.00**

Teapot, cov., Apple patt. **165.00**

Tumbler, juice, Meadow Rose patt., 6 oz......................................**45.00**

Tumbler, Apple patt., 10 oz...........**30.00**

Tumbler, Desert Rose patt., 10 oz..**25.00**

Tumbler, El Patio line, orange glaze..**25.00**

Vegetable bowl, open, round, Apple patt., ca. 1940, 7¾" d., 2" h. **33.00**

Vegetable bowl, open, round, Desert Rose patt., ca. 1941, 8¼" d. **25.00**

Vegetable bowl, open, round, Desert Rose patt., ca. 1941, 9" d. **30.00**

Vegetable bowl, open, oval, divided, Desert Rose patt., 7 x 10¾" **30.00**

FULPER POTTERY

The Fulper Pottery was founded in Flemington, New Jersey, in 1805 and operated until 1935, although operations were curtailed in 1929 when its main plant was destroyed by fire. The name was changed in 1929 to Stangl Pottery, which continued in operation until July of 1978, when Pfaltzgraff, a division of Susquehanna Broadcasting Company of York, Pennsylvania, purchased the assets of the Stangl Pottery, including the name.

Fulper Marks

Candlesticks, wide circular dished base w/angled sides centered by a flaring cylindrical socket angled toward the rim, a sharply angled side handle from the socket rim to the base rim, Mission matte brown glaze, rectangular vertical mark, 2⅜" h., pr. **$193.00**

Center bowl, Effigy-type, a wide shallow bowl w/incurved sides raised on three molded seated figures on a stepped disc base, frothy butterscotch flambé glaze over a mustard yellow matte glaze, the base w/a speckled dark brown matte glaze, early ink mark, 10¾" d., 7½" h. **880.00**

Compote, 8" d., 3¼" h., low pedestal, blue & caramel glazes, ...**115.00**

Moon flask, a footed flattened round form w/the sides tapering to a short cylindrical neck w/a flared mouth flanked by S-scroll handles to the shoulder, fine Flemington green glaze, vertical mark, 10" h. **413.00**

Perfume lamp, cov., figural, modeled as a large green parrot w/orange at the top of its head perched on a brown stump-form base, parrot & upper stump form the cover, perfume escapes through the parrot's beak, impressed oval mark, 9½" h. **2,200.00**

Vase, 4½" h., terraced form w/a broad waist supporting two open stylized handles rising to a wide rim, covered in a rich caramel & tan glossy glaze, impressed mark **165.00**

Vase, 4½" h., ovoid body tapering to a wide, short cylindrical neck, a streaked mirrored black glaze above a Flemington green glaze, rectangular vertical ink stamp mark................................**193.00**

Vase, bud, 5¼" h., 3½" d., a thick footring supporting a wide squatty cushion-form base centered by a tall 'stick' neck,

covered in a cat's-eye flambé
glaze over a matte mustard
yellow ground, early vertical box
ink mark **248.00**

Vase, 6" h., 6" d., a small footring
supports a wide squatty bulbous
onion-form body w/a small rolled
rim flanked by low curved
handles to the shoulder, cat's-
eye flambé glaze, incised
vertical racetrack mark **330.00**

Vase, 7" h., 9½" d., very wide
bulbous tapering body w/a wide
flat mouth flanked by small
squared handles, cucumber
green crystalline glaze, vertical
mark **880.00**

Vase, 7½" h., wide ovoid body
w/a wide rounded shoulder to a
wide, slightly tapering cylindrical
neck blanked by arched handles
to the shoulder, vivid green to
dark green to rose matte glaze,
vertical mark **275.00**

Vase, bud-type, 9" h., 2¾" d.,
baluster-shaped body, covered
in pink & grey 'ashes of roses'
matte glaze, w/original paper
label **275.00**

Vase, 10" h., 5" d., seven-sided
tapering ovoid body, metallic
Chinese flambé glaze dripping
over a mahogany & ivory
flambé glaze, incised mark **605.00**

Vase, 10" h., seven-sided
tapering ovoid body w/a flat
mouth, covered in a thick
oatmeal matte glaze w/blue
highlights & a thick green drip
glaze from the rim down, vertical
ink mark **413.00**

Vase, 11½" h., 9" d., bulbous
lobed baluster-form lotus shape,
fine mirrored black, cat's-eye &
mahogany flambé glaze, vertical
raised racetrack mark **1,430.00**

Vase, 11½" h., 11" d., a wide
bulbous baluster-form w/a short
stepped neck, hammered
surface covered in a mirrored

black & turquoise blue flambé
crystalline glaze, raised
racetrack mark......................**2,970.00**

Vase, 12" h., tall slender baluster-
form body w/disc foot & short
flaring neck, vibrant pale blue,
rose & violet matte glaze,
vertical mark (flake at rim) **385.00**

Vase, 12½" h., 7¾" d., tall slender
ovoid body tapering to a closed-
in mouth, fine mirrored black to
copper dust crystalline flambé
glaze, raised racetrack
mark **1,656.00**

Fulper Baluster-form Vase

Vase, 13" h., simple tall baluster-
form w/a flaring neck, iridescent
surface in a cream & blue
flambé glaze, signed (ILLUS.) ...**690.00**

GAUDY WELSH

*This is a name for wares made in England
for the American market about 1830 to 1860,
with some examples dating much later.
Decorated with Imari-style flower patterns,
often highlighted with copper lustre, it should
not be confused with Gaudy Dutch wares
whose colors differ somewhat.*

Creamer, Vine patt., oblong
footed boat-shaped body
w/scalloped rim & high, wide
arched spout, ornate C-scroll
handle, 4" h. **$138.00**

Cups & saucers, decorated w/floral Imari patt., two pr. (minor wear & stains)............374.00

Oyster Pattern Pitcher

Pitcher, milk, bulbous body tapering to wide cylindrical neck, pinched rim spout & C-form handle, underglaze-blue & polychrome enamel, lustre trim, Oyster patt., minor stains & crazing, 4⅝" h. (ILLUS.) **182.00**

Tea set: cov. teapot, creamer & cov. sugar bowl; Tulip patt., underglaze-blue & polychrome enameling, lustre trim, minor damage & hairline in handle of creamer, 3 pcs. **633.00**

GRUEBY POTTERY

Some fine art pottery was produced by the Grueby Faience and Tile Company, established in Boston in 1891. Choice pieces were created with molded designs on a semi-porcelain body. The ware is marked and often bears the initials of the decorators. The pottery closed in 1907.

GRUEBY

Grueby Pottery Mark

Vase, 3" h., 4" d., squatty bulbous ovoid form w/vertical ribs, tapering to flared lip, covered in fine leathery pale bluish green matte glaze, impressed w/circular "Pottery" mark **$770.00**

Vase, 3" h., 6" d., a wide squatty bulbous body tapering to a short, wide rolled neck, deeply textured green matte glaze, impressed mark........................**880.00**

Vase, 4½" h., bulbous nearly spherical body w/a rounded shoulder to a wide, low molded flat mouth, oatmeal matte glaze, impressed mark (minor chip repair under lip) **413.00**

Vase, 4½" h., 3⅜" d., tapering ovoid body w/a wide rolled short neck, matte pale blue glaze, impressed mark........................**345.00**

Vase, 7" h., 12" d., wide squatty bulbous body tapering to a short wide neck w/flat rim, carved & applied decoration of broad, vertical leaves w/prominent spines, separated by delicate ribbed buds in ivory atop narrow green vertical stems, overall mottled opaque mint green & thick greyish green matte glaze, impressed mark....................**7,150.00**

Vase, 7¾" h., 3¾" d., simple baluster-form body w/a flaring rim, the sides molded in high-relief w/wide leaf blades, matte green glaze, impressed marks & artist's initials, Marie Seaman **1,955.00**

Vase, 8" h., 4¼" d., ovoid form tapering to flared lip, w/tooled & applied leaves alternating w/buds & stems under a rich mottled ochre brown glaze, impressed circular Faience mark & "355 - WP - 1-26-01," by Wilhemina Post, 1901 ....**2,860.00**

Vase, 9½" h., 3½" d., slender ovoid body swelling at the top then tapering slightly to the flaring & lightly scalloped rim, a band of small relief-molded trefoils under the rim, thick rich organic matte green glaze, impressed pottery mark & "RE," by Ruth Erickson (restoration to rim chip)................**2,200.00**

Vase, 13½" h., 7½" d., a narrow footring under a squatty bulbous base tapering to a tall cylindrical neck w/a slightly flared rim, tooled & applied leaves alternating w/buds on tall stems, thick matte green glaze, impressed mark & "RE," by Ruth Erickson, 1906.......................**6,600.00**

HALL

Founded in 1903 in East Liverpool, Ohio, this still-operating company at first produced mostly utilitarian wares. It was in 1911 that Robert T. Hall, son of the company founder, developed a special single-fire, lead-free glaze which proved to be strong, hard and non-porous. In the 1920s the firm became well known for their extensive line of teapots (still a major product) and in 1932 they introduced kitchenwares followed by dinnerwares in 1936 and refrigerator wares in 1938.

The imaginative designs and wide range of glaze colors and decal decorations have led to the growing appeal of Hall wares with collectors, especially people who like Art Deco and Art Moderne design. One of the firm's most famous patterns was the "Autumn Leaf" line, produced as premiums for the Jewel Tea Company. For listings of this ware see "Jewel Tea Autumn Leaf."

Helpful books on Hall include, The Collector's Guide to Hall China *by Margaret & Kenn Whitmyer, and* Superior Quality Hall China - A Guide for Collectors *by Harvey Duke (An ELO Book, 1977).*

HALL CHINA

MADE IN U.S.A.

Hall Marks

Bowl, 9¼" d., 3¼" h., round, vegetable, Blue Bouquet decal on two sides only consisting of rosebud, blue band w/gold lattice design, open roses in pink & yellow, blue band w/gold

Round Vegetable Bowl

lattice design & rosebud, marked in gold, "Hall's Superior Quality Kitchenware, Made in U.S.A." (ILLUS.) **$35.00**

Coffeepot, cov., Daniel shape, Red Poppy patt...........................**55.00**

Coffee set: cov. Daniel shape coffeepot, creamer, cov. sugar bowl & 11¼ x 13¼" platter; Red Poppy patt. the set, (creamer w/hairline)...................**100.00**

Salt shaker, handled, Pert shape, Rose Parade patt. **25.00**

Teapot, cov., Aladdin shape, black w/gold trim.........................**90.00**

Teapot, cover & infuser, Aladdin shape, yellow & gold **50.00**

Teapot, cover & blue infuser, Aladdin shape, Morning Glory patt. **135.00**

Teapot, cov., Boston shape, blue w/gold decoration, 6 cup **45.00**

Teapot, cov., Boston shape, Orange Poppy patt. **185.00**

Teapot, cov., Cleveland shape, Forest green **65.00**

Teapot, cov., French shape, green w/gold trim, 2-cup.............**35.00**

Teapot, cov., Hook Cover, delphinium & gold trim.................**49.00**

Teapot, cov., McCormick shape, maroon **42.00**

Teapot, cov., Medallion shape, Crocus patt., ...**65.00**

Teapot, cov., Melody shape, turquoise w/gold trim **125.00**

Teapot, cov., Moderne shape, cadet...**55.00**

Teapot, cov., New York shape,
8 cup..**250.00**

Teapot, cov., Pert shape,
Chinese red & white **37.00**

Solid Pale Blue Teapot

Teapot, cov., solid pale blue high
gloss w/white interior, complete
w/dipper & spreader, Manhattan
"French Drip Coffee Biggin,"
marked in black "Hall" in a circle
& "Made in U.S.A." outside the
circle (ILLUS.)..............................**95.00**

Teapot, cov., Streamline shape,
Chinese red **125.00**

Teapot, cov., Windshield shape,
Camellia w/gold polka dots..........**55.00**

Teapot, cov., Windshield shape,
canary & gold **85.00**

Tea set: cov. teapot, creamer &
cov. sugar bowl; Philadelphia
shape, cobalt blue w/gold trim
(tiny bubble)..............................**35.00**

Tea set: cov. teapot, creamer &
cov. sugar bowl; Philadelphia
shape, ivory w/gold trim, 3 pcs. ...**35.00**

HARKER POTTERY COMPANY

The Harker Pottery was established in
East Liverpool, Ohio, in 1840 by Benjamin
Harker, Sr. In 1890 the pottery was
incorporated as the Harker Pottery Company.
By 1911 the company had acquired the former
plant of the National China Company and in
1931 Harker purchased the closed pottery of
Edwin M. Knowles in Chester, West
Virginia.

Harker's earliest products were
yellowware and Rockingham-glazed wares
produced from local clay. After 1900
whiteware was made from imported
materials. Perhaps their best-known line is
Cameoware, decorated on solid glazes with
white "cameos" in a silhouette fashion.

There were many other patterns and
shapes created by Harker over the years. In
1972 the pottery was closed after it was
purchased by the Jeanette Glass Company.

Harker Pottery Marks

Bowl, Swirl shape......................**$28.00**

Cake lifter, Amethyst **28.00**

Casserole, cov., Amethyst............**50.00**

Casserole, cov., stacking-type,
Petit Point II patt. **55.00**

Colonial Lady Custard Cup

Custard cup, Colonial Lady
patt., 3¼" h., (ILLUS.)..................**4.00**

Petit Point Pattern Rolling Pin

Pepper shaker, Amethyst **15.00**
Pie baker, Amethyst **32.00**
Plate, 7½" d., Pink-cocoa patt. **8.00**
Platter, 12" l., Amethyst................**25.00**
Platter, Peacock patt. **25.00**
Rolling pin, cadet blue & white.....**80.00**
Rolling pin, Petit Point patt.,
    14½" l. (ILLUS.) **95.00**

HARLEQUIN

The Homer Laughlin China Company, makers of the popular "Fiesta" pottery line, also introduced in 1938 a less expensive and thinner ware which was sold under the "Harlequin" name. It did not carry the maker's trade-mark and was marketed exclusively through F. W. Woolworth Company. It was produced in a wide range of dinnerwares in assorted colors until 1964. Out of production for a number of years, in 1979 Woolworth requested the line be reintroduced using an ironstone body and with a limited range of pieces and colors offered. Collectors also seek out a series of miniature animal figures produced in the Harlequin line in the 1930s and 1940s.

Creamer, novelty, ball-shaped,
    blue...**$45.00**
Cream soup, handled,
    turquoise.....................................**19.00**
Cup, demitasse, light green...........**85.00**
Cup, demitasse, rose **95.00**
Cup, demitasse, green **48.00**
Cup, demitasse, yellow **55.00**
Cup, chartreuse............................**9.00**
Cup, grey.....................................**10.00**
Cup, medium green.......................**9.00**

Cup, rose....................................**9.00**
Cup & saucer, demitasse, rose ..**115.00**
Cup & saucer, demitasse, spruce
    green **195.00**
Cup & saucer, green **13.00**
Egg cup, double, light green **25.00**
Egg cup, double, maroon.............**38.00**
Egg cup, double, rose..................**45.00**
Pitcher, 9" h., ball-shaped w/ice
    lip, spruce green.........................**95.00**
Pitcher, 9" h., ball-shaped w/ice
    lip, yellow...................................**75.00**
Plate, 9" d., medium green **20.00**
Plate, 9" d., yellow **6.00**
Plate, 10" d., blue **35.00**
Sugar bowl, cov., yellow..............**20.00**
Teapot, cov., light green.............**125.00**

HISTORICAL & COMMEMORATIVE WARES

Numerous potteries, especially in England and the United States, made various porcelain and earthenware pieces to commemorate people, places and events. Scarce English historical wares with American views command highest prices. Objects are listed here alphabetically by title of view.

Most pieces listed here will date between about 1820 and 1850. The maker's name is noted in parentheses at the end of each entry.

American Eagle on an Urn
    waste bowl, floral border, dark
    blue, 5½" d., 3" h., Clews
    (unseen flake on foot rim).......**$248.00**

Arms of South Carolina plate,
floral border, dark blue, 6¼" d.,
Mayer (faint scratching) **440.00**

Boston and Bunker Hill platter,
brown, floral border, 13½" l.,
Godwin (two small in-the-making
shoulder separations on the
face) **358.00**

Boston State House plate, floral
border, dark blue, 10¼" d.,
Enoch Wood (minor rim chip,
knife marks) **201.00**

Chateau de Chillon Undertray

**Chateau de Chillon
(Switzerland) undertray,** oval
openwork, Italian Scenery
series, dark blue, 9¼" l., E.
Wood (ILLUS.)..........................**550.00**

City Hall, New York Plate

City Hall, New York plate, floral
border, purple, unseen foot rim
flake, some light mellowing,
10¼" d., Jackson (ILLUS.).........**182.00**

Columbian Star, Oct. 28th, 1840
- Log Cabin (side view) plate,
brown, 7½" d., Ridgway (overall
mellowing, hairline off
the rim) **110.00**

**Commodore MacDonnough's
Victory plate,** shell border, dark
blue, 6½" d. (Wood)..................**303.00**

**Commodore MacDonnough's
Victory plate,** shell border,
irregular center, dark blue, 9" d.
(Enoch Wood) **468.00**

**Doctor Syntax Star Gazing
plate,** raised flowers & scrolls
border, light blue, 8½" d.,
Clews..**350.00**

**Entrance of the Erie Canal into
the Hudson at Albany plate,**
floral border, dark blue, 10" d.
(Wood)......................................**770.00**

**Fairmount Near Philadelphia
soup plate,** spread eagle
border, dark blue, 9¾" d.
(Stubbs) **358.00**

Famous Naval Heroes pitcher,
floral border, vignette scene
of the Monument to the Nautical
Heroes of the War of 1812,
dark blue, 7½" h. (restoration
to chipping around
the rim) **660.00**

**Landing of General Lafayette at
Castle Garden,** New York, 16
August, 1824 plate, floral & vine
border, dark blue, 9" d., Clews
(some facial scratching, small
glaze rub on rim) **187.00**

Marine Hospital, Louisville,
Kentucky plate, shell border,
dark blue, 10¼" d., Enoch Wood
(glaze wear, chips to
base, knife scratches) **316.00**

Mount Vernon Pitcher

Mount Vernon, Washington's
Seat pitcher, floral border, dark
blue, unknown maker, 6¾" h.
(ILLUS.) **1,980.00**

Nahant Hotel, New Boston plate,
spread eagle border, dark blue,
8¼" d., Stubbs (facial wear) **303.00**

**Residence of the Late Richard
Jordan,** New Jersey (The) cup
& saucer, handleless, floral
border, red w/applied blue rim,
J. Heath & Co. (saucer rim
crack)..**116.00**

**Residence of the Late Richard
Jordan,** New Jersey (The) plate,
floral border, purple, 7¾" d., J.
H. & Co. (light overall mellowing,
some inner rim wear)................**154.00**

**Residence of the Late Richard
Jordan,** New Jersey (The) plate,
floral border, black, 10½" d. J. H.
& Co. (initials scratched in
back)..**193.00**

**Residence of the Late Richard
Jordan,** New Jersey (The) plate,
floral border, dark brown,
10½" d., J. H. & Co. **165.00**

State House, Boston custard cup,
flowers in medallions border,
medium dark blue, 2⅝" h.,
Ridgway (restoration to several
tiny rim flakes) **209.00**

Trinity Hall, Cambridge
(England) sauce tureen, cov.,
floral & vignette border, dark
blue, College series, 8¼" l.,
6¼" h. (Ridgway) **660.00**

**Upper Ferry Bridge Over the
River Schuylkill sauce tureen
undertray,** spread eagle & floral
scrolls border, dark blue, 9" l.,
Stubbs (shallow long unseen
chip on interior foot rim)............**358.00**

**View of Trenton Falls - Three
People on Rock plate,** shell
border, dark blue, 7½" d., E.
Wood, (light wear, broken glaze
bubble) **330.00**

HULL

*This pottery was made by the Hull Pottery
Company, Crooksville, Ohio, beginning in
1905. Art Pottery was made until 1950 when
the company was converted to utilitarian
wares. All production ceased in 1986.*

*Reference books for collectors include
Roberts' Ultimate Encyclopedia of Hull
Pottery by Brenda Roberts (Walsworth
Publishing Company, 1992), and Collector's
Guide to Hull Pottery - The Dinnerware
Lines by Barbara Loveless Gick-Burke
(Collector Books, 1993).*

Hull Marks

Tokay Pattern Basket

Basket, Blossom Flite patt.,
No. T-8", 8¼ x 9½" **$115.00**

Basket, Blossom Flite patt.,
No. T-9-10", 10" h......................**100.00**

Basket, Tokay patt., 8" h.
(ILLUS.) **70.00**

Basket, Tokay patt., round
"Moon" form, green & white,
No. 11, 10½" h..............................**75.00**

Butter dish, cov., Little Red Riding
Hood patt.................................**425.00**

Canister set: "Coffee," "Sugar,"
"Flour" & "Tea," Little Red Riding
Hood patt., the set................**2,500.00**

Casserole, cov., Sunglow patt.,
marked "51-7½ Oven Proof
U.S.A.".....................................**55.00**

Cookie jar, cov., Little Red Riding
Hood patt..................................**375.00**

Cookie jar, cov., Little Red Riding
Hood patt., poinsettia decoration
w/gold trim **995.00**

Cookie jar, cov., Little Red Riding
Hood patt., red spray w/gold
bows & red shoes.....................**950.00**

Ewer, Woodland Gloss patt.,
No. W-24-13½", 13½" h.............**195.00**

Flowerpot, Woodland Matte,
pink, No. W-31-5¾" **145.00**

Honey jug, Blossom Flite patt.,
No. T-1-6", 6" h..........................**50.00**

Mustard jar, cov., Little Red
Riding Hood patt......................**350.00**

Model of a duck, No. 80 ....**26.00**

Model of a frog, Novelty Line **60.00**

Model of a hippopotamus,
Novelty Line, green **60.00**

Model of a monkey, Novelty
Line, large.................................**50.00**

Mustard jar, cov., Little Red
Riding Hood patt.......................**475.00**

Early Utility Ware Pitcher

Pitcher, 4½" h., Early Utility ware,
vertical ribs from base to bottom
of handle, white thin horizontal
line, wider dark brown line and a
second thin white line directly
below shoulder, marked "107,"
"H" in a circle & "36"
below it (ILLUS.) **78.00**

Pitcher, 8½" h., No. T-3-8½"
(for watering flowers) **95.00**

Plaque, pierced to hang, round,
Bow-Knot patt., blue,
No. B28-10", 10" d....................**985.00**

Serving dish, three-
compartment, Butterfly patt.,
B23-11½", 11½" **125.00**

Teapot, cov., Woodland patt., No.
W26-6½", 6½" h. (lid
discoloration) **75.00**

Tea set: cov. teapot, creamer &
cov. sugar bowl; Waterlily patt.
white & gold, Nos. L-18-6",
L-19-5", L-20-5", 3 pcs...............**125.00**

Vase, bud, 6" h., Sueno Tulip
patt., No. 104-44-6"
(flea bite top rim) **75.00**

Vase, 6" h., Sueno Tulip patt.,
pink, No. 110-33-6"...................**125.00**

Vase, 6" h., Sueno Tulip patt.,
pink & blue, No. 111-33-6" **150.00**

Vase, 6¼" h., Magnolia Matte
patt., No. 15-6¼" **50.00**

Vase, 7" h., Iris patt., No. 402-7"
(minor restoration) **125.00**

Vase, 7½" h., Woodland Matte
patt., pink, No. W8-7½" **125.00**

Vase, 8" h., Sueno Tulip patt.,
pink, No. 107-33-8"...................**175.00**

Vase, 8" h., Sunglow patt.,
No. 94-8" (minor restoration) **45.00**

Vase, 8½" h., Orchid patt., blue,
No. 309-8" (ILLUS. top
next page) **175.00**

Vase, 8½" h., Water Lily patt., No.
L-8-8½" (tiny repair on base).......**75.00**

Vase, 8½" h., Woodland Gloss
patt., No. 16-8½" **60.00**

Orchid Pattern Vase

Vase, 10½" h., Wildflower No.
   series, No. 77-10½" **270.00**

Vase, 10½" h., Woodland
   Matte, pink, No. W18-10½" h. ...**185.00**

Vase, 12" h., handled,
   Open Rose patt. **225.00**

Wall pocket, Woodland Gloss
   patt., No. W-13, 7½" h. **125.00**

HUMMEL FIGURINES

The Goebel Company of Oeslau, Germany, first produced these porcelain figurines in 1934 having obtained the rights to adapt the beautiful pastel sketches of children by Sister Maria Innocentia (Berta) Hummel. Every design by the Goebel artisans was approved by the nun until her death in 1946. Though not antique, these figurines with the "M.I. Hummel" signature, especially those bearing the Goebel Company factory mark used from 1934 into the early 1940s, are being sought by collectors though interest may have peaked some years ago.

Hummel Marks

Apple Tree Girl, 1940-57,
   4" h. **$112.00**

Apple Tree Girl, 1979-90, 4" h......**80.00**

Begging His Share, w/candle
   hole, 1940-57,
   5½" h. ....**350.00 to 450.00**

Be Patient, 1972-79, 4¼" h. **100.00**

Be Patient, 1963-71,
   6¼" h. ....**175.00 to 200.00**

Boots, 1956-68, 5¼" h. **154.00**

Boots, 1979-90, 5¼" h. **132.00**

Boy with Toothache, 1963-71,
   5½" h. **147.00**

Boy with Toothache, 1979-90,
   5½" h. **138.00**

Builder, 1972-79, 5½" h. **145.00**

Builder, 1979-90, 5½" h. **145.00**

Chef, Hello, green trousers,
   1956-68, 6¼" h. **175.00**

Chick Girl, 1934-49,
   3½" h. ....**350.00 to 400/00**

Chimney Sweep, 1956-68,
   5½" h. ....**140.00 to 150.00**

Chimney Sweep, 1979-90,
   5½" h. **120.00**

Congratulations, 1963-71,
   6" h. **110.00**

Coquettes, 1972-79, 5¼" h. **205.00**

Culprits, 1956-68,
   6¼" h. ....**190.00 to 200.00**

Culprits, 1972-79, 6¼" h. **160.00**

Eventide, 1972-79, 4¾" h. **216.00**

Feeding Time, 1940-57,
   4¼" h. **215.00**

Feeding Time, 1963-71,
   4¼" h. **100.00**

Globe Trotter, 1979-90, 5" h.......**119.00**

Goose Girl, 1940-57, 4" h. **160.00**

Goose Girl, 1972-79, 4" h. **107.00**

Happiness, 1956-68, 4¾" h. **85.00**

Happy Days, 1956-68, 5¼" h......**200.00**

Hear Ye, Hear Ye, 1956-68, 5" h.
   (ILLUS. next page) **120.00**

Hear Ye, Hear Ye, 1979-90,
   6" h. **135.00**

Hear Ye

March Winds

Home From Market, 1963-71,
4 ¾" h. **90.00**

Homeward Bound, 1972-79,
5" h. **280.00**

Just Resting, 1956-68,
3 ¾" h. **112.00**

Kiss Me, without socks, 1979-90,
6" h. **189.00**

Knitting Lesson, 1963-71,
7½" h. **275.00**

Latest News, 1956-68, 5¼" h. **295.00**

Little Cellist, 1972-79, 6" h. **145.00**

Little Fiddler, 1956-68,
11" h. ....**750.00 to 800.00**

Little Gabriel, 1956-68, 5" h. **140.00**

Little Goat Herder, 1940-57,
5¼" h. **295.00**

Little Goat Herder, 1963-71,
5¼" h. **140.00**

Little Hiker, 1956-68,
5½" h. ....**125.00 to 155.00**

Little Hiker, 1979-90, 5½" h. **115.00**

Little Pharmacist, 1972-79,
6" h. ....**150.00 to 200.00**

Little Scholar, 1940-57,
5½" h. ....**175.00 to 225.00**

Little Tooter, 1940-57, 3¾" h.
(part of Nativity set) **135.00**

Lost Sheep, 1972-79, 5½" h. **95.00**

March Winds, 1972-79, 5" h.
(ILLUS.) **109.00**

Max & Moritz, 1979-90,
5¼" h. **144.00**

Merry Wanderer, 1972-79,
4¼" h. **88.00**

Merry Wanderer, 1972-79,
4¾" h. **127.00**

Mischief Maker, 1972-79, 5" h....**160.00**

Mischief Maker, 1979-90, 5" h....**138.00**

On Secret Path, 1972-79,
5⅜" h. **155.00**

Photographer, 1979-90, 4¾" h...**189.00**

Playmates, 1934-49,
4" h...........................**300.00 to 325.00**

Prayer Before Battle, 1979-90,
4¼" h. **107.00**

Retreat to Safety

Retreat to Safety, 1963-71, 4" h.
(ILLUS.) **88.00**

School Boy, 1963-71, 4" h............**70.00**

Sensitive Hunter, 1979-90,
4¾" h. **125.00**

Sensitive Hunter, 1972-79,
5½" h. **163.00**

She Loves Me, 1956-68,
4¼" h.........................**125.00 to 150.00**

Signs of Spring

Signs of Spring, 1956-68, 4" h.
(ILLUS.)....................**145.00 to 155.00**

Silent Night candleholder,
1972-79, 4¾ x 5½" **245.00**

Soldier Boy, 1979-90, 6" h. **126.00**

Spring Dance, 1963-71,
6½" h.........................**450.00 to 500.00**

Stitch in Time, 1963-71,
6¾" h. **175.00**

Stormy Weather, 1956-68, 6¼" h.
(ILLUS. top, next column)..........**345.00**

Strolling Along, 1940-57,
4¾" h.........................**275.00 to 325.00**

Strolling Along, 1979-90,
4¾" h. **100.00**

Sweet Music, 1956-68, 5¼" h.
(ILLUS. bottom, next column)....**154.00**

Telling Her Secret, 1972-79,
5¼" h. **250.00**

Stormy Weather

To Market, 1972-79, 6¼" h. **300.00**

Trumpet Boy, 1940-57,
4¾" h. **140.00**

Umbrella Boy, 1956-68, 5" h. **378.00**

Umbrella Girl, 1972-79, 4¾" h....**378.00**

Umbrella Girl, 1979-90, 4¾" h....**378.00**

Wash Day, 1979-90, 5¾" h. **189.00**

Wayside Devotion, 1956-68,
7½" h. **260.00**

Sweet Music

JEWEL TEA AUTUMN LEAF

Though not antique this ware has a devoted following. The Hall China Company of East Liverpool, Ohio, made the first pieces of Autumn Leaf pattern ware to be given as premiums by the Jewel Tea Company in 1933. The premiums were an immediate success and thousands of new customers, all eager to acquire a piece of the durable Autumn Leaf pattern ware, began purchasing Jewel Tea products. Though the pattern was eventually used to decorate linens, glasswares and tinware, we include only the Hall China Company items in our listing.

Cup, St. Denis style $15.00

Custard cup 4.00

Gravy boat 12.00

Mixing bowl, 1 qt. 15.00

Mixing bowls, nesting-type, two
   6" d., one 7" d. & one 8" d.,
   set of 4......................................150.00

Mug, Irish coffee 95.00

Teapot, cov., Newport shape,
   ca. 1930s 185.00

Teapot, cov., "Rayed," longspout,
   ca. 1935.....................................90.00

JOSEF ORIGINALS

Muriel Joseph George was the talented creator of the whimsical "Josef Originals" figurines. Known in the early 1940s as a jewelry designer, Muriel made items of lucite and ceramic jewelry under the name "Muriel of California." During this time Muriel also enjoyed modeling clay figurines.

In 1946, Muriel and her husband Tom, now home from World War II, talked of opening their own pottery company. Working out of their garage, they produced their first commercial figure, "Pitty Sing," a small Chinese boy in a big coolie hat, sitting asleep, with a cat on his lap. Muriel's father took "Pitty Sing" to a department store, and with an order for two gross, Muriel went to work. It was this first commercial piece that determined the now infamous name, Josef Originals. The printer made an error in the spelling of Joseph, and with a too soon

deadline, "Pitty Sing" and all his descendants, became "Josef Originals." Other figurines were shown and began to sell at a surprising volume.

If imitation is the greatest compliment, then Mrs. George should have been pleased with the flood of "Made in Japan" copies that began to appear on the market during the 1950s. In response to these inferior copies of her work, she produced new designs of unequaled excellence. Consumers wanted the Josef look, however, they did not want the price tag that accompanied the line. In 1959, with sales floundering at an all-time low, Muriel and Tom formed a partnership with George Good, a successful distributor of several California pottery lines. The production of "George Imports" was moved from California to Japan bringing labor costs to a new low. Muriel personally educated the workers at the Katayama Factory in Japan on her "design ways." Returning home, Muriel forwarded new designs to Japan with a final product shipped back to the United States for her approval. There were elegant Victorian ladies, Birthday girls, mice (Muriel is credited with over forty different ones), ostriches, monkeys and more. With production costs down and popular new designs selling, Josef was again a competitive ceramics line.

Retiring in 1981, Muriel continued to design for her former partner, and now company owner, George Good until 1985. Her daughter, Diane, joined in the creativity from 1973-1986. In 1985, George Good sold the company to Applause, Inc. No new designs would be forthcoming under the Josef Originals name. Muriel Joseph George died in 1991.

From 1945 until 1959, Josef Originals were made in California. On the unglazed bottom is an incised script mark of "Josef" or "Josef Originals" and the encircled "C." Some pieces, mostly the animals, were too small for the incised mark. The figurines also carried a ⅝" oval sticker, black with a gold border and the lettering "Josef Originals" and under that "California." Post 1959, the "California" was replaced by a "curl" design and an additional half-inch oval sticker showing Japan was added.

An interesting and helpful hint is that the pre-1980s (Muriel's retirement) girls were all made with black eyes and a glossy finish; most animals with a semi-gloss finish. Prices listed are for perfect figurines; repaired or damaged pieces are not considered collectible.

Bell, figural, "March" **$18.00**

Bell, figural, "September" **26.00**

Candleholders, figural,
Christmas mice, pr. **55.00**

Candle light, model of a privy **36.00**

Figure, "Holiday Lady" **65.00**

Figure, "Little Guest" **50.00**

Figure, "Love Locket," 9" h. **150.00**

Figure, "Mandy" **70.00**

Figure, "Ringbearer" **56.00**

Figure of an angel w/gold club ...**55.00**

Figure of an angel w/paddle **55.00**

Figure of a baby in a cradle **30.00**

Figure of a girl,
"Belle of the Ball" **58.00**

Figure of a girl, Birthday No. 3 .....**30.00**

Figure of a girl, Birthday No. 6 .....**35.00**

Figure of a girl, Birthday No. 8 .....**35.00**

Figure of a girl, Birthday No. 16 ...**38.00**

Figure of a girl, Birthstone
series, January **24.00**

Figure of a girl, Birthstone
series, February, two different
styles, each **46.00**

Figure of a girl, Birthstone
series, April, 3½" h. **36.00**

Figure of a girl, Birthstone
series, August.............................**45.00**

Figure of a girl, Birthstone
series, September **46.00**

Figure of a girl, Birthstone
series, November **24.00**

Figure of a girl, Bridal Party
Bridesmaid **58.00**

Figure of a girl, "Dolls of the
Month," February,
lavender dress...........................**15.00**

Figure of a girl, "Dolls of the
Month," June **35.00**

Figure of a girl, Farmer's
Daughter with Duck **65.00**

Figure of a girl, Farmer's
Daughter with Lamb **65.00**

Figure of a girl, "France," Little
Internationals series, 3¾" h. **32.00**

Figure of a girl,
"Graduation Angel" **30.00**

Figure of a girl, "Holland," Little
Internationals series, 3¾" h. **40.00**

Figure of a girl, "Scotland," Little
Internationals series, 3¾" h. **58.00**

Figure of a girl, "Southern Belle" ..**58.00**

Figure of a girl, "Wedding Belle" ..**58.00**

Figure of a girl w/rose basket **58.00**

Lipstick holder, figure of a girl,
lavender.....................................**28.00**

Model of a cat, "Tawny"...............**22.00**

Elephant with Fly Swatter

Model of an elephant, holding fly
swatter, brown w/pink accents,
2½" h. (ILLUS.)...........................**20.00**

Model of Mother elephant **70.00**

Model of a mouse, brown w/a
peanut, 1¾" h. **20.00**

Music box w/angel, yellow &
green **20.00**

Music box w/boy & girl dancing,
plays Lara's Theme **115.00**

Night light, model of a puppy,
6" h. **10.00**

Pie baker, figural boy or girl chef,
each..**65.00**

Rosary holder, figural nun **95.00**

Josef Originals Owl Salt Shaker

Salt & pepper shakers, model of
owl, brown bodies w/black eyes,
3½" h., pr. (ILLUS. of salt) **30.00**

Sugar shaker, figural hen **18.00**

KAY FINCH CERAMICS

Santta Face Mug

Kay Finch along with her husband, Braden, opened Kay Finch Ceramics in 1939 in Corona del Mar, California. An extremely talented and dedicated artist, Finch is more well known for her animals than any of her other creations. Dogs were a favorite of hers and can be found as figurines, decorating trays, trinket boxes, ashtrays, planters, plates and others. Ideas seemed endless for Finch's creativity. Even in the early days, Kay's ceramics were expensive and have continued to be so today. During a period of production, Kay personally trained twenty-five decorators who assisted her. Braden died in 1963 and the business ceased. Kay used her energies for the good of dog breeding shows. In the mid-1970s, Freeman-McFarlin, another California company, hired Kay to create a set of dog figurines which was later followed with other Finch animal designs. These were done in a gold-leaf treatment and marked in block letters with the Kay Finch name and model numbers in the 800s. However, not all Freeman-McFarlin 800 numbers indicate a Finch creation. Freeman-McFarlin had previously purchased Kay's molds and the working relationship lasted until about 1980. Kay Finch died on June 21, 1993 at the age of eighty-nine.

Figure of a "Godey" man,
standing on round short base,
hat on head, arms across waist,
hands touching, pastel jacket
w/purple, white & blue accents,
9½" h. **$135.00**

Figures of choir boys, pr. **155.00**

Model of a cat, 8" h.....................235.00

Model of a dog, Cocker Spaniel,
black, No. 5201, 8" h. **495.00**

Model of a dog, Pekinese,
No. 154, 14" l. **595.00**

Model of an elephant, walking,
white w/floral trim inside ears,
No. 4626, 5" h...........................**140.00**

Model of a hippopotamus,
standing w/head up & mouth
open, bow tied around neck,
pink body w/polka dots & pastel
accents, Model No. 5019,
5¾" h. **400.00**

Model of a kitten (one flake) **50.00**

Model of an owl, "Tootsie,"
standing, white body w/pink
accents, black eyes, nose &
mouth, Model No. 189,
companion piece to "Hoot," &
"Toot," 3¾" h...............................**75.00**

Model of a pig, "Grumpy," pansy
decoration, 6" h. **325.00**

Model of a rabbit **80.00**

Model of a rooster, gold trim **195.00**

Models of a rooster & hen, "Mr. & Mrs. Banty," Nos. 4844 & 4843, pr. **120.00**

Mug, bulbous w/wreath handle, white ground w/Santa face, red lips & hat w/green holly leaves, pink cheeks, black accents on beard & hat, stamp mark underglaze "Kay Finch California," 2¾" h. (ILLUS. w/introduction) **22.00**

Planter, modernistic leaf-shaped, tan bark glossy glaze, Model No. 205, 6¾" h. **85.00**

Vase, 4¼" h., flared sides w/tan glossy & gold trim, Model No. 479 ....**75.00**

KEELER, BRAD

Model of a Blue Jay

In 1952 Brad Keeler, a talented creator and modeler working in the field of art (particularly ceramics), died at the age of thirty-nine. He has left a legacy for future collectors who are beginning to recognize his enormous talents. At first, the Keeler family used their home garage in Glendale, California to open a small studio and it was there that Brad, at the age of twenty-six, created hand-decorated birds. Riding on the success of his bird line, Brad Keeler leased a small amount of space from Evan Shaw who had taken special interest in Keeler's birds, so much so that he included them in his American Pottery Company line. In 1946, Keeler struck out on his own with Shaw

continuing to help him. Among the lines Brad Keeler produced over the years, his bird line is a favorite among collectors today. This is understandable because they were done in a variety of sizes, shapes and glazes. Many joined soft muted tones of green, pink or tan with more vibrant glazes. Pheasants, flamingos, herons, blue jays, ducks, peacocks and others were quick sellers. He also created a well known lobster dinnerware using the Ming Dragon Blood glaze which he and Andrew Malinovsky, Jr. developed. The lobster line is a large one including chip and dip sets, serving bowls, large divided bowls with a full bodied lobster serving as the divider, and soup bowls with lids. Many collectors like Keeler's whimsical, cute figurines and animals. It must have also been true when Keeler created his Pryde & Joy line. A trait of this line is the 'stitching' scattered in various places over the pieces as if they are being held together with string or thread. When Brad Keeler had his fatal heart attack he was building a large factory in San Juan Capistrano and there was every reason to believe that, with his talent and the success he had already achieved, his products could out perform even the imports that were streaming into the United States. Almost all Keeler products are marked in some fashion. There was a Brad Keeler label and an American Pottery label; in-mold mark with "Brad Keeler," and a model number; a harder-to-find copyright symbol with "B.B.K. made in U.S.A.," stamp on small items or on outside designers' work. (Each designer used their initials to designate their decorating talents).

269
© CMK
MADE IN
U.S.A.

Brad Keeler
W   25

BRAD KEELER
MADE IN U.S.A.
87

Brad Keeler Marks

Figure of a cowboy on round base w/right hand on fence post, stamp mark "Brad Keeler," 7" h. $42.00

Figure of a pioneer woman, stamp mark "Brad Keeler," 6¾" h. 40.00

Model of a blue jay on round base, stamp mark "C.M.K. 269, Made in U.S.A." & copyright symbol, also Brad Keeler sticker, 5" h. (ILLUS. w/introduction) 75.00

Model of a doe, lying down w/head up, No. 878, 6" l., 4" h. 50.00

Model of a duck, standing on a quatrefoil white base, brown body, yellow beak, 5" h. 60.00

Model of a fawn, lying down w/head up, Model No. 879, 4" l., 3" h. 40.00

Model of a flamingo, standing on oval base, head erect, 9" h. 100.00

Model of a flamingo, standing on oval base, head bent, in-mold mark "Brad Keeler 3," 7½" h. 75.00

Model of a sea gull, on ocean wave, head down, wings up, in-mold mark "Brad Keeler 29," 10½" h. 145.00

Salt & pepper shakers, model of a lobster, Ming Dragon Blood glaze, stamp marked "Brad Keeler Made in U.S.A.," 3¼" h., pr. 29.00

LEFTON

Lefton China is one of the most desirable and sought-after collectibles on today's market. The company was founded in the early 1940s by Mr. George Zolton Lefton who had immigrated to the United States from Hungary. In the 1930s he was involved in the designing and manufacturing of sportswear, and his hobby of collecting fine china and porcelain led him to the creation of his own ceramics business.

When the bombing of Pearl Harbor occurred in December of 1941, Mr. Lefton befriended and helped a Japanese-American protect his property from being destroyed. Through this friendship after the war Mr. Lefton learned of the Japanese porcelain factory owned by Kowa Toki K.K. From that point up until 1980 this factory produced thousands of pieces that were sold by the Lefton Company and bore the initials of "KW" before the item number. These items and the many whimsical pieces such as Bluebirds, Dainty Miss, Miss Priss, Cabbage Cutie, Mr. Toodles and the Dutch Girl line

Lefton Figural Book Ends

are eagerly collected today. As with most antiques and collectibles, prices vary depending on location, condition and availability. For additional information on the history of Lefton China, its factories, marks and products, readers should consult the Collector's Encyclopedia of Lefton China *by Loretta DeZozier (Collector Books, 1995).*

Bank, figural elf **$25.00**

Bank, Hubert the Lion **32.00**

Bank, figural mouse **20.00**

Book ends, figural, seated Chinese Boy & Girl, he playing a stringed musical instrument & she playing a flute, white glaze finish w/gold trim, No. 80164) 6" h., pr. (ILLUS. w/introduction) **180.00**

Busts, bisque, figural cherubs, each holding a bouquet of pink roses, white w/blonde hair & gold trim, pr. **90.00**

Classic Elegance Candy Dish

Candy dish, oval, open-handled, Classic Elegance patt., h.p. floral & gold decoration, No. 4808, 8½" l. (ILLUS.) **38.00**

Compote, open, Elegant Rose patt., No. 938, pedestal w/model of a woman's hand w/painted nails, a ring & a rose at the wrist, sponged gold trim on the scalloped rim **60.00**

Cookie jar, cov., figural Bluebird **255.00**

Cookie jar, cov., figural Dutch Girl **275.00**

Cookie jar, cov., figural Little Lady w/blonde hair **135.00**

Cookie jar, cov., figural Little Lady w/grey hair **325.00**

Cookie jar, cov., figural Pig Waitress **175.00**

Cookie jar, cov., figural Mr. Toodles **285.00**

Creamer, figural Dutch Girl **35.00**

Creamer, figural Miss Priss **45.00**

Creamer, figural Thumbelina........**30.00**

Creamer & cov. sugar bowl, Prayer Lady, pink, pr. **150.00**

Decanter, figural Santa Claus, 8" h. **75.00**

Ewer with Applied Rose

Ewer, pink w/large applied yellow rose & ornate handle & trim at neck & base, sponged gold trim, No. 906, 6" h. (ILLUS.) **55.00**

Figurine, Graduate.......................**20.00**

Figurine, Victorian Lady...............**65.00**

Lefton Dancing Couple

Figurines, a dancing girl & boy, each holding a flower, fine pastel painting & applied flowers, round base, No. 4140, 7" h., pr. (ILLUS.)..........................**95.00**

Figurines, Irish boy & girl, pr.........**30.00**

Figurines, Siamese Dancers, white glaze, trimmed w/gold & rhinestones, No. 493, 6½" h., pr. **95.00**

Figurines, three angels playing musical instruments, sitting in delicately detailed pastel flowers, hand applied decoration, No. 1699, 3¼" h., set of 3......................................**120.00**

Lamp with Roses

Lamp, kerosene-type, ovoid chimney tapering to flared pinched rim, bulbous spherical body on cylindrical standard w/domed flaring foot, decorated w/h.p. roses on white ground, gold trim, No. 931, 13½" h. (ILLUS.) **105.00**

Mug, figural Young Lady Head......**60.00**

Lefton Picture Frame

Picture frame, oval, bisque, irregular-shaped border decorated w/ applied roses & gold trim, on white ground, figural cherub applied to each foot, No. 7221, 7¼" h. (ILLUS.) ...**60.00**

Planter, figural rotary telephone **14.00**

Planter, Prayer Lady **165.00**

Salt & pepper shakers, figural Comical Boy & Girl, No. 1646, 4" h., pr. **22.00**

Salt & pepper shakers, figural elf, green, pr. **45.00**

Salt & pepper shakers, figural Miss Cutie Pie, pr. **30.00**

Salt & pepper shakers, figural Thumbelina, pr. **45.00**

Spoon rest, figural bluebird (minor flakes).............................**30.00**

Spoon rest, Mammy, nodder-type **125.00**

Sugar bowl, cov., figural Thumbelina................................**38.00**

Vase, 5" h., china, model of a lyre, decorated w/sponged gold trim & relief-molded pink roses, white ground, No. 955 ....**85.00**

Vase, 6" h., figural bluebird............**75.00**

Vase, 7" h., molded hands on body w/ applied roses & sponged gold trim, No. 280 ....**75.00**

Vases, model of a calla lily w/leaf base decorated w/ applied roses & gold trim, gold sponging on edge of flower, white ground, No. 7093, 8" h., pr. **195.00**

Wall plaques, figural mermaids, pr. **55.00**

Figural Boy with Basket Wall Pocket

Wall pocket, figural boy dressed in black coat & hat, stripped pants carrying a basket w/pink bow on handle, No. 1618, 7" h. (ILLUS.) **95.00**

Wall pocket, figural cat's head......**45.00**

Wall pocket, figural elf **135.00**

Wall pocket, figural girl head **110.00**

Wall pocket, full figure little girl ...**125.00**

Wall pockets, model of a cardinal, pr................................**75.00**

LIMOGES

Numerous factories produced china in Limoges, France, with major production in the 19th century. Some pieces listed below are identified by the name of the maker or are identified by the name of the maker or the mark of the factory. Although the famed Haviland Company was located in Limoges, wares bearing their marks are not included in this listing.

An excellent reference is The Collector's Encyclopedia of Limoges Porcelain, Second Edition, *by Mary Frank Gaston (Collector Books, 1992).*

Berry set: master berry bowl & five small sauce dishes; h.p. decoration, artist-signed, 6 pcs....................................**$225.00**

Bowl, 11½" d., decorated w/h.p. grapes & leaves........................**303.00**

Box, cov., pate-sur-pate, winged girl w/flowers on cobalt, artist-signed, Barbotine (bottom hairline)..**95.00**

Centerpiece, 12" w. octagon-shaped bowl on a separate base w/four gold legs, interior & exterior decorated w/h.p. peaches, 2 pcs. **495.00**

Cup & attached saucer, miniature, decorated w/h.p. flowers, ca. 1896-1900, 1 x 1½"..**60.00**

Dresser set: slightly dished 11" l. oval tray, 3½" d. ring tree, 5¾" d. pin tray, 2¾" d. cov. box & a 5¾" h. lobed, baluster-form candlestick; each piece in white decorated w/purple lilac cluster transfers & gilt trim, the set........**160.00**

Ewer, decorated w/raised gold flowers on beige ground, ca. 1892, 5" h. **125.00**

Fish set: oval platter & eight plates; h.p. fish, 9 pcs...............**750.00**

Game plate, pierced for hanging, h.p. scene of large colorful duck in flight, natural foliage & water in background, scroll-molded gilt rim band, artist-signed, 11¼" d. **225.00**

Game plates, h.p. scene of facing pr. of pheasants on one & pr. of quail on the other, pastel background w/leaves & berries, heavy gold scalloped edges, marked Limoges, pr. (ILLUS. top next page) **225.00**

Game plates, h.p. pheasant on one & a duck in flight on the other, artist-signed, pr. **83.00**

Limoges Game Plates

Ice cream set: 9¼" tray & ten 6½ x 8" dishes; each piece w/ornate scroll & scalloped gilt borders w/blue forget-me-nots & pink rosebuds around the borders, molded end handles on the tray & small central oval gilt & floral medallion, the set (ILLUS. of tray) **425.00**

Pitcher, tankard, 15" h., h.p. grapes & leaves decoration **385.00**

Plate, 9¾" d., a center h.p. scene of an older bearded man sitting by a window, wearing a work apron & examining an artwork or music, the wide border w/a gently scalloped rim in dark cobalt blue w/delicate gilt scrolls & three oval reserves w/a white ground decorated w/a bar of music or flowers & scrolls, artist-signed (ILLUS.) **165.00**

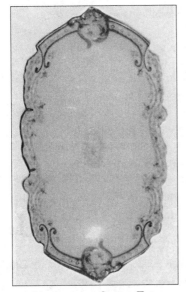

Limoges Ice Cream Tray

Limoges Portrait Plate

Plate, 10¼" d., pierced to hang, round w/ornate molded scroll gilt border band, h.p. w/a large cluster of fruits & leaves including purple grapes, peaches & berries, artist-signed, marked **135.00**

Plate, 12¼" d., heavy gold irregular border, h.p. country scene w/grassy meadow, small pond & trees & lady tending seven sheep, small church in background, marked Limoges ...**195.00**

Large Limoges Plate with Peaches

Plate, 12⅞" d., pierced for hanging, pastel background w/six h.p. peaches & green leaves hanging from branches, heavy gold irregular border & gold highlighting on branches & leaves, green Limoges mark (ILLUS.) **265.00**

Limoges Plates with Fisherman

Plates, pierced for hanging, dull Roman gold scroll-molded borders, detailed colorful h.p. woodland scene w/fisherman & lady on one, hunter, dog & lady on the other, 13¾" d., pr. (ILLUS. of one) **450.00**

Punch set: 13" d., 6" h. punch bowl on round 16" d. tray w/five matching footed cups; decorated w/h.p. purple berries, 7 pcs. **795.00**

Rose bowl, footed, white moriage slipwork, jewelling on turquoise ground, 5¾" h. **250.00**

Vase, 12" h., footed tapering cylindrical body w/short trumpet-form rim, h.p. red roses, green & brown leaves, multicolored ground, wide gold band around shoulder, neck & rim.................**125.00**

LLADRO

Spain's famed Lladro porcelain manufactory creates both limited and non-limited edition figurines as well as other porcelains. The classic simple beauty of the figures and their subdued coloring makes them readily recognizable and they have an enthusiastic following of collectors.

Aggressive Goose, No. 1288, 8¼" h. **$475.00**

Angels Ornaments, miniature, No. 1604, 2" h., 1988, set of 3.....................................**189.00**

Angel Tree Topper Green, No. 5875, 7¼" h..........................**75.00**

Boy with Double Bass, No. 4615, 8½" h. ....**325.00 to 375.00**

Clown, lying on stomach, No. 4618, 6¼" l. ....**225.00 to 250.00**

Coquette, No. 5599, 8¼" h. **108.00**

Comforting Daughter, No. 5142, 10½" h. **295.00**

Donkey in Love, No. 4524, 5" h. **298.00**

Don Quixote, No. 1030, 14½" h. **1,000.00**

Exam Day, No. 5250, 7¾" h. **175.00**

Faithful Steed, No. 5769,
6¾" h. **275.00**

Freedom, No. 5602, 12¼" h.,
limited edition ....**750.00 to 950.00**

Girl with Crossed Arms,
No. 2093, 8" h............................**110.00**

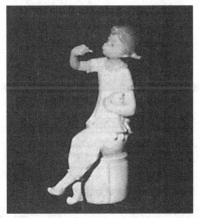

Lladro Girl with Doll

Girl with Doll, No. 1083, 7" h.
(ILLUS.) **250.00**

Girl with Lamb, No. 1010,
8½" h. **180.00**

Happy Birthday, No. 5429,
8¼" h. **93.00**

Lady with Greyhound, No. 4594,
13" h. **895.00**

Little Girl with Cat, No. 1187,
8¼" h. **175.00**

Little Pals, No. S-7600.............**2,200.00**

Musketeer, No. 2059,
27¼" h.....................................**1,000.00**

My Buddy, No. S-7601 ....**350.00**

On the Move, No. 5838, 11" h. ...**237.00**

Pondering, No. 5173, 6½" h. **495.00**

School Days, No. 7604, 1988,
8¼" h. **475.00**

Spring Token, No. 5604,
8½" h. **138.00**

Summer, No. 5219, 7¾" h..........**111.00**

Teresa, No. 5411, 6" h.
(matte finish) **275.00**

Time to Rest (A), No. 5391,
4¾" h. **220.00**

Traveling Artist, No. 5661,
11¼" h. **290.00**

MAJOLICA

Majolica, a tin-enameled glazed pottery, has been produced for centuries. It originally took its name from the island of Majorca, a source of figuline (potter's clay). Subsequently it was widely produced in England, Europe and the United States. Etruscan majolica, now avidly sought, was made by Griffen, Smith & Hill, Phoenixville, Pa., in the last quarter of the 19th century. Most majolica advertised today is 19th or 20th century. Once scorned by most collectors, interest in this colorful ware so popular during the Victorian era has now revived and prices have risen dramatically in the past few years. Also see WEDGWOOD.

Majolica Etruscan Mark

ETRUSCAN

Butter pat, decorated w/lavender,
blue, yellow & pink ribbon in
circles, blue Morning Glories ...**$130.00**

Cake stand, Shell & Seaweed
patt., 9" h. **2,000.00**

Etruscan Cauliflower Pattern Tea Set

Tea set: cov. teapot, cov. sugar
bowl, creamer & 8" d. plate;
Cauliflower patt., small chips,
the set (ILLUS.) **578.00**

GENERAL

Bowl, 8½" w., 4" h., octagonal, &
4 matching 8" plates, h.p.
decoration w/gold & red apples
& leaves, Germany, 5 pcs. **120.00**

Cigar/match caddy, Town Crier
decoration...................................**95.00**

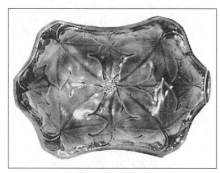

Majolica Leaf Dish

Dish, leaf pattern on basket
ground, Wedgwood, England,
7¼ x 10½" (ILLUS.) **305.00**

Minton Game Dish

Game dish, cov., two-handled,
large relief-molded hare &
mallard duck lying atop ferns &
leaves on cover, the sides
decorated w/green oak leaves
against a brown basketweave
ground, small, Minton, England
(ILLUS.) **2,530.00**

Humidor, cov., figural bust of a
bowler, blue & white, 6" h. **295.00**

Humidor, cov., figural Arab head,
6½" h. **375.00**

Match holder, oblong angled
base w/match striking bands

Tragedy and Comedy Match Holder

along the sides, the tapering
oval body molded at one end
w/a mask of Tragedy & at the
other w/a mask of Comedy,
decorated w/pale blue & golden
yellow (ILLUS.) **770.00**

Match holder, oval base,
turquoise w/white storks
decoration, artist-signed **75.00**

Oyster plate, Wedgwood, 7" d....**285.00**

Pitcher, 6" h., pansy decoration ..**175.00**

Pitcher, 7" h., pale bluish green
ground w/ four exterior panels &
red flowers, green leaves, brown
interior & handle **155.00**

Pitcher, jug-type, 7½" h., figural
Pug dog **245.00**

Pitcher, 7¾" h., bamboo, fern leaf
& cattail decoration, English
Registry dated "1/21/1878".......**375.00**

Pitcher, 8¼" h., cylindrical body
tapering to slightly flared rim,
decorated w/fern fronds in
shaded green, brown & pink,
blue ground w/pink interior,
applied handle (hairline down
one side)...................................**250.00**

Pitcher, 8½" h., gargoyle-
spouted, relief-molded drinking
scene decoration, France..........**195.00**

Pitcher, 9" h, model of a fish
w/the tail up forming the handle,
mouth forms spout, colored
exterior, pink interior, possibly
American, late 19th c.................**225.00**

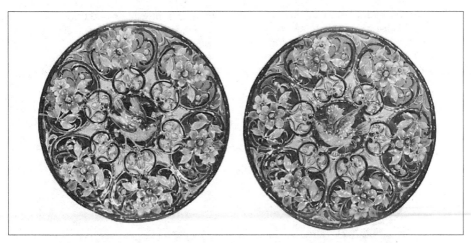

Majolica Plaques

Pitcher, 9½" h., wild roses on a brown tree bark ground, branch handle......................................**300.00**

Pitcher, cov., jug-type, 13" h., waisted cylindrical body decorated w/molded castle wall & relief-molded figures of dancing villages in medieval dress, grape leaf & branch decoration border around base & below rim w/branch handle, court jester finial on cover, ca. 1873, chip to cover thumb rest, spout rim, impressed marks, Minton, England **1,035.00**

Plaques, round, pierced for hanging, center decoration of birds facing each other surrounded by brightly colored flowers & openwork, mark not recognizable, probably French, 13" d., pr. (ILLUS.).....................**615.00**

Plate, 8⅜" d., decorated w/flowers in pink, green & white on a brown basketweave ground **61.00**

Plate, 9" d., Cauliflower patt. **160.00**

Plate, 9¼" d., yellow diamond design w/green foliage & brown trim **116.00**

Majolica Spoon Holder

Spoon holder, egg-shaped, decorated w/cattails & green leaves & laying horizontally on a relief-molded leafy irregular-shaped base, Brown, Westhead & Moore & Co. (ILLUS.) **1,210.00**

Vase, 9" h., scene of bird in flight **100.00**

Vase, figural, lady standing by large tree trunk **175.00**

MARBLEHEAD POTTERY

This pottery was organized in 1904 by Dr. Herbert J. Hall as a therapeutic aid to patients in a sanitarium he ran in Marblehead, Massachusetts. It was later separated from the sanitarium and directed by Arthur E. Baggs, a fine artist and designer, who bought out the factory in 1916 and operated it until its closing in 1936. Most wares were hand-thrown and decorated and carry the company mark of a stylized sailing vessel flanked by the letters "M" and "P."

Marblehead Pottery Mark

Tile, square, molded decoration of a sailing ship under full sail in white against a blue background, in a wide flat oak frame, tile 6½" w. **$385.00**

Vase, 3½" h., simple ovoid body w/a flat closed rim, opaque mustard yellow matte glaze, white interior, impressed mark **242.00**

Small Marblehead Vase

Vase, 3½" h., wide ovoid body tapering slightly to a wide rolled mouth, decorated w/stylized mustard yellow blossoms w/blue centers atop brown branches w/grey & green leaves against a rich tan background, artist-initialed (ILLUS.) **1,045.00**

Vase, 3½" h., wide ovoid body tapering slightly to a wide rolled mouth, matte dark green highlighting on yellow over pale rose, unsigned **173.00**

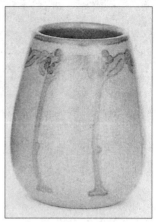

Marblehead Vase

Vase, 4½" h., 3½" d., simple ovoid body tapering slightly to a flat rim, surface-decorated w/a band of stylized green leaves, blueberries & brown stems on a mustard yellow matte ground, impressed mark (ILLUS.) **2,530.00**

Vase, 5½" h., broad circular base supports a narrow cylindrical neck, covered in a grey mottled matte glaze, oval paper labels...**209.00**

Vase, 7" h., swollen cylindrical form w/carved & painted decoration of stylized vertical stems supporting narrow overlapping leaves & berries in matte dark green glaze on green ground, artist's incised initials, tight hairline, impressed mark **1,760.00**

Vase, 7½" h., gently tapering cylindrical body w/a wide flat closed mouth, rich lavender matte glaze, impressed mark (hairline) **154.00**

Vase, 7½" h., simple cylindrical body, medium green flecked matte glaze, impressed mark (base chip)................................**220.00**

MC COY

Collectors are now seeking the art wares of two McCoy potteries. One was founded in Roseville, Ohio, in the late 19th century as the J.W. McCoy Pottery, subsequently becoming Brush-McCoy Pottery Co., later Brush Pottery. The other was founded also in Roseville in 1910 as Nelson McCoy Sanitary Stoneware Co., later becoming Nelson McCoy Pottery. In 1967 the pottery was sold to D.T. Chase of the Mount Clemens Pottery Co. who sold his interest to the Lancaster Colony Corp. in 1974. The pottery shop closed in 1985. Cookie jars are especially collectible today.

A helpful reference book is The Collector's Encyclopedia of McCoy Pottery, *by the Huxfords (Collector Books), and* McCoy Cookie Jars From the First to the Latest, *by Harold Nichols (Nichols Publishing, 1987).*

McCoy Mark

Coffee server w/warmer, El Rancho Bar-B-Que line, ca. 1960s, 2 pcs. **$75.00**

Cookie jar, Old Fashioned Auto (Touring Car), 1962-64 ....**125.00 to 225.00**

Cookie jar, Rocking Chair (Dalmatians), 1961....**325.00 to 375.00**

Dresser caddy, model of a buffalo, brown glaze, produced for Swank Company, 10" l., 5½" h. **45.00**

Iced tea server, barrel-shaped, El Rancho Bar-B-Que line, ca. 1960s ....**150.00 to 200.00**

Jardiniere, bulbous ovoid body w/molded rim, floral decoration, marked "Loy-Nel-Art," 4" h.........**125.00**

Jardiniere, squatty bulbous body w/embossed butterfly decoration, yellow, mark No. 1 (1940) **25.00**

Oil jar, wide ovoid body tapering to a wide rolled rim flanked by small loop strap handles, maroon glaze, 12" h. **125.00**

Planter, the sides modeled as a spread-winged butterfly, green, ca. 1940......................................**60.00**

Planter, figural, Plow boy on horseback by watering trough, dark green & brown glaze, mark No. 7, 1955 ....**85.00**

Planter, figural poodle, standing w/head up & wearing leash, 7½" l., 7½" h., 1956 ....**45.00**

McCoy Swan Planter

Planter, model of a swan, ivory glaze w/brown eyes, orange beak, green outlined leaves on rectangular base, 6½" h., 6½" l., mark No. 4 (ILLUS.) **40.00**

Planter, figural, two quail & baby quail on base w/foliage background, natural colors, mark No. 7, ca. 1955 ....**45.00**

Planter, model of a Wishing Well, mark No. 7, ca. 1950 ....**19.00**

Planter, figural, Pussy at the well, 1956, 7 x 7" **85.00**

Soup tureen, El Rancho Bar-B-Que line, ca. 1960s, 5 qt. **100.00**

Sugar bowl, cov., Pine Cone patt., mark No. 4, 1956................**20.00**

Tea set: cov. teapot, creamer & open sugar bowl; Pine Cone patt., mark No. 4, 1956, 3 pcs. **70.00**

Vase, 5½" h., 7½" w., figural, the sides modeled as a spread-winged butterfly, white glaze, marked "USA"..............................**35.00**

Vase, 6½" h., Wild Rose line, yellow, 1952 (small petal chip) **25.00**

Vase, embossed butterfly decoration, blue, No. 2, ca. 1940 (small nick) **60.00**

Vase, fan-shaped, relief-molded dark green leaves & stem-shaped base handle, chartreuse ground, mark No. 7, ca. 1954....**125.00**

Wall pocket, Blossomtime line, yellow, 1946, 8" h. **80.00**

Wall pocket, leaf-shaped, mark No. 4, ca. 1950 ....**50.00**

Wall pocket, model of a diaper, blue, No. 837 ....**35.00**

MEISSEN

The secret of true hard paste porcelain, known long before to the Chinese, was "discovered" accidentally in Meissen, Germany, by J.F. Bottger, an alchemist working with E.W. Tschirnhausen. The first European true porcelain was made in the Meissen Porcelain Works, organized about 1709. Meissen marks have been widely copied by other factories. Some pieces listed here are recent.

Meissen Mark

Bowl, 11¾" d., shallow, decorated w/polychrome flowers & gilt trim, crossed swords mark **$237.00**

Centerpiece, squatty bulbous oval form w/scenic medallion & floral decoration in reserves around sides, ornate scrolled rim & raised on four ornate scrolled legs, ca. 1881, Crown over D mark, 8½ x 10¼", 6⅜" h. (small amount of restoration around top border)......................................**700.00**

Centerpiece, center bouquet decoration & gilt embossed roses, crossed swords under glaze, 12" d..............................**850.00**

Centerpiece, a tree-form standard flanked by a lady & gentleman in 18th c. attire supporting a deep oval scroll-pierced bowl w/flaring, scalloped rim, all raised on a high scroll-molded footed base, the bowl trimmed in gilt, the standard & base all trimmed in dark rose pink, crossed swords mark in blue enamel, late 19th c., 23¾" h. **4,600.00**

Clock, mantel-type, the cobalt blue-painted & gilded bombé molded case molded in high-relief w/foliage & raised on scrolled feet, the dial surrounded by two cupids, each holding garlands of flowers, ca. 1880-1900, 13 1/8" h. **4,600.00**

Compote, white w/worn gold & blue, crossed swords mark, 12½" d., 6½" h. **83.00**

Dinner service for twelve, Blue Onion patt., the set **4,750.00**

Meissen Ewer

Ewer, applied w/pan playing the pipes & Diana the Huntress, the body decorated w/dogs hunting boar, bear & stag in an extensive landscape, the base w/a putto digging in the soil w/an applied sheaf of wheat-form handle surmounted by a putto w/a basket of fruit, crossed swords mark in underglaze blue, 19th c., 25" h. (ILLUS. previous page).......................**4,950.00**

Figure, allegorical, a representation of Knowledge w/a robed female figure reading from a book, leaning on a pedestal supporting a globe & a stack of books, at her feet an owl, a pipe & a magnifying glass, all raised on a rockwork base, blue underglaze crossed swords mark, late 19th c., 18" h. **4,950.00**

Figure of a jester, in a dancing pose wearing a colorful outfit, early 20th c., marked, 6" h.........**978.00**

Figure of a lady, purple bodice, green striped & floral shirt, yellow collar & white apron, carrying covered tray on top of her head, holding a clam shell in her hand, gold trim around base, underglaze blue crossed swords mark, 6¼" h. **450.00**

Figure of a small girl, placing china doll in colorful red-wheeled doll carriage, colorful blanket & pillow incised numbers, crossed sword mark ..**750.00**

Figure of a youth, standing next to a tree stump topped by a next of eggs set in his hat, 19th c., 7½" h. **633.00**

Figures, one of putto watering flowers in columnar stand, the other of seated putto w/flowers in sack, each w/inscribed base, one inscribed "Te blesse et soulage," the other "Te decouvre tout," factory marks, late 19th c., 5¼" h., pr. **1,035.00**

Figures, a courtly gentleman in 18th c. costume leaning on a scrolled pedestal & holding a small basket of flowers in one hand & holding out a bouquet of flowers w/the other, a standing lady in 18th c. country attire wearing a tri-corner hat, floral-decorated bodice & underskirt & plain folding overskirt, each on a square, scroll-molded base, 19th c., 19" h., pr. **5,750.00**

Figure group, mother & child, the mother in a lavender dress & white apron bending down & guiding her toddling child as he learns to walk, on an oval base, modeled by Schreitmueller, underglaze-blue cross swords mark, impressed "115" & "R169," early 20th c., 7" h...................**2,070.00**

Figure group, two children & a goat, the boy standing wearing a tricorn hat, coat, waistcoat & kneebreeches & playing a flute, the girl seated on the recumbent goat wearing a long flowered dress & holding a bouquet of flowers, on a oval plinth base w/a molded lappet band, early 20th c., factory marks, 6⅛" h. **1,035.00**

Figure group, a shepherd & a shepherdess, both seated barefoot on a rocky base, accompanied by a sheep, she w/a basket of grapes which she feeds to her companion, underglaze-blue crossed swords mark & black-painted numerals, early 20th c., 8¼" h................**1,150.00**

Figure group, allegorical, representing Summer & Fall, one a female cherub on a sheaf of wheat, the other a male cherub w/a bunch of grapes & a goat, on a rockwork base, polychrome decoration, underglaze-blue crossed swords mark, incised "1230," 19th c., 7" l., 9" h. **2,860.00**

Model of a bird, mottled brown body standing on a leafy base, early 19th c., 8" h.......................**575.00**

Model of a bird, the long-billed bird perched on a leafy tree stump w/its head turned, 20th c., 8¾" h. (ILLUS. below, left).........**863.00**

Plate, 10⅛" d., scalloped rim w/a relief-molded gold vine & gold & white double leaves & purple berries running down the center, molded gold leaves & purple berry clusters on each side, dark blue border band, ca. 1760-80 ..**325.00**

Potpourri urn, cover & stand, the large baluster form decorated w/a central scene of a gentleman in 18th c. costume serenading two ladies in a forest setting, the opposite side decorated w/a floral spray, the overall body encrusted w/finely detailed flowers, fruit & insects w/an applied figure of a woman w/a basket of flowers at the scroll-molded base, a figure of a winged putto amid flowers on one side of the body, the stand similarly decorated & the domed cover w/a very tall floral bouquet finial, blue crossed swords mark, vase impressed "109" & enameled "20," late 19th c., overall 36" h..........................**25,300.00**

Soup plate w/flanged rim, Blue Onion patt. **115.00**

Sweetmeat dish, figural, a seated Chinese man wearing a pointed hat & flower sprig-

decorated robe holds a deep shell-shaped dish in front, 20th c., 7½" h. (ILLUS. right) **1,495.00**

Tazza, Indian Flower patt., magenta, blue crossed swords mark, 4½ x 12½" **495.00**

Toothpick holder, Red Dragon patt. **250.00**

METLOX POTTERIES

Metlox Potteries was established in 1927 in Manhattan Beach, California. In 1932, dinnerware was introduced and within two years a complete line of Poppytrail was available. Carl Romanelli joined Metlox as an artware designer and became well-known for his miniature animals and novelties. However, it is the Romanelli figurines, especially nudes and nudes with vases, that are eagerly sought by collectors. After World War II, Evan K. Shaw bought Metlox and dinnerware became a staple for the success of the business. Poppets by Popptrail are piquing the interest of collectors in today's market. They are stoneware flower-holders and planters created in doll-like fashion by Helen Slater. Metlox produced them during the 1960s and 1970s. The shelf sitters and the individual Salvation Army band figures are among the most popular. In 1989, Metlox ceased operations.

METLOX
MADE IN
U. S. A.
Incised or stamped mark

C Romanelli

Carl Romanelli's name found on the base rim of nudes and certain vases.

Miniatures
by METLOX
MANHATTAN BEACH
CALIFORNIA
Paper label in blue on silver.

Meissen Bird & Figural Sweetmeat Dish

Ashtray, California Provincial
patt., 8¼" d. **$65.00**

Ashtray, California Provincial
patt., 10" d. **95.00**

Bowl, soup, 5" d., lug handle,
California Provincial patt.............**25.00**

Bowl, soup, 5" d., lug handle,
Homestead Provincial patt. **22.00**

Bowl, fruit, 5⅜" d., California
Strawberry patt. **10.00**

Bowl, fruit, 6" d., Homestead
Provincial patt., green trim.............**7.00**

Bowl, fruit, 6" d., Provincial Blue
patt. **16.00**

Bowl, fruit, 6" d., Red Rooster
Provincial patt. **7.00**

Bowl, fruit, 6" d., Sculptured
Daisy patt. **12.00**

Bowl, fruit, 6⅜" d., Sculptured
Zinnia patt....................................**6.00**

Bowl, soup, individual, 6¾" d., lug
handles, California Strawberry
patt. **15.00**

Bowl, soup, 6¾" d., California
Strawberry patt. **15.00**

Bowl, cereal, 7" d., Sculptured
Daisy patt. **12.00**

Bowl, 7⅛" d., Red Rooster
Provincial patt.............................**14.00**

Bowl, cereal, 7⅜" d., Sculptured
Zinnia patt.....................................**9.00**

Bowl, low, 24" l., Mosaic patt.,
No. 378......................................**100.00**

Bowl, 3½ x 10 x 24", low, footed,
Tropicana patt. **225.00**

Bread server, Homestead
Provincial patt., 9½"....................**65.00**

Butter dish, cov., Provincial Blue
patt. **75.00**

Candlesticks, Homestead
Provincial patt., pr.......................**60.00**

Canister, cov., "Coffee,"
Homestead Provincial patt. **60.00**

Canister, cov., "Flour,"
Homestead Provincial patt. **80.00**

Canister set, flour, sugar, coffee
& tea, Homestead Provincial
patt., the set...............................**395.00**

Canister set, flour, sugar, coffee
& tea, Provincial Blue patt.,
the set...**395.00**

Canister set, flour, sugar, coffee
& tea, Red Rooster patt.,
the set...**195.00**

Casserole, cov., handled,
Sculptured Daisy patt. 8" d. **85.00**

Casserole, cov., Rooster patt.,
1½ qt. **125.00**

Casserole, cov., handled,
Sculptured Daisy patt. 1½ qt. **90.00**

Coaster, California Provincial
patt., 3¾" d. **22.00**

Coaster, Homestead
Provincial patt.............................**9.00**

Coffeepot, cov., Homestead
Provincial patt., 7 cup **125.00**

Coffeepot, cov., Poppytrail
Gourmetware line,
Flamenco Red **65.00**

Coffeepot, cov., Vernon Della
Robia patt., 8 cup **100.00**

Coffee set: cov. coffeepot,
creamer & cov. sugar bowl; Red
Rooster patt., 3 pcs.
(no rooster)................................**55.00**

Cookie jar, Blue Bird on Stump,
unglazed version **300.00**

Cookie jar, Chicken
(Mother Hen) **95.00**

Cookie jar, Clown, white w/blue
buttons ....**150.00 to 200.00**

Cookie jar, Clown, yellow **90.00**

Cookie jar, Cow-Painted Rex
(Tyrannosaurus Rex).............**1,200.00**

Cookie jar, Cow w/Butterfly,
purple ....**450.00 to 550.00**

Cookie jar, Dinosaur, "Dino" **125.00**

Cookie jar, Downey
Woodpecker **425.00**

Cookie jar, Dutch Boy................**200.00**

Cookie jar,
Egg Basket...............**150.00 to 200.00**

Francine Duck Cookie Jar

Cookie jar, Francine Duck
(ILLUS.) **95.00**

Cookie jar, Frog **125.00**

Cookie jar, Grapes......................**250.00**

Cookie jar, Hippopotamus,
"Bubbles," grey..........**550.00 to 600.00**

Little Pig Cookie Jar

Cookie jar, Little Pig (ILLUS.) **195.00**

Cookie jar, Little Piggy
w/designs **175.00**

Cookie jar, Little Red
Riding Hood............................**2,000.00**

Cookie jar,
Mother Goose ....**300.00 to 350.00**

Cookie jar, Mrs. Rabbit **195.00**

Cookie jar, Penguin, black tie **265.00**

Cookie jar, Pinocchio..................**350.00**

Cookie jar, Pretty Ann.................**200.00**

Cookie jar, Puddles ....**35.00 to 40.00**

Cookie jar, Raccoon Cookie
Bandit **120.00**

Cookie jar, Rag Doll Boy **195.00**

Cookie jar, Rag Doll Girl **125.00**

Cookie jar, Raggedy Andy..........**125.00**

Cookie jar, Raggedy Ann............**140.00**

Cookie jar, Red Rooster patt. **75.00**

Cookie jar, Rooster,
multicolored **300.00**

Cookie jar, Schoolhouse..........**1,100.00**

Cookie jar, Sombrero
(Pancho) Bear **130.00**

Cookie jar, Squirrel on
Pine Cone..................................**125.00**

Cookie jar, Teddy Bear................**45.00**

Cookie jar, Topsy, blue (one tiny
nick on back) **360.00**

Creamer, California Ivy patt. **12.00**

Creamer, California
Strawberry patt. **15.00**

Creamer, Homestead Provincial
patt. w/green trim..........................**9.00**

Creamer, Sculptured Daisy patt. ...**22.00**

Cup & saucer, California
Ivy patt......................................**12.00**

Cup & saucer, Homestead
Provincial patt., green trim.............**8.00**

Cup & saucer, Red Rooster patt.
(no rooster) **8.00**

Cup & saucer, Sculptured
Zinnia patt..................................**10.00**

Dinner service, Antique Grape
patt., assorted pieces including
cov. teapot, 45 pcs. **350.00**

Dish, cov., hen on nest,
Homestead Provincial patt. **125.00**

Dower chest, Homestead
Provincial patt. **215.00**

Egg cup, Provincial Blue patt. **50.00**

Figure of a woman, standing on
a stylized ovoid base, back
arched w/left leg stretched out
behind her & right leg forward
w/knee bent & right foot

Metlox Figure of a Woman

disappearing into plant w/leaves on the base, arms stretched upward holding two birds above her head, long hair cascading behind her & to the base in front of left foot, satin ivory glaze, "C. Romanelli" incised on edge of base & "Poppytrail 1825 C. Romanelli Made in California U.S.A.," on bottom, 10¾" h. (ILLUS.) **285.00**

Poppets "Nick" Figure

Figure, Poppets series, "Nick," organ grinder w/monkey, Nick w/yellow hat & scarf around neck, blue shirt, monkey w/blue hat & white vest, Model No. 649, 6½" h. (ILLUS.) **60.00**

Flowerpot, angel fish decoration ..**45.00**

Gravy boat, Homestead Provincial, green trim, 1 pt...........**45.00**

Gravy boat, Provincial Blue patt., 1 pt. **65.00**

Gravy bowl w/attached underplate, Sculptured Daisy patt. **40.00**

Model of a bird on a branch, Miniature Series, 4 5/8" h. **55.00**

Model of a Scottie dog, Miniature Series **55.00**

Model of a fawn, 5½" h................**50.00**

Models of Clydesdale horse, 9 x 9", pr. **350.00**

Mug, California Provincial patt., 8 oz..**42.00**

Mug, beer, Homestead Provincial patt. **15.00**

Mug, Homestead Provincial patt., 1 pt. **32.00**

Mustard jar, cov., Homestead Provincial patt............................**35.00**

Pickle dish, oval, California Ivy patt., 9¼" l. **22.00**

Pitcher, milk, Homestead Provincial patt., 1 qt. **85.00**

Pitcher, water, California Provincial patt., 2¼ qt. **225.00**

Planter, model of a seal w/two front flippers hugging a round planter, pale blue satin matte, Model No. 456, 5¼" h. **18.00**

Planter, model of a spice box, Homestead Provincial patt. **55.00**

Plate, bread & butter, 6½" d., California Ivy patt.........................**4.00**

Plate, bread & butter, 6¼" d., Sculptured Daisy patt. **8.00**

Plate, bread & butter, 6⅜" d., Homestead Provincial patt **8.00**

Plate, bread & butter, 6⅜" d.,
California Strawberry patt. **7.00**

Plate, salad, 7½" d., Homestead
Provincial, green trim....................**6.00**

Plate, salad, 7½" d., Sculptured
Daisy patt. **10.00**

Plate, salad, 7½" d., Sculptured
Grape patt. **9.00**

Plate, salad, 7½" d., Sculptured
Zinnia patt......................................**7.00**

Plate, salad, 8" d., California
Strawberry patt. **10.00**

Plate, dinner, 10" d., California
Strawberry patt. **15.00**

Plate, dinner, 10" d., Homestead
Provincial patt. **15.00**

Plate, dinner, 10½" d., Sculptured
Daisy patt. **13.00**

Plate, dinner, 10½" d. Sculptured
Grape patt. **12.00**

Plate, dinner, 10½" d., Sculptured
Zinnia patt......................................**9.00**

Plate, buffet server, round,
California Ivy patt., 13½" d. **38.00**

Plate, chop, 13" d., California Ivy
patt. **22.00**

Plate, chop, Camellia patt.
w/brown trim, Prouty line **35.00**

Platter, oval, 11" l., Sculptured
Daisy patt. **40.00**

Platter, oval, 11" l., Sculptured
Zinnia patt......................................**30.00**

Platter, oval, 13" l., California
Ivy patt......................................**35.00**

Platter, 13" l., Provincial
Blue patt. **55.00**

Platter, 13½" l., Homestead patt. ..**55.00**

Platter, 13½" l., Homestead
Provincial, green trim...................**50.00**

Platter, 14½" l., Sculptured
Daisy patt. **45.00**

Platter, 14½" l., Sculptured
Grape patt. **40.00**

Platter, turkey, 22½" l., California
Provincial patt. **495.00**

Salad fork & spoon, Sculptured
Daisy patt., pr. **95.00**

Salt shaker, Red Rooster patt. **6.00**

Salt & pepper shakers,
Sculptured Grape patt., pr. **25.00**

Soup plate w/flanged rim,
Provincial Blue patt., 8" d. **35.00**

Soup plate w/flanged rim, Red
Rooster patt., 8" d.......................**16.00**

Soup tureen, cover & ladle,
Homestead Provincial patt.,
3 pcs...**695.00**

Spice box planter, hanging-type,
Homestead Provincial patt. **125.00**

Sugar bowl, cov., Gigi patt.,
Country French shape, footed
w/grooves in the shape,
4½" h. **22.00**

Sugar bowl, cov., Poppytrail
Gourmetware line,
Flamenco Red **20.00**

Sugar bowl, cov., Sculptured
Daisy patt. **30.00**

Sugar bowl, cov., Vernon Della
Robia patt. **28.00**

Teapot, cov., California Ivy patt.....**90.00**

Teapot, cov., Sculptured Daisy
patt. (tiny nick inside spout).........**95.00**

Vase, 17" h., teardrop-shaped,
Mosaic patt. **95.00**

Vase, 17" h., teardrop-shaped,
Tropicana patt., pineapple
decoration..................................**95.00**

Vegetable bowl, cov.,
Homestead Provincial,
10" d., 1 qt. **85.00**

Vegetable bowl, open, divided,
California Strawberry patt.,
9" d. **40.00**

Vegetable bowl, open, round,
Homestead Provincial, 10" d. **50.00**

Vegetable bowl, open, divided,
rectangular, Homestead
Provincial patt., 12" **60.00**

Vegetable bowl, open, divided,
rectangular, Provincial Blue
patt., 12" l. **65.00**

Vegetable bowl, open, divided, rectangular, Homestead Provincial patt., green trim, 12" l. **50.00**

Vegetable bowl, open, divided, rectangular w/stick handle, Red Rooster patt., 12" l. **32.00**

Vegetable bowl, open, Homestead Provincial patt. **45.00**

Vegetable bowl, open, Sculptured Daisy patt., 8" d. **75.00**

Vegetable bowl, open, Red Rooster patt., basket design, 8⅛" d. **25.00**

Vegetable bowl, open, Sculptured Grape patt., 8½" d. **18.00**

Vegetable bowl, open, Sculptured Zinnia patt., 8½" d. **20.00**

Vegetable bowl, open, Sculptured Grape patt., 9½" d. **27.00**

Vegetable bowl, open, Homestead Provincial patt., green trim, 10" d. **85.00**

Vegetable bowl, open, oval, divided, California Ivy patt., 11" l. **35.00**

MINTON

The Minton factory in England was established by Thomas Minton in 1793. The factory made earthenware, especially the blue-printed variety and Thomas Minton is sometimes credited with invention of the blue "Willow" pattern. For a time majolica and tiles were also an important part of production, but bone china soon became the principal ware. Mintons, Ltd., continues in operation today.

Minton Mark

Flask, pate-sur-pate, pilgrim-style, footed flattened moon-shape w/a short cylindrical neck

& rolled rim flanked by small loop handles to the shoulder, blue ground decorated in white slip w/an angel releasing cherubs from a sack, polychrome slip borders w/gold trim, artist-signed by Louis Solon, impressed printed mark, ca. 1870, 10¼" h. **$8,050.00**

Vase, 20" h., pate-sur-pate, wide classical baluster-form body raised on a stepped pedestal base & tapering to a ringed flaring neck flanked by curved handles to the shoulder, dark brown ground decorated in white slip on one side w/a central classical female figure w/an open book surrounded by three putti, the reverse w/numerous putti in poses of study at a long table, blue & green slip on the neck & base, artist-signed by Louis Solon, printed & impressed marks, ca. 1882 (cover missing, body repaired) **2,875.00**

Vase, 21" h., pate-sur-pate, classical baluster-form w/a short domed foot & slender neck w/flaring rim flanked by thin knotted handles to the shoulder, blue ground decorated in white slip on one side w/a classical female standing among putti, the reverse w/putti figures supporting a seated figure of Cupid, gilt trim on handles, neck & base, artist-signed by Louis Solon, printed & impressed factory marks, ca. 1892 (neck restored) **4,600.00**

Vases, 5¼" h., pate-sur-pate, pilgrim-form, flattened round discs on short squared legs, a short rolled mouth at the top, dark brownish black ground decorated in white slip w/groups of three putti framed by floral borders, artist monogram, possibly by Arthur Morgan,

Fine Minton Pate-Sur-Pate Vases

printed & impressed factory marks, late 19th c., pr. (chips to one foot of each) **2,990.00**

Vases, 7½" h., pate-sur-pate, slender ovoid body raised on a flaring foot & tapering to a rolled rim, leafy scroll gilt handles at the shoulders, brown ground decorated in white slip depicting cupid figures, one chained & one w/a broken chain, gilt trim at rim & foot, artist-signed by Louis Solon, printed factory marks, ca. 1895, pr. **5,463.00**

Vase, 14¾" h., pate-sur-pate, wide urn-form body raised on a short flaring pedestal base, the wide flattened shoulder mounted w/upright loop handles & centered by a short cylindrical neck w/a fitted low cover w/a disc finial, a dark brown background, the body decorated on one side w/three white slip classical maidens in various poses & each holding a lantern, the other side w/a white slip putti

holding torches in a cage, polychrome slip stylized foliate side panels & cover, gilt trim overall, artist-signed by Louis Solon, impressed & printed factory marks, retouched rim nicks, late 19th c. (ILLUS. center) **6,038.00**

Vases, 16¼" h., pate-sur-pate, gently swelled conical body raised on a ringed pedestal base, the angled shoulder w/a tapering swirled gadrooned neck w/a molded rim supporting a domed cover w/a molding, pointed finial, each w/a dark brown ground decorated w/white slip classical female figures surrounded by flying birds & putti, gilt-decorated laurel wreath shoulder handles, gilt decoration on neck & spiral foot, artist-signed by Louis Solon, ca. 1900, impressed & printed factory marks, handles chipped, covers restored, pr. (ILLUS. left & right) **6,325.00**

Various Mocha Pitchers & Bowls

MOCHA

Mocha decoration is found on basically utilitarian creamware or yellowware articles and is achieved by a simple chemical reaction. A color pigment of brown, blue, green or black is given an acid nature by infusion of tobacco or hops. When this acid nature colorant is applied in blobs to an alkaline ground color, it reacts by spreading in feathery seaweed designs. This type of decoration is usually accompanied by horizontal bands of light color slip. Produced in numerous Staffordshire potteries from the late 18th until the late 19th centuries, its name is derived from the similar markings found on mocha quartz. In addition to the seaweed decoration, mocha wares are also seen with Earthworm and Cat's Eye patterns or a marbleized effect.

Bowl or porringer, 5½" d., 2⅝" h., footed squatty bulbous body w/low cylindrical rim & applied leaftip handle, wide dark brown center band w/white spots flanked by blue & white stripes, hairline & chips (ILLUS. top row, center) **$715.00**

Creamer & similar underplate, jug-form creamer w/leaftip handle, both pieces w/a pinkish beige ground decorated w/large black seaweed decoration, stains, hairlines & small chips, creamer 4⅛" h., 2 pcs. (ILLUS. middle row, second from right) **1,265.00**

Pitcher, jug-type, 5⅛" h., D-form leaftip handle, decorated w/a wide tan band divided in the center by two double white bands & incised & tooled green bands, a large zigzagging band of Earthworm patt. in blue, white & dark brown around the body, thin dark brown bands around the top & base, chips, hairline & professional repair (ILLUS. middle row, far right).................**550.00**

Pitcher, jug-type, 5⅝" h., a wide tan center band decorated w/Earthworm patt. in light blue, tan, white & dark brown, three narrow dark & tan stripes at the top & base, professional repair (ILLUS. middle row, far left).......**715.00**

Pitcher, jug-type, 6⅛" h., footed bulbous ovoid body tapering to a tall waisted neck w/rim spout, D-form leaftip handle, wide light brown central band decorated w/a bold Earthworm patt. in blue, white, tan & dark brown, flanked by light brown, dark brown & white stripes & a dark brown neck, wear, small flakes, professional repair (ILLUS. previous page, middle row, second from left) **1,485.00**

Pitcher, jug-type, 6⅝" h., wide center dark brown band decorated w/a double-looping Earthworm patt. in brown, blue & white, tooled blue bands & narrow dark brown bands at the top & base, chips, hairlines, stain in bottom (ILLUS. previous page, bottom row, center) **1,925.00**

Pitcher, jug-type, 7⅛" h., wider light blue bands alternating w/narrow dark brown, tooled green & white stripes, the two top blue bands w/white & orange Cat's-Eye patt., the lower wide blue band decorated w/undulating Earthworm patt. in white, orange & dark brown, chips, hairline in spout, small hole in bottom (ILLUS. previous page, bottom row, far left) **1,155.00**

Pitcher, jug-type, 8" h., D-form leaftip handle, yellow ochre & light blue bands decorated w/one band of undulating Earthworm patt. & another w/a looping Earthworm patt. in blue, white & dark brown, narrow dark brown & white stripes around top & base, handle w/old staple repair, wear, stains, small chips (ILLUS. previous page, bottom row, far right) **1,430.00**

Waste bowl, deep flat flaring sides raised on a low pedestal foot, the sides w/a wide beige band decorated w/the Earthworm patt. in white,

orangish tan & dark brown, short hairlines, rim chip, 4½" d., 2⅝" h. (ILLUS. previous page, top row, far left) **220.00**

Waste bowl, deep flat flaring sides raised on a low pedestal foot, the sides w/a wide reddish orange band decorated w/the Earthworm patt. in white, blue & dark brown, flanked by narrow dark brown stripes & an embossed green rim band, hairlines & chips, 5⅝" d., 2⅞" h. (ILLUS. top row, far right) **275.00**

MOORCROFT

Wisteria Pattern Bowl

William Moorcroft became a designer for James Macintyre & Co. in 1897 and was put in charge of their art pottery production. Moorcroft developed a number of popular designs, including Florian Ware while with Macintyre and continued with that firm until 1913 when they discontinued the production of art pottery.

After leaving Macintyre in 1913, Moorcroft set up his own pottery in Burslem and continued producing the art wares he had designed earlier as well as introducing new patterns. After William's death in 1945, the pottery was operated by his son, Walter.

MOORCROFT

Moorcroft Marks

Bowl, 6¼" d., 2½" h., footed wide rounded form w/a flat rim, Hibiscus patt., peach-colored blossoms on a dark moss green ground, impressed "MOORCROFT - ENGLAND," & a paper label, 1949-73 ....**$220.00**

Bowl, Wisteria patt., wide rounded upright sides w/a closed rim, a creamy white ground decorated w/a wide band of stylized shaded deep red & pale pink & light & dark blue blossoms on shaded green leafy stems, marked w/William Moorcroft's signature in green & impressed "2" & shape number 2267, first quarter 20th c. (ILLUS. w/introduction) **1,870.00**

Candlesticks, Wisteria patt., a wide flattened & cupped socket rim atop a tall, slender ringed standard on a widely flaring disc foot, decorated w/yellow, purple, deep red & green on a cobalt blue ground, impressed factory marks & painted initials of Walter Moorcroft, 10⅛" h., pr. (professionally repaired small rim chip on one)........................**358.00**

Dish, cov., round, Clematis patt., the cover in violet, rose & pink blossoms w/yellow & olive green centers, green & tan leaves against a tan & teal blue ground, the dish base in dark blue, impressed "Made in England, Potter to HM The Queen," incised signature, 6½" d., 4" h...**198.00**

Jar, cov., wide ovoid body w/a rounded shoulder to the short cylindrical neck fitted w/a domed cover, Wisteria patt., decorated w/large purple, red & yellow wisteria blossoms w/pale green leaves on a dark blue ground, impressed "Moorcroft - Made in England - 769," & green script signature mark, 10" h. **770.00**

Lamp base, Leaves & Fruit patt., tall waisted cylindrical body w/a metal base embossed w/a band of buttons, metal top fittings, the design of large hanging yellowish green & reddish orange leaves & clusters of dark blue & red berries around the upper two-thirds, w/a flambé glaze, impressed factory mark & facsimile signature, painted signature & printed paper "Royal Warrent" label, 10⅞" h..............**468.00**

Lamp base, later Cornflower patt., a squatty bulbous base tapering to a very tall, slender ringed neck w/flared rim, decorated in light bluish green w/a full floral design in yellow & red w/blue centers, on a short pedestal foot & fitted on a scalloped, footed gilt-metal base, script signature, 18" d., overall 25" h...............................**715.00**

Vase, 3" h., footed squatty bulbous body tapering to a short neck w/slightly rolled rim, decorated w/blue, rose & yellow flowers against a mottled bluish green ground, impressed factory mark & facsimile signature & "Potter to H.M. the Queen - Made in England" **110.00**

Vase, 4⅛" h., Pomegranate patt., ovoid body tapering to a short, rolled neck, large mottled red fruit w/yellowish green leaves & dark blue & red berries against a cobalt blue ground, impressed factory mark & facsimile signature & "Potter to H.M. the Queen - Made in England" (tiny irregularity in the base) **303.00**

Vase, 4⅞" h., Pansy patt., footed wide squatty bulbous body tapering to a short slightly flaring cylindrical neck, decorated w/large pansy blossoms in shades of deep red, blue & purple w/yellow & green foliage against a mottled cobalt blue ground, impressed factory mark & "Made in England - N 52," painted initials of Walter Moorcroft & small incised circle **220.00**

Vase, 6" h., Anemone patt., decorated w/purple, blue & red flowers w/green & red centers, a dark bluish green to lighter green ground, impressed "W. Moorcroft, Potter to HM the Queen - Made in England" & blue script initials **275.00**

Vase, 6" h., Clematis patt., simple ovoid body w/a short cylindrical neck, large four-petal deep mottled red & blue petals w/yellow & red buds & shaded green leaves against a greenish yellow shaded to cobalt blue ground, impressed "Moorcroft - Made in England," printed paper "Royal Warrent" label **193.00**

Vase, 7½" h., 4" d., slender ovoid body tapering to a short rolled neck, Pomegranate patt., deep red fruit & dark blue berries w/olive green leaves against a cobalt blue ground, impressed "MOORCROFT - BURSLEM - ENGLAND" & script signature ...**440.00**

Vase, 10" h., Pomegranate patt., tall baluster-form w/a short rolled neck, decorated w/red & orange large fruits & small reddish & blue berries & brownish green leaves on a mottled cobalt blue ground, impressed company logo, "Made in England - J," number "72," slightly larger "O" & painted signature of William Moorcroft **990.00**

Vase, 11¾" h., 3¼" d., Florian Ware, a slender cylindrical lower body swelling at the upper half to the gently flared rim, Lilac patt., leafy stems & flower clusters in purple on a pale periwinkle blue ground, script signature & Florian Ware stamp, 1898 ....**1,540.00**

Vase, 12¾" h., 8" d., wide ovoid body tapering to a short wide

rolled neck, purplish blue & yellow fruit & long pointed pale green leaves against a cobalt blue ground, impressed "MOORCROFT - MADE IN ENGLAND" & glaze signature (short rim hairline) **1,210.00**

MULBERRY

Mulberry or Flow Mulberry ironstone wares were produced in the Staffordshire district of England in the period between 1840 and 1870 at many of the same factories which produced its close "cousin," Flow Blue china. In fact, some of the early Flow Blue patterns were also decorated with the dark blackish or brownish purple mulberry coloration and feature the same heavy smearing or "flown" effect. Produced on sturdy ironstone bodies, the designs were either transfer-printed or hand-painted (Brush stroke) with an Asian, Scenic, Floral or Marble design. Some patterns were also decorated with additional colors over or under the glaze; these are designated in the following listings as "w/polychrome."

Quite a bit of this ware is still to be found and it is becoming increasingly sought-after by collectors although presently its values lag somewhat behind similar Flow Blue pieces. The standard references to Mulberry wares is Petra Williams' book, Flow Blue China and Mulberry Ware, Similarity and Value Guide *and* Mulberry Ironstone - Flow Blue's Best Kept Little Secret, *by Ellen R. Hill.*

AMERILLIA (Podmore, Walker & Co., ca. 1850)
Plate, 10" d. **$80.00**

Vegetable dish, cov., oval (ILLUS. next page) **400.00**

ATHENS (W. Adams, ca. 1849)
Plate, 7½" d. **35.00**

Plate, 8½" d. **40.00**

Plate, 9½" d. **50.00**

Plate, 10½" d. **65.00**

Teapot, cov., full-paneled Gothic shape.......................................**300.00**

Amerillia Vegetable Dish

ATHENS (C. Meigh, ca. 1840)

Athens Reticulated Bowl

Bowl, round flaring reticulated
   sides, on paw feet, very rare,
   9" d. (ILLUS.)...........................**1,500.00**

Cup & saucer, handleless **75.00**

Soup plate, 10" d. **90.00**

Teapot, cov., vertically paneled
   Gothic shape (ILLUS.)...............**495.00**

Athens Teapot

AVA (T. J. & J. Mayer, ca. 1850)
Cup & saucer, handleless,
   w/polychrome **65.00**

Ava Sauce Tureen

Sauce tureen, cover & undertray,
   w/polychrome, 3 pcs. (ILLUS.) ..**450.00**

BEAUTIES OF CHINA (Mellor, Venables & Co., ca. 1845)
Plate, 7½" d., w/polychrome..........**40.00**

Plate, 7½" d. **35.00**

Plate, 10½" d., w/polychrome........**85.00**

BOCHARA (James Edwards, ca. 1850)
Cup & saucer, handleless **60.00**

Relish dish, mitten-shaped.........**125.00**

Soup plate, 10½" d. **90.00**

Bochara Vegetable Dish

Vegetable dish, cov., rectangular w/cut corners (ILLUS.)..............**350.00**

CEYLON (C. Meigh, ca. 1840)

Ceylon Footbath

Footbath, deep oval shape w/end handles, w/polychrome (ILLUS.) **2,000.00**

Plate, 10½" d., w/polychrome........**75.00**

Cleopatra Wash Pitcher

CLEOPATRA
(F. Morley & Co, ca. 1850)

Plate, 9½" d. **45.00**

Soup plate, 9" d. **80.00**

Soup tureen w/ladle, 2 pcs. **1,500.00**

Wash pitcher, w/polychrome (ILLUS.) **200.00**

COREAN (Podmore, Walker & Co., ca. 1850)

Cup & saucer, handleless **75.00**

Pitcher, Corean patt., 1½ qt., Podmore, Walker & Co.............**175.00**

Pitcher, Corean patt., 1 qt., Podmore, Walker & Co.............**160.00**

Plate, 7½" d. **30.00**

Plate, 8½" **45.00**

Plate, 9½" **55.00**

Plate, 10½" **75.00**

Platter, small **100.00**

Relish, mitten-shaped **125.00**

Soup plate, 10" d. **75.00**

Corean Teapot

Teapot, cov., full-paneled Gothic shape (ILLUS.) **395.00**

CYPRUS
(Wm. Davenport, ca. 1845)

Cup & saucer, handleless..............**65.00**

Plate, 10½" d. **75.00**

Platter, 14" l.................................**150.00**

DORA
(E. Challinor, ca. 1850)

Dora Teapot

Teapot, cov., Baltic shape
(ILLUS.) **550.00**

FLORA
(T. Walker, ca. 1847)

Creamer, classic Gothic shape ...**175.00**

Sugar bowl, cov., classic
Gothic shape **200.00**

Flora Mulberry Teapot

Teapot, cov., classic Gothic
shape (ILLUS.) **400.00**

JARDINIERE
(V.& Co., ca. 1891)

Cup & saucer, handled.................**50.00**

Jardiniere Water Pitcher

Pitcher, water (ILLUS.) **200.00**
Plate, 7½" **25.00**
Plate, 9½" **30.00**

JEDDO
(Wm. Adams, ca. 1849)

Jeddo Creamer

Creamer, Primary shape
(ILLUS.) **190.00**
Plate, 9½" d. **45.00**
Plate, 10½" d. **65.00**
Teapot, cov., Primary shape **350.00**

KANSU
(T. Walker, ca. 1847)

Kansu Vegetable Dish

Vegetable dish, cov.(ILLUS.) **350.00**

LADY PEEL
(F. Morley & Co., ca. 1850)

Lady Peel Teapot

Teapot, cov., Primary shape
(ILLUS.) **500.00**

LASSO
(W. Bourne, ca. 1850)
Cup & saucer, handleless **60.00**

Lasso Pattern Teapot

Teapot, cov., full-paneled Gothic
shape (ILLUS.) **495.00**

NANKIN
(Wm. Davenport, ca. 1845)

Nankin Wash Pitcher

Wash pitcher, paneled, 11" h.
(ILLUS.) **350.00**

NING PO
(R. Hall, ca. 1840)
Plate, 7½" d. **35.00**

Ning Po Sauce Tureen Set

Sauce tureen, cover, bird-headed
ladle & undertray, 4 pcs.
(ILLUS.) **700.00**
Soup plate, 9" d. **85.00**

PARISIAN GROUPS
(J. Clementson, ca. 1850)
Platter, 21" l., well & tree-type,
w/polychrome **600.00**

Parisian Groups Soup Tureen

Soup tureen, cover & undertray,
w/polychrome, the set
(ILLUS.) **1,200.00**

PELEW
(E. Challinor, ca. 1850)
Cup & saucer, handleless **60.00**
Plate, 7½" d. **35.00**
Plate, 10½" d. **70.00**
Soup plate, 10" d. **80.00**
Teapot, cov., pumpkin-shaped **550.00**

PHANTASIA
(J. Furnival, ca. 1850)

Phantasia Creamer

Creamer, cockscomb handle,
w/polychrome (ILLUS.) **275.00**

RHONE SCENERY
(T. J. & J. Mayer, ca. 1850)

Plate, 9½" d. **60.00**
Plate, 10" d. **70.00**
Platter, 14" l. **150.00**

Rhone Scenery Vegetable Dish

Vegetable dish, cov., Prize
Bloom shape (ILLUS.) **450.00**

SCINDE (T. Walker, ca. 1847)

Scinde Teapot

Teapot, cov., Primary shape
(ILLUS.) **495.00**

TEMPLE (Podmore, Walker & Co., ca. 1850)

Creamer, classic Gothic shape ...**175.00**
Plate, 10½" d. **65.00**

VINCENNES
(J. & G. Alcock, ca. 1840)

Rare Vincennes Casserole

Casserole, cov., rare
(ILLUS.) **1,000.00**

Vincennes Water Pitcher

Pitcher, water, hexagonal
(ILLUS.) **300.00**
Plate, 8½" d. **50.00**
Plate, 10½" d. **65.00**

WASHINGTON VASE (Podmore, Walker & Co., ca. 1850)

Creamer, classic Gothic shape ...**200.00**
Cup & saucer, handleless **75.00**
Plate, 7½" d. **35.00**
Plate, 8½" d. **40.00**
Plate, 9½" d. **45.00**
Plate, 10½" d. **65.00**

Washington Vase Soup Tureen

Soup tureen, cover & undertray,
3 pcs. (ILLUS.) **4,000.00**

Sugar bowl, cov., classic Gothic
shape.......................................**275.00**

Teapot, cov., classic Gothic
shape.......................................**400.00**

WHAMPOA (Mellor, Venables & Co., ca. 1845)

Sauce tureen, cover & undertray,
3 pcs. **400.00**

NEWCOMB COLLEGE POTTERY

This pottery was established in the art department of Newcomb College, New Orleans, Louisiana, in 1897. Each piece was hand-thrown and bore the potter's mark & decorator's monogram on the base. It was always a studio business and never operated as a factory and its pieces are therefore scarce, with the early wares being eagerly sought. The pottery closed in 1940.

Newcomb College Pottery Mark

Bowl-vase, 5" d., 2⅝" h., wide squatty bulbous base w/tapering shoulders to a wide, flat mouth, the matte pale green rim in blue over a light blue body, low-relief stylized floral decoration in pale green, rose & yellow w/cream around the shoulder, clear interior matte glaze, impressed "NC - JM - 70 - MG16," incised artist's initials, possibly Corinne M. Charlaron, ca. 1922 ....**$805.00**

Mug, pear-shaped w/wide flat base & flat mouth, C-form handle, decorated around the upper half w/painted stylized pine cones in light & dark blue on a cream & blue ground, Ada Lonnegan, 1904, impressed "NC - Lonnegan - JM - Q - R15," 5" d., 4¼" h. (handle repair, interior line)................................**825.00**

Trivet, round w/molded rim, a transitional style w/white & yellow flowers on a cobalt blue & bluish green ground, Corinna Luria, 1916, impressed "NC - CL - JM - IC16," 5¾" d. **1,210.00**

Vase, 3½" h., 3⅝" d., wide gently tapering ovoid form w/a wide closed mouth, the matte glaze decorated w/a stylized floral band in white, green & yellow against a blue band on a greenish blue ground, ivory interior, impressed "NC - JM - B - 235," incised "HB - 52" & "GB98," Henrietta D. Bailey, ca. 1912....................................**863.00**

Vase, 3½" h., 4" d., tapering bulbous ovoid body w/a thin footring & flat mouth, decorated w/an abstracted repeating arch design in yellow, dark blue & green on a light blue ground, Sadie Irvine, 1933, impressed "NC - SI - KS - UD5".................**990.00**

Vase, 4" h., 2¾" d., slightly swelled cylindrical form w/rolled rim, decorated w/tall pine trees in blue & bluish green against light green matte ground, impressed "NC - JM - AFS - 238 - HK90," by A.F. Simpson, 1915 (small hairline crack to rim).....**1,100.00**

Vase, 4½" h., 5½" d., squatty bulbous form w/flat rim, decorated w/stylized blue, white & yellow iris blossoms w/green leaves on a shaded blue ground, impressed "NC - SS41 - HB - 75 - JM," by Henrietta Baily, 1931 ....**2,530.00**

Vase, 4¾" h., 2" d., slender ovoid body w/a flat rim, transitional style decorated around the neck w/a band of pink flowers against a blue & pink ground, Leona Nicholson, 1916-17, impressed & ink mark "NC - LN - (?)OK - JM"............................**1,430.00**

Vase, 6" h., gently swelled cylindrical body tapering near the top to a short molded rim, carved decoration of pale blue & green cypress trees atop a blue & green ground backed by calm water & a shoreline of dense brush against a pale blue, yellow & pink sky, impressed "NC - 237 - U95," original paper label (ILLUS.) **2,420.00**

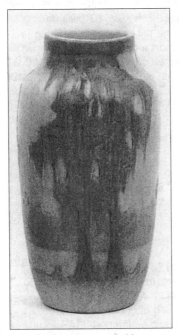

Scenic Newcomb Vase

Vase, 6" h., 4½" d., squatty bulbous base below cylindrical neck w/slightly rolled rim, slip-painted w/stylized poplars in dark blue against a banded light grey, green & dark blue ground, impressed "NC - C90" w/triangle & artist's initials but decorator unknown, 1902 ....**9,075.00**

Vase, 6½" h., 3½" d., tapering ovoid body to a swelled, incurved mouth, matte glaze decorated w/ivory freesia blossoms on greenish blue stems in low-relief, blue ground, cream interior, impressed marks "NC - 90 - JM - mx57" & incised "AFS," Anna Frances Simpson, ca. 1915................................**1,380.00**

Vase, 7¼" h., 4¼" d., gently flaring cylindrical body w/a rounded shoulder tapering to a short cylindrical neck, decorated w/light blue paperwhites on celadon green stems against a blue ground, Henrietta Bailey, 195, impressed & ink mark "NC - HB - 194 - HQ34"..........**3,520.00**

Vase, 7¾" h., cylindrical, deeply carved in the "Espanol" patt., an incised geometric rim band above panels w/narrow arched bands over narrow straight bands, plain rim & base bands, in shades of dark & medium blue w/ pink & green trim, decorated by Anna Frances Simpson, pottery by Joseph Meyer, 1926 (two extremely tight lines from the rim, apparently in the glaze)................................**1,370.00**

Vase, 8½" h., 3¼" d., slightly swelled cylindrical body to a gently tapering cylindrical neck, the neck carved w/pink & green flowers above broad purple leaves on a matte blue ground, impressed "NC - (P)C92 - 92- illegible artist's cypher" **1,320.00**

Vase, 8½" h., 3½" d., tall slender ovoid body tapering to a plain rim band & flat mouth, sharply tooled around the sides w/tall pine trees in dark blue against a bluish green forest & blue sky, transitional type, A.F. Simpson, 1912, impressed "NC - AFS - JM - F189" **7,150.00**

Vase, 8½" h., 4¾" d., ovoid form tapering to cylindrical flat rim, with modeled red flowers & green leaves & stems on a shaded blue matte ground, original paper label & impressed "NC - JM - 161 - RT92 - SI," decorated by Sadie Irvine, 1929 ....**1,650.00**

Vase, 9" h., a short footring supports a tall slender waisted cylindrical body, carved of partially opened crocus blossoms in pastel shades of yellow & green among medium blue decoration stylized vertical stems & leaves on a dark blue ground, early matte glaze, artwork by Alma Mason, thrown by Joseph Meyer, impressed "NC B" **2,860.00**

Vase, 9¾" h., 5¼" d., a wide flat molded mouth above a wide bulbous rounded shoulder above tapering cylindrical sides, decorated around the top & down the sides w/palm trees w/serrated trunks in cobalt blue & gunmetal on a mottled light blue ground, by Sabrina Welles, 1902, impressed "NC - SEW - W5 -U" (minor base bruise) **5,500.00**

NILOAK POTTERY

This pottery was made in Benton, Arkansas and featured hand-thrown varicolored swirled clay decoration in objects of classic forms. Designated Mission Ware, this line is the most desirable of Niloak's production which was begun early in this century. Less expensive to produce, the cast Hywood Line, finished with either high gloss or semi-matte glazes, was introduced during the economic depression of the 1930s. The pottery ceased operation about 1946.

ΝιᴄOΑᴋ
Niloak Pottery Mark

Candlestick, flared base, two original paper labels, 8" h. **$190.00**

Chamberstick, Mission Ware, saucer-type base w/short stepped shaft supporting a cupped candle socket, 4" h. **160.00**

Lamp base, Mission Ware, swirled multicolored clays, 9" h. **275.00**

Vase, 4½" h., Mission Ware, swirled multicolored clays............**90.00**

Vase, 5¾" h., Mission Ware, swirled multicolored clays..........**110.00**

Vase, 6¼" h., Mission Ware, swirled multicolored clays, First Art mark............................**140.00**

Vase, 10½" h., Mission Ware, baluster-form w/wide flattened flaring rim, swirled rust, blue, brown & cream clays, marked ...**253.00**

Vase, 12" h., 6½" d., Mission Ware, tall ovoid body tapering to a short widely flaring neck, swirled dark brown & orange clays, die-stamped "MARIE"......**495.00**

Tall Mission Ware Vase

Vase, 12" h., 6½" d., Mission Ware, tall ovoid body tapering to a short widely flaring neck, swirled dark brown & orange clays, die-stamped "MARIE" (ILLUS.) **495.00**

NIPPON

"Nippon" is a term which is used to describe a wide range of porcelain wares produced in Japan from the late 19th century until about 1921. It was in 1891 that the U.S. implemented the McKinley Tariff Act which required that all wares exported to the United States carry a marking indicating the country of origin. The Japanese chose to use "Nippon," their name for Japan. In 1921 the import laws were revised and the words "Made in" had to be added to the markings. Japan was also required to replace the "Nippon" with the English name "Japan" on all wares sent to the U.S.

Many Japanese factories produced Nippon porcelains and much of it was hand-painted with ornate floral or landscape decoration and heavy gold decoration, applied beading and slip-trailed designs referred to as "moriage." We indicate the specific marking used on a piece, when known, at the end of each listing below. Be aware that a number of Nippon markings have been reproduced and used on new porcelain wares.

Important reference books on Nippon include: The Collector's Encyclopedia of Nippon Porcelain, Series One through Three, *by Joan F. Van Patten (Collector Books, Paducah, Kentucky) and* The Wonderful World of Nippon Porcelain, 1891-1921 *by Kathy Wojciechowski (Schiffer Publishing, Ltd., Atglen, Pennsylvania).*

Ashtray-match holder, an oval dished base centered by an upright rectangular box for holding a small box of matches, Art Deco-style floral & cream border bands inside the base & around the top & base of the match holder, all against a white ground, 3" h. (Rising Sun mark) **$61.00**

Basket, hanging-type, bucket-form, a slightly tapering cylindrical body w/gilt ropework bands near the top & base, the rim w/four squared tab hanging handles above full-relief gilt rams' heads, the body w/an overall floral decoration on an amber & light blue ground, 4" h. (green "M" in Wreath mark) **506.00**

Basket-vase, footed tall slender flattened ovoid form w/the sides tapering to an arched handle w/open scroll loops at the top above an inverted heart-shaped opening, heavy gold trim around the handle & foot, the sides painted w/a lakeside landscape featuring a fisherman in a small boat, 10" h. (blue "M" in Wreath mark)..............................**880.00**

Bowl, 7" d., curved sides w/large gold loop handles, decorated on the exterior w/stylized gold & red designs & on the interior w/a landscape w/a cabin & trees beside a large lake at sunset, a lily pad in the foreground (green "M" in Wreath mark).....................**44.00**

Bowl, 7" square, 2" h., decorated w/yellow roses, yellow base (green "M" in Wreath mark) **25.00**

Bowl, 8" d., footed, "gaudy" pink floral decoration **195.00**

Bowl, 10½" d., intricate scrolled decoration, unmarked................**165.00**

Bread tray, wide oval shallow dish w/fan-molded pointed ends & a lightly scalloped rim w/further molded fans & scrolls, the dished interior decorated w/large clusters of red & yellow chrysanthemum blossoms & green trees w/overall gold trim, 14" l. (blue Maple Leaf mark) **72.00**

Candlestick, tall slightly tapering hexagonal standard w/a flaring socket rim, raised on a low domed hexagonal wide foot, the standard decorated w/a wide stylized landscape scene w/tall trees & water w/pointed arch & panel geometric bands below the scene & around the foot in light blue & gold against a dark mustard yellow ground, 8½" h. (green "M" in Wreath mark) **248.00**

Chocolate pot, cov., tankard-type, footed tall slightly tapering hexagonal body w/an arched short spout & simple arched gold handle, the inset domed cover w/a flaring knob finial, the cover & upper & lower sections decorated w/wide stylized bands of Native American geometric designs in green, red & gold, 11½" h. (blue Maple Leaf mark) **110.00**

Chocolate set: cov. chocolate pot, creamer, sugar bowl, six 7½" d. plates & six cups & saucers; blue & white w/polychrome floral decoration, 22 pcs. **193.00**

Condensed milk can holder, cover & underplate, the holder w/a cylindrical body w/a rolled rim flanked by upswept gilt loop handles, the inset domed cover w/a diamond-shaped gilt finial, the body decorated w/deep red gilt-trimmed bands around the top & halfway down the sides forming square panels decorated w/stylized pink & yellow flowers, the lower section w/a pastel yellow ground trimmed w/a band of heavy gilt cross designs, the matching dished underplate w/a rolled gilt border, 6" h. (green Maple Leaf mark) **165.00**

Cracker jar, cov., bulbous nearly spherical body raised on three short curved peg feet, the wide mouth w/a fitted domed cover w/figural finial, the body decorated w/a large white moriage dragon against a dark black & grey mottled background, 7" h. (green "M" in Wreath mark)............................**413.00**

Cracker jar, cov., bulbous tapering ovoid melon-lobed body raised on three small scroll feet, the low domed cover w/a scrolled loop finial, the cover & upper half of the body w/a pale yellow ground decorated w/heavy gold-outlined large white blossoms w/solid gold leaves above a thin gilt medial band above the plain white lower body & yellow gilt-trimmed feet, 7½" h. (blue "M" in Wreath mark)..............................**55.00**

Cracker jar, cov., decorated w/lavender, green & white flowers, thistles, stems & leaves w/gold trim around base, handle & lid...............................**235.00**

Creamer, gently tapering lobed cylindrical body w/an arched rim spout & simple D-form handles, cobalt blue & heavy gold rim & base bands, the sides decorated w/red & pink roses, 5" h. (blue Maple Leaf mark) **154.00**

Creamer & cov. sugar bowl, a paneled flared foot supporting a flaring, rounded paneled body w/an angled shoulder to a gilt-trimmed opening, the sugar w/a stepped, domed cover w/pointed gold ball finial, angular gilt handles, Wedgwood-style blue & white bands around the foot & shoulder & sugar lid, the paneled sides decorated w/a continuous house in a meadow lakeside landscape, 5" h., pr. (green "M" in Wreath mark) **358.00**

Dish, rounded & gently scalloped four-lobed rim mounted on one side w/a moriage-trimmed rim handle, the interior decorated w/a wide rim band containing a continuous hunting landscape w/horses & riders alternating w/clumps of trees, a center moriage narrow Greek key band, 6" d. (blue Maple Leaf mark) **110.00**

Dresser tray, oval, scenic decoration on cobalt ground, jewel edge **475.00**

Ewer, a footed baluster-form w/a tall slender neck ending in a high, pointed & curved spout, ornate gold C-scroll long handle from the rim to the shoulder, decorated around the middle w/a wide band of large pink roses & green leaves between ornate gold bands flanked by wide dark green bands w/gilt trims, on a green flaring foot w/gilt trim, 12½" h. (blue Maple Leaf mark) **385.00**

Ferner, rectangular, raised on low paneled block feet, the corners gently curved up to the rim & decorated w/black & gold in a teardrop form, the side panels w/white & grey stripes backing clusters of bright red poinsettia & bluish grey leaves above a narrow paneled base band, 3½" h. (green "M" in Wreath mark) **55.00**

Ferner, hexagonal, a squatty bulbous paneled body raised on three tapering outswept gold tab feet, each panel decorated w/stylized colorful blossoms on gilt branching stems w/white & gilt narrow panels at each side angle, all below the low flaring paneled neck w/gilt line trim, 8" w. (green "M" in Wreath mark)..............................**110.00**

Humidor, cov., bulbous cylindrical sides & an overlapping low domed cover w/large knob finial, the cover in grey w/a moriage border band of acorns & leaves, the body painted w/a continuous scene of stag & doe elk in a late autumn woodland, 5½" h. (green "M" in Wreath mark)............................**880.00**

Humidor, cov., h.p. sunset scene w/junks on naturalistic sea, ornate black enameling on cover, finial, top & bottom of base, 3¾" d., 5½" h. (green "M" in Wreath mark).......................**385.00**

Lemonade set: pitcher & five mugs; decorated w/large colorful stylized flowers, marked **295.00**

Loving cup, two-handled, Wedgwood-style, a small conical foot w/a white moriage border band on the blue ground, the widely flaring trumpet-form body decorated on the exterior w/a blue ground & white moriage floral designs of alternating tall daisy stems & shorter lily-of-the-valley stems all below a Greek key border band, the bowl interior w/a blue rim band decorated w/white moriage delicate floral swags, arched D-form handles from the bowl rim to the base of the bowl, 5½" h. (green "M" in Wreath mark).......**303.00**

Matchbox holder w/tray, rose decoration, gold border & trim, 4" l. (green "M" in Wreath mark)..............................**65.00**

Mug, cylindrical body w/an squared loop handle, a wide rim band decorated w/wheel-like devices, the body decorated w/a continuous wintry woodland landscape w/deer, 5" h. ("TN Wreath" mark) **110.00**

Pitcher, 6 x 6½", decorated w/roses over meadow scene (Maple Leaf mark) **150.00**

Pitcher, tankard, 10" h., a tall slender waisted body w/a widely flaring foot & a small flaring rim w/a long pointed spout, a simple C-form gold handle at the center of the side, decorated w/an small oblong reserve of stylized florals on the side completely surrounded from rim to base w/heavy scrolling gold designs on a gold ground (blue Maple Leaf mark) **83.00**

Pitcher, tankard, 13" h., decorated w/roses on cobalt ground w/gold trim, unmarked...**125.00**

Plaque, pierced to hang, decorated w/scene of castle overlooking river, waves crashing on shore, wide border w/alternating reserves of ram's head & flowers, matte finish w/gold beading, 10" d. (blue "M" in Wreath mark) **225.00**

Plaque, rectangular, pierced to hang, scene of cows in stream, trees in background, 8 x 10¼" (green "M" in Wreath mark) **995.00**

Landscape Decorated Plate

Plate, 10¼" d., pierced to hang, h.p. scene of a grove of trees beside a large lake done in shades of brown & cream w/a matte finish, narrow beaded brown border band, green "M" in Wreath mark (ILLUS.) **125.00**

Powder jar, cov., a wide shallow, round dish raised on three gold curved feet, the cylindrical sides decorated w/a cobalt blue band heavily decorated w/gilt grapevines, the fitted low domed cover w/a matching cobalt blue & gold border band framing a large round reserve decorated w/fruits & flowers in shades of orange, yellow, white & green on a shaded yellow ground, 6½" d. (green "M" in wreath mark) **204.00**

Relish dish, oval, windmill scene decoration.................................**125.00**

Salt dip, jeweled w/roses decoration & gold beading..........**65.00**

Sugar shaker, slender ovoid body w/a low domed cover pierced w/holes, a dark cobalt blue ground decorated on the cover & body w/stylized floral bands & clusters, 5" h. ("S&K" mark) **72.00**

Sugar shaker, footed tapering five-sided body w/a molded closed low domed & pointed top pierced w/holes, a high slender arched side handle, the body decorated w/large clusters of colorful roses & green leaves, 5½" h. (blue Maple Leaf mark) ..**127.00**

Tea set: cov. teapot, cov. sugar bowl, creamer, five cups & saucers & five luncheon plates; the teapot & sugar & creamer w/simple tapering cylindrical bodies & domed covers w/gilt button finials, all pieces decorated w/a narrow checked border band above an overall landscape decoration of a white swan on a large lake w/a small cottage & trees in the distance, the set (Paulowania Flowers mark) **193.00**

Toothpick holder, three-handled, a gently rounded & tapering cylindrical body w/low arched gold handles from the rim to the base, decorated overall w/colorful roses & greens leaves, 2" h. (Rising Sun mark) ...**72.00**

Tray, round, a wide gold rim band surrounding a wide Nile River landscape w/large silhouetted palms in the foreground & the river & a sailboat in the mid-ground & low hills & palms in the distance, gold trim, 12" d. ("M" in Wreath mark)............................**220.00**

Urn, cov., bottle-form, a nearly spherical body raised on a cupped band & round flaring foot, a slender tall ringed neck w/a cupped rim supporting a small domed cover w/a small knob finial, the sides w/long, slender C-scroll handles extending from the base of the neck to the lower body, gold-trimmed pale green & white bands around base & upper body & neck, the center of the body w/a wide gold & white band framing a round reserve on each side, one reserve decorated w/a scene of "Peace Bringing Back Abundance," the other w/a cluster of red roses & green leaves, 11½" ("Nippon" in script mark)............................**2,200.00**

Vase, 5" h., wide squatty bulbous body tapering to a short flaring neck, a fine linen tapestry ground decorated w/an overall design of large yellow & pink roses on a greenish yellow ground (blue Maple Leaf mark) **385.00**

Vase, 5½" h., footed squatty bulbous body tapering to a short neck w/molded rim, the sides decorated w/ornate moriage decoration of branches of acorns & oak leaves in red & white against a mottled dark yellow & brown ground (green Maple Leaf mark) **83.00**

Vase, 6" h., a cylindrical body w/a rounded base resting on a footring & rounded shoulders centered by a short rolled neck, a coarse linen tapestry ground decorated at the top & bottom w/gilt-bordered paneled bands w/stylized birds or flowers in each panel, the wide central band decorated w/a continuous rural landscape scene w/a large & cottage among trees (blue Maple Leaf mark) **440.00**

Vase, 6¾" h., footed bulbous body w/short wide slightly flared rim, ornate angled handles from mid-section to rim, decorated

Vase with Hunt Scene

w/relief-molded scene of hounds chasing stag, moriage trim on handles, rim & base (ILLUS.) **795.00**

Vase, 7" h., ovoid body tapering to a short flared neck flanked by upturned angular gold shoulder handles, decorated w/a mottled & swirled tan & dark brown matte ground painted w/undulating gilt thistles around the sides (blue Maple Leaf mark) **440.00**

Vase, 7½" h., footed flattened ovoid body w/a wide undulating shoulder ending in incurved scroll handles which terminate at the short scalloped neck, gilt trim on foot, shoulder, neck & handles, the body decorated w/a wide landscape scene of a house in a meadow in the distance & a lake w/white geese in the foreground (blue Maple Leaf mark) **440.00**

Vase, 8" h., wide baluster-form body w/a rounded shoulder centered by a short cylindrical neck, fine linen tapestry ground in mottled cream & tan, decorated around the upper body w/an Art Deco style narrow gold looped band w/medallions & delicate drops, the shoulder w/a gold wide band w/points sides (blue Maple Leaf mark) **1,265.00**

Vase, 9" h., classical form w/a footed ovoid body w/wide shoulders centered by a tall slender cylindrical neck w/a flaring rim flanked by tall, slender squared open handles, stylized moriage designs on the neck, shoulder & lower body against a dark brown ground, the center decorated w/a continuous landscape scene w/a cottage in a meadow at sunset (green "M" in Wreath mark) **275.00**

Vase, 18½" h., cov., baluster form tall urn shape w/a short flared neck supporting a domed cover w/painted button finial, ornate pierced scroll handles on shoulder, central round floral painted medallion framed by ornate gilding & wide bands w/white blossoms & leafy scrolls on deep red ground flanked by green & white bands trimmed in gold, short pedestal base bolted to a short columnar stand w/scroll-molded feet & decorated to match.................**7,700.00**

Whiskey jug w/stopper, slightly tapering cylindrical body w/a rounded shoulder tapering to a short neck w/a molded rim & rim spout, fitted w/a flattened mushroom stopper, a short C-form shoulder handle, the body decorated w/a continuous seascape scene w/small sailboats & a windmill in the distance, 5½" h. (green "M" in Wreath mark)............................**660.00**

NORITAKE

Noritake china, still in production in Japan, has been exported in large quantities to this country since early in this century. Though the Noritake Company first registered in 1904, it did not use "Noritake" as part of its backstamp until 1918. Interest in Noritake has escalated as collectors now seek out pieces made between the "Nippon" era and World War II (1921-41). The Azalea pattern is also popular with collectors.

Noritake Mark

Bowl, fruit, small, Patt. No. 175...**$12.00**

Casserole, cov., Azalea patt., No. 16..**110.00**

Creamer & cov. sugar bowl, Azalea patt., pr. **50.00**

Cruet w/original stopper, Azalea patt., No. 190.............................**165.00**

Dish, elongated, two-part w/figural bluebird center handle, h.p. Art Deco floral decoration on orange & blue ground, artist-signed................................**110.00**

Luncheon set for six, including cov. teapot, creamer & cov. sugar bowl, Burlington, 21 pcs. **155.00**

Azalea Salt & Pepper & Milk Pitcher

Pitcher, milk, jug-type, Azalea patt., No. 100, 1 qt., 5⅝" h. (ILLUS.) **160.00**

Plate, 6½" d., Alvin patt. **4.00**

Plate, 7⅝" sq., Azalea patt. **75.00**

Plate, 13" d., Azalea patt. **20.00**

Refreshment set, Azalea patt.,
2 pcs. **45.00**

Salt & pepper shakers, Azalea
patt., No. 89, pr.(ILLUS. left,
previous page)...........................**23.00**

Soup plate w/flanged rim,
Patt. No. 175 ....**25.00**

Tea set: cov. teapot, creamer &
cov. sugar bowl; decorated
w/wide borders of flowers &
foliage, black trim, yellow
ground, the set **45.00**

Toothpick holder, Azalea patt.,
No. 192......................................**95.00**

Vase, 5½" h., lobed cylindrical
body w/flaring lobed foot &
flaring rim, colorful lake scene
decoration w/rowboat & trees......**95.00**

OHR (George) POTTERY

George Ohr, the eccentric potter of Biloxi, Mississippi, worked from about 1883 to 1906. The majority of his works were hand-thrown, exceedingly thin-walled items, some of which have a crushed or folded appearance. He considered himself the foremost potter in the world and declined to sell much of his production, instead accumulating a great horde to leave as a legacy to his children. In 1972 this collection was purchased for resale by an antiques dealer.

GEO. E. OHR
BILOXI, MISS.

Ohr Pottery Marks

Bowl, 3" d., 4½" d., round form
pinched into a perfect heart,
covered w/glossy speckled
amber glaze, die-stamped "G.E.
OHR - Biloxi, Miss." (ILLUS.
front row, second from left)...**$1,430.00**

Dish, hand-built, three-part body
w/five feet, with a cobalt, green
& gunmetal mottled flambé over
pink underglaze, die-stamped
"G.E.OHR - Biloxi, Miss.," 3 x 6"
(ILLUS. front row, second
from right) **1,870.00**

Pitcher, 3" h., 6" d., low pedestal
foot supporting a circular rim
tapering to squatty bulbous body
w/twisted applied handle &
broadly rolled rim & pinched
spout, under mottled purple,
cobalt & green flambé glaze,
die-stamped "G.E.Ohr - Biloxi,
Miss." (ILLUS. back row,
far right) **1,430.00**

A Variety of Ohr Pieces

Pitcher, 3¼" h., 5¼" d., squatty bulbous body w/squared shoulder tapering to cylindrical neck w/flat rim & pinched spout, applied handle, all under blistered gunmetal glaze, marked "G.E.OHR - Biloxi, Miss." (ILLUS. previous page, front row, far left) **1,100.00**

Pitcher, 3½" h., 5½" d., ring foot & applied handle, manipulated form w/pinched & dimpled sides, covered in rare pink matte blister glaze, die-stamped "G.E.OHR" (ILLUS. previous page, back row, far left) **2,970.00**

Pitcher, 4" h., 3¾" d., double gourd-shaped pitcher w/pinched spout, under a good mahogany, speckled green & gunmetal drip flambé glaze, die-stamped "G.E.OHR - Biloxi, Miss." (ILLUS. previous page, front row, far right) **1,210.00**

Pitcher, 5½" h., 6" d., bulbous body tapering to widely flaring neck & rim, applied semi-circular handle, under a fine flowing green, red, and gunmetal flambé glaze, die-stamped "G.E.OHR - Biloxi, Miss." (ILLUS. previous page, back row, center) **1,100.00**

PARIS & OLD PARIS

China known by the generic name of Paris and Old Paris was made by several Parisian factories from the 18th through the 19th century; some of it is marked and some is not. Much of it was handsomely decorated.

Figure group, modeled as Turkish lovers, decorated in puce, green & yellow w/gilt trim, 19th c., 6" h. **$55.00**

Plates, 9¼" d., each decorated in the center w/floral designs, one featuring a bouquet of flowers resting upon the corner of a wall, the other showing various

Floral-decorated Paris Plate

flowering plants in a landscapesetting, each within w/diamond band borders in cobalt blue & ornate gold, marked on the back "D'arte Freres a Paris," 19th c., pr. (ILLUS. of one) **748.00**

Paris Porcelain Tea Set

Tea set: cov. teapot, cov. sugar bowl, creamer, cov. coffeepot & four cups & saucers; tall slender ovoid bodies, each piece enameled in tones of brown w/a smoky pedestal on a cream ground within in gilt-rimmed rectangular panel w/incurved corners, flanked by scrolls & clusters of musical instruments & weapons on a periwinkle blue ground, early 19th c., one cup handle off, the set (ILLUS.) **1,265.00**

A Variety of Fine Pate-sur-pate Pieces

PATE-SUR-PATE

Taking its name from the French phrase meaning "paste on paste," this type of ware features designs in relief, obtained by successive layers of thin pottery paste, painted one on top of the other. Much of this work was done in France and England, and perhaps the best-known wares of this type from England are those made by Minton, which see.

Plaque, oval, mottled bluish grey ground decorated in colored slips w/a scene depicting a partially clad classical female holding a lantern as a putto figure lights a torch, titled "La Nouvelle Psyche," attributed to Louis Solon, France, ca. 1870, framed, plaque 11 x 16" (ILLUS. far right) $2,760.00

Vase, cov., 6½" h., a square foot supporting a slender tapering pedestal below a wide, shallow waisted tapering oblong bowl w/double-loop angular end handles, the low domed conforming cover w/a berry finial, a deep teal blue ground w/a gilt-framed grey-ground panel decorated in white slip w/a figure of a reclining maiden, gilt swags & spearpoints around the body & cover, signed by Albione Birks, printed Minton mark, ca. 1900, shallow restored cover chip (ILLUS. front, center) **1,840.00**

Vase, 9½" h., slender ovoid body tapering to a short flaring neck, gilt ring handles on the shoulders, a green ground decorated in white slip w/a maiden in swirling diaphanous clothes caught in a rain storm, gilt trim on the neck shoulder & base, artist-signed by Albione Birks, printed Minton mark, late 19th c., rim gilt wear (ILLUS. previous page, back row, center) **1,725.00**

Vase, cov., 13¾" h., a slender tapering ovoid body raised on a ringed base tapering to a disc foot w/three gilt scroll legs from the base to the foot, the top rim fitted w/a slightly domed widely overhanging cover w/a large pointed finial, the dark brown ground of the body decorated in white slip w/a partially draped female figure holding a flowering branch above her head, the cover, base & foot w/ornate gilt trim, signed by Louis Solon, printed & impressed Minton marks, ca. 1898, cover rim damage, minor gilt wear (ILLUS. previous page far left)............**2,300.00**

PENNSBURY POTTERY

Henry Below and his wife Lee founded the Pennsbury Pottery in Morrisville, Pennsylvania in 1950. The Belows chose the name because William Penn's home was nearby. Lee, a talented artist who designed the well known Rooster pattern, almost the entire folk art designs and the Pennsylvania German blue and white hand-painted dinnerware, had been affiliated with Stangl Pottery of Trenton, New Jersey. Mr. Below had learned pottery making in Germany and became an expert in mold making and ceramic engineering. He, too, had been associated with Stangl Pottery and when he and Lee opened Pennsbury Pottery, several workers from Stangl joined the Belows. Mr. Below's death in 1959 was unexpected and Mrs. Below passed away in 1968 after a long illness. Pennsbury filed for bankruptcy in October, 1970. In 1971 the pottery was destroyed by fire.

During Pennsbury's production years, an earthenware with a high temperature firing was used. Most of the designs are a sgraffito-type similar to Stangl's products. The most popular coloring, a characteristic of Pennsbury, is the smear-type glaze of light brown after the sgraffito technique has been used. Birds are usually marked by hand and most often include the name of the bird. Dinnerware followed and then art pieces, ashtrays and teapots. The first dinnerware line was Black Rooster followed by Red Rooster. There was also a line known as Blue Dowry which had the same decorations as the brown folk art pattern but the decorations were done in cobalt.

Pennsbury
Pottery

Pennsbury

Pottery

morrisville, Pa.

Pennsbury Pottery Marks

Ashtray, motto-type, round, Amish boy & girl kissing w/"Such Schmootzers," 5" d. **$30.00**

Bowl, 6½" d., pie crust edge, Red Rooster patt. **20.00**

Bowl, 9" d., 3" h., Dutch Talk patt., various Dutch emblems & sayings scattered around the piece include, 'Kissin Wears

Dutch Talk Pattern Bowl

Out, Cooking Don't,' 'Borrowing Makes For Sorrowing,' 'Throw The Cow Over The Fence Some Hay,' 'Go Pump Me A Drink' (ILLUS.) **125.00**

Bowl, pretzel, 12" l., 8" w., Barber Shop Quartet patt. w/Luigi, Olson, Schultz & Horowitz **85.00**

Cake stand, Boy & Girl patt., 11" d. **90.00**

Canister, cov., Black Rooster patt., w/black rooster finial, front reads "Flour," 9" h.......................**185.00**

Cookie jar, cov., Harvest patt., 8" h. **275.00**

Red Rooster Cup & Saucer

Cup & saucer, Red Rooster patt., set (ILLUS.) **55.00**

Lamp, pitcher-shaped, Hex patt., 12" h. to the socket **285.00**

Model of a Bluebird, Model No. 103, 4" h..............................**175.00**

Model of a bunny, seated atop a hollowed out gourd, "Slick-Bunny," white gloss, pink eyes, ears back, pink & green gourd, hard-to find, paper label, unmarked, 5½" h. **200.00**

Model of a duck, lying down, white gloss glaze, yellow bill & feet, black eyes, 6½" l. **300.00**

Model of a Hummingbird, perched on a base w/flowers on a tree trunk, white gloss glaze, 3½" h. **245.00**

Models of a rooster & hen, Delft Blue w/white, rooster, 11½" h., hen, 10½" h., pr. **795.00**

Models of a rooster & hen, White Leghorn, rooster Model No. P202, hen Model No. P201, may be found with Model Nos. 127 & 128 respectively, 10½" h., pr. (ILLUS. below) **710.00**

Mother's day plate, "Friendship," 1973 ....**100.00**

Mug, beer-type, Amish patt. **45.00**

Mug, coffee, Black Rooster patt. ...**30.00**

Mug, Eagle patt. **12.00**

Rooster & Hen Models

Pitcher with Eagle on Obverse

Pitcher, 5¼" h., eagle on obverse
w/shield on reverse (ILLUS.) **65.00**

Plaque, shows woman holding
Pennsbury cookie jar, marked "It
is Whole Empty," drilled for
hanging, 4" d. **35.00**

Plaque, Basket of Flowers patt.,
6" d. **47.00**

Plate, salad, 8" d., Red Rooster
patt. **15.00**

Plate, 10" d., Black
Rooster patt................................**50.00**

Red Barn Relish Tray

Relish tray, model of a tree
divided into three sections, Red
Barn patt., 14½" l. (ILLUS.) **225.00**

Salt & pepper shakers, shaped
as small pitchers w/image of
Amish man & woman,
2½" h., pr. **45.00**

Tile, Black Rooster patt., 6" sq. **40.00**

Tile, Hex patt., 6" sq. **50.00**

Tray, octagonal, "Crested Birds,"
3 x 5" **30.00**

Tray, high-relief design of train,
reads "Baltimore & Ohio R.R.
1837 - Lafayette,"
7½" l., 5½" w...............................**60.00**

Wall pocket, donkey & clown
w/dark green border, ivory
center, 6½" sq. **105.00**

PEWABIC POTTERY

A Variety of Pewabic Pieces

Mary Chase Perry (Stratton) and Horace J. Caulkins were partners in this Detroit, Michigan pottery. Established in 1903, Pewabic Pottery evolved from their Revelation Pottery, "Pewabic" meaning "clay with copper color" in the language of Michigan's Chippewa Indians. Caulkins attended to the clay formulas and Mary Perry Stratton was artistic creator of forms & glaze formulas, eventually developing a wide range of colors for her finely textured glazes. The pottery's reputation for fine wares and architectural tiles enabled it to survive the depression years of the 1930s. After Caulkins died in 1923, Mrs. Stratton continued to be active in the pottery until her death, at age ninety-four, in 1961. Her contributions to the art pottery field are numerous.

Pewabic Pottery Mark

Bowl, 5"d., 2¾" h., a small round
foot below the deep flaring
sides, lustered mottled green &
purple glaze, paper label
(ILLUS. right) **$330.00**

Figure of a young girl, standing holding a small dog, wearing a long, pleated shift, iridescent grey & gold glazes, on a raised square foot, artist-signed on base "Gwen Lux," 4¼" w., 11¾" h. (ILLUS. previous page, left).......**440.00**

Tile, fireplace-type, rectangular, originally designed for the Children's room of the City of Detroit's Main Library, one of a series depicting fairy tales, this one about the Tin Soldier, greenish buff partially glazed on the incised decoration w/traditional Pewabic colors including blue, iridescent teal & white, highlighted w/fired-on gold, original paper label from the Architectural League of New York Annual Exhibition, label lists "Pewabic Pottery, 10125 E. Jefferson Avenue, Detroit, Mich." & full titled "Decorative Tile," w/an apparently period old stand, 9¼ X 12⅜" (minor unobtrusive edge chips) **1,210.00**

Vase, 3½" h., hand-thrown, broad ovoid body w/closed rim, a dripping organic turquoise blue glaze over lustre red glazes, produced between 1906 & 1913, impressed Pewabic maple leaf logo & notation "S-2" painted on................................**523.00**

Vase, 4½" h., bulbous ovoid body tapering sharply toward the base, the rounded shoulder narrowing to a wide, short flared neck, tan lustre drip glaze w/violet, blue & pink iridescent highlights over a vivid blue matte glaze, prominent finger marks, impressed marks **605.00**

Vase, 5" h., 5" d., footed bulbous ovoid body w/a rounded shoulder to the wide, short cylindrical neck, overall turquoise & purple lustre glaze, circular die-stamped mark "PEWABIC DETROIT" (ILLUS. previous page, center)..............**495.00**

Vase, 5¼" h., low pedestal foot supporting a gently flaring cylindrical body w/a wide, flat rim, iridescent turquoise blue drippings from the rim down over the greyish green ground, impressed mark "Pewabic Detroit" (pinhead base flakes) ...**550.00**

Vase, 5¼" h., 6¾" d., wide squatty bulbous body w/a sloping shoulder to the short widely flaring neck, covered in an uneven matte brown glaze, original paper label **440.00**

Vase, 6¾" h., 4½" d., gently flaring cylindrical body, interior w/a rich iridescent green glaze, the exterior w/a purple flambé glaze, stamped mark & original label...**880.00**

PICKARD

Pickard, Inc., making fine decorated china today in Antioch, Illinois, was founded in Chicago in 1894 by Wilder A. Pickard. The company now makes its own blanks but once only decorated those bought from other potteries, primarily from the Haviland and others in Limoges, France.

Bowl, 10½" d., nasturtium decoration w/wide gold scalloped beaded rim, ca. 1903-05, artist-signed........**$325.00**

Collar button box, cov., decorated w/lilies, gold trim, ca. 1910-12 ....**80.00**

Cup & saucer, footed tall cylindrical cup, Encrusted Linear patt., blue & white stylized floral panels & bands w/overall heavy gold, cup 1905-10 mark, saucer 1912-18 mark, the set (ILLUS. next page, far left) **150.00**

Cup & saucer, footed rounded cup w/gold D-form handle, decorated w/a cluster of red roses & green leaves against a shaded brown ground w/a

Pickard Cups & Saucers

scalloped gold border band, artist-signed, ca. 1905, the set (ILLUS. second from left) **225.00**

Cup & saucer, deep rounded cup w/gold D-form handle, Modern Conventional patt., black bands & gold scrolls flank tan panels & pale blue leafy scrolls, 1912-18 mark, the set (ILLUS. second from right) **210.00**

Cup & saucer, tall swelled cylindrical cup w/an angular gold handle, Poppies in Gold patt., orange poppy blossoms below a wide gold ground & against a shaded brown to orange ground, artist-signed, 1905-10 mark, the set (ILLUS. far right) **250.00**

Tall Pickard Pitchers

Pitcher, 7¾" h., tall gently swelled ovoid body tapering to a flat rim w/a small spout, D-form gold handle, Modern Conventional patt., black bands w/gold scrolls flanking a tan band w/pale blue leafy scrolls, gold ground, artist-signed, 1905-10 mark (ILLUS. left) **300.00**

Pitcher, 7¾" h., tall gently swelled ovoid body tapering to a flat rim w/a small spout, D-form gold handle, Twin Tulips patt., large orange & white blossoms on pale green leafy stems against a gold shaded to white ground, artist-signed, 1905-10 mark (ILLUS right) **600.00**

Pitcher, 7¾" h., waisted hexagonal body w/a wide rim spout & high looped long gold handle, Convolvulus patt., clusters of trumpet-form white blossoms on tall slender gold leafy stems down the sides, gold rim & base bands, artist-signed, 1912-18 mark **550.00**

Pitcher, 7¾" h., waisted hexagonal body w/a wide rim spout & high looped long gold handle, Wildwood patt., decorated w/a continuous pastel landscap w/pale pink rose bushes in the foreground, gold rim band, 1912-18 mark **600.00**

Plate, 8¾" d., decorated w/a landscape scene in Yosemite w/a waterfall in the background, artist-signed, 1912-18 mark.......**275.00**

Plate, 8¾" d., Wildwood patt., a landscape w/a lake, birch trees & pale pink rose bushes in the foreground, artist-signed, 1912-18 mark **275.00**

Salt & pepper shakers, floral
garlands w/gold trim,
ca. 1910, pr. **60.00**

Cylindrical Pickard Vases

Vase, 10¼" h., cylindrical, Fall
Birches patt., a continuous
landscape w/large trees w/tiny
orange leaves, artist-signed,
1912-18 mark (ILLUS. left) **900.00**

Vase, 11" h., cylindrical,
decorated w/a dancing sylph
w/flowing red hair, her arms
extended behind her head,
wearing a diaphanous flowing
white gown against a white
ground, artist-signed, 1912-18
mark (ILLUS. center) **1,500.00**

Vase, 12" h., gold-footed
cylindrical body, Everglades
patt., decorated w/a continuous
tropical landscape w/tall palm
trees, artist-signed, 1912-18
mark (ILLUS. right) **1,450.00**

PIERCE (Howard) PORCELAINS

Howard Pierce was born in Chicago,
Illinois in 1912. He attended the university
there and also the Chicago Art Institute but
by 1935 he wanted a change and came to
California. That move would alter his life
forever. He settled in Claremont and attended
the Pomona College. William Manker, a well-
known ceramist, hired Mr. Pierce in 1936 to
work for him. That liaison lasted about three
years. After leaving Manker's employment
Howard opened a small studio in Laverne,
California and, not wishing to be in
competition with Manker, began by creating
miniature animal figures, some of which he
made into jewelry. In 1941, he married Ellen
Voorhees who was living in National City,
California. In the 1950s, Mr. Pierce had
national representation through the N.S.
Gustin Company. Polyurethane animals are
high on collectors lists as Howard, after
creating in the early years only a few pieces
using this material, realized he was allergic to
it and had to discontinue its use. He
experimented with various mediums such as a
Wedgwood Jasper Ware type body, then went
into porcelain bisque animals and plants that
he put close to or in open areas of high-gloss
vases. When Mt. St. Helens volcano erupted,
Pierce was one of the first to experiment with
adding the ash to his silica which produced a
rough-textured glaze. Lava, while volcano
associated, was a glaze treatment unrelated to
Mt. St. Helens. Howard described Lava as
"...bubbling up from the bottom..." Pierce
also created some pieces in goldleaf which are
harder to find than the gold treatment he
formulated in the 1950s for Sears. They had
ordered a large number of pieces and wanted
all of them produced in the gold treatment.
Many of these pieces are not marked. Howard
also did what he termed 'tipping' in relation
to glazes. A piece would be high-gloss overall
but, then, the tops, bottoms, sides, etc. would
be brushed, speckled or mottled with a
different glaze, most often brown, black or
grey. For example, a set of three fish made in
the late 1950s or early 1960s were on
individual bases that were 'tipped' as were the
fins with the bodies being a solid brown or
black. Toward the late 1970s, Mr. Pierce
began putting formula numbers on his pieces
and recording the materials used to create
certain glazes. In November 1992, because of
health problems, Howard and Ellen Pierce
destroyed all the molds they had created over
the years. Mr. Pierce began working on a
limited basis producing miniature versions of
past porcelain wares. These pieces are simply
stamped "Pierce." Howard Pierce passed
away in February, 1994.

HP Pierce

HOWARD PIERCE

Howard Pierce Claremont, Calif

Howard Pierce Ceramics Marks

Bowl, 6½" h., ivy-type, small foot rising to a bulbous body w/closed rim, mottled green & black, stamp marked, "Howard Pierce Porcelain," **$35.00**

Figure group, girl w/arm at each side, standing on oval base w/head bent looking at seated dog w/head up, nondescript faces, glossy caramel glaze w/dark brown highlights, marked "Howard Pierce," 1980s, 4½" h. ..**65.00**

Figures of boy & girl ballet dancers, dark brown bodies w/mottled brown & white ballet costumes, arms behind their backs, 1950s, boy, 7" h., girl, 6¾" h., pr. **160.00**

Figures of a native boy & girl, long bodies, short legs, boy w/arms across chest, girl w/arms folded at waist, dark brown glaze w/mottled brown loin cloth on boy & mottled brown skirt on girl, boy, 7½" h., girl, 7" h., pr. ...**150.00**

Model of an eagle, standing on small, rectangular base w/head turned to side, black w/white neck & head, 1950s, 3¼" l., 7½" h. (ILLUS.).........................**110.00**

Model of a pelican, long beak away from body, created only in white body w/dark brown beak & dark brown tipping at lower section of body & base, 1950s, 8" h. **125.00**

Models of a duck family, black w/green speckled chests, 3 pcs. **80.00**

Models of fish, each on a half-circle base, dark brown bodies w/speckled bases & fins, large fish, 6" h., medium fish, 4¾" h. small fish, 3" h., set **125.00**

Models of a rooster & a hen, charcoal-colored, numbered, pr. **165.00**

Pencil holder, figural, two roadrunners, one standing, one running, tan glaze w/dark brown roadrunners, incised initials "HP," 3" d., 3¾" h........................**45.00**

Oblong Vase

Model of Eagle

Vase, 5" h., 6½" l., oblong w/circle in center w/bisque girl w/basket, dog & small platform, chartreuse w/black flecks, incised mark "Howard Pierce 201P Claremont, Calif." (ILLUS.) **125.00**

Vase, bud-type, 9½" h., bulbous lower body rising to a stick neck w/flared rim on one side, multicolor experimental blue, yellow, brown & caramel glazes, stamp mark "Howard Pierce"........**50.00**

Wall pocket, oblong, dusty pink bisque rim & bottom, dark pink center w/five white bisque running deer molded in relief, 7¾" l., 3½" h. **155.00**

REDWARE

Red earthenware pottery was made in the American colonies from the late 1600s. Bowls, crocks and all types of utilitarian wares were turned out in great abundance to supplement the pewter and handmade treenware. The ready availability of the clay, the same used in making bricks and roof tiles, accounted for the vast production. The lead-glazed redware retained its reddish color though a variety of colors could be obtained by adding various metals to the glaze. Interesting effects occurred accidentally through unsuspected impurities in the clay or uneven temperatures in the firing kiln which sometimes resulted in streaks or mottled splotches.

Redware pottery was seldom marked by the maker.

Apple basket, flaring cylindrical body w/pierced sides, yellow slip glaze w/sgraffito decoration on the interior in the form of birds perched on a leafy vine, the base w/an incised & stylized tree, the exterior w/bands of incised circles & flowering vines, inscribed "Sarah Dunn," some wear & losses to glaze, Pennsylvania, ca. 1820, 11" d., 4½" h. (ILLUS.)....................**$9,200.00**

Bank, miniature Empire chest of drawers form w/overall scroddle yellow & brown decoration, probably Philadelphia, ca. 1840, 1⅝ x 3¾", 3" h. **575.00**

Bean pot, flattened bulbous form w/pulled handles & short cylindrical neck, mottled olive-green & orange glaze, Pennsylvania or New England, mid-19th c., 8¾" h. (some old chips & imperfections) **690.00**

Bottle, ovoid body w/molded rim, dark olive amber glaze, old paper label "1882" & sticker from the "Gardner Collection," 7⅞" h. (wear) **77.00**

Bottle, standing squirrel cast in a two-piece mold w/incised eye, tail & paw detail, covered in a mottled & streaky orange & brown glaze, Moravian Potteries, Salem, North Carolina, early 19th c., base restored, 8¼" h **1,725.00**

Redware Apple Basket

Redware Pierced Covered Bowl

Bowl, cov., 4½" d., 4¾" h., cylindrical body w/domed lid, yellow glaze, decorated w/applied solid compass star medallion designs w/yellow, orange, brown & green glaze, the double-walled body decorated w/zigzag everted rim & pierced compass stars & geometric perforations over a solid glazed redware bowl, small chip to rim & lid, possible Henry Grady, Shanksville, Somerset County, Pennsylvania, ca. 1843-80 (ILLUS.) **12,650.00**

Bowl, cup-shaped w/strap handle, dark glaze w/black splotches, 5½" d., 3½" h. (wear & chips on base).......................**160.00**

Coffeepot, cov., cylindrical body w/fine manganese "tortoiseshell" decoration on a red body w/clear lead glaze, domed lid w/flattened finial & applied molded spout & handle, stamped "John Bell, 1800-1880, Waynesboro, Franklin County, Pennsylvania, 1850-1880," 9" h. **7,475.00**

Creamer, baluster-form on a short pedestal & circular foot, applied long S-scroll handle, red body daubed w/manganese, clear lead glaze, Pennsylvania, 19th c., 3½" h. **1,093.00**

Cuspidor, waisted form w/crimped edge, decorated w/impressed stellate devices, leaves, hearts & flowers w/mottled olive-green & orange ground, Pennsylvania, ca. 1820, some age chips & minor losses, 8" d., 5" h. **920.00**

Dish, flattened edge decorated w/sgaraffito tulips & leafage climbing from a double-handled diamond patterned pot, yellowish white glaze daubed w/green copper oxide, incised meandering border, possible Jacob Medinger, Pennsylvania, early 20th c., 9⅞" d................**2,070.00**

Dish, yellowish white slip w/sgraffito decoration in the form of a double eagle w/large central heart & two pendant tulip blossoms, the sides inscribed in ornamental German calligraphy, everted edge, signed "Gemacht von Samuel Paul Im Jahr 1798 vor Maria Helbard," Limerick Township, Montgomery County, 12½" d. (some chips, wear & minor imperfections) **36,800.00**

Flowerpot, footed, inverted bell form w/banded neck, molded lip & applied strap handles, covered w/mottled green, white & brown glaze & decorated w/sgraffito birds perched in flowing branches, gouge-work flowers & initialed "M.M." & dated "1783" on both sides, probably Chester County, Pennsylvania, ca. 1783, some exfoliation & rim chips & hairline crack, 7¼" h. **2,875.00**

Flowerpot w/saucer, tapering cylindrical form w/ruffled rim & saucer & pressed ruffled bands w/applied foliate floral decorations, dark brown & black manganese glaze, attributed to Henry Fahr, Mt. Aetna, Tulpehocken Township, Berks County, Pennsylvania, ca. 1867-85, 8¾" d., 8¼" h., 2 pcs. **250.00**

Jar, cov., cylindrical w/flaring rim, inset cover w/button finial, deep orange w/clear shiny glaze & brown splotchy lines, 6⅜" h. (minor chips on lid) **303.00**

Jar, ovoid, brown glaze w/black splotches, 6" h. (wear & glaze flakes) **61.00**

Jar, footed bulbous ovoid body tapering to wide cylindrical neck, applied scrolled double ear handles & applied & tooled relief-molded flowers on both sides, dark brown glaze, attributed to Baecher, 6½" h. (wear, hairlines & chips, some chipped areas have painted over repair) **1,430.00**

Jar, flared foot w/ovoid body tapering to slightly flaring rim, deep orange w/clear shiny glaze, brown flecks & dark brown sponging, 7" h. (chips) **248.00**

Jar, cylindrical body w/sloping shoulder & flaring neck, green glaze w/amber spots, 7¼" h. (small chips) **138.00**

Jug, ovoid w/ribbed strap handle, dark amber w/brown, 8½" h. (lip chip) **165.00**

Jug, bulbous ovoid w/incised lines at shoulder & bulbous lip, applied strap handle, brown glaze, 8¾" h. (glaze is worn & flaked) **55.00**

Model of a bird, stylized crested long-necked bird w/incised wings covered in a dark brown glaze & mounted on an oval base, 4" l., 3¼" h. **690.00**

Model of a lamb, recumbent sleeping lamb w/incised fur covered in a yellowish white glaze w/daubings of manganese brown & green copper oxide, attributed to S. Bell & Son, Strasburg, Virginia, late 19th c., some wear & exfoliation of glaze, 12" l., 3½" h. (ILLUS.) **20,700.00**

Redware Sleeping Lamb

Mold, food, figural Turk's turban-style, orange interior w/green exterior glaze, 11" d. (small chips) **105.00**

Mug, child's, enameled decoration of flowers, shaded pink, black & green w/black rim, 2¼" h. **94.00**

Redware Sgraffito Mug

Mug, bulbous ovoid form w/applied strap handle, yellow slip w/daubings of brown manganese & copper-green oxide, decorated w/sgraffito tulips & featherleaf motifs, Pennsylvania, early 19th c., some old rim chips & imperfections, 5¾" h. (ILLUS.) **4,025.00**

Pipe holder, cov., three-footed, cylindrical form w/perforated lid & four pipe stands, daubed w/manganese on red body w/clear lead glaze, ca. 1875-96, George A. Wagner Pottery, Weissport, Carbon County, Pennsylvania, 4" h. **2,760.00**

Pitcher, 7" h., slender ovoid body w/flaring rim & strap handle, interior glaze w/rim drips of

yellow slip, worn patina on
exterior (rim chips & hairlines
w/glued rim repair)....................**127.00**

Pitcher, water, 10" h., elongated
baluster-form on a tooled
circular foot w/applied & incised
strap handle & wide flaring
spout, mottled olive-green &
brown manganese glaze,
decorated w/relief-molded
blossoms & leaves, signed
"Anthony Bacher" on base,
Winchester, Virginia,
late 19th c. **5,462.00**

Plate, 12½" d., coggled edge,
yellow slip w/sgraffito checkered
tulips & asters climbing from a
checkered pot within an incised
line border, daubed w/brown &
green, attributed to Jacob
Medinger, Montgomery County,
Pennsylvania, early 20th c.
(rim chips)................................**805.00**

Teapot, cov., oval cylindrical body
w/a straight angled spout, D-
form handle & low domed cover
w/a reeded acorn finial, overall
engine-turned chevron bands,
Staffordshire, England, ca.
1755, impressed pseudo-
Chinese seal marks, 3" h.
(small chips) **345.00**

Umbrella stand, tall cylindrical
form w/a molded tree trunk
design w/a molded ivy vine up
the side, worn original brown &
white paint on exterior, red paint
on interior, 20½" h. **110.00**

Washbowl & pitcher, baluster-
form pitcher w/applied & spurred
strap handles, the matching
bowl w/pierced soap dish,
scrolled crest & mock screws,
both w/creamy white slip glaze
w/daubings of green & red,
attributed to J. Eberly & co.,
Strasburg, Virginia, ca. 1880,
some wear, scratches & old
chips, bowl 13½" d., pitcher
11½" h., the set **5,462.00**

RED WING

*Various potteries operated in Red Wing,
Minnesota from 1868, the most successful
being the Red Wing Stoneware Co., organized
in 1878. Merged with other local potteries
through the years, it became known as Red
Wing Union Stoneware Co. in 1894, and was
one of the largest producers of utilitarian
stoneware items in the United States. After a
decline in the popularity of stoneware
products, an art pottery line was introduced
to compensate for the loss and this was
reflected in a new name for the company, Red
Wing Potteries, Inc., in 1930. Stoneware
production ceased entirely in 1947, but vases,
planters, cookie jars and dinnerwares of art
pottery quality continued in production until
1967 when the pottery ceased operation
altogether.*

Red Wing Marks

ART POTTERY
Planter, canoe-shaped, white
birch pottery, marked "Red Wing
USA," 9¾" l.............................**$145.00**

Planter, swan-shaped, green,
marked "Red Wing USA #259,"
5⅛" l. **28.00**

Planters, model of a bunny,
No. 988, pr..................................**15.00**

Trivet, Minnesota Centennial,
1858-1958, signed "Red Wing
Potteries, Red Wing Minn.,"
6⅝" d. **75.00**

Vase, 7⅜" h., brushed-ware vase
w/cattails, green, rose & white,
stamped "Red Wing Union
Stoneware".................................**55.00**

BRUSHED & GLAZED WARES

Red Wing Cemetery Vase

Vase, 10" h., brushed ware
cemetery vase, green & white,
unmarked (ILLUS.) **40.00**

DINNERWARES & NOVELTIES

Casserole dish, cov., green
rooster-shape, marked "Red
Wing USA, #249," 9¼" l...............**95.00**

Cookie jar, cov., Labriego design,
brown or white, incised peanuts,
no markings...............................**55.00**

Pitcher, water, jug-type w/ice lip,
Rum Rill mark............................**38.00**

STONEWARE & UTILITY WARES

Beater jar, white glazed
stoneware, wire handles, signed
"Red Wing Union Stoneware"......**80.00**

Bean pot, white & brown glazed
stone, advertising marked
"Compliments of D. Theophilus
Grain-Coal Howard S.D." **75.00**

Stoneware Beater Jar

Beater jar, cylindrical w/a molded
rim, white glazed w/blue bands
& advertising in a rectangle on
the front (ILLUS.)......................**145.00**

Bowl, 4" d., spongeware, paneled
stoneware, rare (ILLUS. bottom
left) **350.00**

Bowl, 7" d., spongeware, paneled
stoneware (ILLUS. bottom
right) **145.00**

Bowl/milk pan, white glaze
stoneware, base signed "Red
Wing USA," 13" d. **55.00**

Stoneware Bowls with Sponging

White Glazed Butter Crock

Butter crock, white glazed stoneware, 4" wings, "20 lbs.," rare (ILLUS.)............................**875.00**

Christmas tree holder, white glazed stoneware **650.00**

Union Stoneware Churn

Churn w/wooden cover & dasher, swelled cylindrical body w/eared handles & a molded rim, white-glazed, blue birch leaves over oval & slip-quilled "4," Union Stoneware Co., Red Wing, Minnesota, 4 gal., 20" h. (ILLUS.) **295.00**

Churn, 5 gal. **175.00**

Cooler, iced tea, white glazed stoneware, bailed handles, no wing, 11¾" d., 5 gal. **385.00**

Crock, cov., white glazed stoneware, Nebraska advertising, 3 gal. **525.00**

Crock, white glazed stoneware, two "elephant ears," Union oval stamp, 10¾" d., 3 gal..................**85.00**

Crock, white glazed stoneware, 4" wing, bailed handles, Red Wing oval stamp, 17" d., 12 gal. **110.00**

Filter, cov., white glazed stoneware w/blue bands, blue or black stamp reads "Success - Filter Manufactured by - Union Stoneware Co. - Red Wing, Minn.," w/spigot, 4 gal., 3 pcs....**725.00**

Fruit jar, cov., white glazed stoneware, blue or black stamp reads "Stone - Mason Fruit Jar - Union Stoneware Co. - Red Wing, Minn.," 1 qt. **185.00**

Stoneware Jar

Jar, cov., white glazed stoneware, 4" wing, Red Wing oval stamp, ball lock, 3 gal. (ILLUS.) **210.00**

Jug, molded body, overall Albany slip glaze, 1 gal...........................**65.00**

Jug, beehive-shaped, wing & oval on domed portion, after 1918, 15" h., 4 gal. **575.00**

Koverwate, white glazed stoneware, 5 gal. size................**215.00**

Koverwate, white glazed
stoneware, stamped, 12" d.,
10 gal.......................................**175.00**

Pantry jar, cov., stamped wing
mark, advertising
"Fennimore, WI" **850.00**

Salt box, hanging-type,
Grey Line.............................**1,950.00**

Water cooler, cov., side handles,
large wing mark, 5 gal. **350.00**

ROCKINGHAM WARES

The Marquis of Rockingham first
established an earthenware pottery in the
Yorkshire district of England in around 1745
and it was occupied afterwards by various
potters. The well known mottled brown
Rockingham glaze was introduced about 1788
by the Brameld Brothers and became
immediately popular. It was during the 1820s
that the production of true porcelain began at
the factory and continued to be made until the
firm closed in 1842. Since that time the so-
called Rockingham glaze has been used by
various potters in England and the United
States, including some famous wares
produced in Bennington, Vermont. However,
very similar glazes were also used by potteries
in other areas of the United States including
Ohio and Indiana and only wares specifically
attributed to Bennington should use that
name. The following listings will include
mainly wares featuring the dark brown
mottled glaze produced at various sites here
and abroad.

Bank, squatty bulbous body
w/wide finely beaded center
band below coin slot, topped
w/tall ringed finial & raised on
pedestal base w/wide disc foot,
flint enamel glaze, ca. 1850-60,
Bennington, Vermont, 6½" h. ..**$863.00**

Bowl, 6¼" d., tub-shaped w/ring
handles, mottled brown glaze
(ILLUS. next page, No. 3)..........**303.00**

Bowl, 7⅛" d., shallow, mottled
brown & yellow Rockingham
glaze, Bennington, Vermont,
Fenton's "1849" mark **770.00**

Candlestick, ringed columnar
shape w/flaring foot, Flint
Enamel glaze, Bennington,
Vermont, 6¾" h. **798.00**

Candlestick, ringed columnar
shape w/flaring foot, Flint
Enamel glaze, Bennington,
Vermont, chip on flange at base
of socket, 6⅞" h. **385.00**

Candlestick, ringed columnar
shape w/flaring foot, Flint
Enamel glaze, Bennington,
Vermont, 8¼" h. **880.00**

Candlestick, ringed columnar
shape w/flaring foot, Flint
Enamel glaze, Bennington,
Vermont, 9½" h. **715.00**

Candlestick, ringed columnar
shape w/flaring foot, Flint
Enamel glaze, Bennington,
Vermont, 9⅝" h. **935.00**

Candlestick, ringed columnar
shape w/flaring foot, Flint
Enamel glaze, Bennington,
Vermont, 9⅝" h......................**1,430.00**

Creamer, Alternate Rib patt.,
footed bulbous waisted shape,
arched rim spout, applied C-
scroll handle, Bennington,
Vermont, Fenton's "1849" mark,
pinpoint flakes & short rim
hairline at handle, 5½" h
(ILLUS. next page, No. 2).......**1,100.00**

Crock, footed cylindrical body
w/incurved panels to the rolled
rim, applied cherub head
handles, mottled brown glaze,
6¾" d., 5" h. (ILLUS. next page,
No. 4)..**72.00**

Flask, model of a book, mottled
brown glaze, "Bennington Battle"
impressed on spine, ca. 1849-
58, Bennington, Vermont,
5¾" h. **748.00**

Flask, model of a book, Flint
Enamel glaze, "Ned Buntline's
Bible" impressed on the spine,
Bennington, Vermont, Fenton's
"1849" mark, 6" h....................**2,530.00**

1   2   3   4
5   6   7

Various Rockingham Pieces

Flask, model of a book, Flint Enamel glaze, "Hermit's Life & Suffering" impressed on the spine, Bennington, Vermont, ca. 1849-58, 6" h. **978.00**

Flask, model of a book, Flint Enamel glaze, "Battle of Bennington" impressed on the spine, Bennington, Vermont, lip chips, 6⅞" h. **440.00**

Foot warmer, bell-shaped w/one side flattened w/impressed foot rests, opening at center of top, dark brown slightly mottled glaze, ca. 1847-58, Bennington, Vermont, 9½" h. (large repaired crack) ....**300.00 to 400.00**

Models of lions, head turned slightly to one side, "coleslaw" mane, tongue up, one forepaw raised on a globe, tail draped over its back, standing on a rectangular plinth (appear to be re-attached to bases), covered in a mottled green, rust & cream

Flint Enamel glaze, Bennington, Vermont, 1849-58, one w/hind legs repaired & minor chip to base, break & repairs, 11" l., 9½" h., facing pr. **7,475.00**

Pipkin, bulbous body w/molded rim & applied curved handle, mottled brown glaze, Bennington, Vermont, minor wear & short hairlines in rim, 5½" h., plus handle (ILLUS. No. 5) **358.00**

Pitcher, 7" h., footed bulbous body tapering to high arched spout, applied C-scroll handle, mottled dark brown glaze, decorated w/relief-molded tulips (ILLUS. No. 1) **110.00**

Pitcher, 7¼" h., footed cylindrical body w/wide shoulder below a wide waisted neck, rim spout & applied C-scroll handle, Flint Enamel glaze, small flake on spout, Bennington, Vermont **275.00**

Pitcher, 9½" h., Swirled Alternate Rib patt., bulbous double-gourd shape, rim spout w/molded scrolls & high C-scroll handle, Flint Enamel glaze, chip at end of handle, Bennington, Vermont, impressed 1849 mark A (ILLUS. No. 7) **1,815.00**

Snuff jar, cov., seated figural Mr. Toby holding mug in his hand, hat serves as cover, 1849 mark on base, Bennington, Vermont, 4¼" h. (mismatched cover, base chips) ....**500.00 to 700.00**

Rockingham Tobacco Jar

Tobacco jar, cov., cylindrical sides w/a flaring, ringed foot & rim, the sides w/a continuous molded grapevine design, flattened domed cover w/button finial, mottled dark brown glaze, small chips, 7½" h. (ILLUS.) **220.00**

Toby bottle, seated Mr. Toby, wearing jacket & top hat, straddling barrel & holding a beer mug in his hand, dark brown slightly mottled glaze, mid-19th c., possibly English, 9" h., rim & base chips...............**173.00**

Vegetable dish, open, octagonal w/wide flanged rim, mottled brown & yellow glaze,

Bennington, Vermont, Fenton's "1849" mark, minor glaze wear on rim, 12⅞" l. (ILLUS. No. 6) **1,265.00**

Washbowl & pitcher, washbowl w/wide paneled sides, footed pitcher w/tapering octagonal sides w/wide flaring spout & angled handle, Flint Enamel glaze, each w/1849 mark on base, Bennington, Vermont, ca. 1849-58, bowl 13½" d., pitcher 13" h., the set (glaze wear to interior of bowl, mold crack to pitcher handle).......................**1,093.00**

Water cooler, octagonal w/embossed brick base & Doric columns, Flint Enamel glaze, "Fenton's Enamel pat. 1849, Lyman Fenton Co. Bennington Vermont" impressed in block letters on frieze of entablature, ca. 1848-53, Bennington, Vermont, cracks, lacks cover, 15¾" h. ....**1,700.00 to 2,000.00**

ROOKWOOD

Considered America's foremost art pottery, the Rookwood Pottery Company was established in Cincinnati, Ohio in 1880, by Mrs. Maria Nichols Longworth Storer. To accurately record its development, each piece carried the Rookwood insignia, or mark, was dated, and, if individually decorated, was usually signed by the artist. The pottery remained in Cincinnati until 1959 when it was sold to Herschede Hall Clock Company and moved to Starkville, Mississippi, where it continued in operation until 1967.

A private company is now producing a limited variety of pieces using original Rookwood molds.

Rookwood Mark

Ashtray, figural, modeled as a stylized pelican w/a squatty oblong body & a long pointed wide-open beak, gunmetal black glossy exterior glaze & bright yellow interior, No. 6149, 1930, 4" h. **$385.00**

Book ends, figural, modeled as a Dutch boy leaning on a grey stone wall above a band of pink tulips & green leaves on one & a Dutch girl leaning on a matching wall on the other, the stylized figures decorated in shades of blue & white, Matte glaze, designed by Sallie Toohey, No. 6022, 1945, 5⅝" h., pr. **495.00**

Book ends, figural, modeled as a elephant w/trunk down walking on a molded rectangular base, dark green Matte glaze, No. 2444 D, 1925, 5⅛" h., pr. **605.00**

Book ends, figural, a large frog straddling a domed pile of rounded large pebbles, mottled dark bluish green Matte glaze, No. 2603, 1924, 4½" h., pr. **1,320.00**

Book ends, figural, model of a large rook perched on a rockwork paneled base, rich greenish black Matte glaze, designed by William McDonald, No. 2275, 1925, 5¼" h., pr. **660.00**

Bowl, 5½" d., 4¾" h., inverted bell-shaped body on ring foot, decorated w/red & purple flowers against an orange butterfat ground, No. 2193, impressed w/flame mark & artist's initials, 1924, K. Jones ...**468.00**

Bowl, 6⅜" d., wide flattened bottom w/low incurved sides, the upper rim decorated w/a repeating band of stylized peach-colored flowers & greyish green leaves against a white ground, Vellum glaze, No. 1324, 1909, Lorinda Epply **303.00**

Box, cov., octagonal, the flat paneled sides & fitted flat cover decorated w/a creamy white ground, the cover painted w/a scrolled wreath of deep red & blue blossoms & dark green leaves & brown stems, each side panel w/a similar small floral cluster, glossy glaze, No 2793, 1925, Lorinda Epply, 5⅞" w..**770.00**

Box, cov., wide low cylindrical base w/a molded bottom rim below a continuous molded band of stylized walking classical figures, the overhanging slightly domed cover w/an outer rim band of embossed palmettes centered by a raised disc supporting a seated figural centaur finial, brownish green Matte glaze, turquoise glossy glaze interior, designed by Arthur Conant, No. 2458, 1920, 6⅝" h. **523.00**

Candlesticks, Art Deco style, a slender conical form w/stepped & angled tiers around the upper half, on a stepped, low-domed round foot, Ivory Wax Matte glaze, designed by Louise Abel, No. 6188, 1934, 9¼" h., pr. **550.00**

Candlesticks, figural, a pair of tall standing stylized Egyptian maidens side-by-side holding a flared urn on their shoulders between them, long pleated dresses, raised on a flaring oval pedestal base, overall blue Matte glaze, No. 2304, 1920, retailer's paper tag on the base of one, 11" h., pr. **660.00**

Chocolate pot, cov., slightly tapering tall cylindrical body w/a rim spout & squared loop handle, a flattened fitted lid w/pointed knob finial, pale bluish grey shaded to cream ground decorated w/a long branch of white apple blossoms & green leaves on brown branches up the side, Cameo glaze, No. 251, 1888, Artus Van Briggle, 7¾" h. (few minor glaze scratches) **990.00**

Ewer, squatty bulbous base tapering sharply to a slender flaring neck w/a rolled tricorner rim, applied S-scroll handle, the body decorated w/dark green thistle leaves, stems & buds w/a touch of yellow against a dark brownish green shaded ground, Standard glaze, No. 725 C, 1897, Sallie Toohey, 7½" h. **330.00**

Ewer, footed squatty bulbous base tapering to a tall slender cylindrical neck w/a tricorner rim & long S-scroll handle from rim to top of the body, slip-painted w/yellow honeysuckle & dark green leaves on a shaded brown ground, Art Nouveau scrolling pierced silver overlay down the neck & one side & solid silver around the rim & handle, Standard glaze, No. 468CC, 1893, Josephine Zettel **2,090.00**

Ewer, bulbous nearly spherical body centered by a short cylindrical neck w/a tricorner rim w/the back edge turned down, small C-scroll handle down the neck, shaded dark brown ground decorated on the front w/a bright yellow wild rose blossom & buds & dark shaded green leaves & stems, Standard glaze, No. 62, 1888, Albert Valentien, 8¾" h. (few small glaze bubbles on neck) **605.00**

Inkstand, cov., figural, a wide rounded lily pad-form base w/upturned edges, centered by a bulbous blossom bud-form inkwell w/a small fitted cover w/a tiny knob finial, a large rook stands to one side of the center well, slightly crystalline shaded dark blue Matte glaze, No. 998 1922, 7" h. **2,640.00**

Jar, cov., wide ovoid body w/a small flat mouth fitted w/a flat cover w/small knob finial, Vellum glaze, shaded cream to pale pink ground, No. 1821, 1914, Katherine Van Horne (two chips on cover) **288.00**

Jug w/original stopper, a spherical body w/a D-form shoulder handle & a short flaring cylindrical upright rim spout fitted w/a pointed molded flame-form stopper, the shoulders molded in relief w/a fanned design, fine Matte green glaze, No. 694, 1906, 5¼" d., 8¼" h. **2,090.00**

Loving cup, three-handles, wide cylindrical body w/a flat rim & thick D-form handles, decorated w/a bust portrait of a Native American w/three feathers in his hair & wearing a braided collar on his shirt, dark portrait against a very dark blackish brown ground, Standard glaze, No. 830 E, 1898, Sturgis Laurence, 4¾" h. (minor glaze scratches) **1,100.00**

Mask, half-round bust of a young woman w/pierced-through eye openings, semi-matte white glaze, 1937, small **138.00**

Medallion, round dished form w/low sides, lightly molded on the interior w/a view of the Rookwood Pottery through its gates above the word "Rookwood," green Aventurine glaze, designed for the MacConnell & Company Engineers & Appraisers by Ruben Earl Menzel, 1956, 5⅝" d. **303.00**

Model of a camel, recumbent animal w/its head held high, on a thick rectangular base, overall tan Matte glaze, designed by Louise Abel, No. 6166, 1930, 6½" h. **1,760.00**

Model of a donkey, seated stylized animal in caramel brown w/light brown embossed ribbing, Matte glaze, No. 6243, 1939, E. Abel, 5¾" w., 4¼" h. **330.00**

Model of a rook, large bird perched on a rockwork base, overall glossy black glaze, designed by William McDonald, No. 2636, 1922, 9¼" h............**1,760.00**

Mug, commemorative, wide slightly tapering cylindrical body w/a C-form handle, a shaded very dark brown & green ground embossed w/the image of a railroad mail bag, Standard glaze, 1905, Laura Lindeman, base incised w/notation "Compliments of Fifth Division Railway Mail Service to Delegates Attending Annual Convention Cincinnati, Ohio 1905," 4¾" h. **413.00**

Mug, tankard-type, flared base tapering to cylindrical neck, deeply carved w/arrowroot plants, the broad handle hand-modeled in the shape of an arrowroot leaf, under Matte green & blue glaze, No. 1014C, impressed w/flame mark & artist's initials, 1905, Rose Fescheimer............................**1,200.00**

Paperweight, figural, "Elephant and Clown," molded as a clown standing beside an elephant on a thick rectangular base, rich gunmetal black glaze, designed by William McDonald, No. 2628, 1921 ....**605.00**

Paperweight, figural, model of a standing rooster decorated in pastel tones of greenish yellow, pink & blue on a rectangular thick greenish yellow base, Matte glaze, designed by William McDonald, No. 6030, 1928, 5" h. **550.00**

Paperweight, figural, model of a seal, brown Matte glaze, No. 6071, 1929, 3" h.................**605.00**

Paperweight, figural, a model of a Spanish galleon under full sail on a rectangular base molded w/undulating waves, creamy yellow Matte glaze, No. 2792, 1927, 3⅞" h. **303.00**

Pitcher, 7" h., 9¾" d., Jewel porcelain, bulbous ovoid body w/cylindrical neck & pinched spout, applied handle, decorated w/blue & black cherry blossoms against a light green ground, fringed w/gun metal drip at the rim & pattern at the base, No. 13, impressed w/flame mark & artist's initials, 1925, Sarah Sax...............................**1,870.00**

Plaque, rectangular, a winter landscape w/a partially frozen lake in the foreground between snow-covered banks w/tall fir trees in the background & high mountains in the distance, in shades of dark & light blue, green, purple, white & cream, Vellum glaze, in original wide ogee dark green frame w/a gold edge, 1918, Elizabeth McDermott, 6⅛ X 8" **3,850.00**

Plaque, rectangular, a large mountainous landscape showing a crater lake w/bald mountains in the background & tall pines in the foreground, in tones of brown, blue & green, ca. 1946, E.T. Hurley, in original giltwood shadowbox frame, 9½ X 11½"...............................**5,500.00**

Plaque, rectangular, a wide landscape scene of leafy birch trees surrounding a long, narrow lake, in shades of blues, greens, tans & cream, Vellum glaze, 1947, E.T. Hurley, in new wide beveled frame w/original frame available, 12⅜ X 14⅛"............**9,900.00**

Potpourri jar w/inner & outer covers, ovoid body w/a wide flattened domed cover, the cover decorated w/a large center stylized purple blossom & green leaves on a medium blue ground & w/a border band of white blossoms, the body w/overall stylized purple blossoms & green leaves on the medium blue ground, Matte glaze, No. 1321 E, 1924, Elizabeth Barrett, 4" h...............**495.00**

Ring tray, a small low-sided rounded dish w/a flat rim, the side heavily embossed w/a realistic lizard, fine Matte green glaze, designed by Kataro Shirayamadani, No. 630Z, 1904, 3¼"w., 1" h. **330.00**

Teapot, cov., bulbous ovoid body tapering slightly to a wide flat mouth fitted w/a domed cover & pointed button finial, short curved shoulder spout & angled C-form handle, the sides & sections of the cover painted w/large red & golden yellow blossoms against a very dark shaded green ground, the body, handle, spout & rim covered w/Gorham silver w/pierced leafy scroll silver overlay down & around the front, the cover finial & rim covered & silver w/panels of pierced silver overlay, Standard glaze, No. 615, 1892, 6⅜" h. **1,980.00**

Tile, square, embossed decoration of a pink & tan parrot against green & violet flowers, No. 3077, 1921, 5½" w. **220.00**

Tile, square, incised & decorated w/a beautiful woman w/cocoa & brown hair & a long, flowing dress in rich tan, kneeling & picking flowers w/rich reddish brown blossoms & light green stems from a pasture of olive green ground backed by tall trees w/olive green trunks & mint green leaves & a rich medium blue sky, in a wide flat dark oak frame, 11½" w. **2,530.00**

Trivet, round, molded overall w/flying sea gulls covered w/an Aventurine green glaze over a deep purple mottled ground, No. 2351, 1930, 5¾" d..............**440.00**

Vase, 4½" h., 3½" d., short ovoid body w/a wide rolled rim, decorated w/a wreath of green & yellow flowers outlined in dark blue against a turquoise ground,

Wax Matte glaze, No. 63, 1924, E. Barrett **330.00**

Vase, 4½" h., 4½" d., bulbous ovoid body tapering to a wide flat molded mouth, decorated w/a wide band of stylized pink wild roses & pale green leaves on a shaded turquoise blue butterfat ground, Wax Matte glaze, No. 905E, 1928, Margaret McDonald **660.00**

Vase, 4½" h., 5½" d., squatty bulbous ovoid body w/a wide rounded shoulder to a wide short cylindrical neck, Coramundel aventurine flambé glaze, original paper label, 1932 ....**440.00**

Vase, 5½" h., 3" d., bulbous baluster-form w/a short widely flaring neck, painted white & brown fish on a milky porcelain cream & blue ground, No. 6148, 1943, Jens Jensen **1,100.00**

Vase, 5½" h., 4¼" d., ovoid body tapering to very slightly flared rim, incised w/stylized blossoms in green, brown & dark blue on matte green ground, Matte glaze, No. 914C, impressed w/flame mark & artist's initials, 1919, C.S. Todd **605.00**

Vase, 5¾" h., 3"d., simple ovoid body tapering to a short slightly swelled cylindrical neck w/a closed rim, Sea Green glaze, decorated w/a wild rose sprig in shades of green w/a brown neck & shoulder, No. 920, 1901, Sallie E. Coyne......................**1,725.00**

Vase, 6" h., 3½" d., wide cylindrical body rounded at the bottom rim & shoulder & w/a very short cylindrical neck, the shoulder decorated w/a band of large drooping red flowers & pointed green leaves against a peachish pink ground, Wax Matte glaze, No. 1873V, 1920, Elizabeth Lincoln **660.00**

Vase, 6" h., 3¾" d., ovoid body gently tapering to a flat mouth flanked by small angled loop handles, decorated w/white bulb flowers w/celadon green leaves against a grey shaded to ivory shaded to creamy yellow ground, Iris glaze, No. 104E, 1906, Irene Bishop **825.00**

Vase, 6" h., 4" d., ovoid form tapering to a man & woman wrapped around rim, covered in a smooth Matte glaze, No. 128Z, 1901, A.M. Valentien **2,530.00**

Vase, 6" h., 5" d., bulbous ovoid body tapering to a short cylindrical neck, modeled w/a single large carved peacock feather in blue, orange & black on a sea green ground, Sea Green glaze, No. 531E, 1899, Matthew Daly.........................**7,710.00**

Vase, 6½" h., 3½" d., Jewel Porcelain, slender ovoid body tapering to a short cylindrical neck, decorated w/purple flowers & green leaves on a feathered violet to cream to peach ground, No. 6735, 1939, Kataro Shirayamadani............**1,430.00**

Vase, 6½" h., 5" d., Jewel Porcelain, wide ovoid body w/a wide shoulder to the low molded mouth, decorated w/white & orange flowers w/large green leaves against a shaded blue to ivory ground, No. 6640, 1937, Katiro Shirayamadani **1,650.00**

Vase, 6¾" h., 3" d., Jewel Porcelain, squatty bulbous base below thin slightly swelled cylindrical neck, decorated w/pink & blue cherry blossoms & brown branches on an ivory ground & dark grey base, No. 308, impressed w/flame mark & artist's initials, 1922, Lorinda Epply **605.00**

Vase, 6¾" h., 3" d., slender ovoid body slightly tapering to a gently flared rim, decorated w/sweet pea blossoms, leaves & peas in green & white up the sides against a shaded black to ivory ground, Iris glaze, No. 917D, 1907, Irene Bishop **935.00**

Vase, 7" h., 2¾" d., cylindrical ovoid body w/short cylindrical neck & flat rim, painted pink & white clover blossoms & green leaves on a lavender to olive green ground, Iris glaze, No. 907F, 1902, O.G. Reed ...**1,100.00**

Vase, 7" h., 3" d., cylindrical, decorated around the base w/large triangular leaves in a veined green glaze against a smooth raspberry ground, Matte glaze, No. 1124E, 1905, Sallie Coyne **880.00**

Vase, 7" h., 3½" d., cylindrical body flaring to bulbous shoulder tapering to short flat rim, decorated w/a colorful meadow scene of trees fringed by purple, green & blue mountains, Vellum glaze, No. 935E, impressed w/flame mark & artist's initials, 1921, Fred Rothenbusch........**1,760.00**

Vase, 7¼" h., 3½" d., slender ovoid body w/a short gently tapering neck, decorated w/large white poppies on slender green leafy stems against a shaded grey, green & pink ground, Iris glaze, No. 943E, 1911, Caroline Steinle **880.00**

Vase, 8" h., 4¾" d., wide ovoid body tapering to a short cylindrical neck, decorated w/orange & yellow wild roses & celadon green leaves on a shaded ivory, peach & grey ground, Iris glaze, No. 906D, 1906, Sallie Coyne **1,540.00**

Vase, 8" h., 5" d., ovoid body tapering to a short cylindrical neck, decorated around the shoulder w/white flowers & green leaves on a pink ground, Wax Matte glaze, No. 933D, 1931, L.N. Lincoln **825.00**

Vase, 8" h., 5" d., a wide ovoid lower body below a wide flattened shoulder centered by a wide cylindrical neck w/a widely rolled rim, the lower body embossed w/a band of alternating tall, wide pointed leaves & stems of mistletoe, flowing medium brown Matte glaze, No. 2413, 1928 ....**358.00**

Vase, 8¼" h., 3½" d., ovoid body w/short flared rim, w/carved drooping blue flowers w/green leaves on a raspberry pink ground, Matte glaze, No. 233, impressed w/flame mark & artist's initials, 1917, C.S. Todd **715.00**

Vase, 8¼" h., 4¼" d., slender ovoid body w/a thin rolled rim, decorated w/a banded landscape featuring a wintry greys & blues pond scene against a pale yellow sky, No. 217C, 1912, Fred Rothenbusch..................**1,100.00**

Vase, 8¼" h., 4¼" d., balusterform w/a low flaring foot & tapering to a flaring rim, small loop handles on the lower body, decorated w/amber & yellow pansies on a mahogany ground, rim overlaid w/silver continuing down the sides as pierced Art Nouveau scrolling bands & around the lower body as pierced & arched panels of leafy scrolls, solid silver around the foot, Standard glaze, No. 941W, 1892, Constance Baker..........**1,870.00**

Vase, 9¼" h., 4½" d., a flaring base supporting a tall gently flaring cylindrical body w/a wide angled shoulder tapering up to a low molded rim, decorated w/a snow landscape in dark bluish greys & ivory w/a band of dark blue at the rim, Vellum glaze, No. 1356D, 1918, Sallie Coyne **2,200.00**

Vase, 9¼" h., 5¼" d., swelled cylindrical body w/closed-in rim,

deeply carved w/stylized tulips in light green, blue & yellow, w/dark green leaves, against a raspberry pink ground, carved Matte glaze, No. 1126C, impressed flame mark & artist initials, 1915, C.S. Todd **1,210.00**

Vase, 9½" h., tapering cylindrical body w/a short cylindrical neck, Iris glaze, decorated w/a large iris blossom, buds & foliage in lavender, violet, white, grey, yellow & sea green, the neck mounted w/a silver collar chased w/a band of stylized flowers, No. 907DD, 1904, Charles Schmidt **1,840.00**

Vase, 9½" h., 4" d., cylindrical w/slightly incurved rim, decorated w/a continuous sunset landscape w/tall birch trees in shades of green, blue, white, pink & cream, Vellum glaze, No. 952D, 1911, Katiro Shirayamadani **6,320.00**

Vase, 9½" h., 5¼" d., ovoid form tapering to thick cylindrical neck w/flat rim, brightly painted w/red & yellow tulips & green leaves on a shaded celadon to ivory ground, No. 905C, impressed w/flame mark & artist's initials, 1901, Mary Nourse.................**2,310.00**

Vase, 9¾" h., 4½" d., a small cushion foot on a tall gently flaring cylindrical body w/a wide flattened shoulder centering a small, flat mouth, decorated around the shoulder w/a molded band of stylized wild roses & leaves, the leaves in pale blue & the blossoms & background in deep rose, Matte glaze, No. 1652D, 1913, William Hentschel **990.00**

Vase, 10" h., gently swelled ovoid body on a narrow footring, the rounded shoulder tapering to a short neck w/a widely flaring rim, Standard glaze, decorated w/a large cluster of yellow & green daffodils against a shaded dark to light brown ground, No. 903B, 1901, Sallie E. Coyne...........**1,2565.00**

Vase, 10" h., 4½" d., swelled cylindrical form tapering to slightly flared rim, w/molded & painted green leaves on a shaded burgundy, green & deep blue ground, Matte glaze, No. 1658D, impressed w/flame mark & artist's initials, 1912, W. Hentschel **825.00**

Vase, 10" h., 4½" d., Jewel Porcelain, bulbous baluster-shaped body w/thin neck, w/thick white & red butterfat glaze over blue ground, No. 1778, impressed w/flame mark & artist's initials, 1946, J. Jensen **1,045.00**

Rare Iris Glazed Vase

Vase, 10⅜" h., tall slender swelled cylindrical body w/the narrow shoulder centered by a short rolled neck, decorated w/crocus blossoms & leaves against a shaded dark to light ground, Iris glaze, 1908, Carl Schmidt (ILLUS.) **18,700.00**

Vase, 10½" h., slender baluster-form body w/a short cylindrical neck, decorated w/white iris blossoms & pale green stems & leaves against a shaded dark grey to ivory to pinkish white ground, Iris glaze, No. 667, 1910, Charles Schmidt **9,200.00**

Vase, 14⅞" h., tall slender ovoid body w/a rounded shoulder to the short rolled neck, decorated w/a continuous summertime evening landscape w/woodlands & meadows & a small village w/several buildings & a castle, in shades of blues, greens & creamy yellow, Vellum glaze, No. 614 B, 1926, Fred Rothenbusch (very minor glaze scratches) **6,050.00**

Vase, 15" h., 5¾" d., slightly swelled tall cylindrical form, decorated w/stylized bellflowers & leaves in burgundy, green & blue on a mottled chocolate brown ground, Matte glaze, No. 951, 1914, Wm. Hentschel **4,675.00**

Vase, 15½" h., tall slightly tapering cylindrical body below a short wide cylindrical neck, the body molded w/a band of tall wide & pointed leaves, Matte green glaze, brown traces at base, No. 950A, 1912.............**1,540.00**

Wall pocket, figural, modeled as a large realistic cicada w/wings closed, mottled medium Matte green glaze, No. 1636, 1922, 8¾" l. (tight crack on back near nail hole).......................**1,540.00**

ROSELANE POTTERY

Many potteries in the 1930s started out as home-based operations. Roselane was no exception. William and Georgia Fields opened their pottery in 1938 and in 1940 they moved it to Pasadena, California. "Doc," as he was called, and Georgia produced varied items and treatments in myriad glazes. There were wall pockets, sculptured animals on wood bases, ashtrays, bowls, covered boxes, figurines and vases. They created the Sparkler series in the 1950s. The original Sparklers had glass eyes but later plastic eyes were used. This line has been reproduced so novices would be wise to buy only the marked Sparklers or the ones with a paper label. With experience, it is easier to distinguish between the real thing and a reproduction. In 1968 Roselane was moved again, this time to Baldwin Park, California where it operated for six years. When "Doc" died in 1973, Georgia sold Roselane and it was moved to Long Beach. In 1977 the business closed.

Roselane Marks

Bowl, 9" d., 2" h., gloss grey outside, pink inside w/sgraffito-type fish design, mid-1940s, marked "Roselane" in a scroll....**$65.00**

Bowl, 9" d., 2" h., high-glaze grey underneath, pink inside w/sgraffito-type grey "snowflakes" design, scroll mark, Model No. A-9 (ILLUS.) **55.00**

"Snowflakes" Design Bowl

Candleholders, square center base w/vertical ribs, grey w/maroon candleholder section, marked "Roselane" in-mold, Model No. C1, also w/sticker, 2½" h., pr. **45.00**

Figure of a newsboy, standing, left hand in pocket, newspaper tucked under right arm, knee patch on left trouser, beige & brown, incised on back bottom of left pant leg, "Roselane" & incised on right pant leg bottom "USA" w/copyright symbol, 5" h...**28.00**

Figure of a nurse, holding & feeding baby, beige & brown satin matte, marked w/copyright symbol & "U.S.A.," 4½" h..............**24.00**

Figures of a man & woman, Balinese dancers on bases, high gloss grey; man signed "A.A. Tagaris" on top of base near right foot, man Model No. A401, woman, Model A402, each w/in-mold Roselane mark, woman 11" h., man 12½" h., pr..............**175.00**

Model of a cockatiel on round base, head down almost to bottom of base, tail feathers up, face features non-descript, brown & beige high gloss, marked "Roselane Pasadena, Calif.," 9¾" h. (ILLUS.) **25.00**

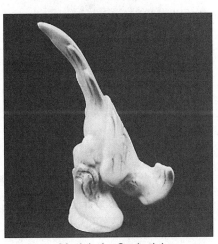

Model of a Cockatiel

Model of a fawn, lying down
w/front legs tucked under head,
left ear over body, white spots &
accents over a satin-matte
brown & beige, brown plastic
eyes, "Sparkler" series,
3¾" l., 2" h. **10.00**

Model of a Dog

Model of a dog, sitting, yellow
glass eyes, marked w/copyright
symbol & "U.S.A.," Sparkler
series, 3" h. (ILLUS.) **16.00**

Model of a goose, seated
w/head & neck over back w/bill
touching back, light & dark grey
satin-matte, incised "USA"
w/copyright symbol,
2¼" l., 3½" h. **18.00**

Roselane "Sparkler" Raccoon

Model of a raccoon, seated
w/ears & tail up, body turned
slightly, front legs out, light &
dark brown bisque w/brown
plastic eyes, "Sparkler" series,
3" h. (ILLUS.)..............................**18.00**

Roselane Running Roadrunner

**Model of a roadrunner on oval
base,** dark caramel gloss
w/black accents, incised
underglaze, "135 Roselane,"
8¾" l., 4½" h. (ILLUS.).................**35.00**

Vase, 6½" h., Chinese Modern
openwork on small square base
rising to straight sides w/tiny
flaring at rim, gloss grey outside,
maroon inside, an often
found item....................................**20.00**

ROSEMEADE

*Laura Taylor was a ceramic artist who
supervised Federal Works Projects in her
native North Dakota during the Depression
era and later demonstrated at the potter's
wheel during the 1939 New York World's
Fair. In 1940, Laura Taylor and Robert J.
Hughes opened the Rosemeade-Wahpeton
Pottery, naming it after the North Dakota
county and town of Wahpeton where it was
located. Rosemeade Pottery was made on a
small scale for only about twelve years with
Laura Taylor designing the items and
perfecting colors. Her animal and bird figures
are popular among collectors. Hughes and
Taylor married in 1943 and the pottery did a
thriving business until her death in 1959. The
pottery closed in 1961 but stock was sold from
the factory salesroom until 1964.*

Rosemeade Mark

Creamer & sugar bowl, model of
a tulip, pr....................................**$50.00**

Flower frog, model of a
seahorse, 9½" h. **80.00**

Model of a foal, lying down,
2" h..**25.00**

Model of a pheasant, 14½" h. **400.00**

Salt & pepper shakers, model of
a brussels sprout, pr. **45.00**

Salt & pepper shakers, model of
a deer, lying down, pr. **125.00**

Salt & pepper shakers, model of
a duck, head up & out,
yellow, pr. **59.00**

Salt & pepper shakers, model of
a green pepper, pr. **45.00**

Salt & pepper shakers, model of
pheasant, pr. **35.00**

Salt & pepper shakers, model of
a quail, pr....................................**35.00**

Salt & pepper shakers, model of
a skunk, large, pr. **60.00**

ROSEVILLE

Roseville Pottery Company operated in Zanesville, Ohio from 1898 to 1954 after having been in business for six years prior to that in Muskingum County, Ohio. Art wares similar to those of Owens and Weller Potteries were produced. Items listed here are by patterns or lines.

Roseville Mark

APPLE BLOSSOM (1948)

White apple blossoms in relief on blue, green or pink ground; brown tree branch handles.

Basket, hanging-type, green
ground, 8" h. **$195.00**

Basket w/low overhead handle,
blue ground, No. 310-10",
10" h..........................**225.00 to 250.00**

Console bowl, pink ground,
No. 331-12", 12" l. .....**145.00 to 155.00**

Jardiniere & pedestal base, pink
ground, No. 302-8",
28" h, 2 pcs...............................**675.00**

Pedestal base, blue ground,
No. 305-8", 8" h. **235.00**

Vase, 7" h., green ground,
No. 373-7" ....**100.00 to 125.00**

Vase, 7" h., asymmetrical rim &
handles, blue ground,
No. 382-7" **140.00**

Vase, 10" h., base handles, green
ground, No. 389-10" **145.00**

Vase, 12½" h., trumpet-shaped,
asymmetrical twig handles,
green ground **495.00**

Vases, 8¼" h., green ground,
No. 385-8", pr. **175.00**

ARTWOOD (late 1940s)

Realistically molded flowers and woody branches framed within cut-outs within geometrically shaped picture planters and vases.

Planter, rectangular upright form
on small knob feet, the bottom
center pierced through w/a
rectangular opening fitted w/a
small curving twig, No. 1054-
8½" w., 8½" l., 6½" h. **105.00**

Planter, low-footed, slightly
everted rim, tree branch within
cut-out, green, No. 1054-8½",
8½" w., 6½" h. **85.00**

Planter, rectangular form on
small knob feet, the bottom
center pierced through w/an
opening fitted w/a small curving
twig, yellow ground,
No. 1056-10", 6½ x 10" **90.00**

AZTEC (1915)

Muted earthy tones of beige, grey, brown, teal, olive, azure blue or soft white with sliptrailed geometric decoration in contrasting colors.

Aztec Jardiniere

Jardiniere, four-handled, bulbous body decorated w/yellow, brown & green flowers on glossy brown ground, 7¾" d., 5¾" h. (ILLUS.) **400.00**

Vase, 12" h., cylindrical body rising to a short projecting collar beneath a flaring rim, squeeze-bag decoration of stylized heart-shaped devices on thin stems around collar in white & sandy tan against a blue ground.....................**435.00 to 450.00**

BANEDA (1933)

Band of embossed pods, blossoms and leaves on green or raspberry pink ground.

Bowl, 11" d., 3" h., hexagonal, two-handled, green ground, No. 234-10"...............**350.00 to 400.00**

Bowl-Vase, 6½ x 6½", footed, bulbous, shoulder-handles, short collared neck, green ground......**385.00**

Candleholder, handles rising from flaring base to nozzle, green ground, 5½" h..................**400.00**

Candlesticks, handles rising from flaring base to nozzle, green ground, pr. **500.00**

Console bowl, green ground, 13" l. ....**275.00 to 300.00**

Jardiniere, No. 626-5", 5" h. **289.00**

Jardiniere & pedestal base, green ground, 14½ x 28½", 2 pcs. ("unchipped" chip at base of pedestal................................**2,860.00**

Jardiniere & pedestal base, raspberry pink ground, 14¼" d., overall 28¼" h., 2 pcs. (2 underbase chips & a line in the base of jardiniere, curving line under the top of the pedestal on the side)................................**2,310.00**

Vase, 4" h., footed squatty bulbous body, tiny rim handles, green ground............**475.00 to 525.00**

Vase, 5" h., footed squatty bulbous body, tiny rim handles, green ground **325.00**

Vase, 6" h., two-handled, tapering cylinder w/short collared neck, raspberry pink ground **420.00**

Vase, 6" h., footed, slender ovoid body w/short collared neck, loop handles from shoulder to rim, green ground, original black paper label................................**275.00**

Vase, 7" h., footed, two handles at shoulder, cylindrical, green ground......................**350.00 to 400.00**

Vase, 7" h., footed trumpet form w/long loop handles from foot to mid-section, raspberry pink ground **1,045.00**

Vase, 7" h., raspberry pink ground, No. 590-7" **389.00**

Vase, 7" h., two-handled, bulbous, green ground, No. 605-7" ....**350.00 to 400.00**

Vase, 10" h., two handles rising from shoulder to beneath rim, raspberry pink ground **825.00**

Vase, 12" h., base handles, green ground................**1,200.00 to 1,250.00**

Vase, 12" h., 10" d., expanding cylinder w/small rim handles, green ground, No. 599-12".....**1,980.00**

Vase, 12" h., expanding cylinder w/small rim handles, raspberry pink ground, No. 599-12"..........**660.00**

BITTERSWEET (1940)

Orange bittersweet pods and green leaves on a grey blending to rose, yellow with terra cotta, rose with green or solid green bark-textured ground; brown branch handles.

Basket, low overhead handle, shaped rim, green ground, No. 810-10", 10" l. .....**185.00 to 200.00**

Basket, low overhead handle, shaped rim, grey ground, No. 810-10", 10" l. .....**180.00 to 195.00**

Basket, yellow ground, No. 811-10", 10" h. **190.00**

Vase, double bud, 6" h., grey ground, No. 873-6" **100.00**

Vase, 7" h., terra cotta ground.......**85.00**

Vase, 14" h., two-handled, grey ground, No. 887-14" **425.00**

Vase, 15½" h., floor-type, baluster-form body w/trumpet neck & flaring foot, shoulder handles, grey ground, No. 888-16" **523.00**

BLACKBERRY (1933)

Band of relief clusters of blackberries with vines and ivory leaves accented in green and terra cotta on a green textured ground.

Jardiniere, two-handled, 4" h......**395.00**
Jardiniere, two-handled, 6" h......**575.00**

Blackberry Vase

Vase, 4" h., squatty bulbous body, angled shoulder handles (ILLUS.) **330.00**

Vase, 6" h., two handles at midsection **303.00**

Vase, 8" h., handles at mid-section, slightly globular base & wide neck **800.00**

Wall pocket, basket-shaped w/narrow base & flaring rim, 6¾" w. at rim, 8½" h. ....**785.00 to 800.00**

BLEEDING HEART (1938)

Pink blossoms and green leaves on shaded blue, green or pink ground.

Candlesticks, conical base, curved handles rising from base to midsection, blue ground, No. 1139-4½", 4½" h., pr. **135.00**

Cornucopia-vase, blue ground, No. 141-6", 6" h. **80.00**

Ewer, blue ground, No. 963-6", 6" h. **195.00**

Jardiniere, small pointed shoulder handles, pink ground, No. 651-3", 3" h. **45.00**

Vase, 4" h., handled, green ground, No. 961-4" **55.00**

Vase, 5" h., rose ground, No. 962-5" **175.00**

BURMESE (1950s)

Sculptured head of an Oriental-type man or woman. Also included in the line are some plain articles.

Candleholder-book end combination, man, green glaze, No. 80-B **100.00**

Candleholders-book ends combination, woman, green glaze, No. 70-B, pr. **235.00**

BUSHBERRY (1948)

Berries and leaves on blue, green or russet bark-textured ground; brown or green branch handles.

Bowl, 4" h., two-handled, globular, blue ground, No. 411-4" **100.00**

Bowl, 4" h., two-handled,
  globular, russet ground,
  No. 411-4" **85.00**

Console bowl, two-handled, blue
  ground, No. 414-10", 10" d. **130.00**

Cornucopia-vase, double, green
  ground, No. 155-8", 6" h. **140.00**

Creamer, green ground, No. 2-C ..**65.00**

Ewer, russet ground,
  No. 1-6", 6" h. **295.00**

Jardiniere, blue ground,
  No. 649-3", 3" h. **100.00**

Jardiniere, two-handled, blue
  ground, No. 657-4", 4" h. **125.00**

Planter, handled, blue ground,
  No. 383-6", 6½" l. **140.00**

Planter, handled, russet ground,
  No. 383-6", 6½" l. **110.00**

Planter, handled, russet ground,
  No. 384-8", 8" l. **195.00**

Vase, 7" h., high-low handles,
  cylindrical, low foot, blue ground,
  No. 32-7" ....**175.00 to 225.00**

Vase, 8" h., cylindrical w/flattened
  disc base above low foot, large
  curving angular handles, blue
  ground, No. 34-8" ......**175.00 to 200.00**

Vase, 9" h., two-handled,
  ovoid, blue ground,
  No. 35-9" ....**225.00 to 240.00**

Vase, 12½" h., large
  asymmetrical side handles,
  bulging cylinder w/flaring foot,
  green ground, No. 38-12" **295.00**

Vase, 12½" h., large
  asymmetrical side handles,
  bulging cylinder w/flaring foot,
  russet ground,
  No. 38-12" ....**235.00 to 250.00**

CAMEO (1920)

Antique ivory bands with embossed figures and trees, or vertical panel with peacock, on dark green or ivory backgrounds.

Jardiniere, bulbous body w/band
  of embossed figures of dancing
  women below rim, ivory ground

Cameo Jardiniere

w/green trim, minor chips to
edges of feet, 13 x 15½"
(ILLUS.) **660.00**

CAPRI (late line)

Various shapes depicting shells, leaves and overlapping petals. Sandlewood (sic) yellow or cactus green matte finishes and a metallic red semi-matte finish.

Ashtray, undulating rim, metallic
  red, No. 597-7", 7" **35.00**

Vase, 10" h., sawtooth rim, cactus
  green, No. C-1016-10" **55.00**

CARNELIAN I (1910-15)

Matte glaze with a combination of two colors or two shades of the same color with the darker dripping over the lighter tone or heavy and textured glaze with intermingled colors and some running.

Console bowl, pink ground
  w/blue drip glaze, scroll handles,
  12" d. **165.00**

Flower frog or candleholder,
  blue & rose, 3½" h.......**75.00 to 100.00**

Vase, 9" h., two-handled,
  cylindrical w/wide collared neck,
  dark & light blue.........................**235.00**

Vase, 15" h., blue & pink glazes ..**525.00**

CARNELIAN II (1915)

Intermingled colors, some with a drip effect.

Carnelian II Floor Vase

Vase, 16½" h., 10" d., floor-type, footed tall ovoid body tapering to a slightly flaring cylindrical neck, intermingled shades of turquoise blue (ILLUS.) ....**1,835.00 to 2,500.00**

CHERRY BLOSSOM (1933)

Cherry Blossom Candlesticks

Sprigs of cherry blossoms, green leaves and twigs with pink fence against a combed blue-green ground or creamy ivory fence against a terra cotta ground shading to dark brown.

Bowl, 3 x 10½", rectangular, handled, terra cotta ground, silver label **275.00**

Bowl-vase, two-handled, globular, terra cotta ground, 6" h. **495.00**

Candlesticks, flared base, loop handles at midsection, terra cotta ground, 4" h., pr. (ILLUS.) **495.00**

Jardiniere, squatty bulbous body, two-handled, terra cotta ground, 4" h. **275.00**

Jardiniere & pedestal base, terra cotta ground, 13½ x 28¼", 2 pcs. **2,310.00**

Jardiniere & pedestal base, pink & blue-green ground, 13½ x 28½", 2 pcs. **5,500.00**

Jug-vase, compressed squatty bulbous body w/a short slightly flared neck flanked by small loop handles, terra cotta ground, 4" h. **193.00**

Lamp, factory-type w/fittings, two-handled, spherical, blue-green ground ....**800.00 to 900.00**

Lamp, factory-type w/fittings, two-handled, spherical, terra cotta ground **600.00**

Vase, 4" h., jug-type, two-handled, terra cotta ground ....**245.00 to 275.00**

Small Cherry Blossom Vase

Vase, 5" h., bulbous ovoid body tapering to a wide flat mouth flanked by small loop handles, blue-green (ILLUS.) **330.00**

Vase, 5" h., two-handled, globular w/wide mouth, terra cotta ground ....**300.00 to 400.00**

Vase, 5" h., two-handled, slightly globular, terra cotta ground......................**225.00 to 250.00**

Vase, bud, 7" h., handles rising from compressed globular base, long slender tapering neck, terra cotta ground, No. 195-7" **90.00**

Vase, 7" h., terra cotta ground......................**425.00 to 500.00**

Vase, 7" h., bulbous ovoid w/tiny loop handles **495.00**

Vase, 7½" h., two-handled, cylindrical, blue-green ground (minute bruise underside of base) **825.00**

Vase, 8" h., handles at midsection, blue-green ground (hairline to rim) **385.00**

Cherry Blossom Vase

Vase, 8" h., two-handled, globular, terra cotta ground (ILLUS.) ....**475.00 to 525.00**

Vase, 10" h., two-handled, ovoid w/short wide neck, terra cotta ground (tight½" bruise on rim) ...**303.00**

Vase, 12½" h., blue-green ground **1,540.00**

Vase, 15" h., floor-type, bulbous ovoid body, small shoulder handles, terra cotta ground, No. 628-15" **2,750.00**

Wall pocket, flaring rim, blue-green ground, 5½" w., 8¼" h........................**875.00 to 925.00**

CLEMANA (1934)

Stylized blossoms with embossed latticework and basketweave on blue, green or tan ground.

Bowl, 6½" d., 4½" h., green ground, No. 281-5"....**160.00 to 200.00**

Urn-vase, two handles at midsection, pedestal base, blue ground, No. 112-7", 7½" h........**350.00**

Vase, 6¼" h., brown ground, No. 750-6", touch-up to minute nick on edge of one handle (ILLUS. right) **275.00**

Clemana Vases

Vase, 6½" h., cylindrical w/handles rising from midsection, blue ground, No. 749-6" (ILLUS. left) **385.00**

Vase, 6½" h., two-handled, expanding cylinder, green ground, No. 750-6" **350.00**

Vase, 7" h., flat pierced handles rising from base, slender rectangular form, blue ground, No. 751-7" **175.00**

Vase, 8½" h., footed cylindrical body, angled shoulder handles, blue ground (flat chip mostly under base) **275.00**

Vase, 9" h., blue ground, No. 755-9" **375.00**

Vase, 10" h, No. 757-10" **295.00**

CLEMATIS (1944)

Clematis blossoms and heart-shaped green leaves against a vertically textured ground - white blossoms on blue, rose-pink blossoms on green and ivory blossoms on golden brown.

Basket w/overhead handle,
pedestal base, brown & gold
ground, No. 389-10", 10" h. **225.00**

Ewer, blue ground, No. 18-15",
15" h. **350.00**

Vase, 6" h., handled, green
ground, No. 186-6" **90.00**

Vase, 7" h., handled, green
w/yellow & pink flowers,
No. 106-7" **75.00**

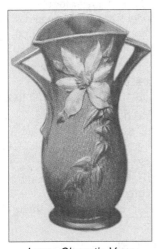

Large Clematis Vase

Vase, 15" h., floor-type, footed tall
slender baluster-form body w/a
widely flaring mouth, long
angular handles down the sides,
terra-cotta ground, No. 114-15"
(ILLUS.) **330.00**

COLUMBINE (1940s)

Columbine blossoms and foliage on shaded ground - yellow blossoms on blue, pink blossoms on pink shaded to green and blue blossoms on tan shaded to green.

Basket, elaborate handle rising
from midsection, green ground,
No. 365-7", 7" h. **180.00**

Basket, tan ground, No. 366-8",
8" h. **325.00**

Basket, blue ground,
No. 367-10", 10" h. **250.00**

Basket, pointed handle rising
from flat base, ovoid w/boat-
shaped top w/shaped rim, pink
ground, No. 368-12", 12" h. **450.00**

Bowl-vase, footed wide squatty
bulbous body w/a wide shoulder
centering a wide low shaped
mouth flanked by tiny angled
handles, shaded blue ground,
No. 655-3", 3" h. ....**65.00 to 75.00**

Urn-vase, 8" h., tan ground,
No. 151-8" **170.00**

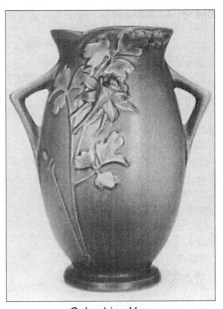

Columbine Vase

Vase, 7½" h., two-handled, ovoid
w/slightly flaring mouth, tan
ground, No. 17-7" (ILLUS.)........**265.00**

Vase, 10" h., ovoid body
w/angular handles rising from
base to midsection, blue ground,
No. 24-10" **365.00**

Vase, floor-type, 14" h.,
No. 26-14", pink........................**565.00**

Vase, 16" h., floor-type, pink
ground, No. 27-16" **450.00**

CORINTHIAN (1923)

Deeply fluted ivory and green body below a continuous band of molded grapevine, fruit, foliage and florals in naturalistic colors, narrow ivory and green molded border at the rim.

Compote, 10" d., 5" h.................**135.00**
Wall pocket, 12" h......................**395.00**

COSMOS (1940)

Embossed blossoms against a wavy horizontal ridged band on a textured ground - ivory band with yellow and orchid blossoms on blue, blue band with white and orchid blossoms on green or tan.

Basket w/overhead handle, tan ground, No. 357-10", 10" h..........................**275.00 to 300.00**
Cornucopia-vase, brown ground, No. 137-8", 8" h. **75.00**
Jardiniere, blue ground, two-handled, No. 649-3", 3" h. **90.00**
Vase, 4" h., two-handled, globular base & wide neck, green ground, No. 944-4".....................**75.00**
Vase, 4½" h., double bud, gate-form, two slender cylinders joined by arched lattice, No. 133-4½" **185.00**
Vase, bud, 7" h., slender, slightly tapering cylinder w/large loop handles at base, green ground, No. 959-7" **115.00**
Vase, 8" h., a small squared foot supports a tall waisted squared body w/the flaring rim notched by four wide pointed tabs, low arched long handles down the sides, blue ground, No. 950-8" ..**225.00**

CREMONA (1927)

Relief-molded floral motifs including a tall stem with small blossoms and arrowhead leaves, wreathed with leaves similar to Velmoss or a web of delicate vines against a background of light green mottled with pale blue or pink with creamy ivory.

Candleholders, squared flaring base, baluster-form candle nozzle, green ground, No. 1068-4", 4" h., pr................**175.00**
Vase, 5" h., pink ground, No. 352-5"................**100.00 to 125.00**
Vase, 7" h., pink ground, No. 354-7"................**125.00 to 150.00**
Vase, 10" h., square body, pink ground, No. 358-10" **150.00**
Vase, 10" h., tall ovoid body w/a narrow flared foot & a small flaring neck flanked by pointed angular handles, pink ground, No. 359-10" **275.00**
Vase, 10" h., baluster-form w/slender neck, flaring mouth & foot, mottled light green ground, No. 360-10" **303.00**
Vase, 10½" h., ovoid w/pointed handles, pink ground, No. 359-10"...............**185.00 to 250.00**
Vase, 12" h., baluster-form w/slender neck & flaring mouth, green ground, No. 361-12" **295.00**
Vase, 12" h., baluster-form w/slender neck & flaring mouth, green ground, No. 361-12" ....**235.00 to 275.00**

DAHLROSE

Band of ivory daisy-like blossoms and green leaves against a mottled tan ground.

Jardiniere & pedestal base, 13½ x 30", 2 pcs.....................**1,540.00**
Vase, triple bud, 6½" h., expanding cylinder flanked by tusk-form tubes ....**125.00 to 150.00**

DAWN (1937)

Incised spidery flowersgreen ground with blue-violet tinted blossoms, pink or yellow ground with blue-green blossoms, all with yellow centers.

Candlesticks, yellow ground, No. 1121-2", 2" h., pr.................**100.00**

Planter, long angular foot supporting a deep boat-shaped bowl w/high stepped end panels, No. 317-10", 10" l. **145.00**

Rose bowl, tab handles at sides, square base, green ground, No. 315-4", 4" d. **80.00**

DELLA ROBBIA, ROZANE (1906)

Incised designs with an overall high-gloss glaze in colors ranging from soft pastel tints to heavy earth tones and brilliant intense colors.

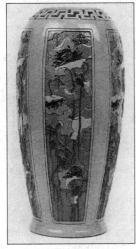

Fine Ovoid Della Robbia Vase

Vase, 17" h., tall slender ovoid body w/a slightly flared foot, a delicate reticulated geometric design surrounded the wide flat mouth, the sides w/five long vertical panels decorated w/large tan, dark brown & white poppies w/olive & greyish green centers & buds atop narrow twisting green stems w/small heart-shaped leaves against a cut-away bluish-grey background, narrow carved line surrounds panels & reticulated work, all on a pale blue background, artist-initialed, exceptional restoration to top (ILLUS.) **7,700.00**

DONATELLO (1915)

Deeply fluted ivory and green body with wide tan band embossed with cherubs at various pursuits in pastoral settings.

Flower frog, No. 14-3½", 3½" d. ....**35.00 to 45.00**

Donatello Jardiniere

Jardiniere, 10" d., 7½" h. (ILLUS.) **66.00**

DUTCH (before 19160

Creamware with colorful decal scenes of Dutch children and adults at various activities.

Lemonade set, pitcher & six tumblers, 7 pcs. (pitcher has spout damage, tumblers are in mint condition) **375.00**

Mug, scene of boy & girl fishing, 5" h. **150.00**

Dutch Plaque

Plaque, round, pierced for hanging, transfer-printed scene of two Dutch men & windmill, small flat chip on back of edge, another inside foot ring, 8½" d. (ILLUS.) **248.00**

Sugar bowl, cov., 4" h..................**85.00**

Tea set, cov. teapot, creamer &
cov. sugar bowl, 3 pcs..............**335.00**

Wash pitcher & bowl, (small chip
to pitcher) the set......................**435.00**

EXPERIMENTALS

Vase, 8¼" h., slightly waisted
cylindrical body w/small loop
handles at shoulder, decorated
w/white blossoms, yellow
centers, green leaves on yellow-
brown ground **1,980.00**

FALLINE (1933)

*Curving panels topped by a semi-scallop
separated by vertical peapod decorations;
blended backgrounds of tan shading to green
and blue or tan shading to darker brown.*

Vase, 6" h., globular w/handles
rising from shoulder to rim, tan
ground....................**800.00 to 1,000.00**

Vase, 6" h., two-handled, swollen
cylinder, tan shading to brown
ground......................**375.00 to 400.00**

Vase, 6" h., 4¾" d., ovoid body
w/flat mouth, C-form shoulder
handles, brown, green, yellow &
blue, unmarked..........................**330.00**

Falline Vase

Vase, 7" h., 6¾" d., wide spherical
body tapering to a stepped
shoulder & a short cylindrical
neck, C-scroll handles from
base of neck to top of the body,
green pods on shaded brown
ground (ILLUS.).......................**625.00**

Vase, 8" h., two-handled,
bulbous, tan shading to blue &
green **525.00**

Vase, 8" h., large handles, brown
ground, No. 651-8" **395.00**

FERELLA (1930)

*Impressed shell design alternating with
small cut-outs at top and base; mottled brown
or turquoise and red glaze.*

Ferella Bowl and Vases

Bowl, 12½" l., 7" h., a small
pierced & tapering round foot
supports a deep & widely flaring
bowl, brown ground,
No. 212-12 x 7" (ILLUS.) **770.00**

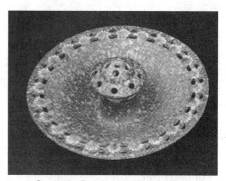

Console Bowl with Flower Frog

**Console bowl w/attached flower
frog,** deep flaring sides, brown
glaze No. 87-8", 8" d.
(ILLUS.) **413.00**

Vase, 4" h., squatty base w/exaggerated handles & narrow neck, turquoise & red glaze, No. 497-4"......................**295.00**

Small Ferella Vase

Vase, 5" h., two-handled, turquoise & red glaze, No. 500-5" (ILLUS.)...**425.00 to 450.00**

Vase, 5" h., two-handled, flaring rim, turquoise & red glaze, No. 503-5" ....**420.00 to 550.00**

Vase, 5½" h., 6½" d., tapering pierced foot supports a ringed bulbous ovoid body tapering slightly to a wide short cylindrical neck, inverted loop handles from shoulder to lower body, turquoise & red glaze, No. 504- 5½" (ILLUS. back right, w/bowl) **605.00**

Vase, 8" h., footed urn-form w/angled handles, brown ground, No. 590-8"....**650.00 to 700.00**

Vase, 9¼" h., 5¼" d., footed slender ovoid body tapering to a short flaring neck, low arched handles down the sides, stylized green & yellow blossoms on reticulated bands on a brown ground, No. 507-9" (ILLUS. back left, w/bowl) ......**550.00 to 575.00**

FOXGLOVE (1940s)

Sprays of pink and white blossoms embossed against a shaded matte finish ground.

Book ends, blue ground, No. 10, pr.................................**200.00**

Cornucopia-vase, blue ground, No. 165-5", 5" h. **125.00**

Cornucopia-vase, green ground, No. 165-5", 5" h. **135.00**

Ewer, blue ground, No. 4-6½", 6½" h. **110.00**

Pedestal base, blue ground........**465.00**

Vase, 6" h., green ground, No. 43-6" **145.00**

Vase, pillow-type, 10½" h., gold ground, No. L4-10" **265.00**

Vase, 12" h., slightly swelled cylindrical body w/rolled neck, loop handles at shoulder, green ground, No. 52-12" (professional base chip restoration)...............**245.00**

FREESIA (1945)

Trumpet-shaped blossoms and long slender green leaves against wavy impressed lines - white and lavender blossoms on blended green; white and yellow blossoms on shaded blue or terra cotta and brown.

Basket, hanging-type, green ground, No. 471-5", 5".............................**200.00 to 250.00**

Basket, domed round foot supporting a flaring ovoid body w/a divided rim w/arched ends, a low arched handle w/angled ends from side to side across the top, terra cotta ground, No. 390-7", 7" h.........**115.00 to 125.00**

Book ends, green ground, No 15, pr....................................**175.00**

Candleholders, tiny pointed handles, domed base, green ground, No. 1160-2", 2" h., pr.......................**90.00 to 110.00**

Freesia Console Bowl

Console bowl, 16½" l. blue ground, No. 469-14" (ILLUS.).....................**140.00 to 165.00**

Cookie jar, cov., blue ground, No. 4-8", 8" h. (imperfection on handle) **300.00**

Ewers, terra cotta ground, No. 21-15", 15" h., pr. **750.00**

Urn-vase, two-handled, terra cotta ground, No. 196-8" **125.00**

Vase, 7" h., base handles, long cylindrical neck, blue ground, No. 119-7" **150.00**

Vase, 9½" h., a short ringed pedestal base supporting a flaring half-round base w/an angled shoulder tapering slightly to a tall, wide cylindrical neck, down-curved angled loop handles from center of neck to rim of lower shoulder, terra cotta ground, No. 123-9"....**135.00 to 170.00**

Vase, 10" h., blue ground, No. 126-10" ....**170.00 to 200.00**

Vase, 18" h., 8¼" d., floor-type, footed tall slender ovoid body tapering to a flared rim, small pointed angular shoulder handles, brown ground, No. 129-18" **375.00**

FUCHSIA (1939)

Coral pink fuchsia blossoms and green leaves against a background of blue shading to yellow, green shading to terra cotta or terra cotta shading to gold.

Bowl, 4" d., two-handled, terra cotta ground, No. 346-4" ....**115.00 to 150.00**

Bowl-vase, terra cotta ground, No. 645-3", 3" h. **80.00**

Ewer, green ground, No. 902-10", 10" h.........................**300.00 to 325.00**

Vase, 6" h., two handles rising from bulbous base to neck, blue ground, No. 891-6" **150.00**

Vase, 7" h., terra cotta ground, No. 894-7" **220.00**

Vase, 7" h., footed baluster-shaped body w/arched loop handles near the rim, blue ground, No. 895-7"....**250.00 to 295.00**

Vase, 7" h., footed baluster-shaped body w/arched loop handles near the rim, terra cotta ground, No. 895-7" **140.00**

Vase, 8" h., handles rising from flat base to shoulder, green ground, No. 897-8" **210.00**

Vase, 8" h., footed ovoid body w/a flattened narrow shoulder w/a short four-lobed neck, long low handles from the shoulder to the base of the body, terra cotta ground, No. 897-8" **303.00**

Vase, 8½" h., pillow-type w/handles rising from base to midsection, terra cotta ground, No. 896-8" **300.00**

Vase, 12" h., two handles rising from above base to neck, terra cotta shading to gold, No. 903-12" ....**475.00 to 500.00**

Fuchsia Floor Vase

Vase, 18" h., 10" d., floor-type, a disc foot supports a tall baluster-form body w/long low C-form handles down the sides, green shading to yellow & brown ground, No. 905-18" (ILLUS.) **545.00**

FUDJI or FUJIYAMA (1906)

Fudji Vase with Tulips

This Rozane line features slip-trailed designs, often florals, against a bisque ground of grey or beige.

Vase, 10¼" h., 3¼" d., baluster form w/flaring foot, decorated w/enameled tulips in brown & green on a bisque matte buff ground , some chipping to base, pinpoint fleck to top rim, marked "Fujiyama" (ILLUS.) **500.00**

Vase, 10½" h., 4¼" d., tall slender corseted form w/a swelled shoulder to a short flaring neck, decorated in enameled slip w/a stylized floral design in long teardrop-form reserves below stylized fanned designs around the shoulder, in amber, teal blue & dark blue on a sandy ground, marked w/Rozane wafer............**990.00**

FUTURA (1928)

Varied line with shapes ranging from Art Deco geometrics to futuristic. Matte glaze is typical although an occasional piece may be high gloss.

Basket w/pointed overhead handle, tall collared neck, terra cotta ground, No. 332-6", 6½" h. w/paper label **695.00**

Futura Jardiniere

Jardiniere, angular handles rising from wide sloping shoulders to rim, sharply canted sides, pink & lavender leaves on grey ground, one chip on bottom rim, small bruise to handle, 9½ x 13½" (ILLUS.) **385.00**

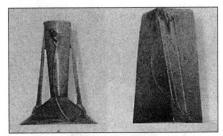

Small Futura Vases

Vase, 6" h., widely flaring conical foot tapering to a slender tall slightly flaring cylindrical body flanked by slender straight handles from near the rim to the foot, stylized floral design in blue & green on a tan shaded to cream ground, No. 422-6" (ILLUS. left) **303.00**

Vase, 6½" h., a tall squared & gently twisted slightly tapering form w/molded stylized foliage in yellow & green (ILLUS. right) **358.00**

Vase, 7" h., square shape tapering to round foot w/green trim, green "vee" design on pink ground **358.00**

Vase, 7" h., sharply canted base, handles rising from shoulder to below rim of long cylindrical stepped neck, grey-green & tan, No. 382-7" ....**350.00 to 400.00**

Vase, 8" h., bottle-shape, variegated green ground w/stepped back bands of pink & green, unmarked **385.00**

Vase, 8" h., ovoid w/short collared neck, lightly embossed floral branch at shoulder, incised rings at midsection, deep rosy beige shading to sand white & black to beige w/touch of blue at branches, No. 428-8".................**425.00**

Vase, 10" h., large spherical body on a small footring, the neck composed of stepped bands, flame-form molded design around the lower half, No. 391-10" **900.00**

Large Futura Vase

Vase, 12¼" h., 5½" d., tall flaring column rising from four spheres & resting on a square base, grey & peach, No. 393-12" (ILLUS.).....................**850.00 to 950.00**

Vase, 14" h., 5½" d., two large handles at lower half, squat stacked base & faceted squared neck, matte glaze in three shades of brown, No. 411-14".........**1,550.00 to 1,600.00**

Bowl, 9" d., 3½" h., thick footring below the widely flaring swirled & lobed sides, decorated w/multicolored circles & a green ribbon on a deep pink ground, No. 187-8" (ILLUS. next page, No. 7).......................................**220.00**

Vase, 8¼" h., 4¼" w., a small stepped triangular base supports the tall slender & slightly flaring triangular body, medium blue ground w/dark blue spearpoints up the corners of the body, No. 383-8" (ILLUS. next page, No. 4).........**550.00**

Vase, 8½" h., 6½" d., a spherical body centered at the top w/a small trumpet neck, raised on four stilts joined to the widely flaring trapezoidal foot, the body decorated w/blue, pink & yellow molded circles on a streaky green ground, No. 404-8" (ILLUS. next page, No. 1).......**1,045.00**

Vase, 8½" h., 6½" d., a spherical body centered at the top w/a small trumpet neck, raised on four stilts joined to the widely flaring trapezoidal foot, the body decorated w/yellow, pink, blue & green circles on a dark blue ground, No. 404-8" (ILLUS. next page, No. 6).......**1,430.00**

Vase, 10" h., 6" d., a narrow flaring foot below the wide ovoid body tapering to a wide, deep flaring neck flanked by small straight handles down to the shoulder, small molded brown pine cones & dark green pine sprigs on the neck & shoulder on the mottled green ground, bruise at rim, two base chips, one nick, No. 433-10" (ILLUS. next page, No. 2).........**413.00**

Vase, 10¼" h., 8" d., large spherical body on a small footring, the neck composed of

2   3   4   5

1   7   6

Various Unusual Futura Pieces

stepped bands, , a swirled glossy bluish green upper half above a dark gunmetal green lower half, No. 391-10" (ILLUS., No. 5) **770.00**

Vase, 14" h., 5½" d., footed squatty bulbous base centered by a four-section stacked body below the tall squared slender & slightly flaring neck, long curved handles from base of the neck to the rim of the squatty base, matte glaze in three shades of brown & some grey, No. 411-14", 14" h. (ILLUS., No. 3) **2,640.00**

GARDENIA (1940s)

Large white gardenia blossoms and green leaves over a textured impressed band on a shaded green, grey or tan ground.

Basket w/overhead handle, shaped rim, No. 608-10", 10" h. **185.00**

Book end, model of a half-open book w/a blossom in the center, grey ground, No. 659 (ILLUS.) ..**100.00**

Gardenia Book End

Console bowl, 12" l., 3" h., No. 630-12" (ILLUS.) **145.00**

Cornucopia-vase, grey ground, No. 621-6", 6" h. **145.00**

Gardenia Console Bowl

IMPERIAL I (1916)

Brown pretzel-twisted vine, green grape leaf and cluster of blue grapes in relief on green and brown back-textured ground.

Basket, upright oval form w/sloping rim & thick overhead handle from side to side, 6¼" h. **83.00**

Jardiniere & pedestal base, overall 28" h., 2 pcs. (hard to find bruise on rim of jardiniere) ..**660.00**

Imperial I Umbrella Stand

Umbrella stand, professional repair of small rim chip, 19½" h. (ILLUS.) **1,430.00**

Vase, triple bud, 8½" h., No. 30-8½" ....**100.00 to 125.00**

Vase, 10" h., semi-ovoid body w/angled handles & tall wide cylindrical neck w/flat rim, unmarked **127.00**

IRIS (1938)

White or yellow blossoms and green leaves on rose blending with green, light blue deepening to a darker blue or tan shading to green or brown.

Basket w/pointed overhead handle, compressed ball form, rose ground, No. 354-8" ....**300.00 to 375.00**

Basket, hanging-type, handled, tan ground, 8" d. **220.00**

Book ends, green ground, No. 5, pr. **125.00**

Bowl, 5" d., two-handled, blue ground, No. 359-5" **225.00**

Candlesticks, blue ground, No. 1134-2", 2" h., pr. **120.00**

Candlesticks, flat disc base, cylindrical nozzle flanked by elongated open handles, tan ground, No. 1135-4½", 4½" h., pr. **200.00**

Console bowl, low oblong shape w/arched sides & small pierced end handles, blue ground, No. 361-8", 10" l., 3" h. **125.00**

Console bowl, 10" d., blue ground, No. 362-10" **185.00**

Flower frog, blue ground, No. 38 ....**135.00**

Pedestal base, tan shading to brown ground, 20½" h. **400.00**

Rose bowl, urn-shaped, blue ground, No. 357-4", 4" h. ....**100.00 to 150.00**

Vase, 15" h., two large handles rising from shoulder to rim, blue ground, No. 929-15" **950.00**

Wall pocket, two handles rising from base to below flaring rim, rose ground, No. 1284-8", 8" h. **695.00**

Wall shelf, rose ground, 8" h.......**475.00**

IXIA (1930s)

Embossed spray of tiny bell-shaped flowers and slender leaves - white blossoms on pink ground; lavender blossoms on green or yellow ground.

Bowl, 6" d., pink ground, No. 326-6" **75.00**

Flower frog, pink ground, No. 34 ....**60.00 to 85.00**

Lamp, blue ground **795.00**

Vase, 8" h., a disc foot supporting a round-bottomed cylindrical body w/a flat rim, tall stepped buttresses from the base halfway up each side, yellow ground, No. 856-8" **165.00**

JONQUIL (1931)

Small Jonquil Bowl-Vase

White jonquil blossoms and green leaves in relief against textured tan ground; green lining.

Bowl-vase, footed bulbous nearly spherical body tapering to a wide low rolled mouth flanked by small C-form handles, 5" d., 4" h. (ILLUS.)....................**138.00**

Bowl, 4" h., squatty bulbous form w/wide flat mouth, small loop handles ....**120.00 to 140.00**

Bowl-vase, down-turned handles, globular, No. 524-4", 4" h. **165.00**

Flowerpot w/frog, No. 94-5½", 5½" h. **350.00**

Jardiniere, two-handled, No. 621-4", 4" h.........**125.00 to 150.00**

Jardiniere, two-handled, No. 621-9", 9" h.........**350.00 to 400.00**

Jardiniere, bulbous, two-handled, 10 x 14" (pinhead glaze nick to one flower)..............................**825.00**

Vase, 4½" h., globular, No. 93-4½" ....**175.00 to 195.00**

Vase, 5" d., 4" h., squatty bulbous body, small loop handles...........**165.00**

Vase, 6½" h., wide ovoid body w/an angled mid-band below the tapering upper section, a wide flat mouth w/arched open handles from the top rim to the mid-band **375.00**

Vase, 6½" h., pear-shaped body tapering to a flat mouth, arched loop handles from the rim down the sides to the widest point **395.00**

Vase, 7" h., base handles ....**170.00 to 195.00**

Vase, 7½" h., squatty bulbous vase w/large loop handles from mid-section to rim **413.00**

Vase, 9½" h., bulbous base w/wide cylindrical neck, slender handles at midsection...............**495.00**

Vase, 12" h., two handles beneath flared rim, slightly ovoid, unmarked....................**1,210.00**

LAUREL (1934)

Laurel branch and berries in low-relief with reeded panels at the sides. Glazed in deep yellow, green shading to cream or terra cotta.

Bowl, 6" d., No. 128-6" **125.00**

Candleholders, No. 1054-4", 4" h., pr. **150.00**

Urn, squatty bulbous body w/closed handles at shoulder, green shading to cream ground, No. 250-6", 6¼ x 7" (ILLUS. right) **495.00**

Vase, 8" h., bulbous ovoid body w/short collared neck, closed handles from shoulder to rim, terra cotta ground, No. 672-8" (ILLUS. left) **413.00**

Laurel Urn and Vase

LOTUS (1952)

Stylized slender lotus petals in vertical relief up the sides of pieces.

Candleholders, No. L5,
2½" h., pr. **110.00**

Planter, brown & beige glossy
finish, No. L9-4", 4" sq., 3½" h.....**75.00**

Planter, blue & white glossy
glaze, No. L7-10½", 10½" h.......**100.00**

Vase, 10" h., cylindrical, cream &
blue high-gloss finish,
No. L3-10" **110.00**

LUFFA (1934)

Relief-molded ivy leaves and blossoms on shaded brown or green wavy horizontal ridges.

Jardiniere & pedestal base,
brown ground, overall 25" h., 2
pcs. (chip to base of jardiniere,
still in place).............................**880.00**

Jardiniere & pedestal base,
green ground, 14½ x 28½", each
piece marked w/silver label,
2 pcs. **2,200.00**

Luffa Vase

Vase, 8½" h, tapering cylindrical
body w/wide molded mouth,
small angled handles rising from
shoulder to beneath rim, green
ground (ILLUS.) ....**325.00 to 350.00**

LUSTRE (1921)

Simple shapes with lustrous glaze in pink, orange and blue.

Console bowl, pink glaze,
No. 6-10", 10" h. **140.00**

**Basket w/tall pointed overhead
handle,** orange glaze,
No. 298-8", 8" h. **99.00**

MAGNOLIA (1943)

Large white blossoms with rose centers and black stems in relief against a blue, green or tan textured ground.

Basket, handled, tan ground,
No. 383-7", 7" h. **95.00**

Book end, blue ground, No. 13.....**85.00**

Bowl, green ground, No. 449-10",
10" l. **110.00**

Candleholders, round base
w/low socket flanked by pointed
angular handles, blue ground,
No. 1156-2½", 2½" h., pr. **110.00**

Console bowl, brown ground,
No. 452-14", 14" l.
(two minor chips) **125.00**

Cornucopia-vase, tan ground,
No. 184-6", 6" h. **110.00**

Creamer, blue ground, No. 4.........**70.00**

Ewer, footed ovoid body w/a wide
shoulder tapering to a slender
forked neck w/a tall, narrow
arched spout & pointed angled
handle, No. 14-10", 10" h. **240.00**

Planter, shell-shaped w/angular
base handles, blue ground,
No. 183-6", 6" l. **125.00**

Tea set: cov. teapot, creamer &
open sugar bowl; blue ground,
No. 4, 3 pcs. **385.00**

Vase, 6" h., handled, tan ground,
No. 446-6" **100.00**

Vase, 9" h., fan-shaped, handles
rising from base to midsection,
brown shading to green ground,
No. 987-9" **220.00**

Magnolia Floor Vase

Vase, 15" h., floor-type, footed,
  ovoid body tapering to wide
  cylindrical neck w/slightly flaring
  rim, angled handles from
  shoulder to neck, brown ground,
  flake at base No. 98-15"
  (ILLUS.) **385.00**

Vase, 16" h., floor-type, green
  ground, No. 99-16" **650.00**

MODERNE (1930s)

*Art Deco style rounded and angular
shapes trimmed with an embossed panel of
vertical lines and modified swirls and circles -
white trimmed with terra cotta, medium blue
with white and turquoise with a burnished
antique gold.*

Vase, 6" h., a round foot tapering
  to a narrow short stem
  supporting a tall conical body,
  two small curved handles from
  foot to lower body, turquoise
  ground, No. 788-6"....**125.00 to 150.00**

Vase, 15" h., 7" d., floor-type, tall
  cylindrical body w/flaring foot,
  small loop handles at base, soft
  cream glaze with a soft orange
  underglaze, impressed mark **413.00**

MONTACELLO (1931)

*White stylized trumpet flowers with black
accents on a terra cotta band light terra cotta
mottled in blue or light green mottled and
blended with blue backgrounds.*

Montacello Console Bowl & Flower Frog

Basket, wide squatty bulbous low
  base centered by a wide
  cylindrical neck w/a rolled rim, a
  long curved upright handle from
  shoulder to shoulder coming to a
  high point above the neck, blue
  ground, No. 332-6",
  6½" h........................**550.00 to 600.00**

Console bowl w/flower frog, low
  long rectangular form w/gently
  rounded ends & the long sides
  coming to soft points at the
  center, the upper half of the
  sides forming a gently sloping
  shoulder to the conforming rim
  w/thick C-form end handles from
  the shoulder to the lower side, a
  round flower frog inside, blue
  ground, No. 225-9", 13" l., 3" h.,
  2 pcs. (ILLUS.) **495.00**

Console bowl, two-handled,
  green ground, No. 225-9", 9" l...**325.00**

Vase, 4" h., sharply compressed
  globular base, handles rising
  from shoulder to rim, terra cotta
  ground, No. 555-4" **160.00**

Vase, 4" h., sharply compressed
  globular base, handles rising
  from shoulder to rim,
  No. 555-4" **275.00**

Vase, 6" h., bulbous ovoid body
  w/wide collared rim, large loop
  shoulder handles, No. 560-6"
  (ILLUS. top next page) **400.00**

Montacello Vase

Vase, 7" h., ovoid w/shoulder handles & collared neck, blue ground, No. 562-7" **650.00**

Vase, 7" h., two-handled, slightly ovoid, wide mouth, terra cotta ground, No. 561-7" **440.00**

Vase, 9" h., two handled, bulbous ovoid, terra cotta ground, No. 564-9" **715.00**

Vase, 10½" h., expanding cylinder w/small base handles, terra cotta ground, No. 565-10" **825.00**

MORNING GLORY (1935)

Two Morning Glory Vases

Stylized pastel morning glory blossoms and twining vines in low relief against a white or green ground.

Bowl-vase, two-handled, green ground, 7" d., 4½" h..................**413.00**

Candleholders, flaring pedestal base tapering to a tall bell-form socket w/small angled handles from the socket to the base, 4½" h., No. 1102-4½", pr..........**450.00**

Urn-vase, two-handled, bulbous body, green ground, 6" h. **770.00**

Vase, 4" h., squatty bulbous, two-handled, white ground, No. 268-4" **275.00**

Vase, 6¾" h., narrow footring support a wide waisted cylindrical body w/a flared rim, low angled handles down the sides, white ground (ILLUS. right) **248.00**

Vase, 7" h., pillow-shaped, base handles, green ground **385.00**

Vase, 7" h., pillow-shaped, base handles, white ground **300.00**

Vase, 7¼" h., an oval disc foot tapers to a tall slightly flaring cylindrical body w/a flared rim & long angled handles from the foot up the sides, green ground (ILLUS. left) **356.00**

Vase, 15" h., shoulder handles, slightly expanding cylinder, green ground (invisible repair to very small chip) **1,210.00**

MOSS (1930s)

Spanish moss draped over a brown branch with green leaves against a background of ivory, pink or tan shading to blue.

Bowl, 4" d., blue ground, No. 289-4" **160.00**

Moss Jardiniere

Jardiniere, wide bulbous ovoid body w/a wide, flat molded mouth flanked by small angled tab handles, tan shading to blue ground, No. 635-7", 7" d., 5½" h. (ILLUS.) **220.00**

Vase, 5" h., blue ground,
No. 773-5" **170.00**

Vase, 6" h., large open angular
handles, blue ground,
No. 774-6" **250.00**

MOSTIQUE (1915)

Incised Indian-type design of stylized flowers, leaves or geometric shapes glazed in bright high-gloss colors against a heavy, pebbled ground.

Bowl, 7" d., low rounded sides,
floral design, sandy beige
ground **115.00**

Jardiniere, geometric floral
design w/arrowhead leaves, tan
ground, No. 606-6", 6" h. **250.00**

Mostique Vase

Vase, 9¾" h., 7" d., bulbous ovoid
body below a slightly tapering
cylindrical neck w/a flat rim, a
triple-ring light brown neck band
above bluish green & pink
blossoms above light brown leaf
clusters on a tan ground
(ILLUS.) **330.00**

Vase, 10¼" h., waisted cylinder
w/flaring mouth, two handles
rising from base to midsection,
arrowhead leaves design, tan
ground, No. 5321-10" **248.00**

PEONY

Peony blossoms in relief against a textured swirling ground yellow blossoms against rose shading to green, brown shading to gold or gold with green; white blossoms against green.

Console bowl, gold ground,
No. 4-10", 10" l. ....**250.00 to 300.00**

Model of a conch shell, gold
ground, No. 436, 9½" w.............**135.00**

Model of a conch shell, rose
ground, No. 436, 9½" w.............**150.00**

Vase, 6" h., pointed handles at
midsection, gold ground,
No. 168-6" **185.00**

Vase, 9" h., No. 65-9" **190.00**

Vase, 18½" h., floor-type,
No. 70-18" ....**550.00 to 600.00**

PINE CONE (1931)

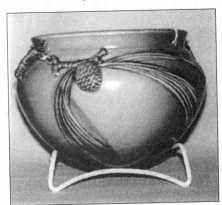

Pine Cone Hanging Basket

Realistic embossed brown pine cones and green pine needles on shaded blue, brown or green ground (Pink extremely rare)

Basket, hanging-type, squatty
bulbous body tapering slightly
toward the base, w/a short wide
cylindrical neck flanked by tiny
branch hanging handles, blue
ground, No. 352-5", 7" d.,
5½" h. (ILLUS.) ....**375.00 to 450.00**

Bowl, 6" d., green ground,
No. 426-6" **195.00**

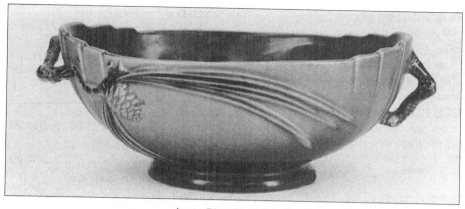

Long Pine Cone Bowl

Bowl, 4 x 11", two-handled, brown ground, No. 279-9" **195.00**

Bowl, 9" l., 4" h., footed oval low body w/fanned sections at each end & small twig end handles, brown ground, No. 279 (ILLUS.) **195.00**

Bowl-vase, squatty nearly spherical body w/a wide short cylindrical neck & small twig loop handles, brown ground, No. 632-3", 3" h. **125.00**

Jardiniere, brown ground, No. 632-3", 3" h. **100.00**

Jardiniere & pedestal base, brown ground, No. 632-12", unmarked, jardiniere 12" h., overall 32" h. (flat chip, mostly underneath, to bottom of jardiniere) **3,575.00**

Jardiniere & pedestal base, blue ground, impressed mark, repair to chip on edge of pedestal, 12" d., 28½", 2 pcs. (ILLUS. next column) **2,200.00**

Lamp base, green ground..........**500.00**

Mug, green ground, No. 960-4", 4" h. ....**200.00 to 225.00**

Planter, single side handle rising from base, blue ground, No. 124-5", 5" h. (ILLUS. top next page) **275.00**

Pine Cone Jardiniere & Pedestal

Planter, single side handle rising from base, brown ground, No. 124-5", 5" h. **220.00**

Planter, brown ground, No. 456-6", 6" l. **160.00**

Vase, 6" h., fan-shaped, green ground, No. 472-6" **195.00**

Vase, 6" h., brown ground, No. 748-6" **175.00**

Vase, 6" h., brown ground, No. 838-6" **200.00**

Pine Cone Planter

Vase, bud, 7" h., green ground,
No. 479-7" **175.00**

Vase, 7" h., blue ground,
No. 704-7" **275.00**

Vase, 9" h., pillow-type, blue
ground, No. 846-9" **450.00**

Vase, 10" h., green ground,
No. 491-10" **288.00**

Vase, 10" h., blue ground,
No. 747-10" ....**400.00 to 450.00**

Vase, 10" h., brown ground,
No. 747-10" ....**400.00 to 450.00**

Vase, 10" h., green ground,
No. 849-10" **595.00**

Pine Cone Double Wall Pocket

Wall pocket, double, two flaring
conical containers joined by an
arched pine cone & needle top
handle, blue ground,
No. 1273-8", 8½" h. (ILLUS.).....**650.00**

Basket, hanging-type, squatty
bulbous body tapering slightly
toward the base, w/a short wide
cylindrical neck flanked by tiny
branch hanging handles, brown
ground, repair to rim,
No. 352-5", 7" d., 5½" h.
(ILLUS. next page, No. 8).........**193.00**

Basket, deeply curved boat-
shape w/overhead branch
handle & open pine needle
handle supports at one end,
blue ground, No. 410-10", 10" l.
(ILLUS. next page, No. 6).........**523.00**

Pitcher, 9½" h., 8¾" d., bulbous
broad ovoid body w/a wide
shoulder tapering up to a small
neck w/a pinched spout, small
arched branch shoulder handle,
green ground, original foil label,
No. 708-9" (ILLUS. next
page, No. 3).............................**495.00**

Vase, 8¼" h., 8" d., disc foot
supporting a wide rounded
squatty base w/a sharp angled
shoulder w/tapering sides to the
tall, wide cylindrical neck,
asymmetrical branch handles,
blue ground, impressed mark
(ILLUS. next page, No. 10)........**715.00**

Vase, 10¼" h., 7¾" d., pedestal-
footed wide urn-form body w/a
sharp shoulder angle tapering to
a slightly flaring deeply forked
neck, angular branch handles
from mid-neck to shoulder rim,
blue ground, blue ground,
impressed mark
(ILLUS. next page, No. 4).........**990.00**

Vase, 10¼" h., 7¾" d., pedestal-
footed wide urn-form body w/a
sharp shoulder angle tapering to
a slightly flaring deeply forked
neck, angular branch handles

1   2   3   4   5
6   7   8   9   10

Large Group of Pine Cone Pieces

from mid-neck to shoulder rim, brown ground, impressed mark (ILLUS., No. 2) **605.00**

Vase, 12½" h., 7" d., a wide squat flaring base w/an angled low shoulder below the tall conical tapering sides w/a slightly flaring rim, asymmetrical twig handles, brown ground (ILLUS., No. 5) ...**495.00**

Vase, 12½" h., 7" d., a wide squat flaring base w/an angled low shoulder below the tall conical tapering sides w/a slightly flaring rim, asymmetrical twig handles, green ground (ILLUS., No. 1) **495.00**

Vases, bud, 7½" h., tall slender cylindrical body w/a rounded base & slightly flaring rim, curving pine cone & pine needle handle from base to mid-body, brown ground, No. 479-7", pr. (ILLUS., No. 9) **413.00**

Wall shelves, rectangular shelf above a long pointed support w/a pine cone & needle bracket green ground, No. 1, 5" w., 8" h., pr. (ILLUS., No. 7) **990.00**

POPPY (1930s)

Embossed full-blown poppy blossoms, buds and foliage yellow blossoms on green, white blossoms on blue or soft pink blossoms on a deeper pink.

Console bowl, handled, pink ground, No. 338-10", 10" d. **275.00**

Ewer, pink ground, No. 876-10", 10" h. **295.00**

RAYMOR (1952)

Modernistic design oven-proof dinnerware.

Bean pot, cov., Autumn brown, No. 193, 3 qt. **70.00**

Bean pot, cov., Autumn brown, No. 194, 2 qt. **50.00**

Bean pot, cov., individual, Autumn brown, No. 195..............**40.00**

Casserole, cov., Autumn brown, No. 183, 11" d.............................**60.00**

Celery/olive dish, Autumn brown, No. 177 ....**40.00**

Creamer, Autumn brown, No. 158......................................**20.00**

Coffeepot, cov., in stand,
No. 176, grey (top repair) **225.00**

Gravy boat, No. 190, grey **30.00**

Pitcher, water, 10" h., Autumn
brown, No. 189 ....**75.00**

ROSECRAFT HEXAGON (1924)

Six-sided form decorated with a simple impressed circular medallion enclosing an elongated stylized flower.

Rosecraft Hexagon Candleholders

Candleholders, orange
decoration on brown ground,
glaze flake to tip of one, 5" d.,
8½" h., pr (ILLUS. of one)..........**605.00**

Vase, double bud, 5" h., gate-
form, blue hi-gloss glaze **550.00**

Vase, 5" h., brown & orange.......**330.00**

Vase, 7 3/8" h., chalice-shaped,
orange & brown **715.00**

ROZANE (1917)

Various forms with pebbled, honeycomb backgrounds in ivory, light green, pink, yellow and blue molded in high-relief w/large clusters of colored blossoms & green leaves .

Jardiniere & pedestal base,
ivory honeycomb ground w/floral

clusters in dark rose, pale yellow
& blue, jardiniere, 14" d., overall
29" h., 2 pcs. (minor roughness
to high points) **440.00**

Urn-vase, short pedestal base
tapering to a flaring rounded
body continuing into upright
inwardly scrolling handles rising
above the rim, ivory
ground, 6½" h. **165.00**

Vase, 7" h., ivory ground **75.00**

Vase, 8" h., baluster-form w/wide
flat mouth....................................**95.00**

Wall pocket, wide bullet-form
w/arched backplate, large floral
cluster on an ivory ground,
7½" h. (tiny firing crack)............**250.00**

ROZANE PATTERN (1940s)

Simple traditional and contemporary shapes decorated with softly blended or mottled matte glazes.

Console bowl, glossy tan glaze,
No. 396-10", 10" d. **60.00**

Console bowl, blue matte glaze,
No. 397-14", 14" l. **65.00**

Vase, 8½" h., pedestal-footed
urn-shape, No. 5-8" **70.00**

RUSSCO (1930s)

Narrow perpendicular panel front and back, stacked handles and octagonal rim openings; solid matte glaze or matte glaze with crystalline overglaze.

Vase, 7" h., brown & gold glaze...**195.00**

Vase, 7" h., flared rim, blue
matte glaze **110.00**

Vase, 8" h., two-handled, gold
w/crystalline overglaze,
green interior **95.00**

Vase, 10½" h., gold glaze............**150.00**

Vase, 14½" h., floor-type, Art
Deco design w/vertical ribbing &
stacked handles, olive green to
buff crystalline flambe glaze
(bruise or "unchipped chip" at
top rim, glaze flake) **220.00**

Vase, 14½" h., floor-type, Art Deco design w/vertical ribbing & stacked handles, persimmon glaze...**295.00**

SAVONA (1924-2

Classical shapes, some with deeply fluted areas at either top or bottom, the smooth areas decorated with cascading grape vines in high-relief; other pieces with fluting covering the entire surface, broken by a horizontal band of beading. High gloss glaze, usually in salmon pink, lime green or light blue.

Savona Vase

Vase, 8½" h., bulbous ovoid body tapering to small flat mouth, one burst bubble near top, light blue glossy glaze (ILLUS.)......................................**413.00**

SILHOUETTE (1952)

Recessed shaped panels decorated with floral designs or exotic female nudes against a combed background.

Candleholders, sloping base, waisted stem, red ground, No. 751-3", 3" h., pr...**125.00 to 150.00**

Planter, footed narrow rectangular form, turquoise ground, No. 731-14", 14" l. ....**100.00 to 125.00**

Vase, 5" h., white ground, No. 779-5" **60.00**

Vase, 5¾" h., 9" d., bulbous, two-handled, female nude, turquoise blue ground **825.00**

Vase, 6" h., handled, blue ground, No. 780-6" **240.00**

Vase, 7" h., fan-shaped, female nudes, white w/turquoise blue panel, No. 783-7"......................**265.00**

Vase, 9" h., double, base w/canted sides supporting two square vases w/sloping rims, joined by a stylized branch-form center post, florals, turquoise blue ground, No. 757-9" **75.00**

SNOWBERRY (1946)

Clusters of white berries on brown stems with green foliage over oblique scalloping, against a blue, green or rose background.

Basket, a wide disc foot supporting a tall trumpet-form body w/an irregular rim joined by an arched handle w/angled ends, shaded rose ground, No. 1BK-10", 10" h. **195.00**

Snowberry Ewer

Ewer, squatty bulbous base below tapering ringed sides to the short cylindrical forked neck w/a high arched spout, angular loop handle from top rim to mid-body, shaded blue ground, No. 1TK-6", 6" h. (ILLUS.) **160.00**

Ewer, shaded rose ground,
No. 1TK-6", 6" h.......................**165.00**

Ewer, shaded blue ground,
No. 1TK-7", 7" h........................**245.00**

Ewer, sharply compressed base
w/long conical neck, shaded
green ground, No. 1TK-10",
10" h. **200.00**

Snowberry Pillow Vase

Vase, 6½" h., pillow-type, a
sloping rectangular foot
supporting a flattened ovoid
form w/the rim curving upward
opposite a stepped tall end tab,
a short C-form handle from the
base to the lower body on one
side & a pointed angled handle
down the opposite side of the
body, shaded green ground,
No. 1FH-6" (ILLUS.) **140.00**

Vase, 6½" h., pillow-type, shaded
rose ground,
No. 1FH-6" ....**75.00 to 100.00**

Vase, 10" h., shaded rose ground,
No. 1V1-10"............................**215.00**

Vase, 15" h. floor-type, shaded
blue ground **450.00**

Wall pocket, wide half-round
form tapering to a pointed base,
low angled handles along the
lower sides, shaded blue
ground, No. 1WP-8",
8" w., 5½" h. (ILLUS.)...............**195.00**

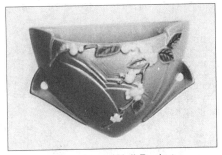

Snowberry Wall Pocket

Wall pocket, angular handles
rising from base, shaded green
ground, No. 1WP-8",
8" w., 5½" h. **195.00**

SUNFLOWER (1930)

Long-stemmed yellow sunflower blossoms framed in green leaves against a mottled green textured ground.

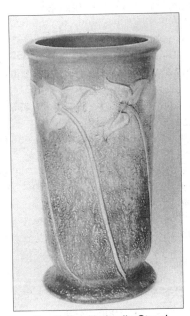

Sunflower Umbrella Stand

Bowl, 5" d., No. 208-5" **650.00**

Jardiniere & pedestal base,
13½" h., overall 28½" h., 2 pcs.
(6 tiny burst bubbles
from firing) **4,400.00**

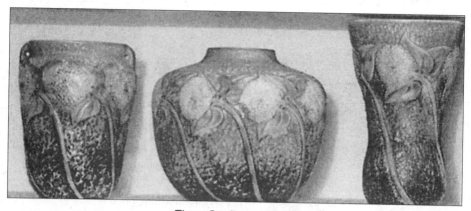

Three Sunflower Vases

Jardiniere & pedestal base,
14" h., overall 29" h., 2 pcs.....**3,850.00**

Umbrella stand, footed tall
cylindrical body w/a thick
molded rim, two small glaze
nicks, one on a leaf & one on a
stem, 11" d., 20¼" h. (ILLUS.
bottom, previous page)...........**6,600.00**

Urn, globular w/small rim handles,
4" h. **550.00**

Urn-vase, 6" h. **850.00**

Vase, 5" h., two-handled,
bulbous......................................**495.00**

Vase, 5" h., two-handled,
cylindrical w/a tapering base **495.00**

Vase, 6" h., cylindrical w/tiny rim
handles (tight hairline at rim) **350.00**

Vase, 6⅛" h., slightly swelled &
flaring cylindrical body w/a short,
wide cylindrical neck flanked by
tiny rim handles (ILLUS. left) **523.00**

Vase, 6⅛" h., 7" d., wide bulbous
ovoid body w/a wide shoulder
tapering to a small flat neck
(ILLUS. center) **660.00**

Vase, 7¼" h., slender trumpet-
form body slightly swelled at the
base (ILLUS. right) **770.00**

Vase, 5¼" h., 4" d., a rounded
bottom below tapering cylindrical
sides w/a molded rim, long low

curved handles down the sides
(ILLUS. next page, No. 7).........**715.00**

Vase, 5¼" h., 5" d., bulbous ovoid
body tapering to a wide flat
mouth flanked by low pointed
shoulder handles
(ILLUS. next page, No. 6).........**660.00**

Vase, 8½" h., 6¾" d., a wide
bulbous ovoid base w/a narrow
rounded shoulder to the tall
slightly tapering cylindrical neck
w/a wide flat rim (ILLUS. next
page, No. 5)...........................**1,320.00**

Vase, 8½" h., 6¾" d., a wide
bulbous ovoid base w/a narrow
rounded shoulder to the tall
slightly tapering cylindrical neck
w/a wide flat rim (ILLUS. next
page, No. 8)...........................**1,100.00**

Vase, 9¼" h., 6½" d., wide ovoid
body tapering to a wide
cylindrical neck flanked by low
curved handles to the shoulder
(ILLUS. next page, No. 1).......**1,320.00**

Vase, 10½" h., 6½" d., tall swelled
cylindrical body tapering slightly
to a wide flat mouth flanked by
tiny loop handles (ILLUS. next
page, No. 2)...........................**1,100.00**

Vase, 10½" h., 6½" d., tall swelled
cylindrical body tapering slightly
to a wide flat mouth flanked by
tiny loop handles (ILLUS. next
page, No. 4)...........................**2,090.00**

1   2   3   4   5

6   7   8

Large & Small Sunflower Vases

Vase, 10½" h., 7½" d., a rounded base below tall wide gently flaring cylindrical sides w/a wide flattened shoulder centered by a wide low molded mouth (ILLUS., No. 3).....................................**2,200.00**

TEASEL (1936)

Gracefully curving long stems and delicate pods.

Vase, 6" h., footed spherical body tapering to a flat closed rim flanked by small curved tab handles, blue ground, No. 348-6" **165.00**

Vase, 7" h., low footed body w/closed handles, beige shading to tan ground, No. 883-7" **115.00**

Vase, 10" h., a conical pedestal foot supporting a tall slightly flaring cylindrical body w/a rolled rim, long slender buttress handles from the mid-body to the foot, shaded blue ground, No. 887-10" ....**150.00 to 165.00**

TOPEO (1934)

Four evenly spaced vertical garlands beginning near the top and tapering gently down the sides.

Bowl, 9" d., 2½" h., sharply canted sides, glossy deep red glaze.....................................**175.00**

Bowl, 11½" d., 3" h., wide low sides w/angled flat shoulder to a wide, low rim, molded around the shoulder w/four small "snails," red glaze **150.00**

Vase, 6" h., 6½" d., bulbous nearly spherical body curving up to a wide low cylindrical neck flanked by four tapering rows of beads, glossy deep red glaze,...**193.00**

Vase, 7" h., slightly bulbous base below straight tapering sides & a short collared mouth, glossy deep red glaze ....**200.00 to 250.00**

Vase, 8" h., wide-mouthed bulbous body, glossy deep red glaze.....................................**275.00**

Vase, 9" h., bulbous body, glossy deep red glaze...........................**195.00**

Vase, 12" h., flared sides, glossy deep red glaze ....**375.00 to 475.00**

Vase, 14" h., bulbous ovoid body tapering to a flaring wide cylindrical neck, matte blue ground w/pastel pink & green tapering bead bands down the sides at the center **825.00**

TOURMALINE (1933)

Produced in various simple shapes and a wide variety of glazes including rose and grey, blue-green, brown or azure blue with green and gold, and terra cotta with yellow.

Console bowl, low pedestal foot tapering to an squatty bulbous oblong body molded w/alternating wide & narrow ribs & tapering slightly to a lightly scalloped rim, mottled green glaze, No. 241-12", 13¼" l., 4¾" h. **120.00**

Ginger jar, cov., mottled tan glaze, 6" h..................................**450.00**

Urn-vase, compressed globular base w/short collared neck, mottled turquoise or mottled blue, No. A-200-4", 4½" h., each ....**100.00 to 125.00**

Vase, 8" h., tall twisted panel hexagonal body, pink & blue mottled glaze, No. A-425-8" **225.00**

Vase, 8" h., a narrow footring below the squatty wide bulbous base w/a wide shoulder ring below the tall, wide trumpet neck, thick C-form handles from the base of the neck to the bottom of the base, mottled rose shading to grey glaze, No. A-332-8"..............................**165.00**

TUSCANY (1927)

Gently curving handles terminating in blue grape clusters and green leaves.

Bowl w/flower frog, 4 x 9 x 15½", mottled pink ground..............................**300.00**

Candleholders, tapering pedestal base supporting a tall waisted candle socket, arched leaf handles on sides of the base, mottled pink ground, 4" h., pr. ...**125.00**

Console bowl, footed widely flaring low rectangular bowl w/rounded, paneled ends, mottled grey ground, 12" l. **150.00**

Console bowl, octagonal, mottled greyish blue ground, 12" l. **150.00**

Console bowl w/flower frog, mottled pink ground, 9 x 15½", 4" h., 2 pcs..............................**300.00**

Flower arranger, a widely flaring ringed low pedestal base supporting a flattened urn-form body w/low curved shoulder to a small, flat mouth, looped leaf handles curve over the shoulder, mottled grey ground, 5" h. **150.00**

Vase, 8" h., handled, mottled pink **100.00**

Vase, 9" h., footed bulbous ovoid body w/a wide shoulder tapering to a cylindrical neck flanked by curved leaf handles ending at the shoulders, mottled pink ground **495.00**

Vase, 12" h., footed tall swelled cylindrical body tapering to a short cylindrical neck flanked by small leaf handles, mottled pink ground **395.00**

WATER LILY (1940s)

Water lily blossoms and pads against a horizontally ridged ground. White lilies on green lily pads against a blended blue ground, pink lilies on a pink shading to green ground or yellow lilies against a gold shading to brown ground.

Water Lily Handled Vase

Basket, conch shell-shaped w/high arched handle, brown ground, No. 381-10", 10" h. **235.00**

Water Lily Ewer

Ewer, disc foot below a tall slender ovoid body tapering to a slender forked neck w/a high arched spout, pointed angled handle from just under rim to mid-body, blended blue ground, No. 12-15", 15" h. (ILLUS.).....................**350.00 to 400.00**

Jardiniere, pink shading to green ground, No. 653-8", 8" h. **410.00**

Vase, 6" h., handled, gold shading to brown ground, No. 72-6" **75.00**

Vase, novelty-type, 6" h., blended blue ground, No. 174-6" **175.00**

Vase, 9" h., a low pedestal foot below the slightly swelled lower body & tapering cylindrical upper body w/a slightly flared rim, long inverted angular handles down the sides, pink shading to green ground, No. 78-9" (ILLUS. previous page)..........................**185.00**

Vase, 9" h., pink shading to green ground, No. 79-9" ......**125.00 to 150.00**

WHITE ROSE (1940)

White roses and green leaves against a vertically combed ground of blended blue, brown shading to green or pink shading to green.

Basket, hanging-type, squatty bulbous form w/incurved rim pierced w/hanging holes, brown shading to green ground, No. 463-5", 5" h.........**190.00 to 250.00**

Basket, pink shading to green ground, No. 364-12", 12" h. **200.00**

Bowl-vase, nearly spherical body w/a wide short neck flanked by small loop shoulder handles, No. 653-3", 3" d., 3" h. **75.00**

Cornucopia-vase, double, pink shading to green ground, No. 145-8", 8" h. **145.00**

White Rose Cornucopia-vases

Cornucopia vases, brown shading to green ground, No. 144-8", 8" h., pr. (ILLUS.)....**248.00**

Ewer, footed wide compressed body tapering to a pierced narrow cylindrical neck w/a long arched spout, loop handle down the side, blue ground, No. 981-6", 6" h. **120.00**

Urn-vase, blended blue ground, No. 387-4", 4" h. **70.00**

Vase, 6" h., footed swelled cylindrical body w/a rounded shoulder centering a four-notched low cylindrical neck, sharply pointed loop shoulder handles, blended blue ground, No. 979-6" **100.00**

Vase, 7" h., handled, blended
blue ground, No. 982-7" **125.00**

Vase, 9" h., blended blue ground,
No. 986-9" **345.00**

Vase, 9" h., fan-shaped, a
tapering rectangular base below
the flatted flaring rectangular
sides w/a wide shaped &
double-notched rim, long low
loop handles from mid-body to
the base, pink shading to green
ground, No. 987-9" **250.00**

Vase, 15½" h., short tapering foot
supports a tall slightly ovoid
body flaring gently at the deeply
forked rim, long low loop
handles down the sides,
blended blue ground,
No. 992-15" **325.00**

WINCRAFT (1948)

*Shapes from older lines such as Pine Cone,
Cremona, Primrose and others, vases with an
animal motif, and contemporary shapes. High
gloss glaze in bright shades of blue, tan,
yellow, turquoise, apricot and grey.*

Book ends, chartreuse ground,
No. 259-6½", 6½" h. pr. **155.00**

Tea set: cov. teapot, creamer &
open sugar bowl; No. 271,
3 pcs. **185.00**

Vase, 10" h., cylindrical, tab
handles, black panther & green
palm trees in relief on shaded
lime green ground, No. 290-10"
(factory flaw on
panther).....................**275.00 to 300.00**

WINDSOR (1931)

*Stylized florals, foliage, vines and ferns on
some, others with repetitive band
arrangement of small squares and rectangles,
on mottled blue blending into green or terra
cotta and light orange blending into brown.*

Jardiniere, bulbous body w/short
wide cylindrical neck, loop
handles from shoulder to rim,
blue, w/ferns, 7" h. (lip repair)...**435.00**

Vase, 7½" h., bulbous body
tapering to short wide cylindrical
neck, loop handles rising from
mid-section to rim, blue ground
w/ green fern decoration...........**275.00**

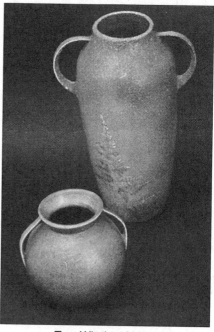

Two Windsor Vases

Vase, 7½" h., 7¾" d., nearly
spherical body tapering to a
short flaring neck w/low loop
handles from rim to shoulder,
fern decoration on brown
ground, No. 551-7"
(ILLUS. left) **440.00**

Vase, 10" h., tall ovoid body
tapering to a wide trumpet neck,
loop handles from neck to
shoulder, mottled terra cotta
ground, No. 554-10" **575.00**

Vase, 15½" h., 10" d., tall swelling
cylindrical form tapering near the
top to a flat molded rim, C-form
loop handles at the shoulders,
yellowish green fern decoration
on a speckled dark blue ground,
glaze fleck to one handle, very
small chip to base
(ILLUS. right) **2,090.00**

WISTERIA (1933)

Lavender wisteria blossoms and green vines against a roughly textured brown shading to deep blue ground, rarely found in only brown.

Roseville Wisteria Vase

Vase, 8" h., 6½" d., bulbous ovoid body tapering to a short cylindrical neck w/a wide flat rim, pointed angled handles from the neck to the shoulder, blue ground (ILLUS.) **550.00**

Vase, 8" h., 6½" d., wide tapering cylindrical body w/small angled handles flanking the flat rim, brown ground, No. 633-8" **495.00**

Vase, 10" h., waisted cylindrical w/wide flaring mouth, angled handles at mid-section (tiny base chip) **600.00**

Console bowl, squatty bulbous rounded rectangular form w/small angled end handles, brown ground, No. 243-12", 3 x 12" (ILLUS. next page, No. 14) **330.00**

Jardiniere, nearly spherical body tapering slightly to a wide flat molded mouth flanked by small angular rim handles, No. 632-5", 5" h. (ILLUS. next page, No. 9) ....\...........**495.00**

Vase, 4" h., low squatty bulbous form w/a wide sloping shoulder to the small molded mouth, tiny angled shoulder handles, mottled green & brown ground, No. 629-4", gold label (ILLUS. next page, No. 11)........**303.00**

Vase, 5¼" h., 6" d., bulbous wide flat-sided spherical body w/a flattened shoulder centered by a flat mouth, tiny angled shoulder handles, No. 632-5", silver foil label, mottled brown, yellow & green ground (ILLUS. next page, No. 13).............................**380.00**

Vase, 5¼" h., 6" d., bulbous wide flat-sided spherical body w/a flattened shoulder centered by a flat mouth, tiny angled shoulder handles, No. 632-5", mottled blue & brown ground (ILLUS. next page, No. 12)........**468.00**

Vase, 6½" h., 4" d., bulbous ovoid body w/a wide shoulder tapering up to a small mouth, small angled shoulder handles, mottled blue & brown ground, No. 630-6" (ILLUS., No. 8) **413.00**

Vase, 6½" h., 4" d., bulbous ovoid body w/a wide shoulder tapering up to a small mouth, small angled shoulder handles, mottled green & blue ground, No. 630-6" (ILLUS., No. 7) **605.00**

Vase, 8" h., 6½" d., wide & slightly tapering waisted cylindrical body w/a wide flat mouth flanked by small angled shoulder handles, mottled yellow, green & brown ground, repair to one handle, No. 633-8" (ILLUS., No. 5) **248.00**

Vase, 8" h., 6½" d., wide & slightly tapering waisted cylindrical body w/a wide flat mouth flanked by small angled shoulder handles, mottled brown & blue ground, No. 633-8" (ILLUS., No. 1) **825.00**

Vase, 8½" h., 4½" d., wide round tapering foot supporting a tall slender trumpet-form body

```
        1              2              3          4          5
6                             7        8          9       10          11
        12            13                          14
```

Roseville Wisteria in a Variety of Forms

curving inward at the shoulder to a wide flat mouth, slender slightly curved buttress handles from the foot to the mid-body, No. 635-8" (ILLUS., No. 6) **715.00**

Vase, 10¼" h., 6¼" d., tall slender swelled cylindrical body tapering slightly at the top to a wide flat mouth flanked by pointed angled shoulder handles, brown ground, No. 639-10" (ILLUS., No. 4) **715.00**

Vase, 10¼" h., 7" d., tall waisted cylindrical body w/a wide flaring mouth, long angled handles at mid-section, tiny base chip, mottled brown & green ground (ILLUS., No. 2) **715.00**

Vase, floor-type, 15" h., tall ovoid body w/a rounded shoulder & a slender tapering cylindrical neck, angled handles from sides of neck to shoulder, mottled green & brown ground, original silver label, No. 641-15" (ILLUS., No. 3) **2,750.00**

ZEPHYR LILY (1946)

Deeply embossed day lilies against a swirl-textured ground. White and yellow lilies on a blended blue ground; rose and yellow lilies on a green ground; yellow lilies on terra cotta shading to olive green ground.

Candleholders, blue ground, No. 1163-4½", 4½" h., pr. **85.00**

Cornucopia-vase, green ground, No. 204-8", 8" h. **125.00**

Urn-vase, terra cotta ground, No. 202-8", 8½" h. **245.00**

Vase, 6" h., blue ground, No. 130-6" **95.00**

Vase, 7" h., pillow-type w/base handles, blue ground, No. 206-7" **149.00**

Vase, 7¼" h., a footed low & wide rounded base w/a flat shoulder centered by a tall cylindrical body, loop handles arching from the body to the rim of the base, blue ground, No. 131-7" **100.00**

Vase, 8" h., two-handled, blue ground, No. 134-8" **170.00**

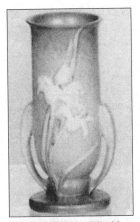

Slender Zephyr Lily Vase

Vase, 8½" h., a disc foot & short pedestal support a tall slightly swelled cylindrical body w/a thin rolled rim, low curved handles from mid-body to the base of the pedestal, terra cotta ground, No. 133-8" (ILLUS.) **110.00**

Vase, 15" h., floor-type, terra cotta ground, No. 141-15" **395.00**

Vase, 18" h., floor-type, green ground, No. 142-18" (unobtrusive firing separation near bottom & a small glaze nick off one of the handles)...............**358.00**

ROYAL BAYREUTH

Good china in numerous patterns and designs has been made at the Royal Bayreuth factory in Tettau, Germany, since 1794. Listings below are by the company's lines, plus miscellaneous pieces. Interest in this china remains at a peak and prices continue to rise. Pieces listed carry the company's blue mark except where noted otherwise.

Royal Bayreuth Mark

CORINTHIAN

Corinthian Pitcher

Pitcher, tankard, 6⅞" h., 3¾" d., orange inside top, classical figures on black satin ground gold bands w/black & white geometric design around neck & base (ILLUS.) **$118.00**

DEVIL & CARDS
Creamer **195.00**

Devil & Cards Match Holder

Match holder, hanging-type, 4" w., 5" h. (ILLUS.) **600.00**

MOTHER-OF-PEARL FINISH
Creamer, Murex Shell patt. **70.00**

ROSE TAPESTRY

Chamberstick, a shaped & flattened base centered by a waisted cylindrical short standard supporting the dished socket w/three rim points, an ornate C-scroll handle down the side, three-color roses, 4¼" h. **860.00**

Chocolate set: cov. chocolate pot w/four matching cups & saucers; three-color roses, 9 pcs. **1,800.00**

Creamer, corset-shaped, three-color roses, 3¾" h......................**175.00**

Dresser box, cov., kidney-shaped, double pink roses, 2 x 5¼" **345.00**

Rose Tapestry Hatpin Holder

Hatpin holder, two-color roses, scroll-molded reticulated gilt-trimmed foot below the baluster-form body w/a flaring gilt-trimmed rim, 4½" h. (ILLUS.) **485.00**

Model of a shoe, decorated w/pink roses & original shoe lace **400.00**

Plate, 7½" d., round w/slightly scalloped rim & four sections of fanned ruffles spaced around the edge, three-color roses **190.00**

Relish dish, open-handled, three-color roses, 4 x 8"......................**275.00**

Vase, 6½" h., decorated w/roses & shadow ferns.........................**325.00**

TOMATO ITEMS

Tomato salt & pepper shakers, pr. **95.00**

MISCELLANEOUS

Ashtray, stork decoration on yellow ground, 3¼ x 5", 1¼" h. ...**100.00**

Ashtray, overhead handle, stork decoration on green ground **135.00**

Bell, nursery rhyme decoration w/Jack & the Beanstalk **400.00**

Box, cov., scene of woman on horse, woman & man w/rake watching, 4¼" d., 2¼" h............**200.00**

Candlestick, oblong dished base w/a standard at one edge flanked by downswept open handles, tulip-form socket w/flattened rim, interior of dished base decorated w/scene of hunter & dogs **200.00**

Creamer, figural Bird of Paradise...................**475.00 to 500.00**

Creamer, figural bull, brown **250.00**

Creamer, figural cat.....................**180.00**

Creamer, figural clown, red **475.00**

Creamer, figural duck.................**295.00**

Creamer, figural frog, unmarked **160.00**

Creamer, figural grape cluster, light green.................................**128.00**

Creamer, figural grape cluster, white **100.00**

Creamer, figural ibex head w/trumpet-form bowl, stirrup-type **750.00**

Creamer, figural lobster (ILLUS.) **110.00**

Figural Lobster Creamer

Creamer, figural Man of the
Mountain, 3½" h. **110.00**

Creamer, figural maple leaf.........**295.00**

Creamer, figural milk maid **650.00**

Creamer, figural pansy................**250.00**

Creamer, figural
parakeet....................**350.00 to 400.00**

Creamer, figural pear **535.00**

Creamer, figural poppy, red **190.00**

Creamer, figural poodle, black
& white...................................**200.00**

Creamer, figural St. Bernard,
brown ....**200.00 to 225.00**

Water Buffalo Creamer

Creamer, figural water buffalo,
black & white
(ILLUS.)....................**125.00 to 150.00**

Creamer, left-handled, scene of
two girls under umbrella,
3½" h. **380.00**

Creamer, scene of girl w/basket,
salmon color...........**800.00 to 1,000.00**

Creamer, "tapestry," wide ovoid
body w/a flaring foot & a long
pinched spout, ornate gilt D-form
handle, "The Bathers" landscape
scene, 3½" h.............................**285.00**

Creamer, "tapestry," footed ovoid
body tapering to a wide rounded
& flaring neck w/a pinched spout
& small C-scroll handle, sheep
in the meadow decoration,
3¾" h. **295.00**

Creamer & cov. sugar bowl,
figural poppy, pr.........................**250.00**

Creamer & cov. sugar bowl,
figural strawberry,
unmarked, pr. **450.00**

Dish, leaf-shaped, nursery rhyme
decoration w/Little Miss Muffet ..**155.00**

Boy & Donkeys Dresser Tray

Dresser tray, rectangular
w/rounded corners, scene of boy
& three donkeys in landscape,
8 x 11" (ILLUS.) **130.00**

**Flower holder w/frog-style
cover,** hunt scene decoration,
3¾" h. **190.00**

Humidor, cov., purple & lavender
floral decoration........................**345.00**

Match holder, hanging-type,
scene of Arab on horseback......**275.00**

Match holder, hanging-type,
"tapestry," sheep in landscape
scene, 4½" l...............................**485.00**

Mustard jar, cov., figural lobster ...**85.00**

Pitcher, 3⅛" h., 2 3/8" w.,
squared waisted body w/short,
wide spout & angled gilt handle,
scene of Arab on horse
(ILLUS. right) **55.00**

Royal Bayreuth Pitcher & Vase

Pitcher, milk, 9½" h., h.p. pasture scene w/three cows **200.00**

Pitcher, milk, figural eagle ....**400.00 to 450.00**

Pitcher, milk, figural elk **275.00**

Pitcher, milk, figural fish head **395.00**

Pitcher, milk, figural poppy **300.00**

Pitcher, milk, figural shell w/seahorse handle, 4¾" h. **315.00**

Pitcher, milk, musicians decoration **128.00**

Pitcher, water, 7¼" h., pinched spout, scenic decoration of cows in pasture **245.00**

Pitcher, sheep scene **125.00**

Plate, 8" d., decorated w/pink & yellow flowers, gold rim, pink ground, blue mark **50.00**

Plate, 9½" d., "tapestry," lady w/horse scene **770.00**

Playing card box, cov., decorated w/a sailing ship scene **195.00**

Salt & pepper shakers, figural shell, pr. **125.00**

Sugar bowl, cov., figural lobster **110.00**

Sugar bowl, cov., figural pansy, purple (tiny rim flake) **225.00**

Sugar bowl, cov., figural poppy, red **225.00**

Toothpick holder, "tapestry," scene of woman w/pony & trees, 2⅖" h. **325.00**

Toothpick holder, three-handled, three feet, nursery rhyme decoration w/Little Boy Blue **165.00**

Vase, 3" h., basket-shaped w/overhead handle, square rim, Babes in Woods decoration **310.00**

Vase, 3¼" h., 1⅞" d., footed, conical body tapering to a silver rim, small tab handles, decorated w/scene of white & brown cows w/green & brown ground (ILLUS. previous page, left w/pitcher) **55.00**

Vase, 3⅝" h., footed conical body tapering to a swelled neck flanked by four loop handles, decorated w/hunting scene, man & woman on horses, unmarked ...**45.00**

Vase, 4½" h., sailing scene decoration **135.00**

Vase, 4¾" h., handled, Babes in Woods decoration, girl holding doll **500.00**

Vase, bud, 4¾" h., "tapestry," rounded body w/a thin tall neck, Lady & Prince scenic decoration **120.00**

Vase, 5" h., "tapestry," bulbous ovoid body tapering to a short slender flaring neck, cottage by a waterfall landscape **295.00**

Vase, 8¼" h., "tapestry," slender ovoid body w/a short cylindrical flaring neck, "The Bathers" landscape scene **435.00**

ROYAL BONN & BONN

Royal Bonn Cracker Jar

Bonn and subsequently Royal Bonn china were produced in Bonn, Germany, in a manufactory established in 1755. Later wares made there are often marked Mehlem or bear the initials FM or a castle mark. Most wares were of the hand-painted type. Clock cases were also made in Bonn.

Royal Bonn & Bonn Mark

Cracker jar, cov., bulbous ovoid
body decorated w/rose, purple &
yellow flowers & green leaves
on a beige & cream ground,
embossed scrolls on shoulder,
silver plate cover, rim & bail
handle, 5¼" d., 6⅝" h.
(ILLUS.) **$195.00**

Vase, 6½" h., portrait-type,
artist-signed.............................**675.00**

Vase, cabinet-type, elaborately
h.p. Art Deco design...................**55.00**

Decorated Royal Bonn Vase

Vase, 13½" h., short pedestal foot
below the tall slender ovoid body
tapering to a short cylindrical
neck, ornate gilt C-scroll
shoulder handles, the neck &
base in green w/black trim, the
creamy white body decorated
overall w/large bluebirds
perched on wild rose vines
w/pink blossoms & green
leaves, incised mark (ILLUS.) ...**300.00**

ROYAL DUX

*This factory in Bohemia was noted for the
figural porcelain wares in the Art Nouveau
style which were exported around the turn of
the century. Other notable figural pieces were
produced through the 1930s and the factory
was nationalized after World War II.*

Royal Dux Marks

Royal Dux Girl & Basket Group

Figure group, a young peasant
girl reclining on a green oblong
base next to a large basket w/a
white cat climbing on the high
handle, delicate hand-painting,
8¼" h. (ILLUS.).........................**$275.00**

Figure group, classical figures of
Perseus & Andromeda, Perseus
in armor & winged helmet
freeing the semi-nude
Andromeda from her shackles
on a tall rock, scrolling waves
around the round base, finely
h.p., signed w/initials "JAH,"
impressed numbers, late 19th -
early 20th c., 24" h. (ILLUS.
next page) **748.00**

Perseus & Andromeda Figure Group

Ornate Royal Dux Lamp

Table lamp, figural, a high oblong tapering base below a footed scroll-molded platform base supporting a figure of a young lady & a young man holding a violin, each dressed in ornate early 19th century costume, finely painted w/naturalistic tones & gilt trim, late 19th c., minor damages, electrified (ILLUS.) **325.00**

ROYAL VIENNA

The second factory in Europe to make hard paste porcelain was established in Vienna in 1719 by Claud Innocentius de Paquier. The factory underwent various changes of administration through the years and finally closed in 1865. Since then, however, the porcelain has been reproduced by various factories in Austria and Germany, many of which have reproduced also the early beehive mark. Early pieces, naturally, bring far higher prices than the later ones or the reproductions.

Royal Vienna Mark

Charger, round, the wide flanged rim decorated w/a red Greek key band alternating w/decorative panels in gold & tan, the center w/a classical landscape scene w/numerous figures of men & women, shield mark in underglaze-blue, titled in German on the back "Alexander d. Gr. u. Thusnelda," late 19th c., 13½" d. **$1,150.00**

Charger, round, a square central panel w/notched corners decorated w/a landscape scene of Apollo & other figures all within wide gilt border on a pink ground, pseudo-shield mark in blue & "Apollo" in red enamel, late 19th c., 13¾" d.................**1,840.00**

Dinner service: forty-one 9½" d. luncheon plates, eighteen 8¼" d. salad plates, fifteen 9¾" d. soup bowls, two 10" sauce bowls & ladles, one 12" l. cov. tureen, one 13¾" l. soup tureen, eight 25" l. (largest) various sized oval vegetable dishes, thirteen 5½" d. bowls, two tiered serving

Royal Vienna Dinner Service

centerpieces & four 10" d. serving bowls; each decorated w/an allegorical painted scene, many marked w/titles & "Angelica Kauffmann," each border band w/Greek key & anthemia trimmed w/gilt on a green & cream ground, various shield marks, late 19th c., the set (ILLUS. of part) **14,950.00**

Plaque, rectangular, a central color scene of an early Grecian interior w/Psyche seated showing jewels to her sisters as Cupid looks on, within a richly gilded border of panels enclosing fantastic creatures, animals & scrolling foliage, inscribed "Fragonard," in a rectangular giltwood & gesso frame, titled in black on the back "Cupid and Psyche," late 19th c., 11¼ x 14" **5,750.00**

Plaque, rectangular, a central classical interior scene of Venus blindfolding Cupid as her attendants hold his bow & arrows, another putto looking over Venus' shoulder, within a richly gilt border of panels

enclosing fantastic creatures, animals & scrolling foliage, in a rectangular giltwood & gesso frame, titled in red "Diana," overglaze blue shield mark, after Titian, late 19th c., 11½ x 14¼" **6,325.00**

Plate, 9½" d., portrait-type, a scene of a chariot w/a cherub & bow & three maidens in burgundy, & gold Tiffany finish, extensive beading & purple, orange, green & aqua, based on an original artwork by Angelica Kauffmann, transfer-printed signature "Kauffmann"...............**300.00**

Plate, 9½" d., decorated in the center w/a color scene of a maiden asleep in a chair, a young admirer standing beside, within a border of arched maroon panels decorated w/landscapes, the back titled in red "Medor un (sic) Angelika," underglaze-blue shield mark, ca. 1900...................................**345.00**

Tray, pierced handles, Mold 82, decorated w/full blossom red & pink roses, 8 x 11⅛" (gold Royal Vienna Mark **250.00**

Urn, cov., the baluster- and inverted-pear-form body decorated w/a wide scenic band depicting a gentleman in 18th c. attire presenting a young woman w/a bird in a cage, a landscape scene on the opposite side, top shoulder, domed cover & lower base & pedestal decorated w/a green lustre glaze w/ornate gilt trim, squared foot w/notched corners, overglaze-red beehive mark, 19th c., overall 14" h......**1,210.00**

Royal Vienna Covered Urn

Urn, cov., a stepped square foot below the square plinth supporting a waisted pedestal & a shouldered ovoid body w/a short wide neck flitted w/a domed cover w/a pointed gilt finial, long angular gilt handles from the shoulders to the lower sides, the cobalt blue & gilt-trimmed background of the body decorated on the front w/an oval reserve painted in color w/a scene of lovers in a forest clearing, surprised by two soldiers, titled Rinaldo & Almida, the square plinth decorated w/a round reserve depicting a maiden w/doves & two putti seated in a floral bower, blue shield mark & "Austria," ca. 1900, 22¾" h. (ILLUS.) **2,875.00**

ROYAL WORCESTER

This porcelain has been made by the Royal Worcester Porcelain Co. at Worcester, England, from 1862 to the present. For earlier porcelain made in Worcester, see WORCESTER. Royal Worcester is distinguished from those wares made at Worcester between 1751 and 1862 that are referred to as only Worcester by collectors.

Royal Worcester Marks

Royal Worcester Butter Dish

Butter dish, cover & drainer, acanthus leaf molding on rim of base & around pine cone finial of the domed cover, typically gilded multicolored flowers, shape No. 1393, ca. 1890, 5¾" h. (ILLUS.)......................**$525.00**

Centerpiece, figural, a young girl & boy in early 19th c. costume walking & carrying between them a large round bowl which also rests on a scrolled tree-trunk-form support, oblong rockwork base, gilt & enamel-decorated, artist-signed, pad mark, boy's neck restored, 13½" l., 10½" h. (ILLUS. next page) **748.00**

Royal Worcester Centerpiece

Cracker jar, cov., cylindrical, jar & cover decorated w/cobalt blue bamboo leaves on a molded white bamboo stalk background, impressed older mark, 5¾" d., 7" h. **55.00**

Ewer, tall baluster-form, the tapering body raised on a ribbed & ringed pedestal on a stepped dome foot, the wide shoulder centered by a short cylindrical neck w/a tricorner curled-up rim w/an ornate arched & pierced scroll handle arching from the rim & branching at the base to attach to the shoulder & side, raised leaf & floral designs in gold and red enamel & gilt trim overall, 1896, 15¾" h. (light gilt wear) **1,495.00**

Figure, "April," signed F. Doughty, No. 3416, 1947 ....**189.00**

Figure, "Funny Fish," boy holding large fish, by Pinder Davis, No. 3493, 1953, 5" h..................**550.00**

Figure, "Grandmother's Dress," designed by F. Doughty, No. 3081, ca. 1935, 6 3/8" h.......................**75.00 to 100.00**

Figure, "January," signed F. Doughty, No. 3452, 1949 ....**189.00**

Figure, "June," signed F. Doughty, No. 3456, 1949 ....**189.00**

Figure, "October," young boy w/squirrels, he is dressed in yellow & blue, signed F. Doughty, No. 3417, 1947, 7¾" h. **189.00**

Figure, Royal Canadian Mounted Policeman................................**850.00**

Figure, Welsh Girl, standing wearing traditional costume & holding a low bowl at her side, overall enamel decoration except on her head & hands, on a squared base w/chamfered corners, signed "Hadley," late 19th c., 6½" h. **690.00**

Figure group, "Babes in the Woods," two young girls, one in pink & purple & the other in blue w/a purple cap, designed by F. Doughty, 1940, No. 3302, 6¼" h. (ILLUS.) **175.00**

"Babes in the Woods" Figure

Pitcher, 11¼" h., jug-type,
bulbous body tapering to tall
slender cylindrical neck, pinched
spout, gold serpent handle,
decorated w/scene of owl on
tree branch, moonlit sky,
ca. 1885.....................................**930.00**

Royal Worcester Dessert Plate

Plate, dessert, 8½" d., scalloped
& beaded gilt rim band,
decorated overall w/a grouping
of peaches & blackberries
among leafy vines, artist-signed,
code-dated 1923, marked
(ILLUS.) **345.00**

Urn, cov., a domed pierced cover
above the globular body painted
w/floral sprays on a
basketweave-molded base,
early 20th c., 11½" h..................**184.00**

Vase, 3¼" h., reticulated sides
w/gilt-trimmed oval panels
w/floral decoration, printed mark,
ca. 1891.....................................**115.00**

Vase, 8½" h., model of a large
nautilus shell, the shell raised on
a colored branching coral
pedestal on a plain rockwork
base w/a flaring ringed foot, the
top side of the shell mounted
w/a realistically modeled colorful
lizard, 19th c. (staining) **230.00**

R.S. PRUSSIA & RELATED WARES

Ornately decorated china marked "R.S. Prussia" and "R.S. Germany" continues to grow in popularity. According to the Third Series of Mary Frank Gaston's Encyclopedia of R.S. Prussia (Collector Books, Paducah, Kentucky), these marks were used by the Reinhold Schlegelmilch porcelain factories located in Suhl in the Germanic regions known as "Prussia" prior to World War I, and in Tillowitz, Silesia, which became part of Poland after World War II. Other marks sought by collectors include "R.S. Suhl," "R.S. " steeple or church marks, and "R.S. Poland."

The Suhl factory was founded by Reinhold Schlegelmilch in 1869 and closed in 1917. The Tillowitz factory was established in 1895 by Erhard Schlegelmilch, Reinhold's son. This china customarily bears the phrase "R.S. Germany" and "R.S. Tillowitz. " The Tillowitz factory closed in 1945, but it was re-opened for a few years under Polish administration. The "R.S. Poland" mark is attributed to that later time period.

Prices are high and collectors should beware of the forgeries that sometimes find their way onto the market. Mold names and numbers are taken from Mary Frank Gaston's books on R.S. Prussia.

We illustrate three typical markings. The "R.S. Prussia" and "R.S. Suhl" marks have been reproduced so buy with care.

Collectors are also interested in the porcelain products made by the Erdmann Schlegelmilch factory. This factory was founded by three brothers in Suhl in 1861. They named the factory in honor of their father, Erdmann Schlegelmilch. A variety of marks incorporating the "E.S." initials were used. The factory closed circa 1935. The Erdmann Schlegelmilch factory was an earlier and entirely separate business from the Reinhold Schlegelmilch factory. The two were not related to each other.

R.S. Prussia Marks

R.S. GERMANY

Bowl, 10" d., decorated w/wild roses, raspberries & blueberries, glossy glaze............................**$125.00**

Bowl, large, Lettuce mold, floral decoration, lustre finish **325.00**

R.S.Germany Cake Plate

Cake plate, double-pierced small gold side handles, decorated w/a scene of a maiden near a cottage at the edge of a dark forest, 10" d. (ILLUS.)................**235.00**

Cup & saucer, demitasse, ornate handle, eight-footed......................**40.00**

Pitcher, 9" h., Mold 343, floral decoration w/overall gilt tracery on cobalt blue (red castle mark)..............................**750.00**

Plate, 7¼" d., poppy decoration **29.00**

Tray, handled, decorated w/large white & green poppies, 15¼" l...**250.00**

R.S. PRUSSIA

Berry set: master bowl & six sauce dishes; five-lobed, floral relief rim w/forget-me-nots & water lilies decoration, artist-signed, 7 pcs. **365.00**

Bowl, 10" d., Mold 85, Summer Season portrait w/mill scene in background (ILLUS. next column)............................**1,400.00**

Bowl, 10" d., Mold 203, pearlized swans & floral decoration **350.00**

Summer Season Portrait Bowl

Bowl, 10¼" d., center decoration of pink roses w/pearlized finish, border in shades of lavender & blue w/satin finish, lavish gold trim (unlisted mold)....................**410.00**

Bowl, 10½" d., Point & Clover mold (Mold 82), decorated w/pink roses & green leaves w/shadow flowers & a Tiffany finish **240.00**

Bowl, 10½" d., handled, four-lobed, decorated w/Art Nouveau relief-molded scrolls & colorful sprays on shaded green ground **200.00**

Bowl, 11" d., 3" h., Sunflower mold, satin finish........................**450.00**

Cake plate, open-handled, Fleur-de-lis mold, Spring Season portrait, 9¾" d. **1,500.00**

Cake plate, open-handled, Mold 259, decorated w/pink & yellow roses, pearl button finish, 10" d. **385.00**

Cake plate, open-handled, Mold 155, hanging basket decoration, 10" d. **345.00**

Cake plate, open-handled, Fleur-de-Lis mold, decorated w/a castle scene in rust, gold, lavender & yellow, 10¼" d. **1,100.00**

Cake plate, open-handled, Medallion mold w/reflecting water lilies decoration, 10½" d...**180.00**

Madame Lebrun-decorated Chocolate Set

Cake plate, open-handled, modified Fleur-de-lis mold, floral decoration, beaded, satin finish, artist-signed, 11" d....................**190.00**

Cake plate, open-handled, Mold 330, decorated w/snapdragons on pastel ground, artist-signed, 11½" d. **345.00**

Cake plate, open-handled, Mold 343, Winter figural portrait in keyhole medallion, cobalt blue inner border, gold outer border, 12½" d. **350.00**

Cake plate, open-handled, ruffled rim, decorated w/peonies & wild roses on satin finish...................**325.00**

Cake plate, open-handled, Carnation mold, decorated w/multicolored roses..................**295.00**

Celery tray, Mold 255, decorated w/Surreal Dogwood decoration, pearlized lustre finish, artist-signed, 12¼" l. **200.00**

Celery tray, open-handled decorated w/soft pink & white flower center w/lily-of-the valley, embossed edge of ferns &pastel colors w/gold highlights, 12½" l. **225.00**

Chocolate set: 10" h. cov. chocolate pot & four cups & saucers; Ribbon and Jewel mold, scene of Dice Throwers decoration on pot & single Melon Eater scene on cups, the set....................................**5,000.00**

Chocolate set: 10" h., cov. chocolate pot & six cups & saucers; Mold 517, Madame Lebrun portrait decoration, the set (ILLUS. above) **8,000.00**

Creamer & cov. sugar bowl, Ribbon and Jewel mold, single Melon Eaters decoration, pr. (ILLUS. below)........................**1,800.00**

Melon Eaters Creamer & Sugar

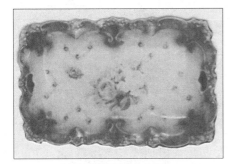

Mold 404 Dresser Tray

Dresser tray, rectangular w/pierced end handles, Mold 404, decorated w/pink & white roses, Tiffany border w/gold clover leaves (ILLUS.) **270.00**

Ferner, six vertical ribs, scalloped, decorated w/lilies of the valley on shaded pastel ground, artist-signed, 3⅞ x 8¼" (¼" underglaze firing crack).......**200.00**

Pitcher, tankard, 13¼" h., Stippled Floral mold (Mold 525), roses decoration, unmarked......**625.00**

Pitcher, tankard, Mold 517, Lebrun II portrait decoration ...**3,000.00**

Plate, 7½" d., Carnation mold, decorated w/pink roses, pink ground, unmarked **165.00**

Plate, 8½" d., Mold 91, decorated w/yellow roses on pink ground ..**180.00**

Plate, 8½" d., Mold 263, pink & white roses decoration **180.00**

Plate, 8¾" d., Mold 278, center decoration of pink poppies on white ground, green border **150.00**

Plate, dessert, Mold 506, branches of pink roses & green leaves against a shaded bluish green to white ground w/shadow flowers & satin finish....................**98.00**

Relish dish, Fleur-de-Lis mold, basket of flowers decoration w/shadow flowers, 8" l. **115.00**

Syrup pitcher, Mold 512, dogwood & pine decoration **175.00**

Toothpick holder, ribbed hexagonal shape w/two handles, decorated w/colorful roses **265.00**

Toothpick holder, three-handled, decorated w/white daisies on blue ground , gold handles & trim on top (slight wear to gold) ...**95.00**

Toothpick holder, urn-shaped, floral decoration, molded star mark **135.00**

Tray, pierced handles, Mold 82, decorated w/full blossom red & pink roses, 8 x 11 1/8" (gold Royal Vienna mark)..................**250.00**

Tray, rectangular, pierced handles, Mold 404, decorated w/pink & white roses, Tiffany border w/gold clover leaves.......**270.00**

Vase, 4½" h., Mold 910, decorated w/pink roses, satin finish w/iridescent Tiffany finish around base, salesman's sample......................................**275.00**

OTHER MARKS

Chocolate pot, cov., Art Nouveau decoration, glossy finish (R.S. Tillowitz - Silesia).......................**55.00**

Coffee set: 6⅝" h., 3¼" d. cov. ovoid coffeepot & two cups & saucers; each piece decorated w/an color oval reserve w/a different romantic scene within a thin gilt border & a deep burgundy panel against a creamy white ground trimmed w/gilt scrolls, a wide red & narrow dark green border band on each, saucers 2¾" d., cups 2¼" h., blue beehive & R.S. Suhl marks, the set **525.00**

Plate, 7¾" d., Sunflower mold, rose pink & yellow roses w/Tiffany finish (Wheelock Prussia) **95.00**

Relish dish, woman's portrait w/shadow flowers & wine border on green ground, 8" (E.S. Germany Royal Saxe) **72.00**

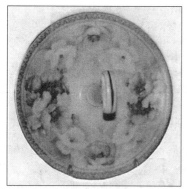

E. Schlegelmilch Handled Server

Server, center-handled, decorated w/orange, white & pink poppies on a shaded bluish grey ground w/a narrow gilt border band, 8½" d., 3¾" h., E. Schlegelmilch - Thuringia (ILLUS.) **100.00**

Serving dish, center-handled, decorated w/lavender & pink roses, gold trim, 11" d. (R.S. Poland) **515.00**

R.S. Tillowitz Pheasant Vase

Vase, 6" h., tapering ovoid body w/slightly flared rim, decorated w/scene of blue & white & brown pheasants, R.S. Tillowitz-Silesia (ILLUS.) **260.00**

Vase, 6⅜" h., 3" d., wide ovoid shouldered body tapering to slender flaring cylindrical neck, Melon Eater decoration

Melon Eaters Vase

surrounded by gold border w/reverse decorated w/heart-shaped area w/dainty pink roses on pastel ground, two-thirds of vase covered in purplish lustre w/fine gold leaves & flowers overall, neck in off white w/fine gold floral decoration, artist-signed in gold, Red Crown "Viersa" mark, Suhl or Tillowitz (ILLUS.) **325.00**

Vase, 9" h., 3" d., tall slender ovoid body tapering to a tall slender trumpet neck, a wide band around the body decorated w/a colored scene of "The Melon Eaters" between narrow gold & white bands, the neck & lower body in deep rose decorated w/gilt leaf sprigs, R.S. Suhl ....**600.00 to 800.00**

Vase, 9½" h., portrait of "Lady with Swallows," gold beading, turquoise on white ground (Prov. Saxe - E.S. Germany) **475.00**

Vase, 10" h., gold Rococo handles, scene of sleeping maiden w/cherub decoration (E.S. Royal Saxe) **350.00**

Vase, 13½" h., portrait of "Lady with Swallows," gold beaded frame, green pearl lustre finish w/gold trim (Prov. Saxe - E.S. Germany) **615.00**

SALTGLAZED WARES

Early Saltglazed Teapot

This whitish ware has a pitted surface texture, which resembles an orange skin as a result of salt being thrown into the hot kiln to produce the glaze. Much of this ware was sold in the undecorated state, but some pieces were decorated. Decorative pieces have been produced in England and Europe since at least the 18th century with later production in the United States. Most pieces are unmarked.

Cup & saucer, handleless, deep rounded & lightly flaring cup raised on a footring, wide dished saucer, both w/incised stylized flowering branches beneath a rim band of shallow swags all highlighted in cobalt blue, Staffordshire, England, ca. 1750 (short cracks on rim, restored chip on saucer) **$460.00**

Cup & saucer, handleless, deep rounded & lightly flaring cup raised on a footring, wide dished saucer, each incised w/stylized 'lollipop' flowers & a chevron center band, low scalloped swags around the borders, all highlighted in cobalt blue, Staffordshire, England, ca. 1765 ....**1,035.00**

Tea canister, cov., a wide cylindrical body w/a sharply angled shoulder to the ring-incised later wooden cylindrical cover, the sides of the body incised w/flowers issuing from rockwork beneath a diaper border on the shoulder, the underside inscribed "Grace Leigh 1754," Staffordshire, England, 3½" h. (short crack) **1,495.00**

Teapot, cov., heart-shaped straight-sided body w/serpentine base & shoulder bands, the gently sloping shoulder to the flat conforming cover w/a button finial, C-scroll handle & swan's-neck serpent-form spout, the body, shoulder & cover molded w/fruiting grapevines, England, ca. 1750, minor nicks to cover & lip of spout, 3¾" h. (ILLUS.) ...**2,530.00**

Teapot, cov., footed squatty bulbous body w/a gently curved faceted spout & applied D-form handle, a short cylindrical neck w/a flattened domed cover w/inverted acorn finial, the sides applied w/a lion, squirrel, fleur-de-lis, acorns, cranes & flowers above a wide crossbanded center band, Staffordshire, England, ca. 1750, 4½" h. (short cracks, minute chips)................**805.00**

SATSUMA

Unusual Satsuma Lamps

These decorated wares have been produced in Japan since the end of the 18th century. The early pieces are scarce and high-priced. Later Satsuma wares are plentiful and, with prices rising, as highly collectible as earlier pieces.

Lamps, kerosene table-type, each w/a vase-shaped body decorated w/male or female figures trimmed w/gilt, set on a gilt-bronze footed base & w/a gilt-bronze pierced connector to the burner & oil cylinder enclosed within a gilt-decorated spherical white glass shade, glass signed "Cristal Superieur Odin, 15," late 19th c., overall 28" h., pr. (ILLUS. previous page).....................**$2,875.00**

Fine Satsuma Teakettle

Teakettle, cov., flattened disc-form raise on small pointed feet, the wide sloping shoulder tapering to a small rolled neck w/inset cover w/button finial, shoulder brackets to support the bail handle, decorated around the shoulder w/a continual design of Japanese figures amid an abundance of flowers, small floral borders above & below, 19th c., 6" d. (ILLUS.).............**1,840.00**

Vase, 5¾" h., an ovoid body tapering inward to a slightly

inverted rim, overall gilt & silver hanging floral sprays, small floral border below rim, all on a muted & flecked greyish brown ground w/slight pink inclusions, four-character Kinkosan signature on base, late 19th c. **748.00**

Vase, 6" h., ovoid body w/a narrow neck & slightly flaring rim, decorated on each side w/panels of women in a garden setting, divided by a blue background w/gold floral scrolling, partially obscured signature on the base, Meiji Period...............................**748.00**

Vase, 12" h., floral decoration w/elaborate beading & raised outlining **195.00**

Vases, 9" h., overall decoration of gold flowers & red leaves, pr. **395.00**

Vases, 12" h., scenic decoration of geishas among stylized flowers, raised gold outlining, scrolled handles, fine crackle finish, pr. **195.00**

SCHAFER & VATER

Figural Astray/Match Holder

Founded in Rudolstadt, Thuringia, Germany in 1890, the Schafer and Vater Porcelain Factory specialized in decorative pieces of porcelain usually in white or colored bisque. They produced many novelty figural items such as creamers, toothpick holders, boxes and hatpin holders and also produced a line of jasper ware with white relief decoration in imitation of the famous Wedgwood jasper wares. The firm also decorated white ware blanks.

The company ceased production in 1962 and collectors now seek out their charming pieces which may be marked with a crown over a starburst containing the script letter "R."

Schafer & Vater Mark

Ashtray w/match holder, figural, oversized smiling feet w/holes in tips of toes, an egg-shaped big-eared bald smiling head w/mouth wide open to form ashtray, 3¼" h. (ILLUS. previous page).........................**$255.00**

Bottle w/original stopper, robed skeleton decoration **200.00**

Figural Bearded Man Bottle

Bottle w/original stopper, figural bearded stocky man standing holding a bowling ball w/another ball between his legs impressed "Gut Holz!," blue glaze, 9" h. (ILLUS. bottom, previous column).....................................**340.00**

Figural Old Woman Bottle

Bottle w/original stopper, figural, a standing old woman w/her hair pulled into a bun, her smiling head forming the stopper, her long neck forming the bottle neck, wearing a cloak & long dress w/her hands held in front, mottled dark brown glossy glaze, 2¾" d., 5¾" h. (ILLUS.)...**125.00**

Bottle w/original stopper, decorated w/a fat-faced red-nosed gentleman & the quote "Don't Let Thy Nose Blush for the Sins of Thy Mouth" **79.00**

Creamer, figural, bust of a Welsh woman, orange shawl & a tall black hat w/a white band, white curls showing under the brim & a white bow, 4¾" h. (ILLUS. top, next page) **190.00**

Welsh Woman Creamer

Figure, novelty, bisque, round base w/Scotsman wearing white pants & hat, red jacket, drinking from a cup & standing by barrel marked "The Thirsty First," unmarked, 2⅛" d., 4¼" h. **145.00**

Humidor, cov., scene of man w/pipe decoration, lavender ground **550.00**

Comical Model of a Dog

Model of a dog, green glossy-glazed dog sitting on a white rectangular base, white eyes & mouth, red tongue out, a white curved rectangular sign at its neck, 2⅜ x 3", 5½" h. (ILLUS.) **135.00**

Mug, elk decoration **45.00**

Plaque, pierced to hang, jasper ware, white relief cherub on a blue ground **30.00**

Vase, 7½" h., jasper ware, decorated w/white relief classical lady on blue ground **45.00**

SCHOOP (Hedi) ART CREATIONS

By far one of the most talented artists working in California in the 1940s and 1950s was Hedi Schoop. Almost every piece in her line she designed and modeled herself. She began her business in 1940 in Hollywood, California. Barker Brothers department store in Los Angeles discovered Schoop's work which encouraged her to open the small Hollywood studio. Shortly after a move to larger quarters, financed by her mother, Hedi began calling her business Hedi Schoop Art Creations. It would remain under that name throughout Schoop's career which was ended when a fire destroyed the operation in 1958. At that time, Hedi decided to free-lance for other companies (see: Cleminson Clay). Probably one of the most imitated artists of the time, other people began businesses using Schoop's designs and techniques. Hedi Schoop decided to sue in court and the results were settled in Schoop's favor. Among those imitators were Kim Ward, and Ynez and Yona. Hedi Schoop saw forms differently than other artists and, therefore, was able to create with ease and in different media. While Hedi made shapely women with skirts that flared out to create bowls as well as women with arms over their heads holding planters, she also produced charming bulky looking women with thick arms and legs. When TV lamps became popular, Hedi was able to easily add her talents to creating those designs with roosters, tragedy and comedy joined together in an Art Deco fashion, and elegant women in various poses. A variety of marks were used by Schoop including her signature (incised or stamped) which also, on occasion, shows "Hollywood, Cal." or "California," and there was also a sticker used but such pieces are hard-to-find.

Hedi Schoop Dutch Boy & Girl Figures

Box, cov., h.p. faux marble
  decoration...............................**$75.00**

Figure of a Dutch boy, standing
  on a thin round white base,
  hands in his pockets, head
  raised & turned to the left, light
  brown hair, glossy brown pants
  & shirt w/yellow accents &
  yellow scarf around his neck &
  onto his left shoulder, brown hat
  w/yellow bill & white clogs
  w/brown & yellow highlights,
  10" h. (ILLUS. right).....................**55.00**

Figure of a Dutch girl standing,
  head bent far to left side
  touching her shoulder, left arm
  straight & slightly away from her
  body, right arm straight &
  against body holding a large pot
  that extends from hand to clogs,
  long gloss brown dress & hat
  w/white body, pot & clogs,
  8½" h. (ILLUS. left).....................**60.00**

Figure of a girl standing, bell-
  shaped skirt w/scalloped edges,

Schoop Sunflower Girl Figure

sunflower-shaped face & yellow
hair, green blouse, yellow skirt,
Model No. 703, 9" h. (ILLUS.) **85.00**

Girl & Bowl Schoop Figure

Woman with Mirror

Figure of a girl standing, holding large, round, plain bowl over her head, left leg raised slightly, right leg on base, white gloss glaze w/blue & green striped skirt, two tied loops at waist on right side, blue scarf around head & tied at neck, blue shoes, incised mark "Hedi Schoop Design, California USA," & copyright symbol, bowl & base, 6¼" d., 13" h. (ILLUS.).................**90.00**

Figure of a girl, standing w/both arms raised over her head holding small slightly scalloped & ribbed bowl, left leg slightly raised w/toes of shoes barely showing, head tilted back & against right shoulder, dark green skirt, white blouse, red scarf over head & tied at neck, white apron w/red trim, inkstamp, "Hedi Schoop, No. Hollywood, Cal." 13" h. **80.00**

Figure of a woman, her arms overhead, long grey & gold dress in a swirl motion indicating a dancer, head down & turned to right, bisque hands, face & neck, delicate porcelain body, inkstamp mark "Hedi Schoop Hollywood, Cal." 12½" h. **100.00**

Figure of a woman, standing on a base w/an oval upright glass mirror behind her, reflecting her back, all black except white hair, blouse, purse & trim on hat & dress, w/mirror in good condition, 4¾" l., 8" h. (ILLUS.) **160.00**

Masks TV Lamp

Lamp, figural, TV-type, Comedy & Tragedy masks on a base w/full comedy, part tragedy conjoined, dark green w/gold trim, ca. 1954, 10¾" l., 12" h. (ILLUS.) **325.00**

Planter, figural group, girl & boy standing on white oval base, each holding small white planter in one hand at side; girl in long brown dress w/white flowers, collar & short sleeve cuffs, rough textured white hair; boy w/head bent to left shoulder, white pants, jacket w/white flowers, white handkerchief, blond hair, inkstamp "Hedi Schoop," 9¼" h. **75.00**

SEVRES & SEVRES STYLE

Some of the most desirable porcelain ever produced was made at the Sevres factory, originally established at Vincennes, France, and transferred, through permission of Madame de Pompadour, to Sevres as the Royal Manufactory about the middle of the 18th century. King Louis XV took sole responsibility for the works in 1759 when production of hard plastic waste began. Between 1850 and 1900, many biscuit and soft-paste pieces were made again. Fine early pieces are scarce and high-priced. Many of those available today are late productions. The various Sevres marks have been copied and pieces listed as "Sevres-Style" are similar to actual Sevres wares, but not necessarily from that factory. Three of the many Sevres marks are illustrated below

Sevres Marks

Bust of Barra, white biscuit, titled in gilt on a cobalt blue ground & inscribed on the hat "Egalité Liberté ou la Mort," impressed & printed marks, ca. 1885, 12¾" h. **$460.00**

Sevres White Biscuit Bust

Bust of a young woman, white biscuit, her hair pulled up into a mound of curls within a wide band, her head tilted slightly downward, a light shawl around her shoulders, impressed mark, base damage, 19th c., 19" h. (ILLUS.) **1,495.00**

Centerpiece, bronze-mounted, an oblong deep dish decorated on the exterior w/a long oval color figural panel opposing a floral panel all on a cobalt blue ground w/ornate scrolling gilt trim, the rim surmounted by a pierced gilt-bronze band flanked by foliate scrolled handles ending in lion masks, the dish raised on a gilt-bronze domed & four-footed base fitted w/two figures of putti playing musical instruments, late 19th c., 15¾" h. **6,325.00**

Cup & saucer, figural, gilt bisquit, the cup in the form of a swimming swan w/its neck curved to form the handle, set in an oval dished saucer, both w/fine gilt border trim, signed "Mve. Imp. le de Sevres," from a service of the Empress Josephine, late 18th - early 19th c. **660.00**

Lovely Masquerade Couple

Figures of masquerade ball couple, each finely modeled in action poses, their costumes & faces delicately painted in polychrome, each on a shaped, marbleized plinth base, marked on the undersides w/"VB" in an applied blue oval, 19th c., 22" h., pr. (ILLUS.) **4,400.00**

Plaque, round, gilt-bronze-mounted, a central circular plaque painted in polychrome w/a scene depicting King Louis XV of France in robes of state standing majestically in front of his throne beside a stool on which rest a crown & scepter within a gilt-bronze bezel set in

an onyx ground interspaced w/eight oval miniatures each painted w/a named portrait of a noble lady of the court & one heraldic shield displaying three fleur-de-lis all within a leaf-tip & swag-cast frame, late 19th c., 21" d. **1,725.00**

Plaques, pate-sur-pate, rectangular, blue ground w/each decorated in white slip w/a scantily draped female, one whipping a suspended putti, the other being whipped by a putti, green slip flowers on the gold-decorated border, artist-signed "Miles," each in carved wood frames, ca. 1865, 4¼ x 8½", pr. **8,050.00**

Sevres Tete-a-Tete Service

Tete-a-tete service: cov. teapot, cov. sugar bowl, two tea cups & saucers, creamer & shaped oblong tray; main pieces w/bulbous bodies, all pieces decorated w/oval reserves in color of couples in landscapes within a jeweled surround, all on a bleu celeste ground, mid-19th c., tray 13" l., the set (ILLUS.) **6,038.00**

Urn, cov., squatty bulbous wide body tapering to a ribbed & stepped domed foot, the shoulder tapering to a short, wide spiral-molded neck supporting a low domed cover centered by a pineapple finial above a radiating circle of leaves, figural gilt swan side handles, the body decorated w/floral garlands flanked by a fishscale pattern band trimmed w/gilt, interlacing "L" mark enclosing "TP" beneath & "France" in red enamel, late 19th c., 13½" h. **2,875.00**

Urn, cov., slender baluster-form w/a tall waisted neck supporting a conical cover w/pineapple finial, raised on a slender ringed pedestal w/a gilt-metal connector on a squared gilt-metal foot, the body decorated w/a portrait of a beautiful young woman w/long flowing hair within a rounded reserve framed by gilt scrolls, on a cream & pink ground w/further gilt trim, the base w/an interlaced "L" mark, 19th c., overall 17" h. **1,540.00**

Urn, cov., gilt-bronze-mounted, the ovoid body painted in polychrome w/a continuous battle scene centrally depicting Napoleon on horseback issuing orders to his surrounding officers, hussars nearby w/battle lines in the distance, the waisted neck beneath a domed cover w/a pine cone finial & spreading foot all decorated in raised gilt on a cobalt blue ground w/the Napoleonic eagle display between oak sprigs & laurel chain borders or an "N" within a laurel & oak leaf wreath, all raised on a slender cobalt blue-ground pedestal on a gilt-bronze plinth, artist-signed, late 19th c., 34½" h. **4,025.00**

Urns, cov., classic baluster-form, the body raised on a ringed, domed pedestal raised on a gilt-metal square plinth w/incurved corners & low-arched feet, the body tapering to a wide waisted neck topped by a stepped & domed high cover w/gilt-metal

border & pineapple finial, high arched tightly looped gilt-metal shoulder handles, each decorated on the front w/a large round reserve depicting a courting couple in a landscape framed by ornate gilt leafy scrolls & lattice, the reverses w/landscape panels, gilt floral wreathes on the necks, bases & covers, all against a Celeste blue ground, each artist-signed, ca. 1880, 16" h., pr. **2,530.00**

Urns, cov., ovoid body w/a domed cover w/a pine cone finial enameled in pink, cream & gilt, each body painted w/a continuous scene in pastel colors, the first w/a bacchante reclining in a bower of flowers w/trailing roses & lilacs attired in diaphanous clinging shift & holding a golden cup & attended by a hovering putto, the second similarly decorated w/a flower maiden & putto playing w/a floral garland, artist-signed, late 19th c., 27½" h., pr. **6,325.00**

Vase, 9¼" h., 3¾" d., footed slender baluster-form w/a narrow angled shoulder tapering to a short trumpet neck, enameled & gilded w/long clusters of purple flowers & delicate green leafy vines against a creamy white ground, by Belet, 1911, ink-stamped "S191 - RF MANUFACTURE NATIONALE - DECORE A SEVRES 1911 - BELET" **1,210.00**

Vase, 12¼" h., simple baluster-form w/a narrow flat footring & narrow flat rim on the flaring neck, white decorated w/chestnuts & leafage in shades of grey, blue, brown & salmon pink, stamped "MANUFACTURE RF NATIONAL - DECORÉ A SEVRES 1908" w/factory hallmark, dated "1906" & impressed "4C5 - Dr." **2,990.00**

Vase, 16" h., tall slender gently flaring cylindrical body w/a gently sloping shoulder to the

Early 20th Century Sevres Vase

short cylindrical neck, decorated w/blackberry blossoms & leafage in shades of pink, green & white reserved against a grey ground, form designed by Alexandre Sandier in 1896, stamped "MANUFACTURE RF NATIONALE - DECORÉ A SEVRES" w/factory mark & dated 1906, impressed "1906 - 1 - BN" (ILLUS.) **2,875.00**

Vases, 8½" h., pate-sur-pate, urn-shaped, a small round domed foot tapering to a short ringed pedestal supporting a wide urn-form body w/a wide tapering neck ending in a flat rim flanked by S-scroll handles, the dark blue ground w/white slip decoration washed in the cafe-au-lait manner, the neck w/a stylized column & urn border w/gilt trim, the main body decorated on each w/a white slip classical female bust, each titled on the reverse & artist-signed, Louis Solon, ca. 1865, one w/a slight rim flake, pr. (ILLUS.) **7,475.00**

Sevres Pate-sur-Pate Vases

Vases, cov., 17" h., 'jeweled' decoration, large classic baluster urn-form w/a wide, short waisted neck supporting a domed, stepped cover w/gadrooned top w/a heart loop finial, raised on a ringed pedestal w/round base on a square foot, the sides flanked by large female term handles w/gilt trim, a celeste blue ground decorated on each side w/a lobed panel, one painted w/classical figures in a landscape, the other w/a floral panel, each panel within an ornate gilt swag & scroll border, bands of small beading around the rim & pedestal base, interlacing "L" mark, late 19th c., pr. (restorations) **2,875.00**

SHAWNEE

The Shawnee Pottery operated in Zanesville, Ohio, from 1937 until 1961. Much of the early production was sold to chain stores and mail-order houses including Sears, Roebuck, Woolworth and others. Planters, cookie jars and vases, along with the popular "Corn King" oven ware line, are among the collectible items which are plentiful and still reasonably priced. Reference numbers used here are taken from Mark E. Supnick's book, Collecting Shawnee Pottery, The Collector's Guide to Shawnee Pottery by Duane and Janice Vanderbilt, or Shawnee Pottery - An Identification & Value Guide by Jim and Bev Mangus.

Bowl, cereal, "Corn King" line, No. 94 ....**$45.00**

Bowl, dessert/fruit, "Corn King" line, No. 92 ....**45.00**

Canister, cov., Snowflake patt., yellow, 2 qt. ....**45.00 to 75.00**

Casserole, cov., "Corn King" line, 1½ qt., No. 74 ....**65.00 to 85.00**

Cookie jar, figural Dutch boy, single stripe..............**175.00 to 200.00**

Cookie jar, figural Dutch girl decorated w/a tulip **155.00**

Cookie jar, figural jug, Pennsylvania Dutch patt............**135.00**

Cookie jar, figural Puss 'n Boots, short tail **185.00**

Cookie jar, figural Puss 'n Boots, long tail......................**175.00 to 225.00**

Cookie jar, figural Winnie Pig, blue collar..................**325.00 to 350.00**

Creamer, "Corn King" line, No. 70, 5" h. ....**25.00 to 35.00**

Creamer, figural elephant..............**35.00**

Creamer, figural Puss 'n Boots, green & yellow ....**65.00 to 75.00**

Creamer, figural Smiley Pig, peach flower **65.00**

Creamer & cov. sugar bowl, "Corn King" line, Nos. 70 & 78, pr. **75.00**

Cup, "Corn King," No. 90 ....**40.00**

Hors d'oeuvre holder, Lobster Ware, Kenwood line, 7½" l. ....**200.00 to 275.00**

Mixing bowl, "Corn King" line, No. 6, 6" d.....................................**23.00**

Mixing bowls, nesting-type, "Corn King" line, 5" d., 6" d. & 8" d., the set **150.00**

Pitcher, ball-type, embossed Snowflake patt., blue **35.00**

Pitcher, tankard, Corn King line, No. 71 (ILLUS.) **60.00**

Corn King Pitcher

Pitcher, figural Chanticleer
Rooster, large ....**75.00 to 125.00**

Pitcher, figural Little Bo Peep,
decals & gold trim **275.00**

Planter, figural automobile,
No. 605 ....**16.00**

Planter, figural dog & jug,
No. 610 ....**22.00**

Plate, 8" l., "Corn King" line,
No. 93 ....**30.00**

Plate, 10" d., "Corn King" line,
No. 68 ....**45.00**

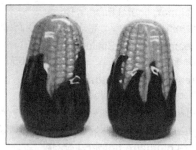

Corn King Salt & Pepper Shakers

Salt & pepper shakers, "Corn
King" line, No. 76, 3¼" h., pr.
(ILLUS.) **28.00**

Salt & pepper shakers, figural
Dutch Boy & Girl, pr. .....**50.00 to 60.00**

Salt & pepper shakers, figural
elephant, teal, pr..........................**30.00**

Salt & pepper shakers, figural
Farmer Pig, pr. **20.00**

Salt & pepper shakers, figural
owl, small, pr. **35.00**

Salt & pepper shakers, figural
Puss 'n Boots, pr. **29.00**

Sugar bowl, cov., figural lobster ...**40.00**

Teapot, cov., embossed
snowflake, blue...........................**28.00**

Teapot, cov., Pennsylvania Dutch
patt., 27 oz..................................**28.00**

Vegetable dish, open, "Corn
Queen" line, No. 95, 9" l.................**75.00**

Wall pocket, figural hand, aqua **75.00**

Wall pocket, figural lady
w/bonnet, 8" h.............................**50.00**

SHELLEY

*Members of the Shelley family were in the
pottery business in England as early as the 18th
century. In 1872 Joseph Shelley formed a
partnership with James Wileman of Wileman &
Co. who operated the Foley China Works. The
Wileman & Co. name was used for the firm for
the next fifty years, and between 1890 and 1910
the words "The Foley" appeared above
conjoined "WC" initials.*

*Beginning in 1910 the Shelley family name
in a shield appeared on wares, although the
firm's official name was still Wileman & Co.
The company's name was finally changed to
Shelley in 1925 and then Shelley China Ltd.
after 1965. The firm changed hands in the 1960s
and became part of the Doulton Group in 1971.
At first only average quality earthenwares were
produced but in the late 1890s new shapes and
better quality decorations were used.*

*Bone china was introduced at Shelley before
World War I and these fine dinnerwares became
very popular in the United States and are
increasingly popular today with collectors. Thin
"eggshell china" teawares, miniatures and
souvenir items were widely marketed during the
1920s and 1930s and are sought-after today.*

Shelley Mark

Ashtray, Harebell patt., 3½".......**$25.00**

Cake plate, Rock Garden patt.....**195.00**

Cake plate, squared shaped
w/notched corners & pointed tab
handles, decorated w/a large
grey tree w/black & yellow
foliage on a white ground, yellow
border trim, 8¼ x 9¾" (ILLUS.
bottom next page, back).............**55.00**

Coffee set: cov. coffeepot,
creamer & cov. sugar bowl & six
cups & saucers; Regency patt.,
15 pcs......................................**500.00**

Cookie plate, footed, Rosebud
patt. **195.00**

Creamer & cov. sugar bowl,
Rock Garden patt., pr. **195.00**

Creamer, cov. sugar bowl & undertray, Stocks patt., 3 pcs....**130.00**

Cup & saucer, demitasse, Begonia patt. **72.00**

Cup & saucer, demitasse, Rose Spray patt. **72.00**

Cup & saucer, demitasse, Summer Glory patt. **135.00**

Cup & saucer, demitasse, conical cup w/ring handle, decorated inside & out w/a bright floral bouquet w/red roses, yellow & red tulip & other yellow, purple & blue florals, thin blue border bands, saucer 4⅞" d., cup 3" d., 2½" h. (ILLUS. front left) **45.00**

Cup & saucer, miniature, Blue Spray patt. **45.00**

Cup & saucer, miniature, Dainty Blue patt. ....**200.00 to 225.00**

Cup & saucer, Blue Heron patt.....**55.00**

Cup & saucer, Daisy patt., blue ..**125.00**

Cup & saucer, Daisy patt., green **95.00**

Cup & saucer, Dainty Blue patt. ...**60.00**

Cup & saucer, Rosebud patt., Dainty shape **60.00**

Cup & saucer, Heather patt..........**45.00**

Cup & saucer, Polka Dot patt., pink..**125.00**

Cup & saucer, Primrose patt. **60.00**

Cup & saucer, decorated w/large clusters of blue flowers w/small pink blossoms, blue-trimmed handle & borders, saucers 5½" d., cup 3¼" d., 2¾" h. **48.00**

Cup & saucer, decorated w/bluebells & a butterfly, cobalt blue trim......................................**55.00**

Cup & saucer, decorated w/grey & black tree, yellow edge & handle, cup 3⅜" d., 3⅞" h, saucer 5⅝" d. **48.00**

Creamer & cov. sugar bowl, Dainty Blue patt., pr. **75.00**

Dessert set: cup & saucer & square dessert plate, each piece w/a grey tree w/black & yellow foliage against a white ground, yellow border bands, cup w/ring handle, plate 6½" w., saucer 5½" d., cup 3¼" d., 2¾" h., the set (ILLUS. right front) **65.00**

Dessert set: cup & saucer & dessert plate; Begonia patt, dainty shape, 3 pcs. **89.00**

A Variety of Shelley Wares

Dessert set: cup & saucer & dessert plate; Crab Apple Blossom patt., Chester shape 3 pcs. **59.00**

Dessert set: cup & saucer & dessert plate; Phlox patt., Regency shape, 3 pcs. **125.00**

Dessert set: cup & saucer & dessert plate; Tall Trees & Sunrise patt., Regency shape, 3 pcs. **99.00**

Muffin dish, cov., Rosebud patt., large **195.00**

Mug, handleless, Blue Rock patt...**38.00**

Plate, 8" d., Blue Rock patt............**35.00**

Plate, dinner, Blue Rock patt.........**65.00**

Plate, Maytime patt........................**89.00**

Plate, Summer Glory patt. **98.00**

Teapot, cov., Blue Iris patt., Queen Anne shape, large **425.00**

SHENANDOAH VALLEY POTTERY

Shenandoah Valley Pitcher

The potters of the Shenandoah Valley in Maryland and Virginia turned out an earthenware pottery of a distinctive type. It was the first earthenware pottery made in America with a varied, brightly colored glaze. The most notable of these potters, Peter Bell, Jr., operated a pottery at Hagerstown, Maryland and later at Winchester, Virginia, from about 1800 until 1845. His sons and grandsons carried on the tradition. One son, John Bell, established a pottery at Waynesboro, Pennsylvania in 1833, working until his death in 1880, along with his sons who subsequently operated the pottery a few

years longer. Two other sons of Peter Bell, Jr., Solomon and Samuel, operated a pottery in Strasburg, Virginia, a town sometimes referred to as "pot town" for six potteries were in operation there in the 1880s. Their work was also continued by descendants, Shenandoah Valley redware pottery, with its colorful glazes in green, yellow, brown and other colors, and the stoneware pottery produced in the area, are eagerly sought by collectors. Some of the more unique forms can be considered true American folk art and will fetch fantastic prices.

Pitcher, 5⅛" h., footed ovoid body w/tooled lines around shoulder & applied strap handle, redware w/cream slip & mottled green & brown glaze (wear & chips) **$578.00**

Pitcher, 6" h., footed ovoid body w/flaring rim, pinched spout & applied strap handle, tooled lines, cream slip on redware w/brown & green glaze, hairline in spout & small chips (ILLUS.) **2,750.00**

Pitcher, 6½" h., footed cylindrical body w/tooling at base & shoulder, pinched spout & applied strap handle, redware w/cream slip & mottled brown & green glaze (wear, hairlines & edge chips) **1,045.00**

Salt dip, ovoid w/flat rim, short flaring foot, cream slip on redware w/green & brown glaze, 3" h. (filled w/wax, chips on base) **1,045.00**

SLIPWARE

This term refers to ceramics, primarily redware, decorated by the application of slip, or semi-liquid paste made of clay. Such wares were made for decades in England and Germany and elsewhere on the Continent, and in the Pennsylvania Dutch country and elsewhere in the United States. Today, contemporary copies of early Slipware items are featured in numerous decorator magazines and offered for sale in gift catalogs.

Slipware Bowl with Bird Decoration

Bowl, 6⅛" d., 2" h., wide shallow sides w/molded edge, redware slip-decorated w/bird perched in a tree trunk surrounded by dots & squiggles of dark manganese brown & thick white lead, possibly Moravian, early 19th ca. (ILLUS.) **$690.00**

Slipware "Moravian" Bowl

Bowl, 13" d., circular, "Moravian" redware, the everted rim w/white slip squiggle decoration, bowl decorated w/alternating bands of green & brown glaze, some minor rim chips, Pennsylvania, 19th c. (ILLUS.) **978.00**

Cuspidor, squatty bulbous base w/trumpet-form neck, redware w/tooled lines at shoulder, cream slip w/mottled green &

brown glaze, 6¾" h. (chips & hairlines, some chips have over paint) **440.00**

Slipware Dish with Large Bird

Dish, molded redware w/coggled edge decorated w/the figure of a large bird surrounded by scrolling pea pods & bud clusters in thick white slip on dark manganese brown ground, Pennsylvania, early 19th c., old repairs, 13⅝" d., 3" h. (ILLUS.) **4,025.00**

Flowerpot w/attached saucer base, flaring sides w/wide finger-crimped rim, wide cylindrical rim on saucer base, redware w/mottled cream slip & clear glaze, impressed "Solomon Bell, Strasburg," 7" d., 4⅜" h. (badly chipped & hole in bottom..............................**1,650.00**

Loaf dish, shallow oblong form, redware w/three parallel triple wavy bands in yellow slip, coggled rim, 13" l. (worn, old chips & scratches) **424.00**

Loaf dish, shallow oblong form, redware w/two diagonal bands of dashes flanking a central diagonal band composed of groups of small S-scrolls all in yellow slip, coggled rim, 16" l. (wear, chips & hairlines)............**374.00**

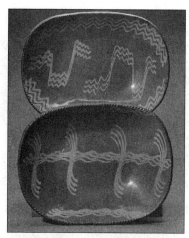

Slipware Loaf Dishes

Loaf dish, rectangular w/coggle wheel rim, redware w/yellow four-quill slip decoration, Pennsylvania, 19th c., 12 x 15¾" (ILLUS., bottom) **1,725.00**

Loaf dish, rectangular w/coggle wheel rim, redware, w/yellow triple-quill zigzag slip decoration, Pennsylvania, 19th c., 11½ x 16 (ILLUS., top) **2,185.00**

Mug, footed wide baluster-form w/a slightly flaring rim & applied C-form handle, yellow ground w/brown slip dots between upper & lower brown bands, Staffordshire, England, ca. 1700, 2⅝" h. **2,070.00**

Pie plate, redware, decorated w/three-line wavy bands of yellow slip, coggled rim, 8" d. (minor wear & old rim chips)......**330.00**

Pie plate, redware, w/three parallel triple wavy bands in yellow slip, coggled rim, 8" d. (minor wear & crazing) **605.00**

Pie plate, redware, three-line yellow slip-quilled decoration, coggled rim, 9½" d. (wear, small chips & short hairline) **330.00**

Pie plate, redware, three-line yellow slip decoration, coggled rim (wear & chips) **149.00**

Pitcher, 7¼" h., squatty bulbous body tapering to cylindrical neck, three rim spouts & applied strap handle, redware w/cream colored slip & mottled brown & green splotches, attributed to J. Eberly (handle repaired, wear & chips)............................**935.00**

Plate, 9" d., redware, decorated w/three-line wavy bands of yellow slip, coggled rim (minor wear & rim chips)......................**495.00**

Plate, 9¾" d., redware w/entwined three-line yellow slip decoration in center flanked by three-line "S" scroll yellow slip bands, coggled rim (wear & minor chips) **358.00**

Plate, redware w/yellow slip glaze, black spiderweb design ..**245.00**

Slipware Tobacco Jar

Tobacco jar, cov., redware, baluster-form w/stand-up incised lip, incised & gouged horizontal & vertical bands w/yellow, white & green slip, the shoulder w/sawtooth design filled in w/yellow, white & green slip decoration, the lid w/horizontal bands of green, yellow & black gouging finished w/a turned finial, probably Pennsylvania, mid-19th c., repair to lid, overall 11" h. (ILLUS.)......................**10,350.00**

Slipware Whistles

Whistle, redware, stylized model of a porcupine on a raised circular foot w/scored bristle & slip decoration, Pennsylvania, late 19th c., 4" l., 2" h. (ILLUS. right) **2,185.00**

Whistle, redware w/orangish brown glaze, stylized bird on a raised circular foot w/incised feather & wing detail heightened w/slip decoration, Pennsylvania, late 19th c., restoration to tail, 4¼" h. (ILLUS. left) **920.00**

SPATTERWARE

Schoolhouse Cup and Saucer

This ceramic ware takes its name from the "spattered" decoration, in various colors, generally used to trim pieces hand-painted with rustic center designs of flowers, birds, houses, etc. Popular in the early 19th century, most was imported from England.

Related wares, called "stick spatter," had free-hand designs applied with pieces of cut sponge attached to sticks, hence the name.

Examples date from the 19th and early 20th century and were produced in England, Europe and America.

Some early spatter-decorated wares were marked by the manufacturers, but not many. 20th century reproductions are also sometimes marked, including those produced by Boleslaw Cybis in the 1940s which sometimes have "CYBIS' impressed.

Cup & saucer, handleless, Peafowl patt., free-hand bird in violet-blue, green, red & black overall green spatter (cup has minor edge damage & stains) **$165.00**

Cup & saucer, handleless, Rainbow spatter (stains & wear, rim of cup has flaked glaze) **72.00**

Cup & saucer, handleless, Rainbow spatter in maroon & blue w/bull's eye center, impressed anchor mark (dark stains)...............................**110.00**

Cup & saucer, handleless, Rooster patt., free-hand bird in black, yellow, blue & red w/red spatter rim (small flake on rim of saucer) **1,375.00**

Cup & saucer, handleless, Schoolhouse patt, free-hand schoolhouse in red, black & green, red spatter border, close mis-match, repair (ILLUS.) **578.00**

Cup & saucer, handleless, Thistle patt., free-hand thistle in red & green w/deep maroon spatter border (stains, cup has chip on table ring) **413.00**

Cup plate, Peafowl patt., free-hand bird in black, blue, yellow & green w/overall red spatter, impressed "P.W. & Co. Stoneware," 4⅛" d. (dark stains)..............................**633.00**

Plate, 8⅛" d., Peafowl patt., free-hand bird in red, yellow, green & black, blue spatter background, impressed "Pearl Stoneware, P.W. & Co" (stains & wear) **358.00**

Plate, 8¼" d., Thistle patt., free-hand red & green thistle w/reddish purple spatter border (small edge flakes **330.00**

Plate, 8¼" d., Rainbow spatter, red & green spatter border & bull's eye design in center (small rim flake & light stains) **770.00**

Plate, 8¼" d., Peafowl patt., free-hand bird in black, blue, green & yellow w/overall red spatter (rim chip & stains)............................**138.00**

Plate, 8⅜" d., Peafowl patt., free-hand bird in red, blue, yellow-ochre & black, blue spatter background (red in tail has bubbled slightly, edge wear & minor stains)............................**303.00**

Tulip Plate and Sugar Bowl

Plate, 8¾" d., Tulip patt., free-hand red, green, yellow & black flower w/blue spatter border, impressed "Cotton and Barlow" (ILLUS.) **413.00**

Plate, 9½" d., Rainbow spatter w/bull's eye design in center, red & green (worn)...........................**182.00**

Platter, 13¾" l., Adam's Rose patt., free-hand rose in red, green & black blue border, (wear, stains & small edge chips, center has scratches & pits) **495.00**

Sauce dish, Tulip patt., free-hand flower in red, yellow, green & black, impressed anchor & "Davenport," green spatter border, 5" d. (chips & hairline) ...**605.00**

Soup plate, w/flanged rim, Dahlia patt., free-hand flower in red, blue, green & black w/purple spatter border, 9⅜" d. (professional repair) **275.00**

Sugar bowl, cov., Tulip patt., free-hand flower in red, green, yellow & black flower w/blue spatter border, stains, rim hairline & chips on inside flange of lid, 5¼" h. (ILLUS. w/plate)....**247.00**

Teapot, cov., squatty bulbous body tapering to flared foot, wide short rolled neck, swan's-neck spout & C-scroll handle, inset cover w/blossom finial, Adam's Rose patt., free-hand rose in red, black & green, blue spatter trim around shoulder & neck, 5½" h. (very minor edge wear & small flake on table ring) **1,485.00**

Stick and Cut Sponge Spatter

Bowl, 14¼" d., "gaudy" floral design & zig zag border in red, green, blue & yellow, marked "Maastricht" (crazing & minor stains) **220.00**

Pitcher, 9" h., cylindrical body tapering to rim, pinched spout & C-form handle (very minor edge flakes) **341.00**

Plate, 9" d., center decoration of a large red rose-type flower surrounded by leaves, w/border of blue stick spatter flowers & leaves (ILLUS.)........................**115.00**

Stick Spatter Plate with Roses

SPONGEWARE

Spongeware's designs were spattered, sponged or daubed on in colors, sometimes with a piece of cloth. Blue on white was the most common type, but mottled tans, browns and greens on yellowware were also popular. Spongeware generally has an overall pattern with a coarser look than Spatterwares, to which it is loosely related. These wares were extensively produced in England and America well into the 20th century.

Bowls, 7" d., brown sponging on yellowware, pr. **$135.00**

Creamer, cylindrical molded ear of corn, tapering to flat rim w/pinched spout, C-form handle, overall light blue sponging on white, 5" h. (stains) **110.00**

Pitcher, 7" h., ovoid body w/pinched spout & C-form handle, coarse blue on white, dark brown Albany slip interior ..**352.00**

Pitcher, 7½" h., bulbous ovoid body w/the upper half angled to a flat mouth w/high, arched spout, simple C-scroll round handle, overall blue sponging on white **193.00**

Pitcher, 8¾" h., bulbous ovoid body w/pinched spout & C-form handle, coarse blue sponging on white, dark brown Albany slip interior **468.00**

Plates, 7½" d., round w/slightly scalloped flanged rim, overall heavy blue sponging on white, pr. **165.00**

Vase, 5½" h., bulbous ovoid body w/molded swirled ribs, tapering to a wide flaring rim, overall finely spattered blue on white (rim chips) **165.00**

Vase, 8¾" h., cylindrical w/molded ribs in zigzag design at rim, blue sponging on white (ILLUS.) **413.00**

Cylindrical Spongeware Vase

Water filter, cov., two-piece, semi-ovoid base w/cylindrical top w/eared handles & slightly flaring rim w/domed cover, overall blue sponging on white, nickel plated spigot, 23¾" h.......**715.00**

STAFFORDSHIRE FIGURES

Small figures and groups made of pottery were produced by the majority of the Staffordshire, England potters in the 19th century and were used as mantel decorations or "chimney ornaments," as they were sometimes called. Pairs of dogs were favorites and were turned out by the carload, and 19th century pieces are still available. Well-painted reproductions also abound and collectors are urged to exercise caution before investing.

Bust of John Wesley, the clergyman w/long curled hair, white collar & black coat, raised on a marbleized socle base, a tablet on the reverse w/intentionally blurred wordings & dates, decorated in grey, black, tan, red, gold & fleshtone, after Enoch Wood, ca. 1870-80, 11⅞" h. (some slight flaking on the robe) **$385.00**

Chicks on Nest Dish

Chicks on nest, bisque, the domed cover w/a group of newly hatched chicks & eggshells painted in polychrome, the molded basketweave oval base painted yellow, 19th c., 7½" l., 6½" h. (ILLUS.)...........................**625.00**

Dog, Poodle in seated position, on a small rectangular hollow base, white decorated w/applied coleslaw main, painted black eyes & pink muzzle, 2" h. (faint hairline off base rim).................**138.00**

Dogs, Poodle standing holding a brightly colored bird in its mouth, standing on a pink & green rectangular pillow raised on a tapering rectangular footed base, applied "coleslaw" mane, tail & ankles, pink lustre trim on the base, 4⅛" h., facing pair......**424.00**

Dogs, Spaniel in seated position, white w/copper lustre spots & trim, 19th c., 5" h., facing pr.......**660.00**

Dogs, Spaniel in standing position holding a small basket of fruit in its mouth, oval base, heavily decorated in rust red, yellow, green & black, 19th c., 4" l., 5" h., facing pr. (some slight enamel loss) **330.00**

Dogs, Whippet, recumbent animal w/front legs crossed on a molded rectangular blue base, painted facial features & narrow collar, 5" l., facing pr. **330.00**

Equestrian group, a man in military uniform astride a prancing white horse, the narrow oval bass w/the raised name "Havelock," well-decorated in orange, green, fleshtone, black & purple, 19th c., 9" h. (in-the-making back separation) **138.00**

Equestrian groups, each showing a man in cavalier dress w/large hat, cape & boots on a prancing horse on an oval base, sparsely decorated in black, fleshtone & gold on white, 19th c., 11¼" h., facing pr.................**187.00**

Equestrian groups, each showing a man dressed in a cavalier outfit mounted stride a prancing white horse draped w/swagged trappings, untitled by identified as The Irish National Forester, 19th c., 13¼" h., facing pr. (one w/neck crack) **495.00**

Figure of an actor, standing in a dramatic pose before a draped pedestal, white w/polychrome highlights, 19th c., 9¾" h. **132.00**

Figure of Benjamin Franklin, standing holding his tricorner hat to his side & a document in the other hand, embossed title "FRANKLIN" across the front of the rectangular base, dressed in a blue coat, black hat & shoes, gold buttons, buckles & fleshtone, red & brown on the face, a sprig-decorated waistcoat, a short stump to one side, early 19th c., 14¼" h. (professional restoration to back of the stump) **1,210.00**

Figure of David Garrick in the role of Richard III, seated w/one hand raised beneath a pointed tent-like canopy, fine decoration in blue, yellow, black, fleshtone, orange, green & red, 19th c., 10¼" h. (long hairline across the back top) **198.00**

Figure of Dick Whittington, young man in medieval costume standing beside a mile post w/raised lettering reading "IV Miles to London," the name

"Dick Whittington" across the front of the oval base, decorated in pinkish red, brown, tan, fleshtone, yellow, black & green, mid-19th c., 17" h. (an in-the-making separation, slight flaking of the black) **275.00**

Figure of a drowsy drinker, a man wearing 18th c. attire curled up & leaning against a large beer keg, polychrome decoration, 19th c., 4¼".............**176.00**

Figure of Garabaldi, standing beside a low draped column, wearing a tall plumed hat, & long orange coat, further decorated w/fleshtone, black, brown, orange & green, mid-19th c., 11¼" h. **468.00**

Figure of a lady in classical dress standing & leaning against a funerary urn atop a tall square pedestal, symbolizing grief, decorated in green, yellow, red & w/a reddish brown urn, square base, early 19th c., 9" h. (minute base flakes) **330.00**

Figure of a lady in classical dress standing & holding a long garland of flowers which drapes over her right shoulder, her long dress decorated w/tiny floral sprigs & larger fleur-de-lis-like sprigs, colored in yellow, brown, orange, green & blue, on a square plinth, early 19th c., 12½" h. (chip on her elbow, chips & flakes on the base, some enamel loss) **248.00**

Figure of a lady in classical dress standing atop a high square plinth trimmed along to corners w/leaves, the figure w/one hand at her hip holding a floral wreath & the other hand holding some sort of instrument near her head, sparsely decorated in fleshtone, brown & gold, 19th c., 13¼" h. (crazing)..**198.00**

Figure of St. Roche, standing holding a dog & wearing a light blue robe, early 19th c., 17" h. (chips) **345.00**

Figure of a Scotsman, in full costume, seated asleep leaning on a basket beside a tree stump, polychrome decoration, 19th c., 10" h. **154.00**

Figures, hunters in fancy dress & feathered hats seated upon recumbent stags w/a large tree stump behind, one stag w/spotted decoration, on oval floral-molded rockwork bases, polychrome trim, 19th c., 10½" h., facing pr. **187.00**

Figures, hunter & huntress, each dressed in 19th c. rural costume, he w/his rifle & a basket of game birds, she holding a basket of game birds, well-decorated in yellow, orange, blue, red, black, brown, fleshtone & gold, on oval bases, 19th c., 15¾" h., pr. (faint hairline of a firing separation in her back) **358.00**

Figures, a lady & man in country attire, each seated upon the back of a recumbent stag, polychrome decoration, 19th c., 6½" h., pr. **176.00**

Figures, a standing man in formal dress w/one hand resting on a low pedestal, titled "Prince," the matching figure of a young woman wearing a long formal gown, titled "Princess," 19th c., 9½" h., pr. **440.00**

Figure group, actors on a couch, a lady wearing a flounced dress seated on the back of a couch beside an man just below her reaching out w/one arm & holding a musical instrument w/the other, he wearing a cap, jacket & kneebreeches, slightly curved & draped footed base, heavy polychrome decoration, 19th c., 10" h. **220.00**

Figure group, pearlware, titled "Christ's Agony," show the kneeling Christ in the garden alongside a squared plinths w/a small kneeling angle offering the suffering Messiah food & drink, on the plinth is printed "Father - Let This - Cup - Pass," the bocage behind consists of three branches w/applied tiny four-petal florets, raised on a high rectangular platform w/a serpentine front & incurved sides, a small medallion on the front reads "Christ's Agony," decorated overall in polychrome in shades of white, black, green, lavender, brick red, yellow, fleshtone, brown & grey, early 19th c., 10½" h. (restoration only to the hands of Christ, several small flakes around base & on tip of one branch) **1,760.00**

Figure group, "Death of Nelson," three figures, the two outer supporting the falling central figure representing Lord Nelson, well decorated in blue, green, red, brown, orange & black, titled in gold script across the base front, 19th c., 8¾" h. **385.00**

Figure group, Emperor Napoleon III of France standing in military uniform next to a seated figure of the Empress Eugenie, titled across the bottom front, polychrome decoration, 19th c., 9¼" h. **330.00**

Figure group, girl hugging sheep, 2½" h. **68.00**

Figure group, lady & man going to market, he walking & carrying a rope-tied bag, dressed in a wide hat, long jacket, vest, kneebreeches & boots, she wearing a long shawl-draped dress & carrying a large bundle on her head, polychrome decoration, oval base, 19th c., 12¼" h. ` **165.00**

Figure group, lovers seated beneath a bower, the young couple seated under a high, arched & pierced branching bower continuing to an oval base, light polychrome trim, 19th c., 14¼" h. **242.00**

Figure group, Mary dressed in country attire standing beside her small sheep, polychrome decoration, 19th c., 6" h.............**121.00**

Figure group, titled "Prodigals: Return," shows the father standing & greeting his young son, each wearing a turban, cloak & long robes, nicely decorated in black, brown, fleshtone, orange, blue, yellow & lavender, 19th c., 13½" h. (tiny firing separation on back, hairline across tip of the father's hand) **385.00**

Figure group, pearlware, The Night Watchmen or The Inebriates, marked on the oval medallion on the base "Vicar and Moses," two intoxicated mean in 18th c. costume, one holding up his friend w/one hand while holding a lantern in the other, the other man clutching a pitcher of ale against his side & a cup in the other hand, carefully decorated & standing on a high rectangular platform base w/overall black splotching & the oval medallion w/title, early 19th c., 11½" h. (small chips on one hat & larger chip on other hat, large chip on upper corner & smaller chips on rim, larger man's black coat w/enamel bubbling & flaking) **825.00**

Figure group, a young couple in country attire, each standing beside a plaid patterned flag, polychrome decoration, oval base, 19th c., 6¼" h...................**176.00**

Figure group, titled "Tam O'Shanter & Sooter Johnny," two men sitting on either side of

Tam O'Shanter & Sooter Johnny

Figural Watch Holder

a barrel, all in natural colors & gold trim, 9½" d., 13" h. (ILLUS.).....................**500.00 to 550.00**

Spill vase, a Spaniel seated beside w tree trunk-form vase, polychrome decoration, 19th c., 13" h. **275.00**

Vase, 18" h., figural, a forester in cavalier dress w/a large feathered hat, jacket, cape, kneebreeches & boots standing beside a tall slender blossom-trimmed trumpet-form tree stump all on a scroll-molded base painted w/the script letters "OR" on the lower front, sparsely decorated overall in black, fleshtone, yellow & gold, 19th c.......................................**198.00**

Vases, 14" h., figural, one w/a Scottish girl standing beside a tall vase formed from a sheaf of wheat, the other a Scottish man beside a matching vase, oval base, decorated in gold, green, red, fleshtone & blue, 19th c., pr. **495.00**

Watch holder, pearlware, figural, in the form of a tall case clock w/a round top w/opening for the watch face, flanked by the figures of a boy & girl, the boy

w/a blue sash covering him, the girl w/a red blouse & bluish green skirt, a hint of pink lustre around dial opening, the lower case of the clock w/a medallion in the form of a ribbon holding a crown done in green, blue, yellow & red, flaking to some paint, 19th c., 7½" h. (ILLUS.) ...**325.00**

Watch holder, modeled as a man & a woman standing & flanking a grape arbor w/an opening for the watch face, 19th c., 12" h. ...**316.00**

Watch holder, model of a castle, paneled towers flanking a lower center section w/a round opening for the watch face, steps & foliage across the front, on an oval base, decorated in orange, yellow, black & green, 19th c., 12" h. (hairline off the rim of one tower) **149.00**

Watch holder, model of a grandfather clock w/the dial opening to display the watch face, the buff face around the opening in decorated w/colored florals & a "moon-phase" dial, the clock case in mahogany red w/brass-colored fittings, 11" h. (fine restoration to lower base) **413.00**

Shepherd Piping Basket and Undertray

STAFFORDSHIRE
TRANSFER WARES

The process of transfer-printing designs on earthenwares developed in England in the late 18th century and by the mid-19th century most common ceramic wares were decorated in this manner, most often with romantic European or Oriental landscape scenes, animals or flowers. The earliest such wares were printed in dark blue but a little later light blue, pink, purple, red, black, green and brown were used. A majority of these wares were produced at various English potteries right up till the turn of the century but French and other European firms also made similar pieces and all are quite collectible. The best reference on this area is Petra Williams' book Staffordshire Romantic Transfer Patterns - Cup Plates and Early Victorian China *(Fountain House East, 1978). Also see ADAMS, CLEWS and other makers and HISTORICAL & COMMEMORATIVE WARES.*

Basket & undertray, the oval basket w/an openwork lattice design & loop end handles, decorated in the bottom w/a landscape scene of a shepherd piping, flower & leaf border, matching oval undertray, medium blue, probably by Riley, basket 10½" l., 2 pcs. (ILLUS.) **$1,210.00**

Creamer, boat-shaped, dark blue, one side w/a decoration of a single swimming swan, the opposite side w/two swimming swans, pseudo-Chinese "Stone China" mark, probably Clews, ca. 1830, 4⅜" h. **204.00**

Creamer, footed tapering octagonal body w/angled handle, Classical Antiquities patt., medium blue, Clementson, 5¼" h. **187.00**

Cup & saucer, handleless, Harvest Home patt., landscapes w/farm harvesting scenes on both cup & saucer, floral & scrolled leaves borders, mulberry, Jackson, ca. 1830 ....**77.00**

Cup & saucer, handleless, The Pet patt., saucer w/central scene of a tent w/a lady & her dog, vignette scenes around exterior of the cup, large leaf borders, mulberry, Adams, ca. 1830 (two minute flakes on cup & saucer) ...**55.00**

Pitcher, 12" h., Corinth patt., brown transfer-printed, ca. 1840s..................................**165.00**

Plate, 5½" d., motto-type, black transfer-printed scene, "Christ Rising From The Grave," ca. 1850...................................**140.00**

Plate, 5½" d., motto-type, black transfer-printed scene, "Sitting Up," ca. 1850   150.00

Plate, 6½" d., Seasons series, black hunting scene titled "November," Adams, ca. 1830 (some mellowing) **83.00**

Plate, 7" d., the flanged rim embossed w/large blossoms & leaves highlighted w/red, blue, green & yellow enamels, the center decorated w/a black transfer-printed scene of a young girl in a garden setting w/two verses, the one above her reading "The Tulip and Butterfly appear in Gayer Clothes than I," the one below her reading "Let me Drest fine as I will, Flies, Worms and Flowers exceed Me Still," early 19th c. (overall mellowing) **127.00**

Plate, 8¼" d., Chinese landscape scene w/people in a small boat in foreground & a cottage in a wooded shore in the background, medium dark blue ...**66.00**

Plate, 8⅞" d., center design of birds & fruit, wide floral border, dark blue, Stubbs (some stacking wear, light overall mellowing) **165.00**

Plate, 10" d., Sheltered Peasants patt., wide flower & fruit border, dark blue, Hall, ca. 1830 (even light wear) **176.00**

Plate, 10" d., center design of birds & fruit, wide floral border, dark blue, Stubbs **248.00**

Plate, 10¾" d., dark blue design w/a central scroll-bordered squared reserve w/a hunting scene framed by a wide floral border & a molded ropetwist rim band, titled "Hunting Series...Starting Out," ca. 1830...................................**330.00**

Plates, India Temple patt., blue, marked "JWR," J. Ridgway, ca. 1850, 10 dinner & 2 luncheon size, group of 12.......................**275.00**

Platter, 16" l., lavender transfer pastoral scene, artist-signed, ca. 1840...................................**160.00**

Platter, 16¾" l., oval, blue printed scene depicting figures w/cows in the foreground & waterfalls & ruins in the background, second quarter 19th c. (minor glaze chips, edge roughness & knife marks) **489.00**

Platter, 16¾" l., oval, dark blue printed scene depicting hunting scene of two men w/long rifle & two dogs, impressed "Clews," small edge flakes & minor scratches) **825.00**

Triumphal Car Pattern Platter

Platter, 17⅛" l., oval w/lightly scalloped rim, Triumphal Car patt., light blue, J. & M.P. Bell and Company, light mottled mellowing, unmarked (ILLUS.) ..**275.00**

Platter, 19¾" l., oblong w/cut corners, an oval center Oriental landscape scene w/boats, water & temples, floral paneled border, light blue, underglaze crown mark & "Mason's Ironstone China".......................................**220.00**

Platter, 20⅛" l., pearlware, oval w/lightly scalloped rim, the center w/an Oriental landscape scene w/a bridge over a river w/boats & temples on the shores, medium blue (shallowrim chip, some knife marks) **270.00**

Soup tureen, cover & undertray, a large bulbous oval paneled body raised on a high flaring foot & w/a narrow shoulder to the flaring rim, a stepped & paneled domed cover w/a large fruit finial, outswept loop end handles on the body, w/a matching oval dished undertray w/molded end handles, The Bridge of Lucano, Italy patt., dark blue, overall 13" h., the set **1,650.00**

Sugar bowl, cov., octagonal baluster-form w/inset paneled conical cover w/florette finial, molded scroll handles, overall design of leafy scrolls & cartouches, dark blue, underglaze mark "Granite China - WRS & Co.," ca. 1840s, 7¼" h. **132.00**

Sugar bowl, cov., octagonal baluster-form w/inset paneled conical cover w/knob finial, outswept loop side handles, Doria patt., light blue, Ridgway, ca. 1840s, 8¾" h.......................**176.00**

Supper set w/tray: comprising a central oval waisted two-handled cov. egg holder fitted w/a liner & inset w/four egg cups & a divided salt cellar; surrounded by two crescent-form cov. dishes & two open spade-form dishes, all printed w/a blue chinoiserie design of island pavilions among trees w/a sampan in the foreground, all fitted into an oval mahogany tray w/upstanding brass carrying handles, England, early 19th c., tray, 22½" l., the set (ILLUS.) **1,840.00**

Unusual Supper Set with Tray

Toddy plate, center landscape scene w/an Eastern temple, floral border, medium dark blue, Riley, 4¾" d. **44.00**

Toddy plate, scene of groom leading out horses, Indian Sporting series, medium dark blue, Clews, 5½" d. (minute pinpoint rim flake) **248.00**

Toddy plate, Scrolls patt., overall medium dark blue design of various scrolls & lattice designs, ca. 1830, 5½" d. (unseen minute flake on back rim) **83.00**

Vegetable dish, cov., rectangular body w/rounded corners & a flanged rim w/scroll-molded end handles, wide flattened domed cover w/loop handle, blue printed design of a landscape w/people & cows in the foreground & waterfalls & ruins in the background, second quarter 19th c., 12" l. (large chips, hairlines) **230.00**

STANGL

Johann Martin Stangl, who first came to work for the Fulper Pottery in 1910 as a ceramic chemist and plant superintendent, acquired a financial interest and became president of the company in 1926. The name of the firm was changed to Stangl Pottery in 1929 and at that time much of the production was devoted to a high grade dinnerware to enable the company to survive the Depression years. One of the earliest solid-color dinnerware patterns was their Colonial line, introduced in 1926. In the 1930s it was joined by their Americana pattern. After 1942 these early patterns were followed by a wide range of hand-decorated patterns featuring flowers and fruits with a few decorated with animals or human figures.

Around 1940 a very limited edition of porcelain birds, patterned after the illustrations in John James Audubon's "Birds of America," was issued. Stangl subsequently began production of less expensive ceramic birds and these proved to be popular during the war years, 1940-46. Each bird was

handpainted and each was well marked with impressed, painted or stamped numerals which indicated the species and the size.

All operations ceased at the Trenton, New Jersey plant in 1978.

Two reference books which collectors will find helpful are The Collectors Handbook of Stangl Pottery *by Norma Rehl (The Democrat Press, 1979), and* Stangl Pottery *by Harvey Duke (Wallace-Homestead, 1994).*

Stangl Mark

DINNERWARES & ARTWARES

Ashtray, oval, Pheasant patt., Sportsmen's Giftware line, No. 3926, 10" l. **$35.00**

Ashtray, oval, Pintail patt., Sportsmen's Giftware line, No. 3926, 10" l. **35.00**

Bowl, fruit, 5½" d., Festival patt.....**10.00**

Bowl, fruit, 5½" d., Provincial patt............................**10.00**

Bowl, fruit, 5½" d., Thistle patt. **12.00**

Bowl, salad, 10" d., Thistle patt.....**40.00**

Bowl, salad, 12" d., Country Garden patt. **45.00**

Candle warmer, Thistle patt. **25.00**

Casserole, cov., individual size, Thistle patt. **15.00**

Celery dish, Country Garden patt. **25.00**

Cigarette box, cov., Daisy decoration, No. 3666 ....**40.00**

Coffeepot, cov., Deco Delight patt., yellow **155.00**

Cup, Magnolia patt. **7.00**

Gravy boat, Fruit patt.....................**30.00**

Mug, pheasant decoration, Sportsmen's Giftware Line, No. 5092.....................................**35.00**

Pitcher, Provincial patt., 1 qt. **35.00**

Plate, 6" d., Festival patt.................**5.00**

Plate, 8" d., Country
Garden patt. **10.00**

Plate, 8" d., Florette patt.................**8.00**

Plate, 9" d., Little Quackers patt.,
Kiddieware line **140.00**

Plate, 10" d., Magnolia patt. **11.00**

Plate, 10" d., Provincial patt. **15.00**

Plate, chop, 12½" d.,
Magnolia patt..............................**25.00**

Platter, Casual, 13¾" l.,
Magnolia patt. **30.00**

Salt & pepper shakers, Roxanne
patt., pr. **15.00**

Server, center handle, Gold
Blossom patt...............................**13.00**

Sugar bowl, cov., Mountain
Laurel patt. **15.00**

Vase, 6" h. scrolled horn-shape,
No. 2056 ....**35.00**

Vegetable bowl, open, Thistle
patt., 8" d. **35.00**

STONEWARE

Stoneware is essentially a vitreous pottery, impervious to water even in its unglazed state, that has been produced by potteries all over the world for centuries. Utilitarian wares such as crocks, jugs, churns and the like, were the most common productions in the numerous potteries that sprang into existence in the United States during the 19th century. These items were often enhanced by the application of a cobalt blue oxide decoration. In addition to the coarse, primarily salt-glazed stonewares, there are other categories of stoneware known by such special names as basalt, jasper and others.

Bottle, cylindrical body w/tapering
neck & molded rim, slip-quilled
cobalt blue "B" on each side &
impressed "P. Pfannebecker"
w/"P" in diamond, 10¾" h.
(stains & small old chips).........**$165.00**

Butter churn, tall swelled
cylindrical body w/eared handles
& molded rim, brushed cobalt
blue primitive tree on the top
front, blue-trimmed handles,
19th c., 16" h. (rim chips)...........**187.00**

Butter churn, wooden dasher
cover, tall swelled cylindrical
body w/eared handles & molded
rim, impressed label "S. Purdy
Portage Co. Ohio 4" w/blue at
handles & label, 4 gal., 18¼" h
(minor chips)..............................**286.00**

Churn, cylindrical w/eared
handles, brushed cobalt blue
flower & "4," 4 gal., 16½" h.
(very minor chips).....................**165.00**

Rare Stoneware Butter Churn

Butter churn, tall swelled
cylindrical body w/eared handles
& a molded rim, cobalt blue slip-
quilled seated lion looking over
its shoulder under a number "6,"
minor base hairline, small chips
inside edge of lip, top
misshapen, 19th c., 6 gal.,
18½" h. (ILLUS.)....................**6,050.00**

Churn, cylindrical body tapering
to wide molded rim, eared
handles, brushed cobalt blue
floral decoration, 19" h. (wear,
stains & some surface
firing chips) **303.00**

Churn, tall swelled cylindrical
body w/wide molded rim, eared
handles, brushed cobalt blue
flowers & "6," 19½" h. (stains) ...**193.00**

Crock, cylindrical body w/eared handles, cobalt blue slip-quilled stylized flower & impressed label "Whites Utica, NY," 7½" h. (stains, glaze flaking & chips) **187.00**

Crock with Smiley-face Flower

Crock, cylindrical w/molded rim & applied eared handles, cobalt blue slip-quilled Smiley-face flower & "2," impressed "J. Burger Rochester, N.,Y.," ca. 1880, 2 gal., few minor glaze flake spots, 8½" h. (ILLUS.)....**1,271.00**

Crock, cylindrical w/eared handles, cobalt blue slip-quilled leafy branch & bird w/long tail, impressed label "N.A. White & Son Utica N.Y. 2," 2 gal., 8¾" h. (interior lime deposits) **495.00**

Crock, cylindrical w/eared handles, slip-quilled cobalt blue feathery leaf decoration & impressed label "J. Burger Jr., Rochester, N.Y. 2," 2 gal., 9" h. (chips) **220.00**

Crock, cylindrical w/eared handles, brushed cobalt blue stylized flower & "3," 3 gal., 10" h. **215.00**

Crock, cylindrical w/eared handles, slip-quilled cobalt blue large bird on flowering branch, impressed "Whites Utica, 3," 10¼" h. (chips & hairline) **182.00**

Crock, cylindrical w/molded rim & applied eared handles, cobalt blue slip-quilled pair of birds on leafy branch decoration, impressed "Ottman Bro's & Co.

Crock with Two Birds

Fort Edward, N.Y.," ca. 1880, 5 gal.,¼" tight through line in back, 12" h. (ILLUS.) **1,876.00**

Crock, cylindrical w/eared handles, cobalt blue stenciled & freehand label "Williams & Reppert, Greensboro, Pa. 4," 4" gal., 13" h. **138.00**

Jar, ovoid body swelling to a wide molded rim, eared handles, slip-quilled cobalt blue stylized floral design & impressed label "J. & F. Norton, Bennington, Vt.," 8½" h. (small chips) **275.00**

Jar, ovoid w/applied ribbed should handles, brushed cobalt blue at handles & impressed label "Stedman & Seymour, New Haven," 9" h. (wear, chips & minor hairlines, lime deposits) **99.00**

Jar, ovoid body swelling to a wide molded rim, eared handles, slip-quilled cobalt blue "2," 2 gal., 9¾" h. (minor chips) **99.00**

Jar, ovoid body swelling to a wide molded rim, cobalt blue stenciled & freehand label "R.T. Williams, New Geneva, Pa." & "2," 2 gal., 10" h......................**198.00**

Jar, ovoid w/applied eared handles & wide molded rim, brushed cobalt blue floral design, 10¼" h..........................**385.00**

Jar, bulbous ovoid w/wide cylindrical neck & flat rim, applied shoulder handles, grey salt glaze w/brown daubing at handles & Albany slip interior, impressed label "W. States" (William States, Stonington, Conn), 11" h. (misshapen & chips) **193.00**

Jar, baluster shaped body w/applied handles & tooled band at neck, two tone brown w/grey band, impressed "Boston 2," 2 gal., 12" h. (hairlines & minor chips) **303.00**

Jar, cylindrical w/applied handles & wide molded rim, large slip-quilled & brushed cobalt blue floral design, impressed label "N.A. White & Son, Utica, N.Y. 2," 2 gal., 11¼" h. **330.00**

Jar, squat semi-ovoid body decorated w/cobalt blue slip-quilled stylized flower, impressed label "J. & E. Norton, Bennington, Vt 2," 2 gal., 11½" h. (rim chips) **275.00**

Jar, bulbous ovoid body tapering to wide flat mouth, applied shoulder handles, brushed cobalt blue floral decoration & impressed "2," 2 gal., 12" h. (small chips) **220.00**

Jar, ovoid body w/wide cylindrical neck, applied shoulder handles w/incised lines, brushed cobalt blue three-part flower decoration & impressed "P.H. Smith 3," 3 gal., 12¾" h. (rim chips & deteriorating repair) **77.00**

Jar, wide cylindrical body w/wide molded rim, incised lines on shoulder, brushed cobalt blue floral design on both sides, attributed to Peter Herman, 13" h. **303.00**

Jar, semi-ovoid w/eared handles, cobalt blue brushed foliage swags, impressed "2" in circle, 2 gal., 13½" h. (chips)...............**231.00**

Jar, ovoid w/applied shoulder handles, incised flower-like design highlighted w/cobalt blue, impressed "Swan & Stains, Stonington," 13¾" h. (some crazing)..........................**193.00**

Jar, ovoid w/applied shoulder handles & tooled neck, brushed cobalt blue floral decoration & impressed "Kelin" in cartouche, 14¾" h. (hairline & chip in base).....................................**193.00**

Jar, swelled cylindrical body w/flat rim, eared handles, brushed cobalt blue flower & "2," 2 gal., 26" h. **182.00**

Jug, ovoid, unmarked, ½ gal. **80.00**

Jug, bulbous semi-ovoid body w/strap handle, cobalt blue design resembles long-horn steer, impressed label "J.B. Caire & Co. Pokeepsie (sic) N.Y.," 9½" h. **242.00**

Jug, ovoid w/molded neck & rim handle, slip-quilled cobalt blue stylized three-petal flower on a stem w/two oblong dotted leaves, impressed "Penn Yan," 19th c., 10¾" h. **209.00**

Jug, bulbous ovoid body tapering to small molded rim & strap handle, impressed cobalt blue label "E.H. Merrill 2" & cobalt blue at handle & lip, 2 gal., 13¼" h. (minor chips) **160.00**

Jug, semi-ovoid body w/molded rim & strap handle, brushed cobalt blue leafy design & blue highlights on impressed label "D.W. Graves, Westmoreland. 2," 13¼" h. **193.00**

Jug, bulbous ovoid body w/molded rim & ribbed strap handle, cobalt blue scalloped design, impressed label "L. Seymour, Troy," 13½" h. (minor crow's foot hairlines).................**176.00**

Jug, bulbous ovoid body w/molded rim & strap handle, cobalt blue brushed flower on front & impressed label "I.M. Mead, Mogadore, Ohio," 14¼" h. (stains & very minor flakes) **413.00**

Jug, bulbous ovoid w/applied strap handle, brushed cobalt blue stylized flower & impressed "3," 3 gal., 15" h. (minor chips & crazing) **165.00**

Jug, bulbous ovoid body w/applied strap handle, concentric tooled rings at neck above brushed cobalt blue leaf & scroll design, 15" h. (small chips) **248.00**

Jug, bulbous ovoid body w/molded rim & strap handle, incised lines, bird on leaf & "3" on neck, 3 gal., 15¾" h. (interior has been weighted to use as a lamp) **358.00**

Jug, bulbous semi-ovoid body, molded rim & strap handle, slip-quilled cobalt blue stylized floral decoration, impressed label "Whites Utica 3," 3 gal., 15½" h. **165.00**

Jug, bulbous ovoid body w/small molded rim, strap handle, red clay w/greenish grey glaze, white slip-quilled wreath at impressed label "Chandler Maker" (Thomas M. Chandler, Drummondtown, Virginia 1810-1854) 16" h...................**2,310.00**

Jug, ovoid body tapering to small molded rim, strap handle, cobalt blue slip-quilled flowers & "3", impressed label "Harrington & Burger, Rochester," 3 gal., 16" h. (stains & chip on base)....**413.00**

Jug, ovoid w/molded rim & strap handle, brushed cobalt blue floral design, impressed label "Elgen Spring Water, S. Allen, Vergennes, Vt. 4," 4 gal., 17" h. (hairline in handle) **297.00**

Pitcher, 7¼" h., wide ovoid body tapering to a wide cylindrical neck w/pinched spout & applied strap handle, brushed cobalt

blue floral design around the front & leaf sprigs around the neck w/blob of green ash on one side **413.00**

Pitcher, 8¾" h., ovoid w/flaring rim & pinched spout, brushed cobalt blue floral design............**358.00**

Pitcher, 8¾" h., footed ovoid body w/tall cylindrical neck, pinched spout & C-form handle, brushed cobalt blue floral design on body beneath spout & brushed leafy design flanking spout & under spout (chips & short hairline on foot).................**550.00**

Preserving jar, ovoid w/applied shoulder strap handles, cobalt blue pinwheel design, brushed stripes & stenciled label "Jas. Hamilton & Co., Greensboro," 9½" h. (small lip flakes) **605.00**

Preserving jar, slightly swelled cylindrical body w/molded rim, stenciled cobalt blue label "James Hamilton & Co., Greensboro, Pa.," 10" h. (hairlines)..................................**110.00**

Water cooler, barrel-shaped w/incised bands trimmed in cobalt blue & an upper panel of incised scrolling foliate designs, impressed mark of Leonard, Benjamin & Clark Chase, Somerset, Massachusetts & "4", 1845-82, 4 gal. minor chips, cracks, 15" h. (ILLUS) **345.00**

Barrel-shaped Water Cooler

TECO POTTERY

Teco Pottery was actually the line of art pottery introduced by the American Terra Cotta and Ceramic Company of Terra Cotta (Crystal Lake), Illinois in 1902. Founded by William D. Gates in 1881, American Terra Cotta originally produced only bricks and drain tile. Because of superior facilities for experimentation, including a chemical laboratory, the company was able to develop an art pottery line, favoring a matte green glaze in the earlier years but eventually achieving a wide range of colors including a metallic lustre glaze and a crystalline glaze. Though some hand-thrown pottery was made, Gates favored a molded ware because it was less expensive to produce. By 1923, Teco Pottery was no longer being made and in 1930 American Terra Cotta and Ceramic Company was sold. A book on the topic is Teco: Art Pottery of the Prairie School, by Sharon S. Darling (Erie Art Museum, 1990).

Teco Pottery Mark

Book ends, modeled as a seated gargoyle w/prominent wings, spiny backbone, pointed ears & open mouth atop a rectangular pedestal, mottled brown, tan & olive dripped glossy glaze, unmarked, 8½" h., pr. (one w/base & wing chips)..............**$440.00**

Bowl-vase, bulbous nearly spherical body w/a short neck & widely flaring rolled rim, matte green glaze, impressed mark twice, No. C180, 4½" d., 3¾" h. **173.00**

Jardiniere, a narrow footring supports a very wide flaring squatty bulbous body w/a rounded shoulder & a wide flat low rolled neck, matte green glaze, stamped twice on base, 26½" d., 13" h. (ILLUS.)..........**4,025.00**

Large Teco Jardiniere

Vase, 4" h., 2¾" d., bulbous ovoid body tapering sharply to a tiny neck w/flared mouth, even matte green glaze, impressed twice w/company mark **413.00**

Vase, 4" h., 3¾" d., bulbous simple ovoid body tapering to a short flaring neck, overall narrow ringed sides under a smooth matte green glaze, die-stamped marks...**330.00**

Vase, 6¾" h., 4¼" d., tall ovoid body tapering to a small trumpet-form neck above small squared buttress shoulder handles, matte green glaze, No. A402 ....**1,093.00**

Vase, 7" h., bulbous base w/cylindrical neck tapering to a flaring rim, mustard matte glaze **500.00**

Vase, 7⅛" h., four upright squared buttresses frame an ovoid lower body & form small open handles around the swelled neck w/a flaring rim, unusual rose-colored matte glaze, marked twice on base (two rim chips, repaired base chip) **550.00**

Vase, 7½" h., 3" d., a ringed foot below a tall cylindrical body w/four slender buttresses up the sides, a flat slightly flaring rim, matte brown glaze, die-stamped marks...................**550.00**

Vase, 8" h., large form w/a swollen base & flared lip w/four buttress handles up the sides, matte green glaze, No. 403A, designed by W. D. Gates **1,495.00**

Vase, 9" h., cylindrical body molded w/jonquils & leafage & glazed in yellow, ca. 1920 ....**431.00**

Rare Teco Vase

Vase, 11½" h., a slightly flared round foot tapering to the oviform body w/an openwork design of overlapping & entwined tall leaves & tulip blossoms & stems curving in at the top, No. 151, faintly stamped twice, designed by William J. Dodd, fine matte green glaze (ILLUS.) **11,500.00**

Vase, 11½" h., a thin footring supports a wide slightly tapering rounded cylindrical body w/thick twisted handles rising from the narrow shoulder to the molded inverted mouth, mint green matte glaze w/heavy charcoaling, No. 257, impressed mark (minor repair to one handle) **1,540.00**

Vase, 25" h., 12" d., tall gently swelled cylindrical body on a narrow footring, a narrow angled shoulder to the short rolled neck, robin's-egg blue matte glaze, No. G60 (chips to base) **935.00**

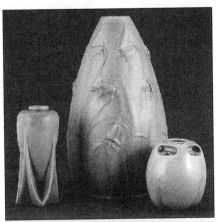

Large & Small Teco Vases

Vase, 6" h., 5½" d., bulbous ovoid lobed body w/short curved buttress handles & cut-out floral designs at the shoulder & short rolled neck, matte green glaze, marked (ILLUS. right) **1,650.00**

Vase, 9" h., 4" d., 'rocketship'-form, a tall tapering ovoid body supported by long curved fins down the sides, the flattened shoulder centering a small molded mouth, smooth matte green glaze, mark stamped twice (ILLUS. left) **3,850.00**

Vase, 17¼" h., 11½" d., tall sharply tapering bulbous ovoid body on a narrow footring, the entire surface embossed w/bellflower blossoms, fine leathery matte green glaze, some restoration to base & rim chips (ILLUS. center).............**4,675.00**

TEPLITZ - AMPHORA

These wares were produced in numerous potteries in the vicinity of Teplitz in the Bohemian area of what is now The Czech Republic during the late 19th and into the 20th century. Vases and figures, of varying quality, were the primary products of such firms as Riessner & Kessel (Amphora), Ernst Wahliss and Alfred Stellmacher. Although originally rather low-priced items, today collectors are searching out the best marked examples and prices are soaring.

Teplitz-Amphora Marks

Basket, porcelain, rope handle, braided & woven ground w/6"" h. angel attached to side holding bunches of flowers under each arm, Czechoslovakia **$495.00**

Bust of beautiful woman w/hair up high, wearing lacy gown, artist-signed, red R St. & K mark at base, 14" h. **1,800.00**

Ewer, decorated w/a portrait of gypsy girl against a grey ground highlighted w/gold butterflies, mark of Reissner, Stellmacher & Kessel......................................**650.00**

Vase, 6" h., portrait of a woman w/long black hair, holding flowers, enameling & jewels **795.00**

Vase, 6¼" h., double-gourd form, the bulbous rounded bottom tapering to a smaller knob w/a short neck, the lower portion of the base & the upper body molded w/a geometric honeycomb design w/gilt trim, a wide smooth center band decorated w/large pale blue flowers & blue & gold leaves on a rich purple ground, dark ground on upper & lower sections, marked "R St & K Turn Teplitz" in red inkstamp & impressed "Amphora - 25" & "3738".................................**193.00**

Vase, 6¾" h., footed, six-sided, reticulated band of green & white diamonds around top, diamond band around bottom, pitted teal glaze, probably Paul Dachsel **475.00**

Vase, 7½" h., a twisted conical body below a broad compressed & angled shoulder w/pointed small tab handles below the short, tapering neck w/a wide molded mouth, fine mustard yellow, olive green, rose, blue, green & cream opaque drip glaze, Amphora wafer mark, impressed "Austria - 0319"........**154.00**

Vase, 10" h., ovoid, decorated w/full figure peacock on top, curled claw feet, peacock on side, Czech mark.......................**650.00**

Vase, 10⅛" h., 8½" w., stylized basket form, molded in high-relief around the upper half w/large clusters of oak leaves above the basket-form lower section, two-handled, gilt leaves w/red & the basket in olive green w/gilding, impressed crown w/"Amphora" & "12025 - G," Austria, ca. 1900 (minor chip) ...**345.00**

Vase, 11¼" h., the compressed body w/a flared cylindrical neck, molded in full-relief at the neck w/a wide-mouthed grouper w/trailing fins, in a semi-gloss marine blue glaze, impressed mark of Reissner, Stellmacher & Kessel **483.00**

Vase, 11½" h., 6½" d., applied handles, decorated w/an iridescent band over a shield centered by a pair of lions, on a molded parcel-gilt base, Amphora mark...........................**184.00**

Vase, 12" h., footed slender ovoid body tapering to a short cylindrical neck w/a molded rim, decorated w/a wide embossed middle band of stylized Art Deco flowers in pink, blue & white w/green leaves & also two large

Three Amphora Dragon Vases

perched barn swallows in black & white w/touches of pink, glossy & matte glazes, base marked w/oval inkstamp reading "Amphora Made in Czechoslovakia" **275.00**

Vase, 12½" h., gourd-form w/long tendril from rim to shoulder & vine-form legs forming base, decorated w/vines, leaves & clusters of cobalt grapes w/frosted effect, marked w/triangle w/swastika mark & "Amphora" underlined below, ca. 1887 (few pieces of vines & leaves missing)......................**3,800.00**

Vase, 12½" h., footed ovoid form w/a swelled, compressed band around the bottom, the sides tapering to a flat, lightly molded rim, the sides divided into large panels w/an embossed scene of two women gathering wheat, one in the foreground, the other in the distance, done in shades of blue, red, grey tan, green & grey glossy & matte glazes within a dark blue mottled border, impressed Amphora crown mark & "Austria" & the numbers "11560 54" (small base chip) **330.00**

Vase, 17½" h., center decoration of embossed full-size chicken, dark blue & light blue ground, artist-signed **850.00**

Vase, 13½" h., ovoid body tapering to a slender neck w/an arched floriform lip, molded in high-relief w/a slender winged dragon wrapped around the body & neck, glazed in matte green, ochre, grey & reddish brown, stamped Amphora marks & incised numbers, ca. 1900 (ILLUS. left) **1,955.00**

Vase, 13½" h., ovoid body tapering to a slender neck w/an arched floriform lip, molded in high-relief w/a slender winged dragon wrapped around the body & neck, glazed matte pale purple, ochre, green & cream w/gilt highlights, impressed Amphora factory mark & numbers, ca. 1900, minor repair to wings (ILLUS. right)............**1,725.00**

Vase, 17" h. the tall ovoid body applied w/a large winged dragon curling around the rim, his wings folded over the body, his head w/open mouth & fierce expression resting on the rim, glazed in matte grey, impressed Amphora mark & numbers, very minor wing restoration, ca. 1900 (ILLUS. center) **3,450.00**

Vase, 17½" h., center decoration of embossed full-sized chicken, dark blue & light blue ground, artist-signed **850.00**

TIFFANY POTTERY

In 1902 Louis C. Tiffany expanded Tiffany Studios to include ceramics, enamels, gold, silver and gemstones. Tiffany pottery was usually molded rather than wheel-thrown, but it was carefully finished by hand. A limited amount was produced until about 1914. It is scarce.

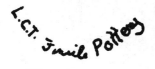

Tiffany Pottery Mark

Bowl-vase, squatty bulbous lobed tomato-form, unglazed bisque exterior w/tomatoes & vine design in relief, green iridescent glazed interior, carved on base "L.C.T.," 12" d., 8" h...........................**$2,300.00**

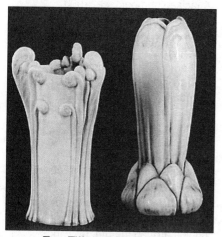

Two Tiffany Pottery Vases

Vase, 9¾" h., 5½" d., a cylindrical form enclosed by three bunches of fiddlehead ferns curling up at the rim, overall ivory glaze, small firing abrasion at the base, signed "PG38 - Tiffany-Favrile Pottery" (ILLUS. left).............**13,200.00**

Vase, 11¼" h., 5" d., the flaring base molded to resemble artichoke leaves w/a tall slender ovoid blossom issuing from the center, greenish ivory glaze, restoration to a hairline, marked "LCT - 7" (ILLUS. right)..........**1,650.00**

TILES

Tiles have been made by potteries in the United States and abroad for many years. Apart from small tea tiles used on tables, there are also decorative tiles for fireplaces, floors and walls and this is where present collector interest lies, especially in the late 19th century American-made art pottery tiles.

Grueby Faience & Tile Company, Boston, Massachusetts, square, decorated w/two bone-white & brown swans on a cocoa brown ground under two stylized trees w/green trunks & leaves backed by pale blue sky & water, 4" w. (minor chips)...........................**$358.00**

Grueby Faience & Tile Company, Boston, Massachusetts, a tapered oval design of cream w/rose border flanked by green leaves on a mustard yellow background, green & rose leaves on border, in a period wide flat oak frame, tile 6" w. **385.00**

Marblehead Pottery, Marblehead, Massachusetts, square, embossed stylized peacock in dark blue & red against green leaves & red berries on a light blue ground, impressed ship mark, in new oak frame, tile 4¾" w. **935.00**

Marblehead Pottery, Marblehead, Massachusetts, square, embossed design of a Spanish galleon under full sail in tan & white on a dark blue rolling sea & a pale blue sky, medium blue border band, matte glazes, marked, 6½" sq. (minor glaze nicks on two corners) **523.00**

Rookwood Pottery, Cincinnati, Ohio, square, deeply sculpted w/a large stylized pink rose blossom atop a short, broad stem surrounded by pale blue narrow stems & broad pointed leaves against a rich cocoa brown ground, Matte glaze, in a wide flat oak frame, 6" w. (minor flakes to high points) **523.00**

Rookwood Pottery, Cincinnati, Ohio, square, a landscape scene of tan & green trees w/lavender & grey trunks on a green, tan & lavender ground, w/olive green brush & a pale blue sky, impressed mark, framed, 17½" w. **3,080.00**

Wheeling Tile Company, Wheeling, West Virginia, square, painted w/a stylized rural landscape w/green, yellow & blue hills w/clusters of green trees, blue water & a small red distant building all under a yellow sky w/flat blue clouds, glossy glaze, signed in one corner "Hortense," embossed company back mark, 6" sq. **248.00**

TOBY MUGS & JUGS

"Martha Gunn" Toby

The Toby is a figural jug or mug usually delineating a robust, genial drinking man. The name has been used in England since the mid-18th century. Copies of the English mugs and jugs were made in America.

For listings of related Character Jugs see DOULTON & ROYAL DOULTON.

Staffordshire "Martha Gunn" pearlware Toby, seated robust woman wearing a feathered hat & holding a small bottle in one hand & a glass in the other, translucent polychrome glazes, ca. 1800, hat repair, 9⅜" h. (ILLUS.) **$1,725.00**

Staffordshire pearlware Toby, seated Mr. Toby wearing a tricorn hat in black trimmed in yellow, a brown jacket, blue vest, orangish ochre breeches & chair on a green base, ca. 1780-1800, 8¾" h. (slight invisible hat restoration) **248.00**

Early Toby Jug

Staffordshire pearlware Toby, seated Mr. Toby wearing a pale brown tricorn hat, green coat, ochre breeches & brown shoes, holding a glass & a foaming jug of ale, ca. 1775, 9½" h. (ILLUS.) **920.00**

Wilkinson "Admiral Beatty" Toby, standing figure of the admiral in uniform his hands flanking a large artillery shell marked "Dread Nought," designed by Sir Francis Carruthers Gould, printed marks, England, ca. 1917, 10½" h. **690.00**

Wilkinson "H.M. King George V" Toby, standing figure of the king in a naval uniform flanked by a small pair of standing lions, designed by Sir Francis Carruthers Gould, entitled "Pro Patria," white-glazed body w/blue suit & black hat brim & shoes, England, printed marks, ca. 1919, 12" h. **431.00**

Wilkinson "Winston Churchill" Toby, standing figure of Churchill holding a model of a naval ship, designed by Clarice Cliff, entitled "And May God Defend the Right" to the front side & "Going Into Action" on the reverse, England, ca. 1941, printed marks, 12" h. **1,380.00**

Yorkshire-type Toby, standing Mr. Toby decorated w/a typical Pratt palette & sponging around the base, England, early 19th c., 4⅝" h. (brim chips & handle restoration) **230.00**

TORQUAY

In the second half of the 19th century several art potteries were established in the South Devon region of England to take advantage of a belt of fine red clay. The coastal town of Torquay gives its name to this range of wares which often featured incised sgraffito decoration or colorful country-style decoration with mottos.

The most notable potteries operating in the Torquay area were the Watcombe Pottery, The Torquay Terra-cotta Company and the Aller Vale Art Pottery, which merged with Watcombe Pottery in 1901 and continued production until 1962. Other firms whose wares are collectible include Longpark Pottery and The Devonmoor Art Pottery.

Torquay Pottery Marks

Bowl, 4½" d., 2¼" h., interior decoration, Black Cockerel patt. **$105.00**

Candlestick, Scandy patt., 7¾" h. **120.00**

Candlesticks, Scandy patt., 4¼" h., pr. **185.00**

Candlesticks, thistle decoration, 5½" h., pr. **155.00**

Creamer, Widecombe Fair, blue ground, 4" h. **110.00**

Creamer & sugar bowl, Shamrock patt., pr. **135.00**

Torquay Cup & Saucer & Mug

Cup & saucer, Motto Ware, Cottage patt., "Daunee be 'Fraid o' it Now," saucer 5½" d., cup 3¼" d., 3" h. (ILLUS. right)...........**40.00**

Cup & saucer, Cottage patt., saucer 8½" d., cup 4" h pr. **145.00**

Mug, ale, Cottage patt., 5" h..........**90.00**

Mug, Cottage patt., 3¾" h..............**65.00**

Mug, Motto Ware, Cottage patt., slightly tapering tall cylindrical body w/a flaring base, C-scroll handle, "No Road Is Long In Good Company," 4" d., 4¾" h. (ILLUS. left) **55.00**

Pitcher, jug-type, Cottage patt.,
4½" h. **125.00**

Plate, 7¼" d., Black Cockerel
patt., blue border **70.00**

Dartmouth Pottery Teapot

Teapot, cov., brown w/tan
embossed scene of men all on a
horse & embossed "Widecombe
Fair," reverse w/sign post
pointing the way to the fair,
embossed leaf design on
handle, Dartmouth Pottery,
5½" d., 5½" h. (ILLUS.)..............**125.00**

Teapot, cov., Motto Ware,
Cottage patt., "Tea Seldom
Spoils When Water Boils,"
4" d., 4" h., Rugby.......................**85.00**

Teapot, cov., Motto Ware,
Cottage patt., "We'll tak a cup o
Kindness for Auld Lang Syne,"
4" d., 4" h. **85.00**

Vase, 3¾" h., four openings,
Black Cockerel patt. **135.00**

VAN BRIGGLE POTTERY

The Van Briggle Pottery was established by Artus Van Briggle, who formerly worked for Rookwood Pottery, in Colorado Springs, Colorado, at the turn of the century. He died in 1904 but the pottery was carried on by his widow and others. From 1900 until 1920, the pieces were dated. It remains in production today, specializing in Art Potttery.

Van Briggle Pottery Mark

Candleholder, shield-back type,
a wide coved & molded
acanthus leaf form w/a small
loop handle at the lower back
near an electric cord hole,
overall burgundy matte glaze,
felt on the base, probably
marked, 4½" w., 6" h. **$220.00**

Jug, "Fire Water" model, bulbous
ovoid body tapering to a short
cylindrical neck w/a small loop
handle on the shoulder, relief-
molded Native American
designs including a spider &
eagle & the words "Fire Water"
around the neck, reddish brown
over pale green matte glaze,
Shape No. 12, 1901, 4⅝" h. ...**2,310.00**

Lamp base, figural owl,
ca. 1910....................................**425.00**

Tray, figural mermaid reclined &
wrapped around one edge, high
gloss jade, designed by Craig
Stevenson, 10" d. **100.00**

Van Briggle Plate & Vase

Plate, 8½" d., flattened round
form w/a swirling large stylized
leafy poppy blossom & stems,
vivid light green matte glaze,
ca. 1902 (ILLUS. right) **1,210.00**

Plate, 9" d., w/stylized Art
Nouveau-style poppy w/swirling
stems, in heavy relief under a
leathery, matte chartreuse
glaze, incised "AA - Van Briggle
- 1920 - III - 20," 1920.............**1,650.00**

Vase, miniature, 3" h., bulbous ovoid body w/a tiny mouth, carved decoration of tiny blossoms w/three petals separated by broad, swirling stylized stems covered in a bluish grey over caramel matte glaze, incised marks, ca. 1920s-30s **220.00**

Vase, 3¾" h., 3¼" d., a bulbous nearly spherical base tapering to a wide cylindrical neck, molded w/large ovoid leaves around the base w/undulating stems up the sides, mottled matte green glaze, Shape No. 823, 1907-11 ....**440.00**

Vase, 3¾" h., 3¾" d., cylindrical form slightly flaring to bulbous angular shoulder tapering to closed-in mouth, decorated w/stylized poppy pods on swirling stems under matte curdled celadon & mauve glaze, incised "AA - Van Briggle - 1905 - 21," 1905 (stilt pulls at base) **413.00**

Vase, 5" h., 3¼" d., bulbous ovoid base tapering to a tall slightly tapering cylindrical neck, feathered greyish blue matte glaze w/red clay exposed, mark indistinct, probably 1906............**440.00**

Vase, 5" h., 3¾" d., a squatty bulbous base tapering to a wide slightly flaring cylindrical neck w/a molded rim, molded in relief around the lower body w/a band of pointed swirled leaves, robin's-egg blue glaze, Shape No. 730, 1907-11 ....**495.00**

Vase, 5" h., 4" d., short foot rim supporting wide base of slightly tapering cylindrical body, decorated w/tall spiked leaves under a flowing green matte glaze, incised "AA - Van Briggle - Colo Springs - 451 - 1906," 1906 (clay showing through leaf edges)..............................**605.00**

Vase, 5" h., 5½" d., wide bulbous ovoid body w/the wide shoulder tapering to a short cylindrical neck, the shoulder embossed w/arrowhead leaves on slender stems down the sides, matte dark blue glaze, 1904 ....**880.00**

Vase, 5½" h., 3¼" d., slightly ovoid body tapering to slightly tapering cylindrical neck w/rolled rim, embossed w/ochre tulips & green stems on a matte ochre ground, incised "AA - Van Briggle - 1903 - 187 - III," 1903 (fine pitting on decoration).........**715.00**

Vase, 7" h., slightly waisted cylindrical body gently swelled at the top w/a closed rim, carved w/a design of stylized blossoms & leaves atop wide stems, deep mustard yellow matte glaze, incised logo & "1903 - III - 132".......................**1,870.00**

Vase, 7" h. slightly tapering cylindrical body swelled around the flat rim, delicately carved w/blossoms w/three petals on broad, vertical stems w/long swirling leaves, dark green matte glaze, incised logo & "1902 - III - 7".........................**2,310.00**

Vase, 7" h., cylindrical form w/a swelled shoulder below the short molded mouth, deeply carved design of twisting vertical leaves stretching from the base to the rim, deep burgundy & dark blue matte glaze, incised marks & "20," ca. 1930s **275.00**

Vase, 7½" h., "Dos Cabezos" model, an ovoid form molded in relief on each side w/a standing Art Nouveau woman reaching around & clinging to the sides of the vase, gun-metal black over green glaze, Shape No. 16, 1916 (two pinhead glaze nicks on one side)............................**2,970.00**

Vase, 7½" h., 3¾" d., tall ovoid form tapering to cylindrical neck w/flat rim, w/embossed lotus blossoms & ribs under a rich matte mustard glaze, "AA - 1916," 1916 ....**715.00**

Vase, 7¾" h., 3½" d., corseted body flaring to angular shoulder sharply tapering to short cylindrical neck w/flat mouth, w/stylized trefoils on long stems under a fine dead matte medium to dark green glaze, incised "AA - Van Briggle - Colo Sprgs - 671," 1907-12 (clay showing through edges) **990.00**

Vase, 8½" h., 3¾" d., corseted form w/rounded shoulder & slightly rounded mouth, w/stylized mistletoe under leathery & veined matte green glaze, incised "AA - Van Briggle - Colo Springs - 379 - 1907," 1907 ....**990.00**

Vase, 9" h., tall slender cylindrical body w/a bulbous swelled shoulder tapering slightly to a molded rim, carved decoration of large blossoms atop vertical stems & leaves covered in a medium blue over pale blue matte glaze, Shape No. 850, ca. 1915 (ILLUS. left w/plate) **715.00**

Vase, 9¼" h., 4" d., bottle-shaped, an ovoid body tapering to a tall slender & gently flaring neck, the sides deeply molded w/tall leaves, matte purple & green glaze, Shape No. 92, 1905........**770.00**

"Lady of the Lily" Vase

Vase, 11" h., figural, "Lady of the Lily," model, a languid female nude reclining against a large lily blossom, embossed florals throughout the base, matte lime green glaze, incised logo & name, date is obscured, shape "No. 4," probably ca. 1904 or earlier, repaired (ILLUS.)......**11,550.00**

Vase, 12" h., Art Nouveau tulip decoration, green matte glaze, ca. 1903...................................**800.00**

Vase, 12" h., a squatty bulbous base tapering sharply to a swelled shoulder & small closed mouth, deeply carved w/a design of low, broad leaves surrounding the base & separated by broad, twisting stems rising to the rim, deep rose & violet matte glaze, incised marks, factory-drilled base hole, ca. 1930s **248.00**

Vase, bulbous base tapering to a wide cylindrical neck, No. 645, Mountain Craig Brown, ca. 1920...................................**110.00**

Bowl-vase, squatty bulbous form tapering gently a small mouth, embossed w/stylized leaves & fruit under a mottled medium green matte glaze, Shape No. 146k, dated "1904" (ILLUS. next page, No. 1).........**935.00**

Tile, square, decorated in cuenca w/a stylized peacock feather in brown, green & blue on a dark green matte ground, one shallow corner chip, some glaze nicks, unmarked, 6" w. (ILLUS. next page, No. 2).........**715.00**

Tile, square, decorated in cuerda seca w/a stylized flower in yellow w/a blue stem & large green leaves on a brick red ground, incised "20 - 8," minor edge nicks (ILLUS. next page, No. 3)......................................**385.00**

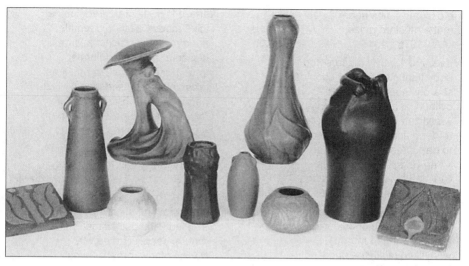

7
10
3   8   4   6   5   1   9   2

A Large Variety of Van Briggle Pieces

Vase, 4" h., 4" d., wide bulbous ovoid body tapering to a small flat mouth, embossed w/crocuses under a light green glaze against a white ground, the beige clay showing through, Shape No. 149, dated "1904" (ILLUS., No. 4) **990.00**

Vase, 6" h., 3" d., simple ovoid form tapering to a tiny mouth flanked by relief-molded trefoils & small in-body handles, khaki matte glaze, Shape No. 169, dated "1904" (ILLUS., No. 5) **660.00**

Vase, 7" h., 3¼" d., slightly tapering cylindrical body w/a swelled shoulder below the wide flat mouth, embossed around the shoulder w/trefoils, the swirling stems going down the sides, dark matte green glaze, dated "1902" (ILLUS., No. 6) ..**1,540.00**

Vase, 10¼" h., 10¼" w., figural, "Lady-of-the-Lily" model, a languid nude female reclining against a large calla lily blossom, matte bluish green & purple glaze, 1925-32 (ILLUS., No. 7) **1,100.00**

Vase, 10¾" h., 4¼" d., tall slender tapering cylindrical form w/small angled handles near the flat, molded mouth, thick leathery matte green glaze over a matte brown base, Shape No. 221, dated "1904" (ILLUS., No. 8) **825.00**

Vase, 13" h., 6½" d., "Despondency" model, wide slightly flaring cylindrical form w/a swelled shoulder supporting the curled-up figure of a nude man, dark blue to burgundy matte glaze, ca. 1928 (ILLUS. No. 9) **1,320.00**

Vase, 13½" h., 6½" d., double-gourd form, a bulbous ovoid lower body molded in relief w/large swirled pointed leaves, slender stems climbing up to the small bulbous top w/a tiny molded mouth, soft matte pink glaze, ca. 1917 (ILLUS., No. 10) **880.00**

VOLKMAR POTTERY

Volkmar Pillow Vase

Charles Volkmar came from an artistic family and was able to study pottery making in Europe where he remained fourteen years before returning home in 1875. At the 1876 Philadelphia Centennial Exposition he was intrigued by the French art pottery exhibited and returned to France for further study.

Volkmar returned to the United States in 1879 and opened his first kiln in Greenpoint, Long Island, New York in 1879. By 1882 he had established his own studio, kilns, salesroom and home at Tremont, New York.

The early Volkmar wares were decorated with applied and underglaze decoration done by Volkmar or an assistant using his designs. During the following years he worked in several partnerships and finally established the Volkmar Keramic Company in Brooklyn in 1895. His last venture was begun in 1902 when he was joined by his son Leon to establish the Volkmar Kilns in Metuchen, New Jersey in 1903. Charles Volkmar died in 1914 and Leon continued pottery production for some years.

Tile, square, a landscape scene of men fishing near a river, painted in heavy slip relief in blue & white, incised "V" on the face, in a flat oak frame, tile 8" w. **$715.00**

Vase, 6" h., bulbous ovoid body tapering to a tiny short cylindrical neck, matte bluish green streaked glaze w/a gloss band at foot, incised "V," ca. 1903.....................................**288.00**

Vase, 6½" h., 4½" d., bulbous baluster-form body, lustred grey & pink iridescent glaze over a crackled white ground, incised "Volkmar - 1938 - 29D".............**440.00**

Vase, 9¾" h., 7 1/4" w., pillow-type, a narrow oval footring on the flattened ovoid body tapering to a narrow oval flat mouth, decorated w/orange & yellow trumpet flowers & green leaves on a textured light blue, pink & brown ground, two small base chips, raised "CV" over "H" mark (ILLUS.) **660.00**

WATT POTTERY

Founded in 1922, in Crooksville, Ohio, this pottery continued in operation until the factory was destroyed by fire in 1965. Although stoneware crocks and jugs were the first wares produced, by 1935 sturdy kitchen items in yellowware were the mainstay of production. Attractive lines like Kitch-N-Queen (banded) wares and the hand-painted Apple, Cherry and Pennsylvania Dutch (tulip) patterns were popular throughout the country. Today these hand-painted utilitarian wares are "hot" with collectors.

A good reference book for collectors is *Watt Pottery, An Identification and Value Guide*, by Sue and Dave Morris (Collector Books, 1933)

Watt Pottery Mark

Bean server, individual, Apple patt., No. 75, 3½" d.................**$350.00**

Tulip Mixing Bowls

Bowl, 5" d., individual
salad/cereal, Rooster patt.,
No. 68...**90.00**

Cookie jar, cov., Starflower patt.,
No. 21.......................................**155.00**

Creamer, Apple (three-leaf) patt.,
No. 62, w/advertising, 4½" h........**90.00**

Creamer, Tulip patt.,
No. 62, 4½" h.............................**225.00**

Mixing bowl, ribbed, No. 4............**75.00**

Mixing bowls, nesting-type, Tulip
patt., Nos. 63, 64 & 65, 6½" d.,
7½" d. & 8½" d., the set
(ILLUS.) **90.00**

Starflower No. 16 Pitcher

Starflower Pie Plate

Pie plate, Starflower patt., five-
petal, No. 33, 9¼" d. (ILLUS.) ...**200.00**

Pitcher, 5½" h., Rooster patt.,
No. 15.......................................**185.00**

Pitcher, 6½" h., Starflower patt.,
four-petal, No. 16 (ILLUS.) **120.00**

Plate, 10" d., Moonflower patt.
(ILLUS. top next page, right) **75.00**

Platter, 15" d., Moonflower patt.,
No. 31 (ILLUS. top next
page, left) **110.00**

Refrigerator pitcher, square-
shaped, Apple patt., No. 69,
8" h., 8½" w. **425.00**

Barrel-shaped Apple Shakers

Moonflower Platter and Plate

Salt & pepper shakers, Apple patt., barrel-shaped, pr. (ILLUS. bottom, previous page)..........................425.00 to 475.00

Sugar bowl, cov., Apple patt., No. 98..375.00

Sugar bowl, cov., Autumn Foliage patt., No. 98..................140.00

Rare Apple Teapot

Teapot, cov., Apple (three-leaf) patt., No. 112, 6" h. (ILLUS.)..**1,800.00**

WEDGWOOD

Reference here is to the famous pottery established by Josiah Wedgwood in 1759 in England. Numerous types of wares have been produced through the years to the present.

BASALT

Bust of Pinder, miniature, classical man's head w/draped shoulders, on a short, slender flaring pedestal w/a round molded base, impressed marks of Wedgwood and Bentley, ca. 1775, 4" h. **$748.00**

Bust of Minerva, classical female warrior wearing a rounded helmet & scaled armor, impressed mark & title, socle pedestal on rounded foot, 19th c., mounted as a lamp, 18" h. (chips restored to nose & helmet rim) **1,160.00**

Bust of Scott, raised on a round socle base, impressed title & mark, mid-19th c., 13" h. (ILLUS. next page) **805.00**

Candlesticks, figural, Triton-style, modeled as a male triton w/curled tail holding a tall candle socket, raised on a rockwork base, 19th c., impressed marks, 9¾" h., pr. **2,415.00**

Crocus pot & undertray, figural, model of a large hump-backed hedgehog, the fur-molded body

Bust of Scott

pierced w/numerous round holes, resting in an oblong tray, impressed marks, ca. 1800, pot 9¾" l. (two foot chips on pot, tray end repaired) **920.00**

Ewers, wine & water, classical-form, the ribbed & ringed pedestal on a molded square foot supporting a tall urn-form body w/a wide shoulder tapering to a high arched spout, water ewer w/the figure of a triton seated on the shoulders & a head of a marine monster below the spout, the wine ewer w/a figure of Bacchus seated on the shoulders w/a ram's head below, the sides of the water ewer molded w/garlands of seaweed, the sides of the wine ewer molded w/grapevines, impressed marks, mid-19th c., 15½" h., pr. (base of water ewer restored) **1,955.00**

Figure of a baby, the recumbent infant on an oblong rockwork base, after Della Robbia, impressed mark, mid-19th c., 5⅛" l. (foot rim chips)................**690.00**

Jardinieres, cylindrical tapering body, decorated w/floral borders & a Neoclassical frieze, late 19th c., 8" h., pr. **518.00**

Medallion, oval, relief-molded profile bust portrait of English king Henry VII, marked "Wedgwood" only, 1⅞ x 2⅛" **135.00**

Model of a bulldog, standing animal w/glass eyes, modeled by E.W. Light, ca. 1915, impressed mark, 4¾" l. (tail repair) **288.00**

Pitcher, dip-type, 6¼" h., tapering cylindrical body, loop handle, white relief medallions w/portrait of Franklin on one side & Washington on other side, black, impressed "Wedgwood - England" (wear & stains) **303.00**

Pitcher, club-type, 6½" h., ovoid body tapering to a short ringed neck w/a wide spout, loop handle from rim to center of the side, decorated w/scattered colored enamel florals, impressed mark, ca. 1860 ....**345.00**

"Death of a Roman Warrior" Plaque

Plaque, rectangular, "Death of a Roman Warrior," a classical scene molded in high-relief w/Roman warriors carrying the body of Meleanger, 19th c., impressed mark, framed, small chips restored, 10¾ x 19¼" (ILLUS.) **2,875.00**

Urn, cov., crater-form, the wide campana-form body raised on a round foot & square base, the flaring rim flanked by high, arched loop handles continuing to the base of the urn, an inset pierced disc cover & insert lid, the sides & lid w/polychrome enamel floral designs & w/iron-red trim, impressed mark, 19th c., 11½" w. (restored rim chips to disc restored, hairline in handle) **1,265.00**

Vase, cov., 7" h., wide squatty bulbous body raised on a slender, short pedestal & square foot, the wide top centered by a short waisted neck w/rolled rim & ribbed, domed cover w/knob finial, the top shoulder decorated w/a molded leaf band above applied drapery swags around the shoulder, impressed wafer mark of Wedgwood and Bentley, ca. 1775 (base chip, finial reglued) **1,150.00**

Vase, cov., 14" h., classical urn-form, the tall body molded in relief w/a scene of Venus & Cupid below the angled shoulder & tapering striped neck w/a rolled rim & domed, ribbed cover w/knob finial, loop handles from the rim to the shoulder & ending in satyr masks, raised on a short flaring pedestal on a square foot, engine-turned detailing, impressed wafer mark of Wedgwood and Bentley, ca. 1775 (handles restored) ...**1,725.00**

Vases, cov., 10½" h., plain ovoid body w/a narrow angled shoulder to the tapering slender neck w/a flattened wide rim centered by a small domed cover w/knob finial, leaf-molded arched handles from the shoulder rim to the lower body terminating in Bacchus-head masks, raised on a short, slender flaring pedestal on a square foot, impressed marks of Wedgwood and Bentley, 18th c., pr. (one handle & rim professionally restored, chip to corner of one base, one cover manufactured) **2,300.00**

Basalt Candlesticks & Ewers

Candlesticks, figural, Triton-style, modeled as a male triton w/curled tail holding a tall candle socket, raised on a rockwork base, impressed marks, 1973, one w/damage to arms & sconce, 10½" h., pr. (ILLUS. center) **690.00**

Ewers, wine & water, classical-form, the ribbed & ringed pedestal on a molded square foot supporting a tall urn-form body w/a wide shoulder tapering to a high arched spout, water ewer w/the figure of a triton seated on the shoulders & a head of a marine monster below the spout, the wine ewer w/a figure of Bacchus seated on the shoulders w/a ram's head below, the sides of the water ewer molded w/garlands of seaweed, the sides of the wine ewer molded w/grapevines, impressed marks, 19th c., 15¼" h., pr.(ILLUS. left & right) **3,335.00**

CANEWARE

Pie dish, cov., a simple low oval dish w/a liner w/a raised basketweave-molded border, the inset oval slightly domed cover molded w/zigzag bands centered by a radiating ring of molded leaves centered by a short cylindrical insert, impressed marks, 1863, 12" l. ...**920.00**

Pitcher & bowl set, a deep rounded bowl on a narrow footring, the jug-form pitcher w/a bulbous body & wide low cylindrical neck w/pinched spout & D-form handle, each decorated in polychrome enamels w/a rim band of zig-zag lines & triangles w/large stylized blossoms on the body, designed by Millicent Taplin, impressed marks, ca. 1930, bowl 7⅜" d., pitcher 5¼" h., the set................**259.00**

Vases, 6¼" h., engine-turned, a bulbous ovoid body w/a tapering ribbed base to a flaring ribbed foot, the wide flattened medial band applied w/a wide rosso antico fruiting grapevine below the wide, short ribbed cylindrical neck w/molded rim, impressed marks, early 19th c., pr. (covers missing, both w/foot rim chip, one w/hairlines) **518.00**

CREAMWARE

Ice pail, deep tapering cylindrical sides w/loop rim handles, body decorated w/narrow bands & a small brown Oliver family crest, late 18th c., 8½" h. (wear, restored rim chip) **546.00**

Early Creamware Tureen

Tureen, cover & undertray, oval, the oval low pedestal foot supporting a long squatty bulbous oval body tapering to an indented neck band below the rolled rim, foliate molded looped end handles, the overhanging stepped & domed cover w/a sunflower finial, set in a fitted oval undertray, impressed marks, slight glaze line in body, finial restored, early 19th c., 13¼" l., the set (ILLUS.) **920.00**

JASPER WARE

Barber bottle w/original stopper, three-color, classical form w/a short pedestal & wide round foot supporting a wide ovoid body tapering to a tall cylindrical neck w/a molded rim & small domed cap w/button finial, decorated around the shoulder w/a wide white relief laurel leaf band & four Bacchus head masks above a band of floral swags separating round figural medallions w/lilac grounds, further white relief swags, leaf & beaded bands on the neck, cap, lower body & base, all on a green ground, impressed mark, mid-19th c., 11" h. (cover insert damage, two Bacchus heads repaired) **633.00**

Box, cov., white relief classical figures on lilac ground, marked "Made in England" **90.00**

Bowl, 4⅝" d., deep nearly straight sides rounded at the bottom, white relief small classical scenes between slender upright leafy scroll panels on crimson, impressed marks, ca. 1920 ....**690.00**

Candle lustres, cut glass & jasper ware, the upper section in cut crystal w/an oval candle socket w/upturned notched bobeche above a flaring notched drip pan suspending long teardrop prisms, an ovoid standard joined by ormolu mounts to the cylindrical jasper ware base w/white relief classical scenes & a leafy scroll top border on dark blue set on an ormolu foot, overall 11½" h., pr. (damage to one bobeche) **1,380.00**

Candlesticks, cylindrical, white relief classical scenes on dark blue, impressed marks, late 19th c., 4¾" h., pr. **288.00**

Candlesticks, white relief classical scene on green ground, 5" h., pr........................**135.00**

Candlesticks, cylindrical, decorated w/white relief classical designs on dark blue, impressed mark, mid-19th c., 7¾" h., pr. **518.00**

Cracker jar, cov., barrel-shaped, white relief figures of hunters on horseback, hounds, fox & horses on dark blue, silver plate rim, cover & bail........................**275.00**

Three-color Jasper Cracker Jar

Cracker jar, cov., waisted cylindrical body, a wide center dark blue band w/white relief classical figures, light blue border bands at top & base, silver plate rim, domed cover & swing arched bail handle, impressed mark, stain spot, ca. 1900, 5" h. (ILLUS.).............**288.00**

Cracker jar, cov., waisted cylindrical body, white relief classical figures on dark blue, silver plated cover, rim & handle, marked "Wedgwood" only, 5¼" d., 6¾" h. **235.00**

Cup & saucer, cylindrical cup w/white D-form handle, decorated w/white relief rams' heads & fruit & flower garlands alternating w/oval medallions decorated w/putti & allegorical designs on charcoal grey, the deep saucer w/matching decoration, marked "Wedgwood" only **715.00**

Egg cup, white relief classical figures on black **65.00**

Jar, cov., wide waisted cylindrical body rounded at the base above a narrow footring, the flared rim supporting a low domed cover w/heavy button finial, the body w/a wide central band w/white relief leafy scrolls centering a small oval medallion w/a classical figure, the lower base band w/white relief scroll swags & drops on light green, the cover w/a wide white relief band of leaves & lappets, impressed mark, late 19th c., 3½" h. (rim chip) **403.00**

Jar, sweetmeat or jam pot, cov., cylindrical w/white relief classical figures on dark blue, silver plated cover, rim & handle, ca. 1892-1915, marked "Wedgwood - England," 3¼" d., 4" h. **145.00**

Jardiniere, cylindrical, white relief garlands of grapes w/lion's head & white relief scenes from mythology on dark blue, ca. 1892-1915, marked "Wedgwood - England," 5⅛" d., 4½" h. **195.00**

Jardiniere, cylindrical, white relief classical scenes on dark blue, impressed mark, mid-19th c. 8" h. **230.00**

Medallion, round, a white relief bust profile of Julius Caesar on light blue, marked "Wedgwood" only, 1½" d. **125.00**

Medallion, oval, white relief bust portrait of George IV, Prince of Wales facing left on solid light blue, impressed title, "1783" date & mark, 19th c., 2⅞ x 3¾" (hairline) **207.00**

Medallion, oval, white relief bust portrait of Admiral Richard Howe facing right on light green, impressed titled & mark, early 19th c., 3½ x 4¼"......................**259.00**

Medallions, oval, one w/white relief bust portrait of Sir John Jervis, the other w/a white relief bust portrait of Admiral Horatio Nelson on light green, impressed titles & marks, early 19th c., 3⅜ x 4⅜", facing pr.......**546.00**

Mug, miniature, three white relief mythology scenes on light blue, ca. 1892-1915, 1⅜" d., 1⅜" h., marked "Wedgwood - England"...................................**145.00**

Jasper Ware Mug & Pitcher

Mug, cylindrical w/sterling silver rim band, ropetwist molded handle, white relief classical ladies & cupids on dark blue, white relief oval medallion on the front w/two soldiers, marked "Wedgwood" only, 3¾" d., 5" h. (ILLUS. left) **125.00**

Pitcher, miniature, 2½" h., white relief classical figures on green ground **65.00**

Pitcher, miniature, jug-form, 1¾" d., 2¾" h., white relief figures of man w/his dog & lady w/her dog, pre-1892, marked "Wedgwood" only **195.00**

Pitcher, 2⅛" d., 2⅝" h., ovoid body w/pinched spout & C-form handle, white relief mythological scenes on dark blue, ca. 1915-30, marked "Wedgwood - Made in England" **69.00**

Pitcher, jug-form, 3½" h., bulbous ovoid body w/small rim spout & D-form handle, white relief classical figural & landscape band around the lower half, impressed marks, ca. 1920 ....**748.00**

Pitcher, tankard, 2½" d., 4" h., white relief classical figures & cupids on dark blue, ca. pre-1892, marked "Wedgwood - Made in England" **88.00**

Pitcher, tankard, 4¼" h., 2¾" d., white relief classical figures & grape border around top edge, dark blue ground, marked "Wedgwood - England"...............**88.00**

Pitcher, tankard, 5½" h., 3½" d., the cylindrical body w/a white relief band of classical ladies & cupids on dark blue w/a white relief band of grapevine around the rim, ropetwist handle, marked "Wedgwood" only (ILLUS. right with mug)..............**118.00**

Pitcher, 9¼" h., three-color, a footed ovoid body tapering to a gently flared rim w/a pinched spout, a C-form handle, a white ground applied w/lilac trophies between floral festoons, impressed mark, late 19th c., repaired chip on spout tip, chip to trim ring (ILLUS. top, next page) **633.00**

Three-color Jasper Pitcher

Plaque, rectangular, white relief scene depicting The Sacrifice to Hymen on solid blue, impressed mark, late 19th c., 6 x 8½" (crazing lines) **460.00**

Plaque, oval, a white relief scene of "Hercules binding Ceberus" on solid light blue, impressed mark, early 19th c., mounted in a molded giltwood oval frame, plaque 6 x 8¾"..........................**978.00**

Plaque, rectangular, white relief classical figures on green, impressed mark, 19th c., mounted in a giltwood frame, plaque 6 x 12"...........................**460.00**

Plaque, rectangular, white relief scene of Achilles w/other classical male & female figures on solid light blue, impressed mark, 19th c., mounted in a giltwood frame, plaque 6½ x 15" (crazing to relief)........................**978.00**

Plaque, rectangular, white relief scene of "The Choice of Hercules" on solid light blue, impressed mark, 19th c., mounted in a wide oak frame, plaque 6½ x 19" (restored) **1,265.00**

Plaques, cut-corner rectangular, each w/white relief classical figures on green, impressed mark, mid-19th c., impressed marks, 3⅝ x 5½", pr. (one w/rim chips) **259.00**

Plaques, round, white relief palmette border centered by a figural frieze from Achilles in Scyros among the Daughters of Lycomedes on each, on solid blue, impressed marks, 19th c., each mounted in an ebonized molded round wood frame, plaques 6¼" d., pr. **1,610.00**

Plates, 8" d., white relief center scene w/George Washington & another rider on horseback on dark blue, a band of white relief starbursts & rim band at the border, impressed marks, ca. 1900, set of 6 (one damaged, one w/slight relief damage to star border) **345.00**

Jasper Potpourri Jar

Potpourri jar, cov., a flaring cylindrical basket-form base w/white loop rim handles, the body w/white relief dancing classical figures on dark blue, the wide low domed cover pierced w/large round holes w/white relief four-petal florets & four long serrated leaves radiating from the central knob finial on dark blue, impressed marks, early 20th c., 4¾" w. handle to handle (ILLUS.) **288.00**

Teapot, cov., squatty bulbous body w/an inset domed cover & button finial, curved spout & C-form handle, white relief classical figures around sides on dark blue, ca. 1892-1915, marked "Wedgwood England," 4½" d., 4½" h. **188.00**

Tobacco jar, cov., cylindrical w/low-domed cover & acorn finial, white relief classical figures around base, white relief zig zag line around finial, marked "Wedgwood - England," 7¾" h. (stains) **110.00**

Urn, cov., waisted cylindrical body raised on a short flaring pedestal on a square foot, domed cover w/knob finial, white loop handles, white relief classical figures around center on lavender, & further white relief designs on lower body, foot & cover, marked "Wedgwood," only, 9¼" h.............................**1,190.00**

Vase, 5" h., 2½" d., footed ovoid body tapering to a slender neck w/a thick rolled rim, white relief classical Cupid figures representing the Four Seasons on dark blue, marked "Wedgwood" only **95.00**

Vase, 5" h., 3½" d., Portland Vase-form, footed bulbous ovoid body tapering to a short neck w/widely flared mouth flanked by arched handles to shoulder, white relief classical figures on bleeding green, marked "Wedgwood" only **195.00**

Vase, 5½" h., white relief classical scene on cobalt ground, marked "Wedgwood" only **90.00**

Vase, cov., 9½" h., tall ovoid body raised on a slender flaring pedestal resting on a square foot, a short flaring neck w/rolled rim supporting a small domed cover w/knob finial, white relief borders on the lid & rim, white relief satyr mask handles on the shoulders joined by a wide lappet & leaf band, the lower body w/a white relief classical band of musicians in a landscape on black, a white relief spearpoint leaf band at the bottom of the body & further band around the base of the pedestal & an acanthus leaf band around the square foot, impressed mark, 19th c. **1,093.00**

Vase, cov., 9¾" h., classical form w/engine-turned borders, white relief figural scene of the Dancing Hours on light blue, impressed mark, 19th c. (cover repair) **690.00**

Fine Portland Vase

Vase, 10½" h., Portland Vase model, wide ovoid body tapering to a short trumpet neck flanked by arched handles to shoulder, white relief continuous classical scene on black, impressed "T. Lovatt," & factory mark, ca. 1877 (ILLUS.)...............**2,000.00 to 2,300.00**

Vases, 10" h., a square plinth w/white relief florets & leaves supports a domed round foot w/further leaves supporting a tall shouldered ovoid body w/a tapering cylindrical neck w/a thick molded rim, arched shoulder handles, the shoulder w/ribbon & trophy white relief drips, the body w/a shoulder white relief leaf band & a wide white relief band of classical figures, all on a green ground, impressed marks, ca. 1900, one w/a hairline, pr. **518.00**

Vases, 10¼" h., cylindrical w/applied silver plate rims, white relief designs of floral festoons & acanthus leaves w/bellflowers on light green, impressed marks, late 19th c., pr..........................**633.00**

Vases, 10½" h., footed ovoid body tapering to a widely flaring trumpet neck, incurved loop shoulder handles, white relief figures of standing Muses between slender foliate upright bars on dark blue, impressed mark, 19th c., pr. (one handle restored on each) **518.00**

Ewer, classical form w/a short round pedestal base below the tall ovoid body tapering to a short ringed cylindrical neck w/a high arched & forked spout, white jasper arched handle from rim to shoulder, white foliate leaf designs, bands & swags on dark blue, early 19th c., 9" h. (ILLUS. center) **633.00**

Pen box, cov., narrow oblong low form, the slightly domed cover w/a large white relief classical maiden walking & carrying a basket of fruit on her head, a narrow ringlet white relief border band, all on dark blue, mid-19th c., impressed mark, 9" l. (ILLUS. left) **546.00**

Vase, cov., 8¼" h., a tripartite base w/three slightly curved buttresses flanking the ovoid body raised on a central pedestal foot, the wide cylindrical neck supports a domed cover w/button finial, ornate white relief classical designs on all sections on a dark blue ground, early 19th c., rim chips, cover restored (ILLUS. right) **1,265.00**

A Group of Diverse Jasper Pieces

Varied Blue Jasper Pieces

Sugar bowl, cov., squatty bulbous body tapering to a wide flat rim, flanged domed cover w/a button finial, the body w/white relief classical figure groups, the cover w/a white relief leaf band on light blue, marked "Wedgwood" only, 4⅜" d., 4" h. (ILLUS. left)...........**110.00**

Ring tree, a narrow footring under a wide slightly dished plate centered by a slender & slightly tapering upright column, tiny white relief classical figure groups & leaf band borders on light blue, marked "Wedgwood - England, " 3⅛" d., 2½" h. (ILLUS. right) **110.00**

Vase, 10¼" h., 3⅝" d., footed tall cylindrical body, tall white relief upright leaves alternating w/slender bellflower clusters below long floral swags joined by small rams' heads, leafy scroll & florette band around the top, all on light blue, marked "Wedgwood" only (ILLUS. center) **265.00**

QUEENSWARE
Bidet, oblong waisted shallow ceramic bowl fitted into a rectangular mahogany stand raised on rod- and ring-turned legs ending in peg feet, early 19th c., 21½" l., 2 pcs. (small stain) **403.00**

Dinner service for twelve, decorated w/cream grapes on lavender ground, 83 pcs. **2,500.00**

Charger, "Rhodian Ware," round w/a wide central overall design of stylized flowerheads & leaves in pink lustre & enamels, the cover band w/alternating rectangular panels of crosshatching & scrolls, impressed mark, ca. 1919, 14⅞" d. **805.00**

Chestnut basket, cov, pierced scrolled foliate molded body w/double entwined handles & a floral finial, impressed mark, 1920, 8½" h. (rim line) **316.00**

Fruit compote, open, the wide pierced loosely woven basketweave body w/a scalloped rim raised on a plain short pedestal w/a widely flaring round foot, potted by Hensleigh Wedgwood, artist-signed & impressed mark, ca. 1930, 7⅛" d. (rim line) **575.00**

Model of a duiker antelope, the small recumbent animal on a rectangular base, glossy glaze, designed by John Skeaping, on an ebonized wood base, artist-signed, impressed marks, ca. 1927, 7" l...........................**230.00**

Model of "Ferdinand the Bull," standing animal w/head raised & tail hanging down, glossy glaze, modeled by Arnold Machin, impressed mark & artist monogram, mid-20th c., 12¼" l. **431.00**

Model of "Taurus the Bull," standing animal w/head lowered & tail curled on his back, glossy glaze, modeled by Arnold Machin, impressed mark, 1967, 15¼" l. **173.00**

Salad bowl, figural, the bowl molded in the form of a large crab raised on realistic shell feet, w/a silver plated rim band & the interior transfer-printed w/ foliate designs, w/a pair of silver plate servers w/long shell-form handles, ca. 1872, 9" d. (light surface wear, chip repair to one handle) **460.00**

Salad bowl, deep half-round bowl w/the exterior relief-molded w/enamel decorated flowers & leafy vines, raised on vegetable-form feet, w/a silver plate rim & a pair of silver plate servers w/vegetable-form handles, impressed mark, ca. 1871, 9¾" d. (surface wear on handles)..............................**230.00**

MISCELLANEOUS

Bowl, 8⅝" d., Dragon Lustre, deep rounded sides on a narrow footring, mottled blue exterior w/a band of large dragons, mother-of-pearl interior, printed mark, ca. 1920s.........................**546.00**

Bowl, 9" octagonal, Fairyland Lustre, Castle on a Road exterior, Fairy in a Cage interior **4,625.00**

Celery dish, bone china, oval, gilt diamond border, first period, printed mark, ca. 1820, 10" l. (foot rim & light gilt wear)...........**173.00**

Center bowl, Hummingbird Lustre, octagonal, decorated in blue lustre glaze w/hummingbirds on the exterior, the interior in bright orange w/a central hummingbird, No. 25294, 8" w. **770.00**

Charger, Crimson Lustre, round dished form decorated w/border bands of large stylized leaves surrounding a central crest, decoration attributed to William De Morgan, impressed mark, ca. 1880, 16¾" d. (surface crazing, glaze wear)............................**1,150.00**

Clock case, earthenware, D-form w/a scalloped top over the conforming case w/outset square pilasters flanking the center panel w/the round hole for the clock face, decorated w/gilt foliage & enamel floral decorations, impressed mark, second half 19th c., impressed mark, 9" h. (no works) **230.00**

Figure of The Weight Thrower, modeled as an athlete standing on one leg, the other raised to the front, his torso curved w/one arm raised straight up & the other holding a shot put ready to be thrown, glossy cream glaze, modeled by Alan Best, impressed mark, ca. 1935, 12" h. (leg restoration) **1,380.00**

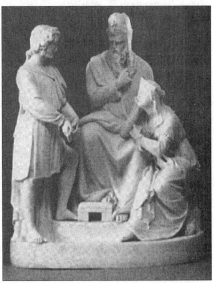

Wedgwood Parian Figure Group

Figure group, parian, "Joseph Before Pharaoh," a young man standing before the bearded ruler who is accompanied by a female companion, on a stepped oval base, modeled by W. Beattie, impressed "S" factory mark, ca. 1860, 20" h. (ILLUS.) **1,150.00**

Gravy boat & liner, Columbia patt. **110.00**

Inkstand, a long, low rectangular tray w/a rectangular raised covered box mounted at the center of the back edge, the box enclosing two inkwells, designed by Keith Murray, ca. 1933, impressed & printed marks, 10" l. **460.00**

Mortar & pestle, vitreous stoneware, the pestle w/a wooden handle, impressed marks & "best composition," mid-19th c., pestle 6" l., mortar 3⅛" d., 2 pcs.............................**201.00**

Mug, cylindrical w/D-form handle, decorates in silver resist lustre w/a floral design surrounding the monogram "HcW," signed on the base "Hensleigh C. Wedgwood Xmas 1950," printed factory mark, 3¾" h. **518.00**

Pilgrim flask, slip-decorated, flattened round body on a low flaring foot & w/a low, widely flaring neck, small loop handles at the shoulders, each side w/a round portrait medallion of a Grecian bust on a drab-colored ground w/off-white & yellow slip, attributed to Frederick Rhead, impressed mark, ca. 1877, 7¼" h. (rim repair, line in base rim) **431.00**

Pitcher, 5" d., Surface Agate, Doric-type, footed bulbous spherical body w/a cylindrical neck w/a mask spout, D-form handle, whirled glaze body in shades of brown, tan & blue agate on a white ground, impressed mark, ca. 1865 ....**316.00**

Pitcher, jug-type, 7" h., Drabware, a bulbous nearly spherical center tapering to a molded foot & to a cylindrical neck w/pinched spout, decorated w/resemble stoneware w/contrasting blue

enameling w/a large central medallion monogrammed "VA," impressed mark, 19th c. **173.00**

Pitcher, tankard, 7½" h., caterer-type, majolica, cylindrical body w/rim spout & angled loop handle, the sides molded w/narrow bands of verse between bands of oval jewels, polychrome decoration, impressed marks, ca. 1870 (foot rim chip, rim wear) **230.00**

Plaque, bone china, round, decorated w/a black transfer-printed design titled "Man Diagram IV," a series of silhouetted standing men within a light square within a larger dark square, by Gleny Barton, printed marks, 1976, 11" d. **1,725.00**

Plate, 9½" d., Dominion of Canada, h.p. coat of arms w/oak & acorn border..............................**70.00**

Platter, 14" l., Columbia patt., blue & gold **55.00**

Platter, 15½" l., Columbia patt. **75.00**

Punch bowl, Poplar Trees exterior, Woodlands Bridge interior w/mermaid center, marked on bottom, "T.W. Twyford Infants Welfare Centre: Hanley, Dec. 9, 1930," 11¼" d., 6" h. **10,550.00**

Sauce tureen, cover & undertray, bone china, the squatty bulbous oval tureen raised on a flaring foot & fitted w/loop end handles, the domed cover w/loop handle, on a dished oval undertray, all decorated w/polychrome large flower blossom clusters, first period, printed mark, ca. 1820, tureen handle to handle 7⅛" l., the set (cover rim chip, gilt rim wear) **345.00**

Teapot, cov., display-type, Pearlware, squatty bulbous body raised on a flaring pedestal foot & tapering to a wide waisted neck w/a rolled rim, stepped domed cover w/pointed finial, swan's-neck spout & D-scroll handle, grey enamel-enhanced gilt decorations w/leaf designs on the spout, banded borders & central knot emblems on the sides, impressed mark & "pearl," ca. 1850, 18½" h. (finial & handle restored, slight gilt wear) **1,380.00**

Tea set: cov. teapot, cov. sugar bowl, creamer, waste bowl & cup & saucer; bone china, squatty bulbous boat-shaped serving pieces, all pieces decorated w/blue transfer-printed Chinese landscape scenes, first period, printed marks, ca. 1820, teapot 11" l., the set (teapot body restored, other pieces w/various hairlines) **431.00**

Tray, rectangular w/cut corners, bone china, Blue Willow patt., late 19th c., printed & impressed marks, 17¼" l. (gilt rim wear) **316.00**

Vase, 7" h., a spherical body molded w/a series of raised, flattened rings tapering to a short, wide cylindrical neck, raised on a low ringed foot, duck-egg blue matte glaze, designed by Keith Murray, 20th c., printed mark..................**345.00**

Vase, 7¼" h., ovoid body w/a narrow footring & a short, slightly flaring cylindrical neck, decorated in silver lustre w/a floral decoration on a black band on the cream-colored body, designed by Louise Powell, impressed mark & artist-signed, ca. 1920....................................**374.00**

Vases, cov., 9½" h., solid agate, a short round pedestal base supporting a wide ovoid vase & cover w/sibyl figural finial in creamware w/traces of gilding, mounted on a square black basalt base, impressed wafer mark of Wedgwood & Bentley,

ca. 1770, gilt rim wear, rim chips on covers, nicks on basalt bases, pr. (ILLUS. of one) **7,475.00**

Rare Early Agate Vase

Veilleuse, cover & undertray, the slightly tapering cylindrical body flanked by long D-form handles from rim to base, low domed cover w/button finial, slightly dished round undertray, decorated w/iron-red & blue enamel lappet banding & trim, impressed mark, early 19th c., 3⅜" h., the set (staining, rim wear, line in base) **460.00**

Vase, 7¾" h., Golconda Ware, squatty bulbous body tapering sharply to a short cylindrical neck, enameled & gilt raised floral & foliate overall designs on a cream ground, impressed mark, rim restoration, surface wear, ca. 1885 (ILLUS. next page, center) **201.00**

Vase, 8½" h., Ivory Vellum porcelain, footed baluster-form w/loop handles on the slender

Decorative Wedgwood Vases

neck, a cream ground decorated
w/enamel & gilt berry & foliate
overall designs, printed &
impressed marks, rim nicks,
ca. 1890 (ILLUS. left) **115.00**

Vase, 9½" h., Ivory Vellum
porcelain, flaring cylindrical body
tapering at the shoulder to a
short cylindrical neck, leaftip &
ring shoulder handles, the body
w/a cream ground decorated
w/gilt-trimmed polychrome bird
on flowering branches, the neck
w/a dark brown ground w/gilt
floral decoration, printed mark,
gilt rim wear, ca. 1885
(ILLUS. right) **345.00**

WELLER

This pottery was made from 1872 to 1945
at a pottery established originally by Samuel
A. Weller at Fultonham, Ohio, and moved in
1882 to Zanesville. Numerous lines were
produced and listings below are by the
pattern or lines.

Reference books on Weller include The
Collectors Encyclopedia of Weller Pottery, by
Sharon & Bob Huxford (Collector Books,
1979) and All About Weller by Ann Gilbert
McDonald (Antique Publications, 1989).

WELLER

Weller Pottery

Weller Marks

ARDSLEY (1928)

Various shapes molded as cattails among
rushes with water lilies at the bottom. Matte
glaze.

Vase, 8" h., fan-shaped, green
w/brown cattails & water lilies at
the base....................................**$90.00**

AURELIAN (1898-1910)

Similar to Louwelsa line but brighter
colors and a glossy glaze.

Vase, 8⅞" h., bulbous nearly
spherical body w/a tiny neck at
the top center, decorated
w/large clusters of dark blue &
orange grapes & dark green &
brown leaves & vines against a
black & yellow mottled ground,
decorated by T. J. Wheatley,

Aurelian Vase

incised "Aurelian TJW" &
impressed "6 - 556," minor glaze
scratches (ILLUS.)....................**770.00**

BALDIN (about 1915-20)
*Rustic designs with relief-molded apples
and leaves on branches wrapped around each
piece.*

Vase, bud **125.00**
Vase, 7½" h., 10" d., bulbous
base w/apple decoration on
green ground.............**300.00 to 325.00**

BARCELONA (late 20s)
*Colorful Spanish peasant-style designs on
buff ground.*

Vase, 9" h. **225.00**

BEDFORD MATT (about 1915)
Umbrella stand, tall wide slightly
waisted cylindrical form w/a
molded band of large knobs
around the base, the lightly
scalloped rim above molded
alternating tulip & sunflower
blossoms w/leaves raised on
slender stems running down to
the base band, matte green
glaze, unmarked, 20⅛" h.
(ILLUS.) **935.00**

Bedford Matt Umbrella Stand

BLUE & DECORATED HUDSON (ca. 1920s)
*A version of the hand-painted Hudson line
with the generally floral decoration painted on
a dark matte blue ground.*

Vase, 9" h., tall swelled cylindrical
body w/a wide flat molded
mouth, dark blue mottled ground
decorated w/a large bluish grey,
pink & white iris & light & dark
green leaves & stalks, marked
(tight two inch line from rim) **413.00**
Vase, 9⅜" h., tall slightly tapering
squared form w/a flat mouth,
dark blue w/a light blue rim band
decorated w/a continuous
branch of leafy white blossoms,
marked (ILLUS.) **385.00**

Square Blue & Decorated Vase

Vase, 13⅛" h., tall slender tapering cylindrical w/a molded foot, dark blue w/a light blue rim band, decorated w/two blue, white & pink birds perched in a flowering tree w/a flying insect nearby, impressed mark.........**1,980.00**

Vases, 10¼" h., bulbous cushion base tapering sharply to a very slender & tall slightly swelled neck, decorated w/tall swirled stems of white lily-of-the-valley on light & dark green stems & leaves on a dark blue ground, marked, pr. **550.00**

BLUE WARE (before 1920)

Classical relief-molded white or cream figures on a dark blue ground.

Jardiniere, 10" h. **250.00**

Vase, 7" h. **200.00**

BONITO (1927-33)

Hand-painted florals and foliage in soft tones on cream ground.

Flowerpot w/saucer .....**90.00 to 100.00**

BOUQUET (late 1930s)

Various molded flowers in color against a light blue, green or ivory ground on simple shapes often accented by lightly molded ribbing.

Bowl-vase, ovoid w/closed-in mouth, 8¾ x 10 14" **140.00**

BRETON (EarlyLate 20s)

Band of roses alternating with smaller flowers around the center. Mottled top and bottom. Matt finish. Middle period

Vase, 8⅞" h., a small foot supporting a widely flaring bulbous ovoid body w/a wide shoulder tapering to a wide cylindrical neck decorated around its base w/a wide band of stylized scrolling flowers, overall matte green glaze, unmarked **248.00**

CLARMONT (ca. 1920)

Generally rounded forms molded with horizontal ribbing or wide bands often molded with abstract florals. Decorated with an overall dark brown glaze.

Vase, 8" h., inverted double-gourd body w/raised roundels around the top section & raised scrolls & berries around the lower section, serrated double-loop handles down the sides **60.00**

COPPERTONE (late 1920s)

Various shapes with an overall mottled green glaze. Some pieces with figural frog or fish handles. Models of frogs also included.

Vase, 6⅝" h., bulbous ovoid body tapering to a widely flaring rim flanked by thick rope-like handles from the rim to mid-body, marked w/an incised "Z" ..**165.00**

Vase, 8" h., a small footring supporting a bulbous ovoid body tapering to a high, widely flaring flat neck, D-form thick handles from neck to center of body, green & brownish black mottled matte glaze, incised "Weller Handmade - 12" (minor rim & base flake) **413.00**

CREAMWARE

Coat of Arms* (about 1915)

Planter, Coat of Arms patt., 5½" sq., 3" h. (no harm chip) **60.00**

Teapot, cov., brown, 6½" h. **60.00**

DICKENSWARE
2nd Line (1900-05)

Various incised "sgraffito" designs usually with a matte glaze.

Vase, 9½" h., 3" d., slender cylindrical body w/slightly flared shoulder tapering to flaring rolled neck & rim, w/incised decoration of a male golfer & a copse of trees, done in yellow, green & brown, incised "LJB - XI8818," by L.J. Burgess **1,210.00**

DUNTON (1915)

Dunton Umbrella Stand

Umbrella stand, tall cylindrical form decorated w/brown, white & blue birds, nests w/eggs among cream branches w/green leaves & pink flowers & buds, glossy black ground, 23" h. (ILLUS.) **2,970.00**

EOCEAN and EOCEAN ROSE (1898-1925)

Early art line with various hand-painted flowers on shaded grounds, usually with a glossy glaze.

Mug, tall slightly tapering cylindrical body w/an angled handle, blackish green shading down to a pale green ground, decorated w/blue, black & red blackberries & pale green leaves & stems, impressed "Weller Ware," incised "9005," 5" h. **248.00**

Pitcher, 6¾" h., a thick & wide cushion-type base tapering slightly to a deeply indented band below the tapering cylindrical sides w/a flat rim, thick rim spout & thick inverted D-form handle from the rim to the edge of the base, dark blackish green ground shading down to pale green & cream,

Eocean Pitcher with Violets

decorated on the upper side w/a bright deep rose wild violet w/pale green leaves & stems, decorated by Mary Pierce, incised "Weller Eocean" (ILLUS.) **330.00**

Pitcher, tankard, 12¼" h., Eocean Rose, decorated w/a dark blackish green shading to pale green shading to rose pink ground & h.p. w/the bust portrait of a smiling round-faced monk, painted by Levi J. Burgess, incised on the base "Eocean Rose Weller" & "S," impressed "580" (small glaze flake off the bottom edge of the spout) **1,430.00**

Vase, 6⅞" h., late-type, footed slender ovoid body tapering to a slender flaring neck, a wide black band around the neck above a mottled greyish green to grey ground, the neck painted w/red cherries on green stems, unmarked **165.00**

Vase, 7⅞" h., late-type, ovoid body tapering to a flaring foot & a wide flaring mouth, dark bluish black upper half over a pale blue lower half, decorated down the side w/stylized purplish pink blossoms w/yellow centers & dark green foliage, unmarked....**385.00**

Vase, 8" h., baluster form w/flaring foot & wide mouth w/slightly flared rim...................**180.00**

Vase, 9¼" h., cylindrical w/a rounded shoulder to the short rolled neck, dark green shading to pale green shading to white ground, decorated w/tall stems of white daffodils w/small yellow centers on pale green leafy stems, incised "Eocean Weller - S" (tight spider crack in glaze on base) **660.00**

Eocean Vase with Daisies

Vase, 10⅛" h., tall slender swelled cylindrical body w/a small shoulder to a short rolled rim, black neck & shoulder shading to dark blue to grey to pale pink, decorated down the sides w/large pale pink daisies w/yellow centers & pale green leafy stems, base incised "Eocean Weller," impressed "X 396" (ILLUS.) **550.00**

Vase, 10¼" h., late-type, swelled flaring base tapering sharply to a slender slightly swelled body w/a tiny mouth, a black neck band above a thin green band above the greyish pink lower body, painted around the neck & down the sides w/colorful stylized trailing florals, marked **193.00**

Vase, 11" h., tall slender cylindrical body w/a rounded shoulder to a short neck w/flattened flared rim, dark grey shading to pinkish white ground, painted w/a large red nasturtium blossom & pale green leaves & stems, company mark & "X - +40" **440.00**

Vase, 11⅝" h., footed slender cylindrical body w/a short waisted neck w/flattened rim flanked by angular loop handles to the shoulder, black shaded to dark green shaded to cream ground at the base, the side painted w/a large white & yellow jonquil & green stems & leaves, unmarked **935.00**

Vase, 11¾" h., tall slender swelled cylindrical body w/a rounded shoulder tapering slightly to a short molded rim, dark blackish green shading to pale green & cream ground, two wary fish painted neck the dark rim, decorated by Levi J. Burgess, incised "Eocean Weller," impressed "X - 315" ..**3,190.00**

Vase, 13" h., tall slender ovoid body tapering gently to a flat molded mouth, a moss green shaded to pale bluish green to cream ground, decorated down the sides w/stems of blue & pink blackberries & white blossoms w/pale green & pink leaves, incised "Eocean Weller," impressed "S - 4 - 476" **1,045.00**

Vase, 13½" h., Eocean Rose, tall cylindrical body w/a bulbous swelled shoulder tapering to a flat slightly molded mouth, dark blackish green shading to green shading to white ground, decorated w/a long bluster of purple wisteria blossoms & leafy vines down the front, decorated by Sarah Reid McLaughlin, base incised "Eocean Rose Weller - 4," impressed "X - 475" **2,750.00**

ETNA (1906)

Similar to Eocean line but designs are molded in low-relief and colored.

Vase, 11⅛" h., bulbous cylindrical body on a narrow footring, the shoulder tapering to a swelled cylindrical neck flanked by loop handles to the shoulder, shaded from dark greyish green to creamy white to pale pink at the base, relief slip-painted pink blossoms on the neck & white & dark pink blossoms down the sides, signed "Weller" in script on the side & impressed "Etna Weller" on the base **275.00**

Vase, 12½" h., wide ovoid body tapering to a molded flat mouth, large heavily slip-painted pink daylilies on slender green stems around the shoulder against a shaded dark green to pale green to lavender ground, marked **715.00**

FLERON (late 20s)

Green glaze, made to look hand turned. Middle period

Bowl, 3" h., squatty tapering sides below a rolled & lobed rim, all-green, No. J-6 ....**80.00**

Vase, 12" h., 10" d., funnel-shaped..........................**750.00**

FOREST (mid-Teens - 1928)

Realistically molded and painted forest scene.

Jardiniere, 8" h. **360.00**

FRU RUSSET

Vase, 4½" h., Arts & Crafts style, tapering bell-form body w/molded rim, the side molded w/large stylized beetles & leaves w/swirled lines, overall dark cranberry matte glaze w/pale grey highlights & black veining, unmarked **550.00**

FUDZI (1904)

Vase, 11¾" h., 3½" d., tall slender cylindrical body w/a rounded shoulder to the small short neck, enameled w/large iris in amber & green against a stippled & shaded brown to ivory ground, die-stamped "607" (very tight in-body line) **275.00**

GARDEN ORNAMENTS (Figural)

Model of "Pop-eyed" Dog, 4" h., marked "Weller Pottery" (by hand) **600.00**

HUDSON (1917-34)

Underglaze slip-painted decoration.

Vase, 6⅛" h., swelled cylindrical body w/a narrow shoulder to the short cylindrical mouth, decorated w/green Virginia creeper leaves & blue berries against a greyish pink ground, artist-initialed by Hester Pillsbury, marked in script "Weller".....................................**275.00**

Vase, 6⅞" h., produced for the Kappa Kappa Gamma Fraternity, slender ovoid body tapering to a molded mouth, decorated in shades of blue & white, the Fraternity colors, w/large iris blossoms & leaves (the fraternity flower), circular base mark "Weller Ware" & Greek letters for Kappa Kappa Gamma, ca. 1930 ....**935.00**

Vase, 7" h., cylindrical w/a rounded base & shoulder w/a wide, flat molded mouth,

Hudson Vase with Clover

medium blue shades to moss green ground, decorated w/red clover & green leaves & blue iris blossoms on slender stalks, artist-signed, semi-circular inkstamp logo mark (ILLUS.) **468.00**

Vase, 7" h., cylindrical w/a rounded shoulder to a wide, flat molded mouth, decorated in pastel tones w/a large cluster of lily-of-the-valley on a dark grey shaded to pale cream ground, impressed mark **348.00**

Vase, 7" h., cylindrical w/a rounded base & shoulder w/a wide, flat molded mouth, medium blue shades to moss green ground, decorated w/red clover & green leaves & blue iris blossoms on slender stalks, artist-signed, semi-circular inkstamp logo mark **468.00**

Vase, 8½" h., simple cylindrical form, painted w/a large white & yellow iris blossom on light & dark green stem & leaves against a lightly shaded medium green to pale yellow ground, decorated by Mae Timberlake, marked **1,210.00**

Vase, 10½" h., tall slender baluster-form w/a short rolled neck, the ground shading from medium grey to dark grey at the base & decorated w/a cluster of large white crocus on green stems, unmarked **385.00**

Vase, 10¾" h., tall slender swelled cylindrical body tapering to a molded mouth, decorated in pastel shades w/lavender & yellow iris blossoms & leaves on a shaded lavender to pale yellow ground, marked **660.00**

Vase, 12⅝" h., tall slender baluster-form w/flared mouth & foot, medium shaded to pale green shaded to pale pink ground decorated w/a large cluster of trailing white & pink

flowers, green leaves & vines, signed by Hester Pillsbury, two base marks............................**880.00**

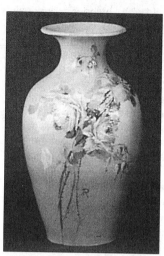

Large Hudson Floor Vase

Vase, 25½" h., 14" d., floor-type, large baluster-form body w/a short neck w/a widely flaring & flattened rim, painted w/white & yellow roses & red bleeding heart on a shaded pink to grey ground, minor firing flaws, signed by Mae Timberlake, company mark (ILLUS.) **15,400.00**

JAP BIRDIMAL (1904)

The outlines of the design on this ware are first incised with a tool and then inlaid with slip that ws squeezed from a tube or heavily painted on with a brush. The designs are then colored and covered with a high-gloss glaze.

Jap Birdimal Vase

Vase, 4⅜" h., squatty bulbous body raised on three short rounded legs, the three-lobed short neck w/a molded rim, greyish blue ground decorated w/slip-trailed bubble-blowing fish in a slip trail sea in blue, yellow & white, artist-initialed, incised "F" & w/impressed number "589" (ILLUS.) **770.00**

LAMAR (1920-25)

A metallic luster ware in a deep raspberry red decorated with black luster scenery. Never marked except with a paper label.

Lamar Scenic Vase

Vase, 7½" h., slender ovoid body w/a small mouth, decorated w/a black silhouetted landscape dotted w/trees & windmills in the distance on a deep rose red ground, unmarked minor glaze scratches & a small glaze bubble at juncture of side & base (ILLUS.) **138.00**

LOUWELSA (1896-1924)

Hand-painted underglaze slip decoration on dark brown shading to yellow ground; glossy glaze.

Jardiniere, very wide & deep bulbous body w/a wide, flat mouth, decorated w/a cluster of large yellow iris & buds on shaded dark green stems & leaves against a dark brown shaded to dark green ground, signed by Frank Ferrell, impressed "Weller Louwelsa," several muddled numbers, 16" d., 12½" h. **248.00**

Mug, tall slightly tapering cylindrical form w/an inverted-D handle, decorated w/a half-length bust profile of a monk dressed in brown, against a brown shaded to golden yellow ground, artist-initialed & impressed marks, 5⅞" h. (minor glaze scratches) **440.00**

Louwelsa Mug

Mug, tankard, slightly tapering cylindrical form w/C-form handle, decorated w/a h.p. bust portrait of a Native American warrior, initialed by artist Levi J. Burgess, impressed shape No. 562, 5⅞" h. (ILLUS.) **990.00**

Vase, 3⅛" h., wide low squatty round body centered by a short, wide trefoil neck w/molded rim, the wide shoulders decorated w/clusters of yellow clover & green leaves & stems against a dark brown ground, decorated by John Butterworth, Louwelsa logo, shape number "239" & notation "M 2" **138.00**

Vase, 9⅝" h., tall ovoid body tapering to a tiny flaring neck, decorated w/a large cluster of orange & yellow trumpet vine w/green leaves hanging down from the top against a dark brown shaded to light green ground, marked " A - L - 110" (two stilt pulls on base) **138.00**

Vase, 11¾" h., ovoid body w/slight flaring rim, decorated w/ acorns & oak leaves on olive & dark brown glaze, incised "C. Bloomeri" & impressed "Louwelsa Weller" (small rim flakes **182.00**

Vase, 12" h., waisted cylindrical form, decorated w/flowers & berries **250.00**

LUSTRE (1922)

Plain metallic luster glaze without decoration. All colors.

Casserole, cov., brown, 5" h. **30.00**

Compote, yellow, 7½" d. **30.00**

MAMMY LINE (1935)

Figural black mammy or black children as handles.

Batter bowl, large **895.00**

MARVO (mid-1920s-33)

Molded overall fern and leaf design on various matte-background colors.

Jardiniere, green, star line, NR base, 6" h. **65.00**

ORRIS (about 1922)

Similar to Greora except melon ribbed.

Jardiniere, 7" h. **60.00**

Wall pocket **200.00**

PARAGON (about 1935)

Allover pattern of stylized flowers and leaves on various background colors. Semigloss finish.

Vase, 4⅜" h., 5¼" d., footed spherical form w/a wide flat mouth, impressed stylized Art

Deco leaf decoration, matte rose glaze, impressed mark, ca. 1934.....................................**173.00**

PEARL (late teens)

Cream color draped with pearl-like beads. Matt finish.

Jardiniere, 6" d., 9" h. (light crazing, one pearly restored).....**200.00**

Vase, 6" h. (one small hairline)......**40.00**

PIERRE (mid 30s)

Utility kitchenware. Basketweave pattern.

Casserole, cov., white, 7" d., 3" h. **30.00**

Pitcher, 5" h., blue.......................**30.00**

Teapot, cov., white, 6½" h. **40.00**

ROCHELLE (early 20s35

Hudson line renamed. Marked only "Weller" High gloss glaze.

Vase, 6⅛" h., swelled cylindrical body w/a tapering shoulder to a short, cylindrical neck, dark brown shaded to gold ground decorated w/clusters of cream & lavender hops & green leafy vines, ca. 1920s, incised mark ..**413.00**

SELMA

Knifewood line with a high-gloss glaze. Occasionally with peacocks, butterflies, and daisies.

Selma Vase

Vase, 4⅜" h., simple ovoid form molded overall w/large yellow-centered white daisies on green leafy stems & w/colored butterflies, all against a finely ribbed mottled brown ground, marked (ILLUS.) **138.00**

SICARDO (1902-07)

Various shapes with iridescent glaze of metallic shadings in greens, blues, crimson, purple or copper tones decorated with vines, flowers, stars or free-form geometric lines.

Vase, 6" h., 4½" d., footed squatty bulbous base tapering to a tall swelled cylindrical neck, a green floral design w/an overall metallic lustre purple glaze, painted mark on side **495.00**

Vase, 6½" h., gently tapering & slightly waisted cylindrical body below an indented neck band below a bulbous neck tapering to a molded rim, small loop handles at the shoulders, overall stylized floral decoration in iridescent shades of blue, purple & green, "Weller Sicard" low on the side, base impressed "Weller - 50 - 2" **935.00**

Vase, 8½" h., 3" d., simple cylindrical form, decorated in the Art Nouveau style w/honeysuckle in a rich lustred bluish green & burgundy iridescent flambé glaze, marked **770.00**

SILVERTONE (1928)

Various flowers, fruits or butterflies molded on a pale purple-blue matte pebbled ground.

Console bowl w/flower frog, round bowl w/deeply flaring sides, domed blossom-molded frog, frog 2½" h., bowl 12" d., 3½" h., 2 pcs.............................**375.00**

SOUEVO (1910 ?)

Indian-type decoration, incised, matte glaze, 1909.

Souevo Jardiniere

Jardiniere, Arts & Crafts style, Native American style design, 13¼" d., 10⅞" h. (ILLUS.)..........**660.00**

STELLAR (1934)

Hand slip decorated with blue stars in a "Comet" design. White background. Matte finish.

Vase, 5¼" h., 5" d., bulbous ovoid body w/a short cylindrical neck, decorated w/white stars on a matte black ground, incised on base "Weller Pottery".................**440.00**

SYDONIA(1931)

Pleated blossom or fan shapes on a leaf-molded foot. Mottled blue or dark green glaze.

Vase, 6½" h., fan-shaped **40.00**

UTILITY WARE

Various simple kitchenware bowls, pitcher, teapots and casseroles, often with simple banded decoration or an overall dark brown glaze.

Teapot, cov., figural pumpkin, 6" h. **125.00**

WHITE & DECORATED

A version of the Hudson line with dark colored floral designs against a creamy white ground.

Vase, 8¾" h., tall slender & gently tapering ovoid body w/a small flat mouth, creamy white ground decorated w/two dark blue bands at the top & w/light & dark blue branches of blossoms hanging down the sides, marked **440.00**

WOODCRAFT (1917)

Rustic designs simulating the appearance of stumps, logs and tree trunks. Some pieces are adorned with owls, squirrels, dogs and other animals.

Vase, 9" h., a flat-rimmed ovoid body tapering to a flaring tree-trunk flanked by slender free-standing smaller tree trunks all joined at the round foot, the body molded w/dense leaves & red berries **200.00**

Vase, 16" h., tall cylindrical tree trunk-form, pierced w/a large hole on one side, a large figural owl to one side of the hole & a cluster of apples & leaves above **1,200.00**

Wall pocket, conical form molded to resemble a tree trunk in green w/twisted brown branches & a full-figure squirrel seated at the base, marked, 9¼" h. **468.00**

WOODROSE (before 1920)

Wall pocket, conical, lilac ground, 6½" l. **85.00**

XENIA (about 1920)

Vase, 4" h., 8½" d., wide squatty bulbous body tapering up to a short cylindrical neck, Arts & Crafts decoration of three burgundy & pink rose blossoms w/outlines & twisting stems in olive green against a bluish grey ground, impressed "Weller" **523.00**

ZONA (about 1920)

Red apples and green leaves on brown branches all on a cream-colored ground; some pieces with molded florals or birds with various glazes.

A line of children's dishes was also produced featuring hand-painted or molded animals. This is referred to as the "Zona Baby Line."

Umbrella stand, cylindrical, decorated w/a row of tall, standing maidens in long dresses holding a continuous garland of pink roses, green ivy vines around the top, all on a cream ground, glossy glaze, 10½" d., 20½" h. (ILLUS.).....................**750.00 to 950.00**

Zona Umbrella Stand

Vase, 4¾" h., 4¼" d., Matte Wares, Arts & Crafts style, wide squatty base tapering sharply to a small molded mouth, molded in high-relief w/large beetles & grapevines under a fine veined matte raspberry to grey glaze (ILLUS. next page, No. 1).........**550.00**

Vase, 6½" h., 4¾" d., Matt Green, bulbous ovoid body tapering to a short cylindrical neck, relief-molded large leaves & branches, veined green glaze, die-stamped mark (ILLUS. next page, No. 5).........**495.00**

Vase, 7¼" h., 3¼" d., Hudson, cylindrical body tapering slightly to a molded flat rim, decorated w/a branch of pink, yellow & blue berries & green leaves on a shaded blue to celadon green ground, artist-initialed by Sara Timberlake & factory-marked (ILLUS. next page, No. 3).........**251.00**

Vase, 7¼" h., 3½" d., Hudson, slender ovoid body w/a molded flat mouth, slip-painted w/milk pods in brown, green & white

Courtesy of Dave Rago

8   6   5   9

2   1   4   3   7

A Variety of Weller Vases in Select Patterns

against a shaded grey to pink ground, artist-initialed & factory-marked (ILLUS., No. 4) **413.00**

Vase, 9¼" h., 4¼" d., Hudson, slender ovoid body w/a rolled & molded mouth, decorated w/a large sprig of lily-of-the-valley in white, yellow, green & lavender on a blue to lavender ground, artist-signed by Claude Leffler, stamped factory mark (ILLUS., No. 2) **495.00**

Vase, 12" h., 4½" d., Eocean, a tall slender ovoid body w/a molded mouth, decorated w/a pear tree branch w/green & purple fruit against a shaded purplish grey to ivory ground, incised "Weller Eocean" & die-stamped "X456" (ILLUS., No. 6) **825.00**

Vase, 13" h., 6½" d., Hudson, large baluster-form w/a short neck & widely flared rim,

decorated w/a large branch of red & yellow hollyhocks w/green leaves against a blue, purple & celadon green ground, signed by Claude Leffler, factory-marked (ILLUS., No. 7) **1,760.00**

Vase, 14½" h., 5½" d., Sicardo, tall slender cylindrical body w/a flaring base & a flattened flaring rim, decorated w/stylized leaves & buds in rich iridescent tones of crimson, turquoise & gold, signed on side "Weller - Sicard" (ILLUS., No. 8) **1,540.00**

Vase, 14½" h., 5½" d., Sicardo, tall slender cylindrical body w/a flaring base & a flattened flaring rim, decorated w/butterflies & stars in iridescent tones of crimson, green, gold & blue, raised "WELLER - 12, " & painted on side "Weller - Sicard" (ILLUS., No. 9) **1,650.00**

WHEATLEY POTTERY

Thomas J. Wheatley was one of the original founders of the art pottery movement in Cincinnati, Ohio in the early 1880s. In 1879 the Cincinnati Art Pottery was formed and after some legal problems it operated under the name T.J. Wheatley & Company. Their production featured Limoges-style hand-painted decorations and most pieces were carefully marked and often dated.

In 1882 Wheatley disassociated himself from the Cincinnati Art Pottery and opened another pottery which was destroyed by fire in 1884. Around 1900 Wheatley finally resumed making art pottery in Cincinnati and in 1903 he founded the Wheatley Pottery Company with a new partner, Isaac Kahn.

The new pottery from this company featured colored matte glazes over relief work designs and green, yellow and blue were the most often used colors. There were imitations of the well-known Grueby Pottery wares as well as artware, garden pottery and architectural pieces. Artwork was apparently not made much after 1907. This plant was destroyed by fire in 1910 but was rebuilt and run by Wheatley until his death in 1917. Wheatley artware was generally unmarked except for a paper label.

Wheatley Pottery Marks

Lamp, table model, kerosene-type, a flaring brass foot ring w/classical motifs below the cylindrical pottery body decorated w/white flowers & green leaves on a striated blue & white ground, domed brass top fittings w/further classical designs at the top, pottery incised "TJWheatley - 1879," electrified, 7" d., overall 16" h. **$440.00**

Vase, 6½" h., 8½" d., squatty bulbous ovoid body tapering to a wide flat neck w/a molded neck ring, carved curved lines under a frothy matte green glaze, unmarked (small rim bruise) **660.00**

Vase, 7½" h., 6½" d., footed bulbous baluster-form w/a short flaring neck, decorated in the Barbotine style w/relief-sculpted & applied dogwood blossoms, pink & green seashells & green seaweed on a mottled blue & white glossy ground, minor damage, incised "TJWheatley - 8 - 1880" **770.00**

Vase, 10½" h., 7" d., wide ovoid body tapering to a wide flaring neck, the shoulder w/an impressed narrow Greek key band, rich feathered matte green glaze, mark covered w/glaze **550.00**

Vase, 11" h., 9¼" d., wide corseted cylindrical body tapering to a short, wide neck, covered in a thick, frothy dripping matte green glaze, marked **1,100.00**

Vase, pillow-type, 13¼" h., 10½" w., a small rectangular foot supports a wide round flattened body w/a short cylindrical neck, decorated w/white daisies & green leaves on a mottled blue ground, small glaze chips at top & bottom rim, incised "TJWheatley - 1879 - ?"....................................**715.00**

WORCESTER

The famed English factory was established in 1751 and produced porcelains. Earthenwares were made in the 19th century. Its first period is known as the "Dr. Wall" period; that from 1783 to 1792 as the "Flight" period; that from 1792 to 1807 as the "Barr and Flight & Barr period. The firm became Barr, Flight & Barr from 1807 to 1813; Flight, Barr & Barr from 1813 to 1840; Chamberlain & Co. from 1840 to 1852, and Kerr and Binns from 1852 to 1862. After 1862, the company became the Worcester Royal Porcelain Company, Ltd., known familiarly as Royal Worcester, which see. Also included in the following listing are examples of wares from the early Chambelains and early Grainger factories in Worcester.

Worcester Marks

Bowl, 6¼" d., 2¾" h., deep footring supporting a deep gently flaring bowl, blue on white transfer-printed floral landscape design, Dr. Wall period crescent mark (minor flakes on table ring) $220.00

Butter tub, cov., low cylindrical body w/scrolled rim handles & a domed cover w/a sculpted blossom finial, the body & cover decorated w/colorful floral sprays below narrow geometric borders, First Period, ca. 1765, 4¼" d., 3¼" h. 489.00

Dish, leaf-form, the molded body painted w/underglaze-blue floral sprays , w/a branch-form handle, First Period, ca. 1765, 8" l. 575.00

Fruit cooler, cylindrical, decorated w/stylized floral reserve, on a stepped round foot, First Period, ca. 1800, 6¼" h. 230.00

Pitcher, 6" h., figural, molded as a head of cabbage w/a mask spout & C-scroll handle, the ovoid form molded w/leaves & decorated w/blue transfer-printed floral clusters, First Period, mid-18th c. 259.00

Plate, 10½" d., three tiny shell feet, center lobed design decorated w/daisies & surrounded by gold scalloped trim, 1¾" reticulated & carved edge, Grainger Worcester 765.00

Plates, 7" d., octagonal, decoration of landscape fan-form reserves against a cobalt blue ground, First Period, mid-18th c., pr. 391.00

Plates, 7½" d., each decorated w/a cartouche & foliate border surrounding a central color floral spray reserve, First Period, ca. 1765, pr. 460.00

Plates, 8" d., each decorated w/transfer-printed blue diaper border surrounding floral sprays, First Period, mid-18th c., pr. 230.00

Tea cup & saucer, handleless, each painted w/a chinoiserie vignette within a blue border, First Period, ca. 1765, cup 2" h. 196.00

Teapot, cov., globular form w/a domed cover & sculpted blossom finial, the body painted w/floral sprays, First Period, ca. 1765, 6½" h. 431.00

Vase, 7¼" h., baluster-form, decorated w/an underglaze-blue floral spray, First Period, ca. 1765...................................374.00

Waste bowl, a floral-molded exterior & floral spray-decorated interior within a lambrequin border, First Period, ca. 1765, 5" d., 2¼" h. 219.00

YELLOWWARE

John Bell Preserving Jar

Yellowware is a form of utilitarian pottery produced in the United States and England from the early 19th century onward. Its body texture is less dense and vitreous (impervious to water) than stoneware. Most, but not all, yellowware is unmarked and its color varies from deep yellow to pale buff. In the late 19th and early 20th centuries bowls in graduated sizes were widely advertised. Still in production, yellowware is plentiful and still reasonably priced.

Bowl, 11½" d., bulbous cylindrical body on a thin footring, the sides tapering to flaring rim, white band w/blue seaweed decoration, dark brown stripes, East Liverpool, Ohio (wear, stains & interior has scratches & surface flakes) **$275.00**

Bowl, 12¾" d, 5¾" h., bulbous cylindrical on a thin footring, sides tapering to flaring rim, white band w/green seaweed decoration & dark brown stripes, East Liverpool, Ohio (wear, stains & interior has scratches & surface flakes) **110.00**

Bowl, 13½" d., 6½" h., bulbous cylindrical body on a thin footring, sides tapering to flaring rim, white band w/blue seaweed decoration, East Liverpool, Ohio (wear & chip on foot) **165.00**

Preserving jar, cov., cylindrical body w/rounded shoulder tapering to slightly flaring rim, inset flat cover w/tab finial, impressed "John Bell," lid fits but color varies, wear & crazing, 5¾" h. (ILLUS.) **550.00**

ZSOLNAY

This pottery was made in Pecs, Hungary, in a factory founded in 1862 by Vilmos Zsolnay. Utilitarian earthenware was originally produced but by the turn of the century ornamental Art Nouveau style wares with bright colors and lustre decoration were produced and these wares are especially sought today. Currently Zsolnay pieces are being made in a new factory.

Ewer, reticulated, aqua & butterscotch, 16¼" h...............**$695.00**

Inkwell, cov., figural, modeled as an upright conch shell w/a high ruffled & flaring rim at one side above the tapering cap, bright crimson & black lustred finish, w/original operculum cap & ceramic insert, embossed bottom mark & "6576," 4½" w., 4¼" h. (repair to cap handle) **330.00**

Unusual Zsolnay Jug

Jug, narrow footring below the wide squatty bulbous body pierced w/oblong raised reserves, tapering to a slender ringed neck below a wide cupped rim, a curved slender shoulder spout w/bracket attaching it to the neck & an angled prong-trimmed handle from top of neck to shoulder, bright aqua green bubbled textured surface, beads around the shoulder & gilt trim overall, impressed "Zsolnay Pecs 768," 9¼" h. (ILLUS.) **260.00**

Vase, 6⅞" h., simple ovoid body tapering to a tall slender neck, iridescent red mosaic glaze w/a mustard yellow ground & interior, silver "Zsolnay - Pecs" stamp, Hungary, early 20th c. ...**173.00**

Vase, 10⅞" h., ovoid body w/a waisted neck, four-handled w/a pierced gilt-metal mount w/buds on interlaced trailing stems, in a gold, green & plum lustred glaze, impressed mark **1,380.00**

CHARACTER COLLECTIBLES

Numerous objects made in the likeness of or named after comic strip and comic book personalities or characters abounded from the 1920s to the present. Scores of these are now being eagerly collected and prices still vary widely.

Alice in Wonderland doll, Madame Alexander's character child, hard plastic head w/Maggie face, large blue sleep eyes w/real upper lashes, painted lower lashes, single-stroke brows, closed mouth, synthetic wig in original set, hard plastic five-piece body, tagged pale lavender taffeta dress, white nylon pinafore, white eyelet-trimmed underclothing, nylon stockings, black one-strap shoes, original bow in hair, 17" **$425.00**

Alice in Wonderland doll, Madame Alexander's character child, composition head, marked "Mme Alexander" on back of head, "by Madame Alexander, N.Y., All Rights Reserved" on dress tag, hazel sleep eyes w/real lashes, feathered brows, eye shadow, painted lower lashes, closed mouth, original human-hair wig, five-piece composition child body dressed in original blue & white print dress, white organdy pinafore, underclothing, socks & black snap shoes, 18" (unplayed-with condition in original box)............**775.00**

Alice in Wonderland tray, glass, advertising Rexall, 1966 ....**35.00**

Baba Looey (Quick Draw McGraw) bank, vinyl..................**35.00**

Barney Google & Spark Plug dolls, wood & cloth, Barney w/a wooden head, large painted black & white eyes, single stroke brows, painted mustache, wooden ears, painted hair, wooden body jointed at shoulders & hips & wearing his original white shirt, black & white checked pants, black felt jacket & wooden hat, Spark Plug w/a jointed wooden body, painted facial features & replaced leather ears, Schoenhut, early 20th c., Barney 7¾" h., Spark Plug 9", pr. (some wear)........**1,035.00**

Brownie Fireplace Andiron

Brownie fireplace andirons, cast iron, cast in the half-round w/a seated Brownie sitting cross-legged on a waisted pedestal w/hands on thighs, wearing a stocking cap, a short fitted jacket & pants, early 20th c., 18¼" h., pr. (ILLUS. of one) **287.00**

Brownie nodders, papier-mâché & wood, modeled after Palmer Cox's Chinaman, Dude & Policeman, Germany, late 19th c., 11", 11 3/8" & 11 1/2" h., set of 3 (scattered paint chipping, damage to lower edge of one head) **3,450.00**

Brownie sketch, pen & ink, by Palmer Cox, a waist-length sketch of the Scotsman Brownie within a circle, signed "Palmer Cox" & dated "New York Jan. 27th 1893," 2¼ x 3⅝" **230.00**

Buster Brown Match Holder

Early Buster Brown Rug

Buster Brown match holder,
wall hanging-type, lithographed
tin, long rectangular plate w/an
arched top w/hanging hole
above a colored scene of Buster
serving bread to his friends
w/advertising for "Buster Brown
Bread," a rectangular match
compartment at the bottom,
paint loss, cracking & fading,
2" w., 7" h. (ILLUS.) **440.00**

Buster Brown pinback button,
advertising "Buster Brown
Bread," shows Buster Brown
holding a dripping paint brush &
Tige standing in front of sign
"Resolved - that the - Best
Bre(a)d - People eat - Buster -
Brown - Bread," done in black,
brown, green & yellow, 1 1/2" d.
(minor scratches).......................**28.00**

Buster Brown rug, machine-
woven, round w/a narrow blue
outer border band w/gold stars
around a golden yellow center
w/large bust portraits of Buster
Brown & Tige in red, white, blue,
gold, tan & brown, soiling & red
stain, some binding loose, early
20th c., 47" d. (ILLUS) **413.00**

**Campbell's Soup Kids trolley
advertisement,** lithographed
cardboard, long rectangular sign
w/a dark green background
printed at one end w/a red &
white can of soup & at the
opposite end w/the standing
figure of a Campbell Soup girl
wiping her hands on her apron,
soup advertising down the
center, self-framed, touch-up
down center & around edges,
13 x 23" (ILLUS. next page) **83.00**

Casper, the Friendly Ghost
lampshade, w/illustrations of
Casper & Friends **45.00**

Charlie McCarthy doll,
composition shoulder head,
painted brown eyes w/red liner,
multi-stroke brows, painted
upper & lower lashes, accented
nostrils, open mouth w/ten lower
teeth painted on lower jaw, pink
cloth body w/composition hands
& feet, stitch-jointed at
shoulders, hips & knees, original
tuxedo, white shirt, tie, vest,
black pants & jacket w/tails, top
hat, marked "Edgar Bergens
Charlie McCarthy, An Effanbee
Product" on back shoulder
plate, 20" **525.00**

Campbell Soup Kids Trolley ad

Charlie McCarthy pin, black & white enamel w/movable mouth & ocular, made under exclusive license from Edgar Bergen & Charlie McCarthy (some enamel loss) **316.00**

Danny O'Day Ventriloquist Dummy

Danny O'Day ventriloquist dummy, plastic head & hands, stuffed-cloth body, wearing tan suit, white shirt w/bow tie &

black & white tennis shoes, marked "Juro Novelty Co., Inc., 1964," w/instruction pamphlet, wear to pamphlet, repair to pants, 30" h. (ILLUS.) **182.00**

Flash Gordon coloring book, 1952 ....**100.00**

Jerry (Tom & Jerry) game, "Throw the Ball," wood **75.00**

Krazy Cat Cloth Doll

Krazy Cat doll, cloth, black velveteen w/black felt ears, white face & hands & yellow felt boots, printed information on soles of boots, Knickerbocker, ca. 1930, 10½" h. (ILLUS.) **1,265.00**

Li'l Abner bank, tin, lithographed, 1953 ....**135.00**

Maggie (Maggie & Jiggs) doll, all-wood, jointed, wearing a cotton floral print blouse & plain skirt, Schoenhut, ca. 1924, 9¼" h. (rolling pin missing, needs restringing).....................**316.00**

Maggie & Jiggs Statue

Maggie & Jiggs (Bringing Up Father comics) statue, chalkware, the couple posing in front of a tree, colorful trim, names molded on front of base, soiling, small chips, touch-up to faces, repair to Jiggs' nose & mouth, ca. 1920s, 12½" h. (ILLUS.) **121.00**

Olive Oyl doll, cloth head w/oilcloth mask face, oversized painted black eyes, single-stroke brows, closed smiling mouth, original mohair wig, unjointed cloth body w/mitten hands, oversized plum colored cloth feet, attached green knit socks, dark green knit sweater, red

shirt w/white strip panties, small yellow felt bonnet w/black ribbon ties, marked "This Is An Original Comic Strip Doll...that all America Loves" on front of paper tag, "Copyright King Features Syndicate Inc., Manufactured and Distributed Exclusively by Columbia Toy Products, Kansas City, Missouri" inside tag, 17"............................**200.00**

Orphan Annie stove, metal, 1930s...**75.00**

Popeye doll, cloth head w/molded cloth mask face, painted blue left eye, right eye closed in wink, single-stroke brows, open-closed mouth w/red wooden pipe, applied ears, unjointed cloth body, pink cloth arms w/mitten hands, oversized purple feet, original red, white & purple striped shirt w/purple felt collar & cuffs at sleeves, blue pants, white hat, marked "This Is An Original Comic Strip Doll...that all America Loves" on front of paper tag, "Copyright King Features Syndicate Inc., Manufactured and Distributed Exclusively by Columbia Toy Products, Kansas City, Missouri" inside tag, 17"............................**250.00**

Popeye toy, battery-operated, Popeye in Rowboat, w/cord & battery control box, w/colorfully lithographed original box, Line Mar, Japan **9,900.00**

Popeye toy, pull-type, "Popeye Spinach Eater," lithographed paper on wood, No. 488, 1939, 9½" h., 8½" l. (paper loss to arms) **230.00**

Popeye toy, windup-tin, Popeye Walker, colorful color decoration, w/key, Chein, overall touch-up, soiling, paint chipping, 6" h. (ILLUS. top next page) **275.00**

Popeye toy, windup tin, Popeye Walker w/Parrot Cages, colorful decoration, Marx Toy Co., King

Popeye Windup Walker Toy

Swee'pea doll, cloth head w/molded mask face, large painted eyes, single-stroke brows, closed smiling mouth to one side, applied felt ears, unjointed cloth body in sitting position, mitten hands, original red baby sleeper w/no opening at feet, trimmed w/white lace at neck & sleeves, pale yellow bonnet w/lace trim, bright yellow ribbon ties, marked "This Is An Original Comic Strip Doll...that all America Loves" on front of paper tag, "Copyright King Features Syndicate Inc., Manufactured and Distributed Exclusively by Columbia Toy Products, Kansas City, Missouri" inside tag, 14".............................**250.00**

Tom & Jerry jewelry box, wood, w/inside mirror, Spain, 1957........**85.00**

CHRISTMAS COLLECTIBLES

Green Tree with Candleholders

Popeye with Parrot Cages Toy

Features Syndicate mark, w/key, 1930s, scratches & soiling, 8¼" h. (ILLUS.)..........................**385.00**

Christmas collecting is extremely popular today, with both old and new Christmas-related pieces being sought by collectors around the country. In the following listing we present a selection of old and scarce Christmas collectibles which are especially desirable and can sometimes be quite expensive.

Artificial & Feather Trees

Tree, blue w/candleholders, square white base, 46" **$425.00**

Tree, green w/red berries, in round white base, 12" **125.00**

Tree, green w/candleholders, square white base, 24" (ILLUS.) ..**250.00**

Candy Containers

Angel, w/bisque doll face w/paperweight eyes & blond mohair wig, German **7,150.00**

Boot, papier-mâché, German........**30.00**

Cornucopia, paper, gold foiled cone...**85.00**

Egg, silk over pressed cardboard **150.00**

Santa in car, celluloid head, cardboard car w/wheels **200.00**

Santa, papier-mâché, slightly-stooped Santa wearing grey suit of plush cloth, 15½" h. **2,860.00**

Santa, papier-mâché, Santa is wearing traditional red robe w/white trim, Germany, 22"h. ..**2,420.00**

Paper Ornaments

Angels, w/tinsel holder, 3"............**15.00**

Miss Liberty, tinsel & cellophane **125.00**

Santa, full-bodied, riding sled (ILLUS., top next page, right) **60.00**

Star w/a scrap angel, tinsel trim, 6" (ILLUS., top next page, left) **40.00**

Dresden Paper Ornaments

Banjo, three-dimensional, 3".......**160.00**

Fox, brown & tan, three-dimensional, 2" **350.00**

Heart, gold, three-dimensional, 3" **85.00**

Jockey on horse, three-dimensional, 3" **525.00**

Santa on Donkey Candy Box

Parrot Ornament

Santa on Donkey, candy box (ILLUS.) **175.00**

Parrot, gold, three-dimensional (ILLUS.) **120.00**

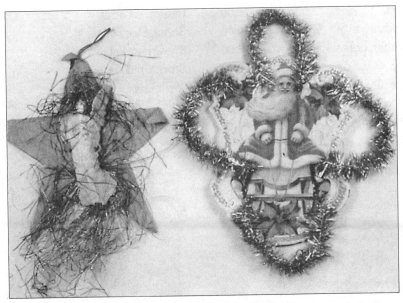

Angel and Santa Ornaments

Pig, gold, three-dimensional,
2" **500.00**

Star, gold, flat, 3" **65.00**

Spun-Glass Ornaments

Angel, paper on clip, w/spun
glass wings..............................**275.00**

Peacock, flat, elaborately
painted, 5" **175.00**

Santa, in circle w/comet tail, 8"....**110.00**

Wax & Waxed Ornaments

Angel, American, ca. 1940s, 4".....**15.00**

Angel, wax, 6" **175.00**

Bird, in metal circle, 5" **220.00**

Soldier, American, ca.
1940s, 4" **15.00**

Pressed Cotton Ornaments

Victorian Boy

Victorian boy, in circle, 5"
(ILLUS.) **40.00**

Victorian Lady

Bell, blue, 3" 25.00

Cow, brass bell, 4"......................170.00

Cucumber, green & yellow, 4" 75.00

Jockey, w/horse head, 4"...........450.00

Orange, 3".....................................65.00

Sailer, w/cap, 4" 300.00

Victorian lady, 3" (ILLUS.)..........170.00

Glass Ornaments
Al Jolsen head, 3¼" 375.00

Automobile and Zeppelin

Automobile, red & silver, 3"
 (ILLUS.) 85.00

Bear, 3".......................................175.00

Bird, owl, standing on clip, 4" 115.00

Bird, game pheasent, 4".............250.00

Boy, whistling, w/hat & scarf, 4" 95.00

Cat, w/fiddle & cap, 3" 225.00

Christ Child head, 3"..................165.00

Devil head, gold, 4"....................425.00

Elephant, 4" 75.00

Fantasy ornament, bells 85.00

Father Christmas, early, 5" 125.00

Frog, on toadstool, 3" 65.00

Horn, silver w/flowers, 4"..............15.00

Indian head, on clip, 2" 195.00

Kite, chenille string, 3"................450.00

Kugel, pear shaped, silver, 3" 200.00

Los Angeles zeppelin, paper
 label, 4" (ILLUS., bottom) 295.00

Mrs. Santa Claus, 4"..................445.00

Pear, matte finish, 4" 45.00

Rabbit, w/carrot, 4".......................45.00

Santa, blue w/tree, 4" 30.00

Snowman, w/broom 4".................25.00

Storks, mother & baby, on
 clip, 5"......................................185.00

Uncle Sam, full-figure, 3" 450.00

Witch, w/cat & broom, 4".............525.00

Italian Glass Ornaments

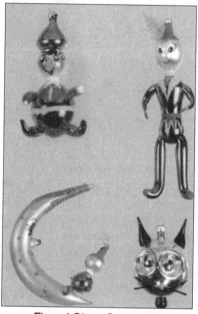

Figural Glass Ornaments

Cat head, 3" (ILLUS., bottom
 right) 50.00

Elf, seated, 6" (ILLUS., top left) 50.00

Man in Moon, 4" (ILLUS., bottom
 left) 75.00

Robin Hood, 6" (ILLUS., top
 right) 85.00

Early Lighting Devices
Candleholder, counterbalance,
 w/clay ball at bottom 15.00

Candleholder, pinch-on, lithographed w/Father Christmas 150.00

Christmas light, quilted milk
 glass 65.00

Christmas light, glass, cranberry **225.00**

Lantern, metal w/glass panels, six-sided **65.00**

Reflector, tin, American **3.00**

Electric Light Bulbs

Aviator, milk glass, boy w/airplane **40.00**

Bird, brown, early European **35.00**

Bubble light, oil, working **50.00**

Bubble light, shooting stars........**100.00**

Clown head, milk glass.................**25.00**

Dick Tracy, milk glass...................**85.00**

Humpty Dumpty, milk glass, large head **35.00**

Pig, w/bowtie, milk glass **65.00**

Rose, clear glass, small, Japan.....**10.00**

St. Nicholas, clear glass, early European....................................**90.00**

Woman in shoe, milk glass **45.00**

Boxed set, glass, Mother Goose characters...............................**190.00**

Santa Figures

Papier-mâché Santa Figures

Belsnickel, red, w/feather branch, 7" (ILLUS., center)........**350.00**

Belsnickel, white, w/feather branch, 11" (ILLUS., right).........**650.00**

Belsnickel, blue, w/feather branch, 12" (ILLUS., left) **725.00**

Celluloid, painted details, Irwin, 12"..................................**250.00**

Cotton, w/paper face, 6" **150.00**

Japan, chenille body over cardboard composition face, 9"..**350.00**

Plaster, in chimney, American, 10" **185.00**

Postcards

Real photo, Santa w/children........**60.00**

Santa riding in train, w/children ...**30.00**

Silk, Santa standing w/sack of toys..**45.00**

Christmas Advertising

Button, celluloid, Santa w/stocking..................................**70.00**

Calendar top, blue Santa w/children **95.00**

Cigar box, Santa w/toys inside cover..**95.00**

Coca-Cola, standing Santa, ca. 1930s...**175.00**

Lion Coffee, Santa w/children chromo **185.00**

Soap box, Fairbank's **400.00**

Greeting Cards

Father Christmas Fold-Out

Fold-out, two-layer, Father Christmas (ILLUS.).....................**70.00**

Cookie Molds, Candy Molds, & Cookie Cutters

Christmas tree, candy mold **45.00**

Santa on Donkey, candy mold,
two-part **225.00**

Games, Puzzles, & Toys

Santa on top of house, 9" **300.00**

Jigsaw puzzle, lantern, Santa
head, American **200.00**

Display, mechanical,
lithographed cardboard & wood,
shows purple-robed Santa
pulling a jumping jack toy from
his bag while three children
look on **7,150.00**

Rolly polly, Santa,
Schoenhut, 7" **850.00**

Wind-up, celluloid Santa, Japan ...**95.00**

Putz (Natvitiy) Related Materials

Animals, wood, assorted,
German **45.00**

Deer, celluloid, Japan, 6" **25.00**

Sheep, composition head, wool
body, 4" **85.00**

Trees, brush, small, Japan **5.00**

Trees, sponge, large Japan...........**12.00**

Miscellaneous Christmas Items

Beaded chains, glass,
German, 12" **15.00**

Handkercheif, family decorating
tree **225.00**

Mask, papier-mâché, early 1900s,
German **350.00**

Snow Baby figure, china, riding
polar bear **225.00**

Tinsel, lead, National Tinsel..........**15.00**

Tree stand, cast iron, Santa
molded on both sides,
Germany...................................**225.00**

Tree stand, wind-up, revolving,
musical, early 1900s, German...**550.00**

CLOCKS

E. Howard Banjo Clock

Banjo clock, wall-type, E. Howard and Co., Boston, Massachusetts, grain-pained case resembling rosewood, the round top w/a glazed door & brass bezel opening to a dial w/Roman numerals above a long slender tapering waist w/an inset eglomisé glazed panel above the rectangular an eglomisé glazed lower section w/curved sides, each glass panel w/maroon & black geometric designs, weight-driven movement, minor imperfections, mid-19th c., 28 ½" h. (ILLUS.) **$1,725.00**

Bracket clock, England, ornate carved oak case, a flat rectangular top over domed sides & a molded cornice above an arched frieze band flanked by carved lion heads above an arched glazed door framed by delicate carved scrolls opening to a large dial w/Roman

Ornate English Bracket

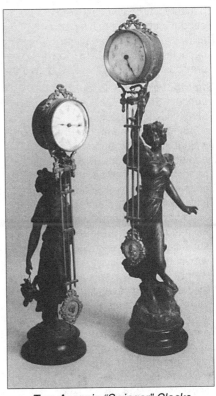

Two Ansonia "Swinger" Clocks

numerals below three small
chapter dials all surrounded by
ornate gilt scrolling, the dials
flanked by carved pilasters
headed by grotesque heads
over leaf bands over florals
above a gadroon-carved mid-
molding over an inset carved
band above the stepped-out
plinth base, springwound triple-
train movement striking
Westminster chimes each
quarter hour on five coil
resonators or "Eight Bell
Chimes" on a nest of eight bells
in graduated sizes, signed
"Peerless" & numbered
"104271," complete w/key &
pendulum, 19th c., 22¼" h.
(ILLUS.) **3,750.00**

Carriage clock, retailed by
Tiffany & Co., New York, New
York, quarter striking-type, brass
case w/handle, dial w/Arabic
numerals above second dial,
striking on two gongs, w/alarm,
6" h. **1,035.00**

Figural "swinger" clock,
Ansonia Clock Co., Connecticut,
a cast-metal bronzed standing
figure of an Art Nouveau-style
maiden in a flowing gown
standing on a rocky outcrop &
holding aloft the round
clockworks w/a round dial
w/Arabic numerals above the
long brass pendulum drop w/a
cast brass pendulum bob w/a
mask portrait, all raised on a
waisted plinth base, late 19th c.
(ILLUS., right) **1,980.00**

Figural "swinger" clock,
Ansonia Clock Co., Connecticut,
a cast metal standing figure of a
maiden looking down, holding
her shoes in one hand w/her
other arm raised above her head
holding the clock's movement
w/a round dial w/Roman
numerals above the long brass

pendulum drop w/a cast brass pendulum bob w/a mask portrait, all raised on a waisted plinth base, late 19th c. (ILLUS., top previous page, left) **2,310.00**

Grandfather, Henry Elliott, London, England, William & Mary style case decorated w/ornate seaweed marquetry walnut, the high stepped & domed pediment above a glazed panel flanked by small colonettes flanking the twelve-inch square brass dial w/silvered chapter ring, matte center, Roman numerals & three subsidiary dials, the spandrels w/putti masks & foliage, signed "Henry Elliott, Londoni Fecit," the tall waisted case w/raised molding in the center w/an oval small window to show the pendulum, stepped out lower case on a plinth base, the six-pillar three-train musical movement w/anchor escapement, striking a nest of eight & a single bell on the quarter hour, the hood & case w/ornate panels of marquetry, late 17th c., 7' 8 ½" h. (case restored, movement possibly associated) **10,925.00**

Grandfather, A. Kennedy Miller, Elizabethtown, New Jersey, Federal inlaid mahogany case, the broken-scroll swan's-neck hood centering three brass ball-and-steeple brass finials, the arched glazed door below opening to a white-painted dial w/Roman numerals, second register & calendar date mechanism, the spandrels & top w/painted classical designs, the dial flanked by small free-standing colonettes, the tall waisted case w/a fan-inlay at the top of the long door over a long beaded inlay oval & lower corner inlaid quarter-fans all flanked by fluted quarter-round columns,

New Jersey Federal Grandfather Clock

the stepped-out base also inlaid w/corner quarter-fans & a central beaded oval, scroll-cut bracket feet, ca. 1800, feet replaced, some repairs to cornice, 9 ½ x 18¼", 8' 2" h. (ILLUS.) **5,750.00**

Grandfather, Stickley Brothers, Mission-style oak case, the rectangular top w/low widely canted cornice overhangs the tall rectangular case two doors, the short upper glazed door opening to the copper dial w/raised Arabic numerals & scrolling brass spandrels, the lower tall door w/a slightly arched glazed panel opening to the weights & large brass pendulum bob, raised on short stile legs w/scalloped toe-boards, original medium-dark finish, unmarked, early 20th c., 15 x 26", 6' 8" h. (ILLUS. top next page) **5,225.00**

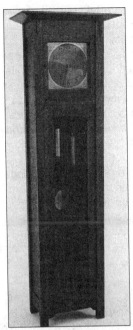

Stickley Brothers Grandfather Clock

Grandfather, Seth Thomas, Thomaston, Connecticut, Arts & Crafts style oak case, the hood w/a down-curved rectangular top w/chamfered ears above slightly incurved sides flanking a door w/a round opening over the metal dial w/raised brass Arabic numerals above a flat, flaring shoulder molding above the tall gently swelled tall case w/a small slender glazed door, on low curved bracket feet, original dark finish, works signed, case unsigned but numbered, early 20th c., 12 x 21 ½", 6' 4 ½" h. (ILLUS. bottom previous column).................................**2,630.00**

Aaron Willard Grandfather Clock

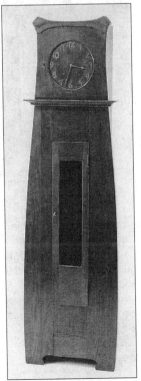

Arts & Crafts Grandfather Clock

Grandfather, Aaron Willard, Boston, Massachusetts, Federal inlaid mahogany case, the arched hood w/pierced fretwork & three slender blocks surmounted by brass ball-and-steeple finials, the hinged arched glazed door below opening to a white-painted dial w/second registers & mounted w/a polychrome-painted rocking ship against a seascape, centering the inscription "Aaron Willard, Boston," the tall waisted case w/a long hinged inlaid door flanked by brass stop-fluted quarter columns, the stepped-out base centering a circular satinwood inlay, shaped apron & slender bracket feet, ca. 1805, 9 1/8 x 19", 8' 7 ½" h (ILLUS. previous page) **31,050.00**

Lantern clock, Charles II period, Nicholas Coxeter, London, England, brass case of typical domed form w/turned finials & brass straps enclosing a bell, w/three pierced crests, the applied chapter ring w/Roman numerals, the center etched w/foliage & signed "Nicholas Coxeter at Ye 3 Chaires in Sothbury, Londini Fecit," w/a single steel hand, the sides w/hinged doors fitted w/wing-shaped projections to accommodate the anchor-shaped pendulum, on brass ball feet, ca. 1660, 6¼" w., 16 ½" h. **4,887.00**

Late Federal 'Acorn' Clock

Shelf or mantel clock, acorn-style Federal case, laminated mahogany & eglomisé, the inverted acorn-shaped top w/a hinged door opening to a white-painted dial w/Roman numerals above a lower deeply waisted case w/a conforming eglomisé glazed panel decorated w/ornate colorful flowers & leaves below a star design, the whole case flanked by slender conforming laminated uprights w/acorn-carved finials, raised on a stepped plinth base, probably Connecticut, ca. 1835, 5 x 14¾", 24 ½" h.(ILLUS. bottom previous column).................................**1,092.00**

Ansonia Mantel Clock

Shelf or mantel clock, Ansonia Clock Company, Connecticut, bronze & glass case, the upright rectangular case w/ornate gilded bronze scrolls at the top & bottom front corners & feet framing the beveled glass sides, round white enameled dial w/Roman numerals w/a brass rhinestone-studded bezel & pendulum, 6 ½ x 7¼", 11¼" h. (ILLUS.) **500.00**

Shelf or mantel clock, Ansonia Clock Company, Connecticut, china case, decorated w/green borders & a cascade of red flowers at sides, 14" l., 11 ½" h. **550.00**

Eiffel Tower Novelty Clock

Shelf or mantel, French novelty clock, parcel-gilt metal, cast in the form of the Eiffel Tower in Paris, the drum case set within the framework, inscribed "Medaille d'Argent, Vincenti, 1855," ca. 1910, 25 ½" h. (ILLUS.) **2,300.00**

Shelf or mantel, Silas Hoadley, Plymouth, Connecticut, Classical style case of carved mahogany veneer, the pediment w/a flat-carved & paint-decorated spread-winged eagle between corner blocks w/carved pineapple finials, the tall rectangular case w/quarter-round side columns flanking the tall two-panel glazed door, the upper panel over the dial

w/Arabic numerals & scroll-decorated spandrels, the lower panel w/a large lakeside landscape w/a large white house to the left, a diamond-form inlaid keyhole escutcheon, on a molded flat base raised on leaf-carved paw front feet, old finish, ca. 1825, 12 x 26¾" (restoration) **1,840.00**

Mills Empire Style Clock

Shelf or mantel, J.B. Mills & Co., New York, New York, Empire style painted & decorated case, the rectangular narrow top w/a cove molding over corner blocks & free-standing columns to lower blocks all flanking the two-panel glazed door, the lower half decorated w/a painted lyre & leaves, the clear upper panel over the white paper dial inscribed "J.B. Mills & Co., New York, A.D. Crane's Patent" within floral spandrels, the ogee shaped front base on a rectangular plinth base, decorated overall in tones of black, yellow & red simulating marble, ca. 1840, 7 x 14", 22¼" h. (ILLUS.) **805.00**

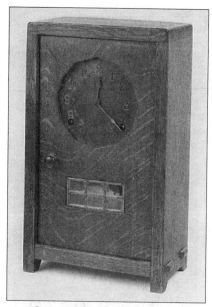

Gustav Stickley Mantel Clock

Shelf or mantel, Gustav Stickley, New Jersey, Mission-style oak case, rectangular upright case w/machine-dovetailed top above a door w/a paneled rounded glazed opening over the metal dial w/Arabic numerals, a small rectangular six-pane leaded glass panel & small knob, flat bottom w/through-tenons, brass pendulum w/Seth Thomas movement, original finish, branded Gustav Stickley signature on the back, early 20th c., 5 x 8 ½", 14" h. (ILLUS.) **6,600.00**

Shelf or mantel, probably Eli Terry, Plymouth, Connecticut, 'box'-style w/a rectangular mahogany case w/a single glazed door opening to a dial w/Arabic numerals & leafy-scroll decorated spandrels w/a spread-winged eagle in the center, the lower door w/a eglomisé scenic panel, old refinish, early 19th c., 14 x 19 3/4" (imperfections, flaking to eglomisé panel) **7,475.00**

Terry 'Pillar & Scroll' Clock

Shelf or mantel, Eli Terry, Plymouth, Connecticut, Federal 'pillar & scroll' style, mahogany & mahogany veneer case w/a broken-scroll pediment centered by a brass urn finial & flanked by matching corner finials above slender colonettes flanking the tall two-panel glazed door, the larger upper panel over the white-painted dial w/Arabic numerals & painted scrolling spandrels w/an American eagle w/shield in the center, the shorter lower panel lithographed cottage scene above an inscription, on a molded base on small bracket feet, round metal door pull, paper label inside, imperfections, early 19th c., 4 3/4 x 17¼", 31 ½" h. (ILLUS.) **2,415.00**

Shelf or mantel, Eli Terry & Son, Connecticut, Federal 'pillar & scroll'-style, mahogany case w/a broken-scroll pediment centered by a brass urn finial & flanked by matching corner finials above slender colonettes flanking the tall two-panel glazed door, the tall upper panel over the painted dial w/Roman numerals & decorated spandrels & the lower panel w/a worn eglomisé landscape scene, ivory diamond-form inlaid keyhole escutcheon, on a molded base w/a scalloped apron & slender French feet, ca. 1830, 17 ½ x 32" (imperfections including foot repairs)..............**1,495.00**

Wall clock, Abiel Chandler, Concord, New Hampshire, Classical-style, ebonized & giltwood frame, the rectangular frame w/ring- and rod-turned split balusters at the sides, top & base joined by corner blocks w/embossed rosettes, the top section w/a rectangular tablet w/red, silver, green & gold leaf-stenciled design around the round iron dial painted white w/black Roman numerals & inscribed "A. Chandler," the lower section enclosing a rectangular mirror plate, the clock w/an eight-day weight-driven brass movement, w/original paper label on the back, ca. 1830.............**11,500.00**

COCA-COLA ITEMS

Coca-Cola promotion has been achieved through the issuance of scores of small objects through the years. These, together with trays, signs, and other articles bearing the name of this soft drink, are now sought by many collectors.

Advertisement, paper w/wood frame, depicts man & woman in sidewalk garden drinking Coca-Cola, 13½" w., 17½" h. **$28.00**

Advertisement, paper w/gesso frame, signed "Henry Hunt," very minor soiling, minor crack to gesso, 23" w., 27" h. (ILLUS. top next column) **28.00**

Coca-Cola Framed Advertisement

Book, "Classic Cooking w/ Coca-Cola" **5.00**

Bottle cap, cork-lined, 1930s **3.00**

Bottle case, red, original wooden twenty-four slot shadow box type, complete & sturdy **25.00**

Bottle case, yellow, original wooden twenty-four slot shadow box type, complete & sturdy **30.00**

Bottle opener, wall-type, cast iron, marked "Starr X," 1925, 2¾" w., 4¼" h. **55.00**

Bottle opener, metal, Coke bottle-shaped, marked "Drink - Coca-Cola - Schutzmarke," 3" l. (minor wear & rust) **22.00**

Bottle opener, metal, reads "Drink - Coca-Cola" across top in raised lettering, 2¾" w., 3¼" h. (scratches, soiling, rust) **55.00**

Bottle, 1940, glass, embossed........**8.00**

Bottle, Geo. Bulldogs Champion-ship, ca. 1980 (slight rust on cap) **80.00**

Calendar, 1918, depicts lady in oval holding drink w/calendar beneath, wooden frame, 10 5/8" w., 13" h. (calendar pad missing, creases & soiling) **176.00**

Calendar, 1925, depicts girl at party draped in white fur w/turban-type wrap on head & holding glass of cola in toast-like position, reads "The typical American girl finds it delicious and refreshing as you will," full pad & cover page **2,750.00**

Calendar, 1933, marked "Coca-Cola" w/"The Village Blacksmith," poem by Henry Wadsworth Longfellow at bottom, 12" w., 25" h. (crease, soiling, edge tears & repairs).....**330.00**

Cards, Airplane Spotter, no envelopes, ca. 1940s, full set of 20................................**1,100.00**

Charm bracelet, NFL, four-charm, 1960s............................**60.00**

Coca-Cola Wall Clock

Clock, wall-type, tin, round, red center reads "Drink Coca-Cola," black dial w/gold numbering, back stamped & dated "Feb. 1954," works, scratches overall, 17½" d. (ILLUS.).......................**143.00**

Clock, wall-type, round, glass & metal, reads "Drink Coca-Cola" in red dial, working condition, ca. 1950s, 14 5/8" d. (minor yellowing) **605.00**

Clock, wall-type, painted metal & wood, electric, reads "Coca-Cola" on center dial, 36" w, 18" h. (scratches, soiling & paint chipping) **440.00**

Clock, wall-type, electric, rectangular, glass front metal face w/wood body, wear to

wood, not working, ca. 1939, 16" w., 16" h. **385.00**

Clock, wall-type, neon lighted, in metal frame, reads "Drink Coca-Cola" in circle, ca. 1942.............**900.00**

Cooler, chest-type, hinged lift off top w/room for crate storage underneath, late 1930s, 24 x 30 x 34"...........................**600.00**

Cooler, chest-type w/handle, metal, marked "Progress Refrigerator Co. Louisville, KY. Pat. 20265336," 8½" deep, 8½" w., 11½" h. (minor paint chips & scratches) **222.00**

Wooden Coca-Cola Cooler

Cooler, wood w/tin sides, scratches & soiling to sides, missing top, small rust spot on edge of one sign, ca. late 1920s, 32" w., 21¼" deep, 29" h. (ILLUS.) **1,870.00**

Dispenser, metal, red soda container w/cream embossed lettering reading " Drink - Coca-Cola," 19" deep, 8½" w., 22" h. **468.00**

Dispenser rack, metal, reads "Coca-Cola - Take home a carton - 25¢," 16½" w., 17" deep, 57½" h. **303.00**

Door push, porcelain w/iron sides, reads "R.J. Dewes Dallas Tex. U.S. Pat. No. 1928149," 34" l., 4" h. (chipping at edges & soiling) **770.00**

Game, Bingo, 1940s **50.00**

Gum jar original lid, Pepsin embossed, (small non-visible crack in bottom) **550.00**

Invitation, party-type, 1950s **8.00**

Knife, pocket-type, 1933 Chicago World's Fair, red metal on white pearlized ground, 2¾" l. (minor rust) **121.00**

Match striker, porcelain, marked "Drink - Coca-Cola - Strike Matches Here" on red ground above striking surface, 4½ x 4½" (chipping at edges & scratches) **275.00**

Menu board, wall-type, plastic & metal, lighted electric, 21½" w., 21½" h. (scratches, soiling & minor wear) **165.00**

Pin, Olympic, 1984 .... **4.00**

Sign, die-cut metal, reads "Drink - Coca-Cola," marked "A.A.W-12-40," 24" w., 20" h. **935.00**

Sign, dispenser-type, two-sided porcelain w/metal frame, reads "Drink - Coca-Cola - Ice Cold," 27" w., 28" h. (chipping to edges, fading, soiling) **935.00**

Sign, figural, "Policeman" crossing guard sign, 1950s, 30½" w., 5'¾" h. **2,500.00**

Sign, metal, "fishtail"-style, painted red w/white lettering "Coca-Cola," 12¼ x 26¼" **275.00**

Sign, metal, button-shaped, reads "Sign of good taste," 18" d. **195.00**

Sign, metal, button-shaped, marked "Drink - Coca-Cola," Canada, ca. 1955, 48" d. (chip to "a" in "Cola") **281.00**

Sign, metal, button-shaped, convex, marked "Coca-Cola" over bottle & "AM-51," 36" d. **302.00**

Sign, metal, reads "Drink - Coca-Cola - Take Home - A Carton," Canada, ca. 1950, 35" w., 53" h. **825.00**

Coca-Cola Neon Sign

Sign, neon & porcelain, original face, new housing, very minor touch up to porcelain, 8" deep, 86" w., 58" h. (ILLUS.) **3,850.00**

Porcelain Coca-Cola Sign

Sign, porcelain, reads "Drink - Coca-Cola - Ice Cold" on dispenser picture, some scratches, 27" w., 28" h. (ILLUS.) **2,090.00**

Sign, porcelain, flange-type, reads "Iced - Coca-Cola - Here," 18" w., 20" h. (minor chips)........ **770.00**

Sign, porcelain, button-shaped, marked "Coca-Cola" over bottle, 23½" d. **660.00**

Sign, porcelain, rectangular, white w/thin green stripes & green "fishtail" logo, 16 x 43½" (chips to edges) **198.00**

Fountain Coca-Cola Sign

Sign, porcelain, rectangular, scratches & chip to "I" in "Fountain," 28" w., 11¾" h. (ILLUS.) **550.00**

Sign, porcelain, rectangular, marked "Drink - Coca-Cola - Ice Cold," 28" w., 20" h. (chipping to edges & mounting holes)...........**495.00**

Sign, porcelain, marked "Made in Canada P&M 49," chipping & touch-up to edges & mounting holes, 58" w., 27½" h.................**495.00**

Sign, tin, Miss Betty, 1941, 20 x 28" **450.00**

Sign, tin, rectangular, top half painted red w/bottom pointing down towards Coke bottle on white ground, top reads "Drink - Coca-Cola" above the bottle, all above "Refresh," 18 x 53½" (minor scratches, some dents) ..**275.00**

Sign, embossed tin, reads "Drink - Coca-Cola," Dasco, 17¾" w., 5¾" h. **187.00**

Thermometer, glass & metal, round, reads "Drink - Coca-Cola - Sign of Good Taste," marked "495 A," 12" d. (scratches to glass) **132.00**

Thermometer, round, white letters read "Drink - Coca-Cola - In Bottles," 12" d. (surface rust, minor soiling) **110.00**

Thermometer, porcelain, oblong, "Thirst knows no season", over silhouette of lady drinking from bottle some touch-up & scratches, 6" w., 18" h. (ILLUS. top next column)........................**468.00**

Thermometer, tin, bottle-shaped, reads "Coca-Cola - Trade Mark Registered," 5½" w., 17" h.

Coca-Cola Thermometer

(denting, paint chipping & scratches) **83.00**

Thermometer, embossed tin, oval-shape w/Coca-Cola bottle in center, marked "Bottle Pat's. Dec. 25, 1923" on bottle, 6¾" w., 16" h. (minor chipping) **176.00**

Trade card, metamorphic, full color image of woman in bath tub w/knees above tub rim, open it shows waitress serving two bald-headed men, ca. 1892, 3½ x 6¼" closed, 5½ x 6¼" open **800.00**

Tray, 1909, oval, St. Louis Fair, 13½ x 16½" **1,500.00**

Tray, 1931, Farm Boy w/Dog by Norman Rockwell **1,100.00**

Tray, 1937, Running Girl, blonde woman in swimwear running on beach w/a Coca-Cola in each hand and a white cape flowing off her back, American Art Works, Inc., Coshocton, Ohio **200.00**

Tray, 1938, Girl in the Afternoon, in yellow dress & large flaring hat sitting w/bottle of Coca-Cola

in hand, American Art Works,
Inc., Coshoctin, Ohio **250.00**

Tray, 1939, Springboard girl,
artwork by Haddon Sundblom,
American Art Works, Inc............**350.00**

1942 Coca-Cola Tray

Tray, 1942, painted metal, depicts
two girls by vehicle drinking
Coca-Cola, scratches, paint
chipping & minor rust,
10½" w.,13" h. (ILLUS.) **138.00**

Tray, 1956, TV Tray Assortment,
relish tray, fruit and Coca-Cola
bottles, 13½ x 18¾".....................**25.00**

Tray, tip, 1913, Hamilton King Girl
in a picture hat holding
a glass **220.00**

Tray, tip, 1914, depicts "Betty" in
white bonnet w/pink flowers,
bow & sash..............................**200.00**

Tumbler glass, Safety Driving
Award, 1950s, 8 oz.....................**55.00**

Vending machine, "Vendo 23,"
working (good condition) **1,250.00**

Vending machine, "Vendo 44,"
completely restored, 16" w., 19"
deep, 4' 10¼" h......................**2,640.00**

COFFEE GRINDERS

PRIMITIVE COFFEE GRINDERS
Box mill, w/brass hopper &
drawer front **$110.00**

Adams Iron Mill

Iron mill, mounted on wooden
handle, signed "ADAMS," 14" l.
(ILLUS.) **120.00**

Iron mill, post-mounted
blacksmith's-type 5" open
hopper **150.00**

SIDE MILLS

Wilson Side Mill

Side mill, w/wood back, "H.
Wilson's Improved Patent Mill"
(ILLUS.) **80.00**

Side mill, w/wood block, marked
"L&S Brighton"............................**60.00**

Side mill, iron, double grinding
gear, Parker Union, unmarked ..**100.00**

BOX MILLS
Box mill, tall wood box w/side
handle & well marked label "Sun
No. 1080," 6½ x 6½" top
(ILLUS. top next page) **100.00**

Box mill, curly maple, tin &
wrought iron, the dovetailed
curly maple base w/a small
drawer & notched rectangular
base, a widely flaring tin hopper

Sun No. 1080

w/a long, curved flat wrought-iron handle w/a turned wood grip, drawer w/a small lacy glass pull, handle marked "A. Keine," 7" w., 7" h. (hopper appears to be old replacement w/inside lip damage) **385.00**

Box mill, walnut base w/small drawer & thin overhanging baseboard, domed cast-iron top w/cast floral design & label "Strobridge Coffee Mill, Logan & Strobridge," long angular top handle w/bulbous wooden knob, overall 8¼" h. (corner chip on drawer) **110.00**

Box mill, tapered wood box w/brass hopper, Austrian, 3½ x 3½" top **170.00**

Box mill, tall wood box w/iron top, cover & handle, w/side crank, top embossed "Arcade Mfg. Co. 1XL" **350.00**

Box mill, wood box w/embossed covered hopper, marked "Logan & Strobridge Pat' Coffee Mill," some damage to box **70.00**

Box mill, wood box w/wood hopper & pivoting wood cover, Peugot Freres, 5½ x 5½" top.....**140.00**

Box mill, wood box w/raised iron hopper & tin dust cover, straight handle, Arcade, unmarked **160.00**

UPRIGHT MILLS

Elgin National No. 44

Upright mill, cast iron, pivoting cover w/spread winged eagle, double 15" wheels, original red paint, embossed "Elgin National Coffee Mill, Woodruff & Edwards Co. Elgin, Ill.," missing tin catcher, eagle replaced, model No. 44 (ILLUS.) **900.00**

Upright mill, cast iron, two-wheel, on a canted wooden base w/a small drawer & turned side handle, marked "Enterprise," original paint, 12½" h. (some paint wear)................................**605.00**

Upright mill, cast iron, single-wheel mill w/wooden drawer & covered tin hopper, on wooden base, Elma, unmarked **160.00**

Upright mill, cast iron, w/wooden drawer & tin covered hopper, painted green w/gold trim, 13" wheel w/gears, embossed "Peugot Freres 2A, Brevetes S.G.D.G." **700.00**

Upright mill, cast iron, covered hopper & double wheels, original red paint & decals, 1898 patent date, wheels embossed "Enterprise Mfg. Co, Philadelphia, U.S.A." **1,000.00**

WALL CANISTER MILLS

Wood Wall Mount Mill

Wall Canister mill, wood & cast-iron, glass front & iron cup, Arcade X-Ray, 14" h. (ILLUS.) ..**200.00**

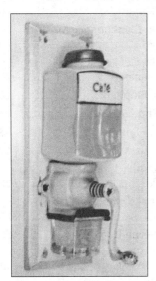

Child's Ceramic Wall Mount Mill

Wall mount, child's, ceramic canister w/glass cup, w/"Cafe" painted on canister, Germany, 5" h. (ILLUS.)............................**300.00**

Wall canister mill, ceramic canister w/glass cup, marked "PeDe".......................................**110.00**

Wall canister mill, ceramic canister w/glass cup & wood backing board, canister marked "KAFFEE," Leinbrock Ideal DRGM **240.00**

Wall canister mill, glass canister & cup embossed "Enterprise No. 100," 16"h **130.00**

Wall canister mill, tin lithographed canister, pictures a young girl wearing white dress, yellow apron & cap, yellow bonnet & dark cap, Bronson-Walton Beauty, 13"h. including cup.........**230.00**

MISCELLANEOUS

Box mill, child's, painted tin, w/brass hopper, 3 x 3" top...........**40.00**

Clamp-on mill, open hopper, original red paint w/label, LF&C No. 01...............................**80.00**

Turkish mill, brass, engraved cylindrical casing w/folding crank...**40.00**

Wall mount mill, cast iron, open hopper & cup, repainted red, embossed "Landers, Frary & Clark," No. 001 ....**80.00**

COOKIE JARS

All sorts of charming and whimsical cookie jars have been produced in recent decades and these are increasingly collectible today. Many well known American potteries such as McCoy, Hull and Abingdon produced cookie jars and their are included in those listings. Below we are listing cookie jars produced by other companies.

Current reference books for collectors include: The Collectors Encyclopedia of Cookie Jars *by Fred and Joyce Roerig (Collector Books, 1991);* Collector's Encyclopedia of Cookie Jars, Book II *by Fred and Joyce Roerig (Collector Books, 1994); and* The Complete Cookie Jar Book *by Mike Schneider (Schiffer, Ltd. 1991). Also see: CERAMICS.*

AMERICAN BISQUE

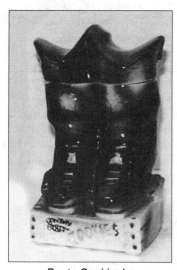

Boots Cookie Jar

Animal Crackers "USA" $20.00

Baby Elephant............................145.00

Bear, flasher-type 495.00

Bear with Hat..............................135.00

Bear with Honey, "Corner Cookie
Jar, 804 USA," flasher-type 585.00

Blackboard Clown (some paint
off blackboard) 245.00

Blackboard Hobo 300.00

Boots, "USA 742" (ILLUS.) 120.00

Boy Bear, blue shirt 45.00

Boy Bear, green shirt 40.00

Candy Baby 145.00

Cat w/paws in pockets, blue &
yellow, bank head, 10½" h.
(crazing) 150.00

Cheerleaders, flasher-type 470.00

Chef, standing 100.00

Chick 100.00

Churn, "USA" 15.00

Churn Boy 205.00

Collegiate Owl 60.00

Cookie Sack 45.00

**Cow Jumped Over the Moon
(The),** flasher-type ....975.00 to 1,000.00

Dog on quilted base 165.00

Dutch Girl 85.00

Elephant w/baseball cap............110.00

Elephant w/beanie 60.00

Elephant w/hands in Pocket 80.00

French Poodle, maroon
decoration...................................85.00

French Poodle, pink 150.00

Girl Bear......................................60.00

Granny 125.00

Hen with Chick, 9½" h................225.00

Jack-in-the-Box 125.00

Kittens on Ball of Yarn 130.00

Lamb with Flower 160.00

Mrs. Rabbit 220.00

Peasant Girl...............................815.00

Poodle, blue 80.00

Popeye 950.00

Rabbit...130.00

Rooster, multicolored (minor
crazing)..70.00

Saddle, light color lid, no
blackboard 300.00

Saddle Blackboard, "Musn't
Forget"..280.00

Saddle Blackboard,
"Remember!" 280.00

Sailor Elephant............................85.00

Sea Bag......................................275.00

Seal on Igloo 330.00

Soldier..120.00

Spaceship, "Cookies Out of the
World"..325.00

Spool of Thread w/thimble
finial 250.00

Toothache Dog, brown..............550.00

Yarn Doll w/yellow dress &
maroon collar..............................145.00

BRUSH - MC COY

Antique Touring Car 1,400.00

Cinderella Pumpkin 495.00

Clown, standing, full figure,
brown pants................................345.00

Clown Bust 385.00
Cookie House 175.00
Covered Wagon 610.00
Cow w/cat finial, black &
  white 1,200.00
Crock with duck finial.................50.00
Crock with praying angel finial...75.00
Davy Crockett...........................310.00
Davy Crockett, gold trim 925.00
Donkey w/Cart, grey 425.00
Elephant w/Ice Cream Cone,
  wearing baby hat.......**400.00 to 500.00**
Formal Pig 375.00
Granny 475.00
Happy Bunny, white 210.00
Humpty Dumpty with Peaked
  Hat..180.00
Lantern......................................65.00

Peter Pan Cookie Jar

Little Boy Blue Cookie Jar

Little Boy Blue, (ILLUS.) 925.00
Little Red Riding Hood 640.00
Old Shoe 120.00
Panda Bear 395.00
Peter Pan, (ILLUS. top next
  column).....................................750.00

Smiling Bear 310.00
Squirrel on Log 120.00
Squirrel w/Top Hat 350.00
Teddy Bear, feet apart 220.00
Teddy Bear, feet apart, green
  apron, gold trim 875.00

CALIFORNIA ORIGINALS
Bear, "G-405" 10.00
Christmas Tree...........................635.00
Cookie Monster, "copyright
  MUPPETS INC., 970".................55.00
Crawling Turtle...........................20.00
Elephant......................................40.00
Elf School House 30.00
Ernie, "copyright
  MUPPETS INC., 973"................70.00
Ernie and Bert Fine Cookies.....475.00
Humpty Dumpty 125.00
Juggler.......................................55.00
Koala Bear 140.00
Oscar the Grouch, "copyright
  MUPPETS INC., 972"..............115.00
Santa Claus 175.00

Scarecrow.....................................365.00
Sheriff, with hole in hat **20.00**
Snowman.....................................375.00
Squirrel on Stump......................90.00
Superman, w/phone booth,
brown ....**250.00 to 300.00**
Superman, w/phone booth,
silver 595.00
Tigger...195.00
Woody Woodpecker in Stump..875.00

DORANNE OF CALIFORNIA
Donkey with Sack of Oats...........**85.00**
Monkey in Barrel,
"USA-CJ43" **65.00**
Pig with Barrel of Pork **70.00**
Pinocchio....................................225.00
Walrus..**40.00**

POTTERY GUILD
Balloon Lady **165.00**
Dutch Boy, blue 25.00
Dutch Boy, red, white & blue 80.00
Elsie in Barrel...........................**300.00**
Red Riding Hood........................**90.00**

REGAL CHINA
Baby Pig w/diaper .....500.00 to 600.00
Cat, tan 260.00
Cat, white...................................470.00
Dutch Girl, peach dress (rare) 995.00
French Chef...............................**475.00**
Goldilocks 290.00
Jim Beam, cylinder 89.00
Majorette, bust 595.00
Peek-a-Boo **1,200.00**

ROBINSON RANSBOTTOM
Dutch Girl 140.00
Hootie Owl 50.00
Jack...180.00
Peter Pumpkin Eater................**375.00**
Whale........................800.00 to 850.00

SIERRA VISTA
Cottage **65.00**
Smiling Train **175.00**
Spaceship..................................575.00
Stagecoach.................................215.00

TREASURE CRAFT
Baseball Boy **30.00**
Bear..**20.00**
Cat with Mouse **30.00**
Chef..**45.00**
Famous Amos **75.00**
Farmer Pig **60.00**
Kitten with Goldfish Bowl **90.00**
Monk **35.00**
Rocking Horse **50.00**
Spice..**60.00**
Stagecoach...................................40.00
Sugar..**60.00**
Truck, red.................................**300.00**

TWIN WINTON
Bambi, beside stump 75.00
Castle..**225.00**
Chipmunk, Twin Winton **20.00**
Cop..**95.00**
Dog on Drum **100.00**
Duck with Drum, Twin Winton....**110.00**
Elephant, grey, Japan..................60.00
Fire Engine, Twin Winton **60.00**
Friar Tuck **58.00**
Noah's Ark................................**145.00**
Ole King Cole **350.00**
Sailor Elephant, Twin Winton.......80.00
Sailor Mouse, Twin Winton..........30.00
Squirrel, Twin Winton (flake on
ear) **20.00**

VANDOR
Betty Boop, head w/top hat **145.00**
Betty Boop, standing **650.00**
Cowboy, head..............................70.00
Popeye Head **425.00**

WISECARVER
Hill Folk, 12½" h...........................**170.00**
Indian Chief, blue decoration......**170.00**
Indian Chief, tan decoration **170.00**
Mammy with Child **130.00**
Pig, 10¾" h................................**150.00**
Raccoons, 10" h. **110.00**

MISCELLANEOUS COMPANIES
Big Bird, Newcor..........................**50.00**
Blue Bird, Lefton.........................**225.00**
Blue Bonnet Sue, "© 1989
Nabisco"..**75.00**
Bum (The), Imperial Porcelain **950.00**
Cactus, "Mirage © Dept. 56" **75.00**
Cat, white, Japan..........................**35.00**
Cathy, "Keep Your Hands Off My
Cookies," copyright George
GOOD Corporation....................**495.00**
Chevrolet, 1957, "Made in
Portugal"....................................**119.00**
Chicken on Nest, Hirsch Mfg
1961 ....**49.00**
Circus Tent, Brayton Laguna......**450.00**
Clown, Lane **250.00**
Clown, Pan American Art..............**60.00**
Clown head, Italy **25.00**
Cookie Monster, Newcor..............**50.00**
Cow, Japan **40.00**
Cross-eyed Bird **595.00**
Dog w/green hat, Japan **15.00**
Dutch Boy, gold trim, unmarked
(crazing) **150.00**
Fred Flintstone, Harry James
Design **150.00**
Frog, Maurice of California..........**195.00**
Frog on Toadstool, Japan **50.00**
Frookie Cookies, made in
Taiwan..**30.00**
Gingerbread House, unknown ...**125.00**
Graduate Owl, Japan....................**18.00**
Grandma's Cookie Jar,
unmarked **30.00**
Granny, Japan **35.00**

Granny, "If All Else Fails, Ask
Grandma," Japan **20.00**
Halo Boy, DeForest of
California **575.00**
Harpo Marx, unmarked **1,150.00**
Jonah on Whale, unmarked **75.00**
Keebler Elf, Fitz & Floyd **40.00**
Keebler Tree House **65.00**
Kermit in TV, Sigma ...450.00 to 500.00
Koo Kee, Chinese Chef, Chinese
writing inside lid **250.00**
Lady with Cat, "© 1989 Animals
& Co. 26 - MP 92" **675.00**
Lion w/green hat, Japan **20.00**
Mammy, yellow, Mosaic Tile **385.00**
Man with Chicken, "© 1989
Animals & Co. 11SG5 192
USA."..**725.00**
Mercedes, Expressive Designs,
made in Taiwan,
1986 ....**250.00 to 300.00**
Monkey, Japan..............................**15.00**
Mopsy, 11½" h. **95.00**
Nestle Toll House Cookies,
unmarked, recipe on back,
believed to be produced by
Holiday Designs **115.00**
Noah's Ark, Japan **60.00**
Nun, DeForest of California.........**220.00**
Pepperidge Farm Ginger Man.....**60.00**
Peter Pumpkin Eater, Japan........**50.00**
Pig Head, Japan............................**25.00**
Planetary Pal, round head,
Sigma **295.00**
Puzzled Monkey, Maurice of
California **95.00**
R2-D2, Roman Ceramics.............**210.00**
Rabbit, brown, Japan **35.00**
Raggedy Andy, Maddux of
California **225.00**
Raggedy Ann, Japan....................**45.00**
Rolls Royce Santa, Fitz &
Floyd ....**800.00 to 875.00**
Runaway (The) **375.00**
Sad Clown, Cardinal China
Company **245.00**

Sailor Cat, Japan **30.00**

Santa Cycle **550.00**

Sherman on the Mount,
American Greeting Corp.,
Cleveland, Ohio.........................**350.00**

Skateboard Nerd, "Nerds®,
©1984 Willie Wonka Brands,
exclusively distributed by United
Silver and Cutlery Co., Made in
Taiwan".......................................**85.00**

Soldier, Cardinal China
Company **425.00**

Spaceship, "Napco," Japan **875.00**

Student Owl, Japan **30.00**

Telephone, Cardinal China
Company **125.00**

Top Cat, marked on box "Henry
James Design," distributed in
England, 1990 Hanna Barbera
Productions, Inc........................**295.00**

Topo Gigio, Maria Perego,
distributed by Ross Products,
Inc., New York **175.00**

Toucan, Himark.............................**35.00**

Turtle, green, Japan......................**35.00**

Winking Cat Head, Japan,
unmarked **60.00**

Ziggy, Korea...............................**390.00**

CURRIER & IVES PRINTS

This lithographic firm was founded in 1835 by Nathaniel Currier with James M. Ives becoming a partner in 1857. Current events of the day were portrayed in the early days and the prints were hand-colored. Landscapes, vessels, sport and hunting scenes of the West all became popular subjects. The firm was in existence until 1906. All prints listed are hand-colored unless otherwise noted. Numbers at the end of the listings refer to those used in Currier & Ives Prints—An Illustrated Checklist, *by Frederick A. Conningham (Crown Publishers).*

American Autumn Fruits, after
F.F. Palmer, large folio, 1865,
framed (foxing) **$1,150.00**

American Country Life,
Pleasures of Winter, after F.F.

Palmer, large folio, N. Currier,
1855 (123) **2,375.00**

American Country Life,
Summer's Evening, after F.F.
Plamer, large folio, N. Currier,
1855 (124) **2,350.00**

American Homestead—Autumn,
mall folio, 1869 (168) **500.00**

Ann Maria, small folio, three-
quarters portrait of woman on
balcony, N. Currier, 1849 (236) ...**95.00**

Barefoot Girl (The), small folio,
full-length portrait of girl at the
seashore w/pail & shovel,
undated (370) **159.00**

**Battle of New Orleans, Jany.
8th, 1815, 1842, (The),** small
folio, N. Currier, 1842 (416).......**210.00**

Beauty of Virginia, small folio,
upright, vignette, undated (473) ..**65.00**

Best Likeness (The), medium
folio, girl looking through empty
frame w/dog beside her 1858
(505) **135.00**

Burial of the Bird, small folio, five
children burying bird, undated
(736) **80.00**

**Burning of the Steamship
"Austria,"** Sept. 13th 1858,
small folio, undated (748) **265.00**

**Camping in the Woods— "A
Good Time Coming,"** after A.F.
Tait, large folio, 1863, (773) ...**4,100.00**

Catterskil Falls, small folio, Falls
in center, stream to right,
undated (858) **235.00**

Central Park— The Bridge,
small folio, undated (949)**370.00**

**Clipper Ship "Comet" of New
York,** large folio, N. Currier,
1855 (1140) **3,475.00**

**Clipper Ship "Queen of
Clippers,"** small folio,
N. Currier, undated (1163) **495.00**

**Coming From the Trot— Sports
on the Home Stretch,** large
folio, 1869, framed (several
tears in margins, staining) **489.00**

Daniel Webster, small folio, half-length portrait, N. Currier, 1851 (1363) **190.00**

Day Before Marriage (The), small folio, full-length portrait of bride trying on jewelry, seated before mirror, N. Currier, 1847 (1459) **110.00**

Easter Flowers, small folio, 1847 (1656) **25.00**

Fall of Richmond, Va (The)— On the Night of April 2nd, 1865, small folio, 1865 (1823) ...**270.00**

Gold Mining in California, small folio, 1871, 2412 (ILLUS. below) **1,575.00**

Home of the Deer (The), medium folio, undated (2867) **565.00**

Hudson Highlands (The), small folio, 1871 (2975) **420.00**

Hungry Little Kitties, small folio, undated (2991) **80.00**

In the Mountains, medium folio, undated (3072) **420.00**

Jesus Blessing the Children, small folio, 1866 (3216) **20.00**

Life and Age of Man (The)— Stages of Man's Life From the

Cradle to the Grave, small folio, undated (3498) **170.00**

Life in the Country— The Morning Ride, large folio, 1859, framed (subtle toning, foxing).....................................**1,955.00**

Little Manly

Little Manly, small folio, three-quarter length portrait, seated, undated, 3663 (ILLUS.) **85.00**

Gold Mining in California

Maiden's Rock— Mississippi River, small folio, undated (3891) **450.00**

Niagara Falls— From the Canada Side, small folio, undated (4461) **150.00**

Presidents of the United State (The), small folio, N. Currier, 1844 (4893) **155.00**

Soldier's Return (The), small folio, N. Currier, 1847 (5608) **100.00**

To The Memory of. . ., small folio, woman kneeling to left of tomb along w/two children, tree at left, river in background, N. Currier, 1845 (6069) **45.00**

Tomb of Washington (The), Mount Vernon, Virginia, medium folio, undated (6110) **165.00**

U.S. Frigate "Constitution," small folio, N. Currier, undated (6303) **535.00**

View of Chicago, small folio, also published as "Chicago As It Was," undated (6393)................**660.00**

View of the Harlem River, N.Y.— The Highbridge in the Distance, large folio, 1852, framed (toning) **920.00**

View on St. Lawrence— Indian Encampment, small folio, undated (6452) **249.00**

Wedding Day (The), small folio, full-length portrait of couple about to enter church, N. Currier, undated (6596) **95.00**

Wild Duck Shooting, small folio, 6666 (ILLUS. below).................**540.00**

Woodcock Shooting

Woodcock Shooting, small folio, 1870, 6775 (ILLUS.) **565.00**

Wreck of the "Atlantic" (The), small folio, 1873 (6787) **295.00**

Yacht "Puritan" of Boston, large folio, 1885 (6810) **1,400.00**

Wild Duck Shooting

DECOYS

Decoys have been utilized for years to lure flying water fowl into target range. They have been made of carved and turned wood, papier-mâché, canvas and metal, and some are in the category of outstanding folk art and command high prices.

New Jersey Brant Decoy

Black-Bellied Plover, by Daniel Lake Leeds, Pleasantville, New Jersey, carved wood w/fine original paint w/minor wear, bill may be later replacement, ca. 1900...............................**$3,020.00**

Black Duck, by Captain Wilbur Corwin, Bellport, Long Island, New York, carved wood w/early worn & weathered working paint, several small body gouges, old & crude bill repair, tight cracks in head, few shot scars, ca. 1873................................**3,520.00**

Black Duck, by Daniel Lake Leeds, Pleasantville, New Jersey, hollow-carved body in swimming pose w/round-bottom style, turned head w/glass eyes, original paint w/minor flaking & wear, thin wash of overpaint on some worn areas....................**1,650.00**

Black Duck, by the Mason Decoy Factory, Detroit, Michigan, Premier grade, carved solid wood body w/snakey head slightly turned, strong original paint w/minor wear, several tiny body dents, small professional tail chip repair, ca. 1905 ....**2,750.00**

Bluebill Drake, by Robert Elliston, Bureau, Illinois, carved wood w/original paint w/very minor wear & good patina, slight wear to bill edges, ca. 1890....**7,425.00**

Bluebill Hen, by Mark Kears, Northfield, New Jersey, hollow-carved body w/original paint in average condition, tight crack on the back, small chip in tail & on side of bill, ca. 1910...................**440.00**

Brant, by Henry Grant, Barnegat, New Jersey, carved wood w/original paint w/minor wear, old in-use tough-up on black area of tail, small chip missing from underside of bill, branded "LB" on underside & in weight, ca. 1900 (ILLUS.) **1,595.00**

Bufflehead Drake, by Doug Jester, Chincoteague, Virginia, carved wood w/original paint w/moderate wear & some flaking, thin crack on back, some damage to to of head w/small nail holding chip in place, ca. 1920s....................................**330.00**

Canada Goose, by Tom Humberstone, New York, carved wood, swimming pose, original paint & glass eyes, 27½" l. **193.00**

Canada Goose Decoy

Canada Goose, Ward Brothers, Crisfield, Maryland, hollow-carved wood, original paint w/fine scratch feathering, all white & black areas w/old repaint, age split in back, several small rough areas in the bottom board, old repairs to neck, made for a hunting club on Deal Island, Virginia, ca. 1931 (ILLUS.) **2,475.00**

Canvasback Hen, by Richard "Fresh-Air" Janson, San Pablo Bay, California, carved wood w/original paint w/minor wear & mellow finish, carved w/the skeg under the tail, ca. 1930...........**1,925.00**

Canvasback Hen & Drake, miniatures, by Elmer Crowell, East Harwich, Massachusetts, carved wood, painted, signed in ink "A.E. Crowell Cape Cod," 2⅝" h., pr. (minor paint wear) **1,093.00**

Canvasback Hen & Drake, by John "Daddy" Holly, Havre de Grace, Maryland, carved wood w/several coats of old working repaint w/wear & flaking, early iron keels, drake w/some neck fractures, hen w/bill repair, ca. mid-to-late 19th c., pr. **715.00**

Curlew, by Daniel Lake Leeds, Pleasantville, New Jersey, carved wood in near mint condition, ca. 1890 ....**14,300.00**

Curlew, by Harry V. Shourds, Tuckerton, New Jersey, carved full-body style, good original paint w/very slight wear & good patina, most of bill a professional replacement, lightly hit by shot **2,750.00**

Eider Drake, oversized, carved wood inlet head, old in-use repaint, several small cracks in neck reinforced w/small nails, light shot marks, slight roughness to tip of tail, Orrs Island, Maine, approximately 27½" l. **3,520.00**

Egret, roothead confidence-type, full-carved solid body, worn natural wood w/a fine patina, mounted on an iron rod & a black wood base, cracks, probably from New Jersey, 15½" l. **57.00**

Greater Yellowlegs, by Thomas Gelston, Quogue, New York, carved wood in running stance,

head slightly cocked & relief wing carving, original paint w/minor shrinkage & wear, several small dents & hairline cracks, small chip at stick hole, several tiny nail holes on underside................................**3,300.00**

Merganser Drake and Hen

Merganser Drake & Hen, by the Mason Decoy Factory, Detroit, Michigan, Challenge grade, carved wood w/strong original paint w/minor wear & good patina, small defect in wood in hen's back, slight roughness on hen's bill & tip of tail, very slight roughness of edge of drake's bill, minor discoloration in white areas, pr. (ILLUS.) **11,550.00**

Pintail Drake

Pintail Drake, attributed to Walter Peizer or possibly Earl Voekler, Milwaukee, Wisconsin, carved wood w/outstanding original paint w/mellowed finish, few dings & some minor damage at tip of bill, ca. mid-to-late 1940s (ILLUS.) **6,600.00**

Pintail Drake, by John Blair, Philadelphia, carved wood w/worn old paint w/traces of original, retains original weight, several small dents & small cracks, body halves joined by small wooden dowels, ca. 1870s...............................**2,475.00**

Plover, full-carved solid body w/shoe button eyes, in an overlook position w/detailed wing carving, retains original spring plumage paint w/minor losses, signed on bottom "R. Birch," mounted on a wood rod & naturalistic wood base, 7¾" l......**287.00**

Redbreasted Merganser Drake, attributed to Samuel Barton, Mathistown, New Jersey, carved wood w/mostly original paint w/some traces of old & thin working overpaint, ca. 1900 or earlier **358.00**

Redhead Drake, carved wood w/high head, good paint, glass eyes, 13¼" l. (age crack in top of block & around neck putty)....**182.00**

Redhead Drake, by Chris Sprague, Beach Haven, New Jersey, carved wood w/original paint w/minor flaking & wear, signed at a later date................**660.00**

Sanderling, by Dan Lake Leeds, Pleasantville, New Jersey, carved wood w/dry original paint w/minor wear, original hardwood inserted bill, ca. 1890-1900 ....**3,300.00**

Sandpiper, by Obediah Verity, Seaford, New York, carved wood w/relief wing carving & carved eyes, original paint w/good patina, minor wear, shot marks **1,870.00**

Yellow legs, Joe Lincoln-type, painted carved wood w/shoe button eyes, ca. 1900 (very minor paint wear)...................**1,495.00**

Wigeon Drake

Wigeon Drake, by Joseph Lincoln, Accord, Massachusetts, carved wood, never rigged, fine original paint w/several slight scuffs, two paint drips on body, tip of bill broken &reattached (ILLUS.) **13,200.00**

Willet, by John Dilley, Quogue, New York, carved wood w/good original paint w/fine detail & good patina, some discoloration on back **10,450.00**

American Eider, full-carved body of solid construction, retains old working paint, minor loss to front of bill, northern coast of Maine, 17" l. (ILLUS. bottom row, center, top next page) **172.00**

American Eider, full-carved wooden body of solid construction, retains most of the original paint, cracks, northern coast of Maine, possibly Orrs Island, 20th c., 17¾" l. (ILLUS. middle row, far right, top next page) **172.00**

Black Duck, full-carved wood of solid construction original paint worn to a fine patina, minor loss to tip of of bill, northern coast of Maine, possible Orrs Island, early 20th c., 21½" l. (ILLUS. top row, right, top next page)...........**115.00**

Canada Goose, full-carved wood body of solid construction, in a swimming position w/carved eyes, remnants of original paint, probably from the Annapolis Valley, Nova Scotia, 25" l. (ILLUS. bottom row, left, top next page) **345.00**

Canvasback Drake, primitive full-carved solid body in high head position w/glass eyes, retains most of the original paint, branded w/an "E," crack down center of back, northeastern Wisconsin, ca. 1930, 17" l. (ILLUS. middle row, center, top next page) **460.00**

Eider Drake, by John McCay, Little Harbor, Nova Scotia, full-

carved solid body, retains some of the original paint, minor loss to bill, signed on base "John McCay, Little Harbor," ca. 1930, 16½ l. (ILLUS. middle row, left) **..172.00**

Eider Hen, by John McCay, Little Harbor, Nova Scotia, full-carved solid body, retains worn original paint, loss to tip of bill, base signed "John McCay, Little Harbor, N.S.," 17" l. (ILLUS. top row, left) **115.00**

Goldeneye Drake, attributed to R. Webber, orthern coast of Maine, full-carved solid body w/an inlet bill, original paint, branded "R. Webber," 20th c., 16¼" l. (ILLUS top row, center) **287.00**

Surf Scoter, full-carved solid body in preening position, retains most of the original paint, carved initials "CENN," cracks & losses, northern coast of Maine, 20¾ l. (ILLUS. bottom row, right) **402.00**

DISNEY COLLECTIBLES

Scores of objects ranging from watches to dolls have been created showing Walt Disney's copyrighted animated cartoon characters, and an increasing number of collectors now are seeking these, made primarily by licensed manufacturers.

Alice in Wonderland movie cel, gouache on celluloid applied to a printed background, Alice stands on the tea part table looking slightly upwards, 1951, 9½" x 12" **$1,840.00**

Bambi movie cel, gouache on trimmed celluloid applied to an airbrushed Courvoiser background, scene of Bambi & Thumper sliding on the ice, 1942, 7 x 9" **4,025.00**

Bambi & Thumper rug, rectangular w/end fringe, meadow scene w/large butterfly in brown, blue, red, yellow, pink & green, 1950s, unused, 22 x 40" (ILLUS.top next page) ...**83.00**

Bambi and Thumper Rug

Disney Characters tumbler,
"The Greedy Pig and Colt,"
enamel on clear w/a farmyard
scene, band around the top
printed "Walt Disney All Star
Parade," scene title at the
bottom, dairy premium, 1939, D.
2166 (ILLUS. right w/Minnie
Mouse tumblers)........................**193.00**

Donald Duck Cartoon Cel

Donald Duck cartoon cel, half-
length portrait of Donald holding
a plate of toast, mulitcolored,
marked "this is an original
handpainted celluloid drawing
actually used in a Walt Disney
Production," ca. 1959, very
minor scratches, dome dent &
creases to paper mat, 9 x 12"
(ILLUS.) **413.00**

Donald Duck toy, pull-type,
"Dapper Donald Duck,"
lithographed paper & wood,
Fisher-Price, No. 460, ca. 1936,
9" h., 6½" l. **374.00**

Donald Duck toy, windup-
celluloid, walker, long-billed
Donald wearing sailor suit
w/bent arms & winking
expression, Japan, ca. 1930s,
3¼" h. (small dent in
arm & tail) **460.00**

Donald Duck toy, windup plastic,
Donald Duck on Tricycle, hard
plastic figure of Donald seated
on a color tin tricycle, a banner
on a stick above the handle bars
reads "Happy Days" below a -
pink balloon, bell ringer on the
back, w/original colorful box,
scratches, 4½" l., 7½" h.
(ILLUS. top next page) **99.00**

Donald Duck toy, windup tin,
"Donald Duck Duet," Donald
Duck wearing sailor suit
standing on snare drum holding
drum sticks, attached to Goofy
on cylindrical base marked
"Donald Duck Duet," Marx, ca.
1946, 10½" h. (replaced
ears) **546.00**

Donald Duck on Tricycle Toy

Donald Duck tumbler, enameled glass, shows Donald in hiking outfit, Mickey Mouse Club series, D2562, 5⅛" h. **18.00**

Donald Duck & Chip 'n Dale rug, rectangular, Donald walking carrying a shoulder yoke w/a bucket hung from each end w/Chip in one & Dale in the other, in a flowered landscape, woven in green, blue, red, white, yellow & brown, end fringe, some soiling, 1950s, 22 x 40" (ILLUS. below)............................**83.00**

Goofy rug, rectangular a colorful scene of Goofy riding on a long,

Donald Duck & Chip 'n Dale Rug

low, small-wheeled wooden vehicle, woven in bright colors of blue, red, white, green, black, pink & yellow, end fringe, 1950s, soiling, 21½ x 40" (ILLUS. below)............................**83.00**

Fantasia movie cel, gouache on celluloid applied to an airbrushed Courvoisier background, the white & black Pegasus parents glide peacefully along, surrounded by their black, yellow, blue & white foals, 1940, Courvoisier Galleries label on back, 7½ x 9½" **3,450.00**

Fantasia movie cel, Sorcerer's Apprentice segment, gouache on celluloid applied to an airbrushed Courvoisier background, Mickey Mouse stands looking stern w/arms crossed & wearing the Sorcerer's cap, 1940, 9 x 9½" **10,925.00**

Ferdinand the Bull cartoon cel, gouache on trimmed celluloid applied to a studio-prepared background, a scene of the Matador trying desperately to get a reaction out of Ferdinand, finally resorting to sticking his tongue out at him, 1938, 8½ x 12½" **2,875.00**

Ferdinand the Bull Windup Toy

Ferdinand the Bull toy, windup tin, lithograph standing bull w/spinning tail, Louis Marx, New York, late 1930s, w/original box, missing one horn, box edge wear & missing one end flap, toy 6" l. (ILLUS.) **288.00**

Colorful Goofy Rug

Jungle Book Movie Cel

Jungle Book movie cel, brown, black & white celluloid image of a seated bear, marked "This is an original handpainted celluloid drawing actually used in a Walt Disney Production," ca. 1959, minor flaking, minor scratches, soiling & creasing to paper frame, 9 x 12" (ILLUS.)..............**385.00**

Lady and the Tramp tumbler, enameled glass, shows Si & Am on one side, D2355, 5¼" h. (colors on back a little off-center) **35.00**

Maleficent (from Sleeping Beauty) drawing, graphite on paper, capturing her in a three-quarters length portrait during a moment of calm, w/full margins, 1959, 12½ x 15½" **920.00**

Mickey Mouse doll, molded stockinette face, felt ears, clothes & tail, black plush head, body & limbs, cloth label, Gund, late 1940s, 13½" h.....................**288.00**

Mickey Mouse drawing, graphite on paper w/red pencil, sketched smiling head of Mickey above handwritten inscription "Greetings From Ecuador - Walt Disney," ca. 1940, 6¾" x 9" **6,900.00**

Mickey Mouse figure, jointed wood, balancing-type, flat circular hands to balance on, fiber tail, "Mickey Mouse" decal on front, ca. 1930, 4¾" h. (flakes on nose & ears) **289.00**

Mickey Mouse figure, wood & cotton rope, pop-up head, wooden body, head, legs & feet, leatherette ears, cotton rope arms, "Mickey Mouse" decal on front (discoloration, missing tail)..**316.00**

Mickey Mouse Hoop-La Game

Mickey Mouse game, "Mickey Mouse Hoop-La Game," flat lithographed figure of Mickey standing w/one arm raised & one to the side, three wooden rings to toss at his body, Marks Bros., Boston, Massachusetts, early 1930s, w/original box in fair condition w/edge wear (ILLUS.) **259.00**

Mickey Mouse lunch box, metal, Mickey Mouse Skating Party **50.00**

Mickey Mouse toy, pull-type, "Mickey Mouse Safety Patrol,"

Fisher-Price, No. 733, ca. 1956, 9½" l. **201.00**

Mickey Mouse toy, pull-type, "Mickey Mouse Xylophone, Fisher-Price, No. 798, 1939, 9 x 11" **289.00**

Mickey Mouse Celluloid toy

Mickey Mouse toy, windup celluloid, walking figure of a pudgy Mickey, Japan, 1930s, missing tail, arms need restringing, 8" h. (ILLUS.) **460.00**

Mickey Mouse toy, windup tin, Mickey on roller skates w/cloth pants, Line Mar, Japan, ca. 1950s, 6¾" h. **690.00**

Minnie Mouse tumbler, black enamel on clear, scene of Minnie walking carrying a polka dot umbrella, name across the bottom, First Dairy Series, 1936, D2013 (ILLUS. below, left) **70.00**

Minnie Mouse tumbler, black enamel on clear, black enamel on clear, scene of Minnie standing & holding her hands together, name vertically down the side, First Dairy Series, 1936, D2013 (ILLUS. below, center) **70.00**

One Hundred and One Dalmatians movie cel, gouache on celluloid applied to a preliminary production background, Pongo sits anxiously waiting for the birth of his & Perdita's puppies, 1961, 8 x 11½" **2,875.00**

Minnie Mouse & Disney Characters Tumblers

Pinocchio Characters Rug

Pinocchio movie cel, gouache on trimmed celluloid applied to an airbrushed Courvoisier background, shows Pinocchio w/donkey ears dropping to the bottom of the sea in search of Geppetto, Courvoisier Galleries label on back, 1940, 8" d. **5,175.00**

Pinocchio, Jiminy Cricket, Cleo & Figaro rug, rectangular, colorful grouping of the characters against a white background w/sea horse & seaweed brackets in the upper corners all within a black band border, end fringe, in yellow, orange, tan, blue & black, soiling, 1950s, 22 x 40" (ILLUS. above) **83.00**

Pluto toy, jointed wood body, twisted fiber legs & tail, felt ears, Geo. Borgfeldt & Co., ca. 1930, original box w/some water staining marked "Pluto the Pup - Mickey Mouse's Dog," toy 5¾" l. **633.00**

Pluto, Thumper & Flower Rug

Pluto tumbler, enameled glass scene of a yellow Pluto banging a drum w/his tail, musical notes around the sides, marked in brown "1937 W.D.Ent.," 4½" h. (tiny in-the-making spot on Pluto's back) **154.00**

Pluto, Thumper & Flower rug, rectangular, colorful scene of Pluto pulling a wagon holding Thumper & Flower, a cottage in the woods in the background, woven in, brown, grey, black, red, blue, green & pink, fringe ends, soiling, 1950s, 22 x 40" (ILLUS. bottom previous page) ...**83.00**

Sleeping Beauty Movie Cel

Sleeping Beauty movie cel, one of the good Fairy Godmothers w/her wand, marked "This is an original handpainted celluloid drawing actually used in a Walt Disney Production," ca. 1959, minor scratches, some creasing to corner of paper mat, 9 x 12" (ILLUS.) **385.00**

Snow White & the Seven Dwarfs dolls, Snow White marked "Walt Disney" on back of composition head, "Knickerbocker Toy Co., New York" on back, hazel eyes w/real lashes, painted lower lashes, eye shadow, single-stroke brows, closed mouth, original black mohair wig, five-piece composition body jointed at shoulders & hips, 15" h., Seven Dwarfs marked "Walt Disney,

Knickerbocker Toy Co." on backs, composition character heads w/painted eyes & features, all but Dopey w/mohair beards, composition bodies jointed at shoulders only, molded & painted shoes, all dressed in original two-piece velvet outfits, velvet hats w/names, each 9" h., "Snow White By Walt Disney" on paper tag, end of box labeled "Knickerbocker Toy Co., Stuffed Animals, 650 Sixth Ave., New York City, No. 3," set of 8 ....**1,800.00**

Snow White & the Seven Dwarfs movie drawing, production graphite & red & green pencil half-length sketch of the Old Witch, stamped in the lower left "Prod 2001 - Seq 13A - Scene 9," 1937, 9½ x 11½".....**920.00**

Snow White & Dwarfs Radio

Snow White & the Seven Dwarfs radio, pressed wood fibre front, two knobs, molded in relief w/scene of Snow White & the Dwarfs below an open window, Emerson, ca. 1939, missing dial, replaced cloth grill, some loss to lower left side, mechanically reconditioned, 5¾ x 7¼", 7¾" h. (ILLUS.).........**489.00**

**Tinker Bell (from Peter Pan)
movie cel,** gouache on full
celluloid applied to a hand-
prepared background, shows
Tinker Bell standing cockily
among leaves w/one hand on
her hip, 1953, 15 x 20" **2,587.00**

Uncle Scrooge tumbler,
enameled glass, Pepsi-Cola
Disney series, 1977, D2596,
mint, 6¼" h. **33.00**

DOLLS

**A.B.G. (Alt, Beck &
Gottschalck) bisque shoulder
head lady** marked "8" on back
of head, marked "1123 1/2 Made
in Germany" on back of shoulder
plate, "JDK - Germany (with
crown & streamers) - Cork
Stuffed" on front of kid body,
turned head w/set brown eyes,
feathered brows, painted upper
& lower lashes, accented
nostrils, open mouth w/six upper
teeth, synthetic wig, kid body
w/gussets at elbows, rivets at
hips & knees, bisque lower
arms, wearing a brown & white
two-piece suit w/ black trim,
underclothing, antique high
button boots, 18" (minor repair
at shoulders, left
thumb chip).............................**$200.00**

**A.B.G. (Alt, Beck &
Gottschalck)** bisque shoulder
head boy marked "880 #8" on
back shoulder plate, pale blue
paperweight eyes, multi-stroke
brows, painted upper & lower
lashes, accented nostrils, closed
mouth w/accent line between
lips, molded & painted blond
curly hair, cloth body w/bisque
lower arms & legs, redressed in
brown velvet two-piece suit,
matching hat, beige lace-
trimmed shirt, new socks &
shoes, 20" (ILLUS. top next
column).....................................**335.00**

Alt, Beck & Gottschalck Boy Doll

**Alexander (Madame) "Baby
McGuffey" composition head
marked "Mme Alexander" on
back,** brown sleep eyes w/real
lashes, single-stroke brows,
painted lower lashes, closed
mouth, original mohair wig, cloth
body w/composition hands &
lower legs, tagged pink dress
marked "Baby McGuffey - By
Madame Alexander, N.Y. - All
Right Reserved," white eyelet
pinafore, matching bonnet,
underclothing, long stockings
w/pink ribbon garters, original
snap shoes, 11"........................**145.00**

**Alexander (Madame) "Boy
Blue" marked "Mme
Alexander" on back,** stamped
Fiction Doll - 'Blue Boy' -
Madame Alexander - New York"
on clothing tag, unjointed
composition head, painted blue
eyes looking to side, single-
stroke brows, painted upper

lashes, closed mouth, original mohair wig, composition body jointed at shoulder & hips, molded & painted socks & shoes, original blue pants w/attached white shirt, blue felt jacket w/white felt collar & two white buttons, blue ribbon tie, blue felt hat, 7" (very light crazing, clothing in good condition) **305.00**

Alexander (Madame) "Bridesmaid" composition head marked "Mme Alexander," brown sleep eyes w/real lashes, eye shadow, single-stroke brows, painted lower lashes, closed mouth, mohair wig in original set, five-piece composition body, original yellow chiffon bridesmaid dress tagged "Madame Alexander - New York - U.S.A.," panties, yellow organdy purse w/purple flowers, matching purple flowers in hair, original shoes, 14" **325.00**

Alexander (Madame) "Butch" composition head marked "Mme Alexander," brown sleep eyes w/real lashes, single-stroke brows, painted lower lashes, closed mouth, original mohair wig, cloth body w/composition hands & lower legs, original tagged romper marked "Butch - Madame Alexander, N.Y. U.S.A." w/peach & white striped top, white shorts, matching white hat, original socks, one-snap shoes, 11" (some light crazing, otherwise excellent condition) ...**140.00**

Alexander (Madame) "Carmen" marked "Mme Alexander" on back, unjointed composition head, painted blue eyes looking to side, single-stroke brows, painted upper lashes, closed mouth, mohair wig in original set, composition body jointed at shoulders & hips, molded & painted socks & shoes, original

satin skirt trimmed w/felt, matching top w/sequins, underclothing, fancy headdress w/fruit & flowers, large plume, attached hoop earrings, 7" (slight wear) **105.00**

Alexander (Madame) "Cissy" hard plastic head doll marked "Alexander," blue sleep eyes w/real lashes, feathered brows, painted lower lashes, closed mouth, earrings, hard plastic body w/vinyl arms, jointed at shoulders, elbows, hips, knees, high heel feet, black velvet dress w/flower-trimmed black taffeta & tulle skirt, diamond ring, bracelet & earrings, flower-trimmed shoes, no slip or panties, dress tagged "Cissy by Madame Alexander," good coloring, hair in original set, 20" **675.00**

Alexander (Madame) "Dionne Quintuplets" in carousel marked "Alexander" on composition heads, marked "Genuine Dionne Quintuplet Dolls - All Rights Reserved - Madame Alexander - N.Y." on clothing tag, painted brown eyes looking to side, single-stroke brows, painted upper lashes, closed mouths, molded & painted hair, bent-limb composition baby bodies, tagged rompers w/matching bonnets, each doll w/own pastel color, no socks or shoes, Cecile, Emelie & Annette name pins, Marie has no pin, dolls on animal seats on wooden carousel w/multi-colored striped canvas top, green carousel frame, center pole, yellow seats & floor, 7½", the set (dolls in good condition w/some general crazing, faded carousel) **900.00**

Alexander (Madame) "Dionne Quintuplets" in swing marked "Alexander" on composition heads, painted brown eyes looking to side, single-stroke brows, painted upper lashes, closed mouths, molded & painted hair, bent-limb baby composition bodies, rompers in different colors for each baby tagged "All Rights Reserved - Madame Alexander, N.Y.," matching bonnets, original socks & center-snap shoes, original gold pin w/name on each doll, long yellow wooden swing w/green wooden frame, each baby's name on swing tray in matching color to each romper, multi-color striped canvas covering top of swing, tiny touch-up on Marie's right eye, craze line on Emilie's right side upper lip, tiny cracks on composition seams in Yvonne's finish, 7½", the set (ILLUS. below)......................**2,300.00**

Alexander (Madame) "Dr. Dafoe" composition head w/character face, painted blue eyes, single-stroke brows, painted upper lashes, closed

smiling mouth, grey mohair wig, five-piece composition body, white doctor outfit w/matching cap tagged "Madame Alexander, New York," original socks & shoes, 13" (end broken off right little finger, clothing lightly soiled)....................................**1,600.00**

Alexander "Easter" marked "© Alexander," vinyl head w/"Mary Ann" face, blue sleep eyes w/real lashes, single-stroke brows, closed mouth, synthetic rooted hair, five-piece vinyl body, yellow lace-trimmed dress tagged "Madame Alexander - All Rights Reserved - New York U.S.A.," matching bonnet, original underclothing, tights & side-snap shoes, 14" (clothing slightly aged) **225.00**

Alexander (Madame) "Flora McFlimsey" marked "13" on back, composition head, blue sleep eyes w/real lashes, eye shadow, single-stroke brows, painted lower lashes, freckles on bridge of nose, open mouth

Madame Alexander "Dionne Quintuplets" in Swing

w/four upper teeth, original red h.h. (human hair) wig, five-piece composition body, green dress tagged "Flora McFlimsey of Madison Square - Madame Alexander, N.Y. U.S.A.- All Rights Reserved," white flower pinafore w/green ribbon trim, one-piece underwear combination, original socks & brown high-snap shoes, green straw bonnet, 13"......................**800.00**

Alexander (Madame) "Jane Withers" composition head w/character face, blue sleep eyes w/real lashes, feathered brows, painted lower lashes, open mouth w/four upper teeth, brunette wig in original set, five-piece composition body, tagged "Jane Withers - All Rights Reserved - Madame Alexander, N.Y." on pink & blue flowered dress, one-piece underwear combination, original socks & shoes, pink hat, marked "Jane Withers" on script pin, 15" (deep cracks in composition forehead, side & back of head, air pockets under finish at inside corners of eyes by nose bridge, deep cracks on front of torso, upper rear torso, left leg, upper right leg & upper right arm, all repairable) **400.00**

Alexander (Madame) "Jeannie Walker" composition head marked "Alexander - Pat.No.2171281" on back, brown sleep eyes w/real upper lashes, painted lower lashes, single-stroke brows, grey eye shadow, closed mouth, original mohair wig, composition body w/wooden walking mechanism at lower torso, dressed on original red plaid dress w/attached half slip & tagged "Jeannie Walker - Madame Alexander - N.Y. U.S.A. - All Right Reserved," underclothing, socks & shoes, navy blue felt

Madame Alexander "Jeannie Walker"

hat, boxed, end of box stamped "Madame Alexander - 3715 - Alexander Doll Company - New York, N.Y., Jeannie Walker," light general crazing, 13" (ILLUS.) **1,175.00**

Alexander (Madame) "Madelaine" composition head marked "Mme Alexander," brown sleep eyes w/real lashes, eye shadow, single-stroke brows, painted lower lashes, closed mouth, h.h. wig in original set, five-piece composition body, coral flowered dress trimmed w/lace & velvet black ribbon & tagged "Madame Alexander - N.Y. U.S.A.," underclothing socks & shoes, bonnet, "Madelaine - An Alexander Product" on front side of paper wrist tag, "Created by Madame Alexander - New York" reverse, 17" (general light crazing, eyes cracked & oiled, light discoloration of legs & clothing) **635.00**

Alexander (Madame) "Marcella" composition head marked "Madame Alexander - New York" on red dress tag, brown sleep eyes w/real lashes, feathered brows, painted lower lashes, open mouth w/four upper teeth, original mohair wig, five-piece composition body, original tagged pink organdy dress w/ribbon trim, matching hat, one-piece underwear combination, socks & shoes, 16" (general light crazing & wear)....**110.00**

Alexander (Madame) "McGuffey Ana" composition head girl marked "Princess Elizabeth - Alexander Doll Co.," hazel sleep eyes w/real lashes & painted lower lashes, feathered brows, open mouth w/four upper teeth, h.h. wig in original set, five-piece composition body, blue & pink flowered dress tagged "McGuffey Ana - Madame Alexander, N.Y. U.S.A. - All Rights Reserved," white eye-let pinafore, one-piece underwear combination , original socks & snap shoes, white straw hat w/red rim, boxed, end of box marked "McGuffey Ana - Madame Alexander, New York," 19" (light crazing on doll, box shows wear) **1,100.00**

Alexander (Madame) Princess Elizabeth composition head marked "Princess Elizabeth - Alexander Doll," blue sleep eyes w/real lashes, feathered brows, painted lower lashes, open mouth w/four upper teeth, h.h. wig in original set, five-piece composition body, peach taffeta dress w/net overlay, tagged "Princess Elizabeth - Madame Alexander, N.Y. U.S.A. - All rights reserved," matching panties, original socks & silver shoes, original tiara on head, boxed, 16" **700.00**

Madame Alexander "Sonja Henie" Doll

Alexander (Madame) "Sonja Henie" composition head w/character face, brown sleep eyes w/real lashes, painted lower lashes, feathered brows, open smiling mouth w/six upper teeth, dimples, original h.h. wig in original set, five-piece composition body, red corduroy jacket w/silver buttons, matching fur-trimmed hat, blue pants w/attached white bodice, white socks, black side-snap shoes attached to wooden skis, ski poles, boxed, marked "Genuine Sonja Henie Doll - Madame Alexander - N.Y. U.S.A." on clothing tag, boxed, "Sonja Henie - Madame Alexander - 3424R" on box label, 17" (ILLUS.)............................**1,250.00**

Alexander (Madame) "Wendy Ann" hard plastic head marked "Alexander," blue sleep eyes w/real lashes, single-stroke brows, painted lower lashes, closed mouth, h.h. wig, five-piece hard plastic body, tagged "Wendy Ann by Madame Alexander - All Rights Reserved" on nylon dress, matching panties, original socks & side-snap shoes, "Wendy Ann - All Rights Reserved" on front of wrist tag, "A Madame Alexander Doll" reverse, 18" (pale facial coloring, clothing in good condition) **315.00**

American Character "Eloise" marked "Eloise - " Eloise Ltd - American Char. Doll Corp. - Brooklyn 32, N.Y." on hand tag, cloth head w/molded mask face, painted eyes, single-stroke brows, painted upper & lower lashes, accented nostrils, closed crooked smiling mouth, original yellow yarn hair, cloth body jointed at shoulders & hips, original white blouse, navy blue pleated skirt, socks & shoes, mint & boxed, 21" **775.00**

American Character "Sweet Sue" marked "Sweet Sue - Queen of Dolls" on front wrist tag, hard plastic head attached to walking mechanism, blue eyes w/real lashes, single-stroke brows, painted lower lashed, closed mouth, original saran hair, hard plastic walking body jointed at knees, original pale blue & white taffeta & nylon dress trimmed w/lace & flowers, underclothing, stockings, shoes & straw bonnet, include pamphlet from American Character w/available dolls pictured & explained, boxed, marked "An American Character Doll - 1015" on end of box label, 14" **475.00**

A.M. (Armand Marseille) bisque socket head girl marked "Made in Germany - 390 - A 11/0 M," blue sleep eyes, single-stroke brows, painted upper & lower lashes, accented

nostrils, open mouth w/four upper teeth, original mohair wig, jointed wood & composition body w/straight wrists, antique white dress w/crocheted top, underclothing, replaced cotton socks, blue cloth French-type shoes marked "2/0" on bottom, 8½" (tiny inherent cut on back of head) **170.00**

A.M. (Armand Marseille) bisque socket head baby marked "A.M. - Germany - 351 2½," tiny blue sleep eyes, softly brushed brows, painted upper & lower lashes, accented nostrils, open mouth w/two lower teeth, lightly molded & painted hair, bent-limb baby composition body, redressed in white nylon & eyelet baby dress, matching bonnet, underclothing, diaper & booties, 10" c., 12"....................**170.00**

A.M. (Armand Marseille) baby marked "A.M. - Germany - 341/8," solid dome bisque flange head, blue sleep eyes, softly blushed brows, very faint painted upper & lower lashes, accented nostrils, closed mouth, lightly molded & painted hair, cloth body w/excelsior stuffing pin-jointed at shoulder & hips, composition hands, long white baby dress w/eyelet trim, underclothing, diaper, new stockings, wool fleecy cape w/feather stitching, flannel blanket w/embroidery trim, 15" c., 23" (generally excellent condition w/perfect head, aged body, slight crazing on hands)...**400.00**

A.M. (Armand Marseille) "Queen Louise" bisque socket head, large brown sleep eyes w/real lashes, feathered brows, painted lower lashes, accented nostrils, open mouth w/accented lips & four upper teeth, synthetic wig, jointed wood & composition body,

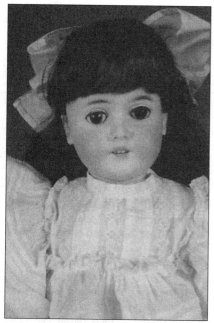

Armand Marseille "Queen Louise" Doll

antique white lace-trimmed low waisted dress, underclothing, new socks & shoes, large white satin bow in hair, small eye chip repair on right eye, general wear, hands repainted, 28" (ILLUS.) **375.00**

Arranbee "Nancy" composition head marked "Nancy," brown sleep eyes w/real lashes, single-stroke brows, painted upper lashes, open mouth w/four upper teeth, original blonde mohair wig, five-piece composition body, original pink nylon taffeta dress, matching underclothing, white fur coat & hat w/matching pink lining, original socks & shoes, 16" (good coloring, clean clothes, eyes crazed).............................**300.00**

Automaton of young woman playing piano, marked "70-1½," bisque head, blue glass eyes inside head, open mouth, blonde mohair wig, wood & wire body, composition hands, lace & silk

costume, wooden piano, paint & paper covered base, early 20th c., 6¹⁄₁₆ x 6⅞", 7½" h. (silk deteriorated, sconces missing from piano, edge wear on base) **575.00**

Baby Bud bisque head marked "Baby Bud - Germany," unjointed head w/character face, painted eyes looking to side, single-stroke brows, accented nostrils, closed smiling mouth w/accent line between lips, molded & painted blue shirt, no other clothing, hands molded w/two fingers up on left hand, one finger up on right hand, 5½" (excellent condition w/some rub on left check) **115.00**

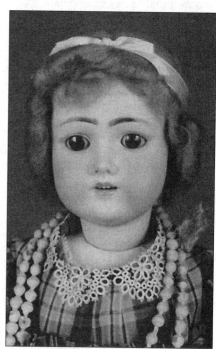

Bergmann Bisque Socket Head Child

Bergmann (C. M.) bisque socket head child marked "C.M. Bergmann - Simon & Halbig - S&H - 3," brown sleep eyes, feathered brows, painted upper & lower lashes, accented nostrils open mouth w/four painted teeth, mohair wig, jointed wood & composition body, red & blue plaid dress, antique underclothing, old socks & shoes, 25" (ILLUS.) **350.00**

Bisque composition Russian girl marked "K&W - 155/10," marked "K&W - 52" faintly on back, painted bisque-type composition head, blue flirty sleep eyes w/tin lids & real lashes, painted lower lashes, open mouth w/two upper teeth, synthetic curly wig, five-piece composition body w/working crier, original flowered sunsuit w/matching dress, socks & red shoes, pearl necklace, 20" (old repaint on body, light wear at joints) **160.00**

Bisque composition Russian toddler marked "PS (intertwined) - 2966 - 11 - 0" on back of head, marked "55" on left shoulder, painted bisque-type composition head, blue sleep eyes w/real lashes, feathered brows, open mouth w/four upper teeth, original synthetic wig, five-piece composition toddler body w/non-working crier, original blue rayon-type dress trimmed in lace, underclothing, socks & red shoes, 23" (cracks in finish under both arms) **165.00**

Bisque socket head German child marked "9H 7X - DEP," set blue eyes, feathered brows, painted upper & lower lashes, accented nostrils, open mouth w/accented lips & four upper teeth, replaced wig, long cloth torso w/child arms & legs, gussets at elbows, hips & knees, dressed in ecru two-piece suit w/lace trim, slip, no pants, replaced socks & shoes, 23" (minor repair on gussets, hands do not match) **125.00**

Bisque socket head German child marked "Made in Germany - B.3.," brown sleep eyes w/real lashes, feathered brows, painted upper & lower lashes, accented nostrils, open mouth w/four upper teeth, auburn mohair wig, jointed wood & composition body, new blue dress, antique underclothing, socks & shoes, 23" (minor repairs at hips, touch-up at neck socket of torso) **240.00**

Bisque socket head German child marked "478,15," brown sleep eyes w/real & painted lashes, molded & feathered brows, accented nostrils, open mouth w/well-accented lips, four upper teeth, pierced ears, h.h. wig, jointed wood & composition body, white dotted Swiss dress, slip, socks & old button shoes, 31" (left eyeball cracked, body repainted & flaking, two fingers off each hand, mismatched arm & thigh parts, damage at hip sockets & toes) **375.00**

Bisque swivel shoulder head lady marked "5" on edge of right shoulder, light blue paperweight eyes, closed mouth, pierced ears, cork pate, red h.h. wig, cloth body & wigs, kid arms & bisque hands, dressed in period dimity dress, ca. 1880, France, 19" (chip to left eye socket, one arm damaged) **920.00**

Buddy Lee composition head boy, unmarked, labeled "Union Made - Lee - Sanforized - Shrunk" on cap & pants, "Lee" snaps on front of pants, unjointed head w/large painted eyes looking to side, single-stroke brows, painted upper & lashes, closed smiling mouth, molded & painted hair, composition body jointed at shoulders only, molded &

"Buddy Lee" Composition Head Doll

painted boots, light crazing, some chipping, 12" (ILLUS.)......**425.00**

Bye-Lo Baby unjointed bisque head marked "20-10" on back, legs & arms, painted blue eyes, softly blushed brows, accented nostrils, closed mouth, lightly molded & painted hair, all bisque body jointed at shoulders & hips, original white dress trimmed in lace & inserts, matching bonnet, slip & diaper, 4" (repair on stringing loop of right leg, otherwise very good condition)....**90.00**

Bye-Lo Baby bisque socket head marked "Copr. by Grace S. Putnam - Made in Germany - 1369 30," brown sleep eyes, softly blushed brows, painted upper & lower lashes, accented nostrils, closed mouth, lightly molded & painted hair, composition bent-limb baby body, short white baby dress, underclothing, no socks or shoes, 12" (numerous chips around neck opening & left little toe) **350.00**

Bye-lo Baby bisque flange head marked "Copr. by Grace S. Putnam - Made in Germany," brown sleep eyes, softly brushed brows, painted upper & lower lashes, accented nostrils, closed mouth w/accent line between lips, lightly molded & painted hair, cloth body, celluloid hands, 15" c., 17" (eyes replaced or rewaxed & reset) **475.00**

Celluloid flange head Russian baby marked "K&R W - 351/4," brown flirty eyes w/separate lids & real lashes, single-stroke brows, painted lower lashes, accented nostrils, open mouth w/two upper teeth, molded & painted hair, cloth body w/celluloid arms & legs, original white blouse, white nylon romper w/red rose buds, green rick-rack trim, white bonnet w/red design embroidered on top, pink booties, 19" (some fading on exposed body parts) ..**165.00**

Cloth black doll, stockinette head, ivory eyes w/shoe button pupils, molded features w/embroidered mouth & eyebrows, black astrakhan hair, cotton twill body & limbs, wearing period dress, late 19th c., American, 20" h. **5,175.00**

Cloth doll, hand-made orange-peel construction head, painted hair & features, cotton sateen body & limbs, painted arms w/stitched fingers, jointed at shoulders, hips & knees, early 20th c., 27" **1,495.00**

Colombian cloth doll marked "Colombian Doll Emma E. Adams Oswego Center N.Y.," muslin, h.p. head & shoulders, dark blonde hair, brown eyes, dressed in period costume, 1891-1906, 28" (paint worn, feet have fabric loss, mark on partially legible) **1,840.00**

Composition head Russian baby marked "SP (intertwined) - 2542/2 1/4," painted bisque-type composition flange head, blue sleep eyes w/real lashes, single-stroke brows, open mouth w/two upper teeth, cloth body w/excelsior-stuffed torso, painted bisque hands, original red & white romper w/red coat, white hat trimmed in red, 15" (clothing slightly aged, otherwise excellent condition)......................**45.00**

Composition head Russian child, unmarked, blue sleep eyes w/real lashes, feathered brows, accented nostrils, closed mouth, mohair wig in original set, five-piece heavy composition body, original peach print dress, babushka, original underclothing, socks & sandals, 26" (excellent condition)..................................**210.00**

"Denny Dimwit" Doll

Denny Dimwit, unmarked, unjointed cloth head w/molded

mask face, blue painted crossed eyes, single-stroke brows, long broad nose, open-closed smiling mouth w/two painted teeth, modeling in face accented by dark lines, applied oversized gold felt ears, blue felt hood attached to head, cloth body jointed at shoulders only, large flannel hands w/three stitched fingers & thumb, unjointed legs w/brown felt feet for shoes, support wires back of legs to help doll stand, red & white striped scarf, red felt pants, dark red knit socks above shoes, gold felt jacket, unplayed with, some surface soil, 18" (ILLUS. previous column) **195.00**

Dressel (Cuno & Otto) bisque socket head child marked "COD - 5," set brown eyes, heavily feathered brows, painted upper & lower lashes, accented nostrils, open mouth w/accented lips & four upper teeth, synthetic wig, jointed wood & composition body, redressed in new brown calico dress, antique underclothing, new socks & shoes, 18" (1" hairline on forehead at crown, repainted body) **175.00**

Dressel (Cuno & Otto) bisque socket head child marked "1913," & **"Made in Germany - (COD cross symbol) - 1912 . 4,"** blue sleep eyes w/real lashes, feathered brows, painted upper & lower lashes, accented nostrils, open mouth w/four upper teeth, h.h. wig, jointed wood & composition body, wearing a white dotted Swiss dress w/ruffle at bottom, underclothing, replaced sock & shoes, 22" (legs do not match, damage to right hip) **130.00**

Effanbee "American Child" marked "Effanbee Anne-Shirley" on back, "I Am An

Effanbee Durable Doll - The Doll With the Satin-Smooth Skin" on paper heart wrist tag, composition head, green sleep eyes w/real upper lashes, painted lower lashes, single-stroke brows, accented nostrils, open mouth w/four upper teeth, original h.h. wig, five-piece composition child body w/large hands, original teal blue dress tagged "Effanbee Durable Dolls - Made in USA" on back, pink eyelet-trimmed pinafore, one-piece underwear combination, original socks & shoes, blue straw hat, 20"..........................**1,100.00**

Effanbee "Anne-Shirley" marked "Effanbee - Anne-Shirley" on back, composition head, blue eyes w/real lashes, feathered brows, painted lower lashes, accented nostrils, closed mouth, h.h. wig in original set, five-piece composition body, original red & white striped dress, white bodice w/blue stars, original underclothing, socks & red shoes, "I Am Little Lady - An Effanbee Durable Doll" on paper wrist tag, "Effanbee Durable Dolls" on gold metal bracelet, 14" (unplayed-with condition).................................**175.00**

Effanbee "Anne-Shirley" 1492 Indian historical replica marked "Effanbee - Anne-Shirley" on back, composition head, painted brown eyes, multi-stroke brows, painted upper & lower lashes, accented nostrils, closed mouth, original auburn h.h. wig in original set, brown five-piece composition body w/large hands, original coral outfit, white blouse w/jabot & full sleeves, underclothing, long stockings & shoes, "Effanbee Durable Dolls" on metal bracelet, 14" (generally excellent condition)..................................**325.00**

Effanbee "Anne-Shirley" 1750 historical replica marked "Effanbee - Anne-Shirley" on back, composition head, painted blue eyes, multi-stroke brows, painted upper & lower lashes, accented nostrils, closed mouth, dark "beauty mark" on right check, original white mohair wig in original set, five-piece composition body w/large hands, original blue quilted skirt w/blue floral overdress lined in red, original underclothing, long stockings & shoes, "Effanbee Durable Dolls" on metal heart bracelet, unplayed condition with in original box, 14"....................**430.00**

Effanbee "Anne-Shirley" 1868 historical replica marked "Effanbee - Anne-Shirley" on back, composition head, painted brown eyes w/much detail, multi-stroke brows, painted upper & lower lashes, accented nostrils, closed mouth, original h.h. wig in original set, five-piece composition body w/large hands, red & white checked dress w/white apron, original underclothing, original long stockings to hips, original shoes, "Effanbee Durable Dolls" on metal heart bracelet, unplayed with condition in original box, 14"..**400.00**

Effanbee "Anne-Shirley" 1872 historical replica marked "Effanbee - Anne-Shirley" on back, composition head, painted blue eyes, multi-stroke brows, painted upper & lower lashes, accented nostrils, closed mouth, h.h. wig in original set, five-piece composition body, original rust colored long gown w/tiered skirt & removable bustle, separate lace-trimmed top w/plain bodice, underclothing, long stockings, shoes, marked "Effanbee

Durable Dolls" on metal bracelet, 14" (few lines of light crazing on face) **450.00**

Effanbee "Anne-Shirley" 1939-today historical replica marked "Effanbee - Anne-Shirley" on back, composition head, painted blue eyes, multi-stroke brows, painted upper & lower lashes, accented nostrils, closed mouth, auburn hair wig in original set, five-piece composition body, "gypsy dress" formal designed by Coco Chanel w/lavender pleated skirt, long sleeve white blouse w/rows of lace, wide green sash, original underclothing , long stockings, shoes, 14" (very light crazing, no fading) **460.00**

Effanbee grumpy Amish man & woman marked "Effanbee Dolls - Walk - Talk - Sleep" on back shoulder plate, composition shoulder heads, painted blue eyes to side, single-stroke brows, closed pouty mouth, original mohair wigs,original beard on man, cloth bodies w/composition arms & feet, molded & painted

shoes on man, composition legs on woman, woman dressed in original white panties, brown flannel slip, blue cotton dress, black apron & shawl, white organdy bonnet under black outer bonnet, socks & shoes, man dressed in original denim pants & jacket, green knit piece on front under-jacket to look like shirt, black felt hat, each paper-tagged "Pennsylvania Dutch Dolls - By Marie Polack - Reg. U.S. Pat. Off." on one side, "Amish" reverse, light crazing on both dolls, otherwise excellent condition, 12", pr. (ILLUS. previous column) **175.00**

Effanbee "Little Lady" marked "I Am Little Lady - An Effanbee Durable Doll" on paper heart wrist tag, composition head, brown sleep eyes w/real lashes, feathered brows, painted lower lashes, accented nostrils, closed mouth, blonde yarn wig in original set, five-piece composition body, original pink chiffon formal

Effanbee Amish Man & Woman

Effanbee "Little Lady" Doll

trimmed w/pink & black rosettes, matching panties, long stockings, shoes, includes "How to make your own glamorous Hair Styles - Little Lady - an Effanbee Doll" booklet, 27" (ILLUS. previous page, right) **400.00**

Effanbee "Patsyette" marked "Effanbee Patsyette Doll" on back, composition head, painted blue eyes to side, single-stroke brows, painted upper lashes, closed "rosebud" mouth, molded & painted hair, five-piece composition body w/bent right arm, pink organdy short dress w/matching underwear, replaced socks & shoes, 9" (general wear, light touch-up on left hand & feet) **300.00**

Effanbee "Wee Patsy" marked "Wee Patsy" on back, unjointed composition head, painted blue eyes, single-stroke brows, closed "rosebud" mouth, molded & painted hair, composition body jointed at shoulders & hips, pale pink organdy dress w/embroidered flowers & bows at shoulders, organdy "panties" sewn on, pink ribbon in hair, molded & painted socks & shoes, 6" (light crazing, small chip on right front of hair) **305.00**

Elizabeth Chitty-style cloth doll, muslin, painted features, applied nose, sewn on red h.h., well defined & stitched hands & feet, dressed in period outfit, late 19th c., 24" (some wear to head & fabric) **1,495.00**

Fulper "Colonial" bisque socket head baby marked "Fulper (vertical) - Colonial Doll - Made in U.S.A." on back, blue sleep eyes, feathered brows, painted upper & lower lashes, accented nostrils, open mouth w/two upper teeth, molded tongue, mohair wig, composition

bent-limb baby body, dressed in old knit baby dress w/matching panties, booties, lacy bonnet, 23" (two minor firing splits on rim, body possibly repainted) **400.00**

Gans & Seyfarth bisque socket head child marked "G&S .5 - Germany," blue sleep eyes, feathered brows, painted upper & lower lashes, accented nostrils, open mouth w/four upper teeth, h.h. wig, jointed wood & composition body, redressed in white dress made from antique clothing, matching bonnet, underclothing, replaced socks & shoes, 23" (repairs at shoulder & hip joints, hands repainted, general wear) **300.00**

Goebel bisque socket head baby marked "(bee) - W on top of G - B 5-6½ - Germany," blue sleep eyes w/real lashes, feathered brows, painted upper & lower lashes, accented nostrils, open mouth w/accented lips & two upper teeth, bent-limb baby body, new baby dress w/eyelet trim, one-piece underwear, socks & shoes, 19" (worn finish on torso, arms & legs repainted).........................**330.00**

Goldsmith (Philip) body w/composition shoulder head lady, set blue eyes, feathered brows, painted upper & lower lashes, accented nostrils, closed mouth w/accented lips & accents line between lips, cloth body by Philip Goldsmith w/red corset, white "lacings" on front, red cloth lower legs, red kid boots as feet, leather lower arms w/stitched fingers, original two-piece suit in off white polished cotton trimmed w/lace & ribbon, original underclothing, 26" (some light wear, otherwise excellent condition)...................**225.00**

Handwerck (Heinrich) bisque socket head girl marked "109 .

7½ - Germany - Handwerck," marked "Heinrich Handwerck" on right hip, large blue sleep eyes, molded & feathered brows, painted upper & lower lashes, accented nostrils, open mouth w/upper accented lips & four upper teeth, pierced ears, mohair wig, jointed wood & composition body, dressed in white blouse w/red & white print jumper, underclothing, replaced socks & shoes, 18" (body shows overall wear, hands repainted) ..**425.00**

Handwerck (Heinrich) bisque socket head girl marked "Germany - Heinrich Handwerck - Simon & Halbig - 1," marked "W" on front of head at crown, "1 - Heinrich Handwerck - Germany" on body, blue sleep eyes w/real lashes, feathered brows, painted lower lashes, accented nostrils, open mouth w/accented lips & four upper teeth, pierced ears, replaced synthetic wig, jointed wood & composition body, redressed in new blue flowered dress, matching hat, eyelet pinafore, lace-trimmed underclothing, stockings & shoes, 18" (very faint ½" hairline from crown on left front, general wear, excellent body, repainted hands & arms) **170.00**

Handwerck (Heinrich) bisque socket head nun marked "109-11 3/4 - DEP - Germany - Handwerck," blue sleep eyes, molded & feathered brows, painted upper & lower lashes, accented nostrils, open mouth w/accented lips & four upper teeth, sparse mohair wig, jointed wood & composition body, dressed in nun's habit, underclothing, old black stockings & shoes, minor repair around neck socket of body, 22" (ILLUS. next column)................**725.00**

Heinrich Handwerck "Nun" Doll

Handwerck (Heinrich) bisque socket head girl marked "14 - Germany - 99 - DEP - Handwerck - 5½," blue eyes, molded & feathered brows, painted upper & lower lashes, accented nostrils, open mouth w/accented lips, four upper teeth, pierced ears, synthetic wig, jointed wood & composition child body, redressed in purple taffeta & velvet, matching purple lace-trimmed taffeta underclothing, brown cotton socks, brown high button shoes, 28" (light wear on body, minor cracks in finish of composition) **725.00**

Handwerck (Heinrich) bisque socket head girl marked "Germany - Handwerck - 9," marked "Heinrich Handwerck - Germany - 9" on lower back, blue sleepy eyes w/real lashes, molded & feathered brows, painted upper & lower lashes, accented nostrils, open mouth w/accented lips & four upper teeth, pierced ears, original h.h. wig, ball jointed composition body, bluish-green taffeta dress, underclothing, socks, 42" (minor crack in each eyeball, body repainted, normal wear) **2,600.00**

Hard plastic socket head Russian girl marked "Sonni," blue sleep eyes w/real lashes, feathered brows, eye shadow, accented nostrils, closed mouth, original wig, five-piece hard plastic body, original pink dress trimmed w/blue flowers, blue panties, replaced socks & shoes, 17" (excellent condition w/bright coloring, good finish, a few minor rubs).........................**115.00**

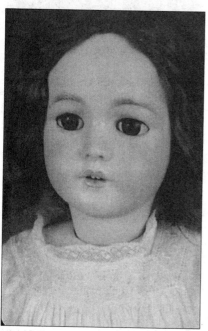

Ernst Heubach Baby Doll

Heubach (Ernst) bisque socket head baby marked "Heubach Koppelsdorf - 342 . 11 - Germany," blue sleep eyes w/real lashes, feathered brows, painted upper & lower lashes, accented nostrils, open mouth w/two upper teeth, dark mohair

wig, bent-limb composition baby body, antique lace-trimmed baby dress, underclothing, socks, oversized lace-trimmed bonnet, body repainted, repair at left hip socket of torso, 27" (ILLUS. previous column) **440.00**

Heubach (Gebruder) unjointed bisque baby marked w/a "Sunburst" on bottom, blue intaglio eyes, single-stroke brows, laughing open-closed mouth, molded w/painted hair, unjointed bisque body in crouched position w/hands in front of feet, unclothed, 6" (some slight rubs marks, otherwise excellent condition)...................**375.00**

Himstedt (Annette) "Neblina" marked "Annette Himstedt - Neblina" on back of head, marked "Annette Himstedt" on back plate, vinyl socket head, brown glass eyes, multi-stroke brows, real upper & lower lashes, closed mouth, original h.h. wig, velveteen body w/vinyl breast plate, vinyl arms & legs, mauve dress, white flowered pinafore, white eyelet underclothing, no socks & shoes, 26"................................**525.00**

Horsman "Groom" composition head, blue sleepy eyes w/real lashes, eye shadow, single-stroke brows, painted lower lashes, accented nostrils, open mouth w/four upper teeth, mohair wig, five-piece composition body, black wool tuxedo, white shirt, white vest, socks & shoes, boxed, stamped "Horsman Doll - Genuine Horsman Art Doll - Made in U.S.A. - Horsman Dolls Inc. - Trenton, New Jersey" on end-of-box label, 20" (eyes cracked & whites have yellowed) **245.00**

Horsman composition head character baby, metal sleep eyes, head w/molded hair, closed mouth, cloth body & legs, composition hands, 1920s, 23" (paint damage on heads & hands) **316.00**

Ideal "Toni" marked "Ideal Doll - Made in USA," on back of head, "Ideal Doll - P-90" on back, hard plastic head, blue sleep eyes w/real lashes, single-stroke brows, painted lower lashes, closed mouth, original nylon wig, five-piece hard plastic body, original pink organdy dress w/embroidery on the bodice, attached half slip, matching panties, original socks & shoes, includes original box with "Play Wave" accessories, 14" **450.00**

Izannah Walker cloth doll, short dark brown painted hair, brown eyes, closed mouth, beige cloth body, painted & stitched hands, painted brown shoes, dressed in period costume, Central Falls, Rhode Island, 1870-80, 17" (fiber loss on head, fiber loss & staining to dress) **6,325.00**

Joy "1939 World's Fair" composition head doll, brown sleep eyes w/real lashes, feathered brows, painted lower lashes, accented nostrils, closed mouth, mohair wig in original set, five-piece composition body, print dress & scarf w/World's Fair scenes, marked "International Doll - Reg. U.S.Pat.Off - Officially Licensed - New York World's Fair - A Joy Doll Product" on dress label, "New York World's Fair 1939 Inc. - Officially Licensed - NYWF" on paper wrist tag, underclothing, socks & shoes, unplayed with in original orange box, 20" **410.00**

Jumeau "Long-Faced" bisque socket head girl marked "13," stamped "Jumeau - Medaille d'Or - Paris" on lower rear torso,

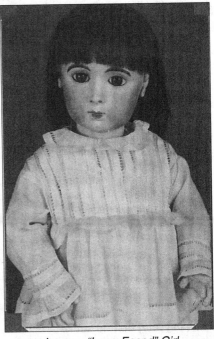

Jumeau "Long-Faced" Girl

bulbous blue paperweight eyes, heavy feathered brows, painted upper & lower lashes, accented nostrils, closed mouth w/accent lips & white space between, pierced & applied ears, replaced h.h. wig, jointed composition body w/straight wrists, antique white dress w/tucks & ruffles, underclothing, antique socks & baby shoes, head professionally repaired from break to forehead, 28" (ILLUS.)...........................**2,500.00**

Jumeau (Emile) bisque head Bebe marked "7 - EJ," blue glass eyes lined w/black & shaded pink, closed mouth, pierced applied ears, blonde mohair wig over cork pate, non-original German jointed & composition body, white cotton dress, cream cotton coat, brown leather shoes, ca. 1885, 19½" (kiln spot on tip of nose & right cheek, flakes from ear pieces, slight wig pull).........................**2,875.00**

Jumeau (Emile) bisque socket head Bebe marked "Depose - E.9.J." on back of head, "Jumeau - Medaille d'Or - Paris" on lower back, large deep brown paperweight eyes, heavy feathered brows, painted upper & lower lashes, accented nostrils, closed mouth w/accented lips & white space between lips, pierced applied ears, replaced h.h. wig, jointed composition body w/straight wrists, slate grey silk dress w/jacket, embroidered lace & ribbon trim, underclothing, brown cotton socks, antique French shoes, lace bonnet w/wide brim, 20" (two small neck chips repaired, tip of nose touched up, normal light wear at joints) **4,200.00**

Jumeau (Tete) bisque socket head girl marked "Depose - Tete Jumeau - Bte S.G.D.G. - 7," dark brown paperweight eyes, heavy feathered brows, long painted upper & lower lashes, accented nostrils, closed mouth w/accented lips & white space between lips, pierced ears, old dark brown h.h. wig, jointed wood & composition body w/straight wrists, hand-made deep blue dress trimmed w/black velvet ribbon, antique underclothing, socks & French shoes, includes cotton jump rope w/wooden handles & old white kid gloves, 16" (normal body wear, short crack at hip socket on torso) **3,500.00**

Jumeau bisque socket head girl marked "1907 - 14," blue paperweight eyes, heavy feathered brows, painted upper & lower lashes, accented nostrils, open mouth w/accented lips & six upper teeth, pierced ears, replaced wig, jointed wood & composition body, redressed in ecru taffeta dress w/lace overlay, silk ribbon trim, underclothing, cotton socks, leather shoes, ecru lace & ribbon trimmed bonnet, 29" (light wear & soil on body, minor break in finish under right arm) **2,300.00**

K&K baby bisque shoulder head marked "42 - K&K - 56 - Made in Germany," blue sleep eyes w/remnants of real lashes, painted upper & lower lashes, accented nostrils, open smiling mouth /four upper teeth, mohair wig, cloth body w/composition lower arms, oil-cloth legs, pink-dotted Swiss dress w/matching hat, underclothing, new socks, old shoes, 18" (lower hands cracked w/finish lifting) **235.00**

K * R (Kammer & Reinhart) bisque socket head toddler marked "K * R - Simon & Halbig - 126, 28" on back & "W" on front of head, blue sleep eyes, feathered brows, painted upper & lower teeth, original h.h. wig, jointed wood & composition toddler body w/joints at elbow & knees, white eyelet blouse, turquoise & white jumper, underclothing, replaced socks & shoes, 13" (general light wear on body & at joints) **700.00**

K * R bisque socket head girl marked "S&H - K * R - 36," brown eyes w/real lashes, painted upper & lower lashes, feathered brows, painted upper teeth, pierced ears, replaced blonde h.h. wig, jointed wood & composition body, beige & blue sailor dress, underclothing, replaced socks & shoes, 14" (lower legs replaced, wear on hands) **300.00**

K * R bisque socket head toddler marked "K * R - Simon & Halbig - 126 - 36," brown sleep eyes, feathered brows, painted upper & lower lashes, accented nostrils, open mouth w/two upper teeth & wobble tongue, original blonde mohair wig, fully-jointed toddler body w/diagonal hip joints, jointed knees & elbows, white dress, knit underclothing, socks & shoes, beige crocheted bonnet, 16" (tiny inherent "pimple" in bisque on nose, teeth replaced, minor wear on hands)...............**825.00**

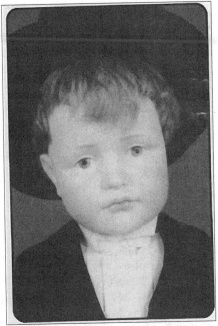

*K * R Groom Doll*

K * R bisque socket head groom marked "K * R - 114 - 46," painted blue eyes, single-stroke brows, accented nostrils, closed pouty mouth, original mohair wig, jointed wood & composition Kammer & Reinhardt body, original tuxedo w/white shirt & vest, black wool jacket w/satin lapels, black wool pants, black satin top hat, socks & shoes, tiny "pick" by left eye, like-new body, 18" (ILLUS.)....**4,700.00**

K * R bisque socket head boy marked "K * R - 101 - 40,"

character face, painted blue eyes w/black accent line, single-stroked brows, accented nostrils, closed pouty mouth, antique h.h. wig, jointed wood & composition toddler body, jointed at shoulders, elbows, wrists, hips & knees, antique plum two-piece wool outfit w/off-white piping, knit off-white cap, socks, black leather shoes, 18" (faint hairline crack from crown of left front through eye into left cheek, general wear).............**2,900.00**

K * R bisque socket head bride marked "Simon & Halbig - K * S - 50," brown flirty eyes, tin lids w/remnants of real lashes, painted upper & lower lashes, molded & feathered brows, accented nostrils, open mouth w/accented lips, four upper teeth, pierced ears, blond mohair wig in original curls, jointed wood & composition Kammer & Reinhardt body, original crepe & lace wedding gown w/long train, underclothing, socks & shoes, head piece from original veil w/wax flowers, pearl necklace, 19" **1,700.00**

K * R bisque socket head girl marked "Simon & Halbig - K * R - 53," marked "W" on front at crown, brown flirty eyes w/tin lids, feathered brows, painted upper & lower lashes, accented nostrils, open mouth w/accented lips & four upper teeth, pierced ears, replaced wig, jointed wood & composition body, redressed in flowered low-waisted dress trimmed w/ribbons & lace, pants, socks & shoes, 20" (faint ½" hairline from crown in front, minor body wear, metal eyelids repainted) **425.00**

K * R bisque head marked "K * R - Simon & Halbig - 403," brown glass sleep eyes, open mouth, pierced ears, blonde mohair wig, composition body, fully jointed arms, straight legs, walking action, 1927, 21" (tiny flakes on ears, some composition damage) **288.00**

K * R bisque socket head toddler marked "K * R - Simon & Halbig - 126 - 56," stamped "ges. geschutzt" on partial label lower back, blue flirty eyes w/tin lids, feathered brows, painted upper & lower lashes, accented nostrils, open mouth, w/two upper teeth & molded tongue, original mohair wig, jointed wood & composition body w/diagonal joints, yellow flowered antique ruffled dress, underclothing, new socks & baby shoes, 24" (2" hairline crack on back of head from crown) **600.00**

*K * R "Flirty Eyes" Doll*

K * R bisque socket head girl marked "K * R - Simon & Halbig - 117N - Germany - 80," brown flirty eyes w/tin lids,

feathered brows, painted upper & lower lashes, accented nostrils, open mouth w/four upper teeth, original blonde mohair wig in bob style, jointed wood & composition flapper body w/diagonal hip joints, high knee joints, rubber hands, white low-waisted dress w/eyelet & tucks, slip, panties, socks & shoes, reglued chip on lower right lid, 30" (ILLUS. previous column) **850.00**

Kestner (J.D.) bisque shoulder head child marked "dep 154 1½," blue sleep eyes w/real lashes, feathered brows, painted lower lashes, accented nostrils, open mouth w/four upper teeth, mohair wig, kid body, bisque lower arms, pin joints at hips, gussets at knees, cloth lower legs, antique pleated light blue & white dress decorated w/feather stitching, underclothing, replaced socks & shoes, 13" (overall soil & wear on body, very tiny chip on left fingers)......**170.00**

Kestner (J.D.) bisque shoulder head child marked "154 dep 5," marked "Made in Germany" on back of shoulder plate, "JDK - Germany" in crown & streamers, "Cork Stuffed" on front of kid body, blue sleep eye w/real lashes, molded & feathered brows, painted lower lashes, accented nostrils, open mouth w/four upper teeth, synthetic wig, bisque lower arms, rivets at hips, cloth lower legs, white dress w/tucks & lace trim, antique underclothing, new socks & white leather shoes, 16" (normal wear & soil, bisque lower arms repaired & repainted) **210.00**

Kestner (J.D.)bisque socket head "Daisy" girl marked "C½ made in Germany 7½ - 171 - 10," marked "Germany - 1½" on rear torso, blue sleep eyes w/real upper lashes, painted lower lashes, feathered brows, accented nostrils, open mouth w/accented lips & four upper teeth, original blonde mohair wig, jointed wood & composition body, antique white dress w/lace trim, underclothing, replaced socks, antique shoes, 18" (balls at hip joints reglued) **675.00**

Kestner (J.D.) bisque shoulder head child marked "9 154 Dep.," brown sleep eyes, molded & feathered brows, painted upper & lower lashes, accented nostrils, open mouth w/accented lips & four upper teeth, synthetic wig, child body w/bisque lower arms, gussets at elbows, hips & knees, antique blue & brown plaid dress w/black rick-rack trim, underclothing, socks, new high-button boots, 20" (overall soil & aging, otherwise excellent condition) **145.00**

Kestner (J.D.) bisque socket head child marked "M½ made in Germany 16½ - 171 - 7," set blue eyes, feathered brows, painted upper & lower lashes, accented nostrils, open mouth w/four upper teeth, synthetic wig, jointed wood & composition body, antique child's dress, underclothing, antique socks & shoes, generally excellent condition w/normal wear & aging of body, 32" (ILLUS. bottom previous column) **875.00**

"Kewpie," all-bisque, marked "Kewpie - Design Pat. - No 43680 - Reg. U.S. Pat. Off." in paper heart label on chest, "Rose O'Neill 1913" in circle on base, unjointed head, painted oversize eyes to side, dot brows, painted upper lashes, closed smiling mouth, molded & painted tufts of hair, composition body jointed at shoulder only, legs molded together standing on blue base, fabric gathered around Kewpie's middle, 12" (few tiny flakes on head & body) **155.00**

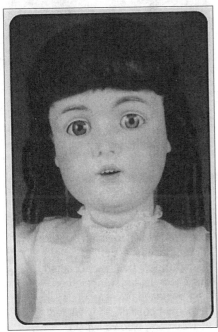

Kestner Child Doll

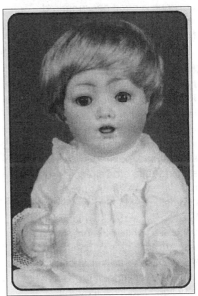

Konig & Wernicke Baby Doll

Konig & Wernicke bisque socket head baby marked "Made in Germany 99/8," stamped "Made in Germany" on left rear shoulder, brown sleep eyes w/real lashes, feathered brows, painted upper & lower lashes, accented nostrils, open mouth w/accented lips, two upper teeth & molded tongue, replaced synthetic wig, composition bent-limb baby body, antique white dress w/eyelet trim, panties, booties, generally excellent w/normal wear, 16½" (ILLUS. bottom previous page)...........................**325.00**

Kruse (Kathe) molded swivel head boy marked "Kathe Kruse - 330730" on left foot, "Made in Germany" on right foot, molded & painted cloth swivel head, painted hazel eyes, single-stroke brows, accented nostrils, closed pouty mouth, original h.h. wig, five-piece cloth body, original red two-piece boy's suit trimmed w/white, matching red cap, white socks & leather shoes, original paper tag on string around neck marked "Kathe Kruse Original gekleidet - Made in U.S. Zone Germany," unplayed with condition, 14"...**1,600.00**

Kruse (Kathe) molded swivel head girl marked "Kathe Kruse - 130869" on bottom of left foot, "Made in Germany - US Zone" on bottom of right foot, molded & painted cloth swivel head, painted hazel eyes, single-stroke brows, accented nostrils, closed pouty mouth, original h.h. wig, five-piece cloth body, original red & white polka dot dress, white pinafore, one-piece underclothing, original socks & white leather shoes, unplayed with condition, 14" very light display soil overall, light wear on shoes) **700.00**

Kruse (Kathe) girl marked "(turtle mark) - T40," marked "(turtle mark) - Modell - Kathe Kruse - T40" on back, celluloid socket head, set blue eyes, lids w/real lashes, single-stroke brows, accented nostrils closed mouth, original h.h. wig in braids, five-piece celluloid body, original blue print dress, underclothing, replaced socks, original shoes, 15" (some slight rubs, clothing somewhat faded) **260.00**

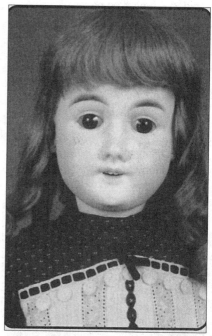

Gebruder Kuhnlenz Child Doll

Kuhnlenz (Gebruder) bisque socket head child marked "Gbr K (in sunburst) - Dep - 44/35," set brown eyes, heavy feathered brows, painted upper & lower lashes, accented nostrils, open mouth w/accented lips & four upper teeth, pierced ears, replaced h.h. wig, unusual heavy composition body jointed at shoulders, elbows, wrists, hips & knees, antique black &

white child's dress, underclothing, long white socks, black & white high button shoes, torso has old repaint w/finish cracked & flaking, lower legs repainted, 37" (ILLUS. previous page)......................**1,500.00**

Lanternier bisque head "Cherie" marked "Limoges Cherie 4," blue glass eyes, open mouth, pierced ears, original blonde mohair wig, fully jointed composition body, 1920s, France, 13¾" (some paint loss) **230.00**

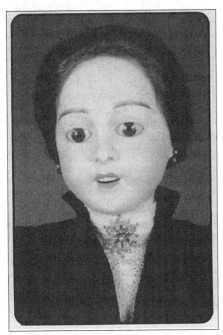

Lanternier French Character Lady

Lanternier bisque French character lady marked "Depose - Fabrication Francaise - Favorite - Ed Tasson - Al & Cie Limoges" on back of bisque socket head, set brown eyes, feathered brows, painted upper & lower lashes, accented nostrils, open mouth w/six upper teeth, pierced ears, synthetic wig, jointed wood & composition body, redressed in black velvet two-piece suite, white eyelet blouse, underclothing, socks & shoes, eyes replaced, few kiln specks in bisque, body repainted, right foot repaired, 31" (ILLUS. previous column) **475.00**

Lenci boy, pressed felt face, painted brown eyes to side, single-stroke brows, painted upper & some lower lashes, accented nostrils, closed mouth, applied felt ears, original mohair wig, cloth torso, felt arms & legs, original white shirt, red felt vest, green felt over vest w/embroidered lamb & edelweiss, brown felt pants & shoes, replaced green felt cap, 14" (overall good condition w/slight soil on hands, repaired shirt) **325.00**

Lenci #1500 "Margarita," unmarked, molded felt pouty face, painted brown eyes to the side, single-stroke brows, painted upper lashes, accented nostrils, closed mouth w/top lip darker than bottom, two white highlights on bottom lip, applied pierced ears, original black mohair wig, five-piece felt body w/hollow torso, jointed at shoulders & hips, original felt outfit w/red & beige checked shirt, beige shorts, red leather sandals, red felt bow in hair, gold hoop earrings, child holding rooster w/yellow body, rust colored wings, multi-colored tail & red comb, 17" (very good condition w/some fading & overall soil) **1,000.00**

Lenci Pierrot, molded felt, wearing black skull cap, bright green clown suit w/pompons down front & at sleeves w/ruffle around neck, shoes w/pompoms, 1930s, 20" (some moth damage, outfit faded) **173.00**

Mattel "Chatty Cathy" Doll

**Mattel "Chatty Cathy" marked
"Chatty Cathy** - Patents
Pending - MCMLX - By Mattel
Inc. - Hawthorne, Calif." on
back, vinyl head, blue sleep
eyes w/real lashes, single-stroke
brows, freckles, open-close
mouth w/two upper teeth, rooted
brunette hair, five-piece rigid
vinyl body, original pink & white
striped dress w/white pinafore
tagged "Chatty Cathy," boxed,
tagged red velvet coat w/fur trim,
matching headband, socks &
shoes, "Mattel's Chatty Cathy -
The Talking Doll" on end of box,
20" (ILLUS.) **260.00**

**Mechanical bisque head pull
toy doll,** glass sleep eyes, open
mouth, wood & wire body, wood
hands, papier-mâché feet, in
original outfit, when toy is pulled
head turns & arm moves baton,
late 19th - early 20th c.,
Germany, 7¼" l., 12¼" h.
(general wear & fading) **460.00**

**Papier- mâché "Milliner's
Model,"** papier-mâché shoulder
head, painted blue eyes, single-
stroke brows, accented nostrils,
closed smiling mouth, molded &
painted hair w/three large curls
on each side of head, braided
bun in back, kid body w/wooden
lower arms & legs, redressed in
two-piece outfit & underclothing,
17" (general light crazing on
face & shoulder plate, paint
worn & flaked off lower arms &
legs)...**900.00**

Ravca-Type Man & Woman

Ravca-type man & woman,
unmarked, soft-sculptured
stockinet faces, well-detailed
painted eyes, multi-colored
brows, closed smiling mouths,
painted "character" lines, original
mohair wigs, stockinet body
w/padded wire armature, hands
w/needle-sculptured fingers,
woman dressed in original black
& blue plaid shirt w/blue buttons,
brown wool plaid skirt, grey
apron, blue plaid taffeta slip,

stockings, wooden shoes, brown plaid scarf, man dressed in original grey & white sweater, brown pants, brown plaid kerchief, dark blue knit cap, wooden shoes, has fish net over shoulder & is carrying a basket, pr. (ILLUS. previous page) **155.00**

R & B composition head "Debu'Teen" marked "Debu'Teen - R&B Quality Doll" on paper tag, blue tin sleep eyes w/real lashes, single-stroke brows, painted lower lashes, eye shadow, closed mouth, red mohair wig in original set, five-piece composition body, original riding outfit w/white blouse, brown flannel jodhpurs, brown oilcloth boots, blue felt hat, boxed, marked "Debu'Teen" on end of box label, 13" (near mint condition) **400.00**

R & B composition head "WAC" marked "R & B," stamped "This Doll Has A Human Hair Wig" on paper wrist tag, blue sleep eyes w/real lashes, single-stroke brows, eye shadow, painted lower lashes, closed mouth, h.h. wig in original set, five-piece composition body, original uniform of the Women's Army Corps, matching hat & shoulder bag w/metal emblems, panties, socks & shoes, 17" (1" damaged area filled w/composition on back of head, repair to lower torso, clothing shows no fading) **330.00**

Redmond (Kathy) bisque shoulder head "Bonnie Blue" marked "Bonnie - R" in cat on back shoulder plate, painted blue eyes w/glaze, feathered brows, painted upper & lower lashes, accented nostrils, closed pouty mouth w/glaze, molded & painted dark hair in long curls hat w/maroon feather, cloth

Kathy Redmond "Bonnie Blue"

w/glaze, molded & painted blue body w/bisque lower arms & legs, molded & painted high-button boots, original blue velvet dress, white lace collar, underclothing, 9" (ILLUS.) **135.00**

Redmond (Kathy) bisque shoulder head child marked w/drawing of cat & "R" in circular torso on back of shoulder plate, head turned & looking up, painted & glazed blue eyes, molded & feathered brows, painted upper & lower lashes, accented nostrils, closed mouth w/accented & glazed lips, accent line between lips, molded, painted & glazed hair, molded & painted bonnet w/molded flowers & glazed blue ribbon, cloth body w/bisque arms & legs, molded & painted shoes w/molded flowers & glazed blue ribbons, original white dress w/tiny blue flowers & trimmed in lace, wide blue ribbon sash at waist, long lace-trimmed pants, 13" **185.00**

Redmond (Kathy) bisque shoulder head child, unmarked, head slightly uplifted, painted & glazed blue eyes, light blush over eyes, molded & feathered brows, painted upper lashes, accented nostrils, closed mouth w/glaze on lips, molded, painted & glazed hair, molded & painted bonnet w/molded & glazed blue flowers & ribbons, cloth body w/bisque lower arms & legs, molded & painted shoes w/glazed blue ribbons, original white dress w/blue flowers, long white lace-trimmed pants, wide blue ribbon sash, 13".................**160.00**

Redmond (Kathy) "Alexandra" bisque shoulder head marked "Alexandra - R" in cat on back of shoulder plate, painted blue eyes w/glaze, feathered brows, accented nostrils, closed mouth w/glazed lips, molded earrings, molded & painted hair w/glaze, molded & painted gold crown, necklace, & bodice, molded white snood w/gold accents, cloth body w/bisque lower arms & lower legs, molded & painted shoes w/glaze, original gold formal dress w/gold trim lace head piece w/gold trim, 15" (excellent condition w/exquisite modeling, detail & color)............**415.00**

Sarg's (Tony) "Mammy Doll" brown composition character head, painted brown eyes w/heavily molded eye lids, single-stroke brows, smiling mouth w/six painted teeth, original mohair wig, large gold hoop earrings, cloth body jointed at shoulders only, large composition hands & feet w/molded & painted shoes, original red & white print dress, white pinafore, red & white bandanna on head, underclothing, white stockings on top of composition shoes, comes w/unmarked 7½"

Sarg's "Mammy Doll"

composition baby w/painted brown hair, jointed at shoulders & hips wearing knit undershirt, flannel diaper, socks tied w/pink ribbons, wrapped in white flannel blanket tied w/pink ribbon, boxed, marked "Tony Sarg's Mammy Doll - Sole Distributors - Geo. Borgfeldt Corp. New York, N.Y." on gold paper label & end of box, 17", pr. (ILLUS.)............................**1,125.00**

Schmidt (Bruno) bisque socket head child marked "Made in Germany - B.S.W. (in heart) - 12," brown sleep eyes w/real lashes, molded & feathered brows, painted lower lashes, accented nostrils, open mouth w/accented lip & two upper teeth, synthetic wig, unusual shaped body w/diagonal hip joints, flat swivel joints at shoulder, large detailed feet, pronounced balls at elbow & knees, old white dress, underclothing, white tights, new shoes, 26" (general overall wear, body possibly repainted)..**350.00**

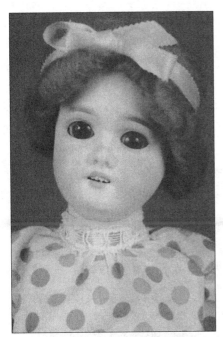

Schoenau & Hoffmeister Child Doll

Schoenau & Hoffmeister bisque socket head child marked "S PB H (in star) - 1909 - 3½ - Germany," marked "Excelsior - Germany - 2½" on rear torso, large brown sleep eyes, feathered brows, painted upper & lower lashes, accented nostrils, open mouth w/four upper teeth, mohair wig, jointed wood & composition body, off-white dress w/gold & grey dots, antique underclothing, socks & shoes, generally excellent condition w/minor inherent flaw on chin, reglued second finger on right hand,19" (ILLUS.) **275.00**

Schoenau & Hoffmeister bisque socket head "Princess Elizabeth" marked "Porzellanfabrik Burggrub - Princess Elizabeth - 5 - Made in Germany," blue sleep eyes, feathered eyes, painted upper & lower lashes, accented nostrils, smiling open mouth w/accented lips, mohair wig, five-piece bent-

limb baby body, embroidered white baby dress, underclothing, socks, 19" (eyes are loose, body repainted & not typical toddler body usually seen on this doll) ..**750.00**

Schoenau & Hoffmeister bisque socket head girl marked "10½ - Germany - S PB (in star) H - 1906 - 5½," blue sleep eyes, feathered brows, painted upper & lower lashes, accented nostrils, open mouth w/four upper teeth, mohair wig, jointed wood & composition body, redressed in rose flowered dress, underclothing, socks, rose-colored shoes, 21" (repainted eyelids, excellent body) **235.00**

Schoenhut wooden socket head "Nature" baby marked "Schoenhut - " on back, marked "Schoenhut Doll - Pat. Jan. 17th 1911 - U.S.A." in oval label on back, painted eyes, single-stroke brows, accented nostrils, closed mouth, mohair wig, wooden bent-limb baby body, white baby dress w/lace inserts, underclothing, 12" (good condition w/repainted eyes & eyebrows, replaced mohair wig, worn body)...............................**145.00**

Schoenhut wooden head "Dolly Face" marked "Schoenhut Doll - Pat. Jan. 17th 1911 - U.S.A." in oval label on back, wooden head, painted eyes, feathered brows, painted upper & lower lashes, accented nostrils, open-close mouth w/four upper teeth, mohair wig, spring-jointed wooden body jointed at shoulders, elbows, wrists, hips, knees & ankles, navy blue sailor-type dress, replaced knit underwear, long black stockings, replaced shoes, 14" (repainted eyes, general wear on body, two fingers broken off right hand) **150.00**

Schoenhut wooden head "Dolly Face" marked "Schoenhut Doll - Pat. Jan. 17th 1911 - U.S.A." in oval label on back, blue decal eyes, feathered brows, painted upper & lower lashes, accented nostrils, open-closed mouth w/four painted teeth, h.h. wig, spring-jointed wooden body jointed at shoulders, elbows, wrists, hips, knees & ankles, redressed in rose polka-dot dress w/matching jacket, panties, socks & shoes, 16" ("washed" coloring, normal wear) **215.00**

Schoenhut wooden head girl marked "Schoenhut Doll - Pat. Jan. 17th 1911 - U.S.A." in oval label on back, brown decal eyes, feathered brows, painted upper & lower lashes, accented nostrils, open-closed mouth w/four teeth, mohair wig, wooden body jointed at shoulders, elbows, wrists, hips, knees & ankles, redressed in knit underwear, pink print dress, stockings, new shoes, 19" (factory repaint, light overall soil) **350.00**

S.F.B.J. bisque composition black girl marked "S.F.B.J. - Paris - 3/0," brown painted bisque head, set brown eyes, single-stroke brows, accented nostrils, closed mouth, original mohair wig, five-piece composition body, original Martinique costume of red plaid taffeta skirt, white blouse, red taffeta cape, yellow plaid head piece, underclothing, no socks or shoes, very good condition w/overall general wear,10" (ILLUS. top, next column)..........**155.00**

Simon & Halbig bisque shoulder head lady marked "S&H - 1160 2/0" on back shoulder plate, "2/0" on front edge of shoulder plate, set

S.F.B.J. Painted Bisque Black Girl

Simon & Halbig Bisque Lady

brown pupilless eyes, single-stroke brows, painted upper & lower lashes, accented nostrils, closed mouth, pierced ears, mohair wig in original set, cloth body w/bisque lower arms & lower legs, molded & painted black four-strap boots, white stockings w/blue garters, original dress w/tiers of lace & trimmed w/tiny silk flowers, original lace-trimmed underclothing, 10" (ILLUS.) **335.00**

Simon & Halbig bisque head lady marked "1159," blue glass sleep eyes, open mouth, ash blonde mohair wig, composition body, slim arms & legs jointed at shoulders, hips & knees, dressed in fur trimmed flannel flapper coat & hat, ca. 1910, 13" **546.00**

Simon & Halbig "Santa" Girl

Simon & Halbig bisque head girl marked "S&H. 1249 - DEP - Germany - Santa - 8," blue sleep eyes, molded & feathered brows, painted upper & lower lashes, accented nostrils, open mouth w/accented lips, small triangular accent on lip, four upper teeth, pierced ears, h.h. wig, jointed wood & composition body, pale blue dress w/white bodice w/tucks & lace trim, underclothing, old socks & black shoes, light wear on lower arms & hands, second finger of right hand replaced, 20" (ILLUS.) **1,050.00**

Simon & Halbig bisque socket head girl marked "S 16 H - 759 - DEP," large set blue threaded eyes, feathered brows, painted upper & lower lashes, accented nostrils, open mouth w/accented lips, six upper teeth, pierced ears, original h.h. wig, heavy jointed wood & composition body w/straight wrists, coral colored dress trimmed w/ruffles, underclothing, socks, 27" (head is slightly "warped," repairs at elbows & knees) **800.00**

Simon & Halbig bisque socket head girl marked "1248 - Germany - Simon & Halbig - S&H - 13½," blue sleep eyes w/real lashes, molded & feathered brows, painted lower lashes, accented nostrils, open mouth w/accented lips & triangular accent on lower lip, pierced ears, original mohair wig, jointed composition body, white antique dress, underclothing, original socks & shoes, 28" (pieces broken off bottom of neck socket, body repainted) **450.00**

Steiff gnomes, marked "ff" on left ear silver buttons, stamped "Made in Germany" on bottom of 12" gnome shoe, molded felt faces w/center seam, inset green glass eyes w/vertical pupils, brows, beards & coarse hair, accented nostrils, inset open-close mouth, applied felt ears, felt bodies jointed at shoulders & hips, feet w/separate big toe, dressed in white shirt, felt shorts, brown felt vest, felt cap, leather clogs w/wooden buttons on two large gnomes, red felt slippers on small gnome, general slight wear & soiling, set of 3 (ILLUS. bottom next page) **550.00**

Steiner Figure C bisque socket head Bebe doll marked "Sie C 3/0," caduceus mark on left hip, set threaded eyes, feathered brows, painted upper & lower lashes, accented nostrils, closed mouth w/accented lips, accented line between lips, pierced ears, original skin wig, jointed composition body w/straight wrists & short stubby fingers, original hand-made long white baby dress w/lace trim at neck, wool slip, white lace-trimmed slip, long pants, pink lacy stockings, original French-style shoes marked "0" on bottom, straw bonnet w/pink trim, 10" **3,000.00**

Steiner Figure C bisque head doll marked "Sie C 3/0" in red ink, lever operated blue eyes, closed mouth, original blonde skin wig over paper pate, jointed wood & composition body w/straight wrists, original clothing comprising cotton underwear & petticoats, teal blue satin dress w/pleated skirt & lace trim, socks & one white shoe, ca. 1885, missing one shoe, 10½" h. (ILLUS. next column) **6,325.00**

Steiner Bisque Figure C Doll

Tea Cozy Russian lady, unmarked, cloth head w/molded mask face, painted blue eyes to side, single-stroke brows, accented nostrils, closed smiling mouth, pierced ears, kerchief over hair, cloth upper body w/cloth arms, mitten hands,

Steiff "Gnomes"

heavy quilted teapot cover for lower body, original peasant-type outfit w/red bodice, large white sleeves, blue & rose print skirt, white apron, left hand stitched in place by face, right hand stitched in place by waist, 20" (excellent condition w/slight general wear) **65.00**

Twiggy, 1967, blonde, pink lips w/painted teeth, rooted eyelashes, bendable legs, original knit dress, cardboard picture cutout from box (several small light colored areas on face, arms are lighter in color than body, faint pink stain on side of right arm, faint dark stain on side & back of right leg) **95.00**

Vogue "Ginny" hard plastic head marked "Vogue" on head & back, blue eyes, single-stroke brows, painted upper lashes, closed mouth, original wig, five-piece hard plastic body, tagged dress w/green & white skirt & panties, grey top & overshirt w/green flocking,

original socks & shoes, Kindergarten series, ca. 1952, 7" (some flocking off dress, otherwise excellent condition) ...**135.00**

Vogue Toddles "Aviator" marked "Vogue" on back of head, marked "Doll Co." on back & "Aviator" on bottom of right shoe, composition head, painted blue eyes to side, single-stroke brows, painted upper lashes, closed mouth, original mohair wig, five-piece composition body, original aviator outfit w/blue jodhpur pants, blue flannel jacket & cap, black patent belt, "boots" made of black tape & snap shoes, red metal airplane pin & gold propeller pin, 7½" (pale coloring, clothing slightly faded) **400.00**

Vogue Toddles "Dutch Boy" composition head marked "Vogue Dolls" on pants tag, painted blue eyes looking to side, single-stroke brows, closed mouth, original mohair wig, five-piece composition body, tagged

Vogue "Jill" & Outfits

Dutch boy outfit w/blue pants, blue jacket w/yellow buttons, matching blue hat, wooden shoes, 7½" (general light crazing on face & body, aged clothing, repair on legs & wooden shoes).......................................135.00

Vogue Toddles "Gretel" composition head marked "Vogue" on back of head, "Doll Co." on back & "Gretel" on bottom of right shoe, painted blue eyes to side, single-stroke brows, painted upper lashes, closed mouth, original mohair wig braids, five-piece composition toddler body, white organdy blouse, red felt skirt w/blue trim & yellow rick-rack, attached panties, blue felt vest w/red flower trim, replaced white socks, red leatherette shoes, 7½" h. (coloring somewhat pale) 160.00

Vogue "Jill" vinyl head doll marked "Vogue," six boxed outfits: #60341 w/tagged red & white one-piece pants & top, white shoes; #60346 w/tagged pink felt coat, matching hat , black shoes & purse; #60746 w/tagged pink fleece jacket, rose slacks, white shoes, necklace; #60340 tagged blue baby-doll pajama set w/white shoes; #60350 w/tagged black flapper skirt & top, black shoes; #60752 w/tagged strapless blue batiste party dress, white shoes, three unboxed outfits not tagged: yellow fuzzy full-length robe; yellow terry cloth top, yellow slacks, green felt purse, yellow & green sunglasses; green felt coat w/leopard accessories, black shoes & necklace; ca. 1962, boxed, marked "Ginny Doll Family, Vogue Dolls Incorporated" on front of box & "Jill" on the end, 10" (ILLUS. bottom previous page)...............300.00

Wax shoulder head girl, unmarked, head reinforced w/plaster-type substance, sad face, brown sleep eyes, brows missing, accented nostrils, closed mouth, original blonde mohair wig, cloth body w/kid arms, gussets at elbows, hips & knees, original long white baby dress w/lace bodice, matching bonnet, original underclothing booties, 12" (overall good condition, nose somewhat flattened, interesting body & original clothing) 230.00

Wax over composition shoulder head girl, unmarked, blue sleep eyes, feathered brows, accented nostrils, closed mouth w/accent line between lips, original blonde mohair wig in original braids & tiny curls, cloth body w/non-working squeaker, wax over composition lower arms, composition lower legs w/molded & painted high button boots, wax over upper part of legs, original white two-piece outfit w/pleats at hem, pleated pocket, 18" (cracks in wax covering, light wear & soil, damage on wax shoulder plate, recovered upper cloth arms & upper cloth legs) 210.00

Wax Over Composition Doll

Wax over composition shoulder head lady, unmarked, reinforced poured wax shoulder head, blue sleep eyes, single-stroke brows, closed mouth, pierced ears, original mohair wig, cloth body, wax over composition lower legs w/molded & painted black & grey boots, dressed in original white lawn dress w/tucks & pale gold silk ribbon trim, underclothing, knit stockings w/ribbon garters, gold flower attached to legs above molded boots, original multi-colored ribbon in hair (ILLUS. bottom previous page)..........................**500.00**

DRUGSTORE & PHARMACY ITEMS

The old-time corner drugstore, once a familiar part of every American town, has now given way to modern, efficient pharmacy. With the streamlining and modernization of this trade, many of the early tools and store adjuncts have become outdated and now fall into the realm of "collectibles." Listed here are the variety of tools, bottles, display pieces and other ephemera once closely associated with the druggist's trade.

Apothecary bottle, cylindrical w/double collar mouth, embossed w/lamb & "Al. S. Lamb, Aspen, Colo." in circle, aqua **$660.00**

Apothecary bottle, square, "Amm. Brom." on label-under-glass, "Pat. Apr. 2 1889, W.T. & Co." on smooth base, tooled lip, ground glass stopper, ca. 1890-1910, cobalt blue, 7⅛" h............**176.00**

Apothecary bottle, cylindrical w/tooled double collar mouth, embossed "Wm H Keith & Co, Apothecaries, San Francisco", aqua **66.00**

Apothecary bottle, calabash, "L. Morp: Hyd:" on painted label, rolled lip, ground pontil, olive amber ground glass stopper, deep purple amethyst, 13⅛" h. **1,320.00**

Apothecary bottle, cylindrical w/vertical ribbing, "Liq: Opii Sed:" on label-under-glass, smooth base, tooled lip, blown & ground glass stopper, yellowish green, 6⅞" h. **242.00**

Apothecary bottle, cylindrical, "Oakland Hydrogen Dioxide" on label-under-glass, "W.T. & Co." on smooth base, tooled lip, ca. 1880-1900, cobalt blue, 7⅝" h. (missing stopper)......................**176.00**

Apothecary bottle, cylindrical w/tooled flanged lip, embossed "Pacific Works" on base, teal blue...**99.00**

Painted Label Apothecary Bottle

Apothecary bottle, round, "Pulv: Marant: O:" on front, "Pot Bromid:" on reverse-painted label, ground pontil, ground glass stopper, black amethyst, 11¾" h. (ILLUS.)......................**440.00**

Apothecary bottle, cylindrical, "Syr. Scillae" on label-under-glass, "W.N. Walton Patd Sept. 23d 1862" on smooth base, tooled lip, ground glass stopper, ca. 1875-1885, cobalt blue, 9¼" h. **138.00**

Apothecary bottle, cylindrical, "Syr: Ficor: C:" on painted label, smooth base, tooled lip, original blown stopper, cobalt blue, 7" h. **165.00**

Label-Under-Glass Apothecary Bottle

Apothecary bottle, cylindrical, "Syr. Glycyrrh." on label-under-glass, "W.T. & Co." on smooth base, tooled lip, period blown stopper, ca. 1880-1890, cobalt blue, 9" h. (ILLUS.) **110.00**

Apothecary bottle, cylindrical, "Tr. Capsici" on label-under-glass, pontil-scarred base, tooled lip, blown glass stopper, ca. 1870-1890, cobalt blue, 11⅜" h. **495.00**

Apothecary bottle, cylindrical, "Tr. Iodine" on label-under-glass, smooth base, tooled lip, ground glass stopper, ca. 1880-1900, cobalt blue, 6¼" h. **121.00**

Apothecary bottle, cylindrical, "Tinct: Iodi. Dec:" on label-under-glass, smooth base, tooled lip, ground glass stopper, yellowish green, 7" h. **88.00**

Apothecary bottle, cylindrical, "Tr. Lobeliae" on label-under-glass, pontil-scarred base, tooled lip, blown glass stopper, ca. 1870-1890, cobalt blue, 11⅜" h. **578.00**

Apothecary bottle, calabash, "Tr. Rhei." on painted label, rolled lip, ground pontil, olive amber ground glass stopper, deep purple amethyst, 12⅝" h...........**413.00**

Apothecary bottle, cylindrical, "Vinum Malaga" on porcelain label, polished pontil, tooled lip, "Etiquettes Porcelain Tissler Paris Btes S.G.D.G." label on base, turquoise blue, 9¾" h.......**198.00**

Apothecary bottle, cylindrical w/flared lip & wide neck, open pontil, periwinkle blue, 5" h........**132.00**

Apothecary bottle, cylindrical w/applied tapered lip, open pontil, puce, 5" h. **242.00**

Apothecary bottle, cylindrical w/tapered lip, open pontil, bluish green, 5¼" h. **220.00**

Apothecary bottle, cylindrical w/flared lip, open pontil, olive green amber, 4¼" h....................**66.00**

Bottle, cylindrical, embossed "Smith & Davis Druggists, Portland, Oregon," applied mouth , smooth base, ca. 1865-1875, aqua, 7¼" h. **209.00**

Bottle, cylindrical, embossed "Strong Cobb & Co Wholesale Druggists, Cleveland, O," applied mouth, "C & I" on smooth base, ca. 1875-1885, cobalt blue, 10⅜" h. **154.00**

FABERGÉ

Carl Fabergé (1846-1920) was goldsmith and jeweler to the Russian Imperial Court and his creations are recognized as the finest of their kind. He made a number of enamel fantasies, including Easter Eggs, for the Imperial Family and utilized precious metals and jewels in other work.

Bookmark, jewelled silver, of shaped rectangular form, the handle chased w/stylized foliage on a matted ground & set w/two cabochon sapphires, the blade engraved w/various signatures, marked "K. Fabergé" in Cyrillic w/Imperial warrant & 88 standard, Moscow, Russia, ca. 1900, 5⅝" l. **$2,875.00**

Brooch, moonstone & diamond, formed as ribbon-bow, set w/two cabochon moonstones & bordered by diamonds, marked w/initials of Workmaster August Holström, St. Petersburg, Russia, ca. 1900, w/original fitted holly wood box, brooch 1⅝" l. **6,037.00**

Cigar lighter, silver, the spherical lighter gimbaled within a frame chased w/acanthus leaves, w/wood handle, marked w/initials of Workmaster Anders Nevainen & 88 standard, St. Petersburg, Russia, ca. 1900, 7⅜" l. **2,587.00**

Faberge Silver Cigarette Case

Cigarette case, silver, rectangular shape, reeded on both sides, the hinged cover applied w/a monogram & w/a gold cat w/emerald eyes, marked "K. Fabergé" in Cyrillic w/Imperial warrant & 84 standard, ca. 1910, 3¾" l. (ILLUS.) **3,220.00**

Cigarette case, silver & jewelled, the cover embossed w/a leafy branch set w/cabochon sapphires, also applied w/a two-color gold jewelled monogram, w/cabochon sapphire thumbpiece, marked "K. Fabergé" in Cyrillic & 84 standard, 3⅜" l. **3,450.00**

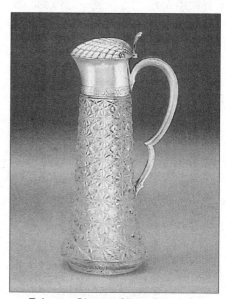

Faberge Glass & Silver Claret Jug

Claret jug, cut glass & silver, the cylindrical body cut w/sunbursts, tapering towards the neck, the hinged silver cover in the form of a shell, w/double-scroll handle, marked w/Cyrillic initials of Workmaster Julius Rappoport & 84 standard, St. Petersburg, Russia, ca. 1890, 12¼" h. (ILLUS.) **5,750.00**

Cracker jar, cov., cut glass & silver, the square boxy form w/ rounded corners, w/plain silver rim mount, the slip-on cover w/flower finial, hinged handle, marked "K. Fabergé" in Cyrillic w/Imperial warrant & 88 standard, Moscow, Russia, ca. 1890, 7¼" h. **5,750.00**

Etui, gold, reeded body of oval section, the hinged cover mounted w/a milky white agate panel engraved w/a calligraphic inscription, the cabochon ruby teardrop-form thumbpiece bordered by diamonds, marked w/Cyrillic initials of Workmaster Michael Perchin & 56 standard, St. Petersburg, Russia, ca. 1890, 3¼" h. **19,550.00**

Frame, enamel & silver, translucent orange over a guilloché ground, the border of the aperture reeded, w/ribbon-ties at intervals, surmounted by a flaming torch, the outer border of the frame chased w/antheniom, w/wood back & silver strut, marked w/initials of Workmaster Anders Johan Nevalainen, 88 standard & w/inventory number, St. Petersburg, Russia, ca. 1890,3⅞" h. **11,500.00**

Jewelled Silver Paper Knife

Paper knife, silver & jewelled, decorated in the Old Russian style w/a country cottage, an owl hovering overhead, set w/two cabochon rubies, marked "K. Fabergé" in Cyrillic w/Imperial warrant & 84 standard, ca. 1900, 7⅜" l. (ILLUS.) **4,025.00**

Pendant, purpupine & gold, purpupine egg w/gold ropework cap, marked w/initials of Workmaster Erik Kollin & 56 standard, St. Petersburg, Russia, ca.1890 ½" l..............**8,625.00**

Pitcher, 8⅝" h., glass & silver, of melon form, the twig-form silver handle extending into leaves & vine encircling the body, marked "K. Fabergé" in Cyrillic w/Imperial warrant & 84 standard, Moscow, Russia **5,462.00**

Salt cellars w/spoons, silver & enamel, in the form of miniature kovshi, enameled w/stylized foliate & vegetable forms in shades of blue & green, the spoons similarly decorated, marked "K. Fabergé" in Cyrillic w/Imperial warrant w/overstriking mark of Feodor Rückert & 88 standard, Moscow, Russia, ca. 1910, 2½" l. **7,475.00**

Scent flask, enamel & silver, tapering ovoid body w/hinged domed cover, rust-orange over a guilloché ground, the rim chased w/leaftips, marked w/Cyrillic initials "K.F." & 56 standard, Moscow, Russia, ca. 1900, 2½" l. (lacks inner stopper) **10,062.00**

Sealing wax case, silver, gold & enamel, upright rectangular shape, translucent green over a guilloché ground, the border chased w/leaftips, w/diamond-set slide, marked w/Cyrillic initials "K.F." & 88 standard, Moscow, Russia, ca. 1900, 2¼" l. (ILLUS. next page) **4,600.00**

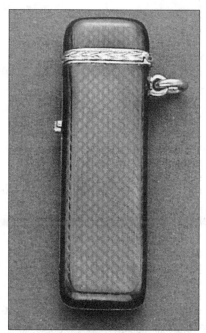

Silver and Gold Sealing Wax Case

Vodka cup, silver & agate, the brown & grey agate cup w/flaring rim carved w/a band of berried leafage, the silver base w/a gadroon border, the silver girdle chased w/a Greek key pattern design, the silver handle decorated w/berried leafage, marked marked "K. Fabergé" in Cyrillic & 84 standard, Moscow, Russia, ca. 1900, 2" h. **6,900.00**

FIREARMS

Carbine rifle, Burnside Third model, .54 caliber, percussion-type, round barrel & wooden forestock, metal all dark brown in finish w/light pitting on lock, walnut stock w/light coat of later varnish, Serial Number 21127, barrel 21" l. (no sling ring) **$990.00**

Carbine rifle, Sharps New Model 1863, barrel reblued, lock w/good signatures & dates, barrel markings think or illegible, walnut stock w/old dark patina & carved initials "J.D." on buttstock, shows inspector's markings, Serial Number C21607, barrel 22" l. **1,128.00**

Carbine rifle, Sharps New Model 1863, round barrel, steel hardware, buttplate made to accept a patch box but stock never had one, wear to stamped signatures, Serial Number 94679, barrel 22" l. **1,325.00**

Carbine rifle, Springfield 1873 saddle model, serial number 145788, w/1879 alterations, adjustable rear sight, barrel 22" l. (receiver probably reblued).....**880.00**

Carbine rifle, Springfield 1873 trapdoor model, walnut stock, clear markings on lock, tang & barrel, serial number 499231, round barrel, barrel 32½" l. (some dents in stock) **330.00**

Derringer pistol, Remington .41 caliber rimfire model, bone grip, one-line signature along flat top of barrel, bright finish, serial number 166, overall 4⅞" l. **303.00**

Derringer pistol, single-short model, approximately .45 caliber, octagonal barrel w/patent breech, back-action lock w/simple engraving, nickel silver hardware includes shield inlay, sideplate & trigger guard, checkered walnut stock w/old repair, one inlay missing, barrel 3¼" l. (ILLUS. fourth row down, left, w/revolvers) **303.00**

Musket, flintlock, 'Brown Bess'-type, third model, stock w/good dark patina & w/inspector's marks, lock stamped w/a crown "G.R." & "Tower," barrel & lock w/crown & arrow marks w/initials "S.G.," bright finish on barrel, barrel 39¼" l. (three short cracks in stock around lock, usual pitting around breech) **990.00**

Musket, flintlock, Harper's Ferry Model 1816, walnut stock w/faint

inspector's markings, lock
stamped w/eagle, "U.S.,"
signature & "1839," barrel
secured w/three bands & w/a
bold eagle head stamp & "1840,"
metal light grey w/areas of light
pitting, barrel 42" l. (short age
crack at lock bolt area
of stock) **1,540.00**

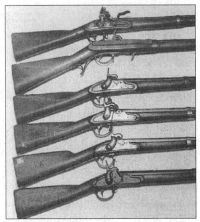

Group of Early Muskets & Rifles

Musket, percussion, Harper's
Ferry Model 1816, metal
carefully cleaned to a light grey,
stock & lock show all markings &
date "1841," small chips ahead
of lock, rear sling swivel missing,
57" l. (ILLUS. fourth from top)....**825.00**

Musket, Potts & Hunt Enfield model,
.58 caliber, round barrel w/three bands,
brass buttplate & trigger guard, steel
w/bright finish, walnut stock w/a few
age splits & area of deterioration near
buttplate, barrel 38" l. **715.00**

Musket, flintlock percussion-
conversion, Remington-Maynard
conversion, round barrel
w/areas of pitting, stock w/good
color & chips & restoration, rear
sight missing, barrel 42" l.,
overall 57" l. (ILLUS. sixth
from top) **715.00**

Musket, flintlock, Springfield
Model 1816, .69 caliber, flintlock
w/good signature w/eagle &

"1832" stamp, walnut stock
w/old finish 7 bold inspector's
marks, ramrod missing, chips in
stock, frizzen spring damage,
57" l. (ILLUS. top.) **550.00**

Musket, flintlock percussion-
conversion, Springfield Model
1816, .69 caliber, arsenal
conversion, old finish, faint
inspector's marks, bold
stampings on lock, dated 1829,
pitting at breech area, 57" l.
(ILLUS. third from top) **880.00**

Musket, flintlock percussion-
conversion, Springfield Model
1816, .69 caliber, arsenal
conversion, walnut stock w/good
patina, faint inspector's marks,
carved "F.A." on buttstock, wrist
stamped "27" (ILLUS. fifth from
top) **660.00**

Musket, flintlock, Whitney Model
1798 U.S. contract, second
model, walnut stock w/original
finish & carved initials "A.F." &
"T.C.," letters "S.C." stamped
ahead of buttplate tang, lock
plate stamped "U. States" &
"New Haven" w/eagle, barrel 43"
l. (small sliver of wood expertly
replaced beneath the lock,
barrel w/areas of pitting).........**1,540.00**

Pistol, Allen and Thurber
'pepperbox' model, .32 caliber,
six-shot w/fluted barrel, scroll-
engraved shield & framed,
hammer pitted, barrel 4" l. **715.00**

Pistol, Sharps 'pepperbox' four-
shot model, .22 caliber, one-line
mark on either side of barrel, "C.
Sharps & Co., Philadelphia, PA,"
& "C. Sharps pat. 1859," brass
frame fitted w/molded gutta
percha grips, Serial Number
5098, 5" l. **495.00**

Pistol, percussion, Johnson
Model 1842, .52 caliber, brass
hardware, walnut stock w/faint
inspector's ovals, age cracks,
bold stampings on lock w/"1854"
date, 14½" l. **550.00**

Pistol, percussion, Germany, large caliber, round barrel, apparently made for cavalry use, bracket in the backstrop for shoulder stock & a ring in the grip, most parts w/inspectors' numbers, trigger guard engraved "3 Rech," signed "Crause in Herzberg" on lock, small repair to breech area, barrel 10" l., overall 18" l. (ILLUS. bottom, w/revolvers).....**440.00**

Pistol, percussion, walnut stock w/swamped round barrel, steel trigger guard engraved & silver grip cap embossed w/a face, barrel 9" l. (small dent in face)...**275.00**

Pistols, percussion, Germany, walnut stock w/relief-carved fluting on grips & 10" l. swamped barrel, adjustable single set trigger & dragon side plates, signed "Jos. Kruse in Munster. Guss. Stahl," w/early walnut case, pr. (one stock w/crack).....**825.00**

Revolver, Allen and Wheelock sidehammer model, .32 caliber, percussion-type, barrel 4" l. (few screws replaced, grip w/shallow chip) **330.00**

Revolver, Colt 1849 pocket model, .31 caliber, percussion-type, octagonal barrel w/brass trigger guard & back strap, top flat of barrel shows bold signature & New York address, cylinder w/faint but complete stagecoach scene, all serial numbers match, Serial Number 327759, hammer will not stand on full cock, barrel 4" l. (ILLUS. below, top left).............**462.00**

Revolver, Colt 1860 Army model, .44 caliber, percussion-type, all matching serial numbers, faint inspector's mark, cylinder shows some engraving, trace of address on barrel, Serial Number 33079,13⅞" l.............**1,760.00**

Revolver, Colt 1862 Police model, .36 caliber, percussion-type, round barrel stamped w/full signature & New York address, walnut grips w/brass grip straps & guard, metal lightly pitted in spots, wedge old replacement, Serial Number 4877, barrel 4½" l. (ILLUS. below, third row down, center) **440.00**

Various Revolvers, a Pistol & a Derringer

Revolver, Colt single-action model, ivory grips, areas of nickel plate remains, two-line patent date mark on framed of 1871-72, single-line signature on the barrel, Serial Number 23066, barrel 7½" l. (ILLUS. second row down, center, previous page) **2,035.00**

Revolver, Remington new Model Army, .44 caliber, percussion-type, walnut grips w/good patina, spots of pitting on cylinder, civilian model, Serial Number 14431 (ILLUS. top right, previous page).................**660.00**

Revolver, Remington New Model Army, .44 caliber, percussion-type, wood grips, crisp signature on flat top of barrel, serial number 124304 ....**990.00**

Revolver, Remington rolling block model, .50 caliber, wood grips, inspector's stamp on grip, traces of case coloring on frame, round barrel 8" l. (dents in grips).....................................**935.00**

Revolver, Remington Model 1875 single-action, .44 caliber, wood grips (metal reblued, small putty repair in grip) **880.00**

Revolver, Remington Navy rolling block model, wood grips, metal w/bright finish & w/an anchor & "J.M.B.C." at breech, frame stamped "P." & "F.C.W.," barrel 7" l. **825.00**

Revolver, Remington-Beals Navy model, .36 caliber, walnut grips w/three notches carved on one side, metal lightly pitted in spots, some letters in signature hard to read, barrel 7⅜" l. (ILLUS. fourth row down, right, previous page) **715.00**

Revolver, Remington-Smoot New Model, .32 caliber, five-shot cylinder, nickel plated finish w/minor wear, hard rubber grips..**138.00**

Revolver, Smith and Wesson Model No. 1, Second Issue, .22 short w/an octagonal barrel, frame & grip straps w/worn silver plate, rosewood grips, good signature, Serial Number 31725, barrel 3³⁄₁₆" l. **413.00**

Rifle, flintlock, fullstock, cherry stock w/checkered wrist, silver wire inlay & engraved brass patchbox, barrel signed "J. Mason," possibly J.C. Mason, Keene, New Hampshire, barrel 40½" l. (restoration) **1,760.00**

Rifle, 1819 Hall-North contract model, .52 caliber, percussion-type, breech block w/North signature w/address & "1830," walnut stock w/good patina & age cracks & fore-end cut, stamped "R. Day" behind the trigger guard, carved "J.B.S." (ILLUS. second from top w/muskets) **853.00**

Rifle, Kentucky half-stock, percussion-type, curly maple stock w/twelve German silver inlays & brass hardware, German silver cap box, octagonal barrel stamped "Postley, Nelson & Co.," top of barrel engraved "C.K.," carefully cleaned, barrel 36" l..................**743.00**

Rifle, Ohio long-rifle, percussion-type, curly maple stock w/old worn finish, brass hardware, lock cast w/detail of a dog & bird, signed "J. Legg," Piqua, Ohio, 1859-78, barrel 37½" l. (old repair at wrist & toe) **633.00**

Rifle, Springfield Model 1870 trapdoor-style, .50-70 caliber, lock dated "1863," breech block & barrel numbered "13730," barrel 32" l. **660.00**

Rifle, Springfield Model 1873, lever-action trapdoor, .45-70 caliber, as-found condition w/some areas of pitting, stock w/good dark patina, Serial No. 67053 ....**495.00**

Rifle, Springfield Model 1873 Cadet variation, .45-70 caliber, bold proofs on barrel, faint eagle signature on lock, stock stamped "509," barrel sling swivel, barrel 29½" l. (ramrod missing) **495.00**

Rifle, Winchester Model 1873, lever-action, .32 W.C.F. caliber, octagonal to round barrel, third model, dark brown finish on metal, Serial Number 290032B, barrel 24" l. (front sight missing) **660.00**

Rifle, Winchester Model 1876, lever-action, .45-60 caliber, round barrel w/full tube magazine, metal w/good amount of original blue w/surface rust in spots, stock & forearm w/dents, late second model, Serial Number 20202, barrel 28" l. ...**1,815.00**

Rifle, half-stock percussion-type, octagonal barrel stamped "J.H. Johnston, Great Western Gun Works, Pittsburgh, PA," walnut stock w/repaired cracks using copper plates, fitted w/brass hardware, barrel 39" l., overall 55¾" l. **220.00**

Rifle, half-stock percussion-type, lock signed "A.W. Spies & Co.," walnut stock w/beavertail cheek piece w/engraved eagle on silver oval, brass hardware, barrel 36" l., overall 51" l. (repaired crack between lock & tang) **220.00**

Shotgun, double-barreled, Westley Richards model, receiver & trigger guard w/fine engraved scrollwork & a dog, checkered walnut stock, damascus barrels marked "W.R.," "J.P.C." & "AB," good bore, barrels 32" l. (two small dents in barrels)........................**330.00**

Shotgun, double-barreled, percussion-type, 10 gauge, barrels w/ornate gold & silver wire inlay at the breech, locks, trigger guard & buttplate w/fine scroll engraving, select grade walnut stock w/old repair at wrist using brass plates, barrels 36¼" l., overall 52" l..................**187.00**

FIRE FIGHTING COLLECTIBLES

Early Leather Fire Bucket

Fire bucket, painted & decorated leather, swelled cylindrical form w/an arched bail leather handle, stitched seams, decorated w/the inscription "No. 37" within a red heart w/"Benj. Marshall 1827" below, green-painted ground, hand distressed, painted worn & chipped, 8" d., 19" h. (ILLUS.) **$460.00**

Fire extinguisher, red glass, "Auto Fyr Stop Co.," light-bulb-shape w/four-leaf clover paper label on body w/paper label around neck, w/holder & original box, 7" d., 7" l.,13½" h. **121.00**

French Fireman's Helmet

Fireman's helmet, brass, the stylized gadrooned plume & flaming urn plaque, w/leather chin strap, inscribed "Sapeyrs Pompiers," 19th c., France, 9" h. (ILLUS.) **431.00**

Early Presentation Silver Pitcher

Pitcher, coin silver, commemorative, classical footed baluster-shaped w/tall waisted neck & high arched spout, high arched C-scroll handle, presentation engraving "...the officers and members of Lyman Engine Company No. 5...Boston October 2nd 1848," reverse engraved w/an early horse-

drawn hand-pumper wagon, Obadiah Rich, Boston, Massachusetts, ca. 1832-50, dents, 12¾" h. (ILLUS.) **1,265.00**

FIREPLACE & HEARTH ITEMS

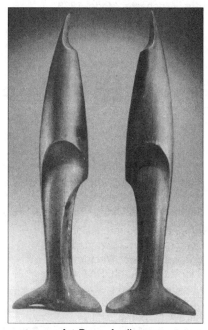

Art Deco Andirons

Andirons, bronze, Art Deco style, each case as a highly stylized upright fish standing on its tail, in lacquered bronze, hinged wrought-iron support, possibly designed by Pierre Legrain, France, ca. 1925, 20¾" h., pr. (ILLUS.) **$10,925.00**

Andirons, cast iron, figural baseball players, each figure cast in profile w/a black cap, white uniform w/black & yellow trim, black belt & black socks & shoes, one standing holding a baseball & posed as a pitcher, the other standing posed as a batter holding a beige bat, each stamped on reverse "RBS 409," late 19th - early 20th c., 19¼" h., pr. **7,475.00**

Andirons, cast iron, figural squirrel seated on a log eating a nut, the log raised on two waisted front legs, American-made, early 20th c., 15¾" h., pr. **2,587.00**

Andirons, cast iron, figural sunflower, each surmounted by a sunburst centering a smiling face, the serpentine support below raised on shaped arched legs, ca. 1880, 9½ x 19", 16½" h., pr. **3,335.00**

Andirons, gilt-bronze, Louis XV-Style, each in the form of arched ornate foliate scrolls supporting at the tops seated monkeys dressed in 18th c. costume, France, 19th c., 11½" h., pr. **4,025.00**

Andirons, gilt-bronze, Louis XVI-Style, a short, reeded columnar upright on a flaring foot supporting a swagged urn w/a large flame finial, the wide extended side bar w/a pierced leafy scroll design & the smaller end columnar upright w/ a swag hanging from the top rim below the large pineapple finial, France, late 19th c., 16" l., pr. (ILLUS.)............................**2,875.00**

Andirons, wrought iron, Arts & Crafts style, heavy gauge iron w/arched heavy legs supporting a tall waisted central shaft w/a pointed drop at the base & a heavy round ring handle at the center front, the rounded top of the shaft topped by a large ball finial, fine original dark patina, Gustav Stickley, early 20th c., 11" w., 20" h., pr. **2,310.00**

Andirons, wrought iron, stepped rectangular upright front bar w/angled flattened top, raised on arched front legs ending in penny feet, tooled decoration, 12½" h., pr. **165.00**

Clock jack, brass cylinder w/bottom hook supporting a rotating cast iron wheel for roasting small game, working, replaced key, late 18th - early 19th c., overall 19" h.................**715.00**

Fireplace bellows, mechanical, brass, wood & leather, the mechanism on a footed walnut board base w/tapering flat end handle, turning the handle on the drive wheel moves the brass pulleys & leather belts to force air through a cannon-shaped brass barrel, ornately detailed in

Louis XVI-Style Andirons

Early Mechanical Fireplace Bellows

black, red & gilt paint w/floral decorations, working, American-made, 19th c., 24½" l. (ILLUS.) **500.00**

Fireplace crane, wrought iron w/scrolled detail, w/attached kettle tilter, 39" w., 41" h. (pitted, rusted) **605.00**

Fireplace fender, brass & wire, Federal style, a long serpentine form w/a brass rim above a conforming vertical wire screen w/a meandering horizontal scrolling wire, ca. 1810-20, 46½" l., 10" h. **1,840.00**

Fireplace fender & grate, brass & steel, the long, low serpentine fender w/a beaded & pierced border of palmettes, the grate w/similar decoration & raised on square tapering legs topped by urn finials, George III period, England, late 18th c., grate 35" l., fender, 4'½" l., 2 pcs. **9,200.00**

Fireplace set, parcel-gilt wrought iron, Art Nouveau style, fender, shovel & tongs, the fender well cast w/anemone blossoms, buds & leafage in gilt & patinated bronze, the pierced design w/two rounded upright enclosing three-leaf sprigs, the shovel & tongs w/the finials cast

w/matching leafage, designed by Louis Majorelle, France, ca. 1900, fender 33" l., the set (ILLUS. top, next page) **10,925.00**

Fireplace set, brass & iron, the andirons in brass w/a bell finial above a faceted sphere w/molded band over a ring-turned base above a hexagonal plinth w/a circular molded base, on spurred cabriole legs w/shod slipper feet & curved billet bars & faceted-turned stops on ring-turned legs, stamped "J.MOLINEUX - BOSTON," together w/a matching set of fire tools including a shovel, poker & tongs each w/faceted brass sphere finials, ca. 1800-10, andirons 32½" h., the set........**6,325.00**

Fireplace tools, silver-mounted steel, each handle w/clusters of triple pierced balls at the top, center & bottom w/slender ring-turned sections between, Europe, in the late 17th c. style, unmarked, tongs, shovel & poker, shovel 34½" l., 3 pcs.(ILLUS. bottom left, next page) **5,462.00**

Roasting spit, cast iron rectangular framework w/two adjustable crossbars w/four wrought spikes each & a bottom

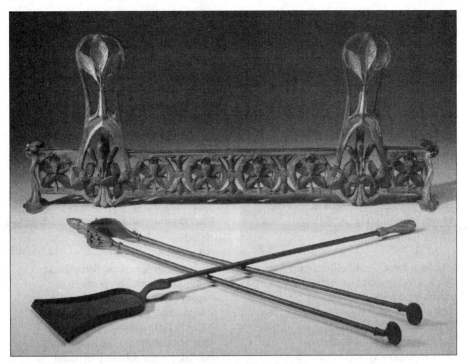

Rare Art Nouveau Fireplace Set

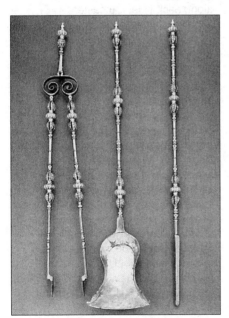

Silver-mounted Fireplace Tools

crossbar w/four spikes & a
slender handle, 31" l.................**165.00**

Fire screen, hand-hammered copper, Arts & Crafts style, a repoussé stylized floral design, decorated w/applied blue stone, hammered copper handle above an arched top, cleaned patina, England, early 20th c., 9 x 19", 30" h. **715.00**

FRAKTUR

Fraktur paintings are decorative birth and marriage certificates of the 18th and 19th centuries and also include drawings, family registers and similar documents. Illuminated family documents, birth and baptismal certificates, religious texts and rewards of merit, in a particular style, are known as "fraktur" because of the similarity to the 16th century type-face of that name. These hand-lettered documents with gay water-color borders, frequently incorporating stylized birds, hearts and flowers, were often executed by local ministers, school masters or itinerant penmen. Most are of Pennsylvania German origin.

Birth announcement for Thomas Weber, pen & ink & water-color on laid paper, a long rectangular form w/a block of stylized flowers in the upper left issuing a floral vine across the top above the German inscription, a wide band of flowering bushes & trees across the bottom, inscription reads "Thomas Weber, January 20, 1798, Lecha County," Pennsylvania, decorated in red, green, yellow, blue, black & brown, attributed to Durs Rudy, framed, fraktur 8¼ x 13⅛" (wear, tears) **$2,475.00**

Birth letter for David Glich, pen & ink & water-color on paper, a scene of a pudgy spotted orange bird w/blue wings & blue & yellow neck rings perched in flowering branches above the bottom edge inscription "David Gilch the 20th day of January 1849," initials "E.B.," in apparently original split-banister & corner block curly maple frame, 6 x 6¼" (ILLUS. bottom w/bird drawing,) **4,025.00**

Birth Letter for Mary Tyson

Birth letter for Mary Tyson, pen & ink & water-color, a central

rectangular narrow panel features the standing profile portrait of an elegantly clad dark-haired lady holding a red & yellow tulip above an inscription flanked by matching long panels w/large stylized red, yellow & green tulips, a horizontal rectangular panel at the bottom encloses the name & English inscription, Montgomery County, Pennsylvania, dated 1814, attributed to John Van Minian, in apparently original molded mahogany frame w/corner blocks, 7½ x 9½" (ILLUS.) **12,650.00**

Birth & baptismal certificate for Levi Zartman, pen & ink & water-color on cut-out paper, a large ovoid central reserve w/long German inscription surrounded by a narrow border w/red, yellow & blue parrots at each corner w/hearts & flowers along each side, Lancaster County, Pennsylvania, dated 1815, attributed to Wilhemus Antonius Faber, 13 x 15 ⅝" **2,875.00**

Birth & baptismal certificate for Tryphena, pen & ink & water-color, an ornate design w/a central rectangular bordered panel w/the lengthy German inscription surrounded by a large heart on each side w/further inscriptions & pairs of long stylized tulips & vining flowers w/quarter-fans in each corner, dated 1808, Berks County, Pennsylvania, tape repairs along folds, 13 x 16" (ILLUS. top, next page) **5,462.00**

Book plate for Maria Messerschmid, water-color & pen & ink on paper, a large central red, yellow & green heart flanked by a pair of red & green birds & vining flowers up the sides, German inscription inside

Large Decorative Birth Certificate

the heart, by Johannes Adam Eyer, dated 1809, in a molded giltwood frame, book plate 4 x 6" (damage along ends) ...**2,012.00**

Drawing, water-color, pen & ink on paper, a stylized leaping stag w/red, yellow & blue spots & w/a sunburst & starburst above & blades of grass below, all within a leafy vine border, late 18th - early 19th c., American school, in early wide beveled frame, drawing 3½ x 4".........................**661.00**

Drawing, water-color, pen & ink on paper, a soldier on horseback in full military uniform including a cap w/a red plume & a blue jacket, in an early wide gilt beveled frame, ca. 1820, drawing 3½ x 4¼"......................**632.00**

Drawing, water-color & pen & ink on paper, a yellow bird w/black wings & blue head perched on a flowering branch, American, ca. 1820, framed, 4 ⅛ x 6 ⅜" (ILLUS. top next column).........**1,150.00**

Bird Drawing & Birth Letter

Fraktur of a Distelfink

Drawing, water-color & pen & ink on paper, a large red, blue & yellow-striped distelfink flanked by tulips on long leafy stems, one stem issuing from a red-outlined heart surrounding an inscription, a starburst in the upper left corner, attributed to Conrad Trewitz, dated 1816, framed, 4¼ x 7" (ILLUS.) **2,012.00**

Drawing, water-color, pen & ink on paper, a long red four-storied 'pyramid' building w/yellow a large yellow arrow weathervane on the peak, multiple windows & yellow doors, American School, 19th c., framed, drawing, 6¼ x 9" **920.00**

Drawing, water-color & pen & ink on laid paper, a stylized tulip blossom on a stem opposite an open heart w/compass designs in each corner, narrow herringbone design band on three sides, in red, green & yellow, modern painted frame, 7¾ x 9¾" (stains)....................**660.00**

Drawing, water-color & pen & ink on paper, two large colorful facing parrots perched on a tall flowering tree w/delicate leafy branches all issuing from a small urn-form vase, starbursts in each corner & a wavy band around the border, American, early 19th c., 8 x 10" (some staining) **5,750.00**

Drawing, water-color & pen & ink on wove paper, a bouquet of stylized tulips & leaves in two shades of blue, yellow, black & faded red, inscribed across the bottom "Maria Cetch 1848," in an early mortised wood frame, 9¾ x 10¾" (stains, fold lines) **495.00**

Verse for Fronica Kinig, water color & pen & ink on paper, a large central heart w/the recipient's name in large ornate letters at the top above a lengthy German inscription, the heart flanked at the top corners by large facing green, yellow, orange & brown parrots w/flowering vines between them, small hearts w/inscriptions & pairs of birds & vines of flowers at the bottom corners, dated 1837, Pennsylvania, attributed to Johannes Kinnig, 12½ x 15½" **1,265.00**

FRAMES

Aluminum, Art Deco style, a narrow rectangular beveled frame w/a beveled glass insert, brushed finish, 12½" w., 14" h. **$55.00**

Cast iron, small rectangular form cast to resemble crisscrossed rough-hewn branches, worn original red & gold paint, each holds an early photograph, late 19th c., 3¾" w., 5¼" h., pr. **165.00**

Copper, hand-hammered, Arts & Crafts style, table model of slightly tapering rectangular sides delicately tooled w/floral blossoms at the corners & hammered designs along the borders, original brown patina, wooden back & supports, early 20th c., 4½" w., 6" h..................**385.00**

Arts & Crafts Copper Frame

Copper, repoussé, Arts & Crafts style, slightly tapering rectangular flat sides w/a gently arched crest at the top center, repoussé designs at the upper corners, embossed across the International Foursome - Played on the Leith Links 1682," original bronze patina, 24½ x 30¼" (ILLUS.) **460.00**

Enamel & silver, rectangular shape w/notched sides, enameled translucent blue over an engine-turned sunburst ground, applied w/ribbon-tied foliate swags, surmounted by a ribbon bow, with silver-gilt strut, Ivan Britzin, St. Petersburg, Russia, ca. 1910, 6⅝" h. **8,625.00**

Leather & copper, Arts & Crafts style, rectangular w/wide mottled brown leather-covered sides w/copper overlay across the top & down one side w/large serrated leaves & clusters of berry clusters, copper w/lightly cleaned patina, back hook for hanging, 8 x 9½" (ILLUS. bottom previous column) **825.00**

Papier-mâché, Arts & Crafts style, flat rectangular form w/off-center rectangular opening, the wider side delicately molded w/a standing woman w/a beaded headband wearing a long flowing gown & slippers among twisting vines, leaves & large blossoms which continue around all the sides, textured background, rich dark brown, impressed "Germany," early 20th c., 7" w., 9½" h....................**66.00**

Papier-mâché, rectangular flat form w/centered rectangular opening, the sides molded w/a design of large blossoms on undulating stems & leaves among water lilies & lily pads against a textured background, rich caramel, early 20th c., 7" w., 9½" h. **358.00**

FRUIT JARS

Arts & Crafts Leather & Copper Frame

Milk Glass Insert Fruit Jar

American - (motif of eagle & flag) - Fruit Jar, cylindrical, ground lip, correct glass lid & lightning closure, smooth base, Australia, ca. 1880-1900, greenish aqua, qt.......................**$94.00**

Ball, ABM lip, correct zinc screw lid, smooth base, ca. 1910-1920, lime green w/darker striations, qt. **105.00**

Eagle, cylindrical, applied groove ring wax sealer, correct glass lid, metal yoke, smooth base, ca. 1870-1890, aqua, qt. (⅜" chip on side of lid) **121.00**

Flaccus Bros. - Steers (motif of steers head) Head - Fruit Jar, ground lip, smooth base, screw band, lid w/milk glass insert w/sunburst in center, ca. 1890-1910, straw yellow w/amber tone, pt. (ILLUS. previous page) **358.00**

Indicator Fruit Jar

Indicator, ground lip, smooth base, ca. 1870-1880, aqua, reproduction 2-pc. metal closure, qt. (ILLUS.) **688.00**

Lafayette (below bust of Lafayette), ground lip, smooth base, original three-piece metal & glass closure, ca. 1880-1890, aqua, qt. **1,265.00**

Ludlow's Patent - June 23 1859 - & August 6 1861, cylindrical, ground lip, smooth base, original glass lid & metal closure, ca. 1861-1865, aqua, ½ gal. (small rim chip on lid) **121.00**

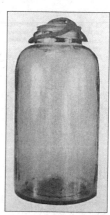

Ludlow's Patent Fruit Jar

Ludlow's Patent - June 28, 1859, ground lip, original glass lid & metal closure, smooth base, ca. 1859-1865, aqua, ½ gal. (ILLUS.) **187.00**

Mason's - Patent - Nov 30th - 1858, zinc screw lid & jar top sealer w/metal wooden handle, lid stamped "J.W.L. Jar Top Sealer K-D Mfg. Co. Lancaster, PA. Pat App'd For" on underside, aqua, 3¼" h., qt. **94.00**

Medford Preserved Fruit - Buffalo, N.Y., cylindrical, applied mouth, smooth base, ca. 1870-1875, deep aqua, ½ gal. (¼" chip side of lip) **193.00**

Potter & Bodine - Air Tight - Fruit Jar - Philada - Patented - April 13th - 1858, barrel-shaped, applied groove ring wax sealer, pontil-scarred base, ca. 1855-1860, aqua, ½ gal. (ILLUS. top left, next page)................**1,595.00**

Safety Valve - Patd May 21 1895 - HC (over triangle), ground lip, original glass lid & metal closure, ground lip, ca. 1875-1890, deep bluish aqua, ½ gal...**50.00**

Barrel-shaped Fruit Jar

Lightning Fruit Jar

Schaffer - Jar - Rochester - N.Y. - J.C.S. (monogram), ground lip, original "finned" glass lid & wire bail, smooth base, ca. 1880-1885, aqua, ½ gal. **303.00**

Stone (A.) & Co - Philada, cylindrical, applied groove ring wax sealer, iron pontil, ca. 1885-1925, aqua, qt. **990.00**

Trade Mark - Advance (over JW monogram) - Pat Apld For, ground lip, original glass lid marked "Advance Fruit Jar, Patent Sep. 18, 1883," coiled wire, smooth base, aqua, qt. **413.00**

Trade (motif of stag) Mark - E.C. Flaccus, cylindrical, ground lip, smooth base, ca. 1890-1910, milk glass, pt. (missing insert & screw band) **154.00**

Trade Mark - Lightning, cylindrical, marked "Patd Apr 25 82 Patd Jan 5 75 - Reisd June 5 77" on correct amber glass lid & lightning closure, embossed "Putnam" on smooth base, ca. 1882-1890, yellowish amber, qt. (break on neck wire) **72.00**

Trade Mark - Lightning, cylindrical, ground lip, original unmarked glass lid & lightning wire closure, smooth base, ca. 1875-1895, yellow w/olive tone, pt. **275.00**

Trade Mark - Lightning - Registered - U.S. Patent Office, cylindrical, ABM lip, original glass lid & lightning closure, smooth base, ca. 1910-1920, cornflower blue, pt. (ILLUS.) **143.00**

Penny-In-Lid Fruit Jar

Wheaton - U.S.A., smooth lip, original glass lid w/circa 1966 penny in lid, lightning-type closure, smooth base marked "Wheaton - U.S.A.," clear, ½ pt. (ILLUS.) **39.00**

Winslow Jar, correct glass lid & wire closure, ground lip, smooth base, aqua, ½ gal. plus one cup..**88.00**

FURNITURE

For our purposes, the general guidelines for dating will be:

Pilgrim Century - 1620-85
William & Mary - 1685-1720
Queen Anne - 1720-50
Chippendale - 1750-85
Federal - 1785-1820
    Hepplewhite - 1785-1820
    Sheraton - 1800-20
American Empire (Classical) - 1815-40
Victorian - 1840-1900
    Early Victorian - 1840-50
    Gothic Revival - 1840-90
    Rococo (Louis XV) - 1845-70
    Renaissance - 1860-85
    Louis XVI - 1865-75
    Eastlake - 1870-95
    Jacobean & Turkish Revival - 1870-95
    Aesthetic Movement - 1880-1900
Art Nouveau - 1890-1918
Turn-of-the-Century - 1895-1910
Mission (Arts & Crafts movement) -
    1900-15
Art Deco - 1925-40

All furniture included in this listing is American unless otherwise noted.

BEDROOM SUITES

French Empire Revival: double bed, armoire & nightstand; ormolu-mounted mahogany, the sleigh-form bed w/the headboard slightly taller than the footboard & each w/a outcurved bar crestrail above a wide panel, the footboard centering by an ornate pierced ormolu bow, arrow & ribbon mount, a lower band & the side rails w/further ormolu mounts, the tall armoire w/a rectangular top above a frieze band decorated w/palmette ormolu mounts above a tall single door w/arched-top mirror & top corner mounts flanked by free-standing colonettes on outset base blocks flanking a central panel w/ormolu mount, the small nightstand w/a square marble top w/outset squared corners over a case w/a small drawer over a small door raised on slender columns resting on a bottom open shelf, all pieces on gilt paw feet, France, ca. 1880, 3 pcs **$7,700.00**

Louis XV-Style Armoire

Louis XV-Style: double bed & armoire; gilt-bronze mounted kingwood, the high bed headboard w/an arched cornice centered by a lion pelt crowned w/berried laurel branches, the lower footboard centered by a flower & laurel wreath, fitted overall w/gilt-bronze scrolled chutes & lion paw sabots; the tall three-section armoire w/a wide arched central cornice mounted w/a gilt-bronze lion pelt finial above an arched central mirrored door flanked by a pair of tall narrow arch-topped cupboard doors inlaid w/urns, each end section raised on three short scrolled legs terminating in gilt-bronze paw feet & a square center back leg, France, late 19th c., armoire, 65½" w., 5' 10¾" h., 2 pcs. (ILLUS. of armoire) **6,900.00**

Signed Bedroom Suite

Victorian Renaissance Revival: high-back double bed & marble-topped chest of drawers; walnut w/burl walnut panels, the bed w/a high headboard topped by a crown crest w/carved palmette over a fan-carved, burl-trimmed shield-shaped panels flanked by scroll-topped curved crestrails over raised burl banding framing a central arched-top inset panel over a lower rectangular burl panel all flanked by squared tall headposts w/raised burl panels, the lower arched footboard w/a molded crestrail over a curved raised burl panel over a recessed oblong panel flanked by rectangular raised burl panels all between low square footposts w/narrow burl panels on the sides between the wide blocked finial & molded square foot, the matching high chest of drawers w/matching arched crestrail above burl-paneled sides w/bracket candle shelves flanking the tall rectangular mirror above a rectangular white marble top above the case of three long graduated drawers each w/raised burl panels & pear-form drops, molded base, stenciled mark of McCracken & Brewster, New Orleans, Louisiana, ca. 1870, bed 18⅞ x 66½", 7' 1¾" h., 2 pcs. (ILLUS.) **2,860.00**

Victorian Renaissance Revival substyle: high-back bed & matched chest of drawers; walnut & burl walnut, each piece w/a high back surmounted by a very ornate crown-form pierce-carved & block crestrail w/a carved sunburst finial on the center section & turned pointed knob finials at the top corners, the bed w/a wide burl inset rectangular panels over narrow

French Campaign Bed

Ornate Renaissance Revival Bed

above burl-paneled sides w/candle shelves flanking the tall rectangular mirror above a rectangular white marble top over a case w/a row of three small drawers over two long drawers, all w/burl veneering & long burl pulls w/bails, molded & double-arched front apron, ca. 1870, 2 pcs. (ILLUS. of the bed, left) **3,850.00**

BEDS

Campaign bed, folding-type, cast iron, straight corner folding upright flat bars w/a pierced diamond design w/a slender curved backrail over slender wire spindles & top endrails over slender spindles, tied wire spring base, raised on hinged flat S-scroll legs, France, 19th c. (ILLUS. above) **468.00**

Classical 'sleigh' bed, twin-size, carved mahogany & mahogany veneer, the matching head- and footboards w/outswept crestrails w/reeded end panels above

rectangular panels flanked by the square sideposts w/blocked knob finials, the low footboard of matching design, the chest of drawers w/matching crestrail

Classical 'Sleigh' Bed

solid panels flanked by free-standing ropetwist-turned columns to corner blocks & the original side rails, raised on "beehive" turned short legs on casters, old refinish, minor imperfections, Mid-Atlantic States, ca. 1825-35, 29½ x 79", 34½" h. (ILLUS. above) **1,265.00**

Classical tall poster bed, carved mahogany, the arched, shaped headboard flanked by turned tapering headposts w/pineapple finials, the footposts w/elaborate foliate carving & pineapple-carved finials, on baluster-turned legs, ca. 1825, 56 x 84⅓", 6' 9¼" h.....................................**460.00**

Classical tall poster tester bed, carved mahogany, the rectangular tester above ring- & baluster-turned headposts surmounted by pineapple-carved finials flanking a shaped headboard, the footposts w/spiral-, floral- & acanthus-carved sections, on ring-turned legs ending in brass sockets w/casters, ca. 1825, 56½" w., 7' 5" h......................**4,140.00**

Decorated Classical Rope Bed

Classical country-style low-poster rope bed, painted & decorated, the baluster- and ring-turned headposts w/double-ring finials flank a wide shaped headboard w/scroll-carve crest, ring- and baluster-turned legs ending in knob feet, simpler footboard w/matching posts, all w/old red ground, the headboard w/black accents & delicate floral & leaf gold stenciled decoration, imperfections, New England, 1830-45, 51" w., 46" h. (ILLUS.) **920.00**

Early Rope Bed

Country-style low-poster rope bed, painted wood, short headposts w/turned knob finials flanking a plain arched low headboard, heavy turned tapering legs, the low footposts w/flattened knob finials above tapering turned legs, original square siderails w/holes for looping rope, original red paint, Connecticut, ca. 1800, 52¼ x 77¼", 32" h. (ILLUS.)................**489.00**

Federal tall poster bed, carved mahogany, the spirally-reeded & beaded acanthus-carved head- and footposts center a shaped & scroll-cut mahogany headboard, turned tapering baluster-form legs ending in peg feet, original side & end rails, Salem, Massachusetts, ca. 1820, 54 x 80", 5' 7" h. **2,070.00**

Federal tall poster bed, stained maple & birch, the plain pencil-post headposts flank a simple arched headboard, the footposts w/a tall swelled & reeded upper section above a baluster-turned section over a small ring-turned

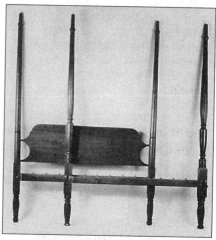

Federal Tall Poster Bed

base section above the knobbed rail, on baluster- and ring-turned legs, original rails for roping, red-stained, restoration, Massachusetts or New Hampshire, ca. 1815-25, 58½ x 81", 6' 11" h. (ILLUS.) **1,725.00**

Federal country-style four-poster bed, turned tiger stripe maple, each head- and footpost w/an acorn finial above reel- and

Federal Tiger Stripe Maple Bed

square spindles, slightly shorter footposts joined by a matching band of spindles, light overcoat on original finish, unmarked, headboard 47½ x 57¼" (ILLUS.) **3,300.00**

Mission-style Twin Bed

vase-turning joined by large maple rails, the headboard of shaped poplar w/a rolled crestrail, the footboard w/reverse-scrolling on the crestrail, raised on tapering turned legs w/ring-turned tapering peg feet, probably Pennsylvania, ca. 1830, 66 x 85", 5' h. (ILLUS.) **4,312.00**

Hired man's bed, ash, rectangular rail construction, old natural color, New England, early 19th c., 38 x 69", 31" h......**345.00**

Mission-style (Arts & Crafts movement) twin bed, oak, upright squared ends w/six flat slats each between square posts, original leather cushion, original finish, signed w/"Stickley & Brandt" decal, early 20th c., 31 x 79", 29" h. (ILLUS.).........**2,310.00**

Fine Mission Double Bed

Mission-style (Arts & Crafts movement) double bed, oak, tall tapering headposts joined by a upper rail over a lower rail above a band of tall slender

Molesworth Twin Bed

Molesworth twin bed, fir, the open rectangular headboard & offset footboard w/brass-tacked upholstered top rails above end panels decorated w/routered figuring & carved in light relief w/a whirling band design framing a central diamond w/Native American good luck symbol, circular hewn legs carved w/an arrow, rails upholstered in rust-colored leather, Thomas Molesworth, ca. 1935, 42½ x 82", 25" h. (ILLUS.) **1,725.00**

Victorian Renaissance Revival Bed

Rustic Pine Bed

Rustic-style double bed, burled pine, the slatted arched rectangular headboard w/burled trim below a heavily burled open H-shaped frame, a conforming offset footboard, designed by Jack Kranenberg, made by Kranenberg & Aiman, ca. 1943, 57 x 95½", 4' 10½" h. (ILLUS.) **3,220.00**

Victorian high-back bed, Renaissance Revival substyle, walnut, the tall headboard w/a molded & rounded arch crestrail w/central carved cartouche above a high rounded panels w/half-round drops down the sides, flanked by tall flattened side posts w/carved & curved finials, original wide sidetails w/arched & shaped corner brackets, the lower footboard w/molded arched crestrail above a recessed oblong panel w/a

raised oblong pointed cartouche & curved corner posts, on casters, ca. 1870, 5' 11" h. (ILLUS.) **935.00**

Patented Belter Rosewood Bed

Victorian high-back bed, Rococo substyle, laminated & carved rosewood, the tall serpentine-shaped headboard w/a molded broken-arch cornice centering an oval medallion flanked by two children holding a garland of flowers, the downswept scrolling returns continuing to molded scrolling rails joining the rounded similarly molded footboard, on molded & scrolled curved bracket feet, patented by John Henry Belter, New York City, ca. 1860, 60 x 84", 5' 11" h. (ILLUS.) ...**17,250.00**

BENCHES

Gothic Revival Bench

Gothic Revival bench, oak, rectangular top w/rounded corners & central handhold decorated w/a carved grapevine border, raised on slightly canted shaped slab legs carved in high-relief w/a pierced Gothic medallion & ending in forked Gothic arch legs, the ends joined by a through-tenon flat rail carved w/Gothic designs & a central florette, carved by Enid Yandell, 1928, 9½ x 17½", 17½" h. (ILLUS.) **431.00**

Hall bench, Mission-style (Arts & Crafts movement), oak, tall tapering square backposts flanking the paneled back & sides w/through-tenon arms above a rectangular lift-seat over a shallow compartment, front posts continue to form legs, original medium finish w/very light overcoat, decal mark of

Mission Oak Hall Bench

Lifetime Furniture, Model No. 511¾, 18½ x 47½", 38½" h. (ILLUS.) **1,210.00**

Renaissance-Style Bench

Hall bench, Renaissance-Style, carved walnut, the arched back boldly carved w/leafy scrollings w/a shell finial & short end blocks w/knob finials above the wide back panel ornately carved w/bold cartouches & scrolls centers by a female mask, downswept arms carved w/scrolls & masks flanking the rectangular plank seat w/beaded border, raised on scroll-carved shaped slab end legs on shoe feet, Italy, 19th c., 71" l., 4' 11" h. (ILLUS.) **1,430.00**

Rococo-Style Bench

Rococo-Style bench, carved giltwood, oblong serpentine upholstered seat above a deep scroll- & shell-carved apron, short cabriole legs w/human figures carved at the knees above the scroll feet, Europe, 19th, 45" l. (ILLUS.) **990.00**

Window bench, Mission-style (Arts & Crafts movement), oak, upright ends w/through-tenoned cross rails above the rectangular cushion seat on a rectangular seat frame raised on square stile legs w/through-tenoned end stretchers & a cross stretcher, original medium finish, unsigned, early 20th c., 17 x 29½", 28⅞" h. **518.00**

BOOKCASES

Baroque-Style bookcase, carved oak, the rectangular top w/a carved flaring cornice surmounted by a large central half-round carved flower-filled urn flanked by winged griffins w/small figural eagles at the top corners above a wide paneled frieze band carved w/scrolling vines alternating w/carved blocks above the pair of tall glazed doors opening to two shelves & separated by three boldly carved pilasters topped by bearded male terms, the side panels w/long scroll-carved

Baroque-Style Bookcase

bands, the slightly stepped-out lower section w/wide rectangular panels carved w/scroll-carved rectangular bands centers by a grotesque face, each panel separated w/a outset block carved w/another grotesque face, thick rounded carved base raised on three compressed grotesque face front feet, Europe, ca. 1870, 20 x 60", 8' h. (ILLUS.) **2,750.00**

Classical bookcase, mahogany veneer, two-part construction: the upper section w/a rectangular top above a deep cove-molded cornice above a pair of 3-pane glazed cupboard doors opening to five shelves above a slightly stepped-out short lower section w/a pair of double-panel cupboard doors on a flat plinth base, old refinish, minor imperfections, New England, ca. 1840, 17¾ x 48½", 7' 10½" h. (ILLUS. top next page) **2,990.00**

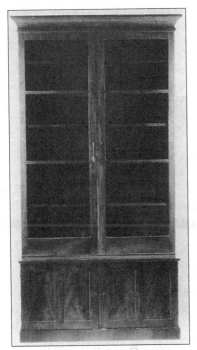

Fine Classical Bookcase

Cherry Country Bookcase

Classical step-back bookcase,
mahogany, two-part construction:
the upper section w/a
rectangular top w/a narrow
coved cornice above a plain
frieze band & narrow molding
over two tall 8-pane glazed
cupboard doors opening to
adjustable shelves; the stepped-
out lower section w/a pair of
paneled cupboard doors, flat
base on heavy knob-turned front
feet, old finish, ca. 1830-50,
cornice 13 x 49¼", 7' 7" h.
(repairs, edge damage, age
crack in one door & pieced
repair to edge of one
top door) **1,155.00**

Country-style bookcase, cherry,
step-back type, a rectangular
top w/a flaring coved cornice
above four long open shelves
above a slightly stepped-out
lower section w/two open
shelves, molded base w/a
narrow scalloped apron & simple

bracket feet, New England, early
19th c., old refinish,
imperfections, 10¼ x 36",
7' 2½" h. (ILLUS.) **2,185.00**

**Mission-style (Arts & Crafts
movement) bookcase,** oak,
single-door, the rectangular top
w/a three-quarters low gallery
w/through-tenons above a single
tall 16-pane glazed door
w/hammered copper hardware
opening to three shelves, panel
back, original finish, shadow of
"The work of..." decal of L. &
J.G. Stickley, Model No. 641,
ca. 1912, 12 x 30", 4' 7" h.......**4,600.00**

**Mission-style (Arts & Crafts
movement) bookcase,** oak,
two-door, the rectangular top
w/the square front posts slightly
extending above the edge above
through-tenons over two tall

Stickley Brothers Bookcase

glaze cupboard doors w/three small panes above to tall vertical panes opening to three shelves, narrow slightly arched double apron, copper plate hardware w/ring pulls, inset side panels, unmarked Stickley Brothers, numbered, Model No. 4692, fine original medium finish, 12 x 49", 4' 7" h. (ILLUS.) **2,310.00**

Lifetime Furniture Bookcase

Mission-style (Arts & Crafts movement) bookcase, oak, two-door, the rectangular top w/a low three-quarter gallery above two long glazed doors w/eight small panes above a long single pane in each, three shelves, flat apron w/angled bracket feet, copper plate & ring hardware, original medium finish, marked "Paine Furniture," Lifetime Model No. 7219, 13 x 42", 4' 7½" h. (ILLUS.) **2,860.00**

Mission-style (Arts & Crafts movement) bookcase, oak, two-door, the rectangular top w/a three-quarters low gallery above a pair of 12-pane glazed doors w/hammered copper hardware opening to three shelves, original medium finish, red decal & paper label of Gustav Stickley, Model No. 719, ca. 1907, 13 x 59¾", 4' 10⅛" h..............................**6,900.00**

Mission-style (Arts & Crafts movement) bookcase, oak, two-door, the rectangular top w/a narrow rectangular backrail, overhanging long corbels on the tall case w/two long 2-pane glazed doors opening to three shelves, light cleaning to original dark finish, paper label of the Charles Limbert Company, Model No. 358, on casters, 14 x 48", 4' 11" h. **3,850.00**

Mission-style (Arts & Crafts movement) book rack, oak, the flat end boards w/semi-circular cut-outs at the top & brackets at the bottom, the top rack of V-form w/exposed keyed tenons, the lower flat shelf also w/keyed tenons, Craftsman paper label of Gustav Stickley, Model No. 74, ca. 1910, 10 x 29¾", 30⅝" h. **1,725.00**

Turn-of-the-Century bookcase, four-section stacking-type, oak, each section w/a long rectangular glass-fronted lift-up door, Grand Rapids, Michigan, ca. 1900-15, 12 x 34", 4' 10" h.................................**578.00**

Victorian Aesthetic Bookcase

Victorian bookcase, Aesthetic Movement substyle, inlaid walnut, two-part construction: the upper section w/a central nearly squared glazed door below a band of carved rosettes flanked by arch-topped open shelved compartments further flanked by free-standing columns headed by a leaftip capital & ending in carved drapery & leaftips; the stepped-out lower section w/an arrangement of eleven long and short drawers fitted w/floral-cast loop handles, overall inlaid w/flowerheads, third quarter 19th c., lacking fee, replacements, 66" w., 6' 3" h. (ILLUS.) **8,050.00**

Victorian bookcase, Rococo substyle, mahogany, the rectangular top w/a flattened flaring cornice above a tall slender glazed door topped w/an gently arched leaf- and scroll-

Victorian Rococo Slender Bookcase

carved band, five shelves, flat plinth base, ca. 1850, 18 x 31", 7' 3" h. (ILLUS.) **1,045.00**

Bird's-eye Maple Bookcase

Victorian bookcase, bird's-eye maple, the rectangular top w/a flaring deep steeped cornice above a pair of tall single-pane glazed doors w/rounded tops opening to two shelves above a medial band & tow shorter glazed doors below opening to one shelf, molded plinth base, ca. 1850 (ILLUS. bottom previous page).......................**1,870.00**

Victorian bookcase, walnut, a rectangular top above a case w/three tall geometrically-glazed cupboard doors opening to shelves, double-paneled ends, on a flaring molded base raised on blocky paw feet, late 19th c., 13 x 64", 4' 6" h. **550.00**

BUREAUX PLAT

Art Nouveau Bureau Plat

Art Nouveau, the rectangular top w/molded edge above an arrangement of three drawers, two small, deep end drawers flanking a long center drawer, applied bronze whiplash foliate mounts, on tapering molded legs, Louis Majorelle, France, ca. 1900, 31¼ x 51½", 29¼" h. (ILLUS.) **1,725.00**

Louis XV-Style, gilt-bronze mounted lacquer, the shaped rectangular top inset w/leather above a conforming apron fitted w/three drawers w/Chinese figural & landscape scenes &

flanked by similar panels all within gilt-bronze foliate-scrolled frames, raised on cabriole legs fitted w/long gilt-bronze scrolling mounts w/similar mounts edging the rim of the top & apron, the legs ending in chutes & sabots, France, late 19th c., 69" l., 31" h. **40,250.00**

CABINETS

Federal Cherry Cellaret

Cellaret (wine cabinet), Federal style, cherry, a rectangular lid lifting above a deep well over a single lower drawer at the base, raised on square tapering legs, replace glass drawer pulls, refinished, restoration, Southern United States, 1780-1800, 17¼ x 25⅝", 36" h. (ILLUS.) **2,185.00**

China cabinet, Mission-style (Arts & Crafts movement), oak, a rectangular top w/rounded front corners & a gently arched crestboard slightly overhanging the case w/a wide single glazed door w/three small panes above a single large pane opening to

Mission-style China Cabinet

three adjustable shelves, the back sides extending out from to a small open shelf on each side supported by curved brackets, door w/original patinated brass hardware, original glass, shelves & pegs, on casters, Limbert branded mark & stenciled Model No. 452, ca. 1906, 16½ x 44¼", 4' 10⅞" h. (ILLUS.) **5,175.00**

China cabinet, turn-of-the-century, golden oak, D-form, the top w/a high superstructure w/a flat crestrail downswept at the ends above a wide panel centered by a shaped beveled mirror flanked by scroll carving, the D-form top above a conforming case w/a tall single-pane center door flanked by curved glass sides, slender curved reeded blocks & slender columns separated each glazed sections, molded base on short front cabriole legs w/paw feet, the interior w/a mirrored section at the top back, four wooden shelves, ca. 1900 (ILLUS. top next column) **1,250.00**

Turn-of-the-Century China Cabinet

Mahogany Veneer China Cabinet

China cabinet, turn-of-the-century, mahogany veneer, the D-form top w/a flattened slightly stepped-out central section, a rounded plain frieze band above the conforming case w/a curved single-panel central door & curved glass sides w/free-standing columns separating each section, molded base, short turned front legs w/heavy paw feet, simple flat cabriole back legs, ca. 1900 (ILLUS. bottom previous page) **1,100.00**

China Cabinet-Sideboard

China cabinet-sideboard, Turn-of-the-Century, golden oak, side-by-side style, the long narrow oval-form crestrail topped by a small scroll-carved crest & ending in scroll-carved ears above a rectangular top w/the left end bowed out above a conforming tall curved glass door opening to four wooden shelves, the right side w/a tall open shelf section backed by a

rectangular beveled mirror w/rounded corners above two long drawers w/wooden knobs above a pair of flat cupboard doors carved w/confronting long slender cornucopia-style designs across the center, the flat apron raised on simple short cabriole front legs & square back legs all on casters, ca. 1900, 18 x 45", 5' 10" h. (ILLUS.) **605.00**

Early Dental Cabinet

Dental cabinet, turn-of-the-century, stained hardwood, the tall case w/a superstructure w/a low flat crestrail above a long narrow breakfront molded top above three conforming glazed small square doors w/frosted glass & small round knobs, the center door w/black & gold label reading "Sterilizer," incurved side brackets flanking a long narrow beveled mirror above a stepped-out rectangular top above the tall case base w/two ranks of very narrow drawers above pairs of deeper drawers above two drawers & a single paneled door at the bottom, paneled sides, on short square stile legs on casters (ILLUS.) **1,100.00**

Mission-style Liquor Cabinet

Liquor cabinet, Mission-style (Arts & Crafts movement), oak, a narrow rectangular overhanging top above a low cabinet w/a double-panel metal-mounted sliding door above a stepped-out lower tall case w/a pair of tall strap-hinged cabinet doors, interior fitted w/a single shelf, original medium finish, unsigned, imperfections, ca. 1910, 16¾ x 24", 39" h. (ILLUS.) **690.00**

Liquor cabinet-bar, Art Deco, bronze-mounted mahogany, the upright rectangular case w/rounded ends raised on tapering turned short legs, the upper mirror section w/sliding glass doors above a pull-out mirrored shelf resting over a pair

of cabinet doors, bronze fittings & sabots, France, ca. 1935, 17 x 44½", 5' 1/1/2" h. **2,990.00**

Modern Style Liquor Cabinet

Liquor cabinet-bar, Modern style, bentwood & mahogany, a flat rectangular topped mahogany cabinet w/a pair of flush-mounted rectangular flat cabinet doors opening to reveal a pair of drawers over two bays w/adjustable shelves, raised on long bentwood rails continuing to form the legs, stamped on the back "AALTO DESIGN ARTEK MADE IN SWEDEN 810," Alvar Aalto, ca. 1940, 15¾ x 39½", 39⅜" h. (ILLUS.) **2,300.00**

Music cabinet, Mission-style (Arts & Crafts movement), oak, a rectangular top a w/three-quarters low gallery above a tall, narrow single door w/ten panels of four square leaded panes, original copper V-pull, slab sides w/through-tenon construction, three original adjustable shelves inside, lightly cleaned original finish, paper label & red decal of Gustav Stickley, Model No. 70, 16 x 20", 46" h. **10,500.00**

Music cabinet, Mission-style (Arts & Crafts movement), oak, a rectangular top w/a three-quarters low gallery above a tall

Mission-style Music Cabinet

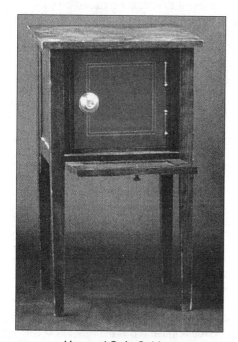

Unusual Safe Cabinet

narrow single door w/ten panels of textured amber glass, hammered copper hardware w/V-pull, the interior w/four adjustable shelves, original medium finish, Gustav Stickley branded mark & partial paper label, Model No. 70, ca. 1912, 16 x 19⅝", 47¼" h. (ILLUS.)...**8,050.00**

Safe cabinet, Arts & Crafts style, oak, a rectangular top overhanging the panel-sided small square case w/a fold-down sliding door opening to the original red-enameled safe, raised on slender square tapering legs, original dark finish, early 20th c., 18" sq., 30" h. (ILLUS. bottom previous column).................................**1,100.00**

Art Nouveau Side Cabinet

Side cabinet, Art Nouveau, inlaid mahogany, the ornate superstructure w/pierced & pointed side crestrails flanking a blossom-form central panel inlaid w/stylized undulating lorals flanked by a pair of large teardrop-form mirrors flanked by downswept pierce-carved side brackets on the serpentine-fronted rectangular top w/scrolled front corner brackets above a single drawer inlaid w/a band of stylized water lily blossoms above the tall 16-pane glazed door w/three leaded glass inverted heart-form devices at the top center & three arched panes along the bottom, undulating carved apron bands flanking a small heart opening, gently arched square legs, brass hardware, Europe, ca. 1900, 14 x 30", 4' 6½" h. (ILLUS.) **863.00**

above a conforming case w/a single center cupboard door painted w/a central landscape scene w/18th c. figures framed by delicate gilt-bronze scroll borders, the sides w/floral marquetry within delicate gilt-bronze scrolling frames, on simple slender cabriole legs w/gilt-bronze mounts & sabots, France, 19th c. (ILLUS.) **8,625.00**

Victorian Side Cabinet

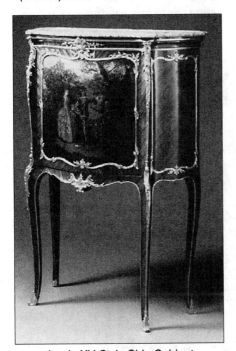

Louis XV-Style Side Cabinet

Side cabinet, Louis XV-Style, gilt-bronze mounted "Vernis Martin" style, the D-form top w/projecting front corners fitted w/a brech d'alep marble top

Side cabinet, Victorian Aesthetic Movement, ebonized & inlaid oak, a high rectangular superstructure w/a floral-carved flat cornice above an arched frieze band decorated w/ornate bird & scrolling leafy vine designs in light wood above the half-round beveled mirror over a wide shelf w/a molded edge raised on four squared post supports to another open shelf overhanging a stepped-back cabinet base w/a wide central door w/rectangular & blossom vine & cluster light wood inlay & flanked by narrow beveled glass side panels all above an narrow oblong opening in the molded plinth base, attributed to R. J. Horner, ca. 1880 (ILLUS.) **3,200.00**

Labeled Renaissance Revival Cabinet

Side cabinet, Victorian Renaissance Revival substyle, parquetry & partial-gilt walnut, the top w/an upright low rectangular central panel w/molded bands at the top & base centering raised panels of veneering, the rectangular top w/incurved & tapering sides above a conforming molded border band over a conforming frieze band w/two long very narrow drawers at the front w/raised diamond-inlay panels & matching inlaid panels at the sides all above the case fronted by a pair of cartouche-form paneled doors w/heavy molding & diamond-inlaid triangular raised panels at each corner, the center of each door w/a large raised oval banding surrounding a delicately inlaid

Ornate Renaissance Revival Cabinet

large bouquet of flowers against a dark ground, the front angled corners w/diamond-inlaid narrow panels carved at the top & base w/classical designs, further inlaid panels on the incurved sides, molded conforming plinth base on squatty disc feet, the back stenciled "Manufactured by Edward Hixon & Co., No. 180 Washington St. Boston," third quarter 19th c., 20¾ x 60", 47½" h. (ILLUS. top, previous page) **4,025.00**

Side cabinet, Victorian Renaissance Revival substyle, carved & gilded walnut & bird's-eye maple, the D-form breakfront top backed by a high crestrail topped by curved panels w/gilt leaf designs centering a shell-carved finial above a narrow shelf & curved sides flanking a small burl veneered drawer w/gilt line trim, the top above a conforming case w/a stepped-out central section w/a drawer over a dentil-, sunburst- and swag-carved band over an inset paneled cupboard door centered w/a round reserve carved w/a nude classical woman & child & flanked by gilt stylized floral & leaf bands, the door flanked by reeded & leaf-carved columns topped by long

blocks w/gilt-incised designs, the side sections w/a plain burled curved frieze panels above an arched, shell-carved opening w/narrow rectangular recessed burl panels & a round plinth at the bottom, the outer sides w/scroll carving & roundels, a wide conforming plinth base w/reeded blocks & some incised gilt trim, ca. 1875 (ILLUS. bottom, previous page)........................**3,080.00**

Side cabinets, Art Deco, lacquered wood & steel, of bisected columnar form, the demi-lune top above a triangular section of which one side is fitted w/a hinged door w/rectangular metal handle & the other fitted w/open shelves, the top w/a rectangular backsplash & angled shelf buttressed by a curved tubular steel post, attributed to Robert Mallet-Stevens, 14 x 25", 35" h., pr. **2,300.00**

Spice cabinet, country-style, painted & decorated pine, long rectangular top w/a molded edge above a case of six rows each w/five graduated small drawers w/small metal pulls, two drawers inscribed "Aaron Page" & "Sarah Page Thourwald,"

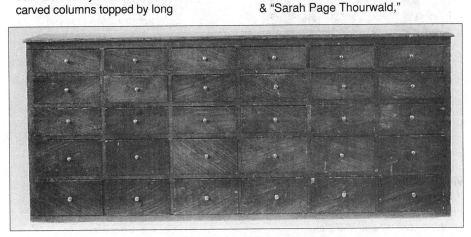

Early Grain-painted Spice Cabinet

overall madder red graining, New England, early 19th c., 8¼ x 48", 20½" h. (ILLUS. bottom previous page)............**4,025.00**

Vitrine cabinet, Art Nouveau, mahogany & wrought iron, the rectangular upright case w/a glass front above burled wood panel, the case carved w/stylized pine cones & acorns, the door applied at the top w/a decorative wrought-iron frieze of pendent leaves & seed pods, on a molded plinth base, branded "Majorelle Nancy," Louis Majorelle, France, ca. 1900, 16½ x 36", 7'½" h. **7,475.00**

door flanked by ebonized columns, the glass sides w/similar divided glazed panels , on a molded base on tapering square legs terminating in ovoid feet, interior shelving of a later date, Austria, first quarter 19th c., 15¾ x 33¼", 5' 4¾" h. (ILLUS.) **3,450.00**

Edwardian Vitrine Cabinet

Biedermeier Vitrine Cabinet

Vitrine cabinet, Biedermeier style, parcel-ebonized walnut, the rectangular top over an angled cornice above a plain frieze band above the stepped-back cabinet w/a divided glazed

Vitrine cabinet, Edwardian, marquetry-inlaid mahogany, the rectangular top w/a narrow molded cornice arched in the center above a frieze band inlaid w/scrolling vines & a central oval device above a pair of tall geometrically-glaze cabinet doors open to two wooden shelves, the lower doors w/panels of scrolling designs matching the frieze band, raise on slender square tall legs, England, early 20th c., 12 x 36", 5' 11" h. (ILLUS.) **660.00**

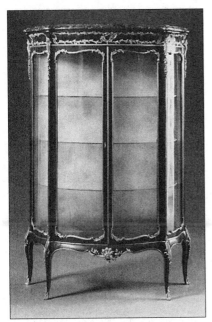

Fine Louis XV-Style Vitrine

Vitrine cabinet, Louis XV-Style, gilt-bronze mounted wood, the shaped D-form dark marble top above an inswept conforming frieze fitted all around w/scrolling gilt-bronze flowers above a pair of single-pane glazed doors opening to three shelves & a mirrored back, curved glass side panels, raised on four simple cabriole legs w/gilt-bronze mounts, scrolling gilt trim around the doors & sides & along the narrow shaped apron centered by a gilt-bronze fanned leaf mount, the legs ending in gilt-bronze sabots, France, late 19th c., 43" w., 5' 3" h. (ILLUS.) **12,650.00**

Vitrine cabinet, Louis XV-Style, gilt-bronze mounted tulipwood, the rectangular top raised on a canted frieze band above the tall conforming case w/a single swelled glazed door flanked by glazed curved side panels above a bombé-form lower case w/a single inlaid cupboard door covered w/ornate gilt-bronze scrolls & swags w/further gilt-bronze scrolling trim around the door, sides & top & continuing down the slender gently outswept legs, the top of the lower cabinet w/small figural gilt-bronze busts, the legs ending in gilt-bronze sabots, France, late 19th c., 27" w., 5' 9" h. **8,625.00**

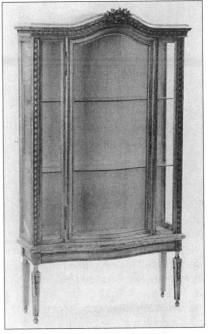

Louis XVI-Style Cabinet

Vitrine cabinet, Louis XVI-Style, giltwood, the rectangular top w/an arched pediment centered by a small carved basket of flowers flanked by an egg-and-dark narrow frieze band above the wide arched single-pane center door flanked by narrow glass panels w/beaded corner bands, narrow glass side panels, a molded slightly serpentine base & plinth raised on squared tapering bellflower-carved legs ending in small knob feet, Europe, second half 19th c., 10 x 39", 5' 6" h. (ILLUS.) **2,860.00**

Modern Style Vitrine

Arts & Crafts Desk Chair

Vitrine cabinet, Modern style, stained mahogany & aluminum, the rectangular top w/rounded front corners above a single-pane glazed door & glazed sides opening to two wooden shelves, a row of small rectangular panels in the lower door above a single drawer at the bottom, raised on a slightly inset plinth w/applied aluminum molding, Austria, ca. 1900, 17¼ x 34", 6' 9¼" h. (ILLUS.) **1,150.00**

CHAIRS

Art Deco "club" chair, upholstered oak, the wide U-form barrel back & arms slope gently to flat arm fronts & a high flat upholstered seatrail & a thick upholstered seat cushion, narrow wooden seatrail raised on short stepped square tapering legs, designed by Jean-Michel Frank, France, ca. 1930, 29½" w., 25½" h. **8,050.00**

Arts & Crafts desk chair, oak & leather upholstery, the square back stiles w/diamond-cut finials joined by two crossbars forming a back panel covered w/leather trimmed w/large hammered brass tacks, curved wooded brackets at base of back on the rectangular leather-covered seat w/further brass hammered tack trim, swiveling above a four-part base w/flat shaped flaring legs, original light finish, marked w/a brass tag inscribed "Santa Barbara County 19016," California, early 20th c., 20¼" w., 42½" h. (ILLUS.) **345.00**

Arts & Crafts hall chair, oak, the tall narrow back w/angular stiles centering a tall flat conforming slat w/painted-yellow stylized flowers, trapezoidal wood seat above an apron band of short square spindles, square legs joined by side stretchers, black paint added to original finish, 4' 1½" h. **660.00**

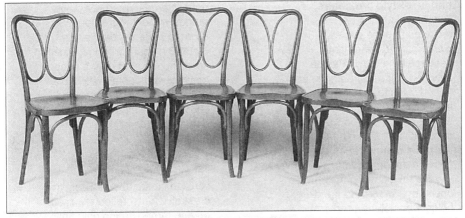

Kohn Bentwood Chairs

Baroque-Style Side Chairs

corners continuing to form side stiles flanking a long curved oval bentwood back loops above the shaped oblong laminated seat, on slender turned & slightly outswept legs w/inverted U-form braces under each side of the seat, original medium to light finish, branded mark & paper label of J. & J. Kohn, Vienna, Austria, Model No. 243, ca. 1916, 34¾" h., set of 8 (ILLUS. above) **690.00**

Baroque-Style side chairs,
carved wood, the tall back w/a pierced & scroll-carved flattened crestrail centered by a cherub figure above a tall caned panel flanked by further bands of vine carving & pierced scroll-carved bands at the bottom centered between block- and spiral-turned stiles topped by small knob finials, the back raised above the caned seat w/pad, block- and ball-turned legs w/a wide pierced scroll-carved front stretcher & spiral-turned H-stretcher & back stretcher, Flanders, 19th c., set of 4 (ILLUS.) **1,650.00**

Bentwood side chairs,
serpentine crestrail w/rounded

Charles II-Style Armchair

Charles II-Style armchairs,
carved walnut, the tall
rectangular base w/a wide
pierce-carved flat crestrail
centered by a crown design
between spiral-twist- and knob-
turned stiles topped by turned
finials, the long central panel
w/wide pierce-carved sides each
centered by a crown design &
flanked a narrow caned panel all
above a bottom matching
pierced rail between the shaped
open arms w/scrolled hand-
holds & baluster-turned arm
supports flanking the over-
upholstered seat, block-, knob-
and ring-turned legs w/carved
feet & joined by a wide pierced
scroll-carved front stretcher w/a
central crown design, red velvet
upholstery, England, 19th c.,
4' 2¼" h., pr. (ILLUS. of one,
bottom, previous page)..........**1,035.00**

Ornate Chinese Armchair

Chinese armchair, carved
hardwood, the wide oblong crest
pierce-carved w/confronted
dragons in clouds, the wide back

panel pierce-carved w/a single
dragon w/pierced side panels
down to the arms carved as
crouching scaly dragons, wide
solid shaped seat over a deep
apron pierce-carved w/a bird &
chilin, raised on heavy carved
cabriole-style legs ending in
dragon claw feet, 19th c., 41" h.
(ILLUS.) **550.00**

Chippendale corner chair,
carved cherry, the reverse-
scrolled crests above a concave
crestrail w/outscrolled terminals
on ring-turned flaring columnar
supports centered by pierced
strapwork splats, the balloon-
form slip-seat below within
conformingly-shaped seatrails,
raised on cabriole legs w/the
front leg carved at the knee w/a
leaf & shell design & ending in a
claw-and-ball foot, the other legs
ending in trifid feet, formerly
fitted w/padded arms & an over-
upholstered seat, repairs to one
splat, both shoes & bottom of
seatrail, the front legs & patches
to trifid feet, restoration to three
knee returns, probably New
England, ca. 1760 ....**3,162.00**

Chippendale Corner Chair

Chippendale corner chair,
cherry, the stepped U-form
crestrail continuing to form flat
shaped arms above to flat back
splats alternating w/three
baluster-turned stiles,
rectangular upholstered seat on
square legs joined by a low
cross-stretcher, probably central
Massachusetts, old finish, ca.
1780, 31" h. (ILLUS. bottom,
previous page)......................**1,840.00**

New England Chippendale Chair

Chippendale side chair, carved
cherry, ox-yoke shaped crestrail
centering a leaf- and flowerhead-
carved reserve w/scrolled
terminals above a pierced
volute-carved vase-form splat,
the shaped seatrail enclosing an
upholstered slip seat, on cabriole
front legs ending in claw-and-ball
feet, square outswept back legs,
legs joined by baluster-turned
box stretchers, New England,
ca. 1775 (ILLUS.)....................**2,587.00**

Chippendale side chair,
transitional-style, maple, the ox-
yoke crest w/molded ears above
a pierced vasiform splat on a
lower rail able the old rush seat,

the baluster- and block-turned
front legs ending in Spanish
feet, double-ball and ring-turned
front stretcher, flat side & back
stretchers, early surface, very
minor imperfections, New
England, 1760-80, 37½" h........**748.00**

Chippendale side chairs, carved
mahogany, a volute-, leaf- and
flower-carved ox-yoke crestrail
w/molded ears above fluted stiles
centering a volute-carved
strapwork splat, the trapezoidal
slip-seat within a conforming
molded & shell-carved arched
seatrail, raised on cabriole front
legs carved w/an exaggerated
pendent leaf device & ending in
delicate claw-and-ball feet,
canted rounded rear legs, appear
to retain old & possibly original
finish, presently unupholstered,
Pennsylvania, ca. 1780, pr.
(repairs to splat & stiles at
juncture w/crestrail)...............**36,800.00**

Chippendale side chairs, cherry,
a simple ox-yoke crestrail w/ears
above a lobed & pierced-cut
vase-form splat between gently
angled stiles, trapezoidal
upholstered seat in molded seat
frame above cabriole legs
ending in pad feet, old refinish,
Connecticut River Valley, 1760-
80, imperfections, 38" h.,
set of 4....................................**8,050.00**

Chippendale Cherry Side Chairs

Classical Side Chairs

Chippendale side chairs, cherry, simple ox-yoke crestrail w/ears raised on slightly outswept stiles flanking the slender loop-pierced waisted back splat, trapezoidal woven rush seat, on square legs joined by box stretchers, Connecticut, ca. 1790, replaced seats, one crest replaced, 37½" h., set of 4 (ILLUS. of part, bottom, previous page)..........**1,437.00**

Classical side chairs, carved mahogany, the scroll-carved crestrail inlaid w/brass stringing above scroll- and shell-carved arched lower rails above the upholstered slip seat, gadroon-carved seatrail raised on sabre legs, old refinish, imperfections, possibly New York, ca. 1820, 34" h., set of 4 (ILLUS. above) **2,415.00**

Classical side chairs, mahogany veneer, the wide gently arched & scroll-ended crestrail above a vase-form back splat above the red velvet-covered slip seat, simple cabriole front legs, old refinish, Boston or New York, ca. 1830-50, imperfections including minor patching, 32½" h., set of 4 ....**748.00**

Classical side chairs, bird's-eye maple, a flat rolled crest bar on the wide crestrail w/rounded ends raised on stiles flanking the wide simple vase-form splat, slightly concave caned rectangular seat, simple flat front sabre legs joined by a flat, curved stretcher, turned side & back stretchers, old refinish, New York State, ca. 1830s, 33½" h., set of 6 (recaned seats, minor repairs) **2,415.00**

Classical side chairs, painted & decorated, wide rectangular & slightly curved crestrail overhanging the ring- and baluster-turned stiles flanking a narrow lower rail, trapezoidal seat w/rounded seatrail raised on ring- and rod-turned front legs joined by a ring-turned stretcher, canted back legs & plain side & back stretchers, the back rails decorated w/gilt-stenciled neoclassical leafy scrolls centering urns against a black-painted ground, Baltimore, Maryland, first half 19th c., 31¼" h., set of 6 (imperfections)......................**1,035.00**

Classical side chairs, mahogany veneer, a rectangular curved crestrail mounted on stiles flanking a wide slat over the upholstered slip-seat, simple curved front & back sabre legs, old refinish, Boston or New York, ca. 1825 , 33" h., set of 7 (imperfections)..........................**978.00**

Old "Ladder-back" Highchair

Country-style child's "ladder-back" highchair, ash, the back w/four arched & shaped slats between simple turned stiles continuing to form back legs, shaped flattened arms on baluster-turned arm supports continuing down to form knob- and rod-turned tall legs, woven rush seat, two baluster-turned stretchers in the front, one badly worn, plain turned stretchers at the sides & back, old seat, refinished, England, 19th c., 37" h. (ILLUS.)..........................**575.00**

Country-style plank-seat side chairs, painted & decorated, the rounded crestrail above a vase-form splat flanked by turned stiles, shaped plank seat on ring- and bamboo-turned front legs & front stretcher, plain side & back stretchers, original black paint w/yellow & gold striping, stenciled decoration of leafy scrolls on the crestrail & splat in red & gold, 19th c., 32¼" h., set of 6 (minor edge wear)..............**726.00**

Danish Modern dining chairs, teak, a narrow curved almond-form crestrail raised on canted round tapering stiles continuing to form the rear legs, the oblong upholstered cushion seat raised on rounded tapering & canted front legs, waisted wide stretchers between the front & rear legs, original finish, branded marks of Carl Hansen & Son, Odense, Denmark, designed by Hans Wegner, mid-20th c., 28½" h., set of 4 ....**546.00**

Early "Ladder-back" Armchair

Early American "ladder-back" armchair, painted hardwood, the tall back composed of five gently arched slats between knob- and rod-turned stiles w/ball finials, narrow shaped arms on baluster- and rod-turned arm supports continuing to form front legs & flanked the damaged woven rush seat, double sausage-turned front stretchers & plain double side stretchers & single rear stretcher, old black paint w/gold accents, old painted splint seat, Long Island or New Jersey, minor imperfections, 1730-1800, 47" h. (ILLUS. bottom previous page) **1,610.00**

ring- and baluster-turned finials, the slender flat arms w/angled hand grips w/crudely carved faces above knob- and rod-turned arm supports continuing down to form the front legs, old splint seat, old dark brown paint, Portsmouth, New Hampshire, late 18th c., rockers added later, imperfections, 46" h. (ILLUS.) **1,955.00**

Long Island" Ladder-back" Rocker

Early "Ladder-back" Rocker

Early American "ladder-back" rocking chair w/arms, painted, four gently arched slats in the back between tall knob- and post-turned stiles w/elongated

Early American "ladder-back" rocking chair w/arms, painted wood, the tall back w/three gently arched slats between baluster- and rod-turned stiles w/ring- and knob-turned finials, serpentine open arms w/ringed medallion-carved handgrips on tapering turned arm rests continuing down to form the baluster- and rod-turned front legs, woven rush seat, double rungs at front & sides, wide inset rockers, old paint, Long Island, New York area, 18th c., imperfections, 4' 1" h. (ILLUS.) **978.00**

Early American "ladder-back" side chair, turned maple, the tall back w/five arched graduated slats flanked by simple turned stiles topped by turned button finials, the square rush seat on simple turned legs joined by a bulbous-turned front stretcher & plain side & back stretchers, the front legs ending in large ball & peg feet, retains old crackled finish, Delaware River Valley, 1770-1800 (old repair to side rail).................**3,450.00**

Federal Mahogany Armchair

Federal armchair, carved mahogany, the tall square back w/a flat narrow reeded crestrail rail & reeded stiles flanking three teardrop-pierced & forked uprights above the reeded base rail, slender curved open arms on set-back incurved molded arm supports above the over-upholstered seat, square tapering reeded front legs & square canted rear legs, old finish, imperfections, probably Portsmouth, New Hampshire, early 19th c., 35½" h. (ILLUS.) **978.00**

Federal "Lolling" Chair

Federal "lolling" armchair, mahogany, the tall rectangular upholstered back w/a serpentine crestrail above long slender shaped arms ending in roundel hand grips above incurved arm supports, deep rectangular upholstered seat raised on square tapering legs joined by flat box stretchers & raised on casters, probably Massachusetts, old refinish, repairs, ca. 1790, 45½" h. (ILLUS.) **1,495.00**

Federal side chair, cherry, an arched crestrail on gently curved stiles flanking the pierced vasiform splat carved w/a central urn, wide trapezoidal upholstered seat raised on square legs joined by an H-stretcher, old surface, Hartford, Connecticut area, possible by Kneeland and Adams, ca. 1795, minor imperfections, 38" h. (ILLUS. top, next page) **748.00**

Federal side chair, carved mahogany, the flat narrow crestrail w/a raised central rectangular panel w/a carved

Federal Cherry Side Chair

Federal Mahogany Side Chair

reeded band, small corner blocks carved w/florettes above the square stiles flanking a row of four slender square spindles curved & forming Gothic arches at the top, overupholstered seat on a flat seatrail & square, tapering reeded legs w/tapering blocked front feet, old refinish, New York City, ca. 1800, overall 35½" h. (ILLUS. bottom, previous column) **690.00**

Federal side chairs, carved mahogany, the arched crestrail centered by a raised panel carved w/drapery against a star-punched background, the beaded square back enclosing eight concave-faced ribs intersecting in arches, on a serpentine over-upholstered seat, imperfections, Salem, Massachusetts, ca. 1790, 36" h., pr. **7,475.00**

Federal side chairs, mahogany, an arched & molded shield-shaped back centering three shaped uprights w/a fan-carved reserve at the base, the rounded & bowed overupholstered seat on square tapering legs joined by box stretchers, on fan reserve replaced, Massachusetts, ca. 1800, set of 6 (ILLUS. top next page) **4,255.00**

Federal country-style child's highchair, painted, the wide flat crestrail above three slender double-baluster-turned spindles on a lower rail flanked by the simple round stiles continuing down to form the rear legs, open rod arms on simple turned supports continuing down to the tall slightly canted front legs, a knob- and baluster-turned front leg support stretcher, plain double stretchers at the side & a single at the back, woven rush seat, old black paint w/mustard

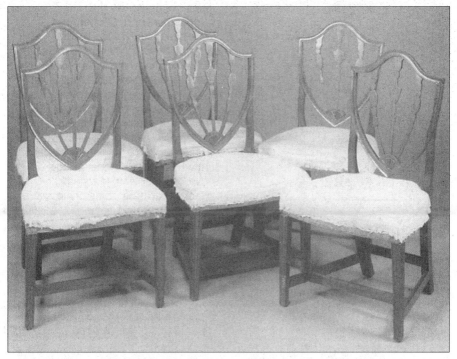

Federal Shield-back Side Chairs

yellow highlights, imperfections, New England, early 19th c., overall 35" h.............................**345.00**

Federal country-style "fancy" side chairs, painted & decorated, a flat slightly curved crestrail above pairs of slender crossed spindles above a lower rail between the tapering & backswept stiles above the

New York "Fancy" Chairs

rounded compass seat on baluster- and ring-turned legs, the original faux tiger maple ground accented w/dark painted striping & stenciled grape clusters centered on the crestrail & seatrail, the seat scored to simulate fine rush, very minor imperfections, New York City, ca. 1805-15, 33½" h., pr. (ILLUS.) **1,725.00**

Federal country-style side chairs, painted & decorated, a flat crestrail flanked by round, canted stiles flanking four arrow slats in the back, shaped seat on slightly canted, ring-turned front legs joined by a turned front stretcher, plain side & back stretchers, decorated w/original brown paint w/yellow striping & a polychrome stenciled fruit & flower design on the crestrail, Pennsylvania, first half 19th c., 33¼" h., set of 6 ....**1,485.00**

Italian Eagle Chair

Italian side chairs, carved walnut, model of a large eagle w/the upright tail feathers forming the rounded back, the round seat above the wing-carved rounded sides w/the bird's neck & turned head reaching down to the notch-carved round foot, Italy, late 19th-early 20th c., 31" h., pr. (ILLUS. of one) **2,530.00**

Mission-style (Arts & Crafts movement) armchair, oak, the tall rectangular back w/a flat slightly curved crestrail above four vertical slats between the square stiles & a lower rail above the shaped flat arms w/corbels on the arm supports continuing to form the front legs, drop-in spring seat, original finish, overcoat on a small part of one post, unmarked L. & J.G. Stickley, 44" h. **935.00**

Mission-style (Arts & Crafts movement) dining chair, oak, the square back panel & over-upholstered square seat covered in the original hard leather w/tack trim, square back stiles continuing to form back legs, square front legs joined by a single flat stretcher w/double stretchers at the sides & a single at the back, fine original black finish, red decal mark of Gustav Stickley, Model No. 1303, 36½" h. (new leather & tack to backside, some dryness & small tears to old leather).............**605.00**

Mission-style (Arts & Crafts movement) dining chairs, oak, square back w/three slats raised above a cushion seat, square legs w/box stretchers, original medium finish, branded mark & paper label of Gustav Stickley, ca. 1912, 36¼" h., set of 5........**1,725.00**

Mission Morris Armchair

Mission-style (Arts & Crafts movement) Morris armchair, oak, the adjustable slatted back w/Naugahyde-upholstered cushion flanked by high flat arms above four slats each, matching seat cushion, through-tenon construction on base rails, partial paper label of J.M. Young, Camden, New York, Model No. 180, 38" h. (ILLUS.) **3,335.00**

Mission-style (Arts & Crafts movement) Morris armchair, oak, the rectangular tall back w/five vertical slats to the floor, short corbels, flat arms over five slats each & through-tenons for the square legs & side rails w/corbels under the arms, original leather back & seat cushions on a slatted foundation, lightly cleaned original dark finish, unmarked, L & J.G. Stickley - Onondaga Shop, Model No. 798, 41" h. ..**4,675.00**

Mission-style (Arts & Crafts movement) rocker w/arms, oak, the wide flat & gently curved crestrail above five vertical slats between square stiles & a lower rail, flat open arms w/corbels above a drop-in spring seat set in a wide frame, unmarked Charles Limbert Company, 35" h. **175.00**

Mission-style (Arts & Crafts movement) rocker w/arms, oak, the wide flat & gently curved crestrail above five vertical slats between square stiles & a lower rail , flat open arms w/corbels above the drop-in spring seat set in a wide frame, unmarked Gustav Stickley, 28 x 27", 37" h. (new finish) **550.00**

Modern style dining chairs, upholstered steel, each w/a circular slate grey steel back & seat raised on four tapering steel beam legs, backs & seats upholstered in faux leopard skin fabric, second half 20th c., set of 10..................................**3,450.00**

Modern style side chair, oak & woven grass, the curving rectangular backrail on three pairs of slender dowel supports above the square seat frame braided w/a grass rope seat, on slightly swollen cylindrical legs & stretchers, designed by George Nakashima, ca. 1970 ....**747.00**

Modern style side chairs, blonde oak plywood, assembled from five separate parts, the curved back & seat joined by a wide bentwood stile, short flattened bentwood U-form legs at the rear & higher matching legs at the front, designed by Charles & Ray Eames for Evans Wood Products, w/earliest Evans logo, ca. 1947, 22 x 23", 27" h., pr....**2,530.00**

Modern style side chairs, "Eiffel Tower" style, wire & upholstery, each wire mesh back & seat supported by a wire "Eiffel Tower" base, upholstered w/black naugahyde seat covers, designed by Charles & Ray Eames, manufactured by Herman Miller Furniture Company, ca. 1952, set of 6 (minor wear & chips)..........**1,840.00**

Molesworth Club Chair

Molesworth club chairs, fir pole & Chimayo wool, a rectangular loose cushion stile back, padded arms above fir pole supports & a loose cushion seat, on pole legs, later upholstered in brass-tacked red leather & Chimayo weaving, the red ground decorated w/a geometric designs, Thomas Molesworth, ca. 1930s, pr. (ILLUS. of one) **5,980.00**

Napoleon III Armchair

Pilgrim Century "Great" Chair

Napoleon III armchairs, gilt-bronze mounted ebonized wood, an simple arched crestrail above the rectangular upholstered back within a twisted ribbon-carved frame continuing to downswept padded open arms on spiral-turned arm supports above the upholstered seat w/a curved front seatrail above fluted tapering round front legs headed by gilt-bronze leaftips, third quarter 19th c., set of four (ILLUS. of one) **5,750.00**

Pilgrim Century "Great" chair, carved oak, an arched, scroll-carved crestrail above heavy flat stiles w/scroll-carved ears above the solid paneled back carved w/an arched design w/lunettes, leaftip & columnar designs, flattened shaped open arms on columnar-turned arm supports above the wide plank seat, flat seatrail w/notch-cut bottom edges, columnar-turned front legs ending in long blocks & knob feet, heavy square back legs, legs joined by flat box

stretchers, England, 17th c., imperfections, 43¼" h. (ILLUS.) **978.00**

Pilgrim Century side chair, turned maple, a baluster-turned top crestrail above plain turned lower rails flanking three baluster- and ring-turned uprights all between simple turned stiles w/inverted acorn-turned finials, woven rush seat, simple turned legs joined by high & low simple turned rungs on front & sides & single low rung at back, old refinish, imperfections, Massachusetts, 1690-1720, 36¾" h. (ILLUS. top next page) **633.00**

Queen Anne armchair, walnut, a simple ox-yoke crestrail w/rounded corners to the tall slightly incurved stiles flanking a vase-form splat, S-scroll open arms on turned incurved arm

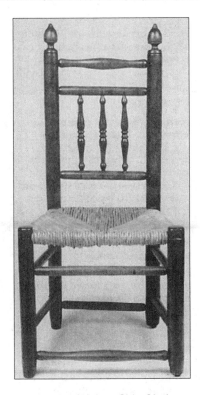

Pilgrim Century Side Chair

English Queen Anne Armchair

supports flanking the over-upholstered seat, cabriole front legs w/scroll-cut brackets ending in pad feet, minor restorations, second quarter 18th c., England, 40½" h. (ILLUS. bottom previous column)....................................**1,265.00**

Queen Anne Mahogany Side Chair

Queen Anne side chair,
mahogany, the spooned yolk crestrail w/curved corners above the flattened gently backswept stiles flanking the vasiform splat, trapezoidal slip seat on front cabriole legs ending in pad feet & w/a scalloped front seatrail, rear raked blocked turned legs joined by swelled & turned box stretchers, refinished, minor imperfections, Massachusetts, ca. 1770, 40¾" h. (ILLUS.) **3,738.00**

Queen Anne side chair, maple & tiger stripe maple, the ox-yoke crestrail w/rounded corners

Queen Anne Maple Side Chair

Queen Anne Side Chairs

continuing to form the gently curved tall stiles flanking the tall vasiform splats, trapezoidal upholstered seat above cabriole front legs ending in pad feet, square canted back legs, legs joined by baluster- and block-turned box stretchers, refinished, imperfections, New England, 18th c., 40½" h. (ILLUS.) **4,600.00**

Queen Anne side chairs, turned & carved, the tall back w/a simple ox-yoke crestrail w/rounded corners above slightly curved stiles flanked the tall vase-form solid splat raised above the woven rush seat, baluster-, block- and knob-turned front legs joined by a double-ball and ring-turned front stretcher & ending in raised pad feet, swelled stretchers at side &

back, old red stained finish, Massachusetts, late 18th c., 41" h., pr. (ILLUS.)..................**4,025.00**

Queen Anne country-style "ladder-back" side chair, an arched slightly bowed crestrail above three similarly shaped graduated slats flanked by cylindrical stiles w/turned finials over a trapezoidal rush seat, on turned legs joined by stretchers, the front stretcher w/bold ball turnings & carrot terminals, on compressed ball feet, Delaware Valley, 18th c., 42¼" h...............**483.00**

Queen Anne country-style side chair, maple, a simple ox-yoke crestrail w/rounded corners above tall flat stiles flanked the slender simple vase-form splat raised above the trapezoidal rush seat, baluster-, block- and ring-turned front legs ending in Spanish feet, a double-knob & ring-turned front high stretcher & flat side & back stretchers, old refinish, minor imperfections, Massachusetts, late 18th c., 40" h. (ILLUS. top next page)....**633.00**

Renaissance-Style armchair, carved wood, the ornate wide tapering back carved in bold

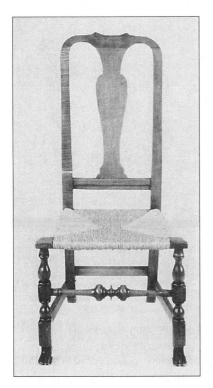

Queen Anne Country Side Chair

Italian Renaissance-Style Chair

relief w/cherubs centering a crown below a scroll- and floral-carved crestrail w/scroll- and animal-head carved sides, the center crown above an armorial crest flanked by winged chimera above a pair of confronted crouching lions at the bottom, long leaf band-carved shaped arms raised on curved animal-head supports above the replaced rectangular seat, a narrow carved seatrail over wide & deep front & back panels, the front boldly carved w/winged beasts over an armorial shield flanked by leafy scrolls above the outswept grotesque animal head feet, Italy, second half 19th c. (ILLUS. bottom previous column)..................................**1,100.00**

Italian Savanarola Chair

Savanarola armchair, walnut, curule-form w/the wide shaped back panel carved w/winged grotesque beasts flanking a roundel surrounding the carved profile bust of a hooded man, the straight squared arms w/florette carving ending in carved lions' heads above the incurved slatted sides flanking the seat above the cross-form & arched & outswept slatted legs ending in paw feet, Italy, 19th c. (ILLUS.) **715.00**

Victorian Steer Horn Chair

Renaissance Revival Armchair

Victorian armchair, longhorn steer horns, the bow-shaped joined double-horn crestrail above similarly shaped shoulders over a back support of four twisting horns flanked by similarly composed arm supports centering a D-shaped overupholstered seat on four twisting cow horn legs terminating in brass claw-and-glass ball feet, the front feet centering opposing twisting horn returns, attributed to Wenzel Friedrich, San Antonio, Texas, ca. 1889, 34" w., 35¼" h. (ILLUS.) **5,175.00**

Victorian armchair, Renaissance Revival substyle, carved & incised walnut, the arched crestrail pierce-carved & centered by an oval medallion & stylized leaf carving continuing down to knob- and scroll-carved ears above side rails flanking the upholstered back flanked by closed upholstered arms w/carved & incurved front supports continuing to the molded bowed seatrail, on ring-turned trumpet-form front legs,

outswept square back legs, on casters, ca. 1875 (ILLUS.)....................**250.00 to 350.00**

Victorian armchair, Renaissance Revival substyle, carved mahogany & walnut, the arched crestrail over a conforming frieze above a suspended padded back flanked by downswept, forward scroll-carved & capped stiles over scroll-carved arms centering a circular medallion & carved bellflower supports above a padded seat, on sabre legs w/carved bulbous feet w/casters, probably New York, ca. 1870-80, 34" h. **460.00**

Victorian armchair, Turkish Revival substyle, the rounded high stuffed & shirred crestrail above a tufted & reclining barrel back continuing to downswept stuffed & shirred arms terminating in scroll supports flanking a bell-shaped over-upholstered seat w/serpentine front rail on a conforming apron on baluster-turned front feet, the whole trimmed overall w/silk cord & at the bottom w/tasseled

Turkish Revival Armchair

fringe, on casters, American-made, third quarter 19th c., 38¼" h. (ILLUS.)....................**2,070.00**

Victorian armchairs, Rococo substyle, carved walnut, the rounded crestrail carved w/a blooming rose, flower & foliate crest above a shaped padded back w/molded surround over padded arms w/serpentine molded supports over an over-upholstered seat, on molded demi-cabriole legs w/casters, mid-19th c., 40¾" h., pr. **518.00**

Victorian side chair, Rococo substyle, carved rosewood, balloon-back style w/the tall tapering oval back frame topped by a high arched floral-carved crest, the scroll-carved stiles joined by overupholstered spring seat w/needlepoint upholstery matching that in the back panels, finger-carved serpentine seatrail continuing to demi-cabriole front legs w/cartouche-carved knees & peg feet, square canted back legs, on casters, attributed to John Henry Belter, New York, ca. 1855, restoration, 37½" h. **978.00**

Victorian side chairs, Aesthetic Movement, carved & ebonized wood, the arched & foliate-carved crestrail w/outset corners over molded stiles w/a carved molded base punctuated by carved rosettes centering a stuffed upholstered back over an upholstered seat w/reeded seatrail w/foliate-carved drop panel & brackets at the sides, on square carved tapering legs & brass feet on casters, attributed to Herter Brothers, New York, City, 1870-90, 35½" h., pr.......**3,680.00**

Victorian side chairs, bamboo-turned figured maple, each w/bamboo-turned ring-set tablet crestrail flanked by turned ball finials above a conforming bamboo-turned lattice back flanked by bamboo-turned stiles over a trapezoidal caned seat on four tapering legs joined by galleried & boxed stretchers, attributed to R. J. Horner & Company, New York City, 1870-85, 36¼" h., set of 4 ....**10,925.00**

Victorian Rosewood Side Chairs

Victorian side chairs, Rococo substyle, carved rosewood, four w/a pierce-carved scrolling crestrail above an entwined pierced scroll back above an over-upholstered balloon seat above a conforming apron

Three Ornate Wicker Chairs

continuing to cabriole front legs & canted square back legs, two matching except w/an arched upholstered crestrail on the back, attributed to John Henry Belter, New York City, ca. 1860, minor repairs & losses, set of 6 (ILLUS. of two) **4,888.00**

Victorian country-style rocking chair, grain-painted, the scrolled serpentine crestrail above a solid vasiform splat flanked by tapering stiles over a cane seat, on turned cylindrical legs joined by an H-stretcher & rockers, 19th c., 42" h. **345.00**

Victorian country-style side chairs, painted & decorated, the gently arched & stepped crestrail above slightly curved stiles joined by a lower shaped rail & centered by a vase-form splat, caned seats on flattened front sabre legs, decorated overall w/gold & brown graining simulating rosewood, old dry surface, replaced caning, minor imperfections, Portland, Maine,

Victorian Country-style Chairs

attributed to the Walter Corey Chair Factory, ca. 1850, 33½" h., set of 6 (ILLUS. of part) **920.00**

Wicker rocker with arms, the tall back w/a gently arched crestrail above a closely woven wicker & knob back panel above a loosely woven diamond lattice lower panel between stiles w/knob finials over narrow tapering side tightly woven wings above wide slightly domed woven arms on baluster-form wicker arm supports, tightly woven wicker trapezoidal seat above a curved, flaring tightly woven arched apron above a loosely woven diamond lattice band, on rockers, Framington Ratan Company, natural finish, late 19th - early 20th century, paper label w/"No. 3893," 39½" h. (ILLUS. center, top previous page) **920.00**

Wicker rocker without arms, the back w/a large oval tightly woven panel framed by a band of tight scrolls over delicate S-scrolls all between tall stiles w/twisted wicker knobs, above a padded tightly woven seats, delicate S-scrolls form the front apron, wicker twisted knobs on the front legs joined to the rockers, a cross-stretcher joining the legs, Wakefield Ratan Co., natural finish, late 19th - early 20th c., w/paper label, 35" h. (ILLUS. left, top previous page) **633.00**

Wicker side chair, the tall narrow back centered by a large tightly woven oval panels above a cluster of delicate scrolls flanked by tall slender curved tightly woven stiles w/tight out-scrolled tips, the stiles continuing down to flanked by wooden rounded seat over a deep tightly woven & rounded seatrail w/a woven diamond design above an pointed arch loosely woven diamond lattice band, on rockers, natural finish, late 19th c., 45" h. (ILLUS. right, top previous page) **403.00**

Wicker armchairs, the back w/a tall, narrow rectangular tightly-woven central panel flanked by arched twisted bands to the seat edge & short quarter-round panels composed of delicate S-scrolls, the oval seat raised on cabriole front legs composed of delicate scrolls joined by an arched apron band, cross-stretchers join the four legs, painted white, late 19th-early 20th c., 35" h., pr. **550.00**

William & Mary country-style "crooked-back" side chairs, carved & stained, the tall back w/scroll-carved ox-yoke crest w/rounded corners above molded stiles flanking a tall vase-form splat raised above the woven rush seat, on block- and baluster-turned front legs w/Spanish feet joined by a knob- and reel-turned front stretcher, flat side & back stretchers, old dark surface, old rush seats, Massachusetts, 1720-50, minor imperfections, 40½" h., pr.......**4,600.00**

William & Mary Side Chair

William & Mary side chair, beech, an arched flat-topped crestrail ending in carved scrolls above tall columnar stiles topped by double-knop turnings & flanking the tall narrow upholstered back panel, the back raised above the woven rush seat on block- and baluster-turned legs, the front legs joined by a high bold double-knob turned stretchers & a high back stretcher, a block- and baluster-turned H-stretcher joins the lower legs, imperfections, probably England, ca. 1700, 46½" h. (ILLUS.) **575.00**

Windsor "braced bow-back" side chair, the arched & molded backrail centering nine swelled spindles supported behind by a brace above a shaped saddle seat, canted knob-, baluster- and rod-turned legs joined by a swelled H-stretcher, branded "M. Bloom - New York, " Mathias Bloom, New York City, 1787-1793, 36" h. **2,760.00**

backrail w/thirteen graduated spindles over the U-form central rail continuing to form flattened, shaped arms, heavier spindles below central rail & canted baluster- and ring-turned arm supports, deeply shaped oblong saddle seat raised on canted baluster- and ring-turned legs joined by a baluster- and ring-turned H-stretcher, old refinish, Hudson River Valley or southern Connecticut, ca. 1780-1800, 46½" h. (ILLUS.).....................**2,990.00**

Windsor "comb-back" armchair, turned & painted, the shaped crestrail w/volute-carved terminals above seven tapered spindles, the U-shaped backrail forming shaped hand holds on incurved arm supports, the peaked plank seat raised on baluster-turned splayed legs joined by swelled H-stretchers, on blunt knob feet, painted black, ca. 1790 ....**4,830.00**

Windsor "Comb-back" Armchair

Windsor "comb-back" armchair, turned wood, a wide narrow serpentine crestrail above six slender spindles continuing down to the arched

"Continuous Arm" Windsor

Windsor "continuous arm" armchair, ash, pine & maple, the high arched crestrail continuing down to form short shaped arms, ten slender swelled & turned back & arm spindles & canted baluster-turned arm supports above the thick shaped saddle seat above four canted baluster- and ring-turned legs joined by a swelled H-stretcher, old refinish, minor imperfections, New England, ca. 1780, 38¼" h. (ILLUS.) **978.00**

Windsor "Fan-back" Side Chair

Windsor "fan-back" side chair, a slender serpentine crestrail w/upturned ears raised on canted bamboo-turned stiles flanking seven bamboo-turned spindles, shaped saddle seat, canted bamboo-turned legs joined by a swelled & bamboo-turned H-stretcher, Connecticut, early 19th c., old black paint, minor imperfections, 34" h. (ILLUS.) **518.00**

Windsor "sack-back" armchair, the arched crestrail above seven slender spindles over a continuous armrail w/scrolled knuckle hand grips above canted ring- and baluster-turned

arm supports over a shaped saddle seat, on canted ring- and baluster-turned legs joined by a swelled H-stretcher, Rhode Island, 1780-1800, 37¾" h.......**5,520.00**

Windsor "sack-back" armchair, an arched crestrail above seven slender spindles continuing through the medial rail that continues to form the arms w/scrolled handgrips, the arms on two short spindles & baluster-turned, canted arm supports, oblong shaped seat raised on canted baluster- and rod-turned legs joined by a swelled H-stretcher, old black paint, Massachusetts, 1760-80, 38½" h. (minor imperfections) **1,265.00**

Windsor "stepped-back" side chairs, painted & decorated, the stepped & scroll-cut narrow crestrail above five slender bamboo-turned spindles & slightly canted bamboo-turned stiles above the shaped saddle seat, raised on slightly canted bamboo-turned legs joined by box stretchers, original simulated rosewood graining decorated on the crest w/a gold-stenciled eagle & further gold striping, northern New England, ca. 1820, minor paint loss, 35½" h., set of 3......**2,530.00**

CHESTS & CHESTS OF DRAWERS

Apothecary chest, Chippendale country-style, cherry, rectangular top above a dovetailed case w/a pair of long drawers w/small turned wood knobs above stacks of 25 small square drawers each w/a wood knob, molded base on scroll-cut bracket feet, originally base of a two-part cupboard, found in Pittsburgh, Pennsylvania area, 17½ x 42½", 47" h. (edge damage, foot repairs & back feet replaced) **3,300.00**

Blanket chest, country-style, painted pine, the rectangular lid w/molded edge opening to a well w/till, dovetailed case w/a molded base on simple bracket feet, old brownish red paint over earlier red, lock w/key, found in Perry County, Pennsylvania, 19th c., 19¾ x 44", 23¾" h. (old repair at one hinge, corner of till lid damaged)...........................**385.00**

Blanket chest, country-style, painted pine, six-board construction, the rectangular top w/molded edges opening to a well w/a missing till, the one-board ends w/arched cut-out feet, original staple hinges & iron lock, old red finish, 18½ x 47½", 24¼" h. **358.00**

Early Blanket Chest

Blanket chest, country-style, painted pine, a rectangular hinged top w/breadboard ends above a case edged in half-round molding & opening to a case w/a deep well w/two small false drawers at the front above a pair of working drawers over a single long drawer at the bottom, each drawer w/pairs of turned wooden knobs, one-board ends w/bootjack feet, old red paint replaced pulls, minor imperfections, New England, early 18th c., 18 x 43", 37¾" h. (ILLUS.) **1,092.00**

Blanket chest, country-style, painted & decorated, six-board construction, the rectangular top w/a molded edge lifting above a well w/a lidded till, on a molded base w/simple bracket feet & a central half-round drop, ornately decorated overall w/swirled graining in gold & burnt sienna on the original painted putty surface, imperfections, New England, early 19th c., 15 x 36¼", 18" h. **2,990.00**

Blanket chest, country-style, painted & decorated, six-board construction, the rectangular top w/molded edges opening to a well w/a lidded till, overall exterior decorated in burnt sienna & gold putty & vinegar painting in a swirled & fanned design, original surface, New England, early 19th c., very minor imperfections, 17 x 40½", 22" h. **2,875.00**

Blanket chest, country-style, painted & decorated, rectangular hinged top opening to a well above a conforming case fitted w/two thumb-molded bottom drawers, the entire surface w/brown & black grain painting, 17 x 40", 36¼" h. **863.00**

Early Painted Blanket Chest

Blanket chest, country-style, six-board construction, painted wood, the rectangular top w/a molded edge lifting above wide plain sides w/pointed bootjack legs, old light blue paint, New England, ca. 1790, 20 x 38½", 26" h. (ILLUS.)......................**2,300.00**

Blanket chest, country-style, decorated cherry & poplar, rectangular hinged lid w/molded edges opening to a till w/two drawers w/spring latches above the dovetailed case decorated w/original green paint w/stenciled band of small stars across the top front above a circle of stars around a sunburst over the date "1859" in white, yellow & red, molded base raised on blocks & double-knob turned removable feet, 20 x 48¼", 26½" h. (minor wear, slight edge damage) **1,650.00**

Blanket chest, country-style, pine, rectangular hinged lid w/a molded edge opening to a well, a conforming case w/the side continuing to shaped bracket feet, 19th c., 15¾ x 43¼", 21¼" h........**184.00**

Gothic-Style Blanket Chest

Blanket chest, Gothic-Style, carved walnut, the heavy rectangular hinged top w/a carved Gothic design border band overhangs the deep case w/two ornately carved panels of Gothic arches & other Gothic designs centering a large iron lock plate above a carved armorial cartouche, flaring molded ball-trimmed base raised on heavy shaped shoe feet, Spain, late 19th c., 21½ x 44¾", 24" h. (ILLUS.)......................**1,725.00**

Cedar chest, matched hardwood patterned veneers, rectangular w/a lift-top above a deep well, carved decoration, made by Roos, ca. 1930-50, 21 x 47", 19" h. **440.00**

Chippendale chest of drawers, carved & figured mahogany, the rectangular top w/a molded edge overhangs a conforming case w/four long graduated thumb-molded drawers, molded base on short angular cabriole legs w/blocky ball-and-claw feet, appears to retain an original, untouched surfaced w/all the cast-brass butterfly pulls & keyhole escutcheons, lacking three & one-half knee returns, distressed drawer lips, repair to left side of case, New England or New York, ca. 1770, 10 x 35", 32" h. **9,775.00**

Chippendale Chest of Drawers

Chippendale chest of drawers, tiger stripe maple, a rectangular top w/molded edges slightly overhanging the case w/four long graduated beaded drawers w/butterfly pulls & keyhole escutcheons, molded base on tall ogee bracket feet, replaced brasses, refinished, imperfections, 19 x 38½", 36½" h. (ILLUS.) **8,625.00**

Chippendale country-style chest of drawers, cherry, rectangular top above a conforming case fitted w/four graduated long drawers, each w/a thumb-molded edge, on a molded base w/bracket feet, 18th c., 19½ x 36½", 35¾" h. (feet later) **1,840.00**

Painted Chippendale Chest

Chippendale country-style chest of drawers, painted maple, a rectangular top w/a molded edge overhanging a case w/four long graduated drawers w/large replaced turned wood pulls, molded base on tall scroll-carved bracket feet, original red wash, imperfections, Newburyport, Massachusetts, 18th c., 18 x 37⅝", 32¾" h. (ILLUS.) **3,335.00**

Chippendale Tall Chest

Chippendale tall chest of drawers, carved maple, a rectangular top w/a wide & deep flaring cornice above a tall case w/three small drawers, the center one fan-carved, above a stack of five long graduated drawers all w/butterfly pulls & keyhole escutcheons, molded base on tall scroll-cut bracket feet, old brasses, some original, refinished, minor imperfections, Sudbury-Concord, Massachusetts area, 18th c., 18½ x 36", 4' 9" h. (ILLUS.) **4,485.00**

Chippendale country-style tall chest of drawers, cherry, a rectangular top above a narrow cove-molded cornice over a pair of small drawers above five long graduated drawers all w/butterfly brasses, molded base on scroll-cut bracket feet, New England, old refinish, 18th c., 19 x 39¾", 4' 2" h. (brasses replaced, restored) **1,380.00**

Country Chippendale Tall Chest

Chippendale country-style tall chest of drawers, painted wood, a rectangular top w/a reeded coved cornice above a pair of drawers above four long graduated drawers, molded base on simple scroll-cut bracket feet, dark brown varnish stain, pulls missing, imperfections, Massachusetts, late 18th c., 17½ x 36", 47¼" h. (ILLUS.) **3,450.00**

Chippendale country-style tall chest of drawers, tiger stripe maple, a rectangular top w/a flaring stepped cornice above a tall dovetailed case w/six long graduated cockbeaded drawers w/butterfly brasses & keyhole escutcheons, molded base on scroll-cut bracket feet, late 18th c., New England, 18¼ x 35¾", 46¼" h. (replaced brasses, restoration) **2,530.00**

Chippendale country-style tall chest of drawers, tiger stripe maple, the rectangular top w/a flaring stepped cornice above a case of six long graduated drawers w/butterfly pulls & keyhole escutcheons, on a molded base raised on tall shaped bracket feet, old finish, replaced brasses, minor imperfections, probably central Massachusetts, late 18th c., 19 x 36", 4' 10" h. **9,200.00**

Classical "Bow-front" Chest of Drawers

Classical (American Empire) "bow-front" chest of drawers, mahogany veneer, a rectangular stepped back compartment w/ovolu reeded corner posts flanking small handkerchief drawers on the rectangular top w/matching ovolu corners above spiral-turned side posts flanking the case of four long bowed drawers all w/turned wood knobs, scalloped apron, baluster- and ring-turned legs w/peg feet, old varnished surface, original pulls, minor imperfections, North Shore, Massachusetts, ca. 1820, 18 x 38", 43½" h. (ILLUS.).........**863.00**

Fine Classical Chest of Drawers

Classical chest of drawers, carved mahogany & figured mahogany veneer, the rectangular to above a slightly outset section w/a pair of drawers each w/two small round brass knobs overhanging the lower case w/three long reverse-graduated drawers w/brass knobs flanked by free-standing spiral-turned columns w/acanthus leaf carving at the top & ring turning at the base, plinth base raised on ring- and baluster-turned short legs ending in peg feet, old refinish, replaced brasses, imperfections, probably Massachusetts, ca. 1825, 21 x 44½", 42¼" h. (ILLUS.)............**1,380.00**

Classical chest of drawers,

grained hardwood, a rectangular top w/ropetwist-carved edge banding above a pair of small, narrow drawers w/small brass ring handles & brass keyhole escutcheons flanked by further ropetwist turnings & set back atop the rectangular top of the case w/ropetwist edge banding above a case of three long, deep graduated drawers flanked by further ropetwist turnings down the front sides, bracket feet, original graining in imitation of rosewood, paneled ends, ca. 1830-50, 17 x 38", 40" h. (replaced oval eagle brasses) ...**660.00**

Signed Classical Chest of Drawers

Classical chest of drawers,

mahogany, the rectangular top surmounted by a paneled backsplash flanked by turned columnar columns w/large double-knob turned finials, the case w/a narrow top frieze band above a pair of long bolection-molded blind drawers outset & supported on free-standing columns flanking inset flat drawers w/a long deep drawer over three long graduated drawers, reverse-breakfront

plinth raised on leaf-carved animal paw front feet & tapering block rear feet on casters, simple turned drawer pulls, appears to retain old & possibly original finish, signed by Sam Skelye, Lansingburgh, New York, ca. 1835, shrinkage cracks in the top, minor veneer losses, chip to foot of one column, 25 x 49", 5' 10" h. (ILLUS.) **920.00**

Classical chest of drawers w/mirror,

carved mahogany, the rectangular beveled mirror w/a veneered frame tilting between acanthus-carved scrolling supports above a frieze of three small drawers over a rectangular case fitted w/a bolection-molded top drawer above two long drawers w/pressed glass pulls flanked by acanthus-carved columns, on acanthus- & acorn-carved feet, New York, ca. 1830, 20¾ x 37", 5' 5" h. **2,185.00**

Classical Chest with Mirror

Classical chest of drawers w/mirror, mahogany veneer, a rectangular mirror within an ogee veneer frame swiveling between scroll-carved slender S-scroll uprights on narrow rectangular stepped-back compartment w/a row of three small drawers w/small glass knobs above a rectangular black marble top above a case of four long drawers w/two original glass pulls each, molded base on bulbous baluster-turned legs, imperfections, New England or New York, ca. 1840, 21 x 39", overall 6' 4½" h. (ILLUS. bottom previous page).......................**2,185.00**

Classical country-style chest of drawers, curly maple, the rectangular top above a row of three small drawers over a single long, deep drawer all overhanging the lower case w/three long, graduated drawers flanked by heavy ogee pilasters, flat apron, on tapering bobbin-turned front feet, paneled ends, simple turned wood knobs, ca. 1840-50, 22¾ x 43", 47¾" h. (refinished, back feet replaced) **880.00**

Decorated Chest-over-Drawers

Country-style chest-over-drawers, painted & decorated pine, the tall case w/a rectangular hinged top w/a molded edge opening above a deep well above a stack of three long graduated drawers, one-board ends w/arched bootjack legs, original black clustered crescent designs on a red ground, minor imperfections, northern New England, late 18th c., 17¾ x 36⅝", 48" h. (ILLUS.) **4,140.00**

Dower chest, painted pine, a rectangular top w/a molded edge opening to a deep well & w/a front butterfly brass keyhole escutcheon, a mid-molding above a row of three small drawers across the bottom above the molded base raised on scroll-cut bracket feet, each drawer w/old butterfly brass, traces of original green paint, old refinish, imperfections, Pennsylvania, late 18th c., 22⅜ x 48⅝", 27¼" h....**1,725.00**

Federal "bow-front" chest of drawers, birch, the rectangular top w/molded edges & bowed front above a conforming case w/four long graduated drawers w/oval brasses & oval brass keyhole escutcheons, molded base raised on tall scroll-cut French feet, original brasses, late 18th - early 19th c., 21¾ x 40½", 36" h. (refinished, stains in top, crack in left front foot) **4,070.00**

Federal "bow-front" chest of drawers, tiger stripe maple, the rectangular top w/a bowed front above a case of four long, graduated cockbeaded drawers w/brass oval keyhole escutcheons & oval brasses, reeded base rail above the scalloped apron continuing to tall French feet, New England, ca. 1800, refinished, original brasses, 16 x 39", 38" h. (imperfections) **4,255.00**

Federal Inlaid Chest of Drawers

Federal chest of drawers, inlaid cherry & mahogany, a rectangular top w/band-inlaid edges above a case of four long graduated drawers each w/a rectangular inlaid panel w/notched corners & diamond-shaped ivory-inlaid keyhole escutcheons & butterfly brasses, raised on tall bracket feet, old refinish, replaced brasses, Concord, New Hampshire, ca. 1795, 18⅝ x 38½", 34½" h. (ILLUS.) **2,185.00**

Federal "serpentine-front" chest of drawers, cherry & inlaid cherry, the rectangular top w/a serpentine front w/a diamond inlaid front edge above a conforming case with four long graduated drawers each w/zipper band edge inlay & leaf & scroll central inlaid designs framing the inset brass keyhole escutcheons, simple bail pulls, the drawers flanked by coved corner bands inlaid w/bands of bellflower & other designs above the molded base raised on a slender curved bracket feet, replaced brasses, refinished, feet replaced, other minor imperfections, Rhode Island, ca. 1810, 22½ x 44⅞", 37" h. **9,775.00**

Federal country-style chest of drawers, walnut, rectangular top above a case of four long graduated drawers w/original oval brasses & inlaid diamond keyhole escutcheons, narrow scalloped apron & French feet, one-board ends, early 19th c., 20½ x 40½", 37¾" h. (feet & apron restoration) **770.00**

Federal country-style chest of drawers, painted pine & poplar, the rectangular top above a case of four long drawers w/small turned pulls, flanked by square corner stiles continuing to short straight legs, old red-painted top, drawer facings & case ends w/black-painted contrasting stiles & drawer separations, minor imperfections, possibly New York, ca. 1800, 19 x 37¾", 43" h. **1,610.00**

Molesworth-decorated Chest

Molesworth chest of drawers, decorated oak, "Cowboy and Friend" design, a rectangular top

Pilgrim Century Chest over Drawers

w/rounded corners above a tall case w/five long graduated drawers w/simple turned knobs, carved & applied down the center in light relief w/a black silhouetted scene of a cowboy standing beside his horse, on shaped bracket feet, decorated by Thomas Molesworth for the "Old Lodge" for George Sumers, ca. 1935-37, 18 x 33¾", 4'¼" h. (ILLUS.) **8,050.00**

Mule chest (box chest w/one or more drawers below a storage compartment), Federal country-style, pine, a rectangular top w/molded edges opening to a deep well fronted by two false long drawers above two long true drawers below, all w/oval brasses, base molding over a deeply scalloped front apron, bootjack end legs, old mellow refinishing, 19th c., 18¼ x 36½", 46¾" h. (pieced repairs, lid & brasses replaced) **968.00**

Pilgrim Century six-board chest over drawers, oak & pine, rectangular top slightly overhanging case w/a deep well w/four-panel front above a medial band over two narrow bottom drawers w/small wooden knobs, molded base, square stile feet, pine top, old refinish, imperfections, Massachusetts, 1690-1720, 18 x 48½", 28½" h. (ILLUS.) **8,050.00**

Queen Anne Tall Chest

Queen Anne tall chest of drawers, pine, a rectangular top w/a molded cornice above a case w/a pair of drawers over four long graduated drawers all w/small butterfly brasses & keyhole escutcheons, stepped molded base raised on high scroll-cut bracket feet, old replaced brasses, refinished, imperfections, 18th c., 17¼ x 35¼", 44" h. (ILLUS. bottom, previous page)......................**1,610.00**

Rustic-style Chest of Drawers

Rustic-style chest of drawers, burled pine, the upright rectangular case fitted w/five long flat drawers each w/two gnarled wood pulls, the edges, top & base of the case w/split burl posts, on casters, designed by Jack Kranenberg, made by Kranenberg & Aiman, ca. 1943, 24 x 46½", 4' 11" h. (ILLUS.) **4,025.00**

Victorian chest of drawers, Renaissance Revival substyle, walnut, the small case w/a high arched & shaped backsplash above the rectangular top w/molded edges above a case

of three long drawers each w/a raised narrow rectangular panel w/notched corners & mounted w/two molded composition fruit pulls, gently scalloped apron & bracket feet, ca. 1870 ....**303.00**

Victorian Chest of Drawers

Victorian chest of drawers, Renaissance Revival substyle, walnut, the rectangular top w/a pair of small hanky drawers centered by a pierce-carved wishbone bracket supporting a swiveling oval mirror within a molded frame, the rectangular top w/molded edge above a case w/a deep long top drawer above three graduated long drawers flanked by top & bottom half-round spindled brackets, each drawer w/a keyhole escutcheon above a raised oval molding band enclosing pairs of molded composition fruit pulls, slightly scalloped apron & simple bracket feet, crest on mirror frame damaged, ca. 1870 (ILLUS.) **495.00**

Ornate Belter Chest of Drawers

Victorian chest of drawers,

Rococo substyle, carved & laminated rosewood, three-part construction: the upper section w/an arched floral- and scroll-carved pediment above a molded arched frame centering a large mirror flanked by two tiered serpentine-shaped small open shelves on C-scroll supports & fronting narrow rectangular mirrors; the lower section w/a serpentine-shaped molded-edge white marble top w/an incurved front above a conforming case w/four long graduated drawers each centered by graduated scroll-carved clusters & foliate-carved pulls, the front corners w/intertwined scroll-carved pilasters above the molded base, on casters, John Henry Belter, New York City, ca. 1855, 23½ x 48", 6' 8" h. (ILLUS.)...**23,000.00**

William & Mary chest of

drawers, hardwood, rectangular top w/a thin cove-molded edge above the case of four long, graduated drawers w/replaced teardrop brasses & oval keyhole escutcheons, raised on bun feet, refinished, New England, early 18th c., 19½ x 36¼", 36½" h. (restored) **1,955.00**

William & Mary Chest of Drawers

William & Mary chest of

drawers, pine, a rectangular top w/molded cornice above a cast w/four long graduated drawers w/small butterfly brasses & keyhole escutcheons, stepped molded base raised on ball feet, original brasses, old refinish, feet old replacements, Massachusetts, ca. 1710-20, 18 x 35½", 36" h. (ILLUS.)......**1,150.00**

William & Mary chest-over-

drawers, painted pine, a rectangular hinged top w/molded edges opening to a deep well fronted by two false drawers w/butterfly brasses & keyhole escutcheons above two long working drawers below w/matching brasses, molded base w/large squatty ball- and peg-turned front feet & flat rear feet, original feet & cleats, early

William & Mary Chest-over-Drawers

black paint over red ground, replaced brasses, old surface, probably western Massachusetts, 1730-50, 17¼ x 36", 41¼" h. (ILLUS.)...**4,025.00**

CRADLES

Early Swinging Cradle

Country-style swinging cradle, a trestle-based frame w/shaped shoe feet supports simple turned uprights w/ball finials joined by an upper rail w/spiral-turned center section, the uprights suspending a narrow

rectangular deep-sided swinging cradle w/tall tapering & round ends w/small holes for the peg supports, original worn red paint, New England, 18th c., 37½" l., 37½" h. (ILLUS.)......................**518.00**

Windsor cradle on rockers, a rectangular flat crestrail above numerous slender knob-turned spindles forming the sides above the plank bottom, raised on simple round canted legs joined by flat side stretchers & swelled end stretchers above the inset wide rockers, early 19th c.....................................**1,725.00**

CUPBOARDS

Classical Clothes Press

Clothes press, Classical, carved & figured mahogany, three-part construction: the removable pitched cornice w/triangular corner brackets above a pair of tall double-paneled hinged doors flanked by reeded side pilasters topped by carved acanthus leaves & opening to an interior w/removable open drawers & three small enclosed drawers below on one side, the right side open & fitted for hanging clothes; the lower section comprising a figured frieze band on ball feet, probably Baltimore or Philadelphia, ca. 1835, 20¼ x 54½", 6' 9" h. (ILLUS.)............**7,475.00**

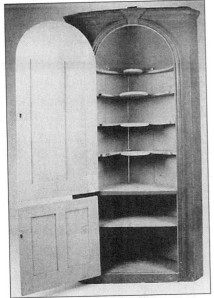

Chippendale Painted Corner Cupboard

Corner cupboard, Chippendale, painted, one-piece construction, the flat top w/a deep molded cornice centered at the front w/a keystone intersecting a raised arched molding flanking to tall round-topped double-paneled door opening to shaped & graduated shelves above a lower short double-paneled door opening to a single shelf, flat base, the top interior w/four green-painted shelves below a red-painted dome, the exterior green paint, original pulls & hardware, imperfections, New England, 18th c., 21½ x 49½", 8' h. (ILLUS.) **2,530.00**

Chippendale Pine Corner Cupboard

Corner cupboard, Chippendale, pine, one-piece construction, the flat top above a deep stepped cornice above an arched hutch opening w/two serpentine-front shelves above a mid-molding above a single raised double-panel cupboard doors on H-hinges & w/a wooden thumblatch, flat base, old refinish, minor imperfections, New England, 18th c., 20 x 45", 7' 4" h. (ILLUS.) **4,600.00**

Corner cupboard, Chippendale, walnut, one-piece construction, the flat top w/a deep molded cornice w/a narrow dentil band above a pair of tall arch-paneled cupboard doors w/exterior-mounted hinges above a mid-molding above a pair of shorter paneled doors, scrolled bracket feet, old worn finish, imperfections, North Carolina, late 18th c., 20 x 41", 7' h. **4,888.00**

Chippendale Walnut Corner Cupboard

Corner cupboard, Chippendale, walnut, one-piece construction, the flat top w/a deep coved cornice above a single 12-pane glaze cupboard door opening to three shelves above double medial bands flanking to small square drawers w/oval pulls above a pair of small paneled doors, a serpentine front apron & simple bracket feet, Mid-Atlantic States, possibly Southern, ca. 1800, 40" w., 7' 3" h. (ILLUS.) **7,475.00**

Corner cupboard, country-style, cherry, one-piece construction, the flat top w/a widely flaring coved & stepped cornice above a pair of tall double-raised-panel doors w/a small square top panel over a long rectangular lower panel, the lower case w/a pair of smaller rectangular raised panel cupboard doors,

gently scalloped apron, early 19th c., cornice 41" w., 5' 10" h. (reconstructed w/repairs to cornice & pierced door repairs, refinished) **1,733.00**

Corner cupboard, country-style, refinished poplar, one-piece construction, the flat top w/a wide flat angled cornice above a pair of tall narrow cupboard doors each w/two long rectangular panes of glass opening to three shelves above a pair of paneled cupboard doors, one w/a wooden knob, deeply scalloped apron & plain bracket feet, 19th c., cornice 49" w., 6' 11½" h. (repaired break at one hinge) **1,870.00**

Federal Cherry Corner Cupboard

Corner cupboard, Federal country-style, cherry, two-part construction: the tall upper section w/a flat top over a deep flaring cornice over the tall 12-

pane glazed cupboard door w/brass thumb latch opening to a three-shelved white interior, the shorter lower section w/a mid-molding over a pair of paneled cupboard doors opening to a two-shelved interior, original red wash on the exterior, minor imperfections, New England or New York state, early 19th c., 20 x 43¼", 7' 6" h. (ILLUS.) **7,475.00**

Victorian Corner Cupboard

Federal Country-style Corner Cupboard

Corner cupboard, Federal country-style, painted, a flat top w/a pointed drop-carved wide cornice & matching notch-carving down the wide side panels, the upper case w/a pair of tall 8-pane glaze cupboard doors opening to three shaped shelves above a pair of raised panel small cupboard doors below, flat base, old paint in poor condition, imperfections, Schoharie County, New York, ca. 1810, 32 x 61", 7' 2½" h. (ILLUS.) **5,462.00**

Corner cupboard, Victorian Aesthetic Movement substyle, two-part construction: the upper section w/a Gothic arch-style cornice enclosing a recessed shelf housing a beveled mirror flanked by side shelves above a pair of side shelves over a pair of glazed door & two side doors; the lower section w/a pair of central multi-paneled decorated cupboard doors flanked by arched recesses housing beveled mirrors & two open shelves, raised on short ring-turned feet, fitted overall w/carved stylized rosettes, third quarter 19th c., 48" w., 7' 6" h. (ILLUS.) **4,600.00**

Corner cupboards, George III-Style, parcel-gilt pine, the sharply curved broken scroll pediment centered by a small platform over a pierced lattice panel over a narrow carved frieze band above the tall single geometrically-glazed cabinet door opening to two shelves

George III-Style Corner Cupboards

over a band of three small drawers, the center one longer, above a geometrically-carved frieze base band continuing down the square front legs ending in block feet, scroll-carved corner brackets at the corners of the legs, very minor losses, England, 19th c., 16 x 28¼", 6' 5½" h., pr. (ILLUS.)...**6,038.00**

Jacobean-Style Court Cupboard

Court cupboard, Jacobean-Style, carved oak, two-part construction: the upper section w/a rectangular top w/a narrow cornice above a carved band of interlocking arches & darts ending in corner blocks w/large knob-turned drops, the top projecting above a recessed back w/a pair of ornately carved rectangular doors center by a diamond device & w/a small wooden knob flanking a smaller rectangular panel also w/a central diamond device, the projecting base cabinet w/a arch-carved frieze band above a pair of tall three-panel cupboard doors w/a horizontal rectangular arch-carved top panel above a pair of narrow upright rectangular panels carved w/looping S-scroll designs, the doors w/exterior-mounted plain winged hinges, flat apron & stile legs, England, 19th w/earlier segments, 23 x 56½", 5' 9¼" h. (ILLUS. bottom, previous column) **1,725.00**

Hanging wall cupboard, cherry, a rectangular top w/a deep flaring stepped cornice above a single 4-pane glazed door w/porcelain knob & small thumb latch above a dovetailed drawer w/two locks, flat base, old worn finish, 19th c., cornice 14¼ x 29", 36½" h. **605.00**

Hanging wall cupboard, painted pine, a rectangular top w/a molded cornice above a tall, narrow raised panel door w/small thumb latch, old dark green repaint, 19th c., cornice 9¾ x 26½", 4' 3" h. (some wear & edge damage) **523.00**

Hutch cupboard, country-style, pine, the rectangular top w/a narrow flaring cornice above a large open compartment w/two serpentine-fronted shelves above a tall cupboard w/two raised panels & H-hinges & a

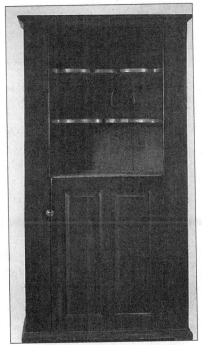

Early Pine Hutch Cupboard

brass thumb latch, old refinish, minor imperfections, New England, last quarter 18th c., 17 x 38", 6' 1¼" h. (ILLUS.) **2,645.00**

Rustic Hutch Cupboard

Hutch cupboard, rustic-style, burled pine, the tall super-structure w/two open shelves framed & trimmed w/burled edging above the stepped-out lower case w/a rectangular top above a case w/a pair of tall narrow side doors flanking a stack of three deep center drawers all above a single long drawer across the bottom, case framed by burled edging, designed by Jack Kranenberg, made by Kranenberg & Aiman, ca. 1943, 23½ x 48", 6' 1" h. (ILLUS. bottom, previous column)..................................**5,520.00**

Hutch cupboard, country step-back style, stained pine, one-piece construction, the rectangular top above canted sides w/molded borders around the three long open shelves over the stepped-out lower case w/a pair of tall paneled doors w/wooden thumb latches & tiny knobs, three lower interior shelves, old red stain, restored, New England, ca. 1830, 17 x 55⅞", 6' 7½" h. **1,610.00**

Jelly cupboard, painted & decorated pine, a rectangular top above a pair of drawers w/simple wood knobs over a pair of tall paneled doors, simple cut-out feet, old worn yellow grained repaint, 19th c., 20¼ x 48¾", 42¼" h. (edge wear, some damage & age cracks) **660.00**

Jelly cupboard, painted & decorated pine, rectangular top w/narrow molded cornice above a long double-paneled door w/thumb latch & beaded frame, on low cut-out feet, original flame graining aged to a dark brown color, 19th c., cornice 20 x 37½", 4' 7" h. **825.00**

Kitchen cupboard, Hoosier-type, maple, the tall superstructure w/a serpentine crestrail above a cupboard section w/a pair of tall

Maple Kitchen Cupboard

w/three long molded graduated drawers, the gadrooned base below on scrolled bracket feet, New Jersey, ca. 1795, 19½ x 49", 6' 5" h. **5,750.00**

Chippendale Gumwood Linen Press

single-pane glazed doors flanked a small paneled door above two small drawers, the lower one w/a deep curved bottom, all above curved side brackets flanking the wide, stepped-out rectangular work surface overhanging the lower cabinet w/a pair of long drawers over a pair of small center drawers flanked by deep curve-bottomed side drawers, raised on slender baluster- and ring-turned legs w/knob feet, ca. 1900-10, 24 x 46", 6' 7" h. (ILLUS.) **770.00**

Linen press, Chippendale, gumwood, two-part construction: the upper section w/a deep flaring molded cornice & reeded tympanum above a pair of tall hinged paneled doors w/Gothic arch-topped panels opening to shelves flanked by fluted pilasters; the lower section

Linen press, Chippendale, gumwood, two-part construction: the upper section w/a rectangular top & molded flaring cornice above a pair of hinged doors each w/scalloped arch raised panels opening to shelves & flanked by fluted pilasters; the lower section w/a pair of short drawers over two long drawers, molded base raised on shaped bracket feet, New Jersey, ca. 1785, 20⅝ x 51", 7' 4½" h. (ILLUS.)...........**6,325.00**

Linen press, Federal, mahogany, two-part construction: the upper section w/a rectangular top & narrow molded cornice above a plain frieze band over a pair of tall paneled doors opening to pull-out shelves above a medial molding; the lower section w/four long graduated beaded drawers w/hexagonal brasses, serpentine apron ending in slender French feet, New York, early 19th c., 22½ x 49", 7' 5" h. (ILLUS. right) **6,325.00**

Linen press, Federal, inlaid mahogany, two-part construction: the upper section w/a molded cornice over a pair of tall paneled doors opening to a shelved interior; the lower stepped-out section w/a long, deep beaded-edge drawer w/astragal line inlay opening to a compartmentalized interior w/six short drawers over eight divided pigeonholes centering an astragal line-inlaid prospect door opening to two divided pigeonholes over one short drawer, the lower section w/a pair of square paneled cupboard doors opening to one long drawer over two pull-out sliding shelves, flat apron on flaring

Federal Linen Press

Early Painted Pewter Cupboard

French feet, Baltimore, 1790-1800, 23 x 43", 7' 7" h. (one bottom cupboard door restored, minor foot repairs) **2,875.00**

Pewter cupboard, painted pine & poplar, the superstructure w/a narrow rectangular top above two long open shelves over a small central open compartment w/incurved sides, the side stiles w/scalloped cutting, the stepped-out lower cupboard w/a pair of raised panel cupboard doors w/L-hinges flanked by fixed rectangular end panels & centered by a narrow fixed double-panel, raised on wide scallop-cut end bracket feet & a narrow tapering center foot, old green paint, height loss to top, surface imperfections, northern New England or Canada, 18th c., 16 x 71½", 5' 10½" h. (ILLUS. bottom, previous page)............**5,463.00**

w/a flat top w/a narrow molded cornice over a pair of narrow raised-panel cupboard doors flanked by wide side boards; the stepped-out lower section w/another pair of shorter raised panel cupboard doors flanked by wide side boards, flat base, three shelves in top section & two in lower section, worn paint & other imperfections, hardware changed, New England, early 19th c., 18½ x 53¾", 5' 3" h. (ILLUS.) **1,150.00**

Painted Walnut Cupboard

Painted Step-back Cupboard

Step-back wall cupboard, country-style, painted, two-part construction: the upper section

Step-back wall cupboard, country-style, painted walnut, two-part construction: the upper section w/a rectangular top over a coved corner above a pair of tall paneled doors opening to three shelves above an open pie shelf; the stepped-out lower section w/a pair of narrow drawers w/wooden knobs above a pair of paneled cupboard doors w/a single wooden knob, flat apron & angled bracket feet, original red paint, some replaced pulls, damage to back & other minor imperfections, Pennsylvania, early 19th c., 19¼ x 44⅛", 7'½" h. (ILLUS.) **1,495.00**

Step-back wall cupboard,
country-style, walnut & poplar, two-part construction: the upper section w/a rectangular top w/a widely flaring stepped cornice over a pair of tall single-pane glazed doors w/beveled framing & cast brass latch w/white porcelain knob, opening to two shelves over an low, arched pie shelf; the lower stepped-out section w/a pair of raised panel drawers w/white porcelain knobs above a pair of raised panel cupboard doors w/beveled framing & a cast brass latch w/white porcelain knob, scalloped apron & short bracket feet, old dark finish, late 19th c., cornice 14½ x 47¾", 7'¾" h. (some edge damage on one drawer, back foot ended out).....**825.00**

Step-back wall cupboard,
Federal country-style, cherry, two-part construction: the upper section w/a rectangular top w/a flat, flaring cornice above a pair of tall double-panel doors above a mid-moldings; the stepped-out lower section w/a long drawer w/two wooden knobs above a pair of paneled doors, one w/a wooden knob, on slender turned & tapering legs, cornice 15¼ x 41", overall 7' 5¼" h. (refinished) **3,300.00**

Step-back wall cupboard,
Federal country-style, painted poplar, two-part construction: the upper section w/a flaring stepped cornice above a pair of 6-pane glazed cupboard doors

opening to two shelves above an arched open pie shelf; the lower stepped-out section w/a rectangular top w/molded edges above a pair of drawers w/simple wooden knobs above a pair of paneled cupboard doors, base molding & ogee bracket feet, dovetailed cases & beading around door & drawer frames, old red repaint, found in Bucks County, Pennsylvania, early 19th c., cornice 13 x 58", 7' 1½" h. (base molding & fee replaced, one pane cracked, one missing, small repairs, edge damage) **2,860.00**

Fine Federal Step-back Wall Cupboard

Step-back wall cupboard,
Federal, walnut & cherry, two-part construction: the upper section w/a rectangular top w/a deep coved cornice over a dentil-carved frieze band above a pair of tall 6-pane glazed cupboard doors w/arched top panes & opening to two shelves above a row of five tiny drawers

w/wooden knobs above a deep pie shelf; the stepped-out lower section w/a row of three drawers, the two outer wider than the middle one, above a pair of raised panel H-hinged end doors flanking a central raised fixed panel, molded base on scroll-cut bracket feet, Pennsylvania, early 19th c., restored & refinished, pulls replaced, 19¼ x 57½", 7' 4" h. (ILLUS.) **6,325.00**

Wall cupboard, country-style, painted pine & poplar, flat rectangular top above a pair of tall paneled doors w/a cast-iron latch w/porcelain knob above a lower pair of shorter paneled doors w/a similar latch, simple cut-out feet, old worn mustard yellow repaint, one-board ends, 19th c., 15¾ x 38¼", 5' 10½" h. (mismatched latches) **880.00**

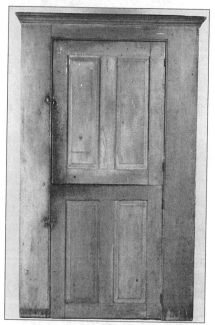

Early Painted Wall Cupboard

Wall cupboard, painted pine, the rectangular top w/a narrow flaring & stepped cornice above

an upper cupboard door w/two tall raised panels & a wooden thumb latch directly above a matching lower door, wide side boards at the front, five-shelved interior, original bluish grey paint, imperfections, New England, early 19th c., 17½ x 47", 6' 5¼" h. (ILLUS.)............**1,840.00**

DESKS

Art Deco desk, East Indian laurel veneer & black lacquer, an asymmetrical form w/a rectangular top above a short drawer over a long door at one end w/a long drawer above the kneehole at the opposite end , the kneehole supported by an angled tubular bar running back to the stack section raised on a black lacquer platform base , the drawers & door w/a three-quarters arc-form chrome segmented pull, designed by Gilbert Rohde, manufactured by Herman Miller, ca. 1930s, 22 x 44", 29" h. **1,760.00**

Art Deco desk, parchment & pearwood, slender rectangular hinged top covered w/panels of creamy parchment & raised on slender square tapering legs headed by narrow parchment panels, the top folding back to reveal small drawers & a parchment-covered writing surfaced lifting to reveal a mirrored surface on the reverse, short drawers numbered "II," "III" & "IV," bottom stamped "7956," Jean-Michel Frank, France, ca. 1934, 24¼ x 42", 32" h. ...**36,800.00**

Chippendale "oxbow serpentine-front" slant front desk, mahogany & mahogany veneer, the narrow top above a wide hinged fall-front opening to an interior fitted w/pairs of narrow drawers over pigeonholes all flanking a central door, the case w/an oxbow serpentine front on the four long graduated cockbeaded drawers w/butterfly brass pulls, molded base on ogee bracket feet, North Shore, Massachusetts, old finish, ca. 1790 (imperfections, replaced brasses) **2,185.00**

Fine Chippendale Desk

Chippendale Slant-front Desk

Chippendale slant-front desk,
cherry, a narrow top above a rectangular hinged thumb-molded slant lid opening to an interior fitted w/a pinwheel-carved prospect door flanked by two valanced pigeonholes above five short drawers over three short drawers, the case w/four long graduated cockbeaded drawers flanked by fluted quarter columns, on ogee bracket feet, Connecticut, I 1760-80, repairs to the feet, 18¾ x 40¾", 42¼" h. (ILLUS.) **1,840.00**

Chippendale slant-front desk,
tiger stripe maple, a narrow rectangular top above a wide hinged slant front opening to a two-tiered interior of open valanced compartments above small drawers, the central pull-out section reveals three

additional drawers, above pull-out supports & four long graduated molded drawers w/original brass bail pulls, molded base on scroll-cut bracket feet, old surface, minor imperfections, New England, 18th c., 17½ x 36¾", 44¾" h. (ILLUS.) **12,650.00**

Country "Stand-up" Desk

Country-style "stand-up" desk,
painted, a narrow rectangular top above the wide slant front

w/breadboard ends opening to a fitted interior well above a long narrow drawer over a pull-out writing surface, raised on slender baluster- and ring-turned legs joined by low rectangular box stretchers, old green paint, replaced pulls, surface imperfections, New England, late 18th c., 24 x 38", 48½" h. (ILLUS.) **5,462.00**

Federal "Butler's" Desk

Federal "butler's" desk, mahogany veneer, a rectangular top above a deep false-front drawer w/a hinged front opening to a desk interior composed of small drawers & valanced compartments flanking an inlaid prospect door concealing an interior cubby & drawer, all above a case of three long cockbeaded & veneer-outlined drawers, oval brasses, shaped aprons & slender bracket feet, old refinish, imperfections, probably New Hampshire, signed "C. Morse 1819, " 21 x 40¼", 43" h. (ILLUS.)..............**3,105.00**

Federal "butler's tambour" desk, inlaid mahogany, a rectangular top w/a reeded edge above a case w/a long fall-front

false drawer opening to a fitted interior above a set-back narrow pair of tambour sliding doors w/diamond-shaped inlaid ivory keyhole escutcheons, the false drawer w/a narrow almond-form inlay reserve & an outer rectangular line-inlaid band w/notched corners, the upper side stiles w/bellflower & line inlay flanking the false drawer, the square tapering legs w/further band inlay, probably Massachusetts, ca. 1790, 24 x 37¼", 40" h. (refinished, restored, some veneer damage) **2,990.00**

Federal Slant-front Desk

Federal slant-front desk, inlaid cherry, a narrow rectangular top above a wide hinged slant front w/line inlay opening to a fitted interior above a case w/a narrow long drawer flanked by pull-out supports above three long graduated drawers all flanked by chamfered, reeded front corners, replaced rectangular brasses, raised on short French feet, refinished, restoration, Connecticut River Valley, early 19th c., 21½ x 39¼", 42½" h. (ILLUS.) **3,335.00**

Louis XVI-Style Desk

Louis XVI-Style desk, cylinder-front style, gilt-bronze mounted mahogany, the low superstructure w/a three-quarter pierced metal gallery above a pair of very narrow drawers above a tambour cylinder opening to reveal a sliding leather-inset writing surface & two drawers, the lower case w/a single frieze drawer w/gilt-bronze mounts, raised on slender square tapering legs, France, late 19th c., 29½" w., 40½" h. (ILLUS.)...................**3,450.00**

Mission-style Desk

Mission-style (Arts & Crafts movement) desk, rectangular

top above a case w/a narrow long drawer above the arched kneehole opening w/a central slat flanked by fixed front panels & open deep end book shelves, original medium finish, shadow of "The Work of..." decal of L.& J.G. Stickley, Model No. 502, ca. 1912, 28 x 48", 29¾" h. (ILLUS.) **1,093.00**

Napoleon III Lady's Desk

Napoleon III lady's desk, inlaid & ormolu-mounted mahogany, a rectangular top shelf w/a low three-quarters ormolu loop border & edge banding raised on S-scroll front supports & a shaped wide back panel inlaid w/an ornate flower & leafy vine designs above a narrow slightly serpentine rectangular top above a conforming case w/two small floral-inlaid drawers on the stepped-out rectangular top w/serpentine edges above a pull-out writing surface w/floral & leafy vine inlay & banding over the serpentine apron, serpentine side aprons continuing to slender squared cabriole legs w/long narrow ormolu knee mounts, second half 19th c. (ILLUS.) **2,420.00**

Victorian Baroque-Style "partners" desk, mahogany, the rectangular top w/molded edges & rounded corners above a swelled frieze band ornately carved w/leafy scrolls centering a long central carved drawer above the kneehole opening w/carved & curved brackets flanked by single drawers above finely carved winged griffin legs on a long shaped platform w/incurved carved edges & raised on compressed gadrooned feet, attributed to Horner, ca. 1900 (ILLUS. below)........................**6,875.00**

School master's desk on frame, country-style, butternut & pine, a narrow rectangular top above the wide hinged slant lid opening to a fitted interior w/pigeonholes w/arched brackets, the case front w/two pull-out support slides, the lower frame w/a deep

apron raised on simple turned & tapering legs w/peg feet, 19th c., 20½ x 31", 38¼" h. (refinished, repairs) **550.00**

Victorian " patent" desk, Renaissance Revival substyle, Wooton model, walnut, the top galleried crestrail w/a raised & pedimented central section w/a pierced scroll-carved crest above a shaped raised burl panels, the shaped corner blocks w/small pierced carved scrolls flanking a narrow shelf above a pair of long doors w/curved & banded burl upper panels above a wide medial band above the flat lower section w/a metal mail slot on each door above an arched-top recessed rectangular panel centered by a conforming raised burl panels, narrow burl panels above the doors & down the block-trimmed sides, deep plinth base raised on heavy arched & molded shoe feet, ca. 1876 (ILLUS. top next page) **8,800.00**

Victorian Baroque-Style "Partners" Desk

Wooton "Patent" Desk

DINING ROOM SUITES

Baroque-Style: round dining table, curved-front china cabinet & five chairs; carved oak, the large table w/a deep curved

Baroque-Style Dining Table

palmette- and scroll-carved apron above four full-figural seated winged griffin supports w/breast shields flanking a heavy central ring-turned column w/a wide central band of large florettes in rings, all raised on a tripartite base w/gadrooned edging, the tall china cabinet w/an oblong top shelf above a wide curved & carved frieze raised on small seated winged griffin supports & a rectangular mirror at the back on the D-form cabinet top w/a wide curved glass door & curved glass sides,

Charles Eames Dining Suite

delicate chain-carved pilasters flanking the door, the molded conforming base raised on heavy paw front feet & block back feet, each chair w/an arched ornately carved crestrail between tall grotesque animal-form finials above a rectangular tufted upholstered back pane over a scroll-carved bottom band & raised above the rectangular upholstered seat on cabriole front legs w/leaf-carved knees & ending in heavy paw feet, square canted rear legs, legs joined by a square H-stretcher, the set (ILLUS. of table) **8,850.00**

Modern style: a round pedestal table & four side chairs; metal & vinyl, the table w/a white Formica top on a steel pedestal w/a four-part steel base, each chair w/a white wire lattice curved back & seat framed covered in blue vinyl upholstery & raised on arched steel legs, designed by Charles Eames , Model DKX-I, made by Herman Miller Furniture Co., ca. 1972, chairs 32½" h., table 48" d., 28⅞" h., the set (ILLUS. bottom previous page)..........................**259.00**

William & Mary-Style Suite

William & Mary-Style: table, china cabinet, pair matching sideboards & six chairs; walnut & walnut veneer, the table w/a

rectangular top w/cut-corners above a burled panel apron raised on heavy baluster-, knob- and block-turned legs joined by shaped flat stretchers, cabinets w/matching veneering, the high-back side chairs w/an arched & scroll-carved crestrail above stiles w/applied half-round spindles centering a pierced vase-form splat, turned legs matching the table, a master chair w/a very tall, narrow needlepoint-upholstered back & a high scroll-carved crestrail, ca. 1935, the set (ILLUS. of part) **440.00**

DRY SINKS

Painted wood, a long rectangular top well w/narrow upright sides slightly overhanging a case w/a stack of three short drawers w/turned wood knobs at one end & a single flat cupboard door near the opposite end, door opens to a fitted interior, painted brown, late 19th c., 21½ x 61½", 33" h. **1,380.00**

GARDEN & LAWN

All pieces cast iron unless otherwise noted.

Settee, the arched crestrail above a pierced splat in a meandering twig form flanked by stiles continuing to arched twig arms & arm supports in a similar twig form over a pierced seat, on scrolling legs w/clover-shaped feet, stamped on seatrail front "JAMES AND KIRKLAND N.Y.," painted green, early 19th c., 16¾ x 35½", 31¼" h. **1,610.00**

Settee, the arched crestrail above a pierced fern leaf cast back continuing to downswept scrolled arms over similar fern

Fern Design Garden Furniture

designs, a pierced interlaced seat, on sabre legs w/ball feet joined by pierced fern leaf-cast stretchers, stamped "KRAMER FOUNDRY, LEAVENWORTH, KANSAS," painted black, late 19th c., 20 x 53", 33½" h. **1,438.00**

Settee & four armchairs, each w/the arched, rounded backs composed of interlacing fern leaves & blackberries curving around to form the arms, pierced scroll seats, on pierced fern design end legs, slate blue paint, indistinct English registry stamp on back of chairs, minor paint imperfections, Coalbrookdale area, England, last quarter 19th c., settee 59½" l., 35¼" h., the set (ILLUS. of part) **5,750.00**

HALL RACKS & TREES

Hall rack, Mission-style (Arts & Crafts movement), oak, the tall narrow rectangular back w/a beveled rectangular mirror flanked by two curved coat hooks on each side above a tall paneled section over the flat & gently curved open arms above the rectangular lift-top seat, a

Mission Oak Hall Rack

curved strap metal umbrella holder extending above one arm above a small drip pan mounted on the lower rim of the apron, new medium finish, possibly by the Stickley Brothers, unmarked, 16¾ x 28", 6' 1½" h. (ILLUS.) **990.00**

Ornate Victorian Iron Hall Rack

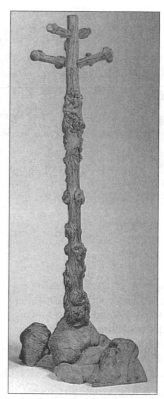

Burled Pine Hall Tree

Hall rack, Victorian Renaissance Revival substyle, gilt-iron, the superstructure w/a central oval small mirror above two seated cherubs within an elaborate foliate-cast pierced ground, the lower section w/a rectangular narrow white marble top above a frieze decorated w/interlacing circles & a single small drawer above an ornate scrolling pierced foliate-cast panel flanked by foliate-scrolled supports, the sides fitted w/umbrella wells, signed "Coalbrookdale" & stamped w/an English registry mark for October 20, 1870, England, late 19th c., 33" w., 7' 5" h. (ILLUS.) **6,325.00**

Hall tree, rustic-style, burled pine, a heavily burled base issuing a cylindrical pole supporting four coat arms, designed by Jack Kranenberg, manufactured by Kranenberg & Aiman, ca. 1943, 5' 5½" h. (ILLUS.) **575.00**

HIGHBOYS & LOWBOYS

HIGHBOYS

Chippendale "bonnet-top" highboy, carved & figured mahogany, two-part construction: the upper section w/a broken swan's-neck pediment surmounted by corkscrew finials centering a ball- and urn-turned finial w/a pinwheel-carved scrollboard below above a row of three small drawers, the deep center one w/fan carving above four long graduated thumb-molded drawers; the lower section w/a mid-molding over a single narrow long drawer above a row of three small drawers, the wider center one w/fan carving, the scroll-cut apron w/a pierced central diamond raised on cabriole legs ending in ball-and-claw feet, Salem, Massachusetts, ca. 1770, appears to retain original finish & brass butterfly pulls & keyhole escutcheons, 22 x 40", 7' 7" h...............................**178,500.00**

Queen Anne "Bonnet-top" Highboy

Queen Anne "bonnet top" highboy, cherry, two-part construction: the upper section w/a molded swan's-neck pediment centering a shaped plinth surmounted by urn- and spire-turned chip-carved finials over reeded plinths above a conforming case fitted w/a deep central thumb-molded fan-carved drawer flanked by small drawers over four long graduated thumb-molded drawers; the lower case w/a mid-molding over a narrow long drawer above a fan-carved center drawer flanked by smaller plain drawers, deeply scalloped apron, raised on cabriole legs ending in pad feet, married, 21 x 39", 7' 1¼" h. (ILLUS.) **8,625.00**

Queen Anne "flat-top" highboy, carved maple, two-part construction: the upper section w/a rectangular top w/a deep flared stepped cornice above a case of five long graduated cockbeaded drawers w/butterfly brasses; the lower section w/a mid-molding above a pair of deep square drawers flanking a shallower fan-carved center drawer all above a deeply scalloped apron w/a central pendent drop, simple cabriole legs ending in pad feet, some original brasses, old refinish, coastal Connecticut, 18th c., 18¾ x 38", 6'¼" h. **14,950.00**

Queen Anne "flat-top" highboy, cherry, two-part construction: the upper section w/a flat top w/a rectangular molded cornice above three small drawers, the central drawer fan-carved, over four long graduated drawers; the lower section w/a long drawer above three small drawers, the central one fan-carved, on cabriole legs ending in pad feet, Connecticut, 18th c., 20⅓ x 37½", 6' 6¼" h. **4,600.00**

Queen Anne "flat-top" highboy, walnut & maple, two-part construction: the upper section w/a rectangular top over a cove-molded cornice above a case of four long graduated drawers; the lower section w/a mid-molding over a single long drawer over a row of three deep drawers, the wider blocked center drawer w/fan carving, a shaped apron w/two drops, raised on cabriole legs ending in raised pad feet, appears to retain original butterfly brasses & keyhole escutcheons & warm brown color, five knee returns replaced, Massachusetts, 1760-80, 20½ x 38¼", 5' 9" h. **20,700.00**

LOWBOYS

Chippendale lowboy, the rectangular thumb-molded top w/notched front corners above one long three short molded drawers, the deeper center drawer carved w/a fluted, flowerhead-carved punchwork-decorated shell flanked by acanthus leaves, fluted quarter-columns flanking, the scalloped apron continuing to shell-carved cabriole legs ending in claw-and-ball feet, appears to retain an old rich brown finish & original rare pierced brass butterfly pulls & escutcheon plate w/one possibly replaced, Philadelphia, ca. 1765, 21⅜ x 37", 30½" h. **74,000.00**

Fine Queen Anne Lowboy

Queen Anne lowboy, carved walnut, the rectangular top w/molded edges & notched corners overhangs a case w/a

single long drawer over a row of three deep drawers, the center slightly shallower, the shaped scrolling apron raised on cabriole legs ending in shod trifid feet, repairs to drawer lips & top presently detached, Pennsylvania, ca. 1760, 22 x 36½", 29½" h. (ILLUS.)...........**9,775.00**

LOVE SEATS, SOFAS & SETTEES

Daybed, Art Deco, burled wood & mahogany, the platform supports w/a rectangular back, one side fitted w/narrow open shelves fitted w/a narrow door, mattresses & cushions upholstered w/lozenge-patterned fabric, 38 x 86", 32" h...............**1,093.00**

Fine Empire-Style Daybed

Daybed, Empire-Style, gilt-metal mounted mahogany, the slightly taller headboard upholstered below the rolled wooden crestrail joining the outswept stiles w/rolled ends terminating in gilt-metal swan head mounts, the lower matching footboard w/stiles terminating in gilt-metal leaf-cast mounts, the long flat side rails mounted at each end w/gilt-metal scroll & acanthus designs & in the center w/scrolls & a pair of facing winged griffins, raised on winged lion head gilt-metal mounted legs ending in gilt-metal paw feet, France, late 19th-early 20th c., 21¼ x 24½" l., 24¾" h. (ILLUS.)........**2,070.00**

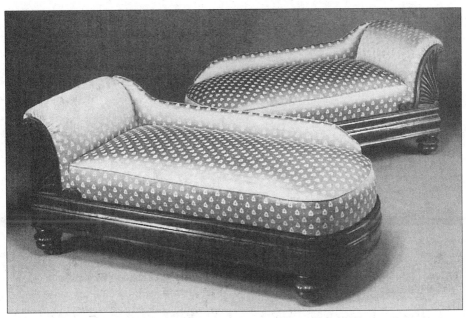

Boston-made Classical Recamiers

Ottoman, Victorian, circular form w/a central conical button-tufted upholstered back support surrounded by a circular upholstered seat, on turned tapering legs on casters, by Neuman & Company, New York, New York, second half 19th c., 68" d., 45½" h. **1,495.00**

Recamiers, Classical, carved mahogany, a low outscrolled upholstered headboard w/a fan-carved front support above a long low upholstered back rail over the long upholstered seat w/a rounded end above a deep ogee-molded conforming seatrail raised on short carved disc feet on casters, Boston, Massachusetts, ca. 1830, 65½" l., pr. (ILLUS.)................**4,600.00**

Recamiers, Regency Revival style, gilt-stenciled mahogany, each w/a outswept scrolled headboard & low upholstered back side ending in large carved scrolls, lower S-scroll footboard w/bolster cushion, long upholstered pad seat & upholstered headboard, the end & back rails w/gilt banding & leafy scrolls, the flat seatrail w/a gilt lattice band, the outswept legs decorated w/gilt classical designs above the carved paw feet, England, late 19th c., 85" l., pr. **11,500.00**

Settee, Classical country-style, bird's-eye maple, the wide, long crestrail w/a flat center section flanked by deeply rounded end sections above a long row of short baluster- and knob-turned spindles, turned round end arms above further turned spindles & turned trumpet-form arm supports flanking the three-cushion seat above a wide flat seatrail ending in long leg blocks above turned tapering legs w/disc-turned ankles, old refinish, imperfections, Pennsylvania or Ohio, ca. 1830-40, 11¾ x 77½", 31" h. (ILLUS. top next page) **748.00**

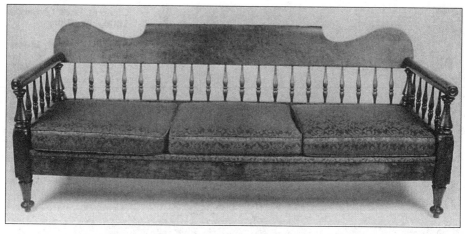

Classical Country-style Settee

Settee, Federal country-style, painted & decorated, pull-out type, the wide flat crestrail decorated w/gold stenciled reserves above two lower rails, one w/further stenciled designs, slender scrolled end arms on baluster-turned arm supports flanking the long hinged seat w/original canvas attached, pull-out section w/long flat seatrail w/gilt stencil designs & flat front stretchers w/further stencil designs, square legs ending in baluster-turned feet, old black-painted ground, imperfections, New England, early 19th c., 21 x 80½", 33¾" h. (ILLUS. below)......................................**1,380.00**

Settee, Molesworth, burled fir & blue Chimayo wool, the

Federal Decorated Settee

rectangular padded double chair back w/brass-tacked upholstered arms & loose double cushion padded seat, on split double burled legs, upholstered in blue leather w/sections of Chimayo weaving, the blue ground decorated w/a geometric Native American motif in red, black & white, Thomas Molesworth, ca. 1937, 36 x 59½", 31" h. **8,050.00**

Settee, Victorian Rococo substyle, carved rosewood, the triple-arched finger-carved crestrail continuing down to form half-arms & curved arm supports continuing into demi-cabriole front legs & a serpentine finger-carved seatrail, the back w/tufted mohair upholstery, ca. 1860, 50" l. **330.00**

Settee, Windsor, a long, narrow flat crestrail above multiple slender bamboo-turned spindles & heavier turned stiles, S-shaped arms on two turned spindles & canted bamboo-turned arm supports, wide plank seat raised on eight slightly canted bamboo-turned legs joined by bamboo-turned stretchers, old black repaint w/yellow striping, 80" l. (one arm replaced) **578.00**

Settee, Windsor, painted & decorated, a long narrow rectangular backrail painted to resemble a double-section back above a long row of slender spindles w/a heavier central spindle & end stiles flanked by S-scroll arms above a spindle & a canted baluster- and knob-turned arm supports, long plank seat raised on three four-leg chair-style supports w/bamboo-turned legs & plain box stretchers, original painted w/olive green & putty black striping, natural mahogany arms, minor surface imperfections, New England, early 19th c., 17¾ x 120½", 34" h. (ILLUS. bottom)............**2,530.00**

Scandinavian Settle-Bed

Settle-bed, painted pine, the wide serpentine back between downswept end arms flanking the long plank seat folding out to form a wooden bed frame, original red paint w/minor wear, Scandinavia, early 19th c., 19 x 73", 35½" h. (ILLUS.)..............**1,150.00**

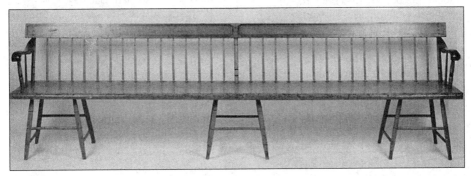

Decorated Windsor Settee

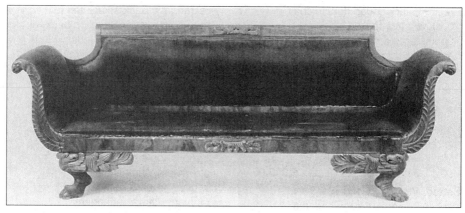

Mahogany Carved Classical Sofa

Sofa, Classical, carved mahogany
& mahogany veneer, the long
narrow flat crestrail centered by
a fruit-carved panel flanked by
veneered panels, the down-
curved side rails join the deep
out-scrolled arms w/acanthus
leaf-carved front supports
continuing into the flat veneered
seatrail centered by a carved
fruit cluster, raise on ankled
heavy paw feet, topped by a
turned eagle head & a
cornucopia issuing fruit & leaves,
Massachusetts, ca. 1820-30,
casters missing, imperfections,
91" l. (ILLUS.) **1,725.00**

Sofa, Federal, carved mahogany,
the horizontal molded crestrail
w/a raised central tablet carved
w/bowknot swags & tassels
above the upholstered back &
over-upholstered seat flanked by
downswept arms w/flowerhead-
carved dies on fluted & reeded
columnar supports continuing to
floral paterae, raised on square
tapering reeded legs ending in
brass caps & casters, attributed
to the firm of Slover & Taylor,
New York City, ca. 1805,
79" l. **3,450.00**

Sofa, Federal, inlaid mahogany,
the gently arched upholstered
back above upholstered end

arms w/reeded downcurved
hand holds above baluster-
turned & reed arm supports
flanking the over-upholstered
seatrail flanked by rectangular-
inlaid end dyes on ring-turned
round tapering legs ending in
vase-form feet, probably
Philadelphia or Middle Atlantic
States, ca. 1815, 82½" l. (some
repairs to rear seatrail & other
repairs) **1,725.00**

Sofa, Mission-style (Arts & Crafts
movement), crib-style, oak, a
wide gently arched crestrail
w/flat even-arms & tall slightly
projecting tapering corner posts
framing the vertical slats of the
back & ends, long loose cushion
on the slatted seat foundation,
light overcoat on original
medium-dark finish, Stickley
Brothers, 30½ x 77", 38½" h......**358.00**

Sofa, Mission-style (Arts & Crafts
movement), oak, an even-arm
form w/flat crestrails above the
slatted back & arms, flat seatrail
& drop-in spring seat, recent
dark finish, unmarked Harden
Company model, 27 x 78",
34½" h. (ILLUS. top next
page) **1,650.00**

Sofa, Modern style,
"Marshmallow" form, the back &
seat composed of original

Mission-style Sofa

orange upholstered round cushions fastened to bars, connected to a black tubular steel frame, designed by George Nelson, manufactured by Herman Miller, ca. 1956, 30 x 51", 33" h. (cushions refoamed) **11,000.00**

Sofa, Modern style, "Sofa Compact," upholstered painted steel & chromed metal, the rectangular back composed of two long horizontal cushions upholstered in purple, orange, green & blue vertically-striped fabric above a matching long single cushion seat all fitted onto a black-painted steel framed raised on narrow angular chromed legs, designed by Charles Eames, manufactured by Herman Miller, Inc., ca. 1954, 74" l. **1,380.00**

Sofa, Molesworth, fir & Chimayo wool "Basket Weave" a rectangular loose cushion reversible padded triple chair back, flat upholstered arms & triple loose cushion reversible padded seat, on circular hewn legs centering green leather

open basketweave side panels, upholstered in brass-tacked brown leather & panels of Chimayo weaving in camel decorated w/geometric Native American designs in green, white, black & grey, Thomas Molesworth, ca. 1946, 34 x 78", 32" h. **8,050.00**

MIRRORS

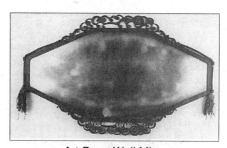

Art Deco Wall Mirror

Art Deco wall mirror, wrought iron, the lozenge-shaped mirror within a conforming wrought-iron narrow frame trimmed w/foliate scrolls on the top & bottom edges & original cloth tassels around the top edges, France, ca. 1925, 42¾" l. (ILLUS.) **1,380.00**

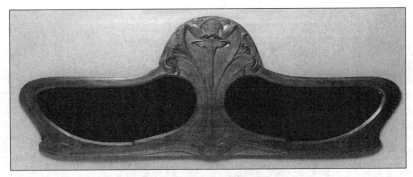

Art Nouveau Wall Mirror

Art Nouveau wall mirror, carved mahogany, the irregular oblong frame in the form of a butterfly fitted w/two conforming mirrors flanking a central carved design of three orchids & trailing stems, whiplash-carved borders, small chip to one mirror, France, ca. 1900, 17¼ x 49" (ILLUS.).....**690.00**

Arts & Crafts cheval mirror, oak, the tall rectangular mirror in a flat frame swiveling between three-quarter length uprights on brass knobs above a trestle-form base w/a wide shaped stretcher on arched & stepped shoe feet on casters, new dark finish, early 20th c., 32½" w., 6' 2¾" h. **715.00**

Chippendale Dressing Mirror

Chippendale dressing mirror, table model, mahogany, a scroll-cut crestrail above an ogee-molded narrow framed swiveling between slender uprights resting an arched shoe feet joined by a bottom flat stretcher, imperfections, America or England, ca. 1790, 13¼" w., 19⅝" h. (ILLUS. bottom, previous column) **518.00**

Chippendale wall mirror, figured maple, the high arched scroll-cut crest flanked by shaped ears above a rectangular mirror w/molded surround & conforming molded frame above a scroll-cut shaped pendent base, American-made, late 18th - early 19th c., 17 x 39½"........**3,450.00**

Chippendale wall mirror, walnut & gilt gesso, the high arched & scroll-cut crest centered by a rounded pierced gilded shell carving above the tall rectangular gilt-lined mirror plate w/rounded & shaped top corners, a scalloped base band flanked by scrolled pierce-cut corner brackets, probably England, minor imperfections, 18th c., 24½" w., 46½" h. (ILLUS. next page) **2,645.00**

Classical overmantel mirror, a wide rectangular flat frame w/rosette-carved corner black surrounded a three-part mirror w/two narrow panels flanking the

Classical Overmantel Mirror

Early Chippendale Mirror

larger central rectangular panels, the reeded end pilasters & slender columns bordered around the sides by eglomisé

tablets of grapevines & flower-filled ewers on a dark grey painted ground, the corner blocks w/ebonized panels, minor imperfections, 19th c., 61¼" l., 32" h. (ILLUS. above) **1,840.00**

Classical pier mirror, gilt & ebonized wood, three-part, the rectangular frame w/applied ring- and baluster-turned pilasters & foliate-carved square corner blocks w/florettes, enclosing a three-part mirror w/a long central section flanked by small rectangular sections, American-made, 1820-40, 61" l., 25" h. **1,150.00**

Classical pier mirror, carved giltwood, the flat molded cornice w/outset corners hung w/egg-and-dart carving over a frieze w/a classical allegorical scene flanked by reeded Corinthian columns embellished w/carved leaves, above a rectangular mirror plate over an elaborately carved base tablet, possibly New York, 1825-35, 29" w., 8' 1½" h. (ILLUS. top next page) **4,600.00**

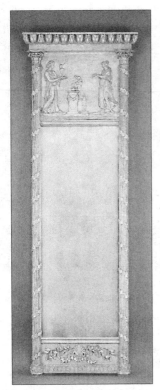

Classical Pier Mirror

Classical wall mirror, giltwood, the narrow rectangular flat crest w/outset corners above a band of small drop balls above a plain frieze band over the long rectangular mirror flanked by slender ring-turned colonettes ending in small blocks on a narrow molded base, minor imperfections, northeastern United States, ca. 1825-40, 34" w., 49" h. (ILLUS.) **891.00**

Classical-Style wall mirror, gilt metal, round, the riband & wreath-form frame enclosing a circular mirror plate, late 19th c., 12¾" **317.00**

Giltwood Federal Mirror

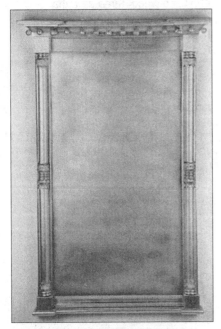

Classical Giltwood Mirror

Federal wall mirror, giltwood, the molded flat cornice w/stepped-out ends above a band of applied spheroids above a rectangular eglomisé reverse-painted tablet showing a girl standing holding a dove in a pastoral landscape, a rectangular concave mirror flanked by flat pilasters w/slender twist-turned pilasters above base blocks, early 19th c., labeled "Parker & Clover:

Looking Glass - and - Picture Frame Makers - 180 Fulton Street - opposite Church Street - New York," 13¾" w., 29½" h. (ILLUS.) **1,840.00**

Georgian-Style shaving mirror, inlaid mahogany, oval plate, serpentine base w/three drawers, on bracket feet, 8 x 18", 23½" h. **288.00**

Mission-style Cheval Mirror

Mission-style (Arts & Crafts movement) cheval mirror, oak, a wide flat board rectangular frame enclosing a rectangular mirror & swiveling between half-length slender square uprights above a paneled base on a trestle-form base, lightened finish w/added varnish, unmarked, early 20th c., 26" w., 4' 9¾" h. (ILLUS.) **550.00**

Mission-style (Arts & Crafts movement) wall mirror, oak, long rectangular flat board frame w/a gently pointed arch crestrail, mounted w/four wrought-iron

curved hanging hooks along the bottom & one on each side, red decal of Gustav Stickley above "gustav stickley," ca. 1909, 42½" l., 28" h. **2,530.00**

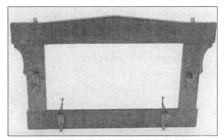

Mission-style Wall Mirror

Mission-style (Arts & Crafts movement) wall mirror, oak, a long "V" shaped crestrail above end corbels & flat sides & baserail mounted w/four curved iron hooks, recent dark finish, unmarked L. & J.G. Stickley Model No. 66, 42½" l., 34¾" h. (ILLUS.) **880.00**

Early Queen Anne Mirror

Queen Anne wall mirror,
japanned wood, the arched &
molded crestrail stepped out
slightly at the top sides &
continuing to for a molded
rectangular frame enclosing an
upper reverse-painted panel of
peonies & an exotic bird above
the rectangular mirror w/a
beaded liner, imperfections,
China, 18th c., 14⅝" w., 26⅛" h.
(ILLUS. bottom, previous
page) **4,888.00**

Victorian Cheval Mirror

Victorian cheval mirror, figured
maple, the bamboo-turned
pagoda-form entablature flanked
by bamboo-turned finials above
a rectangular frieze band set
w/bamboo-turned rosettes over
a tall swiveling rectangular
mirror enclosed by a conforming
frame w/bamboo-turned applied
quarter-molding & flanked by
bamboo-turned cylindrical

supports all above a rectangular
bamboo-turned base on flared
bamboo-turned legs, attributed
to R. J. Horner & Company,
New York City, 1870-85,
32½" w., 5' 11½" h. (ILLUS.) ..**8,050.00**

Victorian Overmantel Mirror

Victorian overmantel mirror,
Renaissance Revival substyle,
giltwood, the broken pediment
centering a bus-carved
cartouche over a projecting
molded cornice w/rectangular
outset corners above carved
frieze over a conforming mirrors
w/fruit-carved spandrels above a
molded & carved base flanked
by pilasters each w/carved
scrolls & acanthus & centered
by foliate- and medallion-carved
elements over an outset square-
carved plinth & a projecting
square molded & carved base,
New York City, ca. 1870-90,
58" w., 7' 4" h. (ILLUS.) **5,175.00**

PARLOR SUITES

Art Nouveau: settee & armchair;
carved cherry, each piece w/a
wide U-form crestrail centered by

Art Nouveau Parlor Suite

a carved Art Nouveau maiden's head w/flowing hair above a wide vase-form flower- and leaf-carved splat flanked on the settee by pierced looping slats & straight slender spindles, the chair w/straight spindles only, the crestrail curving down sharply to form open arms w/scroll-carved hand grips above incurved arm supports, the cushion seat w/curved front above a conforming wide seatrail, angular cabriole front legs w/blocked feet & canted square rear legs, the cushions w/Liberty & Co. upholstery, each w/a metal label of the Karpen Bros. Company, ca. 1900, settee 42¾" l., 36¼" h., the set (ILLUS.) **1,265.00**

Art Nouveau Carved Chairs

Art Nouveau: sofa, armchair & side chair; ornately carved wide framework, the serpentine crestrail on each piece centered by a standing semi-nude Art Nouveau maiden flanked by long undulating floral bands continuing down & around the arms then extending into the short heavy cabriole legs & across the seatrail centered by a floral cluster, tufted velvet back & arm upholstery & smooth upholstered spring seats, attributed to the Karpen firm, ca. 1907, 3 pcs. (ILLUS. of the chairs).....................................**6,050.00**

Bentwood: settee & two armchairs; painted wood, each piece w/a slender U-form crestrail above an upright back composed of sections of vertical & horizontal spindles above caned seats, straight slender spindle legs ending in U-form base rails, painted black, in the style of Josef Hoffmann, Austria, ca. 1908, settee 19 x 49", 30½" h., the set (seats missing) **3,450.00**

Edwardian: settee, two armchairs & four side chairs; mahogany & marquetry, each

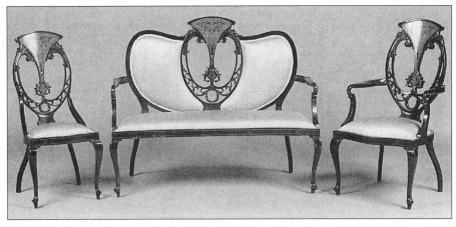

Edwardian Mahogany Parlor Suite

pierced w/an arched triangular crest w/floral marquetry centering a pierced bordered spade-shaped opening, the settee back w/flanking upholstered panels, the settee & armchairs w/shaped open arms on incurved arm supports, upholstered seats on shaped seatrails on simple cabriole front legs ending in peg feet, England, ca. 1900, settee 51" l., the set (ILLUS. of part, above)...........**3,450.00**

Empire style: two armchairs & four side chairs; giltwood, each w/a tall rectangular back w/flat framing w/carved palmette leaves framing the upholstered central panel, the armchairs w/round open arms ending w/ring-turned grips & carved classical profile busts at the end, raised on columnar arm supports w/carved acanthus leaf capitals & continuing down to form the front carved legs, the over-

Louis XV-Style Parlor Suite

French Empire Giltwood Chairs

upholstered seats w/curved fronts above conforming seatrails w/carved leaf bands & a florette, un-upholstered, losses to gilding, France, early 19th c., the set (ILLUS. of part,) **9,488.00**

Louis XV-Style: sofa & two armchairs; giltwood, each w/a shaped scroll-carved frame around the upholstered back, shaped padded open arms above wide over-upholstered seats on serpentine scroll-carved seatrail continuing into floral-carved cabriole legs ending in leaf-tip sabots, upholstered in figural & floral Aubusson tapestry, France, 19th c., the set (ILLUS. bottom, previous page.............**9,200.00**

Louis XVI-Style Armchair

Louis XVI-Style: two settees & four armchairs; giltwood, each w/a curve-topped rectangular upholstered back within a frame decorated w/laurel branches continuing to downswept padded open arms raised on incurved carved arm supports above the rectangular upholstered seat w/a leaftip-carved seatrail, raised on

Modernist Style Settee & Armchair

circular stop-fluted legs, upholstered in figural Aubusson tapestry in tones of cream, rouge & blue, France, late 19th c., the set (ILLUS. of one armchair) **17,250.00**

Modern style: settee & armchair; oak & leather, Bastiano Modernist-type, each of rectangular outline, the settee w/three seat & back cushions & a pair of arm cushions fitted onto a wide angular oak framework, the chair w/matching cushions, all in tan leather upholstery, upholstery cracked & worn, designed by Tobia Scarpa, ca. 1960, settee 83" l., 2 pcs. (ILLUS. bottom previous page) **1,265.00**

Modern style: settee & a pair of matching armchairs; vinyl & metal, the settee w/a shaped rectangular padded & button-tacked back, padded seat & ovoid, downcurved arms, on tapering splayed metal legs, upholstered in chocolate brown vinyl, the chairs matching, designed by Ico Parisi, ca. 1954, the settee 26 x 59", 33" h., the set...................................**3,680.00**

Modern-style Bamboo Sofa

Modern style: sofa, pair of armchairs, lamp table, coffee table & cane-back armchair; curved bamboo w/triple & double clusters tied together to form the framework & crestrails curving

down to form the arms & front legs, cushion back & seat on sofa & cushion seats on the chairs, 1930s, the set (ILLUS. of sofa) ...**495.00**

Aesthetic Movement Sofa

Victorian Aesthetic Movement: two sofas, two side chairs & one armchair; ebonized & upholstered wood, each w/an upholstered back panel above a round of large carved rings, the pieces w/padded arms also over carved rows of rings, over-upholstered seats above carved seatrails & square legs joined w/flat stretchers centered by carved connecting panels, squared flaring paw-form feet, ca. 1880, the set (ILLUS. of sofa)...**1,100.00**

Victorian Renaissance Revival substyle: a triple chair-back settee & a pair of armchairs; carved & incised walnut, each piece w/a carved & pierced crest centering a female portrait bust w/floral- and C-scroll-carved surround above a rectangular padded back, arms & seat, on ring-turned tapering legs, ca. 1875, settee 44¾" h., the set......................................**978.00**

Victorian Renaissance Revival substyle: settee, armchairs & two side chairs; marquetry, gilt-incised rosewood, each piece w/an arched crestrail centered by a small arched leaf-carved

Renaissance Revival Armchair

Two Belter Side Chairs

panel centered by a floral-inlaid oval reserve, squared corners w/small pointed carved finials & carved swags down the side stiles flanking the upholstered back, low flat padded arms w/incised & incurved arm supports flanking the overupholstered seat w/a gently bowed front above a narrow conforming band-inlaid seatrail, turned trumpet-form front legs & slightly canted square back legs all on casters, third quarter 19th c., settee, 64" l., 37" h., the set (ILLUS. of armchair) **1,495.00**

Victorian Rococo substyle: sofa & a pair of side chairs; carved & laminated rosewood, the triple-arch sofa crestrail carved w/three long sections of fruit & flower clusters separated by carved scrolls & continuing to form the incurved frames on the closed arms, serpentine seatrail w/central scroll-carved reserve, on demi-cabriole front legs, the chairs w/matching carved crestrails above the oblong upholstered back panels above the overupholstered seat

w/serpentine seatrail carved w/a central reserve & continuing to cabriole front legs w/carved knees & outswept square back legs, on casters, attributed to John Henry Belter, "Rosalie" patt., ca. 1850, the set (ILLUS. of chairs) **9,000.00**

Victorian Rococo substyle: sofa, open-arm armchair & side chair; carved & laminated rosewood, the triple-back sofa w/a wide pierced crestrail carved w/scrolling grapevines, the high arched central section w/a carved cartouche over a floral cluster w/smaller carved clusters at each end of the top rail that curves down to frame the tufted satin-upholstered back & padded arms w/molded out-curved arm supports flanking the upholstered seat w/serpentine from above the conforming seatrail w/scroll carving & a central carved cartouche, on molded demi-cabriole front legs & square outswept rear legs, chairs w/matching pierce-carved back borders framing shield-form tufted upholstered panels above either arched skirt guards on the side chair on arched & padded open arms on the armchair, "Hawkins" patt. by J. & J.W. Meeks, New York, ca. 1850, the set (ILLUS. of sofa, top, next page) **22,000.00**

Meeks "Hawkins" Sofa

SCREENS

Fire screen, Federal, mahogany, a rectangular screen frame inset w/a chinoiserie-painted silk panel above a delicate ring-turned standard, on a tripod base w/downswept reeded legs w/turned feet, probably American-made, early 19th c., 19" w., 4' 9" h............................**690.00**

Fire screen, Victorian Aesthetic Movement substyle, gilt-bronze & glass, the rectangular screen centered by a panel of small clear beveled glass squares within an ivy-cast border beneath an angular & looped crest, raised on scrolled legs joined by a pierced panel w/an overall undulating pattern, American-made, ca. 1890, 26¼" w., 41¼" h. (ILLUS.)......**6,325.00**

Victorian Aesthetic Fire Screen

Fire screen, Victorian Renaissance Revival substyle, carved walnut, a pierced griffin-carved crest above a molded & floral-carved rectangular frame w/inset glass panel over bracket supports, on quadripartite downswept legs carved w/lion's heads, terminating in paw feet w/casters, mid-19th c., 18¾ x 27", 47⅓" h. **253.00**

Mission Oak & Leather Screen

Folding screen, three-fold, Mission-style (Arts & Crafts movement), oak & leather, the wide center panel w/a large square Moroccan goat leather panel over a pair of tall narrow leather panels flanked by narrow double-panel side panels w/leather & gently curved outer frames, back panels of linen, original finish, branded mark of Charles Limbert Company, Model No. 53-L, overall 68" w., 6' 1" h.(ILLUS.) **3,850.00**

Folding screen, three-fold, Victorian, hand-painted leather panels forming a continuous Oriental style landscape of rockwork, bamboo & figures,

tack trim & wooden framework, late 19th c., each panels 18" w., overall 5' 6¾" h. **460.00**

Fine Painted Canvas Screen

Folding screen, four-fold, painted canvas, each panel w/chinoiserie decoration centered by a large twisted tree-like vine decorated w/small Chinese pavilions, figures, exotic birds, butterflies & large floral blossoms, repairs, repainting, England, 19th c., each panel 27" w., 7' h. (ILLUS.) **8,625.00**

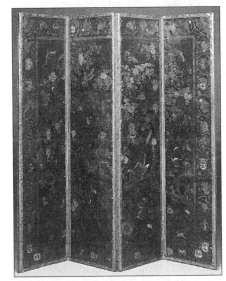

Early Dutch Folding Screen

Large Wallpaper Folding Screen

Folding screen, four-fold, painted leather within a wooden framework, the panels decorated w/a continuous scene of exotic birds amid dense flowers & leaf trees, all framed within a scrolling floral border band around the sides & top, Holland, 18th - 19th century, losses, each panel 22" w., 7' h. (ILLUS. previous page) **5,750.00**

Folding screen, six-fold, wallpaper & wood, composed of six panels of wallpaper from Jean Zuber et Cie., France depicting a continuous seascape view from the series Vues De L'Amerique Du Nord (Scenic America), probably a view of Boston Harbor in the early 19th c., mounted in a wooden framework w/carved fluted columns, ca. 1942 (ILLUS.)....**9,200.00**

Pole screen, Chippendale, mahogany, a tall slender pole w/an adjustable rectangular

Chippendale Pole Screen

needlepoint panel w/notched corners above a narrow rectangular shelf flanked by D-form small drop leaves above a/ knob- and columnar-turned standard on a tripod base w/cabriole legs ending in snake feet, old refinish, restoration, New England, late 18th c., 5' 3½" h. (ILLUS.) **2,070.00**

Pole screen, George III-Style, mahogany, a large rectangular needlework pane, 18th c. or later, depicting an amorous couple w/a musician in a pastoral scene, within a flowerhead-carved frame sliding on a slender pole headed by a finial, the pierced tripod base carved w/bellflowers & raised on cabriole legs ending in scroll-carved feet, England, 19th c., panel 25½" w., overall 5' 7" h....................................**1,380.00**

Chinese Table Screen

Table screen, Chinese porcelain & teak, the rectangular porcelain plaque painted w/male Chinese figures placed upright within a rectangular wooden frame carved w/flowers mounted on an H-shaped stand, the base frieze carved w/fish & flowers between Fu lion feet, damages, China, 19th c., 35" h. (ILLUS.) **920.00**

SECRETARIES

Chippendale secretary-bookcase, carved & figured mahogany, two-part construction: the upper section w/a reverse-breakfront & dentil-molded cornice above a pair of raised cyma-curve paneled doors flanked by Corinthian pilasters, mounted at the sides w/carrying handles; the lower section w/a conformingly-shaped mid-molding & hinged slant lid opening to a raised arched paneled prospect door revealing a valanced drawer & blocked short drawer flanked by columnar document drawers & valanced pigeonholes w/four short drawers below, all above the bombé-form case w/four long graduated drawers within beaded surrounds, the molded base hung w/a central pendant & raised on short cabriole legs ending in claw-and-ball feet, the case also mounted w/side carrying handles, Boston, Massachusetts, ca. 1770, 23½ x 45½", 7' 2½" h. (lacking pediment, minor patch to writing surface, mid-moldings replaced) **42,550.00**

Chippendale country-style secretary-bookcase, cherry, two-part construction: the upper section w/a rectangular top over a deep coved cornice over a pair of tall paneled cupboard doors opening to shelves; the lower section w/a mid-molding above a hinged slant front opening to an interior of nine small drawers,

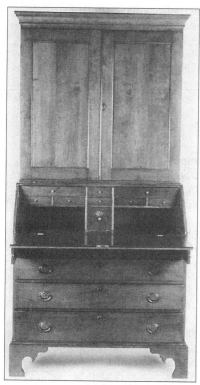

Cherry Chippendale Secretary

the central drawer w/fan carving flanked by compartments above the case w/four long beaded graduated drawers, molded base on dovetailed scroll-cut bracket feet, replaced oval brasses, old refinish, imperfections, probably central Massachusetts, late 18th c., 20 x 40½", 6' 9½" h. (ILLUS.) **5,750.00**

Chippendale country-style secretary-bookcase, carved cherry, two-part construction: the upper section w/a rectangular top w/a deep cove-molded cornice over a pair of tall raised-panel cupboard doors opening to four shelves, a single small wooden door knob; the lower section w/a hinged slant front opening to a desk interior fitted w/open valanced compartments above end-blocked serpentine drawers flanking a fan-carved prospect door w/flanking fluting below pinwheel carving, above a case w/drawer pull-out supports flanking a long drawer over three long drawers w/butterfly brasses, molded base on ogee bracket feet, some brasses original, old refinish, New London County, Connecticut, ca. 1780, 19½ x 41¾", 6' 7" h. (one bracket foot damaged, top may be of different origin).......**9,200.00**

Chippendale country-style secretary-bookcase, inlaid cherry, two-part construction: the upper section w/a rectangular top w/a deep coved cornice over a narrow carved dentil band above a pair of tall cupboard doors w/recessed panels w/serpentine edging, each door w/inlaid stringing & petals; the stepped out lower section w/a hinged rectangular slant front w/inlaid quarter fans & stringing opening to an interior of valanced compartments & a central fan-inlaid drawer flanked by drawers, above the serpentine-fronted case w/four long graduated conforming drawers w/brass florette & ring pulls, a narrow molded base raised on scroll-carved claw-and-ball front feet, original finish, replaced brasses, Connecticut River Valley, probably Massachusetts, ca. 1790, 20 x 40", 6' 4½" h. **33,350.00**

Classical secretary-bookcase, mahogany veneer, two-part construction: the upper section w/a rectangular top w/a narrow cornice widely overhanging the wide frieze band above a pair of paneled pilasters flanked the pair of tall geometrically-glazed cupboard doors w/muntins forming a central Gothic arch &

Massachusetts Federal Secretary

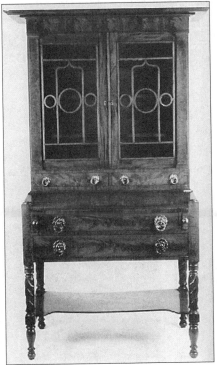

Classical Secretary-Bookcase

three rings & opening to three shelves all above a pair of narrow drawers w/brass ring pulls; the stepped-out lower section w/a fold-out fitted & lined writing surfaced above slide supports & a pair of long narrow drawers w/ring pulls, raised on spiral-carved acanthus leaf supports joined by a wide shaped medial shelf above baluster- and ring-turned legs w/knob feet, old refinish, old replaced brasses, imperfections, probably New York State, ca. 1820-30, 24½ x 38", 6' 1" h. (ILLUS.) **2,990.00**

Federal secretary-bookcase, mahogany & mahogany veneer, two-part construction: the short upper section w/a flat rectangular top w/a molded cornice above a pair of doors w/triple-arched panes enclosing

compartments & drawers; the projecting lower section w/a fold-out writing surface above a pair of pull-out supports & three long cockbeaded graduated drawers flanked by reeded panels, raised on ring- and knob-turned reeded legs, old finish, replaced brass ring brasses, minor imperfections, Massachusetts, ca. 1820, 20 x 39", 4' 6½" h. (ILLUS.) **2,070.00**

Federal secretary-bookcase, inlaid mahogany, two-part construction: the upper section w/a broken-scroll pediment center by an inlaid block topped by a small turned & eagle-topped finial, each scroll w/banded inlay above the narrow coved cornice over a veneered frieze band above a pair of tall geometrically-glazed cupboard doors opening to three shelves; the lower stepped-out section w/a wide, long fold-down writing surfaced veneered to resemble two drawers & opening to a fitted interior above three long graduated lower

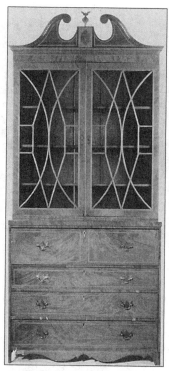

Early Federal Secretary

George III-Style Secretary

drawers each w/banded inlay borders & butterfly brasses, deeply scalloped apron continuing to short bracket feet, refinished, replaced brasses, loss of height, other imperfections, Maryland or Southern United States, ca. 1790, 21 x 46¼', 8' 8" h. (ILLUS.).......................**4,888.00**

George III-Style secretary-bookcase, mahogany, two-part construction: the upper section w/an angled broken scroll pediment centered by an urn-turned finial above a frieze band over a pair of tall narrow geometrically-glazed doors opening to shelves; the lower section w/a mid-molding on the slightly stepped-out case w/four long graduated drawers w/pierced brass butterfly pulls & keyhole escutcheons, a molded base on scroll-cut bracket feet,

restoration, England, late 19th c., 18¼ x 30½", 7' 2" h. (ILLUS.) **2,990.00**

Turn-of-the-Century secretary-bookcase, golden oak, side-by-side style, a high scalloped crestrail centered by a scroll-cut finial over a leafy scroll clusters above a case divided into two sections, the left side w/a rectangular-topped tall bookcase w/a tall single-pane glazed door opening to three wooden shelves, the right side w/a squared mirror w/undulating borders above a narrow shelf above a wide hinged slant-front opening to a fitted interior above a bow-fronted drawer over a rectangular cupboard door at the bottom, the flat apron raised on heavy short cabriole front legs & blocked rear legs, ca. 1900 (ILLUS. top next page) **462.00**

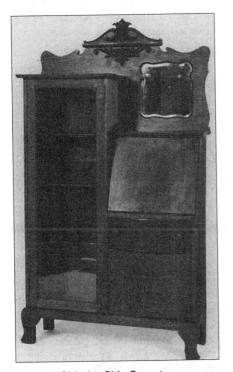

Side-by-Side Secretary

Turn-of-the-Century Secretary

Turn-of-the-Century secretary-bookcase, golden oak, side-by-side style, the high, ornately scroll-carved crestrail w/a large curve-sided & notched beveled mirror atop the right side of the case above impressed scroll carving over a narrow shelf & wide slant-front w/impressed cartouche design opening to a fitted interior above a single drawer & a wide rectangular cupboard door, the left case w/a tall slightly curved single-pane glazed door opening to four wooden shelves, a flat apron raised on tall slender bracket feet, ca. 1900 (ILLUS. below, left) **550.00**

Unusual Side-by-Side Secretary

Turn-of-the-Century secretary-bookcase, oak, side-by-side style, one side w/a high arched & scroll-carved crestrail above an inset compartment w/pierce-carved corner brackets & backed by a square beveled mirror above a drawer above a scroll-carved fold-down writing surfaced opening to a fitted interior above two more drawers above a small cupboard door beside an inset compartment w/an ornate grillwork front, the other side w/a lower spindled gallery top w/corner blocks w/turned finials above a long glazed door flanked by thin beaded bands, the flat front apron w/serrated cut trim, ca. 1900 (ILLUS.) **1,400.00**

Victorian Walnut Secretary

Victorian secretary-bookcase, country-style, carved walnut, two-part construction: the upper section w/a rectangular top over a deep coved & ogee cornice above a pair of tall 3-pane glazed cupboard doors opening to two shelves above a long narrow drop-front w/knob a pair of Gothic arch-paneled cupboard doors below, on wide ogee bracket feet, ca. 1850, 19" w., 7' 8" h. (ILLUS.) **935.00**

Victorian secretary-bookcase, Gothic Revival, walnut, two-part construction: the upper section w/a rectangular overhanging molded cornice above a conforming case fitted w/two glazed cupboard doors above two drawers; the lower section w/a slant lid opening to a baize-lined writing surface & central drawer flanked by pigeonholes all above a molded long drawer over two graduated long drawers, on bracket feet, mid-19th c., 21⅓ x 43⅔", 7' 2" h......................................**1,093.00**

Victorian secretary-bookcase, Renaissance Revival substyle, walnut, one-piece construction: the upper section w/a rectangular molded projecting cornice above a conforming case fitted w/a pair of arched, glazed doors flanked by a pair of similar doors over a over a drawers w/applied molding flanked by a pair of small drawers, on a molded base, ca. 1860, 13½ x 80⅓", 7' 6¼" h. **1,265.00**

SHELVES

Wall shelves, country style, butternut, long rounded tapering sides flanking two shaped open shelves above a lower flat-fronted shelf over two small drawers w/wooden knobs, old refinish, New England, early 19th c., 7½ x 22¼", 3l" h. (ILLUS. left, next page) **1,035.00**

Wall shelves, George III, mahogany, three narrow open shelves above a row of three narrow drawers, a central long drawer flanked by shorter drawers, all between shaped graduated sides, repairs to top shelf, England, late 18th c., 9 x 35", 35" h. (ILLUS. left, next page) **2,587.00**

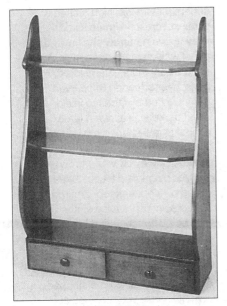

Early Wall Shelves

George III Wall Shelves

SIDEBOARDS

Art Deco buffet, mahogany & marble, in the manner of Dominique, the black Portor marble rectangular top above two center doors w/a circular mirror central escutcheon plate opening to reveal two drawers w/shelving below, raised on a

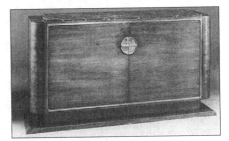

Art Deco Buffet

shaped base trimmed w/brass, France, ca. 1930, 20 x 74", 38½" h. (ILLUS.).....................**2,070.00**

Classical Mahogany Server

Classical server, mahogany & mahogany veneer, the rectangular top above a single long drawer w/brass lion head & ring pulls & a brass keyhole escutcheon flanked by bowed acanthus-carved side blocks above ring- and columnar-turned free-standing columns flanking the pair of paneled cupboard doors w/carved quarter-round lunettes in the upper corners & narrow oval brasses, the reverse-breakfront plinth base raised on large ball-turned feet, some veneer damage, New England, ca. 1825, 22½ x 42", 39" h. (ILLUS.) **978.00**

Canadian Pine Buffet

Country-style buffet, carved
pine, a thin rectangular top
above a case w/a pair of square
paneled cupboard doors
w/wooden thumb latches
flanking a pair of small
rectangular molded panels &
flanked by reeded side pilasters,
the base band of three narrow
molded panels above the deeply
scroll-cut apron w/simple bracket
feet, old refinish, missing top
section, other imperfections,
Canada, early 19th c., 20¾ x
62½", 34½" h. (ILLUS.)...........**2,185.00**

Very Ornate Edwardian Sideboard

Edwardian sideboard, marquetry
& ivory-inlaid rosewood, the high
superstructure w/a high arched &
scroll-cut crest w/ornate scrolling
inlay above a narrow shelf over a
panel w/two small rectangular
mirrors flanking a central inlaid
panel over a reeded & incurved
rail & flanked by tapering inlaid
side brackets all above a large
central shield-shaped mirror
framed by delicate inlay & flanked
at each side by curved narrow
shelves over inlaid frieze bands
raised on slender knob- and rod-
turned spindles to a lower shelf &
backed by rectangular mirrors,
the side mirrors & shelves above
small ornately inlaid panels
flanked by scroll-cut side
brackets; all resting on a stepped-
out lower case w/a rectangular
top w/a deeply incurved concave
central section w/a conforming
frieze of entwined vine band inlay
over an incurved shelf above a
convex narrow door w/a recessed
inlaid panel flanked by narrow
line-inlaid panels, each side of
the lower case w/a narrow drawer
above an arched recess backed
by a rectangular mirror & w/a
short bobbin-turned front rail over
small rectangular doors
w/rectangular inlaid panels
enclosing further ornate inlaid
designs, raised on four short,
slender square & tapering front
legs & three heavier rear legs,
England, ca. 1900, 15 x 60",
7' 2½" h. (ILLUS.) **3,450.00**

Federal server, figured
mahogany, the rectangular top
w/reeded edge above a cast w/a
pair of short drawers above a
long drawer each w/round brass
knobs, reeded swelled supports
below joined by a shaped medial
shelf, on reeded round tapering
legs ending in brass ball feet,
New York, ca. 1810, 19¾ x
35½", 36" h. **4,887.00**

Federal Cherry Server

Federal server, inlaid cherry, a rectangular top above a deep apron w/a pair of string-inlaid drawers w/inlaid diamond keyhole escutcheons above inlaid skirt banding, serpentine front & side aprons, tall slender square tapering legs, old refinish, imperfections, some height loss, probably Piedmont, Virginia area, early 19th c., 20 x 31¾", 27½" h. (ILLUS.)...........**3,737.00**

Federal sideboard, inlaid mahogany, the rectangular top above a case w/a pair of convex end drawers centering a flat long frieze drawer above a case w/a pair of convex hinged end cupboard doors centering a pair of flat bottle drawers & a hinged center door, all w/line-inlaid banding, on line-inlaid square tapering legs ending in crossbanded cuffs, deep brown color, probably Baltimore or Philadelphia, ca. 1800, 27 x 72½", 44¾" h. (restorations, rear of top slightly warped) **6,900.00**

Federal sideboard, inlaid & figured mahogany, a rectangular top w/inlay outlining & a slightly outset flat central section flanked by gently curved side sections, the case w/a deep central butler's drop-front panel centered by a pictorial inlaid oval outlined w/stringing & opening to an interior w/small valanced compartments flanking three smaller drawers, one w/inlaid

Federal Mahogany Sideboard

oak leaf, the curved side sections each w/a single beaded drawer above a large beaded door, stamped oval brasses, arched & line-inlaid central apron, raised on square tapering legs, replaced brasses, old surface, imperfections, Massachusetts or New Hampshire, ca. 1800, 22¾ x 64¼", 38" h. (ILLUS.)..............**9,200.00**

Federal Inlaid Mahogany Sideboard

Federal sideboard, inlaid & figured mahogany, the rectangular top w/a projecting center section & geometric inlaid edge above a conforming case of projecting drawer & two cupboard doors w/borders of geometric stringing inlay & cockbeading flanked by short drawers & cupboard doors, on square double-tapering legs w/string- and bellflower inlay, joined by straight skirt w/geometric inlaid legs, old oval brasses, old finish, minor imperfections, probably Massachusetts, 1790-1800, 20¼ x 67½", 41" h. (ILLUS.)........**11,500.00**

Federal sideboard, inlaid & figured mahogany, demi-lune-form, the D-shaped top w/crossbanded edge above centering a series of crossbanded & line-inlaid panels, a conformingly-shaped case below fitted w/a pair of convex hinged end doors opening to shelves & centering a bowed center section w/four long graduated line-inlaid & crossbanded drawers, on short square tapering inlaid legs, New York, ca. 1800, 28½ x 76", 41¼" h. **1,725.00**

Country-style Sideboard

Federal country-style sideboard, walnut, a rectangular top w/a molded edge above a case w/three deep drawers w/wooden knobs & reeded top & bottom edges above a row of three paneled cupboard doors w/wooden knobs, raised on knob-, ring-, and baluster-turned short legs, imperfections, Meckremburg County, North Carolina, early 19th c., 17¼ x 52", 41" h. (ILLUS.) **1,610.00**

George III-Style sideboard, inlaid mahogany, the rectangular top w/a gently bowed front above a case w/deep end drawers flanked by central long drawer above an arched center apron, raised on square tapering legs ending in spade feet, the drawers & aprons each ornately inlaid w/classical scrolling designs, the long drawer w/an inlaid urn centered by leafy long scrolls, cross-banded veneering around each & further floral inlay down the front legs, England, late 19th c., 24½ x 67", 36¼" h. (ILLUS. top next page) **1,840.00**

Fine George III-Style Sideboard

Mission-style Server

Mission-style (Arts & Crafts movement) server, oak, a low backrail above the rectangular top overhanging a shallow apron w/a pair of small drawers flanking a longer center drawer each w/rectangular copper plate & loop metal pulls, square tall legs joined by a medial shelf, fine original finish, burn mark on lower shelf "Handcraft" decal of L. & J.G. Stickley, Model No. 741, 18 x 44", 40" h. (ILLUS.) **2,420.00**

Mission-style (Arts & Crafts movement) server, oak, a gently arched splashboard on the rectangular base overhanging long corbels & a single long drawer w/rectangular copper pulls above two lower open shelves joining the square legs, light cleaning to the original finish, branded mark of the Charles Limbert Company, 19 x 42", 41" h. **4,675.00**

Mission-style (Arts & Crafts movement) sideboard, oak, a rectangular overhanging top w/an upright plate rack at the back above a case w/three short graduated central drawers flanked by flat cabinet doors w/hammered copper strap hinges & oval brass pulls on drawers & doors, a single long drawer across the bottom, square tapering slender stile legs, branded mark & Craftsman paper label of Gustav Stickley, Model No. 814, ca. 1912, 23¾ x 66", 49⅛" h. (ILLUS. top next page) **5,750.00**

Gustav Stickley Sideboard

Modern-style sideboard, walnut, the rectangular case w/concave front edges, fitted w/four vertically grilled doors opening to reveal three central drawers flanked by cabinets w/adjustable shelf, raised on a set-back plinth base, branded"GEORGE NAKASHIMA" w/Widdicomb Company label, ca. 1970s, 21½ x 68", 29" h. (ILLUS. below) ...**1,150.00**

Modern-style sideboard, bent beechwood & marble, the arched upper frame enclosing a beveled mirror surmounting a shallow center shelf above a tan variegated marble serving counter, a long drawer & two

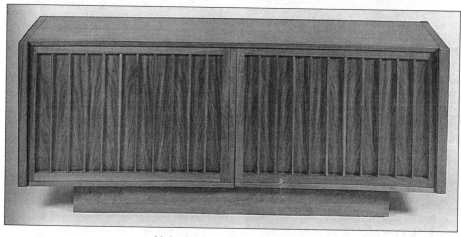

Nakashima Walnut Sideboard

lower shelves centered by a hammered brass kickplate below, Austria, ca. 1900, 22 x 39½", 5' h. (long drawer & marble replaced) **1,150.00**

Victorian Baroque style sideboard, carved oak, the tall superstructure w/a narrow crest topped by a boldly carved, full-relief pair of winged griffins flanking a large central flower-filled urn, smaller carved spread-winged eagles at the top corners above a pair of full-figure seated winged griffin shelf supports flanking a long open shelf w/a long, narrow ornately scroll-carved back panel, this shelf also supported on matching seated winged griffins flanking the top backed by a matching carved panel, the rectangular top w/outset squared sections at the center & ends above grotesque-carved blocks flanking a pair of long scroll-carved drawers above a pair of paneled cupboard doors w/scroll-carved frames centered by an oval medallion w/a carved grotesque face, the doors flanked by three male caryatids down the sides & center, a heavy rounded, carved apron on three short grotesque face front feet, probably Europe, ca. 1870, 46 x 68", 7' 8" h. **2,475.00**

Victorian Gothic Revival sideboard, ebonized oak, the superstructure w/a flat line-incised crestrail above two open graduated shelves between incurved side supports & backed by a solid back w/line-incised bands, the lowest section of the back inset w/a row of figural pottery tiles representing months of the year, the stepped-out rectangular top on the lower case overhangs a pair of long drawers w/strapwork designs & triangular brass keyhole

Victorian Gothic Revival Sideboard

escutcheons & triangular bail pulls above a pair of lower cupboard doors w/ornate Gothic-style strap hinges & large inset pottery tiles flanked an arched open central section w a single shelf, tiles by Minton, Hollins & Co., England, ca. 1880, 21 x 56¼", overall 5' 6" h. (ILLUS.) **575.00**

Fine Victorian Renaissance Sideboard

Victorian Renaissance Revival sideboard, carved walnut & walnut veneer, two-part construction: the superstructure w/a C-scroll & arched molded cornice centering two applied shaped burl panels centering a carved cluster of fruit & vegetables, surmounted by a scrolled cartouche flanked by two turned finials & scrolled returns above a molded edge D-shaped shelf above a molded oval panel flanked by four carved scrolling supports w/turned drop finials; the lower section w/a molded-edge stepped-out rectangular white marble top above a conforming case w/a row of three paneled drawers w/drop pulls above three molded & burl-paneled cupboard doors flanked by two stepped-out fluted & acanthus-carved columns, the center door flanked by applied flat fluted & acanthus-carved pilasters, molded plinth base, American-made, ca. 1870, 25 x 74", 7' 10½" h. (ILLUS.) **3,450.00**

STANDS

Bookstand, Mission-style (Arts & Crafts movement), oak, "Little Journeys" style, a rectangular narrow top overhanging pairs of end slat supports joined by two narrow through-tenoned open shelves forming a trestle base on arched shoe feet, original medium to dark finish, metal tag of the Roycrofters, East Aurora, New York, early 20th c., 14 x 26⅛", 26¼" h. **633.00**

Candlestand, country-style, painted, a small octagonal top w/molded edges raised on a slender ring-, rod- and baluster-turned standard on a tripod base w/a center turned drop & three simple cabriole legs ending in snake feet, old pewter-colored paint w/green accents, Antrim, New Hampshire area, Dunlap

School, late 18th c., 13¾ x 14¼", 26¼" h. (later paint w/losses, other imperfections)................**6,325.00**

Candlestand, Chippendale, walnut, the round slightly dished top tilting above a birdcage mechanism & a turned columnar standard w/a ring- and ball-turned base above the tripod base w/three cabriole legs ending in snake feet, Philadelphia, ca. 1760-90, 18" d., 28¾" h. **24,150.00**

Chippendale Candlestand

Candlestand, Chippendale country-style, painted cherry, nearly square top above a baluster-turned pedestal on a tripod base w/cabriole legs ending in snake feet, painted black w/gilt striping & a drape & tassel design, minor imperfections, probably Connecticut, ca. 1780, 17 x 17½", 27¾" h. (ILLUS.)...........**1,955.00**

Candlestand, Chippendale country-style, maple & birch, small hexagonal top w/a molded edge above a columnar-turned standard raised on a tripod base w/cabriole legs ending in pad

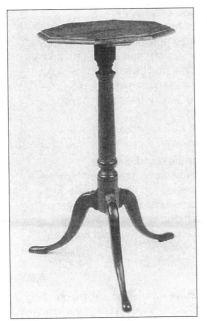

Chippendale Maple & Birch Candlestand

Federal Cherry Candlestand

feet, original surface, very minor imperfections, New Hampshire, 18th c., 13½ x 13¾", 26" h. (ILLUS.) **8,050.00**

Candlestand, Federal, cherry, the shaped top raised on a vase- and ring-turned pedestal on a tripod base w/cabriole legs, New England, 16½ x 17¾", 28" h. (no finish, imperfections)............**920.00**

Candlestand, Federal, cherry, small octagonal top above a ring- & columnar-turned pedestal raised on a tripod base w/three cabriole legs ending in snake feet, probably Massachusetts, Connecticut River Valley, ca. 1790, old refinish, minor imperfections, 15 x 15½", 27" h. (ILLUS. top next column) **2,990.00**

Candlestand, Federal, cherry, a round dished top tilting above a ring-turned vasiform standard above the tripod base w/cabriole legs ending in padded snake feet, early 19th c., 17¼" d., 28⅛" h......................................**920.00**

Federal Inlaid Candlestand

Candlestand, Federal, inlaid bird's-eye maple, the oblong octagonal top w/cross-banded mahogany veneer & outlining cockbeading tilting above a baluster-turned pedestal on a tripod base w/spider legs ending in spade feet, repairs, restoration, Massachusetts or New Hampshire, ca. 1800, 14 x 19¼", 29½" h. (ILLUS.)...........**1,380.00**

Candlestand, Federal, inlaid cherry, the rectangular top w/light wood stringing & fan-inlaid corners above a vasiform standard, tripod base w/cabriole legs ending in padded slipper feet, Connecticut, ca. 1800, 16¼ x 16½", 25¾"h. **2,760.00**

Candlestand, Federal, inlaid mahogany, the circular top w/marquetry depicting a deer beneath a stylized tree above a vasiform standard, on a tripod base w/cabriole legs ending in padded slipper feet, New England, early 19th c., 19⅓" d., 25" h. **1,610.00**

Candlestand, Federal, inlaid mahogany, the oval top w/stringed edge inlay tilting above a ringed columnar-turned standard on a tripod base w/three spider legs w/further stringed inlay & inlaid cuffs, old refinish, Middle Atlantic States, early 19th c., 16½ x 20½", 28½" h. (imperfections) **1,495.00**

Candlestand, Federal, mahogany, nearly square top w/serpentine edges tilting above a vasiform-turned column above the tripod base w/cabriole legs ending in snake feet, old surface, Massachusetts, late 18th c., 19½ x 19¾", 28½" h. (ILLUS. bottom, previous column)..................................**5,175.00**

Candlestand, Federal, mahogany, the hinged lozenge-shaped top tilting above a ring-turned baluster-form pedestal on a tripod base w/spider legs, appears to retain old & possibly original rich brown finish, New England, ca. 1815, 16¼ x 24", 30" h. **4,600.00**

Candlestand, Federal, maple, the oval top above a ring- and urn-turned pedestal over a tripod base w/spider legs, New England, 1790-1810, 15½ x 21¾", 27¾" h. **460.00**

Painted Federal Candlestand

Candlestand, Federal, painted birch, rectangular top w/ovolu corners above a ring- and

Federal Mahogany Candlestand

baluster-turned pedestal raised on a tripod base w/flattened cabriole legs ending in arris pad feet, early black paint, very minor surface wear, probably Portsmouth, New Hampshire, late 18th - early 19th c., top die-stamped "N.R.," 14 x 15", 26" h. (ILLUS.) **4,888.00**

Federal Decorated Candlestand

Candlestand, Federal, painted & decorated, the square top w/notched corners decorated w/a polychrome floral design & egg-and-dart border, accented w/gilt, minor imperfections, possibly central Massachusetts, ca. 1790, 14⅓", 30" h. (ILLUS.) **1,725.00**

Candlestand, Federal, walnut, the round dished one-board top tilting above a ring-turned columnar standard on a tripod base w/spider legs, early 19th c., 20" d., 30" h. (refinished, minor repairs & age crack) **825.00**

Candlestand, Queen Anne, painted wood, the octagonal small top on a baluster- and ring-turned pedestal on a tripod base w/cabriole legs ending in platformed snake feet, painted old black over earlier red, minor imperfections, New England, late 18th f., 15" w., 27" h.........**1,610.00**

English Rosewood Canterbury

Canterbury (music stand), Regency-Style, rosewood, a cross-form lattice w/four slat joined by knob-turned bars & separated by four flat rings, the outer rings carved on the exterior side w/roundels & leaf bands & resting on a scroll-carved band of a short case w/a single drawer w/two turned knobs, the square corner blocks top by inverted acorn-turned finials & raised on tapering ring-turned short legs on casters, 19th c., 13¾ x 18", 22" h. (ILLUS.) **1,610.00**

Canterbury (music stand), tiger stripe maple, the rectangular frame headed by ring-turned ball finials enclosing four concave topped rails between ring-turned corner posts & slat supports over a conforming apron w/a

long drawer, on short ring- and
baluster-turned feet w/socket
casters, New York, mid- to late-
19th c., 12 x 19", 20" h. **6,900.00**

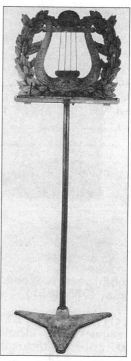

Classical Music Stand

Decorated Pine Stand

Country-style stand, painted &
decorated pine, a nearly square
hinged top above a tall square
pedestal w/a molded base,
original rosewood graining,
minor paint wear, New England,
19th c., 12½ x 13", 32" h.
(ILLUS.) **230.00**

Magazine stand, Mission-style
(Arts & Crafts movement), oak,
the rectangular top w/a three-
quarter high gallery w/a back
slat & cut-out sides w/a top slat
above three lower shelves
between double-slat sides,
three-slat back & square stiles
continuing to form short, square
legs, cleaned original finish,
paper label & red decal mark of
Gustav Stickley, 15 x 20",
36" h. **1,540.00**

Music stand, Classical, painted &
decorated wood & metal, the top
rack pierced-carved as a lute
w/strings topped by a shell-
carved finial & flanked by a leafy
wreath resting on the narrow
music bar, raised on a tall
slender standard on a flattened
three-arm foot, minor
imperfections, England,
ca. 1825-35, 15½" w., 48" h.
(ILLUS.) **1,955.00**

Nightstands, Art Deco,
mahogany veneer & ebonized
wood, each w/a demi-lune
cabinet fitted w/a single door,
general wear, veneer scratching,
probably France, ca. 1935, 15¼
x 17½", 20¾" h., pr. **517.00**

Plant stand, Mission-style (Arts &
Crafts movement), oak, the
square top w/outset square legs
joined by a lower shelf, added
varnish, unmarked L. & J.G.
Stickley, 13½" w., 23¾" h. **770.00**

Plant stand, Turn-of-the-century, oak, a square top w/a molded apron raised on four tall slender slightly canted spool-turned legs joined by a small square medial shelf w/serpentine edges, on glass ball-and-claw feet, ca. 1900, 24" w..........................**105.00**

Plant stand, Victorian Georgian-style, mahogany, circular top above waisted stop-fluted column, raised on three ball-and-claw feet, late 19th c., 56¾" h. **518.00**

Plant stands, stained wood, a square top supported by four slender square supports above a tall paneled base w/molded apron raised on ovoid feet, each side inlaid w/a diamond pattern inlay, stained black, designed by Josef Hoffmann, Austria, ca. 1900, 11" sq., 47¼" h., pr. **3,220.00**

drop leaves w/rounded corners above a case w/two narrow drawers w/old round brass pulls above a deep wooden pull-out bag drawer, baluster-, ring- and knob-turned legs ending in peg feet on casters, New York State, 1815-25, minor imperfections, old refinish, 16⅝ x 18", 27½" h. (ILLUS.) **805.00**

Sewing stand, wicker a domed tightly woven hinged top opening to a deep compartment, the sides w/a flat narrow top band w/continuous wicker scrolls above compressed bombé sides, raised on four slender wicker-wrapped legs w/delicate scroll brackets under the top & joined near the base w/a wooden medial shelf w/a high loosely woven serpentine-topped gallery border, scroll brackets under the medial shelf attached to the slightly outswept lower legs, natural finish, late 19th-early 20th c., 13¼ x 19", 31" h. **518.00**

Federal Sewing Stand

Sewing stand, Federal, cherry, a rectangular top flanked by two

Figural Smoker's Stand

Smoker's stand, painted cast metal, the model of a rustic tree trunk w/a three-root raised base, mounted at the top w/a model of a seated squirrel holding an ashtray, Gotthold P. Schwarz, Bridgeport, Connecticut, ca. 1930, minor paint wear, produced in a limited quantity, 31" h. (ILLUS. bottom previous page) **2,185.00**

Telephone stand, Mission-style (Arts & Crafts movement), oak, a nearly square top overhanging a shallow open inset shelf joining the tall slender square legs, skinned medium finish, metal tag of the Stickley Brothers, 18 x 20", 29½" h.........**550.00**

Country Decorated Washstand

Washstand, country-style, painted & decorated wood, the rectangular top w/a three-quarter gallery ornately scroll-carved at the back center, top overhangs a rectangular case w/a simple flat hinged door, high arched aprons at the front & sides, a divided shelved interior, old comb-graining, imperfections, American-made, late 19th c., 15¾" w., 25" h. (ILLUS.) **460.00**

Federal Corner Washstand

Washstand, Federal corner-style, inlaid mahogany, the downswept splashboard centering a small quarter-round shelf above the bowed top w/three round openings, the two small ones flanking the large central basinhole, the narrow scalloped front apron above the slender square supports to the medial shelf over a bow-fronted single line-inlaid drawer, the tall slender outswept legs joined by a slender lower three-arm flat stretcher, New England, 1790-1810, 15 x 22", 38½" h. (ILLUS.) **575.00**

Washstand, Federal, corner-style, mahogany & flame birch veneer, the high arched splashboard w/a small shelf above the quarter-round top w/a cut-out basin hole, the front apron w/flame birch veneer, raised on three rectangular supports above a quarter-round medial shelf over a conform-ing drawer w/small knob, on three legs joined by a three-arm stretcher above the outswept lower legs, old surface, Boston, ca. 1800, 15¼ x 23", 39½" h. (very minor imperfections) **3,105.00**

Victorian Marble-topped Washstand

Washstand, Victorian Renaissance Revival substyle, walnut, a high rectangular white marble splashboard w/notched corners above the rectangular white marble top w/molded edges above a case w/a small drawer w/a raised oblong burl panels w/two brass diamond & ring pulls & a keyhole escutcheon above a single arch-paneled doors w/keyhole flanked by stepped & reeded side stiles, paneled sides, on a molded plinth base, stenciled mark "MCB" for McCracken and Brewster, New Orleans, Louisiana, ca. 1875 (ILLUS.) **468.00**

Washstand, Victorian Renaissance Revival substyle, walnut, a high rectangular white marble splashboard w/notched corners & mounted w/two small half-round shelves above the rectangular white marble top above a single long drawer w/raised rectangular burl panels w/notched corners & two black pear-shaped pulls above a pair of cupboard doors w/raised rectangular burl panels w/notched corners, raised narrow rectangular burl panels down the front sides, flat apron, on casters, 17 x 31", 39" h........**330.00**

Federal Two-Drawer Stand

Federal two-drawer stand, mahogany, a thin rectangular top above a case w/two narrow drawers w/round brass rosette & ring pulls, on tall slender square tapering legs, New England, 1790-1810, 15 x 16½", 28¾" h. (ILLUS.) **978.00**

Federal country-style stand,
painted cherry, rectangular one-
board top w/ovolu-cut corners
above a deep mortised & pinned
apron, on tall, slender square
tapering legs, old red repaint,
early 19th c., 13¾ x 16½",
27½" h. (age crack in top) **220.00**

**Federal country-style one-
drawer stand,** bird's-eye maple
& birch, rectangular top
w/serpentine edges overhanging
an apron w/a single bird's-eye
maple drawer, on four tall,
slender ring-, baluster- and
tapering rod-turned legs w/knob
feet, refinished, probably Athol,
Massachusetts, attributed to
Spooner, ca. 1820s, 15 x 19¼",
27¾" h. **920.00**

**Federal country-style one-
drawer stand,** cherry, nearly
square top w/ovolu corners
overhanging a narrow apron w/a
single drawer w/old florette
brass pull, raised on knob- and
ring-turned reeded tapering legs
on peg feet, old refinish, New
England, early 19th c., 19½ x
20", 28¾" h. (imperfections) **748.00**

**Federal country-style one-
drawer stand,** cherry & curly
maple, three-board maple top
above a curly maple dovetailed
drawer w/a turned wood knob,
on square tapering cherry legs
w/figured veneer on top posts
of front legs, early 19th c.,
16¼ x 18", 28½" h. (top old
replacement) **248.00**

**Federal country-style one-
drawer stand,** painted &
decorated, rectangular top
overhanging an apron w/a single
drawer w/a large round brass
pull, on ring-, knob- and
baluster-turned legs ending in
peg feet, painted overall in early
yellow w/stenciled dark olive
green leaf cluster bands around
the edge of the top & within a

Painted New England Stand

painted rectangular reserve
w/notched corners on the
drawer, New England, 1800-20,
14 x 16", 27½" h. (ILLUS.)......**1,840.00**

Federal One-Drawer Stand

**Federal country-style one-
drawer stand,** painted pine, the
rectangular top slightly
overhanging the apron w/a
single flat drawer w/a turned
wood knob, raised on tall very

slender tapering square legs, original red surface & pull, minor surface imperfections, New England, early 19th c., 15⅞ x 18", 29¼" h. (ILLUS.)...............**1,093.00**

Federal Tiger Stripe Maple Stand

Federal country-style one-drawer stand, tiger-stripe & bird's-eye maple, rectangular top above a deep apron w/a single drawer trimmed w/cross-banded dark veneer, old replaced brass knob drawer pull, imperfections, New York State, ca. 1820s, 16¾ x 20½", 29" h. (ILLUS.)...............**805.00**

STOOLS

Decorated Classical Stool

Classical stool, painted & decorated, the thick upright scrolled ends joined at the top by a heavy knob-turned stretcher & curving down to form the flat seatrail, rectangular caned seat, raised on ring- and rod-turned tapering legs ending in tall peg feet, decorated overall w/mustard yellow paint w/freehand sepia & black leaf sprig decoration & banding, minor paint wear, New England, first quarter 19th c., 9 x 18", 12½" h. (ILLUS.) **1,610.00**

George II-Style stools, parcel-gilt walnut, the oval upholstered top within a conforming frame raised

Fine George II-Style Stools

on cabriole legs w/large ornately-carved shell knees & medial bands above the boldly-carved claw-and-ball feet, England, 19th c., 6 x 21½", 17" h., pr. (ILLUS. bottom, previous page).....................**5,463.00**

Noguchi Rocking Stool

Modern-style stool, painted wood & metal, rocking-type, a large round dished wooden seat supported on criss-crossed steel "V" supports rising from a smaller circular wooden base w/a rounded bottom, wood painted black, designed by Isamu Noguchi (ILLUS.) **7,150.00**

"Easy Edges" Stools

Modern style stools, "Easy Edges" type, laminated cardboard, compressed scroll form , constructed of laminated

corrugated cardboard sections w/fiberboard ends, design by Frank Gehry, ca. 1972, 15¼ x 17", 16" h. pr. (ILLUS.) **2,875.00**

Piano stool, oak, a round adjustable seat above four canted baluster- and ring-turned legs joined by a cross-stretcher & ending in glass ball and claw feet, ca. 1900.............................**77.00**

Queen Anne stools, oak, a thick rectangular top w/central cut hand-hole overhangs the deep flat apron, raised on simple angular cabriole legs ending in pointed pad feet, England, early 18th c., 13 x 22", 19" h., pr. **7,475.00**

TABLES

Art Deco coffee table, black laminate & chrome, a round black laminate top w/grooved metal edge banding, raised on four legs composed of three square bars arched at the top & joined by ball spacers, 30" d., 20" h. (minor top scratches) **550.00**

Art Deco dining table, mahogany & gilt-bronze, a bowed rectangular top, each end w/three curved tapering flat supports on an arched base w/flared ends, edged in gilt-bronze, attributed to Etienne Martin, France, ca. 1930s, 42½ x 81½", 29½" **1,150.00**

Art Deco Side Table

Art Deco side table, ebene-de-macassar, rectangular top

w/slightly swelling sides on two concave supports spanned by a curving stretcher, France, ca. 1930, minor chipping, 28½ x 72", 28" h. (ILLUS.)......**2,070.00**

Art Nouveau Side Table

Art Nouveau side table, carved mahogany & marquetry, the rectangular top inlaid w/daffodils against a landscape scene, a wide patterned wood apron, raised on slender twisted carved canted legs w/square feet, Louis Majorelle, France, early 20th c., 24¼ x 36½", 28½" h. (ILLUS.) **2,760.00**

Art Nouveau side table, carved mahogany marquetry & gilt-bronze, two-tiered, the rectangular top inlaid w/marquetry design of flower clusters amid leaves, the lobed lower tier w/elaborate marquetry pattern of lotus blossoms & lily pads, w/gilt-bronze floral-cast handles at the ends of the top tier, inlaid signature "L. Majorelle," Louis Majorelle, France, ca. 1900, 24¼ x 36", 31½" h. **5,175.00**

Art Nouveau side table, carved mahogany & marquetry, the square top inlaid w/two large horse chestnut leaves supported on four splayed tapering & fluted legs, the feet carved w/stylized

leaves & berries, the irregularly-edged aprons elaborately inlaid w/chestnut leaves & chestnuts, by Louis Majorelle, France, ca. 1900, 28" w., 30" h............**4,025.00**

Art Nouveau side table, stained hardwood, a carved lobed rounded & reticulated top raised on three slender shaped legs joined by a three-point medial shelf, original black finish on the base, new finish on the top, stamped mark of Charles Rohlfs, 21½" d., 18½" h..........**2,640.00**

Arts & Crafts side table, wrought iron & tiles, the rectangular top inset w/an eight-tile color frieze depicting a Dutch landscape w/houses & windmills all within a black tile border, raised on wrought-iron S-scroll supports on a scrolled iron trestle-form base w/a central vertical support bar w/curled bottom ends, early 20th c., 16¾ x 29", 18" h. **1,210.00**

Chippendale Dining Table

Chippendale dining table, carved mahogany, a rectangular top flanked by wide rectangular drop leaves raised on four square molded stop-fluted legs joined at the top by a valanced apron, refinished, repairs, probably Rhode Island, ca. 1780, 38¼ x 47¾", 29" h. (ILLUS.) **1,725.00**

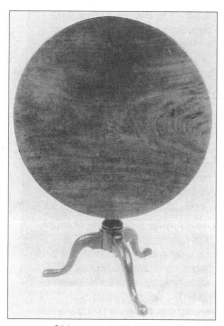

Chippendale Tea Table

Chippendale tea table, walnut, the large round top tilting on a birdcage platform above the vase- and ring-turned pedestal on a tripod base w/cabriole legs ending in pad feet, old finish, minor imperfections, New England, late 18th c., 33¼" d., 29" h. (ILLUS.) **2,300.00**

Classical Breakfast Table

Classical (American Empire) breakfast table, carved mahogany, a rectangular top flanked by a pair of shaped drop leaves above a cockbeaded inlaid apron w/working & faux drawers on a turned acanthus-carved post above four shaped flattened acanthus-carved legs ending in paw feet, refinished, probably New York, ca. 1825, open 40 x 48½", 29" h. (ILLUS.) **1,150.00**

Classical Center Table

Classical center table, mahogany, a round white marble top above a conforming molded apron over a slightly flaring cylindrical pedestal on a flat tripartite base w/acanthus-, lobed- and melon-carved feet w/fitted w/casters, New York City, 1810-20, 36" d., 29" h. (ILLUS.) **5,750.00**

Classical center table, rosewood-inlaid carved & figured mahogany, the round top crossbanded & crotch-figure veneered top tilting above a pineapple-, leaf- and fruit-carved standard w/a gadrooned collar & concave-sided leaf-carved triangular plinth on acanthus-carved paw feet, losses & repairs to veneer, cracks to top & plinth, Philadelphia, ca. 1825, 48" d., 29½" h. **14,950.00**

Classical dressing table, mahogany veneer, a wide rectangular veneered mirror

incurved lower shelf, on squatty knob feet, Boston, ca. 1815, 18½ x 43", 34" h. (imperfections).......................**6,900.00**

Classical Pier Table

Classical pier table, carved mahogany & mahogany veneer, a rectangular white marble top above a projecting frieze drawer over an arched back panel framing a mirror, the front edge supposed on turned & foliate-carved columns on a molded shaped base centering a carved outset three-sided platform, the flanking ends w/recessed panel doors opening to compartments, old finish, minor imperfections, inscribed in pencil under the marble "Williams and Everett," attributed to Williams and Everett, Boston, ca. 1825, 22 x 45", 36½" h. (ILLUS.)......**5,463.00**

Early Pine Side Table

Classical Dressing Table

frame swivels between leaf-carved S-scroll uprights above a narrow top over two small handkerchief drawers on the stepped-out rectangular top, the case w/a pair of drawers above a single long drawer all w/old round glass pulls, raised on four spiral-turned legs joined by a deeply shaped medial shelf above knob- and ring-turned feet, old refinish, imperfections, Massachusetts, ca. 1825-30, 20¼ x 38", 5' 4" h. (ILLUS.) **1,840.00**

Classical pier table, mahogany veneer, original rectangular white marble top above an apron w/corner blocks mounted w/pierced wreath-form ormolu mounts & centered by another long scrolled mount at the center front, the front supported on columnar legs w/ormolu capitals & feet & half-columns at the back flanking a large rectangular mirror fronted by a deeply

Country-style side table, pine, rectangular top widely overhanging the apron w/one long drawer w/a turned wood knob, on square legs w/chamfered corners joined by flat box stretchers, old refinish, some restoration, New England, late 18th c., 20¾ x 31½", 27½" h. (ILLUS. bottom previous page)...........................**690.00**

Country-style work table, painted pine, a rectangular top above a straight apron fitted w/a single drawer, on square tapering legs, painted brown, New England, ca. 1830, 24¼ x 40⅔", 29" h. **863.00**

Early Pennsylvania Work Table

Country-style work table, walnut, the wide rectangular top w/shaped support brackets overhangs a deep apron w/a small & a long drawer each w/wooden knobs, raised on ring- and baluster-turned legs on molded heavy square stretchers on compressed knob feet, old refinish, restoration, Pennsylvania, ca. 1750, 31 x 53¼", 29¾" h. (ILLUS.)...........**1,725.00**

Federal breakfast table, mahogany, a rectangular top flanked by two rectangular drop leaves above an apron w/a singled end drawer w/original bail brass & a scratch bead, raised on tall slender square tapering legs joined by flat cross-stretchers, old refinish, old

replaced stretchers, New York or Connecticut, late 18th c., 19⅝ x 29⅛", 28⅛" h. **1,495.00**

Federal card table, inlaid cherry, a fold-over D-form top w/a banded line-inlaid edge above a conforming apron w/inlaid band & almond-form panels, on square tapering inlaid legs, New Hampshire, 1790-1810, 35¾ x 36", 30¼" h. **920.00**

Federal Card Table

Federal card table, inlaid mahogany, a rectangular fold-over top above a deep veneered apron centered at the front by a rectangular cross-banded panel w/a central oval reserve, raised on slender square tapering legs, old refinish, imperfections, New England, early 19th c., 15¾ x 35½", 29¼" h. (ILLUS.)...........**1,380.00**

Federal dining table, mahogany, a rectangular top flanked by a pair of deep rectangular drop leaves, raised on baluster- and ring-turned reeded tapering legs on casters, old refinish, New England, ca. 1815, open 46 x 59½", 28½" h. (imperfections) ...**748.00**

Federal dining table, mahogany, three-part, each D-form end section w/reeded edging above the conforming apron & raised on four ring- and knob-turned tapering reeded legs ending in

Federal Dining Table

swelled peg feet, the central section w/a rectangular top flanked by two wide drop leaves, all w/reeded edging & raised on matching turned legs w/two swing-out support legs for the leaves, North Shore, Massachusetts, ca. 1820, extended 50 x 103", 29" h. (ILLUS. above) **5,463.00**

Federal dining table, maple, a narrow rectangular top flanked by a pair of hinged rectangular drop leaves, on a beaded-edge apron raised on slender square tapering legs, old refinish, Sudbury-Concord, Massachusetts area, ca. 1800, minor imperfections, 42 x 43" extended, 27½" h. **920.00**

Federal game table, demi-lune form, satinwood-inlaid mahogany, the D-shaped top w/hinged leaf above a line-inlaid figured apron centering oval-inlaid dies, on line-,dot- and bellflower-inlaid square tapering legs ending in crossbanded cuffs, attributed to John and/or Thomas Seymour, Boston, Massachusetts, 1794-1804, 18½ x 36½", 29¼" h. **5,750.00**

Federal game table, serpentine-front, bird's-eye maple & mahogany-inlaid cherry, the oblong top w/serpentine edges & ovolu corners w/a hinged leaf above a center frieze centering an oval bird's-eye maple reserve, on ring-turned & reeded tapering legs ending in ball feet, New England, ca. 1810, 17¼ x 36¼", 30½" h. **5,175.00**

Federal game table, serpentine-front, carved & inlaid mahogany, the hinged top w/a serpentine front, incurved sides & reeded edges above a conforming apron, the ovolu front corners w/ornate scroll carving above ring-turnings & acanthus carving heading the tapering turned & reeded legs ending in ringed cuffs & peg feet on casters, North Shore, Massachusetts, 1815-25, old refinish, 17⅝ x 21⅛", 29½" h. (minor imperfections) **1,725.00**

Federal Pembroke table, cherry veneer, a narrow rectangular top flanked by shallow rectangular drop leaves, the apron w/one working & one simulated end drawer banded in mahogany veneer, original brass pull, old surface, Connecticut, ca. 1800, 19½ x 36", 28½" h. (imperfections)........................**1,035.00**

Federal Pembroke Table

Federal Pembroke table, inlaid mahogany, a rectangular top w/rounded ends flanked by D-form drop leaves all w/inlaid edge banding above bowed drawers at each end, one working, one simulated, each drawer flanked by bookend inlay, raised on square tapering legs w/bellflower, string & cuff inlays, original round ring brasses, old refinish, imperfections, attributed to William Whitehead, New York, 1790-1810, extended 30¾ x 39⅛", 27¾" h. (ILLUS.)..........**8,050.00**

Federal Pembroke table, inlaid mahogany, the rectangular line-inlaid top w/two hinged leaves over a straight apron fitted w/a single drawer centered & flanked by oval inlaid reserves, on square tapering legs w/bellflower inlay, light wood

stringing & cuffs, American-made, 1790-1810, open 31 x 40", 28½" h. **4,600.00**

Federal side table, tiger stripe maple, a long rectangular top w/a deeply bowed central front section & conforming deep apron, on ring- and baluster-turned slender legs, Middle Atlantic States, 1820-30, 17½ x 43", 23" h. **2,530.00**

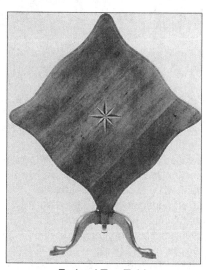

Federal Tea Table

Federal tea table, inlaid cherry, a wide diamond-form squared top w/serpentine edges w/a central compass inlay of contrasting woods & border stringing inlay, raised on a vase- and ring-turned pedestal on a tripod base w/cabriole legs ending in arris pad feet on platforms, refinished, Massachusetts or Connecticut, late 18th c., 31¾" w., 29½" h. (ILLUS.)......**4,313.00**

Federal work table, mahogany, the square top above a conforming case fitted w/three drawers, the top drawer fitted w/five compartments, on ring-turned tapering legs w/turned feet, American-made, ca. 1810, 19 x 20¼", 26¾" h. **575.00**

Federal work table, mahogany, the rectangular top above a case w/two drawers two round brass pulls each raised on ring- and knob-turned reeded legs joined by a rectangular shelf w/a concave front, on baluster-turned feet on brass caps & casters, New York, ca. 1815, 17¼ x 22", 29" h. **1,495.00**

Decorated Federal Dressing Table

Federal country-style dressing table, painted & decorated, the rectangular top w/ovolu front corners & a bowed central section above a conforming apron w/ringed corner sections above the bamboo-turned legs, early sage green paint, the front apron & legs stenciled & free-hand decorated w/large clusters of leaves & plants & small vignettes of cottages, imper-fections, North Shore, Mass-achusetts, early 19th c., 17¾ x 34¼", 28½" h. (ILLUS.)..............**920.00**

Federal country-style side table, inlaid cherry, a widely overhanging rectangular top w'/serpentine edges & canted corners above an apron w/a single drawer, square tapering legs w/inlaid cuffs, the front legs inlaid w/ovals & banding of contrasting woods continuing under the drawer, old refinish, Massachusetts, Connecticut River Valley, ca. 1800, 18½ x 27¾", 28½" h. (ILLUS. top, next column)...................**9,775.00**

Country Federal Side Table

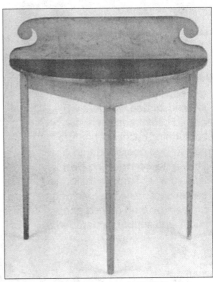

Federal Decorated Side Table

Federal country-style side table, painted & decorated, the high gently arched splashboard w/large scroll-cut terminals above the half-round top overhanging a triangular apron raised on slender square tapering legs, original mustard yellow & brown putty-applied paint, imperfections, New England, ca. 1825, 13¾ x 29¼", overall 34½" h. (ILLUS.) **6,325.00**

George III games table, mahogany & inlay demi-lune, top w/crossbanding & floral & scrolling inlay, baize-lined interior, raised on square tapering legs ending in spade feet, late 18th c., 17¾ x 36", 28¾" (minor damages) **1,495.00**

George III-Style Dressing Table

George III-Style dressing tables, mahogany, the rectangular top w/a gently bowed center section above a conforming case w/a pair of narrow end doors w/a thin oblong applied molding over a small drawer flanking the bowed center section w/three molded drawers over an arched apron, plinth side supports, stamped &

pierced brass pulls & keyhole escutcheons, England, late 19th c., 20 x 39", 31¼" h., pr. (ILLUS. of one) **16,100.00**

"Harvest" table, birch & poplar, long rectangular top flanked by long, wide drop leaves, mortised & pinned apron w/pull-out leaf supports, on slender, square tapering legs, old finish & traces of red, early 19th c., 18½ x 51" plus 11½" leaves, 27½" h. (minor wear, minor top age cracks) **523.00**

Hutch (or chair) table, painted pine, three-board top tilting above one-board ends w/cut-out feet & mortised construction, wide rectangular seat over two dovetailed drawers w/simple metal pulls, late grey paint, found in Berks County, Pennsylvania, 19th c., 39 x 54", 27" h. (age cracks, some damage, pulls replaced).....................................**990.00**

Hutch (or chair) table, painted pine, round top tilting above square uprights continuing to form the legs & framing the rectangular seat, flat box stretchers, original red paint, New England, late 18th c., 44½ x 45½", 27½" h. (imperfections).......................**3,680.00**

Early New England Hutch Table

Hutch (or chair) table, painted pine, the long rectangular three-board top tilting above wide incurved sides on arched bootjack feet joined by a bench-form seat, scrubbed top w/early red paint on the base, imperfections, New England, early 19th c., 37½ x 70¼", 29¼" h. (ILLUS. bottom, previous page)........................**3,105.00**

Hutch (or chair) table, painted poplar, two-board scrubbed rectangular top tilts above one-board, ends w/arched cut-out feet flanking the long seat, old worn yellow repaint over grey, top w/one original steel barn hinge, 19th c., 35½ x 72", 30" h. (one barn hinge missing, minor age cracks in top) **1,760.00**

Hutch (or chair) table, pine & walnut, a wide round top w/braces tilting above simple baluster-turned supports above a square plank seat raised on square legs joined by low square box stretchers, old refinish, remnants of old stain, minor imperfections, New England, ca. 1800, 47½" d., 28½" h. **3,738.00**

Round Oak Dining Table

Mission-style (Arts & Crafts movement) dining table, oak, round divided top raised on a heavy square divided pedestal w/four flattened tapering outswept legs on casters, original medium finish, Paine Furniture retail label, Lifetime Furniture Co., similar to Model No. 9057, early 20th c., 54" d., 29¾" h. (ILLUS.) ....**350.00 to 500.00**

Mission-style (Arts & Crafts movement) dining table, oak, round divided top w/a narrow lip overhanging the short apron raised on shaped brackets to the square tapering split-pedestal supported by four tapering extended serpentine legs, original condition, w/a full rack of leaves, branded mark of Gustav Stickley, 54" d., 30" h. (few small veneer chips to feet) **6,050.00**

Mission style (Arts & Crafts movement) library table, a rectangular top w/molded edge above square legs flanking vertical geometrically-cut panels flanking a long middle drawer over an arched kneehole, open shelves at each end, overcoat to top, otherwise original dark finish, early Charles Limbert piece, 27¾ x 41¾", 29" h........**1,650.00**

Mission-style (Arts & Crafts movement) library table, oak, rectangular top above a narrow apron w/three drawers along the front w/metal plate & bail pulls, each side w/thirteen square spindles above cross stretchers joined by a medial shelf, square legs, red decal & Craftsman paper label of Gustav Stickley, Model No. 659, ca. 1909, 31¾ x 53⅛", 29" h. **6,325.00**

Mission-style (Arts & Crafts movement) side table, oak, square top w/cut-corners raised on slender square legs joined by a cross-stretchers & a small square medial shelf, original medium finish, branded mark "The Work of..." by L. & J.G. Stickley, Model No. 574, ca. 1912, 18" w., 29" h...........**1,093.00**

Mission-style (Arts & Crafts movement) side table, oak, the oval top above flat cross-form supports w/chamfered ends raised on flat & slightly tapering legs joined by an inset oval medial shelf above wide panels w/pairs of oblong cut-outs joining it to each leg, Charles P. Limbert Furniture Co., Model No. 158, 35⅞ x 47½", 28⅞" h. **8,625.00**

Mission Oak Tea Table

Mission-style (Arts & Crafts movement) tea table, oak, a narrow rectangular top flanked by two wide drop leaves, raised on a tall narrow trestle base w/thin rectangular cut-outs & a through-tenoned medial rail above the shoe feet, original medium finish, "The Work of..." decal of L. & J.G. Stickley, Model No. 509, ca. 1910, 24 x 24", 24" h. (ILLUS.).........**1,725.00**

Mission-style (Arts & Crafts movement) tea table, mahogany, round top w/a narrow apron, the square mortised legs flush w/the top rim, lower arched cross-stretchers centered by a small finial, original alligatored finish on base, new finish on top, red decal mark of Gustav Stickley, 36" d., 29½" h. **1,100.00**

Mission-style (Arts & Crafts movement) trestle table, oak, the thick rectangular top overhanging a trestle-form base w/flaring shaped wide sections at the top & bottom & joined by a medial shelf fastened w/keyed through-tenons, original finish, unmarked Gustav Stickley, 29¾ x 48", 28¼" h. **1,320.00**

Modern Style Center Table

Modern style center table, ebonized ash & brass, the rectangular top w/reeded edges above a conforming apron, on four inset heavy square legs ending in brass caps on a brass-mounted & upholstered slightly slanted wide rectangular base, designed by Joseph Hoffmann for J. & J. Kohn, Austria, ca. 1905, 28⅛ x 40", 29¼" h. (ILLUS.) **1,851.00**

Modern style coffee table, teak & glass, the long flat teardrop-form clear glass top raised on a wooden base w/three long tapering radiating support arms joined at the center of the base above three conforming radiating legs, unsigned attributed to Vladimir Kagan, ca. 1952, 59½" l., 15¼" h. **1,035.00**

Modern style conference table, mahogany veneer, aluminum & painted steel, the rounded rectangular top raised on a double support pedestal base, designed by Charles & Ray Eames, manufactured by Herman Miller, w/company plaque, ca. 1960, 53½ x 96", 28½" h. **1,840.00**

Queen Anne dining table, cherry, a rectangular top flanked by w/drop leaves above a flat apron w/a flaring molded edge, on four cabriole legs ending in pad feet, two forming swing-out leaf supports, old repair to one leg, Connecticut River Valley, Massachusetts, first half 18th c., 47 x 48", 27½" h. **3,738.00**

Queen Anne dressing table, walnut, the rectangular molded top w/cusped corners above a conforming case fitted w/three small thumb-molded drawers over two small thumb-molded drawers above a shaped skirt w/a single drawer opening from the back, on cabriole legs ending in Spanish feet, 18th c., 21 x 34½", 30" h. **3,220.00**

Queen Anne Side Table

Queen Anne side table, hardwood, a narrow rectangular top flanked by rectangular drop leaves above a shaped skirt, on straight cabriole legs ending in pad feet, old surface, missing applied skirt shaping, York, Maine area, attributed to Samuel Sewall, late 18th c., 9½ x 31⅛", 26⅝"h. (ILLUS.) **9,200.00**

Queen Anne tea table, cherry, the round top tilting above a columnar-turned pedestal on a tripod base w/three cabriole legs ending in snake feet, refinished, 18th c., Rhode Island, 29¼ d., 28¼" h. (repairs) **805.00**

Queen Anne Tea Table

Queen Anne tea table, mahogany, the rectangular top w/raised cove-molded borders above a delicately scalloped apron, raised on tall slender cabriole legs ending in pad feet, old refinish, restored, probably Massachusetts, ca. 1760, 19½ x 29", 26½" h. (ILLUS.)............**14,950.00**

Queen Anne tea table, mahogany, the circular dished top tilting above a turned & flared pedestal w/a chip-carved base, on a tripod base w/cabriole legs ending in elongated pad feet, Newport, Rhode Island, 1740-60, 34⅝ x 34⅞", 28½" h. **1,380.00**

Queen Anne country-style dining table, cherry, a narrow rectangular top w/rounded ends flanked by half-round drop leaves above a deep apron w/shaped skirt, raised on simple cabriole legs ending in pad feet, old refinish, restoration, Rhode Island, 18th c., 29½ x 33¾", 27¼" h. (ILLUS. top next page) **1,955.00**

Queen Anne Country Dining Table

Early 'Sawbuck' Table

Queen Anne country-style dining table, maple, a narrow rectangular top flanked by deep half-round drop leaves, round tapered legs & a swing-out leg w/duck feet, old refinishing on base, top scrubbed, 18th c., 13¾ x 48½" w/20" w. leaves, 27" h. (repairs to base, top rehinged & w/pieced repairs, feet drilled for casters, one foot repaired) **2,035.00**

Queen Anne country-style dining table, tiger stripe maple, a rectangular top w/rounded ends flanked by a pair of deep half-round drop leaves, serpentine aprons, on nearly straight cabriole legs ending in raised pad feet, refinished, mid-18th c., New England, extended 47½ x 58¼", 28" h. (restoration) **1,725.00**

Queen Anne country-style side table, tiger stripe maple, a slightly oval top raise on a rectangular apron on corner blocks tapering to turned tapering straight legs ending in pad feet, New England, 18th c., 30¼ x 33¾", 27½" (refinished, imperfections) **3,220.00**

"Sawbuck" table, painted pine, the oval scrubbed top raised on an "X" form base in original red paint, all original surfaces & form, coastal Massachusetts or New Hampshire, 23⅛ x 30½", 25" h. (ILLUS.) **3,338.00**

Tavern table, maple, a rectangular top w/breadboard ends widely overhanging an apron w/a single long drawer w/a turned wood knob, on block-knob- and baluster-turned legs joined by flat box stretchers on knob feet, New England, 18th c., refinished, original pull, imperfections, 26 x 42", 25½" h. **1,092.00**

Tavern table, painted pine, one-board rectangular top overhanging an apron w/a single long drawer w/a turned knob, raised on four ring-, baluster- and block-turned legs joined by low rectangular box stretchers, on flaring button feet, old red-painted surface, Massachusetts, early 18th c. **5,463.00**

Tavern table, painted & turned wood, oval top on four block- and rod-turned legs joined by flat apron & base rectangular flat

Early Tavern Table

top above a round heavy divided pedestal raised on a flat quadripartite base w/C-scroll feet, ca. 1900, 48" d. ....**250.00 to 300.00**

Turn-of-the-Century Dining Table

stretchers, painted off-white over earlier red, imperfections, New England, late 18th c., 26 x 30", 26½" h. (ILLUS.) **4,600.00**

Pine Tavern Table

Tavern table, pine, rectangular two-board top w/breadboard ends widely overhanging a deep apron w/a single long drawer w/a small wooden knob, raised on baluster- & knob-turned legs w/blocks joining the flat box stretchers above turned feet, old refinished mellow surface, original drawer pull, two rear feet pieced, northern New England, 18th c., 27 x 39⅛", 27¼" h. (ILLUS.) **3,738.00**

Turn-of-the-century dining table, oak, the round divided

Turn-of-the-century dining table, golden oak, the round divided top w/a deep molded apron raised on a heavy round reeded column above four heavy tapering ornately leaf- and scroll-carved legs ending in large paw feet on casters, hidden compartment in the base, w/two extra leaves, closed 53" d. (ILLUS.) **1,540.00**

Victorian dining table, Renaissance Revival substyle, walnut, divided turtle-top form w/molded edges above the conforming apron, raised on four S-scroll supports continuing into arched & undulating legs w/C-scroll feet & joined at the center by a round disc w/a ring-turned finial, w/two extra leaves, ca. 1860, closed 42 x 54" (ILLUS. top next page) **605.00**

Victorian library table, Aesthetic Movement substyle, walnut, the wide rectangular top above a deep apron carved w/panels of stylized floral & fan carving & w/three long drawers along one side fitted w/large metal animal head & ring pulls, raised on a heavy trestle-form base w/columnar-turned supports

Victorian Walnut Dining Table

flanking leafy scroll-carved panels above heavy shaped outswept feet joined by a line-incised central stretcher centered by a stylized rosette, attributed to Daniel Pabst, Philadelphia, third quarter 19th c., 90" l., 31" h. (ILLUS. below).....................**18,400.00**

Victorian library table,
Renaissance Revival substyle, walnut, the long rectangular top w/chamfered edges above an apron w/a carved sawtooth top band above three drawers w/carved trim all raised on double block-and-column-carved end supports joined by an upper

Fine Aesthetic Movement Library Table

sawtooth-carved stretcher, the
supports ending on a trestle-
form base w/angular outswept
blocked legs trimmed
w/roundels, the lower end
stretchers w/sawtooth bands
below large carved roundels on
angled blocks, the long cross-
stretcher w/a matching large
roundel above a sawtooth band,
ca. 1870, 29 x 47".....................**770.00**

Aesthetic Movement Side Table

Victorian side table, Aesthetic
Movement substyle, ebonized
walnut, the square top flanked
by narrow drop leaves flanking a
narrow frieze drawer all w/burl
walnut w/banded edge trim,
raised on slender ring- and rod-
turned tapering legs joined by a
lower X-form stretcher centered
by a turned finial, attributed to
the Herter Brothers, New York
City, ca. 1880, 35" w., 30¼" h.
(ILLUS.) **8,625.00**

Victorian side table,
Renaissance Revival substyle,
walnut, the round top of
Tennessee brown marble w/a
molded edge supported on a
deep molded apron w/a curved-
front drawer on one side w/a
teardrop pull, apron blocks

Fine Renaissance Revival Side Table

w/half-turned short turned
spindles above slender scroll-cut
& incurved supports continuing
to very slender ring- and knob-
turned spindles all joined to a
central reeded & ring-turned
column by short spindles, heavy
flattened S-scroll downswept
leaves ending in roundels &
raised on casters, Thomas
Brooks, New York, New York,
ca. 1860, 24½" d., 29" h.
(ILLUS.) **3,300.00**

Victorian side table,
Renaissance Revival substyle,
carved, gilded & inlaid
rosewood, the round white
marble top w/a molded edge
above an ornately inlaid apron
divided by four large winged
classical female busts on curved
supports continuing to slender
legs ending in boldly carved paw
feet on casters, a central ring-
and rod-turned & inlaid cross-
stretcher w/a turned pineapple
finial & a slender turned drop
halfway up the legs, a flat round
ribbon- and leaf-carved stretcher

Rare Herter Bros. Table

Southern William & Mary Table

joining the lower legs, produced by the Herter Brothers on commission for the Milton Latham Home, Menlo Park (ILLUS.) **330,000.00**

Wicker side table, the round wooden top above a tightly woven curved apron raised on outwardly carved wicker-wrapped legs w/wicker-wrapped arches between each pair of legs & delicate S-scrolls at the center inside of each legs, the legs tapering down & inward to a small round galleried medial shelf above the outswept lower legs, natural finish, late 19th c., 20¼" d., 31" h. **259.00**

William & Mary side table, walnut & yellow pine, rectangular top w/molded edges overhanging an apron w/a single long molded drawer w/simple wooden pull above a shaped front apron, raised on baluster-turned legs raised on a square, molded heavy H-stretcher above turned ball feet, refinished w/traces of red paint, original pull, Piedmont area, Southern states, 18th c., 16⅝ x 26¾", 27¾" h. (ILLUS. top, next column).................................**5,175.00**

William & Mary tavern table, turned maple & pine, the rectangular top w/breadboard ends widely overhanging an apron w/a single long drawer w/a small wooden knob, raised on baluster-, knob- and block-turned legs w/ball feet joined by a rod-, ball- and block-turned H-stretcher, probably New England, 1720-40, 40" l., 28" h. **3,737.00**

WARDROBES & ARMOIRES

Kas (American version of the Netherlands Kast or wardrobe), gum wood, Queen Anne style, a rectangular top above a deep molded cornice over a pair of molded paneled doors flanked by applied molded panels, above a double-panel long drawer flanked by applied lozenge designs, raised on bulbous feet, Hudson River Valley, mid-18th c., 24 x 68½", 6' 2" h..................................**5,750.00**

Kas, poplar, Queen Anne style, the rectangular top w/a widely flaring deep stepped cornice above a plain frieze band over a narrow molding above a pair of wide doors w/four raised panels each & flanked by three

*Early Queen
Anne Kas*

serpentine-molded pilasters above a lower molding over a row of three drawers w/a small drawer flanked by longer drawers above the deep flaring molded base on short inset bracket feet, New York or Pennsylvania, ca. 1740-60, 27½ x 79", 6' 8" h. (ILLUS. above).......................**5,175.00**

Wardrobe, Classical, diminutive size, ormolu-mounted figured mahogany, the rectangular top above an arched paneled frieze centering a pair of double-paneled tall doors opening to three long shelves & two short shelves & a large compartment flanked on the outer sides w/engaged pilasters, the reverse-breakfront plinth base on turned tapering short legs w/ball feet, New York, ca. 1815, 20 x 41", 4' 7½" h. (ILLUS. right) **3,737.00**

Small Classical Wardrobe

Fine Classical Wardrobe

Wardrobe, Classical, carved
mahogany, a rectangular top
w/a deep molded cornice above
a veneered band over an inset
veneered frieze above a
conforming case fitted w/two tall
double-paneled doors opening
to fitted interiors, one w/seven
shelves, the other w/hanging
space, flanked by turned
colonettes headed by Ionic
scrolled & foliate-carved capitals
over a shaped base, on heavy
carved paw feet w/foliate-carved
knee returns, New York City,
1820-40, 26¼ x 64", 7' 3¼" h.
(ILLUS.) **2,900.00**

Wardrobe, country-style, painted
pine, a flat rectangular top w/a
molded cornice above a tall
double-panel door flanked by
wide side boards, very slightly
arched base, the interior
w/hooks on one side & shelves
on the other, the exterior w/the
original mustard yellow & brown
grained painting, imperfections,
coastal Massachusetts, ca.
1830, 20½ x 44", 6' 6" h. **1,035.00**

Victorian Bamboo-turned Wardrobe

Wardrobe, Victorian, bamboo-
turned figured maple, in three
parts: the top w/rectangular
cornice set w/bamboo-turned
finials flanking a rectangular
bamboo-turned entablature
above a conforming plain frieze;
the middle section w/rectangular
mirrored door enclosing a fitted
interior w/four shelves & eleven
double hooks, the whole flanked
by bamboo-turned engaged
columns above a conforming
separate base fitted w/a single
long drawer w/applied bamboo-
turned moldings & pulls, all on
disc feet w/casters, attributed to
R. J. Horner & Company, New
York City, 1870-85, 21½ x 33",
7' 4½" h. (ILLUS.) **10,925.00**

WHATNOTS & ETAGERES

Federal Mahogany Etagere

Etagere, Federal, mahogany, two open rectangular upper shelves supported on slender ring- and baluster-turned supports topped by small urn-form finials, a third open shelf above a single long drawer w/an old round brass pull above matching supports to a bottom medial shelf on baluster-turned feet w/disc ankles on brass casters, old refinish, imperfections, Mid-Atlantic States, 1815-25, 15½ x 21½", 4' 1½" h. (ILLUS.) **920.00**

Etagere, Victorian Rococo substyle, carved walnut, the tall central arched mirror within a pierce-carved Gothic arch frame topped by an arched crestrail pierce-carved w/a shell finial over grapevines w/pierce-carved

Victorian Rococo Etagere

scrolls & curved supports flanking the mirror & supporting three small graduated open shelves on each side, a panel w/a raised oval reserve below the mirror & above a long serpentine-front open shelf joined by supports to the upper side shelves & resting on long incurved supports joined near the base by a conforming medial shelf on scroll feet, ca. 1850, 50" w., 6' 9" h. (ILLUS.) **1,840.00**

Etagere, Victorian Rococo substyle, carved rosewood, the tall superstructure w/an arched & scroll-carved pediment centering a grape cluster cartouche above ring-turned & serpentine-shaped brackets centering a molded & arched tall central mirror flanked by narrower shaped side mirrors

Philadelphia Rococo Etagere

"Bradley's Infantry Game"

fronted by two shaped open
shelves w/slender ring- and rod-
turned spindle supports
continuing down to the molded
serpentine-fronted top, the lower
section w/a conforming apron
centered by a large carved
stylized shell above shaped
brackets centering at the back a
molded rectangular mirror
framed by four molded cabriole
legs w/small open oblong
shelves halfway down the front
legs & a serpentine-fronted base
shelf below the mirror, on
casters, Philadelphia, ca. 1850.,
20 x 53", 7' 10" h. (ILLUS.) **3,738.00**

GAMES & GAME BOARDS

"Bradley's Infantry Game,"
colorfully lithographed standup
cardboard soldiers, colorful box
top also showing soldiers, Milton
Bradley, early 20th c., missing
instructions (ILLUS top next
column)....................................**$132.00**

"Brownie Horseshoe Game,"
two lithographed tin targets &
stakes, four rubber horseshoes,
M.H. Miller, early 20th c.,
11⅜" d. **144.00**

"Game of India," board-type, box
cover w/tiger hunt scene,
instructions inside cover, playing
board on box bottom, teetotum,
sixteen tokens, Milton Bradley,
late 19th c., 14¼" sq. (cover
soiled, sides of cover & box
damaged) **115.00**

"Home Base Ball Game"

"Home Base Ball Game,"
instructions inside cover, playing
field on box bottom, teetotum,
fourteen wooden disc tokens,
colorful lithographed box cover
showing early batter & catcher,
McLoughlin Bros., 1897, half of
cover side missing, insect
damage on cover & sides, one
red & one yellow token missing,
box 10⅜ x 19⅝" (ILLUS. bottom,
previous page).........................**2,070.00**

**"Improved and Illustrated Game
of Dr. Busby (The),"** set of
twenty hand-colored engraved
cards of Dr. Busby Family,
servants & acquaintances,
contained in a slip case w/label
on front, instructions printed on
the back, Ives, Salem,
Massachusetts, ca. 1843, each
card 2 ⅛ x 3 9/16", the set (slight
edge wear) **173.00**

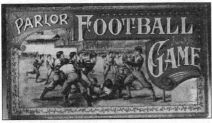

"Parlor Foot-Ball Game"

"Parlor Foot-Ball Game," board-
type, colorful early football game
scene on the box cover,
instructions inside box cover,
playing field on box bottom, two
teetotums, five tokens, one ball
piece, three tokens missing, box
cover side damaged in one
corner, McLoughlin Bros., 1891,
10⅜ x 19¾" (ILLUS. bottom,
previous column) **1,380.00**

Political marble game, a four-
part angled narrow wooden
marble runway supported
between to flat wood figures
cover w/colored lithographed
paper, one figure representing
Uncle Sam, the other John Bull,
American-made, late 19th c.,
20" l., 13" h. (losses to
lithographs)..............................**288.00**

**"The Newport Yacht Race - An
Exciting Game,"** board-type,
colorful box cover scene
w/children in a large rowboat & a
sailing yacht in one corner,
instructions inside box cover,
race course on box bottom,
teetotum, two yachts, box cover
side w/some damage, some
cover soiling, McLoughlin Bros.,
1891, 10⅜ x 19 ⅝"
(ILLUS. below)..........................**489.00**

"The Newport Yacht Race"

Early "Toonerville Trolley Game"

"Toonerville Trolley Game," colorfully lithographed box top showing the trolley & various cartoon strip characters, Milton Bradley, two dice cups, two large die, two characters missing (ILLUS.) **99.00**

GARDEN FOUNTAINS & ORNAMENTS

Ornamental garden or yard fountains, urns and figures often enhanced the formal plantings on spacious lawns of mansion-sized dwellings during the late 19th and early 20th century. While fountains were usually reserved for the lawns of estates, even modest homes often had a latticework arbor or cast-iron urn in the yard. Today garden enthusiasts look for these ornamental pieces to lend the aura of elegance to their landscape.

Garden Armillary

Armillary, wrought iron, painted, raised on wooden base, 7' 5" h. (ILLUS.) **$20,700.00**

Marble Garden Bench

Bench, marble, rectangular seat above scrolled legs, 4' 9" l. (ILLUS.) **5,175.00**

Cannons, cast steel, adjustable barrels on vine, rosette-cast base on wheels, ca. late 19th century, 45" l., 19" h., pr. **5,175.00**

Capitals, stone, leaf-carved Corinthian style in three-quarter round w/block-form back, 30" d., 22" h., pr. **3,163.00**

Figure of boy, marble, curly hair, arms outstretched holding lobed shell & sitting astride rusticated base, late 18th century, 28" h. **3,163.00**

Figure of a maiden, cast stone, standing contraposto w/arms shielding her inclined face, France, 45" h. **1,150.00**

Figure of Venus, marble, ribbon in hair & nude upper torso w/robe falling across bended knee, raised on shaped octagonal base, signed "P. Barzante, Florence," ca. late 19th century, 43¼" h. **8,625.00**

Figures of women, metal, white, classically draped & holding rhyton & circular shelf, H. DuMaige, France, ca. 1830-1888, 12" d., 40½" h., pr. (ILLUS. top next page) **3,450.00**

Fountain, bronze, figural nude of woman w/cupped arms over head, signed "Nanna Matheson Bijan," 26½" h. **6,325.00**

Fountain, cast metal, painted, circular standard w/three storks

Figures of Classical Ladies

among cattails & vining flowers, octagonal basin plumbed for water w/shaped rim decorated w/scallop shells & scrolling branches, raised circular plinth, 32¾" d., 39½" h. **1,495.00**

Marble Figural Garden Fountain

Fountain, marble, base formed as three putti w/sea urchins & raised arms supporting shell-form basin (ILLUS. bottom previous column) **14,950.00**

Marble Wall-Type Garden Fountain

Fountain, marble, wall-type, gadrooned oval dish surmounted by full-maned lion mask w/mouth plumbed for water (ILLUS.) **10,925.00**

Fountain, stone, mermaid-form, each holding a dolphin rising from water weeds, rockwork rectangular base, 44" l., 45" h., pr. **5,175.00**

Fountain, stone, clustering & entwining putti on dolphin above circular shell-shaped basin, supports similar basin centering putto holding cornucopia, France, 7' 10" h. **4,313.00**

Fountain, stone, depicts putto holding fish w/mouth plumbed for water, 4' h. **3,737.00**

Fountain, zinc, figural egret w/mouth plumbed for water, 46" h. **4,887.00**

Fountain back, stone, paneled arch centered by ram's head, France, 19th century, 25" w., 4'¼" h., pr. **1,955.00**

Gate posts, each in the form of a sphere w/cable-twist molded median band above coved circular socle & square plinth, mottled lichen patination, 18" h., pr. **1,610.00**

Jardiniere, terra-cotta, glazed & decorated w/alternating bands w/cherub masks & rosettes, 31" h. (repairs & missing handles)....................................**805.00**

Jardiniere, marble, sarcophagus-form, welled body hung w/berried & ribbon-tied ivy garlands centering satyr masks on opposing sides, each corner w/ram mask, 36" l. **10,925.00**

Jardiniere, stone, octagonal-form, allegorical panels decorating all sides, ca. 1900, 15½" h. **2,875.00**

Bacchus Marble Garden Mask

Mask, carved marble, bearded Bacchus w/open mouth & grapes leaves in wavy hair, 19th century, 15" h. (ILLUS.) **2,300.00**

Model of deer, cast iron, painted, 5' h...**6,325.00**

Model of monkey & cat, wrought iron, one modeled as monkey, one modeled as cat, Rococo-style w/each raised on carved limestone foliate & rockwork base, 21" h., pr. **17,250.00**

Models of lions, marble, each roaring, full-maned & advancing on rectangular plinth, 42" l., pr. **8,050.00**

Models of lions, stone, each seated on rectangular base, 43" h., pr. **3,450.00**

Pedestal, marble, oval-ended top w/coved frieze above panel-engraved front on conforming plinth, Italy, late 19th century, 17" d., 28½" w., 44½" h., 3 pcs. **3,263.00**

Pedestals, marble, circular coved top carved w/stylized foliage above ringed column, France, ca. late 19th century, 33" h., pr. **1,150.00**

Pedestals, stone, figural putti, one carrying basket of grapes, the second playing tambourine, both w/draped torso & sitting on globes, fluted tapering columnar form pedestals on stepped square plinths, 27½" h., pr.......**518.000**

Planters, cast iron, square-form w/pierce panels, corner supports w/leaftips ending in pine cone finials, 31" h., pr.....................**9,775.00**

Planters, wrought iron, scrolls headed by crown-form jardiniere & raised on scrolled legs, traces of paint, 4' 1" h., pr.................**5,175.00**

Seat, cast iron, painted w/fern patt., stamped "James W. Carr, Richmond VA.," 38" l. **3,737.00**

Seat, porcelain, decorated w/overall scrolls & flowers on pink ground, inscribed "England, 588," England, 20½" h...........**1,380.00**

Torchere, carved marble, white, three female figures supporting floral & gargooned circular dish raised on triangular rams heads,

laurel leaf-carved base, Greek
key-carved plinth, 6' 6½" h. **4,600.00**

Urn, cov., stone, inverted bell-
shape w/stepped domed &
lobed cover w/ovoid finial, lower
section cast w/Vitruvian
scrollwork over spiraling
acanthus, raised on spreading
circular socle cast w/foliage,
square plinth w/overhanging
projecting from capital & base,
on pedestal, 8' 2" h. **5,175.00**

Urn, cast stone, decorated
w/foliate swags, 23" h.............**6,325.00**

Cast-Iron Urn

Urns, cast-iron, each w/fluted
everted rim above lobed body &
leopard's head masks,
spreading circular socle on
square base, France, late 19th
century, 21" d., 15" h., pr........**1,495.00**

Urns, cast-iron, each w/deep
cavetto over lobed lower portion,
handles formed as grotesque
winged chimera, raised on
circular leaf-cast base, painted
dark green, France, ca. late 19th
century, 16½" h., pr. **1,093.00**

Urns, iron, each w/lobed body
beneath angular open handles
on beaded circular base,
France, late 19th century,
21" w., 19¼" h., pr. **2,070.00**

Neoclassical Garden Urn

Urn, cast stone, waisted inverted
bell-form w/gadrooned base,
raised on tinged socle on square
base, Neoclassical style, ca.
19th century, 29¼" h.
(ILLUS.) **2,588.00**

Urn, marble, gadrooned body
w/campana form, outswept rim
on waisted circular foot & square
base, 34" h. **6,900.00**

Urn, cast iron, painted, foliate-
cast body flanked w/scrolled
handles, on stand, 41" h.
(ILLUS. top next column)........**1,840.00**

Urns, cast iron, gadrooned body
flanked w/mask & ring handles,
12¾" h., pr. **1,725.00**

Urns, cast iron, tulip-form w/leaf-
tip rim over lobed vessel, raised
on molded lobe socle & square
plinth, late 19th century,
17¼" d., 20½" h., pr...............**2,185.00**

Urns, cast iron, painted, shaped
rims w/body centered by
cartouche flanked by scrolled
angular handles, stepped
square base w/egg & dart
borders, 23" h., pr..................**2,585.00**

Urns, marble, rim modeled w/two
satyrs & two rams masks hung
w/foliate swags, 28" d., 25" h.,
pr. **12,650.00**

GLASS

Also see: Antique Trader Books American Pressed Glass & Bottles Price Guide *and* American & European Decorative & Art Glass Price Guide.

AGATA

Agata was patented by Joseph Locke of the New England Glass Company in 1887. The application of mineral stain left a mottled effect on the surface of the article. It was applied chiefly to the Wild Rose (Peach Blow) line but sometimes was applied as a border on a pale opaque green. In production for a short time, it is scarce. Items listed below are of the Wild Rose line unless otherwise noted.

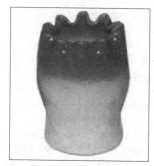

Fine Agata Spooner

Spooner, deeply ruffled lavender rim, 4½" h. (ILLUS.)................**$865.00**

Tumbler, even color & mottling, 3¾" h. **620.00**

Tumbler, dark mottling and gold tracery **785.00**

AKRO AGATE

This glass was made by the Akro Agate Company in Clarksburg, West Virginia between 1932 and 1951. The company was famous for their marble production but also produced many novelty items in various colors of marbleized glass and offered a popular line of glass children's dishes in plain colors and marbleized glass. Most articles bear the company mark of a crow flying through a capital letter A.

Akro Agate Mark

GENERAL LINE

Rare Apple Powder Jar

Ashtray, square, marbleized green & white, 3" w.....................**$7.00**

Ashtray, square, marbleized red & white, 3" w. **9.00**

Ashtray w/wood holder, square, marbleized blue & white, pr. **20.00**

Bowl, 9" d., tab-handled, green.....**50.00**

Candlesticks, tall, ribbed, green, 4¼" h., pr. **210.00**

Candlesticks, ink well-shaped, marbleized green & white, 2" h....**45.00**

Cornucopia vase, marbleized green & white, 3¼" h. **5.00**

Cosmetic container, model of a bell, No. 725, crystal...................**22.00**

Flowerpot, Graduated Dart patt., white, 4" h.................................**20.00**

Flowerpot, scalloped rim, Graduated Dart patt., No. 305, pumpkin, 4" h.............................**30.00**

Flowerpot, Stacked Disc patt., white, 2½" h.................................**13.00**

Jardiniere, square-mouthed, Ribs & Flutes patt., lime green, 5" h. ...**48.00**

Match holder, marbleized oxblood & white...........................**12.00**

Planter, oval, scalloped rim, Graduated Dart patt., ivory, 8½" l. **25.00**

Powder jar, cov., model of an apple, pumpkin orange (ILLUS. previous page.) **300.00**

Mexicali Powder Box

Powder box, hat-shaped cover, Mexicali patt., marbleized orange & white (ILLUS.).............................**45.00**

Urn, beaded top, square, footed, marbleized green & white, 3¼" h...**6.00**

Urn, Grecian, six-sided foot, marbleized green & white, 3¼" h...**6.00**

Urn, Grecian, six-sided foot, marbleized green, blue & white, 3¼" h. **6.00**

Vigil light, transparent red, 1⅞" h. **23.00**

CHILDREN'S DISHES

Boxed set: Octagonal patt., small, 21 pcs. **295.00**

Bowl, cereal, Concentric Ring patt., blue opaque.......................**25.00**

Creamer, Stacked Disc patt., green lustre, small **12.00**

Cup, Stacked Disc patt., blue **14.00**

Cup, Concentric Ring patt., rose, large **35.00**

Cup, open-handled, Octagonal patt., yellow, small **25.00**

Pitcher, cobalt blue, 2½" h. **35.00**

Pitcher, Stacked Disc, transparent green, 2¾" h............**15.00**

Plate, dinner, Interior Panel patt., marbleized blue & white **16.00**

Plate, dinner, Interior Panel patt., marbleized red & white **15.00**

Saucer, Interior Panel patt., marbleized red & white **12.00**

Sugar bowl, cov., Octagonal patt., pumpkin w/beige top, large, 1½" h. **25.00**

Sugar bowl, Interior Panel patt., green luster, small, 1¼" h. **15.00**

Teapot, cov., Interior Panel patt., marbleized blue & white, small....**45.00**

Teapot, cov., Octagonal patt., open-handled, turquoise..............**35.00**

Teapot, cov., Stacked Disc & Interior Panel patt., transparent blue (cobalt), large....................**125.00**

Teapot, cov., Trans Optic patt., topaz...**25.00**

Tea set: open-handled teapot w/lid, creamer & covered sugar bowl; Octagonal patt., turquoise, 3 pcs. **75.00**

AMBERINA

Amberina was developed in the late 1880s by the New England Glass Company and a pressed version was made by Hobbs, Brockunier & Company (under license from the former). A similar ware, called Rose Amber, was made by the Mt. Washington Glass Works. Amberina-Rose Amber shades from amber to deep red or fuchsia and cut and plated (lined with creamy white) examples were also made. The Libbey Glass Company briefly revived blown Amberina, using modern shapes, in 1917.

Amberina Mark

Bowl, 5½" d., ruffled rim **$200.00**

Bowl, 7⅛" sq., 2⅛" h., pressed
Daisy & Button patt....................**375.00**

Bowl, 8" d., 3½" h., Plated
Amberina **7,500.00**

Amberina Bowl & Mug

Bowl, 5¾" d., 3¾" h., squatty
bulbous body w/swirled molded
ribbing below the deeply ruffled
& crimped rim (ILLUS. right) **135.00**

Bowl, 6½" d., 6¾" h., deeply
ruffled flaring amber rim, applied
amber handles, applied amber
base forming feet.......................**350.00**

Bowls, individual berry, 5" d.,
square, pressed Daisy & Button
patt., set of 6.............................**500.00**

Butter dish, round blown cover in
Inverted Thumbprint patt.,
pressed Daisy & Button
underplate **198.00**

Castor set: four bottle w/mustard
jar, shaker, oil & vinegar cruets,
& one stopper; each bottle
engraved in Silver plate frame,
the set.......................................**985.00**

Celery vase, Diamond Quilted
patt., New England Glass Co.,
6½" h. **375.00**

**Cruet w/amber faceted
matching stopper,** smooth
applied amber handle, Inverted
Thumbprint patt., 6" h. **425.00**

**Cruet w/original mold-blown
amber ball stopper,** wide flat
base w/rounded cylindrical body
w/swirled optic ribbing to the
cylindrical neck w/pinched
spout, applied amber handle,
4¼" d., 8⅝" h. (ILLUS.)..............**225.00**

Large Amberina Cruet

Cruet w/original stopper, Plated
Amberina **8,500.00**

Dish, sawtooth rim, pressed
Daisy & Button patt., Gillinder
Glass Co., 4¼" d., 6⅛" l. **375.00**

Finger bowls, squared rim above
a rounded Hobnail bowl,
polished pontil, 4¼" w., 2⅞" h.,
the set.......................................**450.00**

Goblet, rose to amber w/ribbing
effect, 3⅜" d., 6⅛" h. **125.00**

Ice bucket, Diamond Optic patt.
w/cut star on base, tab handles,
6¾" d., 5" h. **700.00**

Lamp globe, 6½" across at
widest, 6½" deep, 3" d. fitter......**145.00**

Unusual Amberina Hall Lantern

Lantern, hall-type, kerosene, the large teardrop-form shade w/an Inverted Thumbprint design, brass fittings at the top & bottom, 6¾" d., 12½" h. (ILLUS. bottom previous page)..............**350.00**

Mug, barrel-shaped swirled optic-ribbed body on an applied disc foot, amber twisted rope handle w/end curl, heavily decorated w/gold flowers & leaves, 2¾" d., 4⅝" h. (ILLUS. left, with bowl) ...**150.00**

Mug, barrel-shaped body w/wafer foot, cranberry to golden amber, applied amber rope handle, 2⅝" d., 4¾" h. **65.00**

Tall Amberina Mug

Mug, tall cylindrical body swelled at the base, wide swirled ribs up the sides to a plain rim, applied amber ropetwist C-form handle, decorated w/gilt stems w/flowers & leaves, 2½" d., 5½" h. (ILLUS.) **165.00**

Pitcher, milk, tricorner rim, applied amber handle, Inverted Honeycomb patt., Mt. Washington Glass Co., 5" h. **150.00**

Pitcher, 6" h., tricorner rim, Inverted Thumbprint patt. **400.00**

Pitcher, 6¾" h., ten-panel tankard form w/applied amber reeded handle.......................................**450.00**

Pitcher, 8" h., tricorner rim, Inverted Thumbprint patt., ...**475.00**

Plate, 4¾" d., flared rim, Diamond Quilted patt., Mt. Washington Glass Co..................**95.00**

Plate, 7" d., Inverted Thumbprint patt. **160.00**

Punch cup, applied threaded handle, New England Glass Co...**90.00**

Punch cup, eighteen optic ribs, New England Glass Co., 2½" h...**185.00**

Salt shaker w/original two piece lid, Baby Thumbprint patt., bulging dual mold-blown body, 2½" h. **235.00**

Spooner, Diamond Quilted patt., New England Glass Co., 4½" h. **235.00**

Toothpick holder, square mouth, Diamond Quilted patt., New England Glass, Co. **190.00**

Trinket dish, wide flared rim, Diamond Quilted patt., Mt. Washington Glass Co., 4¾" d. ..**195.00**

Tumbler, flat, Inverted Thumbprint patt., 2¾" d., 3¾" h. **65.00**

Vase, 5" h., 5¾" w. jack-in-the-pulpit form, signed "Libbey" **1,200.00**

Vase, 5¼" h., 3⅝" d., bulbous ovoid body w/dimpled sides tapering to a short neck w/a flaring crimped rim, decorated w/enameled white blossoms, blue leaves & gold vines............**225.00**

Vase, 6¾" h., 3⅞" d., a narrow cushion foot below the wide cylindrical body w/an optic ribbed swirled design, finely enameled w/white blossoms & green leaves (ILLUS. top next page) **195.00**

Vase, 7" h., trumpet-form, wafer foot **550.00**

Cylindrical Amberina Vase

Vase, 7½" h., cylindrical, elongated, Inverted Thumbprint patt. **175.00**

Water set: tall pitcher & eight matching tall tumblers; the cylindrical pitcher w/an optic rib design to the rounded shoulder & the wide cylindrical neck w/a pinched spout, applied amber handle, each tumbler w/matching optic ribbing, pitcher, 4¾" d., 10" h., tumbler 2⅝" d., 5¼" h., the set (ILLUS. below)..........................**495.00**

ANIMALS

Americans evidently like to collect glass animals and, for the past sixty years, American glass manufacturers have turned out a wide variety of animals to please the buying public. Some were produced for long periods and some were later reproduced by other companies, while others were made for only a short period of time and are rare. We have not included late productions in our listings and have attempted to date the productions where possible. Evelyn Zemel's book, American Glass Animals A to Z, *will be helpful to the novice collector. Another helpful book is* Glass Animals of the Depression Era *by Lee Garmon and Dick Spencer (Collector Books, 1993).*

Angelfish, amber, Viking Glass Co., 1957, 6½" h......................**$43.00**

Bear, mama, clear, New Martinsville Glass Mfg. Co., 6" l., 4" h. **225.00**

Bunny "Cotton Tail" dispenser, ears down, Paden City Glass Co., clear **95.00**

Bunny "Cotton Tail" dispenser, ears down, Paden City Glass Co., pink **125.00**

Duck ashtray, clear, Duncan & Miller Glass Co., large, 6" d........**40.00**

Duck, orange, Viking Glass Company, 1960s, 9" h. **65.00**

Large Amberina Water Set

Eagle book end, clear, Cambridge Glass Co., 4" base d., 6" w. wing spread, 6" h. **53.00**

Eagle book end, clear, Fostoria Glass Co., 1938-44, 3 x 4½" base, 7¼" h. **125.00**

Fish on base, dark medium blue, Viking Glass Co., 1960s, 10" h. **28.00**

Gazelle, clear, A.H. Heisey & Co., 1947-49, 3¼" l., 10¾" h. **1,450.00**

Goose (The Fat Goose), clear, Duncan & Miller Glass Co., 6" l., 6½" h. **275.00**

Goose girls, pigtailed little girl w/two geese on oval base, clear, L.E. Smith Glass Co., 7¾", the set..............**75.00**

Goose, wings down, A.H. Heisey & Co., not signed, 2" h., 10¼" l. **225.00**

Hen, head down, New Martinsville Glass Mfg. Co., crystal, 5" h. **45.00**

Horse, head up, clear, New Martinsville Glass Mfg. Co., 8" h. **90.00**

Horse, Plug (Sparky), clear, A.H. Heisey & Co., 1941-46, 4" l., 4" h. **115.00**

Horse, pony standing, clear, A.H. Heisey & Co., 1942-52, 1½ x 2¼" base, 3" l., 5" h. **95.00**

Horse, pony standing, tall, Paden City Glass Co., 4½" chest to tail, 3 x 5½" base, 12" h. **95.00**

Horse Head book ends, clear, A.H. Heisey & Co., 1937-55, 6¼" l., 7¼" h., pr. **125.00**

Horse Head book ends, frosted clear, A.H. Heisey & Co., 1937-55, 2¾ x 4¼" base, 7¼" h., pr. ...**165.00**

Horse Head bookends, clear, A.H. Heisey & Co., 1937-55, 2¾ x 4¼" base, 7¼" h., pr. **165.00**

Horse jumping book end, clear, hollow base, American Glass Co., 8" h.....................**35.00**

Horse rearing book ends, L.E. Smith Glass Co., 3 x 5½" base, 8" h., the set **110.00**

Horse w/cart (same as donkey & cart), K.R. Haley Glass Co., 9⅜" l., 4⅛" h. **35.00**

Owl book ends, owl on tree limb, clear, Fostoria Glass Co., 1943, 7½" h., pr. **250.00**

Panther, walking, amber, Indiana Glass Co., 7" l., 3½" h. **195.00**

Piglet, standing, clear, New Martinsville Glass Mfg. Co., 2" l., 1¼" h. **145.00**

Pouter Pigeon, Paden City Glass Co., crystal, 5" h. **85.00**

Ringneck Pheasant, clear, standing in grass w/blossoms, A.H. Heisey & Co., 1942-53, 11" l., 4¾" h. **145.00**

Rooster, head down, K.R. Haley Glassware Co., green, 9" h. **55.00**

Seal, baby w/ball, clear, New Martinsville Glass Mfg. Co., 2¼" w., 4¾" h. **65.00**

Sparrow, clear, A.H. Heisey & Co., 1942-45, 4" l., 2¼" h. at raised tail **145.00**

Squirrel book end, clear, New Martinsville Glass Mfg. Co., 6¼ x 2¼" base, 5½" h., ...**45.00**

Squirrel, running, olive green, Fostoria Glass Co., No. 2631/703 "B", 1965-73 ....**35.00**

Squirrel, sitting, olive green, Fostoria Glass Co., No. 2631/1702A, ca. 1965-73, ...**28.00**

Swan dish, Janice Line, New Martinsville Glass Mfg. Co., clear, 12" l...................**55.00**

Swan dish, large, clear, L.E. Smith Glass Co., 1930s, 8½" h. ..**23.00**

Swan, open, chartreuse, Duncan & Miller Glass Co., 7" l...............**65.00**

APPLIQUÉD

Simply stated, this is an art glass form with applied decoration. Sometimes master glass craftsmen applied stems or branches to an art glass object and then added molded glass flowers or fruit specimens to these branches or stems. At other times a button of molten glass was daubed on the object and a tool pressed over it to form a prunt in the form of a raspberry, rosette or other shape. Always the work of a skilled glassmaker, applied decoration can be found on both cased (two-layer) and single layer glass. The English firm of Stevens and Williams was renowned for the appliquéd glass they produced.

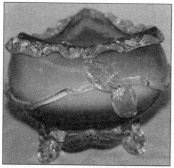

Cranberry & Vaseline Appliqued Bowl

Bowl, 5⅜" d., 4¾" h., squatty bulbous wide body in light cranberry opalescent tapering to a tricorner rim applied w/a vaseline ruffle, a vaseline vine & leaves wrapped around the sides & the base raised on vaseline wishbone feet (ILLUS.) **$295.00**

Bowl, 6" d., 4¼" h., a small footring supports w/wide rounded base w/slightly flaring cylindrical sides, blue overshot on a clear ground, applied amber rigaree around the rim, applied blue & white blossoms, green leaves & a pale purple branch around the lower body (ILLUS. below, right)..................**225.00**

Bowl, 6" d., 5" h., Diamond Quilt patt., white w/flared rim, citron applied Matsu-no-ke style decoration w/leaves & daisy-shaped flowers on twisted tree stems, brown stems supporting bowl, single frosted rosette on pontil **600.00**

Bowl, 12½" d., 7" h., bulbous body w/applied glass strawberries, green leaves, amber stems, handles & feet on pinkish blue background, pink opalescent ruffled rim **2,475.00**

Box w/hinged cover, round, squatty bulbous opalescent base raised on gilt brass feet & w/gilt brass mounts, the domed cover applied w/a red blossoms in the center of curved lavender vines & green leaves w/a red bud at the tip, 5½" d., 4½" h. **495.00**

Pitcher, 8¾" h., ovoid body w/heart-shaped ruffled rim, rose

Appliqued Bowl & Vase

to pink exterior w/white interior, applied glass ruffled leaf in amber & cranberry, crystal handle.................................**1,020.00**

Vase, 3" h., 3⅛" d., ball-shaped , chartreuse green ground applied overall w/rows of crystal leaves **115.00**

Vase, 3¾" h., 2½" d., rounded egg shaped, amber ground decorated overall w/applied clear leaves & raised on applied amber leaf feet **145.00**

Vase, 4¾" h., 3⅛" d., bulbous cylindrical body on a small base & tapering to a wide, short cylindrical neck, the white body w/an applied amber rim, an applied amber branch w/large blue leaves & plum on the sides (ILLUS. bottom previous page, left) **125.00**

Vase, 5" h., 3" d., ovoid body tapering to a four-lobed rim, rose pink cased in white, clear applied thorny rim band, clear applied flowers & leaves around the body, raised on slender applied clear feet **118.00**

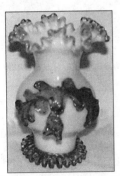

White & Amber Appliqued Vase

Vase, 7⅛" h., 4¼" d., bulbous baluster-form w/a deeply ruffled & crimped rim, opaque white w/a thin applied amber rim band, two large cranberry & amber applied leaves & an amber bellflower, an applied crimped band around the foot (ILLUS.) **135.00**

Vase, 9¼" h., 6" d., the amber optic-ribbed conical body flaring to a wide tapering shoulder centered by a short cylindrical neck, clear applied rigaree around the shoulder & down the sides, the smooth panels enameled w/dainty blue, white & gold blossoms & green leaves w/additional gold trim, raised on applied slender clear legs...**195.00**

Tall Squared Appliqued Vase

Vase, 14¼" h., 5¼" d., tall squared form w/a bulbous base & tall neck, pale pink opalescent optic ribbed body applied w/large vaseline leaves & vines & an oversized tulip-form vaseline opalescent blossom (ILLUS.)......................**550.00**

ART GLASS BASKETS

Popular novelties in the late Victorian era, these ornate baskets of glass were usually hand-crafted of free-blown or mold-blown glass. They were made in a wide spectrum of colors and shapes. Pieces were highlighted with tall applied handles and often applied feet, however fancier ones might also carry additional appliquéd trim.

Blue, wide squatty bulbous body w/a swirled optic rib design tapering up to a wide rolled & crimped rim w/one side turned up, an applied clear handle from side to side, 5½" d., 6" h.........**$135.00**

Cased, flared ribbed bowl w/clear applied handle, white exterior, deep rose interior, clear edging around ruffled rim, 5" d., 4¼" h. **69.00**

Spangled Art Glass Basket

Cranberry Art Glass Basket

Cranberry, ovoid body w/a deeply ruffled & crimped flaring rim w/a shaped applied clear handle, 4½" d., 6¼" h. (ILLUS.) **150.00**

Opaline, applied sapphire blue edge at ruffled rim, applied leaf & flower on front & looped handle, 5¾" d., 9½" h. **385.00**

Spangled, spherical body w/a four-lobed rim pulled into points, amber w/cream & brown spatter & gold aventurine over deep cranberry, applied amber handle, 4½" d., 6½" h. **355.00**

Spangled, melon-lobed body w/a widely flaring crimped & ruffled rim, yellow, white & maroon spangled interior, white exterior,

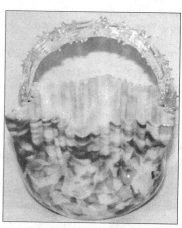

Spatter Art Glass Basket

applied clear loop handle, 5½ x 6½", 7½" h. (ILLUS. top) **150.00**

Spatter, swirled body w/crimped rim, light blue w/white spatter, applied blue thorn handle, 5" d., 6" h. **165.00**

Spatter, spherical body w/an upright crimped & ruffled rim, white interior, aqua, oxblood, light brown & white spatter exterior, applied clear thorn handle, 5" d., 6¼" h. (ILLUS. bottom) **175.00**

Spatter, conical crimped body in blue & white spatter in clear,

clear applied handle, 4⅝" d.,
5½" h. **85.00**

Vaseline opalescent, slender
swelled cylindrical body w/large
applied leaves around the rim &
a pointed applied handle, optic
swirled design in the basket,
2¾" d., 6" h. **125.00**

Cased, the footed body w/a
squatty wide base tapering to a
wide crimped & ruffled rim,
opaque white exterior & deep
pink interior, an applied amber
rim band & a large amber &
cranberry ruffled applied leaf
around the center, applied
amber handle, attributed to
Stevens & Williams, 6" d., 7½" h.
(ILLUS. below center)................**265.00**

Green, a tapering bulbous body
w/an optic ribbed design applied
around the rim w/large ribbed &
pointed clear petals, applied
twisted loop pointed handle,
4⅝" d., 6¾" h. (ILLUS.
below left) **110.00**

Spatter, a short cylindrical body
w/two widely rolled sides, dark
green w/fine white spatter on the
exterior, raised on clear applied
petal feet, clear applied pointed
loop handle, 4¼" d., 6" h.
(ILLUS. right) **95.00**

BLOWN THREE MOLD

Miniature Blown-Three-Mold Creamer

This type of glass was entirely or partially blown in a mold and was popular from about 1820 to 1840. The object was formed and the decoration impressed upon it by blowing the glass into a metal mold, usually of three but sometimes more sections, hinged together. Mold-blown glass actually dates back to ancient times. Recent research reveals that certain geometric patterns were reproduced in the 1920s and some new pieces, usually sold through museum gift shops, are still available.

Varied Art Glass Baskets

Collectors are urged to read all recent information available. Reference numbers are from George L. and Helen McKearin's book, American Glass.

Bottle, geometric, barrel-shaped w/a slender tall cylindrical neck w/applied sloping flat double collar, attributed to Keene, New Hampshire, olive green, pint (GII-7) **$1,210.00**

Bowl, 4¼" d., 1⅝" h., geometric, widely flaring sides w/a small base, folded rim, clear (GII-18)..**132.00**

Bowl, 5⅞" d., 1⅜" h., geometric, widely flaring shallow sides w/a folded rim, rayed base w/pontil, clear (GIII-6) **143.00**

Bowl, 8¾" d., 1¾" h., wide round shallow form w/upright sides w/a folded rim, rayed base w/a pontil, clear (GIII-20).................**440.00**

Carafe, geometric, ovoid body w/wide bands of vertical wide ribbing alternating w/bands of wide rings at the base & shoulder, short cylindrical neck w/flaring rim, attributed to the Mount Vernon Glass Works, quart, bluish green (GI-29) **1,430.00**

Celery vase, geometric, cylindrical body w/flared rim, on applied solid foot w/iron pontil, clear, GIII-34 (shallow lip flake) **1,650.00**

Creamer, miniature, geometric, wide ovoid body tapering to a flared tooled rim w/pinched spout, rayed base w/pontil, applied solid handle w/end curl, 3" h. ,GIII-21 (ILLUS. previous page) **468.00**

Creamer, Baroque, cylindrical body w/a tapering ribbed shoulder to the tall widely flaring neck w/a wide spout, applied strap handle w/medial rib, end curl missing, clear, 4½" h. (GV-8) **330.00**

Creamer, geometric, wide ovoid body tapering to a high flaring neck w/pinched spout & tooled rim, applied solid ribbed strap handle w/end curl, clear, 4" h., GIII-6 (small chip inside spout)..**605.00**

Creamer, geometric, tapering cylindrical body w/a widely flaring rim & spout, applied handle w/end curl, purplish blue, 4¼" h. (GIII-26).....................**2,420.00**

Decanter w/period pressed waffle stopper, miniature, geometric, bulbous body on a disc foot, tapering to a ringed neck w/flanged rim, probably blown from a stopper mold, 3½" h. (GII-18)..........................**880.00**

Rare Blue Baroque Decanter

Decanter w/original hollow blown unpatterned stopper,. baroque patt., tapering ribbed & scroll-molded body w/a flanged rim, hint of stain on interior bottom, tiny open bubble on rim, sapphire blue, quart, GV-8 (ILLUS.) **2,475.00**

Decanter w/original ribbed hollow stopper, geometric, wide upper & lower bands of ribbing flanking a central narrow horizontal band embossed w/"BRANd/y," tall cylindrical neck w/flanged rim, smooth base w/pontil, clear, quart, GI-8 (stem of stopper cracked, slight residue in base) **440.00**

Decanter w/pattern molded hollow stopper, geometric, wide ovoid body tapering to a slender neck w/a flanged rim, rayed base w/pontil, clear, quart (GII-24) **303.00**

Decanter w/pattern molded acorn stopper, geometric, ovoid body tapering to a slender neck w/a flanged rim, clear, quart (GIII-5) **220.00**

Decanter w/blown patterned hollow stopper, geometric, bulbous ovoid body tapering to a slender neck w/three applied ribbed rings & a flanged mouth, diamond base w/pontil, clear, 10½" h. (GII-18) **187.00**

Decanter w/no stopper, geometric, ovoid body tapering to a tall tapering neck w/flat mouth, rayed base w/pontil, olive green, pint (GIII-16)...........**385.00**

Decanter w/no stopper, geometric, ovoid body w/spiraling ribs up the shoulder to the slender cylindrical neck w/flanged rim, smooth base w/tubular pontil, attributed to the Mount Vernon Glass Company, olive green, quart, GIII-2, high spot wear, small flake on edge of lip **2,200.00**

Decanters w/original blown patterned stoppers, geometric, ovoid body tapering to a triple-ring neck w/flanged rim, clear, pint, pr. (GII-18) **275.00**

Dish, geometric, wide flaring shallow sides w/a folded rim, ribbed base w/pontil, clear, 4⅞" d. (GIII-24) **77.00**

Dish, geometric, shallow low-sided round form w/folded rim &

rayed base w/pontil, clear, 6" d. (GIII-24) **66.00**

Dish, geometric, shallow round form w/upright sides w/a folded rim, rayed base w/pontil, clear, small (GII-1).............................**154.00**

Flip glass, geometric, tapering cylindrical form, tooled rim, rayed base w/pontil, clear, 4⅞" h., GIII-14 (rim slightly ground) **121.00**

Flip glass, geometric, slightly tapering cylindrical form, elongated tooled rim, smooth base w/pontil, clear, 4¼" d., 6" h.(GIII-22) **275.00**

Flip glass, geometric, cylindrical w/tooled rim, 15-diamond base w/pontil, clear, some flat open bubbles on the interior, 4½" d., 6" h. (GIII-18) **110.00**

Model of a top hat, geometric, slightly tapering cylindrical form w/a rolled, folded rim, 'pinwheel' pattern base w/faint pontil, clear, 2¼" h. (GII-13).........................**110.00**

Model of a top hat, geometric, tapering cylindrical sides w/a wide rolled rim, sapphire blue, 2¼" h. (GII-18).........................**715.00**

Model of a top hat, geometric, rolled rim, cobalt blue, 2½" d., 2⅜" h. (GIII-23).........................**495.00**

Mug, geometric, cylindrical w/applied strap handle, rayed base w/cylindrical pontil, clear, 2¼" d., 2¾" h. (GIII-13)..............**715.00**

Mug, geometric, cylindrical w/tooled rim & applied ribbed strap handle, clear, 3" d., 3½" h. (GIII-18) **330.00**

Mustard bottle w/tam stopper, geometric, cylindrical, slightly tapering at the short neck to a flaring, flattened rim supporting the wide stopper flange, rayed base w/pontil, clear, 4½" h. (GIII-28) **385.00**

Pitcher, miniature, 2" h., geometric, ovoid body tapering to a widely flaring rim & spout, applied solid handle w/end curl, clear (GIII-5) **825.00**

Pitcher, 4⅝" h., geometric, ovoid body tapering to a widely flaring neck w/wide spout & tooled rim, applied hollow ribbed strap handle w/end curl, 16-diamond base w/pontil, clear (GII-18) **358.00**

Salt dip, geometric, model of a top hat, cylindrical slightly tapering sides to a wide flattened folded brim, rayed base w/pontil, clear, 1½" h. GIII-4) **159.00**

Salt dip, geometric, bulbous body w/a galleried rim raised on a short pedestal & diamond design round foot, clear, 2½" h. (GII-18) **248.00**

Rare Blown Three Mold Salt

Salt dip, geometric, tapering inverted bell-form bowl w/incurved galleried rim, on a flaring ribbed foot, sapphire blue, 2½" h., GIII-13 (ILLUS.)...**1,045.00**

Salt dip, geometric, tapering inverted bell-form bowl on a flaring foot, sapphire blue (GIII-23) **770.00**

Shaker w/original metal pressure cap, cylindrical body tapering to the cap, clear, 4¾" h. (GII-44) **83.00**

Shakers w/original copper pressure caps, smooth base

without pontils, clear, 4 ¼" h. GIV-4 , pr. (unseen flaking under caps)....................................**132.00**

Shot glass, geometrical, flaring cylindrical form, plain rim, clear, 2¼" h. (GII-19).........................**88.00**

Sugar bowl, cov., geometric, squatty bulbous body tapering to a wide galleried rim w/an inset domed cover w/button finial, the rayed applied solid base w/a pontil, clear, 5¾" h. (GII-22) ...**4,950.00**

Toilet bottle w/original solid tam stopper, ribbed, tapering ovoid body w/ringed neck, swirled narrow ribbing, folded flanged lip, cobalt blue, 6 ¼" h. (GI-3, type 2) **209.00**

Tumbler, geometric, barrel-shaped w/plain rim, rayed base w/pontil, clear, 2½" h. (GIII-21)..**209.00**

Tumbler, geometric, cylindrical, tooled rim, rayed base w/pontil, 2½" d., 2¾" h. (GIII-13)..............**154.00**

Tumbler, geometric, flaring cylindrical form, sheared plain rim, plain base w/pontil, clear, 3¾" h. (GII-33) **110.00**

Wine, geometric, tapering cylindrical bowl applied to a ringed cylindrical slender stem on an applied round foot, 4¼" h. (GII-22) **550.00**

BRIDE'S BASKETS & BOWLS

These berry or fruit bowls were popular late Victorian wedding gifts, hence the name.

Cased bowl, apricot shaded to white interior w/enameling, white exterior, deeply scalloped rim, satin finish, Meridan silver plate frame w/birds, 15" d.,..............**$795.00**

Cased bowl, blue satin interior w/white satin exterior, oval bowl w/pleated rim , applied frosted ribbon edge, ornate silver plated footed Forbes frame, 12½" h., 10½" d. **250.00**

Green Cased Lattice Design Bowl

Cased Pink Decorated Bride's Basket

Cased bowl, dark green shaded to white satin interior w/an embossed lattice design around the ruffled rim, white exterior, 11½" d., 3⅝" h. (ILLUS.)............**225.00**

Cased bowl, dark pigeon blood shaded to a soft cranberry to a creamy custard interior w/white exterior, flared, ribbed bowl, very ornate high footed frame, resilvered, overall 11½" x 14" h. **350.00**

Shaded Lavender Bride's Bowl

Cased bowl, lavender shaded to yellow interior decorated w/delicate gilt florals & leaves, yellow exterior, crimped rim sections w/two sides folded inward, 10 x 10⅝", 4" h. (ILLUS.) **295.00**

Cased bowl, pink shaded to white interior decorated w/ornate white enameled flowers & large gold leaves on vines, deeply fluted crimped rim, white exterior, in a simple silver plate resilvered framed w/a conical foot, bowl 11" d., overall 4" h. (ILLUS.) **495.00**

Cased bowl, pink mother-of-pearl satin Herringbone patt. exterior & yellow interior, decorated w/yellow chrysanthemums, lobed bulbous body w/scalloped rim, silver plate holder supported by three cupids, inscribed "1897," 10½" d., 13" h.............**2,380.00**

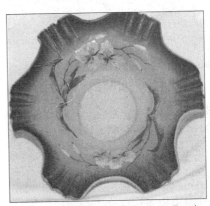

Shaded Purple Satin Bride's Bowl

Cased bowl, purple shaded to white satin interior decorated w/white & yellow enameled orchids w/green & brown leaves, six-lobed crimped rim, white exterior, 10¼" d., 3¼" h. (ILLUS.) **295.00**

Pink Bride's Bowl on Silver Stand

Pink shaded to white satin interior, applied clear rim band, flaring ribbed sides w/deeply fluted & crimped edges, white exterior, raised on a silver plate pedestal base w/flaring foot, 7¾" d., 5½" h. (ILLUS.)..............**210.00**

BURMESE

Burmese is a single-layer glass that shades from pink to pale yellow. It was patented by Frederick S. Shirley and made by the Mt. Washington Glass Co. A license to produce the glass in England was granted to Thomas Webb & Sons, which called its articles Queen's Burmese. Gundersen Burmese was made briefly about the middle of this century, and the Pairpoint Crystal Company is making limited quantities at the present time.

Bowl, squatty bulbous body w/floral decoration, footring, 6¼" d., 3¾" h. **$1,110.00**

Bowl, ruffled rim, 9" d. **350.00**

Bowls, butterfly rim folds tapering to short cylindrical base, interior decorated w/orange flowers & gold leaves, silver plated footed frame tapering to twining calla lilies to form handle, calla lily handles on matching spoons, Thos Webb & Sons Patented, 5¾" d., 3 ¼" h., pr. (one bowl slightly darker) **1,675.00**

Cruet w/original mushroom stopper, melon-ribbed body, Mt. Washington Glass Co., 6¾" h. **1,085.00**

Custard cup, flared rim, applied yellow handle, glossy finish, Mt. Washington Glass Co., 2⅞" h. ..**450.00**

Mustard pot w/silver plate hinged lid, collar & bail handle, barrel-shaped w/vertical ribbing, Mt. Washington Glass Co., 4½" h. **375.00**

Pitcher, tankard-type, Mt. Washington Glass Co., 9½" h. **895.00**

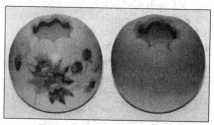

Two Miniature Rose Bowls

Rose bowl, miniature, spherical w/an eight-crimp top, satin finish decorated w/enameled lavender five-petal flowers w/green & brown leaves, attributed to Thomas Webb, 2⅜" d., 2⅜" h. (ILLUS. left) **335.00**

Rose bowl, miniature, spherical w/an eight-crimp top, satin finish, attributed to Thomas Webb, 2½" d., 2½" h. (ILLUS. right) **195.00**

Rose bowl, miniature, spherical w/an eight-crimp top, satin finish, 3" d., 3" h.......................**210.00**

Tazza, bowl on short stem joined by a glass wafer, 7" d., 4½" h. **550.00**

Toothpick holder, Diamond Quilted patt., satin finish, Mt. Washington Glass Co...............**385.00**

Tumbler, enameled yellow roses decoration, Mt. Washington Glass Co., 3¾" h. **465.00**

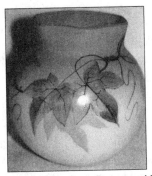

Decorated Miniature Burmese Vase

Vase, miniature, 2½" h., scalloped top, signed Webb **525.00**

Vase, miniature, 3¾" h., 3¼" d., spherical body tapering to a short hexagonal neck, the sides enameled w/green, yellow & brown ivy leaves, satin finish, attributed to Thomas Webb (ILLUS.) **395.00**

Vase, miniature, 3¾" h., 4¼" d., eight deep lobed sections continue to the flaring rim, decorated w/ivy in shades of green **480.00**

Vase, 8" h., double gourd-shaped, decorated w/peach-colored roses & turquoise-colored for-get-me-not blossoms, Mt. Washington Glass Co.............**1,250.00**

Vase, 12" h., decorated w/a scene of pyramids, sacred ibis & desert oasis, Mt. Washington Glass Co. (drilled ⅜" hole in base) **2,750.00**

Vase, 23½" h., lily-form, Mt. Washington Glass Co.............**1,250.00**

Vases, 6½" h., two-handled, footed, rare ginkgo leaf decoration, Mt. Washington Glass Co., pr. **2,100.00**

Vases, 12" h., swelled cylindrical form w/flaring neck & footring, decorated w/flowering vines & two small birds on each, pr.....**5,030.00**

Whisky taster, satin finish, probably Webb, 2½" d., 2⅞" h...**150.00**

CAMBRIDGE

The Cambridge Glass Company was founded in Ohio in 1901. Numerous pieces are now sought, especially those designed by Arthur J. Bennett, including Crown Tuscan. Other productions included crystal animals, "Black Amethyst," "blanc opaque," and other types of colored glass. The firm was finally closed in 1954. It should not be confused with the New England Glass Co., Cambridge, Massachusetts.

NEAR CUT

Cambridge Marks

Ashtray, pressed Caprice patt., yellow, 3" d. **$14.00**

Ashtray, three-footed, shell-shaped, pressed Caprice patt., Moonlight blue, 2¾" d.................**15.00**

Basket, handled, tall waisted body w/two sides of the rim pulled up & joined by the high arched handle, etched Rose Point patt., No. 119, Crystal, 7" h. **525.00**

Basket, two-handled, footed, etched Wildflower patt., Crystal, 6" h. **45.00**

Bonbon, square, footed, pressed Caprice patt., Moonlight blue, 6" d. **37.00**

Bonbon, two-handled, footed, etched Wildflower patt., Crystal, 6" d. **23.00**

Bouillon cup w/saucer, two-handled, etched Cleo patt., Decagon line, green, 2 pcs..........**40.00**

Bowl, fruit, 5" d., crimped rim, pressed Caprice patt., Moonlight blue..**95.00**

Bowl, fruit, 5" d., pressed Caprice patt., Moonlight blue **50.00**

Bowl, fruit, 5¾" d., flat rim, Decagon line, green **15.00**

Bowl, 9" d., four-footed, etched
Rose Point patt., No. 3400,
Crystal **72.00**

Bowl, 10½" d., crimped-edge,
footed, pressed Caprice patt.,
Crystal **30.00**

Bowl, flower or fruit, 10½" l.,
footed, Statuesque line, Flying
Lady patt., seashell bowl w/nude
lady at one end, No. 30011/40,
Crystal (ILLUS.) **468.00**

Bowl, 12" d., four-footed,
handled, Corinth (No. 3900) line,
Crystal **125.00**

Bowl, 12½" d., bell-shaped, four-
footed, pressed Caprice patt.,
Moonlight blue **125.00**

Bowl, 13" d., crimped-edge, four-
footed, pressed Caprice patt.,
Moonlight blue **110.00**

Bowl, vegetable, 9½" l., oval,
Decagon line, etched Cleo patt.,
pink...**115.00**

**Candelabrum w/bobeches &
prisms,** two-light, etched Rose
Point patt., Crystal, the set **195.00**

Candlestick, three-light, pressed
Caprice patt., No. 74, Crystal **35.00**

Candlestick, three-light, Decagon
line, green.................................**35.00**

Candlesticks, Martha
Washington line, Crystal,
9" h. pr. **60.00**

Candlesticks, Mt. Vernon line,
Crystal, 4" h., pr. **30.00**

Candlesticks, one-light, keyhole
stem, gold-encrusted etched
Rose Point patt., 5" h., pr. **75.00**

Candlesticks, two-light, etched
Wildflower patt., shape No. 647,
Crystal, pr. **95.00**

Candy box, cov., etched Rose
Point patt., No. 3400/9, Crystal,
7" d. **175.00**

Candy box, cov., etched gold-
encrusted Rose Point patt.,
No. 3500/57, Crystal, 8" d. **150.00**

Candy box, cov., etched Rose
Point patt., No. 3500/57, Crystal,
8" d. **105.00**

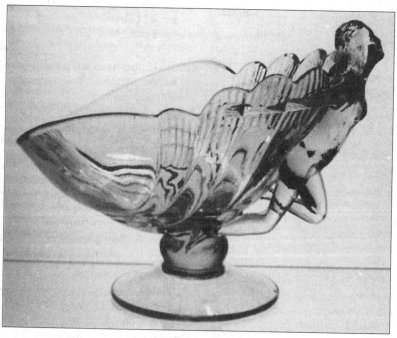

Flying Lady Flower Bowl

Candy dish, cov., pressed Alpine Caprice patt., Crystal.................**60.00**

Candy dish, cov., three-footed, pressed Alpine Caprice patt., Moonlight blue **100.00**

Cheese & cracker set: 5½" d. comport & 11½" d. plate; etched Rose Point patt., Crystal, the set.......................................**115.00**

Cigarette box, cov., triangular, pressed Caprice patt., Moonlight blue, 3 x 3"................................**65.00**

Clarets, Line #1066, red, 4½ oz., set of 6.......................................**135.00**

Coaster, pressed Caprice patt., Crystal, 3½" d. **13.00**

Cocktail, Amethyst in Farberware holder **13.00**

Cocktail, etched Apple Blossom patt., No. 3130, yellow, 3 oz. **24.00**

Cocktail, blown Caprice patt., No. 300, Moonlight blue, 3 oz......**40.00**

Cocktail, green in Farberware holder **15.00**

Cocktail, Gadroon (No. 3500) line, Crystal, 3 oz. **25.00**

Cocktail, etched Portia patt., No. 3121, Crystal, 3 oz. **15.00**

Cocktail, etched Portia patt., No. 3126, Crystal, 3 oz. **15.00**

Cocktail, etched Portia patt., No. 3130, Crystal, 3 oz. **15.00**

Cocktail, etched Rose Point patt., No. 3121, Crystal, 3 oz. **36.00**

Cocktail, etched Rose Point patt., No. 3500, Crystal, 3 oz. **38.00**

Cocktail, Tally Ho line, Royal blue, 3 oz. **35.00**

Cocktail shaker, cov., Pristine line, Crystal...............................**89.00**

Cocktail shaker w/glass stopper, etched Rose Point patt., No. 101, Crystal, 32 oz. **160.00**

Compote, low-footed, pressed Caprice patt., Crystal, 7" h...........**19.00**

Compote, cheese, gold-encrusted etched Chantilly patt. ..**30.00**

Compote, blown, etched Wildflower patt., Crystal, 5⅜" d. ..**75.00**

Console bowl, pressed Alpine Caprice patt., Crystal..................**32.00**

Console bowl, oblong, four-footed, fancy rim, etched Rose Point patt., No. 3400/160, Crystal, 12" l. **100.00**

Cordial decanter w/stopper, etched Wildflower patt., No. 3400, Crystal, 12 oz. **295.00**

Cordial, blown Caprice patt., No. 300, Crystal, 1 oz. **50.00**

Cordial, etched Daffodil patt., Crystal, 1 oz. **55.00**

Cordial, etched Diane patt., Crystal, 1 oz. **65.00**

Cordial, Line No. 3121, Crystal, 1 oz. **75.00**

Creamer, footed, etched Cleo patt., pink.................................**20.00**

Creamer & open sugar bowl, pressed Caprice patt., Crystal, medium, pr. **22.00**

Creamer & open sugar bowl, pressed Caprice patt., Crystal, large, pr. **28.00**

Creamer & open sugar bowl, pressed Caprice patt., Mocha, pr. **50.00**

Creamer & open sugar bowl, etched Rose Point patt., No. 3500, Crystal, pr. **55.00**

Creamer & open sugar bowl w/undertray, pressed Caprice patt., Crystal, 3 pcs.....................**40.00**

Crown Tuscan ashtray, footed, No. SS33, 4"................................**11.00**

Crown Tuscan cigarette box, cov., No. 101 ....**78.00**

Crown Tuscan cigarette box, cov., dolphin-footed, No. SS35....**27.00**

Cruets w/original stoppers, vinegar & oil, silvered metal base, Chantilly patt., the set **135.00**

Cup & saucer, etched Apple Blossom patt., Crystal **25.00**

Cup & saucer, etched Apple
Blossom patt., yellow...................**28.00**

Cup & saucer, etched Cleo patt.,
Moonlight blue **25.00**

Cup & saucer, Tally Ho line,
Amber...**15.00**

Decanter w/stopper, Mt. Vernon
line, Crystal................................**50.00**

Decanter w/stopper, pressed
Caprice patt., Crystal, 35 oz. **275.00**

Goblet, water, etched Apple
Blossom patt., No. 3130, yellow ..**26.00**

Goblet, water, Decagon line,
black, 9 oz. **25.00**

Goblet, water, Decagon line,
Cobalt blue, 9 oz. **30.00**

Goblet, water, Heirloom line,
Crystal, 9 oz. **9.00**

Hurricane lamp, etched Rose
Point patt., Crystal, small...........**250.00**

Ice bucket, Decagon line, Ebony ..**35.00**

Ice bucket, Tally Ho line,
Crystal **150.00**

Ice bucket, Tally Ho line, Royal
blue...**175.00**

**Ice bucket w/liner & chrome
handle,** etched Elaine patt.,
Crystal **75.00**

**Ice bucket w/liner & chrome
handle,** etched Portia patt.,
Crystal **75.00**

Ivy ball, pressed Caprice patt.,
No. 232, Crystal, 5" h. **75.00**

Ivy ball, footed, Mt. Vernon line,
Crystal, 4½" d. **25.00**

Jelly dish, square, two-handled,
pressed Caprice patt., 5" d.,
Mandarin gold.............................**28.00**

Mayonnaise bowl, footed, two-
handled, etched Cleo patt.,
green **39.00**

Mayonnaise bowl, underplate &
ladle, etched Rose Point patt.,
Crystal, 3 pcs..............................**65.00**

Mustard, cov., Cobalt blue insert
in Farberware holder **40.00**

Oyster cocktail, low, blown
Caprice patt., No. 300, Crystal,
4½ oz...**18.00**

Oyster cocktail, Gadroon (No.
3500) line, Crystal, 4½ oz...........**50.00**

Parfait, blown Caprice patt.,
Crystal, No. 300, 5 oz. **95.00**

Pickle dish, etched Rose Point
patt., No. 477, Crystal, 9½" l........**57.00**

Pitcher, etched Apple Blossom
patt., Crystal, 76 oz. **395.00**

Pitcher, ball-shaped, Emerald
w/Crystal handle, 9" h.................**50.00**

Pitcher, tall Doulton-style,
pressed Caprice patt., Moonlight
blue, 90 oz. **4,200.00**

Pitcher, etched Rose Point patt.,
Crystal, 20 oz. **275.00**

Pitcher, martini, etched Rose
Point patt., Crystal, small........**1,100.00**

Plate, bread & butter, 6" d.,
etched Apple Blossom patt.,
Crystal **9.00**

Plate, bread & butter, 6" d.,
etched Rose Point patt.,
Crystal **10.00**

Plate, bread & butter, 6½" d.,
pressed Caprice patt., Crystal **9.00**

Plate, 7" d., etched Cleo patt.,
Moonlight blue **20.00**

Plate, 7" d., Line No. 3400,
Crystal **15.00**

Plate, tea, 7½" d., etched Apple
Blossom patt., Crystal **15.00**

Plate, salad, 7½" d., pressed
Caprice patt., Crystal **15.00**

Plate, salad, 8" d., etched Diane
patt., Crystal **15.00**

Plate, luncheon, 8½" d., pressed
Caprice patt., Mocha **30.00**

Plate, salad, 8½" d., Decagon
line, green...................................**9.00**

Plate, salad, 8½" d., Decagon
line, pink **12.00**

Plate, 12" d., four-footed, "Happy
Anniversary" silver overlay

decoration, pressed Caprice patt., Crystal **35.00**

Plate, cabaret, 14" d., four-footed, pressed Caprice patt., Moonlight blue...**95.00**

Platter, 11½" d., etched Apple Blossom patt., yellow..................**65.00**

Platter, 12" d., etched Cleo patt., Moonlight blue **150.00**

Relish dish, three-part, pressed Caprice patt., No. 124, Crystal **35.00**

Relish dish, three-part, pressed Caprice patt., Moonlight blue, 8" l. **38.00**

Relish dish, three-part, etched Elaine patt., No. 3500/112, Crystal, 15" l. **150.00**

Relish dish, two-part, Gadroon (No. 3500) line, Crystal, 5½" l......**40.00**

Relish dish, five-part, Mt. Vernon line, Crystal, 12" l........................**35.00**

Relish dish, three-part, etched Rose Point patt, No. 3500/69, Crystal, 6½" l. **40.00**

Relish dish, four-part, two-handled, etched Rose Point patt., Crystal, 7½" l. **65.00**

Relish dish, two-part, etched Wildflower patt., No. 124, Crystal, 7" l. **25.00**

Salt & pepper shakers, ball-shaped, pressed Caprice patt., No. 91, Crystal, pr. **35.00**

Salt & pepper shakers, glass tops, pressed Caprice patt., No. 96, Moonlight blue, pr...............**110.00**

Salt & pepper shakers, individual, flat, pressed Caprice patt., No.92, Moonlight blue pr. **125.00**

Salt & pepper shakers, handled, etched Chantilly patt., Crystal, small, pr. **38.00**

Salt & pepper shakers, etched Wildflower patt., Crystal, pr. **40.00**

Server, center-handled, Decagon line, Moonlight blue **35.00**

Server, center-handled, Decagon line, pink **20.00**

Sherbet, blown Caprice patt., No. 300, Crystal, 6 oz. **15.00**

Sherbet, tall, etched Cleo patt., Moonlight blue, 6 oz. **35.00**

Sherbet, Gadroon (No. 3500) line, Crystal, 7 oz. **25.00**

Sherbet, Heirloom line, Crystal, 6 oz..**8.00**

Sherbet, engraved Lynbrook patt., Crystal **10.00**

Sherbet, tall, etched Rose Point patt., No. 3121, Crystal, 6 oz. **30.00**

Sugar bowl, open, etched Candlelight patt., Crystal **22.00**

Sugar bowl, open, scalloped edge, Decagon Line, green **7.00**

Tray, creamer & sugar, pressed Caprice patt., Crystal **18.00**

Tray, oval, Decagon Line, pink, 15" l. **25.00**

Tray, square-shaped, Gadroon (No. 3500) line, 6" w. **140.00**

Tray, two-handled, square-shaped, gold-encrusted etched Rose Point patt.........................**160.00**

Tumbler, footed, etched Apple Blossom patt., No. 3130, yellow, 8 oz...**19.00**

Tumbler, iced-tea, footed, etched Candlelight patt., Crystal, 12 oz...**28.00**

Tumbler, juice, footed, pressed Caprice patt., Crystal, 5 oz. **14.00**

Tumbler, footed, pressed Caprice patt., No. 300, Moonlight blue, 12 oz...**40.00**

Tumbler, flat, pressed Caprice patt., No. 184, Moonlight blue, 12 oz...**45.00**

Tumbler, iced-tea, flat, blown Caprice patt., No. 301, Crystal, 12 oz...**18.00**

Tumbler, iced-tea, footed, etched Chantilly patt., Crystal, 12 oz.......**20.00**

Tumbler, footed, Decagon Line, Moonlight blue, 5 oz. **14.00**

Tumbler, footed, Decagon Line,
Moonlight blue, 8 oz. **18.00**

Tumbler, Gadroon (No. 3500)
line, Crystal, 10 oz. **33.00**

Tumbler, footed, Heirloom line,
Crystal, 12 oz. **10.00**

Tumbler, iced-tea, footed, Line
No. 3121, Crystal, 12 oz. **35.00**

Tumbler, iced-tea, footed,
engraved Lynbrook patt.,
Crystal, 12 oz. **15.00**

Tumbler, iced-tea, etched Rose
Point patt., No. 3500, Crystal,
12 oz. **32.00**

Tumbler, flat, Tally Ho line,
Carmen, 10 oz. **20.00**

Tumbler, iced-tea, etched
Wildflower patt., Crystal, 12 oz. **28.00**

Urn w/cover, Mt. Vernon line,
Crystal, 8" d. **45.00**

Vase, 4½" h., crimped edge,
pressed Caprice patt., No. 344,
Amber.......................................**125.00**

Vase, 8" h., etched Rose Point
patt., No. 1430, Crystal..............**125.00**

Vase, 8½" h., ball-shaped,
pressed Caprice patt., Cobalt
blue...**295.00**

Wine, blown Caprice patt., No.
300, Crystal, 2½ oz. **25.00**

Wine, blown Caprice patt., No.
300, Moonlight blue, 2½ oz. **65.00**

Wine, gold-encrusted etched
Portia patt., No. 3126, 2½ oz.......**22.00**

CARNIVAL GLASS

Earlier called Taffeta glass, the Carnival glass now being collected was introduced early in this century. Its producers gave it an iridescence that attempted to imitate that of some Tiffany glass. Collectors will find available books by leading authorities Donald E. Moore, Sherman Hand, Marion T. Hartung and Rose M. Presznick.

For a more extensive listing of Carnival Glass, please refer to the forthcoming second edition of Antique Trader Books American Pressed Glass & Bottles Price Guide

ACORN BURRS (Northwood)

Berry set: master bowl & 4 sauce
dishes; purple,
5 pcs. ....**$375.00 to 425.00**

Butter dish, cov.,
green.........................**350.00 to 400.00**

Butter dish, cov., marigold **178.00**

Butter dish, cov.,
purple ....**275.00 to 375.00**

Creamer, marigold **150.00**

Creamer, purple **220.00**

Pitcher, water, green ..**875.00 to 900.00**

Pitcher, water, marigold **325.00**

Pitcher, water,
purple ....**425.00 to 500.00**

Punch bowl & base, purple,
2 pcs. **1,100.00**

Punch cup, blue...........................**85.00**

Punch cup, green...........**60.00 to 65.00**

Punch cup, ice green...**100.00 to 150.00**

Punch cup, marigold.....................**27.00**

Punch cup, purple ....**35.00 to 40.00**

Punch cup, white **80.00**

Punch set: bowl, base & 5 cups;
green, 7 pcs..............................**1,800.00**

Punch set: bowl, base & 6 cups;
green, 8 pcs. ....**2,000.00 to 2,250.00**

Punch set: bowl, base & 6 cups;
marigold, 8 pcs. **1,250.00**

Punch set: bowl, base & 6 cups;
purple, 8 pcs. ......**1,360.00 to 1,375.00**

Acorn Burrs Punch Set

Punch set: bowl, base & 6 cups; white, 8 pcs. (ILLUS. bottom previous page) **4,000.00**

Sauce dish, green **49.00**

Sauce dish, marigold **36.00**

Sauce dish, purple ....**40.00 to 50.00**

Spooner, green ....**170.00 to 180.00**

Spooner, marigold **100.00**

Spooner, purple ....**250.00 to 275.00**

Sugar bowl, cov., marigold **160.00**

Sugar bowl, cov., purple **290.00**

Table set: cov. sugar bowl, creamer, spooner & cov. butter dish; marigold, 4 pcs. ....**895.00 to 925.00**

Table set, purple, 4 pcs. **1,000.00**

Tumbler, green ....**65.00 to 70.00**

Tumbler, marigold **50.00**

Tumbler, purple **65.00**

Water set: pitcher & 4 tumblers; marigold, 5 pcs. ....**600.00 to 650.00**

Water set: pitcher & 4 tumblers; purple, 5 pcs. ....**700.00 to 775.00**

Water set: pitcher & 6 tumblers; green, 7 pcs. **1,200.00**

Water set: pitcher & 6 tumblers; purple, 7 pcs. ....**955.00 to 975.00**

COIN DOT

Bowl, 6" d., green **25.00**

Bowl, 6" d., ice cream shape, red **1,500.00**

Bowl, 6½" d., lavender **30.00**

Bowl, 6½" d., stippled, purple **32.00**

Bowl, 7" d., green **30.00**

Bowl, 7" d., red **1,700.00**

Bowl, 7" d., ribbon candy rim, green (ILLUS. top next column) **50.00**

Bowl, 7" d., ribbon candy rim, purple **35.00**

Bowl, 7½" d., blue **55.00**

Bowl, 8" d., piecrust rim, purple **20.00**

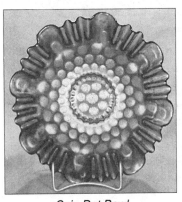

Coin Dot Bowl

Bowl, 8" to 9" d., amber **65.00**

Bowl, 8" to 9" d., green ...**45.00 to 50.00**

Bowl, 8" to 9" d., stippled green **25.00**

Bowl, 8" to 9" d., lavender **75.00**

Bowl, 8" to 9" d., marigold ....**35.00 to 40.00**

Bowl, 8" to 9" d., stippled marigold **75.00**

Bowl, 8" to 9" d., peach opalescent **149.00**

Bowl, 8" to 9" d., purple **48.00**

Bowl, 8" to 9" d., ruffled, vaseline **55.00**

Bowl, 9" d., three-in-one edge, purple **97.00**

Bowl, 9½" d., ruffled, purple ....**60.00 to 65.00**

Bowl, 9½" d., stippled, purple **35.00**

Bowl, 10" d., green **35.00**

Bowl, 10" d., stippled, marigold **28.00**

Bowl, 10"d., ruffled, peach opalescent **158.00**

Bowl, aqua **65.00**

Bowl, green **70.00**

Bowl, purple **77.00**

Bowl, red **1,700.00**

Compote, celeste blue opalescent **100.00**

Compote, ice blue **450.00**

Compote, purple **60.00**

Plate, 9" d., aqua 80.00

Plate, 9" d., purple 90.00

Rose bowl, green ....70.00 to 75.00

Rose bowl, stippled, green 75.00

Rose bowl, marigold.......40.00 to 50.00

Rose bowl, large, marigold 78.00

Rose bowl, purple........................52.00

Rose bowl, stippled,
  purple ....65.00 to 70.00

Rose bowl, vaseline...................100.00

FRUITS & FLOWERS
(Northwood)

Berry set: master bowl & 6 sauce
  dishes; marigold, 7 pcs..............200.00

Bonbon, stemmed, two-handled,
  amber 375.00

Bonbon, stemmed, two-handled,
  aqua opalescent........475.00 to 525.00

Bonbon, stemmed, two-handled,
  blue ....170.00 to 200.00

Bonbon, stemmed, two-handled,
  blue w/electric iridescence 214.00

Bonbon, stemmed, two-handled,
  green.........................100.00 to 125.00

Bonbon, stemmed, two-handled,
  ice blue 575.00

Bonbon, stemmed, two-handled,
  ice blue opalescent...................875.00

Bonbon, stemmed, two-handled,
  ice green ....550.00 to 600.00

Bonbon, stemmed, two-handled,
  lavender....................................650.00

Fruits & Flowers Bonbon

Bonbon, stemmed, two-handled,
  marigold (ILLUS. bottom
  previous column)........80.00 to 100.00

Bonbon, stemmed, two-handled,
  olive green................................135.00

Bonbon, stemmed, two-handled,
  pastel marigold 113.00

Bonbon, stemmed, two-handled,
  purple ....125.00 to 150.00

Bonbon, stemmed, two-handled,
  white ....300.00 to 350.00

Bowl, 6" d., ruffled, green.............48.00

Bowl, 6" d., ruffled, marigold 60.00

Bowl, 6" d., ruffled, purple 39.00

Bowl, 7" d., blue 85.00

Bowl, 7" d., blue w/electric
  iridescence ....275.00 to 300.00

Bowl, 7" d., green........................52.00

Bowl, 7" d., stippled green 325.00

Bowl, 7" d., ruffled,
  blue ....200.00 to 275.00

Bowl, 7" d., ruffled, Basketweave
  exterior, green...........100.00 to 110.00

Bowl, 7" d., ruffled, ice green 350.00

Bowl, 7" d., stippled, marigold.....250.00

Bowl, 9½" d., ruffled,
  Basketweave exterior, green.......70.00

Bowl, 9½" d., ruffled,
  Basketweave exterior,
  marigold.....................................145.00

Bowl, master berry, 10" d.,
  green.........................110.00 to 125.00

Bowl, master berry, 10" d.,
  ice green..................................750.00

Bowl, master berry, 10" d.,
  marigold......................................65.00

Bowl, 10" d., ruffled, purple 153.00

Bowl, piecrust rim, purple............225.00

Bowl, ruffled, stippled,
  marigold......................................50.00

Plate, 7" d., green.......................170.00

Plate, 7" d., marigold 178.00

Plate, 7" d., purple 170.00

Plate, 7½" d., handgrip,
  green 165.00

Plate, 7½" d., handgrip,
purple **175.00**

Plate, 9½" d., marigold **250.00**

Sauce dish, purple **36.00**

IMPERIAL GRAPE (Imperial)

Basket, marigold **75.00**

Basket, purple **60.00**

Basket, smoky.............................**118.00**

Berry set: master bowl & 4 sauce
dishes; green, 5 pcs. .**125.00 to 150.00**

Bowl, 6" d., marigold **35.00**

Bowl, 6" d., ruffled, purple **70.00**

Bowl, 7" d., 2½" h., green.............**41.00**

Bowl, 7" d., 2½" h.,
marigold ....**30.00 to 35.00**

Bowl, 7" d., 2½" h., ruffled,
purple **70.00**

Bowl, 8" to 9" d., aqua...................**75.00**

Bowl, 8" to 9" d., green..................**48.00**

Bowl, 8" to 9" d.,
marigold ....**35.00 to 40.00**

Bowl, 8" to 9" d.,
purple ....**100.00 to 115.00**

Bowl, 9" d., low, amber **400.00**

Bowl, 10" d., green ....**60.00 to 70.00**

Bowl, 10" d., marigold **45.00**

Bowl, 10" d., purple **158.00**

Bowl, 10" d., smoky.......................**33.00**

Bowl, 11" d., ruffled,
purple **125.00**

Bowl, 11½" d., ruffled, aqua........**650.00**

Bowl, low, ruffled, green...............**65.00**

Compote, amber **65.00**

Compote, clambroth **35.00**

Compote, green.............**45.00 to 55.00**

Compote, lavender swirled
w/amber......................................**140.00**

Compote, smoky **35.00**

Cup & saucer, amber **65.00**

Cup & saucer, green **85.00**

Cup & saucer, marigold (ILLUS.
top next column) ....**75.00 to 80.00**

Imperial Grape Cup and Saucer

Decanter w/stopper,
green........................**125.00 to 150.00**

Decanter w/stopper,
marigold ....**95.00 to 100.00**

Decanter w/stopper,
purple ....**200.00 to 250.00**

Goblet, aqua teal..........................**90.00**

Goblet, clambroth..........................**75.00**

Goblet, green **35.00**

Goblet, marigold...........................**36.00**

Goblet, purple ....**85.00 to 90.00**

Goblet, smoky..............**75.00 to 100.00**

Pitcher, water, amber..................**650.00**

Pitcher, water, marigold **95.00**

Pitcher, water,
purple ....**300.00 to 400.00**

Pitcher, water,
smoky.......................**300.00 to 400.00**

Plate, 6" d., amber ......**140.00 to 150.00**

Plate, 6" d., green..........................**53.00**

Plate, 6" d., marigold.......**35.00 to 40.00**

Plate, 6" d., purple **150.00**

Plate, 7" d., green..........................**75.00**

Plate, 7" d., marigold.......**25.00 to 30.00**

Plate, 8" d., stippled, clambroth.....**75.00**

Plate, 8" d., green..........................**63.00**

Plate, 8" d., marigold **50.00**

Plate, 8" d., purple.........**75.00 to 100.00**

Plate, 9" d., ruffled, clambroth **75.00**

Plate, 9" d., flat, green **75.00**

Plate, 9" d., ruffled, green...........**156.00**

Plate, 9" d., flat,
marigold ....**85.00 to 100.00**

Plate, 9" d., ruffled,
marigold ....**65.00 to 75.00**

Plate, 9" d., ruffled, purple **113.00**

Plate, 9" d., ruffled, smoky.............**95.00**

Plate, 9" d., ruffled, white...............**55.00**

Plate, flared, stippled, amber.......**400.00**

Rose bowl, amber......................**675.00**

Rose bowl, purple **68.00**

Rose bowl, white **70.00**

Sauce dish, amber ....**30.00 to 35.00**

Sauce dish, green.........................**25.00**

Sauce dish, ruffled, marigold **20.00**

Sauce dish, purple **35.00**

Tray, center handle, amber **30.00**

Tray, center handle, clambroth......**45.00**

Tray, center handle, marigold........**80.00**

Tray, center handle, smoky **35.00**

Tumbler, amber **98.00**

Tumbler, lilac **59.00**

Tumbler, marigold **20.00**

Tumbler, purple ....**40.00 to 50.00**

Tumbler, smoky............**90.00 to 100.00**

Water bottle, green ....**100.00 to 125.00**

Water bottle,
marigold ....**135.00 to 175.00**

Water bottle, purple....**200.00 to 225.00**

Water bottle, smoky...................**525.00**

Water set: pitcher & 4 tumblers;
marigold, 5 pcs..........**175.00 to 200.00**

Water set: pitcher & 6 tumblers;
marigold, 7 pcs. **210.00**

Water set: pitcher & 6 tumblers;
purple, 7 pcs. ....**625.00 to 675.00**

Water set: pitcher & 8 tumblers;
marigold, 9 pcs. **250.00**

Wine, clambroth **18.00**

Wine, green....................**25.00 to 30.00**

Wine, marigold **25.00**

Wine, purple **37.00**

Wine, smoky.................................**50.00**

Wine set: decanter w/stopper &
6 wines; marigold,
7 pcs ....**200.00 to 250.00**

Wine set: decanter w/stopper &
6 wines; purple, 7 pcs...............**575.00**

Wine set: decanter w/stopper &
7 wines; purple, 8 pcs...............**450.00**

PEACOCKS ON FENCE
(Northwood Peacocks)

Peacocks on the Fence Bowl

Bowl, 8" to 9" d., piecrust rim,
aqua opalescent
(ILLUS.)...............**2,700.00 to 2,900.00**

Bowl, 8" to 9" d., piecrust rim,
blue...**485.00**

Bowl, 8" to 9" d., piecrust rim,
blue, stippled w/ribbed back **795.00**

Bowl, 8" to 9" d., piecrust rim,
blue w/electric
iridescence ....**600.00 to 625.00**

Bowl, 8" to 9" d., piecrust rim,
green...................**1,575.00 to 1,625.00**

Bowl, 8" to 9" d., piecrust rim,
ice blue................**1,400.00 to 1,450.00**

Bowl, 8" to 9" d., piecrust rim,
ice green...............................**1,850.00**

Bowl, 8" to 9" d., piecrust rim,
lavender....................................**550.00**

Bowl, 8" to 9" d., piecrust rim,
marigold....................................**265.00**

Bowl, 8" to 9" d., piecrust rim,
stippled, marigold......**300.00 to 325.00**

Bowl, 8" to 9" d., piecrust rim,
pastel marigold.........**320.00 to 350.00**

Bowl, 8" to 9" d., piecrust rim,
purple ....**450.00 to 475.00**

Bowl, 8" to 9" d., piecrust rim,
stippled, Renniger blue..............**700.00**

Bowl, 8" to 9" d., piecrust rim,
white **1,025.00**

Bowl, 8" to 9" d., ruffled rim,
aqua opalescent..**1,075.00 to 1,100.00**

Bowl, 8" to 9" d., ruffled rim,
blue...**505.00**

Bowl, 8" to 9" d., ruffled rim,
green **1,100.00**

Bowl, 8" to 9" d., ruffled rim,
ice blue **1,750.00**

Bowl, 8" to 9" d., ruffled rim,
ice green................................**1,400.00**

Bowl, 8" to 9" d., ruffled rim,
marigold....................................**250.00**

Bowl, 8" to 9" d., ruffled rim,
purple ....**350.00 to 400.00**

Bowl, 8" to 9" d., ruffled rim,
smoky **2,500.00**

Bowl, 8" to 9" d., ruffled rim,
white **725.00**

Bowl, 9" d., stippled, green **1,100.00**

Bowl, ruffled, ribbed exterior,
aqua opalescent **1,700.00**

Bowl, ruffled, lime green
opalescent **4,000.00**

Plate, 8" d., blue.......**900.00 to 1,000.00**

Plate, 8" d., ice green..**475.00 to 500.00**

Plate, 9" d., stippled,
cobalt blue.................**700.00 to 750.00**

Plate, 9" d., blue w/electric
iridescence **875.00**

Plate, 9" d., green.....................**1,535.00**

Plate, 9" d., ice
blue ....**1,650.00 to 1,750.00**

Plate, 9" d., ice
green.......................**500.00 to 575.00**

Plate, 9" d., lavender **1,020.00**

Plate, 9" d., marigold...**400.00 to 450.00**

Plate, 9" d., dark marigold **550.00**

Plate, 9" d., stippled,
marigold ....**450.00 to 500.00**

Plate, 9" d., purple.......**575.00 to 600.00**

Plate, 9" d., white ....**650.00 to 750.00**

Plate, 9" d., white,
decorated **1,100.00**

STIPPLED RAYS

Stippled Rays Bonbon

Bonbon, two-handled,
celeste blue...............**275.00 to 300.00**

Bonbon, two-handled, green
(ILLUS.) **50.00**

Bonbon, two-handled,
ice green ....**145.00 to 150.00**

Bonbon, two-handled,
lime green.................................**200.00**

Bonbon, two-handled, marigold **38.00**

Bonbon, two-handled,
purple ....**40.00 to 50.00**

Bonbon, two-handled, red **350.00**

Bonbon, two-handled, vaseline **75.00**

Bowl, 5" d., Amberina.................**175.00**

Bowl, 5" d., blue **50.00**

Bowl, 5" d., green ....**20.00 to 30.00**

Bowl, 5" d., marigold **25.00**

Bowl, 5" d., purple **30.00**

Bowl, 5" d., red ....**400.00 to 450.00**

Bowl, 6" d., Amberina.................**260.00**

Bowl, 6½" d., ruffled, red.............**395.00**

Bowl, 6½" d., ruffled, reverse
Amberina **295.00**

Bowl, 6½" d., stippled, Scale
Band exterior, blue **225.00**

Bowl, 6¾" d., dome-footed,
aqua **300.00**

Bowl, 7" d., dome-footed, green....**32.00**

Bowl, 7" d., red...........................**250.00**

Bowl, 7" d., ruffled rim, red..........**450.00**

Bowl, 8" to 9" d., blue **225.00**

Bowl, 8" to 9" d., green.................**60.00**

Bowl, 8" to 9" d., ribbon candy
rim, green **75.00**

Bowl, 8" to 9" d., marigold............**32.00**

Bowl, 8" to 9" d., purple................**48.00**

Bowl, 8" to 9" d., ribbon candy
rim, purple **70.00**

Bowl, 8" to 9" d., teal blue **50.00**

Bowl, 10" d., amber.....................**42.00**

Bowl, 10" d., green.......................**65.00**

Bowl, 10" d., ruffled, lavender **75.00**

Bowl, 10" d., ruffled, marigold **80.00**

Bowl, 10" d., piecrust rim,
purple ....**75.00 to 85.00**

Bowl, 10" d., white......................**175.00**

Bowl, 10" w., tricornered, crimped
rim, green **85.00**

Bowl, 11" d., Basketweave
exterior, ruffled, marigold............**60.00**

Bowl, 11" sq., dome-footed,
ribbon candy rim, green.............**115.00**

Bowl, dome-footed, Greek Key &
Scales exterior, purple................**90.00**

Bowl, Wild Rose exterior,
green **75.00**

Bowl, Wild Rose exterior,
purple **110.00**

Creamer & sugar bowl,
individual size, blue, pr. **55.00**

Creamer & sugar bowl,
blue, pr. ....**75.00 to 100.00**

Creamer & sugar bowl,
marigold, pr. **50.00**

Plate, 6" to 7" d., green................**110.00**

Plate, 6" to 7" d.,
marigold ....**35.00 to 40.00**

Plate, 6" to 7" d., red................**1,250.00**

Rose bowl, purple.........................**70.00**

Sherbet, Amberina **275.00**

Sugar bowl, individual size,
marigold......................................**10.00**

Sugar bowl, open, blue...............**25.00**

Sugar bowl, open, marigold..........**24.00**

VINTAGE or VINTAGE GRAPE

Bonbon, two-handled, blue
(Fenton) ....**60.00 to 70.00**

Bonbon, two-handled, green
(Fenton) **50.00**

Bonbon, two-handled, marigold
(Fenton) **30.00**

Bonbon, two-handled, purple
(Fenton) **45.00**

Bowl, 5" d., purple **28.00**

Bowl, 6" d., blue (Fenton).............**40.00**

Bowl, 6" d., ruffled., celeste
blue...**1,100.00**

Bowl, 6" d., green (Fenton) **38.00**

Bowl, 6" d., purple
(Fenton) ....**25.00 to 30.00**

Bowl, 6" d., ruffled, vaseline........**120.00**

Bowl, 6½" d., ice cream shape,
green **43.00**

Bowl, 7" d., fluted, aqua
opalescent (Fenton) **925.00**

Bowl, 7" d., fluted, blue **42.00**

Bowl, 7" d., green ....**70.00 to 75.00**

Bowl, 7" d., fluted, green.
(Fenton) **33.00**

Bowl, 7" d., purple
(Millersburg) ....**60.00 to 70.00**

Bowl, 7" d., ruffled,
vaseline.....................**115.00 to 125.00**

Bowl, 7½" d., ice cream shape,
blue..**36.00**

Bowl, 7½" d., ice cream shape,
green **32.00**

Bowl, 7½" d., ice cream shape,
purple **35.00**

Bowl, 8" d., piecrust rim, blue......**110.00**

Bowl, 8" d., ribbon candy rim, aqua opalescent..**1,600.00 to 1,900.00**

Bowl, 8" d., ribbon candy rim, blue ....**95.00 to 100.00**

Bowl, 8" d., ribbon candy rim, Wide Panel exterior, blue **55.00**

Bowl, 8" d., ribbon candy rim, green **100.00**

Bowl, 8" to 9" d., aqua opalescent...........**1,000.00 to 1,200.00**

Bowl, 8" to 9" d., ruffled, aqua opalescent.............**850.00 to 1,000.00**

Bowl, 8" to 9" d., footed, blue (Fenton) ....**40.00 to 50.00**

Bowl, 8" to 9" d., ruffled, blue........**70.00**

Bowl, 8" to 9" d., green (Fenton).....................................**49.00**

Bowl, 8" to 9" d., green (Millersburg) **39.00**

Bowl, 8" to 9" d., marigold (Fenton).....................................**35.00**

Bowl, 8" to 9" d., footed, purple (Fenton).....................................**38.00**

Bowl, 8" to 9" d., ruffled, footed, purple **52.00**

Bowl, 8" to 9" d., ruffled, red......................**2,800.00 to 3,000.00**

Bowl, 8" to 9" d., fluted teal blue...................................**75.00**

Bowl, 8" to 9" d., vaseline............**200.00**

Bowl, 9" d., three-in-one edge, green **65.00**

Bowl, 9" d., purple **100.00**

Bowl, 9" d., ruffled, purple (Fenton)....................................**90.00**

Bowl, 9½" d., green......................**85.00**

Bowl, 9½" d., ruffled, dome-footed, marigold **67.00**

Bowl, 10" d., blue............**55.00 to 75.00**

Bowl, 10" d., green, Hobnail exterior (Millersburg) **950.00**

Bowl, 10" d., marigold, Hobnail exterior (Millersburg) **575.00**

Bowl, 10" d., ruffled, green..........**118.00**

Bowl, 10" d., ruffled, purple **55.00**

Bowl, 10" d., ruffled, red..........**3,250.00**

Bowl, 10" d., ruffled, vaseline w/marigold overlay **110.00**

Bowl, 10" d., ice cream shape, blue..**200.00**

Bowl, 10" d., ice cream shape, red (Fenton) ....**1,300.00 to 1,900.00**

Bowl, 10" d., ice cream shape, vaseline (Fenton).......................**225.00**

Bowl, 11" d., ice cream shape, marigold...................................**600.00**

Bowl, ruffled, domed base, celeste blue **825.00**

Compote, 7" d., fluted, aqua opalescent **925.00**

Compote, 7" d., blue (Fenton).......**90.00**

Compote, 7" d., fluted, green (Fenton) ....**55.00 to 60.00**

Compote, 7" d., marigold (Fenton) ....**50.00 to 60.00**

Compote, 7" d., purple (Fenton) ...**45.00**

Cuspidor, marigold **2,300.00**

Epergne, blue (Fenton) ....**155.00 to 165.00**

Epergne, green, large **258.00**

Epergne, green (Fenton) ....**250.00 to 300.00**

Epergne, marigold (Fenton) ....**250.00 to 300.00**

Small Vintage Epergne

Epergne, purple, small
  (ILLUS. bottom previous
  page) ....**110.00 to 125.00**

Epergne, purple, large **365.00**

Fernery, footed, blue
  (Fenton) ....**75.00 to 100.00**

Fernery, footed, green
  (Fenton) ....**60.00 to 70.00**

Fernery, footed, marigold
  (Fenton).....................................**50.00**

Fernery, footed, purple (Fenton) ...**57.00**

Fernery, footed, red
  (Fenton) ....**1,400.00 to 1,600.00**

Ice cream set: master ice cream
  bowl & four 6" d. bowls; cobalt
  blue, 5 pcs. **575.00**

Nut dish, footed, blue, 6" d.
  (Fenton) ....**80.00 to 90.00**

Nut dish, footed, green, 6" d.
  (Fenton).....................................**100.00**

Nut dish, footed, purple, 6" d.
  (Fenton).....................................**62.00**

Plate, 5" d., blue **75.00**

Plate, 6" d., blue **140.00**

Plate, 6" d., purple **65.00**

Plate, 7" d., blue
  (Fenton) ....**65.00 to 75.00**

Plate, 7" d., green
  (Fenton) ....**225.00 to 250.00**

Plate, 7" d., marigold (Fenton).....**150.00**

Plate, 7" d., purple
  (Fenton) ....**250.00 to 350.00**

Plate, 7" d., purple **70.00**

Plate, 8" d., blue **128.00**

Plate, 9" d., flat, purple **4,500.00**

Plate, 8" d., green.......................**183.00**

Powder jar, cov., marigold
  (Fenton).....................................**80.00**

Powder jar, cov., marigold **95.00**

Powder jar, cov., purple
  (Fenton) ....**150.00 to 175.00**

Plate, 7" d., blue
  (Fenton) ....**65.00 to 75.00**

Plate, 7" d., blue
  (Millersburg) ....**190.00 to 225.00**

Plate, 7" d., green (Fenton) **170.00**

Plate, 7" d., marigold (Fenton).....**125.00**

Plate, 7" d., purple
  (Fenton) ....**125.00 to 150.00**

Plate, 7" d., purple **70.00**

Plate, 8" d., blue **125.00**

Plate, 8" d., green.......................**183.00**

Powder jar, cov., marigold
  (Fenton).....................................**80.00**

Powder jar, cov., marigold **70.00**

Powder jar, cov., purple
  (Fenton) ....**150.00 to 175.00**

Sandwich tray, handled, aqua
  opalescent **90.00**

Sandwich tray, handled,
  clambroth ....**30.00 to 35.00**

Sandwich tray, handled,
  marigold.....................................**35.00**

Sauce dish, blue **30.00**

Sauce dish, green.........................**27.00**

Sauce dish, marigold (Fenton) **20.00**

Sauce dish, ice cream shape,
  Hobnail exterior, marigold
  (Millersburg) **700.00**

Tumbler, marigold (Fenton) **25.00**

Wine, marigold (Fenton)...............**28.00**

Wine, purple (Fenton) .....**35.00 to 45.00**

WIDE PANEL

Banana bowl, amber **40.00**

Basket, green................................**80.00**

Bowl, 8" to 9" d., purple................**60.00**

Bowl, 8½" d., Ragged Robin,
  3 in 1 rim, blue..........................**135.00**

Bowl, 10" d., console, blue...........**40.00**

Bowl, 10" d., console, smoky **55.00**

Bowl, 10" d., console, vaseline **40.00**

Bowl, 12" d., marigold **45.00**

Candy dish, cov., marigold **30.00**

Candy dish, cov., red..................**350.00**

Candy dish, cov., white **55.00**

Compote, miniature, green **60.00**

Compote, miniature, marigold.......**35.00**

Wide Panel Epergne

Compote, purple 400.00

Epergne, four-lily, green
(ILLUS.) **1,125.00**

Epergne, four-lily, ice blue **225.00**

Epergne, four-lily,
marigold ....**550.00 to 600.00**

Epergne, four-lily, purple.............**950.00**

Epergne, four-lily, white **2,075.00**

Goblet, marigold ....**25.00 to 35.00**

Goblet, red **175.00**

Plate, 8" d., marigold **45.00**

Plate, 8" d., red.............................**57.00**

Plate, chop, 12" d., vaseline **50.00**

Plate, chop, 14" d.,
marigold ....**80.00 to 100.00**

Plate, chop, 14" d., red **195.00**

Plate, chop, 14" d., smoky.............**53.00**

Plate, chop, 14" d., white...............**28.00**

Rose bowl, clambroth **40.00**

Rose bowl, marigold **25.00**

Rose bowl, purple **29.00**

Salt dip, marigold **50.00**

Salt set: master pedestal salt dip
& 6 individual size salt dips;
marigold (Northwood), 7 pcs. **150.00**

Vase, 6" h., marigold **55.00**

Vase, 8½" h., 7½" d., smoke over
milk white glass **185.00**

Vase, 9" h., aqua **85.00**

Vase, 9" h., marigold overlay.......**150.00**

Vase, 11" h., marigold **30.00**

Vase, 13" h., funeral, white..........**220.00**

Vase, 15" h., marigold **110.00**

Vase, 16" h., funeral, marigold **180.00**

CRANBERRY

Gold was added to glass batches to give this glass its color on reheating. It has been made by numerous glasshouses for years and is currently being reproduced. Both blown and molded articles were produced. A less expensive type of cranberry was made with the substitution of copper for gold.

Bottle w/clear facet-cut stopper,
squatty bulbous body w/optic
ribbing tapering to a tall slender
cylindrical neck w/a tricorner
mouth, the body enameled
w/small white dotted flowers &
gilt trim, 3½" d.,
7¼" h......................**$125.00 to 150.00**

Cranberry Box with Sheep

Box w/hinged cover, round, the
cover enameled in white & gold
w/a scene of a sheep standing
amid bushy trees, further white
bands down the sides, 5¼" d.,
3¼" h. (ILLUS.) **295.00**

Unique Cranberry Claret Set

Claret set: tall tapering cylindrical jug w/embossed French pewter neck, hinged dome cover & C-scroll handle, seven small tumblers & a dished round tray; each piece finely threaded up the sides, tray 11¼" d., jug 4¼" d., 11" h., the set (ILLUS.) **395.00**

Cologne bottle w/clear facet-cut stopper, squatty bulbous body tapering to a short cylindrical neck w/a flaring rim, the sides decorated w/gold flowers, leaves & a lattice band, 3½" d., 5¼" h. **145.00**

Cruet w/original stopper, Inverted Thumbprint patt. **169.00**

Cruet w/original stopper, enameled w/serpent, attributed to Moser **599.00**

Decanter w/clear facet-cut teardrop stopper, the double gourd-form body w/pinched indentations around the lower section, short cylindrical neck w/pinched spout, applied clear handle on upper section, decorated on each segment w/lacy gold enamel decoration & deep red flowers, 3⅝" d., 11¼" h. **198.00**

Decanter w/clear facet-cut stopper, jug-form, thick cushion foot below the tall slender ovoid body tapering to a slender cylindrical neck w/a curved rim spout, applied clear handle from rim to shoulder, decorated w/large gold roses & leaves & gilt banding, 4" d., 13" h. **195.00**

Epergne, jack-in-the-pulpit shape on the three trumpets & three vases, applied crystal on center trumpet & three side vases, crimped bowl base measuring 11½" d. **2,075.00**

Classical Cranberry Ewer

Ewer, classical form w/a round cushion foot supporting a slender short pedestal below the flaring conical body w/a wide flattened shoulder tapering sharply to the tall slender & slightly flaring cylindrical neck w/a wide arched spout, clear applied S-scroll handle from rim to shoulder, decorated around the shoulder w/delicate white enamel bands, the lower body decorated w/a wide band of white beaded coralene flowers & leafy vines, 16¼" h. (ILLUS.).....**920.00**

Pitcher, cov., tankard, wide optic-ribbed slightly tapering cylindrical body fitted w/a silver plated spouted rim & hinged cover, applied clear C-form handle, 5¼" d., 11" h. **265.00**

Cranberry Pitcher with Ice Bladder

Pitcher, 10¼" h., 5¼" d., bulbous ovoid body w/an indented ice bladder at the back, tapering to a cylindrical neck w/a small pinched spout, applied long clear handle w/end curl (ILLUS.) **195.00**

Rose bowl, spherical w/optic-ribbed sides, six-crimp rim, gilt trim at rim, 3¾" d., 3¾" h. **85.00**

Salt dip, short swelled cylindrical form w/wide mouth, applied band of rigaree around the middle, 2⅜" d., 1⅞" h. **75.00**

Sugar bowl, cov., footed nearly spherical body w/light optic ribbing, fitted low domed cover w/optic ribbing & an applied clear teardrop & knob finial, clear applied foot, 4" d., 6⅛" h...**110.00**

Sweetmeat jar in frame, cov., textured surface decorated w/heavy enamel, resilvered metal frame, 4¾" h., 4½" d. **250.00**

Vase, 13¾" h., vertical optic ribbed design, decorated w/gold flowers & raised enamel **180.00**

Small Decorated Cranberry Vases

Vases, 4⅜" h., 2⅝" d., footed optic-ribbed ovoid body tapering to a short cylindrical neck, decorated w/white enameled dot flowers & long green leaves, pr. (ILLUS.) **145.00**

CROWN MILANO

This glass, produced by Mt. Washington Glass Company late last century, is opal glass decorated by painting and enameling. It appears identical to a ware termed Albertine, also made by Mt. Washington.

Crown Milano Mark

Atomizer, swirled body, trumpet vine decoration, 6½" h.............**$595.00**

Creamer, square, applied ribbed handle, gold enameled flowers, berries & leaves........................**275.00**

Creamer & cov. sugar bowl, each of squatty bulbous form, the creamer w/silver plate rim & high curved metal spout, the sugar bowl w/small loop silver plate handles, knop finial & marked "M.W. 2039" on lid, each decorated w/blue flowers on pale pinkish yellow background, pr. **800.00**

Ornate Crown Milano Jar

Jar, cov., bulbous ovoid body tapering to a small domed cover w/a ribbed & pointed finial, creamy white ground ornately decorated w/ivy leaves & vine in heavy green & brown enamel outlined in gold w/light brown scrolls outlined in gold around the base & cover, unmarked, 10½" h. (ILLUS.) **2,375.00**

Crown Milano Vase with Dahlias

Vase, 7" h., 6¾" d., squatty bulbous swirl-molded body tapering to a short neck flaring into four fluted lobes, decorated w/dahlia flowers in yellow & burgundy, the leaves & stems w/heavy gold trim, tan shadow leaves in the backgeround, gold trim on foot & rim, unmarked (ILLUS.) **2,030.00**

Vase, 11¾" h., footed bulbous base tapering to long stick neck, decorated w/nine gulls flying over salmon-colored background highlighted w/moon & stars in gold.......................**2,795.00**

CUSTARD GLASS

For an expanded listing of Custard Glass see Antique Trader Books American & European Decorative & Art Glass.

This ware takes its name from its color and is a variant of milk white glass. It was produced largely between 1890 and 1915 by the Northwood Glass Co., Heisey Glass Company, Fenton Art Glass Co., Jefferson Glass Co., and a few others. There are 21 major patterns and a number of minor ones. The prime patterns are considered Argonaut Shell, Chrysanthemum Sprig, Inverted Fan and Feather, Louis XV and Winged Scroll. Most custard glass patterns are enhanced with gold and some have additional enameled decoration or stained highlights. Unless otherwise noted, items in this listing are fully decorated.

Northwood

Northwood Script Mark

ARGONAUT SHELL (Northwood)

Bowl, master berry or fruit, 10½" l., 5" h. **$205.00**

Butter dish, cov. **338.00**

Compote, jelly, 5" d., 5" h...........**145.00**

Creamer **155.00**

Cruet w/original stopper **850.00**

Pitcher, water, excellent gold trim...................................**465.00**

Sauce dish, gold trim, decorated **60.00**

Spooner **150.00**

Sugar bowl, cov. (ILLUS. top next page) **190.00**

Argonaut Shell Sugar Bowl

Table set, cov. butter dish, cov.
sugar bowl, creamer & spooner,
4 pcs. 560.00

Toothpick holder.......................385.00

Tumbler.....................................115.00

Water set, pitcher & 6 tumblers,
7 pcs. 910.00

CHRYSANTHEMUM SPRIG
(Northwood's Pagoda)

Chrysanthemum Sprig Master Berry

Bowl, master berry or fruit, 10½"
oval, decorated (ILLUS.) 165.00

Bowl set: master berry & 6
individual dishes, 7 pcs. 590.00

Butter dish, cov. 297.00

Celery vase................................755.00

Compote, jelly,
decorated ....100.00 to 125.00

Compotes, jelly, goofus trim,
set of 7......................................385.00

Compote, undecorated 55.00

Condiment tray ....570.00 to 610.00

Creamer.....................100.00 to 150.00

Cruet w/original
stopper ....300.00 to 400.00

Pitcher, water, decorated...........457.00

Pitcher, water, undecorated.......225.00

Salt & pepper shakers
w/original tops, decorated
w/gold trim 145.00

Sauce dish...................................55.00

Sauce dish, blue trim 140.00

Spooner.....................100.00 to 150.00

Sugar bowl, cov.,
decorated ....175.00 to 250.00

Sugar bowl, cov.,
undecorated ....150.00 to 180.00

Table set, cov. sugar bowl,
creamer, cov. butter dish, &
spooner, 4 pcs. 740.00

Toothpick holder w/gold trim &
paint, signed.............250.00 to 350.00

Toothpick holder, decorated......225.00

Toothpick holder,
undecorated 175.00

Tray, round, footed 275.00

Tumbler ....75.00 to 100.00

Water set, pitcher & 6 tumblers,
7 pcs. ....675.00 to 775.00

GENEVA (Northwood)

Banana boat, four-footed,
11" oval......................................105.00

Banana boat, four-footed, green
stain, 11" oval 145.00

Bowl, master berry or fruit, oval,
8½" d., four-footed.......................95.00

Bowl, master berry or fruit, round,
8½" d., three-footed.................135.00

Butter dish, cov. 200.00

Compote, jelly 75.00

Creamer ....80.00 to 100.00

Cruet w/ original stopper 300.00

Pitcher, water 225.00

Salt & pepper shakers
w/original tops, pr. 245.00

Geneva Sauce Dish

Sauce dish, oval (ILLUS.) 55.00

Sauce dish, round 40.00

Spooner 95.00

Sugar bowl, open 75.00

Syrup pitcher w/ original
top 285.00

Table set, 4 pcs. ....450.00 to 500.00

Toothpick holder, decorated......125.00

Toothpick holder, decorated,
green stain, goofus trim 240.00

Tumbler 50.00

Tumbler w/green trim 55.00

INTAGLIO (Northwood)
Berry set: 9" d. master berry
bowl, compote-style, footed & 6
sauce dishes, 7 pcs. 392.00

Berry set: green & gold,
6 pcs. 850.00

Bowl, fruit 7½" d. master berry
bowl, compote-style, footed.......132.00

Bowl, master berry w/green
decoration.................................165.00

Butter dish, cov. ....200.00 to 260.00

Butter dish, cov., gold w/blue
decoration.................................130.00

Butter dish, cov., gold w/green
decoration.................................285.00

Compote, decorated 175.00

Compote, jelly 115.00

Creamer & cov. sugar bowl,
pr. 275.00

Cruet w/original stopper 310.00

Pitcher, water 373.00

Salt shaker w/original top 98.00

Salt & pepper shakers
w/original tops, pr. 200.00

Intaglio Sauce Dish

Sauce dish (ILLUS.) 58.00

Table set, green stain,
4 pcs. 540.00

Tumbler..58.00

Tumbler, blue decoration 85.00

JACKSON or FLUTED SCROLLS WITH FLOWER BAND (Northwood)
Bowl, master berry or fruit.............85.00

Creamer 85.00

Pitcher, water, undecorated........275.00

Salt shaker w/original top,
undecorated 60.00

Salt & pepper shakers
w/original tops, pr. 135.00

Tumbler..45.00

Water set: pitcher & 4 tumblers,
5 pcs. ....365.00 to 385.00

Water set: pitcher & 6 tumblers,
7 pcs ....425.00 to 475.00

LOUIS XV (Northwood)
Butter dish, cov. 150.00

Bowl, master berry or
fruit w/gold trim 295.00

Bowl, berry or fruit, 7¾ x 10"
oval..135.00

Butter dish, cov., ...150.00 to 200.00
Creamer 75.00
Cruet w/original stopper 450.00
Pitcher, water ....200.00 to 250.00
Sauce dish, footed, 5" oval 40.00
Spooner........................50.00 to 75.00
Sugar bowl, cov. ....120.00 to 175.00
Table set, 4 pcs.........................525.00
Tumbler ....45.00 to 60.00

NORTHWOOD GRAPE, GRAPE & CABLE or GRAPE & THUMBPRINT

Northwood Grape Master Berry Bowl

Banana boat 325.00
Bowl, 6½" d., ruffled rim, nutmeg
   stain...40.00
Bowl, 7½" d., ruffled rim 45.00
Bowl, master berry or fruit, 11" d.,
   ruffled, footed (ILLUS.) 450.00
Butter dish, cov. 250.00
**Cologne bottle w/original
   stopper** 540.00
Cracker jar, cov.,
   two-handled ....575.00 to 600.00
Creamer......................125.00 to 150.00
Creamer & open sugar bowl,
   breakfast size, pr.......100.00 to 125.00
Dresser tray ....275.00 to 325.00
Dresser tray, nutmeg
   decoration...................................150.00
Humidor, cov..............................650.00
Pin dish......................................160.00
Plate, 7¾" d. 60.00

Plate, 8" d. 55.00
Plate, 8" w., six-sided 65.00
Punch cup 75.00
Sauce dish, flat............................35.00
Sauce dish, footed.......................40.00
Spooner 135.00
Sugar bowl, cov. 150.00
Sugar bowl, open, breakfast
   size 65.00
Tumbler......................................47.00
Water set, pitcher & 6 tumblers,
   7 pcs. 850.00

WINGED SCROLL or IVORINA VERDE

Winged Scroll Celery Vase

Berry set, master bowl & 4 sauce
   dishes, undecorated, 5 pcs. 275.00
Berry set, master bowl & 5 sauce
   dishes, 6 pcs. 445.00
Bowl, fruit, 8½" d.,
   undecorated 125.00
Butter dish, cov. ....190.00 to 220.00
Celery vase (ILLUS.) 350.00
Cigarette jar...............................160.00
Creamer, decorated 105.00
Cruet w/original stopper,
   undecorated 100.00
Match holder ....190.00 to 225.00
Pitcher, water, 9" h., bulbous 230.00

Pitcher, water, tankard,
   decorated **340.00**

Pitcher, water, tankard,
   undecorated **230.00**

**Salt & pepper shakers
   w/original tops,** pr. **150.00**

Sauce dish, 4½" d.......................**36.00**

Spooner **84.00**

Sugar bowl, cov. decorated........**225.00**

Sugar bowl, cov., undecorated.....**95.00**

Table set, cov. butter dish,
   creamer & spooner, 3 pcs. **250.00**

Toothpick holder.......................**130.00**

Tumbler......................................**72.00**

CUT GLASS

Cut glass most eagerly sought by collectors is American glass produced during the so-called "Brilliant Period" from 1880 to about 1915. Pieces listed below are by type of article in alphabetical order.

BASKETS

High tiered base, notched rim &
   double notched handle, satin
   roses & deeply cut leaves on
   basket, 4" x 8" d., 12½" h. **$245.00**

Hunt's Royal patt., set off by
   florals **255.00**

Tuthill, unsigned, intaglio floral
   w/cutting on sides, 14" h.........**2,000.00**

BOWLS

American Cut Glass Co.,
   rectangular, Radiant Star patt.,
   center hobstar surrounded by
   pointed arches w/hobstars
   above fan cutting, outer boarder
   of zipper cut ribbing, large **950.00**

Clark signed, vertical leaves &
   Cosmos-type satin flowers on
   body w/deep cut horizontal
   leaves around the bottom, ray
   cut rim & base, 5½" h. **135.00**

Clark's Lapidary patt.,
   hexagonal block centering a six-
   arm star, surrounded by six plain
hexagonal blocks, each
   centered by a single button,
   border band of four arm stars in
   diamonds alternating w/small
   hobstars, notched rim, 8" d.....**2,300.00**

Hawkes signed, Centauri patt.,
   large twelve-arm center hobstar
   within six-arm star w/small
   hobstar tips, outer boarder
   cutting w/pairs of fans below
   small hobstars alternating
   w/small eight point stars,
   scalloped & notched rim, 8" d....**195.00**

Hawkes' Chrysanthemum patt.,
   variant, nailhead cutting
   alternates w/cane cutting in two
   of four loops, low bowl, 9" d.......**295.00**

Hawkes' Grecian patt., center
   hobstar in bottom, surrounded
   by eight point star w/crosshatch
   rays, the sides have wide panels
   of Russian cut w/fan cut rim
   alternating w/long teardrop
   panels, 9" square...................**1,800.00**

Hawkes signed, Panel patt.,
   sharp cutting on brilliant white
   blank, 8" d.............................**2,300.00**

Hawkes signed, St. Louis patt.,
   diamond & intaglio design,
   5" d. **170.00**

Hawkes Signed Bowl

Hawkes signed, blown-out thick
& heavy blank (ILLUS.) **2,100.00**

Hoare's Croesus patt., plain cornucopia radiating panels from center, below a wide band of fans alternating w/cane handcut blocks, 9" d. **1,500.00**

Hoare's Oxford patt., 8" d. **150.00**

Libbey's Comet patt., large center hobstar surrounded by long swirled arms enclosing small hobstars, border band of large twelve point flashed hobstars, 9" d. **1,100.00**

Libbey's Ellsmere patt., center hobstar w/large six point star surrounded by six smaller hobstars alternating w/panels of cane cutting outer boarder of fine notched ribbing, 9" d. **1,100.00**

Libbey signed, Princess patt., orange-type, cradle-shaped, large center multi-rayed star, surrounded by alternating panels of cross-cut diamond & strawberry diamond within a border of large fans, 7½" d. x 11" l. **310.00**

Libbey signed, oblong, Strawberry patt., 13" l, 8½" w. **175.00**

Libbey signed, Sultana patt., center hobstar surrounded by four crossed elipticals alternating w/outer band of large hobstars & fan-cut panels, 8" d. **250.00**

Maple City's Alsatia patt., 8" d. ...**45.00**

Meriden's Alhambra patt., 8" d. **1,300.00**

Meriden's Alhambra patt., 9" d. **1,800.00**

Monroe's Olga patt., 8" d. **1,250.00**

Mt. Washington's Patt. No. 60, triangular, sides 10" l., 2½" h....**400.00**

Pairpoint's Myrtle patt., hobstar centered in triangular design surrounded by pinwheels, 9¾" d. **450.00**

Straus, hobstar, cane & strawberry diamond cuts w/sterling rim, 10" d., 5" deep...**550.00**

Tuthill's Primrose patt., 9½" d., 4¼" h. **950.00**

CELERY TRAYS & VASES

Tray, Libbey signed, Leota patt., 12" l, 4" w...............................**120.00**

Tray, Sunburst patt., 12" l.............**90.00**

Vase, Russian cut, scalloped sawtooth rim, 6½" h..................**245.00**

COMPOTES

Fan hobstars & diamond point, cranberry cut to clear, pr. **1,250.00**

Gladys patt. w/petticoat base, 4" w., 7" h.. ....**200.00**

Hoare signed, Caroline patt., ruffled top, petticoat base, small, 6½" d., 5¼" h. **145.00**

Hobstars in arches of cut buttons, cut pedestal stem, cut rayed base, unusual shape w/sawtooth rim turned in to form a "cup-like" bowl, 5" d., 4" h.......**135.00**

Jelly, teardrop stem cut in long feathers, bowl in flashed stars, zippers & fans, 10" h. **225.00**

Three-part, hobstar & cane w/prism, hobstar & cross-cut diamond petticoat foot, 15" h., 10" d. **3,600.00**

CREAMERS & SUGAR BOWLS

Creamer, hobstars, cross-cut diamonds & fans, notched lip & handle, heavy blank **110.00**

Hawkes signed, creamer & sugar bowl on sterling silver pedestal base, engraved satin bands, pr. **125.00**

Libbey signed, creamer & sugar bowl, oval, prism cut, pr.............**400.00**

CRUETS

Chrysanthemum patt., triple-notched handle..........................**160.00**

Dorflinger's Renaissance patt., miniature size (no stopper)........**175.00**

Sinclaire signed, original stopper, cutting of gooseberries & daisies on body & stopper, 7¾" h. **185.00**

DISHES, MISCELLANEOUS

Bonbon, Hawkes signed, yellow cut to clear w/gold decorative border, gilt-metal handle............**300.00**

Bonbon servers, Meriden Cut Glass Co., overall cut & cut center upright stick-handle w/faceted ball top, pr. **295.00**

Butter plate, Unger Brothers' Emerald patt., 4" d. **50.00**

Butter plate, center cut upright stem handle w/faceted ball top, fine cutting of pineapples & hobstars, sawtooth rim, 5" d., 4½" h. **225.00**

Cake plate, J. Hoare's Nassau patt., three peg feet, 10" d. **375.00**

Candy dish, Bergen's Arcadia patt. on petticoat standard, apidary knob on lid, 9" h. **550.00**

Cheese, cov., Strauss signed w/signed underplate, pinwheel w/crossing tusks of cane, 2 pcs. **700.00**

Finger bowls, Libbey signed, Ellsmere patt., set of 9............**1,000.00**

Ice cream plates, Festoon patt., 7" d., set of 6 ....**1,185.00**

Nut dish, Tuthill signed, intaglio cutting, footed, 6" d...................**450.00**

Salts, J. Hoare, hobnails & pillars, 3½" w., 4½" h. **1,000.00**

Vegetable, cov., Taylor Brothers, hobstars & cross-cut diamond motif on bowl, cover w/lapidary stopper, rare shape on extra fine blank....................................**1,100.00**

FLOWER HOLDERS

Cut Glass Flower Holder

Flower center, Libbey's Empress patt., 6½" h. **500.00**

Pot, Meridan Cut Glass Co., Florence Hobstar patt., flashed hobstars alternating w/strawberry diamond points, silver plated liner, 4" d., 4" h. **165.00**

Roman chariot, cut glass yoke, wheels & cart w/two vases, sterling ram's head & liner (ILLUS.) **5,600.00**

Rose bowl, Libbey's Ellsmere patt., prism cutting on fine blank....................................**2,000.00**

Rose globe, Strauss' Rossette patt., 7" d. **200.00**

Rose globe, Hawkes signed, pedestal-style cut w/chain of hobstar & strawberry diamond, 6" d., 7" h. **450.00**

GOBLETS

Hawkes signed, water, Brunswick patt., set of 6 ....**1,650.00**

Hawkes' Gravic Iris patt., water, clear blanks w/lapidary knob on stems, square pedestal feet, set of 4....................................**1,100.00**

Libbey signed, Colonna patt., teardrop stems, 6⅛" h., set of 8....................................**1,200.00**

Russian-style cutting, water, set of 7....................................**650.00**

Sinclair signed, shrimp chain of hobstars & flute, 5" h., 5" d., set of 6 ....**660.00**

St. Louis Diamond patt., set of 6....................................**375.00**

JARS

Cherry, Strauss' Venetian cut, pattern-cut lid, 6" h. **375.00**

Diamond Prism patt., sterling embossed lid, 2½" d. **80.00**

Tobacco, cov., cranberry cut to clear, ray lid & base, polished leaf & berry design, 6" h. **600.00**

LAMPS

Hobstar Cut Glass Lamp

Boudoir, overall Russian cut.......**575.00**

Pairpoint, mushroom-shaped cut
shade w/twenty-eight prisms on
tall cut base, 11" d., 20" h.......**3,650.00**

Table, Bergen's Harvard patt.
w/five lights, 28" h..................**8,300.00**

Table, intaglio, hobstar &
mushroom shade lamp, 25" h.
(ILLUS.) **4,600.00**

NAPPIES

Hawkes' Iris patt., 8" d. **225.00**

Hawkes signed, leaf-shaped
w/hobstars, 7" d........................**175.00**

Pitkin & Brooks signed, Flashed
Hobstar patt., triple-notched
handle, 5" d. **80.00**

Tuthill signed, Vintage patt.,
intaglio cutting, 6" d. **250.00**

PERFUME & COLOGNE BOTTLES

Cologne, overall hobstars
w/rayed base, faceted stopper,
4" d. **165.00**

Cologne, Dorflinger's Hob Lace
patt., cranberry cut to clear,
matching stopper, 7" h..............**600.00**

Cologne, Hawkes signed,
Venetian patt., band of hobstars
alternating w/fans above split
vesicas, faceted stopper, 4½" d.,
8" h. **495.00**

Perfume w/original square-cut
stopper w/long dauber, square
cut shape w/blue cut to clear
basket of flowers on the front,
4" d., 5" h. **160.00**

PITCHERS

Averbeck's Genoa patt.,
10½" h. **200.00**

Champagne, Bullseye patt.,
twenty-four point hobstar base,
3" w. sterling rim, triple-notch
handle, 12½" h. **375.00**

Cider, Egginton-style patt., triple-
notched handle, 8½" h.,
4" d. **325.00**

Quaker City's Wilmot patt.,
bulbous, 7¾" h...........................**295.00**

Sinclaire's Bengal patt.,
9½" h. **1,000.00**

Tankard, Blackmer's Oregon
patt., 9" h. **175.00**

PLATES

7" d., Libbey signed, Aztec patt...**975.00**

7" d., Libbey signed, Wedgemere
patt. **800.00**

8" d., Dorflinger's Star & Diamond
patt., set of 12......................**1,020.00**

10" d., oval, Hawkes signed,
Imperial patt..........................**1,300.00**

10" d., Hawkes signed, Napoleon
patt. **625.00**

10" d., Pairpoint's Baltic patt.,
cheese & cracker (tiny nicks on
base) **248.00**

10" d., Sinclaire Stars & Pillar
patt., twenty-four point star
center, rayed to band of hobs....**565.00**

PUNCH BOWLS, CUPS & SETS

Gorham signed, Libbey's Colonna patt., bowl & ladle w/cut teardrop handle, the set **500.00**

Gorham signed, bowl & ladle, ladle w/teardrop handle, shell-form bowl in sterling silver, the set......................................**440.00**

Hawkes signed, Kensington patt., bowl, brilliant-cut chains of hobstars & cane **2,000.00**

Pairpoint signed, bowl & ladle, large handle cut w/hobstar design on ladle, the set **500.00**

Parshe & Co.'s Empire patt., cups, set of 3 ....**30.00**

VASES

Corning's Rock Crystal patt., bud, 7" h. **125.00**

Egginton, wide serrated edge tapering to solid green ovoid body, clear pedestal & disc base, floral cut, 16" h..............**1,300.00**

Fry signed, Trojan patt., center w/eight-point hobstar within square w/large hobnail cut vesicas from each corner separated by short rows of notched prism cutting below buzzstars, 14" h.........................**800.00**

Geometric hobstars & vesicas, honeycomb-cut pedestal, rayed base, 12" h. **1,200.00**

Hawkes, chain of hobstars ring top & bottom, alternating columns of bull's-eyes & horizontal cut areas, 10" h.........**200.00**

Hawkes signed, slim bowling pin-shape, overall florals & leaves including under base, 12" h. **155.00**

Hawkes signed, Brunswick patt. variant, trumpet-shaped, hobstar cut foot.........................**295.00**

Hawkes signed, intaglio floral cutting, including the base, 12" h. **110.00**

Hawkes signed, lemon yellow enamel on engraved flowers, swags & ribbons w/gold on rim & shoulder, Steuben blank, 8½" h. **195.00**

Pitken & Brooks signed, Prism patt. w/chain of hobstars at base & top, 13" h...............................**400.00**

Quaker City's Empress patt., sharply cut on fine white blank, 23¾" h. **3,900.00**

Tuthill signed, Woodlily patt., 5" h. **525.00**

CZECHOSLOVAKIAN

At the close of World War I, Czechoslovakia was declared an independent republic and immediately developed a large export industry. Czechoslovakian glass factories produced a wide variety of colored and hand-painted glasswares from about 1918 until 1939, when the country was occupied by Germany at the outset of World War II. Between the wars, fine quality blown glasswares were produced along with a deluge of cheaper, vividly colored spatterwares for the American market. Subsequent production was primarily limited to cut crystal or Bohemian-type etched wares for the American market. Although it was marked, much Czechoslovakian glass is mistaken for the work of Tiffany, Loetz, or other glass artisans it imitates. It is often misrepresented and overpriced.

With the recent break-up of Czechoslovakia into two republics, such wares should gain added collector appeal.

Liquor set: decanter w/stopper & six footed tumblers; Art Deco style, the decanter of flattened ovoid form w/a flat shoulder centering a short cylindrical neck w/flattened rim & fitted w/a tall flattened diamond stopper, each tumbler w/a heavy conical foot tapering to an inverted conical bowl, all of clear glass w/intaglio-cut panels w/a deep amber background on the decanter front & stopper & on each tumbler, each cut w/a

stylized flower & leaf design,
tumblers 2¾" h., the decanter
5½" w., 11" h., the set.............**$775.00**

Vase, 6⅛" h., mottled colors
cased in white, applied three-
footed pedestal base **65.00**

Vase, 7" h., cased blue body
w/applied jet black rim, signed **45.00**

Wine set: decanter w/stopper &
three stemmed wines; all ruby-
stained & etched w/leafy
grapevines, signed, decanter
10" h., the set **75.00**

DAUM NANCY

This fine glass, much of it cameo, was made by Auguste and Antonin Daum, who founded a factory in 1875 in Nancy, France. Most of their cameo and enameled glass was made from the 1890s into the early 20th century.

Daum Nancy Marks

Cameo bowl-vase, footed
spherical body tapering to a
molded flat mouth, grey
internally mottled w/aubergine &
yellow, overlaid w/brown & cut
w/hydrangea leaves & applied
w/feasting beetles, signed in
cameo, beetles applied at a later
date, ca. 1900, 9" h. **$1,840.00**

Cameo lamp, table model, the
10½" d. domed mushroom-form
shade w/a turned-up rim pulled
into four points above the very
slender baluster-form lamp
pedestal w/a knobbed bottom
resting on a shaped wide disc
foot, the base & shade each in

Fine Daum Cameo Lamp

grey mottled w/yellow & overlaid
in orange & green, each cut w/a
leafy river landscape, simple
four-arm mount, shade signed in
cameo & w/the Cross of
Lorraine, ca. 1900, overall
20¼" h. (ILLUS.).................**10,325.00**

Cameo-vase, 10½" h., simple
ovoid form tapering to a short
neck w/a inverted ringed rim,
bright lemon yellow overlaid in
opalescent white, cut w/a
landscape w/tall conifers in the
foreground, signed in cameo
"DAUM - NANCY," w/the Cross
of Lorraine, ca. 1900 ....**4,140.00**

Cameo vase, 11¾" h., flattened
ovoid body w/a flat mouth &
flaring foot, grey over purple, the
grey layer cut w/a large thistle
plant & several Crosses of
Lorraine, on a rough acid-etched
ground, trimmed in gilt, signed in
gilt "Daum Nancy" w/a Cross of
Lorraine, gilt rubbed, ca. 1900...**920.00**

Cameo vase, 12" h., a cushion
foot below a bulbous base
tapering gently to a very tall
cylindrical neck w/a slightly

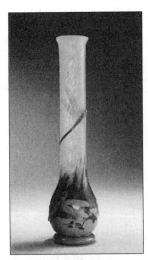

Rare Daum Cameo Vase

flared rim, grey shaded w/pale blue & aubergine, overlaid in green & yellow, cut around the button w/waterlilies & leafage & applied w/two wheel-carved large dragonflies, signed in cameo & w/the Cross of Lorraine, ca. 1900 (ILLUS.) ..**19,550.00**

Cameo vase, 17¼" h., a disc foot & squatty knob stem support a swelled slender body tapering to a tall cylindrical neck w/a flared rim, grey internally striated w/orange & salmon, overlaid w/deep navy blue & green, finely wheel-carved w/thorny prunus branches laden w/berries, signed in cameo **9,200.00**

Daum Enameled Jar & Tumbler

Jar, cover & underplate, squatty bulbous body w/a fitted low domed cover w/button finial, on a match round underplate, each in grey internally mottled w/yellow & pink, cut w/chrysanthemums & enameled in light blue, purple & charcoal, the jar sides applied w/faceted hemispheres internally shaded green, each back by gold foil, all sections trimmed in gold, jar & underplate signed in gilt "DAUM - NANCY" w/the Cross of Lorraine, 6" h., the set (ILLUS. left previous column).............**11,500.00**

Tumbler, domed foot w/wide ringed stem supporting a slightly flaring cylindrical bowl, grey cut & enameled w/designs of a fleur-de-lis, Cross of Lorraine, rampant lions & scrollwork, all reserved against textured grounds, enameled in shades of grey, ivory, black & brown, trimmed w/gold, signed in enamel "DAUM - NANCY" w/the Cross of Lorraine, 5¾" h. (ILLUS. right previous column) **4,600.00**

Vase, 6⅜" h., a thick round cushion foot below a small bulbed base flaring sharply to form a wide ovoid body w/a wide flat closed rim, grey mottled w/pale blue & white, cut w/an early fall landscape w/leafy trees amid a verdant meadow, enameled in shades of amber, charcoal brown, green & ochre, signed in enamel "DAUM - NANCY" & the Cross of Lorraine, ca. 1900................................**4,025.00**

Vase, 9¾" h., footed wide spherical body w/a short cylindrical neck w/a tapering rim, charcoal grey internally mottled w/random bubbles & black specks, cut w/geometric bands resembling overlapping feathers, inscribed "DUAM NANCY FRANCE" w/a Cross of Lorraine, ca. 1925 (ILLUS. top next page) **3,105.00**

Acid-etched Daum Nancy Vase

Vase, 14¾" h., cushion-footed baluster-form w/a swelled, incurved rim, grey streaked w/orange & cranberry, cut w/a woodland landscape enameled in umber & charcoal, signed in enamel "DAUM NANCY" & the Cross of Lorraine, ca. 1900..................................**3,737.00**

DEPRESSION

For an extensive listing of Depression Glass patterns see the forthcoming second edition of Antique Trader Books American Pressed Glass & Bottles Price Guide.

The phrase "Depression Glass" is used by collectors to denote a specific kind of transparent glass produced primarily as tablewares, in crystal, amber, blue, green, pink, milky-white, etc., during the late 1920s and 1930s when this country was in the midst of a financial depression. Made to sell inexpensively, it was turned out by such producers as Jeannette, Hocking, Westmoreland, Indiana and other glass companies. We compile prices on all the major Depression Glass patterns. Collectors should consult Depression Glass references for information on those patterns and pieces which have been reproduced.

AMERICAN SWEETHEART, MacBeth - Evans Glass Co., 1930-36 (Process-etched)

Bowl, berry, 3¾" d., pink **$63.00**

Bowl, cream soup, 4½" d., Monax......................................**112.00**

Bowl, cream soup, 4½" d., pink.....**85.00**

Bowl, cereal, 6" d., Monax **15.00**

Bowl, cereal, 6" d., pink................**15.00**

Bowl, berry, 9" d., Monax **61.00**

Bowl, berry, 9" d., pink **50.00**

Bowl, soup w/flanged rim, 9½" d., Monax..**75.00**

Bowl, soup w/flanged rim, 9½" d., pink..**68.00**

Bowl, 11" oval vegetable, Monax..**80.00**

Bowl, 11" oval vegetable, pink **65.00**

Console bowl, Monax, 18" d. **425.00**

Creamer, footed, blue **95.00**

Creamer, footed, Monax **12.00**

Creamer, footed, pink...................**14.00**

American Sweetheart Creamer and Sugar Bowl

Creamer, footed, ruby red (ILLUS. right) **106.00**

Cup & saucer, Monax..................**12.00**

Cup & saucer, pink **20.00**

Cup & saucer, ruby red **117.00**

Lamp shade, Monax **560.00**

Pitcher, 7½" h., 60 oz., jug-type, pink..**615.00**

Pitcher, 8" h., 80 oz., pink...........**622.00**

Plate, bread & butter, 6" d., Monax..**5.00**

Plate, bread & butter, 6" d., pink......**5.00**

Plate, salad, 8" d., blue...............**110.00**

Plate, salad, 8" d., Monax...............**9.00**

Plate, salad, 8" d., pink.................**11.00**

Plate, luncheon, 9" d., Monax **12.00**

Plate, dinner, 9¾" d., Monax **24.00**

Plate, dinner, 9¾" d., pink **38.00**

Plate, dinner, 10¼" d., Monax **20.00**

Plate, chop, 11" d., Monax **16.00**

Plate, salver, 12" d., Monax...........**19.00**

Plate, salver, 12" d., pink..............**21.00**

Plate, 15½" d., w/center handle,
Monax....................................**223.00**

Platter, 13" oval, Monax **64.00**

Platter, 13" oval, pink **52.00**

Salt & pepper shakers, footed,
Monax, pr. **318.00**

Salt & pepper shakers, footed,
pink, pr....................................**218.00**

Sherbet, footed, pink, 3¾" h..........**21.00**

Sherbet, footed, Monax, 4¼" h. **18.00**

Sherbet, footed, pink, 4¼" h..........**17.00**

Sherbet, metal holder, clear **14.00**

Sugar bowl, open, Monax..............**9.00**

Sugar bowl, open, pink.................**13.00**

Sugar bowl, open, ruby red
(ILLUS. w/creamer) **90.00**

Tidbit server, two-tier, pink...........**56.00**

Tidbit server, three-tier,
ruby red **575.00**

Tumbler, pink, 3½" h., 5 oz. **87.00**

Tumbler, pink, 4¼" h., 9 oz. **78.00**

Tumbler, pink, 4¾" h., 10 oz. **95.00**

CHERRY BLOSSOM
Jeannette Glass Co., 1930-38
(Process-etched)

Bowl, berry, 4¾" d., Delphite.........**15.00**

Bowl, berry, 4¾" d., green.............**18.00**

Bowl, berry, 4¾" d., pink **17.00**

Bowl, cereal, 5¾" d., green **37.00**

Bowl, cereal, 5¾" d., pink..............**43.00**

Bowl, soup, 7¾" d., green **57.00**

Bowl, soup, 7¾" d., pink................**72.00**

Bowl, berry, 8½" d., green.............**44.00**

Bowl, berry, 8½" d., pink **47.00**

Bowl, 9" d., two-handled,
Delphite **32.00**

Bowl, 9" d., two-handled, green **57.00**

Bowl, 9" d., two-handled, pink.......**46.00**

Bowl, 9" oval vegetable, green......**46.00**

Bowl, 9" oval vegetable, pink **44.00**

Bowl, fruit, 10½" d., three-footed,
green **79.00**

Bowl, fruit, 10½" d., three-footed,
pink..**84.00**

Butter dish, cov., green **80.00**

Butter dish, cov., pink..................**84.00**

Cake plate, three-footed, green,
10¼" d. **31.00**

Cake plate, three-footed, pink,
10¼" d. **29.00**

Coaster, green **13.00**

Coaster, pink **15.00**

Creamer, Delphite **20.00**

Creamer, green **18.00**

Creamer, pink..............................**20.00**

Cup, Delphite...............................**18.00**

Cup & saucer, Delphite **23.00**

Cup & saucer, green **24.00**

Cup & saucer, pink **25.00**

Cherry Blossom Mug

Mug, green, 7 oz. (ILLUS.) **177.00**

Pitcher, 6¾" h., 36 oz., overall
patt., Delphite **92.00**

Pitcher, 6¾" h., 36 oz., overall
patt., green **58.00**

Pitcher, 6¾" h., 36 oz., overall
patt., pink...................................**59.00**

Pitcher, 8" h., 36 oz., footed,
cone-shaped, patt. top, green **59.00**

Pitcher, 8" h., 36 oz., footed,
cone-shaped, patt. top, pink........**67.00**

Pitcher, 8" h., 42 oz., patt.
top, green **56.00**

Pitcher, 8" h., 42 oz., patt.
top, pink **55.00**

Plate, sherbet, 6" d., green..............**8.00**

Plate, sherbet, 6" d., pink **8.00**

Plate, salad, 7" d., green **21.00**

Plate, salad, 7" d., pink..................**21.00**

Plate, dinner, 9" d., Delphite..........**18.00**

Plate, dinner, 9" d., green..............**23.00**

Plate, dinner, 9" d., pink **23.00**

Plate, grill, 9" d., green **26.00**

Plate, grill, 9" d., pink....................**24.00**

Platter, 11" oval, green..................**43.00**

Platter, 11" oval, pink **44.00**

Platter, 13" oval, green..................**63.00**

Platter, 11" oval, pink **64.00**

Platter, 13" oval, divided, pink.......**68.00**

Salt & pepper shakers, green,
pr. **1,085.00**

Sandwich tray, handled,
Delphite, 10½" d. **23.00**

Sandwich tray, handled, green,
10½" d. **27.00**

Sandwich tray, handled, pink,
10½" d. **26.00**

Sherbet, green **18.00**

Sherbet, pink...............................**17.00**

Sugar bowl, cov., green...............**36.00**

Sugar bowl, cov., pink **33.00**

Sugar bowl, open, Delphite **19.00**

Sugar bowl, open, green **16.00**

Sugar bowl, open, pink.................**13.00**

Tumbler, patt. top, green, 3½" h.,
4 oz..**25.00**

Tumbler, patt. top, pink, 3½" h.,
4 oz..**22.00**

Tumbler, juice, footed, overall
patt., Delphite, 3¾" h., 4 oz. **18.00**

Tumbler, juice, footed, overall
patt., green, 3¾" h., 4 oz. **23.00**

Tumbler, juice, footed, overall
patt., pink, 3¾" h., 4 oz...............**18.00**

Tumbler, footed, overall patt.,
Delphite, 4½" h., 8 oz. **20.00**

Tumbler, footed, overall patt.,
green, 4½" h., 8 oz. **33.00**

Tumbler, footed, overall patt.,
pink, 4½" h., 8 oz........................**33.00**

Tumbler, patt. top, green, 4¼" h.,
9 oz...**23.00**

Tumbler, patt. top, pink, 4¼" h.,
9 oz...**23.00**

Tumbler, footed, overall patt.,
Delphite, 4½" h., 9 oz. **23.00**

Tumbler, footed, overall patt.,
green, 4½" h., 9 oz. **31.00**

Tumbler, footed, overall patt.,
pink, 4½" h., 9 oz.......................**32.00**

Tumbler, patt. top, pink, 5" h.,
12 oz...**67.00**

Water set: pitcher & 6 tumblers;
green, 7 pcs.............................**165.00**

Water set: pitcher & 6 tumblers;
pink, 7 pcs. **126.00**

JUNIOR SET:

Creamer, Delphite **43.00**

Creamer, pink..............................**50.00**

Cup, Delphite...............................**31.00**

Cup, pink **35.00**

Cup & saucer, Delphite **44.00**

Cup & saucer, pink **43.00**

Plate, 6" d., Delphite....................**12.00**

Plate, 6" d., pink **13.00**

Saucer, Delphite............................**6.00**

Saucer, pink **8.00**

Sugar bowl, Delphite **42.00**

Sugar bowl, pink..........................**43.00**

14 pc. set, Delphite **322.00**

14 pc. set, pink...........................**322.00**

DOGWOOD or Apple Blossom or Wild Rose, MacBeth-Evans, 1929-32 (Process-etched)

Bowl, cereal, 5½" d., green...........**27.00**

Bowl, cereal, 5½" d., pink..............**30.00**

Bowl, berry, 8½" d., Cremax **31.00**

Bowl, berry, 8½" d., Monax **44.00**

Bowl, berry, 8½" d., pink **58.00**

Bowl, fruit, 10¼" d., green...........**223.00**

Cake plate, heavy solid foot,
green, 13" d. **125.00**

Cake plate, heavy solid foot,
pink, 13" d.................................**119.00**

Creamer, thin, green, 2½" h. **46.00**

Creamer, thin, pink, 2½" h.............**18.00**

Creamer, thick, footed, pink,
3¼" h. **19.00**

Cup & saucer, Cremax **35.00**

Cup & saucer, green **39.00**

Cup & saucer, Monax **39.00**

Dogwood Pattern Pieces

Cup & saucer, pink (ILLUS.).........**22.00**

Pitcher, 8" h., 80 oz., American
Sweetheart style, pink **565.00**

Pitcher, 8" h., 80 oz., decorated,
pink..**172.00**

Plate, bread & butter, 6" d.,
green **8.00**

Plate, bread & butter, 6" d., pink..... **8.00**

Plate, luncheon, 8" d., clear............**4.00**

Plate, luncheon, 8" d., green **8.00**

Plate, luncheon, 8" d., pink.............**8.00**

Plate, dinner, 9¼" d., pink **34.00**

Plate, grill, 10½" d., overall patt.
or border design only, green **18.00**

Plate, grill, 10½" d., border
design, pink **18.00**

Plate, grill, 10½" d., overall patt.,
pink (ILLUS. w/cup & saucer)......**20.00**

Plate, salver, 12" d., Monax...........**19.00**

Plate, salver, 12" d., pink..............**26.00**

Platter, 12" oval, pink **481.00**

Sherbet, low foot, pink **34.00**

Sugar bowl, open, thin, green,
2½" h. **31.00**

Sugar bowl, open, thin, pink,
2½" h. **17.00**

Sugar bowl, open, thick, footed,
pink, 3¼" h.................................**18.00**

Tumbler, decorated, pink, 3½" h.,
5 oz..**298.00**

Tumbler, decorated, green, 4" h.,
10 oz..**83.00**

Tumbler, decorated, pink, 4" h.,
10 oz..**38.00**

Tumbler, decorated, green,
4¾" h., 11 oz. **116.00**

Tumbler, decorated, pink,
4¾" h., 11 oz. **47.00**

Tumbler, decorated, pink,
5" h., 12 oz. **60.00**

Tumbler, molded band, pink **18.00**

FLORENTINE or Poppy No. 2, Hazel Atlas Glass Co., 1932-35 (Process-etched)

Bowl, berry, 4½" d., clear **11.00**

Bowl, berry, 4½" d., green............**12.00**

Bowl, berry, 4½" d., pink **15.00**

Bowl, berry, 4½" d., yellow............**18.00**

Bowl, cream soup, plain rim,
4¾" d., clear **11.00**

Bowl, cream soup, plain rim,
4¾" d., green **15.00**

Bowl, cream soup, plain rim,
4¾" d., pink.................................**14.00**

Bowl, cream soup, plain rim,
4¾" d., yellow **21.00**

Bowl, 5½" d., yellow **41.00**

Bowl, cereal, 6" d., green 23.00

Bowl, cereal, 6" d., yellow 41.00

Bowl, 8" d., clear 20.00

Bowl, 8" d., green 25.00

Bowl, 8" d., pink 31.00

Bowl, 8" d., yellow 32.00

Bowl, cov. vegetable, 9" oval, clear..47.00

Bowl, cov. vegetable, 9" oval, green 54.00

Florentine Vegetable Bowl

Bowl, cov. vegetable, 9" oval, yellow (ILLUS.) 60.00

Bowl, 9" oval vegetable, green......23.00

Bowl, 9" oval vegetable, yellow.....21.00

Butter dish, cov., clear 93.00

Butter dish, cov., green 99.00

Butter dish, cov., yellow 148.00

Candlesticks, green, 2¾" h., pr. ...53.00

Candlesticks, yellow, 2¾" h., pr. ..60.00

Candy dish, cov., clear 94.00

Candy dish, cov., green.............105.00

Candy dish, cov., pink 124.00

Candy dish, cov., yellow.............148.00

Coaster, clear, 3¼" d. 12.00

Coaster, green, 3¼" d. 13.00

Coaster, pink, 3¼" d.....................18.00

Coaster, yellow, 3¼" d. 21.00

Coaster-ashtray, clear, 3¾" d. 18.00

Coaster-ashtray, green, 3¾" d. 18.00

Coaster-ashtray, yellow, 3¾" d. ...25.00

Coaster-ashtray, green, 5½" d. 22.00

Coaster-ashtray, yellow, 5½" d. ...35.00

Compote, 3½", ruffled, clear 22.00

Compote, 3½", ruffled, cobalt blue...50.00

Compote, 3½", ruffled, green........21.00

Compote, 3½", ruffled, pink 21.00

Condiment set: creamer, cov. sugar bowl, salt & pepper shakers & 8½" d. tray; yellow, 5 pcs. 145.00

Creamer, clear 6.00

Creamer, green 10.00

Creamer, yellow 12.00

Cup & saucer, clear........................9.00

Cup & saucer, green 13.00

Cup & saucer, pink 12.00

Cup & saucer, yellow....................14.00

Custard cup, green.......................70.00

Custard cup, yellow......................77.00

Gravy boat, yellow 51.00

Gravy boat w/platter, yellow, 11½" oval...................................99.00

Pitcher, 6¼" h., 24 oz., cone-shaped, yellow...........................134.00

Pitcher, 7½" h., 28 oz., cone-shaped, clear...............................28.00

Pitcher, 7½" h., 28 oz., cone-shaped, green 43.00

Pitcher, 7½" h., 28 oz., cone-shaped, yellow...........................29.00

Pitcher, 7½" h., 48 oz., straight sides, pink 126.00

Pitcher, 7½" h., 48 oz., straight sides, yellow 168.00

Pitcher, 8¼" h., 76 oz., clear.........58.00

Pitcher, 8¼" h., 76 oz., green 85.00

Pitcher, 8¼" h., 76 oz., pink 235.00

Pitcher, 8¼" h., 76 oz., yellow.....400.00

Plate, sherbet, 6" d., clear 4.00

Plate, sherbet, 6" d., green.............4.00

Plate, sherbet, 6" d., yellow 6.00

Plate, 6¼" d., w/indentation, yellow 30.00

Plate, salad, 8½" d., clear..............7.00

Plate, salad, 8½" d., green **11.00**

Plate, salad, 8½" d., yellow **11.00**

Plate, dinner, 10" d., clear **11.00**

Plate, dinner, 10" d., green...........**15.00**

Plate, dinner, 10" d., yellow **15.00**

Plate, grill, 10¼" d., clear..............**12.00**

Plate, grill, 10¼" d., green **14.00**

Plate, grill, 10¼" d., yellow **13.00**

Platter, 11" oval, clear **8.00**

Platter, 11" oval, green.................**17.00**

Platter, 11" oval, yellow................**20.00**

Platter, 11½" , for gravy boat,
yellow **37.00**

Relish dish, three-part or plain,
clear, 10" **13.00**

Relish dish, three-part or plain,
green, 10".....................................**22.00**

Relish dish, three-part or plain,
pink, 10".......................................**24.00**

Relish dish, three-part or plain,
yellow, 10" **29.00**

Salt & pepper shakers, clear,
pr. **39.00**

Salt & pepper shakers, green.,
pr **43.00**

Salt & pepper shakers, yellow,
pr **47.00**

Sherbet, clear................................**10.00**

Sherbet, green **11.00**

Sherbet, yellow **11.00**

Sugar bowl, cov., clear **24.00**

Sugar bowl, cov., green.................**19.00**

Sugar bowl, cov., yellow...............**34.00**

Sugar bowl, open, clear..................**9.00**

Sugar bowl, open, green **9.00**

Sugar bowl, open, yellow **11.00**

Tray, yellow, 8½" d. **87.00**

Tumbler, footed, clear, 3¼" h.,
5 oz...**13.00**

Tumbler, footed, green, 3¼" h.,
5 oz...**14.00**

Tumbler, footed, yellow, 3¼" h.,
5 oz...**14.00**

Tumbler, juice, clear, 3½" h.,
5 oz...**9.00**

Tumbler, juice, green, 3½" h.,
5 oz...**13.00**

Tumbler, juice, pink, 3Z\x" h.,
5 oz...**12.00**

Tumbler, juice, yellow, 3½" h.,
5 oz...**18.00**

Tumbler, footed, clear, 4" h.,
5 oz...**12.00**

Tumbler, footed, green., 4" h.,
5 oz...**14.00**

Tumbler, footed, yellow, 4" h.,
5 oz...**16.00**

Tumbler, blown, clear, 3½" h.,
6 oz...**16.00**

Tumbler, blown, green, 3½" h.,
6 oz...**14.00**

Tumbler, water, clear, 4" h.,
9 oz...**11.00**

Tumbler, water, cobalt blue, 4" h.,
9 oz...**51.00**

Tumbler, water, green., 4" h.,
9 oz...**15.00**

Tumbler, water, pink, 4" h.,
9 oz...**16.00**

Tumbler, water, yellow, 4" h.,
9 oz...**20.00**

Tumbler, footed, green, 4½" h.,
9 oz...**24.00**

Tumbler, footed, yellow, 4½" h.,
9 oz...**35.00**

Tumbler, blown, clear, 5" h.,
12 oz..**20.00**

Tumbler, blown, green., 5" h.,
12 oz..**16.00**

Tumbler, iced tea, clear, 5" h.,
12 oz..**24.00**

Tumbler, iced tea, green,
5" h., 12 oz. **33.00**

Tumbler, iced tea, yellow,
5" h., 12 oz. **43.00**

Vase (or parfait), 6" h., clear **28.00**

Vase (or parfait), 6" h., green.......**37.00**

Vase (or parfait), 6" h., yellow **58.00**

IRIS or Iris & Herringbone
Jeannette Glass Co., 1928-32
(Press-mold)

Berry set: 9½" d. ruffled fruit bowl & 6 sauce dishes; clear, 7 pcs.....**68.00**

Bowl, berry, 4½" d., beaded rim, amber iridescent..........................**10.00**

Bowl, berry, 4½": d., beaded rim, clear..**44.00**

Bowl, cereal, 5" d., clear **129.00**

Bowl, sauce, 5" d., ruffled rim, amber iridescent..........................**27.00**

Bowl, sauce, 5" d., ruffled rim, clear..**9.00**

Bowl, soup, 7½" d., amber iridescent......................................**70.00**

Bowl, soup, 7½" d., clear **161.00**

Bowl, berry, 8" d., beaded rim, amber iridescent..........................**23.00**

Bowl, berry, 8" d., beaded rim, clear..**92.00**

Bowl, salad, 9½" d., amber iridescent......................................**14.00**

Bowl, salad, 9½" d., clear.............**15.00**

Bowl, fruit, 11" d., straight rim, clear..**57.00**

Bowl, fruit, 11" d., straight rim, amber iridescent..........................**16.00**

Bowl, fruit, 11" d., straight rim, clear..**14.00**

Butter dish, cov., amber iridescent......................................**48.00**

Butter dish, cov., clear **48.00**

Candlesticks, two-branch, amber iridescent, pr.............................**45.00**

Candlesticks, two-branch, clear, pr. **41.00**

Candy jar, cov., clear **170.00**

Coaster, clear.............................**103.00**

Creamer, footed, amber iridescent......................................**13.00**

Creamer, footed, clear **13.00**

Cup & saucer, demitasse, clear..**193.00**

Cup & saucer, demitasse, ruby ..**288.00**

Cup & saucer, amber iridescent ...**23.00**

Cup & saucer, clear.....................**26.00**

Goblet, wine, amber iridescent, 4¼" h., 3 oz. **31.00**

Goblet, wine, clear, 4¼" h., 3 oz. ..**15.00**

Goblet, cocktail, clear, 4¼" h., 4 oz...**24.00**

Goblet, clear, 5¾" h., 4 oz.............**24.00**

Lamp shade, blue **70.00**

Lamp shade, clear **82.00**

Lamp shade, clear frosted **87.00**

Lamp shade, pink **79.00**

Lamp shade, pink frosted **85.00**

Nut set: 11½" d. ruffled bowl in metal holder, w/nutcracker & picks; amber iridescent, the set.....................................**120.00**

Nut set: 11½" d. ruffled bowl in metal holder, w/nutcracker & picks; clear, the set **68.00**

Pitcher, 9½" h., footed, amber iridescent......................................**38.00**

Pitcher, 9½" h., footed, clear.........**39.00**

Plate, sherbet, 5½" d., amber iridescent......................................**13.00**

Plate, sherbet, 5½" d., clear **13.00**

Plate, luncheon, 8" d., clear.........**113.00**

Plate, dinner, 9" d., amber iridescent......................................**43.00**

Plate, dinner, 9" d., clear **54.00**

Plate, sandwich, 11¾" d., amber iridescent......................................**29.00**

Plate, sandwich, 11¾" d., clear **40.00**

Sherbet, footed, amber iridescent, 2½" h.........................**13.00**

Sherbet, footed, clear, 2½" h. **24.00**

Sherbet, footed, clear, 4" h. **20.00**

Sugar bowl, cov., footed, amber iridescent......................................**27.00**

Sugar bowl, cov., footed, clear **26.00**

Sugar bowl, open, footed, amber iridescent......................................**10.00**

Sugar bowl, open, footed, clear....**12.00**

Tumbler, clear, 4" h.....................**136.00**

Tumbler, footed, amber iridescent, 6" h............................**18.00**

Tumbler, footed, clear, 6" h...........**18.00**

Tumbler, footed, clear, 6½" h........**33.00**

Vase, 9" h., amber iridescent.........**24.00**

Vase, 9" h., clear **28.00**

Water set: pitcher & 7 tumblers;
clear, in original box, 8 pcs. **225.00**

MAYFAIR or Open Rose, Hocking Glass Co., 1931-37 (Process-etched)

Bowl, cream soup, 5", pink............**48.00**

Bowl, cereal, 5½", blue **49.00**

Bowl, cereal, 5½", pink..................**26.00**

Bowl, vegetable, 7", blue...............**52.00**

Bowl, vegetable, 7", pink...............**26.00**

Bowl, vegetable, 7", pink frosted...**18.00**

Bowl, 9½" oval vegetable, blue **72.00**

Bowl, 9½" oval vegetable, pink **34.00**

Bowl, 10", cov. vegetable, blue ...**130.00**

Bowl, 10", cov. vegetable, pink ...**114.00**

Bowl, 10", open vegetable, blue....**74.00**

Bowl, 10", open vegetable, pink....**25.00**

Bowl, 11¾" d., low, blue...............**82.00**

Bowl, 11¾" d., low, green **38.00**

Bowl, 11¾" d., low, pink **60.00**

Bowl, fruit, 12" d., deep,
scalloped, blue **91.00**

Bowl, fruit, 12" d., deep,
scalloped, green. **40.00**

Bowl, fruit, 12" d., deep,
scalloped, pink............................**55.00**

Butter dish, cov., blue **306.00**

Butter dish, cov., pink..................**69.00**

Cake plate, footed, blue, 10".........**68.00**

Cake plate, footed, pink, 10" **25.00**

Cake plate, handled, blue, 12" **64.00**

Cake plate, handled, pink, 12" **35.00**

Cake plate, handled, pink frosted,
12" **31.00**

Candy jar, cov., blue **299.00**

Candy jar, cov., pink **55.00**

Candy jar, cov., pink frosted **38.00**

Celery dish, blue, 10" l.................**51.00**

Celery dish, pink, 10" l.................**48.00**

Celery dish, two-part, blue, 10" l...**62.00**

Celery dish, two-part, pink,
10" l. **209.00**

Cookie jar, cov., blue **300.00**

Cookie jar, cov., green...............**541.00**

Cookie jar, cov., pink **53.00**

Creamer, footed, blue **84.00**

Creamer, footed, pink...................**25.00**

Creamer, footed, pink frosted........**16.00**

Cup & 5¾" underplate, blue **76.00**

Cup & 5¾" underplate, pink **36.00**

Cup & saucer w/cup ring, pink **36.00**

Decanter w/stopper, pink,
10" h., 32 oz. **176.00**

Decanter, no stopper, pink,
10" h., 32 oz. **84.00**

Goblet, wine, pink, 4½" h., 3 oz. ...**81.00**

Goblet, cocktail, pink, 4" h.,
3½ oz...**85.00**

Goblet, water, pink, 5¾" h., 9 oz. ..**63.00**

Goblet, water, thin, blue, 7¼" h.,
9 oz..**209.00**

Pitcher, juice, 6" h., 37 oz., blue..**156.00**

Pitcher, juice, 6" h., 37 oz., pink....**51.00**

Pitcher, 8" h., 60 oz., jug-type,
blue...**195.00**

Pitcher, 8" h., 60 oz., jug-type,
pink.. **57.00**

Pitcher, 8½" h., 80 oz., jug-type,
pink..**106.00**

Plate (or saucer), 5¾", blue..........**24.00**

Plate (or saucer), 5¾", pink..........**12.00**

Plate, sherbet, 6½" d., pink **14.00**

Plate, sherbet, 6½ d., off-center
indentation, blue **26.00**

Plate, sherbet, 6½ d., off-center
indentation, pink **14.00**

Plate, luncheon, 8½", blue.............**54.00**

Plate, luncheon, 8½", pink.............**26.00**

Plate, dinner, 9½", blue **78.00**

Plate, dinner, 9½", pink (ILLUS.
top next page) **50.00**

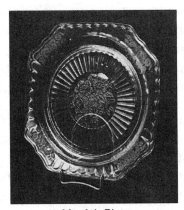

Mayfair Plate

Plate, grill, 9½", blue.....................**65.00**

Plate, grill, 9½", pink.....................**39.00**

Platter, 12" oval, open handles, blue...**72.00**

Platter, 12" oval, open handles, pink...**28.00**

Platter, 12½" oval, closed handles, yellow.........................**200.00**

Relish, four-part, blue, 8⅜" **65.00**

Relish, four-part, pink, 8⅜"............**33.00**

Salt & pepper shakers, flat, blue, pr. **309.00**

Salt & pepper shakers, flat, pink, pr. **66.00**

Salt & pepper shakers, flat, yellow, pr. **1,175.00**

Sandwich server w/center handle, blue, 12".......................**81.00**

Sandwich server w/center handle, green, 12" **36.00**

Sandwich server w/center handle, pink, 12" **40.00**

Sandwich server w/center handle, pink frosted, 12".............**23.00**

Sherbet, flat, blue, 2¼" h.............**134.00**

Sherbet, flat, pink, 2¼" h.............**153.00**

Sherbet, footed, pink, 3" h.............**16.00**

Sherbet, footed, blue, 4¾" h. **84.00**

Sherbet, footed, pink, 4¾" h..........**88.00**

Sugar bowl, open, footed, blue.....**81.00**

Sugar bowl, open, footed, pink.....**28.00**

Sugar bowl, open, footed, pink frosted **16.00**

Tumbler, whiskey, pink, 2¼" h., 1½ oz...**73.00**

Tumbler, juice, footed, pink, 3¼" h., 3 oz...**80.00**

Tumbler, juice, blue, 3½" h., 5 oz...**100.00**

Tumbler, juice, pink, 3½" h., 5 oz...**46.00**

Tumbler, water, blue, 4¼" h., 9 oz...**112.00**

Tumbler, water, pink, 4¼" h., 9 oz...**32.00**

Tumbler, footed, blue, 5¼" h., 10 oz...**152.00**

Tumbler, footed, pink, 5¼" h., 10 oz...**36.00**

Tumbler, water, blue, 4¾" h., 11 oz...**139.00**

Tumbler, water, pink, 4¾" h., 11 oz...**129.00**

Tumbler, iced tea, pink, 5¼" h., 13½ oz. **51.00**

Tumbler, iced tea, footed, blue, 67½" h., 15 oz. **183.00**

Tumbler, iced tea, footed, pink, 67½" h., 15 oz. **47.00**

Vase, 5½ x 8½", sweetpea, hat-shaped, blue.............................**114.00**

Vase, 5½ x 8½", sweetpea, hat-shaped, pink **157.00**

Wine set: decanter, 5 wines, pink, 6 pcs **525.00**

MOONSTONE, Anchor Hocking Glass Corp., 1941-46 (Press-mold)

Bonbon, heart-shaped, w/handle, 6½" w...**11.00**

Bowl, berry, 5½" d.........................**15.00**

Bowl, dessert, 5½" d., crimped rim **9.00**

Bowl, 6" w., three-part, cloverleaf-shaped.......................................**12.00**

Bowl, 6½" d., two-handled, crimped rim.................................**13.00**

Bowl, 7¾" d., flat **13.00**

Bowl, 9½" d., crimped rim **21.00**

Candleholder................................**10.00**

Candleholders, pr.........................**17.00**

Candy dish, cov., two-handled,
  6" d...**26.00**

Cigarette box, cov., rectangular ...**22.00**

Creamer, footed **10.00**

Cup & saucer................................**14.00**

Dinner set, service for four, 23
  pcs...**275.00**

Moonstone Goblet

Goblet, 10 oz. (ILLUS.) **20.00**

Plate, sherbet, 6¼" d. **6.00**

Plate, luncheon, 8" d. **14.00**

Plate, sandwich, 10" d., crimped
  rim **24.00**

Puff box, cov., 4¾" d.....................**23.00**

Relish bowl, divided, 7¾" d. **9.00**

Sherbet, footed **8.00**

Sugar bowl, footed **9.00**

Vase, bud, 5½" h. **12.00**

PARROT or Sylvan, Federal Glass Co., 1931-32 (Process-etched)

Bowl, berry, 5" sq., amber.............**21.00**

Bowl, berry, 5" sq., green..............**27.00**

Bowl, soup, 7" sq., amber **33.00**

Bowl, soup, 7" sq., green **45.00**

Bowl, large berry, 8" sq., green.....**58.00**

Bowl, 10" oval vegetable, green....**58.00**

Butter dish, cov., green **356.00**

Creamer, footed, green **51.00**

Cup & saucer, amber **39.00**

Cup & saucer, green **61.00**

Hot plate, green, scalloped
  edge **888.00**

Jam dish, amber, 7" sq. **34.00**

Plate, sherbet, 5¾" sq., amber **21.00**

Plate, sherbet, 5¾" sq., green **28.00**

Plate, salad, 7½" sq., green **38.00**

Plate, dinner, 9" sq., amber...........**40.00**

Plate, dinner, 9" sq., green **54.00**

Plate, grill, 10½" sq., amber **30.00**

Platter, 11¼" oblong, green **51.00**

Salt & pepper shakers, green,
  pr. **246.00**

Sherbet, footed, cone-shaped,
  amber **23.00**

Sherbet, footed, cone-shaped,
  green **24.00**

Sugar bowl, cov., green.............**183.00**

Tumbler, footed, amber, 5½" h.,
  10 oz..**150.00**

Tumbler, footed, cone-shaped,
  amber, 5¾" h. **116.00**

Tumbler, footed, cone-shaped,
  green, 5¾" h. **151.00**

PATRICIAN or Spoke, Federal Glass Co., 1933-37 (Process-etched)

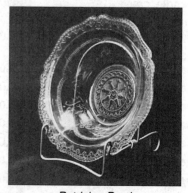

Patrician Bowl

Bowl, cream soup, 4¾" d.,
amber **15.00**

Bowl, cream soup, 4¾" d., pink.....**19.00**

Bowl, berry, 5" d., amber..............**10.00**

Bowl, berry, 5" d., clear **11.00**

Bowl, berry, 5" d., green...............**12.00**

Bowl, berry, 5" d., pink **14.00**

Bowl, cereal, 6" d., amber **23.00**

Bowl, cereal, 6" d., clear **20.00**

Bowl, cereal, 6" d., green **21.00**

Bowl, cereal, 6" d., pink................**25.00**

Bowl, large berry, 8½" d., amber...**43.00**

Bowl, large berry, 8½" d., clear **37.00**

Bowl, large berry, 8½" d., green....**32.00**

Bowl, large berry, 8½" d., pink
(ILLUS.) **29.00**

Bowl, 10" oval vegetable, amber...**30.00**

Bowl, 10" oval vegetable, clear **30.00**

Bowl, 10" oval vegetable, green....**33.00**

Butter dish, cov., amber **87.00**

Butter dish, cov., clear **86.00**

Butter dish, cov., green **98.00**

Butter dish, cov., pink.................**213.00**

Cookie jar, cov., amber.................**81.00**

Cookie jar, cov., clear **78.00**

Creamer, footed, clear **11.00**

Creamer, footed, green **14.00**

Creamer, footed, pink...................**12.00**

Cup & saucer, amber **18.00**

Cup & saucer, green **19.00**

Jam dish, amber, 6"......................**29.00**

Jam dish, green, 6".......................**30.00**

Pitcher, 8" h., 75 oz., molded
handle, amber **110.00**

Pitcher, 8" h., 75 oz., molded
handle, clear.............................**107.00**

Pitcher, 8" h., 75 oz., molded
handle, green **148.00**

Pitcher, 8" h., 75 oz., molded
handle, pink **119.00**

Pitcher, 8¼" h., 75 oz., applied
handle, clear.............................**128.00**

Plate, sherbet, 6" d., amber...........**10.00**

Plate, sherbet, 6" d., green.............**7.00**

Plate, sherbet, 6" d., pink **8.00**

Plate, salad, 7½" d., amber **15.00**

Plate, salad, 7½" d., clear.............**14.00**

Plate, salad, 7½" d., green **16.00**

Plate, luncheon, 9" d., amber **11.00**

Plate, luncheon, 9" d., clear...........**11.00**

Plate, luncheon, 9" d., green **14.00**

Plate, luncheon, 9" d., pink............**13.00**

Plate, dinner, 10½" d., amber..........**7.00**

Plate, dinner, 10½" d., clear **8.00**

Plate, dinner, 10½" d., green........**39.00**

Plate, dinner, 10½" d., pink **32.00**

Plate, grill, 10½" d., amber **13.00**

Plate, grill, 10½" d., clear..............**13.00**

Plate, grill, 10½" d., green **15.00**

Platter, 11½" oval, amber..............**30.00**

Platter, 11½" oval, clear **28.00**

Platter, 11½" oval, green..............**26.00**

Salt & pepper shakers, amber,
pr. **59.00**

Salt & pepper shakers, clear,
pr. **62.00**

Salt & pepper shakers, green,
pr. **64.00**

Salt & pepper shakers, pink, pr. ..**81.00**

Sherbet, amber **11.00**

Sherbet, clear...............................**12.00**

Sherbet, green **14.00**

Sherbet, pink................................**13.00**

Sugar bowl, cov., amber...............**63.00**

Sugar bowl, cov., clear **54.00**

Sugar bowl, open, amber **8.00**

Sugar bowl, open, clear..................**8.00**

Sugar bowl, open, green **11.00**

Sugar bowl, open, pink................**11.00**

Tumbler, amber, 4" h., 5 oz. **34.00**

Tumbler, green, 4" h., 5 oz. **26.00**

Tumbler, pink, 4" h., 5 oz. **33.00**

Tumbler, footed, amber, 5¼" h.,
8 oz...**47.00**

Tumbler, footed, clear, 5¼" h.,
8 oz...**34.00**

Tumbler, footed, green, 5¼" h.,
8 oz..53.00

Tumbler, amber, 4½" h., 9 oz. 29.00

Tumbler, clear, 4½" h., 9 oz..........28.00

Tumbler, green, 4½" h., 9 oz. 27.00

Tumbler, pink, 4½" h., 9 oz. 31.00

Tumbler, iced tea, amber, 5½" h.,
14 oz...47.00

ROYAL LACE, Hazel Atlas Glass Co., 1934-41 (Process-etched)

Royal Lace Butter Dish

Bowl, cream soup, 4¾" d., blue 42.00

Bowl, cream soup, 4¾" d., clear ...13.00

Bowl, cream soup, 4¾" d., green ..30.00

Bowl, cream soup, 4¾" d., pink.....27.00

Bowl, berry, 5" d., clear.................13.00

Bowl, berry, 5" d., pink 32.00

Bowl, berry, 10" d., blue 87.00

Bowl, berry, 10" d., green..............34.00

Bowl, berry, 10" d., pink 34.00

Bowl, 10" d., three-footed, rolled
edge, pink..................................85.00

Bowl, 10" d., three-footed, ruffled
edge, clear.................................42.00

Bowl, 10" d., three-footed, ruffled
edge, pink..................................80.00

Bowl, 10" d., three-footed,
straight edge, blue......................86.00

Bowl, 10" d., three-footed,
straight edge, clear.....................13.00

Bowl, 11" oval vegetable, blue 61.00

Bowl, 11" oval vegetable, clear 21.00

Bowl, 11" oval vegetable, green....33.00

Bowl, 11" oval vegetable, pink 34.00

Butter dish, cov., blue 565.00

Butter dish, cov., clear (ILLUS.) ...66.00

Butter dish, cov., green 251.00

Butter dish, cov., pink................145.00

Candlesticks, rolled edge, blue,
pr. 203.00

Candlesticks, rolled edge, clear,
pr. 49.00

Candlesticks, rolled edge, pink,
pr. 52.00

Candlesticks, ruffled edge, clear,
pr. 28.00

Candlesticks, straight edge,
blue, pr. 143.00

Candlesticks, straight edge,
clear, pr. 32.00

Candlesticks, straight edge,
green, pr. 63.00

Cookie jar, cov., blue 441.00

Cookie jar, cov., clear 35.00

Cookie jar, cov., green.................88.00

Cookie jar, cov., pink 62.00

Creamer, footed, blue 57.00

Creamer, footed, clear 12.00

Creamer, footed, green 30.00

Creamer, footed, pink...................21.00

Cup & saucer, blue......................47.00

Cup & saucer, clear.....................15.00

Cup & saucer, green 30.00

Cup & saucer, pink 24.00

Pitcher, 48 oz., straight sides,
blue..180.00

Pitcher, 48 oz., straight sides,
clear...39.00

Pitcher, 48 oz., straight sides,
green 96.00

Pitcher, 48 oz., straight sides,
pink..92.00

Pitcher, 8" h., 64 oz., without ice
lip, blue 196.00

Pitcher, 8" h., 64 oz., without ice
lip, green....................................80.00

Pitcher, 8" h., 64 oz., without ice lip, pink **116.00**

Pitcher, 8" h., 68 oz., w/ice lip, clear..**40.00**

Pitcher, 8" h., 68 oz., w/ice lip, pink..**98.00**

Pitcher, 8" h., 86 oz., without ice lip, green.......................................**146.00**

Pitcher, 8" h., 86 oz., without ice lip, pink **78.00**

Pitcher, 8½" h.,96 oz., w/ice lip, blue...**289.00**

Pitcher, 8½" h.,96 oz., w/ice lip, clear..**56.00**

Pitcher, 8½" h.,96 oz., w/ice lip, green **153.00**

Pitcher, 8½" h.,96 oz., w/ice lip, pink...**90.00**

Plate, sherbet, 6" d., blue **14.00**

Plate, sherbet, 6" d., clear **5.00**

Plate, sherbet, 6" d., green............**12.00**

Plate, sherbet, 6" d., pink **10.00**

Plate, luncheon, 8½" d., blue.........**37.00**

Plate, luncheon, 8½" d., green **19.00**

Plate, luncheon, 8½" d., pink.........**20.00**

Plate, dinner, 9⅞" d., blue **48.00**

Plate, dinner, 9⅞" d., clear **16.00**

Plate, dinner, 9⅞" d., green...........**28.00**

Plate, dinner, 9⅞" d., pink **31.00**

Plate, grill, 9⅞" d., blue..................**27.00**

Plate, grill, 9⅞" d., clear...................**9.00**

Plate, grill, 9⅞" d., green **29.00**

Plate, grill, 9⅞" d., pink..................**20.00**

Platter, 13 " oval, blue **57.00**

Platter, 13 " oval, clear **15.00**

Platter, 13 " oval, green.................**44.00**

Platter, 13 " oval, pink **38.00**

Salt & pepper shakers, blue, pr. **302.00**

Salt & pepper shakers, clear, pr. **42.00**

Salt & pepper shakers, green, pr. **124.00**

Salt & pepper shakers, pink, pr. ..**74.00**

Sherbet, footed, blue...................**48.00**

Sherbet, footed, clear...................**15.00**

Sherbet, footed, green **28.00**

Sherbet, footed, pink....................**22.00**

Sherbet in metal holder, amethyst.....................................**34.00**

Sherbet in metal holder, blue **28.00**

Sugar bowl, cov., clear **28.00**

Sugar bowl, cov., green................**85.00**

Sugar bowl, cov., pink **67.00**

Sugar bowl, open, blue................**38.00**

Sugar bowl, open, clear..................**8.00**

Sugar bowl, open, green **24.00**

Sugar bowl, open, pink.................**13.00**

Toddy or cider set: cookie jar w/metal lid, 8 roly-poly tumblers, metal tray/ladle; blue, 11 pcs.....**195.00**

Tumbler, blue, 3½" h., 5 oz...........**57.00**

Tumbler, clear, 3½" h., 5 oz..........**12.00**

Tumbler, green, 3½" h., 5 oz. **32.00**

Tumbler, pink, 3½" h., 5 oz...........**22.00**

Tumbler, blue, 4⅛" h., 9 oz...........**45.00**

Tumbler, clear, 4⅛" h., 9 oz..........**14.00**

Tumbler, green, 4⅛" h., 9 oz. **33.00**

Tumbler, pink, 4⅛" h., 9 oz. **26.00**

Tumbler, blue, 4⅞" h., 10 oz.......**151.00**

Tumbler, blue, 5⅜" h., 12 oz.......**102.00**

Tumbler, clear, 5⅜" h., 12 oz........**30.00**

Tumbler, green, 5⅜" h., 12 oz. **42.00**

Tumbler, pink, 5⅜" h., 12 oz........**54.00**

Water set: 68 oz. pitcher & six 9 oz. tumblers; blue, 7 pcs. **360.00**

Water set: pitcher & 6 tumblers; clear, 7 pcs. **138.00**

SIERRA or Pinwheel, Jeannette Glass Co., 1931-33 (Press-mold)

Bowl, cereal, 5½" d., green **14.00**

Bowl, cereal, 5½" d., pink.............**13.00**

Bowl, berry, 8½" d., green............**30.00**

Bowl, berry, 8½" d., pink **30.00**

Bowl, 9½" oval vegetable, green...**91.00**

Bowl, 9½" oval vegetable, pink **41.00**

Butter dish, cov., green **70.00**

Butter dish, cov., pink..................**59.00**

Creamer, green **21.00**

Creamer, pink..............................**16.00**

Cup & saucer, green **21.00**

Cup & saucer, pink **18.00**

Pitcher, 6½" h., 32 oz., green **115.00**

Plate, dinner, 9" d., green.............**20.00**

Plate, dinner, 9" d., pink **18.00**

Platter, 11" oval, green................**41.00**

Platter, 11" oval, pink **36.00**

Salt & pepper shakers, green,
pr. **38.00**

Salt & pepper shakers, pink, pr. ..**43.00**

Serving tray, two-handled,
green **21.00**

Sugar bowl, cov., green...............**36.00**

Tumbler, footed, green, 4½" h.,
9 oz..**83.00**

Tumbler, footed, pink, 4½" h.,
9 oz..**67.00**

WINDSOR DIAMOND or WindsorJeannette Glass Co., 1936-46 (Press-mold)

Windsor Diamond Butter Dish

Ashtray, Delphite, 5¾" d. **43.00**

Ashtray, green, 5¾" d. **45.00**

Ashtray, pink, 5¾" d.....................**35.00**

Ashtray, w/patterned rim, pink **475.00**

Bowl, berry, 4¾" d., clear **6.00**

Bowl, berry, 4¾" d., green............**11.00**

Bowl, berry, 4¾" d., pink **8.00**

Bowl, 5" d., pointed edge, clear **5.00**

Bowl, 5" d., pointed edge, pink......**18.00**

Bowl, cream soup, 5" d., green **26.00**

Bowl, cream soup, 5" d., pink........**21.00**

Bowl, cereal, 5⅛" or 5⅜" d., clear ...**7.00**

Bowl, cereal, 5⅛" or 5⅜" d.,
green **24.00**

Bowl, cereal, 5⅛" or 5⅜" d.,
pink..**22.00**

Bowl, 7" d., three-footed, clear........**7.00**

Bowl, 7" d., three-footed, pink **23.00**

Bowl, 8" d., pointed edge, clear **12.00**

Bowl, 8" d., pointed edge, pink......**35.00**

Bowl, 8" d., two-handled, clear........**6.00**

Bowl, 8" d., two-handled, green **21.00**

Bowl, 8" d., two-handled, pink.......**19.00**

Bowl, berry, 8½" d., clear **11.00**

Bowl, berry, 8½" d., green............**15.00**

Bowl, berry, 8½" d., pink **20.00**

Bowl, 9½" oval vegetable, clear **9.00**

Bowl, 9½" oval vegetable, green...**27.00**

Bowl, 9½" oval vegetable, pink **22.00**

Bowl, 10½" d., pointed edge,
clear...**25.00**

Bowl, 10½" d., pointed edge,
pink...**154.00**

Bowl, 7 x 11¾" boat shape, clear..**17.00**

Bowl, 7 x 11¾" boat shape,
green **37.00**

Bowl, 7 x 11¾" boat shape, pink...**32.00**

Bowl, fruit, 12½" d., clear **26.00**

Bowl, fruit, 12½" d., pink **106.00**

Butter dish, cov., clear **25.00**

Butter dish, cov., green **87.00**

Butter dish, cov., pink (ILLUS.) **48.00**

Cake plate, footed, clear, 10¾" d....**8.00**

Cake plate, footed, green,
10¾" d. **18.00**

Cake plate, footed, pink,
10¾" d. **21.00**

Candlestick, pink, 3" h. **47.00**

Candlesticks, clear, 3" h., pr. **19.00**

Candlesticks, pink, 3" h., pr..........**95.00**

Candy jar, cov., clear **11.00**

Coaster, clear, 3¼" d. **6.00**

Coaster, green, 3¼" d. **15.00**

Coaster, pink, 3¼" d.....................**13.00**

Creamer, flat, clear..........................**6.00**

Creamer, flat, green **15.00**

Creamer, flat, pink.......................**12.00**

Creamer, footed, clear **7.00**

Cup & saucer, clear.......................**7.00**

Cup & saucer, green **17.00**

Cup & saucer, pink **15.00**

Pitcher, 4½" h., 16 oz., clear **20.00**

Pitcher, 4½" h., 16 oz., pink........**117.00**

Pitcher, 6¾" h., 52 oz., clear.........**12.00**

Pitcher, 6¾" h., 52 oz., pink..........**29.00**

Plate, sherbet, 6" d., clear **3.00**

Plate, sherbet, 6" d., green..............**8.00**

Plate, sherbet, 6" d., pink **5.00**

Plate, salad, 7" d., green **19.00**

Plate, salad, 7" d., pink..................**16.00**

Plate, dinner, 9" d., clear **7.00**

Plate, dinner, 9" d., green.............**23.00**

Plate, dinner, 9" d., pink **24.00**

Plate, sandwich, 10¼", handled,
    clear..**7.00**

Plate, sandwich, 10¼", handled,
    green **20.00**

Plate, sandwich, 10¼", handled,
    pink **17.00**

Plate, chop, 13⅝" d., clear **10.00**

Plate, chop, 13⅝" d., green **40.00**

Plate, chop, 13⅝" d., pink.............**41.00**

Platter, 11½" oval, clear **8.00**

Platter, 11½" oval, green..............**22.00**

Platter, 11½" oval, pink **18.00**

Powder jar, cov., clear **14.00**

Relish, divided, clear, 11½"...........**10.00**

Relish, divided, pink, 11½"..........**163.00**

Salt & pepper shakers, green,
    pr. **48.00**

Salt & pepper shakers, pink, pr. ..**36.00**

Sherbet, footed, clear......................**5.00**

Sherbet, footed, green **15.00**

Sherbet, footed, pink....................**12.00**

Sugar bowl, cov., flat, clear **9.00**

Sugar bowl, cov., flat, green.........**33.00**

Sugar bowl, cov., flat, pink **28.00**

Sugar bowl, cov., footed, clear **6.00**

Sugar bowl, cov., no lip, pink......**107.00**

Sugar bowl, open, clear..................**4.00**

Sugar bowl, open, green **13.00**

Sugar bowl, open, pink.................**11.00**

Tray, pink, 4" sq., w/handles **10.00**

Tray, clear, 4" sq., without
    handles..**7.00**

Tray, pink, 4" sq., without
    handles...**37.00**

Tray, green, 4⅛ x 9", w/handles....**15.00**

Tray, pink, 4⅛ x 9", w/handles **15.00**

Tray, clear, 4⅛ x 9", without
    handles...**10.00**

Tray, pink, 4⅛ x 9", without
    handles...**44.00**

Tray, clear, 8½ x 9¾", w/handles **5.00**

Tray, green, 8½ x 9¾",
    w/handles **29.00**

Tray, pink, 8½ x 9¾", w/handles ...**23.00**

Tray, clear, 8½ x 9¾", without
    handles...**13.00**

Tray, pink, 8½ x 9¾", without
    handles...**75.00**

Tumbler, clear, 3¼" h., 5 oz..........**10.00**

Tumbler, green, 3¼" h., 5 oz. **33.00**

Tumbler, pink, 3¼" h., 5 oz. **23.00**

Tumbler, clear, 4" h., 9 oz...............**6.00**

Tumbler, green, 4" h., 9 oz. **31.00**

Tumbler, pink, 4" h., 9 oz. **19.00**

Tumbler, footed, clear, 4" h., 9 oz. **7.00**

Tumbler, footed, clear, 5" h., 11 oz. ..**9.00**

Tumbler, clear, 5" h., 12 oz.............**9.00**

Tumbler, green, 5" h., 12 oz. **46.00**

Tumbler, pink, 5" h., 12 oz. **31.00**

Tumbler, footed, clear, 7¼" h........**17.00**

Water set: pitcher & 7 tumblers;
    pink, 8 pcs. **150.00**

DUNCAN & MILLER

Duncan & Miller Glass Company, a successor firm to George A. Duncan & Sons Company, produced a wide range of pressed wares and novelty pieces during the late 19th century and into the early 20th century. During the Depression era and after, they continued making a wide variety of more modern patterns, including mold-blown types and also introduced a number of etched and engraved patterns. Many colors, including opalescent hues, were produced during this era and especially popular today are the graceful swan dishes they produced in the Pall Mall and Sylvan patterns. The numbers after the pattern name indicate the original factory pattern number. The Duncan factory was closed in 1955. Also see ANIMALS and PATTERN GLASS in the Glass section.

Teardrop Wine & Champagne

Ashtray, square, Early American Sandwich patt. (No. 41), clear **$8.00**

Basket, Early American Sandwich patt., 7" h....................**94.00**

Bonbon, heart-shaped, handled, Early American Sandwich patt., clear, 5" l....................................**14.00**

Bonbon, heart-shaped, ring-handled, Early American Sandwich patt., clear, 6" l. **20.00**

Bowl, fruit, 5" d., Early American Sandwich patt., clear **10.00**

Bowl, grapefruit, 6" d., rimmed edge, Early American Sandwich patt., clear..................................**15.00**

Bowl, 10" d., 3¾" h., flared rim, footed, etched First Love patt., clear....................................**50.00**

Bowl, fruit, 12" d., flared rim, Early American Sandwich patt., clear....................................**35.00**

Bowl, 12" d., flared rim, Hobnail patt. (No. 118), clear..................**25.00**

Bowl, flower, 14" d., Sanibel patt. (No. 130), blue opalescent **90.00**

Butter dish w/silvered metal cover, Teardrop patt. (No. 5301),¼ lb. **27.00**

Cake stand, plain pedestal base, Early American Sandwich patt., clear, 13" d. **75.00**

Candelabra, one-light w/prisms, Early American Sandwich patt., 10" h., pr. **250.00**

Candleholder, open-back swan-shaped, milk glass body w/ruby neck, 7" h....................................**200.00**

Candy dish, cov., Caribbean patt. (No. 115), blue, 4 x 7"................**95.00**

Candy jar, cov., footed, Early American Sandwich patt., clear, 8½" d. **55.00**

Champagne, Early American Sandwich patt., clear, 5¼" h., 5 oz...**10.00**

Champagne, saucer-type, etched First Love patt. (No. 5111½), clear, 5" h., 5 oz...........................**17.00**

Champagne, Teardrop patt., clear, 5" h., 5 oz. (ILLUS. right) **8.00**

Cheese dish, cov., Early American Sandwich patt., clear, 8" d. **90.00**

Claret, Teardrop patt., clear, 5½" h, 4 oz...**18.00**

Cocktail, etched First Love patt. (No. 5111½), clear, 4½" h., 3½ oz...**18.00**

Condiment set, Canterbury patt. (No. 115), clear, 5 pcs. **70.00**

Condiment set: two cruets, salt & pepper, four-part tray; Early American Sandwich patt., clear, 5 pcs. **90.00**

Cup & saucer, Early American Sandwich patt., clear **29.00**

Deviled egg plate, Early American Sandwich patt., clear, 12" d. **87.00**

Epergne, fruit, three-part, Early American Sandwich patt., clear, 12" d. **250.00**

Goblet, water, Canterbury patt., chartreuse, 9 oz..................**10.00**

Goblet, water, etched First Love patt. (No. 5111½), clear, 6¾" h., 10 oz..................**23.00**

Goblet, water, Early American Sandwich patt., clear, 6" h., 9 oz..................**15.00**

Goblet, water, Teardrop patt., clear, 7" h., 9 oz..................**11.00**

Marmalade, cov., Teardrop patt., clear, 4" d. **27.00**

Mayonnaise set: 7" d. underplate, ladle & 5" d. bowl; Early American Sandwich patt., clear, 3 pcs. **28.00**

Mayonnaise set: bowl, ladle, underplate, Canterbury patt. (No. 115), clear, 3 pcs. **38.00**

Model of a swan, Pall Mall patt. (No. 30), clear, 3" l..................**30.00**

Model of a swan, Pall Mall patt., clear, 7" l..................**35.00**

Model of a swan, Pall Mall patt., clear, 7½" l..................**12.00**

Model of a swan, Pall Mall patt., ruby, 10½" l. **75.00**

Nappy, Sanibel patt., pink opalescent, 6" d. **24.00**

Nappy, two-part, Early American Sandwich patt., clear, 6" d. **14.00**

Novelty, model of a top hat, Hobnail patt., blue opalescent, 4" h. **40.00**

Novelty, model of a top hat, Hobnail patt., pink opalescent, 4" h. **40.00**

Oyster cocktail, etched First Love patt., clear, 3¾" h., 4½ oz....**22.00**

Pitcher w/ice lip, Early American Sandwich patt., 8" h., 64 oz.......**115.00**

Plate, bread & butter, 6" d., Early American Sandwich patt., green ...**9.00**

Plate, dessert, 7" d., Early American Sandwich patt., clear.....**6.00**

Plate, salad, 7½" d., Spiral Flutes patt., amber **4.00**

Plate, salad, 8" d., Early American Sandwich patt., green **15.00**

Plate, salad, 8½" d., Sanibel patt., pink opalescent **32.00**

Plate, 11" d., two-handled, Teardrop patt., clear **30.00**

Plate, 11½" d., two-handled, Early American Sandwich patt., clear..................**35.00**

Plate, service, 13" d., Early American Sandwich patt., clear ...**62.00**

Plate, 16" d., lazy Susan-type w/turntable, Early American Sandwich patt., clear **45.00**

Punch bowl, Mardi Gras patt., clear, 14½" h., 2 gal..................**150.00**

Punch cup, handled, Caribbean patt., red **14.00**

Relish dish, oval, two-part, two-handled, Canterbury patt., clear, 7" l. **15.00**

Relish dish w/silver overlay, three-part, three-handled, Canterbury patt., clear, 8" l. **25.00**

Relish dish, three-part, three-handled, Canterbury patt., clear, 8" l..................**18.00**

Relish dish, five-part, two-handled, etched First Love patt., clear, 10½" l. **70.00**

Relish dish, Sanibel patt., pink opalescent, 13" l. **45.00**

Relish dish, two-part, ring-handled, Early American Sandwich patt., clear, 5½" l. **15.00**

Relish dish, three-part, oblong, Early American Sandwich patt., clear, 10" l..................**30.00**

Relish dish, three-part, rectangular, Early American Sandwich patt., clear, 10½" l.......**26.00**

Relish dish, three-part, three-handled, Teardrop patt., clear, 9" l. **28.00**

Relish dish, round, five-part, Teardrop patt., clear, 2" d...........**29.00**

Sherbet, Early American Sandwich patt., clear, 4¼" h., 5 oz..**9.00**

Tray, celery, oval, Early American Sandwich patt., clear, 10" l. **22.00**

Tray, creamer & sugar-type, Early American Sandwich patt., clear..**31.00**

Tray, pickle, oval, Early American Sandwich patt., clear, 7" l. **22.00**

Tumbler, iced-tea, flat, Early American Sandwich patt., clear, 5¼" h., 13 oz......................**16.00**

Tumbler, juice, footed, Early American Sandwich patt., clear, 3¾" h., 5 oz........................**11.00**

Tumbler, juice, footed, Teardrop patt., clear, 3½", 5 oz..................**12.00**

Vase, 3" h., footed, crimped rim, Early American Sandwich patt., clear...**20.00**

Vase, 4" h., crimped rim, Hobnail patt., blue opalescent **30.00**

Vase, flower arranger, 5½" h., Canterbury patt., blue opalescent....................................**65.00**

Vase, 10" h., Early American Sandwich patt., clear **60.00**

Wine, ball stem, footed, Caribbean patt., 3½" h., 3½ oz. ..**17.00**

Wine, Teardrop patt., clear, 4¾" h., 3 oz. (ILLUS. left w/Champagne) **16.00**

FENTON

Fenton Art Glass Company began producing glass at Williamstown, West Virginia, in January 1907. Organized by Frank L. and John W. Fenton, the company *began operations in a newly built glass factory with an experienced master glass craftsman, Jacob Rosenthal, as their factory manager. Fenton has produced a wide variety of collectible glassware through the years, including Carnival. Still in production today, their current productions may be found at finer gift shops across the country. William Heacock's three-volume set on Fenton, published by Antique Publications, is the standard reference in this field.*

Fenton Mark

Basket, 11" d., Vasa Murrhina, No. 6437, ca. 1964-68, Aventurine green w/blue............**$97.00**

Basket, Burmese, No. 7437, w/decorated roses, ca. 1971-80, medium size **135.00**

Basket, crystal handle, Silver Crest, 6½" h...............................**25.00**

Basket, Hobnail patt., cranberry opalescent, 4½" h........................**53.00**

Basket, oval, handled, four-footed, Hobnail patt., milk white ..**30.00**

Basket, Silver Crest, 7" h. **25.00**

Bell, Bicentennial, No. 8467, Patriot red.....................................**53.00**

Bonbon, Apple Blossom Crest, No. 7333.....................................**45.00**

Bonbon, Water Lily & Cattails patt., green opalescent...............**55.00**

Bowl, 7½" d., crimped rim, Gold Crest...**30.00**

Bowl, 11" d., double-crimped rim, Silver Crest.................................**30.00**

Bowl, 11" d., rolled rim, Burmese, h.p. w/one dogwood & one rose, ca. 1970s................................**140.00**

Bowl, 12" d., footed, Silver Crest...**40.00**

Bowl, 8" d., crimped rim, Hobnail patt., milk white..........................**20.00**

Bowl, chip & dip, low, Silver
Crest...**54.00**

Bowl, desert, deep, ruffled rim,
Silver Crest, No. 7221 ....**30.00**

Cake plate, low-footed, Diamond
Lace patt., French Opalescent
w/applied aqua rim **80.00**

Candleholder, handled, Hobnail
patt., No. 3870, milk white **15.00**

Candlestick, cornucopia-form,
Hobnail patt., blue opalescent,
large **40.00**

Candlesticks, cornucopia-form,
Ivory Crest, pr.............................**75.00**

Candlesticks, cornucopia-form,
Ming Rose line, No. 950, pink,
5½" h., pr. **70.00**

Candlesticks, low, Hobnail patt.,
French Opalescent, pr. **40.00**

Candy box, cov., footed, Silver
Crest...**125.00**

Candy jar, cov., wide low form,
Hobnail patt., milk white,
No. 3880.....................................**35.00**

Centerpiece bowl, oval, Ming
Rose line, No. 1663, ca. 1935,
pink, 12" d..................................**75.00**

Cigarette holder, hat-shaped,
Daisy & Button patt., blue
opalescent, 3¾" h.......................**40.00**

Compote, open, 8" d., footed,
Gold Crest **30.00**

Compote, open, crimped rim,
footed, Silver Crest....................**68.00**

Compote, open, double crimped
rim, Hobnail patt., blue
opalescent **50.00**

Condiment set: salt & pepper
shakers, creamer & open sugar
bowl, oil cruet, cov. mustard dish
& tray; Hobnail patt., No. 3809,
milk white, 7 pcs. **50.00**

Console set: bowl & pair of
candlesticks; Hobnail patt.,
blue opalescent, 3 pcs.................**90.00**

Cookie jar, cov., Big Cookies
patt., Ebony, 7" h.......................**120.00**

Creamer, 4½" h., squat-form,
Hobnail patt., cranberry
opalescent **60.00**

Creamer, Aqua Crest,
No. 1924.......................................**45.00**

Cruet w/original stopper, Coin
Dot patt., cranberry
opalescent **175.00**

Cruet w/original stopper,
Hobnail patt., milk white, 7 oz.....**28.00**

Decanter w/original stopper, Rib
Optic, No. 1667, cranberry
opalescent, 13½" h. **225.00**

Epergene, single lily, Burmese ...**295.00**

Epergne, three-lily, Diamond
Lace patt., French Opalescent
w/applied aqua rim, No. 1948,
ca. 1948-54 ....**150.00**

Goblet, Lincoln Inn patt., cobalt
blue..**45.00**

Goblet, water, Hobnail patt., milk
white **12.00**

Hurricane shade, Snow Crest,
green **95.00**

Jam & jelly set: two footed ovoid
jars w/domed covers w/spoon
holes resting on a center-
handled oval tray; Hobnail patt.,
milk white, the set........................**35.00**

Lamp, daybreak pillar-style,
Burmese, 90th anniversary.
collection, 33" h. **550.00**

Lamp, Peacock patt., chimney
shade w/flaring ruffled rim
centered on a low wide
cushion-form base, No. G-70,
satin black & crystal, 10½" h. **175.00**

Lemonade set: ovoid-shaped
pitcher w/applied handle & wide
ruffled rim & six glasses;
Hanging Heart patt., custard,
7 pcs...**303.00**

Liquor tray, rectangular
w/notched corners, reverse-
etched flower-design, No. 1934,
light blue w/satin finish, 12" l. **125.00**

Model of a top hat, Hobnail patt.,
French Opalescent, 2½" h..........**25.00**

Mustard jar, cov., Hobnail patt.,
milk white......................................**15.00**

Oil lamp font, Hobnail patt.,
cranberry opalescent, 7" d...........**35.00**

Pitcher, cream, 4" h., Dot Optic
patt., No. 1924, cranberry
opalescent.....................................**60.00**

Pitcher, jug-type, water, ruffled
rim, Dot Optic, cranberry
opalescent.....................................**295.00**

Pitcher, jug-type, 5½" h., Hobnail
patt., cranberry opalescent, ...**80.00**

Pitcher, Jacqueline line, No.
9166, honey amber, 48 oz.........**135.00**

Plate, 6" square, Hobnail patt.,
French Opalescent **25.00**

Plate, bread & butter, 6½" d.,
Aqua Crest **15.00**

Plate, 6½" d., Silver Crest **14.00**

Plate, 12½" d., Silver Crest,
No. 7211..**48.00**

Puff box w/wooden cover,
Hobnail patt., French
Opalescent **33.00**

Relish dish, divided, Silver Crest,
9½" l. **57.00**

Rose bowl, Beaded Melon patt.,
ivy green cased in white **50.00**

**Salt & pepper shakers
w/original tops,** Hobnail patt.,
cranberry opalescent,
3½" h., pr. **85.00**

Salt & pepper shakers, Block &
Star patt., No. 5606, milk white,
pr. **25.00**

Sherbet, Silver Crest....................**20.00**

Sugar shaker w/original top,
Dot Optic patt., cranberry
opalescent **95.00**

Tidbit tray, two-tier, Emerald
Crest, No. 7296, ca. 1954-55 ......**65.00**

Tumbler, Hobnail patt., milk
white, 3½", 8 oz. **8.00**

Tumbler, footed, Stars & Stripes
patt., cranberry opalescent..........**50.00**

Vase, 3½" h., 6" d., hat-shaped,
Spiral Optic patt., No. 1923,
French Opalescent......................**25.00**

Vase, 4" h., Hobnail patt., French
Opalescent **28.00**

Vase, 5½" h., short ovoid ribbed
body w/octagonal crimped rim,
Vasa Murrhina, Aventurine
green w/blue **35.00**

Vase, 5½" h., bulbous base
w/crimped rim, Hobnail patt.,
cranberry opalescent...................**70.00**

Vase, 6½" h., ovoid body
w/ground rim, Hanging Heart
patt., bittersweet, variation of
shape No. 0003, Robert Barber
Collection (minor flakes)............**275.00**

Vase, 7" d.,Burmese, No. 7252,
roses decoration **95.00**

Vase, 7½" h., footed, rounded
cylindrical body w/flaring trumpet
neck, Hanging Heart patt., white
on black amethyst, Fenton mark
& etched "Don Fenton 8-7-81".....**94.00**

Vase, 8" h., ribbed baluster body
w/deeply ruffled rim, Vasa
Murrhina, No. 6456, Aventurine
green w/blue **50.00**

Vase, 8" h., Diamond Optic patt.,
No. 1758, blue opalescent...........**60.00**

Vase, 8" h., Hobnail patt.,
cranberry opalescent...................**80.00**

Vase, 8" h., Peach Crest,
No. 7258, decorated w/roses **57.00**

Vase, 8" h., Polka Dot patt.,
No. 2251, cranberry opalescent ..**95.00**

Vase, 9½" h., Coin Dot patt.,
cranberry opalescent...................**95.00**

Vase, 10" h., Hanging Heart patt.,
No. 0007, Robert Barber
Collection, ca. 1975-76..............**135.00**

Vase, 10½" h., footed bulbous
ovoid body tapering to a slender
neck w/a tricorner rolled rim,
Spiral Optic patt., No. 894, blue
opalescent **130.00**

Vase, 11" h., tall ribbed ovoid
body w/deeply ruffled rim, Vasa
Murrhina, No. 6458, ca. 1964-
68, Aventurine green w/blue........**60.00**

Vase, 11" h., swelled cylindrical
form with long flaring neck,

Sophisticated Lady patt. w/deep etched design, amethyst, Fenton mark & signed "Richard Delaney, 1-12-82".....................**220.00**

Water set: pitcher w/four ten-row tumblers; Hobnail pattern, cranberry opalescent, 5 pcs. **750.00**

Wine bottle w/clear pointed & ribbed stopper, slender tapering triple-gourd form, Rib Optic patt., No. 1667, cranberry opalescent, ca. 1953-62, 13½" h. **155.00**

FOSTORIA

Fostoria Glass company, founded in 1887, produced numerous types of fine glassware over the years. Their factory in Moundsville, West Virginia closed in 1986.

Fostoria Mark

Appetizer set: tray w/six inserts; American patt., clear, 10½"d., 7 pcs......................**$250.00**

Ashtray, Mayfair patt., Topaz (early gold tint)............................**13.00**

Bonbon, three-footed, Colony patt., clear, 7" d. **14.00**

Bouillon cup & saucer, Fairfax patt., Orchid (early lavender).......**17.00**

Bowl, jelly, 3¾" d., footed, Coin patt., No. 448, clear **14.00**

Bowl, fruit, 5" d., Century patt., clear..**15.00**

Bowl, 5" d., two-handled, Colony patt., clear...................................**11.00**

Bowl, fruit, 5" d., Fairfax patt., Rose (pink) **12.00**

Bowl, 5½" d., Cameo etching, clear..**35.00**

Bowl, 6" w., square, Baroque patt., blue...................................**35.00**

Bowl, 6½" d., rimmed, Vesper etching, green (avocado).............**20.00**

Bowl, 7" d., round, cupped,three-footed, Baroque patt., Azure **48.00**

Bowl, 8½" l., boat-shaped, American patt., green **150.00**

Bowl, 9" l., oval, Coin patt., olive...**30.00**

Bowl, 9" d., lily pond-type, Century patt., clear **40.00**

Bowl, 10" l., oval, two-part, American patt., clear **35.00**

Bowl, 10½"d., low footed, Colony patt., clear.................................**70.00**

Bowl, 11" d., Sunray patt., clear....**37.00**

Bowl, 12" d., 2⅞" h., flared sides, Buttercup etching, clear...............**56.00**

Cake plate, two-handled, American patt., clear, 10" d. **25.00**

Cake plate, two-handled, Century patt., clear, 10" d. **27.00**

Cake plate, two-handled, Navarre etching, Line No. 2496, clear, 10" d. **45.00**

Cake plate, two-handled, Chintz etching, clear **42.00**

Cake salver, footed, Colony patt., clear, 12" d. **70.00**

Candleholders, three-light, Buttercup etching, clear, 8" h., pr. **70.00**

Candleholders, mushroom-shaped, Versailles etching, Rose, pr. **130.00**

Candlestick, scroll-shaped, June etching, Topaz, 5" h....................**89.00**

Candlestick, mushroom-shaped, Versailles etching, Line No. 2375, green **44.00**

Candlesticks, octagonal, footed, American patt., clear, 6" h., pr. **55.00**

Candlesticks, Baroque patt., Azure, 5½" h., pr........................**72.00**

Candlesticks, three-light, Baroque patt., clear, 6" h., pr.......**48.00**

Candlesticks, Colony patt., clear, 3½" h., pr. **24.00**

Candlesticks, Pioneer patt.,
Rose, pr. **48.00**

Celery dish, Baroque patt., clear,
11" l. **24.00**

Celery dish, June etching, Azure,
11½" l. **95.00**

Celery dish, Lafayette patt.,
Wisteria (delicate lavender),
11½" l. **95.00**

Celery dish, Mayfair patt., Topaz,
11" l. **30.00**

Celery dish, Raleigh patt., clear,
10½" l. **21.00**

Centerpiece bowl, 12" d.,
mushroom-shaped, Versailles
etching, Rose **78.00**

Champagne, Holly cutting, clear,
6 oz. **11.00**

Champagne, saucer-shaped,
Navarre etching, Line No. 6106,
clear, 5½ oz. **23.00**

Cheese & cracker server,
Colony patt., clear, 12½" d. **60.00**

Claret, Holly Cutting, clear,
3½ oz. **22.00**

Cocktail, American patt., 3 oz. **10.00**

Cocktail, June etching, clear,
3 oz. **20.00**

Cocktail, Versailles etching,
Line No. 5299, Topaz **28.00**

Compote, 4⅜" h., Century
patt., clear.................................**19.00**

American Pattern Jelly Compote

Compote, cov., jelly, 6¾" h.,
American patt., clear (ILLUS.
bottom previous column) **30.00**

Console bowl, Baroque patt.,
clear, 12" d. **35.00**

Console bowl, June etching,
Azure, 12" d. **140.00**

Console bowl, Mayflower
etching, Rose, 12" d. **96.00**

Cordial, Holly cutting, clear,
1 oz. **25.00**

Cream soup bowl & underplate,
footed, double-handled
w/paneled underplate, June
etching, Rose, 7½" d., 2 pcs. **30.00**

Cream soup & underplate,
Fairfax patt., Azure, 2 pcs. **37.00**

Creamer & open sugar bowl,
Hermitage patt., clear, pr. **17.00**

Creamer & open sugar bowl,
Lafayette patt., Navarre etching,
clear, pr. **48.00**

Creamer & open sugar bowl,
individual size, Baroque patt.,
Azure, pr. **60.00**

Creamer & open sugar bowl,
individual size, Mayfair patt.,
Ebony (black), pr. **37.00**

Creamer & open sugar bowl,
individual size, Mayfair patt.,
Topaz, pr. **24.00**

Cruet w/original stopper, Colony
patt., clear, 4½ oz. **42.00**

Cup & saucer, demitasse, Fairfax
patt., Topaz **13.00**

Cup & saucer, Baroque patt.,
clear..**12.00**

Cup & saucer, Colony patt.,
clear..**12.00**

Cup & saucer, Mayfair patt.,
Topaz **16.00**

Cup & saucer, Mayflower
etching, Rose **25.00**

Decanter w/stopper, American
patt., clear, 24 oz, 9¼" h..............**75.00**

Decanter w/stopper, Cameo
etching, clear **155.00**

Dinner bell, Navarre etching,
clear......................................**65.00**

Domino tray, Cameo etching,
clear......................................**190.00**

Figure of a Madonna w/base,
Silver mist, 1950s, 10" h.............**62.00**

Fingerbowl & underplate,
Versailles etching, Azure,
2 pcs...**68.00**

Goblet, American patt., clear,
9 oz...**12.00**

Goblet, water, Century patt.,
clear, 10 oz...............................**23.00**

Goblet, water, June etching,
Topaz, 9 oz...............................**22.00**

Goblet, water, labeled, Century
patt., clear, 10 oz.......................**25.00**

Goblet, Wheat cutting, clear,
10½ oz.......................................**12.00**

Handkerchief box, cov.,
American patt., clear,
4⅝" x 5⅝"................**280.00 to 390.00**

Hurricane lamp base, American
patt., clear..................................**55.00**

**Ice bucket w/metal handle &
tongs,** Mayflower etching, Line
No. 2560, clear, 2 pcs. **50.00**

Ice tub, Cameo etching,
clear..**195.00**

Ice tub, Hermitage patt.,
amber **48.00**

Mayonnaise bowl, footed,
Pioneer patt., amber...................**24.00**

Mayonnaise bowl & underplate,
Century patt., clear, 2 pcs. **32.00**

Mayonnaise set: bowl,
underplate & ladle; Holly cutting,
clear, 3 pcs. **48.00**

Mustard jar, cover & spoon,
American patt., clear, 3 pcs. **35.00**

Olive dish, oblong, Colony patt.,
clear, 7" l...................................**17.00**

Oyster cocktail, American patt.,
clear, 4½ oz................................**18.00**

Oyster cocktail, Corsage
etching, clear, 4 oz. **12.00**

Pickle castor, cov., clear Victoria
patt. insert, ornate silver plate
frame, cover & tongs, ca.
1890s......................................**225.00**

Pickle dish, Raleigh patt., clear,
8" l. **17.00**

Pickle dish, handled, Sunray
patt., clear, 6" l...........................**30.00**

Plate, 6" d., Mayfair patt.,
green **7.00**

Plate, 6" d., Vesper etching,
amber **7.00**

Plate, salad, 7" d., American patt.,
clear..**10.00**

Plate, salad, 7" d., Colony patt.,
clear..**7.00**

Plate, salad, 7" d., Midnight Rose
etching, Line No. 2440, clear.......**10.00**

Plate, salad, 7½" d., Fairfax patt.,
Rose **5.00**

Plate, 7½" d., Holly cutting, clear.....**6.00**

Plate, salad, 7½" d., Navarre
etching, clear **15.00**

Plate, crescent salad, 7⅜" l.,
Hermitage patt., amber...............**25.00**

Plate, luncheon, 8" d., Baroque
patt., Azure **23.00**

Plate, 8" d., Mayfair patt.,
Topaz **18.00**

Plate, 8" d., Rose cutting, clear **15.00**

Plate, luncheon, 8½" d., Century
patt., clear..................................**12.00**

Plate, breakfast, 8¾" d.,
Versailles etching, Rose..............**20.00**

Plate, dinner, 9" d., Colony patt.,
clear..**27.00**

Plate, dinner, 10½" d., Vesper
etching, green.............................**32.00**

Plate, torte, 13" round, Buttercup
etching, clear **58.00**

Plate, torte, 14" d., June etching,
Azure **145.00**

Plate, torte, 14" d., Pioneer patt.,
green **68.00**

Plate, torte, 20" d., American
patt., clear..................................**125.00**

Platter, 10½" oval, American
patt., clear....................................**45.00**

Platter, 13" round, Baroque patt.,
Azure **85.00**

Platter, 15" oval, Acanthus
etching, amber..........................**125.00**

Preserve, cov., Century patt.,
clear, 6" d. **31.00**

Punch bowl & undertray, Sunray
patt., clear, 2 pcs. **115.00**

Punch set: 14" d. bowl, base &
12 cups; American patt., clear,
14 pcs. **325.00**

Relish dish, divided, handled,
Baroque patt., clear, 6" l. **17.00**

Relish dish, three-part, Baroque
patt., Azure, 10" l. **39.00**

Relish dish, two-part, Century
patt., clear, 7⅜" l.......................**13.00**

Relish dish, oval, four-part, two-
handled, Colony patt., clear.........**32.00**

Relish dish, three-part, Fairfax
patt., green, 8½" l. **15.00**

Relish dish, three-part, Holly
cutting, clear, 10" l. **30.00**

Relish dish, two-part, handled,
Lafayette patt., Ruby (red),
6½" d. **34.00**

Relish dish, four-part, Mayfair
patt., amber, 8½" l. **38.00**

Relish dish, three-part, Pioneer
patt., pink...................................**26.00**

Relish dish, three-part, Pioneer
patt., Topaz **22.00**

Ring holder, American patt.,
clear...**950.00**

Salt & pepper shakers
w/original tops, Baroque patt.,
Topaz, pr. **70.00**

Salt & pepper shakers
w/original tops, Century patt.,
clear, pr. **17.00**

Salt & pepper shakers
w/original tops, Jamestown
patt., green, pr. **35.00**

Salt & pepper shakers
w/original glass tops, Mayfair
patt., Topaz, pr. **68.00**

Salt & pepper shakers
w/original tops & tray, Colony
patt., clear, 3 pcs. **35.00**

Sauceboat, Pioneer patt., green ...**55.00**

Sherbet, American patt., clear,
5 oz...**9.00**

Sherbet, Baroque patt., clear,
5 oz...**15.00**

Sherbet, Jamestown patt.,
amber, 4½" h., 6½ oz. **6.00**

Sherbet, Manor etching, Line
No. 6003, Wisteria base, clear
bowl **30.00**

Sherbet, Rose cutting, clear..........**15.00**

Sherbet, tall, Trojan etching,
Rose **30.00**

Sherbet, low stem, Versailles
etching, Azure **26.00**

Sherbet, tall stem, Versailles
etching, Topaz, 6" h....................**18.00**

Sherbet, tall stem, Willowmere
etching, clear **22.00**

Shrimp bowl, American patt.,
clear, 12¼" **395.00**

Snack set: plate & cup, Century
patt., clear, 8" d., 2 pcs...............**35.00**

Sweetmeat, cov., Baroque patt.,
Topaz, 9" d. **135.00**

Syrup jug, cov., square crystal
body w/wide band of tiny
diamond point, applied handle,
Hartford patt., ca. 1900, clear......**95.00**

Toothpick holder, American
patt., clear.................................**25.00**

Tray, center-handle, Century
patt., clear, 11½" d. **45.00**

Tumbler, footed, Navarre etching,
Line No. 6016, clear, 13 oz. **32.00**

Tumbler, iced tea, footed,
American patt., clear, 12 oz.........**14.00**

Tumbler, iced tea, footed,
Century patt., clear, 12 oz. **25.00**

Tumbler, juice, Colony patt.,
clear, 5 oz.................................**16.00**

Tumbler, juice, footed,
Jamestown patt., amber, 5 oz. **9.00**

Tumbler, water, footed, Navarre
etching, Line No. 6106, clear,
10 oz..**30.00**

Tumbler, water, Watercress cutting, clear **16.00**

Vase, bud, 6" h. Century patt., clear..**18.00**

Vase, 7" h., footed, Baroque patt., Topaz **100.00**

Vase, 7" h., cupped, footed, Colony patt., clear **40.00**

GALLÉ

Gallé glass was made in Nancy, France, by Emile Gallé, a founder of the Nancy School and a leader in the Art Nouveau movement in France. Much of his glass, both enameled and cameo, is decorated with naturalistic motifs. The finest pieces were made in the last two decades of the 19th century and the opening years of the present one. Pieces marked with a star preceding the name were made between 1904, the year of Gallé's death, and 1914.

Gallé
Nancy
Déposé
Gallé
*Gallé

Gallé Marks

Cameo bowl, 7" d., short tapering cylindrical foot supports a wide deep rounded bowl w/an incurved rim, frosted grey overlaid in red & cut w/lotus blossoms & lily pads on the surface of still water, signed in intaglio, ca. 1900 ....**$1,495.00**

Cameo lamp base, miniature, slender baluster-form body on a widely flaring foot, the wide rounded shoulder tapering to a short cylindrical neck, grey mottled w/peach & overlaid in periwinkle blue, amber & green, cut w/a mountain landscape w/trees in the foreground, signed in cameo, ca. 1900, lip reduced, 6" h. (ILLUS. far right) **345.00**

Cameo vase, 6⅝" h., slender tapering ovoid body w/a small closed rim, white, green & red mottled grey sides overlaid in olive green shading to forest green, cut w/a tree-lined lake scene, signed in cameo, original paper label, ca. 1900 (ILLUS. second from right) **1,035.00**

Gallé Cameo Lamp Base & Vases

Cameo vase, 8⅝" h., tall slender ovoid body w/a flat mouth, grey banded w/wide patches of lemon yellow, overlaid in pale blue, deep purple & russet & finely cut w/a forest & lake at the base of towering mountains, signed in intaglio, ca. 1900 (ILLUS. bottom previous page, far left) **3,450.00**

Cameo vase, 9½" h., slender elongated teardrop form, grey touched w/pink, overlaid in light green shading to olive green, cut w/a lake landscape scene, signed in cameo, ca. 1900 (ILLUS. bottom previous page, second from left w/lamp) **1,610.00**

Cameo vase, 12½" h., a small footring supports a compressed spherical small body below a very tall, slender waisted neck w/flaring top, opaque bone white overlaid in deep red & cameo cut w/berries on twisting stems & branches w/broad, curled leaves, early fire-polished example, Chinese-style signature................................**4,125.00**

HEISEY

Numerous types of fine glass were made by A.H. Heisey & Co., Newark, Ohio, from 1895. The Company's trade-mark an H enclosed within a diamond has become known to most glass collectors. The company's name and molds were acquired by Imperial Glass Co., Bellaire, Ohio, in 1958, and some pieces have been reissued. The glass listed below consists of miscellaneous pieces and types. Also see ANIMALS and PATTERN GLASS under Glass.

Heisey Mark

Ashtray, Lariat patt., clear, 4" d. **$15.00**

Bowl, mint, 5½" d., footed, Queen Ann patt., Orchid etching, clear **35.00**

Bowl, mint, 5½" d., footed, Rose etching, clear **40.00**

Bowl, jelly, 6" d., two-handled, footed, Empress patt., Sahara (yellow) **19.00**

Bowl, mint, 6" d., dolphin-footed, Empress patt., Flamingo (pink) ...**26.00**

Bowl, jelly, 7" d., footed, Waverly patt., Rose etching, clear............**70.00**

Bowl, nasturtium, 8" d., Twist patt., Flamingo (pink)..................**68.00**

Bowl, console, 12" d., Lariat patt., clear...**33.00**

Bowl, floral, 12" l., oval, Ridgeleigh patt. ....**50.00 to 60.00**

Bowl, console, 13" d., scalloped-rim, Sunflower patt., clear...........**50.00**

Butter dish, cov., Waverly patt., Orchid etching, clear, 6" d. **190.00**

Butter dish, cov., Waverly patt., Rose etching, clear, 6" d. **185.00**

Cake plate, footed, Waverly patt., Rose etching, clear, 15" d. **275.00**

Candlesticks, Little Squatter, Flamingo, pr. **99.00**

Candlesticks, Twist patt., Moongleam (green), 2" h., pr.....**160.00**

Candlesticks, two-light, Lariat patt., clear, pr. **60.00**

Champagne, Minuet etching, clear, 6 oz. **29.00**

Champagne, New Era patt., clear, 6 oz. **12.00**

Cheese dish, cov., footed, Lariat patt., clear, 5" d. **40.00**

Chip & dip set, Kohinoor patt., clear, 11" d., 2 pcs. **35.00**

Cocktail, Lariat patt., Moonglo cutting, clear, 3½ oz. **18.00**

Cocktail, New Era patt., clear, 3½ oz..**35.00**

Compote, 6½" d., low, Waverly
patt., Orchid etching, clear **42.00**

Cordial, Orchid etching, clear,
1 oz. **145.00**

Creamer & covered sugar bowl,
hotel-type, Petal patt., Flamingo,
pr. **90.00**

Heisey Twist Cruet

Cruet w/original stopper, Twist
patt., green, 4" h., 2½ oz.
(ILLUS.) ....**85.00 to 90.00**

Cup & saucer, Crystolite patt.,
clear..**27.00**

Goblet, water, Charter Oak patt.,
Flamingo, 8 oz. **47.00**

Goblet, water, Duquesne patt.,
Tangerine, 9 oz. **200.00**

Goblet, water, Kohinoor patt.,
clear, 9 oz. **25.00**

Goblet, water, pressed, Lariat
patt., clear, 9 oz. **20.00**

Goblet, water, blown, Lariat patt.,
clear, 10 oz. **22.00**

Goblet, water, Yeoman patt.,
clear, 10 oz. **35.00**

Goblets, water, footed, Ipswitch
patt., clear, 8 pcs. **110.00**

Ice bucket w/silver overlay,
Queen Ann patt., clear **50.00**

Mayonnaise set: 5" d. bowl, 7" d.
underplate & ladle; Lariat patt.,
clear, 3 pcs. **45.00**

Pitcher w/ice lip, Old Sandwich
patt., clear w/silver overlay,
½ gal......................................**250.00**

Pitcher, Old Sandwich patt.,
Sahara (yellow), ½ gal..............**175.00**

Plate, sherbet, 6" d., Empress
patt., yellow **13.00**

Plate, salad, 8" d., Rose etching,
clear..**35.00**

Plate, salad, 8" d., Waverly patt.,
Rose etching, clear.....................**30.00**

Plate, salad, 8½" d., Crystolite
patt., clear....................................**17.00**

Plate, sandwich, 14" d., center
handle, Waverly patt., Rose
etching, clear **215.00**

Relish dish, three-part, Lariat
patt., clear, 11" l..........................**24.00**

Relish dish, three-part, Waverly
patt., clear...................................**20.00**

Relish dish, four-part, Waverly
patt., Rose etching, clear, 9" l....**110.00**

Salt & pepper shakers, Waverly
patt., Rose etching, pr. **70.00**

Sherbet, blown, Lariat patt., clear,
5½ oz. **14.00**

Sugar bowl, open, individual,
Whirlpool patt., clear, 2½" h. **22.00**

Syrup jug, w/original hinged lid,
Plain Band, clear, ca. 1900 ....**95.00**

Toothpick holder, Fancy Loop
patt., clear w/gold, ca. 1900 ......**120.00**

Tumbler, fruit, Minuet etching,
clear, 5 oz. **32.00**

Vases, 7½" h., footed, crimped
rim, Lariat patt., clear, pr. **55.00**

Wine, Duquesne patt.,
Tangerine **200.00**

Wine, Minuet etching, clear,
2½ oz..**65.00**

IMPERIAL

Imperial Glass Company, Bellaire, Ohio,
was organized in 1901 and was in continuous
production, except for very brief periods, until
its closing in June 1984. It had been a major

producer of Carnival Glass earlier in this century and also produced other types of glass, including an Art Glass line called "Free Hand Ware" during the 1920s and its "Jewels" about 1916. The company acquired a number of molds of other earlier factories, including the Cambridge and A.H. Heisey Companies, and reissued numerous items through the years. Also see CARNIVAL GLASS and ANIMALS under glass.

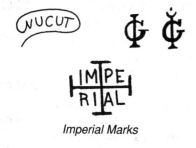

Imperial Marks

CANDLEWICK PATTERN

Ashtray-bonbon, heart-shaped, No. 400/174, clear, 6½" d. **$10.00**

Ashtray-bonbon, heart-shaped, No. 400/174, milk white, 6½" d. **45.00**

Ashtray set, round, No. 400/550, clear, 3 pcs. **25.00**

Bowl, 5½" d., heart-shaped, No. 400/53H, clear **20.00**

Bowl, 6" d., three-footed, No. 400/183, clear **75.00**

Bowl, mint, 6" d., handled, No. 400/51F, clear **14.00**

Candleholders, mushroom-shaped, No. 400/86, clear, pr. **85.00**

Coaster, No. 400/78, clear, 4" d. **8.00**

Cocktail, No. 3400, clear, 4 oz. **14.00**

Compote, 5½" d., low ball stem, No. 400/66B, clear **30.00**

Creamer & open sugar bowl, plain footed, No. 400/31, clear, pr. **22.00**

Deviled egg server, center handle, No. 400/154, clear, 12" d. **170.00**

Ladle, mayonnaise, No. 400/135, clear, 6¼" l. **15.00**

Marmalade set: cov. bowl, underplate & spoon; clear, 3 pcs. **45.00**

Nappy, round, No. 400/5F, clear, 7" d. **45.00**

Party set: oval plate w/indent & cup; No. 400/98, clear, 2 pcs.......**20.00**

Pitcher, Liliputian-type, No. 400/19, clear, 16 oz. **325.00**

Pitcher, Colonial patt., clear, 6¾" h., 40 oz. **110.00**

Plate, 5½" d., two-handled w/star cutting, No. 400/42D, clear..........**30.00**

Plate, canapé, 6" d., No. 400/36, clear..**9.00**

Plate, salad, 7" d., No. 400/3D, clear..**6.00**

Plate, 8½" d., two-handled, No. 400/62D, clear **9.00**

Plate, 10" d., two-handled, No. 400/72D, clear **14.00**

Relish dish, oval, two-handled, No. 400/217, clear, 10" l. **30.00**

Salad fork & spoon w/vertical ribs, No. 701, clear, 2 pcs. **30.00**

Sauceboat undertray, No. 400/169, clear....................................**35.00**

Sherbet, No. 400/190, clear, 6 oz..**12.00**

Tray, wafer, No. 400/51T, clear, 6" l. **25.00**

Tray, No. 400/68D, clear w/floral cutting, 11½" l. **95.00**

Tray, No. 400/68D, clear w/star cut decoration, 11½" l. **85.00**

Tumbler, No. 400/19, clear, 12 oz..**16.00**

Vase, bud, 5¾" h., bead-footed, No. 400/107, clear **40.00**

Vase, bud, 7" h., footed No. 400/186, clear............................**240.00**

Vase, 8½" h., bead-footed, flared rim, No. 400/21, clear ....**200.00 to 225.00**

Wine, No. 3800, clear, 4 oz. **20.00**

CAPE COD PATTERN

Bottle w/stopper, condiment, No.
160/224, clear, 6 oz. **65.00**

Bowl, finger, 4½" d.,
No. 1604½A **7.00**

Bowl, fruit, 9" d., footed, No.
160/67F, clear **66.00**

Bowl, console, 13" d., No.
160/75L, clear............................**60.00**

Cake stand, footed, No. 160/67D,
clear, 10½" d. **55.00**

Claret, No. 1602, Azalea (pink),
5 oz...**40.00**

Compote, cov., 6" d., No.
160/140, clear............................**60.00**

Creamer & sugar bowl, footed,
No. 160/31, clear, pr. **30.00**

**Creamer & open sugar bowl
w/undertray,** No. 160/29/30,
clear, 3 pcs. **35.00**

Goblet, dinner, No. 1602, clear,
11 oz..**10.00**

Goblet, dinner, No. 1602, Verde
green, 11 oz. **15.00**

Plate, 7" d., No. 160/3D, clear **5.00**

Plate, 8" d., cupped, (liner for
gravy), No. 160/203, clear **74.00**

Relish dish, five-part, No.
160/102, clear............................**65.00**

Salad fork & spoon, No.
160/701, pr. **30.00**

Salt & pepper shakers,
stemmed, footed, No. 160/243,
clear, pr. **43.00**

Sherbet, tall, No. 1602, clear,
6 oz...**7.00**

Tumbler, juice, footed, No. 1602,
Amber, 6 oz. **16.00**

Tumbler, juice, footed, No. 1602,
Azalea (pink), 6 oz......................**35.00**

Tumbler, iced-tea, footed, No.
1600, clear, 12 oz. **20.00**

Tumbler, iced-tea, footed, No.
1602, Verde green, 12 oz. **12.00**

Whiskey, No. 160, clear,
2½ oz..**12.00**

LACY

Lacy Glass is a general term developed by collectors many years ago to cover the earliest type of pressed glass produced in this country. "Lacy" refers to the fact that most of these early patterns consisted of scrolls and geometric designs against a finely stippled background which gives the glass the look of fine lace. Formerly this glass was often referred to as "Sandwich" for the Boston & Sandwich Glass Company of Sandwich, Massachusetts which produced a great deal of this ware. Today, however, collectors realize that many other factories on the East Coast and in the Pittsburgh, Pennsylvania and Wheeling, West Virginia areas also made lacy glass from the 1820s into the 1840s. All pieces listed are clear unless otherwise noted. Numbers after salt dips refer to listings in Pressed Glass Salt Dishes of the Lacy Period, 1825-1850, *by Logan W. and Dorothy B. Neal. Also see CUP PLATES and SANDWICH GLASS.*

Bowl, miniature toy-size, 1¼" d.,
1" h., hexagonal decorated sides
on a conforming foot (mold
roughness, lines on the foot) ...**$143.00**

Bowl, 5¼" d., 1¼" h., Riverboat
patt., boat design in center &
repeating scroll clusters around
the flanged rim, Midwestern, ca.
1830-35, clear w/aquamarine
tint...**550.00**

Bowl, 8" d., 1¼" h., Shield &
Anchor patt. (two tipped
scallops) **176.00**

Compote, open, 6¼" d., 4¼" h.,
Flowers & Leaves patt. in bowl,
ribbed standard attached
w/wafers to lacy floral foot, New
England (two tipped rim scallops
& one tipped on base) **523.00**

Dish, round w/deep sides, a
bull's-eye rim around designs of
stylized blossoms, zigzags, S-
scrolls, shells & beading around
a central starburst, probably
Pittsburgh, clear, 9¼" d. (one
scallop damaged, eight others
tipped) **715.00**

Lamp, table model, whale oil, free-blown shouldered conical font tapering to old metal burner, attached w/a wide disc wafer to an inverted lacy cup plate foot, ca. 1830, 6¾" h. (some light interior font stain & exterior scratches) **935.00**

Plate, 5¾" d., a wide border of faint leafy scrolls, center ring inscribed in the mold "T & J Robinson - Pittsbg.," attributed to Pittsburg, ca. 1830s (one tipped scallop) **220.00**

Plate, 6¼" d., central design of a starburst composed of stippled diamonds, points & fans, the lightly scalloped border w/fans & diamonds, attributed to New England, ca. 1830-45 (minor rim flakes, some green slag in one small rim area).........................**330.00**

Basket of Flowers Lacy Plate

Plate, 7⅜" w., octagonal, Basket of Flowers patt., leafy scroll borders w/outer border of tiny bull's-eyes, Midwestern, ca. 1835, tipping & flaking to the points & bull's-eyes (ILLUS.) **220.00**

Salt dip, eagle salt, boat-shaped w/a molded figure of an eagle at each corner joined by a looped top border band on each side, on scroll feet, attributed to Sandwich (EE-3b) **176.00**

Salt dip, model of a boat, the sidewheeler steamer w/the sidewheels marked "Lafayet," base embossed "Sandwich, " Boston & Sandwich, ca. 1830s, sapphire blue w/light fiery opalescence, BT-5, 3½" l., 1½" h. (minor flake on rudder, few very minor table ring flakes) ...**1,250.00**

Salt dip, cov., model of a Grecian sofa w/ beaded scroll ends & S-scroll beaded feet, pots of flowers on sides, fitted rectangular tapering domed cover w/pine cone finial & scroll designs, probably Boston & Sandwich, clear, CD-2 (two small chips) **880.00**

Salt dip, oval, on a narrow foot below rounded sides composed of scroll-patterned roundels, deep blue (OL-11) **523.00**

Salt dip, pedestal-type w/a round bowl w/small scallops around the rim, the sides w/six panels alternating w/scenes of sailing ships or eagles, low pedestal foot, probably Boston & Sandwich, ca. 1830-40, clear, EE-8a (one scallop half missing) **495.00**

Salt dip, rectangular sides w/corner posts ending in small knob feet, strawberry diamond design on sides, lightly scalloped rim w/tiny bull's-eyes, fiery opalescent (SD-11)............**413.00**

Salt dip, rectangular sides w/corner posts ending in small knob feet, strawberry diamond design on sides, lightly scalloped rim, attributed to Sandwich, violet blue, SD-9 (shallow chip on upper rim & mold roughness).......................**385.00**

Sugar bowl, cov., Acanthus Leaf & Shield design, attributed to the Providence Flint Glass Works, Providence, Rhode Island, ca. 1830-33 (mold roughness on cover, shallow chip on beaded

base rim under galleried rim,
one base scallop chipped & two
flakes on galleried rim) **715.00**

Toddy plate, Harp & Star patt.,
probably an Eastern factory, ca.
1830s, brilliant peacock blue,
4⁵⁄₁₆" d. (two slightly disfigured
scallops, unseen chip on table
ring) **275.00**

Toddy plate, Eagle patt., leaf
band borders, probably
Sandwich, ca. 1830, 4½" d. **77.00**

Tray, miniature toy-size, oval, a
pair of heart-shaped scrolls in
the center, border of tiny florals,
probably Boston & Sandwich,
ca. 1835-50, canary, 2½" l.
(minute bottom flakes, one
scallop missing) **330.00**

LALIQUE

Lalique "Amour" Book End

Fine glass, which includes numerous extraordinary molded articles, has been made by the glasshouse established b René Lalique early in this century in France. The firm was carried on by his son, Marc, until his death in 1977 and is now headed by Marc's daughter, Marie-Claude. All Lalique glass is marked, usually on, or near, the bottom with either an engraved or molded signature. Unless

otherwise noted, we list only those pieces marked "R. Lalique" produced before the death of René Lalique in 1945.

R. Lalique France N=3152

R LALIQUE
FRANCE

Lalique Marks

Book ends, "Amour," frosted
clear figural form molded as a
nude putto w/long curly locks &
short wings, seated on a small
mound w/a rectangular base,
each inscribed "R. LALIQUE -
FRANCE," introduced in 1929,
7½" h., pr. (ILLUS.
of one) **$2,530.00**

Bowl, 8½" d., "Volubilis," wide
shallow form raised on three
short legs each molded as the
center of a spreading trumpet
blossom when seen from above,
lemon yellow-tinted
opalescence, molded in reverse
"R. LALIQUE" & inscribed
"France," introduced in 1921 .....**690.00**

Clock, "Naiades," square
opalescent front plate molded
w/six mermaids w/long flowing
beaded hair, enclosing the
circular clock face w/ black
handles, silvered & enameled
dial & applied silvered baton
numerals, eight-day movement
w/lever escapement, plate
molded "R. LALIQUE,"
introduced in 1926, 4½" h.
(minor chipping & wear) **1,840.00**

Hood ornament, "Tete d'Aigle,"
frosted clear molded stylized
head of an eagle, molded mark,
introduced in 1928, 4½" h.........**690.00**

**Perfume bottle w/original
stopper,** "Vers le Jour" by
Worth, the flattened spherical
vessel & stopper in clear w/light

amber shading to dark, molded in low-relief w/chevrons, molded "WORTH" & "R. LALIQUE - FRANCE," introduced in 1926, 4¼" h. **632.00**

Vase, 7" h., "Saint-Francois," flaring trumpet-form grey body molded in high-relief w/plump opalescent finches & in low-relief w/the delicate leafy branches on which they perch, minute traces of the original blue patine, stamped "R. LALIQUE," introduced in 1955 ....**1,725.00**

Vase, 8¼" h., "Escargot," a footed flattened disc form w/a small flaring neck, grey ground molded in low-relief on the front & back w/a spiraling snail's shell, original green patine, molded mark "R. LALIQUE," introduced in 1920 ....**1,840.00**

Vase, 9¾" h., "Perruches," frosted green, ovoid body molded w/pairs of lovebirds perched in flowering branches, traces of original white patine, inscribed mark, introduced in 1919 (drilled) **1,840.00**

LIBBEY

In 1878, William L. Libbey obtained a lease on the New England Glass Company of Cambridge, Massachusetts, changing the name to the New England Glass Works, W.L. Libbey and Son, Proprietors. After his death in 1883, his son, Edward D. Libbey, continued to operate the company at Cambridge until 1888 when the factory was closed. Edward Libbey moved to Toledo, Ohio, and set up the company subsequently known as Libbey Glass Co. During the 1880s, the firm's master technician, Joseph Locke, developed the now much desired colored art glass lines of Agata, Amberina, Peach Blow and Pomona. Renowned for its Cut Glass of the Brilliant Period (see CUT GLASS), the company continues in operation today as Libbey Glassware, a division of Owens-Illinois, Inc.

Compote, 11" d., Silhouette patt., white opalescent figural elephant stem, signed **$975.00**

Cordial, Silhouette patt., figural kangaroo stem..........................**110.00**

Cordial, Silhouette patt., figural monkey stem **150.00**

Dinner bell, etched "1893 World's Fair" & molded w/"1893 World's Columbian Xposition (sic.)," frosted handle & metal clapper, 5¾" h. **285.00**

Punch cup, pressed glass petal-form marked "World's Fair 1893," impressed "Libbey Glass Co., Toledo, Ohio," & "World's Fair" inside..................................**75.00**

Vase, 11" h., Amberina, patt. #3304 ....**750.00**

Wine, Silhouette patt., opalescent figural kangaroo stem, signed, 6" h. **135.00**

Wine, Silhouette patt., opalescent figural monkey stem, signed, 6" h. **125.00**

Wine, Silhouette patt., black figural polar bear stem, signed, 6" h. **125.00**

LOETZ

Iridescent glass, some of it somewhat resembling that of Tiffany and other contemporary glasshouses, was produced by the Bohemian firm of J. Loetz Witwe of Klostermule and is referred to as Loetz. Some cameo pieces were also made. Not all pieces are marked.

Loetz,
tustria

Loetz Mark

Bowl-vase, paperweight-type, spherical w/flattened sides below the narrow angled shoulder to the wide, flat mouth, grey shaded lime green & metallic blue at the shoulders & rim, the whole encased in clear, unsigned, ca. 1900, 7" d.......**$2,300.00**

Vase, 4½" h., tapering ovoid body w/a rounded shoulder tapering to a short flaring neck, iridescent pale yellow w/a hooked & pulled feather decoration in silvery blue, signed "Loetz - Austria".............**770.00**

Vase, 5⅞" h., ovoid body w/a pinched-in neck w/a tri-lobed widely ruffled rim, clear decorated w/salmon pink & silvery blue horizontal lines further embellished w/large randomly placed dots of silvery blue iridescence, inscribed "Loetz - Austria," ca. 1901 ......**4,600.00**

Vase, 8³⁄₁₆" h., squatty bulbous base tapering to a slender swelled body w/a flaring, flattened rim, deep cobalt blue decorated w/concentric swirling trailings & three applied salmon pink & silvery blue striped long drops w/pulled trailings, inscribed "Loetz - Austria," ca. 1900..............................**13,800.00**

Vase, 9¹⁄₁₆" h., footed sharply tapering slender ovoid waisted body w/a short flaring neck, salmon pink decorated w/pulled silvery blue feathers between swirled borders in purple & deep aubergine & amber, inscribed "Loetz - Austria," ca. 1900 ....**21,850.00**

Vase, 12⅝" h., very tall sender baluster-form body swelled just below the widely flaring, flattened mouth, clear decorated w/bands of salmon pink, golden amber & gunmetal black w/swirled silvery blue trailings, the foot, rim & swelled neck decorated w/scrolling foliate silver mounts, designed by Franz Hofstatter, ca. 1900, unsigned..............................**11,500.00**

MARY GREGORY

Glass enameled in white with silhouette-type figures, primarily of children, is now termed "Mary Gregory" and was attributed to the Boston and Sandwich Glass Company. However, recent research has proven conclusively that this was not decorated by Mary Gregory, nor was it made at the Sandwich plant. Miss Gregory was employed by Boston and Sandwich Glass Company as a decorator; however, records show her assignment was the painting of naturalistic landscape scenes on larger items such as lamps and shades, but never the charming children for which her name has become synonymous. Further, in the inspection of fragments from the factory site, no paintings of children were found.

It is now known that all wares collectors call "Mary Gregory" originated in Bohemia beginning in the late 19th century and were extensively exported to England and the United States well into this century.

For further information, see The Glass Industry in Sandwich, Volume #4, *by Raymond E. Barlow and Joan E. Kaiser, and the book,* Mary Gregory Glassware, 1880-1900, *by R.& D. Truitt.*

Box w/hinged cover, glove-type, rectangular w/beveled edges, sapphire blue, lid depicts children in white lawn bowling, white floral swags on base, metal feet & trim, 10" l., 4½" w., 5" h. (ILLUS. top next page) **$2,400.00**

Dresser jar, cov., cylindrical, cover w/a tall tulip-shaped finial w/gold trim, amethyst, white enameled little girl blowing bubbles, 8¼" h..........................**150.00**

Lamp, banquet-style, kerosene-type, a thick cushion foot supporting a tapering cylindrical ringed pedestal below the ringed short cylindrical font all in blue w/a white opalescent swirl design, the pedestal decorated w/a white enameled seated girl fishing, bands of white dot flowers around the foot & font,

Long Mary Gregory Glove Box

the brass burner supporting a tulip-form blue w/white opalescent swirls satin-finished shade w/a deeply crimped & ruffled rim, h.p. w/ornate gold scroll cartouches trimmed w/white flowers & green leaves, clear chimney, complete, overall 16½" h. **1,500.00**

Pitcher, 8" h., 3½" d., an applied blue disc foot supports a tall ovoid amber body w/a cylindrical neck & pinched spout, applied angled blue handle, the body w/a white enameled young girl in a garden **225.00**

Pitcher, 10¾" h., blue, white enameled girl w/tinted hair & design on dress **395.00**

Tea warmer, square, brass w/four ruby-stained panels depicting various scenes, a white enameled boy doffing hat, girl w/hoop, girl w/flowers, & boy w/butterfly net, 5¼" sq., 4" h......**940.00**

Urn, black w/white enameled young girl holding basket & young boy picking apples from tree, gold trim on base & rim, 4½" d. pedestal base., 5⅜" d., 9¾" h. **300.00**

Vase, 4" h., bulbous bottom & ruffled rim, cranberry, white enameled boy holding flowers ...**225.00**

Vase, 10" h., 3⅝" d., sapphire blue, cushion foot below an ovoid body tapering to a ringed tapering neck w/a widely flaring deeply crimped & ruffled rolled rim, white enameled young boy blowing bubbles.........................**275.00**

Vase, 12" h., 3½" h. honey amber, applied clear pedestal base, white enameled girl w/rod & hoop **235.00**

Black Amethyst Mary Gregory Vases

Vases, 11½" h., 5" d., black amethyst, footed baluster-form w/flaring neck, one w/a white enameled girl wearing a hat & holding a basket of flowers looking up at a bird, the other w/a girl holding a stick & hoop, facing pr. (ILLUS. bottom previous page)...........................**650.00**

Wine, lavender-stained, flaring cylindrical bowl on a tapering light amber-stained stem & round foot, white enamel boy in garden, 2½" d., 5" h. **95.00**

McKEE

Red Ships Butter Dish

The McKee name has been associated with glass production since 1834, first producing window glass and later bottles. In the 1850s a new factory was established in Pittsburgh, Pennsylvania, for production of flint and pressed glass. The plant was relocated in Jeannette, Pennsylvania in 1888 and operated there as an independent company almost continuously until 1951 when it sold out to Thatcher Glass Manufacturing Company. Many types of collectible glass were produced by McKee through the years including Depression, Pattern, Milk White and a variety of utility kitchenwares.

McKee PRESCUT
McKee Marks

Beater bowl w/rolled rim spout, milk white w/Red Ships patt., 4½" h. **$48.00**

Butter dish, cov., milk white w/Red Ships patt. (ILLUS.)..........**28.00**

Canister, cov., marked "Sugar," Seville Yellow **95.00**

Canister, cov., round, Skokie Green, 10 oz.............................**20.00**

Canister w/clear cover, milk white w/Red Ships patt., 3½" h., 24 oz.....................................**33.00**

Cocktail glass spoon, amber, 8½" l. **25.00**

Console bowl, paneled foot below a short knobbed pedestal & a shallow, widely flaring bowl w/pointed scallops, caramel **45.00**

Console bowl, paneled foot below a short knobbed pedestal & a shallow, widely flaring bowl w/pointed scallops, Skokie Green **65.00**

Console bowl, paneled foot below a short knobbed pedestal & a shallow, widely flaring bowl w/pointed scallops, Seville Yellow...**95.00**

Jardiniere, three-footed, Skokie Green **35.00**

Measuring cup, Seville Yellow, 4 cup......................................**100.00**

Measuring cup, Skokie Green, 2 cup...**30.00**

Mixing bowl, French Ivory, 11½" d. **95.00**

Refrigerator dish, open, milk white w/Red Ships patt., 4 x 5"......**7.00**

Refrigerator dish, open, milk white w/Red Ships patt., 5 x 8"......**9.00**

Salt & pepper shakers, Roman Arch style, milk white w/Red Ships patt., pr. **29.00**

Tom & Jerry set: bowl & 11 cups, Jade Green w/black lettering & decoration, ca. 1930s, 12 pcs....**225.00**

Tumbler, whiskey, w/coaster base, "Bottoms Up," Skokie Green, the set...........................**170.00**

MILK WHITE

This is opaque white glass that resembles the color of and was used as a substitute for white porcelain. Opacity was obtained by adding oxide of tin to a batch of clear glass. It has been made in numerous forms and shapes in this country and abroad from about the first quarter of the last century. It is still being produced, and there are many reproductions of earlier pieces.

Animal covered dish, Boar's Head, Atterbury, marked "Patented May 29, 1888," 9½" l. **$1,700.00**

Animal covered dish, Cat on wide rib base, blue & white..........**70.00**

Animal covered dish, Cow, oblong base, Vallerysthal, original paint, 7" l, 4¼" w. **125.00**

Animal covered dish, Crawfish on two-handled oblong base, 7¼" handle to handle, 4¼" h. **200.00**

Animal covered dish, Deer on Fallen Tree, marked "E.C. Flaccus Co. Wheeling W. Va.," 6⅝" l., 5" h. **300.00**

Animal covered dish, Mouse On Egg, 5" l. **575.00**

Animal covered dish, Pig on Drum, marked "PV.," Vallerysthal, 3" h.......................**110.00**

Animal covered dish, Rabbit, Portieux, France, 6" l. **375.00**

Animal covered dish, Turtle on two-handled oblong base, 7¼" handle to handle, 4¼" h. **250.00**

Animal covered dish, Walking Elephant **250.00**

Animal covered dish, Wavy Base Duck, glass eyes, Tiffin Glass Co., 8" l.............................**60.00**

Bowl, 7¾" d., 4" h., crimped rim, Lacy Edge patt. **45.00**

Bowl, 6½" d., Wicket patt. **24.00**

Bowl, 7½" d., round, footed, Scroll patt. **24.00**

Bowl, 7½" d., Scroll & Eye patt. **30.00**

Bowl, model of a swan, tureen-style, open neck w/diamond design on wings & breast, 11½" l., 6½" h. (hairline crack on front) **3,000.00**

Compote, Open Hand patt., 9⅛" d., 8¾" h. **35.00**

Covered dish, Cruiser Warship, 6" l., 4" h. **68.00**

Covered dish, Prairie Schooner, 5⅞" l. **135.00**

Covered dish, Stagecoach, L.E. Smith Company, 5" l., 4¼" h. **175.00**

Covered jar, cov., Queen Victoria bust w/medallion, 8¼" h. **80.00**

Egg-shaped globe, marked "More Chicken" below a relief-molded smiling black face peeking through the side of the egg, 4⅜" h. **375.00**

Inkwell, model of a boat w/original pewter cover, marked "Pat. Aug. 9, 1876," 5½" l. (slight edge roughness) **200.00**

Bull's Head Mustard Jar

Mustard jar, cover & ladle, figural Bull's Head, Atterbury, ca. 1888, the set (ILLUS.) **195.00**

Nappies, Maple Leaf patt., set of four **55.00**

Plate, 7" d., smooth center w/raised owls, an eagle,

crescent moon & frog on pad around the edges, w/gold decoration....................................**65.00**

Plate, 7" d., William Howard Taft 1908 Campaign, President Taft surrounded by eagles, flags & stars (factory-flaw in border)........**45.00**

Plate, 7" d., Three Kittens patt., worn paint, Westmoreland Specialty Company **35.00**

Plate, Indian Chief patt., lacy edge **65.00**

Platter, Fish, Atterbury, clear border embossed "Give Us This Day Our Daily Bread," patented Nov. 23, 1875, 12⅞" l., 9" w. ..**1,700.00**

Shaker w/original top, figural General Shafter, ...**900.00**

Shaker w/original top, figural Columbus w/beard **1,100.00**

Sugar bowl, open, Fish, English, ca. 1882....................................**100.00**

Syrup pitcher w/original lid, model of ear of corn with husk, 7½" h. **60.00**

Toothpick holder, figural Corset, Bellaire Goblet Co. **85.00**

Toothpick holder, Monkey with Hat...**130.00**

MT. WASHINGTON

Decorated Mt. Washington Cracker Jar

A wide diversity of glass was made by the Mt. Washington Glass Company of New Bedford, Massachusetts, between 1869 and 1900. It was succeeded in 1900 by the Pairpoint Corporation. Miscellaneous types are listed below.

Boudoir bottles w/original blown stoppers, decorated w/large shaded yellow roses, 9¼" h., pr. **$145.00**

Cracker jar, cov., barrel-shaped, yellow to peach background decorated w/copper-colored outlined leaves & shaded white blossoms, resilvered rim, cover & bail handle, unmarked (ILLUS.) **815.00**

Cruet w/original thorn stopper, applied frosted twig handle, apricot Diamond Quilted satin glass (chip on stopper) **450.00**

Photo box, decorated overall w/gold scrolls & enameled blue forget-me-nots, satin finish, 3¾" x 5" **135.00**

Powder box, cov., round, h.p. violets on base & cover **75.00**

Rose bowl, crystal w/optic ribbing, the rim highlighted in gold, green ivy leaf decoration w/rust-colored stems w/ petite pink & yellow blossoms **485.00**

Salt shaker, egg-shaped, reclining-type w/a flat base, decorated w/a spray of h.p. pink & blue violets **185.00**

Salt shaker, egg-shaped, stand up-type w/h.p. pecking hen, 2½" h. **350.00**

Salt & pepper shakers w/original lids, pillar ribbing, floral decoration, resilvered handled frame, pr. **310.00**

Sweetmeat jar, cov., spangle glass w/gold mica & decorated w/dogwood blossoms in ivory, burgundy & pink blossoms, pink lining, original silver plated rim & repousse cover.........................**285.00**

Toothpick holder, floral
decoration..................................**175.00**

Vase, 5½" h., melon-ribbed body
w/ruffled rim, apricot mother-of-
pearl satin Raindrop patt., white
lining **250.00**

Vase, bud, 5¾" h., footed,
Fireglow w/h.p. blue florals &
strawberries w/a firefly, on
applied high curled feet **110.00**

Vase, 13½" h., pinched-form,
white opal ground decorated
w/enameled flowers in pink,
gold, & brown, marked at base
w/numbers & letter "P"..............**550.00**

NEW MARTINSVILLE

*The New Martinsville Glass Mfg. Co.
opened in New Martinsville, West Virginia
in 1901 and during its first period of
production came out with a number of colored
opaque pressed glass patterns. They also
developed an art glass line they named
"Muranese," which collectors refer to as
"New Martinsville Peach Blow." The factory
burned in 1907 but reopened later that year
and began focusing on production of various
clear pressed glass patterns, many of which
were then decorated with gold or ruby
staining or enameled decoration. After going
through receivership in 1937, the factory
again changed the focus of its production to
more contemporary glass lines and figural
animals. The firm was purchased in 1944 by
The Viking Glass Company (now Dalzell-
Viking) and some of the long-popular New
Martinsville patterns are now produced by
this still active firm.*

Berry set: one master bowl & six
individual sauce dishes, Old
Colony patt. (No. 97 Line),
7 pcs......................................**$150.00**

Bonbon, cov., Radiance patt.
(No. 4233 Line), amber **275.00**

Cake salver, low, Radiance patt.,
ice blue **175.00**

Chambersticks, saucer base
w/scalloped rim, centered by
paneled shaft w/short ring-side

handle & flaring socket, No. 18,
cobalt blue, 6" h., 7" w., pr.........**175.00**

Compote, footed, Moondrops
patt., cobalt blue **175.00**

Cordial, Moondrops patt., amber
w/silver decoration, 3" h. **25.00**

Cordial, Moondrops patt., amber ..**17.00**

Cordial, Radiance patt., amber,
2⅝" h. **15.00**

Cordial, Radiance patt., red,
2⅝" h. **25.00**

Creamer & open sugar bowl,
Radiance patt., ice blue **65.00**

Creamer, footed, Prelude etching,
clear..**13.00**

Cruets w/original stoppers, oil &
vinegar, Janice patt., blue, pr. ...**150.00**

Cup, footed, Moondrops patt.,
red **15.00**

Honey jar, cov., Radiance patt.,
amber **275.00**

Plate, 7½" d., Fancy Squares
patt. (No. 35 Line), Jade green......**8.00**

Plate, 14" d., Florentine etching **20.00**

Punch bowl & underplate,
Radiance patt., red, 14" d...........**85.00**

Punch ladle, Radiance patt.,
amber **75.00**

Shot glass, round, handled,
Moondrops patt. **11.00**

Tumbler, Moondrops patt., red.,
9 oz...**15.00**

Vase, 11" h., footed, Prelude
etching......................................**125.00**

Wine, Moondrops patt., red **12.00**

NORTHWOOD

*Harry Northwood (1860-1919) was born
in England, the son of noted glass artist John
Northwood. Brought up in the glass business,
Harry immigrated to the United States in
1881 and shortly thereafter became manager
of the La Belle Glass Company, Bridgeport,
Ohio. Here he was responsible for many
innovations in colored and blown glass. After
leaving La Belle in 1887 he opened The*

Northwood Glass Company in Martins Ferry, Ohio in 1888. The company moved to Ellwood City, Pennsylvania in 1892 and Northwood moved again to take over a glass plant in Indiana, Pennsylvania in 1896. One of his major lines made at the Indiana, Pennsylvania plant was Custard glass (which he called "ivory"). It was made in several patterns and some pieces were marked on the base with "Northwood" in script.

Harry and his family moved back to England in 1899 but returned to the U.S. in 1902 at which time he opened another glass factory in Wheeling, West Virginia. Here he was able to put his full talents to work and under his guidance the firm manufactured many notable glass lines including opalescent wares, colored and clear pressed tablewares, various novelties and probably best known of all, Carnival glass. Around 1906 Harry introduced his famous "N" in circle trademark which can be found on the base of many, but not all, pieces made at his factory. The factory closed in 1925.

In this listing we are including only the clear and colored tablewares produced at Northwood factories. Specialized lines such as Custard glass, Carnival and Opalescent wares are listed under their own headings in our Glass category.

Northwood Script & Circle Marks

Berry set: master bowl & four sauce dishes; Goofus decoration w/ruby colored berries on gold branches, 5 pcs. **$150.00**

Berry set: master bowl w/four sauce dishes; Leaf Medallian (Regent) patt., purple w/gold trim, the set **150.00**

Bowl, cov. Plums & Cherries patt., clear w/color stain.............**175.00**

Butter dish, cov., Leaf Mold patt., lime green.................................**195.00**

Celery vase, Chrysanthemum Swirl patt., speckled canary.......**145.00**

Celery vase, Leaf Umbrella patt., cased blue **250.00**

Creamer, Chrysanthemum Swirl, cranberry speckled **165.00**

Creamer, Leaf Mold patt., canary, satin finish **245.00**

Pitcher, water, Leaf Umbrella patt., cased blue **375.00**

Rose bowl, Leaf Mold patt., canary w/cranberry spatter, satin finish **285.00**

Salt & pepper shakers, Leaf Mold patt., canary w/cranberry splatter, pr. **150.00**

Sugar bowl, cov., Leaf Mold patt., lime green........................**165.00**

Sugar bowl, cov., Regal patt., green opalescent........................**90.00**

Sugar shaker w/original lid, Leaf Mold patt., transparent frosted light blue **295.00**

Sugar shaker w/original lid, Leaf Umbrella patt., blue spatter **425.00**

Sugar shaker w/original lid, Ribbed Pillar patt., cranberry & white spatter **235.00**

Syrup w/original lid, Wild Rose patt., clear.................................**65.00**

Table set: creamer, cov. sugar bowl, cov. butter dish & spooner; Leaf Medallion patt., cobalt blue w/gold trim, 4 pcs. **725.00**

Tumbler, Memphis patt., green w/gilt trim, signed........................**45.00**

Water set: pitcher & three tumblers; Peach patt., green w/gold trim, 4 pcs. ....**400.00 to 425.00**

OPALESCENT

(For an expanded listing of Opal-escent Glass see Antique Trader Books American & European Decorative & Art Glass Price Guide.)

Presently, this is one of the most popular areas of glass collecting. The opalescent effect was attained by adding bone ash chemicals to areas of an item while still hot and refiring the object at tremendous heat. Both pressed and mold-blown patterns are available to collectors and we distinguish the types in our listing below. Opalescent Glass from A to Z *by the late William Heacock is the definitive reference book for collectors.*

MOLD-BLOWN OPALESCENT PATTERNS

COIN SPOT

Coin Spot Syrup Pitcher

Compote, jelly, green **$35.00**

Pitcher, 8"h., crimped rim blue **175.00**

Pitcher, water, square top mold, cranberry **150.00**

Sugar shaker w/original top, Northwood mold, white..............**110.00**

Sugar shaker, w/original top, tapered mold, blue.....................**150.00**

Syrup pitcher w/original top, nine-panel mold, green (ILLUS.) **275.00**

Tumbler, cranberry **50.00**

DAISY & FERN

Lamp, banquet-type, white..........**500.00**

Pitcher, water, cranberry **245.00**

Rose bowl, cranberry...................**65.00**

Rose bowl, white **45.00**

Syrup pitcher w/original metal top, blue...................................**265.00**

Water set: pitcher & six tumblers; cranberry, 7 pcs. ....**500.00 to 550.00**

RIBBED OPAL LATTICE

Celery vase, blue **90.00**

Ribbed Opal Lattice Salt

Salt shaker, w/original top, cranberry (ILLUS.) ....**300.00 to 350.00**

Toothpick holder, blue...............**135.00**

Toothpick holder, white **75.00**

SPANISH LACE

Spanish Lace Bowl

Bowl, 5½" d., canary **35.00**

Bowl, 6½"d., ruffled rim, white.......**48.00**

Bowl, w/upturned rim, canary,
7" d., (ILLUS. bottom previous
page) **95.00**

Pitcher, water, 9½" h., ruffled rim
blue..**300.00**

Rose bowl, canary **40.00**

Salt shaker, w/original top,
canary...**95.00**

Sugar shaker, w/original top,
cranberry ....**425.00 to 450.00**

Tumbler, canary **48.00**

Vase, 6" h., canary **75.00**

Vase, blue...................................**225.00**

PRESSED OPALESCENT PATTERNS

DIAMOND SPEARHEAD

Diamond Spearhead Butter Dish

Butter dish cov., green
(ILLUS.)......................**225.00 to 250.00**

Mug, green **50.00**

Mug, canary..................................**55.00**

Table set, green 4 pcs. **575.00**

EVERGLADES

Bowl, oblong master berry,
blue..**214.00**

Butter dish, cov., canary **250.00**

Compote, jelly, blue **80.00**

Compote, jelly, blue w/gold trim....**95.00**

Compote, jelly, canary **110.00**

Pitcher, water, canary **525.00**

Table set, blue, 4 pcs. **550.00**

Table set, canary,
4 pcs. ....**500.00 to 525.00**

Tumbler, canary w/gold trim **50.00**

Tumbler, white **45.00**

Water set: pitcher & five
tumblers, white, 6 pcs...............**675.00**

FLUTED SCROLLS

Berry set, master bowl & six
sauce dishes; canary, 7 pcs. **285.00**

Butter dish, cov., blue **175.00**

Butter dish, cov., c anary **155.00**

Creamer, blue **65.00**

Cruet w/original stopper,
canary......................................**225.00**

Pitcher, water, canary **240.00**

Salt & pepper shakers
w/original tops, canary, pr. **140.00**

Sauce dish, blue **38.00**

Table set, blue, 4 pcs. **525.00**

Table set, canary,
4 pcs. ....**450.00 to 500.00**

Water set: pitcher & six tumblers;
canary, 7 pcs.............**675.00 to 725.00**

INVERTED FAN & FEATHER

Bowl, master berry, 10" d., blue ..**245.00**

Candy dish, green **285.00**

Creamer, blue **125.00**

Rose bowl, canary **40.00**

Sauce dishes, white, set of 6......**125.00**

Spooner, blue **150.00**

IRIS WITH MEANDER

Bowl, 9" d., footed, blue **45.00**

Bowl, 9" d., footed, green.............**40.00**

Compote, jelly, canary ....**50.00 to 75.00**

Creamer, blue **125.00**

Sauce dish, blue **30.00**

Sugar bowl, cov., white **50.00**

Toothpick holder, blue................**85.00**

Toothpick holder, green **85.00**

SWAG WITH BRACKETS

Compote, jelly, blue **40.00**

Compote, jelly, canary **35.00**

Compote, jelly, green...................**35.00**

Creamer, blue **105.00**

Pitcher, water, amethyst **125.00**

Spooner, blue **110.00**

Sugar bowl, cov., canary **115.00**

Sugar bowl, cov., green..............**125.00**

Toothpick holder, canary,
2½" h. **165.00**

Tumber, canary............................**55.00**

TOKYO

Bowl, 7" d., ruffled rim, blue **40.00**

Bowl, master berry, green.............**70.00**

Creamer, blue **70.00**

Cruet w/original stopper, blue...**165.00**

WREATH & SHELL

Salt dip, blue **110.00**

Sauce dish, blue **32.00**

Spooner, blue **85.00**

Wreath & Shell Sugar Bowl

Sugar bowl, cov., blue
(ILLUS.)....................**175.00 to 200.00**

Table set, blue, 4 pcs..................**690.00**

Toothpick holder, blue..............**200.00**

Toothpick holder, white **150.00**

Toothpick Holder, slightly
tapering cylindrical form w/an
applied clear reeded handle,
cranberry **165.00**

PATE DE VERRE

Pate de Verre, or "paste of glass," was molded by very few artisans. In the pate de verre technique, powdered glass is mixed with a liquid to make a paste which is then placed in a mold and baked at a high temperature. These articles have a finely-pitted or matte finish and are easily distinguished from blown glass. Duplicate pieces are possible with this technique.

A WALTER
NANCY

G·ARGY ROUSSEAU

Pate De Verre Marks

Bowl-vase, miniature, flared cup-
shape, molded in low- and
medium-relief w/ivy leaves &
berries in shades of grey, red,
violet & green, molded mark
"G. Argy-Rousseau,"
ca. 1919, 3½" h. **$5,462.00**

Figure, a standing cowled maiden
holding a long amphora, grey
shaded pale yellow & molded in
full-relief, impressed "A. WALTER
- NANCY," ca. 1900, 9" h. **2,530.00**

Paperweight, figural, modeled as
a greyish brown field mouse
crouching on vegetation in
shades of green, inscribed
"DAUM - NANCY" w/the Cross
of Lorraine, 2 ¼" h. **2,070.00**

Vase, 6½" h., a high flaring foot
supporting a slender trumpet-
form body w/a wide flat rim, deep
blue foot molded w/tiny blossoms
w/yellow centers, the body
molded w/delicate broad leaves
in blue & green & clusters of
reddish brown berries suspended
from a band of green leaves &
reddish brown berries around the

Pate de Verre Vase with Leaves & Berries

rim against an opaque to medium blue ground, signed on the base by A. Walter, artist's signature at the rim (ILLUS.) **2,860.00**

Vase, 8¾" h., swelled cylindrical form w/a wide, flat mouth, grey mottled w/deep amber, yellow & brick red, molded in low- and medium-relief w/three striding lions amid stylized scrolling designs, molded "G. ARGY-ROUSSEAU - FRANCE," ca. 1926...............**26,450.00**

Vase, 9¼" h., "Les Loups dans la Neige," gently swelled ovoid form, grey molded in low- and medium-relief w/a pack of black wolves striding along a snowy ledge, in shades of frosty white, black, green purple & blue, molded "G. Argy-Rousseau," ca. 1926...............................**32,200.00**

Veilleuse (night light), tall egg-shaped shade on a narrow wrought-iron base w/tiny ball feet, the shade in grey streaked w/amber & purple, cast in medium-relief w/three grotesque masks between zig-zag-decorated borders, above a brickwork ground in shades of raspberry, chocolate brown & charcoal, hammered wrought-iron base, molded "G. ARGY ROUSSEAU," ca. 1923, 5¼" h. **6,037.00**

PATTERN GLASS

For an expanded listing of Pattern Glass, see Antique Trader Books American Pressed Glass & Bottles Price Guide.

Though it has never been ascertained whether glass was first pressed in the United States or abroad, the development of the glass pressing machine revolutionized the glass industry in the United States and this country receives the credit for improving the method to make this process feasible. The first wares pressed were probably small flat plates of the type now referred to as "lacy," the intricacy of the design concealing flaws.

In 1827, both the New England Glass Co., Cambridge, Massachusetts and Bakewell & Co., Pittsburgh, took out patents for pressing glass furniture knobs and soon other pieces followed. This early pressed glass contained red lead which made it clear and resonant when tapped (flint.) Made primarily in clear, it is rarer in blue, amethyst, olive green and yellow.

By the 1840s, early simple patterns such as Ashburton, Argus and Excelsior appeared. Ribbed Bellflower seems to have been one of the earliest patterns to have had complete sets. By the 1860s, a wide range of patterns was available.

In 1864, William Leighton of Hobbs, Brockunier & Co., Wheeling, West Virginia, developed a formula for "soda lime" glass which did not require the expensive red lead for clarity. Although "soda lime" glass did not have the brilliance of the earlier flint glass, the formula came into widespread use because glass could be produced cheaply.

An asterisk (*) indicates a piece which has been reproduced.

ACTRESS

Bowl, cov...................................$110.00
Bowl, 6" d., flat 45.00
Bowl, 6" d., footed 50.00
Bowl, 7" d., footed 60.00
Bowl, 8" d., Adelaide Neilson 65.00
Bread tray, Miss Neilson,
   12½" l. ....50.00 to 75.00
Butter dish, cov.,
   Fanny Davenport &
   Miss Neilson..............100.00 to 125.00
Cake stand, Maude Granger &
   Annie Pixley, 10" d., 7" h. 119.00
Cake stand, frosted
   stem ....150.00 to 165.00

Actress Celery Vase

Celery vase, Pinafore scene
   (ILLUS.) 160.00
Cheese dish, cov., "Lone
   Fisherman" on cover,
   "The Two Dromios"
   on underplate ....200.00 to 225.00
Compote, cov., 6" d., 10" h. 100.00
Compote, cov., 7" d., 8½" h. 165.00
Compote, cov., 8" d.,
   12" h. ....175.00 to 200.00
Compote, open, 7" d., 7" h.,
   Miss Neilson 150.00

Compote, open, 7" d., 7" h.,
   Maggie Mitchell & Fanny
   Davenport 100.00
Compote, open, 8" d., 5" h............75.00
Compote, open, 10" d., 6" h..........80.00
Creamer, clear 72.00
Creamer, frosted........200.00 to 250.00
Goblet, Lotta Crabtree & Kate
   Claxton......................70.00 to 100.00
Marmalade jar, cov., Maude
   Granger & Annie Pixley 110.00
*Pickle dish, Kate Claxton,
   "Love's Request is Pickles,"
   5 1/4 x 9 1/4" 36.00
Pitcher, water, 9" h., Miss
   Neilson & Maggie
   Mitchell ....275.00 to 325.00
Platter, 7 x 11½", Pinafore
   scene...107.00
*Relish, Miss Neilson, 5 x 8" 40.00
Relish, Maude Granger,
   5 x 9" ....75.00 to 95.00
Salt shaker w/original
   pewter top 56.00
Sauce dish, Maggie Mitchell &
   Fanny Davenport,
   4½" d., 2½" h. 19.00
Spooner, Mary Anderson &
   Maude Granger 83.00
Sugar bowl, cov., Lotta Crabtree
   & Kate Claxton 118.00

ATLANTA (Lion or Square Lion's Head)

Bowl, 5 x 8" oblong, flat................50.00
Butter dish, cov.2 ....105.00
Cake stand................................110.00
Celery vase ....80.00 to 100.00
Compote, cov., 5" sq., 6" h. 95.00
Compote, cov., 7" sq., high
   stand ....175.00 to 200.00
Compote, open, 4 1/4" sq.,
   4" h. 46.00
Compote, open, 6" sq., 7½" h. 75.00
Creamer 68.00

Egg cup......................................95.00

*Goblet 78.00

Relish, boat-shaped 28.00

Salt dip, individual size 35.00

Salt dip, master size ...100.00 to 125.00

Sauce dish 35.00

Spooner 52.00

Sugar bowl, cov., engraved........160.00

Sugar bowl, cov., plain 97.00

Syrup pitcher
   w/original top..........200.00 to 250.00

Toothpick holder.........................60.00

Tumbler, engraved......................39.00

Tumbler, plain 35.00

Wine ....15.00 to 20.00

BANDED PORTLAND

(Portland w/Diamond Point Band, Virginia (States series), Portland Maiden Blush (when pink-stained))

Clear & colors stained on - blue, yellow & gold are higher value. Maiden Blush is pink-stained. Non-flint.

Berry set: master bowl & 4 sauce
   dishes; pink-stained,
   5 pcs. 175.00

Bowl, berry, 9" d. 30.00

Butter dish, cov., pink-stained....173.00

Candlesticks, pr. 88.00

Celery tray, pink-stained,
   10" oval 75.00

Celery tray, 5 x 12" 28.00

Celery vase ....30.00 to 35.00

Cologne bottle w/original
   stopper 49.00

Compote, cov., 8" d., high
   stand..105.00

Compote, open, 8¼" d., 8" h.,
   scalloped rim ....35.00 to 40.00

Creamer & sugar bowl,
   individual size, pink-stained,
   pr. 70.00

Cruet w/original stopper,
   pink-stained 400.00

Dresser jar, cov., clear,
   3½" d. 36.00

Dresser set: large tray, oval pin
   tray, cov. jar, cologne bottle
   w/original stopper &
   ring tree; 5 pcs..........................215.00

Goblet, clear................................52.00

Goblet, pink-stained 64.00

Goblet, yellow stained..................85.00

Pitcher, water, 9½" h.....................95.00

Pitcher, tankard, 11" h.,
   pink-stained..............225.00 to 250.00

Pitcher, child's.............................32.00

Pomade jar, cov. 28.00

Punch cup, clear...........................11.00

Punch cup, pink-stained 31.00

Relish, pink-stained, 4 x 6½".........28.00

Ring tree, gold-stained.................50.00

Banded Portland Sauce Dish

Salt shaker w/original top,
   pink-stained 65.00

Salt & pepper shakers
   w/original tops, clear, pr. 60.00

Sauce dish, 4½" d........................15.00

Sauce dish, pink-stained,
   4½" d. 24.00

Spooner, pink-stained...................75.00

Sugar bowl, cov., pink-stained ...112.00

Sugar bowl, individual size 24.00

Sugar shaker w/original top,
   clear...50.00

Sugar shaker w/original top,
   pink-stained (ILLUS.)................135.00

Toothpick holder, clear
   w/gold 25.00

Toothpick holder,
   pink-stained...................50.00 to 55.00

Tumbler, clear................................27.00

Tumbler, pink-stained 44.00
Vase, 6" h., flared, clear 32.00
Vase, 6" h., flared, pink-stained.....35.00
Vase, 9" h. 42.00
Wine, clear 29.00
Wine, pink-stained ....60.00 to 70.00

BEADED TULIP
Bowl, 6⅝ x 9½" oval.....................20.00
Creamer 65.00
Goblet 35.00
Pitcher, milk, 1 qt. 75.00
Pitcher, water ....55.00 to 60.00
Plate, dinner, 6" d. 19.00
Sauce, 4" d. 8.00
Tray, wine, 9" d............................35.00
Wine...............................25.00 to 35.00

BIRD & STRAWBERRY (Bluebird)
Berry set, master bowl & 5 sauce
  dishes; w/color, 6 pcs. 525.00
Bowl, 5½" d., clear..........30.00 to 35.00
Bowl, 5½" d., w/color....................35.00
Bowl, 7½" d., footed, w/color.........70.00
Bowl, 9" d., flat, w/color................75.00
Bowl, 9½" l., 6" w., oval, footed.....60.00
Bowl, 10" d., flat, clear....60.00 to 70.00
Bowl, 10" d., flat, w/color &
  gold trim.....................................115.00
Butter dish, cov., clear 125.00
Butter dish, cov.,
  w/color......................175.00 to 225.00
Cake stand, 9" to
  9½" d.............................60.00 to 70.00
*Celery tray, 10" l. ....50.00 to 60.00
Compote, cov., 6" d., low stand 57.00
*Compote, cov., 6½" d.,
  9½" h.........................145.00 to 155.00
Compote, cov., jelly 130.00
Compote, open, 6" d., ruffled rim,
  w/color......................100.00 to 125.00
Creamer, clear ....60.00 to 70.00

Creamer, w/color........................115.00
Dish, heart-shaped ....55.00 to 60.00
Pitcher, water, clear....285.00 to 300.00
Pitcher, water,
  w/color.......................400.00 to 425.00
Plate, 12" d. 80.00
Punch cup 24.00
Sauce dish, flat or footed,
  clear ....25.00 to 30.00
Sauce dish, w/color 40.00
Spooner, clear 60.00
Spooner, w/color ....100.00 to 125.00
Sugar bowl, cov. 65.00
Tumbler, clear ....50.00 to 55.00

Bird & Strawberry Tumbler

Tumbler, w/color (ILLUS.) 95.00
Wine................................55.00 to 75.00

BLOCK & FAN
Bowl, berry, 8" d., footed...............28.00
Bowl, 9¾" d. 32.00
Butter dish, cov. ....50.00 to 60.00
Cake stand, 9" to 10" d...40.00 to 50.00
Carafe, water ....55.00 to 65.00

Celery tray 25.00

CABBAGE ROSE

Butter dish, cov. 95.00

Cake stand, 9½" to
12½" d. ....55.00 to 75.00

Celery vase...............................50.00

Champagne 75.00

Compote, cov., 6" d., low stand 95.00

Compote, cov., 6" d., high
stand..110.00

Compote, cov., 7½" d., high
stand..105.00

Compote, cov., 8½" d., high
stand..95.00

Compote, open, 7" d., low
stand..30.00

Compote, open, 7½" d., high
stand..60.00

Compote, open, 8½" d., high
stand ....75.00 to 85.00

Creamer, applied handle..............55.00

Egg cup......................................34.00

***Goblet**..40.00

Cabbage Rose Pickle Dish

Pickle dish, 7½" to 8½" l.
(ILLUS.).........................25.00 to 35.00

Salt dip, master size 30.00

Sauce dish ....30.00 to 35.00

***Spooner** (ILLUS. top next
column)......................................30.00

Sugar bowl, cov. 62.00

Tumbler, bar 43.00

Cabbage Rose Spooner

Cabbage Rose Tumbler

Tumbler (ILLUS.) 42.00

Wine...............................40.00 to 50.00

CARDINAL BIRD

Cardinal Sauce Dish

Butter dish, cov. 95.00

Butter dish, cov., three
unidentified birds 98.00

Creamer ....35.00 to 45.00

Goblet ....40.00 to 45.00

Sauce dish, flat or footed, each
(ILLUS. bottom previous page) ...**14.00**

Spooner.........................25.00 to 35.00

Sugar bowl, cov............................**55.00**

COTTAGE (Dinner Bell or Finecut Band)

Cottage Goblet

Butter dish, cov., clear **47.00**

Cake stand, amber **75.00**

Cake stand, clear.........................**37.00**

Celery vase, amber.......................**85.00**

Celery vase, clear **32.00**

Champagne **65.00**

Compote, cov., 8" d., high stand,
amber **180.00**

Compote, open, jelly, 4½" d.,
4" h., clear **22.00**

Compote, open, jelly, 4½" d.,
4" h., green **48.00**

Creamer, amber **60.00**

Creamer, clear **27.00**

Cruet w/original stopper **65.00**

*Goblet, amber..............................**52.00**

*Goblet, blue ....65.00 to 70.00

*Goblet, clear (ILLUS.) **28.00**

Pitcher, milk, clear **35.00**

Pitcher, water, 2 qt. ....55.00 to 65.00

Plate, 6" d. **14.00**

Plate, 7" d. **20.00**

Plate, 10" d. **43.00**

Salt shaker w/original top **35.00**

Sauce dish, amber.......................**25.00**

Sauce dish, clear **15.00**

Tray, water, clear...........................**48.00**

Tray, water, green **65.00**

*Wine, amber..................................**53.00**

DAHLIA

Dahlia Blue Pitcher

Bread platter, 8 x 12" .....35.00 to 40.00

Butter dish, cov., clear **54.00**

Cake stand, amber, 9½" d. **73.00**

Cake stand, blue, 9½" d...............**53.00**

Cake stand, clear, 9½" d..............**35.00**

Champagne **75.00**

Compote, open, 8" d., high
stand...**50.00**

Cordial **40.00**

Creamer, clear **30.00**

Egg cup, double ....45.00 to 50.00

Goblet 35.00

Mug, amber 45.00

Mug, blue....................................60.00

Mug, clear....................................30.00

Mug, child's...................................20.00

Pitcher, milk, canary 65.00

Pitcher, milk, applied handle........51.00

Pitcher, water, blue
  (ILLUS.)......................95.00 to 100.00

Pitcher, water, clear 55.00

Plate, 7" d. 35.00

Plate, 9" d., w/handles, apple
  green 38.00

Plate, 9" d., w/handles,
  canary...38.00

Plate, 9" d., w/handles, clear.........18.00

Relish, apple green, 5 x 9½" 25.00

Relish, blue, 5 x 9½" 25.00

Sauce dish, flat, amber.................22.00

Sauce dish, footed, clear 7.00

Spooner, amber 48.00

Spooner, apple green 65.00

Spooner, blue 50.00

Spooner, canary 55.00

Spooner, clear 28.00

Sugar bowl, cov., canary 60.00

Wine, amber 57.00

Wine, clear 46.00

DAISY & BUTTON

Banana boat, green 30.00

Berry set: master bowl & 12
  sauce dishes; canary, 13 pcs. ...225.00

Bowl, 7 x 9½", sapphire blue.........30.00

Bowl, 8" d., flat 15.00

Bowl, 8" w., tricornered, canary 38.00

Bowl, 8" w., tricornered, clear 45.00

Bowl, berry or fruit, 8½" d.............35.00

Bowl, 9" sq., amber.........30.00 to 35.00

Bowl, 9" sq., Amberina................183.00

*****Bowl,** 10" oval, blue 65.00

Bowl, 10 x 11" oval, 7¾" h.,
  flared, canary...............................95.00

Bowl, 11" d., amber......................38.00

Bowl, 12" l., 9" w., shell-shaped
  oval, blue 75.00

*****Bread tray,** amber 35.00

*****Bread tray,** canary 25.00

*****Butter chip,** round, amber 12.00

*****Butter chip,** round, blue 15.00

Butter chip, square, amber..........14.00

Butter chip, square, Amberina 75.00

Daisy & Button Canoe

Butter chip, square, blue **16.00**

Butter chip, square, canary **20.00**

Butter chip, square, clear **7.00**

Butter dish, cov., square,
canary......................................**80.00**

Butter dish, cov., square,
green **60.00**

Butter dish, cov., triangular,
amber **60.00**

*Butter dish, cov., model of
Victorian stove, apple **215.00**

Cake stand, blue......................**50.00**

Cake stand, clear, 9" sq., 6" h. **45.00**

Cake stand, clear.........................**30.00**

Canoe, canary, 4" l. **18.00**

Canoe, amber, 8" l.....................**115.00**

Canoe, blue, 8" l. (ILLUS.
bottom previous page)................**46.00**

Canoe, canary, 8" l. **100.00**

Canoe, clear, 10" l. **20.00**

Canoe, amber, 11" l.....................**39.00**

Canoe, blue, 11" l. **60.00**

Canoe, amber, 12" l. ....**60.00 to 65.00**

Canoe, clear, 12" l. **28.00**

Canoe, green, 13" l.......................**54.00**

Canoe, canary, 14" l. **85.00**

Canoe, clear, 14" l. **26.00**

Castor set, 3-bottle, amber, clear
& blue, in clear glass frame **120.00**

Castor set, 4-bottle, blue, in glass
frame **375.00**

Celery tray, flat, boat-shaped,
4½ x 14", clear............................**90.00**

Celery tray, flat, boat-shaped,
14" l., canary.............................**125.00**

Celery vase, square.....................**35.00**

Celery vase, triangular, amber......**65.00**

Cheese dish, cov., canary **165.00**

Cheese dish, cov., clear **62.00**

Comb case, hanging-type,
blue, 8½" l.................................**100.00**

Creamer, child's, amber **25.00**

*Creamer, amber..........................**27.00**

*Creamer, blue **40.00**

*Creamer, clear...............**10.00 to 15.00**

Creamer, pedestal base,
canary, 7" h. **30.00**

*Cruet w/original stopper,
blue...**95.00**

*Cruet w/original stopper,
clear..**45.00**

Dish, canary, shallow, 5" sq. **20.00**

*Dish, fan-shaped, amber,10" w......**8.00**

Dresser tray, amber, 8 x 11".........**53.00**

*Goblet, amber............................**36.00**

*Goblet, blue **25.00**

*Goblet, clear **24.00**

*Hat shape, amber,
2½" h..............................**25.00 to 30.00**

*Hat shape, blue,
2½" h..............................**40.00 to 50.00**

*Hat shape, canary, 2½" h. **38.00**

*Hat shape, clear, 2½" h. **18.00**

*Hat shape, amber, from tumbler
mold, 4" widest diameter **40.00**

*Hat shape, clear, from tumbler
mold, 4½" widest diameter **55.00**

*Hat shape, blue, from tumbler
mold, 4¾" widest diameter **45.00**

Hat shape, canary yellow, from
tumbler mold, 5" widest
diameter, 3¾" h. **48.00**

Hat shape, clear, 8 x 8", 6" h.........**60.00**

*Ice cream dish, cut corners,
6" sq. **9.00**

Ice cream set: 2 x 7 x 9½" ice
cream tray & two square sauce
plates; amber, 3 pcs. **85.00**

Ice cream set: 2 x 7 x 9½"
ice cream tray & six small
bowls; w/amber stain,
7 pcs. **150.00**

Ice tub, amber, 4¼ x 6¾" **53.00**

Inkwell w/original insert, cat
seated on cover........................**210.00**

Inkwell, canary **175.00**

*Match holder, cauldron
w/original bail handle, blue **25.00**

Match holder, wall-hanging
scuff, blue **85.00**

Match holder, wall-hanging scuff,
clear...**65.00**

Mustard, amber ....**15.00 to 20.00**

*Pickle castor, amber insert,
w/silver plate frame & tongs **198.00**

*Pickle castor, canary insert,
w/silver plate frame & tongs **185.00**

*Pickle castor, sapphire blue
insert, w/silver plate frame &
tongs...**238.00**

Pitcher, water, tankard, 9" h.,
amber **125.00**

Pitcher, water, bulbous, applied
handle, clear................................**95.00**

Plate, 7" sq., blue **18.00**

Plate, 9" d., canary **40.00**

*Plate, 10" d., scalloped rim,
amber **26.00**

*Plate, 10" d., scalloped rim,
blue...**35.00**

*Plate, 10" d., scalloped rim,
canary...**40.00**

Platter, 9 x 13" oval, open
handles, amber ....**30.00 to 35.00**

Platter, 9 x 13" oval, open
handles, canary **53.00**

Powder jar, cov., amber,
3¾" d., 2" h. **30.00**

Powder jar, cov., blue **38.00**

Relish, "Sitz bathtub," amber **125.00**

Relish, "Sitz bathtub," canary **80.00**

Relish, "Sitz bathtub,"
clear ....**90.00 to 100.00**

*Rose bowl, canary.......................**38.00**

*Rose bowl, clear..........................**17.00**

*Salt dip, canoe-shaped, amber,
2 x 4" **20.00**

*Salt dip, canoe-shaped, canary,
2 x 4" **12.00**

*Salt dip, canoe-shaped, clear,
2 x 4" **15.00**

*Salt dip, master size, canary,
3½" d. **23.00**

*Salt shaker w/original top,
corset-shaped, amber **25.00**

***Salt & pepper shakers
w/original tops,** canary, pr. **58.00**

*Sauce dish, amber,
4" to 5" sq. **13.00**

*Sauce dish, Amberina,
4" to 5" sq. **115.00**

*Sauce dish, blue, 4" to 5" sq. **16.00**

*Sauce dish, canary, 4" to
5" sq. **20.00**

Sauce dish, w/amber-stained
buttons..**20.00**

Sauce dish, tricornered,
canary...**16.00**

*Slipper, "1886 patent," amber......**46.00**

*Slipper, "1886 patent,"
blue...**47.00**

*Slipper, "1886 patent,"
canary...**50.00**

*Slipper, "1886 patent,"
clear..**40.00**

*Slipper, "1886 patent," canary **15.00**

*Slipper, apple green **35.00**

*Slipper, canary **15.00**

*Spooner, amber...........................**33.00**

Spooner, Amberina,
5" h. ....**110.00 to 125.00**

Spooner, amethyst.......................**30.00**

*Spooner, clear **32.00**

Toothpick holder, fan-shaped,
amber **35.00**

Toothpick holder, fan-shaped,
blue...**40.00**

Toothpick holder, square,
blue...**24.00**

Toothpick holder, three-footed,
Amberina **170.00**

* Toothpick holder, three-footed,
electric blue **55.00**

Toothpick holder, urn-shaped,
canary...**30.00**

Toothpick holder, urn-shaped,
clear..**23.00**

Tray, clover-shaped, amber **75.00**

Tray, canary, 10 x 12" **57.00**

Tray, ice cream, 9 x 14".................**40.00**

Tray, water, triangular,
canary ....**75.00 to 80.00**

Tumbler, water, amber.................**26.00**

Tumbler, water, blue **30.00**

Tumbler, water, canary...**25.00 to 30.00**

Tumbler, water, clear **19.00**

Tumbler, water, ruby-stained
buttons...**35.00**

Waste bowl, canary **30.00**

Whimsey, "canoe," wall
hanging-type, ruby-stained
buttons,11" l..............................**110.00**

*Whimsey, "dustpan,"
light blue **43.00**

*Whimsey, "sleigh," amber,
4½ x 7¾" **225.00**

Whimsey, "umbrella," original
metal handle, canary **425.00**

Whimsey, "wheel barrow,"
canary.......................................**125.00**

*Whimsey, "whisk broom" dish,
blue...**75.00**

*Whimsey, "whisk broom" dish,
canary..**33.00**

*Wine..**20.00**

DIAMOND QUILTED

Diamond Quilted Champagne

Bowl, 6" d., turquoise blue **11.00**

Bowl, 7" d., amber.....................**25.00**

Bowl, 7" d., canary **18.00**

Celery vase, amber.....................**38.00**

Celery vase, blue **50.00**

Celery vase, deep amethyst **68.00**

Champagne, amethyst.................**38.00**

Champagne, canary **26.00**

Champagne, turquoise blue
(ILLUS.) **52.00**

Claret, canary.............................**18.00**

Diamond Quilted Compote

Compote, open, 6" d., 6" h.,
amber (ILLUS.) ....**20.00 to 25.00**

Compote, open, 6" d., 6" h.,
clear..**23.00**

Compote, open, 6" d., 6" h.,
canary...**25.00**

Compote, open, 7" d., low stand,
amber **18.00**

Compote, open, 8" d., low stand,
amethyst.....................................**45.00**

Compote, open, 8" d., low stand,
turquoise blue.............................**30.00**

Compote, open, 9" d., low stand,
canary...**37.00**

Compote, open, 9" d., high stand,
amethyst......................................**35.00**

Cordial, amber **33.00**

*Goblet, amber..............................**48.00**

*Goblet, amethyst ....**30.00 to 35.00**

*Goblet, blue **37.00**

*Goblet, canary **33.00**

Relish, amber, 4½ x 7½"..............**14.00**

Relish, leaf-shaped, canary,
5½ x 9" **20.00**

*Salt dip, amber, master size,
rectangular **32.00**

*Salt dip, amethyst, master size,
rectangular **22.00**

Sauce dish, flat or footed, amber,
each..**12.00**

Sauce dish, flat or footed,
turquoise blue, each **11.00**

Sauce dish, flat or footed,
canary, each ....**10.00 to 15.00**

Spooner, amber **28.00**

Spooner, canary **37.00**

Sugar bowl, cov., amber...............**68.00**

Sugar bowl, cov., amethyst **85.00**

Sugar bowl, cov., canary **55.00**

Tray, water, cloverleaf-shaped,
amethyst, 10 x 12" ....**30.00 to 35.00**

Tray, water, cloverleaf-shaped,
amethyst, 10 x 12"......................**45.00**

Tray, water, cloverleaf-shaped,
canary 10 x 12"...........................**35.00**

*Tumbler, amber **30.00**

*Tumbler, canary **33.00**

Waste bowl, blue, 4½" d. **38.00**

*Wine, amber................................**21.00**

*Wine, amethyst **42.00**

*Wine, blue **36.00**

*Wine, canary **38.00**

*Wine, clear **17.00**

EYEWINKER
Banana boat, flat, 8½" **90.00**

Banana stand **115.00**

Bowl, cov., 9" d. **85.00**

Bowl, 6½" d. **25.00**

Bowl, master berry or fruit,
9" d., 4½" h. **70.00**

*Butter dish, cov. ....**80.00 to 85.00**

Cake stand, 8" d. ....**65.00 to 70.00**

Cake stand, 9½" d. **85.00**

Celery vase, 6½" h.......................**55.00**

*Compote, cov., 6" d., high
stand...**50.00**

Compote, open, 4" d., 5" h.,
scalloped rim ....**30.00 to 35.00**

Compote, open, 5½" d., high
stand..**60.00**

* Compote, open, 7½" d., high
stand, flared rim ....**75.00 to 80.00**

Compote, open, 8½" d., high
stand..**75.00**

Compote, open, 9½" d., high
stand ....**125.00 to 150.00**

Compote, open, 10" d., high
stand ....**140.00 to 160.00**

Creamer **45.00**

*Goblet **30.00**

Pitcher, milk **70.00**

*Pitcher, water **80.00**

Plate, 7" sq., 1½" h., turned-up
sides **24.00**

Eyewinker Salt Shaker

Salt shaker w/original top
(ILLUS.) **35.00**

*Sauce dish, round **34.00**

Spooner........................**35.00 to 40.00**

*Sugar bowl, cov. **52.00**

Syrup pitcher w/silver plate
top...**135.00**

*Tumbler **28.00**

FINECUT & BLOCK

Finecut & Block Celery Tray

Bowl, round, handled, pink
blocks **50.00**

Butter dish, cov., two-handled......**55.00**

Celery tray, clear w/amber
blocks, 11" l. (ILLUS.).................**85.00**

Champagne, amber **70.00**

Cordial **35.00**

Cordial, clear w/blue blocks **105.00**

***Creamer,** clear **30.00**

Creamer, clear w/amber blocks **63.00**

Creamer, clear w/pink blocks **75.00**

Egg cup, single, clear w/amber
blocks **453.00**

Egg cup, single, clear w/pink
blocks **55.00**

Egg cup, double **29.00**

***Goblet,** amber..............................**53.00**

***Goblet,** clear **35.00**

Goblet, clear w/blue blocks **70.00**

Goblet, clear w/pink blocks **62.00**

Goblet, clear w/yellow blocks........**52.00**

Pitcher, water, clear w/amber
blocks **85.00**

Pitcher, water, clear w/blue
blocks **125.00**

Pitcher, water, clear w/pink
blocks **110.00**

Punch cup, clear w/yellow
blocks **55.00**

Salt dip......................................**12.00**

Sauce dish, amber......................**16.00**

Sauce dish, clear w/amber
blocks **13.00**

Sauce dish, clear w/blue
blocks **23.00**

Sauce dish, clear w/yellow
blocks **18.00**

Spooner, clear **40.00**

Spooner, clear w/amber blocks **45.00**

Sugar bowl, cov., clear w/yellow
blocks........................**100.00 to 125.00**

Waste bowl, amber......................**55.00**

***Wine,** amber................................**58.00**

***Wine,** blue **58.00**

***Wine,** clear **24.00**

Wine, clear w/amber blocks **48.00**

Wine, clear w/ blue blocks............**45.00**

Wine, clear w/pink blocks **44.00**

Wine, clear w/yellow blocks..........**35.00**

FROSTED LION (Rampant Lion)

Bread tray, oval, lion handles,
frosted or non-frosted,
10" l. **125.00**

***Bread plate,** rope edge, closed
handles, 10½" d......................**85.00**

Bread plate, rope edge, closed
handles, blue,
10½" d. ....**150.00 to 200.00**

Bread plate, rope edge, closed
handles, canary,
10½" d. ....**150.00 to 200.00**

Bread plate, rope edge, closed
handles, clear, 10½" d................**85.00**

***Butter dish,** cov., collared base,
frosted lion's head finial **110.00**

Butter dish, cov., collared base,
rampant lion finial......**165.00 to 170.00**

Butter dish, cov., crouched lion
finial..........................**125.00 to 140.00**

Butter dish, cov.,
child's ....**125.00 to 150.00**

***Celery vase,** each (ILLUS. top
next page) **110.00**

Cheese dish, cov., rampant lion
finial **750.00**

**Cologne bottle
w/stopper** ....**1,000.00 to 1,200.00**

Compote, cov., 3⅞ x 6⅞" oval,
collared base, crouched
lion finial **125.00**

Frosted Lion Celery Vases

Frosted Lion Goblet

Compote, cov., 4⅝ x 7⁷⁄₁₆" oval, collared base, crouched lion finial **150.00**

Compote, cov., 5" d., 8½" h. **175.00**

Compote, cov., 5⅕ x 8⅞" oval, collared base, crouched lion finial **140.00**

Compote, cov., 6" d., high stem, rampant lion finial ......**200.00 to 250.00**

Compote, cov., 6" d., high stem, lion head finial **125.00**

Compote, cov., 6" d., high stem, crouched lion finial ....**150.00 to 175.00**

*Compote, cov., 6¾" oval, 7" h., collared base, rampant lion finial...........................**150.00 to 175.00**

Compote, cov., 7" d., 8" h. to top of base, high stem, lion head finial **150.00**

Compote, cov., 5½ x 8¾" oval, 8¼" h., rampant lion finial...........................**170.00 to 180.00**

Compote, open, 7" d., 6¼" h.......**125.00**

Compote, open, 7" oval, 7½" h. ..**140.00**

Compote, open, 8" d. **175.00**

Creamer ....**85.00 to 95.00**

*Egg cup **125.00**

*Goblet (ILLUS. next column) **110.00**

Marmalade jar, cov., rampant lion finial **135.00**

Marmalade jar, cov., lion's head finial **155.00**

Paperweight, embossed "Gillinder & Sons, Centennial" ...**225.00**

Paperweight, round, lion's head ....**110.00 to 125.00**

*Pitcher, water ....**550.00 to 750.00**

Powder jar, cov., (very rare) ....**1,500.00 to 1,750.00**

Salt dip, master size, collared base, rectangular......................**350.00**

*Sauce dish, 4" & 6" d. ...**20.00 to 25.00**

*Spooner ....**55.00 to 65.00**

Spooner, child's, clear & frosted ....**110.00 to 125.00**

*Sugar bowl, cov., collared base, frosted lion's head finial **100.00**

Sugar bowl, cov., hotel-typed (plain base)...................................**65.00**

Sugar bowl, cov., crouched lion finial..........................**100.00 to 125.00**

Table set, cov. sugar bowl, creamer & spooner, 3 pcs. **225.00**

HAND (Pennsylvania, Early)
Bread plate, 8 x 10½" oval............**38.00**

Butter dish, cov. **125.00**

Cake stand ....**45.00 to 50.00**

Cake stand, 12¼" d., engraved ..**175.00**

Celery vase ....35.00 to 40.00
Claret..85.00
Compote, cov., 7" d., high stand...95.00
Compote, open, 7¾" d., 6¾" h......40.00
Cordial 85.00
Creamer.......................30.00 to 40.00

Hand Goblet

Goblet (ILLUS.) 39.00
Marmalade jar, cov........50.00 to 55.00
Mug 95.00
Pickle castor, w/silver plate
  frame & tongs 110.00
Pitcher, water ....85.00 to 95.00
Relish 23.00
Sauce dish, 4½" d.........................13.00
Spooner 45.00
Sugar bowl, cov. ....55.00 to 60.00
Tumbler, water..............................97.00
Wine..............................45.00 to 55.00

HUMMINGBIRD (Flying Robin or Bird & Fern)

Butter dish, cov., blue 110.00
Celery vase....................................33.00
Creamer, amber............75.00 to 100.00
Creamer, blue 85.00

Creamer, clear ....40.00 to 45.00
Goblet, amber.................60.00 to 65.00
Goblet, blue....................................69.00
Goblet, clear ....55.00 to 60.00
Pitcher, water, amber..................150.00
Pitcher, water, blue 145.00
Spooner 30.00
Sugar bowl, cov., blue 110.00
Tray, water 50.00
Tumbler, amber 60.00
Tumbler, blue.................................75.00
Tumbler, clear ....40.00 to 50.00
Waste bowl 120.00
Wine...............................75.00 to 85.00

JACOB'S LADDER (Maltese)

Bowl, 7½ x 10¾" oval....................25.00
Bowl, 9" d., flat 40.00
Butter dish, cov., Maltese Cross
  finial 55.00
Cake stand, 8" to 12" d. 52.00
Celery vase ....40.00 to 45.00
Compote, cov., 8¼" d., high
  stand...128.00
Compote, open, 6" d., high
  stand..24.00
Compote, open, 7" d., high
  stand..35.00
Compote, open, 8" d., high
  stand..42.00
Compote, open, 9" d., low
  stand..52.00
Compote, open, 10" d.,
  5" h....................................30.00 to 35.00
Compote, open, 10" d., high
  stand..55.00
Compote, open, 13½" d., high
  stand..75.00
Creamer 32.00
Cruet w/original stopper,
  footed 85.00
Dish, 8" oval 18.00
Goblet ....55.00 to 60.00
Honey dish, open 9.00

Marmalade jar, cov.....125.00 to 135.00

Pickle dish, Maltese Cross
handle..**18.00**

Pitcher, water, applied handle **185.00**

Plate, 6" d., amber........................**105.00**

Plate, 6" d., clear **35.00**

Plate, 6" d., purple **110.00**

Relish, Maltese Cross handles,
5½ x 9½" oval.............................**16.00**

Salt dip, master size,
footed ....35.00 to 40.00

Sauce dish, flat or footed,
blue...**20.00**

Sauce dish, flat or footed,
canary..**72.00**

Sauce dish, flat or footed, clear **6.00**

Spooner..........................25.00 to 30.00

Sugar bowl, cov. **65.00**

**Syrup jug w/metal
top** ....100.00 to 125.00

Wine **25.00**

KING'S CROWN (Also see Ruby Thumbprint)

King's Crown Punch Cup

Banana stand **110.00**

Bowl, berry or fruit, 8¼" d.,
flared rim **27.00**

Bowl, 9¼" oval, scalloped rim,
round base **68.00**

Bowl, berry or fruit, 10½" d.,
4" h. **22.00**

Butter dish, cov. **65.00**

Cake stand, 9" d. **85.00**

Castor bottle, w/original top **17.00**

Castor set, salt & pepper
shakers, oil bottle w/stopper &
cov. mustard jar in original
frame, 4 pcs.................................**325.00**

Celery vase, engraved.................**60.00**

Celery vase, plain **62.00**

*Compote, cov., 5" d., 5½" h.,
engraved **33.00**

Compote, cov., 7" d., 7" h. **95.00**

Compote, cov., 11" d. **145.00**

Compote, open, jelly. **38.00**

Compote, open, 7½" d., high
stand..**45.00**

Compote, open, 8½" d., high
stand..**85.00**

Compote, open, 9" d., low stand...**46.00**

*Cordial **50.00**

Creamer **48.00**

*Creamer, individual size, clear.....**19.00**

Creamer, individual size, w/green
thumbprints..................................**35.00**

Goblet, clear...................................**25.00**

Goblet, clear w/amber
thumbprints..................................**22.00**

Goblet, clear w/engraved moose,
doe & dog **95.00**

Goblet, w/green thumbprints,
souvenir.......................................**18.00**

Lamp, kerosene-type, low hand-
type w/finger hold......170.00 to 200.00

*Lamp, kerosene-type, stem
base, 10" h. **180.00**

Mustard jar, cov. ....40.00 to 50.00

Pitcher, tankard, 8½" h. **100.00**

Pitcher, tankard, 11" h. **110.00**

Pitcher, tankard, 13" h.,
engraved...................135.00 to 145.00

Pitcher, tankard, 13" h., plain......**195.00**

Pitcher, bulbous. **125.00**

*Plate, 8" sq................................**57.00**

Punch bowl, footed. ...225.00 to 250.00

Punch cup (ILLUS.) **23.00**

Salt dip, individual size **30.00**

Salt & pepper shakers
  w/original tops, pr. ......65.00 to 70.00

Sauce dish, boat-shaped.............**21.00**

*Sauce dish, round **17.00**

Spooner **39.00**

Toothpick holder,
  clear ....**20.00 to 25.00**

Toothpick holder, rose stain,
  souvenir ....**30.00 to 35.00**

Tray, square **29.00**

*Tumbler **22.00**

Wine, clear **21.00**

Wine, cobalt blue ....**100.00 to 150.00**

Wine, cobalt blue, souvenir **165.00**

Wine, w/amethyst thumbprints **18.00**

MASCOTTE

Bowl, cov., 7" d. **90.00**

Butter dish, cov., engraved **85.00**

Butter pat......................................**11.00**

Cake basket w/handle **76.00**

Cake stand, 10" d. **48.00**

Celery vase..................................**35.00**

Compote, cov., 5" d. **44.00**

Compote, cov., 8" d.,
  12" h..............................**85.00 to 90.00**

Compote, open, jelly **33.00**

Mascotte Creamer

Creamer (ILLUS.) **36.00**

Goblet, engraved ....**30.00 to 40.00**

Goblet, plain.................................**30.00**

Jar, cov., globe-type, embossed
  patent date, milk white..............**265.00**

Marmalade jar, cov., cranberry-
  stained, engraved date,
  4½" d., 8" h. **42.00**

Pitcher, water ....**120.00 to 130.00**

Salt shaker w/original
  top ....**25.00 to 30.00**

Sauce dish, flat or footed,
  engraved, each...........................**12.00**

Spooner, canary **135.00**

Spooner, clear, engraved **38.00**

Spooner, clear, plain....................**30.00**

Table set, 4 pcs..........................**165.00**

Tray, water, engraved **65.00**

Tray, water, plain.........................**59.00**

Tumbler, engraved......................**36.00**

Tumbler, plain **24.00**

Wine, engraved **36.00**

Wine, plain..................................**26.00**

OAKEN BUCKET (Wooden Pail)

Butter dish, cov., amber **70.00**

Butter dish, cov., canary **110.00**

Creamer, amber.............**50.00 to 55.00**

Creamer, amethyst ....**55.00 to 75.00**

Creamer, blue **65.00**

Creamer, canary ....**65.00 to 75.00**

Creamer, clear ....**25.00 to 30.00**

Oaken Bucket Match Holder

Match holder w/original wire
  handle, 2⅝" d., 2⅝" h., amber
  (ILLUS.) **28.00**

Pitcher, water, amber....................**85.00**

Pitcher, water,
   amethyst ....**185.00 to 195.00**

Pitcher, water, canary **120.00**

Pitcher, water, clear **80.00**

Spooner, amber............**35.00 to 40.00**

Spooner, blue ....**45.00 to 55.00**

Spooner, clear **35.00**

Sugar bowl, cov., canary **105.00**

Sugar bowl, cov. **45.00**

Sugar bowl, open, amethyst.........**35.00**

Toothpick holder, amber **30.00**

Toothpick holder, clear...............**17.00**

PALMETTE

Butter dish, cov. ....**60.00 to 65.00**

Celery vase...................................**53.00**

Compote, open, 8" d., high
   stand ....**80.00 to 85.00**

Compote, open, 8" d., low
   stand..**24.00**

Creamer, applied
   handle ....**55.00 to 60.00**

Cruet **95.00**

Cup plate, 3⅜" d. **45.00**

Egg cup ....**30.00 to 35.00**

Palmette Goblet

Goblet (ILLUS.)..............**35.00 to 40.00**

Lamp, kerosene-type, table
   model w/stem, clear **79.00**

Pitcher, water, applied
   handle ....**100.00 to 125.00**

Relish **18.00**

Salt dip, master size, footed **25.00**

Sauce dish......................................**8.00**

Spooner **35.00**

Tumbler, water, flat **75.00**

Wine..............................**75.00 to 100.00**

PANELED THISTLE

Paneled Thistle Wine

Bowl, 7" oval, 1¾" h. **35.00**

*Bowl, 8" d.....................................**19.00**

*Bowl, 8" d., w/bee **35.00**

*Butter dish, cov., w/bee **50.00**

Cake stand....................................**38.00**

Celery vase...................................**53.00**

Compote, open, 5" d., low stand...**19.00**

*Compote, open, 6" d., high
   stand...**45.00**

*Creamer **45.00**

*Creamer, w/bee **60.00**

Cruet w/stopper ....**40.00 to 50.00**

*Goblet **37.00**

*Honey dish, cov., square **60.00**

Honey dish, open **10.00**

Pitcher, milk...................**50.00 to 55.00**

*Plate, 7" sq. **28.00**

*Plate, 7" sq., w/bee **34.00**

Plate, 9½" d. **26.00**

Rose bowl, 5" d., 2¾" h. 40.00

Salt dip, individual size 16.00

*Salt & pepper shakers
w/original tops, pr. 65.00

*Sauce dish, flat or footed,
each..14.00

*Spooner, handled 45.00

*Sugar bowl, cov. 45.00

Toothpick holder.........................30.00

*Tumbler, clear 30.00

Vase, 13½" h., pulled top rim.........45.00

*Wine (ILLUS.) 24.00

*Wine, w/bee 30.00

RIBBON CANDY (Bryce or Double Loop)

Ribbon Candy Creamer

Butter dish, cov., flat ......35.00 to 40.00

Butter dish, cov.,
footed ....50.00 to 55.00

Cake stand, child's, 6½" d.,
3" h 25.00

Cake stand, 8" to 10½" d. 47.00

Celery vase.....................................5.00

Creamer (ILLUS.).........................35.00

Cruet w/faceted stopper............225.00

Doughnut stand 32.00

Goblet ....50.00 to 75.00

Pitcher, milk...................30.00 to 35.00

Plate, 8½" d. 26.00

Relish, 8½" l. 13.00

Spooner ....25.00 to 30.00

Sugar bowl, cov. 448.00

Wine 95.00

ROSE IN SNOW

Bitters bottle w/original
stopper 100.00

Bowl, 8½ x 11½" oval...................48.00

Butter dish, cov., round 60.00

Butter dish, cov., square 50.00

Cake plate, handled, amber,
10" d. 50.00

Cake plate, handled, blue, 10" d. ...65.00

Cake plate, handled, clear,
10" d. 23.00

Cake stand, 9" d. ....100.00 to 125.00

Cologne bottle w/original
stopper 95.00

Compote, cov., 6" d., 8" h. 85.00

Compote, cov., 7" d., 8" h. 95.00

Compote, cov., 7" d., low
stand...125.00

Compote, cov., 8" d., 10" h.,
canary...155.00

Compote, open, 5" d., blue 110.00

Compote, open, 6" d., canary 42.00

Compote, open, 6" d., low stand...50.00

Compote, open, 8" sq., low
stand..110.00

Compote, open, 8" d., high
stand..70.00

Creamer, round..............40.00 to 45.00

Creamer, square, clear 32.00

Dish, 8½ x 11" oval, 1½" h. 130.00

*Goblet, amber.............................45.00

*Goblet, blue..................70.00 to 75.00

*Goblet, clear.................40.00 to 45.00

*Goblet, canary ....35.00 to 45.00

Marmalade jar, cov., 5¾" d..........55.00

Mug, blue, large........................110.00

Mug, clear, 3½" h. 40.00

*Mug, applied handle, "In Fond
Remembrance," clear.................50.00

Pitcher, water, applied handle,
  canary....................................**16.00**

Pitcher, water, applied handle,
  clear ....**125.00 to 135.00**

Plate, 5" d. **26.00**

Plate, 6" d. **30.00**

Plate, 9" d., blue **80.00**

*Plate, 9" d., clear ....**25.00 to 30.00**

*Relish, 5½ x 8" oval, clear **23.00**

Relish, 6¼ x 9¼" **18.00**

Sauce dish, flat or footed..............**10.00**

Spooner, square **28.00**

*Sugar bowl, cov., square **47.00**

Tumbler...**41.00**

SHELL & TASSEL

Shell & Tassel Compote

Bowl, 7½" l., shell-shaped, three
  applied shell-shaped feet **55.00**

Bowl, 9" oval, clear.......................**50.00**

Bowl, 10" oval, amber **90.00**

Bowl, 10" oval, clear.....................**59.00**

Bowl, 6½ x 11½" oval, amber **90.00**

Bowl, 6½ x 11½" oval, blue.........**125.00**

Bowl, 6½ x 11½" oval, clear..........**50.00**

Bowl, 8" d., cov., collared base,
  canary...**120.00**

Bread tray, 9 x 13" **55.00**

Bride's basket, 5 x 10" oval
  amber bowl in silver plate
  frame.......................**250.00 to 275.00**

Bride's basket, 8" oval blue bowl
  in silver plate frame...**320.00 to 350.00**

Cake stand, shell corners,
  9" sq. **94.00**

Cake stand, shell corners,
  10" sq. ....**100.00 to 125.00**

Celery vase, round, handled........**90.00**

Compote, cov., 4¼" sq., 8" h. **45.00**

Compote, cov., 5¼" sq.................**60.00**

Compote, open, jelly **85.00**

Compote, open, 6½" sq.,
  6½" h. **50.00**

Compote, open, 7½" sq., 7½" h. **95.00**

Compote, open, 8" sq., 7½" h. **56.00**

Compote, open, 8½" sq., 8" h.
  (ILLUS.).........................**50.00 to 55.00**

Compote, open. 9½" d., 9" h.........**90.00**

Compote, open, 10" sq., 8" h. **70.00**

Creamer, round...............**35.00 to 45.00**

Creamer, square.............**55.00 to 60.00**

Dish, 7 x 10" rectangle **35.00**

Doughnut stand, 8" sq., signed..**225.00**

*Goblet, round, knob
  stem ....**45.00 to 55.00**

Mug, miniature, blue....................**100.00**

Oyster plate, 9½" d.....................**250.00**

Pickle jar, cov. ....**150.00 to 175.00**

Pitcher, water, round....................**150.00**

Pitcher, water, square.................**110.00**

Plate, shell-shaped w/three shell-
  shaped feet, large........................**70.00**

Platter, 8 x 11" oblong..................**54.00**

Platter, 9 x 13" oval **51.00**

Relish, amber, 5 x 8"....................**95.00**

Relish, blue, 5 x 8"......**100.00 to 110.00**

Relish, canary, 5 x 8" **125.00**

Salt dip, shell-shaped **18.00**

Salt & pepper shakers
  w/original tops, pr. **260.00**

Sauce dish, flat or footed,
  4" to 5" d. **15.00**

Sauce dish, footed, w/shell
  handle..**15.00**

Spooner, round..............**40.00 to 45.00**

Spooner, square **52.00**

Sugar bowl, cov., round, dog
finial **110.00**

Tray, ice cream.........................**125.00**

Tumbler, clear.............................**40.00**

Vase ....**155.00 to 165.00**

SNAIL (Compact)

Snail Goblet

Banana stand, 10" d.,
7" h. ....**160.00 to 170.00**

Bowl, 7" d., low.............................**35.00**

Bowl, berry, 8" d., 4" h..................**34.00**

Bowl, 5¼ x 8", oval.......................**35.00**

Bowl, cov., vegetable, 5½ x 8"....**125.00**

Bowl, 9" d., 2" h. ....**45.00 to 50.00**

Butter dish, cov. **95.00**

Butter dish, ruby-
stained ....**135.00 to 145.00**

Cake stand, 10" d. **125.00**

Celery vase ....**30.00 to 40.00**

Cheese dish, cov. **125.00**

Compote, cov., 7" d., 8" h.,
engraved **160.00**

Compote, cov., 7" d., 11½" h. **145.00**

Compote, open, 8" d., 6" h............**85.00**

Cracker jar, cov., 8" d., 9" h. **295.00**

Creamer, clear) **58.00**

Creamer, ruby-stained **70.00**

Cruet w/original stopper **145.00**

Goblet (ILLUS.)............**95.00 to 120.00**

Pitcher, milk, bulbous, applied
handle, large ....**195.00 to 215.00**

Pitcher, water,
tankard ....**125.00 to 130.00**

Pitcher, wine, tankard **295.00**

Punch cup **33.00**

Relish, 9" oval **32.00**

Rose bowl, miniature, 3" h...........**36.00**

Rose bowl, 4½" h.........................**43.00**

Rose bowl, double, miniature **35.00**

Rose bowl, medium **55.00**

Rose bowl, large...........................**71.00**

Salt dip, individual size **25.00**

Salt dip, master size, 3" d. **40.00**

Salt shaker w/original top,
clear...**40.00**

Salt shaker w/original top,
ruby-stained.............................**65.00**

Sauce dish **18.00**

Spooner, clear **40.00**

Spooner, ruby-stained **85.00**

Sugar bowl, cov., individual size ..**75.00**

Sugar bowl, cov., plain **69.00**

Sugar bowl, cov., ruby-
stained ....**135.00 to 145.00**

Sugar shaker w/original top......**115.00**

Syrup jug w/original brass
top ....**135.00 to 150.00**

Tumbler.......................................**45.00**

Vase, 12½" h., scalloped rim **80.00**

THOUSAND EYE

Bowl, 8" d., 4½" h., footed,
amber **35.00**

Bread tray, amber.......................**32.00**

Bread tray, apple green **52.00**

Bread tray, clear **28.00**

Butter dish, cov., amber **115.00**

Butter dish, cov., blue **135.00**

Butter dish, cov., clear ...**75.00 to 85.00**

Cake stand, blue, 8½" to 10" d. ..**105.00**

Celery vase, three-knob stem,
clear (ILLUS. top next page) **40.00**

Thousand Eye Celery Vase

Celery vase, three-knob stem, clear to opalescent w/purple tint..............**110.00 to 125.00**

Celery vase, plain stem, amber **45.00**

Cologne bottle w/matching stopper **26.00**

Compote, cov., 12" h. **115.00**

***Compote**, open, 6" d., low stand, blue..**38.00**

Compote, open, 7½" d., 5" h.........**35.00**

Compote, open, 8" d., 3¾" h., apple green **40.00**

Compote, open, 8" d., 6" h., three-knob stem, amber **39.00**

Compote, open, 8" d., 6" h., three-knob stem, apple green **65.00**

Compote, open, 8" d., 6" h., three-knob stem, blue..................**65.00**

Compote, open, 8" d., high stand, three-knob stem, canary.............**58.00**

Compote, open, 8" sq., low stand, apple green......................**65.00**

Compote, open, 9½" d., low stand, amber **31.00**

Creamer, amber **42.00**

***Creamer**, clear **35.00**

Cruet w/original three-knob stopper, amber **105.00**

Cruet w/original three-knob stopper, apple green ....**90.00 to 95.00**

Cruet w/original three-knob stopper, blue ....**125.00 to 150.00**

Cruet w/original three-knob stopper, canary ....**110.00 to 115.00**

Egg cup, amber **65.00**

Egg cup, blue................................**65.00**

Egg cup, clear...............................**25.00**

***Goblet**, amber **28.00**

***Goblet**, apple green **40.00**

***Goblet**, blue **42.00**

***Goblet**, canary **34.00**

***Goblet**, clear **25.00**

Hat shape, blue, small **30.00**

Lamp, kerosene-type, pedestal base, amber, 14" h. to collar......**225.00**

Lamp, kerosene-type, pedestal base, blue font, amber base, 12" h. **195.00**

Lamp, kerosene-type, pedestal base. blue, 12" h.......................**155.00**

Lamp, kerosene-type, flat base, ring handle, amber **325.00**

Lamp, kerosene-type, flat base, ring handle, clear.......................**110.00**

***Mug**, amber, 3½" h.......................**25.00**

***Mug**, blue, 3½" h. **27.00**

***Mug**, canary, 3½" h. **32.00**

***Mug**, clear, 3½" h. **28.00**

***Mug**, miniature, amber **30.00**

Pickle dish, apple green **25.00**

Pitcher, water, three-knob stem, amber.......................**150.00 to 155.00**

Pitcher, water, three-knob stem, blue..**95.00**

***Pitcher**, water, clear.....................**65.00**

Plate, 6" d., amber........................**21.00**

Plate, 6" d., apple green **17.00**

Plate, 6" d., blue **18.00**

***Plate**, 6" d., clear.........................**15.00**

Plate, 8" d., amber ....**30.00 to 35.00**

Plate, 8" d., canary **32.00**

Plate, 8" d., clear **28.00**

Plate, 10" sq., w/folded corners.....**27.00**

Salt dip, cart shape,
amber, 3½" **90.00**

**Salt & pepper shakers
w/original tops,** blue, pr. **75.00**

**Salt & pepper shakers
w/original tops,** clear, pr. **65.00**

Sauce dish, flat or footed,
amber **11.00**

Sauce dish, flat or footed,
blue..**16.00**

* Sauce dish, flat or footed,
clear..**10.00**

Spooner, three-knob stem,
amber **52.00**

Spooner, three-knob stem,
canary..**42.00**

Spooner, three-knob stem, clear ..**30.00**

Sugar bowl, cov., three-knob
stem, amber **55.00**

*Sugar bowl, open, three-knob
stem..**25.00**

**Syrup pitcher w/original pewter
top,** footed, apple
green.......................**185.00 to 190.00**

*Toothpick holder, amber **38.00**

*Toothpick holder, blue **40.00**

*Toothpick holder, canary **37.00**

*Toothpick holder,
clear ....**20.00 to 25.00**

Tray, water, amber, 12½" d. **65.00**

Tray, water, blue,
12½" d. ....**95.00 to 100.00**

Tray, water, clear,
12½" d. ....**40.00 to 45.00**

Tray, apple green, 14" oval **60.00**

Tray, blue, 14" oval.......................**70.00**

*Tumbler, apple green **39.00**

*Tumbler, blue **38.00**

Waste bowl, ...**45.00**

*Wine, amber................................**20.00**

*Wine, apple green........................**43.00**

*Wine, blue...................................**43.00**

*Wine, canary **38.00**

*Wine, clear **20.00**

VALENCIA WAFFLE (Block & Star)

Butter dish, cov., apple green **55.00**

Celery vase, clear **34.00**

Compote, cov., 7" sq., low
stand, blue ....**50.00 to 75.00**

Compote, cov., 7" sq., low stand,
clear..**40.00**

Compote, cov., 8" sq., low stand,
clear..**125.00**

Compote, open, 6" sq., low
stand, blue.................................**30.00**

Compote, open, 7" sq., low
stand, amber **33.00**

Compote, open, 7" sq., light
blue..**55.00**

Compote, open, 8" d., 8" h.,
amber **60.00**

Compote, open, 9" d., high
stand...**65.00**

Goblet, amber **40.00**

Goblet, apple green **44.00**

Goblet, blue ....**40.00 to 45.00**

Goblet, clear ....**20.00 to 25.00**

Pitcher, water, 7½" h.,
amber...........................**60.00 to 65.00**

Pitcher, water, blue **72.00**

Relish, amber, 5⅜ x 9".................**23.00**

Salt dip, master size, blue............**45.00**

Salt shaker w/original top, apple
green **30.00**

Salt shaker w/original top,
blue..**45.00**

Sauce dish, footed, blue **13.00**

Spooner, amber **38.00**

Spooner, canary **35.00**

Tray, water **25.00**

WASHINGTON CENTENNIAL

Bowl, 7" oval **18.00**

Bowl, 8½" oval **21.00**

Bread platter, Carpenter's
Hall center................**100.00 to 115.00**

Bread platter, George
　Washington center,
　frosted ....**100.00 to 115.00**

Bread platter, Independence Hall
　center **85.00**

Bread platter, Independence Hall
　center, frosted **95.00**

Cake stand,
　8½ to 11½" d. ....**55.00 to 75.00**

Celery vase **55.00**

Champagne **68.00**

Egg cup...**39.00**

Goblet ....**40.00 to 45.00**

Pitcher, milk **350.00**

Pitcher, water..............................**110.00**

Relish, bear paw handles,
　dated 1876 ....**30.00 to 35.00**

Salt dip, master size **60.00**

Sauce dish, flat or footed, each **10.00**

Spooner **35.00**

Sugar bowl, cov. **73.00**

Tumbler...**58.00**

WILDFLOWER

Basket, cake, oblong w/metal
　handle......................................**130.00**

Bowl, 5¾" sq., canary **33.00**

Bowl, 5¾" sq., clear **20.00**

Bowl, 6½" sq., amber **24.00**

Bowl, 6½" sq., blue **35.00**

Bowl, 7" sq., clear **18.00**

Bowl, 8" sq., 5" h., footed,
　amber **23.00**

Bowl, 8" sq., 5" h., footed, apple
　green **33.00**

Butter dish, cov., flat, blue............**50.00**

Butter dish, cov., collared base,
　canary ....**70.00 to 80.00**

Cake stand, 9½" to 11" **46.00**

Cake stand, blue, w/bail handle..**225.00**

Celery vase, ambe.......................**50.00**

Celery vase, apple green..............**65.00**

Celery vase, blue **75.00**

Celery vase, canary **80.00**

Celery vase, clear **32.00**

Compote, cov., 6" d. **49.00**

Compote, cov., 7" d., canary........**80.00**

Compote, cov., 8" d., high stand
　blue...**125.00**

Compote, cov., 8" d.,
　clear ....**75.00 to 100.00**

Compote, open, 10½" d., 7½" h.,
　blue...**125.00**

*Creamer, amber..........................**30.00**

*Creamer, blue **45.00**

Wildflower Creamer

*Creamer, clear
　(ILLUS.).........................**35.00 to 45.00**

*Goblet, amber.............................**36.00**

*Goblet, apple green.......**30.00 to 40.00**

*Goblet, blue **37.00**

*Goblet, canary **40.00**

*Goblet, clear (ILLUS.) **26.00**

Pitcher, water, amber....................**60.00**

Pitcher, water, canary **76.00**

Pitcher, water, clear........**40.00 to 50.00**

Plate, 10" sq., blue **45.00**

Plate, 10" sq., canary **27.00**

Plate, 10" sq., clear **21.00**

Platter, 8 x 11", apple green.........**48.00**

Platter, 8 x 11", blue.....................**45.00**

Platter, 8 x 11", canary.................**48.00**

Relish, amber................................**17.00**

Relish, apple green **22.00**

Relish, canary **28.00**

*Salt dip, turtle-shaped, amber **45.00**

*Salt shaker w/original top,
amber **35.00**

Salt shaker w/original top, apple
green.............................**45.00 to 55.00**

Salt shaker w/original top, blue ..**55.00**

Salt & pepper shakers
w/original tops, canary, pr. **130.00**

*Sauce dish, flat or footed,
apple green **23.00**

*Sauce dish, flat or footed, blue....**15.00**

*Sauce dish, flat or footed,
canary...**15.00**

*Sauce dish, flat or footed, clear...**12.00**

Spooner, amber **30.00**

Spooner, blue **35.00**

Spooner, canary **40.00**

Spooner, clear **22.00**

*Sugar bowl, cov., blue.................**50.00**

Syrup pitcher w/original top,
blue...**350.00**

Syrup pitcher w/original top,
canary ....**265.00 to 275.00**

Tray, water, amber, 11 x 13" **45.00**

Tray, water, blue,
11 x 13" ....**75.00 to 100.00**

Tray, water, amber, 11 x 13" **45.00**

Tray, water, blue,
11 x 13" ....**75.00 to 100.00**

Tumbler, amber ....**30.00 to 35.00**

Tumbler, apple green...................**40.00**

Tumbler, blue...............................**45.00**

Tumbler, canary **35.00**

Waste bowl, amber......................**48.00**

Waste bowl, clear **28.00**

*Wine...**50.00**

PEACH BLOW

Several types of glass lumped together by collectors as Peach Blow were produced by half a dozen glasshouses. Hobbs, Brockunier & Co., Wheeling, West Virginia, made Peach Blow as a plated ware that shaded from red at the top to yellow at the bottom and is referred to as Wheeling Peach Blow. Mt. Washington Glass Works produced an homogeneous Peach Blow shading from a rose color at the top to pale blue in the lower portion. The New England Glass Works' Peach Blow, called Wild Rose, shaded from rose at the top to white. Gunderson-Pairpoint Co. also reproduced some of the Mt. Washington Peach Blow in the early 1950s and some glass of a somewhat similar type was made by Steuben Glass Works, Thomas Webb & Sons and Stevens & Williams of England. New England Peach Blow is one-layered glass and the English is two-layered.

Another single layered shaded art glass was produced early in this century by the New Martinsville Glass Mfg. Co. Originally called "Muranese," collectors today refer to it as "New Martinsville Peach Blow."

NEW ENGLAND

Peach Blow Tumbler

Creamer, ribbed w/applied white
handle, 3½" d.,
2¾" h. ....**$250.00 to 300.00**

Cuspidor, lady's, bulbous base
narrowing in the middle then
flaring to a wavy rim **750.00**

Pitcher, 4½" h., squatty bulbous
w/tricorner rim, satin finish,
applied crystal ribbed handle.....**865.00**

Tumbler, cylindrical, satin finish,
3¾" h. (ILLUS.)..........................**475.00**

WEBB

Webb Peach Blow Bowl

Bowl, 3⅞" d., 2⅝" h., small gilt footring below the wide squatty rounded body w/a wide incurved rim, decorated around the sides w/heavy gold prunus blossoms on branches, gold pine needles, satin finish, glossy white interior (ILLUS.) **365.00**

Cracker jar, cov., barrel-shaped, decorated w/daisies in light blue & white, matching glass cover w/metal finial, white interior, 7¾" h. **830.00**

Finger bowl w/underplate, round bowl w/a tightly crimped rim, ruffled underplate, bowl shaded both inside & out w/creamy opaque layer between, underplate w/typical coloring on top, creamy color on bottom, glossy finish, decorated w/gold prunus flowers & butterflies, plate 6¼" d., bowl 4¼" d., 2¾" h., pr. **600.00**

Vase, 3¼" h., 2¾" d., round short pedestal base below the bulbous nearly spherical body tapering to a short, wide rolled mouth, heavy gold decoration of flowers w/a butterfly on the reverse, gold rim trim, creamy white lining, satin finish **325.00**

Vase, 5⅛" h., 3¼" d., baluster-form, decorated w/gold & silver florals & leaves, creamy white interior (ILLUS. next column) **295.00**

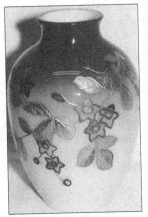

Silver- & Gold-Decorated Vase

Vase, 5⅞" h., 3" d., tapering ovoid body w/a wide cylindrical neck, decorated w/heavy gilt leaves & vining blossoms & an insect highlighted w/white enamel, white interior **295.00**

Vase, 8¼" h., pinch-sided bulbous body w/stick neck.........**300.00**

Vases, 8½" h., 4" d., tapering cylindrical body w/short neck, applied creamy white wafer foot, creamy white interior, pr. **395.00**

WHEELING

Tumbler, glossy finish, 3¾" h.......**485.00**

Vase, baluster-form w/a short flaring neck, shape No. 6 ....**400.00 to 500.00**

PILGRIM CAMEO GLASS

The Pilgrim Glass Corporation of Ceredo, West Virginia has been producing good quality commercial glassware for many years and continues in operation today. In 1986 they began a new venture with the formation of a division to produce specially designed cameo-cut art glass pieces. Under the careful leadership of Kelsey Murphy, chief designer and Director of the Art Glass Division, the production of cameo wares has grown in quality and sophistication over the years. Some pieces are one-of-a-kind originals while others are produced in limited editions. Many of the discontinued designs have seen a remarkable growth in value on the secondary market. The size of an edition and the elaborateness of the design, with layers ranging from one to ten colors, help determine the growth potential of a piece. The following is a listing of various releases offered over the past decade. The pieces are listed alphabetically by the factory title and each listing includes the number of glass layers, the company Registry Number and the original issue price and, finally, the current market value.

Three Pilgrim Cameo Vases

The Rhododendron vase, four-layer cameo, Reg. No. 901005, second edition, issue price $1,200. (ILLUS. front right) **1,534.00**

Grape Handkerchief vase, Reg. No. 902539, issue price $500....**750.00**

Hyacinth paperweight, four-layer cameo, Reg. No. 902725, original edition, issue price $770. ....**1,050.00**

Cattail Scent Bottles

Fairie vase, assorted colors, two-layer cameo, Reg. No. 903503, open edition, issue price $140., each.......................................**$190.00**

Cattail scent bottles, various shapes, four-layer cameo, Reg. No. 902984, original edition, issue price $572., each (ILLUS. of group) **680.00**

Fuschia Venus vase, three-layer cameo, Reg. No. 901002, second edition, issue price $400. (ILLUS. top next column, front left) **720.00**

Ladies in the Aviary vase, three-layer cameo, Reg. No. 901006, second edition, issue price $550. (ILLUS. top next column, back left) **1,320.00**

Cameo Mallard Duck

Mallard duck figure, five-layer cameo, five-layer cameo, Reg. No. 903450, issue price $2,900. (ILLUS.) **2,900.00**

Midnight Ladies vase, three-layer cameo, Reg. No. 901030, second edition, issue price $1,200. (ILLUS. top next page) **1,300.00**

Midnight Ladies Vase

Moon Over West Virginia vase,
Reg. No. 901032, issue price
$995. ....**1,300.00**

Morning Vineyard vase, Reg.
No. 901014, issue price
$1,500. ....**2,250.00**

Rhododendron Blue, three-layer
cameo, Reg. No. 901028,
second edition, issue
price $475. ....**1,200.00**

Rondell clock, three-layer
cameo, Reg. No. 902807,
original edition, issue price
$800. ....**1,200.00**

Rare Super Noma Vase

Super Noma vase, ten-layer
cameo, Reg. No. 997028
(ILLUS.) **12,000.00**

**Swan Amongst the Flowers
vase,** four-layer cameo, Reg.
No. 900801, original edition,
issue price $2,500 ....**5,000.00**

Wellman's Vintage Year vase,
Reg. No. 900871, issue price
$600 ....**900.00**

POMONA

First produced by the New England Glass Company under a patent received by Joseph Locke in 1885, Pomona has a frosted ground on clear glass decorated with mineral stains, most frequently amber-yellow, sometimes pale blue. Some pieces bore smooth etched floral decorations highlighted with staining. Two types of Pomona were made. The first Locke patent covered a technique whereby the piece was first covered with an acid resistant coating which was then needle-carved with thousands of minute criss-crossing lines. The piece was then dipped into acid which cut into the etched lines giving the finished piece a notable "brilliance."

A cheaper method, covered by a second Locke patent on June 15, 1886, was accomplished by rolling the glass piece in particles of acid-resistant material which were picked up by it. The glass was then etched by acid which attacked areas not protected by the resistant particles. A favorite design on Pomona was the cornflower.

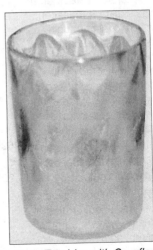

Pomona Tumbler with Cornflower

Champagne, amber-stained rim, second patent, 3⅝" d., 4¼" h...**$325.00**

Creamer & open sugar bowl, first patent, amber stain on ruffled edges, pr. **485.00**

Finger bowl, first patent, brilliant gold stain, 2½" h. **75.00**

Goblets, second patent, set of 6.....................................**150.00**

Toothpick holder, ruffled rim & applied rigaree around body......**195.00**

Tumbler, cylindrical, blue cornflower decoration, second patent, 2⅝" d., 3¾" h. (ILLUS. w/introduction)............................**145.00**

QUEZAL

In 1901, Martin Bach and Thomas Johnson , who had worked for Louis Tiffany, opened a competing glassworks in Brooklyn, New York. The Quezal Art Glass and Decorating Co. produced wares closely resembling those of Tiffany until the plant's closing in 1925.

Quezal

Quezal Mark

Lamp, table model two-light, the baluster-form body in cased white decorated w/feathered trailings in blue & iridescent silver & in iridescent gold, w/reeded & foliate-cast metal mounts, two curving arms fitted w/a pair of paneled opalescent floriform shades w/iridescent gold interiors & gold feathering on the exterior, each shade signed, ca. 1925, overall 25¾" h. **$690.00**

Plate, 6½" d., gold iridescence w/purple highlights.....................**225.00**

Vase, 6¼" h., bulbous ovoid body w/a rounded shoulder to the cylindrical neck w/a flared, ruffled rim, amber iridescent ground overlaid around the neck

Two Silver-Overlay Quezal Vases

& shoulder w/stylized interlacing sterling silver designs, inscribed mark, ca. 1920 (ILLUS. left) ...**1,035.00**

Vase, 9⅜" h., slender footed ovoid body w/constricting neck & flaring lip, amber iridescence shading to yellow & violet, pontil inscribed "Quezal," ca. 1920 .....**402.00**

Vase, 9⅞" h., bulbous ovoid base tapering to a tall slender & slightly flaring 'stick' neck, amber iridescence overlaid in sterling silver & cut w/blossoms, leaves & whiplash strapwork, pontil inscribed "Quezal," ca. 1910 (ILLUS. right) **1,150.00**

ROSE BOWLS

These decorative small bowls were widely popular in the late 19th and early 20th centuries. Produced in various types of glass, they are most common in satin glass or spatter glass. They are generally a spherical shape with an incurved crimped rim, but ovoid or egg-shaped examples are also popular.

Their name derives from their reported use, to hold dried rose petal potpourri or small fresh-cut roses.

Amber, miniature "jewell"-type, vertically ribbed sides w/optic ribbing on each rib & small controlled air bubbles, engraved "Rd. 55693, England, 12-crimp top, 2½" d., 2¼" h. **$125.00**

Cameo, morning glory flowers & leaves in white cut to pink cut to yellow, white interior, English, 2¾" d., 2¼" h. **1,315.00**

Satin Ribbon Pattern Rose Bowl

Cased satin, spherical, heavenly blue mother-of-pearl Ribbon patt., white interior, nine-crimp top, 3⅝" d., 2⅝" h. (ILLUS.).......**245.00**

Cased satin, spherical, shaded brown mother-of-pearl Diamond Quilted patt., white interior, eight-crimp top, 3" d., 3" h. **395.00**

Cased satin, spherical, shaded chartreuse green embossed w/flowers & leaves, white interior, eight-crimp top, 4" d., 3½" h. **125.00**

Cased satin, spherical, blue, white & brown flower decoration w/brown & yellow leaves, white interior, 8-crimp top, 4¼" d., 4" h. **125.00**

Cased satin, spherical, shaded heavenly blue decorated w/white, brown & cream flowers & leaves, white interior, eight-crimp top, 4⅜" d., 4" h. **125.00**

Cranberry glass, spherical body, Optic patt., five-crimp top, 4⅜" d., 4¼" h. **90.00**

Green shading to clear, intaglio-cut lily & leaves, 2½" d. **240.00**

Shaded & Appliqued Rose Bowls

Green shading to cranberry, spherical, finely threaded exterior, eight-crimp top, 3½" d., 3" h. (ILLUS. left) **110.00**

Purple cased appliqué, spherical, shaded exterior w/optic rib design, large applied white spatter blossom w/applied clear leaf & vine, light white interior, 4" d., 3⅞" h. (ILLUS. right w/shaded green bowl) **135.00**

Sapphire blue, miniature, "jewell"-type, spherical w/molded ribbing & interior optic ribbing on each rib & small controlled air bubbles, ground pontil engraved "Rd. 55693, " English, 12-crimp top, English, 2½" d., 2¼" h. **135.00**

Spangled, egg-shaped, rose exterior w/mica flakes in coral, white interior, 3⅜" d., 3¾" h.......**110.00**

RUBINA CRYSTAL

This glass, sometimes spelled "Rubena," is a flashed ware, shading from ruby to clear. Some pieces are decorated.

Condiment set: salt & pepper shakers, cov. mustard jar & oblong tray; the long clear tray w/rounded ends cut w/a button & half-daisy design, the swelled squared containers cut w/hobstar & starburst designs, tray 6¾" l., each container 2⅜" w., 3½" h., the set) **$165.00**

Cruet w/original stopper, enamel decoration of various colorful blossoms, 7" h. **375.00**

Rubina Decorated Decanter

Decorated Rubina Tumbler

Tumbler, cylindrical w/optic-ribbed design, decorated w/enameled blue violets, yellow flowers & roses & green & yellow leaves, 2¾" d., 3¾" (ILLUS.) **55.00**

Water set: 13¼" h. tankard pitcher & six 5" h. matching tumblers; molded floral & scrolling leaf design outlined in gold, ornate white enamel scrollwork around the top of the pitcher, applied crystal pitcher handle, the set **920.00**

SANDWICH

Numerous types of glass were produced at The Boston & Sandwich Glass Works in Sandwich, Massachusetts, on Cape Cod, from 1826 to 1888. Those listed here represent a sampling. Also see PATTERN GLASS and LACY in the "Glass" section.

All pieces are pressed glass unless otherwise noted. Numbers after salt dips refer to listings in Pressed Glass Salt Dishes of the Lacy Period, 1825-1850, *by Logan W. and Dorothy B. Neal.*

Candlestick, hexagonal tulip-form candle socket attached by a wafer to a matching ringed & flaring hexagonal pedestal base w/a flaring foot, severe mold

Decanter w/original teardrop bubble stopper, ovoid body tapering to a slender neck w/a high, arched spout & applied arched gilt handle, the sides decorated w/an overall design of gold ribbon streamers outlined in enamel, clear stopper w/gold trim, 3⅝" d., 11⅜" h. (ILLUS.)....**195.00**

Liqueur set: tankard pitcher w/hinged silver plate rim, flat cover & angled handle & two matching liqueur glasses; each cylindrical piece w/an embossed swirl design w/the ribs trimmed in gold, glasses 1⅛" d., 1⅞" h., pitcher 2½" d., 7⅜" h., the set **245.00**

Pitcher, 4" h., miniature, applied smooth crystal handle, Inverted Thumbprint patt., Hobbs............**150.00**

Pitchers, 8⅝" h., 5⅛" d., ovoid melon-lobed body tapering to a wide cylindrical neck w/a pinched spout, applied clear handle, polished pontil, pr. **350.00**

Sandwich Hexagonal Candlestick

roughness around edges of
socket, medium amethyst,
7⅝" h. (ILLUS.) $550.00

Candlestick, figural dolphin stem
supporting a petal socket, on a
square single-step base, pale
lime green socket attached to a
clambroth base, 10¼" h. (one
petal off & reglued, crack off
another petal) 523.00

Candlestick, figural dolphin stem
supporting a petal socket, an
opaque soft starch blue socket
attached to an opaque white
single-step base, 10¼" h.
(unseen chip under base, short
crack on tip of tail) 605.00

Compote, open, miniature, 6" d.,
pierced ribbon-edge w/flaring
sides & shoulder pedestal foot,
amethyst, mid-19th c. (few base
chips) 1,150.00

Jar, cov., slightly tapering
cylindrical base w/a matching
domed cover w/knob finial,
overall Basketweave patt.,
applied gold bands around rims
& finial, opaque jade green,
3¼" d., 4⅝" h. 495.00

Lamp, sparking-type, a clear
spherical free-blown font w/tin
drop-in whale oil burner & an
applied solid handle w/end curl,
applied to a slender ringed stem
attached to an inverted
miniature lacy cup plate foot,
4" h. (some mold roughness,
small flakes under foot) 1,210.00

Lamp, table model, Acanthus
patt. font, attached to a baluster-
form acanthus leaf stem on a
double-step square base,
opaque jade green font, opaque
clambroth base, sand or crizzled
finish, w/slightly crooked brass
collar, 11⅝" h........................1,980.00

Pomade jar, cov., model of a
bear, fiery opalescent, small
size, 3¾" h. (minor flakes
around head & base, small chip
on back of one ear) 495.00

Salt shaker w/original metal lid,
"Christmas" salt, barrel-shaped,
1877 patent date on lid, cobalt
blue, 2½" h. (small rim chip
under lid) 66.00

Salt shaker w/original metal lid,
"Christmas" salt, barrel-shaped,
1877 patent date on lid,
opalescent white h.p. w/a winter
landscape scene w/tree & fence,
2½" h. 275.00

Spooner (spillholder), Sandwich
Star patt., footed, polished
pontil, electric blue, 5" h. (usual
mold roughness along base) ..1,320.00

Vase, 10" h., Leaf patt., the
tapering bowl w/a swirled rib
design manipulated to form four
receptacles for flowers, attached
by a wafer to the flaring eight-
lobed leaf-patterned pedestal
base, ca. 1840-50, usual mold
roughness, flakes under base,
clear...413.00

Vases, 9¾" h., tulip-form, paneled
sides w/flaring rim on an
octagonal pedestal base, deep
green, mid-19th c., pr. (minor
base chips) 4,485.00

SATIN

Satin glass was a popular decorative glass developed in the late 19th century. Most pieces were composed of two layers of glass with the exterior layer usually in a shaded pastel color. The name derives from the soft matte finish, caused by exposure to acid fumes, which gave the surface a "satiny" feel. Mother-of-pearl satin glass was a specialized variety wherein air trapped between the layers of glass provided subtle surface patterns such as Herringbone and Diamond Quilted. A majority of satin glass was produced in England, Bohemia and America, but collectors should be aware that reproductions have been produced for many years.

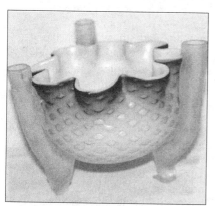

Mother-of-Pearl Satin Footed Bowl

Basket, deep rose mother-of-pearl Diamond Quilted patt. on the interior, white on the exterior, applied twisted clear satin thorn handle, 7¼" d., 8¾" h. **$795.00**

Bowl, 5⅞" d., 4½" h., deep bulbous rounded sides w/a flaring eight-lobed rim, shaded blue mother-of-pearl Diamond Quilted exterior, white interior, supported between three applied heavy frosted clear thorn legs (ILLUS.) **395.00**

Cracker jar, cov., shaded pinkish white decorated w/yellow flowers & lavender stems, silver plate bail handle, rim & cover w/matching etched designs, 9¼" h. **525.00**

Cracker jar, cov., shaded blue mother-of-pearl Diamond Quilted patt., decorated w/yellow flowers, silver plate rim, cover & bail handle, overall 9½" h., ...**1,020.00**

Creamer, clear frosted footring supports a squatty spherical body w/a heart-form rim in blue mother-of-pearl Ribbon patt., applied frosted clear handle, 2¾" d., 2⅛" h. **245.00**

Creamer, spherical blue body w/an eight-crimp rim in mother-of-pearl Seaweed patt., applied frosted clear handle, 3¼" d., 2¾" h. **265.00**

Satin Mother-of-Pearl Ewer

Ewer, a cushion foot w/a short pedestal supporting the squatty bulbous body tapering to a cylindrical neck w/a tricorner crimped rim, shaded apricot mother-of-pearl Herringbone patt., applied angular clear frosted thorn handle, 4¼" d., 7" h. (ILLUS.)...........................**265.00**

Jam dish in frame, wide squatty flaring bowl w/a yellow exterior decorated w/gold floral vines & butterflies, white interior, set in a silver plate frame on ball feet & an arched bail handle, 5½" d., 5½" h. **245.00**

Rose bowl, molded Seashell patt., shaded yellow, decorated w/small orange enameled florets..**85.00**

Sugar shaker w/original lid, raspberry shading to pink mother-of-pearl Raindrop patt. (small in-making burst bubble on base) **495.00**

Vase, 3" h., 2¾" d., applied clear frosted disc foot supports an inverted bell-form body w/a squared rim, pink mother-of-pearl Ribbon patt., white interior **188.00**

Vase, 5¾" h., pink mother-of-pearl Hobnail patt., white interior **500.00**

Herringbone Mother-of-Pearl Vase

Vase, 6½" h., 2⅞" d., ovoid melon-lobed body below a tall slightly flaring cylindrical neck w/a fanned & crimped neck, shaded pink mother-of-pearl Herringbone patt. (ILLUS.) **175.00**

Vase, 6¾" h., mother-of-pearl Federzeichnung patt., marked "Rd. 76057" **1,350.00**

SPANGLED

Spangled glass incorporated particles of mica or metallic flakes and variegated colored glass particles imbedded in the transparent glass. Usually made of two layers, it might have either an opaque or transparent casing. The Vasa Murrhina Glass Company of Sandwich, Massachusetts, first patented the process for producing Spangled glass in 1884 and this factory is known to have produced great quantities of this ware. It was, however, also produced by numerous other American and English glasshouses. This type, along with Spatter, is often erroneously called "End of the Day."

A related decorative glass, Aventurine, features a fine speckled pattern resembling gold dust on a solid color ground. Also, see ART GLASS BASKETS and ROSE BOWLS under Glass.

Ewer, cushion-footed inverted bell-form body w/the wide shoulder tapering to a short cylindrical neck w/a widely flaring crimped tricorner rim, transparent light blue w/silver mica flakes, white interior, applied angled clear thorn handle from rim to shoulder, 3⅜" d., 7⅜" h. **$115.00**

Ewer, squatty bulbous body w/a tall ringed neck & three-petal rim, applied crimped handle, pink w/silver spangles on white cased in crystal, 9½" h. **250.00**

Pitcher, 4⅜" h., 3¼" d., bulbous ovoid molded swirl design body w/a wide cylindrical neck & pinched spout, cased turquoise blue w/silver mica flecks, applied clear ribbed handle **195.00**

Rose bowl, spherical, sapphire blue w/white spatter & scattered tiny silver mica flecks, eight-crimp top, 3⅝" d., 3¼" h. **85.00**

Rose bowl, spherical, swirled rib clear exterior casing on reverse-swirled layer of beige, pink & maroon spatter & mica flecks lined w/white, 3¾" d., 3⅜" h. **110.00**

Spangled Tumbler

Tumbler, cylindrical, deep amber w/Inverted Thumbprint patt. & white spatter w/silver mica flecks, 2¾" d., 3¾" h. (ILLUS.) **45.00**

Vase, 13½" h., 5¼" d., cylindrical body tapering slightly to a cylindrical neck w/molded rim, cobalt blue w/overall dense silver mica flecks, enamel-decorated w/pink flowers, green & brown leaves & two blue, white & green birds sitting on branches, gargoyle-like heads on three ormolu feet **375.00**

STEUBEN

Most of the Steuben glass listed below was made at the Steuben Glass Works, now a division of Corning Glass, between 1903 and about 1933. The factory was organized by T.G. Hawkes, noted glass designer, Frederick Carder, and others. Mr. Carder devised many types of glass and revived many old techniques.

AURENE

Steuben Marks

AURENE

Steuben Aurene Goblet

Bonbon, triangular shape w/turned in edges, gold iridescence, signed "Aurene 531," 5" d. **$250.00**

Bowl, 5" d., 4" h., blue iridescence, signed "Aurene 2799" **850.00**

Dish, a wide flat round rim centered by a small round indentation, vivid gold iridescence w/violet, pink, green & orange highlights, signed "Steuben - Aurene - 2361," 6½" d., 1" h. **176.00**

Goblet, domed footed, short stem, gold iridescence, signed "Steuben 2814," 4½" h. **235.00**

Goblet, a round disc foot centered by a twisted, swelled stem supporting a tall inverted bell-form bowl, iridescent gold w/vivid violet, blue & orange highlights, signed "Aurene 2361," 6" h. (ILLUS.)..................**275.00**

Vase, 6½" h., a baluster-form body w/a rounded, stepped shoulder & short flaring neck, pulled decoration on a pale blue iridescent ground w/violet & gold highlights, signed "Aurene," paper label...............................**935.00**

BUBBLY

Bowl, centerpiece, 12" d., 2" h., clear bubbly w/green threading on outer rim, green crystal flower frog, signed **375.00**

Compote, 6" d, 4½" h., bowl w/ruffled rim, clear bubbly w/yellow threading, signed, ...**165.00**

Compotes, 8" h., shallow bowl w/upturned lip raised on a tall swollen cylindrical stem w/a shallow domed foot, pale transparent green decorated w/overall controlled bubbles & applied w/threading, unsigned, set of 4......................................**575.00**

CALCITE

Bowl, 5½" d. , 2½" h., white interior wide rolled stretched rim, gold Aurene exterior w/green & red iridescence **550.00**

Compote, 7¼" d., 3¼" h., gold Aurene stretched interior w/rolled rim, white exterior.........**575.00**

IVRENE

Cornucopia-vase, white iridescence, very graceful cornucopia resting on a domed round foot, shape No. 7579, signed "Steuben" **425.00**

Vase, 8" h., fanned Grotesque ribbed shape w/undulating rim, the sides tapering sharply to a domed round foot (ILLUS. below, right) ....**1,500.00 to 2,000.00**

JADE

Garniture set: tall open compote & a pr. of candlesticks; each w/a Jade green top on a swirled Alabaster foot, the compote w/a wide shallow bowl w/a flattened rim raised on a

An Ivrene Vase & Jade Garniture Set

swelled slender stem, each
candlestick w/a swirled ovoid
socket w/a wide flatted rim
attached w/a wafer to a slender
swelled tall standard, each piece
signed, ca. 1925, compote 7" h.,
candlesticks 10" h., the set
(ILLUS. bottom, previous page,
left w/Ivrene vase) **1,150.00**

Vase, 6" h., three-trunk-style, a
cluster of three staggered thorny
ribbed stump-form cylindrical
vases attached to a round disc
foot, green Jade, signed
"Steuben".....................................**231.00**

VERRE DE SOIE

Verre de Soie Threaded Bowl

Bowl, 8½" d., flaring sides, green
threading around the rim
(ILLUS.) **225.00**

Candlesticks, satiny glass w/blue
threading, signed "Steuben,"
5" h., pr. **475.00**

STEVENS & WILLIAMS

*This long-established English glasshouse
has turned out a wide variety of artistic
glasswares through the years. Fine satin glass
pieces and items with applied decoration
(sometimes referred to as "Matsu-No-Ke")
are especially sought after today. The
following represents a cross-section of its
wares.*

Bowl, 4⅞" d., 3¼" h., squatty
bulbous form w/a wide three-
lobed rolled rim, deep pink
interior w/applied amber rim
band above the white exterior

applied w/a wide ruffled
cranberry, amber & green leaf
wrapping around the sides,
raised on applied amber petal
feet, clear berry pontil **$135.00**

Cracker jar, cov., barrel-shaped
w/narrow ribbing, swirling blue,
crystal & white stripes, silver
plate cover, rim & bail handle,
8" h. to top of handle **420.00**

Finger bowl & under plate,
emerald green & clear glass,
intaglio-cut grapes, branches &
leaves in frosted green, plate
6⅜" d., bowl 4¾" d., 2½" h.,
2 pcs. **295.00**

Rose bowl & underplate, light
blue mother-of-pearl Ribbon
patt. rose bowl, light green
mother-of-pearl Ribbon patt. lily
pad underplate w/folded edges,
rose bowl 2¾" d., underplate
5" d., 2 pcs..............................**400.00**

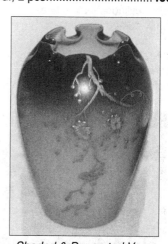

Shaded & Decorated Vase

Vase, 5⅛" h., 3½" d., simple
ovoid body w/an incurved
crimped rim, shaded brown
exterior decorated w/heavy gold
prunus branches & blossoms,
creamy white interior
(ILLUS.) **425.00**

Vase, 7¼" h., 5¼" d., bulbous
ovoid melon-lobed body tapering
to a tall rim pulled into four

points w/inwardly-curled tips,
cased light blue exterior & white
interior, the exterior w/large
applied clear ruffled leaves &
wishbone feet **325.00**

Vase, 8" h., 5¼" d. at shoulder,
gourd-shaped, mother-of-pearl
satin Swirl patt., reverse Rubina
Verde coloring, ground pontil
(three small blemishes) **350.00**

Vase, 9" h., 5½" d., deep rose
shaded to pink, decorated
w/applied cherries, flowers &
vines in rose, amber-yellow &
white **485.00**

Vase, 15½" h., jack-in-the-pulpit
type w/trumpet-shaped w/ruffled
rim, white opaque & cranberry
striped w/clear base **305.00**

TIFFANY

*This glassware, covering a wide diversity
of types, was produced in glasshouses
operated by Louis Comfort Tiffany, America's
outstanding glass designer of the Art
Nouveau period, from the last quarter of the
19th century until the early 1930s. Tiffany
revived early techniques and devised many
new ones.*

Various Tiffany marks

Bowl, 7½" d., 3" h., wide rounded
ribbed sides tapering to a small
foot, the broad incurved rim
slightly scalloped, gold
iridescence w/violet, blue &
orange highlights, signed "L.C.T.
Favrile" (minor scratches to
interior) **$440.00**

Bowl, centerpiece, 4" deep, 9" d.,
five-lobed, cobalt glass w/heavy
iridescent vertical mottling,
signed "L.C.T. 0071920".........**1,895.00**

Bowl, 2½" x 8½" d., iridized rim,
lemon yellow w/white opal pulls
to center, pastel........................**635.00**

Champagne glass, iridescent
gold, long fragile stem, Tiffany
signed, 5½" h.............................**285.00**

Compote, open, 4" h., 8" d., a
round, wide slightly domed foot
centered by a short, waisted
pedestal supporting a wide
shallow flaring bowl, iridescent
gold w/pink, blue, violet &
orange highlights, signed "L.C.T.
- 7587" **468.00**

Compote, open, 5" h., floriform, a
round foot centered by a short,
slender stem supporting a
bulbous tapering bowl w/a wide
flaring, flattened & deeply ruffled
rim, stretched blue iridescent
finish w/violet & gold highlights,
signed "L.C. Tiffany - Favrile -
1529-4388L" **1,045.00**

Cup & saucer, cup has seven
large applied lily pads & stems
pulled into foot, gold
iridescence, Tiffany signed........**425.00**

Dish, small round flaring form w/a
deeply crimped & fluted incurved
rim, iridescent blue w/violet &
green highlights, signed "L.C.T.,"
2½" d., 1" h................................**165.00**

Dish, a thin footring supports a
wide shallow ribbed bowl w/a
deeply fluted rim, iridescent blue
w/gold, violet & pink highlights,
signed "L.C. Tiffany - Favrile -
X305," 4" d., 1½" h. **220.00**

Rose water sprinkler, the
bulbous nearly spherical body
w/a tall slender undulating neck
flaring to a gooseneck lip, green
decorated w/silvery blue
peacock feathers w/five pea
'eyes' in gold & dark blue,
inscribed "X L.C.T.," 14" h. ...**31,625.00**

Sherbet, deep slightly flaring wide cylindrical bowl w/ applied prunts around the outside raised on a short cylindrical stem on a flaring round foot w/ delicate crimped decoration, overall gold iridescence w/pink, violet, blue, green & orange highlights, signed "L.C.T.," 3½" h. **297.00**

Shot glass, dimpled, rose gold iridescence, Tiffany signed, 1¾" h. **135.00**

Tumbler, baluster-form w/wide, slightly flaring mouth, the sides decorated w/applied stylized lily pad prunts, overall gold iridescence w/light blue, pink, violet & orange highlights, signed "L.C.T. - M7380," 4" h. ...**495.00**

Vase, miniature, 2½" h., ovoid body tapering to a narrow neck w/a tiny mouth, narrow rim in iridescent gold w/violet, pink & blue highlights, the body w/a pulled feather design in vivid green below a white upper half, signed "L.C. Tiffany - Favrile - 4948K".....................................**715.00**

Vase, miniature, 3¼" h., "Cypriote," bulbous nearly spherical body tapering to a small, short cylindrical neck, amber externally textured w/violet, blue & silvery iridescence, indistinctly inscribed "L.C. Tiffany - 8508 K," ca. 1916.................................**3,162.00**

Vase, 4¼" h., ovoid body w/tiny loop shoulder handles, tapering to a small flaring neck, brilliant red exterior cased over white, inscribed "L.C. Tiffany - Favrile - 1615 K," ca. 1916 ....**2,875.00**

Vase, 5" h., floriform, a round foot centered by a short, slender stem supporting a tapering squatty bulbous bowl w/a very widely flaring & fluted rim, the base & interior in iridescent gold w/blue & violet highlights, the exterior of the bowl w/green

pulled feather designs on a white ground, signed "L.C. Tiffany - Favrile - 4244 C".........**880.00**

Vase, 6" h., footed ovoid body tapering to a short cylindrical neck, opalescent ivory w/iridized interior, decorated on the exterior w/an overall design of iridescent amber heart-shaped leaves & tendrils & applied tendrils & silvery blue flowerheads (cracked) **2,587.00**

Vase, 6" h., bottle-form, a small cushion foot supporting a bulbous ovoid body tapering to a tall, slender 'stick' neck w/a flaring rim, iridescent gold w/pink, orange & pale blue highlights, signed "L.C. Tiffany - Favrile - 394L" **715.00**

Vase, 9" h., baluster-form w/a broad shoulder below a short cylindrical double-ringed neck, the shoulder decorated w/an intaglio design of deeply carved blossoms w/detailed centers atop thorny branches & broad, jagged leaves w/prominent spines, the neck w/a stylized leaf & berry design, all in iridescent gold w/orange, violet & blue highlights, signed "L.C. Tiffany - Favrile - #7540G" **2,970.00**

Vase, 9⅛" h., "Tel el Amarna," the slender shouldered baluster-form w/a flaring foot & a gently flaring cylindrical neck, bright cobalt blue cased over white, the neck in navy blue w/a band of Egyptian chain design in sea foam green & fine-lined metallic silvery pink, inscribed "L.C. Tiffany, Favrile - 4668 G," ca. 1912.................................**7,475.00**

Vase, 18" h., floriform, the tall slender swelled cup in amber w/iridized interior & white shading in the upper section, decorated around the bottom w/green leafage, raised on a very slender green stem on a

Group of Tiffany Vases

domed iridized amber foot, inscribed "L.C.T. - 8691," ca. 1905 (ILLUS. right) **9,775.00**

Vases, bud, 13¼" h., very slender cylindrical body w/a small flared rim in iridescent amber subtly decorated w/pulled green leafage, set into a short cylindrical stem on a knobbed gilt-bronze foot, partial intaglio finish, gilt & brown base patina, one inscribed "L.C.T.," each base inscribed "TIFFANY STUDIOS - NEW YORK - 717," early 20th c., pr. (ILLUS. left) **3,105.00**

TIFFIN

A wide variety of fine glasswares were produced by the Tiffin Glass Company of Tiffin, Ohio. Beginning as a part of the large U.S. Glass Company early in this century, the Tiffin factory continued making a wide range of wares until its final closing in 1984. One popular line is now called "Black Satin" and included various vases with raised floral designs. Many other acid-etched and hand-cut patterns were also produced over the years and are very collectible today. The three "Tiffin Glassmasters" books by Fred Bickenheuser, are the standard references for Tiffin collectors.

Ashtray, cloverleaf-shaped, Twilight cutting, clear, 3" d.........**$25.00**

Ashtray, cloverleaf-shaped, Twilight cutting, clear, 5" d...........**45.00**

Basket, flower-type, No. 6553, Copen blue & clear, 13" h..........**165.00**

Bowl, console, etched Cerise patt., clear....................................**65.00**

Bowl, 11½" d., etched Flanders patt., yellow **46.00**

Candlelight garden set, five-lobed candleholder, Dawn patt., No. 9153-110, Twilight cutting, pr. **195.00**

Candlestick, two-light, etched Fuchsia patt., No. 5209, clear **75.00**

Candlesticks, stylized frog head w/a long, slender neck, sitting on a dome-shaped base, etched Princess patt., No. 69, Black Satin, pr. **250.00**

Celery dish, etched Cherokee Rose patt., No. 5902, clear, 10½" l **75.00**

Centerpiece, etched Fontaine patt., green, 13" d. **85.00**

Champagne, cut Festival patt., clear..**12.00**

Champagne, etched Fuchsia patt., No. 15083, clear **14.00**

Champagne, etched June Night patt., No. 17378, clear **23.00**

Champagne, etched Persian Pheasant patt., clear **16.00**

Champagne, saucer-type, etched Cadena patt., yellow & crystal **44.00**

Claret, etched Flanders patt., clear..**55.00**

Claret, etched June Night patt., clear, 4 oz. **45.00**

Claret, etched Persian Pheasant patt. No. 17358, clear **30.00**

Cocktail, etched Cordelia patt., clear..**10.00**

Cocktail, etched Cherokee Rose patt., No. 17399, clear **18.00**

Cocktail, etched June Night patt.,
3½ oz., 5¼" h., clear...................**24.00**

Cocktail, liquor, etched Fuchsia
patt., clear....................................**18.00**

Comport, blown, etched Persian
Pheasant, clear, 6" h. **85.00**

Console bowl, black amethyst
w/satin finish, 12" d......................**39.00**

Cordial, etched Cordelia patt.,
No. 15047, clear **22.00**

Cordial, etched June Night patt.,
No. 17392, clear **45.00**

Cordial, etched Persian Pheasant
patt., clear....................................**55.00**

**Cordial decanter w/original
stopper,** pheasant-shaped, Era
Line, etched Princess patt.,
ca 1942-57, clear.......................**175.00**

Cup & saucer, blown, etched
Fontaine patt., Twilight, pr. **125.00**

Flower arranger, Empress line,
No. 6568, Twilight & Smoke,
17" l. **295.00**

Flower floater set: undulating
oblong shallow dish w/three
short candle sockets at wide end
& 10" h. removable stylized fawn
at narrow end, clear, late 1940s,
14½" l., 2 pcs. **85.00**

Goblet, water, Athlone patt.,
clear...**12.00**

Goblet, water, gold-encrusted
etched Bouquet patt., clear **19.00**

Goblet, water, etched Cherokee
Rose patt., No. 17399, clear,
9 oz...**25.00**

Goblet, water, etched Flanders
patt., clear....................................**30.00**

Goblet, water, etched Fuchsia
patt., No. 15083, clear **24.00**

Goblet, water, etched June Night
patt., clear, 9 oz. **28.00**

Goblet, water, cut Lord Nelson
patt., clear....................................**18.00**

Goblet, water, cut Mt. Vernon
patt., clear....................................**18.00**

Goblet, water, Twilight,
No. 17492.....................................**35.00**

Mayonnaise dish, footed, etched
Fuchsia patt., clear **50.00**

Oyster cocktail, etched Cerise
patt., No. 15072, clear **12.00**

Oyster cocktail, etched June
Night etching, clear......................**12.00**

Pitcher, water, etched Princess
patt., clear..................................**125.00**

Pitcher, cov., jug-type, footed,
etched Psyche patt., ca. 1926-
31, clear w/green trim, 2 qt. **450.00**

Plate, 6" d., etched Cadena patt.,
yellow **10.00**

Plate, 6" d., etched Julia patt.,
amber **20.00**

Plate, 7½" d., etched Cadena
patt., yellow **14.00**

Plate, salad, 8" d., etched
Cherokee Rose patt., clear..........**13.00**

Plate, 8" d., etched Classic patt.,
clear...**12.00**

Plate, 8" d., etched Flanders patt.,
clear...**12.00**

Plate, 8" d., etched Julia patt.,
amber **25.00**

Plate, 8" d., etched June Night
patt., clear....................................**17.00**

Plate, 9½" d., etched Flanders
patt., yellow **60.00**

Plate, 10" d., etched Julia patt.,
amber **45.00**

Plate, dinner, 10½" d., etched
Classic patt., clear **125.00**

Plate, sandwich, 14" d., etched
Cherokee Rose patt., clear..........**80.00**

Salt & pepper shakers, etched
Fuschia patt., clear, pr. **75.00**

Tumbler, seltzer, footed,
etched La Fleure patt., No. 185,
clear...**19.00**

Sundae, etched Byzantine patt.,
clear...**12.00**

Sundae, etched Cordelia patt.,
clear, 3¾" h. **8.00**

Sundae, tall stem, cut Liege patt.,
clear...**18.00**

Sundae, tall stem, etched June
Night patt., clear, 5½ oz. **20.00**

Sundae, tall-stem, etched
Flanders patt., clear....................**28.00**

Sugar bowl, open, flat-bottom,
etched Flanders patt., yellow.......**75.00**

Tumbler, etched Princess patt.,
clear, 12 oz. **14.00**

Tumbler, iced-tea, etched Classic
patt., No. 354, clear, 12 oz. **50.00**

Tumbler, iced-tea, footed, etched
Fuschia patt., clear **38.00**

Tumbler, iced-tea, footed, etched
June Night patt., clear **27.00**

Tumbler, water, etched Flanders
patt., clear..................................**25.00**

Tumbler, water, etched Flanders
patt., yellow **22.00**

Tumbler, water, footed, etched
Cadena patt., clear, 5¼" h..........**29.00**

Vase, bud, 6" h., etched
Cherokee Rose patt., clear.........**29.00**

Vase, bud, 6" h., etched June
Night patt., clear **45.00**

Vase, bud, 10" h., etched June
Night patt., clear **40.00**

Water set: pitcher & six tumblers;
etched Cadena patt., clear,
7 pcs. **220.00**

Whiskey, etched Flanders patt.,
clear...**55.00**

Wine, cut Athlone patt., clear,
2½ oz..**8.00**

Wine, cut Liege patt., clear, 4 oz. ..**18.00**

Wine, etched Cherokee Rose
patt., clear, 3½ oz. **18.00**

Wine, etched Flanders patt.,
clear...**38.00**

Wine, etched June Night patt.,
No. 17403, clear, 2 oz. **45.00**

Wine, gold encrusted etched
Bouquet patt., clear **16.00**

VENETIAN

Venetian glass has been made for six centuries on the island of Murano, where it continues to be produced. The skilled glass artisans developed numerous techniques, subsequently imitated elsewhere.`

Bowl, 9" d., 6" h., "iridato"-style, a
small round foot supports a
wide, deep rounded bowl
w/delicate swirled ribbing below
a tightly crimped flaring rim,
applied S-scroll leaf handles at
the sides, handles & base
contain fine gold leaf, remains of
paper label, Barovier & Toso,
ca. 1940..................................**$880.00**

Bowl, 13" l., 4½" h., "rugiadoso"-
style, a free-blown oblong boat-
shape w/irregular side rims &
wide pulled-out arched &
pierced end handles, on a small
applied foot, the interior applied
w/glass shards containing gold

Barovier & Toso Boat-shaped Bowl

leaf patches, Barovier & Toso, ca. 1940 (ILLUS. previous page) **1,430.00**

Figure of a woman, clear standing figure w/long hair & wearing a long dress flaring to form the base, on hand on her hip, the other at her side holding a jug, gold leaf applications, Barovier & Toso, ca. 1940, 8½" h. **385.00**

Figures of girls, one girl w/blouse & ribbed ankle length skirt, the other w/form-fitting slacks, each holding a hat & on swirl pedestal, orange & heavy gold, 12" h., pr. **500.00**

Venetian Model of a Bird

Model of a bird, "sgraffito"-style, duck-type bird w/angled ribbed ovoid body & an upturned head w/open bill, internally decorated w/deep blue powders & gold leaf in a swag design, Barovier & Toso, ca. 1952, 6" h. (ILLUS.) ...**550.00**

Vase, 6½" h., cornucopia-form, curled tail & widely flaring rim, composed of green & white filigrana w/an applied leaf-form foot w/deep amethyst specks & gold leaf, Alberto Toso, 1950s (ILLUS. top next column)...........**138.00**

Vase, 8¾" h., "pezzati," simple tapering cylindrical body, decorated w/bands of alternating orangish red & opalescent white

Cornucopia-form Venetian Vase

rectangular tessarae, designed by Ercole Barovier, Barovier & Toso, after 1956 ....**4,600.00**

Vase, 11½" h., "a lenti," tapering cylindrical form in clear applied w/large raised hemispheres & internally decorated w/gold foil inclusions, inscribed "MURANO - VENEZIA," designed by Ercole Barovier, Barvoier & Toso, ca. 1940................................**4,600.00**

VENINI

Founded by former lawyer Paolo Venini in 1925, this Venetian glasshouse soon developed a reputation for its fine quality decorative glass and tableware's. Several noted designers have worked for the firm over the years and their unique pieces in the modern spirit, made using traditional techniques, are increasingly popular with collectors today. The factory continues in operation.

Bottle w/stopper, "fasce"-style, a tall cylindrical body tapering at the top to a narrow trumpet-form neck fitted w/a stopper w/a short pedestal supporting a large ball finial, grey body w/applied lattimo white bands & a round white ball finial on the clear stopper, acid-stamped mark "venini murano italia," designed by Paolo Venini, ca. 1950s, 16½" h. **$990.00**

Bowl, 3½" d., 1½" h., "filigrana"-style, wide shallow form w/thick sides, clear containing spiraling light green filigrana threading, designed by Carlo Scarpa, acid-stamped "venini murano - MADE IN ITALY," ca. 1930s **187.00**

Bowl, 8¾" d., 2½" h., "murrina"-style, a wide shallow form, clear w/wavy radiating bands of yellow & white & black & white, includes distinctive Venini murrina in spider form, acid-stamped mark "venini murano ITALIA," designed by Riccardo Licata, ca. 1956 ....**1,980.00**

Compote, open, 7" h., shallow widely flaring flat-sided bowl in pale lavender above a foliate-form stem composed of two clusters of red blossoms emerging from graduated flaring pale green "pulegoso" leaves, on a pale lavender disc foot, designed by Napoleone Martinuzzi, 1928-30 ....**1,725.00**

Figure, "Comedia dell'Arte"-type, 'Tartaglia,' delicately posed figure of a man standing on one leg w/the other raised resting on a short tree trunk, wearing high boots, striped britches below a pleated kilt & white jacket & patterned cape, a conical hat on head, white w/black applications, designed by Fulvio Bianconi, ca. 1950, acid-stamped mark "venini murano ITALIA," 13" h. **1,430.00**

Screen, floor-type, four-fold, each panel composed of variously sized panels in clear glass internally streaked w/amorphous trailings in cobalt blue & black, fitted in a white-painted iron frame, unsigned, ca. 1955, 72" l., 5' h.............................**8,050.00**

Vase, 6½" h., "cappello del Doge," spherical body tapering sharply on the upper half to a tiny flat mouth, translucent orange overlaid w/mustard yellow & black, designed by Thomas Sterns, stamped "venini -

murano - ITALIA" w/remnants of original paper label, ca. 1962...**6,900.00**

Venini "Con Machie" Vase

Vase, 8¾" h., "con machie"-style, tapering ovoid body w/a flat rim, clear shading to pale yellow w/blue & deep amethyst mirroring figures on the front & back, designed by Fulvio Bianconi, acid-stamped "venini - murano - ITALIA," ca. 1950 (ILLUS.) **5,175.00**

Vase, 10¾" h., spherical body tapering to a short small & thick flaring neck, decorated overall w/applied pointed prunts, designed by Carlo Scarpa, ca. 1936, unsigned......................**7,475.00**

Vase, 19½" h., "inciso"-style, a very tall & slightly swelled cylindrical body, clear cased over amber & blue w/fine horizontally incised lines, acid-stamped mark "venini murano ITALIA," designed by Paolo Venini, ca. 1950.....................**2,530.00**

VICTORIAN COLORED GLASS

There are, of course, many types of colored glassware of the Victorian era and we cover a great variety of these in our various glass categories. However, there are some pieces of pressed, mold-blown and free-blown Victorian colored glass which don't fit well into other specific listings, so we have chosen to include a selection of them here.

Victorian Colored Bottles

Bottle w/original stopper,
tapering cylindrical body w/a
wide shoulder to a tall cylindrical
neck w/a flared rim, dark
sapphire blue enameled w/white
& yellow daisies & green stems
& leaves, olive amber teardrop
stopper, 3⅜" d., 8⅝" h.
(ILLUS. left) **$165.00**

Bottle w/original stopper, tall
slender waisted body below a
squatty bulbous shoulder
tapering to a short cylindrical
neck w/a flared & ruffled rim, line
green decorated around the
shoulder & down the sides
w/dainty pink strawberries,
green leaves & gold trim, clear
pointed stopper, 3¼" d., 11½" h.
(ILLUS. right) **135.00**

Cruet w/original stopper,
tapering conical optic-ribbed
body below a spherical optic-
ribbed shoulder tapering to a tall
cylindrical neck w/a high arched
spout, pale blue decorated
w/dainty pink & coral flowers,
applied reeded amber handle &
amber facet-cut stopper, 3½" d.,
9" h. **145.00**

Decanter w/original stopper,
flattened bulbous nearly
spherical optic-ribbed body w/a
short cylindrical neck & arched
spout, dark amethyst shaded to
clear body & ball stopper, clear
applied handle, 4¾" d., 8½" h. ..**175.00**

Lamp, candle-type, model of a
lighthouse, blue opaque,
6¼" h. **250.00**

Liqueur set: a ringed barrel-
shaped container w/a metal
spigot at one end supported in a
metal wire framework also
suspending six matching liqueur
cups; all in sapphire blue
decorated w/rust-colored
flowers, green leaves & gold
trim, keg 6½" d., 6½" h.,
the set **225.00**

Pitcher, tankard, 8½" h., Inverted
Thumbprint patt., cylindrical body,
clear twisted neck ring & handle,
sapphire blue **310.00**

Sugar shaker w/original lid,
tapered cylinder, Inverted
Thumbprint patt., amber **129.00**

Vase, 6½" h., cylindrical body,
sapphire blue, bird & floral
enameling **125.00**

Vase, 7⅞" h., 3⅜" d., footed
slightly flaring cylindrical body,
optic-ribbed amethyst decorated
on the exterior w/large creamy
white & yellow jonquils w/gold
stems & leaves **175.00**

Cobalt Blue Decorated Vase

Vase, 8¾" h., 4¼" d., a wide cushion foot supporting a tall bulbous ovoid body tapering to a short waisted cylindrical neck w/a flattened rim, cobalt blue decorated w/large sanded gold flying birds above white enameled grasses & foliage, two sanded gold cattails (ILLUS. bottom previous page)...............**110.00**

WAVE CREST

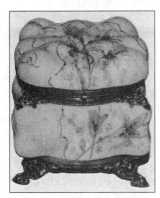

Ornate Wave Crest Box

Now much sought after, Wave Crest was produced by the C.F. Monroe Co., Meriden, Connecticut, in the late 19th and early 20th centuries from opaque white glass blown into molds.

It was then hand-decorated in enamels and metal trim was often added. Boudoir accessories such as jewel boxes, hair receivers, etc., were predominant.

WAVE CREST WARE

Wave Crest Mark

Ash receiver, squared body w/slight ribbing, floral decoration on a creamy white background, applied gilt metal rim band, pierced handles, 5" d..............**$495.00**

Bonbon, cov., Rococo mold, metal rim & twisted bail handle, 8" d. **925.00**

Box w/hinged lid, Hexagonal mold w/applied pink ceramic flowers surrounded by green leaves on light green background, 4½" d. **1,250.00**

Box w/hinged lid, Shell mold, blue w/pink flowers on cover, 4½" d., 3" h..............................**310.00**

Box w/hinged cover, Helmschmeid Swirl mold, pale blue, h.p. flowers, 4½" d., 3" h...**350.00**

Box w/hinged cover, Baroque Shell mold, scene of Niagara Falls bordered by white enamel dots & blue forget-me-nots, cream background, 5¼" d. **790.00**

Box w/hinged lid, Egg Crate mold, enameled floral decoration on the lid & gilt "Collars & Cuffs" on side, 6½" w. **1,350.00**

Box w/hinged lid, Egg Crate mold, creamy ground w/lovely h.p. pink flowers, 6½" w.............**495.00**

Box w/hinged lid, Egg Crate mold, yellow lilies on white ground w/light blue panels, all trimmed w/lavender & gold enamel, 6¾" w., 6½" h. (ILLUS.) **1,570.00**

Broom holder, blue & lavender floral decoration on creamy white ground, ornate gilt-metal frame **1,220.00**

Card holder w/gilt metal insert, narrow upright rectangular form w/oblong scalloped side panels, pink floral decoration in scroll on creamy white background **450.00**

Cracker jar, cov., Egg Crate mold, twisted bail handle, hand-tinted flowers, 7⅜" w., 5" h. **370.00**

Cracker jar, cov., barrel-shaped, embossed Egg Crate mold, h.p. flowers w/robin blue ground, silver plate cover, rim & bail handle, overall 10¼" h...............**885.00**

Cracker jar, cov., barrel-shaped, satin finish w/fern decoration on pale yellow background, metal cover, rim & bail handle, 10½" to top of handle..............................**280.00**

Creamer & cov. sugar bowl, smooth body, squatty bulbous body decorated w/cupid amid floral scrolls, sugar w/silver plated rim, cover & twisted bail handle, ring finial, creamer w/silver plated rim & bail handle, pr. **475.00**

Creamer, Helmschmeid Swirl mold, mushroom garden decoration....................................**75.00**

Ewers, bulbous rounded melon-lobed body decorated w/yellow florals, top fitted w/tall metal arching forked spout & a large S-scroll handle, raised on tapering pedestal above a flaring scroll molded cast-metal footed base w/grotesque masks at each corner, pr. **650.00**

Ferner, low cylindrical body on narrow footed ring base w/gilt-metal rim insert, light overall scrolling w/h.p. green & brown fern leaves on shaded yellow ground **650.00**

Humidor w/hinged lid, cylindrical body w/scroll-embossed domed cover, floral decoration on blue & cream background, "Tobacco" across front, 5¼" h.. ....**575.00**

Jardiniere, bulbous body tapering to a short cylindrical rim w/gold lacy trim, body decorated w/h.p. mums & foliage...........................**850.00**

Match holder, decorated w/flowers & beading on top & bottom, four gilt-metal ornate feet **195.00**

Photo receiver, Egg Crate mold, upright rectangular form, floral decoration on creamy white background w/gilt-metal rim on a gilt-metal footed base **525.00**

Ring box, cov., green ground, transfer portrait of woman on lid w/white background, 2" d., 2½" h. **960.00**

Salt shaker w/original lid, Scroll Wave mold, pink to white w/blue flowers, ...**75.00**

Spooner, paneled cylindrical-shape w/silver plate rim & handles, decorated w/floral transfers **285.00**

Sugar bowl, cov., Helmschmeid Swirl mold, silver plate cover & two-handled rim, decorated w/flowers & three mushrooms on each side, unsigned **175.00**

Sugar shaker w/original top, Helmschmeid Swirl mold, panels alternate w/blue scrolls & yellow flowers **485.00**

Syrup jug, cov., Ribbed Skirt mold, h.p. blue florals, tall..........**165.00**

Toothpick holder, h.p. yellow daisies, footed ormolu frame, Red Banner mark **275.00**

Vase, 5¾" h., slender baluster-form w/ovoid body & tall slender flaring cylindrical neck, fitted w/gilt-medal rim & shoulder bands, joined by openwork scrolling handles raised on short pedestal above domed scrolled-cast metal base, decorated w/delicate florals on front...........**428.00**

Vase, 8" h., bottle-form, spherical footed body tapering to a tall stick neck w/flared rim, gilt-metal feet, dark green free-form lines, blue forget-me-nots & pink scrolls filled w/tiny white dots **495.00**

Vase, 12¼" h., footed tapering bulbous body, Rococo mold w/gilt-metal fittings, daisies in shaded rust background, olive green flare around bottom **1,850.00**

WEBB

This glass is made by Thomas Webb & Sons of Stourbridge, one of England's most prolific glasshouses. Numerous types of glass, including cameo, have been produced by this firm through the years. The company also produced various types of novelty and "art" glass during the late Victorian period. Also see in "Glass" BURMESE, ROSE BOWLS, and SATIN & MOTHER-OF-PEARL.

Cameo bowl, 6" d., 1½" h., shallow, blue cut to white w/a butterfly hovering over a branch laden with foxglove blossoms **$750.00**

Bowl, 5" d., 3⅝" h., squatty bulbous body w/a six-crimp rim, shaded brown satin decorated w/heavy gold blossoms, branches & a dragonfly, white interior, raised on gold reeded pointed legs **495.00**

Bowl, 5½ x 13¼", 7" h., oval foot supporting a long squatty bulbous body tapering to a upright ruffled rim w/pulled-down ends attached to the shoulder, shaded dark blue to white decorated w/an ornate scene of a silver & gold large butterfly among flowering leafy branches in silver & dotted gold **650.00**

Perfume, lay-down teardrop-shape, shaded blue mother-of-pearl Diamond Quilted patt., 5½" l. **575.00**

Small Decorated Webb Vase

Vase, 4¾" h., 4¼" d., footed squatty bulbous body w/a short flaring cylindrical neck, shaded

blue exterior decorated w/gilt-trimmed blue flowers & gold leafy branches (ILLUS. previous column) **175.00**

Vase, 7½" h., 2⅞" d., footed bottle-form, the ovoid body tapering to a tall slender 'stick' neck, glossy ivory opaque decorated w/long gold prunus blossoms & branches & gold berries & a bee down the sides, gilt rim & foot band **175.00**

Ornate Webb Burmese Vases

Vases, 12" h., Burmese, footed swelled cylindrical body w/a narrow shoulder to the wide, short neck, ornately enameled w/flowering vines & two birds in naturalistic colors, pr. (ILLUS.) **5,030.00**

WESTMORELAND

Westmoreland Cat on Lacy Base Dish

Westmoreland Specialty Company was founded in East Liverpool, Ohio in 1889 and relocated in 1890 to Grapeville, Pennsylvania where it remained until its closing in 1985.

During its early years Westmoreland specialized in glass food containers and novelties but by the turn of the century they had a large line of milk white items and clear tableware patterns. In 1925 the company name was shortened to The Westmoreland Glass Company and it was during that decade that more colored glasswares entered their line-up. When Victorian-style milk glass again became popular in the 1940s and 1950s, Westmoreland produced extensive amounts in several patterns which closely resemble late 19th century wares. These and their figural animal dishes in milk white and colors are widely collected today but buyers should not confuse them for the antique originals. Watch for Westmoreland's "WG" mark on some pieces. A majority of our listings are products from the 1940s through the 1970s. Earlier pieces will be indicated.

Westmoreland Marks

Animal covered dish, miniature, Hen on basket, blue head, milk white, 2" h. **$65.00**

Animal covered dish, Cat on lacy base, milk white, copied from antique original (ILLUS.) ...**100.00**

Animal covered dish, Dove in hand on lacy base, milk white, copied from antique original **155.00**

Animal covered dish, Mother Eagle on basket, milk white, copied from antique original **105.00**

Animal covered dish, Rooster, standing w/hand-painted accents, milk white, copied from antique original **50.00**

Appetizer set: three-part relish dish, round fruit cocktail & ladle; Paneled Grape patt., milk white, 9" d., 3 pcs.................................**55.00**

Banana bowl, bell-footed, Paneled Grape patt., milk white, 12" d. **125.00**

Bowl, cov., 7" h., square, flared-rim, footed, Beaded Grape patt., milk white.....................................**40.00**

Bowl, 9" d., belled, low footed, Doric patt., milk white **30.00**

Bowl, 9" d., 5½" h, oval, diamond-footed, English Hobnail patt., milk white.....................................**25.00**

Cake salver, pattern around top rim of plate, skirted foot, Paneled Grape patt., milk white, 10" d. **100.00**

Candleholder, handled, round, Paneled Grape patt., milk white, 5" h. **35.00**

Candlesticks, lace-edge, Doric patt., milk white, 4½" h., pr. **35.00**

Candlesticks, skirted bottom, Paneled Grape patt., milk white, 4" h., pr. **15.00**

Candlesticks, Wedding Bowl patt., milk white, 4½" h., pr. **45.00**

Candy dish, cov., barrel-shaped, low footed, Paneled Grape patt., milk white, 6½" h. **30.00**

Candy dish, cov., square-footed, English Hobnail, clear, 9" d. **35.00**

Cheese dish, cov., Old Quilt patt., milk white, 4½" d. **35.00**

Chocolate box, cov., Paneled Grape patt., milk white, 6½" d. **48.00**

Cocktail, Paneled Grape patt., blue opalescent **24.00**

Compote, 6" d., ruffled rim, footed, Paneled Grape patt., milk white....................................**40.00**

Cookie jar, cov., Maple Leaf (Bramble) patt., milk white, 8" d. **115.00**

Creamer & covered sugar bowl,
Paneled Grape patt., milk white,
large, pr. **50.00**

Cruet w/original stopper,
Paneled Grape patt., milk white,
2 oz...**40.00**

Cup & saucer, English Hobnail
patt., milk white...........................**14.00**

Cup & saucer, Old Quilt patt.,
milk white.....................................**38.00**

Cup, Beaded Edge patt. w/fruit
decoration No. 64-2.....................**11.00**

Epergne, one-lily, lipped-edge
bowl w/ 8½" h. lily vase, Paneled
Grape patt., milk white, 9" d. **180.00**

Goblet, water, Della Robbia patt.,
milk white, trimmed in gold,
8 oz...**18.00**

Goblet, water, footed, Old Quilt
patt., milk white, 8 oz. **19.00**

Honey dish, cov., low-footed,
square, Old Quilt patt., milk
white **28.00**

Ivy ball, square, footed, English
Hobnail patt., 6½" h. **28.00**

Mayonnaise dish, bell-rimed,
footed, Paneled Grape patt.,
milk white, 4" d. **25.00**

Mayonnaise set: round fruit
cocktail, saucer & ladle; Paneled
Grape patt., milk white, 3½" d.,
3 pcs. **30.00**

Nappy, round, footed, Old Quilt
patt., milk white, 4½" d. **30.00**

Nappy, round, Paneled Grape
patt., milk white, 4½" d. **22.00**

Nappy, bell-shaped, footed, Old
Quilt patt., milk white, 5½" d. **30.00**

Nut bowl, oval, Paneled Grape
patt., milk white, 6" l.....................**25.00**

Perfume bottle w/stopper, flat,
Paneled Grape patt., milk white,
5 oz...**50.00**

Pickle dish, oval, English Hobnail
patt., milk white, 8" d. **13.00**

Pitcher, Old Quilt patt., milk
white, pt. **30.00**

Planter, oblong, Paneled Grape
patt., milk white, 5" x 9" **35.00**

Plate, bread & butter, 6" d., Old
Quilt patt., milk white **30.00**

Plate, salad, 7" d., Beaded Edge
patt. No. 64-2 fruit decoration on
milk glass.....................................**12.00**

Plate, 8½" d. Old Quilt patt., milk
white **40.00**

Plate, 10½" d., Old Quilt patt.,
milk white......................................**75.00**

Puff box, cov., square, Beaded
Grape patt., milk white, 4" w........**25.00**

Punch set: 13" d. belled eight-
quart punch bowl, skirted
pedestal base, twelve punch
cups & ladle; Paneled Grape
patt., milk white, 15 pcs. **595.00**

Salt & pepper shakers, footed,
English Hobnail patt., milk white,
pr. **24.00**

Sherbet, tall, American Hobnail,
milk white.....................................**10.00**

Snack server, center-handled,
two-tier, Paneled Grape patt.,
milk white, base 10½" d..............**75.00**

Tumbler, iced-tea, flat, Old Quilt
patt., milk white 11 oz. **30.00**

Tumbler, iced-tea, footed, Della
Robbia patt., milk white, 11 oz. ...**18.00**

Tumbler, juice, Paneled Grape
patt., milk white, 5 oz. **30.00**

Vase, 7½" h., Lily of the Valley
patt. **15.00**

Vase, 9" h., bell-rimmed, footed,
Old Quilt patt., milk white.............**55.00**

Vase, 9½" h., straight-sided,
footed, Paneled Grape patt.,
milk white......................................**25.00**

Vase, 12" h., swung-type, flat,
English Hobnail patt., milk white..**25.00**

Vase, 15" h., swung-type, flat,
Paneled Grape patt., milk
white, ...**45.00**

Wedding bowl, cov., Wedding
Bowl patt., milk white, 8" w. **35.00**

Wine, Della Robbia patt., milk
white, 4⅝" h.................................**18.00**

GLOBE MAPS

J.Wilson Celestial Globe

Celestial globe, table model, lithographed paper globe, grass meridians, walnut stand, J. Wilson and Sons, Albany, New York, 1851, imperfections, 18" h. (ILLUS.) **$2,185.00**

Celestial globe, floor model, the globe set within flat brass rings & raised on an ebonized socle w/a stepped foot, signed "A. Bouvard, Astronome Par CH. Dien 1853," Louis Philippe period, France, 23½" h. (minor damages to parchment globe) **4,600.00**

American 1850s Terrestrial Globe

Terrestrial globe, table model, the globe set within a wooden medial ring & raised on a scrolled cast-iron three-legged base, marked "Franklin," by Merriam, Moore & Co., Troy, New York, ca. 1852, globe 6" d. (ILLUS.) **2,415.00**

Terrestrial globe, floor model, the globe raised on a baluster-shaped stem supported by three cast-iron foliate scrolled legs, w/a cartouche inscribed "S. Chedlers Terrestrial Globe, Jersey City, New Jersey copywrited (sic) 1889," globe 8" d., overall 40¼" h. (restorations) **1,380.00**

Victorian Terrestrial Globe

Terrestrial globe, floor model, the globe fitted within wooden rings & raised on three canted slender swelled ebonized legs ending in double-knob feet, ca. 1880, restorations, globe 22" d., overall 42" h. (ILLUS.) **7,475.00**

Terrestrial & Celestial globes, floor models, w/the Cary's mark, the terrestrial globe corrected to 1827, the celestial to 1800, each set within wooden rings & raised on foliate-carved turned legs joined by turned cross-stretchers, ca. 1830, each globe 12" d., height to meridian 18" h., pr. (ILLUS. top next page) **4,140.00**

Cary's Terrestrial & Celestial Globes

GRANITEWARE

This is a name given to metal (customarily iron) kitchenware covered with an enamel coating. Featured at the 1876 Philadelphia Centennial Exposition, it became quite popular for it was lightweight, attractive, and easy to clean. Although it was made in huge quantities and is still produced, it has caught the attention of a younger generation of collectors and prices have steadily risen over the past few years. There continues to be a constant demand for the wide variety of these utilitarian articles turned out earlier in this century and rare forms now command high prices.

BLUE & WHITE SWIRL

Blue Swirl Coffee Biggin

Baking pan, wire handles, 8¼" w,
12" 1½" depth **$175.00**

Bowl, mixing, 10"d.,3½" h **100.00**

Bread raiser, tin cov., footed,
16" d., 9½" h **475.00**

Coffee biggin, tin biggin &
cover, 4" d., 9" h., (ILLUS.) **800.00**

Colander, footed, 9½" d., 7¾" h... **250.00**

Cream can, tin cov., 6½", 11" h... **425.00**

Dipper, windsor, 6¼" d., 6¼"
handle **120.00**

Bulbous Shaped-Funnel

Funnel, bulbous shape, 4½"d,
3½" h. (ILLUS.) **190.00**

Ladle, soup, 3½"d, 10½" handle ... **75.00**

Muffin pan, Columbian Ware,
8 cup **1,200.00**

Mug, 3½" d, 3" h. **60.00**

Pail, water, 11½" d., 9" h. **150.00**

Pie pan, 10¾" d., 1¼" h **60.00**

Pitcher, 9" h., 6" d., water, ... **275.00**

Salt Box with Wooden Cover

Salt box, wooden cover, marked
"Sel." 6" d., 9¾" h. (ILLUS.) **500.00**

Soup bowl, white interior, 9¼" d.,
1½" h. **150.00**

Strainer, 7¾" d., 5½" handle **225.00**

Teapot, tin cov., bulbous, 5" d,
5" h., ...**275.00**

Wash basin, 13¾" d., 3¾" h **100.00**

BLUE DIAMOND WARE
(Iris Blue & White Swirl)

Diamond Ware Measuring Cup

Berry bucket, cov., 5" d., 5½" h...**400.00**

Bowl, mixing, 5" d., 2" h. **75.00**

Coffee boiler, cov., 9½" d., 12" h ..**300.00**

Cream can, 5" d., 9" h. **575.00**

Kettle, cov. Berlin-style, 8¼" d.,
7" h. **200.00**

Measuring cup, 3" d., 4½" h.
(ILLUS.) **625.00**

Mug, miner's, 6" d., 4¾" h. **225.00**

Roaster, cov., oval, flat top,
17½" w., 7½" h., 11¾" depth **250.00**

Soup bowl, white interior, 9¼" d.,
1½" h. **165.00**

Bulbous Teapot

Teapot, cov., bulbous body
5½" d., 6" h. (ILLUS.).................**700.00**

BROWN & WHITE SWIRL

Berry bucket, cov., wood & wire
handle, 10½" d., 11½" h **400.00**

Coffeepot, cov., goose neck,
5½" d., 9½" h **425.00**

Dish pan, oval, 14" w., 17¾" l.,
7" h..**280.00**

Measuring cup, 4" d., 6¼" h **425.00**

Roaster, cov., round, 12" d.,
8½" h **300.00**

Hanging Soap Dish and Insert

Soap dish, hanging, w/insert, 6"
w., 3¼" h., 4¼" depth, 3 pcs.
(ILLUS.) **240.00**

Brown Swirl Spooner

Spooner, 4" d., 5¼" h. (ILLUS.)..**1,100.00**

Sugar bowl, cov., 4¼" d., 6 "h **900.00**

CHRYSOLITE & WHITE SWIRL
(Dark Green & White Swirl)

Bowl, mixing, 10" d., 4" h. **125.00**

Butter churn, granite storage
cover, 10¼" d., 19" h **2,000.00**

Cream can, tin cov., 5" d., 9½" h ..**550.00**

Green & White Swirl Cup & Saucer

Cup & saucer, 4" d., 2"h. cup, 6" d. saucer (ILLUS.) **125.00**

Lunch bucket, oval, 9" w., 7" h., 6¾" d...**1,100.00**

Plate, 9" d., ¾" h..........................**125.00**

Skimmer, 4¾" d., 11" handle **200.00**

Chrysolite Tea Steeper

Tea steeper, cov., 4¼" d., 5" h. (ILLUS.) **400.00**

COBALT BLUE & WHITE SWIRL

Chamber pail, cov., 10¾" d., 12"h **300.00**

Coffeepot, cov., wooden handle, 5¾" d., 9½" h. (ILLUS. top next column)....................................**350.00**

Creamer, 3½" d., 5" h..................**875.00**

Double boiler, cov., 6¾" d., 8" h., 3 pcs......................................**400.00**

Grocer's scoop, 6½" w., 13½" l., 2¼" depth **400.00**

Coffeepot with Wooden Handle

Muffin pan, 9 cup **1,000.00**

Pitcher, water 10" h., 7¼" d. **750.00**

Sauce pan, lipped, 6" d., 3" h., 6" handle **95.00**

Soup bowl, 9" d., 1½" h. **150.00**

Spoon, 2½" d., 11½" l **125.00**

Teapot, cov., bulbous body, 4½" d., 6" h. **1,000.00**

Wash basin, 12¾" d., 3½" h. **125.00**

EMERALD WARE
(Green & White Swirl)

Cream can, cov., wood & wire handle, 5" d., 9¼" h. (ILLUS. top next page) **850.00**

Jelly roll pan, 9" d., 1¼" h **100.00**

Lunch bucket, round, 7¼" d., 10" h., 3 pcs...........................**1,100.00**

Emerald Ware Cream Can

Molasses pitcher, cov., 3½" d.,
6" h **1,100.00**

Sauce pan, cov., Berlin-style,
9" d., 6½" h **250.00**

Teakettle, cov., 9" d., 7½" h **600.00**

Wash basin, 11" d., 3" h **125.00**

RED & WHITE SWIRL

Red Swirl Coffeepot

Baking pan, 10¼" w., 15¼" l.,
2¼" depth **2,000.00**

Chamber pot, 9" d., 5" h **1,800.00**

Coffeepot, cov., goose neck,
unattached cover, light weight,
ca. 1960s, 5" d., 8" h. (ILLUS.)..**100.00**

Cup & saucer, 4¼" d., 2¼" h.
cup, 6" d. saucer......................**800.00**

Mug, miner's, 6¼" d., 5" h **800.00**

Plate, swirl inside & out light
weight, ca. 1950s to 1960s,
10¼" d., 1" h **30.00**

Sauce pan, wooden handle, swirl
inside & out, light weight, ca.
1950s, 13" w., 17½" l., 1¼"
depth **140.00**

GRAY (Mottled)

Biscuit Cutter

Biscut cutter, 3½" d., 2¼" h.
(ILLUS.) **550.00**

Butter carrier, cov., oval w/strap
handle, 8" w. 6½" h., 6" depth......**250.00**

Candlestick, 6¼" d., 2" h **280.00**

Coffee flask, cov., round
w/screw-on cover, 4¾" d., 5" h..**475.00**

Coffeepot, cov., 7½" d., 11¼" h....**75.00**

Colander, footed, 10½" d., 4" h.....**75.00**

Cream can, tin cov., 5¼" d., 9"h..**110.00**

Cuspidor, 7¼" d., 3¾" h..............**120.00**

Grater, 4½" w., 11"h **200.00**

Match holder, double pocket,
3¾" d., 4" h..............................**550.00**

Molasses pitcher, cov., 4" d.,
6" h. **225.00**

Mold, oval fluted w/corn design,
4¾" w., 6" l., 2½" h. (ILLUS. top
next column) **180.00**

Plate, dinner, 9½" d. **30.00**

Platter, oval, 8½" w., 13" l,
1¼" depth **100.00**

Scoop, thumb, 2¾" w., 4½" l **140.00**

Skimmer, hand, 5" w., 5¼" l........**200.00**

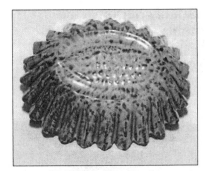

Mold with Corn Design

Pewter Trimmed Sugar Bowl

Sugar bowl, cov., pewter
scalloped rim, pewter cover &
trim, 5" d., 8" h. (ILLUS.)............**375.00**

SOLID COLORS

Berry bucket, cov., cream
w/green trim, 4½" d., 5" h **70.00**

Butter churn, cov., solid blue,
9½" d., 18" h............................**800.00**

Candlestick, cream w/green trim,
6½" d., 1½" h..............................**95.00**

Coffeepot, cov., cream w/green
trim, 5½" d., 7¾" h......................**50.00**

Colander, footed, solid yellow
w/black trim, 10" d., 5 "h..............**35.00**

Cup & saucer, cream w/green
trim, 4½" d., 2¼ h., 6" saucer **55.00**

Double boiler, cov., red w/black
trim, 6" d., 7½" h., 3 pcs **55.00**

Dust pan, solid red, 10½" w.,
13¼" h.....................................**200.00**

Ladle, white w/black trim &
handle, 3" d., 9" handle **30.00**

Blue Hanging Bracket Lamp

Lamp, hanging bracket lamp w/tin
reflector solid blue, 5½" d.,
10½" h. (ILLUS.)......................**225.00**

Mold, white, oval, fluted melon
shape, 7½" w., 11¼" l., 3¼"
depth **95.00**

Pail, water, cream w/green trim,
10½" d., 9¼" h............................**60.00**

Pie pan, solid red, 9" d.,
1¼" h **25.00**

Platter, 10" w., 14" l., 1" depth,
oval, cream w/green trim **20.00**

Salt box, cov., hanging, solid red,
white lettering, wood cover,
5¾" d., 8" h **150.00**

Skillet, white w/cobalt blue trim,
6" d., 5" handle **45.00**

Strainer, triangular sink, yellow
w/black trim, 10¾" d., 3½" h. **35.00**

Tumbler, solid blue w/black trim,
3¼" d., 4¼" h. **65.00**

Wash basin, cream w/green trim,
12" d., 3¼" h **50.00**

CHILDREN'S ITEMS, MINIATURES & SALESMAN'S SAMPLES

Bowl, child's feeding, cream w/green trim "Dickory Dickory Dock," 8" d. **40.00**

Egg pan, miniature, blue w/white specks, 5 eyes & handle, 2½" d., ½" h. **150.00**

Funnel, miniature, solid blue, marked Germany, 1¾" d., 2¼" h. **60.00**

Mold, miniature, solid blue, Turk's head, 2¼" d., 1"h. **200.00**

Mug, child's, red w/white interior, "Little Jack Horner," marked Sweden, 3" d., 3" h. **35.00**

Pail, water, miniature, solid blue w/bail handle, 2¾" d., 2¼" h. **125.00**

Roaster, salesman's sample, oval, blue & white mottled, w/insert, marked "LISK," 4" w., 5¾" l., 2½" h. **1,000.00**

Spatula, miniature, blue w/white specks, perforated, 1¾" w., 5½" l. **100.00**

Miniature Blue Teakettle

Teakettle, cov., miniature, blue, w/lid, bell-shaped, 3" d., 2½" h. (ILLUS.) **400.00**

Tea set, miniature: cov. teapot, four cups, four saucers, creamer, open sugar; white w/red floral & leaf design, teapot 3¾" h., 13 pcs............................**450.00**

MISCELLANEOUS GRANITEWARE & RELATED ITEMS

Multicolored End of Day Teapot

Berry bucket, cov., Bluebell Ware, blue shading to lighter blue back to blue, 7¼" d., 7½" h. **150.00**

Bread raiser, tin cov., cobalt & white mottled, 17¼" d., 11" h.....**275.00**

Candlestick, "Snow on the Mountain," white w/light blue swirl, 5¼" d., 2¼" h. **300.00**

Colander, footed, blue & white mottled inside & out, 10" d., 3½" h. **160.00**

Creamer, Thistle Ware, deep violet shading to a light violet, 3¼" d., 5¼" h. **175.00**

Ladle, soup, Onyx Ware, brown & white mottled, 3½" d., 9½" handle..**35.00**

Molasses pitcher, Bluebelle Ware, blue shading to a lighter blue back to blue, 3½" d., 6" h...**250.00**

Roaster, Bonny Blue, white decorated w/a scalloped blue design, oval, 10" w., 15¼" l., 7½" h., 2 pcs.............................**150.00**

Strainer, triangular sink, blue & white mottled, 10"d., 2½" h........**300.00**

Teapot, cov., End of Day, multicolored, red, yellow, cobalt blue & black swirl, 4½" d., 4½" h. (ILLUS.) **475.00**

Tea strainer, blue & white mottled, screen bottom, 4½" d., 6¾" h. **155.00**

ICONS

Icon is the Latin word meaning likeness or image and is applied to small pictures meant to be hung on the iconostasis, a screen dividing the sanctuary from the main body of Eastern Orthodox churches. Examples may be found all over Europe. The Greek, Russian, and other Orthodox churches developed their own styles, but the Russian contribution to this form of art is considered outstanding.

Christ Pantocrator

Christ Pantocrator, the Saviour holding an open book of Gospels, Russia, 19th c., 12¼ x 14" (ILLUS.) **$1,035.00**

Hodigitria Mother of God, the elaborate frame carved & gilded w/foliage, Balkan-area, 18th c., 22 x 30" **2,530.00**

St. Nicholas, w/a repoussé & chased w/a border of Strapwork, contained within a giant kiot, Moscow, Russia, 1864, 10 x 12" **3,737.00**

The Virgin & Child Triptych, the wings painted w/Ss. George & Dmirtri, also w/two chosen saints, Greece, 18th c., 10¾ x 15⅜"...........................**2,415.00**

Vladimir Mother of God, the gilded silver oklad engraved w/a border of flowers & scrolling foliage, the robes sewn w/seed pearls, Moscow, Russia, 19th c., 10⅜ x 12¼ "............................**1,725.00**

INDIAN ARTIFACTS & JEWELRY

Indian Baby Wrap

Baby wrap, Northern Woodlands, black velvet body w/spot-stitch floral beading, leather lacing, muslin lining, 21" l. (ILLUS.) **$160.00**

Basket, Apache, oval, polychrome w/yucca root, martynia & willow, ca. 1910, 10½" x 14" (one rim stitch missing) **440.00**

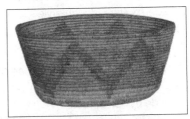

Jicarilla Apache Indian Basket

Basket, Jicarilla Apache, deep oval shape w/faded aniline red & green zig-zag design, slight wear on bottom, 19¼" l., 8½" h. (ILLUS.) **236.00**

Bow case, tanned leather case w/long fringe, yarn & horse hair decoration, black & white painted geometric design, 5" x 67" (stains & some minor damage) **138.00**

Bow, Lower Colorado River Indian design, yard binding at ends in cochineal red & dark indigo blue, painted geometric design red & black inside convex side, 41⅝" l. **224.00**

Bowl, Hopi, basketry w/yellow, brown & black coil design encircling body, 9" d., 4" h. **103.00**

Bowl, Isleta, pottery, umber & red ochre design over creamy white slip body, 7¼" d., 3¾" h. (overall minor spaling) **91.00**

Bowl, Laguna, pottery, dough-style, red ochre & umber on pale cream slip, ca. 1880-90, 8⅞" d., ⁴⁄₁₄" h. (wear & small rim chips) **853.00**

Bowl, Pima, basketry w/martynia & willow design, 5⅛" d., 3¾" h. ...**79.00**

Bowl, San Ildefonso, pottery, black design on polished redware w/tan back, ca. 1800s, 10⅝" d., 3⅝" h. (wear & smudging to rim)......................**495.00**

Bowl, Southwestern Anasazi, pottery, black & buff design on polished red interior, 4⅞" d., 2¼" h. (two 1" hairline cracks) **55.00**

Bowl, Zuni, pottery, dough-style, polychrome prayer-stick design, ca. 1880, marked "Valencia Co., N.M." on bottom, 14⅞" d., 6⅝" h. **1,045.00**

Buckle, silver w/turquoise & coral set, made by "Small Bear, Ponca," 3" x 6¼".....................**303.00**

Canteen, Acoma, pottery, umber avian design on white slip, ca. 1900s, 7½" d., 9" h. **193.00**

Canteen, Hopi, pottery, red ochre & umber on smoked creamy slip, 6" x 6", 4" h. **303.00**

Concho belt, Navaho, German silver stamped conchos w/turquoise blue center stones on black leather, 51" l. **515.00**

Concho belt, Navaho, oval & butterfly shaped, stamped nickel silver conchos set w/turquoise blue stones, includes buckle, 38" l. **484.00**

Dance rattle, Plains, green & yellow painted head, 12" l. (wear) **91.00**

Dance Ornament & Indian Moccasins

Dance ornament, Plains, hair-pipe bone, leather, brass bead design w/ribbon, beads & velvet, restrung, 24½" l., framed 18½" w. x 34" h. (ILLUS. center) **91.00**

Doll, Hopi, Kachina-type, simple painted figure w/ruff of fiber wrapped in string, wool & leather top, 9¾" h. **105.00**

Plains Indian Flageolet

Flageolet, Plains, marked "Lakota 1870" & "92," early 1900s, 21" l. (ILLUS.) **220.00**

Gloves, beaded blue, oranges & reds on cuffs & back of hand, elkhide, 14" l. **484.00**

Hand drum, Plains, painted blue, green & red depicting frizzy-haired man, thunderbird & Plains cross on one side, painted edge circle on reverse, 18½" d., 2½" h. **1,760.00**

Jar, Acoma, pottery, umber & red ochre geometric design over white slip, early 1900s, 9½" d., 8" h. **1,331.00**

Jar, Hopi, pottery, umber on polished orange body, signed w/corn emblem for Lena Chio, 6½" d., 6¼" h. (minor spaling) ...**272.00**

Jar, Southern California Cahullia, Agua Caliente basketry w/fine patina to juncos body, 10" d., 9" h. **295.00**

Jar, Taos, pottery, plain micaceous clay, 7⅛" d., 6¼" h. ...**55.00**

Knife w/sheath, Sioux, knife w/bone handle, sheath front w/lazy-stitch beaded in dark & medium blue, green yellow & translucent red w/white ground, 10" tassels ending in tin cones, sheath 9" l., knife 12½" l., 2 pcs. **105.00**

Ladle, Anasazi, pottery, black & grey, marked "Red Lake Ariz" on back w/illegible numbers, 3¾" x 6" **72.00**

Leggings, Sioux, women's, green, white-heart red & blue on white bead ground, 11¼ x 12 3/8" (replaced ties, leather wear & repair, missing rows of beads) **726.00**

Moccasins, Crow/Flathead, yellow ochre-stained leather, dark blue & red tradecloth, simple beading in green blues & white, 8" l. **309.00**

Moccasins, Pawnee, low-folded cuff beaded w/white edging, orange, blue & white strip, 9¼" l. **79.00**

Moccasins, Plains, leather w/multi-color mix beads, areas of cut-faceted metallic beads,

ca. 1920s, 9½" l. (ILLUS. right w/dance ornament)....................**151.00**

Moccasins, Sioux, beaded in green & white w/blue, yellow & white-heart pinks, orange & red trade cloth cuff, 10⅜" l. (leather damage, slight bead damage) ...**272.00**

Moccasins, Sioux, child's, sky blue, Cheyenne pink, white-heart red & yellow beads, sinew sewn, 6" l. (ILLUS. left w/dance ornament) **393.00**

Necklace, Navaho, coral & sterling silver, squash blossom design w/silver leaf encircling stones **339.00**

Painting, oil, depicts Saint Liberata on framed canvas, Mexico, 11⅝" w., 15½" h. **484.00**

Parfleche container, Plains, buffalo hide w/red, yellow & green geometric design w/red wool edge binding, 16" w., 14¼" h. **121.00**

Plateau pouch, Blackfoot, floral design in blue, yellow translucent maroon, white & green beads, 5" x 5½" **24.00**

Rifle case, Plains, red, blue, yellow & green geometric design, red wool binding w/long buckskin fringe, 43" l. **103.00**

Navaho Wool Rug

Rug, Navaho, deep red, dark brown & carded grey handspun wool w/fine sheen, ca. 1910-15, 4' 6" x 7" (ILLUS.) **526.00**

Rug, Navaho, serrate design
w/red, gold, grey black & natural
heavy wool, ca. 1950s,
3' 10" x 5' 9".............................**236.00**

Rug, Navaho, stepped terrace in
natural color w/unusual green
center, ca. 1925, 3' 3" x 4' 11"
(several small holes & wear at
one end) **454.00**

Rug, Navaho, West Reservation
design finely woven stripe, band
in gold, red, black, grey &
natural, 2' 10" x 6' **339.00**

Serape, striped w/long fringe,
Mexico, 4' 1" x 6' 10" **12.00**

Skull cracker, Plains, sinew
sewn orange, white-heart red,
dark blue, yellow, green & white
beads, 17" l. (slight bead loss) ..**260.00**

Trade ax, Norse-style hammer
poll & Osage orange haft,
8" w., 18" l................................**193.00**

Tobacco bag, Plains, twin-
shaped w/simple lazy stitch
bands in sky blue, dark blue,
white-heart red, metallic gold &
orangish white-heart red beads,
bottom fringe tabs, ca.
1890-1900, 13" l. **194.00**

Tomahawk, brass pipe-style,
handle set w/small brass tacks,
ca. early 1900s, 7" w., 13" l. **50.00**

Tray, Apache, basketry w/willow
& martynia star design, ca.
1900, 13⅞" d. **605.00**

Tray, Papago, basketry
w/stepped whirling fret design in
marynia & willow, 14" d., 3½" h.
(minor rim damage) **163.00**

Water jar, Acoma, pottery,
curvilinear design w/hatching in
umber over creamy white slip,
red-ochre bottle bottom, ca.
1900, 9¾" d., 5⅝" h. (small slip
chips, minor wear & scratches,
paint specks) **1,452.00**

Water jug, Santo Domingo, black
design on grey slip over red
ochre band, orangish-buff bottle
bottom, 10½" d., 10" h. (design
runs, minute wear, glaze hairline
cracks) **460.00**

Acoma Water Olla

Water olla, Acoma, pottery,
polychrome design, red ochre
birds, red ochre & umber
geometric design on creamy
white slip over concave red
ochre base, minute wear at rim,
10½" d., 10" h. (ILLUS.)..........**1,595.00**

Weaving, Navaho, corn & yei
figures in grey, black & red on
natural, ca. 1930, 16" x 33" **42.00**

Wedding jar, Acoma, pottery,
ochre & umber avian design on
white slip w/double spout, ca.
1930s, 5¾" d., 12" h. (roughness
& wear at spout tips).................**242.00**

JEWELRY

ANTIQUE (1800-1920)

Victorian Bar Pin

Bar pin, pearl & yellow gold
(18k), suspending alternating
conch pearl & rosette drops from
scalloped top, wire-twist &
beadwork, signed "Tiffany
& Co.," Victorian (ILLUS.) **$1,610.00**

Bar pin, ruby & diamond, alternately set w/square-cut rubies & rose-cut diamonds, set in 18k yellow gold, ca. 1920 ...**1,150.00**

Bar pin, yellow gold (18k), Japanese-style w/foliate overlay in platinum & green gold, signed "Tiffany & Co.," Victorian, (replaced pin stem)...................**575.00**

Bracelet, bangle-type, coral, rose & yellow gold (14k), hinged design, front set w/four coral beads, applied wire-twist & beadwork, flanked by black enamel geometric motifs, Victorian (minor crack to one bead) **978.00**

Bracelet, bangle-type, silver & green gold, hinged wide design, front w/rose & green gold foliate motifs & beaded edge, marked "Standard," Victorian **288.00**

Bracelet, bangle-type, yellow gold (14k), archeological style w/mythological animal head terminals w/wire-twist & beadwork, Etruscan Revival ...**3,105.00**

Bracelet, blue stones & yellow gold (14k), Arts & Crafts-style, composed of foliate links spaced by cabochon blue stones, hallmark for Evald Nielson, Denmark................................**1,093.00**

Bracelet, citrine & yellow gold (14k), openwork scrolling & foliate oval links alternately set w/citrine, enhanced w/beadwork, Victorian **978.00**

Bracelet, garnet, enamel & yellow gold (18k), composed of seven oval black enamel plaques w/scrolling gold centers, gold mounts w/French hallmarks & maker's mark "J.W.," possibly for Wiese, Victorian **1,610.00**

Bracelet, onyx & silver, Arts & Crafts-style in alternating rectangular plaque links set w/applied floral & acorn motifs in 14k yellow gold, attributed to Edward Oakes........................**1,610.00**

Bracelet, pearl & yellow gold (18k), braided mesh design, the front w/seed pearl buckle, Victorian **805.00**

Bracelet, sapphire & yellow gold (14k), Art Nouveau-style, composed of openwork scrolling links, round sapphire w/each collet-set, hallmark for Solace & Co. **1,265.00**

Brooch, amethyst & diamond, quatrefoil design centered by clipped-corner 16 x 14 mm amethyst in pierced diamond-set frame, platinum mount, fitted box marked "Jays of London," Edwardian **5,462.50**

Brooch, Art Nouveau-style w/flower in shades of pink & yellow enamel w/green leaves, attributed to Whiteside & Blank (minor enamel loss) **690.00**

Brooch, Art Nouveau-style, flower w/carved grossularite garnet blossoms centered by two diamonds on 18k yellow gold vine w/pave-set rose-cut diamonds, European hallmarks **1,380.00**

Brooch, coral & yellow gold (15k), designed as coral cabochon suspending a snake chain tassel, set in a wire-twist & beaded circular frame, reverse w/compartment, Victorian (minor wear) **1,380.00**

Brooch, demantoid garnet & diamond, harp & wreath motif, centered by harp w/green garnets, surrounded by wreath of diamond-set clovers, surmounted by enamel crown, platinum & 14K yellow mount, Edwardian (solder) **1,840.00**

Victorian Diamond Brooch

Brooch, diamond, bow-shaped w/prong-set & pave-set round diamonds, platinum mounts (ILLUS.) **23,000.00**

Brooch, garnet, pearl, diamond & yellow gold (14k), Art Nouveau-style, centered by oval abalone pearl within scrolling openwork frame, enhanced by collet-set green demantoid garnets & old mine-cut diamonds in gold, hallmarked, pearl measures 9/16 x 1¼" **1,265.00**

Brooch, gem-set, gold (14k yellow), woven basket w/flowers & sprays, set w/demantoid & hessonite garnets, seed pearls, diamonds, sapphire & ruby in platinum-topped gold mount, Edwardian (minor loss).............**575.00**

Etruscan Revival Brooch

Brooch, gold (18k yellow), applied scarab in reeded frame, suspending amphora & two drops, surmounted by rosette & two bird heads, overall wire-twist decoration, ca. 19th century, Etruscan Revival, signed "Carli for Antonio Carli," (ILLUS.) **2,760.00**

Brooch, malachite & enamel, cabochon malachite center flanked by falcon wings in shades of pink & green enamel, enhanced by pink stones, silver gilt mounting, Egyptian Revival......................................**518.00**

Brooch, porcelain, depicting double image of classical figures in rose-cut diamond foliate frame, suspending diamond & pearl drop in 18k rose gold mount, fitted Boucheron box (pin stem replaced)........................**3,910.00**

Brooch, scarf-type sapphire, diamond & yellow gold (18k), Art Nouveau-style, designed as falcon wings centering sapphire cabochon & rose-cut diamond, platinum accents **1,092.00**

Cameo brooch, coral, depicting Mercury in openwork foliate & beadwork frame, Victorian, (minor damage & solder to frame) **920.00**

Cameo brooch, hardstone, classical male in profile in applied wire-twist, 14k yellow gold frame (minor solder) **633.00**

Cameo Brooch

Cameo brooch, hardstone, front facial view of male w/wrinkled brow & open mouth, wire & bead frame flanked by scrolls in 14k yellow gold, fitted box (ILLUS.) **2,415.00**

Cameo brooch, onyx, classical female in profile in 18k yellow gold simple round frame, Victorian **920.00**

Chain, slide-type, pearl, enamel & yellow gold (14k), composed of beaded splayed circular links w/shield-shape slide, highlighted by seed pearls & black enamel tracery, swivel hook, Victorian, 62" l. **1,955.00**

Chain, textured oval trace link design w/turquoise-set beaded clasp, Georgian, 30" **1,265.00**

Cuff links, diamond & yellow gold (14k), Art Nouveau-style, designed as griffins, accented w/collet-set diamonds, pr. (some wear) **690.00**

Cuff links, enamel & yellow gold (14k), oblong octagonal-form w/reeded top & blue enamel edges, marked "Carrington and Company," pr............................**201.00**

Cuff links, mosaic, centered by beetle in circular frame in half-circle & triangular mosaic elements, 18k yellow gold mount, Italian hallmark, pr. **2,185.00**

Cuff links, ruby, sapphire & yellow gold (18k), double oval link design, front set w/circular ruby & sapphire, triangular-set accents, European hallmarks, Edwardian, pr. **230.00**

Earpendants, diamond, two sections set w/five collet-set diamonds, spaced by diamond leaves suspending collet-set diamond tassels, button pearl & diamond parts, platinum mount, Edwardian (ILLUS. bottom previous column) **6,900.00**

Earrings, diamond, plique-a-jour & yellow gold (18k), Art Nouveau-style, each suspending foliate drop in shades of purple & green enamel, kite-shape frame w/scrolling diamond accented cap, gold mount, signed "Masriera," pr. **2,875.00**

Locket, diamond & yellow gold (14k), Art Nouveau-style, circular locket depicting profile of mythological figure in repousse, accented by a round diamond, monogrammed on back.............**690.00**

Locket, yellow gold (14k) & enamel, Art Nouveau-style, repousse design depicting a woman in naturalistic setting, accented by small round diamond (minor dents) **518.00**

Necklace, coral & yellow gold (18k), suspending three carved angel-skin coral rose motif drops from beaded rosette links, completed by flexible mesh chain, Victorian..........................**988.00**

Edwardian Diamond Earpendants

Emerald & Gold Necklace

Necklace, emerald & gold,
pierced gold chain collet-set
w/foil back emeralds, bow &
pendoloque terminal, 14k & 18k,
17" l. (ILLUS. bottom previous
page) **2,530.00**

Necklace, garnet & yellow gold
(14k), composed of scrolling
chased links centering on
openwork plaque, highlighted by
garnet clusters & suspending
half-drops, Victorian (missing
center drop) **633.00**

Necklace, peridot & tourmaline,
designed as fringe of navette-
shape peridot alternating w/bar
drops, set w/oval pink tourmaline
flanked by circular blue stones,
suspended from yellow gold
(14k) fine link chain,
Edwardian **690.00**

Necklace, plique-a-jour, Art
Nouveau-style, composed of
flower & leaf links, shades of
green, blue & rose enamel in
silver mount, French hallmarks,
19½" l. **748.00**

Pendant, crystal & yellow gold
(18k), depicting bird in
naturalistic setting in polychrome
enamel, set within beaded frame
in platinum & gold, reverse
w/compartment, Victorian.......**1,610.00**

Pendant, pearl & yellow gold
(15k), Arts & Crafts-style,
centered by an oval turquoise
within an openwork free-form
frame suspending a collet-set
pearl **633.00**

Pendant, tassel-type, enamel &
yellow gold (18k), Arts & Crafts-
style, latticework cap w/blue &
peach marble enamel ground
w/foliate border, yellow gold
(14k) link chain w/bead & leaf
finials, attributed to Edward
Oakes, 32" l. (ILLUS. top next
column)...................................**3,450.00**

Pendant/brooch, pearl & yellow
gold (14k), Art Nouveau-style,
designed as cluster of

Arts & Crafts Pendant

Art Nouveau Pendant Brooch

freshwater pearls, enhanced by
blue stone cabochon eye,
suspending a freshwater pearl
drop, pendant loop (ILLUS.) **805.00**

Pin, diamond & yellow gold (14k),
cluster set w/round diamonds,
gold mount, Victorian..............**1,265.00**

Pin, porcelain, plaque w/putto,
14k yellow gold frame
suspended from 18k yellow gold
bar, both w/applied twists, beads
& scrolls (solder, minor repair)...**460.00**

Art Nouveau Pin

Pin, yellow gold (18k) & enamel, portrait in Art Nouveau-style, asymmetrical form w/female in profile, enamel face & background in shades green accented w/diamonds (ILLUS.) **1,093.00**

Pin, yellow gold (14k), Art Nouveau-style, shaped as feather w/textured openwork design set w/a cabochon opal, hallmark for Riker Bros. **317.00**

Ring, diamond, sapphire & yellow gold (18k), navette design set w/three round sapphires in frame of rose-cut diamonds, gold mount, Edwardian..............**460.00**

Ring, moonstone, measuring 12.50 mm, Arts & Crafts-style, shoulders set w/pearls & collet-set sapphires, foliate 18k yellow gold mount, attributed to Edward Oakes (some scratches to moonstone) **1,840.00**

Ring, mosaic yellow gold (18k), polychrome enamel depicting swan, set within foliate shoulders & completed by reeded shank, Victorian.............**748.00**

Ring, opal & yellow gold (14k), Arts & Crafts-style, pear-shaped black opal within a butterfly & foliate designed mount (crazing) **863.00**

Ring, sapphire, diamond & yellow gold (18k), designed as row of alternating sapphires & diamonds in navette shape mount, flanked by engraved shoulders, English hallmarks, Victorian **345.00**

Watch chain, yellow gold (14k), curb-link chain w/swivel hook & T-bar, Victorian, 14" l.................**345.00**

Watch chain, yellow gold (14k), link chain w/swivel hook & two 18k yellow gold cylindrical slides, engraved w/applied floral & red stone decoration, 67" l.....................**2,185.00**

SETS

Bar pin & earrings: turquoise, pearl & yellow gold (18k), comprising bar pin suspending channel-set turquoise circle & bead drops, enhanced by openwork scroll motifs & seed pearl accents, matching earrings, Victorian, the set (kidney wires in 14k gold)..........**489.00**

Brooch & ear pendants: 14k gold, brooch highlighted w/black enamel foliate tracery, beadwork & faceted pendant drop, matching ear pendants, Victorian, the set (solder, enamel loss) **374.00**

Brooch & earrings: amethyst & yellow gold (14k), comprising a brooch w/matching ear pendants, each set faceted circular amethyst in scrolling frame, enhanced by suspended geometric & foliate motif drops, Victorian, the set (minor solder) **978.00**

Necklace & ear pendants: peal drops suspended from tulip-form diamond tops, collet-set diamond knife edge platinum chain, matching ear pendants, Edwardian, the set (ILLUS. top next page) **19,550.00**

Edwardian Pearl Necklace &
Earpendants

MODERN (1920s - 1960s)

Bar pin, diamond, Art Deco-style, centering old mine-cut diamond, flanked by ten diamonds w/smaller diamond accents, platinum mount..........................**920.00**

Bracelet, diamond, Art Deco-style, alternating semi-circle links of 113 baguettes & 404 round diamonds, accented by 6 marquise diamonds, centered by 2-ct. emerald-cut diamond, platinum mount (missing one baguette) **20,700.00**

Art Deco Bracelet

Bracelet, diamond & emerald, Art Deco-style, geometric plaques set w/two square emeralds, each flanked by square-cut diamonds in pave-set diamond open links, platinum mounts (ILLUS.) **19,550.00**

Bracelet, diamond & sapphire, Art Deco-style, round diamonds & sapphires in platinum box-links, No. 18932.....................**3,335.00**

Brooch, amethyst & enamel, Art Deco-style, surrounded by seed pearls, framed by black, orange & green enamel in stylized foliate designs, pierced 14k yellow gold mount, amethyst measuring 23x18.50 mm (slight enamel abrasion).....................**575.00**

Brooch, silver, disc w/raised stylized dragon design, ca. 1940s, hallmarked & signed "Spratling, Mexico" **345.00**

Necklace, Egyptian Revival, pendant set w/amethyst scarab dating 1700 BC, flanked by vultures w/small carnelian sun disc, lotus blossom symbol of rebirth suspended from bark, cartouche marked "Tutankhamun," suspended from trace link chain w/semi-precious stone & gold beads in manner of Tut's jewels, 18k yellow gold mount, ca. 1925, in fitted box marked "Cairo," 18" l **3,680.00**

Pin, sterling silver, modeled as open blossom w/four wide ruffled petals, blue lapis button surrounded by tiny beading, impressed "Georg Jensen # 189 B - Sterling - Denmark," 1¼" d. **385.00**

Ring, diamond, jade & platinum, Art Deco-style, centered by oval jade, flanked by marquise diamonds, completed by channel-set diamond baguette shoulders, platinum mount **4,025.00**

Ring, diamond & onyx, Art Deco-style, onyx plaque accented by kite-shaped & round diamond, flanked by splayed diamond-set shoulder, platinum mount, signed "Tiffany & Co.".............**920.00**

Ring, jade & diamond, 15 x 11 mm oval jade button, diamond-set platinum lattice-work mount (ILLUS. top next page) **12,050.00**

Ring, peridot, diamond & platinum, Art Deco-style, pear-shaped peridot flanked by tapered baguette diamonds, signed "Cartier".....................**1,725.00**

Jade & Diamond Ring

the fashions from which it was made became passé, a great deal of costume jewelry has survived and is being avidly sought by collectors.

Instead of imitating precious jewelry designs, costume jewelry designs were original. Glass beads, plastic bracelets and gold-plated pins were all affordable in their time, and still are for the collector. No matter if costume jewelry has little or no intrinsic value, the enjoyment of its fine design and craftsmanship is the secret of its appeal.

Music Box Charm Bracelet

SETS

Brooch & earclips: yellow gold(18k) & ruby, flower w/serpent in petals centered by dome-set rubies, earclips, marked "Italy," the set **690.00**

Hair comb barrette & earrings: sterling silver & enamel, Art Deco-style, barrette designed w/blue enamel foliate motifs & black stripe accents, matching earrings, French hallmarks for David, the set **1,725.00**

Necklace & earclips: carved opal, earclips w/small round diamond centers, matching pendant, 14k gold fine link chain & findings, the set **575.00**

Necklace & bracelet: sterling silver, each composed of linked rectangular segments w/bead & linear decoration, designed by Hector Aguilar, Mexico, impressed marks, 7" & 15½" l., 2 pcs. **920.00**

COSTUME JEWELRY

The term Costume Jewelry refers to jewelry designs made of inexpensive, non-precious material. Originally made to complement designer's dress collections, it is today recognized as a combination of art, design and craftsmanship, and representative of the fashions and history of its time. Although it was meant to be discarded when

Bar pin, blue cloisonné enamel on copper w/floral design, 2¾" w.......................................**30.00**

Bar pin, gold-filled, key motif, 2⅝" w.......................................**55.00**

Bracelet, Bakelite bangle-style, moss green & black, wave motifs, ½" w. **85.00**

Bracelet, Bakelite bangle-style, green, oval cut-outs & applied brass leaves on carving on two sides, unusual, 1⅛" w...............**225.00**

Bracelet, hinged bangle-style, textured gold-plate horse head set w/rhinestones, closure w/ring inserts into mouth, signed "Castlecliff," ⅞" w......................**125.00**

Bracelet, hinged bangle-style, gold-plate ribbed design, signed "Ciner," ½" w..............................**40.00**

Bracelet, hinged bangle-style, textured gold-plate, signed "KJL," 2⅝" w. **175.00**

Bracelet, hinged bangle-style, brushed gold, crown-style front, tiny rhinestone flowers, signed "Joseph Mazer," ¾" w. **65.00**

Bracelet, hinged bangle-style, sterling silver, Art Nouveau-style, bamboo & bird design, ⅝" w. **125.00**

Bracelet, charm-type, music box charm on gold-plated chain bracelet, plays "Anniversary Waltz," signed "Holiday," mint condition in box (ILLUS.) **90.00**

Bracelet, charm-type, five gold-plated horse motif charms **30.00**

Bracelet, rhinestones, large links in clear rhinestones w/large oval red stone centers, clear & red stone accents, signed "Kramer," ⅞" w. **150.00**

Bracelet, tennis-style, white metal set w/large lavender rhinestones, ¼" w. **35.00**

Clip, Bakelite, black, highly carved raised leaves, 1⅝" h. **45.00**

Clip, rhinestone, Art Deco-style, square centers w/pave rhinestone trim, large red & green glass button ends, 2" w. **40.00**

Clip, rhinestone set w/overlapping scallops, Art Deco-style, 1½" h....**15.00**

Clip, rhinestone, topaz color, drop shape, Czechoslovakia, 2" h. **30.00**

Clips, Bakelite, yellow translucent w/brown inlaid Art Deco-style design, 2" h., pr. **75.00**

Clips, chatelaine-style, pink gold fur-type connected w/chains, rhinestone set keys applied to pink gold hearts, pr. **65.00**

Clips, duette, rhinestone openwork in an Art Deco design, Clip-Mates, old Trifari mark, 1½ x 2½" **125.00**

Clips, gold on sterling silver fur-type, flying bird design, pave

rhinestone set wings & upper bodies, Corocraft, 1¼ & 1½", pr............................**175.00**

Earrings, clip-on, gold-plate coil design, signed "Alva," 1⅜" d., pr. **30.00**

Earrings, clip-on, curved gold-plate hoops, Christian Dior, Germany, 1⅛", pr. **40.00**

Earrings, clip-on, elongated hoops, red, white & blue enamel, Trifari, 1", pr. **45.00**

Earrings, clip-on, rhinestone, large green stones, clear trim, fleur-de-lis shape, Eisenberg, 1⅛", pr. **75.00**

Earrings, ornate filigree tops, large amber-yellow crystals handing from chains, 1¾", pr.......**35.00**

Earrings, pearl ball drops on chains, ca. 1955, 1½" h., pr.........**35.00**

Earrings, rhinestones, large clear round & triangular stones, flower design, small rhinestone trim, Eisenberg, 1" d., pr.....................**65.00**

Earrings, screw-on crystal drops, large yellow pear-shape, ca. 1925, 2", pr. **45.00**

Earrings, screw-on, textured gold-plate hoops, Monet, ¾" d., pr. **35.00**

Earrings, white glass drop, large hanging bead, ca. 1955 1", pr. **30.00**

Necklace, bib-style, six rows of gold-plate half-circles, Matisse **35.00**

Necklace, blue enamel on chrome, blue Bakelite & chrome cylindrical drop, Art Deco-style, 20" l. **40.00**

Necklace, brass flat chain, center-carved carnelian stone, four yellow, black & orange enamel Chinese writing designs alternating w/two smaller carnelian stones, Art Deco-style, 1930s, short length (ILLUS. top next page) **75.00**

Art Deco-Style Necklace

Necklace, collar-style, fringes of tiny beads, blue iridescent glass, turquoise, clear **85.00**

Necklace, copper, turquoise enamel links, Matisse, short **60.00**

Necklace, enamel on sterling silver orchid, pastel colors, freshwater pearl center, sterling silver chain, Art Nouveau-style, 24" l. **150.00**

Necklace, gold collar-type, ancient Egyptian-style, sighed "BSK," 1½" w. **50.00**

Necklace, gold-plate snakechain, rhinestone-set acorn & leaves, Coro..**45.00**

Necklace, graduated clear crystal beads strung on chain, ca. 1930, 16½" l............................**45.00**

Necklace, green Peking glass beads strung on chain, graduated, ca. 1935, short **30.00**

Necklace, grey pearls, matching grey enamel head of wildcat center, rhinestone trim, signed "KJL" for Avon, 18½" l. **95.00**

Necklace, monkey design, gold-plated, each connected w/triple chains, Judith Leiber, 44" l. **150.00**

Necklace, multi-chain w/apple green large twist glass beads, adjustable, signed "Kramer" **40.00**

Necklace, ornate pendant on large gold-plate chain, large turquoise stone design, Hattie Carnegie Exclusive Italy, 28" l.................................**100.00**

Necklace, pressed amber breads, graduated, yellow & brown, 29" l.................................**85.00**

Necklace, rhinestone, blue, amber & citrine w/large raised center amber stone, Weiss, short **65.00**

Trifari Aquamarine Rhinestone Necklace

Necklace, rhinestone, faux aquamarine squares alternating w/chrome square, Trifari design, short (ILLUS.) **90.00**

Necklace, sterling silver w/three cabochon bluish-black gemstones in ornate marcasite settings, ca. 1935, short **150.00**

Necklace, sterling silver w/leaves & flower links, signed "Cini" & "Black, Starr & Gorham," 17" l. ...**275.00**

Necklace, V-shaped bibbed rows of crystal & black beads, Art Deco-style, ca. 1935, short..........**55.00**

Pin, black Bakelite, highly carved raised flowers w/leaves set in gold-plated metal, twist frame, 2⅜" **150.00**

Pin, brass, enameled turquoise butterfly motif watch pin, 1" w......**55.00**

Pin, brass, head bearded man wearing turban, signed "Joseph Hollywood," 2" **175.00**

Pin, celluloid, Dutch girl motif w/hanging basket, 2⅛" **55.00**

Pin, chatelaine-type, silver plated shells connected by double chains, hanging charms at each shell **95.00**

Pin, gold-plated crown set w/pearls & grey rhinestones, signed "DeNicola," 2" w. **110.00**

Pin, gold-plated rooster, ornate cut-out fancy metalwork tail feathers, signed "Janmax 1971," 3¼" h. **75.00**

Pin, gold-plated large openwork butterfly, pearl trim, sighed "Jeanne," 4½" w., 3½" h. **115.00**

Pin, enamel on sterling sliver multi-color abstract design, signed "Balle," 1¾ x 4¼" **75.00**

Art Nouveau Sash Pin

Pin, enamel on sterling silver, Art Nouveau-style, red w/green leaf center, green trim, 2¼" (ILLUS.) **165.00**

Pin, enameled daisy style, ca. 1955, 1½" d. **30.00**

Pin, enameled, "Socks the Cat" style, black white, rhinestone collar, original pouch, signed "Carolee," 1½" h. **45.00**

Trifari Enamel Bow-Style Pin

Pin, enameled white bow-style, signed "Trifari," 3" w. (ILLUS. bottom previous column) **40.00**

Pin, intaglio-cut classic face in brown marbleized glass, gold crown top, drop of six chains w/faux coins, signed "Florenza," 3½" h. **45.00**

Pin, rhinestone pale blue baguettes, marquise, Retro-style ribbon design w/two pear-shaped drops, Corocraft, 1½ x 2" **50.00**

Pin, rhinestone, three-dimensional design, square, marquise oval cabochon stones in lavender shades, signed "Schreiner," 2¼" d. **175.00**

Pin, Russian silver, dome center w/bar across opening, twists & beaded ball design, hallmarked, 2½" d. **295.00**

Pin, shell cameo, "Three Graces" design, sterling frame w/marcasites, hallmarked, 1¼" **150.00**

Pin, sterling silver, gold-plated snowflake design w/blue & clear rhinestones, Coro, 1¾" d. **75.00**

Pin, sterling silver, three-dimensional design, gold-plated flower over leaf w/realistic details, Napier, 2½" h. **70.00**

Pin, sterling silver, gold-plated Retro-style flower designs w/pink & blue crystals, Boucher, 2½" **250.00**

Pin, sterling silver, grapes inside ball frame, signed "McClelland Barclay," 1½" **200.00**

Pin, sterling silver, grinning man holding three hanging keys, ca. 1940, 3" h. **95.00**

Pin, sterling silver, inlaid Aztec influenced Art Deco design w/green stone background, five matching drops, Mexico, signed "B" **195.00**

Pin, sterling silver, scallop shell design w/flying bird inside, large real pearl, 1 x 1½" **110.00**

Pin, white metal, three dimensional design, orchid motif set w/grey & clear rhinestones, signed "Reinad, 4" (ILLUS.).......**150.00**

SETS

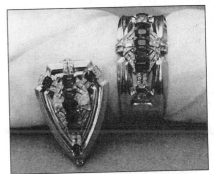

Art Deco-Style Clip & Bracelet

Flower & Leaf Cini Pin

Pin, sterling silver, spray of flowers & leaves w/bow at base, signed "Gugliermo Cini," 3⅝" h. (ILLUS.)..........................**250.00**

Pin, sword w/chain on inside scabbard design, signed " Manrey," sword can be removed, 3½" h. **95.00**

Bracelet & clip: blue emerald-cut rhinestones & clear trim on gold-plate, Art Deco-style, shield-shaped clip, hinged bangle bracelet, signed "McClelland Barclay," clip 2½" h., bracelet 1¼" w., set (ILLUS.) **495.00**

Bracelet & ring combination: brass filigree flowers, green stone centers, extended flower on chain leading to ring, ca 1925, set....................................**65.00**

Reinad Rhinestone Orchid Pin

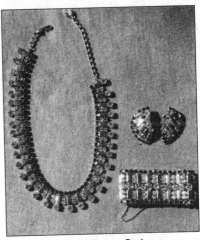

Hobe Retro-Style Topaz & Rhinestone Set

Bracelet, earrings & necklace: collar-style necklace w/gold bars alternating w/two large clear rhinestones, larger citrine colored stones form lower border, row of amber stones on inside collar, top & bottom of bracelet, Retro-style, signed "Hobe," bracelet 1⅜" w., clip earrings 1½", the set (ILLUS. bottom previous page)..............**375.00**

Earrings & ring: pave-set rhinestones in a raised gold-plate oval design, signed "Kenneth Lane," 1" clip earrings, small size matching ring, the set..**65.00**

Necklace & earrings: green glass "jade" in gold rhinestone-set design pendant, green beads, matching clip earrings, signed "Kramer," necklace 24" l., earrings ¾", the set **85.00**

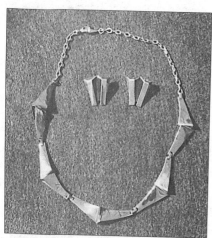

Renoir Copper Necklace & Earring Set

Necklace & earrings: copper, three-dimensional design, Retro-style, signed "Renoir," ca. 1950s, the set (ILLUS.) **65.00**

Pin & earrings: rhinestone baguette-set flowers & coiled ribbon design, citrine color, Retro-style, signed "Corocraft," the set..**80.00**

Pin & earrings: rhinestone-set butterfly pin, four trembling wings on springs, white, topaz & citrine colors, signed "Schreiner, pin 2", clip earrings 1½", the set......................................**275.00**

Pin & earrings: pave-set red Aurora Borealis stones, umbrella design, pin 3½", clip earrings 1¾", the set **60.00**

Pin, fur clip, earrings & cuff bracelet: copper, three-leaf design, Rebajes, the set...........**165.00**

KITCHENWARES

Also see: METALS

Spongeware Bowl

Apple corer, tin T-shaped..........**$18.00**

Apple parer, Reading "78" turntable **75.00**

Bake board, tin, S-curved bottom to hold pin................................**295.00**

Bowl, blue painted rim w/white interior, exterior blue & white sponge-painted, w/short foot, unmarked (ILLUS.) **350.00**

Can opener, aluminum w/steel blade, marked "MARVEL" (ILLUS. bottom next page, No. 2)..**65.00**

Can opener, cast iron, adjustable clamp-on style, Blue Streak (ILLUS. bottom next page, No. 1 ....**85.00**

Can opener, cast iron, adjustable, unmarked (ILLUS. bottom next page, No. 3)............**60.00**

Can opener, cast iron, adjustable, marked "WORLD'S BEST, DILLSBURG, PA," (ILLUS. below, No. 4) **40.00**

Can opener, cast iron, "DELMONICO, PAT FEB 11 1898" (ILLUS. below, No. 7) **30.00**

Can opener, steel, marked "USE BAKER'S COAL, F.H. BAKER, MT. JOY, PA" (ILLUS. below, No. 5) **35.00**

Can opener, cast iron, Never Slip, "PAT MAY 17, 92," available (ILLUS., No. 6) **25.00**

Can opener, wooden handle, marked cap lifter & can opener, (ILLUS., No. 8) **5.00**

Cookie sheet, tin, marked "Kreamer" **25.00**

Cornstick pan, aluminum "Griswold," No. 803, in original carton **25.00**

Cottage cheese mill, wooden dovetailed box covered w/mesh, iron turn handle & wood

cylinder, marked "The Star," 5 ¾" sq. **155.00**

Metal Dish Drainer

Dish drainer, tin & wire, (ILLUS.) **50.00**

Flour sifter, electric, plug-in, marked "Miracle" in original box...**35.00**

Fork ejector, wood handle, push top projection to eject **65.00**

Fly swatter, wire handle & wire mesh w/three protrusions to keep fly from hitting against wall **40.00**

Grater, tin, primitive hand-punched semi-circle mounted on

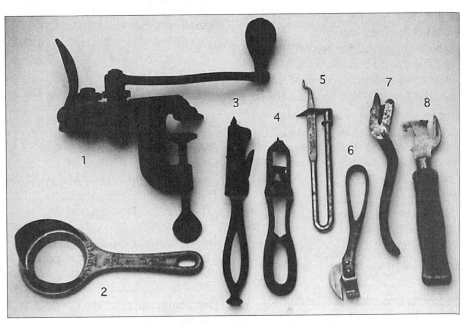

Various Can Openers

walnut board w/hanging hole,
board 24" l. **65.00**

Lemon squeezer, cast iron
w/white porcelain interior,
marked "E.M. Sammis," pat.
Sept. 1878 ....**25.00**

Meat tenderizer, beige crockery
w/black painted wood handle,
marked "Pat. Dec. 25, 1877,"
8½" l. **85.00**

Mold, jelly, copper, circular bundt
shape w/nine ornate pillars,
5½" w., 6⅛" h. **60.00**

Nutmeg grater, wood & brass,
Champion, Boston, MA, Pat.
Oct 9, 1866, ...**375.00**

Pastry blender, wire w/tin
handle, ...**12.00**

Pie crimper, brass, wheel on one
end, shaft on other, shaft
marked "Pat. Sept. 11, 1866,"
6" l. **140.00**

Potato masher, wooden,
simple design **150.00**

Raisin seeder, wire w/wood
handle, marked "Everett"............**50.00**

Rolling pin, wood, mounted
wooden hopper across top that
enclosed mesh corked tube to
hold flour, marked "Harlowe's
Do Not Stick," 20" l. **225.00**

Scoop, tin, ice cream-type, cone-
shaped disher w/tin handle & top
turn key, marked "V. Clad, Phila"
& "Pat. May 3, 1878,"
No. 5 ....**95.00**

Sifter, tin, two-cup measure
w/wood handle, marked
"Calumet Baking
Powder"......................................**38.00**

Spoon, wire mesh center, wood
handle...**18.00**

Spoon-fork combination, twisted
wire three prong fork on one
end, wire spoon on other............**45.00**

Spoon Holder

Spoon holder, tin, oval shaped
seven holes & ridge around
edge, w/hook, placed on side of
kettle for drippings from
spoon, unmarked (ILLUS.) **35.00**

Sugar auger, hand-wrought iron,
twirled iron in center shaft
divides into one straight prong,
two beautifully curved swirls at
bottom, wooden handle,
mid-1800s, 20" l.........................**175.00**

Vegetable strainer, wire base,
wood handle **18.00**

Wafer iron, cast iron, Griswold
No. 955, w/stand **320.00**

EGGBEATERS

Eggbeaters are a very popular kitchen collectible ranging in price from less than $10.00 to hundreds of dollars.

Cyclone, cast iron, rotary marked
"Cyclone Pat. 6-25 and 7-16
1901," 11½" h. **75.00**

Dover, cast iron, rotary marked
"Dover Egg Beater Pat. May 31,
1870," 12½" h. **200.00**

Dover, cast iron, nickel-plated, D-
handle, rotary marked "Genuine
Dover, Dover Stamping Co.,"
11¼" h. **50.00**

Hand-held, plastic handle,
marked "Patent
No. 2906510"................................**5.00**

Holt-Lyon, cast iron, side-handle, marked "Holt's Egg Beater & Cream Whip Pat. Aug. 22-'98 Apr. 3-00," 8½" h. **200.00**

Jaquette Bros., scissors-type, cast iron, marked "Jaquette Bros No. 1," 7½" l. **400.00**

Ladd, metal rotary, marked "No. 0 Ladd Beater Pat'd July 7, 1908 Feb. 2, 1915 United Royalties Corp.," 9¾" h. **20.00**

Ladd, tumbler model, metal rotary, marked "No. 5 Ladd Ball Bearing Beater Oct. 18, 1921," 11½" h. **35.00**

Monroe, cast-iron rotary, shelf mount, marked "EP Monroe patented April 19, 1859," 10½" h **700.00**

P-D-&-Co., cast-iron rotary w/spring dasher bottom w/the word "E-A-S-Y" cut-out on spokes of main gear wheel & marked "Pat Sept. 28 26," 9¾" h **500.00**

S&S Hutchinson, cast-iron rotary (w/Hutchinson cut-out in wheel) marked "Hutchinson new York Pat. apld For," glass apron on bowl embossed "130 Worth St. New York J. Hutchinson S&S Trade Mark," 9½" h...................**450.00**

Taplin, cast-iron rotary, marked "The Taplin Mfg. Co. New Britain Conn, U.S.A. Light Running Pat. Nov. 24 '08," 12½" h...................**50.00**

Taplin, cast-iron rotary, wood handle, marked "Pattern Improved April 14, 1903," 11¾" h. **30.00**

EGG TIMERS

A little glass tube filled with sand and attached to a figural base measuring between 3" and 5" in height was once a commonplace kitchen item. Many beautiful timers were produced in Germany in the 1920s and later Japan, reaching their heyday in the 1940s. These small egg timers were commonly made in a variety of shapes in bisque, china, *chalkware, cast iron, tin, brass, wood or plastic. Although egg timers were originally used to time a 3-minute egg, some were also used to limit the length of a telephone call as a cost saving measure.*

Bellhop, ceramic, green, Japan, 4½" h. **70.00**

Bellhop on phone, ceramic, Japan, 3" h. **45.00**

Black Chef Egg Timer

Black chef, wooden, unmarked, 4" h. (ILLUS.)..............................**95.00**

Black chef sitting w/raised hand holding timer, ceramic, many sizes & shadings, Germany....................................**100.00**

Black chef standing w/large fish w/timer in fish's mouth, ceramic, Japan, 4 ¾" h. **145.00**

Boy, ceramic, stands on plastic head & fills w/sand, marked "Cooly Lilly" on sticker, 3 ¾" h. **65.00**

Boy w/red cap, stands & holds glass tubes in each hand, wooden, unmarked, 4½" h. **35.00**

Cat standing by grandfather clock, ceramic, Germany 4½" h. **75.00**

Chef in blue & white apron, towel over right arm & timer in jug under left arm, Japan, 4 ½" h. **50.00**

Chef holding plate w/hole to hold removable time, ceramic, Japan.........................**50.00**

Chef winking, ceramic, wearing white clothes, timer built in back & turns upside down to tip sand, 4" h. **50.00**

Chefs, ceramic, double man & woman, Goebel, Germany, 4" h. **100.00**

Chicken, ceramic, wings holding tube, Germany, 2 ¾" h. **65.00**

Chicken on nest, plastic, green, England, 2½" h. **25.00**

Golliwog Egg Timer

Chimney Sweep Egg Timer

Chimney sweep carrying ladder, ceramic, Germany, 3¼" h. (ILLUS.)..........................**85.00**

Clown on phone, ceramic, standing in yellow suit, Japan, 3 ¾" h. **65.00**

Colonial man in knickers, ceramic, wearing ruffled shirt, Japan, 4 ¾" h..........................**75.00**

Dutch boy kneeling, ceramic, Japan, 2½" **50.00**

Dutch girl walking w/flowers, chalkware, unmarked, 4½" h. **55.00**

Friar Tuck, ceramic, single, Goebel, Germany, 4" h...............**75.00**

Golliwog, bisque, England, 4½" h. (ILLUS. top next column) **150.00**

Lady Egg Timer

Lady in yellow bonnet, ceramic, Germany, 4½" h. (ILLUS.) **85.00**

Leprechaun w/shamrock base, brass, Ireland, 3¼" h. **35.00**

Lighthouse, ceramic, blue, cream & orange lustreware, Germany, 4½" h. **85.00**

Mammy, tin, lithographed picture of Mammy cooking, includes pot holder hooks, unmarked, 7 ¾" h. **125.00**

Mexican boy playing guitar, ceramic, Germany, 3 ½" h. **55.00**

Mouse, chalkware, yellow & green, Josef Originals, Japan, ca. 1970s, 3¼"..........................**35.00**

Mr. Pickwick, ceramic, green, double, Goebel, Germany, 4" h. **165.00**

Native Egg Timer

Native, ceramic, Japan, 5" h. (ILLUS.) **140.00**

Newspaper boy, ceramic, Japan, 3 ¼" h. **65.00**

Parlor maid w/cat, ceramic, Japan...........................**65.00**

Penguin, chalkware, England, 3 ¾" h. **65.00**

Pixie, ceramic, Enesco, Japan, 5½" h. **40.00**

Rabbits, ceramic, double, various color combinations, Goebel, Germany, 4" **100.00**

Sailor, ceramic, blue, Germany...........................**85.00**

Santa Claus Egg Timer

Santa Claus w/present, ceramic, Sonsco, Japan, 5½" h. (ILLUS. bottom previous column) **85.00**

Scotsman w/bagpipes, plastic, England, 4½" h. **65.00**

Telephone, black glaze on clay, Japan, 2" h. **25.00**

Telephone, wooden, candlestick tube on base w/cup timer, Cornwall Wood Products, South Paris, Maine **25.00**

Veggie man or woman, bisque, Japan, 4½" h. **75.00**

Windmill, ceramic, yellow w/bird on top, unmarked, 4" h. **75.00**

Windmill Egg Timer

Windmill w/dog on base, ceramic, Japan, 3 ¾" h. (ILLUS.) **95.00**

Windmill w/kissing Dutch couple, ceramic, Japan, 4" h. **65.00**

Wind mill w/pigs on base, ceramic, Japan, 3 ¾" h. **95.00**

NAPKIN DOLLS

These lovely ladies never fail to be the talk of the table. Until about two years ago they were a relatively obscure collectible and those lucky enough to have gotten in on the ground floor will be amazed at their increasing value and desirability. Although most commercially made napkin dolls probably date to the 1950s, they were apparently a popular project in ceramic craft classes from the 1930s through the 1980s.

Napkin Doll With Shakers

Ceramic, pink figure of woman w/4 ¾" shakers, toothpick tray held in front, marked "Japan," shakers represent 50% of the value, 9¾" h. (ILLUS.) **125.00**

Ceramic, green & white figure of bartender w/tray holding candle, 8¾" h. **100.00**

Woman & Poodle Napkin Doll

Ceramic, green figure of woman holding poodle, jewel-decorated, hat masks candleholder, marked "Kreiss & Co.," 10¾" h. (ILLUS.) **85.00**

Ceramic, yellow & white figure of Spanish dancer holding tambourine, marked "#460 California Originals USA," 8¾" h. **85.00**

Ceramic, yellow & white figure of Spanish dancer holding tambourine, marked "#460 California Originals USA," 13" h. **100.00**

Ceramic, yellow & white figure of Spanish dancer holding tambourine, marked "#460 California Originals USA," 15" h. **135.00**

Candleholder Napkin Doll

Ceramic, blue & white figure of woman clasping hands in front, candleholder in hat, ca. 1954, 13" h. (ILLUS.) **95.00**

Ceramic, black model of rooster w/yellow & red trim, 10¼" h. (ILLUS. top next page) **35.00**

Ceramic, green figure of woman, fan masks candleholder, jewel-decorated, marked "Kreiss & Co.," 8¾" h. (ILLUS. middle next page, right) **65.00**

Ceramic, pink figure of woman, fan masks candleholder, jewel-decorated, marked "Kreiss & Co.," 10½" (ILLUS. middle next page, left)............................**85.00**

Rooster Napkin Doll

Ladies With Fans Napkin Dolls

Peasant Woman Napkin Doll

Ceramic, figure of peasant woman, pink w/floral design, holding toothpick tray on head, jeweled eyes, 9 ¼" h. (ILLUS.) **60.00**

Baker Girl Napkin Doll

Ceramic & metal, half-doll figure of baker doll girl holding pie & loaf of bread w/holes for toothpicks, wire bottom, 7" h. (ILLUS.) **100.00**

Ceramic & wood, half-figure of native woman w/wood base & wires to hold napkins, marked "Goebel, W. Germany," 9" h. **200.00**

Woman With Strawberry Napkin Doll

Wood, pink & blue figure of woman, strawberry on head w/holes for toothpicks, 8" h. (ILLUS. bottom previous page) **55.00**

Half-Figure Napkin Holder

Wood, red half-figure, base marked "Napkins," ca. 1952, 11½" h. (ILLUS.) **35.00**

Wood, figure of black native girl, basket of fruit on head w/moveable arms, 6 ¾" h. **85.00**

PIE BIRDS

A pie bird can be described as small, hollow device usually between 3½" to 6" long, glazed inside and vented from the top. Its function is to raise the crust of a pie to allow steam to escape, thus preventing juices from bubbling over onto the oven floor while providing a flaky, dry crust.

Originally, in the 1880s, pie birds were funnel-shaped vents used by the English for their meat pies. Not until the turn of the century did figurals appear, first in the form of birds, followed by elephants, chefs, etc. By the 1930s, many shapes were found in America. Today the market is flooded by many reproductions and newly created pie birds, usually in many whimsical shapes and subjects. It is best to purchase from knowledgeable dealers and fellow collectors.

Benny the Baker Pie Bird

Benny the Baker, Cardinal China, New Jersey, USA (ILLUS.) **125.00**

Black Bird Pie Bird

Bird, black, perched on log, England (ILLUS.) **95.00**

Bird, black on white base, yellow feet & beak, Nutbrown, England **45.00**

Bird, two-headed, Barn Pottery, Devon, England **95.00**

Bird, blue & white on white funnel two-piece, Royal Worcester, England **85.00**

Bird, grey, England **95.00**

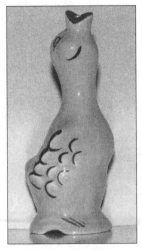

Yellow Pie Bird

Brown Chef Pie Bird

Bird, yellow w/red beak, black
feather-detailing,
England (ILLUS.) **95.00**

Black Chef Pie Bird

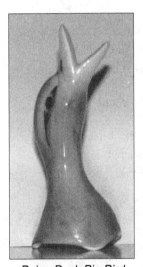

Beige Duck Pie Bird

Black chef, full-figure, yellow
smock w/white hat, USA
(ILLUS.) **95.00**

Brown chef, half-figure, England
(ILLUS. top next column)...........**115.00**

Dragon, Creician Pottery, Wales,
U.K. **110.00**

Duck, long neck, blue, pink or
yellow, USA **50.00**

Duck, yellow beak, beige w/black
detailing, England
(ILLUS.) **100.00**

Duck head, beige w/black detail,
England **125.00**

Elephant, incised "ccc" on back,
USA (ILLUS. top next page) **100.00**

Elephant, dark grey w/yellow
glaze inside, England **100.00**

Elephant, grey, Nutbrown,
England ....**100.00+**

Elephant, white, Nutbrown,
England **55.00**

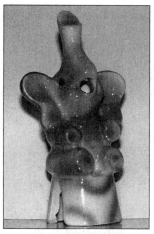

Elephant Pie Bird

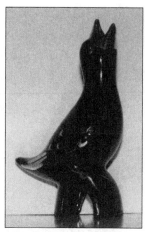

Black Songbird Pie Bird

Funnel, plain white,
England **22.00**

Howling bear, USA......................**95.00**

Mammy w/outstretched arms,
USA...**95.00**

Morton Pottery "Patches,"
USA...**35.00**

"Pillsbury" bird, USA...................**45.00**

Rooster, multicolored,
Cleminson, USA **50.00**

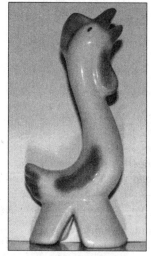

Rooster Pie Bird

Rooster, Pearl China, USA
(ILLUS.) **95.00**

Songbird, black w/gold detailing,
Lapiere, Ohio (ILLUS.) **100.00**

Songbirds, beige, blue & pink,
USA **35.00**

Seal, black, Japan **125.00**

Walrus, black, Japan..................**125.00**

REAMERS

One a staple in the American household during the 1920s-40s, manual juice reamers have again gained popularity as a hot commodity in today's collectible market. although some wooden reamers date to the mid-1800s, the majority found today were produced during the reamer's heyday. They range from American-made depression glass and pottery, to exquisitely painted ceramics and uniquely-shaped- figurals from far off places like Japan, France, Germany and Czechoslovakia. Lovely silverplate and sterling examples that once graced elegant Victorian tables now command hefty prices. And even the early electric and deco chrome models of the 1950s have found a collectible niche.

Ceramic, yellow, marked "U.S.A.
Zippy Trademark Patent Applied
For Wolverine Products in.,
Detroit, Mich.," 3 ¼" h.,
6½" d **95.00**

Ceramic, green with model of
yellow and white kitten and pink,

Ceramic Reamer with Kitten

yellow and green cone, marked
"Made in Japan," 4" h.,
(ILLUS.) **85.00**

Ceramic, luster with red and
yellow flowers, marked
"Made in Japan," 2" h. **125.00**

Clown Reamers

Ceramic figure of clown, white,
blue green and yellow, with blue
and white top, marked "Made in
Japan," 6" h (ILLUS. right).........**100.00**

Same, 8" h. (ILLUS. left)..............**135.00**

Ceramic, sauce-boat shaped,
blue chintz/multicolored flowers,
marked "Crown Ducal, Made in
England," 3½" h., 8" l.................**350.00**

Ceramic model of house, tan
with green and red trees, green
trim and blue windows, marked
"Made in Japan," with six 3¼"
matching cups, 5½" h., the set
(ILLUS. of part) **165.00**

*Ceramic Model of a House with
Matching Cup*

Ceramic, orange luster with white
cone, two-piece, marked
"Czechoslovakia," 3¾" h..............**65.00**

Manx Cat Reamer

Ceramic, beige with model of
black cat, two-piece, "Manx Cat
From The Isle of Man." marked
"Crown Devon, Made in
England," 3½" h (ILLUS.) **95.00**

Figural Mexican Man

Ceramic, figure of Mexican man with cactus, unmarked, 5½" h., (ILLUS. bottom previous page)...**275.00**

Ceramic, model of orange with yellow and blue flowers and green leaves, "Orange For Baby," marked "Goebel GW Co., Germany," 3½" h...............**135.00**

Ceramic and wood, blue and white cone, 8¾" wooden handle, Germany......................**275.00**

Glass, blue Fry with white opal trim, 4" d. **165.00**

Glass, pink, Jeanette Glass co., 5¼" d. **100.00**

Cobalt Blue Glass Reamer

Glass, cobalt blue criss-cross, Hazel Atlas Glass Co., 6⅛" d. (ILLUS.) **275.00**

Glass, crystal, two-piece, Westmoreland Specialty Co., 4 ⅝" h. **65.00**

Glass, white milk glass, embossed with fleur-de-lis, 6 ¼" d. **95.00**

Federal Glass Amber Reamer

Glass, amber, ribbed with loop handle, Federal Glass Co., 6¼" d. (ILLUS.)...........................**20.00**

"Speakeasy Cocktail Shaker"

Glass and metal, green "Speakeasy Cocktail Shaker" Paden City, 9¼" h. (ILLUS.) **75.00**

Metal and Glass Sunkist Jucit

Metal and glass, green with white milk glass bowl, ceramic cone, marked "Sunkist Jucit Refined," electric, 8¾" h. (ILLUS.) **45.00**

Metal, hand-held, marked "Lemon Squeezer," 6¾" l...............**8.00**

Silverplate, model of bird, marked "Muss Bach, 4½" l. **20.00**

Silverplate, marked "T&T NS, 30-
66 Hand Hammered,
7 ⅛" d. **125.00**

Sterling silver with glass cone,
24" d. **250.00**

Wood, hand-held, 6 ¼" l. **35.00**

Wood, hinged, hand-held, 10" l. **45.00**

STRINGHOLDERS

Before the invention of cellophane tape, string was used to tie up packages in country stores as well as during food preparation in the home kitchen. Today we admire string holders for their decorative nature. Made in cast iron, plaster of Paris (chalkware) and ceramic, many different subjects are depicted.

Apples & berries, chalkware **35.00**

Apple w/face, ceramic, PY **125.00**

Babies, ceramic, one laughing &
one crying, Lefton, pr.................**250.00**

Bird, ceramic, "String Nest Pull"....**40.00**

Bird in bird cage, chalkware **125.00**

**Bird on branch w/scissors in
head,** ceramic **85.00**

**Bonzo the dog w/bee on
chest,** ceramic **135.00**

Boy, chalkware, top hat & pipe
w/eyes to side............................**65.00**

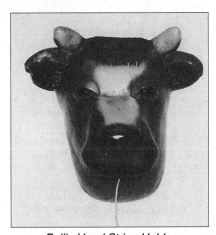

Bull's Head String Holder

Bull's head, chalkware
(ILLUS.) **250.00**

Butler, ceramic, black man
w/white lips & eyebrows (ILLUS.
w/Mammy)..............................**300.00+**

Chef, chalkware............................**65.00**

Chef String Holder

Chef, chalkware, Rice Crispy
(ILLUS.) **145.00**

Cherries, chalkware **135.00**

Clown w/string around tooth,
chalkware **125.00**

Dog String Holder

Dog, ceramic, Schnauzer
(ILLUS.) **135.00**

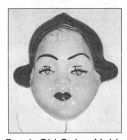

Dutch Girl String Holder

Dutch girl head w/hat,
chalkware (ILLUS.)......................**65.00**

Elephant, ceramic, yellow,
England **75.00**

Girl in bonnet, chalkware, eyes
to side..**65.00**

Granny in rocking chair,
ceramic, PY **125.00**

Heart String Holder

Heart, ceramic, puffed, marked
"You'll Always Have A 'Pull' With
Me," Cleminsion (ILLUS.) **125.00**

House, ceramic, Cleminsion **125.00**

Iron w/flowers, ceramic **75.00**

Jester, chalkware........................**95.00**

Kitten w/ball of yarn, ceramic,
home-made **40.00**

Kitten w/ball of yarn,
chalkware **65.00**

Little "Blue" Riding Hood

Little "Blue" Riding Hood,
chalkware (ILLUS.).................**250.00+**

Maid, ceramic, Sarsaparilla, ca.
1984 ....**85.00**

Mammy & Butler String Holders

Mammy, ceramic, full-figured
w/plaid & dotted dress
(ILLUS. left) **135.00**

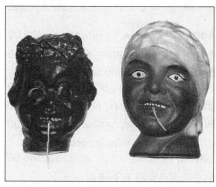

Mammy Face String Holders

Mammy face, chalkware, many
variations (ILLUS.)..................**250.00+**

Knitting Mammy String Holder

Mammy w/knit stocking,
ceramic (ILLUS.) **250.00**

Mouse sitting, ceramic, Josef
Original **85.00**

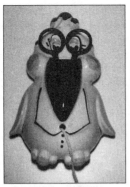

Penguin String Holder

Penguin w/scissors in nose,
  (ILLUS.) **70.00**

Pig w/flowers, ceramic **145.00**

Pirate & gypsy, wood fiber, pr. ...**150.00**

Rooster, ceramic, Royal
  Bayreuth ....**350.00+**

Rose String Holder

Rose, chalkware (ILLUS.) **135.00**

Rosie the Riveter, chalkware **125.00**

Sailor boy **125.00**

Senor, chalkware **65.00**

Senora, chalkware **75.00**

Soldier head, chalkware **75.00**

Southern Belle w/full skirt,
  ceramic **65.00**

**Southern gentleman w/two
ladies,** ceramic **85.00**

Witch in pumpkin winking,
  ceramic **150.00**

Woman w/turban, chalkware **150.00**

LAUNDRY ROOM ITEMS

The "good old days" weren't really all that good when Monday "wash day" and Tuesday "ironing day" came around. There was a lot of hard work involved in scrubbing clothes on the washboard and smoothing out the wrinkles with the hefty flatiron or "sadiron" (sad = heavy). Today collectors can look back with some nostalgia on those adjuncts of the laundry room, curious relics of the not too distant past.

IRONS

Box Iron with Brass Trivet

Box Iron, brass body, single post
  & swing gate, Germany **$150.00**

Box Iron, iron body w/brass trivet,
  drop in slug, wood handle,
  Belgium (ILLUS. above) **650.00**

Charcoal iron, marked "Queen
  Carbon Sad Iron" **300.00**

Little iron, model of a cross rib,
  2 ½" **35.00**

Tailor iron, cast iron, marked
  "Sensible" w/removable wood &
  iron handle, 20 lb. **200.00**

Electric iron, Art Deco-style,
  streamlined body w/black handle
  & red & black cord, marked
  "Petipoint" (ILLUS. top next
  page) **175.00**

Electric iron, General Mills
  w/steam attachment **45.00**

Art Deco-style Electric Iron

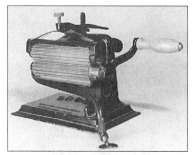

Crown Fluter

Fluter, crank, cast iron, w/C-clamp, marked "Crown" on base, Pat. Nov. 2, 1875 (ILLUS.) **125.00**

Sears Fuel Iron

Fuel iron, iron base w/round tank mounted on top of iron, wood handle, Sears (ILLUS.)..............**175.00**

Sad iron, detachable handle, bentwood, marked "Bless & Drake"......................................**190.00**

Sleeve iron, 'duck bill' model, marked "Geneva" on body & "GENEVA Pat. applied for" on toe **275.00**

SPRINKLING BOTTLES

To remove wrinkles from clothes, water was distributed through the fabric and rolled up. Clothes were then ready to be ironed. Although many people used a soda bottle with an attached sprinkler head, other whimsical bottles produced for this purpose were either purchased or created in ceramics class. The variety of subjects depicted as figural sprinkler bottles runs from objects related to ironing to the people who did the ironing.

Cat Sprinkling Bottle

Cat, ceramic w/amber marble eyes, American Bisque (ILLUS.) **200.00**

Cat, ceramic, tan, Siamese **135.00**

Cat, ceramic, home-made in variety of colors & designs, each...**75.00**

Chinese man, yellow & green ceramic, marked "Sprinkle Plenty," Cardinal China Company **30.00**

Chinese man, ceramic, blue shirt & white pants, home-made, marked "Me Sprinkle Clothes," each (ILLUS. left & right, top next page) **45.00**

Chinese man, ceramic, white & aqua w/paper shirt tag marked "Your Number One Sprinkle Boy," Cleminson (ILLUS. middle, top next page).................**85.00**

Chinese Men Sprinkling Bottles

Chinese Men Sprinkling Bottles

Chinese man, ceramic, home-
made, marked, each
(ILLUS.) **45.00**

Chinese man, white & aqua,
Cleminson **40.00**

Chinese man holding iron,
white, green & brown, marked
"Sprinkle Plenty" **150.00**

**Chinese man w/removable
head,** marked "Sprinkle Plenty"
(ILLUS. top next column)...........**175.00**

Clothespin, ceramic, aqua,
yellow & pink w/smiling
face...**150.00**

Clothespin, ceramic, home-
made, each (ILLUS.
center next column).....................**95.00**

Clothespin, plastic, red, yellow or
green **25.00**

Dearie is Weary, ceramic,
Enesco **200.00**

Removable Head Sprinkling Bottle

Clothespin Sprinkling Bottle

Dutch Boy & Girl Sprinkling Bottles

Dutch boy, ceramic, green & white (ILLUS. left, bottom previous page)............................**150.00**

Dutch girl, ceramic, white w/green & pink trim, Dutch boy mate, (ILLUS. right, bottom previous page)............................**150.00**

Elephant Sprinkling Bottle

Elephant, American Bisque (ILLUS.) **250.00**

Elephant, ceramic, pink & grey **55.00**

Elephant, ceramic, white & pink w/clover on tummy **75.00**

Emperor, ceramic, home-made in variety of colors & designs, each...**100.00**

Iron, ceramic, blue flowers **75.00**

Iron, plastic, green.........................**25.00**

Iron, ceramic, depicts lady ironing..**65.00**

Iron, ceramic, depicts farm couple (ILLUS. top next column)...........**125.00**

Iron, ceramic, souvenir of Aquarena Springs, San Marcos, Texas (ILLUS. middle next column).....................................**125.00**

Iron, ceramic, pink flamingo, souvenir of Florida....................**125.00**

Iron, ceramic, souvenir of Wonder Cave **125.00**

Mammy, ceramic, unmarked.......**250.00**

Mary Poppins, ceramic, Cleminson (ILLUS. bottom, next column)....................................**225.00**

Farm Couple On Ceramic Iron

Iron Souvenir Sprinkling Bottle

Mary Poppins Sprinkling Bottle

Merry maid, plastic, all colors,
Reliance, each.............................**25.00**

Myrtle by Pfaltzgraff

Myrtle, ceramic, Pfaltzgraff
(ILLUS.) **225.00**

Poodle, ceramic, grey, white &
pink, each (ILLUS. below) **165.00**

Queen or king, ceramic, Tilso,
Japan, each **100.00**

Rooster, ceramic, red & green **125.00**

LIGHTING DEVICES

LAMPS

FAIRY LAMPS

These are candle burning night lights of the Victorian era. Best known are the Clarke Fairy Lamps made in England, but they were also made by other firms. They were produced in two sizes, each with a base and a shade. Fairy Pyramid lamps usually have a clear glass base and are approximately 2 7/8" d. and 3 1/4" h. The Fairy Lamps are usually at least 4" d. and 5" h. when assembled. These may or may not have an additional saucer or bottom holder to match the shade in addition to the clear base.

Acid-Cut Blue Fairy Lamp

Ceramic Poodle Sprinkling Bottles

Blue glass shade, frosted & acid-cut overall w/flowers & leaves, on a clear ribbed marked "Clarke" base, 3⅝" d., 4¾" h. (ILLUS.) $175.00

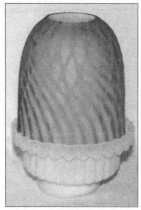

Blue Satin Fairy Lamp

Satin glass mother-of-pearl heavenly blue Diamond Quilted patt. shade w/embossed swirls, on a marked footed frosted "Clarke"base, 4" d., 4¾" h. (ILLUS.) 245.00

FIGURAL FAIRY LAMPS

Baby Head Fairy Lamp

Glass, frosted emerald green shade molded as a two-faced baby, one face smiling, the

opposite side crying, on a clear signed "Clarke" base, 2⅝" d., 4½" h. (ILLUS.) **175.00**

HANDEL LAMPS

The Handel Company of Meriden, Connecticut (1885-1936) began as a glass and lamp shade decorating company. Following World War I they became a major producer of decorative lamps which have become very collectible today.

Handel Lamp with Surface-Painted Shade

Table lamp, 14" d. domical surface-painted shade decorated w/branches of yellow & brown oak leaves & acorns against a speckled green ground, raised on a slender bronze floriform base covered in a pristine dark original patina, the base w/a "HANDEL" cloth tag, shade die-stamped on ring & painted "Handel - 6294- R.G.," overall 20½" h. (ILLUS.) **3,025.00**

Table lamp, a 16" domical reverse-painted shade w/a chipped-ice exterior decorated on the interior w/a landscape of clusters of dark & light green leaves w/delicate yellow blossoms on twisting brown branches, backed by a bluish grey shoreline, against a pale blue lake backed by distant bluish grey mountains & a cloudy sky of pale blue & white, on a slender bronzed-metal base swelled at the top & then tapering to a flaring, lobed foot, rich dark brown patina, shade signed "Handel 5939 R," overall 24" h. **3,575.00**

patina, shade signed in enamel "HANDEL - 5784," upper ring impressed "HANDEL - PAT'D. NO. 979664," base impressed "HANDEL," 23" h. **8,625.00**

Arts & Crafts Design Handel Lamp

Handel Lamp with Bordered Shade

Table lamp, 18" d. domical reverse-painted shade w/a leafy scrolling wide border band in peach, rust, blue & green, the upper portion in mottled peach & green, raised on a bronzed-metal base w/three long slender leafy scroll supports flanking a slender central column all raised on a thick disc foot w/a reeded rim, base w/original patina & signed w/a label, shade signed & numbered, overall 23" h. (ILLUS.) **6,050.00**

Table lamp, 18" d. domical reverse-painted shade in grey w/a chipped ice & sand-textured exterior, painted on the interior & exterior w/a pine forest before a ground of rolling hills, in shades of forest green, grass green & blue, the bulbous pear-form patinated bronze base also cast w/a forest scene w/a brown

Table lamp, 18" d. conical chipped ice shade decorated overall in brown enamel giving an icing effect, further decorated w/an Arts & Crafts looping design in chocolate brown all on a mustard yellow ground, raised on a slender waisted bronzed-metal base w/a wide gently lobed foot, shade signed "Handel - 5342," overall 24" h. (ILLUS.) **3,300.00**

Table lamp, 18" d. domical reverse-painted shade decorated w/a landscape of evergreens lining a stream, dark brown trunks & foliage against a peach-colored sky w/pale yellow moon reflecting in the stream, raised on a bronzed-metal baluster-form base cast w/ribs of stylized long leaves tapering to a wide, round disc foot, shade signed & numbered, overall 24" h...........................**6,600.00**

Handel Lamp with Scenic Shade

Table lamp, 18" d. domical gently ribbed reverse-painted shade w/chipped ice effect, decorated w/a seaside landscape of tall trees w/gnarled trunks in tan & brown, w/clumps of teal, green, blue & brown leaves atop brush-covered green & brown ground w/yellow & orange highlights, boats w/lavender sails atop calm royal blue water w/teal & white waves, white sea gulls hovering overhead, all backed by a lavender & pale green sky w/billowing white clouds, slender baluster-form bronzed-metal base w/a flaring slightly swirled & undulating foot & original patina, shade signed "Handel 6749" & artist-initialed, base w/cloth label, overall 25" h. (ILLUS.) **8,800.00**

Table lamp, 18" d. conical open-topped four-paneled reverse-painted shade, two panels painted w/a red & black flying macaw above brown grasses, grasses in the other two panels, raised on a slender bronzed-metal ring- and baluster-turned pedestal on a triangular platform w/three small paw feet, unsigned, overall 29" h. **2,200.00**

MINIATURE LAMPS

Our listings are arranged numerically according to the numbers assigned to the various miniature lamps pictured in Frank R. & Ruth E. Smith's book Miniature Lamps, *now referred to as Smith's Book I, and Ruth Smith's Sequel,* Miniature Lamps II, *All references are to Smith's Book I unless otherwise noted.*

Shaded Blue Ribbed Lamp

Pink satin Artichoke shade on a bulbous squared base tapering to a cushion foot, clear chimney, Nutmeg burner, 7¾" h., No. II, color, center (chips on shade rims) **105.00**

Milk glass Artichoke ball shade on a squatty bulbous ribbed base tapering to small foot, fired-on decoration in pink & green, Nutmeg burner, No. III, far left, 8⅞" h. (small chips to top of chimney, base of shade repaired) **105.00**

Green "Handy" footed font, brass insert collar & Acorn burner, "Handy" on the side, clear chimney, 7¼" h., No. 5...**55.00**

Milk glass paneled umbrella-form font & matching conical shade w/embossed ribs, painted light blue, Acorn burner, clear chimney, base marked "Germany," 7⅜" h., No. 130 ....**110.00**

Milk glass footed ovoid lobed **font** w/molded large blossoms & scrolls in each lobe, matching chimney-form shade, decorated in yellow & gold, Acorn burner, 8" h., No. 156..............................**85.00**

Milk glass ovoid font w/stepped round foot & a matching egg-shaped shade, painted stain w/enameled flowers in red, blue, yellow, green & brown, Acorn burner, 7¼" h., No. 186 ....**90.00**

Blue opaque bulbous squared tapering font w/embossed acanthus leaves at each corner, matching ball shade, clear chimney, Nutmeg burner, 9½" h., No. 240 (slight nicks to shade top rim) **190.00**

Milk glass squared base & puffy-molded Artichoke variant shade, Nutmeg burner, by Consolidated Lamp & Glass Co., Pittsburgh, No. 380 ....**470.00**

Blue satin glass w/beaded panels w/embossed scrolls & flowers, Nutmeg burner, 7¾" h., No. 396 ....**430.00**

Blue opaline conical font w/embossed scrolls around the base below a waffle design, matching ball shade, foreign burner, no chimney, 6⅞" h., No. 410 (nicks on base, shade may have been ground) **520.00**

Milk glass figural recumbent elephant font trimmed in yellow, gold & a trace of red, embossed swirled ball shade, clear chimney, Nutmeg burner, 7⅝" h., No. 488.................**270.00**

Shaded sapphire blue tall square font w/slight molded ribbing & a frosted finish, a matching ribbed ball shade, clear chimney, 10" h., similar to No. 509 (ILLUS.) **450.00**

Pink mother-of-pearl satin Diamond Quilted patt. bulbous baluster-form font, burner & shade ring, base only, 3¾" h., No. 599 ....**350.00**

Blue clear glass embossed pedestal base w/embossed matching shade, Nutmeg burner, font identical to "Cathedral lamp" made by McKee & Bros., Pittsburgh, Pennsylvania, 8" h., Book II No. 228 ....**525.00**

Brass ringed foot & shoulder w/a cylindrical milk glass font, font h.p. w/a house in a snow scene, clear chimney, Hornet burner, 5" h. (Book II, No. 158)..**150.00**

PAIRPOINT LAMPS

"Puffy" Rose Bouquet Lamp

Table lamp, 13" d. "Puffy" domical 'Rose Bouquet' reverse-painted shade, grey molded & painted w/a bouquet of roses & leafage in shades of white, pink, yellow, brown & green, stamped in gilt "PAT. APPLIED FOR," on a modern slender ribbed baluster-form brass base, ca. 1915 (ILLUS.) **8,625.00**

Table lamp, 15" d. "Puffy" flat-topped mushroom-form 'Palermo' reverse-painted shade, grey painted to simulate fabric w/rows of floral medallions within laced lozenges, above a scrolling floral border, the top also w/an elaborate floral design, enameled in shades of red, green, orange, teal blue & yellow, on a gilt-metal slender urn-form base w/cast swags raised on three slender scroll legs on a tripartite foot, base impressed "PAIRPOINT MFG. CO. - B 3014," ca. 1915, 20½" h. **2,185.00**

Table lamp, 16" d. reverse-painted 'Exeter' shade, grey painted on the interior w/a scrolling floral design w/two large exotic birds in shades of pink, yellow, blue, orange & green reserved against black, brown patina, raised on a slender baluster- and knob-cast patinated metal base w/a stepped square plinth raised on four paw feet, base impressed "PAIRPOINT D3075," early 20th c., 21" h. (shade chips) **3,162.00**

TIFFANY LAMPS

Desk lamp, Favite glass & bronze, counter-balance-type, 7" d. domical iridescent bluish purple glass shade w/iridescent rainbow ware & scroll decoration, supported by flattened circular base ascending to a gooseneck arm w/a weighted ball, shade engraved "L.C.T." & base stamped "TIFFANY STUDIOS NEW YORK 416," 13¾" h. **8,625.00**

Floor lamp, "Lily," twelve-light, Favrile glass & gilt-bronze, each gently paneled lily-form golden iridescent shade pendent from a socket cast w/petals, raised on a slender rod standard fitting into a base cast w/lily pads & leafage, eleven shades inscribed "L.C.T - Favrile," one impressed "L.C.T.," base

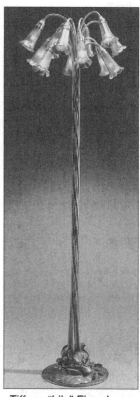

Tiffany "Lily" Floor Lamp

impressed "TIFFANY STUDIOS - NEW YORK - 685," overall 4' 8" h. (ILLUS) **41,400.00**

Floor lamp, "Turtleback," 23¼" d. domical leaded glass shade w/beaded border, w/sixteen iridescent green turtleback tiles & w/partial tiles between them, the bronze floor base cast w/pods & raised on four petal feet, the standard surmounted by an oil canister cast in relief w/a band of pods, stamped "TIFFANY STUDIOS NEW YORK 379," 56" h. **31,050.00**

Lily lamp, eighteen-light, Favrile glass & gilt-bronze, 18 gold iridescent lily-form glass shades attached to arched tall stems clustered on a lily pad foot, sixteen shades inscribed "L.C.T.," two inscribed "L.C.T.

Eighteen-Light Lily Lamp

Favrile," base impressed
"TIFFANY STUDIOS - NEW
YORK - 333," overall 21¼" h.
(ILLUS.) **37,950.00**

Tifffany Student Lamp

Student lamp, Favrile glass &
bronze, two-arm, each 9⅞" d.
domical gently paneled shade in
amber damascene glass cased
over white, pendent from an
adjustable curved bronze arm
on a slender central standard
raised on a round reeded &

incised domed foot, brown
patina, shades inscribed
"L.C.T.," base impressed
"TIFFANY STUDIOS - NEW
YORK - 316," overall 26¼" h.
(ILLUS.) **6,900.00**

Rare Tiffany Butterfly Lamp

Table lamp, "Butterfly," 20" d.
leaded glass umbrella-form
shade w/an overall pattern of
small butterflies in flight in
shades of mottled & striated
amber, lemon yellow,
opalescent & cypriote glass,
reserved against a ground
shading from cobalt blue to pale
blue striated w/opalescence, the
swirled metal shade supports
tapering to a bronze ring above
the bulbous ovoid bronze base
w/undulating leaf-form bands
around the top & base, dark
brown patina, shade unsigned,
base impressed "TIFFANY
STUDIOS -25918," overall
23¾" h. (ILLUS.)..................**90,500.00**

Table lamp, "Dragonfly," 14⅛" d.
domical leaded shade decorated
w/six dragonflies, their bodies in
mottled yellow & their wings in
striated yellow & green

w/delicate openwork bronze overlay, set w/emerald green cabochon 'jewels,' against mottled moss green ground, on cast bronze mushroom-shaped base, shade stamped "TIFFANY STUDIOS NEW YORK," base stamped "TIFFANY STUDIOS NEW YORK 337," 17¾" h. ...**36,800.00**

Table lamp, "Mandarin," the 26½" w. shallow mushroom-form shade composed of green & white stiated opalescent glass tiles shading to mottled opalescent tiles at the outer rim, raised on a reeded standard & base, further raised on five ball feet, pierced finial, greenish brown patina, shade impressed "TIFFANY STUDIOS - NEW YORK," base impressed "TIFFANY STUDIOS 6863, 25" h. **43,125.00**

Unique Tiffany "Peacock" Lamp

Table lamp, "Peacock," 18½" d. open-topped domical leaded glass shade w/two rows of pea 'eyes' in cobalt blue, emerald green & amber, reserved against a ground shading from amberish green to sky blue, striated cobalt & deep purple, all within mottled amber glass tile borders, the lower section w/stylized geometric feathering

in lime green glass, raised on a three-arm support above an oil font insert cast w/rows of overlapping feathers, the baluster-form base blown w/six sections of reticulated mottled blue glass w/swirling amber inclusions, set between large feathered plumes continuing to the base, each centered by a pea 'eye' inset w/green & blue iridescent glass, greenish brown patina, shade impressed "TIFFANY STUDIOS - NEW YORK - 1472-8," oil font each impressed "TIFFANY STUDIOS - NEW YORK - 26999," overall 25½" h. (ILLUS.).................**101,500.00**

Table lamp, "Woodbine," 14" d. domical leaded glass shade w/a pattern of woodbine leaves in striated shades of olive, sea and grass green reserved against a background of striated bluish green glass mottled w/white, bronze reeded base w/a slender waisted standard above a domed base w/a ropetwist edge band & raised on four ball feet, shade impressed "TIFFANY STUDIOS - NEW YORK," base impressed "TIFFANY STUDIOS - NEW YORK - S 995," overall 19" h. **17,825.00**

LAMPS, MISCELLANEOUS

Fine Early Argand Lamp

Argand lamps, two-light, ormolu & clear glass, each w/a lantern-form fluid receptacle above a gadrooned prism support & double scrolled wick supports, the clear glass lower section raised on an ormolu wreath, each of the socket arms fitted w/a clear frosted & floral-etched shade, ca. 1830, ormolu wreath on base of one lamp, 24" h., pr. (ILLUS. of one) **5,462.00**

Art Deco table lamps, figural, modeled as an upright cluster of three alabaster tulip blossoms for the shades & raised on silvered-bronze stems w/a scrolled leafage foot, Albert Cheuret, France, one inscribed "Albert Cheuret," ca. 1925, 15" h., pr. **16,100.00**

Art Nouveau table lamp, jeweled patinated brass, the domed shade w/impressed stylized foliage & a blackened bronze patina set around the top w/synthetic amber jewels above a scalloped apron also set w/oval jewels, raised on angular arms above the skeletal two-stem shaft on a round foot, base w/bronze patina, three sockets w/two beaded acorn pulls, unsigned, Austria, ca. 1905, wear, shaded 15¾" d., overall 25½" h. **1,150.00**

Banquet lamp, cranberry onion-form font cut w/ovals w/brass connectors to the red marble ovoid stem & square platform on a gilt-metal scroll-cast base, original burner & ring support a frosted cranberry ball shade embossed overall w/leafy scrolls & blossoms, clear chimney, 6" d., 21½" h. (ILLUS. top next column) **650.00**

Benedict Studios table lamp, hand-hammered copper, Arts & Crafts style, the tapering baluster-form base on a domed,

Cranberry Glass Banquet Lamp

stepped round foot, applied band around the middle, w/a three-socket fixture supporting a conical copper-framed shade w/wide panels of mica below the large button finial, original patina & mica, ca. 1910, shade 21" d., overall 30" h. **3,300.00**

Bradley & Hubbard desk lamps, Arts & Crafts-style, wrought iron, each w/four sided, faceted base & a flaring, four sided pink & green slag glass shade, both marked w/raised B & R mark, overall 18½" h., pr. **1,980.00**

Cranberry glass & silvered metal table lamp, the silvered metal stepped & domed round foot & short pedestal w/embossed decorative bands below the onion-form optic-ribbed cranberry font highlighted w/a band of gilt scrolls, brass collar & burner supporting a dark cranberry glass tulip-form shade w/a flaring fluted rim & decorated w/a gilt wreath & leaf band, clear chimney, 5⅜" d., overall 10½" h. **395.00**

Duffner & Kimberly table lamp, a 19" d. domical leaded glass shade composed of graduated geometric bands of mottled amber & white & vivid green & white slag glass, raised on a bronzed-metal base w/a slender reeded cylindrical standard on a domed & ringed round foot all in a rich brown & green patina, overall 22" h. (a few glass segments cracked) **1,650.00**

Gone with the Wind kerosene table lamp, milk glass base & matching ball shade painted in shades of green, rococo design cast brass foot & mounts, glass chimney, late 19th c., 24½" h. ...**285.00**

Kerosene table lamp, Goddess of Liberty figural base in black w/clambroth, berry pattern clear font, 10¼" h. **325.00**

Kerosene table lamp, figural Goddess of Liberty base frosted w/a clear font, 11" h. **360.00**

Dolphin & Column Kerosene Lamp

Kerosene table lamp, blue opaline pressed round stepped & blocked foot below a columnar reeded pedestal wrapped w/a figural dolphin, metal connector to the short clear cylindrical font w/brass collar & shaped ring supporting a frosted clear ball shade acid-etched w/large blossoms & leaves, Europe, late 19th c., electrified, chips, overall 24" h. (ILLUS.) **460.00**

Lard lamp, tin, a horizontal cylindrical font w/top opening raised on a slender cylindrical stem w/side strap handle above a wide shallow dished foot, 7½" h. **154.00**

Moe Bridges Table Lamp

Moe Bridges table lamp, 15" d. domical reverse-painted shade w/chipped ice finish, decorated w/a landscape of trees & a lake in blues & greens against a red & yellow sky, leaf-carved baluster-form base w/rounded square foot, painted green, overall 21" h. (ILLUS.) **2,530.00**

Peg lamp, satin glass font, shaded pink mother-of-pearl Swirl patt., original brass fittings & burner, 3⅜" d., 6" h. (ILLUS. top next page) **165.00**

Satin Mother-of-Pearl Peg Lamp

Fine Suess Leaded Glass Lamp

Suess leaded glass table lamp, a wide umbrella-form leaded glass shade w/uneven lower rim, composed of segments forming large red mottled peonies w/yellow centers, green leaves on a white ground, raised on a bronzed-metal telescoping base w/four slender reeded legs ending in paw feet on a round disc foot, original patina, shade 22" d., overall 29" h. (ILLUS.) **6,600.00**

Stickley table lamp, Arts & Crafts-style, w/oak pyramidal base, square shaft & original fittings & silk-lined wicker shade, w/original fittings & clean original dark brown finish, w/branded mark, Gustav Stickley, overall 19" h. **1,760.00**

Whale oil lamps, japanned tin, petticoat-form w/a double-tier conical form w/a small strap handle on the lower section, original brown japanning, old whale oil burners, 19th c., 4" h. plus burners, pr. (minor scratches) **165.00**

OTHER LIGHTING DEVICES

CHANDELIERS

Art Deco style, chrome & glass, five-light, slender angular brushed chrome arms & sockets extending from a central cylindrical shaft, each socket fitted w/a saucer-shaped frosted cream glass shade, original finish, unsigned, 25" d., 40" h. **770.00**

Art Deco style, wrought iron & glass, the central shade & eight satellite shades in grey glass mottled w/orange pendent from a ornate round stepped frame wrought w/bands of scrolls & grape clusters, designed by Edgar Brandt, Model No. 2053, central shade inscribed "Daum - Nancy - France" w/a Cross of Lorraine, France, ca. 1925, 36" d. **19,550.00**

Brass, eight-light, the shaped baluster standard w/looped finial above a bulbous pendant fitted w/eight scrolled candlearms ending in leaf-cast supports & circular drip pans centering cylindrical candle cups, probably late 18th c., 28⅛" h. (ILLUS. top next page) **3,450.00**

Brass Eight-Light Chandelier

Early French Empire Chandelier

Empire style, ormolu & cut glass, twelve-light, the short candlearms w/cast swans' heads extending from a wide leaf-cast central ring interspaced by addorsed swans surmounted by flower-filled baskets, the whole hung w/swags of facet cut glass drops & pear-shaped pendants, France, first quarter 19th c., some pendants replaced, 40" h. (ILLUS.) **29,900.00**

Louis XVI-Style, gilt-bronze & glass, nine-light, the central glass standard supporting scrolled arms each ending in a candle cup, hung overall w/beaded swags, chains, drops & flowerheads, late 19th - early 20th c., 45" h. **5,750.00**

Tiffany "Hydrangea" Chandelier

Tiffany-signed, "Hydrangea," the 29" d. wide conical leaded glass shade w/an overall pattern of bull-blown hydrangea blossoms in opalescent rippled & striated glass mottled w/emerald green & sea green & opalescent leafage, striated w/cobalt blue, emerald green & wintergreen, reserved against a partially fractured glass ground in translucent pale mauve striated w/opalescence & lemon yellow, the bronze fittings w/a greenish brown patina, impressed "TIFFANY STUDIOS - NEW YORK - 167-6" (ILLUS.) **34,500.00**

Victorian style, brass & enamel, six-light, the long slender central ringed-knob standard w/enameled pottery inserts, issuing six square downswept arms headed by florettes & ending in shade rings hung w/prisms around the socket, each upper arm decorated w/an attached half-round frame enclosing a lotus-form device,

Ornate Victorian Chandelier

angled & scroll-tipped flat bands extending to the top w/stylized fanned devices at the top just below the flaring ceiling cap, w/five wide acid-etched tulip-shaped shades, ca. 1880 (ILLUS.) **3,520.00**

LANTERNS

Large Early Candle Lantern

Candle lantern, wood & glass, an upright wooden framework w/small stile feet, flat top & base w/a bentwood handle at the top, one side forms a door, 19th c., 10" h. plus handle (one pane cracked)....................................**468.00**

Candle lantern, wood & glass, an upright heavy wooden post framework w/a flat base & top w/tenoned side posts, the top w/a round opening covered by an arched tin heat shield, wire bail handle, one side hinged for a door, tin candle socket, handle replaced, 15" h. (ILLUS.) **385.00**

Candle lantern, Paul Revere-type, punched tin, cylindrical w/curved side door, conical top w/top ring handle replaced, pierced w/circles, quarter-circles & starflowers, 19th c., 16¼" h. (some battering & old repair).....**220.00**

Ornate Gilt-Bronze Hall Lantern

Hall lantern, gilt-bronze & glass, the large ovoid body fitted w/six oval glass panels above a band of egg-shaped glass inserts over the scroll-pierced squatty bulbous base terminal w/flat pierced finial drop, another band of egg-shaped glass inserts around the domed top & below the scrolled crown-form top rim, 19th c., 29" h. (ILLUS.)...........**3,737.00**

Kerosene lantern, pole or smoke stack-type, tin & glass, a tall rectangular tin lantern w/a hinged side door & large round front lens, the four-sided domed top w/vent opening & carrying handle, fitted w/iron bracket for mounting, interior burner assembly w/kerosene burner, large reflector & mismatched chimney, 19th c., 22" h. plus handle (front glass cracked) **303.00**

Kerosene lantern, post-type, tin & glass, tin top & base w/clear glass globe marked "Dietez Tubular Globe #3," tin w/old worn green paint, original brass burner, late 19th - early 20th c., 26" h. (light rust, some loose pieces) **220.00**

Post lantern, painted metal, flaring squared glazed sides w/a tapering metal top w/round, stepped cap w/curled over scalloped top below the pointed ovoid finial, each bottom corner raised on an S-scroll bracket, four-light candleholder inside, square flat base platform, Regency period, England, early 19th c., 39" h., pr. **2,875.00**

Whale oil lantern, glass & tin, a cylindrical pierced tin top w/a conical cap & wide hanging ring, a clear blown ball globe above a low pierced cylindrical tin base, worn black paint, rust on base, no font or burner, 8½" h. plus ring handle (ILLUS. bottom previous column) **182.00**

Whale oil lantern, tin & glass, a pierced cylindrical top w/a conical cap & wide ring handle above the ovoid blown cobalt blue globe above a short pierced cylindrical base w/a flared & slightly domed foot, worn brown japanning, removable whale oil font, probably New England Glass Co., 11½" h. plus handle (font chips resoldered) **495.00**

MAGAZINES

Vintage Norman Rockwell Illustration

Early Whale Oil Lantern

The most sought after elements in many of the old magazines (especially pre-1930 issues) are the ILLUSTRATOR/or Artists who designed magazine covers, advertisements, and story illustrations for numerous periodicals. These are especially apparent in the pre-photographic period which was from *about 1895 to the mid-1930s in general. Also most issues which featured movie stars, personalities, sports and specialty articles are in great demand by collectors who have interest in a particular person or subject matter.*

The most valuable issues are those with multiple value, such as a cover by an important iillustrator, auto or other advertising, articles, story illustrations. Most often older issues are parted by dealers for their overall sale content. The magazine values given here are for those sold to the individual who usually only buys 1 or 2 at a time, or just those issues in their area of collecting interest. Dealers pay much, much less because they buy in quantity and expect large discounts for doing so.

The prices given here are for clean, undamaged and complete magazines.

Below are the top selling American Illustrators. Values in general are given here for various magazine Illustrations.

EACH

MP = Maxfield Parrish
(1895-1936) ....**$12.00 to 200.00**

RA = Rolf Armstrong
(1914-1932) ....**8.00 to 100.00**

E = Erté
(1916-1936) ....**12.00 to 125.00**

GP = Petty
(1932-1955) ....**7.00 to 90.00**

NR = Norman Rockwell
(1914-1975) ....**1.00 to 500.00**

HF = Harrison Fisher
(1890-1935) ....**7.00 to 70.00**

RO = Rose O'Neill
(1896-1935) ....**4.00 to 150.00**

VA = Vargas
(1920-1974) ....**4.00 to 175.00**

JCL = J.C. Leyendecker
(1896-1954) ....**4.00 to 100.00**

FXL = F.X. Leyendecker
(1896-1924) ....**3.00 to 90.00**

JWS = Jessie Wilcox Smith
(1900-1934) ....**4.00 to 50.00**

CP = Coles Phillips
(1907-1927) ....**3.00 to 50.00**

GENERAL CIRCULATION MAGAZINES

General issues, high and low value range: Ar=Articles; C=Covers; I=Illustrations; A= Advertising; COW=Cream Of Wheat ad.

Where there are three columns of values ON ONE LINE: the 1st is the value of the average issue, with nothing on cover or within that can be sold to a collector; second column shows values at the lowest level of saleable items, far right column maximum value

V1, first editions always bring a premium value for most publications

Agricultural Digest,
1930s $2.00;10.00;65.00
Nov. 1934, MP Cover 65.00

Air Progress,
1930s-1940s Ar..................5.00; 55.00
Dec. 1928, Graf Zeppelin Ar........12.00

Airbrush Action,
1980s-1990s 1.00; 12.00
Mar/Apr., 1988, A. Varga.............12.00
Dec. 1993, Olivia cover 8.00

American Boy,
1899-1930s Ar (C-I-A)
NR-RA-MP-JCL 6.00; 9.00; 90.00
Nov. 1918, H. Cady Cartoon 11.00
Aug. 1916, New Autos.................21.00

American Detective,
1930s ....7.00 to 8.00
Jan. 1936, V4, #2, Crime Cases ...7.00

American Magazine (The),
1920s-1930s
Ar (C-I-A)..................4.00; 7.00; 45.00
Oct. 1934, Henry Ford...................7.00

Antique Automobile,
1940s-1980s 4.00; 4.00; 15.00

Argosy,1880s-1970s
Ar (I) 5.00; 7.00; 38.00

Arizona Highways,
1920s-1980s Ar........2.00; 4.00; 20.00
Mar. 1935, Turquoise Ar.............11.00
Nov. 1980, Schoonover, Wyeth.....7.00
Dec. 1980 ....6.00

Atlantic Monthly, 1918-1960
 (C-I-A) MP NR..........**3.00; 6.00; 85.00**
 Aug. 1973, Marilyn Monroe **12.00**
 Nov. 1933, Wyeth Poster **20.00**
Audubon, 1890s-1950s
 Ar (I) **6.00; 7.00; 125.00**
Avante Garde, 1968-1971
 Ar **20.00; 25.00; 60.00**
 Mar. 1968, #2
 Marilyn Monroe...........................**60.00**
 1969, #8 Picasso **45.00**

Baseball Digest,
 1940s-1980s **2.00; 45.00**
 Sept. 1943, Musial......................**18.00**
 Jan. 1949, Hegan **12.00**
 Apr. 1951, DiMaggio...................**50.00**
 June 1963, Kaline.......................**13.00**
 Sept. 1967, McCarver **6.00**
 June 1970, Stottemyre **6.00**
 July 1987, Witt.............................**5.00**
Baseball Magazine,
 1940s-1950s **9.00; 9.00; 95.00**
Basketball Illustrated,
 1940s Ar..........................**20.00; 30.00**
 1948, LSU **30.00**
Better Homes & Gardens,
 1922-1960 Ar (C-I-A)
 NR.............................**3.00; 5.00; 30.00**
 Sept. 1935 ....**24.00**
 Dec. 1943, Vernon Grant,
 Junket ad...................................**10.00**
Boys Life 1912-1960
 (C-I-A) NR **3.00; 5.00; 155.00**
 June 1937, H. Cady Cover **17.00**
 July 1937, HC Christy Cover **16.00**
 Apr. 1966, Willie Mays.................**22.00**
 June 1969, Mantle......................**27.00**
 June 1985, Pete Rose..................**7.00**

Christian Herald, 1878-1980s
 (A) NR **1.00; 5.00; 35.00**
 Apr. 1909, RO Jello Ad B&W **9.00**
Circus, 1940s-1950s
 (C-A) **10.00; 11.00; 25.00**
College Humor, 1920s-1930s
 Ar (C-I) **12.00; 65.00**
 Dec. 1925, RA Cover **50.00**
 Feb. 1932, RA Cover...................**55.00**
 Nov. 1934, Mencken **11.00**
Collier's, 1888-1957 Ar (C-I-A)
 MP-JCL-FXL-NR **6.00; 8.00; 175.00**

Collier's September 22, 1906 with
F. X. Leyendecker Cover

Sept 12, 1903, C.D Gibson,
2 pg. B&W **20.00**
May 14, 1904,
F. Remington FO **14.00**
Nov. 25, 1905, J.W Smith
Cover..**38.00**
Dec. 9, 1905, E. Penfield
Cover..**22.00**
Oct. 1920, Jemina ad **10.00**
July 2, 1927, CP Cover **45.00**
Oct. 31, 1931, Twelvetrees
Cover..**15.00**
Mar. 7, 1936, Merle Oberon **10.00**
May 25, 1940, Mussolini...............**5.00**
June 1945, Truman **7.00**
Jan. 1947, L. Wood Cover..........**11.00**
Aug. 21, 1953, Brooklyn
Dodgers......................................**20.00**
Oct. 16, 1953, M. Monroe
Cover..**75.00**
Nov. 1955, Bette Davis Cover **21.00**
Cosmopolitan, 1886-1960 Ar
 (C-I-A) HF-JWS
 MP-NR **5.00; 6.00; 85.00**
 June 1894, Buffalo Bill.................**50.00**
 Mar. 1899, Indian Ar...................**27.00**
 Aug. 1903, RO Illus **28.00**
 May 1905, E. Barrymore Ar.........**13.00**
 Mar. 1909, HF Cover...................**25.00**
 July 1913, HF Cover....................**25.00**
 June 1916, HF Cover **23.00**
 Sept. 1928, HF, RO, Gibson **40.00**

Nov. 1930, HF Cover, O'Neill **26.00**
Sept. 1931, HF Cover,O'Neill **42.00**
July 1936, Crandall Cover **13.00**
Oct. 1955, A. Hepburn Ar **10.00**
Country Gentleman, 1853-1935
Ar (C-I-A) NR **6.00; 7.00; 130.00**
Dec. 23, 1911, R. Robinson
Cover **20.00**
Sept. 1, 1917, CP Auto ad...........**30.00**
July 26, 1919, H. Cady B&W **7.00**
Sept. 1925, N.C Wyeth Cover **35.00**

Delineator The, 1873-1937
(C-I-A-P) RO-MP-
JCL-NR **7.00; 10.00; 120.00**
Dec. 1905, JCL Illus. **80.00**
Mar. 1912, Chester PD................**35.00**
Aug. 1914, RA Cover **45.00**
July 1917, Stars PD.....................**70.00**
June 1920, CP Adams
Gum Ad **14.00**
May 1928, RO Kewpie page **30.00**

Esquire, 1933-1970s (C-I-A)
V-GP **4.00; 8.00; 150.00**
Fall 1933, V1, #1 ....**95.00**
Sept 1934, R. Kent, 3 Illus.
B&W **15.00**
Dec. 1939, GP FO **55.00**
Dec. 1940, AV FO & Calendar ..**100.00**
Sept.1951, Monroe gatefold **110.00**
Dec. 1955, A. Huxley Ar **8.00**
Nov. 1960, Lenny Bruce Ar **14.00**
Aug. 1971, Bonanno Ar **5.00**

Film Fun Pin-up Cover

Film Fun, 1930s-1940s
(C-I) **20.00; 35.00**
Mar. 1935, Pin-up Cover **30.00**
Feb. 1937, Pin-up Cover **29.00**

Forbes, Teens-1980s
Ar **1.00; 2.00; 12.00**
Fortune , 1930-1960
(C-I-A) **5.00; 7.00; 100.00**
Sept 1930, Golf Issue..................**42.00**
Aug. 1932, Grant Wood Illus. **18.00**
Feb. 1933, Cigar Bands Issue.....**75.00**
Nov. 1933, R. Kent 2 pg. ad **18.00**
Dec. 1934, Rockwell soup ad......**18.00**
Jan. 1937, Packards....................**22.00**
May 1938, Binder Cover..............**16.00**
Frank Leslie's, 1855-1915
Ar **9.00; 10.00; 40.00**
Jan. 4, 1879, Tiffany's **14.00**
Apr. 28, 1883, Brooklyn Bridge ...**16.00**
Apr. 18, 1885, Tom Thumb **18.00**
June 22, 1889, Johnstown
Flood **12.00**
Apr. 26, 1890,
General Sherman **13.00**
Mar. 24, 1900, Boer War **11.00**
Sept 21, 1901, McKinley shot......**16.00**
Feb. 2, 1905, Asian War.............**13.00**

Godey's Magazine,
1830-1898 (I)...................**15.00; 85.00**
1867, 12 fashion plates **60.00**
Golfing, 1930s-1960s **5.00; 22.00**
Good Housekeeping, 1885-1960
(C-I-A-P) CP-JWS-
NR..........................**4.00; 15.00; 65.00**
June 1912, CP Cover **45.00**
Jan. 1915, O'Neill Kewpie **26.00**
Aug. 1917, CP Cover **40.00**
Feb. 1929, Fangel Frig. ad **9.00**
Dec. 1932, J.W. Smith Illus. **16.00**
Feb. 1933, J.W. Smith Cover **25.00**
Disney Cartoon pgs.
1934-1944 ....**12.00; 20.00**
Oct. 1937, Pearl Buck,
Petty ad **20.00**
July 1969, Marilyn Monroe
Cover...**18.00**
Harper's Bazar, 1867-1960
(C-I-A) RO-E-MP.....**5.00; 9.00; 250.00**
Nov. 2, 1867, #1, (I) Nast **26.00**
Nov. 2, 1867, Winslow Homer
Illus. **20.00**
Dec. 1911, H.C. Christy...............**22.00**
Apr. 1918, Erté Cover...............**125.00**
Oct. 1922, Erté Cover...............**110.00**

Erté Cover for July 1917

Harper's Monthly, 1890s-Teens*
(C) MP...................**12.00; 9.00; 210.00**
June 1882, A.B. Frost Illus. **19.00**
Aug. 1901, H.C. Christy Illus. **10.00**
Mar. 1906, E.S, Green, 5 Illus:
B&W **14.00**
Aug. 1907, H. Pyle, 9 Illus. **32.00**
Jan. 1920, Newell, 6 Illus:
B&W **12.00**
Harper's Round Table, 1890s
(C) MP..................**10.00; 9.00; 150.00**
Harper's Weekly, 1857-1916
(C-I-A) Ar RO-MP **16.00; 125.00**
Jan. 3, 1857, V1, #1 ....**60.00**
Aug. 30, 1862,
Stonewall Jackson.......................**40.00**
May 20, 1865, Lincoln dies..........**54.00**
Sept 30, 1871, Nast cover...........**20.00**
July 22, 1876, Custers Last
Stand **55.00**
Jan. 29, 1881, Nast Cartoon **15.00**
July 9, 1887, Pyle Illus.................**22.00**
Aug. 20, 1892, Columbian
Exposition.....................................**18.00**
Dec. 1894, E. Penfield Cover **34.00**
Nov. 27, 1897, Newel Cover
B&W **23.00**
Aug. 1907, A.B. Stephens,
3 Illus. **11.00**
Feb. 8, 1913, R. Robinson
Cover...**36.00**
House Beautiful, 1896-1970 Ar
(C-I-A) NR-MP..........**2.00; 7.00; 50.00**

Oct. 1923, CP Varish ad.............**35.00**
Oct. 1959, F.L.Wright Ar...............**9.00**
Jack & Jill, 1930s-1960s
(Paperdolls)..............**2.00; 3.00; 16.00**
May 1961, Roy Rogers Cover **20.00**

Grace Drayton Cover for Judge,
April 12, 1913

Judge, 1881-1939 (C-I-A) JCL-
NR..........................**6.00; 8.00; 175.00**
July 4, 1891, Baseball cartoons ..**20.00**
Dec. 1, 1917, FXL Cover.............**65.00**
Oct. 14, 1922, Baseball Ar **20.00**
Dec. 8, 1928, Skiing Cover..........**20.00**

Ladies' Home Journal, 1883-
1960(C-I-A-P) NR-RO-MP-CP-
JWS **4.00; 8.00; 250.00**
May 1893, Palmer Cox,
Brownies.......................................**20.00**
Mar. 1896, Louis Rhead
Cover...**50.00**
June 1895, Stephens Cover........**11.00**
Oct. 1901, J.W. Smith Ivory Soap
ad **16.00**
Nov. 1901, Will Bradley B&Ws **15.00**
Oct. 1903, HF Cover **35.00**
Apr. 1905, J.W. Smith Cover,
HF Ad. **50.00**
Oct. 22, 1904, COW **18.00**
Aug. 1908, Henry Hutt B&W.........**7.00**
Feb. 1909, J.M. Flagg COW.......**20.00**
Sept 1909, HF Cover...................**35.00**
Jan. 1910, Young PD **40.00**
Feb. 1911, CP Cover...................**40.00**
Apr. 1918, Pogany Cover **25.00**
July 1920, Schoonover, 2 Illus. ...**14.00**

Cream of Wheat Advertisement, "The Connoisseurs"

July 1922, Brewer COW
(ILLUS.) **20.00**
Oct. 1921, CP Cover **32.00**
Jan. 1923, Kay PD **24.00**
June 1924, Pogany Djer-Kiss
ad **25.00**
Aug. 1925, Fangel Cover **28.00**

Rose O'Neill's Kewpieville Story from 1927

Apr. 1927, RO Kewpies
(ILLUS.) **18.00**
June 1937, Fangel COW.............**16.00**
Sept. 1939, Paperdoll Cutout **17.00**
Jan. 1960, Pat Boone...................**5.00**

July 1973, Marilyn Monroe Ar......**13.00**
Life (Old), 1883-1935(C-I-A-P)
  NR-MP-RA-FX **7.00; 8.00; 180.00**
Dec. 1899, MP Cover **165.00**
Mar. 3, 1901, MP Cover **145.00**
Feb. 2, 1905, MP Cover **165.00**
Feb. 20, 1908, CP Cover............**47.00**
Oct. 14, 1909, CP Cover **38.00**
June 13, 1912, CP Cover **38.00**
May 10, 1917, NR Cover.............**60.00**
Sept. 13, 1917, MP Fisk Ad.........**70.00**
Mar. 13, 1919, NR Cover & Ad....**75.00**
July 21, 1921, FXL Cover............**60.00**
Feb. 2, 1921, FXL Cover **75.00**
Jan. 18, 1923, John Held Cover..**30.00**
Jan. 31, 1924, MP Cover & Ad..**190.00**
Nov. 25, 1926, John Held
Cover...**27.00**
Life (New). 1936-1960 Ar (A)
  NR-GP-MP-V **6.00; 4.00; 150.00**
Nov. 11, 1936, V1, #1 ....**160.00**
Feb. 7, 1938, Gary Cooper,
Fair...**20.00**
June 20, 1938, Rudolph
Valentino **35.00**
May 1, 1939, Dimaggio, Petty **85.00**
June 3, 1941, Statue of Liberty **9.00**
Mar. 3, 1941, JCL Coffee ad **12.00**
Oct. 16, 1941, B. Crandell ad **9.00**
Nov. 16, 1942, N.C. Wyeth
corn ad **16.00**
Apr. 16, 1945, Eisenhower **12.00**
Nov. 17, 1947, Howard Hughes ..**18.00**
June 20, 1949, High School **7.00**
Nov. 13, 1952, Monroe ad,
Stars...**25.00**
Feb. 27, 1956, Eskimos.................**6.00**
Apr. 20, 1959, Monroe,
Mantle Ad **65.00**
Sept. 28, 1959, Ducks **6.00**
Apr. 13, 1962, Baseball Card **110.00**
Mar. 1, 1963, Snakes **5.00**
Sept. 6, 1963, Rockwell ad..........**18.00**
May 22, 1964, Streisand,
Baseball......................................**32.00**
July 30, 1965, Mickey Mantle **40.00**
Jan. 1, 1966, Sean Connery........**15.00**
Jan. 14, 1966, Ho Chi Minh...........**5.00**
Mar. 6, 1970, Skier **5.00**
Mar. 19, 1971, Ali/Frazier **18.00**
Sept. 8, 1972, Marilyn Monroe **22.00**
May 1979, Three Mile Island **3.00**

Dec. 1981, Brook Shields..............**2.00**
Mar. 1984, Daryl Hannah **2.00**
Oct. 1986, Coke Smoker **1.00**
Sept. 1987, Elvis, Prince C...........**7.00**
June 1989, A Bra.......................**1.00**
Look, 1937-1970s Ar, Stars,
Sports.......................**7.00; 8.00; 90.00**
May 1937, V1, #5, Jean Harlow
Ar.....................................**42.00**
Oct. 1937, Barclay Cover **33.00**
Jan. 12, 1943, J. Stewart Cover ..**16.00**
Oct. 15, 1946, Ted Williams **85.00**
Sept. 9, 1952, Monroe Cover **80.00**
June 1, 1954, Jackie Gleason **14.00**
Dec. 24, 1957, V. Grant ad...........**9.00**
Feb. 12, 1963, Grace Kelly
Cover....................................**25.00**
Dec. 3, 1963, Kennedys **10.00**
Feb. 6, 1967, JFK.......................**7.00**
Jan. 9, 1963, Beatles Ar **28.00**
Sept. 8, 1970, Garbo **8.00**

McCalls, 1873-1970 Ar (C-I-P)
JWS-MP-NR **2.00; 6.00; 60.00**
Aug. 1921, Cummins PD.............**24.00**
Jan. 1924, Hader PD..................**24.00**
July 1931, NC Wyeth 3 Illus. **23.00**
Aug. 1951, Betsy PD..................**14.00**
Apr. 1960, Marilyn Monroe **20.00**
May 1968, Raquel Welch **6.00**
Oct. 1984, Sally Field **1.00**
Modern Priscilla, 1887-1930
(C-I-A) MP-NR-RO **12.00; 75.00**
Jan. 1914, COW ad....................**19.00**
Feb. 1919, CP Jell-O ad..............**25.00**
June 1919, E. Christy Cover **36.00**
Nov. 1919, COW ad **19.00**
June 1921, Lawlor Cover **16.00**
Dec. 1921, E. Bolles Cover **35.00**
July 1925, Flapper Cover **19.00**
Aug. 1914, Ray Cover **14.00**
Modern Screen, 1930-1976
Movie Magazine,
Stars.....................**15.00; 20.00; 65.00**
Dec. 1930, V1, #1
Kay Francis C.............................**65.00**
Apr. 1933, Colbert C...................**42.00**
Oct. 1948, Judy Garland C..........**35.00**
May 1951, J. Crain C...................**19.00**
May 1954, E. Williams C **15.00**
Jan. 1956, James Dean **35.00**
June 1961, Liz Taylor C **12.00**

Aug. 1971, Jackie O C **7.00**
Mother Earth News, 1960s-
1980s Ar...................**4.00; 4.00; 10.00**
Motion Picture, 1913-1987
Movie Stars **9.00; 15.00; 135.00**
Oct. 1913, Bronco Billy..............**130.00**
Aug. 1916, Mary Pickford C **90.00**
Jan. 1920, M. Murray C..............**45.00**
Jan. 1928, LaPlante C................**35.00**
Mar. 1933, K. Hepburn C **27.00**
July 1943, Hayworth C **22.00**
Apr. 1949, Wyman C **19.00**
July 1958, Natalie Wood C..........**20.00**
Sept 1961, Doris Day C..............**11.00**
Jan. 1972, Jackie O.....................**8.00**
Oct. 1977, Bisset C **7.00**

National Geographic, 1888-1960
Ar (A) NR **6.00; 15.00; 4,000.00**
#1, 1888 ....**5,000.00**
V1, 2 thru V1, 4, each.............**2,500.00**
1890 thru 1900, each ...**100.00; 400.00**
Jan. 1905.................................**85.00**
Oct. 1909, North Pole.................**45.00**
Apr. 1913, Peru **18.00**
Jan. 1926, Pigeons......................**8.00**
Dec. 1939, Cathedrals..................**5.00**
Nov. 1951, Minerals **8.00**
Sept 1962, Brazil.........................**3.00**
Aug. 1963, Walt Disney Issue **10.00**
Aug. 1976, Venezuela...................**1.00**
NeedleCraft, 1909-1940
(A-I) NR-RO, COW....**4.00; 5.00; 30.00**
Feb. 1919, RO Jell-O Ad **25.00**
Oct. 1924, NR Quaker ad...........**28.00**
May 1933, Winter Cover..............**12.00**
Newsweek, 1930s-1980s
Ar **2.00; 5.00; 75.00**
Feb. 17, 1933, V1, #1 ....**35.00**
Mar. 27, 1939, Supreme Court......**5.00**
Feb. 26, 1940, War News.............**6.00**
Sept. 14, 1946, Ted Williams **80.00**
Nov. 21, 1955, Railroads.............**4.00**
July 1, 1957, Stan Musial **30.00**
Dec. 1965, Christie on Cover **4.00**
Dec. 1970, J. Nicholson Cover......**3.00**
Oct. 1972, Marilyn Monroe
Cover.....................................**15.00**
Apr. 3, 1976, Nuclear **50**
June 16, 1975, Nolan Ryan.........**20.00**
Jan. 1, 1979, Chris Reeves..........**1.00**

Outdoor Life,
  1890s-1980s **2.00; 6.00; 16.00**
  Apr. 1967, Ar Fishermans Report..**2.00**
  Jan. 1978, Ar Grizzly **2.00**
  Aug. 1982, AR Deer stories...........**2.00**

Peterson's, 1842-1898 (I)..**18.00; 24.00**
  Jan. 1842, V1, #1 ....**22.00**
  June 1865, Fashions, 70 pp. **30.00**
Pictorial Review, 1899-1939
  (C-I-A-P)
  RA-RO-MP-NR **7.00; 9.00; 110.00**
  Oct. 1913, Drayton PD **55.00**
  Sept 1918, Drayton PD **45.00**
  Feb. 1926, Twelvetrees Cover **16.00**
  Dec. 1927, Jesus..........................**6.00**
  Feb. 1930, Drayton PD, COW **34.00**
  Mar. 1931, Mary Pickford, Ads **17.00**
  May 1934, Dottie Darlings PD **22.00**
  Apr. 1935, Ads, Fashions **5.00**
Playboy, 1953-1990s,
  Mens **4.00; 5.00; 7.00; 400.00**
  Dec. 1953, #1,
  Marilyn Monroe......................**7,500.00**
  Jan. 1955, Bettie Page **1,000.00**
  Jan. 1957, June Blair................**175.00**
  Jan. 1960, Stella Stevens............**85.00**
  Dec. 1963, Donna Michelle **65.00**
  Nov. 1966, Lisa Baker **25.00**
  Dec. 1972, Mercy Rooney **20.00**
  Sept. 1980, Lisa Welch **12.00**
Police Gazette,
  1927-1960s **3.00; 7.00; 13.00**
  Apr. 1940, Carol Landis
  on Cover.....................................**8.00**
  Jan. 1959, Monroe Ar..................**15.00**
Popular Mechanics, 1902-1960
  Ar **4.00; 6.00; 35.00**
  Dec. 1941, Mosquito boats...........**4.00**
Popular Science, 1872-1970s
  Ar (C) NR **3.00; 8.00; 185.00**
  Oct. 1920, NR Cover **225.00**
  Apr. 1929, H. Paus cover **14.00**
  Mar. 1957, Antennas **2.00**
  Mar. 1976, Wind power **2.00**
  Nov. 1985, Technology **50**
Puck, 1877-1918 Ar (C-I-A)
  RA-RO-FXL.........**16.00; 18.00; 130.00**
  Sept. 29, 1880, Douglas..............**22.00**
  Oct. 10, 1883, Cowboys **30.00**
  Dec. 4, 1884, N.Y. Tribune **12.00**
  Feb. 16, 1887, Railroads **15.00**

*Rolf Armstrong Cover for
March 27, 1915 Puck*

  June 11, 1891, Scandal-
  mongers **12.00**
  Sept. 15, 1897, RO Cover **100.00**
  Feb. 16, 1898, HF Cover &
  Illus. **80.00**
  Apr. 16, 1902, Autos....................**18.00**
  Apr. 20, 1904, RO Illus. **40.00**
  Feb. 1914, Cartoon Cover...........**16.00**

Reader's Digest, 1890-1970s
  Ar NR **1.00; 3.00; 15.00**
Redbook, 1903-1980 (I), Movie
  ads, Stars.................**1.00; 6.00; 50.00**
  Nov. 1934, Herbert Hoover **7.00**
  June 1936, Tunney & Louis........**12.00**
  Mar. 1947, Movie Ads **8.00**
  Sept. 1948, Dennis Day **3.00**
  Jan. 1951, Howard Hughes.........**10.00**
  Mar. 1953, Monroe Cover & Ar ...**65.00**
  Nov. 1954, Grace Kelly Cover.....**18.00**
  Nov. 1955, Mrs. Billy Graham **2.00**
  Mar. 1957, Tony Curtis Ar **4.00**
  Apr. 1960, Monroe Pic...................**8.00**
  Oct. 1990, Monroe Article..............**3.00**
Rolling Stone, 1970s-1980s
  Ar **3.00; 5.00; 75.00**
  #1, 1967, John Lennon................**70.00**
  #37, 1969, Elvis.........................**21.00**
  #198, 1975, Bob Dylan..................**9.00**
  #415, 1984, Beatles **7.00**
  #486, 1986, Billy Joel **3.00**

Saturday Evening Post, 1821-
1960 (C-I-A) CP-NR-
MP-HF-JCL-FX 7 ....**9.00; 500.00**
Mar. 11, 1899, HF Cover & Ills: ...**40.00**
Nov. 10, 1900, HF Cover **42.00**
June 13, 1908, HF Cover **38.00**
Feb. 17, 1912, HF Cover.............**33.00**
Dec. 8, 1923, JCL 2 pg.
Interwoven.................................**25.00**
Mar. 15, 1930, Fangel Milk ad.....**16.00**
Dec. 25, 1943, Mead Schaeffer
Cov. **16.00**
May 1, 1954, Stan Musial...........**40.00**
Apr. 20, 1957, Yogi Berra...........**24.00**
Dec. 26, 1959, Christ...................**1.00**
May 11, 1963, Leo Durocher.......**15.00**
Sept. 28, 1963, Vietnam...............**4.00**
Feb. 2, 1964, Sophia Loren...........**8.00**
June 29, 1968, Sex Education **1.00**
May 1976, Chris Evert...................**1.00**

Scribners, 1890s-
1930s **7.00; 9.00; 210.00**
Aug. 1879, Whistler **12.00**
Feb. 1880, Edison's Light............**24.00**
Jan. 1899, C.D. Gibson Illus........**19.00**
Feb. 1899, A.B. Frost 9 Illus.......**20.00**
Aug. 1904, J. Guerin Illus. **17.00**
Oct. 1906, N.C. Wyeth Illus. **30.00**
Feb. 1907, JCL, HF, Flagg **60.00**
Feb. 1928, Rockwell Kent
Cover......................................**17.00**
Dec. 1929, Rockwell Kent
Cover......................................**17.00**

Sports Illustrated, Baseball,
Football, swimsuit & many
Personality issues have
premium value, that is higher
then average values.
Dell Issues: #1, Feb. 1949, Ralph
Beard....................................**110.00**
June 1949, Dodgers **70.00**
1950s **9.00; 25.00**
1960s **5.00; 20.00**
1970s **4.00; 15.00**
1980s **3.00; 10.00**
1990s **2.00; 4.00**
Dec. 1953, Dummy Issue **285.00**
Aug. 16, 1954, V1, #1
with cards **385.00**
Aug. 23, 1954, Yankee cards **400.00**
Jan. 3, 1955, R. Banister............**42.00**
Mar. 21, 1955, P. O'Brien...........**16.00**

Apr. 11, 1955, Baseball card **255.00**
Apr. 23, 1956, Billy Martin **27.00**
May 12, 1958, America's Cup **16.00**
Jan. 11, 1960, Jerry Lucas **19.00**
Mar. 6, 1961, Reds.....................**22.00**
July 2, 1962, Mickey Mantle **120.00**
June 22, 1964, Tom O'Hara **10.00**
Mar. 7, 1966, Adolp Rupp **10.00**
Jan. 15, 1968, Swimsuit Issue.....**39.00**
Mar. 2, 1970, New York
Rangers...................................**14.00**
Mar. 13, 1972, Johnny Bench **19.00**
Jan. 21, 1974, Super Bowl VII.....**20.00**
Mar. 22, 1976, Tracy Austin **10.00**
Feb. 27, 1978, Leon Spinks **10.00**
Feb. 4, 1980, Christie Brinkley **40.00**
Aug. 2, 1982, Ray Mancini **50.00**
Apr. 23, 1984,
Darrell Strawberry **11.00**
Dec. 1, 1986, Mike Tyson............**16.00**
Mar. 21, 1988, Larry Bird.............**11.00**
Aug. 6, 1990, Joe Montana **11.00**

Time, 1923-1980 Ar (C-A) GP-
MP-NR **2.00; 6.00; 200.00**
Mar. 3, 1923, V1, #1 ....**90.00**
Apr. 15, 1935, Dizzy Dean **66.00**
Oct. 5, 1936, Gehrig **128.00**
Oct. 10, 1941, Joe Louis **26.00**
Aug. 3, 1942, Artzbasheff Cover ...**9.00**
Oct. 4, 1948, Dimaggio..............**85.00**
May 29, 1950, Viet Nam................**3.00**
July 26, 1954, Willie Mays
Cover......................................**12.00**
Oct. 3, 1955, Casy Stengal **32.00**
Feb. 22, 1963, Cassius Clay **42.00**
July 7, 1966, DeGaulle Cover **2.00**
June 25, 1965, Bundy Cover.........**1.00**
Aug. 18, 1966, Stock Market.........**1.00**
July 12, 1968, TV Commercials **3.00**
Mar. 8, 1971, Ali/Frazer.............**18.00**
July 16, 1973, Marilyn Monroe
Ar..**9.00**
Aug. 18, 1985 ....**5.00**

True Confessions,
1930s-1950s **7.00; 40.00**
May 1936, Colbert Cover **15.00**
Feb. 1938, Lombard Cover;
Mozert **38.00**
Sept. 1945, Marie Denham **8.00**
Feb. 1954, AR **8.00**

TV Guide, 1953-1990
Ar **1.00; 6.00; 220.00**

Apr. 3, 1953, #1 ....**230.00**
May 22, 1953, #8.....................**50.00**
Sept. 27, 1955 ....**42.00**
1958 Averages **6.00; 50.00**
1960 ....**5.00; 32.00**
1962 ....**5.00; 12.00**
1964 ....**2.00; 6.00**
Most other years for common issues
depending on Star
content & programs:.............**2.00; 5.00**
Some values to: **20.00; 45.00**

Vanity Fair, 1859-1960 (C-A)
FXL-NR **5.00; 9.00; 85.00**
Dec. 31, 1859, V1, #1 ....**45.00**
Sept. 1913, Babe Ruth cover **80.00**
Feb. 1914, FXL Cover **80.00**
Jan. 1917, JCL B&W ad, Golf **20.00**
Apr. 1920, Rockwell Kent **55.00**
Nov. 1929, Deco cover **38.00**
Vogue, 1892-1960 (C-I-A)
E-FXL **6.00; 7.00; 95.00**
Oct. 10, 1895, Golf Issue.............**70.00**
Mar. 15, 1913, FXL cover **85.00**
May 15, 1924, CP ad B&W **10.00**
Nov. 1, 1927, Bolin Cover **35.00**
Oct. 1, 1937, GP Ad **12.00**
Jan. 1940, Swimsuit Cover..........**14.00**
Apr. 1, 1961, Your Clothes **3.00**
Fall/Winter 1964, Fall Knitting **4.00**

Woman's Day,
1930s-1980s **50; 2.00; 6.00**

Woman's Home Companion
December 1904 Cover

Woman's Home Companion,
1873-1960 (C-I-A-P) RO-JCL-
NR-MP **3.00; 7.00; 110.00**
Aug. 1898, J.W. Smith Cover **50.00**

Sept. 1898, JCL Cover **80.00**
Feb. 1904, Edison's Home **18.00**
Sept. 1910, RO Kewpie **35.00**
Aug. 1914, Fangle Illus:..............**12.00**
Apr. 1916, RA Cover, CP Ad.......**60.00**
Sept. 1916, CP Fashion page **40.00**
May 1917, J.W. Smith,
B&W Soap ad.............................**11.00**
Oct. 1925, Our Gang PD **48.00**
Nov. 1926, Cowboy PD **35.00**
Mar. 1938, COW **8.00**
Jan. 1939, Fangle Cover **25.00**
July 1953, Dietrich on Cover **12.00**

Youths Companion, 1827-1929
(A) MP-NR **8.00; 9.00; 65.00**
Oct. 16, 1919, Pogany
Soap ad **23.00**
July 6, 1916, COW, unsigned......**15.00**

METALS

BRASS

Brass Hanukah Lamp

Andirons, plinth engraved
w/foliate design, lemon top, ca.
1800, 25" h., pr. **$748.00**

Bedwarmer, round pan w/hinged
domed lid decorated at the top
w/stamped & chased scrolls &
rosettes, w/a long flat iron
handle ending in a hooked
terminal, first half 18th c.,
38¾" l. **1,840.00**

Bedwarmer, engraved lid &
turned wooden handle w/traces
of old graining, 40¾" l. **259.00**

Cooking pot, three-footed, cast design in handle, 10¼" d. **193.00**

Hanukah lamp, tapering cylindrical standard supports eight curved candle arms molded w/flowers & leaves terminating into horizontal support, servant light in center, quadrangular base, Germany, 17th c., 19¾" h. (ILLUS.) **3,737.00**

Kettle, spun brass w/iron bale handle, labeled "The American Brass Kettle Manufactury," 15" d. **61.00**

Mortar & pestle, bell metal, 3⅜" h., 2 pcs................................**72.00**

Oil can, tall upright oval body w/a flat top w/arched flat handle from side to side & looped handgrip handle at the back rim, angled long pouring spout at front rim, marked "10 QT," overall 16½" h. **104.00**

Teakettle, cov., a low cylindrical dovetailed inset cooper bottom for fitting into stove burner, body of ringed bell-form w/shaped & pointed top swing handle, angled goose neck spout, 9¾" h. plus handle (old soldered repair) **83.00**

Teakettle, cover & trivet, arched hinged handle above swelled body, serpentine spout, lid & hinged tab, oblong Queen Anne pierced oval brass trivet decorated w/stylized C-scrolls, four cabriole legs & pad feet, ca. late 1700s, kettle 13½" w., 13½" h., 2 pcs........................**1,035.00**

Vase, hand-hammered, Arts & Crafts style, gently swelled cylindrical body on a thin footring, the top tapering to a gently flaring flat mouth, original greenish brown patina, impressed mark of F.J. Wildenhofer, early 20th c., 8½" h. **248.00**

Wall sconces, domed & stepped circular wall plate w/removable serpentine candle arms, dished drip plates & cylindrical candle cups, England, late 1770s, 14" l., pr. **3,737.00**

BRONZE

Birdcage, gilt-bronze, domed top w/berried & feather finial, central door & sides fitted w/feeders, dentelled base w/single drawer releasing liner, raised on bun feet, signed "FR.OT.ST.," 43" h. (ILLUS.) **9,200.00**

Gilt-Bronze Birdcage

Candlesticks, Renaissance Revival style, the wide low-domed foot cast w/bold floral swags, a wide disc ring at the bottom of the tapering shaft w/a bulbous gadrooned knop below the tapering column cast w/further swags, a wide drip pan below the urn-form candle socket cast w/satyr masks, 19th c., 8" h., pr. **546.00**

Censer, figural, ovoid animal body, standing foursquare w/spiral ornaments inlaid in silver on flanks beneath collar of stiff lappets, lion-like head forms cover w/open jaws revealing fangs, China, 18th c., 12½" h. **5,175.00**

Ewers, baluster form w/arched handles surmounted by winged putto, each body decorated w/bacchic cherubs in relief & raised on circular feet, decorated w/vintage patt., 35" h. **2,880.00**

Jardiniere, gilt finish, gadrooned oval boat-shaped body w/tapering shoulders cast w/floral swags below the rolled rim, each end cast w/the figure of a mermaid forming a handle, raised on a leafy scroll legs on a shaped oblong plinth base, France, 19th c., 21" l. **2,760.00**

Matchbox holder, Modeled patt., original patina, marked "Tiffany Studios New York - 112," 4½" w., 3½" h. **121.00**

Vase, the shaped triangular vessel w/a very tall slender neck above the bulbous bifurcated base, the body composed of three hammered scarab shields, each decorated w/two free-form crimson & umber patinated spots, signed "L. GAILLARD," Lucien Gaillard, France, early 20th c., 16" h. **14,950.00**

CHROME

Ashtray, Art Deco style, a ball-shaped sphere encircled by a copper-trimmed disc & stars, raised on a low round black base, Chase, 4" d., 3½" h..........**176.00**

Candlesticks, Faberware Statuesque Line, 8½" h., pr. **55.00**

Lamp, desk, Art Deco style, the circular base intersected by three small circular discs, supporting a cylindrical standard issuing an adjustable shade w/ball finial, designed by Donald Deskey, ca. 1931, 15" h. **299.00**

Teapot, cov., electric, Art Deco style w/"ivory" insulated swivel handle & finial, by Chase, 1930s..**60.00**

COPPER

Bedwarmer, tooled lid & wooden handle w/worn black & red graining, 42" l............................**358.00**

Bowl, hand-hammered, flaring w/red patina, impressed square mark, 4½" d., 2" h. **468.00**

Bowl, hand-hammered, Arts & Crafts style, wide & deep rounded & tapering sides w/a wide closed rim, applied initial "W" in silver on the side, dark brown original patina, impressed "KALO," Kalo Shop, Chicago, Illinois, early 20th c., 8½" d., 3½" h. **1,100.00**

Bowl, hand-hammered, Arts & Crafts style, flaring 'lotus' bowl w/high sides & a flaring notched rim, the interior w/original reddish brown patina, die-stamped open box mark, Dick van Erp, 17½" d., 4½" h.............**880.00**

Box, cov., hand-hammered, Arts & Crafts style, rectangular w/a hinged domed cover on a riveted strap & panel-constructed base, impressed mark of Gustav Stickley, early 20th c., 4⅝ x 8⅝", 2¾" h. (cleaned) **805.00**

Box, cov., rectangular, the deep sides w/rolled & riveted corner brackets continuing to form short legs w/rolled tips, the fitted rectangular cover w/a heavy gauge applied angled loop handle riveted to a raised oval, original dark brown patina, impressed mark of Benedict Studios, early 20th c., 6½ x 10", 6" h. **468.00**

Candle sconce, wall-type, Arts & Crafts style, tall flat backplate w/an arched crest w/hanging hole & pointed corners, impressed banding around the rim & a pointed arch in the center, a small rectangular shelf holding the cylindrical candle

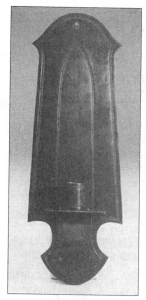

Arts & Crafts Candle Sconce

socket above the waisted flaring base drop w/further banded trim, original bronze patina, Robert Jarvie, Chicago, early 20th c., 4⅞" w., 13⅜" h. (ILLUS.).......**1,150.00**

Cauldron, cylindrical form, tapering rounded lip w/bail handle, ca. 1880s, 21½" d., 15½" h. **403.00**

Jardiniere, hand-hammered, wide bulbous ovoid body w/a wide flattened flaring rim, the sides w/riveted applied handles w/acorn straps, original dark brown patina, impressed "The Turchin Co., N.Y.," 14" d., 10" h. **605.00**

Lamp, table model, hand-hammered copper, Arts & Crafts style, bulbous ovoid copper base on a narrow footring tapers gently to the socket supporting a tall conical shade w/a copper frame enclosing four wide panels of mica, new patina, impressed mark of Dirk van Erp, early 20th c., shade 14" d., overall 15" h..........................**8,250.00**

Matchbox holder, hand-hammered, Arts & Crafts style, rounded rectangular small uprights forming a narrow "U" to hold a box, raised on a short flat support centered on a round dished base, original patina, Dirk van Erp mark, 5" d., 3" h...........**495.00**

Sauce pan, dovetailed w/cast iron handle, "Wrought Iron Range Co." cast label marking, 7¼" d. **83.00**

Teakettle, cov., dovetailed w/cast brass handle & gooseneck spout, 10½" h. **121.00**

Teakettle, cov., oval tall upright sides w/a domed top & small inset cover w/angled loop handle, large swing handle from shoulder to shoulder, swan's-neck spout, handle marked "Thomas Bishop, Clyde Place, Glasgow," Scotland, 11" h. (minor dents) **138.00**

Gustav Stickley Copper Tray

Tray, hand-hammered, Arts & Crafts style, round form w/a flat flanged rim decorated w/four repousse' oblong lobes alternating w/curved leaf-form devices, dished center, impressed Gustav Stickley mark, Model No. 346, patina loss, 20⅞" d. (ILLUS.) **4,025.00**

Vase, hand-hammered, Arts & Crafts style, squatty bulbous form w/original medium-dark patina, Harry Dixon, 5¼" d., 4" h. **905.00**

Vase, bud, hand-hammered, Arts & Crafts style, a four-sided base supports a nicely riveted heavy gauge upright brace & ring in original dark brown & black patina w/cylindrical glass tube flower holder, marked "KK, Karl Kipp," early 20th c., 8" h. **330.00**

Copper Candle Scounce

Wall sconce, candle-type, rectangular form, backplate w/rounded corners repoussé w/two vinters carrying large cluster of grapes below fruiting grapevine, Dutch, minor losses, 9¼" h. (ILLUS.)..........**2,070.00**

IRON

Andirons, painted cast, figural Hessian Soldiers marching in review w/head turned over left shoulder & sword held upright, ca. early 1900s, 19⅔" h., pr.......**518.00**

Andirons, cast, figural liberty holding flaming torch & standing on shell, naturalistic base, ca. 1800s, 17½" h., pr. **230.00**

Candleholder, hand-wrought, standing holder w/circular candlecup & spring action holder mounted on cylindrical shaft, arched tripod legs w/scrolled feet, 28" h. **288.00**

Griddle, fifteen-sided griddle w/raised rim & spout, 22" d. (some edge damage) **138.00**

Hitching post, cast, painted full-bodied figural boy wearing white shirt & blue overalls standing on square base, ca. early 1900s, 44⅓" h. **748.00**

Kettle, gypsy-style w/relief design of bears, marked "Camp-Fire, Keep The Faith Tho I Go Empty," 11" d., 8½" h................**495.00**

Early Iron Kettle Stand

Kettle stand, hand-wrought w/cast rectangular decorative grill top, raised on four simple cabriole-style legs, 9½ x 15" (ILLUS.) **358.00**

Mask, wall-type, cast, a large lion's mask cast in the half-round w/realistic features & a slightly open mouth, retains traces of old polychrome, on a rod in a white metal base, American-made, late 19th c., 12½" w., 26½" h. **3,737.00**

Model of a Setter dog, cast, life-sized recumbent animal looking straight ahead, cast in the round, probably New York, late 19th c., 39½" l., 19½" h. **8,050.00**

Spoon, figural, wrought & cast, the bowl fashioned as an rounded open hand & continuing to a long slender faceted stem terminating in a small teardrop-form spoon, early 19th c., 10" h. **690.00**

PEWTER

Baptismal bowl, deep gently flaring sides, stamped w/"BX" quality mark, Boardman, Hartford, Connecticut or New York, New York, 19th c., 9" d., 4⅜" h. **920.00**

Beaker, cylindrical, Timothy Boardman & Co., New York, New York, ca. 1825, 5⅛" h. **633.00**

Beakers, cylindrical w/ringed foot & flaring rim, two w/incised mid-bands, attributed to Thomas D. Boardman Company, Hartford, Connecticut, 1805-50, 5¼" h., set of 4.....................................**575.00**

Bowl-vase, Arts & Crafts style, a short wide foot supporting a wide short cylindrical bowl w/rolled rim & angular side handles, the sides decorated w/a repeated decoration of embossed three-rose clusters on vertical stems, tiny butterflies flying among the blossoms, a band around the base reads "And The Woodbine Spices Are Wafted Abroad And The Musk Of The Rose Is Blown," original patina, impressed "Tudric - 011," England, early 20th c., 12" d., 4½" h. **990.00**

Candlestick, altar-type, cylindrical flaring shallow cup w/candleholder above a ring-and-baluster-turned stem over a circular stepped foot, unmarked, England, 19th c., 19" h. (repairs to base) **58.00**

Candlesticks, baluster-form w/flared candle socket, Roswell Gleason, Dorchester, Massachusetts, 1822-71, 8¾" h., pr. (minor dents)............**978.00**

Candlesticks, Art Nouveau style, a three-sided domed base w/small tab feet & indented oval reserves w/whiplash floral designs below the three-side slightly tapering standard supporting a narrow neck w/thin loop handles framing it below the three-sided candle socket w/upturned flaring three-sided rim, original patina, Kayserzinn mark, Germany, early 20th c., 12" h., pr. **770.00**

Chandelier, four-light, shaped standard w/a ring finial & four scrolled candlearms ending in baluster-shaped candle cups w/drip pans, 18th c., 18½" h. ...**3,737.00**

Charger, partial touch may be part of Danforth mark, 12¼" d. (wear, scratches & two splits)....**110.00**

Unusual Pewter Ciborium

Ciborium, cov., wide short ringed cylindrical body w/a flattened dished cover w/a cross finial, molded foot, Homan & Company, Cincinnati, Ohio, ca. 1880, 5⅞" h. (ILLUS.)................**460.00**

Clock, desk-type, pewter case decorated w/a stylized Art Nouveau design in low-relief & blue enamel hearts in high-relief, silver dial w/black hands & numerals, impressed "TUDRIC 0482 - MADE IN ENGLAND," early 20th c., 4" w., 4" h............**748.00**

Communion service: cov. flagon & two chalices; the flagon w/a round flaring ringed foot & a ringed cylindrical pedestal below the body w/a squatty bulbous base tapering to a tall slightly flaring cylindrical upper body, high stepped, domed cover w/domed finial, wide rim spout & long C-scroll handle, each pedestal-footed chalice of matching shape, Hiram Yale & Company, Wallingford, Connecticut, 1825-35, chalices 7⅛" h., flagon 13¾" h., the set **2,530.00**

Dish, Samuel Danforth, Hartford, Connecticut, marked "Laughlin," ca. 1795-1816, touchmarks on base, 11¾" h. **431.00**

Dish, Samuel Danforth, Hartford, Connecticut, marked "Laughlin," ca. 1795-1816, touchmarks on base, 13¼" d. **489.00**

Flagon, cov., flaring ringed base tapering to a medial ring on the tall gently tapering cylindrical body w/a long rim spout, stepped & domed cover w/urn-form finial, shaped C-scroll long handle, Thomas & Samuel Boardman, Hartford, Connecticut, ca. 1825, 14⅛" h. **3,450.00**

Ice bucket w/handle, Continental, Angle touch, 8" h. ...**440.00**

Lamp, added tin flange foot, whale oil burner, 8½" h. **165.00**

Plate, flanged rim, Blakslee Barns, Philadelphia, 1812-17, 7⅞" d. (worn) **140.00**

Plates, flanged rim, marked "James Dixon & Sons, Sheffield," England, 19th c.,10⅛" d., pr. (dents) **187.00**

Spoons, marked "WT & Co.," 19th c., 8" l., set of 6 ....**230.00**

Stuffing spoon, wide deep oval bowl w/long flat oblong handle, anchor mark & stamped "DEP," bright-cut decoration, Europe, 14" l. **110.00**

Tankard, tapering cylindrical body w/a scrolled strap handle, Frederick Basset, Hartford, Connecticut, 1780-1810, 6" h. **2,300.00**

Teapot, cov., flaring foot on the wide, short slightly tapering cylindrical body w/a low angled rim, pyramidal hinged cover w/a button finial, swan's-neck spout, C-scroll metal handle, Morey & Obert, Boston, 1852-55, 6¼" h. (some wear) **220.00**

Teapot, battered, marked "H.B. Ward," Wallingford Connecticut, 8½" h. **275.00**

Teapot, cov., pedestal-footed pigeon-breasted body w/a tapered band at the base of the waisted neck w/a widely flaring rim, stepped, domed cover w/a wooden disc finish, swan's-neck spout & black-painted metal C-scroll handle, marked "Wm. McQuilkin - 1," Philadelphia, 1839-53, 9⅞" h. (minor denting on side).....................................**400.00**

Teapot, cov., domed low foot below the double-swelled tapering cylindrical body w/a flaring rim, hinged high-domed cover w/wooden finial button missing, angled C-scroll handle, tall swan's-neck spout, Thomas D. Boardman, Hartford, Connecticut, 1830s, 11¾" h. (handle dented, repair to top of spout where it attaches to body) **325.00**

Vegetable dish, cov., oval, cover w/pear finial, Angle touch, Europe, 13½" l. **220.00**

SHEFFIELD PLATE

Candelabra, three-light, each on a domed oblong reeded foot supporting a tall ring-turned cylindrical standard w/a flared reeded medial ring issuing to long slender scrolled arms ending in wide scroll-edged drip pans & urn-form candle sockets w/rolled embossed rims, the center shaft topped by another reeded ring below the central

One Sheffield Plate Candelabrum

urn-form candle socket, early
19th c., rosing, 20" h., pr.
(ILLUS. of one) **1,725.00**

Candlesticks, paneled baluster
ovoid form, separate bobeches,
early 19th c., 11⅜" h., pr.
(rosing) **403.00**

Entree dishes, cov., rectangular
body & cover w/gadrooned &
shell rims, each cover engraved
w/an armorial, mounted w/ring
handles, ca. 1820,
12¾" l., pr. **747.00**

Meat platter, oval form, engraved
border w/crest at side, scalloped
rim applied w/leaf-capped scrolls
alternating w/shells, ca. mid
1800s, 17¼" l...........................**230.00**

Tray, rectangular form, shaped
rim & two handles applied
w/scrolling foliage, engraved
center w/wide band of
conforming decoration centering
engraved armorial, ca. early
1800s, 29½" l............................**805.00**

Tureens, cov., deep oval bombé
body w/fluting around the lower
half, the rolled rim cast w/a leafy
band, upright & everted scroll-
cast loop end handles, the inset
stepped & domed cover w/a
band of gadrooning & a large
upright wreath-form ring handle,

raised on four winged paw legs,
unmarked, ca. 1820,
overall 9¼" l., pr......................**1,265.00**

SILVER, AMERICAN
(Sterling & Coin)

Ornate Gorham Bonbon Scoops

Basket, cylindrical form w/flared
rim & upright handle, reticulated
& engraved decoration, 1919,
Gorham Mfg. Company,
Providence, Rhode Island,
12" h. **230.00**

Bonbon scoops, oblong chased
& reticulated German
Renaissance design w/arched &
pierced handle, Gorham Mfg.
Company, Providence, Rhode
Island, engraved monogram &
dates, 9¾" l., pr.
(ILLUS.) **1,035.00**

Bowl, rounded sides on a small
raised foot, 1947-56, Tiffany &
Co., New York, New York,
6¾" d. **115.00**

Bowl, lotus blossom form,
hammer textured, engraved
name & date, ca. 1886, Whiting
Mfg. Co., 8⅜" d.........................**345.00**

Bowl, Chrysanthemum patt.,
footed oval w/deep gently
rounded sides chased & applied
w/a band of flowers, the shaped
rim applied w/flowers, gilt
interior, Black, Starr & Frost,
early 20th c., 9½" l....................**517.00**

Bread tray, rectangular form
w/applied pierced floral rim,
engraved ribbon monogram,

Redlick, retailed by Gorham Mfg. Company, Providence, Rhode Island, 14" l. **633.00**

Button hook, figural cherub handle, 2¼" l. **42.00**

Cake plate, reticulated floral & scroll rim, engraved monogram, Howard Sterling Co., Providence, Rhode Island, 20th c., 11½" d. **489.00**

Candlesticks, square base w/flaring square stem, globular candle cup fitted w/shaped square nozzle, weighted, marked "Gorham Mfg. Co.," ca. 1916, 7¾" h. **517.00**

Cann, baluster form, engraved w/contemporary arms in rococo cartouche flanked by floral sprays w/shell below , leaf-capped double-scroll & cast molded foot, "Ann Willing Morris" engraved on base & marked "IB" in oval, ca. 1760, 4⅛" h. **4,887.00**

Coaster, wine, round form w/ border of blossoms, Unger Brothers, ca. 1900, 6⅜" d. **173.00**

Coffeepot, cov., Medallion patt., a low footring below the squatty bulbous body tapering to a tall cylindrical slightly flaring neck w/a hinged flat cover w/a helmet-form finial, a long slender upright spout from the shoulder, a stepped long angular handle

Medallion Pattern Coffeepot

from the rim to the shoulder & fitted at the top w/a classical head, a spearpoint engraved band around the upper neck, the lower body w/a profile bust of a bearded classical man within a large classical cartouche medallion, Ball, Black & Company, mid-19th c., 10¼" h. (ILLUS.) **1,150.00**

Coffee set: cov. coffeepot, open sugar, creamer & oval tray, Colonial Revival, each urn form w/urn, swag & Greek key details, Gorham Mfg. Co., Providence, Rhode Island, coffeepot 9½" h., tray 13⅛" l., 4 pcs. **1,035.00**

Dish, Arts & Crafts style, circular w/a shallow incurved rim pinched into four points, stamped "Sterling Hand Wrought at The Kalo Shops Chicago and New York J 179 L," 1914-18, 14" d. **2,185.00**

Dishes, each modeled as cockerel standing w/spread tail on ground, maker's mark of Durgin & Co. on one, 9½" l, pr. **805.00**

Fruit bowl, Art Nouveau style, round form w/applied base-relief-shaped hollyhock rim, monogram, Unger Brothers, ca. 1900, 11½" d. **489.00**

Gravy boat, chased landscaped & floral design, marked "S. Kirk & Son, Co.," ca. 1900, 7¾" l. **633.00**

Ice pail, circular form, slightly flaring on banded foot, fitted w/strainer pierced w/scrolling foliage & strapwork, Tiffany & Co., ca. 1907-47, 8½" d. **862.00**

Mug, child's, cylindrical, the upper half panel decorated w/a parade of children in low-relief, impressed marks of Tiffany & Company, New York, New York, engraved "Walter," 2⅞" d., 3¼" h. **316.00**

Mug, coin, cylindrical w/a molded rim band & incurved base raised on a thin embossed footring, ornate C-scroll handle, the sides embossed w/a strawberry & leaf design, inscribed "Laura H. Jack," Hyde & Goodrich, New Orleans, Louisiana, ca. 1850, 3⅝" h. **385.00**

Kirk Repousse Water Pitcher

Pitcher, water, ovoid body w/a C-scroll leaf-embossed handle, overall decoration of chased & repoussé leaf decoration, the sides tapering to a short neck w/a wide arched spout, engraved monogram on bottom, Samuel Kirk & Sons, Baltimore, 1880-90, 7⅜" h. (ILLUS.)........**1,093.00**

Pitcher, water, ovoid form w/hammered surface, mounted w/cast grapevine handle & rims, marked "Gorham Mfg. Co.," retailed by Spaulding & Co., Chicago, ca. 1900, 10" h. **1,265.00**

Porringer, wide circular form, keyhole handle engraved w/script initial "L" marked near center interior w/"Revere" in a rectangle, Paul Revere Jr., Boston, Massachusetts, ca. 1790, 5⅝" d. **13,800.00**

Punch bowl & ladle, domed & swirled lobed base w/applied foliage around the rim supporting a widely flaring bowl w/a wide shaped rim applied w/swirled foliage, marked "Mauser Mfg. Co.," ladle w/lobed bowl & applied handle w/swirling foliage, engraved w/monogram, ladle marked by Dominick & Haff and Mauser Mfg. Co., ca. 1900, 17" l., 2 pcs. **6,035.00**

Punch ladle, beveled border & shell design w/engraved accents & Old English "R," Dominick & Haff, ca. 1913 ....**259.00**

Salad serving set: bowl w/domed foot & hammered surface, two matching salad servers, all impressed w/stylized circular & sectioned banded decoration, maker's mark of Durgin Mfg. Co., ca. 1900s, monogrammed, bowl 10" d., set of 3 ....**632.00**

Sugar cube rack, Arts & Crafts style, a smoothly formed trough design w/two end supports w/a reticulated design w/angled tops, marked "Sterling - Kalo," Kalo Shop, Chicago, Illinois, early 20th c., 1½ x 7½", 1½" h. **468.00**

Sugar urn, cov., coin, classical urn form w/a tall tapering cover w/a ringed tip topped by a pineapple finial, raised on a short flaring pedestal resting on a square foot, beaded bands, engraved initials "HL" on one side & "LD to HD" on the bottom, Joseph Jr. & Nathaniel Richardson, Philadelphia, ca. 1790, 8½" h. **1,495.00**

Tea caddy, cov., applied grapevine design, monogrammed, late 19th - early 20th c., retailed by A. Stowell & Co., Frank W. Smith Silver Co., Inc., Gardner, Massachusetts, 5" h. (dents) **230.00**

Tea & coffee set: cov. teapot & coffeepot, cov. sugar, creamer & waste bowl; each of swelled baluster form w/ribbed rim & base detail, coffeepot & teapot w/wooden handles,

monogrammed, early 20th c.,
Towle Silversmiths,
Newburyport, Massachusetts,
coffeepot 7" h., 5 pcs.................**633.00**

Tray, round form w/shaped
applied scroll & floral rim,
engraved monogram, Gorham
Mfg. Company, Providence,
Rhode Island, 14⅜" d. (dents) ...**230.00**

Tray, oval, applied Classical
Revival urn & swag border,
engraved monogram & dates in
center, 1917, Gorham Mfg. Co.,
Providence, Rhode Island,
18¾" l. **489.00**

Vase, coin, classical baluster-
form, low round foot, tall waisted
neck w/a flaring beaded rim
w/gently curved long handles
from the rim to the angled
shoulder, boldly chased overall
w/a vintage grape design,
Jones, Ball & Poor, Boston,
1846, 7⅛" h. (slight denting)......**978.00**

Sterling Silver American Vase

Vase, slightly flaring trumpet-form
body on a low stepped round
foot, plain wide cupped top
w/flattened rim, the sides
chased & reticulated overall w/a
pansy design, engraved
monogram, Mauser, early
20th c., 14⅞" h. (ILLUS.) **1,840.00**

SILVER, ENGLISH & OTHERS

Brazier, pierced w/two bands of
strapwork & raised on three
scroll & claw supports w/wood
terminals, straight turned wood
handle & removable liner, base
inscribed, marked on body &
handle, liner marked, William
Pearson, London, England,
1711, 6½" d. **1,840.00**

George III Silver Cake Basket

Cake basket, circular form, deep
rounded wirework sides rising
from stiff leaves w/ropework
swing handle, center engraved
w/contemporary arms on
drapery mantle, George III
period, marked "John Wakelin &
William Taylor, London, 1731,"
11⅜" d. (ILLUS.) **7,475.00**

Centerpiece, circular form
w/domed base on four scrolling
acanthus supports, pierced
w/shells & scrolling foliage, putto
wearing scarf w/hair in floral
braid supporting circular dish,
pierced, lobed lower body below
pierced band pairs of swans
w/scrolling foliage, fitted w/blue
glass liner, Austria, 11" h.
(repairs to stand & liner) **1,495.00**

Coffee set: 8½" h. cov. coffeepot,
cov. sugar bowl & creamer;
each piece in a footed bulbous
form, the coffeepot w/a swelled
base below tall slightly tapering

sides & a flat hinged cover, each piece w/C-form wooden handles w/scrolled silver body attachments, ball finials, William Spratling, Mexico, mid-1940s, 3 pcs. **2,875.00**

Coffeepot, cov., pear-shaped, embossed & chased w/rococo ornament, the duck's head spout rising from a bacchic mask, shaped foot cast shellwork, the handle terminals cast w/shellwork & leafy sprays, marked on base & cover, Aymé Videu, London, England, 1758, 10¾" h. **8,050.00**

Creamer, in the form of a Chinese Export porcelain creamer, bamboo-style handle engraved w/contemporary monogram "JAW," John Scofield, London, England, 1783, 5⅝" h. **2,070.00**

Cruet, egg, rectangular form w/raffia & ovolo borders, angles mounted w/caducei above winged shell feet, cups w/gilt interiors, George III period, marked "Emes & Barnard, London, 1808," includes six King's Husk patt. egg spoons marked "Charles Marsh, Dublin, 1825," 7¾" l., 13 pcs..............**1,265.00**

Spanish Silver Dish

Dish, oval, embossed w/flowers & scrolling foliage, wide lobed border chased w/band of stylized leaves, marked "Gregorio Yzquierdo, Madrid" & "Parraga," Spain, ca. 1700, 18½" l. (ILLUS.) **2,587.00**

Gravy boat w/attached tray, double-lipped oval bowl w/chased rim scrolls & loop side rim handles, the oval tray w/a wide flat flanged rim chased w/rococo decoration, Austria, hallmarked, 19th c., 9¹³⁄₁₆" l., 6⅞" h. **546.00**

Ice bowl, the flared flat rim decorated w/pendent icicles, the foot cast w/a husky dog barking at a bear on a rocky surface, mid-19th c., France, 10½" d. ..**4,025.00**

Mug, plain tapered cylindrical form, scrolled handle w/shaped shield terminal engraved w/contemporary initials "AN" surrounded by stars, w/maker's mark "IK" crowned, Jonah Kirk, London, England, 1694, 5" h. **2,645.00**

Platter, shaped gadroon rim decorated w/demi-lions in foliage alternating w/foliage, engraved twice w/contemporary arms, William Brown, London, England, 1823, 20" l. **4,312.00**

Punch strainer, circular body pierced w/strapwork, mounted w/pair of shaped handles pierced w/strapwork, engraved w/crest, Queen Anne period, maker's mark of John Albright, London, early 18th c., 6¾" over handle length.............................**747.00**

Salver, round, the shaped rim pierced & chased w/panels of grapevine between bacchic masks, the center engraved w/contemporary arms in rococo cartouche, on four scrolled panel feet cast w/vine leaves, George Wickes, London, England, 1743, 11⅝" d. **12,650.00**

Samovar, cov., plain cylindrical form, the angular handles w/turned ivory grips, w/a pierced ivory spigot, the domed base raised on four bun feet, the top w/ivory insulators, maker's mark

Russian Silver Samovar

Art Nouveau Tea & Coffee Service

of E.K., St. Petersburg, Russia, 1892, 18½" h. (ILLUS.)..........**8,625.00**

Soup tureen, cov., bombé form, engraved w/arms & partly chased w/rococo ornament, on four acanthus-headed paw feet, marked on base & cover, George Fenwick, Edinburgh, Scotland, 1822, 10" h. **6,325.00**

Spice box, cov., shaped rectangular cartouche form w/fluted corners, double-hinged cover w/molded rim, flat-chased w/scrolls & trelliswork, stippled ground w/shell at both ends & four scroll feet, Elias Adam, Augsburg, Germany, 1736-37, 2¾" l. **2,645.00**

Stirrup cups, each in the form of a stag's head & engraved on the inner rim "St. Hubertus," retailed by Tiffany & Co., Germany, 20th c., 7" h., pr. **5,175.00**

Sugar bowl, cov., inverted pear-shape, engraved w/arms in baroque cartouche, marked on base & cover, Thomas Parr II, London, England, 1752, 4¼" h. **2,875.00**

Tankard, cov., tapered cylindrical form engraved w/later arms, flat hinged cover, the handle initialed "EB," fully marked Robert Cooper, London, England, 1707, 7" h. **6,900.00**

Tea & coffee service: cov. teapot, cov. coffeepot, cov. sugar bowl, creamer & tray; Art Nouveau design , each piece w/a tall swirled paneled designs w/long loops & cast sprigs of leaves & berries, looped C-form handles, pointed domed covers w/flat pierced finials, long slender swan's-neck spouts, the oblong lobed tray w/a molded rim & asymmetric large loop end handles, Wurttembergishe Metallewaren Fabrik, Germany, impressed "WMF" beehive mark & "ALLEMAGNE," ca. 1909, tray 24" l., coffeepot 11" h., the set (ILLUS.) **4,312.00**

Tea caddy, cov., octagonal form, sliding base & slip-on cap, marked on body, base & neck, John Chartier, London, England, 1710, 5" h. **3,162.00**

Teapot, cov., flattened inverted pear-form w/wide band of rocaille on stripped ground, cartouche on either side engraved w/crest, spout modeled & chased as zoomorphic beast, everted rim applied w/chased band of acanthus, hinged & domed cover w/blossom finial, mounted w/leaf-capped scroll handle, domed foot w/conforming decoration, William IV period, England, 12¼" l. **1,745.00**

Vase, clear glass & silver, flared rim, reticulated collar & base, the flared rim vase wheel-cut

overall w/floral & scroll
decoration, hallmarked, late 19th
- early 20th c., Europe,
9½" h. **374.00**

SILVER PLATE (Hollowware)

Castor set: a quadruple-plate
footed stand w/central loop
handle & center rim w/openings
holding five clear engraved
bottles w/stoppers, silver by
James W. Tufts, ca. 1880s, the
set...**225.00**

Centerpiece, Louis XV-Style,
oval form w/upright ornately
decorated & pierced sides
trimmed w/four full-figure
caryatids continuing down to
form short legs, the side panels
w/ornate scrolling decoration &
flowers, musical instruments, &
birds centered by wreath-framed
oval h.p. reserves, w/scroll-
supported fruit-filled urns at the
center top rims, ornate scrolled
outswept end handles, w/a
metal liner w/crenulated top rim,
19th c., 10 x 20", 7" h. **1,540.00**

Cigar stand, figural, modeled as
a three-wheeled tricycle w/a
wide shaped dish over the back
two wheels, a seat w/driver fitted
above the front wheel, the driver
wearing kneebritches & a top
hat, one hand at his hat, the
other holding aloft a candle
socket, late 19th c. **275.00**

Coffee set: cov. coffeepot & ten
cylindrical tumblers; Art Deco
style, the tall cylindrical pot
raised on a ribbed base & flat
foot, the domed cover w/a
conforming knob, C-form strap
handle, short angled rim spout
w/stopper, the cover knob &
spout stopper set w/octagonal
mustard yellow Bakelite
decoration, the matching
cylindrical tumblers w/a flared
rim, each stamped "Barbour

Art Deco Coffee Set

6733," cups also stamped
"PATD JAN 11 1927," coffeepot
11⅛" h., the set (ILLUS.) **863.00**

Communion service: a cov.
flagon & three chalices; the
tapering cylindrical flagon w/a
stepped, hinged cover w/molded
finial & shaped spout, on a
circular foot, the chalices each
of tapering cylindrical form w/a
ring stem & a circular molded
foot, Reed & Barton, Taunton,
Massachusetts, 1860-80, flagon
14½" h., the set **115.00**

Document box, cov., rectangular,
ornate repoussé decoration
on the top of delicate leafy
scrolls centering an oval
reserve, the sides w/a
continuous band of marching
figures, the edge of the cover &
the base bands of ornate leaf &
scroll designs, on six small knob
feet, Meriden mark, ca. 1880,
6" h. **413.00**

Hot water kettle on stand, the
large bulbous tapering melon-
lobed pot w/each lobe engraved
w/a rococo scroll cartouche, a
paneled swan's-neck spout,
scroll-trimmed arched overhead
swing handle, supported by
Gothic trefoil scroll supports on
each side above a round
shallow tray w/an alcohol
burner, all raised on four leafy
scroll feet, England, late 19th c.,
overall 15¾" h.............................**805.00**

Tea set: cov. teapot, spooner, cov. sugar, creamer, waste bowl & cov. butter dish; Renaissance Revival style, each of squatty baluster form on a low ringed foot, low domed covers w/ribbed button finials, acid-etched & engraved Elizabethan figural decoration, style No. 3284, ca. 1885, Reed & Barton, Taunton, Massachusetts, butter knife missing teapot, 6⅞" h., the set (ILLUS. below)............................**259.00**

Tray, rectangular w/a chased center design & shell, scroll & gadroon border, loop end handles, Gorham Mfg. Company, Providence, Rhode Island, late 19th c., 22" l. **225.00**

Vase, bud, baluster-form w/figural deer head handles, Gorham Mfg. Company, Providence, Rhode Island, late 19th c., 5¹³⁄₁₆" h. **230.00**

Water set: covered porcelain-lined ice water pitcher tilting within an arched stand w/ornate pierced side supports & a small side shelf supporting a matching chalice-form goblet,

Ice Water Pitcher with Stand

Renaissance Revival design w/ornate band & florette bands around the pitcher, the base of the stand & on the goblet, Reed & Barton, ca. 1880-90, overall 19" h. (ILLUS.)..........................**288.00**

Wine cooler, campana-form, the flaring cylindrical body w/a wide rolled rim of full-relief grapevine above looped & ribbed branch handles trimmed w/further grapevine continuing around the base & up the sides, raised on a short slender pedestal on a flaring, scalloped & pierced foot, 10" d., 11" h. **880.00**

Reed & Barton Victorian Tea Set

TIN & TOLE

Bowl, tole, oval upright sides w/a deeply scalloped rim, wrought loop end handles, old red repaint w/gilt stencil leaf band, 11" l. (some bottom rust) **143.00**

Candle screen, tin, adjustable, a wide oblong shiny tin screen adjusting on a tall slender iron upright w/a round foot, overall 25½" h. **248.00**

Candle mold, tin, ten-tube mold w/double ear handles, 11¾" h. (battered & several tubes loose at base) **127.00**

Cheese mold, tin, heart-shaped, pierced overall w/drain holes, solid old resoldering, 4½" l. **248.00**

Chestnut urns, cov., classical tapering oval urn-form on a slender pedestal base w/a flaring foot, the upward-curved rim of the base fitted w/a conforming cover w/a tall slender pyramidal center w/an acorn finial, decorated w/continuous floral bandings flanked by lion mask handles suspending loops , the cover decorated w/floral sprays, later decorated, Georgian period, England, late 18th - early 19th c., 12¾ h., pr. **690.00**

Coffeepot, cov., tole, tall tapering cylindrical body w/a flared base band, gooseneck angled spout, C-shaped ribbon handle, hinged domed cover w/brass knob finial, the black ground decorated on the cover w/a yellow star design, the rim of the cover & gallery rim on base decorated w/a yellow feather-like design, further decorated w/yellow band rim band w/a black squiggled line, the sides decorated w/large round reserves w/a cream ground decorated w/red, yellow & green floral designs, early 19th c., 6¼" d., 10½" h. **950.00**

Coffeepot, cov., tin, footed low-waisted body w/a flaring lower section below the tall, tapering cylindrical upper section, angled goose-neck spout, C-form strap handle w/grip, domed cover w/brass button finial, tooled & beaded band decoration, 19th c., 11¼" h. **215.00**

Early Tin Dutch Oven

Dutch oven, tin, large half-round form w/curved top hinged lid w/rectangular incised decoration, on looped strap front feet & low strap handles at the top sends, w/an interior spit, 19" l. (ILLUS.) **347.00**

Early Tole Plate Warmer

Plate warmer, tole, upright rectangular box w/a flat round-edged top above an open back & a hinged front door w/rounded top corners, raised on long slender cabriole legs w/penny feet, brass scroll mounts w/ring handles at the top sides, original black ground decorated w/gilt flower & leaf stenciling around the front sides & the edge of the door, England or America, ca. 1815, missing one handle, 10½ x 13", 26" h. (ILLUS.)................**546.00**

Sugar shaker, cov., tole, cylindrical w/a fitted cover & small side strap handle, black ground decorated w/yellow & red feather-like design, 19th c., 3" d., 3¾" h. (some wear)..........**210.00**

Tray, tole, rectangular w/curved flanged rim & rounded corners, black ground w/a stenciled floral decoration in gold, blue, red & cream, rim w/a band of gold scrollwork & outer rim band, late 19th c., 8¾ x 11¾" (some wear)..**45.00**

Wall sconce, tin, candle-type, a tall arched backplate pierced at the top w/a heart within an arch above a panel w/a group of three punched hearts & tiny diamonds & stars, all above a panel w/two bands of narrow ribbing above the half-round tray centered by a candle socket, American-made, 18th c., 13½" h. (imperfections) **3,738.00**

NUTTING (Wallace) COLLECTIBLES

In 1898, Wallace Nutting published his first hand-tinted pictures and these were popular for more than 20 years. An "assembly line" subsequently colored and placed a signature and (sometimes) a title on the mat of these copyrighted photographs. Interior scenes featuring Early American furniture are considered the most collectible of these photographs.

Nutting's photographically illustrated travel books and early editions of his antiques reference books are also highly collectible.

The following material was submitted by Michael Ivankovich, who is generally regarded as the country's leading authority on Wallace Nutting pictures, books, furniture and memorabilia, and is the author of The

Collector's Guide to Wallace Nutting Pictures: Identification and Value. *His quarterly Wallace Nutting Catalog Auctions are considered to be the national center of Wallace Nutting collecting activity.*

You may contact Mr. Ivankovich by writing to P. O. Box 2458, Coylestown, Pennsylvania, 18901. He would be happy to answer any general questions you may have, but cannot provide any "value" information unless you include a good quality close-up photograph which includes the picture's frame, and a self-addressed, stamped envelope.

BOOKS

"Windsor Chairs" Book

"Connecticut Beautiful," first edition, green cover..................**$45.00**

"Cruise of the 800 (The)," 1905, first edition **110.00**

"England Beautiful," first edition..**55.00**

"Ireland Beautiful," first edition....**50.00**

"Maine Beautiful," second edition, brown cover **35.00**

"Massachusetts Beautiful," first edition..**35.00**

"New Hampshire Beautiful," first edition..**40.00**

"New York Beautiful," second edition..**45.00**

"Pathways of the Puritans," 1930, first edition **55.00**

"Pennsylvania Beautiful," first edition..**40.00**

"Vermont Beautiful," first edition .**45.00**

"Virginia Beautiful," second edition.......................................**40.00**

"Windsor Chairs," first edition with dust jacket (ILLUS.).......................**75.00 to 150.00**

"Clock Book," second edition **40.00**

"Furniture of the Pilgrim Century," 1921, first edition ....**75.00 to 150.00**

"Furniture Treasury," first edition, three volume set **300.00**

"Furniture Treasury," 1954 edition, blue cover, Vol. I-II.........**35.00**

"Photographic Art Secrets"......**125.00**

"Wallace Nutting Biography" **85.00**

FURNITURE

General Guidelines:

Chairs represent the most common form of Wallace Nutting Furniture, especially Windsor chairs.

"Case" pieces, i.e., highboys, lowboys, chests of drawers, secretary desks, blanket chests, etc., represent the rarest Nutting forms.

The more difficult a piece was to produce, the higher the original cost and the fewer pieces Nutting produced. Today these are the rarest pieces.

Script branded furniture may be worth anywhere from 25-35 per cent less than an identical piece bearing a paper label or block branded signature.

Nutting furniture can generally be dated based upon its markings:

Paper label: 1918-22

Script branded signature: 1922-24

Paper label and block branded signature: 1925-26

Block branded signature only: 1927-1930s

As with all other forms of antiques, condition is extremely important. Those items in the best condition will bring the best prices. Those showing normal wear will bring less,

and those in poor or damaged condition will be the least desirable pieces.

No. 17 Windsor tripod candlestand, block brand.........**525.00**

No. 21 Maple screw (Whirling) candlestand, block brand.........**990.00**

No. 22 Cross-based candlestand, block brand.........**575.00**

No. 28 Treenware open salt dish, impressed brand, 1½"d. ...**155.00**

No. 31 Curly maple candlestick (single), unmarked.....................**95.00**

No. 31 Curly maple candlestick (single), impressed brand.........**175.00**

No. 101 Windsor round stool, block brand...............................**300.00**

No. 102 Windsor oval stool, paper label.................................**250.00**

No. 164 Brewster rushed three-legged stool, script brand **385.00**

No. 166 Rushed maple stool, block brand, 15" h......................**300.00**

No. 168 Rushed maple stool, block brand, 22" h......................**425.00**

No. 301 Windsor side chair, block brand...............................**525.00**

No. 305 Windsor bent-rung bow-back side chair, bamboo turnings, block brand **800.00**

No. 401 Windsor continuous-arm armchair, block brand.....................**650.00 to 1,200.00**

No. 411 Brewster armchair, script brand............................**1,000.00**

No. 412 Pennsylvania Windsor comb-back armchair, block brand **1,400.00**

No. 414 Windsor low-back armchair, block brand & pape label...**525.00**

No. 420 Windsor bow-back armchair, paper label (ILLUS. top next column) ....**750.00 to 1,500.00**

Windsor Bow-back Armchair

No. 421 Windsor rocking armchair, script brand **1,100.00**

No. 440 Windsor writing armchair, Pennsylvania turnings w/drawer, block brand **2,800.00**

No. 615 Maple trestle table with pine top, block branded signature ....**600.00 to 1,000.00**

No. 616 Pine trestle table, block brand **750.00**

No. 619 Maple crane bracket table, script brand **685.00**

No. 761 Gold three-feather mirror, impressed brand **575.00**

No. 809 low post bed, block brand signature **330.00**

No. 6288 Mahogany Pembroke table, block brand signature......**715.00**

Treenware pen & pencil tray, impressed brand........................**250.00**

PRINTS

Afternoon Tea (An), 14 x 17", interior scene **175.00**

"Angel" Garden (The), 12 x 20", foreign exterior scene **198.00**

At the Finder, (sic) 10 x 12", interior scene **110.00**

Attiring the Bride, 11 x 14", interior scene **110.00**

Barre Brook (A), 13 x 16", exterior scene.............................**125.00**

Basket Running Over (A), 16 x 20", floral scene **1,155.00**

Beech Borders, 16 x 20", foreign exterior scene.............................**110.00**

Birch Brook, 13 x 16", exterior scene..**132.00**

Birch Strand (The), 14 x 17", exterior scene...........................**275.00**

Birthday Flowers, 10 x 16", interior scene...............................**77.00**

Bit of Sewing (A), 11 x 14", interior scene...............................**95.00**

Book Settle (The), 10 x 16", interior scene.............................**132.00**

Breakfast Hour (The), 7 x 13", exterior scene...........................**319.00**

Call For More (A), 11 x 14", interior scene.............................**143.00**

Century of Age (A), 13 x 17", exterior scene...........................**143.00**

Chair for John (A), 12 x 16", interior scene.............................**195.00**

Cluster of Zinnias (A), 13 x 16", floral scene **413.00**

Colonial Days, 14 x 17" **1,125.00**

Comfort and a Cat, 14 x 17", interior scene.............................**325.00**

Coming from Confession, 10 x 14", exterior scene.............**660.00**

Coming Out of Rosa (The), 14 x 17", exterior scene.............**195.00**

Rare Print with Dogs

Dog-On-It, 7 x 11", exterior scene, very rare (ILLUS.)..............**1,000.00 to 1,500.00**

Dutch Maids, 8 x 10", foreign
exterior scene............................**220.00**

Early Foliage, 10 x 16", exterior
scene..**44.00**

Early June Brides, 14 x 20",
exterior scene............................**110.00**

Embroidering, 16 x 20", interior
scene..**220.00**

Eventful Journey (An) **650.00**

Floral Scene, 8 x 10",
signed ....**500.00 to 750.00**

For the Honored Guest,
11 x 17", interior scene.............**165.00**

Four O'clock, 14 x 17".............**1,275.00**

Fruit Luncheon (A), 16 x 20",
interior scene.............................**295.00**

Garden of Larkspur (A),
13 x 16", foreign exterior scene...**85.00**

Grace, 14 x 17", exterior scene ...**110.00**

Great Expectations, 11 x 14",
interior scene...........................**1,073.00**

Greeting (A), 11 x 14", foreign
exterior scene............................**165.00**

Gruelling Process (A), 14 x 17",
interior scene.............................**220.00**

Happy Valley Road, 13 x 16",
exterior scene ....**90.00 to 95.00**

Hollyhocks, 8 x 10", floral scene ..**525.00**

Home Hearth (The), 12 x 20",
interior scene..............................**55.00**

Home Room (The), 14 x 17",
interior scene..............................**90.00**

Honeymoon Cottage, 17 x 25",
exterior scene..............................**88.00**

Honeymoon Drive, 16 x 20",
exterior scene............................**105.00**

Informal Call (An), 16 x 20",
interior scene.............................**132.00**

In the Brave Days of Old,
13 x 16", interior scene.............**242.00**

Intimates, 14 x 17", interior
scene..**99.00**

Into the West, 8 x 14", exterior
scene..**88.00**

Ladies in White Satin, 9 x 11",
exterior scene..............................**77.00**

LaJolla, 13 x 16", exterior
scene..**275.00**

Lane's End, 10 x 14", exterior
scene..**44.00**

Larkspur, 11 x 14", foreign
exterior scene..............................**75.00**

Lined with Petals, 17 x 21",
exterior scene............................**165.00**

Little Helper (A), 14 x 17",
interior scene.............................**523.00**

Maine Surf, 12 x 20", exterior
scene..**330.00**

Maple Sugar Cupboard (The),
14 x 17", interior scene.............**150.00**

Market Place (A), 16 x 20",
foreign exterior scene...............**688.00**

Mary's Little Lamb, 13 x 16",
exterior scene............................**250.00**

May Drive (A), 11 x 17", exterior
scene..**55.00**

Mountain Born, 10 x 12", exterior
scene..**99.00**

Mount Tom, 10 x 16", exterior
scene..**110.00**

Natural Bridge (The), 10 x 13",
exterior scene............................**132.00**

Nest (The), 12 x 15", exterior
scene..**150.00**

New England Shore (A),
11 x 14", exterior scene.............**176.00**

New Hampshire October (A),
11 x 13", exterior scene...............**60.00**

Off Shore, 10 x 16", exterior
scene..**495.00**

Old Parlor Corner (An), 14 x 17",
interior scene (ILLUS. top
next page) ....**275.00 to 375.00**

Old Salt, 14 x 17", exterior
scene..**660.00**

Overflowing Cup (An), 20 x 30",
exterior scene............................**220.00**

Patchwork Siesta (A), 16 x 20",
interior scene.............................**578.00**

Pergola, Amalfi (The), 13 x 16",
foreign exterior scene...............**160.00**

An Old Parlor Corner Print

Process print, Bonnie Dale, 16 x 20" foreign exterior scene...**17.00**

Process print, Decked as a Bride, 16 x 20", exterior scene...**20.00**

Process print, Barre Brook (A), 12 x 15", exterior scene...............**15.00**

Quilting Party (The), 18 x 22", interior scene.............................**220.00**

Returning from a Walk, 13 x 17", interior scene................**99.00**

Revealing a State Secret, 14 x 16", interior scene.............**275.00**

River Grasses, 12 x 15", exterior scene...**121.00**

Sea Ledges, 10 x 16", exterior scene...**265.00**

Side Hill Cottage, 12 x 16", foreign exterior scene...............**176.00**

Sip of Tea (A), 14 x 17", interior scene...**154.00**

Springfield Lane (A), 9 x 11", exterior scene.............................**72.00**

Stairs at Positano and Amalfi, 13 x 20", foreign exterior scene...**303.00**

Still Depths, 11 x 14", exterior scene...**50.00**

Stitch in Time (A), 14 x 17", interior scene............................**220.00**

Sunshine and Music, 13 x 16", interior scene............................**225.00**

Swimming Pool (A), 11 x 17", exterior scene............................**165.00**

Tea at Uncle Jonathan's, 14 x17", interior scene.............**550.00**

Tea for Two, 13 x 16", interior scene...**225.00**

Three Chums, 16 x 20", interior scene...**495.00**

Trousseau Trimmings, 13 x 16", interior scene............................**165.00**

Very Satisfactory, 14 x 17", interior scene..............................**28.00**

Waiting for Jacob, 10 x 16", interior scene............................**308.00**

Warm Spring Day (A), 11 x 17", exterior scene ....**325.00 to 375.00**

Watersmeet, 13 x 16", exterior scene...**125.00**

Way It Begins (The), 13 x 16", interior scene ....**350.00 to 550.00**

Way It Begins (The), 14 x 17", interior scene.............................**625.00**

Wayside in May (The), 10 x 16", exterior scene.............................**121.00**

We Are Young Again, 11 x 14",
exterior scene **83.00**

Where Bees are Humming,
13 x 17", exterior scene **66.00**

Wine Carrier, 7 x 13", foreign
exterior scene **248.00**

Winslow Water, 14 x 17", exterior
scene **176.00**

MISCELLANEOUS MEMORABILIA

Advertising sign, glass,
8 x 10" **550.00**

Advertising sign, paper,
11 x 16" **125.00**

Calendar in thin metal
frame **75.00**

Colorist's photograph,
8 x 10" **110.00**

Furniture catalog, supreme
edition, 1930 ....**110.00**

Furniture catalog, final edition,
1937 ....**125.00**

Greeting card w/exterior scene,
4 x 5" **75.00**

Miniature, exterior scene,
4 x 5" **65.00**

Miniature, interior scene,
4 x 5" **110.00**

Miniature, floral scene,
4 x 5" **175.00**

Pirate print, swimming pool,
unsigned.....................................**10.00**

Silhouette, girl by garden urn,
4 x 4" **40.00**

Silhouette, lamb follows girl to
school, 7 x 8" **65.00**

Silhouette, girl sits at vanity,
4 x 4" **35.00**

Silhouette, girl stands by chevel
mirror, 5 x 5" **45.00**

Silhouette, Christmas card,
Dr. & Mrs. Nutting.......................**72.00**

Silhouette, Mother's Day
card **45.00**

Silhouettes, Abraham & Mary
Todd Lincoln, 4 x 5", pr..............**176.00**

Silhouettes, George & Martha
Washington, pr. ....**85.00 to 110.00**

ORIENTALIA

The following is a special section covering a wide range of popular Oriental antiques specially prepared for us by Sandra Andacht, Oriental expert and long-time columnist for the "East Meets West" column of The Antique Trader Weekly. *Mrs. Andacht is also Editor and Publisher of* The Orientalia Journal *and her new book,* Collectors' Value Guide to Oriental Decorative Arts, *will be released by Antique Trader Books in the fall of 1997.*

Oriental Carpets and Rugs

Asfar bagface, south Persia,
early 20th c., large hooked
diamond & four small diamonds
in red, light blue, gold, reddish
brown & bluish green on a
midnight blue field, ivory
arabesque leaf & double vine
border, overall good condition,
2' 2" x 2' 9" ....**$600.00 to 800.00**

Bahktiari carpet

Bahktiari carpet, Persia, early
20th c., evenly worn, 12' 5" x
19' 5" (ILLUS.) ..**14,000.00 to 16,000.00**

Bordjalou Kazak prayer rug,
southwest Caucasus, late 19th
c., two diamond & two hexagons
in navy blue, ivory, gold & deep
bluish green on a red field, ivory
wine glass border, good
condition,
3' 9" x 6' 4............**1,200.00 to 1,500.00**

Heriz carpet, northwest Persia, early 20th c., concentric gabled square medallion & vines in sky blue & dark blue, rose, gold, purple & bluish green on a reddish rust field, light blue spandrels, midnight blue rosette border, evenly worn, 7' 2" x 10' 8" ....**5,000.00 to 7,000.00**

Kurd rug, northwest Persia, first quarter 20th c., four columns of "dragons tooth" designs in blue, red, apricot, ivory, gold, purple, & bluish green on a navy blue field, blue floral meander border, evenly worn, two corners rewoven, 4' 4" x 7' 6" ....**900.00 to 1,200.00**

Sarouk rug, west Persia, early 20th c., cruciform palmette motifs & floral sprays in dark red, light blue, camel, & tannish gold on a dark blue field, red floral meander border, 3' 5" x 4' 10" ....**800.00 to 1,200.00**

Seichour mat, northeast Caucasus, late 19th c., overall pattern of abstract floral motifs in rust, rose, royal blue, ivory & dark green on a navy blue field, evenly worn, 2' 4" x 3' ....**600.00 to 800.00**

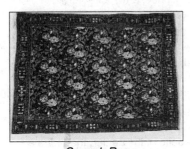
Sennah Rug

Sennah rug, northwest Persia, late 19th c., good overall condition, 5' x 7' (ILLUS.)................**10,000 to 12,000.00**

Serabend runner, northwest Persia, ca. 1900, staggered rows of filigree-style boteh in red, rose, ivory, gold, & bluish green on a navy blue field, ivory rosette & vine border, 2' 10" x 15'..........**1,000.00 to 1,500.00**

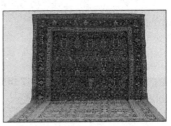
Shirvan Rug

Shirvan long rug, east Caucasus, last quarter 19th c., small areas of minor wear, 3' 9" x 8' 2" (ILLUS.).......**3,000.00 to 4,000.00**

Yamud Chuval, west Turkestan, mid-19th c., nine *chuval guls* in deep blue, red, ivory & bluish green on a purple field, gotshak border & flowering plant elem, moth damage & worn areas, 2' 8" x 3' 8" ....**400.00 to 600.00**

Artwork

Chinese Paintings
Attributed to Ma Yuan (act. 1190-1225); Scholar in a mountain landscape, hanging scroll, ink & light color on silk, signed "Ma Yuan," 9¼" x 10½"...............**20,000.00 to 25,000.00**

Gao Jianfu (1879-1951); Bat, ink on paper; one seal of the artist, dated 1936, 10⅞ x 13½" ....**1,200.00 to 1,500.00**

Ning Fucheng (1897-1966); Flower & Rock, hanging scroll, ink & color on paper, w/two seals of the artist, 13½ x 54"............**2,000.00 to 3,000.00**

Pu Ru (1896-1963); Pine & Rock, hanging scroll, ink on paper, w/three seals of the artist, 13 x 37½"............**3,000.00 to 5,000.00**

Qian Hui'an (1833-1910); Zhong
Kui , hanging scroll, ink & color
on paper, signed & dated spring
1888, one seal of the artist
24¼ x 51½" ....**2,500.00 to 3,200.00**

Tang Yifen (1778-1853);
Landscape, hanging scroll, ink
on paper, signed & dated 1844
w/three seals of the artist & one
collector's seal .....**5000.00 to 7,000.00**

Wang Zhen (1867-1938); Portrait
of a monk, hanging scroll, ink &
color on paper, signed & dated
spring 1933, three seals of the
artist, 26 x 60" .....**3,000.00 to 4,500.00**

Zhai Dakun (act. 1782-1797);
Landscape, hanging scroll, ink &
color on paper, signed & dated
1784, two seals of the artist,
19½ x 38½" ....**3,000.00 to 5,000.00**

Japanese Paintings

Painting, Daikoku, colors on silk,
framed & glazed, ca. 1955,
framed size 11 x 14" ...**75.00 to 100.00**

Hanging scroll, painting on
paper, ink & colors, five cranes,
three flying, two wading in water,
late 19th-early 20th c.,
remounted ca. 1960,
27½" l. ....**350.00 to 550.00**

Hanging scroll, painting on silk,
colors & ink, Samurai on
Horseback, late 19th c., foxed,
toned, creases,
33" l. ....**500.00 to 750.00**

Hanging scroll, painting on silk,
colors & ink, bird on branch
w/flowers & foliage, foxed &
creased, ca. 1955,
39" l. ....**175.00 to 250.00**

Hanging scroll, painting on silk,
colors & ink, the rising sun,
attributed to Kogyo,
creased & water
stained, 41" l. ....**800.00 to 1,200.00**

Hanging scroll, painting on silk,
woman holding a drum while
standing in a boat under a
willow, signed "Genkei" (1747-
1797), condition problems,
13½ x 36½" ....**300.00 to 500.00**

Jewelry

Bangle bracelet, Chinese, apple
green jadeite w/paler
green tone,
52.9 mm dia. .....**7,800.00 to 11,000.00**

Brooch, Chinese, silver gilt,
turquoise & enamel, circular
form w/four turquoise
cabochons, 1½" dia.....**75.00 to 100.00**

Ear ornaments, south Indian,
Tamil Nadu, abstract form, each
w/geometric shapes including
spheres, faceted disks, cubes &
diamonds, the separately cast
sections joined together
w/hinges & fastening
screws, pr., 3" l....**4,000.00 to 6,000.00**

Necklace, Indian, enameled gold,
Jaipur, cresscentic form
composed of 23 individual
plaques enameled in green w/a
rose-cut tear-shaped colorless
stone at the center of each, the
reverse delicately enameled in
red, white & green w/a pair of
birds perched on flowering
branches, a row of emerald
beads below suspending seed
pearls & green glass
beads, 5" w. ....**1,500.00 to 2,000.00**

Pendant, Chinese, aquamarine,
19th c., carved w/squirrel &
grapes, 1½" l. ....**300.00 to 400.00**

Pendant, jadeite, Art Deco, ca.
1925, w/chain, carved Chinese
jadeite in the center, the stone a
shade of apple green carved
w/fruit in relief on both sides, set
in platinum & adorned w/black
enamel on the top & bottom &
ornamented with 50 small
diamonds, total carat weight 2.5,
the platinum chain w/black onyx
links, pendant 2¼" l. (ILLUS.
top next page) .....**7,000.00 to 9,000.00**

Chinese Jade Pendant

Ring, Chinese, jadeite, oval shaped cabochon of mottled apple green, 5.9 mm x 10.8 mm x 14.7 mm ....**1,000.00 to 1,300.00**

Ring, Chinese, jadeite & diamonds, center marquise diamond approx. 3 cts, set within two plaques of apple green suffused w/emerald green tone jadeite edged by small round diamonds, set in white gold, size 6 ......**23,000.00 to 26,000.00**

Snuff Bottles

Amber (cherry), double gourd-form ....**40.00 to 60.00**

Cameo agate, rectangular form w/reddish brown scene of fisherman in a boat, 19th c. ....**350.00 to 450.00**

Cinnabar lacquer, ovoid carved w/horse motif, 20th c. ....**125.00 to 175.00**

Glass, amber hue, ovoid form ca. 1900 ....**80.00 to 120.00**

Glass, interior painted, figural landscape design, early 20th c. ....**100.00 to 175.00**

Glass, ruby red, ovoid form, 19th c. ....**100.00 to 200.00**

Hornbill, in beak form w/engraved figural design, conforming stopper ...**150.00 to 200.00**

Ivory, melon-form w/relief carving of a child climbing up the side of a melon ....**100.00 to 150.00**

Jadeite, light green, ovoid form w/carving of sage & crane on both sides, 19th c......**300.00 to 400.00**

Jadeite, white, flattened rounded shape, carved in low relief w/a *qin* on each side superimposed by a diaper patterned cloth, ca. 1750-1850...........**2,500.00 to 4.000.00**

Lapis lazuli, form of temple jar w/crane & cloud design in relief, 20th c. ....**150.00 to 200.00**

Nephrite, grey, double gourd-form, late 19th c. ....**150.00 to 200.00**

Porcelain, blue & red underglaze cylindrical form, landscape motif, 19th c. ....**150.00 to 200.00**

Porcelain, blue & white, figural form, early 20th c., (chipped) ....**60.00 to 80.00**

Porcelain, Chinese snuff bottles (ILLUS. left to right next page): **Famille Rose,** flattened pear-shape, both sides decorated w/a grasshopper in shades of green, red & purple, slightly worn, late 19th c. ....**600.00 to 800.00**

Blue ground bottle, compressed spherical form w/waisted neck, each side decorated w/stylized floral motif, yellowish green leaves & scrolling stems w/longevity character on each shoulder beneath a bat, early 19th c. ....**1,200.00 to 1,600.00**

Gold enameled bottle, cylindrical form, waisted neck, continuous motifs of floral scrolls between ruyi borders, last half 19th c. ....**700.00 to 900.00**

Porcelain, Famille Rose, molded in relief w/dragon & cloud design, late 19th c. ....**200.00 to 300.00**

Group of Chinese Snuff Bottles

Pottery, Yixing, flask-form w/landscape design on each side, early 20th c. ....**250.00 to 350.00**

Rock crystal (clear quartz), ovoid form w/flat sides, carved w/bat on each side in low relief, late 19th c. ....**150.00 to 200.00**

Rock crystal, double gourd-shape, well hollowed, carved in low-relief on each side w/the character "da" on the upper portion & "ji" on the lower, also carved w/stylized flowerheads, possibly Beijing Palace workshops, ca. 1740-1830...........**6,000.00 to 9,000.00**

Smoky quartz, hexagonal shape, carved w/continuous scene around the body w/eight cranes in flight & cranes also wading in a pond, ca. 1800-1900...........**1,500.00 to 2,000.00**

Soapstone, pear-shape carved in low-relief w/a sage ....**100.00 to 150.00**

Netsuke

Bone netsuke, a frog on a folded lotus leaf, ca. 1900....**200.00 to 250.00**

Horn, in the form of tengu emerging from an egg, late 19th-early 20th ....**250.00 to 350.00**

Ivory, in the form of an elderly man reclining, late 18th-19th c. ....**125.00 to 175.00**

Ivory, in the form of Okame mask, ca. 1900.........**150.00 to 200.00**

Ivory, figure of a farmer w/axe, post WW II ....**40.00 to 60.00**

Ivory, manju, carved bamboo, w/farmer, late 19th c. ....**125.00 to 200.00**

Ivory, in the form of a boar...........................**150.00 to 200.00**

Ivory, model of Sennin Chokaro, 19th c. ....**800.00 to 1,200.00**

Ivory, figure of Ebisu, eyes inlaid, 19th c. ....**1,200.00 to 1,800.00**

Porcelain, an elder holding his beard, late 19th c. .....**150.00 to 200.00**

Wood, a manju w/dragon in relief, 19th c. ....**200.00 to 300.00**

Wood, model of a squirrel & eggplant, ca. 1900 ....**125.00 to 175.00**

Wood, in the form of a coiled snake ....**125.00 to 175.00**

Wood, figure of Sarumawashi w/a monkey, 19th c....**1,800.00 to 2,200.00**

Wood, figure of an oni stirring a bowl of mochi, early 19th c. ....**800.00 to 1,200.00**

Wood, model of a pod w/movable seeds, minor crack, 19th c. ....**140.00 to 225.00**

PARRISH (Maxfield) ARTWORK

Magazine covers, internal illustrations & ads.

These are mint condition without mailing labels.

Values for each item or items per issue listed include complete magazine. Values are higher depending on internal contents of each issue. Items are in color unless noted; B&W=Black & White.

AMERICAN ARTIST
Oct. 1973, Cover & 15 Illus. $19.00

AMERICAN HERITAGE
Feb. 1962: Pictures.....................25.00
Dec. 1970: 14 Illus. 44.00

AMERICAN MAGAZINE
Sept. 1918: Djer-Kiss Perfume
Ad..110.00
July 1921: Hires Root Beer
Ad..52.00

AMERICAN MONTHLY REVIEW
Feb. 1918: EM Ad 90.00

ANTIQUE TRADER (THE)
Feb. 18, 1981: Cover, Illus. &
Article 11.00

ARCHITECTURAL DIGEST
Dec. 1984: Print 13.00

ARTIST
1898: 2 B&W 68.00

BOOKNEWS
Oct. 1895: Cover.......................135.00
Dec. 1895: Cover 100.00
Jan. 1896: Cover 100.00
Apr. 1897: Cover 95.00
June 1897: Cover 135.00

CHRISTIAN HERALD
Mar. 1919: Ferry Seed Ad.........120.00

COLLECTORS SHOWCASE
Sept./Oct. 1981: Article 8.00

COLLIER'S:
Dec. 3, 1904: Cover 135.00
Nov. 18, 1905: Cover...............138.00
Sept. 1, 1906: Frontispiece
Illustration 70.00
Sept 12, 1908: Cover...............140.00
Apr. 24, 1909: Cover 88.00
May 29, 1909: Cover...................88.00

"The Idiot" or "The Booklover,"
September 10, 1910 Cover

July 30, 1910: Cover 110.00
Nov. 16, 1912: Cover...............120.00
May 17, 1913: Cover.................88.00
Nov. 30, 1929: Cover...............100.00
Oct. 24, 1936: Cover...............110.00
Dec. 26, 1936: Cover 110.00

COSMOPOLITAN
Feb. 1924: Jell-O Ad 85.00

COUNTRY GENTLEMAN
June 27, 1925: Edison-Mazda
Ad=EM...55.00
Aug. 22, 1925: EM Ad 55.00

COUNTRY LIFE
Mar. 1904: Royal Baking
Powder 50.00
Sept. 1917: Fisk Tire Ad..........100.00
May 1922: Jell-O Ad 85.00

DELINEATOR
Aug. 1921: Djer-Kiss................155.00
Mar. 1922: Jell-O Ad 140.00

FARM JOURNAL (THE)
Sept. 1925: EM Ad...................115.00

FARMER'S WIFE (THE)
Nov. 1922: Jell-O Ad................127.00

HARPER'S YOUNG PEOPLE
Apr. 1895: Cover 240.00

HEARST'S
June 1912: Cover 230.00
Nov. 1912: Cover......................230.00
Mar. 1922: Jell-O Ad 95.00

LADIES' HOME JOURNAL
July 1896: Cover 200.00

June 1901: Cover 135.00
Dec. 1912: Cover 110.00
May 1913: Cover.........................95.00
Dec. 1916: Djer-Kiss Ad...........170.00
Jan. 1919: EM Ad 160.00
Nov. 1921: Ham Ad 170.00
July 1925: Coffee Ad 40.00
Jan. 1931: Cover 95.00

LIFE
Dec. 1899: Cover 215.00
Sept. 13, 1917: Fisk Tire Ad
(ILLUS. below)............................95.00

*"The Modern Magic Shoes" Fisk Tire
Advertisement*

Dec. 2, 1920: Cover 145.00
Jan. 5, 1922: Cover 145.00
Mar. 1, 1923: Cover 135.00
Jan. 31, 1924: Cover + Jell-O
Ad 195.00

McCALLS
Mar. 1922: Jell-O Ad 148.00
Apr. 1919: Djer-Kiss Ad 95.00

MODERN PRISCILLA
Jan. 1924: Jell-O Ad 140.00

**NEBRASKA EDUCATIONAL
JOURNAL**
Oct. 1928: Cover.........................70.00

**NEW HAMPSHIRE
TROUBADOUR**
1938: Yearbook, Cover 55.00
1939: Fair Edition, Cover 60.00
1940: Yearbook, Cover 75.00

PICTORIAL REVIEW
Jan. 1922: Jell-O Ad 145.00
Feb. 1924: Jell-O Ad 145.00

PRINT MAGAZINE
May/June 1991: Article & Illus. ...11.00

PROGRESSIVE FARMER
June 1952: Cover 65.00

SATURDAY EVENING POST
Nov. 22, 1913: Ad, B&W,
Subscription Card....................220.00
Dec. 27, 1924: GE Ad 35.00
Dec. 1974: Prints & Article 19.00

SPINNING WHEEL
Nov. 1973: Cover & Article 18.00

STUDIO INTERNATIONAL
Aug. 1964: B&W 8.00

TIME
Feb. 17, 1936: Article.................14.00

WORLDS WORK
Dec. 1919: Fisk Tire Ad 65.00
June 1921: Hires Ad 55.00
July 1921: Hires Ad 55.00

YANKEE
Dec. 1935: Cover 50.00
Dec. 1979: Cover 15.00

YOUTHS COMPANION
Feb. 20, 1919: Ferry Seed Ad...135.00

Edison-Mazda Calendars:
1918: Night Is Fled or Dawn
Large, Complete 3,650.00
Small, Complete 1,350.00

1919: Spirit of Night
Large, Complete 4,700.00
Small, Complete 1,625.00

1920: Prometheus
Large, Complete 4,100.00
Small, Complete 1,450.00

1921: Primitive Man
Large, Complete 3,350.00
Small, Complete 1,550.00

1922: Egypt
Large, Complete 4,600.00
Small, Complete 1,750.00

1923: Lampseller of Bagdad
Large, Complete 3,525.00
Small, Complete 1,350.00

1924: The Venetian Lamplighter
Large, Complete 2,900.00
Small, Complete 950.00

1925: Dreamlight
Large, Complete 2,700.00
Small, Complete 950.00

"Enchantment" 1926 Calendar

1926: Enchantment
Large, Complete 2,850.00
Small, Complete 950.00

1927: Reveries
Large, Complete 2,150.00
Small, Complete 610.00

1928: Contentment
Large, Complete 2,200.00
Small, Complete 665.00

1929: Golden Hours
Large, Complete 1,900.00
Small, Complete 620.00

"Solitude" 1932 Calendar

1930: Ecstasy
Large, Complete **2,000.00**
Small, Complete **580.00**

1931: Waterfall
Large, Complete **2,000.00**
Small, Complete **570.00**

1932: Solitude
Small, Complete **840.00**

1933: Sunrise
Large, Complete **2,700.00**
Small, Complete **700.00**

1934: Moonlight
Small, Complete **900.00**

Books:
All books listed here are the first editions with Parrish unless otherwise noted.

AMERICAN ART BY AMERICAN ARTISTS
Collier's: 11 picture plates
100 Favorite Paintings; N.Y.:
1898-1914 ....**600.00**

ARABIAN NIGHTS
1909: Wiggins & Smith. 12
Plates **285.00**
1912: 2nd Edition **210.00**

COLLECTION OF COLOUR PRINTS (A)
Jansen, J., Guerin & Parrish illus.:
1920s..**410.00**

DREAM DAYS
Grahame, K., John Lane:
1898 ....**175.00**
N.Y. & London, B&W

GOLDEN AGE (THE)
Grahame, K., John Lane:
1899-1900 ....**185.00**
B&Ws: 1904 ....**135.00**

KNAVE OF HEARTS (THE)
Sanders: 1925
Hardbound; Boxed **1,750.00**
Hardbound without box **1,575.00**
Softbound **865.00**

KNICKERBOCKERS HISTORY OF NY
Irving, W., Dodd & Mead:
1900 ....**400.00**
1903 thru 1915 ....**300.00**

MAXFIELD PARRISH
Ludwig, C., Bio. & Illus.; 1st Edition:
1973 ....**100.00**
Watson-Guptil: 1970s thru
1980s ....**40.00 to 65.00**

MAXFIELD PARRISH (THE)
EARLY YEARS
Skeeters, P. Nash: 1973 ....**325.00**
Japanese Edition: 1974.............**110.00**

MOTHER GOOSE IN PROSE
Baum, Frank L. Way & Williams:
1897 ....**1,850.00**
George Hill, Chicago: 1901 ....**600.00**
Bobbs-Merrill: 1905, 4th
Edition **135.00**

POEMS OF CHILDHOOD
Field, E., Scribner's: 1904 ....**285.00**
English Edition.........................**275.00**
2nd Edition: 1920 ....**175.00**

SONG OF HIAWATHA
Longfellow, H., Houghton-Mufflin:
1911 ....**145.00**

WONDERBOOK OF
TANGLEWOOD TALES
Hawthorne, H., Duffield, 10 plates:
1910 ....**275.00**
Duffield: 1929 ....**220.00**
Dodd-Mead: 1934 & 1938 ....**190.00**

YOUNG MAXFIELD PARRISH
Stuart, J., 1995, softbound **25.00**
Limited Edition Of 300,
slipcased **65.00**

Art Prints
House of Art - Reinthal & Newman -
Crane printing

CANYON: 1924
Blonde girl clinging to rocky cliffs
edge, below her is a raging river.
6 x 10" **175.00**
12 x 15" **355.00**

CLEOPATRA: 1917
Cleopatra in a bed of roses,
riding in a barge, with rowers &
servants.6½ x 7½" **395.00**
15 x 16" **800.00**
24½ x 28".................................**2,275.00**

"Cleopatra" Print

DAYBREAK: 1922
Young nude is leaning over a
reclined blonde woman, open
temple, pool.
6 x 10" **140.00**
10 x 18" **270.00**
18 x 30" **550.00**

DREAMING: 1928
Nude sitting on the roots of huge
tree.
6 x 10" **275.00**
10 x 18" **650.00**
18 x 30" **1,700.00**

EVENING: 1922
Nude sitting on rock within a dark
pool.
6 x 10" **200.00**
12 x 15" **365.00**

GARDEN OF ALLAH: 1918
Three women reclining by
reflecting pool.
9 x 18" (R) **220.00**
15 x 30" (R) **585.00**

HILLTOP: 1927
Two girls upon knoll, sitting under
big oak.
6 x 10" **175.00**
12 x 20" **435.00**
18 x 30" **1,000.00**

MORNING: 1926
Blonde girl sitting on rocks with
her arms around her legs, high
on mountain peak.
6 x 10" **175.00**
12 x 15" **300.00**

PRINCE (THE): 1928
A prince lying down in a field of
flowers, bridge in background
10 x 12" (R) **325.00**

ROMANCE: 1925
Knave & maiden on pillared
balcony, castles & mountains in
background.12 x 24"...............**1,450.00**

RUBIAYAT: 1917
Outdoor scene showing man with
book on far right, woman with
book on the far left.
4 x 14" **340.00**
8 x 30" **900.00**

STARS: 1927
Nude woman on a rock,
stargazing, darkest blues.
6 x 10" **325.00**
12 x 20" **875.00**
18 x 30" **1,650.00**

WILD GEESE:1924
Blonde lady lying on her stomach,
upon rock, dark mountains.
12 x 15" **300.00**

Posters
CENTURY:1897
Nude on grass holding her knees,
14 x 20" **2,250.00**

FERRY SEEDS:Print Sizes: 19 x
19", overall 21 x 28" Peter
Pumpkin Eater,1918...............**1,700.00**
Peter Piper,1919 ....**1,700.00**
Mary, Mary,1921 ....**1,675.00**
Jack & the Beanstalk,1923.....**1,950.00**

NATIONAL AUTHORITY ON AMATEUR SPORT
1897 Harpers, overall 14½ x
18½".....................................**1,850.00**

NEW HAMPSHIRE STATE PLANNING
Thy Templed Hills, 1936, 24 x
29"...**800.00**
N.H. Winter Paradise, 1939, 24 x
29" **950.00**

SCRIBNER'S
Cover Poster, 1897, Fiction Number,
August, 14 x 22" **2,650.00**

SCRIBNER'S
Cover Poster, "Scribner Christmas
Dinner,"1897..........................**2,950.00**

PERFUME, SCENT & COLOGNE BOTTLES

BOTTLES & FLASKS

Corset-waisted Cologne Bottle

Amber glass, football form,
polished screw lip, original metal
screw cap, smooth base, ca.
1865-1875, 1⅞" h. **$99.00**

Bluish-grey opaque glass,
tapering column on pedestal,
tooled lip, pontil-scarred base,
France, ca. 1845-1865,
8½" h. **440.00**

Canary yellow glass, corset-
waisted w/vertical ribbing, tooled
lip, long cylindrical neck, smooth
base, ca. 1860-1870, 4⅞" h.
(ILLUS.) **1,595.00**

Clear glass, arrowhead-shape in
sunburst design, sheared &
tooled lip, pontil-scarred base,
ca. 1840-1855, 2½" h. **110.00**

Cobalt blue glass, tapering ovoid
body, flared lip, original blown
stopper, pontil-scarred base, ca.
1820-1830, 5½" h. **55.00**

Cobalt blue glass, twelve-sided
w/slightly tapering body, rolled
lip, sloped shoulders, smooth
base, ca. 1865-1880, 7¼" h. **165.00**

Cobalt blue glass, light cobalt
blue w/darker striations in lower

half, arrowhead-shape in sunburst design, sheared lip, pontil-scarred base, ca. 1845-1855, 2⅞" h. **209.00**

Plume & Crown Design Scent Bottle

Cobalt blue w/purple tone,
plume & crown design, sheared lip, pontil-scarred base, ca. 1845-1855, 2⅞" h. (ILLUS.).......**253.00**

Cranberry glass, tapering ovoid body, cylindrical neck, wafer rim, decorated w/enameled gold leaves, vine & bunches of grapes, clear faceted original stopper, 2⅞" d., 7¾" h. **145.00**

Cranberry glass, ovoid body w/long cylindrical neck, decorated w/gold stars, original clear faceted stopper, 2 ¾" d., 8¼" h. **145.00**

Green opaline glass, bell-shaped bottom & tulip-form rim, enameled gold florals & decoration, original gold enameled stopper, polished pontil, ca. 1870, 8" h. **195.00**

Lavender blue glass, overall diamond & sunburst pattern, ground lip, original metal screw cap, smooth base, ca. 1865-1875, 3⅝" h. **138.00**

Milk glass, tapering cylindrical w/vertical ribbing, partially flared lip, ringed shoulder, smooth base, ca. 1870-1880, 7½" h. **110.00**

PIN-UP ART

The illustrated pin-up is an American phenomena. Its golden age was only a 20 year period from the mid-1930s to about 1955. Some works can be found earlier and in later years, but it is in this time period the bulk of the great work was done by the masters of the genre. Pin-up works were usually of a beautiful young girl, scantily clad, but with a girlie innocence. Colors on most calendars, prints and mutoscope cards were bright and primary, creating eye-catching flash and hot color appeal.

A great bulk of the pin-ups were printed by Brown & Bigelow and can be identified by their trademarkB&B, which is always printed in the lower corner of the illustration.

When dates are not given or known exactly, and the item is not a reprint you may usually assume correctly that most were printed in the 1940s and/or through the early 1950s.

*Indicates the image has been verified on a mutoscope card and it is listed as such with value for card.

UNDERLINED ITEMS ARE ALL CALENDARS with prints thereon, overall size given first, followed by print size.

A Description is given with title when known, plus, any prints, cards, illustrations done with this title are listed.

Calendar Notepads (CN) were done in many years, each pad was good for one month and sometimes a year. Each had an illustrated cover, size about 2 3/4 x 4 1/2", 3 1/2 x 6", and 3 3/4 x 9". One Month Calendar (OMC) about 5 x 10" & cardboard.

Ink blotters (IB) usually measured 3 1/2 x 25" up to 4 x 9" overall, mutoscope cards about 3 x 5" to 4 1/4 x 5 1/4". In most instances when the size 3 x 5" is used it denotes a mutoscope card. Most cards had blank backing, some had postcard backing.

—Denis Jackson

Artist's and Their Works

Rolf Armstrong:
"Adorable" 1950: brunette on her side, red & white gown
16 x 33", 16 x 20" **$160.00**
8"x10" Print................................**40.00**

*A Winning Combination:girl
holding flag, all red, white & blue
Mutoscope card **13.00**

"Betty": portrait girl, ornate silk
headdress
1925: 8 x 10" **65.00**
1970s reproduction calendar
Large **22.00**
Small **16.00**

"Cleopatra" 1929, B&B: blonde,
shield, Egyptian scene in
background
12 x 16½" print **360.00**

"Here We Go" Dec. 1952, B&B:
girl bathing chicks
11" x 23" **45.00**
18 x 27", 14 x 18" print **75.00**

*Hell-o Everybody: redhead
seated on floor, wearing black &
gold **12.00**
IB: **13.00**

"Lady of the Evening" 1928:
black hair, back to you, mostly
blacks and golds 8 x 10", plus
borders & pad **140.00**

""Lovely to Look At": girl on
back, arms back of head
1937: 13½ x 16½", 8 x 11½" **130.00**
1938: 23 x 28", 23 x 35" **310.00**
8 x 11½" print **50.00**

"Queen of Hearts"
Feb./Apr. 1948: 4 x 9" IB **16.00**

"Service with Pleasure" tennis
girl 11 x 15½", for Cleo Cola,
1930s **80.00**

**College Humor Magazine: with
Armstrong covers**
Jan. 1927, girl with lacy black
mask **60.00**
May 1927, brunette with white
kitten **45.00**
Oct. 1929, blonde in white furs....**50.00**
Mar. 1932, brunette in white & black
gown **45.00**
Sept. 1932, blonde in ermine & white
veil **45.00**

Salute: Cover
Mar. 1948: Rolf with pastels &
model **35.00**

The New Movie:
Sept. 1931, blue-eyed blonde, red
background **46.00**

Sheet Music:
Dream Girl, 1919: brunette, black
background **22.00**
Girl of Mine, 1919: lady in flowered
bonnet **24.00**
My Sunshine Rose, 1920, lady's
portrait **24.00**

Billy DeVorss:

"Alluring," 1951: lady, low cut
gown, on bed 16 x 32", 16 x 20"
print **70.00**
11 x 14", 9 x 12" print **38.00**

"Happy Landing" 1944: blonde
in pink ski suit
8 x 10", print only **15.00**
16 x 33", 16 x 20" print **70.00**
11 x 22", 11 x 14 print **40.00**

*Look of the Month: portrait of
puckering blonde **9.00**

"Nice Party" 1948: brunette,
head on arm, white blouse,
yellow skirt above knees, blue
background
33 x 16", print 16 x 20" **85.00**
12 x 21", print 10 x 12" **50.00**

"Winter Queen," 1945: red &
white outfitted skier
11 x 22", 11 x 13" print **55.00**
11 x 22", 11 x 14", same lady
skiing **60.00**

"Youthful Charm," 1937: blonde
looking over shoulder, white
dress with red ribbon, blue
background
8 x 10" **34.00**

Esquire Publishing items: 1930s through mid-1950s (18)

Many pin-up illustrators worked for this publication. Including George Petty and Alberto Varga, each one should be inspected closely for multiple values. Prices range per each issue from $4.00 to $160.00

Esquire Calendars: Sizes 8½ x
12" to 11 x 16", with envelopes,

some foldouts, most have 12
pinup pages
1948: Ben-Hur-Baz, Willis, Demera,
Wick......................................**55.00**
1949: Al Moore (see Moore
Area now) **42.00**
1953: Chiriaka **38.00**

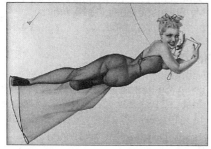

Esquire Foldout by George Petty

Gill Elvgren:

Pieces are from the 1940s & 1950s unless noted otherwise. Where prices are not given, these titles have been done as mutoscope cards, unless noted by IB, about 3¾ x 9"

*And The Wind Blew: IB **15.00**

"A Neat Package," 1963: black-
haired girl on floor, black skirt,
hose tops, wrapping package......**65.00**
16 x 20" print, 16 x 33" overall

Belle Wringer: redhead caught in
wringer, clothes basket:*IB..........**16.00**
3 x 4" print **8.00**
7½ x9½" print **20.00**
7 x 9", 9 x 15" overall..................**55.00**

*Catch On: blonde on pier,
fishing, dog, sea gull...................**16.00**
IB: June 1945 ....**16.00**
5 x 6" print **9.00**
5 x 7" **11.00**
7 x 9" **15.00**

"Enchanting," 1955: nude
blonde on rock with toes in the
water
8 x 10¾", overall 10 x 17½",........**80.00**

"It's Easy," 1957: magic girl &
poodle
16 x 33" overall............................**68.00**

Keeping Posted, 1949: redhead
swamped with mail
16 x 33", 16 x 20"......................**115.00**
8 x 10" print **24.00**

"Miss Sylvania" a series of these
were done, some follow:
Miss Betty Sylvania: letter, mailbox,
she's caught in picket fence
1951: 16 x 34¼", 16 x 20".........**155.00**
1953: Miss S. on door: blonde on
make-up stool 16 x 34½",
16 x 20" **95.00**
1957: Miss S.: red-headed queen,
basket red roses, S mirror 16 x 34",
16 x 20" **100.00**
1960: Miss S: blonde leaving horse
carriage 16 x 34", 16 x 20".........**65.00**

Rarin' To Go, 1953: cowgirl
putting on boot, buckskins
16 x 20", 16 x 33" overall.............**75.00**
one 22 x 45" overall....................**125.00**

*Slip Off Shore: stranded girl,
boat adrift, dog **12.00**
11 x 14" **40.00**
IB: May 1945 ....**15.00**

*Thar She Blows: blonde in
green dress which is blowing up
at funhouse.................................**17.00**

*Weight Control.........................**12.00**

"Weight Control": redhead,
black undies, legs in pulley
5 x 6½" **8.00**
7½ x 9½" **17.00**
IB: **14.00**

Earl MacPherson:

1943: Artist's Sketch pad, 9 x 14",
12 illus. pages **110.00**
1949: "The MacPherson Model,":
blonde in two-piece swimsuit,
sitting on table edge 16 x 33" **80.00**

1954: Artist's Sketch pad
"The Butcher Takes the Best Cuts
Home"......................................**100.00**

"Just Making Sure" OMC: **12.00**

Limited edition Prints: "Marilyn
Monroe Sex Goddess"
12 x 19", hand-signed...............**125.00**

Magazines:
Popular Photography, Jan.
  1950: four page pictorial..............**20.00**
Escapade, Oct. 1956: article &
  pinups...**22.00**

Earl Moran:

Various Earl Moran Pin-up Illustrations

*All In Favor Of This Motion Say
  "Ah": brunette, two piece white
  outfit **12.00**
  IB:..**15.00**

*Boy, You Can See A Lot From
  Here!: girl on chimney with
  binoculars watching plane **10.00**
  10 x 15", print 4¼" x 5¼".............**55.00**
  1944 IB:.......................................**14.00**

"Follies of 1937": redhead, top
  hat, dancing
  7½ x 16" card, 5½ x 11" **50.00**
  8 x 15", 5 x 7" **40.00**
  11 x 15" print **48.00**
  8 x 10" print **25.00**

Maybe I Wiggled When I Should
  Have Waggled: blonde, ship,
  signal flags
  1944 IB:.....................................**14.00**

*Popular Number (A): blonde
  seated, talking on phone **14.00**
  5 x 6" print **11.00**
  CN: 1/1943 ....**13.00**

"Reflections": nude wearing red
  hat, sitting on stool in front of
  mirror
  22 x 27" Calendar top/print........**175.00**
  15 x 19" **100.00**

*Sitting Pretty: girl in all red, red
  rose in hair.....................................**9.00**
  1946: 11 x 15½", 7½ x 10¼"
  print **40.00**

"Why Not?": seated blonde in
  gold, yellow phone
  1950: 16 x 33", 16 x 20" print **80.00**
  8 x 10" **20.00**

*You're The Top: brunette sailor
  girl, bow, sea gulls.......................**14.00**
  1937: 22 x 45" **185.00**
  8 x 15", 5 x 7" **40.00**

Earl Moran: Calendars, most with 12 pages, Brown & Bigelow
  1946: "Heavenly Bodies,"
  8½" x 14½" **85.00**
  1949: "Nursery Nifties" **135.00**
  1952: "Earl Moran's Girls of 1952" 12
  pgs., 12 images, with Marilyn Monroe
  pinup, 8½ x 14½" **140.00**

Zoe Mozert:
"Anytime," Apr. 1951, B&B:
  strapless white gown & flower
  11 x 23" **52.00**
  16 x 33", 16 x 20" print **80.00**

"Fairest Flower," 1946: nude
  blonde sitting in field of flowers
  11 x 23" overall..........................**155.00**
  10 x 17", with print 7½x10½".....**105.00**
  8 x 10" print **40.00**

"How's This?," 1948: girl in
  bathing suit 12½ x 14½",
  print 8 x 11" **85.00**

*It's Corn But They Love It,
  brunette in shorts, roosters
  (ILLUS. next page, left) **7.00**
  1945: 4½ x 8", calendar..............**22.00**

"Just For You," 1949: lady,
gown, dozen roses
4 x 6" **9.00**
8 x 10" **14.00**
10 x 17½", 7½ x 10" print **46.00**
22 x 27" **68.00**

Two Illustrations by Zoe Mozert

*My Calves Took First Place:
farm girl holding blue ribbon and
pitch fork **10.00**
IB: Sept. 1945 (ILLUS. right) **13.00**

"Right You Are," 1952: brunette
in bikini sitting on brick wall
11 x 23" **48.00**
16 x 33" **80.00**

"Shirley" for Texaco: bathing
suit, beach towel
1942: 8 x 10" **20.00**
1941: 9 x 19", 9 x 8" **35.00**

"You Started Me Dreaming,"
1942: blonde in low cut wine
dress, black background **55.00**
12 x 14", 12 x 21" overall

Mozert: Magazine covers

Motion Picture
Jan. 1937, Garbo.........................**65.00**
July 1937, Jean Harlow **80.00**
Apr. 1938, Loretta Young **55.00**

Movie Story
May 1938, Clark Gable &
Myrna Loy...................................**45.00**
Feb. 1938, Joan Crawford...........**40.00**

Walt Otto:
(Well known for his Pin-up girl
bowling themes)
"A Sure Strike": girl throwing ball
12 x 15" print **40.00**

"Bubbles," 1946 Calendar: girl in
red swimwear, fish......................**35.00**
"Right Down Your Alley," 1946:
brunette throwing ball, low white
neckline, red background
16 x 33", 16 x 20" **80.00**
12 x 21", print 12 x 16" **50.00**

POP CULTURE

*The collecting of pop culture memorabilia
is not a new phenomenon; fans have been
collecting music-related items since the
emergence of rock and roll in the 1950s. But it
was not until the 'coming of age' of the post-
war generation that the collecting of popular
culture memorabilia became a recognized
movement.*

*The most sought-after items are from the
1960s, when music, art, and society were at
their most experimental. This time period is
dominated by artists such as The Beatles, The
Rolling Stones and Bob Dylan, to name a few.
From the 1950s, Elvis Presley is the most
popular.*

*Below we offer a cross-section of popular
culture collectibles ranging from the 1950s to
the present day.*

Acid Test poster, includes "Acid
Test" membership card, ca.
1966, 22" x 17" **$3,620.00**

Aerosmith signed guitar,
Gibson-Epiphone Les Paul
model six-string electric guitar,
signed "Tom Hamilton, Brad
Whitford, Joe Perry, & Steve
Tyler" in black marker...............**920.00**

**Allman Brothers signed
acoustic guitar,** Ibanez
Performance acoustic, ebony
finish, signed "Gregg Allman,
Jaimoe, Butch Trucks, & Dickey
Betts" in silver marker.............**1,150.00**

**Barbra Streisand album cover
artists' proof w/signature,**
William Shirley artwork for
"Butterfly" album cover, matted
& framed w/black pen & ink
signature, inscribed "Happy
Days! Barbra Streisand," 26" l.,
22" w. (ILLUS. next page) **2,875.00**

Barbra Streisand Album Cover

The Beatles Autograph

Beach Boys signed drum head,
Remo drum head signed "Brian
Wilson, Carl Wilson, Bruce
Johnston, Mike Love, & Al
Jardine" in bold blue marker,
14" d. **230.00**

Beach Boys signed guitar,
acoustic guitar signed by all five
w/Brian Wilson, inscribed "I wish
they all could be California girls"
w/Mike Love, Al Jardine, Carl
Wilson, & Bruce Johnston **2,070.00**

**Beatles (The) "gold" album
award for "Sgt. Pepper's
Lonely Hearts Club Band,"**
RIAA award to commemorate
550,000+ Capital Records
album, cassette & C.D. sales,
mounted & framed, 21" x 17".....**805.00**

**Beatles (The) autograph
w/"gold" single,** four signatures
in blue pen & ink on blue
autograph paper, matted &
framed w/black & white picture
of Beatles & "gold" single for "I
Want To Hold Your Hand,"
18 x 22" **1,160.00**

Beatles (The) autograph, all four
signatures on autograph album
page signed in blue pen, matted
& famed w/black & white picture
from "Meet The Beatles" album,
ca. 1963, 14" x 18" (ILLUS.
next column **2,415.00**

Beatles (The) biscuit set,
ceramic portraits w/cup, the
set..**125.00**

**Beatles (The) cardboard
Christmas display,** Capitol
Records tiered cardboard store
display w/Beatles in holiday
attire, titled "Happy Holidays
From The Beatles".................**3,220.00**

The Beatles Drum Head

Beatles (The) drum head,
original Ludwig bass, used by
Ringo Starr at Cow Palace
concert in San Francisco August
19, 1964 (ILLUS.) **14,950.00**

Beatles (The) headband **35.00**

Beatles (The) stockings, Vroom
& Dressman, in original
package......................................**45.00**

Beatles (The) tile, includes four
portraits, England, framed **35.00**

Beatles (The) UK fan club flexi discs, includes 1963-69 w/original sleeves, set of 7 .....**2,070.00**

Beatles (The) wall plaques, ceramic, figural, set of 4 ....**275.00**

Bob Dylan signed album cover, "The Band" album cover signed "Planet Waves" in blue & black markers by Dylan, Robbie Robertson, Levon Helm, Rick Danko & Garth Hudson, 13" x 13" **517.00**

Bob Marley signed photograph, pen & ink signature of legendary musician on a photograph, framed, 11¼" l., 9¼" w. **1,035.00**

Bobby Rydell candy tin, includes colorful portrait, Holland **110.00**

Bruce Springsteen Poster

Bruce Springsteen poster from "The Hopkins Center," original black, orange, & yellow poster for Bruce Springsteen at Dartmouth College in Hanover, N.H., framed, ca. 1974, 24½" l., 20½" w. (ILLUS.) **632.00**

Buddy Holly signed album cover, marked "Coral" & "Buddy Holly" on front cover, blue pen & ink inscription reads "Love, Buddy Holly" **1,600.00**

Creedence Clearwater Revival signed electric guitar, Fender

Squier stratocaster, black finish, signed on pickguard "John Fogerty" & on body by "Stu Cook & Doug 'Cosmo' Clifford" **460.00**

Crosby, Stills, Nash & Young signed acoustic guitar, full-sized KIMA acoustic guitar signed by "David Crosby, Stephen Stills, Graham Nash, & Neil Young" in blue marker **1063.00**

Doors (The) "gold" album award for "The Doors," RIAA award presented to Doors to commemorate 500,00+ copy sale of album, cassette & C.D. of "The Doors," matted & framed, 21" x 17"...................**1,035.00**

Elton John Signed Jacket

Elton John stage-worn signed jacket, "Yellow Brick Road" worn tails-style jacket in black material, enhanced w/neon yellow, orange & green piping, lining, & striped lapels, "Elton John" embroidered on sleeves & front w/Annie Reave London tagging on inter lining, also signed & inscribed in black marker on inside lining (ILLUS.) **6,900.00**

Elvis Presley audiotape, ¼"
audiotape includes songs "King
Creole," "Dixieland Rock,"
"Crawfish," "Lover Doll" & many
more, original "Tape Legend"
handwritten label **1,759.00**

Elvis Presley jacket, red, worn in
the movie "Double Trouble" **6,000.00**

Elvis Presley Jumpsuit

Elvis Presley jumpsuit, stage-
worn outfit w/photographs of
"The King" wearing outfit,
includes supporting
documentation for garment &
Las Vegas menu (ILLUS.) **60,250.00**

Elvis Presley Director's Chair

**Elvis Presley "Kid Galahad"
director's chair,** orange & red
director's chair w/script pouch,
back painted in black & white
w/"Kid Galahad" on one side &
Elvis on the other, ca. 1961
(ILLUS.) **1,840.00**

Elvis Presley signed stationery,
inscribed "TCB" & "Thanks Elvis"
in black felt tip pen...................**920.00**

Eric Clapton handwritten-poem,
blue ink on notebook paper, full
page initialed at end "EC" &
titled by Clapton at top "No. 3,"
matted & framed w/color picture
of Clapton, ca. 1980, 14" x
18" **1,300.00**

Everly Brothers candy tin,
includes colorful portrait **110.00**

**Fleetwood Mac autograph
collection,** signatures on two
large album pages, signed "Mick
Fleetwood, John McVie, Stevie
Nicks, Christine McVie, &
Lindsey Buckingham" in blue
ink, mounted on board w/color
picture of band, includes 8x10"
black & white promo photo,
ca. 1970s, 2 pcs. **575.00**

**James Brown worn stage
jacket,** silver eyelash lame
swallow-tail stage jacket, worn
at The Apollo Theater in Harlem,
New York, ca. 1960s **3,162.00**

Janis Joplin cigarette holder,
metal w/red tip, used by Joplin,
includes photo of Joplin smoking
& using holder **1,150.00**

Jim Morrison autograph, black
pen & ink signature on white
paper, matted & framed w/black
& white picture & "gold" single
for "Light My Fire," 13" x 17"......**690.00**

Jimi Hendrix signature, bold
signature in black felt-tip on
album page, ca. 1968, matted &
framed w/black & white picture
of Hendrix, 14" x 18"
(ILLUS. next page) **1,150.00**

John Lennon bronze bust,
Gerrit Timmerman bronze
sculpture cast in limited edition
(25/500), shows Lennon wearing
signature glasses, on a marble
base w/plaque, ca. 1981,
12" h. **575.00**

Jimi Hendrix Signature

John Lennon eyeglasses case,
for round eyeglasses, includes
facsimile signature....................**225.00**

**John Lennon signed publishing
agreement for "Mother
Nature's Son,"** signed in black
felt tip pen, dated October 15,
1968 ....**2,760.00**

John Lennon & Yoko Ono Photograph

**John Lennon & Yoko Ono
photograph,** black & white
photograph taken & signed
by Jack Mitchell on reverse,
ca. 1980, 11" x 14"
(ILLUS.) **575.00**

Led Zeppelin autographs,
includes album cover for "Led
Zeppelin II," signed "Jimmy
Page, Robert Plant, & John Paul
Jones" in silver & red marker,
album flat for "No Quarter" by
"Jimmy Page and Robert Plant"
in red pen, Robert Plant solo
album "Pictures At Eleven"
signed in blue, black & white
photo of Jimmy Page w/guitar
signed in blue, 4 pcs.................**690.00**

Signed Madonna Photograph

**Madonna signed color picture
w/lipstick kiss,** blue felt-tip pen
signed color picture, matted &
framed w/pink lipstick kiss on
white paper, 13" l., 17" w.
(ILLUS.) **1,380.00**

**Monkees (The) signed electric
guitar,** white Fender Squier
stratocaster signed "Peter Tork,
David Jones, & Mickey Dolenz"
in blue marker & signed
"Michael Nesmith" in black
marker on pickguard.................**690.00**

**Moody Blues (The) signed
electric guitar,** white Fender
Squire stratocaster signed "John
Lodge, Ray Thomas, Graeme
Edge, & Justin Hayward" in blue
marker **805.00**

**Nirvana "gold" album award for
"Nevermind,"** RIAA award
presented to Kurt Cobain to
commemorate 500,000+ copy
sales of DGC Records album,

cassette, & C.D. "Nevermind," mounted & framed, 21" l., 17" w...........................**690.00**

Paul McCarthy signed fan club card, blue pen & ink signature on top of fan club card, matted & framed w/color picture of Beatles performing & "gold" single for "Yesterday," 17" x 20½" **345.00**

Paul Stanley jacket, KISS performer's black bolero-style jacket w/rhinestone trim design, worn on stage.......................**2,185.00**

Pearl Jam "platinum" album award for "VS," RIAA award presented to Pearl Jam to commemorate 1,000,000+ copy sales of Epic album, cassette, & C.D. "VS," mounted & framed, 21" l., 17" w..............................**517.00**

Pearl Jam signed electric guitar, Montaya "Les Paul" style electric guitar, tobacco sunburst finish, signed "Eddie Vedder, Mike McReady, Dave Abruzesse, & Jeff Ament," inscribed "Hard Rock Café Sucks" in blue Sharpie **1,380.00**

Pink Floyd autograph collection, includes album cover "Dark Side of the Moon," signed "David Gilmour, Rick Wright, & Nick Mason" in silver marker, promotion portrait of Roger Waters signed in blue metallic marker & ink signature of original band members, Syd Barrett on small sheet of lined paper, mounted w/early group photo, 3 pcs. **690.00**

Rick Griffin poster, featuring "The Who at the Hollywood Palladium," ca. 1969, 16" x 22⅝" **460.00**

Rolling Stones "platinum" album award for "Tattoo You," RIAA award presented to Mick Jagger to commemorate 1,000,000+ copy sales of Rolling

Stones record album "Tattoo You," mounted & framed, 21" l., 17" w.....................................**1,092.00**

Rolling Stones Poster

Rolling Stones poster, original h.p. poster for Rolling Stones, hung on wall of Cavern Club, also includes early photograph of band performing at Cavern Club w/Rolling Stones poster visible on wall, 2 pcs. (ILLUS.) **4,887.00**

Rolling Stones signed Christmas card, various ink signatures of Mick Jagger, Keith Richards, Charlie Watts, Brian Jones, & Bill Wyman on black & white card, opens to reveal black & white picture of the Stones **977.00**

Roy Orbison first recording acetate, never released version of "Oozy Doughboy" & other songs w/mullet-page letter documenting session from Sid King **1,150.00**

Sex Pistols signed electric guitar, Crestwood "strat-style" electric guitar, ivory finish, signed "Johnny Rotten, Glen Matlock, Steve Jones, & Paul Cook" in blue Sharpie................**632.00**

Stevie Ray Vaughan "gold" album award for "Soul to Soul," RIAA album award presented to Stevie Ray Vaughan to commemorate 500,000+ copy sales of album, cassette & C.D. "Soul to Soul," mounted & framed, 17" x 21".....**575.00**

Sting signed electric guitar, full-scale bass guitar by Crestwood, white finish signed in blue marker, inscribed "If you love somebody, set them free, Sting." **690.00**

The Cure signed electric guitar, Bentley "strat style" electric guitar, black finish, signed "Simon, Perry, Jason, & Robert Smith" in red/silver metallic markers **805.00**

Who (The) signed color picture, large color portrait of band from "Fab" magazine, autographed in ink by all four original members Pete Townshend, Roger Daltrey, John Entwistle, & Keith Moon, matted & framed, ca. 1966, 18" l., 13½" w..........................**2,700.00**

Who (The) signed electric guitar, Bently "Les Paul Style" guitar, tobacco sunburst finish, signed by Roger Daltrey & John Entwistle in black Sharpie, also signed on pickguard by Pete Townshend, 2 pcs. **1,150.00**

Yardbirds (The) signed printed photo, black & white portrait signed "Jimmy Page, Jeff Beck, Chris Dreja, Keith Relf, & Jim McCarty" in black felt-tip, matted & framed, ca. 1966 ....**1,150.00**

Yoko Ono postcard to John Lennon, sent by Ono from Paris to Lennon in Kenwood, black pen & ink w/some lines crossed out, stamped & postmarked, matted w/black & white photo of couple, ca. 1968, 16" x 22½"....**690.00**

RUGS - HOOKED & OTHER

HOOKED

Bird on branch, a long-tailed blue bird perched on a flowering branch w/wide wavy borders down the ends, worked in reds, greys, brown & black, 26 x 40" **$248.00**

Cats, two facing dark brown cats seated in the center of a background of stylized scrolls w/a scrolled blossom in each corner, ovoid chain border band, worked in shades of brown, blue, red, green & beige, wear, holes, repairs, 19th c., 32½ x 46" **1,150.00**

Dogs in landscape, a large white & brown dog & a smaller brown dog running through a hilly landscape w/a corner of a rail fence in the background, standing & cut-down trees on the hillsides & a stream in the foreground, worked in shades of blue, green, brown & white, 40 x 49" (some wear & fading w/light stains) **506.00**

Florettes & geometric blocks, nine large squares w/large blossoms surrounded by leaves alternating w/crossed-block design squares w/a row of pinwheel squares at each end, worked in green, blue, beige, red, pink & brown fabric, blossoms in pink, end pinwheels in blue & beige, early 20th c., 37 x 51" **920.00**

Horses & apple tree, closely hooked w/a tiny horse at the left border & a standing dark horse in the center nibbling from an apple tree, worked in reds, greys, brown, green, etc., signed "E.W. 1984," a wide dark border w/an undulating inner border, 26" sq. (ILLUS. top, next page)..............**358.00**

Horses & Apple Tree Rug

Ship in Harbor Hooked Rug

Ship in harbor scene, a large steamship in the foreground w/scattered village houses on the hills in the background, worked in red, green, orange, blue, brown, beige & grey, mounted on a stretcher, some wear & holes, late 19th c., 23½ x 9½" (ILLUS.) **2,300.00**

Townscape, titled "Our Town," a large rectangular bird's-eye view of a small town w/a factory & water tower in the background w/various houses & vehicles in the mid-ground & further homes & a large church by a roadway w/vehicles in the foreground, worked in a variety of green, pale red, yellow, blue, dark brown & cream chenille yarns, mounted on a stretcher, by Mrs. Turnley, La Grange County, Indiana, ca. 1930, 26 x 42" (some fading, minor edge fraying) **4,255.00**

OTHER

Appliqued, rectangular, appliqued overall w/arranged designs of cut-out stars, three-leaf clovers, & circles in blues, olive green, grey, white, red & brown on a goldenrod ground, 19 x 36" (wear, stains, small holes & tears, rebacked w/burlap) **440.00**

Appliqued & pieced rug, rectangular w/pointed ends, composed of colorful wool hexagons pieced together & highlighted w/contrasting embroidery, general wear w/some fabrics very worn, red yarn edging replaced, 42 x 83" **110.00**

Ingrain carpet runner, woven w/a delicate overall feathery scroll & blossom design down the center w/large flowerhead bands down each side, worked in green, gold & white, 19th c., 1' 10" w., 19' 8" l. **237.00**

Woven rag runner, worked in various silk, cotton & wool fabrics & colors in horizontal geometric bands, one side w/fringe, Shaker-made, New York, ca. 1860, 24 x 109½" **1,035.00**

SIGNS & SIGNBOARDS

Fine Winchester Tin Sign

Bread, "Bond Bread," porcelain, rectangular, black letters read "Bond - Bread - The home-like loaf" on yellow ground, 14 x 19" (some shipping & crazing) **$66.00**

Cartridges & guns, "Winchester," lithographed tin, rectangular, depicting in color a rack of firearms & hanging wild game above the wording "We Recommend and Sell WINCHESTER Cartridges and Guns," from a painting by Alexander Pope, copyrighted by Winchester in 1914, 30 x 36" (ILLUS.) **1,331.00**

Chocolate drink, "Ovaltine," tin, painted image of runners jumping over hurdles above image of Ovaltine container, marked "Ovaltine - for Health - Strength and Energy," in red, blue, white, green & bluish green, made in England, 12 x 18" (scratches & dents) **187.00**

Coffee, "Arbuckles' " tin, rectangular, embossed & painted "Pure - Wholesome - Arbuckles' - Coffee," done in blue, red & white on an orange ground, 5½ x 19½" **143.00**

Credit card, "American Express," flange-type, shield-shaped, two toned, top reads "American Express" above logo, all above "Credit - Cards," 18½ x 23¾" (minor surface rust at top) **138.00**

Flour, "King Arthur Flour," porcelain, blue ground w/white lettering & a round central medallion w/a knight on horseback w/banner below "King Arthur Flour," across the bottom edge "Sands, Taylor & Wood Co.," fading, chipping & ragged edges, 36 x 40"..........................**204.00**

Ice Cream, "Meadow Gold," light-up-type, yellow & cream on blue reverse-painted glass front reads "Meadow Gold - 'Smooth-Freeze' - Ice Cream," metal exterior, 3½ x 14½", 4¼" h. (minor surface rust) **121.00**

Insurance, "State Farm Insurance," porcelain, rectangular, "State Farm - Insurance Companies - Agency - Automobile - Life -- Fire" to the right of State Farm logo, in red & black on white ground, 13 x 22" (minor chipping, one grommet missing) **204.00**

Medicine, "Venos Cough Cure," porcelain, rectangular, blue lettering reads "Venos - Lightning - Cough - Cure - For - Coughs, Colds, - Bronchitis, Asthma, - Children's Coughs - The Ideal Family Remedy," on orange ground, 20 x 30" (minor chipping, fading & crazing to some of the porcelain)................**83.00**

Motor oil, "Wm. Penn Motor Oils," flange-type, silhouette of William Penn above "Wm. Penn - Motor Oils," done in red, green & yellow, 13½ x 18" (scratches & chips to edges) **385.00**

No smoking, porcelain, white lettering "Smoking - or - Carrying Lighted Cigars, Cigarettes or - Pipes On The Cars, Stations Or - Station Stairways Of The - Subway - Is Unlawful - Offenders Are Liable To Arrest - By Order Of The Board Of Health," on blue ground, 21 x 27½" **132.00**

Paint, "Sherwin-Williams," die-cut 3-D porcelain, the famous 'Cover The Earth' logo on a world globe dripping w/paint pouring from a can printed w/"SWP," in red, yellow, green, white & black, chipping at holes, to bottom 'paint drips' bent at bottom, 19" w., 34½" h. (ILLUS. top next page) **176.00**

Patent medicine, "Scofill's Sarsaparilla or Blood & Live Syrup," heavy paper, reads "A Good Angel's Visit - A Tale of

Sherwin-Williams Paint Sign

Scofill's Sarsaparilla or Blood & Liver Syrup" above two women dressed in 19th c. attire, one holding a bottle of the medicine, above testament to the medicine, 3 x 5" (minor soiling).....................**28.00**

Shoes, "Brown Shoe Co.," painted tin, black image of hand pointing to bottom of shoe to the left of "The Brown Shoe Co.'s - Star-Five-Star - $250 and $350 - Shoes - For Men and Women - Sold By - J. C. Baker," all on orange ground, 13¾ x 19¾" (minor soiling, dents & scratching, folds at corners) **143.00**

Soap, "Wright's Coal Tar Soap," porcelain, rectangular, centered w/a shield marked "Wright's - Coal Tar - Soap - The Nursery Soap - per 4D Tablet," green & blue on white, 12 x 18" (chip on one hole & chipped at edges)....**121.00**

Soft drink, "Cherry-Cheer," cardboard, rectangular, w/image of young woman holding a glass of soda w/bottle of Cherry-Cheer to the lower left, surrounded by vines & berries, reads "Cheer Up - Drink - Cherry-Cheer - 5¢ - It's Good," in red, yellow & green, in wood frame, 10 x 14" ...**286.00**

Soft drink, "Hires," tin, rectangular, center brown rectangle reads "Hires" w/"Drink" above & "In Bottles" below, all on an orange ground, 5 x 13¾" (some denting, minor scratches) **72.00**

Soft drink, "Whistle," tin, rectangular, colorfully painted & embossed image of two elves building a billboard sign that reads "Whistle" w/another elf wheeling in bottle of Whistle soda, 36 x 59½" (minor scratches & denting).................**660.00**

Steamship company, "American Red Star Line," lithographed metal, rectangular tapering to rounded end, colorful scene of ship, w/sailboats in background, reads "American Line Red Star Line - New York–Southampton (London) Cherbourg (Paris) - Philadelphia–Liverpool via Queenstown" & "New York–Antwerp - Philadelphia–Antwerp," bottom reads "International Navigational Company 73 Broadway New York," 3 x 12".............................**253.00**

Early Tailor's Trade Sign

Tailor, early carved & gilded wood trade sign, in the form of a giant pair of scissors w/molded finger hold, the blades inscribed in black "Adj. POULIOT" & "TAILLEUR," New York, late 19th c., 64½" l. (ILLUS.) **8,050.00**

Tea, "Nectar Tea," porcelain, in the shape of a tea cup & saucer, cup reads "Nectar - Tea," 12½ x 21" (scratches & chips).............**242.00**

SPORTS MEMORABILIA

BASEBALL GAME-USED ITEMS

1930 Oscar Melillo, St. Louis Browns game flannel...........**$1,300.00**

1941 Red Ruffing, New York Yankees flannel......................**1,090.00**

1942 Tommy Bridges, Detroit Tigers road flannel.................**2,500.00**

1947 St. Louis Browns uniform, Rawlings away w/shirt & pants worn by pitcher Nelson Potter, excellent condition.................**3,450.00**

1949 Whitey Kurowski, St. Louis Cardinals flannel jersey **950.00**

1958 Elston Howard, Yankee jersey, World Champion road grey w/"Howard '58" in collar, original Wilson 44 w/professionally resorted #32, much wear.............................**1,265.00**

1959 Dodgers team-signed bat, Norm Larker game-used H&B w/24 signatures ranging from 2/10-7/10, Alston, Furillo & Hodges rates 7/10, "5" in marker on knob....................................**518.00**

1960 Whitey Ford, New York Yankees jersey **5,825.00**

1961 Mickey Mantle bat **7,500.00**

1965 Maury Wills, game-used spikes & bat, well-worn black leather spikes, "30" in black marker on inside of tongue, Wills-model H&B bat w/strong game use...............................**1,265.00**

1965-66 Mickey Mantle, game-used bat, P104 of the type w/some burn damage & crack on top of handle.....................**1,955.00**

1967 Ferguson Jenkins, All-Star bat, signed by entire team, includes Tom Seaver as a rookie, Don Drysdale, Pete Rose, Ernie Banks & Bob Gibson (ILLUS. below) **910.00**

1969 Ron Swoboda, New York Mets World Series flannel jersey....................................**8,200.00**

1976 Pat Kelly, softball-style Chicago White Sox jersey **1,550.00**

1978 Johnny Bench, Cincinnati Reds jersey **1,000.00**

1978 Steve Carlton, Philadelphia Phillies jersey **1,145.00**

1979 Willie Mays, Mets jersey, grey Rawlings pullover w/familiar blue & orange coloring & 2-button collar, "Mays 24" dominates back w/"Mets" sprawled above number on front, circular team logo on left sleeve, all original tags on inside read "Set 1...42...79...24" **805.00**

1982 Gaylord Perry, Seattle Mariners jersey, 300th win season....................................**400.00**

1984 Darrel Evans, road World Series Tigers jersey.................**670.00**

1984 George Brett bat **530.00**

1985 Rod Carew, California Angels jersey............................**575.00**

1986 Greg Maddux, rookie home pinstripe Cubs uniform (ILLUS. top, next page) **7,200.00**

1988 Dwight Gooden, signed road jersey, well-worn grey gamer from playoff year w/"Rawlings Set 1...88...16...44" on requisite tags in tail, blue & orange lettering reads "New

Ferguson Jenkins All-Star Bat

Greg Maddux Rookie Uniform

York" across front & "Gooden"
on back above familiar "16,"
signed "Doc Gooden" below
lettering on front in NRMT blue
Sharpie **518.00**

1988 Nolan Ryan, Houston
Astros jacket.........................**1,335.00**

1988 Nolan Ryan, Houston
Astros warm-up sweater.........**1,090.00**

1988 Pete Rose, Cincinnati Reds
manager jersey..........................**660.00**

1989 Mike Schmidt, home
Phillies jersey **1,050.00**

1990 Lance Johnson, Chicago
White "Turn Back the Clock"
complete uniform, 1919 style
uniform includes jersey &
pants.....................................**1,070.00**

1991 Nolan Ryan, Texas
Rangers jersey **1,985.00**

1993 Cal Ripken, "Turn Back the
Clock" uniform **3,220.00**

1993 George Brett, 3,008th hit
ball, historic ball hit by Brett on
April 9, 1993 ....**605.00**

1993 Ryne Sandberg, Chicago
Cubs road jersey **1,000.00**

1994 Ozzie Smith jersey **2,375.00**

1995 Hideo Nomo glove **3,080.00**

1996 Frank Thomas, Black
Sunday jersey........................**1,250.00**

1996 Hideo Nomo, complete
Dodgers uniform, includes
jersey w/name on back, pants,

Dodgers blue jacket w/name on
back, batting helmet, Nike Air
Blue spikes, player hat, batting
helmet, batting gloves, socks,
Louisville Slugger C243 model
33" bat w/Nomo on barrel,
uncracked **5,000.00**

Albert Belle glove **1,515.00**

Alex Rodriguez bat, signed........**770.00**

Carlton Fisk, Boston Red Sox
catcher's mitt **2,665.00**

Carlton Fisk, Red Sox bat **1,020.00**

Carlton Fisk, road Chicago
White Sox jersey **1,175.00**

**Coach Bill Martin, Oakland
jersey** **950.00**

Eddie Murray's, first baseman's
mitt, signed inside glove
w/player number **3,080.00**

Greg Maddux bat **1,100.00**

Hack Wilson bat **1,615.00**

Hank Aaron bat **970.00**

Honus Wagner bat **1,540.00**

Joe Cronin, Red Sox player
glove...**665.00**

Joe Garagiola, St. Louis
Cardinals player jacket **800.00**

John Smoltz, Atlanta Braves
home jersey **800.00**

Johnny Bench, Cincinnati Reds
batting practice jersey **245.00**

Johnny Bench, third baseman's
glove...**705.00**

Johnny Sain, Yankees pinstripe
flannel jersey **1,600.00**

Michael Jordan, Worth/Wilson
bat, special bat made for Jordan
during baseball career............**1,760.00**

Nolan Ryan, Houston Astros
jersey.....................................**3,135.00**

Nolan Ryan, Houston Astros
jersey w/rainbow design **4,000.00**

Ozzie Smith, glove (ILLUS. top,
next page) **4,070.00**

Paul Molitor's, 1982 season
glove...**500.00**

Ozzie Smith Baseball Glove

Pete Rose bat **730.00**

Pete Rose, Philadelphia Phillies pants...**425.00**

Stan Musial's glove, signed "My Game Glove, Stan Musial." **3,325.00**

AUTOGRAPHED BASEBALLS

1913 Philadelphia A's & New York Giants signed World Series game ball, from World Series game #4 on October 10, 1913, signed by 23 members of both teams, signatures include Jim Thorpe, Chief Bender, Connie Mack, John McGraw, Christy Mathewson, Fred Merkle, Eddie Collins & Eddie Plank **10,000.00**

1920s Babe Ruth signed baseball, Ruth on sweet spot in blue ink, ball & signature rate 7/10 overall............................**2,185.00**

1924 World Series ball, signed by Hall of Famers Walter Johnson & Ross Youngs **1,750.00**

1925 Kennesaw Mountain Landis single-signed baseball, OAL signed ball, black ink signature on sweet spot reads "K.M. Landis, Balboa, Feb 1, 1925," rates 7/10, framed 4x6" photo of Landis in Balboa, ball used in game between Mexico & Panama along w/LOA **1,495.00**

1927 Yankees team-signed baseball, Murderer's Row on off-white Ban Johnson OAL ball, "Ruth" on sweet spot, includes Gehrig (6/10), Coombs (9/10), Pennock, Lazzerri, Hoyt & Muesel, legible & varied signatures, some scuffing on ball...**1,380.00**

1928 New York Yankees World Championship ball w/25 signatures, signed by Babe Ruth in quotations on sweetspot, includes Lou Gehrig, Leo Durocher, Tony Lazzerri, Benny Bengough, Bill Dickey & Herb Pennock **1,250.00**

1928 Ruth, Gehrig & Cobb signed baseball, on shellacked OAL Barnard ball w/Ruth (8/10) on sweet spot, Gehrig (6/10), Cobb (8/10), Speaker (7/10) & Collins (7/10), each on own panel, toned & stained in places, legible black ink signatures **3,450.00**

1928 Yankees team-signed baseball, 26 Bombers on consistently aged OAL ball, "Babe Ruth" (5/10) on sweet spot w/Gehrig (5/10) on side, includes Combs, Dickey & Hoyt, visible signatures...................**2,530.00**

1930 Babe Ruth single-signed baseball, signed across sweet spot in black fountain ink w/parts of "Babe" slightly traced over, signature is overall 8/10 w/bold "1930" on side **2,300.00**

1930 Babe Ruth, Lou Gehrig & All-Stars baseball, dark & crisp Ruth on sweet spot, lighter Gehrig on side w/35 signatures including L.Waner, Pennock, Vance, Lopez, Dickey, Traynor, Combs, Ruffing, Lazzeri & Hubbell, tanned "National League" ball w/dark signatures..............................**2,415.00**

1930 Philadelphia A's World Championship ball w/23 signatures, features Lefty Grove & Jimmie Fox on the sweet spot, includes Connie Mack, Eddie Collins & Mickey Cochran **1,180.00**

**1931 Cincinnati Reds team ball
w/24 signatures,** includes Edd
Rousch, Epa Rixey & Tony C....**870.00**

**1931 New York Yankees team
ball w/9 signatures,** includes
Babe Ruth on sweet spot, Lou
Gehrig, Earle Combs, Ben
Chapman, Earl Sewell, Billy
Dickey & Red Ruffing **1,450.00**

**1931 Ruth & Gehrig Yankee
signed ball,** "Official League"
ball w/strong "Babe Ruth" (8/10)
on sweet spot & "Lou Gehrig"
(9/10) on side, also includes
Lazzeri, Sewell & Combs
w/Spalding baseball box.........**2,990.00**

**1931 St. Louis Cardinals team
ball from World Championship
team w/22 signatures,** includes
Frankie Frisch, Jim Bottomley &
Wild Bill Hallahan **1,320.00**

**1933 Yankee team-signed
baseball,** dated 8/8/33 below
big & bold "Babe Ruth" (8.5/10)
on sweet spot, 18 signatures
include Gehrig, Lazzeri ,
Gomez, Dickey & Crosetti, OAL
ball rates EX-MT, signatures
average 7/10 ....**2,760.00**

**1934 American League All-Star
baseball w/19 signatures,**
includes Lou Gehrig, Lefty
Gomez, Ben Chapman, Joe
Cronin, Charlie Gehringer,
Heinie Manusch, Left Grove,
School Boy Rowe &
Al Simmons **3,630.00**

**1935 Babe Ruth single-signed
baseball,** white ONL Frick ball
signed on sweet spot by Ruth
during final year in baseball
w/Braves, bold black ink 9+/10
signature, in original box **9,775.00**

**1935 Yankees team-signed
baseball,** OAL ball w/21
signatures, Gehrig (8/10) on
sweet spot, includes Gomez,
Rolfe, Combs, Chapman,
Crosetti, Hoag, Dickey, Lazzeri
& Sewell, black ink signatures
rate 7/10 overall.....................**2,185.00**

**1938 New York Yankees
autographed team baseball
w/Lou Gehrig,** Gehrig signature
slightly to left of the sweet spot,
22 signatures (56) on "Official
Joe DiMaggio League Ball,"
includes Gehrig, Sundra,
Andrews, Chandler, Beggs,
Henrich, Hoag, Dickey, Hadley,
DiMaggio, Crosetti, Murphy,
Powell, Knickerbocker, Gordon,
Glenn, Pearson, Dahlgren,
Rolfe, Selkirk, Gomez, Jorgens,
signatures somewhat light &
perfectly readable **1,089.00**

1940 Dodgers reunion baseball,
ONL Frick ball w/28 signatures
signed by both 1916 & 1920 NL
Championship teams during
1940 reunion, includes Wheat,
Marquard, Miller, Griffith,
Bressler & Vance in clear black
ink, signatures rate strong
NRMT, ball is NRMT **2,185.00**

**1941 American League All-Star
baseball w/27 signatures,**
includes Joe and Dom
DiMaggio, Jimmie Fox, Bill
Dickey, Bob Feller, mint
condition **1,810.00**

**1946 Boston Red Sox All
Champs autographed baseball
w/25 signatures,** includes
Williams, Cronin, Doerr, Persku
& DiMaggio **806.00**

**1947 Dodgers team-signed
baseball w/30 signatures,**
includes Robinson on sweet spot,
Hodges, Reese, Snider, Furillo,
Branca, Casey & Edwards, black
ink signatures range from 7/10 -
10/10 on "Official League Ball,"
EX-MT **1,265.00**

**1949 Dodgers team-signed
baseball,** slightly toned ONL
Frick ball w/25 signatures,
includes Reese, Snider, Furillo,
Cox , Robinson, Hodges,
Newcombe, Roe & Campy,
overall signatures rate solid
8/10, many stronger **1,265.00**

1949 NL All-Star team-signed baseball, ONL Frick ball w/25 signatures in bold blue ink, includes Robinson, Campy, Snider, Reese, Musial, Kiner, Spahn, Roberts, Slaughter, Maglie & Roe, signatures rate 9/10 overall, several stronger, ball is EX-MT **1,610.00**

1952 Dodgers team-signed baseball, ONL Giles specimen w/26 signatures on near flawless ball, includes Robinson, Hodges, Snider, Roe, Black, Campy, Erskine, Furillo, Reese, Branca & Pafko w/Dressen on sweet spot, 9/10 signature ratings, ball is NRMT-MT...............................**1,840.00**

1955 Dodgers team-signed baseball, ONL Giles w/21 signatures by Robinson, Hodges, Reese, Snider, Newcombe, Campanella & others, blue ink signatures rate NRMT-MT w/ball to match......**4,600.00**

1955 New York Yankees team ball w/23 signatures, includes Mickey Mantle, Billy Martin, Casey Stengel, Elston Howard, Don Larsen, Whitey Ford & Phil Rizzuto **1,070.00**

1956 Brooklyn Dodgers baseball, ONL w/23 signatures, include Alston, Hodges, Gilliam, Koufax, Newcombe, Labine, Drysdale, Robinson, Campy, Erskine, Snider, Reese & Furillo, rates EX-MT **1,265.00**

1956 Yankees team-signed baseball, includes Mantle (ss), Berra (ss), Bauer, Howard, Martin, Ford & 20 more on excellent OAL ball, signatures rate EX-MT w/many stronger...**1,380.00**

1961 American League All-Star baseball w/27 signatures, includes Mickey Mantle & Yogi Berra on sweet spot, also includes Elston Howard, Roger

Maris, Frank Crosetti, Norm Cash & many others.................**660.00**

1961 Roger Maris baseball, from historic 61st home run game, on Joe Cronin American League baseball, signed "Yankee Stadium 10-1-61" across sweetspot, side panel reads "Game Ball 10-1-61" **6,050.00**

1967 National League All-Star baseball w/31 signatures, includes Roberto Clemente, WIllie Mays, Don Drysdale, Jimmy Wynn, Fergie Jenkins, Pete Rose, Bob Gibson, Lou Brock & Tom Seaver **590.00**

1968 World Champion Cardinals ball, 25 signatures on ONL ball w/"St Louis Cardinals 1968 National Champions," Schoendienst & Cepeda on sweet spot w/strong Maris on side, NRMT **920.00**

1969 Mets champion team-signed baseball, white ONL Giles w/25 signatures rating 7 overall, includes Seaver, Koosman, Hodges, Berra, Agee, Grote, Jones & Otis (no Ryan)...**920.00**

1970 Pittsburgh Pirates autographed team baseball w/25 signatures (89) on official NL baseball, includes Gibbon, Guisti, Clemente, Stargell, Dal Canton, Alley, Murtaugh, Walker, Sanguillen, Veale, Jeter, Clines, Cash, Mazeroski, Robertson, Pagan, Oliver, Ellis, Lamb, Blass, Cambria, Patek, Moose & Ricketts **730.00**

1975 Cincinnati Reds autographed baseball w/29 signatures, includes Rose, Bench, Morgan, Concepcion, Pere, Anderson, Kluszewski, Gullett & Geronimo **430.00**

1976 Yankee team-signed baseball, 30 signatures on OAL w/Martin on sweet spot, includes Munson, Howard, Berra, Hunter, Guidry & Nettles, NRMT-MT...**1,495.00**

1977 Yankees team-signed baseball, white OAL ball w/26 mixed ink signatures, Includes Munson, Rivers, Guidry, Piniella & the rest (no Jackson), signatures rate NRMT overall.....................................**1,380.00**

Babe Ruth & Lou Gehrig signed baseball, blue & red stitched OAL signed during West Coast swing of Babe's Larrupin' Lou's tour, "Babe Ruth" on sweet spot, signatures rate NRMT, clear shellac, overall 8/10................**6,325.00**

Babe Ruth single-signed Harridge baseball, black ink "Babe Ruth" signature on the sweet spot of white 9.5/10 OAL Harridge ball **12,650.00**

Babe Ruth & Lou Gehrig signed baseballs (2), Babe Ruth on the sweet spots & Lou Gehrig on sides, clear & dark signatures, quality 1920s Spalding balls imprinted "Made Especially for Nat C. Strong," well-browned.................................**3,450.00**

Babe Ruth-Mickey Cochrane signed baseball, Ruth on sweet spot w/Cochrane on side panel of "Official League" ball, signed at hometown parade for Mickey, "August 1947 Billings, Montana," EX..**2,645.00**

Cy Young Signed Baseball

Cy Young single-signed baseball (ILLUS.)...................**5,500.00**

Hall of Fame baseball by Tris Speaker, signed on sweet spot,

includes Lefty Grove, Mel Ott, Home Run Baker & Jimmie Foxx on one side, Ty Cobb, Paul Waner, Dazzy Vance & Bill Dickey on reverse...................**1,650.00**

Honus Wagner single-signed baseball **640.00**

Larry Lajoie autographed ball **1,185.00**

Lou Gehrig single-signed & dated home run ball, signed by Gehrig on the sweet spot, dated June 3, 1932.........................**3,750.00**

Mel Ott single-signed baseball, well-kept ONL w/EX-MT, inscription reads "To Dale, Best Wishes, Mel Ott" in light blue ink **1,725.00**

Mickey Mantle day game-used ball, black stitched OAL ball used on Mantle Day August 25, 1996 at The Stadium, unique "New York Mickey Mantle 7" logo below league label, facsimile on sweet spot of AL president Gene Budig & signed on side panels by four umpires of game signed.........................**805.00**

Napoleon Lajoie signed baseball, Larry Lajoie 4-4-55" is solid 8/10 on side panel of Official "Cleveland Baseball Federation" ball, includes two stamped signatures on slightly-toned ball **2,875.00**

Tony Lazzeri autographed ball **1,997.00**

Ty Cobb single-signed baseball, blue & red stitched ball signed on aside panel in dark brown ink, browned condition **1,610.00**

Walter Johnson & Clark Griffith signed baseball **2,450.00**

Walter Johnson single-signed baseball **1,650.00**

World Champions 1936 N.Y. Yankees baseball, OAL ball w/22 signatures, Gehrig on sweet spot, includes Lazzeri, Dickey, Crosetti, Gomez, Ruffing, Rolfe & DiMaggio, near-white ball w/overall strong signatures & wear, rates 7/10 ....**2,415.00**

BASEBALL CARDS

1880s baseball player tobacco cards (6), includes 1887 N28 Allen & Ginter World's Champions Cap Anson (VG), John Clarkson (GVG), Timothy Keefe (VGEX), Joseph Mulvey (VG), John Ward (EX, _" paper off reverse), 1887 N184 Kimball Champions Dell Darling (VG, reverse staining) **1,533.00**

1888 John Ward, shortstop, New York Giants, issued by G & B Chewing Gum of New York **3,158.00**

1909 T204 Johnny Evers, well-centered w/sharp corners, bright gold coloring, excellent/mint condition, light bend on top border **990.00**

1909 T204 Ramly Miller Huggins, well-centered w/sharp corners & perfect focus, mint, scratch on the photo at Huggins' right ear, excellent/mint condition **770.00**

1909-11 T206 white border Ty Cobb, green background PSA 5 excellent condition card, Sweet Caporal reverse w/rich deep green background **1,099.00**

1910 Piedmont unopened tobacco pack of intact cards **3,900.00**

1911 T3 Turkey Red collection of 10 cabinet cards, includes 5 Crawford, 21 Kleinow, 24 Mitchell, 25 McIntyre, 88 Coveleski, 91 Downey, 96 Groom, 105 Lobert, 106 Lord, 112 Paskert/ Cinn. & Phila **932.00**

1915 Cracker Jack #57 Walter Johnson, well-centered w/sharp corners, white borders & perfect focus, near mint condition **1,771.00**

1933 Goudey baseball card of Lou Gehrig #392, mint condition **3,630.00**

1949 Bowman set of 240 cards **3,061.00**

1950 Bowman set of 252 cards **1,252.00**

1951 Bowman Mickey Mantle card **3,450.00**

1952 Topps #311 Mickey Mantle card, centered 80/20 side to side & 65/35 top to bottom very good/excellent w/soft corners & light creasing along lower left & right border, reverse is clean & without staining **4,012.00**

1952 Topps #311 Mickey Mantle card, mint condition **12,00.00**

1953 Topps Jackie Robinson card **220.00**

1953 Topps Mickey Mantle

1953 Topps Mickey Mantle card (ILLUS.) **2,500.00**

1953 Topps #82 Mickey Mantle, centered 65/35 side to side & 50/50 top to bottom w/strong corners, sharp focus & full gloss, few minor "dings" along the side borders, very solid excellent plus condition **1,317.00**

1953 Topps Willie Mays card **1,179.00**

1954 Bowman #66 Ted Williams card, centered 65/35 in both directions w/decent corners, white borders & perfect photographic clarity, excellent condition 1,132.00

1954 Bowman complete set of 224 cards............................1,012.00

1954 Topps baseball set, excellent to near-mint condition 1,770.00

1955 Bowman #202 Mickey Mantle card 425.00

1955 Topps set of 206 cards...1,064.00

1956 Topps #125 Mickey Mantle card..815.00

1956 Topps baseball set, all cards near mint or better 5,300.00

1957 Topps #95 Mickey Mantle card, centered 55/45 in both directions w/rich color, white borders & sharp corners, upper left corner has minuscule "ding," solid near mint condition............730.00

1961 Topps Mickey Mantle MVP #475 card 90.00

1963 Fleer complete set of 66 cards plus checklist, includes 4 Robinson (EX), 5 Mays (VG), 8 Yaz (VG), 41 Drysdale (EX), 42 Koufax (VG), 43 Wills (EXMT), 45 Spahn (EXMT), 46 Adcock (EXMT), 56 Clemente (VGEX), 61 Gibson (GD), NNO Checklist SP (EXMT), very good to excellent/mint 779.00

1965 Kahn's Weiners complete set of 45 cards, laser-sharp & crystal clean, mint condition ...1,288.00

1965 Topps #477 Steve Carlton card..160.00

1968 Topps Babe Ruth Look 'N See card 200.00

1972 Topps, 2 packs, high numbers from series #6 & #7 ....120.00

1972 Topps, 8 wax packs 200.00

1973 Topps, 4 rack packs, high series w/each rack pack containing 54 cards 180.00

1975 Topps mini wax pack box, 36 packs 850.00

1982 Fleer Cal Ripken test cards..410.00

1991 Topps Frank Thomas Desert Shield card..................100.00

Joe Jackson WG-4 polo grounds card, mint condition, perfectly centered 880.00

T205 1911 Gold Borders set, complete set of 208 T205 tobacco cards in overall good to very good condition 2,956.00

Turkish Red unopened tobacco pack w/cards intact 1,045.00

BASEBALL-MISCELLANEOUS

1916 World Series program, Red Sox vs. Brooklyn game #2 at Boston, neatly scored in ink, very solid copy graded very good/excellent condition w/great eye appeal 1,089.00

1917 Chicago White Sox panorama, includes all eight Black Sox players w/Joe Jackson, Buck Weaver, Cicotte, Collins, Gandil, Faber, Shalk & others, 20 x 40" 3,025.00

1936 Lou Gehrig signed original art, charcoal portrait on green artist paper shows uniformed Gehrig following through after throwing, subtle background, signed to artist Jon Anderson "With Kindest Personal Regards, Lou Gehrig," matching black frame, 17 x 25" 6,900.00

Photo, George Burke image shows Ruth posing in Dodgers uniform, signed "To My Old Pal Press, From Babe Ruth," 9/10 black ink signature, image NRMT w/slight damage to back, 3½ x 6" 2,185.00

1947 Babe Ruth signed ticket stub, World Series game #2 at Yankee Stadium signed across front by attendee "Babe Ruth" in mint black signature, ticket is NRMT & fresh w/tiny tear **1,380.00**

1952 Dodgers autographed team photo, team photo at Ebbets Field w/N.L. Champs banner in background, 37 signatures including Jackie, Campy, Snider, Hodges, Reese, Dressen, Furillo, Roe & Black, legible signatures range from 6/10-10/10, professional matting & framing, 13 x 16" **2,645.00**

1955 Brooklyn Dodgers black bat, H&B bat w/names engraved in gold, 30 signatures featuring Jackie, Campy, Koufax, Hodges, Snider & Furillo, includes half signatures/half block letters w/"Brooklyn Dodgers World Champions 1955" in green block next to label **2,415.00**

1955 signed Dodgers vs. Yankees World Series program, full set of players signatures from two all-time classic teams, includes Mantle, Robinson, Campanella, Reese, Koufax, Berra & more, NRMT signatures in blue ink beneath program photos, 24 signatures from Dodgers, 27 from Yanks, additional personalized Erksine & Hoak signature on cover & full set of signatures from Dodgers coaches **4,313.00**

1958 N.Y. Yankees World Series ring, 14k gold w/center diamond, "New York Yankees World Champions" encircles top w/team logo below, "1958" on either side, no name in ring **2,300.00**

1962 Mets team-signed yearbook, full team-signed yearbook w/all 25 signatures on cover, includes Stengel, Hodges, Thomas, Ashburn, Throneberry, Jackson, & Lavagetto, signatures rate NRMT overall, yearbook w/famed Mets baby image rates EX-MT **1,495.00**

1963 Dodgers championship ring, 14k gold ring engraved "Los Angeles Baseball Club" around Dodger blue stone, "Dodgers 4 Straight" engraved on one side w/"J. Redfern 1963" on reverse **1,955.00**

1969 Mets team-signed yearbook, signed by 37 members w/most signatures on own color photos, signatures rate MT overall **1,725.00**

1973 Oakland Athletics World Series team trophy, gold wrap-around trophy reads "Oakland A's -1973 World Champions" **10,678.00**

1981 Cal Ripken contract, assigned from the Orioles to Minor Leagues w/seven listed players, includes Calvin Ripken Jr., dated March 24, 1981 ....**900.00**

Babe Ruth signed photo, 3 x 5¾", Ruth in usual spring training baseball gear, matted & cleanly autographed "Babe Ruth" at top left, signature is solid 8/10 w/perfect image, 9 x 11" **1,840.00**

Brooklyn Dodgers signed bat, "Cooperstown Bat Co." bat w/picture of Ebbets Field on barrel surrounded by 45 signatures from Dodger legends, includes Snider, Reese, Black, Furillo, Podres, Drysdale, Shuba, Stanky, Erskine, Maglie, Newcombe & Herman, NRMT signatures in different pens & many include both date signed & date played **1,035.00**

Jackie Robinson's first pro game program, some chipping, otherwise very good condition **1,495.00**

Lou Gehrig signed Goudey premium, mint ink signature signed boldly & clearly across pinstripes, light corner creases **2,645.00**

Mickey Mantle & Joe DiMaggio
signed photo 290.00

Mickey Mantle game-ready bat,
blond H&B M110 dates 1965-68,
not used, 34½" **2,300.00**

Roger Maris early 1960s batting
helmet, h.p. w/crude white "NY"
on front, taped "9 MARIS" inside
w/size 7½ American baseball
cap label **4,025.00**

Shoeless Joe Jackson mini
decal bat, mint condition........**1,650.00**

FOOTBALL GAME-USED ITEMS

1960s Gayle Sayers, Chicago
Bears jersey **2,420.00**

1977 Rod Perry, Los Angeles
Rams Riddell helmet **515.00**

Walter Payton Memorial Game Jersey

1983 Walter Payton/George
Halas, Memorial Game jersey
worn by Payton after Bears
famous owner & Hall of Fame
George Halas passed away,
features 2" wide black memorial
band on left sleeve (ILLUS.)...**2,420.00**

1992 Dennis Byrd, New York
Jets jersey **1,320.00**

1992 Steve Young, first game
San Francisco 49ers jersey **1,060.00**

1993 Steve Young, jersey
w/team letter **970.00**

1996 Brett Favre, Green Bay
Packers jersey **1,210.00**

John Elway, Denver Broncos
game helmet............................**2,475.00**

Ray Nitschke, Green Bay
Packers helmet......................**2,000.00**

Reggie White, Philadelphia
Eagles helmet............................**806.00**

FOOTBALL AUTOGRAPHED ITEMS

1962 Baltimore Colts, team-
signed football, Johnny Unitas
MacGregor F-709 football w/31
signatures **442.75**

1963 Chicago Bears,
championship-signed football,
34 signatures including Ditka,
Morris, O'Bradivich, Pyle &
Petinone **880.00**

1965 Green Bay Packers,
autographed football, signed by
47 members of 1965 NFL
Champions including Vince
Lombardi, Tom Fears, Bart Starr,
Henry Jordan, Paul Hornung,
Don Chandler, Fuzzy Thurston,
Davis, Jerry Kramer, Ray
Nitschke, Elijah Pitts, Jim Taylor,
Boyd Dowler, Lionel Aldridge,
Willie Wood, Herb Adderley,
Zeke Bratkowski, Marv Fleming,
Max McGee, Forrest Gregg,
Dave Robinson & Dale **4,327.00**

1966 Green Bay Packers,
autographed football, signed by
47 members of the World
Champions including Paul
Hornung, Jim Taylor, Jim
Bradkowski, Willie Wood, Herb
Adderley, Bob Hyland, Marv
Fleming, Boyd Dowler, Dave
Robinson, Jerry Kramer, Willie
Davis, Fuzzy Thurston, Bart
Starr, Lionel Aldridge, Forrest
Gregg, Zeke Bratkowski, Gail
Gillingham, Henry Jordan, Dave
Hanner, Travis Williams, Elijah
Pitts & Ray Nitschke...............**2,443.00**

1967 Green Bay Packers, team-
signed Super Bowl I football, 51
signatures includes Vince
Lombardi, Bart Starr, Jerry
Kramer, Willie Davis & Elijah
Pitts (ILLUS. top, next page)...**7,590.00**

1967 Green Bay Packers Super Bowl Football

1968 New York Jets, autographed football, signed by 38 members of Jets after Super Bowl, includes Joe Namath, Emerson Boozer & Don Maynard **1,035.00**

1969 Chicago Bears, team ball w/Brian Piccolo, features 40+ signatures including Dick Butkus **650.00**

1972 Miami Dolphins, perfect season team-signed football, white-panel Wilson ball painted "Miami Dolphins World Champs, 1972, 17-0-0," 45+ signatures including Don Shula, Bob Griese, Larry Csonka, Mercury Morris, Paul Warfield & Jim Kiick **4,490.00**

1972 Oklahoma, team-signed football, signed after Oklahoma State beat Penn State in Sugar Bowl, features 60+ signatures ...**220.00**

1984 Chicago Bears, team-signed football, 40+ signatures including Jim McMahon, Mike Singletary, Richard Dent & Walter Payton **265.00**

1985 Super Bowl Champion Chicago Bears, team-signed football, over 40 signatures including Walter Payton, Steve McMichael & Mike Singletary ...**3,145.00**

Bart Starr signed football **585.00**

Vince Lombardi, signed yearbook, 1962 Packers yearbook signed by Lombardi in upper right corner of cover **814.00**

Vince Lombardi single-signed football **665.00**

BASKETBALL GAME-USED ITEMS

Anfernee Hardaway, McDonald's classic 1990 high school jersey......................................**3,200.00**

Charles Barkley, 1994 All-Star jersey..**900.00**

Dennis Rodman, 1995-96 Chicago Bulls jersey..............**1,650.00**

Grant Hill ,1995-96 game jersey w/team letter.........................**1,750.00**

Kareem Abdul Jabaar, early 1980s Laker jersey **1,200.00**

Karl Malone, Dream Team One jersey......................................**1,950.00**

Larry Bird, Boston Celtics game jersey......................................**1,405.00**

Magic Johnson, 1979 rookie home jersey, gold Lakers **5,340.00**

Magic Johnson, 1989 game jersey, home gold sand knit version...................................**2,055.00**

Magic Johnson, Olympic game jersey, road blue uniform........**7,040.00**

Magic Johnson, signed game-worn shoes, size 14...................**735.00**

Mark Jackson, 1990 Knicks jersey..**350.00**

Meadowlark Lemon, Harlem Globetrotters jersey **1,270.00**

Michael Jordan Rookie Jersey

Michael Jordon, 1986-87 game jersey, sand knit size 44+ w/Bulls exclusive tag (ILLUS.) **9,100.00**

Michael Jordan, autographed
1989 home jersey, sandknit size
44+2" home white Chicago
Bulls silk screened jersey **6,500.00**

Michael Jordan, 1994-95 #45
jersey, Champion size
46+ 3" **8,500.00**

Michael Jordan, 1995-96 game
shoes **4,250.00**

Reggie Miller, Dream Team
Two jersey **1,100.00**

Scottie Pippen, 1992 Dream
Team One jersey **3,800.00**

Shaquille O'Neal, road rookie
jersey, size 52+ **1,330.00**

Shaquille O'Neal, home rookie
jersey......................................**2,245.00**

Shaquille O'Neal, 1994-95
complete uniform, road black
uniform, jersey size 54+4,"
boldly autographed shorts sized
at 48+2+4," shows wear **2,200.00**

Shaquille O'Neal, freshman
college jersey, LSU jersey,
uniform #33, customized Russell
size 48+2".............................**5,740.00**

Shawn Kemp, rookie jersey **1,810.00**

Spud Webb, rookie Atlanta
Hawks jersey **605.00**

BASKETBALL MISCELLANEOUS
1984 United States Olympic,
team-signed basketball, signed
by Jordan, Chris Mullin, Patrick
Ewing & 12 others **2,900.00**

Joe Dumars, 1989-90 NBA
Finals MVP Award Sport
Magazine trophy **1,020.00**

John Starks Road, Knicks 1990
warm-up jacket **445.00**

Kevin Garnett, game high school
jersey.......................................**900.00**

Larry Bird's, rookie shooting shirt
w/family letter **2,420.00**

Leroy Neiman's, final sketch of
Michael Jordan, once personally
owned by Jordan, professionally
framed, 15 x 19" **18,000.00**

Magic Johnson's, last complete
road warm-up, purple Laker
jacket, pants tagged 1992-93,
size 38=38-1, both have player
number, jacket has name on
back..**950.00**

Magic Johnson, match charity
uniform, signed, bright red mesh
complete uniform from "Magic
Mint Match" tournament, "Earvin
Magic Johnson" on back &
retired number 32 perfectly
autographed, mint condition **400.00**

Magic Johnson's, Mesh "Pepsi"
Tour uniform, autographed,
white mesh w/colorful
Pepsi logo................................**550.00**

Magic Johnson's, Pepsi Tour
complete signed uniform, jersey
& shorts from "Pepsi" sponsored
Magic Tour basketball
tournament **500.00**

Michael Jordan, National
Association of Black Colleges
basketball jersey, from NABC
Charity Tournament, red w/white
& blue trim, nylon jersey Russell
size 48 w/4" added length tag,
faded Russell tag, MJ/45 written
in black Sharpie.....................**3,300.00**

Michael Jordan, Number 45
charity jersey **2,200.00**

Michael Jordan, prototype Space
Jam jersey, "Tune Squad" silk-
screened across front, #23 on
back.......................................**2,000.00**

Wilt Chamberlain's, 1959 White
Harlem Globe Trotters jersey,
worn by Chamberlain before he
turned pro **7,850.00**

TEXTILES

COVERLETS
Jacquard, single weave, one-
piece, a star in the center within
ring bands & larger starburst
framed by flowering vines & a
large spread-winged eagle at

each corner, scrolls, harps & cornucopias around the border band, edge label "Made by Wm. Ney, Myerstown, N. Labanono Co., Pa.," green, red, gold & natural white, 82" sq. **$550.00**

Diamond Medallions & Stars & Leaves Coverlet

Jacquard, single weave, two-piece, rows of checked diamond medallions framed by leafy ovals alternating w/rows of four-point stars & four leaves & two blossoms medallions, trellis & bird borders, corners labeled "John Richin Rome, S.C., Ohio, 1854," navy blue, tomato red & natural white, wear, top edge worn w/incomplete fringe, 69 x 82" (ILLUS.) **413.00**

Jacquard, single weave, two-piece, rows of large four-pod clusters framing heart-shaped stems & small tulip-like blossoms alternating a narrow band of delicate florals, the border w/a band of flower & leaf bands, corners dated "1855," red, navy blue, olive gold & natural white, 70 x 88" **275.00**

Jacquard, single weave, two-piece, rows of ovals formed by pairs of leaves surrounding four-blossom medallions centered by a lacy diamond all alternating w/small starbursts & pairs of small blossoms, eagles & grapevine borders, corners labeled "John Hartman,

Lafayette, Ohio, 1857," navy blue, teal green, deep red & natural white & olive green, very minor stains, 78 x 88" **1,018.00**

Jacquard, single weave, two-piece, rows of large eight-petal flowers alternating w/rows of smaller floral clusters within grapevine & double-bird borders, corner block signed & dated, Ohio, 1851, 68 x 90" (wear & edge damage).............**275.00**

Jacquard, single weave, two-piece, rows of oval four-rose medallions alternating w/rows of large four-leaf clusters within vining borders of birds, corners labeled "John King, Andrew Kump, Damask Coverlet Manufacturer, Hanover, York County, Pa. 1846," medium blue, tomato red & natural white, 76 x 92" (minor wear) **523.00**

Rose Medallions Jacquard Coverlet

Jacquard, single weave, two-piece, rows of four-rose medallions each framed by pairs of large pointed leaves alternating w/smaller starbursts, vining & snowflake borders, signed "Joseph Deavler, Mary Buch, 1841," Lancaster County, Pennsylvania, navy blue, sage green, red & natural white, 81 x 106" (ILLUS.) **550.00**

Jacquard, double woven, two-piece, rows composed of nine large floral medallions alternating w/diamonds, navy blue, salmon red & natural white, 82 x 90" (some wear & stains) **275.00**

Overshot, two-piece, geometric block optical pattern in medium blue & white, 68 x 96" (minor stains, no fringe) **220.00**

Overshot, one-piece, snowflake in lattice design w/pine tree border, medium blue & natural white, late, 88 x 106" (minor wear) **220.00**

QUILTS

Early Appliqued Eagle Quilt

Appliqued Carolina Lily patt., composed of vivid red, green & orange cotton patches arranged as three-blossom clusters on leafy stems, arranged as three rows of three clusters each all within double narrow bands framed by a wide white diamond quilted border band, early 20th c., 41 x 80"..........................**575.00**

Appliqued Eagle patt., a large central spread-winged eagle w/stars across its chest & wings & holding flower stems in its talons centered in an almond-shaped reserve framed by flaring stems w/large blossoms & leaves, a wide outer border band of vining flowers & leaves,

worked in solid red, blue & yellow calico, worn, some of the blues in tatters, 19th c., 80 x 92" (ILLUS. previous column) **715.00**

Appliqued Floral Medallions patt., a total of nine large squared flower & leaf clusters around a central floral ring, in shades of red & green, well-quilted, 70" sq............................**330.00**

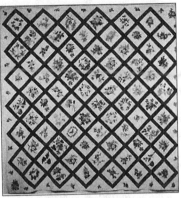

Early Appliqued Friendship Quilt

Appliqued Friendship quilt, composed of lattice bands around squares signed & dated between 1844 & 1847, each square w/cut chintz flowers & birds appliqued onto a white ground, the trellis design in printed green cotton, 104 x 106" (ILLUS.) **2,300.00**

Appliqued Oak Leaf Medallions patt., composed of sixteen oak leaf clusters in red & green calico w/a solid red border stripe, all on a white plain quilted ground, 72 x 75" (wear, stains w/small holes)..........................**413.00**

Appliqued Rose Wreath patt., composed of four large swirling round wreaths w/a large blossom in the center w/smaller blooms & leaf sprigs around the edges of each, a four-arm central leaf & berry pinwheel, all within borders composed of long vining roses & leaves issuing

Appliqued Rose Wreath Quilt

from small urn-form vases, worked in red & green, parallel line quilting in the background, scattered staining, American, 19th c., 84 x 88" (ILLUS.) **1,035.00**

Appliqued Tulip & Rose Wreath variation patt., composed of red, green & yellow cotton patches arranged as stylized tulip clusters alternating w/rose wreathes & scattered small leaves on a white ground all within a continuous tulip & vine border enclosed by red binding, overall diamond & foliate quilting, Pennsylvania, 19th c., 87¼ x 89" **805.00**

Appliqued Urns of Flowers Quilt

Appliqued Urns of Flowers & Berries patt., four large urns overflowing w/vining branches w/blossoms, berries & serrated

leaves, all within a border of pairs of large scrolled & serrated leaves flanking a flowerhead, done in green, red & yellow solid & printed calico, on a white cotton ground w/channel & diamond quilting, mid-19th c., some minor fading & staining, 80 x 82" (ILLUS.) **1,495.00**

Crib quilt, pieced Basket patt., composed of purple & black patches, Amish, 20th c., 34 x 48" **230.00**

Pieced Basket patt., a design of twenty baskets of flowers in squares on an ivory ground w/yellow banding, diamond-quilted ground, 72 x 86"............**330.00**

Carpenter's Wheel Pieced Quilt

Pieced Carpenter's Wheel patt., composed of red, teal blue & mustard yellow cotton blocks enclosed by a triple border band in red, teal blue & mustard yellow within a red cotton binding, overall princess feather & diamond quilting, Amish, Pennsylvania, ca. 1870, 80¼" sq. (ILLUS.) **4,600.00**

Pieced Checkerboard patt., overall design of small squares in multi-colored calico within narrow red & white borders, 73" sq. (minor stains)................**300.00**

Pieced Diamond-in-Square patt., composed of red & white calico patches in a sawtooth-

Diamond-in-Square Pieced Quilt

edged design framed by a red calico border, white calico binding, w/diamond & ocean waves quilting, 1830-50, 80½ x 81½" (ILLUS.) **1,150.00**

Pieced Fan & Stripes patt., a large multi-colored central striped cross centered by a block w/a multi-colored round fan design, a large round multi-colored fan in each quadrant of the cross, done in blue, deep pink, yellow, purple & green on white, w/embroidered detail, 85 x 86" **344.00**

Feathered Diamond Pieced Quilt

Pieced Feathered Diamond patt., composed of dark green & purple patches arranged w/sawtooth borders on the inner designs, Amish, 19th c. (ILLUS.) **1,840.00**

Pieced Flowerpot patt., composed of thirty-two pots in

green, green gingham, lavender & floral prints on a white ground w/green grid & two-tone green border, 72 x 90" (overall wear) ..**220.00**

Pieced Flying Geese patt., composed of bands of multi-colored prints & solids w/red calico bar borders, 78 x 88" (minor stains)..........................**275.00**

Star-of-Bethlehem Quilt

Pieced Star-of-Bethlehem patt., composed of multiple calico fabrics & chintz blocks enclosed by an alternating red & olive green triple border, overall princess feather, diamond & ocean waves quilting, ca. 1830-40, 73¾ x 74¾" (ILLUS.) **1,495.00**

Pieced Sunshine-and-Shadow patt., composed of a multitude of small square blocks in green, cranberry, blue, teal, orange, yellow, pink & red cotton, all enclosed by a double border of red & green cotton w/cranberry binding, overall diamond & ocean waves quilting, Amish, Lancaster County, Pennsylvania, ca. 1870, 76 x 78¼" **2,875.00**

SAMPLERS
Alphabet above pious verses above a grouping of family genealogy notes for the Wells family noting birthdates in the 1780s, zigzag borders across the top & down the sides & a

basket of flowers flanked by the initials "G.- W" at the bottom, dated 1785, framed, some discoloration, 11⅞ x 21" **690.00**

Alphabets in rows above the inscription "Melissa Berker Stone, aged 8 years Nov 8th, 1830, Belpre, Washington County, Ohio," a row of small trees, buildings & animals across the bottom & vining borders at the sides, silk on homespun linen work in green, red, pale blue, white & yellow, matted & framed, 13½ x 21" (some fading & darkening of linen, small hole in margin).....**2,805.00**

Early Adam & Eve Sampler

Alphabets & numerals above a scene of "Adam & Eve in the Garden of Eden" above the signature & date "Matilda Wikoff's Sampler, August 27, 1801," baskets, trees & a bird across the top & meandering floral vines down the sides, worked in green, blue, pink, cream & brown stitches on a linen ground, Monmouth County, New Jersey, framed, 10¼ x 16" (ILLUS.) **8,050.00**

Numerals flanking a church building above an inscription & signature, "Remember me when

this you see, Catharine Fulton 1834," all above large clusters of florals in the lower two-thirds w/an urn of flowers flanked by birds at the bottom, vining floral border on three sides, wool & silk on linen homespun worked in faded green, blue, pink, white & yellow, matted & framed, 23 x 27" (wear, holes, some poorly executed repairs).......................**385.00**

Pious verses above varied oblong reserves over a landscape scene w/a large two-story house centered atop a hill flanked by pine trees w/flowers & animals on the hillside, signed at the top "Sarah W. West's Work wrought at Bennington School in the Year 1824 and in the Eleventh year of her age," probably New Jersey, some staining, tear, framed, 20 x 24½" **4,600.00**

Pot of flowers & floral sprigs above a long pious inscription above the name & date "Mary Haynes Aged 9, Anno Domini 1818," flowers across the bottom, within a narrow vining floral border band, silk on homespun linen worked in green, brown, gold, white & black, framed, 16¾ x 18" (wear, many small holes, edge damage, color bleeding) **303.00**

TOYS

Toy Automobile

Airplane, "Spirit of St. Louis," pressed steel, Metalcraft Corp., St. Louis, Missouri, Model No. 800, late 1920s, wing span 11½" **$104.00**

Automobile, Hubley # 5, aluminum, red & silver, paint chips, distressed tires, missing back left tire rubber, ca. late 1930s, 9½" l.(ILLUS.) **1,320.00**

Automobile, "Irwin Mechanical Super Racing Car," red & yellow plastic, windup, No. 105, boxed, 12⅛" l., 3" h. **94.00**

Automobile, Ohlsson & Rice Inc. #35, metal, red, 10¼" l. **253.00**

Automobile, Vis-A-Vis, Bing, Gebrüder, Nuremberg, Germany, ca. 1902.................**7,920.00**

Automobile, limousine, Bing, Gebrüder, Nuremberg, Germany, ca. 1908.................**4,400.00**

Battery-operated, astronaut, lithographed, metallic blue w/plastic dome, gun in right hand, rear tank battery box, Daiya, ca. 1955-1960, 14" h. (some bubbling on battery box, plastic dome cracked) **1,380.00**

Apollo-Z Space Toy

Battery-operated, "Apollo-Z," tin & plastic, clean battery compartment, some scratches & soiling, 12" l. (ILLUS.).................**66.00**

Battery-operated, motor boat w/motor, stand & box, metal & wood, marked "Sakan," 15⅝" l. (minor scratches & wear) **154.00**

Battery-operated, "Space Dog," metallic blue w/lithographic detail, remote control decorated w/image of space dog, antenna head, hinged ears, flashing light on back & spring tail, marked "KO," ca. 1950s, 6" l. (some wear on remote control) **2,300.00**

"Trick Pony" Bell Ringer

Bell ringer toy, "Trick Pony," cast iron, Gong Bell Co., ca. 1880s, soiling, paint loss & rust, 7¾" l. (ILLUS.) **523.00**

Boat, "PT-109," plastic w/instructions, Revell, copyright 1963, box side marked "Commanded in the South Pacific by Lt. J.G./J.F. Kennedy, USNR," 13⁵⁄₁₆" l. **33.00**

Bread truck, cast iron, Hathaway, replaced driver & rubber tires, soiling & paint chipping, 9½" l. **2,310.00**

Bride, "Anxious Bride Nanni," bride passenger pulled by "Motor Rad Cycle," Lehmann, EPL # 470 ....**1,610.00**

Bus, Greyhound, partial "Arcade" toys decal on bottom, ca. 1930s, 9" l., 2½" h. (touch up to paint) ...**176.00**

Chinese men, lithographed tinplate, two figures carrying tea chest, Lehmann "Kadi" **1,265.00**

Circus cage truck, "Overland Circus," cast iron, red w/gold trim, pressed steel wheels, w/driver, Kenton Hardware Co., Kenton, Ohio, ca. 1925, 7¼" ..**1,035.00**

Circus train, floor-type, lithographed tin, locomotive & three cars w/wooden wheels, Toyland, ca. 1930s, 16 ½" l. (slight surface rust) **86.00**

Circus set: cotton tent w/pendants, bare-back rider, lion tamer & whip, black dude, clown, elephant, giraffe, donkey, horse, horse w/platform, lion, two chairs, two stools, ball, barrel, two ladders, poles, acrobat swing, "Humpty Dumpty Circus," Schoenhut, boxed (some paint wear, tent slightly soiled, cover damaged) **1,955.00**

Clockwork mechanism, boy on swing, painted tin figure w/cotton costume, wooden base, Ives, Bridgeport Connecticut, ca. 1870s, 14¼" h. (clockwork missing, replaced base) **3,737.00**

Clockwork mechanism, double acrobats, wood & papier-mâché, wooden figure w/h.p. papier-mâché heads, remnants of original silk costumes, Ives, Bridgeport, Connecticut, ca. 1875, 5¾ x 6", 8" h. **2,300.00**

Clockwork mechanism, girl on velocipede, painted tin, iron & papier-mâché, tin & iron velocipede, girl w/papier-mâché head & painted features, molded hair, original clothes, Stevens & Brown, New York, New York, ca. 1870, 11½" l., 9" h. **1,840.00**

German Monoplane Toy

Clockwork mechanism, monoplane, tinplate, white finish w/red & yellow lining, German, probably Gunterman, ca. 1910, 9½" l. (ILLUS.)......................**1,150.00**

Clockwork mechanism, rowboat "Mary," painted tin, green hull, red deck, wood oars & oarsman, original blue fabric clothes, Ives, Bridgeport, Connecticut, ca. 1869, oars 7" l., boat 13" l. **4,312.00**

Clockwork mechanism, "Zulu," tinplate, ostrich-mail finish in

yellow lithography, Lehmann, EPL #721....................................**690.00**

Clown w/car, tinplate, Lehmann "Mixtum," EPL #775...............**1,092.00**

Fire truck, Tonka suburban #46, ca. 1957....................................**150.00**

Fire pumper, h.p., Guntherman S.G., Nuremberg, Germany, ca. 1898 ....**4,510.00**

Cast-Iron Fire Pump Wagon

Fire pump wagon, cast iron, painted red & cream, three horse-drawn wagon w/four ladders, two figures & bell beneath driver, 31" l. (ILLUS.)...**862.00**

Fortune wheel, "Cracker Jacks" ...**55.00**

Garage, tinplate, EPL #772 w/two opening doors, includes mechanical cars "Galop" EPL #760 & "Sedan" EPL #765, Lehmann, set of 3.....................**805.00**

Gum truck, embossed metal, Buddy L. Wrigley's Spearmint Chewing Gum, marked "Railway Express Agency" on both sides & "Buddy L" on door, 24½" l. (missing front grill, some wear)...**231.00**

Log wagon, cast iron, black driver w/oxen, paint loss, rust & small piece off wheel center, 14¾" **935.00**

Motor boat, "Sea-Fury," plastic w/metal motor, h.p., ca. 1948, 16" l. **171.00**

Motorcycle, cast iron, blue w/white rubber tires, Champion, 5" l., 3" h. **413.00**

Pedal car, Chevrolet Bel Air Convertible, 1955, promotional scale model w/colorful decals in imitation of the famous Indy car race **4,510.00**

Pedal car, Austin Pathfinder, 1949, ermine white body w/red flame accents outlined in yellow on front & behind seat, red "7" outlined in black & shadowed in grey on both rear sides, pneumatic tires, leather straps hold down hood, chrome rear bumper guard & exhaust, chrome hub caps, red upholstered interior, chrome pull brake on side, 23" w., 62" l., 25" h. (steering wheel loose, minor abrasion on rear) **2,558.00**

Pedal car, Packard, 1923, creamy yellow, American National Co., Toledo, Ohio (unrestored condition) **7,370.00**

U.S. Mail Truck

Pedal vehicle, mail truck, metal, painted red, white & blue, rubber tires, marked "Air Mail - U.S. Mail Truck," scratches, soiling, 18" w., 43" l. (ILLUS.) **550.00**

Penny toy, windup boat, lithographed tin, launch penny-type w/cream body & blue trim (dents, scratches & soiling) **303.00**

Penny toy, donkey w/cart, lithographed, marked "Germany" on belly of donkey, 4¾" l. (scratches & small rust spots) ...**110.00**

Pull toy, cannon & ammunition cart, painted wood, gold cannon w/blue body & wheels w/red striping, Germany, early 20th c., 48" l. (one lid hinge missing) **633.00**

Pull toy, donkey, pressed steel, flywheel mechanism, nodding head, yellow on red platform, Dayton Toy & specialty Co., Dayton, Ohio, 10¾" l. **86.00**

German Wooden Horse

Pull toy, horse on mechanized wheeled platform, carved wooden horse w/saddle, bridle, iron wheels & key-wind power source, marked "GS Made in Germany," 16" l., 14" h. (ILLUS.) **440.00**

Pull toy, man in canoe, papier-mâché, wood & wire, boat of papier-mâché, man w/papier-mâché head & wood & wire body & oars, man wears original outfit, Germany, late 19th - early 20th c., 11" l. (some damage & discoloration) **173.00**

Pull toy, "Rooster & Rabbit - Chanticleer," painted lithographed tinplate, gyroscope mechanism, Lehmann EPL # 370................................**805.00**

Robot, "Earth Man," yellow lithographed tin, Normura, Boogaerts #174, Tin Toy Dreams #144, ca. 1950s, unboxed, 9½" h. **977.00**

Robot, "Machine Man," battery-powered, lithographed panels, red w/green lighting eyes, ears & mouth, bump & go action arms, on/off switch, ca. 1950s, unboxed, 15" h. (ILLUS. top, next page) **42,550.00**

Machine Man Robot

Robot, "Mars King," battery-operated, lithographed dark silver, T-V screen on torso, Horikawa, Boogaerts #37, Tin Toy Dreams #133, cardboard box, ca. 1960s, 9¼" h. **460.00**

Robot, "Mr. Mercury," battery-operated tin & plastic, light blue finish, unboxed, ca. 1955-1960s, 13" h. **1,150.00**

Robot, "Radicon," steel grey textured body, torso inset w/gauge & electric light, red eyes, radio remote control & cardboard box, Masudaya, marked "Tin Toy Dreams," ca. 1950s, crazing to base, slight wear to control) 14½" h. **21,850.00**

Robot, "Space Hopper," red w/lithographed details, plastic antenna, Yonezawa, Boogaerts #271, ca. 1970-1975, unboxed, 3¾" h. **201.00**

Scooter, "Felix the Cat," tin, ca. 1930, 7½" l. **575.00**

Sled, child's size, carved & painted pine & wrought iron, shaped platform painted red & inscribed in block letters "Vigilant" in yellow & gold letters outlined in black, the whole mounted on shaped wood runners w/wrought-iron blades, American-made, third quarter 19th c., 39½" l., 4¼" h. (some paint loss, stress cracks) **2,012.00**

Squeak toy, cat, seated, painted papier-mâché, Pennsylvania, late 19th c., 7" h. (replaced leather on bellow) **920.00**

Squeak toy, robin & dog, painted papier-mâché, robin on wire spring & tree trunk, wood & leather bellows, late 19th c., 6¾" l., 5" h. (slight flaking) **863.00**

Squeak toy, St. Bernard w/sleeping child, painted papier-mâché, dog w/opening mouth, wood & leather bellows, late 19th c., 6½" l., 4¼" h. (dog missing one leg, replaced leather, slight wear) **978.00**

Steamboat, side-wheeler type, gold paint w/red stacks, A.C. Williams Co., Ravenna, Ohio, 1912-1920s, 7⅝" l. **230.00**

Stove, "Baby," cast iron, includes shovel, pan, kettle, burners & handle, two steel coal buckets, stove pipe & wood box, Ideal, early 20th c., 7 x 16", 16" h. (slight surface rust) **690.00**

Train set: carved & painted wood, black engine w/stack & tender, red, grey & black freight car, grey, black & red coal car & black, red & gold open passenger car, early 20th c., 75½" l., the set.......................**1,265.00**

Train set: painted tin, consists of locomotive w/red cab & blue roof w/green base, two yellow passenger cars & one orange passenger car, America, ca. 1880, each car 5" l., the set.......**316.00**

Tricycle, carved & painted wood, model of long-bodied white rooster w/blue-painted eyes, yellow bill & red comb & wattle, back flattened as seat surmounted by metal horseshoe-shaped steering device w/red rubber handles, rounded tail feathers above two white legs w/yellow spurred feet, three wire & rubber wheels w/black rubber pedals, ca. 1930, 9 x 32½", 25" h. **2,760.00**

Truck, stake-type, pressed steel, light blue cab, red chassis & fenders & green body, wooden wheels, electric headlights, Louis Marx Co., New York, New York, ca. 1930s, 10½" **230.00**

Truck, cast iron, oil pumper-type, red w/rubber tires, marked "1559," (paint chips, cracking & soiling to tires) **220.00**

Truck, Tonka pickup #302, ca. 1963 ....**65.00**

Wagon, painted wood, green w/yellow striping, red wheels & frame, removable panels, seat, wooden spoked wheels, snow sled attachment, early 20th c., 25 x 45", 27" h. **1,150.00**

Windup tin automobile, lithographed, Marx, 14" l., 3½" h. (dents & scratches) **204.00**

Windup tin bus, Greyhound "Limited 228," bright blue, rubber tires, Keystone Mfg. Co., Boston, Massachusetts, late 1930s, 18⅜" l. (some wear & rust) **259.00**

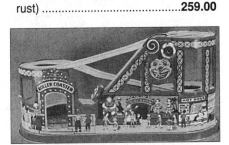

Windup Circus Roller Coaster

Windup tin circus roller coaster w/car, lithographed circus scenes, scratches, soiling & denting, 19" l., 10" h. (ILLUS.) ...**143.00**

Windup tin clown musicians, h.p. tin, musical, one clown

playing violin, one playing bells, green wooden base, Gunthermann, S.G., Nuremberg, Germany, ca. 1890s **1,380.00**

Windup Coal Truck

Windup tin coal truck, lithographed, Lehman, marked "EHE & Co." & "Made in Germany," scratches, oiling, paint chipping & fading, 6½" l. (ILLUS.) **440.00**

Windup tin drum major, Wolverine #27, 13½" h. **220.00**

Windup tin Dutch girl, lithographed, young girl dressed in traditional Dutch costume, w/moving glass eyes, Germany, early 20th c., 5¾" h....................**201.00**

Tin Monkey With Cart

Windup tin monkey w/cart, lithographed, German, ca. 1910, soiling & paint chipping, 12½" l. (ILLUS.) **440.00**

Windup tin roadster, lithographed, Louis Marx & Co., New York, New York, ca. 1930, 8½" l. **230.00**

Windup tin run-about, lithographed auto & painted driver, rubber tires, Guntherman, ca. 1900, 6¾" l. (missing carriage lamps & one tire) **2,530.00**

Windup tin taxi, "Yell-O-Taxi," lithographed, Ferdinand Strauss Corp., New York, New York, ca. 1920s, w/original box, 8" l.........**805.00**

Windup trainer & bear, trainer w/bisque head, wooden body, composition hands & legs, wearing Russian-style wool hat & cotton outfit, fully-jointed mohair bear w/glass eyes, all on wood base, Germany, late 19th - early 20th c., 6½" l., 6½" h.........**575.00**

VENDING & GAMBLING DEVICES

Pace "Batum" Slot Machine

Gambling, Caille "Superior" slot machine, 5-cent play w/four reel payout, ca. 1930...................**$2,300.00**

Gambling, Jennings "Club Chief" payout slot machine, 5-cent play, ca. 1940s, includes original stand......................................**1,250.00**

Gambling, Jennings "Sun Chief" slot machine, 25-cent play, ca. 1947................................**1,800.00**

Gambling, Mills "Cherry Front" slot machine, 5-cent play, ca. 1930s..............................**1,150.00**

Gambling, Pace "Batum" slot machine, 1-cent play, ca. 1930s, restored (ILLUS.)...................**1,275.00**

Gambling, Pace "Pace's Race" slot machine, payout floor model, ca. 1937.....................**7,500.00**

Gambling, Watling, front vendor slot machine, 5-cent play, marked "Superior Mints" on front, ca. 1930s.....................**4,000.00**

Gambling, Watling "Treasury" payout slot machine, 25-cent play, ca. 1935........................**3,250.00**

Roulette Wheel

Roulette wheel, G. Caro, Paris, ca. 1890, 32" d. (ILLUS.)........**2,200.00**

Trade stimulator, Atlas Mgf. Co. "Little Midget," cast aluminum, 5-cent play, marked "36 - Lucky Spot - Midget" on front, ca. 1920s..................................**750.00**

Trade stimulator, Caille "Good Luck," oak case w/original decals, ca. 1906 ....**650.00**

Trade stimulator, Field Mgf. Co. "Baby Vendor" w/gumball vendor, cast aluminum, ca. 1920-1930s......................**1,000.00**

Trade stimulator, Mills "Little Perfection," oak w/"gold" horseshoe on front, ca. 1901-1933 ....**600.00**

Trade stimulator, Mills "New Target Practice," cast aluminum, 1-cent play, label marked "A Game of Skill" on front, ca. 1920-1930s **325.00**

Trade stimulator, Royal "Royal Reels" w/gumball vendor, cast aluminum, ca. 1934 ....**500.00**

Trade stimulator, Trip-L-Jacks payout-style, cast aluminum & oak, 1-cent play, ca. 1930s **850.00**

"Nickel Tickler" Trade Stimulator

Trade stimulator, Western Automatic Weighing Company "Nickel Tickler," oak casing, 5-cent play, ca. 1892 (ILLUS.)...**4,000.00**

WEATHERVANES

Early Airplane Weathervane

Airplane, carved & painted pine & metal biplane, the stylized plane fashioned from several carved planks joined by iron wires on rotating wheels, retains traces of gilding & silver paint, now mounted on a rod & a black metal base, ca. 1920, 37½" l., overall 19¼" h. (ILLUS.) **$1,150.00**

Arrow & banner, copper, zinc & iron, silhouetted form w/an arrow tip on a forked scroll at the end of a swelled oblong pierced banner w/cut-out scrolls &

palmette & a forked fishtail terminal, w/directionals, verdigris finish, 35½" l., 24½" h.............**3,220.00**

Banner, lyre-form, gilt copper, verdigris & bole surface, 19th c., 65" l. (old repairs) **3,450.00**

Cod fish, gilt copper, full-bodied style, 20th c., regilt, repaired, 31½" l. **2,645.00**

Cow, standing, molded copper, the swell-bodied animal w/cast zinc horns & applied tail, retaining old yellow polychrome, probably L.W. Cushing & Co., Waltham, Massachusetts, third quarter 19th c., now mounted on a black metal base, 24½" l., 13" h. **1,840.00**

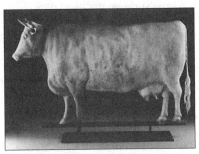

Harris & Co. Cow Weathervane

Cow, standing, molded copper, swell-bodied w/sheet copper ears & zinc horns, overall verdigris, retains some minor traces of gilding, mounted on a later black metal rod & black metal rectangular base, Harris & Company, Boston, Massachusetts, third quarter 19th c., 33½" l., 18½" h. (ILLUS.) **2,587.00**

Cow, standing, cut-out wood, the silhouetted animal painted white w/large black spots, New England, late 19th c., 34" l., 20½" h. (breaks, repairs) **805.00**

'Dr. Hex,' carved & painted pine, a silhouetted figure of the flying Dr. Hex wearing a black top hat, blue coat & black boots, fashioned from a single plank, painted on both sides, Bucks County, Pennsylvania, ca. 1860, 26½" l., 13½" h. **4,600.00**

Horse, trotting, copper & cast iron, swelled body, gilt & verdigris surface, late 19th c., 29" l. **2,760.00**

Horse, trotting, copper, swelled body, trail straight out, old finish, early 20th c., 42" l., 22" h........**1,955.00**

Merino ram, copper & zinc, swelled-body style w/tightly curled horns, fine verdigris surface, 19th c. (repaired bullet holes)....................................**6,900.00**

Rooster, gilt copper, full-bodied w/wide arched tail, gilt & verdigris surface, traces of dark red paint, late 19th c., 21" h. (imperfections, repair) **1,955.00**

Rooster, gilt copper, full-bodied, comb & wattle painted red, late 19th c., 24½" h. **2,875.00**

Rooster, molded copper, swell-bodied bird w/molded feather, wing & tail detail, molded zinc feet, mounted on a rod over an orb & a later wood base, late 19th c., 27" l., 26" h. (one toe broken, repairs, holes & repaired holes)....................................**1,955.00**

Rooster, molded copper, standing swelled-body bird w/articulated neck, wing & tail feathers, on spurred legs, on a rectangular black base, retains traces of gilding & yellow paint, late 19th c., 26½" l., 30½" h....**3,450.00**

Stag, leaping, molded copper, full-bodied animal w/extended back legs & articulated main, tail & antlers, w/original gilding, on a rectangular black base, late 19th c., 30½" l., 23½" h. **4,025.00**

Surrey, molded copper, a full-figural buggy set on four wire wheels w/springs mounted on a rod & weathered to an overall verdigris, A.B. & W.T. Westervelt, New York, New York, third quarter 19th c., 31" l., 22" h. **10,925.00**

INDEX

I-J-K

L-M-N

O-P-Q

R-S

T-Z